BUTTERWORTHS
STONE'S
JUSTICES' MANUAL
2018
KEY MATERIALS
& SUPPLEMENT

BUTTERWORTHS STONE'S JUSTICES' MANUAL 2018 KEY MATERIALS & SUPPLEMENT

One Hundred and Fiftieth Edition

edited by

A J TURNER

Barrister, Chambers of Adrian Turner, Eastbourne

A J KELLY

District Judge (Magistrates' Courts)

N J WATTAM

District Judge (Magistrates' Courts)

R K INYUNDO

District Judge (Magistrates' Courts)

B P BRANDON

Barrister, 3 Raymond Buildings, Gray's Inn

Members of the LexisNexis Group worldwide

United Kingdom	Reed Elsevier (UK) Limited trading as LexisNexis, 1-3 Strand, London WC2N 5JR
Australia	Reed International Books Australia Pty Ltd trading as LexisNexis, Chatswood, New South Wales
Austria	LexisNexis Verlag ARD Orac GmbH & Co KG, Vienna
Benelux	LexisNexis Benelux, Amsterdam
Canada	LexisNexis Canada, Markham, Ontario
China	LexisNexis China, Beijing and Shanghai
France	LexisNexis SA, Paris
Germany	LexisNexis Deutschland GmbH, Munster
Hong Kong	LexisNexis Hong Kong, Hong Kong
India	LexisNexis India, New Delhi
Italy	Giuffrè Editore, Milan
Japan	LexisNexis Japan, Tokyo
Malaysia	Malayan Law Journal Sdn Bhd, Kuala Lumpur
New Zealand	LexisNexis NZ Ltd, Wellington
Singapore	LexisNexis Singapore, Singapore
South Africa	LexisNexis Butterworths, Durban
USA	LexisNexis, Dayton, Ohio

© Reed Elsevier (UK) Ltd 2018
Published by LexisNexis

This is a Butterworths title

ISBN for this volume: 9781474307673

ISBN for the set: 9781474307628

Printed and bound by CPI Group (UK) Ltd, Croydon, CR0 4YY

Visit LexisNexis at http://www.lexisnexis.co.uk

PUBLISHER'S NOTE

This is *Butterworths Stone's Justices' Manual 2018 Key Materials & Supplement.*

There have been amendments made to the material contained in the Key Materials.

The Criminal Procedure Rules 2015 have been updated to take in amendments made by the Criminal Procedure (Amendment) (No 2) Rules 2018, SI 2018/847.

The Magistrates' Court Sentencing Guidelines have been updated to include all the guidelines issued in 2018.

A number of new Acts have been included in the supplement: Finance Act 2017, The Finance (No 2) Act 2017, The Data Protection Act 2018, the Laser Misuse (Vehicles) Act 2018, and the Sanctions and Anti-Money Laundering Act 2018

There have been a number of new Statutory Instruments included in the supplement: The Animal Welfare (Licensing of Activities Involving Animals) (England) Regulations 2018, SI 2018/486, The Package Travel and Linked Travel Arrangements Regulations 20181, SI 2018/634, The Breaching of Limits on Ticket Sales Regulations 20181, SI 2018/735, The Non-Road Mobile Machinery (Type-Approval and Emission of Gaseous and Particulate Pollutants) Regulations 2018, 2018/764, Social Workers Regulations 20181, SI 2018/893, Housing Administration (England and Wales) Rules 20181 (2018/719)

The latest revised 2018 versions of the Police and Criminal Evidence Act 1984 Codes of Practice: Codes C, E, F and H have been included in the supplement.

Material in the supplement is set out under the Part headings used in *Stone*, using the relevant paragraph numbers. The contents of the supplement have been incorporated into the accompanying CD.

06100901

CONTENTS

Contents

CRIMINAL PRACTICE DIRECTIONS 2015[1]

[1] [2015] EWCA 1567 (Crim). Amendment Number 1 [2016] EWCA 97 (Crim) was handed down by the Lord Chief Justice on 23rd March, 2016 and came into force on the 4th April, 2016. Amendment Number 2 [2016] EWCA 1714 (Crim) was handed down by the Lord Chief Justice on 16th November, 2016 and came into force on 16th November, 2016. Amendment Number 3 [2017] EWCA 30 (Crim) was handed down by the Lord Chief Justice on 31st January 2017 and came into force on 31st January 2017. Amendment Number 4 [2017] EWCA 310 (Crim) was handed down by the Lord Chief Justice on 28th March, 2017 and came into force on 3rd April, 2017. Amendment Number 5 [2017] EWCA 1076 (Crim) was handed down by the Lord Chief Justice on 26th July 2017 and came into force on 2nd October 2017. Amendment Number 6 was handed down by the Lord Chief Justice on 22nd March 2018 and came into force on 2nd April 2018. Amendment Number 7 was handed down by the Lord Chief Justice on 26th July 2018 and came into force on 1st October 2018.

CPD	Division	CPD ref	Title of CPD, if applicable
CPD	III Custody and bail	14F	Forfeiture of monies lodged as security or pledged by a surety/estreatment of recognizances
CPD	III Custody and bail	14G	Bail during trial
CPD	III Custody and bail	14H	Crown Court judge's certification of fitness to appeal and applications to the Crown Court for bail pending appeal
CPD	IV Disclosure	15A	Disclosure of unused material
CPD	V Evidence	16A	Evidence by written statement
CPD	V Evidence	16B	Video recorded evidence in chief
CPD	V Evidence	16C	Evidence of audio and video recorded interviews
CPD	V Evidence	17A	Wards of Court and children subject to current Family proceedings
CPD	V Evidence	18A	Measures to assist a witness or defendant to give evidence
CPD	V Evidence	18B	Witnesses giving evidence by live link
CPD	V Evidence	18C	Visually recorded interviews: memory refreshing and watching at a different time from the jury
CPD	V Evidence	18D	Witness anonymity orders
CPD	V Evidence	18E	Use of s 28 Youth Justice and Criminal Evidence Act 1999; Pre-recording of cross-examination and re-examination for witnesses captured by s 16 YJCEA 1999
CPS	V Evidence	19A	Expert evidence
CPS	V Evidence	19B	Statements of understanding and declarations of truth in expert reports
CPS	V Evidence	19C	Pre-hearing discussion of expert evidence
CPD	V Evidence	21A	Spent convictions
CPD	V Evidence	22A	Use Of Ground Rules Hearing When Dealing With s 41 Youth Justice And Criminal Evidence Act 1999 (YJCEA 1999) Evidence Of Complainant's Previous Sexual Behaviour
CPD	V Evidence	23A	Cross-Examination Advocates
CPD	VI Trial	24A	Role of the justices' clerk/legal adviser
CPD	VI Trial	24B	Identification for the court of the issues in the case
CPD	VI Trial	25A	Identification for the jury of the issues in the case
CPD	VI Trial	26A	Juries: introduction
CPD	VI Trial	26B	Juries: preliminary matters arising before jury service commences
CPD	VI Trial	26C	Juries: eligibility
CPD	VI Trial	26D	Juries: precautionary measures before swearing
CPD	VI Trial	26E	Juries: swearing in jurors
CPD	VI Trial	26F	Juries: ensuring an effective jury panel
CPD	VI Trial	26G	Juries: preliminary instructions to jurors
CPD	VI Trial	26H	Juries: discharge of a juror for personal reasons
CPD	VI Trial	26J	Juries: views
CPD	VI Trial	26K	Juries: Directions, written materials and summing up
CPD	VI Trial	26L	Juries: jury access to exhibits and evidence in retirement
CPD	VI Trial	26M	Jury Irregularities
CPD	VI Trial	26N	Open justice
CPD	VI Trial	26P	Defendant's right to give or not to give evidence
CPD	VI Trial	26Q	Majority verdicts
CPD	VII Sentencing	A	Pleas of guilty in the Crown Court
CPD	VII Sentencing	B	Determining the factual basis of sentence
CPD	VII Sentencing	C	Indications of sentence: *R v Goodyear*

CPD	Division	CPD ref	Title of CPD, if applicable
CPD	VII Sentencing	D	Facts to be stated on pleas of guilty
CPD	VII Sentencing	E	Concurrent and consecutive sentences
CPD	VII Sentencing	F	Victim Personal Statements
CPD	VII Sentencing	G	Families bereaved by homicide and other criminal conduct
CPD	VII Sentencing	H	Community Impact Statements
CPD	VII Sentencing	I	Impact Statements for Businesses
CPD	VII Sentencing	J	Binding over orders and conditional discharges
CPD	VII Sentencing	K	Committal for sentence
CPD	VII Sentencing	L	Imposition of life sentences
CPD	VII Sentencing	M	Mandatory life sentences
CPD	VII Sentencing	N	Transitional arrangements for sentences where the offence was committed before 18 December 2003
CPD	VII Sentencing	P	Procedure for announcing the minimum term in open court
CPD	VII Sentencing	Q	Financial information required for sentencing
CPD	VII Sentencing	R	Medical reports for sentencing purposes
CPD	VIII Confiscation		[empty]
CPD	IX Appeal	34A	Appeals to the Crown Court
CPD	IX Appeal	39A	Appeals against conviction and sentence – the provision of notice to the prosecution
CPD	IX Appeal	39B	Listing of appeals against conviction and sentence in the Court of Appeal Criminal Division (CACD)
CPD	IX Appeal	39C	Appeal notices and grounds of appeal
CPD	IX Appeal	39D	Respondents' notices
CPD	IX Appeal	39E	Loss of time
CPD	IX Appeal	39F	Skeleton arguments
CPD	IX Appeal	39G	Criminal Appeal Office summaries
CPD	IX Appeal	44A	References to the European Court of Justice
CPD	X Costs		[Costs Practice Direction]
CPD	XI Other proceedings	47A	Investigation orders and warrants
CPD	XI Other proceedings	48A	Contempt in the face of the magistrates' court
CPD	XI Other proceedings	50A	Extradition: General matters and case management
CPD	XI Other proceedings	50B	Extradition; Management of Appeal to the High Court'
CPD	XI Other proceedings	50C	Extradition: Representation Orders
CPD	XI Other proceedings	50D	Extradition: Applications
CPD	XI Other proceedings	50E	Extradition: Court Papers
CPD	XI Other proceedings	50F	Extradition: Consequences of non compliance with directions
CPD	XII General application	A	Court dress
CPD	XII General application	B	Modes of address and titles of judges and magistrates
CPD	XII General application	C	Availability of judgments given in the Court of Appeal and the High Court
CPD	XII General application	D	Citation of authority and provision of copies of judgments to the Court
CPD	XII General application	E	Preparation of judgments: neutral citation
CPD	XII General application	F	Citation of Hansard
CPD	XIII Listing	A	Judicial responsibility and key principles
CPD	XIII Listing	B	Classification

A.1

I GENERAL MATTERS

THE OVERRIDING OBJECTIVE

A.1   The Lord Chief Justice has power, including power under section 74 of the Courts Act 2003 and Part 1 of Schedule 2 to the Constitutional Reform Act 2005, to give directions as to the practice and procedure of the criminal courts. The following directions are given accordingly.

A.2   These Practice Directions replace the Criminal Practice Directions given on 7th October, 2013 [2013] EWCA Crim 1631; [2013] 1 WLR 3164 as amended by the Directions given on (i) 10th December, 2013 [2013] EWCA Crim 2328; [2014] 1 WLR 35, (ii) 23rd July, 2014 [2014] EWCA Crim 1569; [2014] 1 WLR 3001, (iii) 18th March, 2015 [2015] EWCA Crim 430; [2015] 1 WLR 1643 and (iv) 16th July, 2015 [2015] EWCA Crim 1253; [2015] 1 WLR 3582, (No 2) [2016] EWCA Crim 1714, (No 3) [2017] EWCA Crim 30, (No 4) [2017] EWCA Crim 310, (No 5) [2017] EWCA Crim 1076 (Crim), (No 6) [2018] EWCA Crim 516 .

A.3   Annexes D and E to the Consolidated Criminal Practice Direction of 8th July, 2002, [2002] 1 W.L.R. 2870; [2002] 2 Cr. App. R. 35, as amended, which set out forms for use in connection with the Criminal Procedure Rules, remain in force. See also paragraph I 5A of these Practice Directions.

A.4   These Practice Directions supplement many, but not all, Parts of the Criminal Procedure Rules, and include other directions about practice and procedure in the courts to which they apply. They are to be known as the Criminal Practice Directions 2015. They come into force on 5th October, 2015. They apply to all cases in all the criminal courts of England and Wales from that date.

A.5   Consequent on the rearrangement of the Criminal Procedure Rules in the Criminal Procedure Rules 2015, SI 2015/1490:

(a)   the content of these Practice Directions is arranged to correspond. Within each division of these Directions the paragraphs are numbered to correspond with the associated Part of the Criminal Procedure Rules 2015. Compared with the Criminal Practice Directions given in 2013, as amended, the numbering and content of some divisions is amended consequentially, as shown in this table:

Derivations	
Divisions of 2015 Directions	*Divisions of 2013 Directions*
I General matters	I General matters; II Preliminary proceedings 16A – C
II Preliminary proceedings	II Preliminary proceedings 9A, 10A, 14A – B
III Custody and bail	III Custody and bail
IV Disclosure	IV Disclosure
V Evidence	V Evidence
VI Trial	VI Trial
VII Sentencing	VII Sentencing
VIII Confiscation and related proceedings [empty]	VIII Confiscation and related proceedings [empty]
IX Appeal	X Appeal
X Costs [Criminal Costs Practice Direction]	XI Costs [Criminal Costs Practice Direction]
XI Other proceedings	II Preliminary proceedings 6A, 17A – F; IX Contempt of court
XII General application	XII General application
XIII Listing	XIII Listing

(b)   the text of these Practice Directions is amended:
     (i)   to bring up to date the cross-references to the Criminal Procedure Rules and to other paragraphs of these Directions which that text contains, and
     (ii)   to adopt the abbreviation of references to the Criminal Procedure Rules ('CrimPR') for which rule 2.3(2) of the Criminal Procedure Rules 2015 provides.

A.6   In all other respects, the content of the Criminal Practice Directions 2015 reproduces that of the Criminal Practice Directions 2013, as amended.

CRIMPR PART 1 THE OVERRIDING OBJECTIVE

CPD I General matters 1A: The overriding objective

1A.1   The presumption of innocence and an adversarial process are essential features of English and Welsh legal tradition and of the defendant's right to a fair trial. But it is no part of a fair trial that questions of guilt and innocence should be determined by procedural manoeuvres. On the contrary, fairness is best served when the issues between the parties are identified as early and as clearly as possible. As Lord Justice Auld noted, a criminal trial is not a game under which a guilty defendant should be provided with a sporting chance. It is a search for truth in accordance with the twin principles that the prosecution must prove its case and that a defendant is not obliged to inculpate himself, the object being to convict the guilty and acquit the innocent.

1A.2   Further, it is not just for a party to obstruct or delay the preparation of a case for trial in order to secure some perceived procedural advantage, or to take unfair advantage of a mistake by someone else. If courts allow that to happen it damages public confidence in criminal justice. The Rules and the Practice Directions, taken together, make it clear that courts must not allow it to happen.

CRIMPR PART 3 CASE MANAGEMENT

CPD I General matters 3A: Case management

3A.1 CrimPR 1.1(2)(e) requires that cases be dealt with efficiently and expeditiously. CrimPR 3.2 requires the court to further the overriding objective by actively managing the case, for example:

(a) When dealing with an offence which is triable only on indictment the court must ask the defendant whether he or she intends to plead guilty at the Crown Court (CrimPR 9.7(5));
(b) On a guilty plea, the court must pass sentence at the earliest opportunity, in accordance with CrimPR 24.11(9)(a) (magistrates' courts) and 25.16(7)(a) (the Crown Court).

3A.2 Given these duties, magistrates' courts and the Crown Court therefore will proceed as described in paragraphs 3A.3 to 3A.28 below. The parties will be expected to have prepared in accordance with CrimPR 3.3(1) to avoid unnecessary and wasted hearings. They will be expected to have communicated with each other by the time of the first hearing; to report to the court on that communication at the first hearing; and to continue thereafter to communicate with each other and with the court officer, in accordance with CrimPR 3.3(2).

3A.3 There is a Preparation for Effective Trial form for use in the magistrates' courts, and a Plea and Trial Preparation Hearing form for use in the Crown Court, each of which must be used as appropriate in connection with CrimPR Part 3: see paragraph 5A.2 of these Practice Directions. Versions of those forms in pdf and Word, together with guidance notes, are available on the Criminal Procedure Rules pages of the Ministry of Justice website.

Case progression and trial preparation in magistrates' courts

3A.4 CrimPR 8.3 applies in all cases and requires the prosecutor to serve:

(i) a summary of the circumstances of the offence;
(ii) any account given by the defendant in interview, whether contained in that summary or in another document;
(iii) any written witness statement or exhibit that the prosecutor then has available and considers material to plea or to the allocation of the case for trial or sentence;
(iv) a list of the defendant's criminal record, if any; and
(v) any available statement of the effect of the offence on a victim, a victim's family or others.

The details must include sufficient information to allow the defendant and the court at the first hearing to take an informed view:

(i) on plea;
(ii) on venue for trial (if applicable);
(iii) for the purposes of case management; or
(iv) for the purposes of sentencing (including committal for sentence, if applicable).

Defendant in custody

3A.5 If the defendant has been detained in custody after being charged with an offence which is indictable only or triable either way, at the first hearing a magistrates' court will proceed at once with the allocation of the case for trial, where appropriate, and, if so required, with the sending of the defendant to the Crown Court for trial. The court will be expected to ask for and record any indication of plea and issues for trial to assist the Crown Court.

3A.6 If the offence charged is triable only summarily, or if at that hearing the case is allocated for summary trial, the court will forthwith give such directions as are necessary, either (on a guilty plea) to prepare for sentencing, or for a trial.

Defendant on bail

3A.7 If the defendant has been released on bail after being charged, the case must be listed for the first hearing 14 days after charge, or the next available court date thereafter when the prosecutor anticipates a guilty plea which is likely to be sentenced in the magistrates' court. In cases where there is an anticipated not guilty plea or the case is likely to be sent or committed to the Crown Court for either trial or sentence, then it must be listed for the first hearing 28 days after charge or the next available court date thereafter.

Guilty plea in the magistrates' courts

3A.8 Where a defendant pleads guilty or indicates a guilty plea in a magistrates' court the court should consider whether a pre-sentence report – a stand down report if possible – is necessary.

Guilty plea in the Crown Court

3A.9 Where a magistrates' court is considering committal for sentence or the defendant has indicated an intention to plead guilty in a matter which is to be sent to the Crown Court, the magistrates' court should request the preparation of a pre-sentence report for the Crown Court's use if the magistrates' court considers that:

(a) there is a realistic alternative to a custodial sentence; or
(b) the defendant may satisfy the criteria for classification as a dangerous offender; or
(c) there is some other appropriate reason for doing so.

3A.10 When a magistrates' court sends a case to the Crown Court for trial and the defendant indicates an intention to plead guilty at the Crown Court, then that magistrates' court must set a date for a Plea and Trial Preparation Hearing at the Crown Court, in accordance with CrimPR 9.7(5)(a)(i).

Case sent for Crown Court trial: no indication of guilty plea

3A.11 In any case sent to the Crown Court for trial, other than one in which the defendant indicates an intention to plead guilty, the magistrates' court must set a date for a Plea and Trial

Preparation Hearing, in accordance with CrimPR 9.7(5)(a)(ii). The Plea and Trial Preparation Hearing must be held within 28 days of sending, unless the standard directions of the Presiding Judges of the circuit direct otherwise. Paragraph 3A.16 below additionally applies to the arrangements for such hearings. A magistrates' court may give other directions appropriate to the needs of the case, in accordance with CrimPR 3.5(3), and in accordance with any standard directions issued by the Presiding Judges of the circuit.

Defendant on bail: anticipated not guilty plea

3A.12 Where the defendant has been released on bail after being charged, and where the prosecutor does not anticipate a guilty plea at the first hearing in a magistrates' court, then it is essential that the initial details of the prosecution case that are provided for that first hearing are sufficient to assist the court, in order to identify the real issues and to give appropriate directions for an effective trial (regardless of whether the trial is to be heard in the magistrates' court or the Crown Court). In these circumstances, unless there is good reason not to do so, the prosecution should make available the following material in advance of the first hearing in the magistrates' court:

- (a) A summary of the circumstances of the offence(s) including a summary of any account given by the defendant in interview;
- (b) Statements and exhibits that the prosecution has identified as being of importance for the purpose of plea or initial case management, including any relevant CCTV that would be relied upon at trial and any Streamlined Forensic Report;
- (c) Details of witness availability, as far as they are known at that hearing;
- (d) Defendant's criminal record;
- (e) Victim Personal Statements if provided;
- (f) An indication of any medical or other expert evidence that the prosecution is likely to adduce in relation to a victim or the defendant;
- (g) Any information as to special measures, bad character or hearsay, where applicable.

3A.13 In addition to the material required by CrimPR Part 8, the information required by the Preparation for Effective Trial form must be available to be submitted at the first hearing, and the parties must complete that form, in accordance with the guidance published with it. Where there is to be a contested trial in a magistrates' court, that form includes directions and a timetable that will apply in every case unless the court otherwise orders.

3A.14 Nothing in paragraph 3A.12-3A.13 shall preclude the court from taking a plea pursuant to CrimPR 3.9(2)(b) at the first hearing and for the court to case manage as far as practicable under Part 3 CrimPR.

Exercise of magistrates' court's powers

3A.15 In accordance with CrimPR 9.1, sections 49, 51(13) and 51A(11) of the Crime and Disorder Act 1998, and sections 17E, 18(5) and 24D of the Magistrates' Courts Act 1980 a single justice can:

- (a) allocate and send for trial;
- (b) take an indication of a guilty plea (but not pass sentence);
- (c) take a not guilty plea and give directions for the preparation of trial including:
    - (i) timetable for the proceedings;
    - (ii) the attendance of the parties;
    - (iii) the service of documents;
    - (iv) the manner in which evidence is to be given.

Case progression and trial preparation in the Crown Court

Plea and Trial Preparation Hearing

3A.16 In a case in which a magistrates' court has directed a Plea and Trial Preparation Hearing, the period which elapses between sending for trial and the date of that hearing must be consistent within each circuit. In every case, the time allowed for the conduct of the Plea and Trial Preparation Hearing must be sufficient for effective trial preparation. It is expected in every case that an indictment will be lodged at least 7 days in advance of the hearing. Please see the Note to the Practice Direction.

3A.17 In a case in which the defendant, not having done so before, indicates an intention to plead guilty to his representative after being sent for trial but before the Plea and Trial Preparation Hearing, the defence representative will notify the Crown Court and the prosecution forthwith. The court will ensure there is sufficient time at the Plea and Trial Preparation Hearing for sentence and a Judge should at once request the preparation of a pre-sentence report if it appears to the court that either:

- (a) there is a realistic alternative to a custodial sentence; or
- (b) the defendant may satisfy the criteria for classification as a dangerous offender; or
- (c) there is some other appropriate reason for doing so.

3A.18 If at the Plea and Trial Preparation Hearing the defendant pleads guilty and no pre-sentence report has been prepared, if possible the court should obtain a stand down report.

3A.19 Where the defendant was remanded in custody after being charged and was sent for trial without initial details of the prosecution case having been served, then at least 7 days before the Plea and Trial Preparation Hearing the prosecutor should serve, as a minimum, the material identified in paragraph 3A.12 above. If at the Plea and Trial Preparation Hearing the defendant does not plead guilty, the court will be expected to identify the issues in the case and give appropriate directions for an effective trial. Please see the Note to the Practice Direction.

3A.20 At the Plea and Trial Preparation Hearing, in addition to the material required by paragraph 3A.12 above, the prosecutor must serve sufficient evidence to enable the court to case manage effectively without the need for a further case management hearing, unless the case falls within paragraph 3A.21. In addition, the information required by the Plea and Trial Preparation Hearing form must be available to the court at that hearing, and it must have been discussed between the parties in advance. The prosecutor must provide details of the availability of likely prosecution witnesses so that a trial date can immediately be arranged if the defendant does not plead guilty.

Further case management hearing

3A.21 In accordance with CrimPR 3.13(1)(c), after the Plea and Trial Preparation Hearing there will be no further case management hearing before the trial unless:

(i)   a condition listed in that rule is met; and
(ii)   the court so directs, in order to further the overriding objective.

The directions to be given at the Plea and Trial Preparation Hearing therefore may include a direction for a further case management hearing, but usually will do so only in one of the following cases:

(a)   Class 1 cases;
(b)   Class 2 cases which carry a maximum penalty of 10 years or more;
(c)   cases involving death by driving (whether dangerous or careless), or death in the work-place;
(d)   cases involving a vulnerable witness;
(e)   cases in which the defendant is a child or otherwise under a disability, or requires special assistance;
(f)   cases in which there is a corporate or unrepresented defendant;
(g)   cases in which the expected trial length is such that a further case management hearing is desirable and any case in which the trial is likely to last longer than four weeks;
(h)   cases in which expert evidence is to be introduced;
(i)   cases in which a party requests a hearing to enter a plea;
(j)   cases in which an application to dismiss or stay has been made;
(k)   cases in which arraignment has not taken place, whether because of an issue relating to fitness to plead, or abuse of process or sufficiency of evidence, or for any other reason;
(l)   cases in which there are likely to be linked criminal and care directions in accordance with the 2013 Protocol.

3A.22 If a further case management hearing is directed, a defendant in custody will not usually be expected to attend in person, unless the court otherwise directs.

Compliance hearing

3A.23 If a party fails to comply with a case management direction, that party may be required to attend the court to explain the failure. Unless the court otherwise directs a defendant in custody will not usually be expected to attend. See paragraph 3A.26-3A.28 below.

Conduct of case progression hearings

3A.24 As far as possible, case progression should be managed without a hearing in the courtroom, using electronic communication in accordance with CrimPR 3.5(2)(d). Court staff should be nominated to conduct case progression as part of their role, in accordance with CrimPR 3.4(2). To aid effective communication the prosecution and defence representative should notify the court and provide details of who shall be dealing with the case at the earliest opportunity.

Completion of Effective Trial Monitoring form

3A.25 It is imperative that the Effective Trial Monitoring form (as devised and issued by Her Majesty's Courts and Tribunals Service) is accurately completed by the parties for all cases that have been listed for trial. Advocates must engage with the process by providing the relevant details and completing the form.

Compliance courts

3A.26 To ensure effective compliance with directions of the courts made in accordance with the Criminal Procedure Rules and the overriding objective, courts should maintain a record whenever a party to the proceedings has failed to comply with a direction made by the court. The parties may have to attend a hearing to explain any lack of compliance.

3A.27 These hearings may be conducted by live link facilities or via other electronic means, as the court may direct.

3A.28 It will be for the Presiding Judges, Resident Judge and Justices' Clerks to decide locally how often compliance courts should be held, depending on the scale and nature of the problem at each court centre.

Note to the Practice Direction

In 3A.16 and 3A.19 the reference to 'at least 7 days' in advance of the hearing is necessitated by the fact that, for the time being, different circuits have different timescales for the Plea and Trial Preparation Hearing. Had this not been so, the paragraphs would have been drafted forward from the date of sending rather than backwards from the date of the Plea and Trial Preparation Hearing.

CPD General matters 3B: Pagination and Indexing of Served Evidence

3B.1 The following directions apply to matters before the Crown Court, where

(a)   there is an application to prefer a bill of indictment in relation to the case;
(b)   a person is sent for trial under section 51 of the Crime and Disorder Act 1998 (sending cases to the Crown Court), to the service of copies of the documents containing the evidence on which the charge or charges are based under Paragraph 1 of Schedule 3 to that Act; or
(c)   a defendant wishes to serve evidence.

3B.2 A party who serves documentary evidence in the Crown Court should:

(a)   paginate each page in any bundle of statements and exhibits sequentially;
(b)   provide an index to each bundle of statements produced including the following information:

     (i)   the name of the case;
     (ii)   the author of each statement;
     (iii) the start page number of the witness statement;
     (iv) the end page number of the witness statement.
  (c)   provide an index to each bundle of documentary and pictorial exhibits produced, including the following information:
     (i)   the name of the case
     (ii)   the exhibit reference;
     (iii) a short description of the exhibit;
     (iv) the start page number of the exhibit;
     (v)   the end page number of the exhibit;
     (vi) where possible, the name of the person producing the exhibit should be added.

3B.3   Where additional documentary evidence is served, a party should paginate following on from the last page of the previous bundle or in a logical and sequential manner. A party should also provide notification of service of any amended index.

3B.4   The prosecution must ensure that the running total of the pages of prosecution evidence is easily identifiable on the most recent served bundle of prosecution evidence.

3B.5   For the purposes of these directions, the number of pages of prosecution evidence served on the court includes all

  (a)   witness statements;
  (b)   documentary and pictorial exhibits;
  (c)   records of interviews with the defendant; and
  (d)   records of interviews with other defendants which form part of the served prosecution documents or which are included in any notice of additional evidence,

but does not include any document provided on CD-ROM or by other means of electronic communication.

CPD I General matters 3C: Abuse of process stay applications

3C.1   In all cases where a defendant in the Crown Court proposes to make an application to stay an indictment on the grounds of abuse of process, written notice of such application must be given to the prosecuting authority and to any co-defendant as soon as practicable after the defendant becomes aware of the grounds for doing so and not later than 14 days before the date fixed or warned for trial ("the relevant date"). Such notice must:

  (a)   give the name of the case and the indictment number;
  (b)   state the fixed date or the warned date as appropriate;
  (c)   specify the nature of the application;
  (d)   set out in numbered sub-paragraphs the grounds upon which the application is to be made;
  (e)   be copied to the chief listing officer at the court centre where the case is due to be heard.

3C.2   Any co-defendant who wishes to make a like application must give a like notice not later than seven days before the relevant date, setting out any additional grounds relied upon.

3C.3   In relation to such applications, the following automatic directions shall apply:

  (a)   the advocate for the applicant(s) must lodge with the court and serve on all other parties a skeleton argument in support of the application, at least five clear working days before the relevant date. If reference is to be made to any document not in the existing trial documents, a paginated and indexed bundle of such documents is to be provided with the skeleton argument;
  (b)   the advocate for the prosecution must lodge with the court and serve on all other parties a responsive skeleton argument at least two clear working days before the relevant date, together with a supplementary bundle if appropriate.

3C.4   Paragraphs XII D.17 to D.23 of these Practice Directions set out the general requirements for skeleton arguments. All skeleton arguments must specify any propositions of law to be advanced (together with the authorities relied upon in support, with paragraph references to passages relied upon) and, where appropriate, include a chronology of events and a list of dramatis personae. In all instances where reference is made to a document, the reference in the trial documents or supplementary bundle is to be given.

3C.5   The above time limits are minimum time limits. In appropriate cases, the court will order longer lead times. To this end, in all cases where defence advocates are, at the time of the preliminary hearing or as soon as practicable after the case has been sent, considering the possibility of an abuse of process application, this must be raised with the judge dealing with the matter, who will order a different timetable if appropriate, and may wish, in any event, to give additional directions about the conduct of the application. If the trial judge has not been identified, the matter should be raised with the Resident Judge.

CPD I General matters 3D: Vulnerable people in the courts

3D.1   In respect of eligibility for special measures, 'vulnerable' and 'intimidated' witnesses are defined in sections 16 and 17 of the Youth Justice and Criminal Evidence Act 1999 (as amended by the Coroners and Justice Act 2009); 'vulnerable' includes those under 18 years of age and people with a mental disorder or learning disability; a physical disorder or disability; or who are likely to suffer fear or distress in giving evidence because of their own circumstances or those relating to the case.

3D.2   However, many other people giving evidence in a criminal case, whether as a witness or defendant, may require assistance: the court is required to take 'every reasonable step' to encourage and facilitate the attendance of witnesses and to facilitate the participation of any person, including the defendant (CrimPR 3.9(3)(a) and (b)). This includes enabling a witness or defendant to give their best evidence, and enabling a defendant to comprehend the proceedings and engage fully with his or her defence. The pre-trial and trial process should, so far as necessary, be adapted to meet those ends. Regard should be had to the welfare of a young defendant as required by section 44 of the Children and Young Persons Act 1933, and generally to Parts 1 and 3 of the Criminal Procedure Rules (the overriding objective and the court's powers of case management).

3D.3   Under Part 3 of the Rules, the court must identify the needs of witnesses at an early stage (CrimPR 3.2(2)(b)) and may require the parties to identify arrangements to facilitate the giving of evidence and participation in the trial (CrimPR 3.11(c)(iv) and (v)). There are various statutory special measures that the court may utilise to assist a witness in giving evidence. CrimPR Part 18 gives the procedures to be followed. Courts should note the 'primary rule' which requires the court to give a direction for a special measure to assist a child witness or qualifying witness and that in such cases an application to the court is not required (CrimPR 18.9).

3D.4   Court of Appeal decisions on this subject include a judgment from the Lord Chief Justice, Lord Judge in *R v Cox* [2012] EWCA Crim 549, [2012] 2 Cr. App. R. 6; *R v Wills* [2011] EWCA Crim 1938, [2012] 1 Cr. App. R. 2; and *R v E* [2011] EWCA Crim 3028, [2012] Crim L.R. 563.

3D.5   In *R v Wills*, the Court endorsed the approach taken by the report of the Advocacy Training Council (ATC) 'Raising the Bar: the Handling of Vulnerable Witnesses, Victims and Defendants in Court' (2011). The report includes and recommends the use of 'toolkits' to assist advocates as they prepare to question vulnerable people at court:

http://www.advocacytrainingcouncil.org/vulnerable-witnesses/raising-the-bar

3D.6   Further toolkits are available through the Advocate's Gateway which is managed by the ATC's Management Committee:

http://www.theadvocatesgateway.org/

3D.7   These toolkits represent best practice. Advocates should consult and follow the relevant guidance whenever they prepare to question a young or otherwise vulnerable witness or defendant. Judges may find it helpful to refer advocates to this material and to use the toolkits in case management.

3D.8   'Achieving Best Evidence in Criminal Proceedings' (Ministry of Justice 2011) describes best practice in preparation for the investigative interview and trial:

http://www.cps.gov.uk/publications/docs/best_evidence_in_criminal_proceedings.pdf

CPD I General matters 3E: Ground rules hearings to plan the questioning of a vulnerable witness or defendant

3E.1   The judiciary is responsible for controlling questioning. Over-rigorous or repetitive cross-examination of a child or vulnerable witness should be stopped. Intervention by the judge, magistrates or intermediary (if any) is minimised if questioning, taking account of the individual's communication needs, is discussed in advance and ground rules are agreed and adhered to.

3E.2   Discussion of ground rules is required in all intermediary trials where they must be discussed between the judge or magistrates, advocates and intermediary before the witness gives evidence. The intermediary must be present but is not required to take the oath (the intermediary's declaration is made just before the witness gives evidence).

3E.3   Discussion of ground rules is good practice, even if no intermediary is used, in all young witness cases and in other cases where a witness or defendant has communication needs. Discussion before the day of trial is preferable to give advocates time to adapt their questions to the witness's needs. It may be helpful for a trial practice note of boundaries to be created at the end of the discussion. The judge may use such a document in ensuring that the agreed ground rules are complied with.

3E.4   All witnesses, including the defendant and defence witnesses, should be enabled to give the best evidence they can. In relation to young and/or vulnerable people, this may mean departing radically from traditional cross-examination. The form and extent of appropriate cross-examination will vary from case to case. For adult non vulnerable witnesses an advocate will usually put his case so that the witness will have the opportunity of commenting upon it and/or answering it. When the witness is young or otherwise vulnerable, the court may dispense with the normal practice and impose restrictions on the advocate 'putting his case' where there is a risk of a young or otherwise vulnerable witness failing to understand, becoming distressed or acquiescing to leading questions. Where limitations on questioning are necessary and appropriate, they must be clearly defined. The judge has a duty to ensure that they are complied with and should explain them to the jury and the reasons for them. If the advocate fails to comply with the limitations, the judge should give relevant directions to the jury when that occurs and prevent further questioning that does not comply with the ground rules settled upon in advance. Instead of commenting on inconsistencies during cross-examination, following discussion between the judge and the advocates, the advocate or judge may point out important inconsistencies after (instead of during) the witness's evidence. The judge should also remind the jury of these during summing up. The judge should be alert to alleged inconsistencies that are not in fact inconsistent, or are trivial.

3E.5   If there is more than one defendant, the judge should not permit each advocate to repeat the questioning of a vulnerable witness. In advance of the trial, the advocates should divide the topics between them, with the advocate for the first defendant leading the questioning, and the advocate(s) for the other defendant(s) asking only ancillary questions relevant to their client's case, without repeating the questioning that has already taken place on behalf of the other defendant(s).

3E.6   In particular in a trial of a sexual offence, 'body maps' should be provided for the witness' use. If the witness needs to indicate a part of the body, the advocate should ask the witness to point to the relevant part on the body map. In sex cases, judges should not permit advocates to ask the witness to point to a part of the witness' own body. Similarly, photographs of the witness' body should not be shown around the court while the witness is giving evidence.

CPD I General matters 3F: Intermediaries

Role and functions of intermediaries in criminal courts

3F.1   Intermediaries facilitate communication with witnesses and defendants who have communication needs. Their primary function is to improve the quality of evidence and aid understanding between the court, the advocates and the witness or defendant. For example, they commonly advise on the formulation of questions so as to avoid misunderstanding. On occasion, they actively assist and intervene during questioning. The extent to which they do so (if at all) depends on factors such as the communication needs of the witness or defendant, and the skills of the advocates in adapting their language and questioning style to meet those needs.

3F.2	Intermediaries are independent of parties and owe their duty to the court. The court and parties should be vigilant to ensure they act impartially and their assistance to witnesses and defendants is transparent. It is however permissible for an advocate to have a private consultation with an intermediary when formulating questions (although control of questioning remains the overall responsibility of the court).

3F.3	Further information is in *Intermediaries: Step by Step* (Toolkit 16; The Advocate's Gateway, 2015) and chapter 5 of the *Equal Treatment Bench Book* (Judicial College, 2013).

Links to publications

- www.theadvocatesgateway.org/images/toolkits/16intermediariesstepbystep060315.pdf
- www.judiciary.gov.uk/wp-content/uploads/2013/11/5-children-and-vulnerable-adults.pdf

Assessment

3F.4	The process of appointment should begin with assessment by an intermediary and a report. The report will make recommendations to address the communication needs of the witness or defendant during trial.

3F.5	In light of the scarcity of intermediaries, the appropriateness of assessment must be decided with care to ensure their availability for those witnesses and defendants who are most in need. The decision should be made on an individual basis, in the context of the circumstances of the particular case.

Intermediaries for prosecution and defence witnesses

3F.6	IIntermediaries are one of the special measures available to witnesses under the Youth Justice and Criminal Evidence Act 1999 (YJCEA 1999). Witnesses deemed vulnerable in accordance with the criteria in s.16 YJCEA are eligible for the assistance of an intermediary when giving evidence pursuant to s.29 YJCEA 1999. These provisions do not apply to defendants.

3F.7	An application for an intermediary to assist a witness when giving evidence must be made in accordance with Part 18 of the Criminal Procedure Rules. In addition, where an intermediary report is available (see 3F.4 above), it should be provided with the application.

3F.8	The Witness Intermediary Scheme (WIS) operated by the National Crime Agency identifies intermediaries for witnesses and may be used by the prosecution and defence. The WIS is contactable at wit@nca.x.gsi.gov.uk / 0845 000 5463. An intermediary appointed through the WIS is defined as a 'Registered Intermediary' and matched to the particular witness based on expertise, location and availability. Registered Intermediaries are accredited by the WIS and bound by Codes of Practice and Ethics issued by the Ministry of Justice (which oversees the WIS).

3F.9	Having identified a Registered Intermediary, the WIS does not provide funding. The party appointing the Registered Intermediary is responsible for payment at rates specified by the Ministry of Justice.

3F.10	Further information is in *The Registered Intermediaries Procedural Guidance Manual* (Ministry of Justice, 2015) and Intermediaries: Step by Step (see 3F.3 above).

Link to publication

- www.theadvocatesgateway.org/images/procedures/
registered-intermediary-procedural-guidance-manual.pdf

Intermediaries for defendants

3F.11	Statutory provisions providing for defendants to be assisted by an intermediary when giving evidence (where necessary to ensure a fair trial) are not in force (because s.104 Coroners and Justice Act 2009, which would insert ss. 33BA and 33BB into the YJCEA 1999, has yet to be commenced).

3F.12	The court may direct the appointment of an intermediary to assist a defendant in reliance on its inherent powers (*C v Sevenoaks Youth Court* [2009] EWHC 3088 (Admin)). There is however no presumption that a defendant will be so assisted and, even where an intermediary would improve the trial process, appointment is not mandatory (*R v Cox* [2012] EWCA Crim 549). The court should adapt the trial process to address a defendant's communication needs (*R v Cox* [2012] EWCA Crim 549). It will rarely exercise its inherent powers to direct appointment of an intermediary but where a defendant is vulnerable or for some other reason experiences communication or hearing difficulties, such that he or she needs more help to follow the proceedings than her or his legal representatives readily can give having regard to their other functions on the defendant's behalf, then the court should consider sympathetically any application for the defendant to be accompanied throughout the trial by a support worker or other appropriate companion who can provide that assistance. This is consistent with CrimPR 3.9(3)(b) (see paragraph 3D.2 above); consistent with the observations in R v Cox (see paragraph 3D.4 above), *R (OP) v Ministry of Justice* [2014] EWHC 1944 (Admin) and *R v Rashid* [2017] EWCA Crim 2; and consistent with the arrangements contemplated at paragraph 3G.8 below.

3F.13	The court may exercise its inherent powers to direct appointment of an intermediary to assist a defendant giving evidence or for the entire trial. Terms of appointment are for the court and there is no illogicality in restricting the appointment to the defendant's evidence (*R v R* [2015] EWCA Crim 1870), when the 'most pressing need' arises (I [2014] EWHC 1944 (Admin)). Directions to appoint an intermediary for a defendant's evidence will thus be rare, but for the entire trial extremely rare keeping in mind paragraph 3F.12 above.

3F.14	An application for an intermediary to assist a defendant must be made in accordance with Part 18 of the Criminal Procedure Rules. In addition, where an intermediary report is available (see 3F.4 above), it should be provided with the application.

3F.15	The WIS is not presently available to identify intermediaries for defendants (although in OP v Secretary of State for Justice [2014] EWHC 1944 (Admin), the Ministry of Justice was ordered to consider carefully whether it were justifiable to refuse equal provision to witnesses and defendants with respect to their evidence). 'Non-registered intermediaries' (intermediaries appointed other than through the WIS) must therefore be appointed for defendants. Although training is available, there is no accreditation process for non-registered intermediaries and rates of payment are unregulated.

3F.16 Arrangements for funding of intermediaries for defendants depend on the stage of the appointment process. Where the defendant is publicly funded, an application should be made to the Legal Aid Agency for prior authority to fund a pre-trial assessment. If the application is refused, an application may be made to the court to use its inherent powers to direct a pre-trial assessment and funding thereof. Where the court uses its inherent powers to direct assistance by an intermediary at trial (during evidence or for the entire trial), court staff are responsible for arranging payment from Central Funds. Internal guidance for court staff is in *Guidance for HMCTS Staff: Registered and Non-Registered Intermediaries for Vulnerable Defendants and Non-Vulnerable Defence and Prosecution Witnesses* (Her Majesty's Courts and Tribunals Service, 2014).

3F.17 The court should be satisfied that a non-registered intermediary has expertise suitable to meet the defendant's communication needs.

3F.18 Further information is in *Intermediaries: Step by Step* (see 3F.3 above).

Ineffective directions for intermediaries to assist defendants

3F.19 Directions for intermediaries to help defendants may be ineffective due to general unavailability, lack of suitable expertise, or non-availability for the purpose directed (for example, where the direction is for assistance during evidence, but an intermediary will only accept appointment for the entire trial).

3F.20 Intermediaries may contribute to the administration of justice by facilitating communication with appropriate defendants during the trial process. A trial will not be rendered unfair because a direction to appoint an intermediary for the defendant is ineffective. 'It would, in fact, be a most unusual case for a defendant who is fit to plead to be so disadvantaged by his condition that a properly brought prosecution would have to be stayed' because an intermediary with suitable expertise is not available for the purpose directed by the court (*R v Cox* [2012] EWCA Crim 549).

3F.21 Faced with an ineffective direction, it remains the court's responsibility to adapt the trial process to address the defendant's communication needs, as was the case prior to the existence of intermediaries (*R v Cox* [2012] EWCA Crim 549). In such a case, a ground rules hearing should be convened to ensure every reasonable step is taken to facilitate the defendant's participation in accordance with CrimPR 3.9. At the hearing, the court should make new, further and / or alternative directions. This includes setting ground rules to help the defendant follow proceedings and (where applicable) to give evidence.

3F.22 For example, to help the defendant follow proceedings the court may require evidence to be adduced by simple questions, with witnesses being asked to answer in short sentences. Regular breaks may assist the defendant's concentration and enable the defence advocate to summarise the evidence and take further instructions.

3F.23 Further guidance is available in publications such as Ground Rules Hearings and the Fair Treatment of Vulnerable People in Court (Toolkit 1; The Advocate's Gateway, 2015) and General Principles from Research - Planning to Question a Vulnerable Person or Someone with Communication Needs (Toolkit 2(a); The Advocate's Gateway, 2015). In the absence of an intermediary, these publications include information on planning how to manage the participation and questioning of the defendant, and the formulation of questions to avert misunderstanding (for example, by avoiding 'long and complicated questions . . . posed in a leading or 'tagged' manner' (*R v Wills* [2011] EWCA Crim 1938, [2012] 1 Cr App R 2))

Links to publications

- www.theadvocatesgateway.org/images/toolkits/
  1groundruleshearingsandthefairtreatmentofvulnerablepeopleincourt060315.pdf
- www.theadvocatesgateway.org/images/toolkits/2generalprinciplesfromresearchpolicyand
  guidance-planningtoquestionavulnerablepersonorsomeonewith
  communicationneeds141215.pdf

Intermediaries for witnesses and defendants under 18

3F.24 Communication needs (such as short attention span, suggestibility and reticence in relation to authority figures) are common to many witnesses and defendants under 18. Consideration should therefore be given to the communication needs of all children and young people appearing in the criminal courts and to adapting the trial process to address any such needs. Guidance is available in publications such as *Planning to Question a Child or Young Person* (Toolkit 6; The Advocate's Gateway, 2015) and *Effective Participation of Young Defendants* (Toolkit 8; The Advocate's Gateway, 2013).

Links to publications

- http://www.theadvocatesgateway.org/images/toolkits/
  6planningtoquestionachildoryoungperson141215.pdf
- http://www.theadvocatesgateway.org/images/toolkits/8YoungDefendants211013.pdf

3F.25 For the reasons set out in 3F.5 above, the appropriateness of an intermediary assessment for witnesses and defendants under 18 must be decided with care. Whilst there is no presumption that they will be assessed by an intermediary (to evaluate their communication needs prior to trial) or assisted by an intermediary at court (for example, if / when giving evidence), the decision should be made on an individual basis in the context of the circumstances of the particular case.

3F.26 Assessment by an intermediary should be considered for witnesses and defendants under 18 who seem liable to misunderstand questions or to experience difficulty expressing answers, including those who seem unlikely to be able to recognise a problematic question (such as one that is misleading or not readily understood), and those who may be reluctant to tell a questioner in a position of authority if they do not understand.

Attendance at ground rules hearing

3F.27 Where the court directs questioning will be conducted through an intermediary, CrimPR 3.9 requires the court to set ground rules. The intermediary should be present at the ground rules hearing to make representations in accordance with CrimPR 3.9(7)(a).

Listing

3F.28 Where the court directs an intermediary will attend the trial, their dates of availability should be provided to the court. It is preferable that such trials are fixed rather than placed in warned lists.

Photographs of court facilities

3F.29 Resident Judges in the Crown Court or the Chief Clerk or other responsible person in the magistrates' courts should, in consultation with HMCTS managers responsible for court security matters, develop a policy to govern under what circumstances photographs or other visual recordings may be made of court facilities, such as a live link room, to assist vulnerable or child witnesses to familiarise themselves with the setting, so as to be enabled to give their best evidence. For example, a photograph may provide a helpful reminder to a witness whose court visit has taken place sometime earlier. Resident Judges should tend to permit photographs to be taken for this purpose by intermediaries or supporters, subject to whatever restrictions the Resident Judge or responsible person considers to be appropriate, having regard to the security requirements of the court.

CPD I General matters 3G: Vulnerable defendants

Before the trial, sentencing or appeal

3G.1 If a vulnerable defendant, especially one who is young, is to be tried jointly with one who is not, the court should consider at the plea and case management hearing, or at a case management hearing in a magistrates' court, whether the vulnerable defendant should be tried on his own, but should only so order if satisfied that a fair trial cannot be achieved by use of appropriate special measures or other support for the defendant. If a vulnerable defendant is tried jointly with one who is not, the court should consider whether any of the modifications set out in this direction should apply in the circumstances of the joint trial and, so far as practicable, make orders to give effect to any such modifications.

3G.2 It may be appropriate to arrange that a vulnerable defendant should visit, out of court hours and before the trial, sentencing or appeal hearing, the courtroom in which that hearing is to take place so that he or she can familiarise him or herself with it.

3G.3 Where an intermediary is being used to help the defendant to communicate at court, the intermediary should accompany the defendant on his or her pre-trial visit. The visit will enable the defendant to familiarise him or herself with the layout of the court, and may include matters such as: where the defendant will sit, either in the dock or otherwise; court officials (what their roles are and where they sit); who else might be in the court, for example those in the public gallery and press box; the location of the witness box; basic court procedure; and the facilities available in the court.

3G.4 If the defendant's use of the live link is being considered, he or she should have an opportunity to have a practice session.

3G.5 If any case against a vulnerable defendant has attracted or may attract widespread public or media interest, the assistance of the police should be enlisted to try and ensure that the defendant is not, when attending the court, exposed to intimidation, vilification or abuse. Section 41 of the Criminal Justice Act 1925 prohibits the taking of photographs of defendants and witnesses (among others) in the court building or in its precincts, or when entering or leaving those precincts. A direction reminding media representatives of the prohibition may be appropriate. The court should also be ready at this stage, if it has not already done so, where relevant to make a reporting restriction under section 39 of the Children and Young Persons Act 1933 or, on an appeal to the Crown Court from a youth court, to remind media representatives of the application of section 49 of that Act.

3G.6 The provisions of the Practice Direction accompanying Part 6 should be followed.

The trial, sentencing or appeal hearing

3G.7 Subject to the need for appropriate security arrangements, the proceedings should, if practicable, be held in a courtroom in which all the participants are on the same or almost the same level.

3G.8 Subject again to the need for appropriate security arrangements, a vulnerable defendant, especially if he is young, should normally, if he wishes, be free to sit with members of his family or others in a like relationship, and with some other suitable supporting adult such as a social worker, and in a place which permits easy, informal communication with his legal representatives. The court should ensure that a suitable supporting adult is available throughout the course of the proceedings.

3G.9 It is essential that at the beginning of the proceedings, the court should ensure that what is to take place has been explained to a vulnerable defendant in terms he or she can understand and, at trial in the Crown Court, it should ensure in particular that the role of the jury has been explained. It should remind those representing the vulnerable defendant and the supporting adult of their responsibility to explain each step as it takes place and, at trial, explain the possible consequences of a guilty verdict and credit for a guilty plea. The court should also remind any intermediary of the responsibility to ensure that the vulnerable defendant has understood the explanations given to him/her. Throughout the trial the court should continue to ensure, by any appropriate means, that the defendant understands what is happening and what has been said by those on the bench, the advocates and witnesses.

3G.10 A trial should be conducted according to a timetable which takes full account of a vulnerable defendant's ability to concentrate. Frequent and regular breaks will often be appropriate. The court should ensure, so far as practicable, that the whole trial is conducted in clear language that the defendant can understand and that evidence in chief and cross-examination are conducted using questions that are short and clear. The conclusions of the 'ground rules' hearing should be followed, and advocates should use and follow the 'toolkits' as discussed above.

3G.11 A vulnerable defendant who wishes to give evidence by live link, in accordance with section 33A of the Youth Justice and Criminal Evidence Act 1999, may apply for a direction to that effect; the procedure in CrimPR 18.14 to 18.17 should be followed. Before making such a direction, the court must be satisfied that it is in the interests of justice to do so and that the use of a live link would enable the defendant to participate more effectively as a witness in the proceedings. The direction will need to deal with the practical arrangements to be made, including the identity of the person or persons who will accompany him or her.

3G.12 In the Crown Court, the judge should consider whether robes and wigs should be worn, and should take account of the wishes of both a vulnerable defendant and any vulnerable witness. It is generally desirable that those responsible for the security of a vulnerable defendant who is in custody, especially if he or she is young, should not be in uniform, and that there should be no recognisable police presence in the courtroom save for good reason.

3G.13 The court should be prepared to restrict attendance by members of the public in the courtroom to a small number, perhaps limited to those with an immediate and direct interest in the outcome. The court should rule on any challenged claim to attend. However, facilities for reporting the proceedings (subject to any restrictions under section 39 or 49 of the Children and Young Persons Act 1933) must be provided. The court may restrict the number of reporters attending in the courtroom to such number as is judged practicable and desirable. In ruling on any challenged claim to attend in the courtroom for the purpose of reporting, the court should be mindful of the public's general right to be informed about the administration of justice.

3G.14 Where it has been decided to limit access to the courtroom, whether by reporters or generally, arrangements should be made for the proceedings to be relayed, audibly and if possible visually, to another room in the same court complex to which the media and the public have access if it appears that there will be a need for such additional facilities. Those making use of such a facility should be reminded that it is to be treated as an extension of the courtroom and that they are required to conduct themselves accordingly.

CPD I General matters 3H: Wales and the Welsh language: Devolution issues

3H.1 These are the subject of Practice Direction: (Supreme Court) (Devolution Issues) [1999] 1 WLR 1592; [1999] 3 All ER 466; [1999] 2 Cr App R 486, to which reference should be made.

CPD I General matters 3J: Wales and the Welsh language: Applications for evidence to be given in Welsh

3J.1 If a defendant in a court in England asks to give or call evidence in the Welsh language, the case should not be transferred to Wales. In ordinary circumstances, interpreters can be provided on request.

CPD I General matters 3K: Wales and the Welsh language: Use of the Welsh language in courts in Wales

3K.1 The purpose of this direction is to reflect the principle of the Welsh Language Act 1993 that, in the administration of justice in Wales, the English and Welsh languages should be treated on a basis of equality.

General

3K.2 It is the responsibility of the legal representatives in every case in which the Welsh language may be used by any witness or party, or in any document which may be placed before the court, to inform the court of that fact, so that appropriate arrangements can be made for the listing of the case.

3K.3 Any party or witness is entitled to use Welsh in a magistrates' court in Wales without giving prior notice. Arrangements will be made for hearing such cases in accordance with the 'Magistrates' Courts' Protocol for Listing Cases where the Welsh Language is used' (January 2008) which is available on the Judiciary's website: http://www.judiciary.gov.uk/NR/exeres/ 57AD4763-F265-47B9-8A35-0442E08160E6. See also CrimPR 24.14.

3K.4 If the possible use of the Welsh language is known at the time of sending or appeal to the Crown Court, the court should be informed immediately after sending or when the notice of appeal is lodged. Otherwise, the court should be informed as soon as the possible use of the Welsh language becomes known.

3K.5 If costs are incurred as a result of failure to comply with these directions, a wasted costs order may be made against the defaulting party and / or his legal representatives.

3K.6 The law does not permit the selection of jurors in a manner which enables the court to discover whether a juror does or does not speak Welsh, or to secure a jury whose members are bilingual, to try a case in which the Welsh language may be used.

Preliminary and plea and case management hearings

3K.7 An advocate in a case in which the Welsh language may be used must raise that matter at the preliminary and/or the plea and case management hearing and endorse details of it on the advocates' questionnaire, so that appropriate directions may be given for the progress of the case.

Listing

3K.8 The listing officer, in consultation with the resident judge, should ensure that a case in which the Welsh language may be used is listed

  (a)   wherever practicable before a Welsh speaking judge, and
  (b)   in a court in Wales with simultaneous translation facilities.

Interpreters

3K.9 Whenever an interpreter is needed to translate evidence from English into Welsh or from Welsh into English, the court listing officer in whose court the case is to be heard shall contact the Welsh Language Unit who will ensure the attendance of an accredited interpreter.

Jurors

3K.10 The jury bailiff, when addressing the jurors at the start of their period of jury service, shall inform them that each juror may take an oath or affirm in Welsh or English as he wishes.

3K.11 After the jury has been selected to try a case, and before it is sworn, the court officer swearing in the jury shall inform the jurors in open court that each juror may take an oath or affirm in Welsh or English as he wishes. A juror who takes the oath or affirms in Welsh should not be asked to repeat it in English.

3K.12 Where Welsh is used by any party or witness in a trial, an accredited interpreter will provide simultaneous translation from Welsh to English for the jurors who do not speak Welsh. There is no provision for the translation of evidence from English to Welsh for a Welsh speaking juror.

3K.13 The jury's deliberations must be conducted in private with no other person present and therefore no interpreter may be provided to translate the discussion for the benefit of one or more of the jurors.

Witnesses

3K.14 When each witness is called, the court officer administering the oath or affirmation shall inform the witness that he may be sworn or affirm in Welsh or English, as he wishes. A witness who takes the oath or affirms in Welsh should not be asked to repeat it in English.

Opening / closing of Crown Courts

3K.15 Unless it is not reasonably practicable to do so, the opening and closing of the court should be performed in Welsh and English.

Role of Liaison Judge

3K.16 If any question or problem arises concerning the implementation of these directions, contact should in the first place be made with the Liaison Judge for the Welsh language through the Wales Circuit Office:

HMCTS WALES / GLITEM CYMRU
3rd Floor, Churchill House / 3ydd Llawr Tŷ Churchill
Churchill Way / Ffordd Churchill
Cardiff / Caerdydd CF10 2HH
029 2067 8300

CPD I General Matters 3L: Security of Prisoners at Court

3L.1 High-risk prisoners identified to the court as presenting a significant risk of escape, violence in court or danger to those in the court and its environs, and to the public at large, will as far as possible, have administrative and remand appearances listed for disposal by way of live link. They will have priority for the use of video equipment.

3L.2 In all other proceedings that require the appearance in person of a high-risk prisoner, the proceedings will be listed at an appropriately secure court building and in a court with a secure (enclosed or ceiling-high) dock.

3L.3 Where a secure dock or live link is not available the court will be asked to consider an application for additional security measures, which may include:

(a) the use of approved restraints (but see below at 3M.6);
(b) the deployment of additional escort staff;
(c) securing the court room for all or part of the proceedings;
(d) in exceptional circumstances, moving the hearing to a prison.

3L.4 National Offender Management Service (NOMS) will be responsible for providing the assessment of the prisoner and it is accepted that this may change at short notice. NOMS must provide notification to the listing officer of all Category A prisoners, those on the Escape-list and Restricted Status prisoners or other prisoners who have otherwise been assessed as presenting a significant risk of violence or harm. There is a presumption that all prisoners notified as high-risk will be allocated a hearing by live link and/or secure dock facilities. Where the court cannot provide a secure listing, the reasons should be provided to the establishment so that alternative arrangements can be considered.

Applications for use of approved restraints

3L.5 It is the duty of the court to decide whether a prisoner who appears before them should appear in restraints or not. Their decision must comply with the requirements of the European Convention on Human Rights, particularly Article 3, which prohibits degrading treatment, see *Ranniman v Finland* (1997) 26 EHRR 56.

3L.6 No prisoner should be handcuffed in court unless there are reasonable grounds for apprehending that he will be violent or will attempt to escape. If an application is made, it must be entertained by the court and a ruling must be given. The defence should be given the opportunity to respond to the application: proceeding in the absence of the defendant or his representative may give rise to an issue under Article 6(1) of the European Convention on Human Rights: *R v Rollinson* (1996) 161 JP 107, CA. If an application is to be made ex parte then that application should be made inter partes and the defence should be given an opportunity to respond.

Additional security measures

3L.7 It may be in some cases that additional dock officers are deployed to mitigate the risk that a prisoner presents. When the nature of the risk is so serious that increased deployment will be insufficient or would in itself be so unobtrusive as to prejudice a fair trial, then the court may be required to consider the following measures:

(a) reconsider the case for a live link hearing, including transferring the case to a court where the live link is available;
(b) transfer the case to an appropriately secure court;

(c)   the use of approved restraints on the prisoner for all or part of the proceedings;

(d)   securing the court room for all or part of the proceedings; and

(e)   the use of (armed) police in the court building.

3L.8   The establishment seeking the additional security measures will submit a Court Management Directions Form setting out the evidence of the prisoners identified risk of escape or violence and requesting the courts approval of security measures to mitigate that risk. This must be sent to the listing officer along with current, specific and credible evidence that the security measures are both necessary and proportionate to the identified risk and that the risk cannot be managed in any other way.

3L.9   If the court is asked to consider transfer of the case, then this must be in accordance with the Listing and Allocation Practice Direction XIII F.11-F.13 post. The listing officer will liaise with the establishment, prosecution and the defence to ensure the needs of the witnesses are taken into account.

3L.10   The Judge who has conduct of the case must deal with any application for the use of restraints or any other security measure and will hear representations from the Crown Prosecution Service and the defence before proceeding. The application will only be granted if:

(a)   there are good grounds for believing that the prisoner poses a significant risk of trying to escape from the court (beyond the assumed motivation of all prisoners to escape) and/or risk of serious harm towards those persons in court or the public generally should an escape attempt be successful; and

(b)   where there is no other viable means of preventing escape or serious harm.

High-risk prisoners giving evidence from the witness box

3L.11   High-risk prisoners giving evidence from the witness box may pose a significant security risk. In circumstances where such prisoners are required to move from a secure dock to an insecure witness box, an application may be made for the court to consider the use of additional security measures including:

(a)   the use of approved restraints;

(b)   the deployment of additional escort staff or police in the courtroom or armed police in the building. The decision to deploy an armed escort is for the Chief Inspector of the relevant borough: the decision to allow the armed escort in or around the court room is for the Senior Presiding Judge (see below);

(c)   securing the courtroom for all or part of the proceedings;

(d)   giving evidence from the secure dock; and

(e)   use of live link if the prisoner is not the defendant.

CPD I General Matters 3M: Procedure for Applications for Armed Police Presence in the Royal Courts of Justice, Crown Courts and Magistrates' Court Buildings

3M.1   This Practice Direction sets out the procedure for the making and handling of applications for authorisation for the presence of armed police officers within the precincts of any Crown Court and magistrates' court buildings at any time. It applies to an application to authorise the carriage of firearms or tasers in court. It does not apply to officers who are carrying CS spray or PAVA incapacitant spray, which is included in the standard equipment issued to officers in some forces and therefore no separate authorisation is required for its carriage in court.

3M.2   This Practice Direction applies to all cases in England and Wales in which a police unit intends to request authorisation for the presence of armed police officers in the Crown Court or in the magistrates' court buildings at any time and including during the delivery of prisoners to court.

3M.3   This Practice Direction allows applications to be made for armed police presence in the Royal Courts of Justice.

Emergency situations

3M.4   This Practice Direction does not apply in an emergency situation. In such circumstances, the police must be able to respond in a way in which their professional judgment deems most appropriate.

Designated court centres

3M.5   Applications may only be made for armed police presence in the designated Crown Court and magistrates' court centres (see below). This list may be revised from time to time in consultation with the Association of Chief Police Officers (ACPO) and HMCTS. It will be reviewed at least every five years in consultation with ACPO armed police secretariat and the Presiding Judges.

3M.6   The Crown Court centres designated for firearms deployment are:

(a)   Northern Circuit: Carlisle, Chester, Liverpool, Preston, Manchester Crown Square & Manchester Minshull Street.

(b)   North Eastern Circuit: Bradford, Leeds, Newcastle upon Tyne, Sheffield, Teesside and Kingston-upon-Hull.

(c)   Western Circuit: Bristol, Winchester and Exeter.

(d)   South Eastern Circuit (not including London): Canterbury, Chelmsford, Ipswich, Luton, Maidstone, Norwich, Reading and St Albans.

(e)   South Eastern Circuit (London only): Central Criminal Court, Woolwich, Kingston and Snaresbrook.

(f)   Midland Circuit: Birmingham, Northampton, Nottingham and Leicester.

(g)   Wales Circuit: Cardiff, Swansea and Caernarfon.

3M.7   The magistrates' courts designated for firearms deployment are:

(a)   South Eastern Circuit (London only): Westminster Magistrates' Court and Belmarsh Magistrates' Court.

Preparatory work prior to applications in all cases

3M.8 Prior to the making of any application for armed transport of prisoners or the presence of armed police officers in the court building, consideration must be given to making use of prison video link equipment to avoid the necessity of prisoners' attendance at court for the hearing in respect of which the application is to be made.

3M.9 Notwithstanding their designation, each requesting officer will attend the relevant court before an application is made to ensure that there have been no changes to the premises and that there are no circumstances that might affect security arrangements.

Applying in the Royal Courts of Justice

3M.10 All applications should be sent to the Listing Office of the Division in which the case is due to appear. The application should be sent by email if possible and must be on the standard form.

3M.11 The Listing Office will notify the Head of Division, providing a copy of the email and any supporting evidence. The Head of Division may ask to see the senior police office concerned.

3M.12 The Head of Division will consider the application. If it is refused, the application fails and the police must be notified.

3M.13 In the absence of the Head of Division, the application should be considered by the Vice-President of the Division.

3M.14 4The relevant Court Office will be notified of the decision and that office will immediately inform the police by telephone. The decision must then be confirmed in writing to the police.

Applying to the Crown Court

3M.15 All applications should be sent to the Cluster Manager and should be sent by email if possible and must be on the standard form.

3M.16 The Cluster Manager will notify the Presiding Judge on the circuit and the Resident Judge by email, providing a copy of the form and any supporting evidence. The Presiding Judge may ask to see the senior police officer concerned.

3M.17 The Presiding Judge will consider the application. If it is refused the application fails and the police must be informed.

3M.18 If the Presiding Judge approves the application it should be forwarded to the secretary in the Senior Presiding Judge's Office. The Senior Presiding Judge will make the final decision. The Presiding Judge will receive written confirmation of that decision.

3M.19 The Presiding Judge will notify the Cluster Manager and the Resident Judge of the decision. The Cluster Manager will immediately inform the police of the decision by telephone. The decision must then be confirmed in writing to the police.

Urgent applications to the Crown Court

3M.20 If the temporary deployment of armed police arises as an urgent issue and a case would otherwise have to be adjourned; or if the trial judge is satisfied that there is a serious risk to public safety, then the Resident Judge will have a discretion to agree such deployment without having obtained the consent of a Presiding Judge or the Senior Presiding Judge. In such a case:

(a) the Resident Judge should assess the facts and agree the proposed solution with a police officer of at least Superintendent level. That officer should agree the approach with the Firearms Division of the police.

(b) if the proposed solution involves the use of armed police officers, the Resident Judge must try to contact the Presiding Judge and/or the Senior Presiding Judge by email and telephone. The Cluster Manager should be informed of the situation.

(c) if the Resident Judge cannot obtain a response from the Presiding Judge or the Senior Presiding Judge, the Resident Judge may grant the application if satisfied:
  (i) that the application is necessary;
  (ii) that without such deployment there would be a significant risk to public safety; and
  (iii) that the case would have to be adjourned at significant difficulty or inconvenience.

3M.21 The Resident Judge must keep the position under continual review, to ensure that it remains appropriate and necessary. The Resident Judge must make continued efforts to contact the Presiding Judge and the Senior Presiding Judge to notify them of the full circumstances of the authorisation.

Applying to the magistrates' courts

3M.22 All applications should be directed, by email if possible, to the Office of the Chief Magistrate, at Westminster Magistrates' Court and must be on the standard form.

3M.23 The Chief Magistrate should consider the application and, if approved, it should be forwarded to the Senior Presiding Judge's office. The Senior Presiding Judge will make the final decision. The Chief Magistrate will receive written confirmation of that decision and will then notify the requesting police officer and, where authorisation is given, the affected magistrates' court of the decision.

Urgent applications in the magistrates' courts

3M.24 If the temporary deployment of armed police arises as an urgent issue and a case would otherwise have to be adjourned; or if the Chief Magistrate is satisfied that there is a serious risk to public safety, then the Chief Magistrate will have a discretion to agree such deployment without having obtained the consent of the Senior Presiding Judge. In such a case:

(a) the Chief Magistrate should assess the facts and agree the proposed solution with a police officer of at least Superintendent level. That officer should agree the approach with the Firearms Division of the police.

(b) if the proposed solution involves the use of armed police officers, the Chief Magistrate must try to contact the Senior Presiding Judge by email and telephone. The Cluster Manager should be informed of the situation.

(c) if the Chief Magistrate cannot obtain a response from the Senior Presiding Judge, the Chief Magistrate may grant the application if satisfied:

(i)   that the application is necessary;
(ii)   that without such deployment there would be a significant risk to public safety; and
(iii)   that the case would have to be adjourned at significant difficulty or inconvenience.

3M.25   The Chief Magistrate must keep the position under continual review, to ensure that it remains appropriate and necessary. The Chief Magistrate must make continued efforts to contact the Senior Presiding Judge to notify him of the full circumstances of the authorisation.

CPD I General Matters 3N: Use of Live Link and Telephone Facilities

3N.1   Where it is lawful and in the interests of justice to do so, courts should exercise their statutory and other powers to conduct hearings by live link or telephone. This is consistent with the Criminal Procedure Rules and with the recommendations of the President of the Queen's Bench Division's *Review of Efficiency in Criminal Proceedings* published in January 2015. Save where legislation circumscribes the court's jurisdiction, the breadth of that jurisdiction is acknowledged by CrimPR 3.5(1), (2)(d).

3N.2   It is the duty of the court to make use of technology actively to manage the case: CrimPR 3.2(1), (2)(h). That duty includes an obligation to give directions for the use of live links and telephone facilities in the circumstances listed in CrimPR 3.2(4) and (5) (pre-trial hearings, including pre-trial case management hearings). Where the court directs that evidence is to be given by live link, and especially where such a direction is given on the court's own initiative, it is essential that the decision is communicated promptly to the witness: CrimPR 18.4. Contrary to a practice adopted by some courts, none of those rules or other provisions require the renewal of a live link direction merely because a trial has had to be postponed or adjourned. Once made, such a direction applies until it is discharged by the court, having regard to the relevant statutory criteria.

3N.3   It is the duty of the parties to alert the court to any reason why live links or telephones should not be used where CrimPR 3.2 otherwise would oblige the court to do so; and, where a direction for the use of such facilities has been made, it is the duty of the parties as soon as practicable to alert the court to any reason why that direction should be varied CrimPR 3.3(2)(e) and 3.6.

3N.4   The word 'appropriate' in CrimPR 3.2(4) and (5) is not a term of art. It has the ordinary English meaning of 'fitting', or 'suitable'. Whether the facilities available to the court in any particular case can be considered appropriate is a matter for the court, but plainly to be appropriate such facilities must work, at the time at which they are required; all participants must be able to hear and, in the case of a live link, see each other clearly; and there must be no extraneous noise, movement or other distraction suffered by a participant, or transmitted by a participant to others. What degree of protection from accidental or deliberate interception should be considered appropriate will depend upon the purpose for which a live link or telephone is to be used. If it is to participate in a hearing which is open to the public anyway, then what is communicated by such means is by definition public and the use of links such as Skype or Facetime, which are not generally considered secure from interception, may not be objectionable. If it is to participate in a hearing in private, and especially one at which sensitive information will be discussed – for example, on an application for a search warrant – then a more secure service is likely to be required.

3N.5   There may be circumstances in which the court should not require the use of live link or telephone facilities despite their being otherwise appropriate at a pre-trial hearing. In every case, in deciding whether any such circumstances apply the court will keep in mind that, for the purposes of what may be an essentially administrative hearing, it may be compatible with the overriding objective to proceed in the defendant's absence altogether, especially if he or she is represented, unless, exceptionally, a rule otherwise requires. The principle that the court always must consider proceeding in a defendant's absence is articulated in CrimPR 3.9(2)(a). Where at a pre-trial hearing bail may be under consideration, the provisions of CrimPR 14.2 will be relevant.

3N.6   Such circumstances will include any case in which the defendant's effective participation cannot be achieved by his or her attendance by such means, and CrimPR 3.2(4) and (5) except such cases from the scope of the obligation which that rule otherwise imposes on the court. That exception may apply where (this list is not exhaustive) the defendant has a disorder or disability, including a hearing, speech or sight impediment, or has communication needs to which the use of a live link or telephone is inimical (whether or not those needs are such as to require the appointment of an intermediary); or where the defendant requires interpretation and effective interpretation cannot be provided by live link or telephone, as the case may be. In deciding whether to require a defendant to attend a first hearing in a magistrates' court by live link from a police station, the court should take into account any views expressed by the defendant, the terms of any mental health or other medical assessment of the defendant carried out at the police station, and all other relevant information and representations available. No single factor is determinative, but the court must keep in mind the terms of section 57C(6A) of the Crime and Disorder Act 1998 (Use of live link at preliminary hearings where accused is at police station) which provides that 'A live link direction under this section may not be given unless the court is satisfied that it is not contrary to the interests of justice to give the direction.'

3N.7   Finally, that exception sometimes may apply where the defendant's attendance in person at a pre-trial hearing will facilitate communication with his or her legal representatives. The court should not make such an exception merely to allow client and representatives to meet if that meeting can and should be held elsewhere. However, there will be cases in which defence representatives reasonably need to meet with a defendant, to take his or her instructions or to explain events to him or her, either shortly before or immediately after a pre-trial hearing and in circumstances in which that meeting cannot take place effectively by live link.

3N.8   Nothing prohibits the member or members of a court from conducting a pre-trial hearing by attending by live link or telephone from a location distant from all the other participants. Despite the conventional view that the venue for a court hearing is the court room in which that hearing has been arranged to take place, the Criminal Procedure Rules define 'court' as 'a tribunal with jurisdiction over criminal cases. It includes a judge, recorder, District Judge (Magistrates' Court), lay justice and, when exercising their judicial powers, the Registrar of Criminal Appeals, a justices' clerk or assistant clerk.' Neither CrimPR 3.25 (Place of trial), which applies in the Crown Court, nor CrimPR 24.14 (Place of trial), which applies in magistrates' courts, each of which requires proceedings to take place in a courtroom provided by the Lord Chancellor, applies for the purposes of a pre-trial hearing. Thus for the purposes of such a hearing there is no legal obstacle to the judge, magistrate or magistrates conducting it from elsewhere, with other participants assembled in a courtroom from which the member or members of the court are physically absent. In principle, nothing prohibits the conduct of a pre-trial hearing by live link or telephone with each participant, including the member or members of the court, in a different location (an arrangement sometimes described as a 'virtual hearing'). This is dependent upon there being means by which that hearing can be witnessed by the public – for example, by public attendance at a courtroom or other venue from which the participants all can be seen and heard (if by live link), or heard (if by telephone). The principle of open justice to which paragraph 3N.17 refers is relevant.

3N.9 Sections 57A to 57F of the Crime and Disorder Act 1998 allow a defendant who is in custody to enter a plea by live link, and allow for such a defendant who attends by live link to be sentenced. In appropriate circumstances, the court may allow a defendant who is not in custody to enter a plea by live link; but the same considerations as apply to sentencing in such a case will apply: see paragraph 3N.13 beneath.

3N.10 The Crime and Disorder Act 1998 does not allow for the attendance by live link at a contested trial of a defendant who is in custody. The court may allow a defendant who wishes to do so to observe all or part of his or her trial by live link, whether she or he is in custody or not, but (a) such a defendant cannot lawfully give evidence by such means unless he or she satisfies the criteria prescribed by section 33A of the Youth Justice and Criminal Evidence Act 1999 and the court so orders under that section (see also CrimPR 18.14 – 18.17); (b) a defendant who is in custody and who observes the trial by live link is not present, as a matter of law, and the trial must be treated as taking place in his or her absence, she or he having waived the right to attend; and (c) a defendant who has refused to attend his or her trial when required to do so, or who has absconded, must not be permitted to observe the proceedings by live link.

3N.11 Paragraphs I 3D to 3G inclusive of these Practice Directions (Vulnerable people in the courts; Ground rules hearings to plan the questioning of a vulnerable witness or defendant; Intermediaries; Vulnerable defendants) contain directions relevant to the use of a live link as a special measure for a young or otherwise vulnerable witness, or to facilitate the giving of evidence by a defendant who is likewise young or otherwise vulnerable, within the scope of the Youth Justice and Criminal Evidence Act 1999. Defence representatives and the court must keep in mind that special measures under the 1999 Act and CrimPR Part 18, including the use of a live link, are available to defence as well as to prosecution witnesses who meet the statutory criteria. Defence representatives should always consider whether their witnesses would benefit from giving evidence by live link and should apply for a direction if appropriate, either at the case management hearing or as soon as possible thereafter. A defence witness should be afforded the same facilities and treatment as a prosecution witness, including the same opportunity to make a pre-trial visit to the court building in order to familiarise himself or herself with it. Where a live link is sought as a special measure for a young or vulnerable witness or defendant, CrimPR 18.10 and 18.15 respectively require, among other things, that the applicant must identify someone to accompany that witness or defendant while they give evidence; must name the person, if possible; and must explain why that person would be an appropriate companion for that witness. The court must ensure that directions are given accordingly when ordering such a live link. Witness Service volunteers are available to support all witnesses, prosecution and defence, if required.

3N.12 Under sections 57A and 57D or 57E of the Crime and Disorder Act 1998 the court may pass sentence on a defendant in custody who attends by live link. The court may allow a defendant who is not in custody and who wishes to attend his or her sentencing by live link to do so, and may receive representations (but not evidence) from her or him by such means. Factors of which the court will wish to take account in exercising its discretion include, in particular, the penalty likely to be imposed; the importance of ensuring that the explanations of sentence required by CrimPR 24.11(9), in magistrates' courts, and in the Crown Court by CrimPR 25.16(7), can be given satisfactorily, for the defendant, for other participants and for the public, including reporters; and the preferences of the maker of any Victim Personal Statement which is to be read aloud or played pursuant to paragraph VII F.3(c) of these Practice Directions.

Youth defendants

3N.13 In the youth court or when a youth is appearing in the magistrates' court or the Crown Court, it will usually be appropriate for the youth to be produced in person at court. This is to ensure that the court can engage properly with the youth and that the necessary level of engagement can be facilitated with the Youth Offending Team worker, defence representative and/or appropriate adult. The court should deal with any application for use of a live-link on a case-by-case basis, after consultation with the parties and the Youth Offending Team. Such hearings that may be appropriate, include, onward remand hearings at which there is no bail application or case management hearings, particularly if the youth is already serving a custodial sentence.

3N.14 It rarely will be appropriate for a youth to be sentenced over a live link. However, notwithstanding the court's duties of engagement with a youth, the overriding welfare principle and the statutory responsibility of the youth offending worker to explain the sentence to the youth, after consultation with the parties and the Youth Offending Team, there may be circumstances in which it may be appropriate to sentence a youth over the live-link:

(a) If the youth is already serving a custodial sentence and the sentence to be imposed by the court is bound to be a further custodial sentence, whether concurrent or consecutive;

(b) If the youth is already serving a custodial sentence and the court is minded to impose a non-custodial sentence which will have no material impact on the sentence being served;

(c) The youth is being detained in a secure establishment at such a distance from the court that the travelling time from one to the other will be significant so as to materially affect the welfare of the youth;

(d) The youth's condition-whether mental or otherwise- is so disturbed that his or her production would be a significant detriment to his or her welfare.

3N.15 Arrangements must be made in advance of any live link hearing to enable the youth offending worker to be at the secure establishment where the youth is in custody. In the event that such arrangements are not practicable, the youth offending worker must have sufficient access to the youth via the live link booth before and after the hearing.

Conduct of participants

3N.16 Where a live link is used, the immediate vicinity of the device by which a person attends becomes, temporarily, part of the courtroom for the purposes of that person's participation. That person, and any advocate or legal representative, custodian, court officer, intermediary or other companion, whether immediately visible to the court or not, becomes a participant for the purposes of CrimPR 1.2(2) and is subject to the court's jurisdiction to regulate behaviour in the courtroom. The substance and effect of this direction must be drawn to the attention of all such participants.

Open justice and records of proceedings

3N.17 The principle of open justice to which CrimPR 6.2(1) gives effect applies as strongly where electronic means of communication are used to conduct a hearing as it applies in other circumstances. Open justice is the principal means by which courts are kept under scrutiny by the public. It follows that where a participant attends a hearing in public by live link or telephone then that person's participation must be, as nearly as may be, equally audible and, if applicable, equally visible to the public as it would be were he or she physically present. Where electronic means of communication are used to conduct a hearing, records of the event must be maintained in the usual way: CrimPR 5.4. In the Crown Court, this includes the recording of the proceedings: CrimPR 5.5.

CRIMPR PART 3 CASE MANAGEMENT

CPD I General matters 3A: Case management

3A.1 CrimPR 1.1(2)(e) requires that cases be dealt with efficiently and expeditiously. CrimPR 3.2 requires the court to further the overriding objective by actively managing the case, for example:

(a) When dealing with an offence which is triable only on indictment the court must ask the defendant whether he or she intends to plead guilty at the Crown Court (CrimPR 9.7(5));

(b) On a guilty plea, the court must pass sentence at the earliest opportunity, in accordance with CrimPR 24.11(9)(a) (magistrates' courts) and 25.16(7)(a) (the Crown Court).

3A.2 Given these duties, magistrates' courts and the Crown Court therefore will proceed as described in paragraphs 3A.3 to 3A.28 below. The parties will be expected to have prepared in accordance with CrimPR 3.3(1) to avoid unnecessary and wasted hearings. They will be expected to have communicated with each other by the time of the first hearing; to report to the court on that communication at the first hearing; and to continue thereafter to communicate with each other and with the court officer, in accordance with CrimPR 3.3(2).

3A.3 There is a Preparation for Effective Trial form for use in the magistrates' courts, and a Plea and Trial Preparation Hearing form for use in the Crown Court, each of which must be used as appropriate in connection with CrimPR Part 3: see paragraph 5A.2 of these Practice Directions. Versions of those forms in pdf and Word, together with guidance notes, are available on the Criminal Procedure Rules pages of the Ministry of Justice website.

Case progression and trial preparation in magistrates' courts

3A.4 CrimPR 8.3 applies in all cases and requires the prosecutor to serve:

(i) a summary of the circumstances of the offence;

(ii) any account given by the defendant in interview, whether contained in that summary or in another document;

(iii) any written witness statement or exhibit that the prosecutor then has available and considers material to plea or to the allocation of the case for trial or sentence;

(iv) a list of the defendant's criminal record, if any; and

(v) any available statement of the effect of the offence on a victim, a victim's family or others.

The details must include sufficient information to allow the defendant and the court at the first hearing to take an informed view:

(i) on plea;

(ii) on venue for trial (if applicable);

(iii) for the purposes of case management; or

(iv) for the purposes of sentencing (including committal for sentence, if applicable).

Defendant in custody

3A.5 If the defendant has been detained in custody after being charged with an offence which is indictable only or triable either way, at the first hearing a magistrates' court will proceed at once with the allocation of the case for trial, where appropriate, and, if so required, with the sending of the defendant to the Crown Court for trial. The court will be expected to ask for and record any indication of plea and issues for trial to assist the Crown Court.

3A.6 If the offence charged is triable only summarily, or if at that hearing the case is allocated for summary trial, the court will forthwith give such directions as are necessary, either (on a guilty plea) to prepare for sentencing, or for a trial.

Defendant on bail

3A.7 If the defendant has been released on bail after being charged, the case must be listed for the first hearing 14 days after charge, or the next available court date thereafter when the prosecutor anticipates a guilty plea which is likely to be sentenced in the magistrates' court. In cases where there is an anticipated not guilty plea or the case is likely to be sent or committed to the Crown Court for either trial or sentence, then it must be listed for the first hearing 28 days after charge or the next available court date thereafter.

Guilty plea in the magistrates' courts

3A.8　Where a defendant pleads guilty or indicates a guilty plea in a magistrates' court the court should consider whether a pre-sentence report – a stand down report if possible – is necessary.

Guilty plea in the Crown Court

3A.9　Where a magistrates' court is considering committal for sentence or the defendant has indicated an intention to plead guilty in a matter which is to be sent to the Crown Court, the magistrates' court should request the preparation of a pre-sentence report for the Crown Court's use if the magistrates' court considers that:

(a)　there is a realistic alternative to a custodial sentence; or
(b)　the defendant may satisfy the criteria for classification as a dangerous offender; or
(c)　there is some other appropriate reason for doing so.

3A.10　When a magistrates' court sends a case to the Crown Court for trial and the defendant indicates an intention to plead guilty at the Crown Court, then that magistrates' court must set a date for a Plea and Trial Preparation Hearing at the Crown Court, in accordance with CrimPR 9.7(5)(a)(i).

Case sent for Crown Court trial: no indication of guilty plea

3A.11　In any case sent to the Crown Court for trial, other than one in which the defendant indicates an intention to plead guilty, the magistrates' court must set a date for a Plea and Trial Preparation Hearing, in accordance with CrimPR 9.7(5)(a)(ii). The Plea and Trial Preparation Hearing must be held within 28 days of sending, unless the standard directions of the Presiding Judges of the circuit direct otherwise. Paragraph 3A.16 below additionally applies to the arrangements for such hearings. A magistrates' court may give other directions appropriate to the needs of the case, in accordance with CrimPR 3.5(3), and in accordance with any standard directions issued by the Presiding Judges of the circuit.

Defendant on bail: anticipated not guilty plea

3A.12　Where the defendant has been released on bail after being charged, and where the prosecutor does not anticipate a guilty plea at the first hearing in a magistrates' court, then it is essential that the initial details of the prosecution case that are provided for that first hearing are sufficient to assist the court, in order to identify the real issues and to give appropriate directions for an effective trial (regardless of whether the trial is to be heard in the magistrates' court or the Crown Court). In these circumstances, unless there is good reason not to do so, the prosecution should make available the following material in advance of the first hearing in the magistrates' court:

(a)　A summary of the circumstances of the offence(s) including a summary of any account given by the defendant in interview;
(b)　Statements and exhibits that the prosecution has identified as being of importance for the purpose of plea or initial case management, including any relevant CCTV that would be relied upon at trial and any Streamlined Forensic Report;
(c)　Details of witness availability, as far as they are known at that hearing;
(d)　Defendant's criminal record;
(e)　Victim Personal Statements if provided;
(f)　An indication of any medical or other expert evidence that the prosecution is likely to adduce in relation to a victim or the defendant;
(g)　Any information as to special measures, bad character or hearsay, where applicable.

3A.13　In addition to the material required by CrimPR Part 8, the information required by the Preparation for Effective Trial form must be available to be submitted at the first hearing, and the parties must complete that form, in accordance with the guidance published with it. Where there is to be a contested trial in a magistrates' court, that form includes directions and a timetable that will apply in every case unless the court otherwise orders.

3A.14　Nothing in paragraph 3A.12-3A.13 shall preclude the court from taking a plea pursuant to CrimPR 3.9(2)(b) at the first hearing and for the court to case manage as far as practicable under Part 3 CrimPR.

Exercise of magistrates' court's powers

3A.15　In accordance with CrimPR 9.1, sections 49, 51(13) and 51A(11) of the Crime and Disorder Act 1998, and sections 17E, 18(5) and 24D of the Magistrates' Courts Act 1980 a single justice can:

(a)　allocate and send for trial;
(b)　take an indication of a guilty plea (but not pass sentence);
(c)　take a not guilty plea and give directions for the preparation of trial including:
　　(i)　timetable for the proceedings;
　　(ii)　the attendance of the parties;
　　(iii)　the service of documents;
　　(iv)　the manner in which evidence is to be given.

Case progression and trial preparation in the Crown Court

Plea and Trial Preparation Hearing

3A.16　In a case in which a magistrates' court has directed a Plea and Trial Preparation Hearing, the period which elapses between sending for trial and the date of that hearing must be consistent within each circuit. In every case, the time allowed for the conduct of the Plea and Trial Preparation Hearing must be sufficient for effective trial preparation. It is expected in every case that an indictment will be lodged at least 7 days in advance of the hearing. Please see the Note to the Practice Direction.

3A.17　In a case in which the defendant, not having done so before, indicates an intention to plead guilty to his representative after being sent for trial but before the Plea and Trial Preparation Hearing, the defence representative will notify the Crown Court and the prosecution forthwith. The court will ensure there is sufficient time at the Plea and Trial Preparation Hearing for sentence and a Judge should at once request the preparation of a pre-sentence report if it appears to the court that either:

    (a)   there is a realistic alternative to a custodial sentence; or
    (b)   the defendant may satisfy the criteria for classification as a dangerous offender; or
    (c)   there is some other appropriate reason for doing so.

3A.18   If at the Plea and Trial Preparation Hearing the defendant pleads guilty and no pre-sentence report has been prepared, if possible the court should obtain a stand down report.

3A.19   Where the defendant was remanded in custody after being charged and was sent for trial without initial details of the prosecution case having been served, then at least 7 days before the Plea and Trial Preparation Hearing the prosecutor should serve, as a minimum, the material identified in paragraph 3A.12 above. If at the Plea and Trial Preparation Hearing the defendant does not plead guilty, the court will be expected to identify the issues in the case and give appropriate directions for an effective trial. Please see the Note to the Practice Direction.

3A.20   At the Plea and Trial Preparation Hearing, in addition to the material required by paragraph 3A.12 above, the prosecutor must serve sufficient evidence to enable the court to case manage effectively without the need for a further case management hearing, unless the case falls within paragraph 3A.21. In addition, the information required by the Plea and Trial Preparation Hearing form must be available to the court at that hearing, and it must have been discussed between the parties in advance. The prosecutor must provide details of the availability of likely prosecution witnesses so that a trial date can immediately be arranged if the defendant does not plead guilty.

Further case management hearing

3A.21   In accordance with CrimPR 3.13(1)(c), after the Plea and Trial Preparation Hearing there will be no further case management hearing before the trial unless:

    (i)   a condition listed in that rule is met; and
    (ii)   the court so directs, in order to further the overriding objective.

The directions to be given at the Plea and Trial Preparation Hearing therefore may include a direction for a further case management hearing, but usually will do so only in one of the following cases:

    (a)   Class 1 cases;
    (b)   Class 2 cases which carry a maximum penalty of 10 years or more;
    (c)   cases involving death by driving (whether dangerous or careless), or death in the work-place;
    (d)   cases involving a vulnerable witness;
    (e)   cases in which the defendant is a child or otherwise under a disability, or requires special assistance;
    (f)   cases in which there is a corporate or unrepresented defendant;
    (g)   cases in which the expected trial length is such that a further case management hearing is desirable and any case in which the trial is likely to last longer than four weeks;
    (h)   cases in which expert evidence is to be introduced;
    (i)   cases in which a party requests a hearing to enter a plea;
    (j)   cases in which an application to dismiss or stay has been made;
    (k)   cases in which arraignment has not taken place, whether because of an issue relating to fitness to plead, or abuse of process or sufficiency of evidence, or for any other reason;
    (l)   cases in which there are likely to be linked criminal and care directions in accordance with the 2013 Protocol.

3A.22   If a further case management hearing is directed, a defendant in custody will not usually be expected to attend in person, unless the court otherwise directs.

Compliance hearing

3A.23   If a party fails to comply with a case management direction, that party may be required to attend the court to explain the failure. Unless the court otherwise directs a defendant in custody will not usually be expected to attend. See paragraph 3A.26-3A.28 below.

Conduct of case progression hearings

3A.24   As far as possible, case progression should be managed without a hearing in the courtroom, using electronic communication in accordance with CrimPR 3.5(2)(d). Court staff should be nominated to conduct case progression as part of their role, in accordance with CrimPR 3.4(2). To aid effective communication the prosecution and defence representative should notify the court and provide details of who shall be dealing with the case at the earliest opportunity.

Completion of Effective Trial Monitoring form

3A.25   It is imperative that the Effective Trial Monitoring form (as devised and issued by Her Majesty's Courts and Tribunals Service) is accurately completed by the parties for all cases that have been listed for trial. Advocates must engage with the process by providing the relevant details and completing the form.

Compliance courts

3A.26   To ensure effective compliance with directions of the courts made in accordance with the Criminal Procedure Rules and the overriding objective, courts should maintain a record whenever a party to the proceedings has failed to comply with a direction made by the court. The parties may have to attend a hearing to explain any lack of compliance.

3A.27   These hearings may be conducted by live link facilities or via other electronic means, as the court may direct.

3A.28   It will be for the Presiding Judges, Resident Judge and Justices' Clerks to decide locally how often compliance courts should be held, depending on the scale and nature of the problem at each court centre.

Note to the Practice Direction

In 3A.16 and 3A.19 the reference to 'at least 7 days' in advance of the hearing is necessitated by the fact that, for the time being, different circuits have different timescales for the Plea and Trial Preparation Hearing. Had this not been so, the paragraphs would have been drafted forward from the date of sending rather than backwards from the date of the Plea and Trial Preparation Hearing.

CPD General matters 3B: Pagination and Indexing of Served Evidence

3B.1   The following directions apply to matters before the Crown Court, where

(a)   there is an application to prefer a bill of indictment in relation to the case;
(b)   a person is sent for trial under section 51 of the Crime and Disorder Act 1998 (sending cases to the Crown Court), to the service of copies of the documents containing the evidence on which the charge or charges are based under Paragraph 1 of Schedule 3 to that Act; or
(c)   a defendant wishes to serve evidence.

3B.2   A party who serves documentary evidence in the Crown Court should:

(a)   paginate each page in any bundle of statements and exhibits sequentially;
(b)   provide an index to each bundle of statements produced including the following information:
    (i)   the name of the case;
    (ii)   the author of each statement;
    (iii)   the start page number of the witness statement;
    (iv)   the end page number of the witness statement.
(c)   provide an index to each bundle of documentary and pictorial exhibits produced, including the following information:
    (i)   the name of the case
    (ii)   the exhibit reference;
    (iii)   a short description of the exhibit;
    (iv)   the start page number of the exhibit;
    (v)   the end page number of the exhibit;
    (vi)   where possible, the name of the person producing the exhibit should be added.

3B.3   Where additional documentary evidence is served, a party should paginate following on from the last page of the previous bundle or in a logical and sequential manner. A party should also provide notification of service of any amended index.

3B.4   The prosecution must ensure that the running total of the pages of prosecution evidence is easily identifiable on the most recent served bundle of prosecution evidence.

3B.5   For the purposes of these directions, the number of pages of prosecution evidence served on the court includes all

(a)   witness statements;
(b)   documentary and pictorial exhibits;
(c)   records of interviews with the defendant; and
(d)   records of interviews with other defendants which form part of the served prosecution documents or which are included in any notice of additional evidence,

but does not include any document provided on CD-ROM or by other means of electronic communication.

CPD I General matters 3C: Abuse of process stay applications

3C.1   In all cases where a defendant in the Crown Court proposes to make an application to stay an indictment on the grounds of abuse of process, written notice of such application must be given to the prosecuting authority and to any co-defendant as soon as practicable after the defendant becomes aware of the grounds for doing so and not later than 14 days before the date fixed or warned for trial ("the relevant date"). Such notice must:

(a)   give the name of the case and the indictment number;
(b)   state the fixed date or the warned date as appropriate;
(c)   specify the nature of the application;
(d)   set out in numbered sub-paragraphs the grounds upon which the application is to be made;
(e)   be copied to the chief listing officer at the court centre where the case is due to be heard.

3C.2   Any co-defendant who wishes to make a like application must give a like notice not later than seven days before the relevant date, setting out any additional grounds relied upon.

3C.3   In relation to such applications, the following automatic directions shall apply:

(a)   the advocate for the applicant(s) must lodge with the court and serve on all other parties a skeleton argument in support of the application, at least five clear working days before the relevant date. If reference is to be made to any document not in the existing trial documents, a paginated and indexed bundle of such documents is to be provided with the skeleton argument;
(b)   the advocate for the prosecution must lodge with the court and serve on all other parties a responsive skeleton argument at least two clear working days before the relevant date, together with a supplementary bundle if appropriate.

3C.4   Paragraphs XII D.17 to D.23 of these Practice Directions set out the general requirements for skeleton arguments. All skeleton arguments must specify any propositions of law to be advanced (together with the authorities relied upon in support, with paragraph references to passages relied upon) and, where appropriate, include a chronology of events and a list of dramatis personae. In all instances where reference is made to a document, the reference in the trial documents or supplementary bundle is to be given.

3C.5   The above time limits are minimum time limits. In appropriate cases, the court will order longer lead times. To this end, in all cases where defence advocates are, at the time of the preliminary hearing or as soon as practicable after the case has been sent, considering the possibility of an abuse of process application, this must be raised with the judge dealing with the matter, who will order a different timetable if appropriate, and may wish, in any event, to give additional directions about the conduct of the application. If the trial judge has not been identified, the matter should be raised with the Resident Judge.

CPD I General matters 3D: Vulnerable people in the courts

3D.1 In respect of eligibility for special measures, 'vulnerable' and 'intimidated' witnesses are defined in sections 16 and 17 of the Youth Justice and Criminal Evidence Act 1999 (as amended by the Coroners and Justice Act 2009); 'vulnerable' includes those under 18 years of age and people with a mental disorder or learning disability; a physical disorder or disability; or who are likely to suffer fear or distress in giving evidence because of their own circumstances or those relating to the case.

3D.2 However, many other people giving evidence in a criminal case, whether as a witness or defendant, may require assistance: the court is required to take 'every reasonable step' to encourage and facilitate the attendance of witnesses and to facilitate the participation of any person, including the defendant (CrimPR 3.9(3)(a) and (b)). This includes enabling a witness or defendant to give their best evidence, and enabling a defendant to comprehend the proceedings and engage fully with his or her defence. The pre-trial and trial process should, so far as necessary, be adapted to meet those ends. Regard should be had to the welfare of a young defendant as required by section 44 of the Children and Young Persons Act 1933, and generally to Parts 1 and 3 of the Criminal Procedure Rules (the overriding objective and the court's powers of case management).

3D.3 Under Part 3 of the Rules, the court must identify the needs of witnesses at an early stage (CrimPR 3.2(2)(b)) and may require the parties to identify arrangements to facilitate the giving of evidence and participation in the trial (CrimPR 3.11(c)(iv) and (v)). There are various statutory special measures that the court may utilise to assist a witness in giving evidence. CrimPR Part 18 gives the procedures to be followed. Courts should note the 'primary rule' which requires the court to give a direction for a special measure to assist a child witness or qualifying witness and that in such cases an application to the court is not required (CrimPR 18.9).

3D.4 Court of Appeal decisions on this subject include a judgment from the Lord Chief Justice, Lord Judge in *R v Cox* [2012] EWCA Crim 549, [2012] 2 Cr. App. R. 6; *R v Wills* [2011] EWCA Crim 1938, [2012] 1 Cr. App. R. 2; and *R v E* [2011] EWCA Crim 3028, [2012] Crim L.R. 563.

3D.5 In *R v Wills*, the Court endorsed the approach taken by the report of the Advocacy Training Council (ATC) 'Raising the Bar: the Handling of Vulnerable Witnesses, Victims and Defendants in Court' (2011). The report includes and recommends the use of 'toolkits' to assist advocates as they prepare to question vulnerable people at court:

http://www.advocacytrainingcouncil.org/vulnerable-witnesses/raising-the-bar

3D.6 Further toolkits are available through the Advocate's Gateway which is managed by the ATC's Management Committee:

http://www.theadvocatesgateway.org/

3D.7 These toolkits represent best practice. Advocates should consult and follow the relevant guidance whenever they prepare to question a young or otherwise vulnerable witness or defendant. Judges may find it helpful to refer advocates to this material and to use the toolkits in case management.

3D.8 'Achieving Best Evidence in Criminal Proceedings' (Ministry of Justice 2011) describes best practice in preparation for the investigative interview and trial:

http://www.cps.gov.uk/publications/docs/best_evidence_in_criminal_proceedings.pdf

CPD I General matters 3E: Ground rules hearings to plan the questioning of a vulnerable witness or defendant

3E.1 The judiciary is responsible for controlling questioning. Over-rigorous or repetitive cross-examination of a child or vulnerable witness should be stopped. Intervention by the judge, magistrates or intermediary (if any) is minimised if questioning, taking account of the individual's communication needs, is discussed in advance and ground rules are agreed and adhered to.

3E.2 Discussion of ground rules is required in all intermediary trials where they must be discussed between the judge or magistrates, advocates and intermediary before the witness gives evidence. The intermediary must be present but is not required to take the oath (the intermediary's declaration is made just before the witness gives evidence).

3E.3 Discussion of ground rules is good practice, even if no intermediary is used, in all young witness cases and in other cases where a witness or defendant has communication needs. Discussion before the day of trial is preferable to give advocates time to adapt their questions to the witness's needs. It may be helpful for a trial practice note of boundaries to be created at the end of the discussion. The judge may use such a document in ensuring that the agreed ground rules are complied with.

3E.4 All witnesses, including the defendant and defence witnesses, should be enabled to give the best evidence they can. In relation to young and/or vulnerable people, this may mean departing radically from traditional cross-examination. The form and extent of appropriate cross-examination will vary from case to case. For adult non vulnerable witnesses an advocate will usually put his case so that the witness will have the opportunity of commenting upon it and/or answering it. When the witness is young or otherwise vulnerable, the court may dispense with the normal practice and impose restrictions on the advocate 'putting his case' where there is a risk of a young or otherwise vulnerable witness failing to understand, becoming distressed or acquiescing to leading questions. Where limitations on questioning are necessary and appropriate, they must be clearly defined. The judge has a duty to ensure that they are complied with and should explain them to the jury and the reasons for them. If the advocate fails to comply with the limitations, the judge should give relevant directions to the jury when that occurs and prevent further questioning that does not comply with the ground rules settled upon in advance. Instead of commenting on inconsistencies during cross-examination, following discussion between the judge and the advocates, the advocate or judge may point out important inconsistencies after (instead of during) the witness's evidence. The judge should also remind the jury of these during summing up. The judge should be alert to alleged inconsistencies that are not in fact inconsistent, or are trivial.

3E.5   If there is more than one defendant, the judge should not permit each advocate to repeat the questioning of a vulnerable witness. In advance of the trial, the advocates should divide the topics between them, with the advocate for the first defendant leading the questioning, and the advocate(s) for the other defendant(s) asking only ancillary questions relevant to their client's case, without repeating the questioning that has already taken place on behalf of the other defendant(s).

3E.6   In particular in a trial of a sexual offence, 'body maps' should be provided for the witness' use. If the witness needs to indicate a part of the body, the advocate should ask the witness to point to the relevant part on the body map. In sex cases, judges should not permit advocates to ask the witness to point to a part of the witness' own body. Similarly, photographs of the witness' body should not be shown around the court while the witness is giving evidence.

CPD I General matters 3F: Intermediaries

Role and functions of intermediaries in criminal courts

3F.1   Intermediaries facilitate communication with witnesses and defendants who have communication needs. Their primary function is to improve the quality of evidence and aid understanding between the court, the advocates and the witness or defendant. For example, they commonly advise on the formulation of questions so as to avoid misunderstanding. On occasion, they actively assist and intervene during questioning. The extent to which they do so (if at all) depends on factors such as the communication needs of the witness or defendant, and the skills of the advocates in adapting their language and questioning style to meet those needs.

3F.2   Intermediaries are independent of parties and owe their duty to the court. The court and parties should be vigilant to ensure they act impartially and their assistance to witnesses and defendants is transparent. It is however permissible for an advocate to have a private consultation with an intermediary when formulating questions (although control of questioning remains the overall responsibility of the court).

3F.3   Further information is in *Intermediaries: Step by Step* (Toolkit 16; The Advocate's Gateway, 2015) and chapter 5 of the *Equal Treatment Bench Book* (Judicial College, 2013).
Links to publications

- www.theadvocatesgateway.org/images/toolkits/16intermediariesstepbystep060315.pdf
- www.judiciary.gov.uk/wp-content/uploads/2013/11/5-children-and-vulnerable-adults.pdf

Assessment

3F.4   The process of appointment should begin with assessment by an intermediary and a report. The report will make recommendations to address the communication needs of the witness or defendant during trial.

3F.5   In light of the scarcity of intermediaries, the appropriateness of assessment must be decided with care to ensure their availability for those witnesses and defendants who are most in need. The decision should be made on an individual basis, in the context of the circumstances of the particular case.

Intermediaries for prosecution and defence witnesses

3F.6   IIntermediaries are one of the special measures available to witnesses under the Youth Justice and Criminal Evidence Act 1999 (YJCEA 1999). Witnesses deemed vulnerable in accordance with the criteria in s.16 YJCEA are eligible for the assistance of an intermediary when giving evidence pursuant to s.29 YJCEA 1999. These provisions do not apply to defendants.

3F.7   An application for an intermediary to assist a witness when giving evidence must be made in accordance with Part 18 of the Criminal Procedure Rules. In addition, where an intermediary report is available (see 3F.4 above), it should be provided with the application.

3F.8   The Witness Intermediary Scheme (WIS) operated by the National Crime Agency identifies intermediaries for witnesses and may be used by the prosecution and defence. The WIS is contactable at wit@nca.x.gsi.gov.uk / 0845 000 5463. An intermediary appointed through the WIS is defined as a 'Registered Intermediary' and matched to the particular witness based on expertise, location and availability. Registered Intermediaries are accredited by the WIS and bound by Codes of Practice and Ethics issued by the Ministry of Justice (which oversees the WIS).

3F.9   Having identified a Registered Intermediary, the WIS does not provide funding. The party appointing the Registered Intermediary is responsible for payment at rates specified by the Ministry of Justice.

3F.10   Further information is in *The Registered Intermediaries Procedural Guidance Manual* (Ministry of Justice, 2015) and Intermediaries: Step by Step (see 3F.3 above).
Link to publication

- www.theadvocatesgateway.org/images/procedures/
registered-intermediary-procedural-guidance-manual.pdf

Intermediaries for defendants

3F.11   Statutory provisions providing for defendants to be assisted by an intermediary when giving evidence (where necessary to ensure a fair trial) are not in force (because s.104 Coroners and Justice Act 2009, which would insert ss. 33BA and 33BB into the YJCEA 1999, has yet to be commenced).

3F.12   The court may direct the appointment of an intermediary to assist a defendant in reliance on its inherent powers (*C v Sevenoaks Youth Court* [2009] EWHC 3088 (Admin)). There is however no presumption that a defendant will be so assisted and, even where an intermediary would improve the trial process, appointment is not mandatory (*R v Cox* [2012] EWCA Crim 549). The court should adapt the trial process to address a defendant's communication needs (*R v Cox* [2012] EWCA Crim 549). It will rarely exercise its inherent powers to direct appointment of an intermediary but where a defendant is vulnerable or for some other reason experiences communication or hearing difficulties, such that he or she needs more help to follow the proceedings than her or his legal representatives readily can give having regard to their other functions on the defendant's behalf, then the court should consider sympathetically any application for the defendant to be accompanied throughout the trial by a support worker or other appropriate companion who can provide that assistance. This is consistent with CrimPR 3.9(3)(b) (see paragraph 3D.2 above); consistent with the observations in R v Cox (see paragraph 3D.4 above), *R (OP) v Ministry of Justice* [2014] EWHC 1944 (Admin) and *R v Rashid* [2017] EWCA Crim 2; and consistent with the arrangements contemplated at paragraph 3G.8 below.

3F.13   The court may exercise its inherent powers to direct appointment of an intermediary to assist a defendant giving evidence or for the entire trial. Terms of appointment are for the court and there is no illogicality in restricting the appointment to the defendant's evidence (*R v R* [2015] EWCA Crim 1870), when the 'most pressing need' arises (I [2014] EWHC 1944 (Admin)). Directions to appoint an intermediary for a defendant's evidence will thus be rare, but for the entire trial extremely rare keeping in mind paragraph 3F.12 above.

3F.14   An application for an intermediary to assist a defendant must be made in accordance with Part 18 of the Criminal Procedure Rules. In addition, where an intermediary report is available (see 3F.4 above), it should be provided with the application.

3F.15   The WIS is not presently available to identify intermediaries for defendants (although in OP v Secretary of State for Justice [2014] EWHC 1944 (Admin), the Ministry of Justice was ordered to consider carefully whether it were justifiable to refuse equal provision to witnesses and defendants with respect to their evidence). 'Non-registered intermediaries' (intermediaries appointed other than through the WIS) must therefore be appointed for defendants. Although training is available, there is no accreditation process for non-registered intermediaries and rates of payment are unregulated.

3F.16   Arrangements for funding of intermediaries for defendants depend on the stage of the appointment process. Where the defendant is publicly funded, an application should be made to the Legal Aid Agency for prior authority to fund a pre-trial assessment. If the application is refused, an application may be made to the court to use its inherent powers to direct a pre-trial assessment and funding thereof. Where the court uses its inherent powers to direct assistance by an intermediary at trial (during evidence or for the entire trial), court staff are responsible for arranging payment from Central Funds. Internal guidance for court staff is in *Guidance for HMCTS Staff: Registered and Non-Registered Intermediaries for Vulnerable Defendants and Non-Vulnerable Defence and Prosecution Witnesses* (Her Majesty's Courts and Tribunals Service, 2014).

3F.17   The court should be satisfied that a non-registered intermediary has expertise suitable to meet the defendant's communication needs.

3F.18   Further information is in *Intermediaries: Step by Step* (see 3F.3 above).

Ineffective directions for intermediaries to assist defendants

3F.19   Directions for intermediaries to help defendants may be ineffective due to general unavailability, lack of suitable expertise, or non-availability for the purpose directed (for example, where the direction is for assistance during evidence, but an intermediary will only accept appointment for the entire trial).

3F.20   Intermediaries may contribute to the administration of justice by facilitating communication with appropriate defendants during the trial process. A trial will not be rendered unfair because a direction to appoint an intermediary for the defendant is ineffective. 'It would, in fact, be a most unusual case for a defendant who is fit to plead to be so disadvantaged by his condition that a properly brought prosecution would have to be stayed' because an intermediary with suitable expertise is not available for the purpose directed by the court (*R v Cox* [2012] EWCA Crim 549).

3F.21   Faced with an ineffective direction, it remains the court's responsibility to adapt the trial process to address the defendant's communication needs, as was the case prior to the existence of intermediaries (*R v Cox* [2012] EWCA Crim 549). In such a case, a ground rules hearing should be convened to ensure every reasonable step is taken to facilitate the defendant's participation in accordance with CrimPR 3.9. At the hearing, the court should make new, further and / or alternative directions. This includes setting ground rules to help the defendant follow proceedings and (where applicable) to give evidence.

3F.22   For example, to help the defendant follow proceedings the court may require evidence to be adduced by simple questions, with witnesses being asked to answer in short sentences. Regular breaks may assist the defendant's concentration and enable the defence advocate to summarise the evidence and take further instructions.

3F.23   Further guidance is available in publications such as Ground Rules Hearings and the Fair Treatment of Vulnerable People in Court (Toolkit 1; The Advocate's Gateway, 2015) and General Principles from Research - Planning to Question a Vulnerable Person or Someone with Communication Needs (Toolkit 2(a); The Advocate's Gateway, 2015). In the absence of an intermediary, these publications include information on planning how to manage the participation and questioning of the defendant, and the formulation of questions to avert misunderstanding (for example, by avoiding 'long and complicated questions . . . posed in a leading or 'tagged' manner' *(R v Wills* [2011] EWCA Crim 1938, [2012] 1 Cr App R 2))

Links to publications

* www.theadvocatesgateway.org/images/toolkits/
  1groundruleshearingsandthefairtreatmentofvulnerablepeopleincourt060315.pdf
* www.theadvocatesgateway.org/images/toolkits/2generalprinciplesfromresearchpolicyand
  guidance-planningtoquestionavulnerablepersonorsomeonewith
  communicationneeds141215.pdf

Intermediaries for witnesses and defendants under 18

3F.24   Communication needs (such as short attention span, suggestibility and reticence in relation to authority figures) are common to many witnesses and defendants under 18. Consideration should therefore be given to the communication needs of all children and young people appearing in the criminal courts and to adapting the trial process to address any such needs. Guidance is available in publications such as *Planning to Question a Child or Young Person* (Toolkit 6; The Advocate's Gateway, 2015) and *Effective Participation of Young Defendants* (Toolkit 8; The Advocate's Gateway, 2013).

Links to publications

- http://www.theadvocatesgateway.org/images/toolkits/
  6planningtoquestionachildoryoungperson141215.pdf
- http://www.theadvocatesgateway.org/images/toolkits/8YoungDefendants211013.pdf

3F.25   For the reasons set out in 3F.5 above, the appropriateness of an intermediary assessment for witnesses and defendants under 18 must be decided with care. Whilst there is no presumption that they will be assessed by an intermediary (to evaluate their communication needs prior to trial) or assisted by an intermediary at court (for example, if / when giving evidence), the decision should be made on an individual basis in the context of the circumstances of the particular case.

3F.26   Assessment by an intermediary should be considered for witnesses and defendants under 18 who seem liable to misunderstand questions or to experience difficulty expressing answers, including those who seem unlikely to be able to recognise a problematic question (such as one that is misleading or not readily understood), and those who may be reluctant to tell a questioner in a position of authority if they do not understand.

Attendance at ground rules hearing

3F.27   Where the court directs questioning will be conducted through an intermediary, CrimPR 3.9 requires the court to set ground rules. The intermediary should be present at the ground rules hearing to make representations in accordance with CrimPR 3.9(7)(a).

Listing

3F.28   Where the court directs an intermediary will attend the trial, their dates of availability should be provided to the court. It is preferable that such trials are fixed rather than placed in warned lists.

Photographs of court facilities

3F.29   Resident Judges in the Crown Court or the Chief Clerk or other responsible person in the magistrates' courts should, in consultation with HMCTS managers responsible for court security matters, develop a policy to govern under what circumstances photographs or other visual recordings may be made of court facilities, such as a live link room, to assist vulnerable or child witnesses to familiarise themselves with the setting, so as to be enabled to give their best evidence. For example, a photograph may provide a helpful reminder to a witness whose court visit has taken place sometime earlier. Resident Judges should tend to permit photographs to be taken for this purpose by intermediaries or supporters, subject to whatever restrictions the Resident Judge or responsible person considers to be appropriate, having regard to the security requirements of the court.

CPD I General matters 3G: Vulnerable defendants

Before the trial, sentencing or appeal

3G.1   If a vulnerable defendant, especially one who is young, is to be tried jointly with one who is not, the court should consider at the plea and case management hearing, or at a case management hearing in a magistrates' court, whether the vulnerable defendant should be tried on his own, but should only so order if satisfied that a fair trial cannot be achieved by use of appropriate special measures or other support for the defendant. If a vulnerable defendant is tried jointly with one who is not, the court should consider whether any of the modifications set out in this direction should apply in the circumstances of the joint trial and, so far as practicable, make orders to give effect to any such modifications.

3G.2   It may be appropriate to arrange that a vulnerable defendant should visit, out of court hours and before the trial, sentencing or appeal hearing, the courtroom in which that hearing is to take place so that he or she can familiarise him or herself with it.

3G.3   Where an intermediary is being used to help the defendant to communicate at court, the intermediary should accompany the defendant on his or her pre-trial visit. The visit will enable the defendant to familiarise him or herself with the layout of the court, and may include matters such as: where the defendant will sit, either in the dock or otherwise; court officials (what their roles are and where they sit); who else might be in the court, for example those in the public gallery and press box; the location of the witness box; basic court procedure; and the facilities available in the court.

3G.4   If the defendant's use of the live link is being considered, he or she should have an opportunity to have a practice session.

3G.5   If any case against a vulnerable defendant has attracted or may attract widespread public or media interest, the assistance of the police should be enlisted to try and ensure that the defendant is not, when attending the court, exposed to intimidation, vilification or abuse. Section 41 of the Criminal Justice Act 1925 prohibits the taking of photographs of defendants and witnesses (among others) in the court building or in its precincts, or when entering or leaving those precincts. A direction reminding media representatives of the prohibition may be appropriate. The court should also be ready at this stage, if it has not already done so, where relevant to make a reporting restriction under section 39 of the Children and Young Persons Act 1933 or, on an appeal to the Crown Court from a youth court, to remind media representatives of the application of section 49 of that Act.

3G.6   The provisions of the Practice Direction accompanying Part 6 should be followed.

The trial, sentencing or appeal hearing

3G.7   Subject to the need for appropriate security arrangements, the proceedings should, if practicable, be held in a courtroom in which all the participants are on the same or almost the same level.

3G.8   Subject again to the need for appropriate security arrangements, a vulnerable defendant, especially if he is young, should normally, if he wishes, be free to sit with members of his family or others in a like relationship, and with some other suitable supporting adult such as a social worker, and in a place which permits easy, informal communication with his legal representatives. The court should ensure that a suitable supporting adult is available throughout the course of the proceedings.

3G.9   It is essential that at the beginning of the proceedings, the court should ensure that what is to take place has been explained to a vulnerable defendant in terms he or she can understand and, at trial in the Crown Court, it should ensure in particular that the role of the jury has been explained. It should remind those representing the vulnerable defendant and the supporting adult of their responsibility to explain each step as it takes place and, at trial, explain the possible consequences of a guilty verdict and credit for a guilty plea. The court should also remind any intermediary of the responsibility to ensure that the vulnerable defendant has understood the explanations given to him/her. Throughout the trial the court should continue to ensure, by any appropriate means, that the defendant understands what is happening and what has been said by those on the bench, the advocates and witnesses.

3G.10   A trial should be conducted according to a timetable which takes full account of a vulnerable defendant's ability to concentrate. Frequent and regular breaks will often be appropriate. The court should ensure, so far as practicable, that the whole trial is conducted in clear language that the defendant can understand and that evidence in chief and cross-examination are conducted using questions that are short and clear. The conclusions of the 'ground rules' hearing should be followed, and advocates should use and follow the 'toolkits' as discussed above.

3G.11   A vulnerable defendant who wishes to give evidence by live link, in accordance with section 33A of the Youth Justice and Criminal Evidence Act 1999, may apply for a direction to that effect; the procedure in CrimPR 18.14 to 18.17 should be followed. Before making such a direction, the court must be satisfied that it is in the interests of justice to do so and that the use of a live link would enable the defendant to participate more effectively as a witness in the proceedings. The direction will need to deal with the practical arrangements to be made, including the identity of the person or persons who will accompany him or her.

3G.12   In the Crown Court, the judge should consider whether robes and wigs should be worn, and should take account of the wishes of both a vulnerable defendant and any vulnerable witness. It is generally desirable that those responsible for the security of a vulnerable defendant who is in custody, especially if he or she is young, should not be in uniform, and that there should be no recognisable police presence in the courtroom save for good reason.

3G.13   The court should be prepared to restrict attendance by members of the public in the courtroom to a small number, perhaps limited to those with an immediate and direct interest in the outcome. The court should rule on any challenged claim to attend. However, facilities for reporting the proceedings (subject to any restrictions under section 39 or 49 of the Children and Young Persons Act 1933) must be provided. The court may restrict the number of reporters attending in the courtroom to such number as is judged practicable and desirable. In ruling on any challenged claim to attend in the courtroom for the purpose of reporting, the court should be mindful of the public's general right to be informed about the administration of justice.

3G.14   Where it has been decided to limit access to the courtroom, whether by reporters or generally, arrangements should be made for the proceedings to be relayed, audibly and if possible visually, to another room in the same court complex to which the media and the public have access if it appears that there will be a need for such additional facilities. Those making use of such a facility should be reminded that it is to be treated as an extension of the courtroom and that they are required to conduct themselves accordingly.

CPD I General matters 3H: Wales and the Welsh language: Devolution issues

3H.1   These are the subject of Practice Direction: (Supreme Court) (Devolution Issues) [1999] 1 WLR 1592; [1999] 3 All ER 466; [1999] 2 Cr App R 486, to which reference should be made.

CPD I General matters 3J: Wales and the Welsh language: Applications for evidence to be given in Welsh

3J.1   If a defendant in a court in England asks to give or call evidence in the Welsh language, the case should not be transferred to Wales. In ordinary circumstances, interpreters can be provided on request.

CPD I General matters 3K: Wales and the Welsh language: Use of the Welsh language in courts in Wales

3K.1   The purpose of this direction is to reflect the principle of the Welsh Language Act 1993 that, in the administration of justice in Wales, the English and Welsh languages should be treated on a basis of equality.

General

3K.2   It is the responsibility of the legal representatives in every case in which the Welsh language may be used by any witness or party, or in any document which may be placed before the court, to inform the court of that fact, so that appropriate arrangements can be made for the listing of the case.

3K.3   Any party or witness is entitled to use Welsh in a magistrates' court in Wales without giving prior notice. Arrangements will be made for hearing such cases in accordance with the 'Magistrates' Courts' Protocol for Listing Cases where the Welsh Language is used' (January 2008) which is available on the Judiciary's website: http://www.judiciary.gov.uk/NR/exeres/ 57AD4763-F265-47B9-8A35-0442E08160E6. See also CrimPR 24.14.

3K.4   If the possible use of the Welsh language is known at the time of sending or appeal to the Crown Court, the court should be informed immediately after sending or when the notice of appeal is lodged. Otherwise, the court should be informed as soon as the possible use of the Welsh language becomes known.

3K.5   If costs are incurred as a result of failure to comply with these directions, a wasted costs order may be made against the defaulting party and / or his legal representatives.

3K.6   The law does not permit the selection of jurors in a manner which enables the court to discover whether a juror does or does not speak Welsh, or to secure a jury whose members are bilingual, to try a case in which the Welsh language may be used.

Preliminary and plea and case management hearings

3K.7 An advocate in a case in which the Welsh language may be used must raise that matter at the preliminary and/or the plea and case management hearing and endorse details of it on the advocates' questionnaire, so that appropriate directions may be given for the progress of the case.

Listing

3K.8 The listing officer, in consultation with the resident judge, should ensure that a case in which the Welsh language may be used is listed

    (a)   wherever practicable before a Welsh speaking judge, and
    (b)   in a court in Wales with simultaneous translation facilities.

Interpreters

3K.9 Whenever an interpreter is needed to translate evidence from English into Welsh or from Welsh into English, the court listing officer in whose court the case is to be heard shall contact the Welsh Language Unit who will ensure the attendance of an accredited interpreter.

Jurors

3K.10 The jury bailiff, when addressing the jurors at the start of their period of jury service, shall inform them that each juror may take an oath or affirm in Welsh or English as he wishes.

3K.11 After the jury has been selected to try a case, and before it is sworn, the court officer swearing in the jury shall inform the jurors in open court that each juror may take an oath or affirm in Welsh or English as he wishes. A juror who takes the oath or affirms in Welsh should not be asked to repeat it in English.

3K.12 Where Welsh is used by any party or witness in a trial, an accredited interpreter will provide simultaneous translation from Welsh to English for the jurors who do not speak Welsh. There is no provision for the translation of evidence from English to Welsh for a Welsh speaking juror.

3K.13 The jury's deliberations must be conducted in private with no other person present and therefore no interpreter may be provided to translate the discussion for the benefit of one or more of the jurors.

Witnesses

3K.14 When each witness is called, the court officer administering the oath or affirmation shall inform the witness that he may be sworn or affirm in Welsh or English, as he wishes. A witness who takes the oath or affirms in Welsh should not be asked to repeat it in English.

Opening / closing of Crown Courts

3K.15 Unless it is not reasonably practicable to do so, the opening and closing of the court should be performed in Welsh and English.

Role of Liaison Judge

3K.16 If any question or problem arises concerning the implementation of these directions, contact should in the first place be made with the Liaison Judge for the Welsh language through the Wales Circuit Office:

HMCTS WALES / GLITEM CYMRU
3rd Floor, Churchill House / 3ydd Llawr Tŷ Churchill
Churchill Way / Ffordd Churchill
Cardiff / Caerdydd CF10 2HH
029 2067 8300

CPD I General Matters 3L: Security of Prisoners at Court

3L.1 High-risk prisoners identified to the court as presenting a significant risk of escape, violence in court or danger to those in the court and its environs, and to the public at large, will as far as possible, have administrative and remand appearances listed for disposal by way of live link. They will have priority for the use of video equipment.

3L.2 In all other proceedings that require the appearance in person of a high-risk prisoner, the proceedings will be listed at an appropriately secure court building and in a court with a secure (enclosed or ceiling-high) dock.

3L.3 Where a secure dock or live link is not available the court will be asked to consider an application for additional security measures, which may include:

    (a)   the use of approved restraints (but see below at 3M.6);
    (b)   the deployment of additional escort staff;
    (c)   securing the court room for all or part of the proceedings;
    (d)   in exceptional circumstances, moving the hearing to a prison.

3L.4 National Offender Management Service (NOMS) will be responsible for providing the assessment of the prisoner and it is accepted that this may change at short notice. NOMS must provide notification to the listing officer of all Category A prisoners, those on the Escape-list and Restricted Status prisoners or other prisoners who have otherwise been assessed as presenting a significant risk of violence or harm. There is a presumption that all prisoners notified as high-risk will be allocated a hearing by live link and/or secure dock facilities. Where the court cannot provide a secure listing, the reasons should be provided to the establishment so that alternative arrangements can be considered.

Applications for use of approved restraints

3L.5 It is the duty of the court to decide whether a prisoner who appears before them should appear in restraints or not. Their decision must comply with the requirements of the European Convention on Human Rights, particularly Article 3, which prohibits degrading treatment, see *Ranniman v Finland* (1997) 26 EHRR 56.

3L.6 No prisoner should be handcuffed in court unless there are reasonable grounds for apprehending that he will be violent or will attempt to escape. If an application is made, it must be entertained by the court and a ruling must be given. The defence should be given the opportunity to respond to the application: proceeding in the absence of the defendant or his representative may give rise to an issue under Article 6(1) of the European Convention on Human Rights: *R v Rollinson* (1996) 161 JP 107, CA. If an application is to be made ex parte then that application should be made inter partes and the defence should be given an opportunity to respond.

Additional security measures

3L.7 It may be in some cases that additional dock officers are deployed to mitigate the risk that a prisoner presents. When the nature of the risk is so serious that increased deployment will be insufficient or would in itself be so unobtrusive as to prejudice a fair trial, then the court may be required to consider the following measures:

(a) reconsider the case for a live link hearing, including transferring the case to a court where the live link is available;
(b) transfer the case to an appropriately secure court;
(c) the use of approved restraints on the prisoner for all or part of the proceedings;
(d) securing the court room for all or part of the proceedings; and
(e) the use of (armed) police in the court building.

3L.8 The establishment seeking the additional security measures will submit a Court Management Directions Form setting out the evidence of the prisoners identified risk of escape or violence and requesting the courts approval of security measures to mitigate that risk. This must be sent to the listing officer along with current, specific and credible evidence that the security measures are both necessary and proportionate to the identified risk and that the risk cannot be managed in any other way.

3L.9 If the court is asked to consider transfer of the case, then this must be in accordance with the Listing and Allocation Practice Direction XIII F.11-F.13 post. The listing officer will liaise with the establishment, prosecution and the defence to ensure the needs of the witnesses are taken into account.

3L.10 The Judge who has conduct of the case must deal with any application for the use of restraints or any other security measure and will hear representations from the Crown Prosecution Service and the defence before proceeding. The application will only be granted if:

(a) there are good grounds for believing that the prisoner poses a significant risk of trying to escape from the court (beyond the assumed motivation of all prisoners to escape) and/or risk of serious harm towards those persons in court or the public generally should an escape attempt be successful; and
(b) where there is no other viable means of preventing escape or serious harm.

High-risk prisoners giving evidence from the witness box

3L.11 High-risk prisoners giving evidence from the witness box may pose a significant security risk. In circumstances where such prisoners are required to move from a secure dock to an insecure witness box, an application may be made for the court to consider the use of additional security measures including:

(a) the use of approved restraints;
(b) the deployment of additional escort staff or police in the courtroom or armed police in the building. The decision to deploy an armed escort is for the Chief Inspector of the relevant borough: the decision to allow the armed escort in or around the court room is for the Senior Presiding Judge (see below);
(c) securing the courtroom for all or part of the proceedings;
(d) giving evidence from the secure dock; and
(e) use of live link if the prisoner is not the defendant.

CPD I General Matters 3M: Procedure for Applications for Armed Police Presence in the Royal Courts of Justice, Crown Courts and Magistrates' Court Buildings

3M.1 This Practice Direction sets out the procedure for the making and handling of applications for authorisation for the presence of armed police officers within the precincts of any Crown Court and magistrates' court buildings at any time. It applies to an application to authorise the carriage of firearms or tasers in court. It does not apply to officers who are carrying CS spray or PAVA incapacitant spray, which is included in the standard equipment issued to officers in some forces and therefore no separate authorisation is required for its carriage in court.

3M.2 This Practice Direction applies to all cases in England and Wales in which a police unit intends to request authorisation for the presence of armed police officers in the Crown Court or in the magistrates' court buildings at any time and including during the delivery of prisoners to court.

3M.3 This Practice Direction allows applications to be made for armed police presence in the Royal Courts of Justice.

Emergency situations

3M.4 This Practice Direction does not apply in an emergency situation. In such circumstances, the police must be able to respond in a way in which their professional judgment deems most appropriate.

Designated court centres

3M.5 Applications may only be made for armed police presence in the designated Crown Court and magistrates' court centres (see below). This list may be revised from time to time in consultation with the Association of Chief Police Officers (ACPO) and HMCTS. It will be reviewed at least every five years in consultation with ACPO armed police secretariat and the Presiding Judges.

3M.6 The Crown Court centres designated for firearms deployment are:

(a) Northern Circuit: Carlisle, Chester, Liverpool, Preston, Manchester Crown Square & Manchester Minshull Street.

(b) North Eastern Circuit: Bradford, Leeds, Newcastle upon Tyne, Sheffield, Teesside and Kingston-upon-Hull.
(c) Western Circuit: Bristol, Winchester and Exeter.
(d) South Eastern Circuit (not including London): Canterbury, Chelmsford, Ipswich, Luton, Maidstone, Norwich, Reading and St Albans.
(e) South Eastern Circuit (London only): Central Criminal Court, Woolwich, Kingston and Snaresbrook.
(f) Midland Circuit: Birmingham, Northampton, Nottingham and Leicester.
(g) Wales Circuit: Cardiff, Swansea and Caernarfon.

3M.7 The magistrates' courts designated for firearms deployment are:

(a) South Eastern Circuit (London only): Westminster Magistrates' Court and Belmarsh Magistrates' Court.

Preparatory work prior to applications in all cases

3M.8 Prior to the making of any application for armed transport of prisoners or the presence of armed police officers in the court building, consideration must be given to making use of prison video link equipment to avoid the necessity of prisoners' attendance at court for the hearing in respect of which the application is to be made.

3M.9 Notwithstanding their designation, each requesting officer will attend the relevant court before an application is made to ensure that there have been no changes to the premises and that there are no circumstances that might affect security arrangements.

Applying in the Royal Courts of Justice

3M.10 All applications should be sent to the Listing Office of the Division in which the case is due to appear. The application should be sent by email if possible and must be on the standard form.

3M.11 The Listing Office will notify the Head of Division, providing a copy of the email and any supporting evidence. The Head of Division may ask to see the senior police office concerned.

3M.12 The Head of Division will consider the application. If it is refused, the application fails and the police must be notified.

3M.13 In the absence of the Head of Division, the application should be considered by the Vice-President of the Division.

3M.14 4The relevant Court Office will be notified of the decision and that office will immediately inform the police by telephone. The decision must then be confirmed in writing to the police.

Applying to the Crown Court

3M.15 All applications should be sent to the Cluster Manager and should be sent by email if possible and must be on the standard form.

3M.16 The Cluster Manager will notify the Presiding Judge on the circuit and the Resident Judge by email, providing a copy of the form and any supporting evidence. The Presiding Judge may ask to see the senior police officer concerned.

3M.17 The Presiding Judge will consider the application. If it is refused the application fails and the police must be informed.

3M.18 If the Presiding Judge approves the application it should be forwarded to the secretary in the Senior Presiding Judge's Office. The Senior Presiding Judge will make the final decision. The Presiding Judge will receive written confirmation of that decision.

3M.19 The Presiding Judge will notify the Cluster Manager and the Resident Judge of the decision. The Cluster Manager will immediately inform the police of the decision by telephone. The decision must then be confirmed in writing to the police.

Urgent applications to the Crown Court

3M.20 If the temporary deployment of armed police arises as an urgent issue and a case would otherwise have to be adjourned; or if the trial judge is satisfied that there is a serious risk to public safety, then the Resident Judge will have a discretion to agree such deployment without having obtained the consent of a Presiding Judge or the Senior Presiding Judge. In such a case:

(a) the Resident Judge should assess the facts and agree the proposed solution with a police officer of at least Superintendent level. That officer should agree the approach with the Firearms Division of the police.
(b) if the proposed solution involves the use of armed police officers, the Resident Judge must try to contact the Presiding Judge and/or the Senior Presiding Judge by email and telephone. The Cluster Manager should be informed of the situation.
(c) if the Resident Judge cannot obtain a response from the Presiding Judge or the Senior Presiding Judge, the Resident Judge may grant the application if satisfied:
 (i) that the application is necessary;
 (ii) that without such deployment there would be a significant risk to public safety; and
 (iii) that the case would have to be adjourned at significant difficulty or inconvenience.

3M.21 The Resident Judge must keep the position under continual review, to ensure that it remains appropriate and necessary. The Resident Judge must make continued efforts to contact the Presiding Judge and the Senior Presiding Judge to notify them of the full circumstances of the authorisation.

Applying to the magistrates' courts

3M.22 All applications should be directed, by email if possible, to the Office of the Chief Magistrate, at Westminster Magistrates' Court and must be on the standard form.

3M.23 The Chief Magistrate should consider the application and, if approved, it should be forwarded to the Senior Presiding Judge's office. The Senior Presiding Judge will make the final decision. The Chief Magistrate will receive written confirmation of that decision and will then notify the requesting police officer and, where authorisation is given, the affected magistrates' court of the decision.

Urgent applications in the magistrates' courts

3M.24   If the temporary deployment of armed police arises as an urgent issue and a case would otherwise have to be adjourned; or if the Chief Magistrate is satisfied that there is a serious risk to public safety, then the Chief Magistrate will have a discretion to agree such deployment without having obtained the consent of the Senior Presiding Judge. In such a case:

(a)   the Chief Magistrate should assess the facts and agree the proposed solution with a police officer of at least Superintendent level. That officer should agree the approach with the Firearms Division of the police.

(b)   if the proposed solution involves the use of armed police officers, the Chief Magistrate must try to contact the Senior Presiding Judge by email and telephone. The Cluster Manager should be informed of the situation.

(c)   if the Chief Magistrate cannot obtain a response from the Senior Presiding Judge, the Chief Magistrate may grant the application if satisfied:

(i)   that the application is necessary;

(ii)   that without such deployment there would be a significant risk to public safety; and

(iii) that the case would have to be adjourned at significant difficulty or inconvenience.

3M.25   The Chief Magistrate must keep the position under continual review, to ensure that it remains appropriate and necessary. The Chief Magistrate must make continued efforts to contact the Senior Presiding Judge to notify him of the full circumstances of the authorisation.

CPD I General Matters 3N: Use of Live Link and Telephone Facilities

3N.1   Where it is lawful and in the interests of justice to do so, courts should exercise their statutory and other powers to conduct hearings by live link or telephone. This is consistent with the Criminal Procedure Rules and with the recommendations of the President of the Queen's Bench Division's *Review of Efficiency in Criminal Proceedings* published in January 2015. Save where legislation circumscribes the court's jurisdiction, the breadth of that jurisdiction is acknowledged by CrimPR 3.5(1), (2)(d).

3N.2   It is the duty of the court to make use of technology actively to manage the case: CrimPR 3.2(1), (2)(h). That duty includes an obligation to give directions for the use of live links and telephone facilities in the circumstances listed in CrimPR 3.2(4) and (5) (pre-trial hearings, including pre-trial case management hearings). Where the court directs that evidence is to be given by live link, and especially where such a direction is given on the court's own initiative, it is essential that the decision is communicated promptly to the witness: CrimPR 18.4. Contrary to a practice adopted by some courts, none of those rules or other provisions require the renewal of a live link direction merely because a trial has had to be postponed or adjourned. Once made, such a direction applies until it is discharged by the court, having regard to the relevant statutory criteria.

3N.3   It is the duty of the parties to alert the court to any reason why live links or telephones should not be used where CrimPR 3.2 otherwise would oblige the court to do so; and, where a direction for the use of such facilities has been made, it is the duty of the parties as soon as practicable to alert the court to any reason why that direction should be varied CrimPR 3.3(2)(e) and 3.6.

3N.4   The word 'appropriate' in CrimPR 3.2(4) and (5) is not a term of art. It has the ordinary English meaning of 'fitting', or 'suitable'. Whether the facilities available to the court in any particular case can be considered appropriate is a matter for the court, but plainly to be appropriate such facilities must work, at the time at which they are required; all participants must be able to hear and, in the case of a live link, see each other clearly; and there must be no extraneous noise, movement or other distraction suffered by a participant, or transmitted by a participant to others. What degree of protection from accidental or deliberate interception should be considered appropriate will depend upon the purpose for which a live link or telephone is to be used. If it is to participate in a hearing which is open to the public anyway, then what is communicated by such means is by definition public and the use of links such as Skype or Facetime, which are not generally considered secure from interception, may not be objectionable. If it is to participate in a hearing in private, and especially one at which sensitive information will be discussed – for example, on an application for a search warrant – then a more secure service is likely to be required.

3N.5   There may be circumstances in which the court should not require the use of live link or telephone facilities despite their being otherwise appropriate at a pre-trial hearing. In every case, in deciding whether any such circumstances apply the court will keep in mind that, for the purposes of what may be an essentially administrative hearing, it may be compatible with the overriding objective to proceed in the defendant's absence altogether, especially if he or she is represented, unless, exceptionally, a rule otherwise requires. The principle that the court always must consider proceeding in a defendant's absence is articulated in CrimPR 3.9(2)(a). Where at a pre-trial hearing bail may be under consideration, the provisions of CrimPR 14.2 will be relevant.

3N.6   Such circumstances will include any case in which the defendant's effective participation cannot be achieved by his or her attendance by such means, and CrimPR 3.2(4) and (5) except such cases from the scope of the obligation which that rule otherwise imposes on the court. That exception may apply where (this list is not exhaustive) the defendant has a disorder or disability, including a hearing, speech or sight impediment, or has communication needs to which the use of a live link or telephone is inimical (whether or not those needs are such as to require the appointment of an intermediary); or where the defendant requires interpretation and effective interpretation cannot be provided by live link or telephone, as the case may be. In deciding whether to require a defendant to attend a first hearing in a magistrates' court by live link from a police station, the court should take into account any views expressed by the defendant, the terms of any mental health or other medical assessment of the defendant carried out at the police station, and all other relevant information and representations available. No single factor is determinative, but the court must keep in mind the terms of section 57C(6A) of the Crime and Disorder Act 1998 (Use of live link at preliminary hearings where accused is at police station) which provides that 'A live link direction under this section may not be given unless the court is satisfied that it is not contrary to the interests of justice to give the direction.'

3N.7   Finally, that exception sometimes may apply where the defendant's attendance in person at a pre-trial hearing will facilitate communication with his or her legal representatives. The court should not make such an exception merely to allow client and representatives to meet if that meeting can and should be held elsewhere. However, there will be cases in which defence representatives reasonably need to meet with a defendant, to take his or her instructions or to explain events to him or her, either shortly before or immediately after a pre-trial hearing and in circumstances in which that meeting cannot take place effectively by live link.

3N.8 Nothing prohibits the member or members of a court from conducting a pre-trial hearing by attending by live link or telephone from a location distant from all the other participants. Despite the conventional view that the venue for a court hearing is the court room in which that hearing has been arranged to take place, the Criminal Procedure Rules define 'court' as 'a tribunal with jurisdiction over criminal cases. It includes a judge, recorder, District Judge (Magistrates' Court), lay justice and, when exercising their judicial powers, the Registrar of Criminal Appeals, a justices' clerk or assistant clerk.' Neither CrimPR 3.25 (Place of trial), which applies in the Crown Court, nor CrimPR 24.14 (Place of trial), which applies in magistrates' courts, each of which requires proceedings to take place in a courtroom provided by the Lord Chancellor, applies for the purposes of a pre-trial hearing. Thus for the purposes of such a hearing there is no legal obstacle to the judge, magistrate or magistrates conducting it from elsewhere, with other participants assembled in a courtroom from which the member or members of the court are physically absent. In principle, nothing prohibits the conduct of a pre-trial hearing by live link or telephone with each participant, including the member or members of the court, in a different location (an arrangement sometimes described as a 'virtual hearing'). This is dependent upon there being means by which that hearing can be witnessed by the public – for example, by public attendance at a courtroom or other venue from which the participants all can be seen and heard (if by live link), or heard (if by telephone). The principle of open justice to which paragraph 3N.17 refers is relevant.

3N.9 Sections 57A to 57F of the Crime and Disorder Act 1998 allow a defendant who is in custody to enter a plea by live link, and allow for such a defendant who attends by live link to be sentenced. In appropriate circumstances, the court may allow a defendant who is not in custody to enter a plea by live link; but the same considerations as apply to sentencing in such a case will apply: see paragraph 3N.13 beneath.

3N.10 The Crime and Disorder Act 1998 does not allow for the attendance by live link at a contested trial of a defendant who is in custody. The court may allow a defendant who wishes to do so to observe all or part of his or her trial by live link, whether she or he is in custody or not, but (a) such a defendant cannot lawfully give evidence by such means unless he or she satisfies the criteria prescribed by section 33A of the Youth Justice and Criminal Evidence Act 1999 and the court so orders under that section (see also CrimPR 18.14 – 18.17); (b) a defendant who is in custody and who observes the trial by live link is not present, as a matter of law, and the trial must be treated as taking place in his or her absence, she or he having waived the right to attend; and (c) a defendant who has refused to attend his or her trial when required to do so, or who has absconded, must not be permitted to observe the proceedings by live link.

3N.11 Paragraphs I 3D to 3G inclusive of these Practice Directions (Vulnerable people in the courts; Ground rules hearings to plan the questioning of a vulnerable witness or defendant; Intermediaries; Vulnerable defendants) contain directions relevant to the use of a live link as a special measure for a young or otherwise vulnerable witness, or to facilitate the giving of evidence by a defendant who is likewise young or otherwise vulnerable, within the scope of the Youth Justice and Criminal Evidence Act 1999. Defence representatives and the court must keep in mind that special measures under the 1999 Act and CrimPR Part 18, including the use of a live link, are available to defence as well as to prosecution witnesses who meet the statutory criteria. Defence representatives should always consider whether their witnesses would benefit from giving evidence by live link and should apply for a direction if appropriate, either at the case management hearing or as soon as possible thereafter. A defence witness should be afforded the same facilities and treatment as a prosecution witness, including the same opportunity to make a pre-trial visit to the court building in order to familiarise himself or herself with it. Where a live link is sought as a special measure for a young or vulnerable witness or defendant, CrimPR 18.10 and 18.15 respectively require, among other things, that the applicant must identify someone to accompany that witness or defendant while they give evidence; must name the person, if possible; and must explain why that person would be an appropriate companion for that witness. The court must ensure that directions are given accordingly when ordering such a live link. Witness Service volunteers are available to support all witnesses, prosecution and defence, if required.

3N.12 Under sections 57A and 57D or 57E of the Crime and Disorder Act 1998 the court may pass sentence on a defendant in custody who attends by live link. The court may allow a defendant who is not in custody and who wishes to attend his or her sentencing by live link to do so, and may receive representations (but not evidence) from her or him by such means. Factors of which the court will wish to take account in exercising its discretion include, in particular, the penalty likely to be imposed; the importance of ensuring that the explanations of sentence required by CrimPR 24.11(9), in magistrates' courts, and in the Crown Court by CrimPR 25.16(7), can be given satisfactorily, for the defendant, for other participants and for the public, including reporters; and the preferences of the maker of any Victim Personal Statement which is to be read aloud or played pursuant to paragraph VII F.3(c) of these Practice Directions.

Youth defendants

3N.13 In the youth court or when a youth is appearing in the magistrates' court or the Crown Court, it will usually be appropriate for the youth to be produced in person at court. This is to ensure that the court can engage properly with the youth and that the necessary level of engagement can be facilitated with the Youth Offending Team worker, defence representative and/or appropriate adult. The court should deal with any application for use of a live-link on a case-by-case basis, after consultation with the parties and the Youth Offending Team. Such hearings that may be appropriate, include, onward remand hearings at which there is no bail application or case management hearings, particularly if the youth is already serving a custodial sentence.

3N.14 It rarely will be appropriate for a youth to be sentenced over a live link. However, notwithstanding the court's duties of engagement with a youth, the overriding welfare principle and the statutory responsibility of the youth offending worker to explain the sentence to the youth, after consultation with the parties and the Youth Offending Team, there may be circumstances in which it may be appropriate to sentence a youth over the live-link:

(a) If the youth is already serving a custodial sentence and the sentence to be imposed by the court is bound to be a further custodial sentence, whether concurrent or consecutive;

(b) If the youth is already serving a custodial sentence and the court is minded to impose a non-custodial sentence which will have no material impact on the sentence being served;

(c) The youth is being detained in a secure establishment at such a distance from the court that the travelling time from one to the other will be significant so as to materially affect the welfare of the youth;

(d) The youth's condition-whether mental or otherwise- is so disturbed that his or her production would be a significant detriment to his or her welfare.

3N.15 Arrangements must be made in advance of any live link hearing to enable the youth offending worker to be at the secure establishment where the youth is in custody. In the event that such arrangements are not practicable, the youth offending worker must have sufficient access to the youth via the live link booth before and after the hearing.

Conduct of participants

3N.16 Where a live link is used, the immediate vicinity of the device by which a person attends becomes, temporarily, part of the courtroom for the purposes of that person's participation. That person, and any advocate or legal representative, custodian, court officer, intermediary or other companion, whether immediately visible to the court or not, becomes a participant for the purposes of CrimPR 1.2(2) and is subject to the court's jurisdiction to regulate behaviour in the courtroom. The substance and effect of this direction must be drawn to the attention of all such participants.

Open justice and records of proceedings

3N.17 The principle of open justice to which CrimPR 6.2(1) gives effect applies as strongly where electronic means of communication are used to conduct a hearing as it applies in other circumstances. Open justice is the principal means by which courts are kept under scrutiny by the public. It follows that where a participant attends a hearing in public by live link or telephone then that person's participation must be, as nearly as may be, equally audible and, if applicable, equally visible to the public as it would be were he or she physically present. Where electronic means of communication are used to conduct a hearing, records of the event must be maintained in the usual way: CrimPR 5.4. In the Crown Court, this includes the recording of the proceedings: CrimPR 5.5.

CPD I General Matters 3P: Commissioning of Medical Reports

General observations

3P.1 CrimPR 24.3 and 25.10 concern procedures to be followed in magistrates' courts and in the Crown Court respectively where there is doubt about a defendant's mental health and, in the Crown Court, the defendant's capacity to participate in a trial. CrimPR 3.28 governs the procedure where, on the court's own initiative, a magistrates' court requires expert medical opinion about the potential suitability of a hospital order under section 37(3) of the Mental Health Act 1983 (hospital order without convicting the defendant), the Crown Court requires such opinion about the defendant's fitness to participate at trial, under section 4 of the Criminal Procedure (Insanity) Act 1964, or either a magistrates' court or the Crown Court requires such opinion to help the court determine a question of intent or insanity.

3P.2 Rule 3.28 governs the procedure to be followed where a report is commissioned at the instigation of the court. It is not a substitute for the prompt commissioning of a report or reports by a party or party's representatives where expert medical opinion is material to that party's case. In particular, those representing a defendant may wish to obtain a medical report or reports wholly independently of the court. Nothing in these directions, therefore, should be read as discouraging a party from commissioning a medical report before the case comes before the court, where that party believes such a report to be material to an issue in the case and where it is possible promptly to commission it. However, where a party has commissioned such a report then if that report has not been 4 received by the time the court gives directions for preparation for trial, and if the court agrees that it seems likely that the report will be material to what is in issue, then when giving directions for trial the court should include a timetable for the reception of that report and should give directions for progress to be reviewed at intervals, adopting the timetable set out in these directions with such adaptations as are needed.

3P.3 In assessing the likely materiality of an expert medical report to help the court assess a defendant's health and capacity at the time of the alleged offence or the time of trial, or both, the court will be assisted by the parties' representations; by the views expressed in any assessment that may already have been prepared; and by the views of practitioners in local criminal justice mental health services, whose assistance is available to the court under local liaison arrangements.

3P.4 Where the court requires the assistance of such a report then it is essential that there should be (i) absolute clarity about who is expected to do what, by when, and at whose expense; and (ii) judicial directions for progress with that report to be monitored and reviewed at prescribed intervals, following a timetable set by the court which culminates in the consideration of the report at a hearing. This is especially important where the report in question is a psychiatric assessment of the defendant for the preparation of which specific expertise may be required which is not readily available and because in some circumstances a second such assessment, by another medical practitioner, may be required.

Timetable for the commissioning, preparation and consideration of a report or reports

3P.5 CrimPR 3.28 requires the court to set a timetable appropriate to the case for the preparation and reception of a report. That timetable must not be in substitution for the usual timetable for preparation for trial but must instead be incorporated within the trial preparation timetable. The fact that a medical report is to be obtained, whether that is commissioned at a party's instigation or on the court's own initiative, is never a reason to postpone a preparation for trial or a plea and trial preparation hearing, or to decline to give the directions needed for preparation for trial. It follows that a trial date must be set and other directions given in the usual way.

3P.6 In setting the timetable for obtaining a report or reports the court will take account of such representations and other information that it receives, including information about the anticipated availability and workload of medical practitioners with the appropriate expertise. However, the timetable ought not be a protracted one. It is essential to keep in mind the importance of maintaining progress: in recognition of the defendant's rights and with respect for the interests of victims and witnesses, as required by CrimPR Part 1 (the overriding objective). In a magistrates' court account must be taken, too, of section 11 of the Powers of Criminal Courts (Sentencing) Act 2000, which limits the duration of each remand 5 pending the preparation of a report to 3 weeks, where the defendant is to be in custody, and to 4 weeks if the defendant is to be on bail.

3P.7 Subject, therefore, to contrary judicial direction the timetable set by the court should require:

(a) the convening of a further pre-trial case management hearing to consider the report and its implications for the conduct of the proceedings no more than 6 – 8 weeks after the court makes its request in a magistrates' court, and no more than 10 – 12 weeks after the request in the Crown Court (at the end of Stage 2 of the directions for pre-trial preparation in the Crown Court);

(b) the prompt identification of an appropriate medical practitioner or practitioners, if not already identified by the court, and the despatch of a commission or commissions accordingly, within 2 business days of the court's decision to request a report;

(c) acknowledgement of a commission by its recipient, and acceptance or rejection of that commission, within 5 business days of its receipt;

(d) enquiries by court staff to confirm that the commission has been received, and to ascertain the action being taken in response, in the event that no acknowledgement is received within 10 business days of its despatch;

(e) delivery of the report within 5 weeks of the despatch of the commission;

(f) enquiries into progress by court staff in the event that no report is received within 5 weeks of the despatch of the commission.

3P.8 The further pre-trial case management hearing that is convened for the court to consider the report should not be adjourned before it takes place save in exceptional circumstances and then only by explicit judicial direction the reasons for which must be recorded. If by the time of that hearing the report is available, as usually should be the case, then at that hearing the court can be expected to determine the issue in respect of which the report was commissioned and give further directions accordingly. If by that time, exceptionally, the report is not available then the court should take the opportunity provided by that hearing to enquire into the reasons, give such directions as are appropriate, and if necessary adjourn the hearing to a fixed date for further consideration then. Where it is known in advance of that hearing that the report will not be available in time, the hearing may be conducted by live link or telephone: subject, in the defendant's case, to the same considerations as are identified at paragraph 3N.6 of these Practice Directions. However, it rarely will be appropriate to dispense altogether with that hearing, or to make enquiries and give further directions without any hearing at all, in view of the arrangements for monitoring and review that the court already will have directed and which, by definition therefore, thus far will have failed to secure the report's timely delivery.

3P.9 Where a requirement of the timetable set by the court is not met, or where on enquiry by court staff it appears that the timetable is unlikely to be met, and in any instance in which a medical practitioner who accepts a commission asks for more time, then court staff should not themselves adjust the timetable or accede to such a request but instead should seek directions from an appropriate judicial authority. Subject to local judicial direction, that will be, in the Crown Court, the judge assigned to the case or the resident judge and, in a magistrates' court, a District Judge (Magistrates' Courts) or justice of the peace assigned to the case, or the Justices' Clerk, an assistant clerk or other senior legal adviser. Even if the timetable is adjusted in consequence:

(a) the further pre-trial case management hearing convened to consider the report rarely should be adjourned before it takes place: see paragraph 3O.13 above;

(b) directions should be given for court staff henceforth to make regular enquiries into progress, at prescribed intervals of not more than 2 weeks, and to report the outcome to an appropriate judicial authority who will decide what further directions, if any, to give.

3P.10 Any adjournment of a hearing convened to consider the report should be to a specific date: the hearing should not be adjourned generally, or to a date to be set in due course. The adjournment of such a hearing should not be for more than a further 6 – 8 weeks save in the most exceptional circumstances; and no more than one adjournment of the hearing should be allowed without obtaining written or oral representations from the commissioned medical practitioner explaining the reasons for the delay.

Commissioning a report

3.11 Guidance entitled 'Good practice guidance: commissioning, administering and producing psychiatric reports for sentencing' prepared for and published by the Ministry of Justice and HM Courts and Tribunals Service in September 2010 contains material that will assist court staff and those who are asked to prepare such reports: http://www.ohrn.nhs.uk/resource/policy/GoodPracticeGuidePsychRepo rts.pdf

The guidance includes standard forms of letters of instruction and other documents.

3.12 CrimPR 3.28 requires the commissioner of a report to explain why the court seeks the report and to include relevant information about the circumstances. The HMCTS Guidance contains forms for judicial use in the instruction of court staff, and guidance to court staff on the preparation of letters of instruction, where a report is required for sentencing purposes. Those forms and that guidance can be adapted for use where the court requires a report on the defendant's fitness to particpate, in the Crown Court, or in a magistrates' court requires a report for the purposes of section 37(3) of the Mental Health Act 1983.

3.13 The commission should invite a practitioner who is unable to accept it promptly to nominate a suitably qualified substitute, if possible, and to transfer the commission to that person, reporting the transfer when acknowledging the court officer's letter. It is entirely appropriate for the commission to draw the recipient's attention to CrimPR 1.2 (the duty of the participants in a criminal case) and to CrimPR 19.2(1)(b) (the obligation of an expert witness to comply with directions made by a court and at once to inform the court of any significant failure, by the expert or another, to take any step required by such a direction).

3.14 Where the relevant legislation requires a second psychiatric assessment by a second medical practitioner, and where no commission already has been addressed to a second such practitioner, the commission may invite the person to whom it is addressed to nominate a suitably qualified second person and to pass a copy of the commission to that person forthwith.

Funding arrangements

3.15 Where a medical report has been, or is to be, commissioned by a party then that party is responsible for arranging payment of the fees incurred, even though the report is intended for the court's use. That must be made clear in that party's commission.

3.16 Where a medical report is requested by the court and commissioned by a party or by court staff at the court's direction then the commission must include (i) confirmation that the fees will be paid by HMCTS, (ii) details of how, and to whom, to submit an invoice or claim for fees, and (iii) notice of the prescribed rates of fees and of any legislative or other criteria applicable to the calculation of the fees that may be paid.

Remand in custody

3.17 Where the defendant who is to be examined will be remanded in custody then notice that directions have been given for a medical report or reports to be prepared must be included in the information given to the defendant's custodian, to ensure that the preparation of the report or reports can be facilitated. This is especially important where bail is withheld on the ground that it would be otherwise impracticable to complete the required report, and in particular where that is the only ground for withholding bail.

CPD I Annex

Guidance on Establishing and Using Live Link and Telephone Facilities for Criminal Court Hearings

1. This guidance supplements paragraph I 3N of these Practice Directions on the use of live link and telephone facilities to conduct a hearing or receive evidence in a criminal court.

2. This guidance deals with many of the practical considerations that arise in connection with setting up and using live link and telephone facilities. However, it does not contain detailed instructions about how to use particular live link or telephone equipment at particular locations (how to turn the equipment on; how, and exactly when, to establish a connection between the courtroom and the other location; etc.) because details vary from place to place and cannot practically all be contained in general guidance. Those details will be made available locally to those who need them. Nor does this guidance contain detailed instructions about the individual responsibilities of court staff, police officers and prison staff because those are matters for court managers, Chief Constables and HM Prison Governors.

Installation of live link and telephone facilities in the courtroom

3. Everyone in the courtroom must be able to hear and, in the case of a live link, see clearly those who attend by live link or telephone; and the equipment in the courtroom must allow those who attend by live link or telephone to hear, and in the case of a live link see, all the participants in the courtroom. If more than one person is to attend by live link or telephone simultaneously then the equipment must be capable of accommodating them all. (These requirements of course are subject to any special or other measures which a court in an individual case may direct to prevent a witness seeing, or being seen by, the defendant or another participant, or members of the public.)

4. Some of the considerations that apply to the installation and use of equipment in other locations will apply in a courtroom, too. They are set out in the following paragraphs. In the case of a live link, attention will need to be given to lighting and to making sure that those attending by live link can see and hear clearly what takes place in the courtroom without being distracted by the movement of court staff, legal representatives or members of the public, or by noise inside the courtroom. The sensitivity and positioning of the courtroom microphones may mean that even the movement of papers, or the operation of keyboards, while barely audible inside the courtroom itself, is clearly audible and distracting to a witness or defendant attending by live link or telephone.

Installation and use of live link and telephone facilities in a live link room

5. Paragraph 6 applies to the installation and use of equipment in a building or in a vehicle which is to be used regularly for giving evidence by live link. It applies to a room within the court building, but separated from the courtroom itself, from which a witness can give evidence by live link; it applies to such a room at a police station or elsewhere which has been set aside for regular use for such a purpose; and it applies to a van or other vehicle which has been adapted for use as a mobile live link room. However, that paragraph does not apply to the courtroom itself; it does not apply to a place from which a witness gives evidence, or a participant takes part in the proceedings, by live link or telephone, if that place is not regularly used for such a purpose (but see paragraph 7 beneath); and it does not apply in a prison or other place of detention (as to which, see paragraph 12 beneath). The objective is to ensure that anyone who participates by live link or telephone is conscious of the gravity of the occasion and of the authority of the court, and realises that they are required to conduct themselves in the same respectful manner as if they were physically present in a courtroom.

6. A live link room should have the following features:

(a) the room should be an appropriate size, neither too small nor too large.

(b) the room should have suitable lighting, whether natural or electric. Any windows may need blinds or curtains fitted that can be adjusted in accordance with the weather conditions outside and to ensure privacy.

(c) there should be a sign or other means of making clear to those outside the room when the room is in use.

(d) arrangements should be made to ensure that nobody in the vicinity of the room is able to hear the evidence being given inside, unless the court otherwise directs (for example, to allow a witness' family to watch the witness' evidence on a supplementary screen in a nearby waiting room, as if they were seeing and hearing that evidence by live link in the courtroom).

(e) arrangements should be made to minimise the risk of disruption to the proceedings by noise outside the room. Such noise will distract the witness and may be audible and distracting to the court.

(f) the room should be provided with appropriate and comfortable seating for the witness and, where the witness is a civilian witness, seating for a Witness Service or other companion. A waiting area/room adjacent to the live link room may be required for any other persons attending with the witness. There must be adequate accommodation, support and, where appropriate, security within the premises for witnesses. If both prosecution and defence witnesses attend the same facility, they should wait in separate rooms. It may be inappropriate for defence witnesses to give evidence in police premises (for example in a trial for assaulting a police officer) and in that case parties and the court should identify an alternative venue such as a court building (not necessarily the location of the hearing), or arrange for evidence to be given from elsewhere by Skype, etc. Care must be taken to ensure that all witnesses, whether prosecution or defence, are afforded the same assistance, respect and security.

(g) the equipment installed (monitor, microphone and camera, or cameras) in the room must be good enough to ensure that both the picture and sound quality from the room to the court, and from the court to the room, is fit for purpose. The link must enable all in the courtroom to see and hear the witness clearly and it must enable the witness to see and hear clearly all participants in the courtroom.

(h) unless the court otherwise directs, the witness usually will sit to take the oath or affirm and to give evidence. The camera(s) must be positioned to ensure that the witness' face and demeanour can be seen whether he or she sits or stands.

(i) the wall behind the witness, and thus in view of the camera, should be a pale neutral colour (beige and light green/blue are most suitable) and there should be no pictures or notices displayed on that wall.

(j) the Royal coat of arms may be displayed to remind witnesses and others that when in use the room is part of the courtroom.

(k) a notice should be displayed that reminds users of the live link to conduct themselves in the same manner as if they were present in person in the courtroom, and to remind them that while using the live link they are subject to the court's jurisdiction to regulate behaviour in the courtroom.

(l) the room should be supplied with the same oath and affirmation cards and Holy books as are available in a courtroom. The guidance for the taking of oaths and the making of affirmations which applies in a courtroom applies equally in a live link room. Holy books must be treated with the utmost respect and stored with appropriate care.

(m) unless court or other staff are on hand to operate the live link or telephone equipment, clear instructions for users must be in the live link room explaining how, and when, to establish a connection to the courtroom.

Provision and use of live link and telephone facilities elsewhere

7. Where a witness gives evidence by live link, or a participant takes part in proceedings by live link or telephone, otherwise than from an established live link room, the objective remains the same as explained in paragraph 5 above. In accordance with that objective, the spirit of the requirements for a live link room should be followed as far as is reasonably practicable; but of course the court will not expect adherence to the letter of those requirements where, for example, a witness who is seriously ill but still able to testify is willing to do so from his or her sick bed, or a doctor or other expert witness is to testify by live link from her or his office. In any such case it is essential that the parties anticipate the arrangements and directions that may be required. Of particular and obvious importance is the need for arrangements that will exclude audible and visible interruptions during the proceedings, and the need for adequate clarity of communication between the remote location and the courtroom.

Conduct of hearings by live link or telephone

8. Before live link or telephone equipment is to be used to conduct a hearing, court staff must make sure that the equipment is in working order and that the essential criteria listed in paragraph I 3N.4 of the Practice Directions ('appropriate' facilities) are met.

9. If a witness who gives evidence by live link produces exhibits, the court must be asked to give appropriate directions during preparation for trial. In most cases the parties can be expected to agree the identity of the exhibit, whatever else is in dispute. In the absence of agreement, documentary exhibits, copies of which have been provided under CrimPR 24.13 (magistrates' court trial) or CrimPR 25.17 (Crown Court trial), and other exhibits which are clearly identifiable by reference to their features and which have been delivered by someone else to the court, may be capable of production by a witness who is using a live link.

10. Where a witness who gives evidence by live link is likely to be referred to exhibits or other material while he or she does so, whether or not as the producer of an exhibit, the court must be asked to give directions during preparation for trial to facilitate such a reference: for example, by requiring the preparation of a paginated and indexed trial bundle which will be readily accessible to the witness, on paper or in electronic form, as well as available to those who are in the courtroom. It is particularly important to make sure that documents and images which are to be displayed by electronic means in the courtroom will be accessible to the witness too. It is unlikely that the live link equipment will be capable of displaying sufficiently clearly to the witness images

displayed only on a screen in the courtroom; and likely to be necessary to arrange for those images to be displayed also at the location from which the witness gives evidence, or made available to him or her by some other means. It is likewise important that there should be readily accessible to the witness, on paper or in electronic form, a copy of his or her witness statement (to which she or he may be referred under CrimPR 24.4(5), in a magistrates' court, or under CrimPR 25.11(5), in the Crown Court) and transcript of his or her ABE interview, if applicable.

Conduct of those attending by live link or telephone: practical considerations

11. A person who gives evidence by live link, or who participates by live link or telephone, must behave exactly as if he or she were in the courtroom, addressing the court and the other participants in the proper manner and observing the appropriate social conventions, remembering that she or he will be heard, and if using a live link seen, as if physically present. A practical application of the rules and social conventions governing a participant's behaviour requires, among other things, the following:

(1) in the case of a professional participant, including a police officer, lawyer or expert witness:
   (a) a participant should prepare themselves to communicate with the court with adequate time in hand, and especially where it will be necessary first to establish the live link or telephone connection with the court.
   (b) on entering a live link room a participant should ensure that those outside are made aware that the room is in use, to avoid being interrupted while in communication with the court.
   (c) a participant should ensure that they have the means to communicate with court staff by some means other than the proposed live link or telephone equipment, in case the equipment they plan to use should fail. They should have to hand an alternative contact number for the court and, if using a mobile phone for the purpose, they should ensure that it is fully charged.
   (d) immediately before using the live link or telephone equipment to communicate with the court the person using that equipment and any other person in the live link room must as a general rule switch off any mobile telephone or other device which might interfere with that equipment or interrupt the proceedings. If the device is essential to giving evidence (for example, an electronic notebook), or if it is the only available means of communication with court staff should the other equipment fail, then every effort must be made to minimise the risk of interference, for example by switching a mobile telephone to silent and by placing electronic devices at a distance from the microphone.
   (e) a person who gives evidence by live link, or who takes part in the proceedings for some other purpose by live link, must dress as they would if attending by physical presence in the courtroom.
   (f) each person in a live link room, whether he or she can be seen by the court or not, and each person present where a telephone conference or loudspeaker facility is in use, must identify themselves clearly to the court.
   (g) a person who participates by telephone otherwise than from a room specially equipped for that purpose must take care to ensure that they cannot be interrupted while in communication with the court and that no extraneous noise will be audible so as to distract that participant or the court.
   (h) a person who participates by telephone in a call to which he or she, the court and others all contribute must take care to speak clearly and to avoid interrupting in such a way as to prevent any other participant hearing what is said. Particular care is required where a participant uses a hands-free or other loudspeaker phone.
   (i) a witness who gives evidence by live link may take with him or her into the live link room a copy of her or his written witness statement and (if a police officer) his or her notebook. While giving evidence the witness must place the statement or notes face down, or otherwise out of sight, unless the court gives permission to refer to it. The witness must take the statement or notes away when leaving the live link room.
   (j) where successive witnesses are due to give evidence about the same events by live link, and especially where they are due to do so from the same live link room; where the events in question are controversial; or where there is any suggestion that arrangements are required to guard against the accidental or deliberate contamination of a witness' evidence by communication with one who has already given evidence, then the court must be asked to give directions accordingly. Subject to those directions, the usual arrangement should be that a witness who has been released should remain in sight of the court, by means of the live link, in the live link room while the next witness enters, and then should leave: so that the court will be able to see that no inappropriate communication between the two has occurred.
(2) in the case of any other participant:
   (a) the preparation of any live link room and the use of the equipment will be the responsibility of court staff, or of the staff present at that live link room if it is outside the court building. Where the participant is a witness giving evidence pursuant to a special measures direction, detailed arrangements will have been made accordingly.
   (b) mobile telephones and other devices that might interfere with the live link or telephone equipment must be switched off.
   (c) a witness or other participant should take care to speak clearly and to avoid interrupting or making a sound which prevents another participant hearing what is said, especially where a hands-free or other loudspeaker phone is in use.
   (d) the party who calls a witness, or the witness supporter, or court or other staff, as the case may be, must supply the witness with all he or she may need for the purpose of giving evidence, in accordance with the relevant rules and Practice Directions. This may, and usually will, include a copy of the witness' statement, in case it becomes necessary to ask him or her to refer to it, and copies of any exhibits or other material to which he or she may be asked to refer: see also paragraph 10 above.

Prison to court video links

12. The objective of the guidance in the preceding paragraphs applies. It is essential that the authority and gravity of the proceedings is respected, by defendants and by their custodians. Detailed instructions are contained in the information issued jointly by the National Offender Management Service and by HM Courts and Tribunals Service, with which prison and court staff must familiarise themselves. The principles set out in that guidance correspond with those of the Criminal Practice Directions, as elaborated in this guidance.

13. Where a defendant in custody attends court by live link it is likely that he or she will need to communicate with his or her representatives before and after the hearing, using the live link or by telephone. Arrangements will be required to allow that to take place.

14. Court staff are reminded that a live link to a prison establishment is a means of communication with the defendant. It does not provide an alternative means of formal communication with that establishment and it may not be used in substitution for service on that establishment of those notices and orders required to be served by the Criminal Procedure Rules.

Part 4 Service of documents

[No Practice Directions]

CrimPR Part 5 Forms and court records

CPD I General matters 5A: Forms

5A.1 The forms at Annex D to the Consolidated Criminal Practice Direction of 8th July, 2002, [2002] 1 WLR. 2870; [2002] 2 Cr App R 35, or forms to that effect, are to be used in the criminal courts, in accordance with CrimPR 5.1.

5A.2 The forms at Annex E to that Practice Direction, the case management forms, must be used in the criminal courts, in accordance with that rule.

5A.3 The table at the beginning of each section of each of those Annexes lists the forms and:

(a) shows the rule in connection with which each applies;
(b) describes each form.

5A.4 The forms may be amended or withdrawn from time to time, or new forms added, under the authority of the Lord Chief Justice.

CPD I General matters 5B: Access to information held by the court

5B.1 Open justice, as Lord Justice Toulson re-iterated in the case of *R (Guardian News and Media Ltd) v City of Westminster Magistrates' Court* [2012] EWCA Civ 420, [2013] QB 618, is a 'principle at the heart of our system of justice and vital to the rule of law'. There are exceptions but these 'have to be justified by some even more important principle.' However, the practical application of that undisputed principle, and the proper balancing of conflicting rights and principles, call for careful judgments to be made. The following is intended to provide some assistance to courts making decisions when asked to provide the public, including journalists, with access to or copies of information and documents held by the court, or when asked, exceptionally, to forbid the supply of transcripts that otherwise would have been supplied. It is not a prescriptive list, as the court will have to consider all the circumstances of each individual case.

5B.2 It remains the responsibility of the recipient of information or documents to ensure that they comply with any and all restrictions such as reporting restrictions (see Part 6 and the accompanying Practice Direction).

5B.3 For the purposes of this direction, the word document includes images in photographic, digital including DVD format, video, CCTV or any other form.

5B.4 Certain information can and should be provided to the public on request, subject to any restrictions, such as reporting restrictions, imposed in that particular case. CrimPR 5.5 governs the supply of transcript of a recording of proceedings in the Crown Court. CrimPR 5.8(4) and 5.8(6) read together specify the information that the court officer will supply to the public; an oral application is acceptable and no reason need be given for the request. There is no requirement for the court officer to consider the non -disclosure provisions of the Data Protection Act 1998 as the exemption under section 35 applies to all disclosure made under 'any enactment ... or by the order of a court', which includes under the Criminal Procedure Rules.

5B.5 If the information sought is neither transcript nor listed at CrimPR 5.8(6), rule 5.8(7) will apply, and the provision of information is at the discretion of the court. The following guidance is intended to assist the court in exercising that discretion.

5B.6 A request for access to documents used in a criminal case should first be addressed to the party who presented them to the court or who, in the case of a written decision by the court, received that decision. Prosecuting authorities are subject to the Freedom of Information Act 2000 and the Data Protection Act 1998 and their decisions are susceptible to review.

5B.7 If the request is from a journalist or media organisation, note that there is a protocol between NPCC, the CPS and the media entitled 'Publicity and the Criminal Justice System':

http://www.cps.gov.uk/publications/agencies/mediaprotocol.html www.cps.gov.uk/publication/publicity-and-criminal-justicesystem

There is additionally a protocol made under CrimPR 5.8(5)(b) between the media and HMCTS:

www.newsmediauk.org/writ/jMediaUploads/PDF%20DocsjProtocol_for _Sharing_ Court_Documents.pdf

This Practice Direction does not affect the operation of those protocols. Material should generally be sought under the relevant protocol before an application is made to the court.

5B.8 An application to which CrimPR 5.8(7) applies must be made in accordance with rule 5.8; it must be in writing, unless the court permits otherwise, and 'must explain for what purpose the information is required.' A clear, detailed application, specifying the name and contact details of the applicant, whether or not he or she represents a media organisation, and setting out the reasons for the application and to what use the information will be put, will be of most assistance to the court. Applicants should state if they have requested the information under a protocol and include any reasons given for the refusal. Before considering such an application, the court will expect the applicant to have given notice of the request to the parties.

5B.9   The court will consider each application on its own merits. The burden of justifying a request for access rests on the applicant. Considerations to be taken into account will include:

(i)   whether or not the request is for the purpose of contemporaneous reporting; a request after the conclusion of the proceedings will require careful scrutiny by the court;
(ii)   the nature of the information or documents being sought;
(iii)   the purpose for which they are required;
(iv)   the stage of the proceedings at the time when the application is made;
(v)   the value of the documents in advancing the open justice principle, including enabling the media to discharge its role, which has been described as a 'public watchdog', by reporting the proceedings effectively;
(vi)   any risk of harm which access to them may cause to the legitimate interests of others; and
(vii)   any reasons given by the parties for refusing to provide the material requested and any other representations received from the parties.

Further, all of the principles below are subject to any specific restrictions in the case. Courts should be aware that the risk of providing a document may reduce after a particular point in the proceedings, and when the material requested may be made available.

Documents read aloud in their entirety

5B.10   If a document has been read aloud to the court in its entirety, it should usually be provided on request, unless to do so would be disruptive to the court proceedings or place an undue burden on the court, the advocates or others. It may be appropriate and convenient for material to be provided electronically, if this can be done securely.

5B.11   Documents likely to fall into this category are:

(i)   Opening notes
(ii)   Statements agreed under section 9 of the Criminal Justice Act 1967, including experts' reports, if read in their entirety
(iii)   Admissions made under section 10 of the Criminal Justice Act 1967.

Documents treated as read aloud in their entirety

5B.12   A document treated by the court as if it had been read aloud in public, though in fact it has been neither read nor summarised aloud, should generally be made available on request. The burden on the court, the advocates or others in providing the material should be considered, but the presumption in favour of providing the material is greater when the material has only been treated as having been read aloud. Again, subject to security considerations, it may be convenient for the material to be provided electronically.

5B.13   Documents likely to fall into this category include:

(i)   Skeleton arguments
(ii)   Written submissions
(iii)   Written decisions by the court

Documents read aloud in part or summarised aloud

5B.14   Open justice requires only access to the part of the document that has been read aloud. If a member of the public requests a copy of such a document, the court should consider whether it is proportionate to order one of the parties to produce a suitably redacted version. If not, access to the document is unlikely to be granted; however open justice will generally have been satisfied by the document having been read out in court.

5B.15   If the request comes from an accredited member of the press (see *Access by reporters* below), there may be circumstances in which the court orders that a copy of the whole document be shown to the reporter, or provided, subject to the condition that those matters that had not been read out to the court may not be used or reported. A breach of such an order would be treated as a contempt of court.

5B.16   Documents in this category are likely to include:

(i)   Section 9 statements that are edited

Jury bundles and exhibits (including video footage shown to the jury)

5B.17   The court should consider:

(i)   whether access to the specific document is necessary to understand or effectively to report the case;
(ii)   the privacy of third parties, such as the victim (in some cases, the reporting restriction imposed by section 1 of the Judicial Proceedings (Regulation of Reports) Act 1926 will apply (indecent or medical matter));
(iii)   whether the reporting of anything in the document may be prejudicial to a fair trial in this or another case, in which case whether it may be necessary to make an order under section 4(2) of the Contempt of Court Act 1981.

The court may order one of the parties to provide a copy of certain pages (or parts of the footage), but these should not be provided electronically.

Statements of witnesses who give oral evidence

5B.18   A witness statement does not become evidence unless it is agreed under section 9 of the Criminal Justice Act 1967 and presented to the court. Therefore the statements of witnesses who give oral evidence, including ABE interview and transcripts and experts' reports, should not usually be provided. Open justice is generally satisfied by public access to the court.

Confidential documents

5B.19   A document the content of which, though relied upon by the court, has not been communicated to the public or reporters, nor treated as if it had been, is likely to have been supplied in confidence and should be treated accordingly. This will apply even if the court has made reference to the document or quoted from the document. There is most unlikely to be a sufficient reason to displace the expectation of confidentiality ordinarily attaching to a document in this category, and it would be exceptional to permit the inspection or copying by a member of the public or of the media of such a document. The rights and legitimate interests of others are likely to outweigh the interests of open justice with respect these documents.

5B.20 Documents in this category are likely to include:

(i)   Pre-sentence reports
(ii)   Medical reports
(iii) Victim Personal Statements
(iv) Reports and summaries for confiscation

Prohibitions against the provision of information

5B.21 Statutory provisions may impose specific prohibitions against the provision of information. Those most likely to be encountered are listed in the note to rule 5.8 and include the Rehabilitation of Offenders Act 1974, section 18 of the Criminal Procedure and Investigations Act 1996 ('unused materia' disclosed by the prosecution), sections 33, 34 and 35 of the Legal Aid, Sentencing and Punishment of Offenders Act 2012 ('LASPO Act 2012') (privileged information furnished to the Legal Aid Agency) and reporting restrictions generally.

5B.22 Reports of allocation or sending proceedings are restricted by section 52A of the Crime and Disorder Act 1998, so that only limited information, as specified in the statute, may be reported, whether it is referred to in the courtroom or not. The magistrates' court has power to order that the restriction shall not apply; if any defendant objects the court must apply the interests of justice test as specified in section 52A. The restriction ceases to apply either after all defendants indicate a plea of guilty, or after the conclusion of the trial of the last defendant to be tried. If the case does not result in a guilty plea, a finding of guilt or an acquittal, the restriction does not lift automatically and an application must be made to the court.

5B.23 Extradition proceedings have some features in common with committal proceedings, but no automatic reporting restrictions apply.

5B.24 Public Interest Immunity and the rights of a defendant, witnesses and victims under Article 6 and 8 of the European Convention on Human Rights may also restrict the power to release material to third parties.

Other documents

5B.25 The following table indicates the considerations likely to arise on an application to inspect or copy other documents.

Document	Considerations
Charge sheet Indictment	The alleged offence(s) will have been read aloud in court, and their terms must be supplied under CrimPR 5.8(4)
Material disclosed under CPIA 1996	To the extent that the content is deployed at trial, it becomes public at that hearing. Otherwise, it is a criminal offence for it to be disclosed: section 18 of the 1996 Act.
Written notices, applications, replies (including any application for representation)	To the extent that evidence is introduced, or measures taken, at trial, the content becomes public at that hearing. A statutory prohibition against disclosure applies to an application for representation: sections 33, 34 and 35 of the LASPO Act 2012.
Written decisions by the court, other than those read aloud in public or treated as if so read	Such decisions should usually be provided, subject to the criteria listed in CrimPR 5.8(4)(a) (and see also paragraph 5B.31 below).
Sentencing remarks	Sentencing remarks should usually be provided to the accredited Press, if the judge was reading from a prepared script which was handed out immediately afterwards; if not, then permission for a member of the accredited Press to obtain a transcript should usually be given (see also paragraphs 26 and 29 below).
Official recordings	See CrimPR 5.5.
Transcript	See CrimPR 5 .5 (and see also paragraphs 5B.3 2 to 36 below).

Access by reporters

5B.26 Under CrimPR Part 5 , the same procedure applies to applications for access to information by reporters as to other members of the public. However, if the application is made by legal representatives instructed by the media, or by an accredited member of the media, who is able to produce in support of the application a valid Press Card (http://www.ukpresscardauthority.co.uk/) then there is a greater presumption in favour of providing the requested material, in recognition of the press' role as 'public watchdog' in a democratic society (*Observer and Guardian v United Kingdom* (1992) 14 E.H.R.R. 153, Times November 27, 1991). The general principle in those circumstances is that the court should supply documents and information unless there is a good reason not to in order to protect the rights or legitimate interests of others and the request will not place an undue burden on the court (*R(Guardian News and Media Ltd)* at [87]). Subject to that, the paragraphs above relating to types of documents should be followed.

5B.27 Court staff should usually verify the authenticity of cards, checking the expiry date on the card and where necessary may consider telephoning the number on the reverse of the card to verify the card holder. Court staff may additionally request sight of other identification if necessary to ensure that the card holder has been correctly identified. The supply of information under CrimPR 5.8(7) is at the discretion of the court, and court staff must ensure that they have received a clear direction from the court before providing any information or material under rule 5.8(7) to a member of the public, including to the accredited media or their legal representatives.

5B.28 Opening notes and skeleton arguments or written submissions, once they have been placed before the court, should usually be provided to the media. If there is no opening note, permission for the media to obtain a transcript of the prosecution opening should usually be given (see below). It may be convenient for copies to be provided electronically by counsel, provided that the documents are kept suitably secure. The media are expected to be aware of the limitations on the use to which such material can be put, for example that legal argument held in the absence of the jury must not be reported before the conclusion of the trial.

5B.29 The media should also be able to obtain transcripts of hearings held in open court directly from the transcription service provider, on payment of any required fee. The service providers commonly require the judge's authorisation before they will provide a transcript, as an additional verification to ensure that the correct material is released and reporting restrictions are noted. However, responsibility for compliance with any restriction always rests with the person receiving the information or material: see CPD I General matters 6B, beneath.

5B.30 It is not for the judge to exercise an editorial judgment about 'the adequacy of the material already available to the paper for its journalistic purpose' (*Guardian* at 82) but the responsibility for complying with the Contempt of Court Act 1981 and any and all restrictions on the use of the material rests with the recipient.

5B.31 Where the Criminal Procedure Rules allow for a determination without a hearing there may be occasions on which it furthers the overriding objective to deliver the court's decision to the parties in writing, without convening a public hearing at which that decision will be pronounced: on an application for costs made at the conclusion of a trial, for example. If the only reason for delivering a decision in that way is to promote efficiency and expedition and if no other consideration arises then usually a copy of the decision should be provided in response to any request once the decision is final. However, had the decision been announced in public then the criteria in CrimPR 5.8(4)(a) would have applied to the supply of information by the court officer; and ordinarily those same criteria should be applied by the court, therefore. Moreover, where considerations other than efficiency and expedition have influenced the court's decision to reach a determination without convening a hearing then those same considerations may be inimical to the supply of the written decision to any applicant other than a party. Reporting restrictions may be relevant, for example; as may the considerations listed in paragraph 5B.9 above. In such a case the court should consider supplying a redacted version of the decision in response to a request by anyone who is not a party; or it may be appropriate to give the decision in terms that can be supplied to the public, supplemented by additional reasons provided only to the parties.

Transcript

5B.32 CrimPR 5.5 does not require an application to the court for transcript, nor does the rule anticipate recourse to the court for a judicial decision about the supply of transcript in any but unusual circumstances. Ordinarily it is the rule itself that determines the circumstances in which the transcriber of a recording mayor may not supply transcript to an applicant.

5B.33 Where reporting restrictions apply to information contained in the recording from which the transcript is prepared then unless the court otherwise directs it is for the transcriber to redact that transcript where redaction is necessary to permit its supply to that applicant. Having regard to the terms of the statutes that impose reporting restrictions, however, it is unlikely that redaction will be required frequently. Statutory restrictions prohibit publication 'to the public at large or any section of the public', or some comparable formulation. They do not ordinarily prohibit a publication constituted only of the supply of transcript to an individual applicant. However, any reporting restrictions will continue to apply to a recipient of transcript, and where they apply the recipient must be alerted to them by the endorsement on the transcript of a suitable warning notice, to this or the like effect:

"WARNING: reporting restrictions may apply to the contents transcribed in this document, particularly if the case concerned a sexual offence or involved a child. Reporting restrictions prohibit the publication of the applicable information to the public or any section of the public, in writing, in a broadcast or by means of the internet, including social media. Anyone who receives a copy of this transcript is responsible in law for making sure that applicable restrictions are not breached. A person who breaches a reporting restriction is liable to a fine and/or imprisonment. For guidance on whether reporting restrictions apply, and to what information, ask at the court office or take legal advice."

5B.34 Exceptionally, court staff may invite the court to direct that transcript must be redacted before it is supplied to an applicant, or that transcript must not be supplied to an applicant pending the supply of further information or assurances by that applicant, or at all, in exercise of the judicial discretion to which CrimPR 5.5 (2) refers. Circumstances giving rise to concern may include, for example, the occurrence of events causing staff reasonably to suspect that an applicant intends or is likely to disregard a reporting restriction that applies, despite the warning notice endorsed on the transcript, or reasonably to suspect that an applicant has malicious intentions towards another person. Given that the proceedings will have taken place in public, despite any such suspicions cogent and compelling reasons will be required to deny a request for transcript of such proceedings and the onus rests always on the court to justify such a denial, not on the applicant to justify the request. Even where there are reasons to suspect a criminal intent, the appropriate course may be to direct that the police be informed of those reasons rather than to direct that the transcript be withheld. Nevertheless, it may be appropriate in such a case to direct that an application for the transcript should be made which complies with paragraph 5B.8 above (even though that paragraph does not apply); and then for the court to review that application with regard to the considerations listed in paragraph 58.9 above (but the usual burden of justifying a request under that paragraph does not apply).

5B.35 Some applicants for transcript may be taken to be aware of the significance of reporting restrictions, where they apply, and, by reason of such an applicant's statutory or other public or quasi-public functions, in any event unlikely to contravene any such restriction. Such applicants include public authorities within the meaning of section 6 of the Human Rights Act 1998 (a definition which extends to government departments and their agencies, local authorities, prosecuting authorities, and institutions such as the Parole Board and the Sentencing Council) and include public or private bodies exercising disciplinary functions in relation to practitioners of a regulated profession such as doctors, lawyers, accountants, etc. It would be only in the most exceptional circumstances that a court might conclude that any such body should not receive unredacted transcript of proceedings in public, irrespective of whether reporting restrictions do or do not apply.

5B.36 The rule imposes no time limit on a request for the supply of transcript. The assumption is that transcript of proceedings in public in the Crown Court will continue to be available for as long as relevant records are maintained by the Lord Chancellor under the legislation to which CrimPR 5.4 refers.

CPD I GENERAL MATTERS: 5C ISSUE OF MEDICAL CERTIFICATES

5C.1 Doctors will be aware that medical notes are normally submitted by defendants in criminal proceedings as justification for not answering bail. Medical notes may also be submitted by witnesses who are due to give evidence and jurors.

5C.2 If a medical certificate is accepted by the court, this will result in cases (including contested hearings and trials) being adjourned rather than the court issuing a warrant for the defendant's arrest without bail. Medical certificates will also provide the defendant with sufficient evidence to defend a charge of failure to surrender to bail.

5C.3 However, a court is not absolutely bound by a medical certificate. The medical practitioner providing the certificate may be required by the court to give evidence. Alternatively the court may exercise its discretion to disregard a certificate which it finds unsatisfactory: *R V Ealing Magistrates' Court Ex P. Burgess* [2001] 165 J.P. 82

5C.4 Circumstances where the court may find a medical certificate unsatisfactory include:

(a) Where the certificate indicates that the defendant is unfit to attend work (rather than to attend court);
(b) Where the nature of the defendant's ailment (e.g. a broken arm) does not appear to be capable of preventing his attendance at court;
(c) Where the defendant is certified as suffering from stress/anxiety/depression and there is no indication of the defendant recovering within a realistic timescale.

5C.5 It therefore follows that the minimum standards a medical certificate should set out are:

(a) The date on which the medical practitioner examined the defendant;
(b) The exact nature of the defendants ailments
(c) If it is not self-evident, why the ailment prevents the defendant attending court;
(d) An indication as to when the defendant is likely to be able to attend court, or a date when the current certificate expires.

5C.6 Medical practitioners should be aware that when issuing a certificate to a defendant in criminal proceedings they make themselves liable to being summonsed to court to give evidence about the content of the certificate, and they may be asked to justify their statements.

CRIMPR PART 6 REPORTING, ETC. RESTRICTIONS

CPD I General matters 6A: Unofficial sound recording of proceedings

6A.1 Section 9 of the Contempt of Court Act 1981 contains provisions governing the unofficial use of equipment for recording sound in court.

Section 9(1) provides that it is a contempt of court

(a) to use in court, or bring into court for use, any tape recorder or other instrument for recording sound, except with the permission of the court;
(b) to publish a recording of legal proceedings made by means of any such instrument, or any recording derived directly or indirectly from it, by playing it in the hearing of the public or any section of the public, or to dispose of it or any recording so derived, with a view to such publication;
(c) to use any such recording in contravention of any conditions of leave granted under paragraph (a).

These provisions do not apply to the making or use of sound recordings for purposes of official transcripts of the proceedings, upon which the Act imposes no restriction whatever.

6A.2 The discretion given to the court to grant, withhold or withdraw leave to use equipment for recording sound or to impose conditions as to the use of the recording is unlimited, but the following factors may be relevant to its exercise:

(a) the existence of any reasonable need on the part of the applicant for leave, whether a litigant or a person connected with the press or broadcasting, for the recording to be made;
(b) the risk that the recording could be used for the purpose of briefing witnesses out of court;
(c) any possibility that the use of the recorder would disturb the proceedings or distract or worry any witnesses or other participants.

6A.3 Consideration should always be given whether conditions as to the use of a recording made pursuant to leave should be imposed. The identity and role of the applicant for leave and the nature of the subject matter of the proceedings may be relevant to this.

6A.4 The particular restriction imposed by section 9(1)(b) applies in every case, but may not be present in the mind of every applicant to whom leave is given. It may therefore be desirable on occasion for this provision to be drawn to the attention of those to whom leave is given.

6A.5 The transcript of a permitted recording is intended for the use of the person given leave to make it and is not intended to be used as, or to compete with, the official transcript mentioned in section 9(4).

6A.6 Where a contravention of section 9(1) is alleged, the procedure in section 2 of Part 48 of the Rules should be followed. Section 9(3) of the 1981 Act permits the court to 'order the instrument, or any recording made with it, or both, to be forfeited'. The procedure at CrimPR 6.10 should be followed.

CPD I General matters 6B: Restrictions on reporting proceedings

6B.1 Open justice is an essential principle in the criminal courts but the principle is subject to some statutory restrictions. These restrictions are either automatic or discretionary. Guidance is provided in the joint publication, Reporting Restrictions in the Criminal Courts issued by the Judicial College, the Newspaper Society, the Society of Editors and the Media Lawyers Association. The current version is the fourth edition and has been updated to be effective from May 2015.

6B.2 Where a restriction is automatic no order can or should be made in relation to matters falling within the relevant provisions. However, the court may, if it considers it appropriate to do so, give a reminder of the existence of the automatic restriction. The court may also discuss the scope of the restriction and any particular risks in the specific case in open court with representatives of the press present. Such judicial observations cannot constitute an order binding on the editor or the reporter although it is anticipated that a responsible editor would consider them carefully before deciding what should be published. It remains the responsibility of those reporting a case to ensure that restrictions are not breached.

6B.3 Before exercising its discretion to impose a restriction the court must follow precisely the statutory provisions under which the order is to be made, paying particular regard to what has to be established, by whom and to what standard.

6B.4 Without prejudice to the above paragraph, certain general principles apply to the exercise of the court's discretion:

(a) The court must have regard to CrimPR Parts 6 and 18.
(b) The court must keep in mind the fact that every order is a departure from the general principle that proceedings shall be open and freely reported.
(c) Before making any order the court must be satisfied that the purpose of the proposed order cannot be achieved by some lesser measure e.g. the grant of special measures, screens or the clearing of the public gallery (usually subject to a representative/s of the media remaining).
(d) The terms of the order must be proportionate so as to comply with Article 10 ECHR (freedom of expression).
(e) No order should be made without giving other parties to the proceedings and any other interested party, including any representative of the media, an opportunity to make representations.
(f) Any order should provide for any interested party who has not been present or represented at the time of the making of the order to have permission to apply within a limited period e.g. 24 hours.
(g) The wording of the order is the responsibility of the judge or Bench making the order: it must be in precise terms and, if practicable, agreed with the advocates.
(h) The order must be in writing and must state:
    (i) the power under which it is made;
    (ii) its precise scope and purpose; and
    (iii) the time at which it shall cease to have effect, if appropriate.
(i) The order must specify, in every case, whether or not the making or terms of the order may be reported or whether this itself is prohibited. Such a report could cause the very mischief which the order was intended to prevent.

6B.5 A series of template orders have been prepared by the Judicial College and are available as an appendix to the Crown Court Bench Book Companion; these template orders should generally be used.

6B.6 A copy of the order should be provided to any person known to have an interest in reporting the proceedings and to any local or national media who regularly report proceedings in the court.

6B.7 Court staff should be prepared to answer any enquiry about a specific case; but it is and will remain the responsibility of anyone reporting a case to ensure that no breach of any order occurs and the onus rests on such person to make enquiry in case of doubt.

CPD I General matters 6C: Use of live text-based forms of communication (including twitter) from court for the purposes of fair and accurate reporting

6C.1 This part clarifies the use which may be made of live text-based communications, such as mobile email, social media (including Twitter) and internet-enabled laptops in and from courts throughout England and Wales. For the purpose of this part these means of communication are referred to, compendiously, as 'live text-based communications'. It is consistent with the legislative structure which:

(a) prohibits:
    (i) the taking of photographs in court (section 41 of the Criminal Justice Act 1925);
    (ii) the use of sound recording equipment in court unless the leave of the judge has first been obtained (section 9 of the Contempt of Court Act 1981); and
(b) requires compliance with the strict prohibition rules created by sections 1, 2 and 4 of the Contempt of Court Act 1981 in relation to the reporting of court proceedings.

General Principles

6C.2 The judge has an overriding responsibility to ensure that proceedings are conducted consistently, with the proper administration of justice, and to avoid any improper interference with its processes.

6C.3 A fundamental aspect of the proper administration of justice is the principle of open justice. Fair and accurate reporting of court proceedings forms part of that principle. The principle is, however, subject to well-known statutory and discretionary exceptions. Two such exceptions are the prohibitions, set out in paragraph 6C.1(a), on photography in court and on making sound recordings of court proceedings.

6C.4 The statutory prohibition on photography in court, by any means, is absolute. There is no judicial discretion to suspend or dispense with it. Any equipment which has photographic capability must not have that function activated.

6C.5 Sound recordings are also prohibited unless, in the exercise of its discretion, the court permits such equipment to be used. In criminal proceedings, some of the factors relevant to the exercise of that discretion are contained in paragraph 6A.2. The same factors are likely to be relevant when consideration is being given to the exercise of this discretion in civil or family proceedings.

Use of Live Text-based Communications: General Considerations

6C.6 The normal, indeed almost invariable, rule has been that mobile phones must be turned off in court. There is however no statutory prohibition on the use of live text-based communications in open court.

6C.7 Where a member of the public, who is in court, wishes to use live text-based communications during court proceedings an application for permission to activate and use, in silent mode, a mobile phone, small laptop or similar piece of equipment, solely in order to make live text-based communications of the proceedings will need to be made. The application may be made formally or informally (for instance by communicating a request to the judge through court staff).

6C.8 It is presumed that a representative of the media or a legal commentator using live text-based communications from court does not pose a danger of interference to the proper administration of justice in the individual case. This is because the most obvious purpose of permitting the use of live text-based communications would be to enable the media to produce fair and accurate reports of the proceedings. As such, a representative of the media or a legal commentator who wishes to use live text-based communications from court may do so without making an application to the court.

6C.9 When considering, either generally on its own motion, or following a formal application or informal request by a member of the public, whether to permit live text-based communications, and if so by whom, the paramount question for the judge will be whether the application may interfere with the proper administration of justice.

6C.10 In considering the question of permission, the factors listed in paragraph 6A.2 are likely to be relevant.

6C.11 Without being exhaustive, the danger to the administration of justice is likely to be at its most acute in the context of criminal trials e.g., where witnesses who are out of court may be informed of what has already happened in court and so coached or briefed before they then give evidence, or where information posted on, for instance, Twitter about inadmissible evidence may influence members of the jury. However, the danger is not confined to criminal proceedings; in civil and sometimes family proceedings, simultaneous reporting from the courtroom may create pressure on witnesses, by distracting or worrying them.

6C.12 It may be necessary for the judge to limit live text-based communications to representatives of the media for journalistic purposes but to disallow its use by the wider public in court. That may arise if it is necessary, for example, to limit the number of mobile electronic devices in use at any given time because of the potential for electronic interference with the court's own sound recording equipment, or because the widespread use of such devices in court may cause a distraction in the proceedings.

6C.13 Subject to these considerations, the use of an unobtrusive, hand-held, silent piece of modern equipment, for the purposes of simultaneous reporting of proceedings to the outside world as they unfold in court, is generally unlikely to interfere with the proper administration of justice.

6C.14 Permission to use live text-based communications from court may be withdrawn by the court at any time.

CPD I General matters 6D: Taking Notes in Court

6D.1 As long as it does not interfere with the proper administration of justice, anyone who attends a court hearing may quietly take notes, on paper or by silent electronic means. If that person is a participant, including an expert witness who is in the courtroom under CrimPR 24.4(2)(a)(ii) or 25.11(2)(a)(ii), note taking may be an essential aid to that person's own or (if they are a representative) to their client's effective participation. If that person is a reporter or a member of the public, attending a hearing to which, by definition, they have been admitted, note taking is a feature of the principle of open justice. The permission of the court is not required, and the distinctions between members of the public and others which are drawn at paragraphs 6C.7 and 6C.8 of these Practice Directions do not apply.

6D.2 However, where there is reason to suspect that the taking of notes may be for an unlawful purpose, or that it may disrupt the proceedings, then it is entirely proper for court staff to make appropriate enquiries, and ultimately it is within the power of the court to prohibit note taking by a specified individual or individuals in the court room if that is necessary and proportionate to prevent unlawful conduct. If, for example, there is reason to believe that notes are being taken in order to influence the testimony of a witness who is due to give evidence, perhaps by briefing that witness on what another witness has said, then because such conduct is unlawful (it is likely to be in contempt of court, and it may constitute a perversion of the course of justice) it is within the court's power to prohibit such note taking. If there is reason to believe that what purports to be taking notes with an electronic device is in fact the transmission of live text-based communications from court without the permission required by paragraph 6C.7 of these Practice Directions, or where permission to transmit such communications has been withdrawn under paragraph 6C.14, then that, too, would constitute grounds for prohibiting the taking of such notes.

6D.3 The existence of a reporting restriction, without more, is not a sufficient reason to prohibit note taking (though it may need to be made clear to those who take notes that the reporting restriction affects how much, if any, of what they have noted may be communicated to anyone else). However, if there is reason to believe that notes are being taken in order to facilitate the contravention of a reporting restriction then that, too, would constitute grounds for prohibiting such note taking.

CRIMINAL PRACTICE DIRECTIONS 2015 DIVISION II
Preliminary proceedings

CRIMPR PART 8 INITIAL DETAILS OF THE PROSECUTION CASE

CPD II Preliminary proceedings 8A: Defendant's record

Copies of record

8A.1 The defendant's record (previous convictions, cautions, reprimands, etc) may be taken into account when the court decides not only on sentence but also, for example, about bail, or when allocating a case for trial. It is therefore important that up to date and accurate information is available. Previous convictions must be provided as part of the initial details of the prosecution case under CrimPR Part 8.

8A.2 The record should usually be provided in the following format:

Personal details and summary of convictions and cautions – Police National Computer ["PNC"] Court / Defence / Probation Summary Sheet;

Previous convictions – PNC Court / Defence / Probation printout, supplemented by Form MG16 if the police force holds convictions not shown on PNC;

Recorded cautions – PNC Court / Defence / Probation printout, supplemented by Form MG17 if the police force holds cautions not shown on PNC.

8A.3 The defence representative should take instructions on the defendant's record and if the defence wish to raise any objection to the record, this should be made known to the prosecutor immediately.

8A.4 It is the responsibility of the prosecutor to ensure that a copy of the defendant's record has been provided to the Probation Service.

8A.5 Where following conviction a custodial order is made, the court must ensure that a copy is attached to the order sent to the prison.

Additional information

8A.6 In the Crown Court, the police should also provide brief details of the circumstances of the last three similar convictions and / or of convictions likely to be of interest to the court, the latter being judged on a case-by-case basis.

8A.7 Where the current alleged offence could constitute a breach of an existing sentence such as a suspended sentence, community order or conditional discharge, and it is known that that sentence is still in force then details of the circumstances of the offence leading to the sentence should be included in the antecedents. The detail should be brief and include the date of the offence.

8A.8 On occasions the PNC printout provided may not be fully up to date. It is the responsibility of the prosecutor to ensure that all of the necessary information is available to the court and the Probation Service and provided to the defence. Oral updates at the hearing will sometimes be necessary, but it is preferable if this information is available in advance.

CRIMPR PART 9 ALLOCATION AND SENDING FOR TRIAL

CPD II Preliminary proceedings 9A: Allocation (mode of trial)

9A.1 Courts must follow the Sentencing Council's guideline on Allocation (mode of trial) when deciding whether or not to send defendants charged with "either way" offences for trial in the Crown Court under section 51(1) of the Crime and Disorder Act 1998.

CRIMPR PART 10 THE INDICTMENT

CPD II Preliminary proceedings 10A: Preparation and Content of the Indictment

Preferring the indictment

10A.1 Section 2 of the Administration of Justice (Miscellaneous Provisions) Act 1933 allows Criminal Procedure Rules to "make provision ... as to the manner in which and the time at which bills of indictment are to be preferred". CrimPR 10.2(5) lists the events which constitute preferment for the purposes of that Act. Where a defendant is contemplating an application to the Crown Court to dismiss an offence sent for trial, under the provisions to which CrimPR 9.16 applies, or where the prosecutor is contemplating discontinuance, under the provisions to which CrimPR Part 12 applies, the parties and the court must be astute to the effect of the occurrence of those events: the right to apply for dismissal is lost if the defendant is arraigned, and the right to discontinue is lost if the indictment is preferred.

Printing and signature of indictment

10A.2 Neither Section 2 of the Administration of Justice (Miscellaneous Provisions) Act 1933 nor the Criminal Procedure Rules require an indictment to be printed or signed. Section 2(1) of the Act was amended by section 116 of the Coroners and Justice Act 2009 to remove the requirement for signature. For the potential benefit of the Criminal Appeal Office, CrimPR 10.2(7) requires only that any paper copy of the indictment which for any reason in fact is made for the court must be endorsed with a note to identify it as a copy of the indictment, and with the date on which the indictment came into being. For the same reason, CrimPR 3.22 requires only that any paper copy of an indictment which in fact has been made must be endorsed with a note of the order and of its date where the court makes an order for joint or separate trials affecting that indictment or makes an order for the amendment of that indictment in any respect.

Content of indictment; joint and separate trials

10A.3 The rule has been abolished which formerly required an indictment containing more than one count to include only offences founded on the same facts, or offences which constitute all or part of a series of the same or a similar character. However, if an indictment charges more than one offence, and if at least one of those offences does not meet those criteria, then CrimPR 3.21(4) cites that circumstance as an example of one in which the court may decide to exercise its power to order separate trials under section 5 (3) of the Indictments Act 1915. It is for the court to decide which allegations, against whom, should be tried at the same time, having regard to the prosecutor's proposals, the parties' representations, the court's powers under the 1915 Act (see also CrimPR 3.21(4)) and the overriding objective. Where necessary the court should be invited to exercise those powers. It is generally undesirable for a large number of counts to be tried at the same time and the prosecutor may be required to identify a selection of counts on which the trial should proceed, leaving a decision to be taken later whether to try any of the remainder.

10A.4 Where an indictment contains substantive counts and one or more related conspiracy counts, the court will expect the prosecutor to justify their joint trial. Failing justification, the prosecutor should be required to choose whether to proceed on the substantive counts or on the conspiracy counts. In any event, if there is a conviction on any counts that are tried, then those that have not been proceeded with can remain on the file marked "not to be proceeded with without the leave of the court or the Court of Appeal". In the event that a conviction is later quashed on appeal, the remaining counts can be tried.

10A.5 There is no rule of law or practice which prohibits two indictments being in existence at the same time for the same offence against the same person and on the same facts. However, the court will not allow the prosecutor to proceed on both indictments. They cannot be tried together and the court will require the prosecutor to elect the one on which the trial will proceed. Where different defendants have been separately sent for trial for offences which properly may be tried together then it is permissible to join in one indictment counts based on the separate sendings for trial even if an indictment based on one of them already exists.

Draft indictment generated electronically on sending for trial

10A.6 CrimPR 10.3 applies where court staff have introduced arrangements for the charges sent for trial to be presented in the Crown Court as the counts of a draft indictment without the need for those charges to be rewritten and served a second time on the defendant and on the court office. Where such arrangements are introduced, court users will be informed (and the fact will become apparent on the sending for trial).

10A.7 Now that there is no restriction on the counts that an indictment may contain (see paragraph 10A.3 above), and given the Crown Court's power, and in some cases obligation, to order separate trials, few circumstances will arise in which the court will wish to exercise the discretion conferred by rule 10.3 (1) to direct that the rule will not apply, thus discarding such an electronically generated draft indictment. The most likely such circumstance to arise would be in a case in which prosecution evidence emerging soon after sending requires such a comprehensive amendment of the counts as to make it more convenient to all participants for the prosecutor to prepare and serve under CrimPR 10.4 a complete new draft indictment than to amend the electronically generated draft.

Draft indictment served by the prosecutor

10A.8 CrimPR 10.4 applies after sending for trial wherever CrimPR 10.3 does not. It requires the prosecutor to prepare a draft indictment and serve it on the Crown Court officer, who by CrimPR 10.2(7)(b) then must serve it on the defendant. In most instances service will be by electronic means, usually by making use of the Crown Court digital case system to which the prosecutor will upload the draft (which at once then becomes the indictment, under section 2 of the Administration of Justice (Miscellaneous Provisions) Act 1933 and CrimPR 10.2(S)(b)(ii)).

10A.9 The prosecutor's time limit for service of the draft indictment under CrimPR 10.4 is 28 days after serving under CrimPR 9.15 the evidence on which the prosecution case relies. The Crown Court may extend that time limit, under CrimPR 10.2(8). However, under paragraph CrimPD I 3A.16 of these Practice Directions the court will expect that in every case a draft indictment will be served at least 7 days before the plea and trial preparation hearing, whether the time prescribed by the rule will have expired or not.

Amending the content of the indictment

10A.10 Where the prosecutor wishes to substitute or add counts to a draft indictment, or to invite the court to allow an indictment to be amended, so that the draft indictment, or indictment, will charge offences which differ from those with which the defendant first was charged, the defendant should be given as much notice as possible of what is proposed. It is likely that the defendant will need time to consider his or her position and advance notice will help to avoid delaying the proceedings.

Multiple offending: count charging more than one incident

10A.11 CrimPR 10.2(2) allows a single count to allege more than one incident of the commission of an offence in certain circumstances. Each incident must be of the same offence. The circumstances in which such a count may be appropriate include, but are not limited to, the following:

 (a) the victim on each occasion was the same, or there was no identifiable individual victim as, for example, in a case of the unlawful importation of controlled drugs or of money laundering;

 (b) the alleged incidents involved a marked degree of repetition in the method employed or in their location, or both;

 (c) the alleged incidents took place over a clearly defined period, typically (but not necessarily) no more than about a year;

(d) in any event, the defence is such as to apply to every alleged incident. Where what is in issue differs in relation to different incidents, a single "multiple incidents" count will not be appropriate (though it may be appropriate to use two or more such counts according to the circumstances and to the issues raised by the defence).

10A.12 Even in circumstances such as those set out above, there may be occasions on which a prosecutor chooses not to use such a count, in order to bring the case within section 75(3)(a) of the Proceeds of Crime Act 2002 (criminal lifestyle established by conviction of three or more offences in the same proceedings): for example, because section 75(2)(c) of that Act does not apply (criminal lifestyle established by an offence committed over a period of at least six months). Where the prosecutor proposes such a course, it is unlikely that CrimPR Part 1 (the overriding objective) will require an indictment to contain a single "multiple incidents" count in place of a larger number of counts, subject to the general principles set out at paragraph 10A.3.

10A.13 For some offences, particularly sexual offences, the penalty for the offence may have changed during the period over which the alleged incidents took place. In such a case, additional "multiple incidents" counts should be used so that each count only alleges incidents to which the same maximum penalty applies.

10A.14 In other cases, such as sexual or physical abuse, a complainant may be in a position only to give evidence of a series of similar incidents without being able to specify when or the precise circumstances in which they occurred. In these cases, a 'multiple incidents' count may be desirable. If on the other hand the complainant is able to identify particular incidents of the offence by reference to a date or other specific event, but alleges that in addition there were other incidents which the complainant is unable to specify, then it may be desirable to include separate counts for the identified incidents and a 'multiple incidents' count or counts alleging that incidents of the same offence occurred 'many' times. Using a 'multiple incidents' count may be an appropriate alternative to using 'specimen' counts in some cases where repeated sexual or physical abuse is alleged. The choice of count will depend on the particular circumstances of the case and should be determined bearing in mind the implications for sentencing set out in R v Canavan; R v Kidd; R v Shaw [1998] 1 W.L.R. 604, [1998] 1 Cr. App. R. 79, [1998] 1 Cr. App. R. (S.) 243. In R v A [2015] EWCA Crim 177, [2015] 2 Cr.App.R.(S.) 115(12) the Court of Appeal reviewed the circumstances in which a mixture of multiple incident and single incident counts might be appropriate where the prosecutor alleged sustained sexual abuse.

Multiple offending: trial by jury and then by judge alone

10A.15 Under sections 17 to 21 of the Domestic Violence, Crime and Victims Act 2004, the court may order that the trial of certain counts will be by jury in the usual way and, if the jury convicts, that other associated counts will be tried by judge alone. The use of this power is likely to be appropriate where justice cannot be done without charging a large number of separate offences and the allegations against the defendant appear to fall into distinct groups by reference to the identity of the victim, by reference to the dates of the offences, or by some other distinction in the nature of the offending conduct alleged.

10A.16 In such a case, it is essential to make clear from the outset the association asserted by the prosecutor between those counts to be tried by a jury and those counts which it is proposed should be tried by judge alone, if the jury convict on the former. A special form of indictment is prescribed for this purpose.

10A.17 An order for such a trial may be made only at a preparatory hearing. It follows that where the prosecutor intends to invite the court to order such a trial it will normally be appropriate to proceed as follows. A draft indictment in the form appropriate to such a trial should be served with an application under CrimPR 3.15 for a preparatory hearing. This will ensure that the defendant is aware at the earliest possible opportunity of what the prosecutor proposes and of the proposed association of counts in the indictment.

10A.18 At the start of the preparatory hearing, the defendant should be arraigned on all counts in Part One of the indictment. Arraignment on Part Two need not take place until after there has been either a guilty plea to, or finding of guilt on, an associated count in Part One of the indictment.

10A.19 If the prosecutor's application is successful, the prosecutor should prepare an abstract of the indictment, containing the counts from Part One only, for use in the jury trial. Preparation of such an abstract does not involve "amendment" of the indictment. It is akin to where a defendant pleads guilty to certain counts in an indictment and is put in the charge of the jury on the remaining counts only.

10A.20 If the prosecutor's application for a two stage trial is unsuccessful, the prosecutor may apply to amend the indictment to remove from it any counts in Part Two which would make jury trial on the whole indictment impracticable and to revert to a standard form of indictment. It will be a matter for the court whether arraignment on outstanding counts takes place at the preparatory hearing, or at a future date.

CPD II Preliminary proceedings 10B: Voluntary bills of indictment

10B.1 Section 2(2)(b) of the Administration of Justice (Miscellaneous Provisions) Act 1933 and paragraph 2(6) of Schedule 3 to the Crime and Disorder Act 1998 allow the preferment of a bill of indictment by the direction or with the consent of a judge of the High Court. Bills so preferred are known as 'voluntary bills'.

10B.2 Applications for such consent must comply with CrimPR 10.3.

10B.3 Those requirements should be complied with in relation to each defendant named in the indictment for which consent is sought, whether or not it is proposed to prefer any new count against him or her.

10B.4 The preferment of a voluntary bill is an exceptional procedure. Consent should only be granted where good reason to depart from the normal procedure is clearly shown and only where the interests of justice, rather than considerations of administrative convenience, require it.

10B.5 Prosecutors must follow the procedures prescribed by the rule unless there are good reasons for not doing so, in which case prosecutors must inform the judge that the procedures have not been followed and seek leave to dispense with all or any of them. Judges should not give leave to dispense unless good reasons are shown.

10B.6   A judge to whom application for consent to the preferment of a documents submitted by the prosecutor and any written submissions made by the prospective defendant, and may properly seek any necessary amplification. CrimPR 10.3(4)(b) allows the judge to set a timetable for representations. The judge may invite oral submissions from either party, or accede to a request for an opportunity to make oral submissions, if the judge considers it necessary or desirable to receive oral submissions in order to make a sound and fair decision on the application. Any such oral submissions should be made on notice to the other party and in open court unless the judge otherwise directs.

(a)   on making an application for consent to preferment of a voluntary bill, give notice to the prospective defendant that such application has been made;

(b)   at about the same time, serve on the prospective defendant a copy of all the documents delivered to the judge (save to the extent that these have already been served on him or her);

(c)   inform the prospective defendant that he or she may make submissions in writing to the judge, provided that he or she does so within nine working days of the giving of notice under (a) above.

10B.7   Prosecutors must follow these procedures unless there are good reasons for not doing so, in which case prosecutors must inform the judge that the procedures have not been followed and seek leave to dispense with all or any of them. Judges should not give leave to dispense unless good reasons are shown.

10B.8   A judge to whom application for consent to the preferment of a voluntary bill is made will, of course, wish to consider carefully the documents submitted by the prosecutor and any written submissions made by the prospective defendant, and may properly seek any necessary amplification. The judge may invite oral submissions from either party, or accede to a request for an opportunity to make oral submissions, if the judge considers it necessary or desirable to receive oral submissions in order to make a sound and fair decision on the application. Any such oral submissions should be made on notice to the other party and in open court.

CRIMINAL PRACTICE DIRECTIONS 2015 DIVISION III

Custody and bail

CRIMPR PART 14 BAIL AND CUSTODY TIME LIMITS

CPD III Custody and bail 14A: Bail before sending for trial

14A.1   Before the Crown Court can deal with an application under CrimPR 14.8 by a defendant after a magistrates' court has withheld bail, it must be satisfied that the magistrates' court has issued a certificate, under section 5(6A) of the Bail Act 1976, that it heard full argument on the application for bail before it refused the application. The certificate of full argument is produced by the magistrates' court's computer system, Libra, as part of the GENORD (General Form of Order). Two hard copies are produced, one for the defence and one for the prosecution. (Some magistrates' courts may also produce a manual certificate which will usually be available from the justices' legal adviser at the conclusion of the hearing; the GENORD may not be produced until the following day.) Under CrimPR 14.4(4), the magistrates' court officer will provide the defendant with a certificate that the court heard full argument. However, it is the responsibility of the defence, as the applicant in the Crown Court, to ensure that a copy of the certificate of full argument is provided to the Crown Court as part of the application (CrimPR 14.8(3)(e)). The applicant's solicitors should attach a copy of the certificate to the bail application form. If the certificate is not enclosed with the application form, it will be difficult to avoid some delay in listing.

Venue

14A.2   Applications should be made to the court to which the defendant will be, or would have been, sent for trial. In the event of an application in a purely summary case, it should be made to the Crown Court centre which normally receives Class 3 work. The hearing will be listed as a chambers matter, unless a judge has directed otherwise.

CPD III Custody and bail 14B: Bail: Failure to surrender and trials in absence

14B.1   The failure of defendants to comply with the terms of their bail by not surrendering, or not doing so at the appointed time, undermines the administration of justice and disrupts proceedings. The resulting delays impact on victims, witnesses and other court users and also waste costs. A defendant's failure to surrender affects not only the case with which he or she is concerned, but also the court's ability to administer justice more generally, by damaging the confidence of victims, witnesses and the public in the effectiveness of the court system and the judiciary. It is, therefore, most important that defendants who are granted bail appreciate the significance of the obligation to surrender to custody in accordance with the terms of their bail and that courts take appropriate action, if they fail to do so.

14B.2   A defendant who will be unable for medical reasons to attend court in accordance with his or her bail must obtain a certificate from his or her general practitioner or another appropriate medical practitioner such as the doctor with care of the defendant at a hospital. This should be obtained in advance of the hearing and conveyed to the court through the defendant's legal representative. In order to minimise the disruption to the court and to others, particularly witnesses if the case is listed for trial, the defendant should notify the court through his legal representative as soon as his inability to attend court becomes known.

14B.3   Guidance has been produced by the British Medical Association and the Crown Prosecution Service on the roles and responsibilities of medical practitioners when issuing medical certificates in criminal proceedings: link. Judges and magistrates should seek to ensure that this guidance is followed. However, it is a matter for each individual court to decide whether, in any particular case, the issued certificate should be accepted. Without a medical certificate or if an unsatisfactory certificate is provided, the court is likely to consider that the defendant has failed to surrender to bail.

14B.4   If a defendant fails to surrender to his or her bail there are at least four courses of action for the courts to consider taking:-

(a)   imposing penalties for the failure to surrender;
(b)   revoking bail or imposing more stringent conditions;
(c)   conducting trials in the absence of the defendant; and
(d)   ordering that some or all of any sums of money lodged with the court as a security or pledged by a surety as a condition on the grant of bail be forfeit.

The relevant sentencing guideline is the Definitive Guideline Fail to Surrender to Bail. Under section 125(1) of the Coroners and Justice Act 2009, for offences committed on or after 6 April 2010, the court must follow the relevant guideline unless it would be contrary to the interests of justice to do so. The guideline can be obtained from the Sentencing Council's website:http://sentencingcouncil.judiciary.gov.uk/guidelines/guidelines-to-download.htm

CPD III Custody and bail 14C: Penalties for failure to surrender

Initiating Proceedings – Bail granted by a police officer

14C.1   When a person has been granted bail by a police officer to attend court and subsequently fails to surrender to custody, the decision whether to initiate proceedings for a section 6(1) or section 6(2) offence will be for the police / prosecutor and proceedings are commenced in the usual way.

14C.2   The offence in this form is a summary offence although section 6(10) to (14) of the Bail Act 1976, inserted by section 15(3) of the Criminal Justice Act 2003, disapplies section 127 of the Magistrates' Courts Act 1980 and provides for alternative time limits for the commencement of proceedings. The offence should be dealt with on the first appearance after arrest, unless an adjournment is necessary, as it will be relevant in considering whether to grant bail again.

Initiating Proceedings – Bail granted by a court

14C.3   Where a person has been granted bail by a court and subsequently fails to surrender to custody, on arrest that person should normally be brought as soon as appropriate before the court at which the proceedings in respect of which bail was granted are to be heard. (There is no requirement to lay an information within the time limit for a Bail Act offence where bail was granted by the court).

14C.4   Given that bail was granted by a court, it is more appropriate that the court itself should initiate the proceedings by its own motion although the prosecutor may invite the court to take proceedings, if the prosecutor considers proceedings are appropriate.

Timing of disposal

14C.5   Courts should not, without good reason, adjourn the disposal of a section 6(1) or section 6(2) Bail Act 1976 offence (failure to surrender) until the conclusion of the proceedings in respect of which bail was granted but should deal with defendants as soon as is practicable. In deciding what is practicable, the court must take into account when the proceedings in respect of which bail was granted are expected to conclude, the seriousness of the offence for which the defendant is already being prosecuted, the type of penalty that might be imposed for the Bail Act offence and the original offence, as well as any other relevant circumstances.

14C.6   If the Bail Act offence is adjourned alongside the substantive proceedings, then it is still necessary to consider imposing a separate penalty at the trial. In addition, bail should usually be revoked in the meantime. Trial in the absence of the defendant is not a penalty for the Bail Act offence and a separate penalty may be imposed for the Bail Act offence.

Conduct of Proceedings

14C.7   Proceedings under section 6 of the Bail Act 1976 may be conducted either as a summary offence or as a criminal contempt of court. Where proceedings are commenced by the police or prosecutor, the prosecutor will conduct the proceedings and, if the matter is contested, call the evidence. Where the court initiates proceedings, with or without an invitation from the prosecutor, the court may expect the assistance of the prosecutor, such as in cross-examining the defendant, if required.

14C.8   The burden of proof is on the defendant to prove that he had reasonable cause for his failure to surrender to custody (section 6(3) of the Bail Act 1976).

Sentencing for a Bail Act offence

14C.9   A defendant who commits an offence under section 6(1) or section 6(2) of the Bail Act 1976 commits an offence that stands apart from the proceedings in respect of which bail was granted. The seriousness of the offence can be reflected by an appropriate and generally separate penalty being imposed for the Bail Act offence.

14C.10   As noted above, there is a sentencing guideline on sentencing offenders for Bail Act offences and this must be followed unless it would be contrary to the interests of justice to do so. Where the appropriate penalty is a custodial sentence, consecutive sentences should be imposed unless there are circumstances that make this inappropriate.

CPD III Custody and bail 14D: Relationship between the bail act offence and further remands on bail or in custody

14D.1   The court at which the defendant is produced should, where practicable and legally permissible, arrange to have all outstanding cases brought before it (including those from different courts) for the purpose of progressing matters and dealing with the question of bail. This is likely to be practicable in the magistrates' court where cases can easily be transferred from one magistrates' court to another. Practice is likely to vary in the Crown Court. If the defendant appears before a different court, for example because he is charged with offences committed in another area, and it is not practicable for all matters to be concluded by that court then the defendant may be remanded on bail or in custody, if appropriate, to appear before the first court for the outstanding offences to be dealt with.

14D.2 When a defendant has been convicted of a Bail Act offence, the court should review the remand status of the defendant, including the conditions of that bail, in respect of all outstanding proceedings against the defendant.

14D.3 Failure by the defendant to surrender or a conviction for failing to surrender to bail in connection with the main proceedings will be significant factors weighing against the re-granting of bail.

14D.4 Whether or not an immediate custodial sentence has been imposed for the Bail Act offence, the court may, having reviewed the defendant's remand status, also remand the defendant in custody in the main proceedings.

CPD III Custody and bail 14E: Trials in absence

14E.1 A defendant has a right, in general, to be present and to be represented at his trial. However, a defendant may choose not to exercise those rights, such as by voluntarily absenting himself and failing to instruct his lawyers adequately so that they can represent him.

14E.2 The court has a discretion as to whether a trial should take place or continue in the defendant's absence and must exercise its discretion with due regard for the interests of justice. The overriding concern must be to ensure that such a trial is as fair as circumstances permit and leads to a just outcome. If the defendant's absence is due to involuntary illness or incapacity it would very rarely, if ever, be right to exercise the discretion in favour of commencing or continuing the trial.

Trials on Indictment

14E.3 Proceeding in the absence of a defendant is a step which ought normally to be taken only if it is unavoidable. The court must exercise its discretion as to whether a trial should take place or continue in the defendant's absence with the utmost care and caution. Due regard should be had to the judgment of Lord Bingham in *R v Jones* [2002] UKHL 5, [2003] 1 A.C. 1, [2002] 2 Cr. App. R. 9. Circumstances to be taken into account before proceeding include:

(a) the conduct of the defendant,
(b) the disadvantage to the defendant,
(c) the public interest, taking account of the inconvenience and hardship to witnesses, and especially to any complainant, of a delay; if the witnesses have attended court and are ready to give evidence, that will weigh in favour of continuing with the trial,
(d) the effect of any delay,
(e) whether the attendance of the defendant could be secured at a later hearing, and
(f) the likely outcome if the defendant is found guilty.

Even if the defendant is voluntarily absent, it is still generally desirable that he or she is represented.

Trials in the Magistrates' Courts

14E.4 Section 11 of the Magistrates' Courts Act 1980 applies. If either party is absent, the court should follow the procedure at CrimPR 24.12. Subject to the provisions of the statute, the principles outlined above are applicable. Benches and legal advisers will note that the presumption at rule 24.12(3)(a) does not apply if the defendant is under 18 years of age.

CPD III Custody and bail 14F: Forfeiture of monies lodged as security or pledged by a surety/estreatment of recognizances

14F.1 A surety undertakes to forfeit a sum of money if the defendant fails to surrender as required. Considerable care must be taken to explain that obligation and the consequences before a surety is taken. This system, in one form or another, has great antiquity. It is immensely valuable. A court concerned that a defendant will fail to surrender will not normally know that defendant personally, nor indeed much about him. When members of the community who do know the defendant say they trust him to surrender and are prepared to stake their own money on that trust, that can have a powerful influence on the decision of the court as to whether or not to grant bail. There are two important side-effects. The first is that the surety will keep an eye on the defendant, and report to the authorities if there is a concern that he will abscond. In those circumstances, the surety can withdraw. The second is that a defendant will be deterred from absconding by the knowledge that if he does so then his family or friends who provided the surety will lose their money. In the experience of the courts, it is comparatively rare for a defendant to fail to surrender when meaningful sureties are in place.

14F.2 Any surety should have the opportunity to make representations to the defendant to surrender himself, in accordance with their obligations.

14F.3 The court should not wait or adjourn a decision on estreatment of sureties or securities until such time, if any, that the bailed defendant appears before the court. It is possible that any defendant who apparently absconds may have a defence of reasonable cause to the allegation of failure to surrender. If that happens, then any surety or security estreated would be returned. The reason for proceeding is that the defendant may never surrender, or may not surrender for many years. The court should still consider the sureties' obligations if that happens. Moreover, the longer the matter is delayed the more probable it is that the personal circumstances of the sureties will change.

14F.4 The court should follow the procedure at CrimPR 14.15. Before the court makes a decision, it should give the sureties the opportunity to make representations, either in person, through counsel or by statement.

14F.5 The court has discretion to forfeit the whole sum, part only of the sum, or to remit the sum. The starting point is that the surety is forfeited in full. It would be unfortunate if this valuable method of allowing a defendant to remain at liberty were undermined. Courts would have less confidence in the efficacy of sureties. It is also important to note that a defendant who absconds without in any way forewarning his sureties does not thereby release them from any or all of their responsibilities. Even if a surety does his best, he remains liable for the full amount, except at the discretion of the court. However, all factors should be taken into account and the following are noted for guidance only:

(i)   The presence or absence of culpability is a factor, but is not in itself a reason to reduce or set aside the obligations entered into by the surety.
(ii)   The means of a surety, and in particular changed means, are relevant.
(iii)   The court should forfeit no more than is necessary, in public policy, to maintain the integrity and confidence of the system of taking sureties.

CPD III Custody and bail 14G: Bail during trial

14G.1   The following should be read subject to the Bail Act 1976.

14G.2   Once a trial has begun the further grant of bail, whether during the short adjournment or overnight, is in the discretion of the trial judge or trial Bench. It may be a proper exercise of this discretion to refuse bail during the short adjournment if the accused cannot otherwise be segregated from witnesses and jurors.

14G.3   An accused who was on bail while on remand should not be refused bail during the trial unless, in the opinion of the court, there are positive reasons to justify this refusal. Such reasons might include:

(a)   that a point has been reached where there is a real danger that the accused will abscond, either because the case is going badly for him, or for any other reason;
(b)   that there is a real danger that he may interfere with witnesses, jurors or co-defendants.

14G.4   Once the jury has returned a guilty verdict or a finding of guilt has been made, a further renewal of bail should be decided in the light of the gravity of the offence, any friction between co-defendants and the likely sentence to be passed in all the circumstances of the case.

CPD III Custody and bail 14H: Crown court judge's certificaton of fitness to appeal and applications to the crown court for bail pending appeal

14H.1   The trial or sentencing judge may grant a certificate of fitness for appeal (see, for example, sections 1(2)(b) and 11(1A) of the Criminal Appeal Act 1968); the judge in the Crown Court should only certify cases in exceptional circumstances. The Crown Court judge should use the Criminal Appeal Office Form C (Crown Court Judge's Certificate of fitness for appeal) which is available to court staff on the HMCTS intranet.

14H.2   The judge may well think it right to encourage the defendant's advocate to submit to the court, and serve on the prosecutor, before the hearing of the application, a draft of the grounds of appeal which he will ask the judge to certify on Form C.

14H.3   The first question for the judge is then whether there exists a particular and cogent ground of appeal. If there is no such ground, there can be no certificate; and if there is no certificate there can be no bail. A judge should not grant a certificate with regard to sentence merely in the light of mitigation to which he has, in his opinion, given due weight, nor in regard to conviction on a ground where he considers the chance of a successful appeal is not substantial. The judge should bear in mind that, where a certificate is refused, application may be made to the Court of Appeal for leave to appeal and for bail; it is expected that certificates will only be granted in exceptional circumstances.

14H.4   Defence advocates should note that the effect of a grant of a certificate is to remove the need for leave to appeal to be granted by the Court of Appeal. It does not in itself commence the appeal. The completed Form C will be sent by the Crown Court to the Criminal Appeal Office; it is not copied to the parties. The procedures in CrimPR Part 39 should be followed.

14H.5   Bail pending appeal to the Court of Appeal (Criminal Division) may be granted by the trial or sentencing judge if they have certified the case as fit for appeal (see sections 81(1)(f) and 81(1B) of the Senior Courts Act 1981). Bail can only be granted in the Crown Court within 28 days of the conviction or sentence which is to be the subject of the appeal and may not be granted if an application for bail has already been made to the Court of Appeal. The procedure for bail to be granted by a judge of the Crown Court pending an appeal is governed by CrimPR Part 14. The Crown Court judge should use the Criminal Appeal Office Form BC (Crown Court Judge's Order granting bail) which is available to court staff on the HMCTS intranet.

14H.6   The length of the period which might elapse before the hearing of any appeal is not relevant to the grant of a certificate; but, if the judge does decide to grant a certificate, it may be one factor in the decision whether or not to grant bail. If bail is granted, the judge should consider imposing a condition of residence in line with the practice in the Court of Appeal (Criminal Division).

CRIMINAL PRACTICE DIRECTIONS 2015 DIVISION IV

Disclosure

CRIMPR PART 15 DISCLOSURE

CPD IV Disclosure 15A: Disclosure of unused material

15A.1   Disclosure is a vital part of the preparation for trial, both in the magistrates' courts and in the Crown Court. All parties must be familiar with their obligations, in particular under the Criminal Procedure and Investigations Act 1996 as amended and the Code issued under that Act, and must comply with the relevant judicial protocol and guidelines from the Attorney-General. These documents have recently been revised and the new guidance will be issued shortly as *Judicial Protocol on the Disclosure of Unused Material in Criminal Cases* and the *Attorney-General's Guidelines on Disclosure.* The new documents should be read together as complementary, comprehensive guidance. They will be available electronically on the respective websites.

15A.2   In addition, certain procedures are prescribed under CrimPR Part 15 and these should be followed. The notes to Part 15 contain a useful summary of the requirements of the CPIA 1996 as amended.

CRIMINAL PRACTICE DIRECTIONS 2015 DIVISION V
Evidence

CRIMPR PART 16 WITNESS STATEMENTS

CPD V Evidence 16A: Evidence by written statement

16A.1 Where the prosecution proposes to tender written statements in evidence under section 9 of the Criminal Justice Act 1967, it will frequently be necessary for certain statements to be edited. This will occur either because a witness has made more than one statement whose contents should conveniently be reduced into a single, comprehensive statement, or where a statement contains inadmissible, prejudicial or irrelevant material. Editing of statements must be done by a Crown Prosecutor (or by a legal representative, if any, of the prosecutor if the case is not being conducted by the Crown Prosecution Service) and not by a police officer.

Composite statements

16A.2 A composite statement giving the combined effect of two or more earlier statements must be prepared in compliance with the requirements of section 9 of the 1967 Act; and must then be signed by the witness.

Editing single statements

16A.3 There are two acceptable methods of editing single statements. They are:-

(a) By marking copies of the statement in a way which indicates the passages on which the prosecution will not rely. This merely indicates that the prosecution will not seek to adduce the evidence so marked. The original signed statement to be tendered to the court is not marked in any way.

The marking on the copy statement is done by lightly striking out the passages to be edited, so that what appears beneath can still be read, or by bracketing, or by a combination of both. It is not permissible to produce a photocopy with the deleted material obliterated, since this would be contrary to the requirement that the defence and the court should be served with copies of the signed original statement.

Whenever the striking out / bracketing method is used, it will assist if the following words appear at the foot of the frontispiece or index to any bundle of copy statements to be tendered:

'The prosecution does not propose to adduce evidence of those passages of the attached copy statements which have been struck out and / or bracketed (nor will it seek to do so at the trial unless a notice of further evidence is served)'.

(b) By obtaining a fresh statement, signed by the witness, which omits the offending material, applying the procedure for composite statements above.

16A.4 In most cases where a single statement is to be edited, the striking out/ bracketing method will be the more appropriate, but the taking of a fresh statement is preferable in the following circumstances:

(a) When a police (or other investigating) officer's statement contains details of interviews with more suspects than are eventually charged, a fresh statement should be prepared and signed, omitting all details of interview with those not charged except, insofar as it is relevant, for the bald fact that a certain named person was interviewed at a particular time, date and place.

(b) When a suspect is interviewed about more offences than are eventually made the subject of charges, a fresh statement should be prepared and signed, omitting all questions and answers about the uncharged offences unless either they might appropriately be taken into consideration, or evidence about those offences is admissible on the charges preferred. It may, however, be desirable to replace the omitted questions and answers with a phrase such as: *'After referring to some other matters, I then said, "* . . . . *"',* so as to make it clear that part of the interview has been omitted.

(c) A fresh statement should normally be prepared and signed if the only part of the original on which the prosecution is relying is only a small proportion of the whole, although it remains desirable to use the alternative method if there is reason to believe that the defence might itself wish to rely, in mitigation or for any other purpose, on at least some of those parts which the prosecution does not propose to adduce.

(d) When the passages contain material which the prosecution is entitled to withhold from disclosure to the defence.

16A.5 Prosecutors should also be aware that, where statements are to be tendered under section 9 of the 1967 Act in the course of summary proceedings, there will be a need to prepare fresh statements excluding inadmissible or prejudicial material, rather than using the striking out or bracketing method.

16A.6 Whenever a fresh statement is taken from a witness and served in evidence, the earlier, unedited statement(s) becomes unused material and should be scheduled and reviewed for disclosure to the defence in the usual way.

CPD V Evidence 16B: Video recorded evidence in chief

16B.1 The procedure for making an application for leave to admit into evidence video recorded evidence in chief under section 27 of the Youth Justice and Criminal Evidence Act 1999 is given in CrimPR Part 18.

16B.2 Where a court, on application by a party to the proceedings or of its own motion, grants leave to admit a video recording in evidence under section 27(1) of the 1999 Act, it may direct that any part of the recording be excluded (section 27(2) and (3)). When such direction is given, the party who made the application to admit the video recording must edit the recording in accordance with the judge's directions and send a copy of the edited recording to the appropriate officer of the Crown Court and to every other party to the proceedings.

16B.3 Where a video recording is to be adduced during proceedings before the Crown Court, it should be produced and proved by the interviewer, or any other person who was present at the interview with the witness at which the recording was made. The applicant should ensure that such a person will be available for this purpose, unless the parties have agreed to accept a written statement in lieu of attendance by that person.

16B.4 Once a trial has begun, if, by reason of faulty or inadequate preparation or for some other cause, the procedures set out above have not been properly complied with and an application is made to edit the video recording, thereby necessitating an adjournment for the work to be carried out, the court may, at its discretion, make an appropriate award of costs.

CPD V Evidence 16C: Evidence of audio and video recorded interviews

16C.1 The interrogation of suspects is primarily governed by Code C, one of the Codes of Practice under the Police and Criminal Evidence Act 1984 ('PACE'). Under that Code, interviews must normally be contemporaneously recorded. Under PACE Code E, interviews conducted at a police station concerning an indictable offence must normally be audio-recorded. In practice, most interviews are audio-recorded under Code E, or video-recorded under Code F, and it is best practice to do so. The questioning of terrorism suspects is governed separately by Code H. The Codes are available electronically on the Home Office website.

16C.2 Where a record of the interview is to be prepared, this should be in accordance with the current national guidelines, as envisaged by Note 5A of Code E.

16C.3 If the prosecution wishes to rely on the defendant's interview in evidence, the prosecution should seek to agree the record with the defence. Both parties should have received a copy of the audio or video recording, and can check the record against the recording. The record should be edited (see below) if inadmissible matters are included within it and, in particular if the interview is lengthy, the prosecution should seek to shorten it by editing or summary.

16C.4 If the record is agreed there is usually no need for the audio or video recording to be played in court. It is a matter for the discretion of the trial judge, but usual practice is for edited copies of the record to be provided to the court, and to the jury if there is one, and for the prosecution advocate to read the interview with the interviewing officer or the officer in the case, as part of the officer's evidence in chief, the officer reading the interviewer and the advocate reading the defendant and defence representative. In the magistrates' court, the Bench sometimes retire to read the interview themselves, and the document is treated as if it had been read aloud in court. This is permissible, but CrimPR 24.5 should be followed.

16C.5 Where the prosecution intends to adduce the interview in evidence, and agreement between the parties has not been reached about the record, sufficient notice must be given to allow consideration of any amendment to the record, or the preparation of any transcript of the interview, or any editing of a recording for the purpose of playing it in court. To that end, the following practice should be followed.

(a) Where the defence is unable to agree a record of interview or transcript (where one is already available) the prosecution should be notified at latest at the Plea and Case Management Hearing ('PCMH'), with a view to securing agreement to amend. The notice should specify the part to which objection is taken, or the part omitted which the defence consider should be included. A copy of the notice should be supplied to the court within the period specified above. The PCMH form inquires about the admissibility of the defendant's interview and shortening by editing or summarising for trial.

(b) If agreement is not reached and it is proposed that the audio or video recording or part of it be played in court, notice should be given to the prosecution by the defence as ordered at the PCMH, in order that the advocates for the parties may agree those parts of the audio or video recording that should not be adduced and that arrangements may be made, by editing or in some other way, to exclude that material. A copy of the notice should be supplied to the court.

(c) Notice of any agreement reached should be supplied to the court by the prosecution, as soon as is practicable.

16C.6 Alternatively, if, the prosecution advocate proposes to play the audio or video recording or part of it, the prosecution should at latest at the PCMH, notify the defence and the court. The defence should notify the prosecution and the court within 14 days of receiving the notice, if they object to the production of the audio or video recording on the basis that a part of it should be excluded. If the objections raised by the defence are accepted, the prosecution should prepare an edited recording, or make other arrangements to exclude the material part; and should notify the court of the arrangements made.

16C.7 If the defendant wishes to have the audio or video recording or any part of it played to the court, the defence should provide notice to the prosecution and the court at latest at the PCMH. The defence should also, at that time, notify the prosecution of any proposals to edit the recording and seek the prosecution's agreement to those amendments.

16C.8 Whenever editing or amendment of a record of interview or of an audio or video recording or of a transcript takes place, the following general principles should be followed:

(i) Where a defendant has made a statement which includes an admission of one or more other offences, the portion relating to other offences should be omitted unless it is or becomes admissible in evidence;

(ii) Where the statement of one defendant contains a portion which exculpates him or her and partly implicates a co-defendant in the trial, the defendant making the statement has the right to insist that everything relevant which is exculpatory goes before the jury. In such a case the judge must be consulted about how best to protect the position of the co-defendant.

16C.9 If it becomes necessary for either party to access the master copy of the audio or video recording, they should give notice to the other party and follow the procedure in PACE Code E at section 6.

16C.10 If there is a challenge to the integrity of the master recording, notice and particulars should be given to the court and to the prosecution by the defence as soon as is practicable. The court may then, at its discretion, order a case management hearing or give such other directions as may be appropriate.

16C.11 If an audio or video recording is to be adduced during proceedings before the Crown Court, it should be produced and proved in a witness statement by the interviewing officer or any other officer who was present at the interview at which the recording was made. The prosecution should ensure that the witness is available to attend court if required by the defence in the usual way.

16C.12 It is the responsibility of the prosecution to ensure that there is a person available to operate any audio or video equipment needed during the course of the proceedings. Subject to their other responsibilities, the court staff may be able to assist.

16C.13 If either party wishes to present audio or video evidence, that party must ensure, in advance of the hearing, that the evidence is in a format that is compatible with the court's equipment, and that the material to be used does in fact function properly in the relevant court room.

16C.14 In order to avoid the necessity for the court to listen to or watch lengthy or irrelevant material before the relevant part of a recording is reached, counsel shall indicate to the equipment operator those parts of a recording which it may be necessary to play. Such an indication should, so far as is possible, be expressed in terms of the time track or other identifying process used by the interviewing police force and should be given in time for the operator to have located those parts by the appropriate point in the trial.

16C.15 Once a trial has begun, if, by reason of faulty preparation or for some other cause, the procedures above have not been properly complied with, and an application is made to amend the record of interview or transcript or to edit the recording, as the case may be, thereby making necessary an adjournment for the work to be carried out, the court may make at its discretion an appropriate award of costs.

16C.16 Where a case is listed for hearing on a date which falls within the time limits set out above, it is the responsibility of the parties to ensure that all the necessary steps are taken to comply with this Practice Direction within such shorter period as is available.

CRIMPR PART 17 WITNESS SUMMONSES, WARRANTS AND ORDERS

CPD V Evidence 17A: Wards of court and children subject to current family proceedings

17A.1 Where police wish to interview a child who is subject to current family proceedings, leave of the Family Court is only required where such an interview may lead to a child disclosing information confidential to those proceedings and not otherwise available to the police under Working Together to Safeguard Children (March 2013), a guide to inter-agency working to safeguard and promote the welfare of children: www.workingtogetheronline.co.uk/chapters/contents.html

17A.2 Where exceptionally the child to be interviewed or called as a witness in criminal proceedings is a Ward of Court then the leave of the court which made the wardship order will be required.

17A.3 Any application for leave in respect of any such child must be made to the court in which the relevant family proceedings are continuing and must be made on notice to the parents, any actual carer (e.g. relative or foster parent) and, in care proceedings, to the local authority and the guardian. In private proceedings the Family Court Reporter (if appointed) should be notified.

17A.4 If the police need to interview the child without the knowledge of another party (usually a parent or carer), they may make the application for leave without giving notice to that party.

17A.5 Where leave is given the order should ordinarily give leave for any number of interviews that may be required. However, anything beyond that actually authorised will require a further application.

17A.6 Exceptionally the police may have to deal with complaints by or allegations against such a child immediately without obtaining the leave of the court as, for example

(a) a serious offence against a child (like rape) where immediate medical examination and collection of evidence is required; or

(b) where the child is to be interviewed as a suspect.

When any such action is necessary, the police should, in respect of each and every interview, notify the parents and other carer (if any) and the Family Court Reporter (if appointed). In care proceedings the local authority and guardian should be notified. The police must comply with all relevant Codes of Practice when conducting any such interview.

17A.7 The Family Court should be appraised of the position at the earliest reasonable opportunity by one of the notified parties and should thereafter be kept informed of any criminal proceedings.

17A.8 No evidence or document in the family proceedings or information about the proceedings should be disclosed into criminal proceedings without the leave of the Family Court.

CRIMPR PART 18 MEASURES TO ASSIST A WITNESS OR DEFENDANT TO GIVE EVIDENCE

CPD V Evidence 18A: Measures to assist a witness or defendant to give evidence

18A.1 For special measures applications, the procedures at CrimPR Part 18 should be followed. However, assisting a vulnerable witness to give evidence is not merely a matter of ordering the appropriate measure. Further directions about vulnerable people in the courts, ground rules hearings and intermediaries are given in paragraphs I 3D to 3G.

18A.2 Special measures need not be considered or ordered in isolation. The needs of the individual witness should be ascertained, and a combination of special measures may be appropriate. For example, if a witness who is to give evidence by live link wishes, screens can be used to shield the live link screen from the defendant and the public, as would occur if screens were being used for a witness giving evidence in the court room.

CPD V Evidence 18B: Witnesses giving evidence by live link

18B.1 A special measures direction for the witness to give evidence by live link may also provide for a specified person to accompany the witness (CrimPR 18.10(f)). In determining who this should be, the court must have regard to the wishes of the witness. The presence of a supporter is designed to provide emotional support to the witness, helping reduce the witness's anxiety and stress and contributing to the ability to give best evidence. It is preferable for the direction to be made well before the trial begins and to ensure that the designated person is available on the day of the witness's testimony so as to provide certainty for the witness.

18B.2 An increased degree of flexibility is appropriate as to who can act as supporter. This can be anyone known to and trusted by the witness who is not a party to the proceedings and has no detailed knowledge of the evidence in the case. The supporter may be a member of the Witness Service but need not be an usher or court official. Someone else may be appropriate.

18B.3 The usher should continue to be available both to assist the witness and the witness supporter, and to ensure that the court's requirements are properly complied with in the live link room.

18B.4 In order to be able to express an informed view about special measures, the witness is entitled to practise speaking using the live link (and to see screens in place). Simply being shown the room and equipment is inadequate for this purpose.

18B.5 If, with the agreement of the court, the witness has chosen not to give evidence by live link but to do so in the court room, it may still be appropriate for a witness supporter to be selected in the same way, and for the supporter to sit alongside the witness while the witness is giving evidence.

CPD V Evidence 18C: Visually recorded interviews: memory refreshing and watching at a different time from the jury

18C.1 Witnesses are entitled to refresh their memory from their statement or visually recorded interview. The court should enquire at the PTPH or other case management hearing about arrangements for memory refreshing. The witness's first viewing of the visually recorded interview can be distressing or distracting. It should not be seen for the first time immediately before giving evidence. Depending upon the age and vulnerability of the witness several competing issues have to be considered and it may be that the assistance of the intermediary is needed to establish exactly how memory refreshing should be managed.

18C.2 If the interview is ruled inadmissible, the court must decide what constitutes an acceptable alternative method of memory refreshing.

18C.3 Decisions about how, when and where refreshing should take place should be court-led and made on a case-by-case basis in respect of each witness. General principles to be addressed include:

(i) the venue for viewing. The delicate balance between combining the court familiarisation visit and watching the DVD, and having them on two separate occasions, needs to be considered in respect of each witness as combining the two may lead to 'information overload'. Refreshing need not necessarily take place within the court building but may be done, for example, at the police ABE suite.

(ii) requiring that any viewing is monitored by a person (usually the officer in the case) who will report to the court about anything said by the witness.

(iii) whether it is necessary for the witness to see the DVD more than once for the purpose of refreshing. The court will need to ask the advice of the intermediary, if any, with respect to this.

(iv) arrangements, if the witness will not watch the DVD at the same time as the trial bench or judge and jury, for the witness to watch it before attending to be cross examined, (depending upon their ability to retain information this may be the day before).

18C.4 There is no legal requirement that the witness should watch the interview at the same time as the trial bench or jury. Increasingly, this is arranged to occur at a different time, with the advantages that breaks can be taken as needed without disrupting the trial, and cross-examination starts while the witness is fresh. An intermediary may be present to facilitate communication but should not act as the independent person designated to take a note and report to the court if anything is said.

18C.5 Where the viewing takes place at a different time from that of the trial bench or jury, the witness is sworn (or promises) just before cross-examination and, unless the judge otherwise directs:

(a) it is good practice for the witness to be asked by the prosecutor, (or the judge/magistrate if they so direct), in appropriate language if, and when, he or she has watched the recording of the interview;

(b) if, in watching the recording of the interview or otherwise the witness has indicated that there is something he or she wishes to correct or to add then it is good practice for the prosecutor (or the judge/magistrate if they so direct) to deal with that before cross-examination provided that proper notice has been given to the defence.

CPD V Evidence 18D: Witness anonymity orders

18D.1 This direction supplements CrimPR 18.18 to 18.22, which govern the procedure to be followed on an application for a witness anonymity order. The court's power to make such an order is conferred by the Coroners and Justice Act 2009 (in this section, 'the Act'); section 87 of the Act provides specific relevant powers and obligations.

18D.2 As the Court of Appeal stated in *R v Mayers and Others* [2008] EWCA Crim 2989, [2009] 1 W.L.R. 1915, [2009] 1 Cr. App. R. 30 and emphasised again in *R v Donovan and Kafunda* [2012] EWCA Crim 2749, unreported, 'a witness anonymity order is to be regarded as a special measure of the last practicable resort': Lord Chief Justice, Lord Judge. In making such an application, the prosecution's obligations of disclosure 'go much further than the ordinary duties of disclosure' (*R v Mayers*); reference should be made to the Judicial Protocol on Disclosure, see paragraph IV 15A.1.

Case management

18D.3 Where such an application is proposed, with the parties' active assistance the court should set a realistic timetable, in accordance with the duties imposed by CrimPR 3.2 and 3.3. Where possible, the trial judge should determine the application, and any hearing should be attended by the parties' trial advocates.

Service of evidence and disclosure of prosecution material pending an application

18D.4 Where the prosecutor proposes an application for a witness anonymity order, it is not necessary for that application to have been determined before the proposed evidence is served. In most cases, an early indication of what that evidence will be if an order is made will be consistent with a party's duties under CrimPR 1.2 and 3.3. The prosecutor should serve with the other prosecution evidence a witness statement setting out the proposed evidence, redacted in such a way as to prevent disclosure of the witness' identity, as permitted by section 87(4) of the Act. Likewise the prosecutor should serve with other prosecution material disclosed under the Criminal Procedure and Investigations Act 1996 any such material appertaining to the witness, similarly redacted.

The application

18D.5 An application for a witness anonymity order should be made as early as possible and within the period for which CrimPR 18.3 provides. The application, and any hearing of it, must comply with the requirements of that rule and with those of rule 18.19. In accordance with CrimPR 1.2 and 3.3, the applicant must provide the court with all available information relevant to the considerations to which the Act requires a court to have regard.

Response to the application

18D.6 A party upon whom an application for a witness anonymity order is served must serve a response in accordance with CrimPR 18.22. That period may be extended or shortened in the court's discretion: CrimPR 18.5.

18D.7 To avoid the risk of injustice, a respondent, whether the Prosecution or a defendant, must actively assist the court. If not already done, a respondent defendant should serve a defence statement under section 5 or 6 of the Criminal Procedure and Investigations Act 1996, so that the court is fully informed of what is in issue. When a defendant makes an application for a witness anonymity order the prosecutor should consider the continuing duty to disclose material under section 7A of the Criminal Procedure and Investigations Act 1996; therefore a prosecutor's response should include confirmation that that duty has been considered. Great care should be taken to ensure that nothing disclosed contains anything that might reveal the witness' identity. A respondent prosecutor should provide the court with all available information relevant to the considerations to which the Act requires a court to have regard, whether or not that information falls to be disclosed under the 1996 Act.

Determination of the application

18D.8 All parties must have an opportunity to make oral representations to the court on an application for a witness anonymity order: section 87(6) of the Act. However, a hearing may not be needed if none is sought: CrimPR 18.18(1)(a). Where, for example, the witness is an investigator who is recognisable by the defendant but known only by an assumed name, and there is no likelihood that the witness' credibility will be in issue, then the court may indicate a provisional decision and invite representations within a defined period, usually 14 days, including representations about whether there should be a hearing. In such a case, where the parties do not object the court may make an order without a hearing. Or where the court provisionally considers an application to be misconceived, an applicant may choose to withdraw it without requiring a hearing. Where the court directs a hearing of the application then it should allow adequate time for service of the representations in response.

18D.9 The hearing of an application for a witness anonymity order usually should be in private: CrimPR 18.18(1)(a). The court has power to hear a party in the absence of a defendant and that defendant's representatives: section 87(7) of the Act and rule 18.18(1)(b). In the Crown Court, a recording of the proceedings will be made, in accordance with CrimPR 5.5. The Crown Court officer must treat such a recording in the same way as the recording of an application for a public interest ruling. It must be kept in secure conditions, and the arrangements made by the Crown Court officer for any transcription must impose restrictions that correspond with those under CrimPR 5.5(2).

18D.10 The hearing of an application for a witness anonymity order usually should be in private: CrimPR 18.18(1)(a). The court has power to hear a party in the absence of a defendant and that defendant's representatives: section 87(7) of the Act and rule 18.18(1)(b). In the Crown Court, a recording of the proceedings will be made, in accordance with CrimPR 5.5. The Crown Court officer must treat such a recording in the same way as the recording of an application for a public interest ruling. It must be kept in secure conditions, and the arrangements made by the Crown Court officer for any transcription must impose restrictions that correspond with those under CrimPR 5.5(2).

18D.11 Where confidential supporting information is presented to the court before the last stage of the hearing, the court may prefer not to read that information until that last stage.

18D.12 The court may adjourn the hearing at any stage, and should do so if its duty under CrimPR 3.2 so requires.

18D.13 On a prosecutor's application, the court is likely to be assisted by the attendance of a senior investigator or other person of comparable authority who is familiar with the case.

18D.14 During the last stage of the hearing it is essential that the court test thoroughly the information supplied in confidence in order to satisfy itself that the conditions prescribed by the Act are met. At that stage, if the court concludes that this is the only way in which it can satisfy itself as to a relevant condition or consideration, exceptionally it may invite the applicant to present the proposed witness to be questioned by the court. Any such questioning should be carried out at such a time, and the witness brought to the court in such a way, as to prevent disclosure of his or her identity.

18D.15 The court may ask the Attorney General to appoint special counsel to assist. However, it must be kept in mind that, 'Such an appointment will always be exceptional, never automatic; a course of last and never first resort. It should not be ordered unless and until the trial judge is satisfied that no other course will adequately meet the overriding requirement of fairness to the defendant': *R v H* [2004] UKHL 3, [2004] 2 A.C. 134 (at paragraph 22), [2004] 2 Cr. App. R. 10. Whether to accede to such a request is a matter for the Attorney General, and adequate time should be allowed for the consideration of such a request.

18D.16 The Court of Appeal in *R v Mayers* 'emphasise[d] that all three conditions, A, B and C, must be met before the jurisdiction to make a witness anonymity order arises. Each is mandatory. Each is distinct.' The Court also noted that if there is more than one anonymous witness in a case any link, and the nature of any link, between the witnesses should be investigated: 'questions of possible improper collusion between them, or cross-contamination of one another, should be addressed.'

18D.17 Following a hearing the court should announce its decision on an application for a witness anonymity order in the parties' presence and in public: CrimPR 18.4(2). The court should give such reasons as it is possible to give without revealing the witness' identity. In the Crown Court, the court will be conscious that reasons given in public may be reported and reach the jury. Consequently, the court should ensure that nothing in its decision or its reasons could undermine any warning it may give jurors under section 90(2) of the Act. A record of the reasons must be kept. In the Crown Court, the announcement of those reasons will be recorded.

Order

18D.18 Where the court makes a witness anonymity order, it is essential that the measures to be taken are clearly specified in a written record of that order approved by the court and issued on its behalf. An order made in a magistrates' court must be recorded in the court register, in accordance with CrimPR 5.4.

18D.19 Self-evidently, the written record of the order must not disclose the identity of the witness to whom it applies. However, it is essential that there be maintained some means of establishing a clear correlation between witness and order, and especially where in the same proceedings witness anonymity orders are made in respect of more than one witness, specifying different measures in respect of each. Careful preservation of the application for the order, including the confidential part, ordinarily will suffice for this purpose.

18D.20 Should the judge grant the anonymity then the following should be considered by the judge with the assistance of the court staff, so that the practical arrangements (confidentially recorded) are in place to ensure that the witness's anonymity is not compromised:

i. Any pre-trial visit by the anonymous witness;
ii. How the witness will enter and leave the court building;
iii. Where the witness will wait until they give evidence;
iv. Provision for prosecution counsel to speak to the anonymous witness at court before they give evidence;
v. Provision for the anonymous witness to see their statement or view their ABEs;
vi. How the witness will enter and leave the court room;
vii. Provisions to disguise the identity of the anonymous witness whilst they give evidence (voice modulation and screens);
viii. Provisions for the anonymous witness to have any breaks required;
ix. Provisions to protect the anonymity of the witness in the event of an emergency such as a security alert.

Discharge or variation of the order

18D.21 Section 91 of the Act allows the court to discharge or vary a witness anonymity order: on application, if there has been a material change of circumstances since the order was made or since any previous variation of it; or on its own initiative. CrimPR 18.21 allows the parties to apply for the variation of a pre-trial direction where circumstances have changed.

18D.22 Should the application for anonymity be refused, consideration will be given as to whether the witness to whom the application related can be compelled to give evidence despite any risk to their safely and what special measures could support them to give their evidence.

18D.23 The court should keep under review the question of whether the conditions for making an order are met. In addition, consistently with the parties' duties under CrimPR 1.2 and 3.3, it is incumbent on each, and in particular on the applicant for the order, to keep the need for it under review.

18D.24 Where the court considers the discharge or variation of an order, the procedure that it adopts should be appropriate to the circumstances. As a general rule, that procedure should approximate to the procedure for determining an application for an order. The court may need to hear further representations by the applicant for the order in the absence of a respondent defendant and that defendant's representatives.

Retention of confidential material

18D.25 If retained by the court, confidential material must be stored in secure conditions by the court officer. Alternatively, subject to such directions as the court may give, such material may be committed to the safe keeping of the applicant or any other appropriate person in exercise of the powers conferred by CrimPR 18.6. If the material is released to any such person, the court should ensure that it will be available to the court at trial.

Arrangements at trial

18.26 At trial the greatest possible care must be taken to ensure that nothing will compromise the witness' anonymity. Detailed arrangements may have been proposed by the applicant under CrimPR 18.19(1)(b) and directed by the court on determining the application for the order. Such arrangements must take account of the layout of the courtroom and of the means of access for the witness, for the defendant or defendants, and for members of the public. The risk of a chance encounter between the witness and someone who may recognise him or her, either then or subsequently, must be rigorously excluded. Subject to contrary direction by the trial judge, the court staff and those accompanying the witness must adopt necessary measures to ensure that the witness is neither seen nor heard by anyone whose observation would, or might, render nugatory the court's order. Further HMCTS guidance for court staff can be found in Guidance for Criminal Courts for England and Wales for Anonymous/Protected Witnesses.

CPD V Evidence 18E: Use of s 28 Youth Justice and Criminal Evidence Act 1999; Pre-recording of cross-examination and re-examination for witnesses captured by s 16 YJCEA 1999

18E.1   When Section 28 of the Youth Justice and Criminal Evidence Act 1999 (s 28 YJCEA 1999) is bought into force by Statutory Instrument for a particular Crown Court, under that SI, a witness will be eligible for special measures under s. 28 if

(i)   he or she is under the age of 18 at the time of the special measures hearing; or
(ii)   he or she suffers from a mental disorder within the meaning of the Mental Health Act 1983, or has a significant impairment of intelligence and social functioning, or has a physical disability or a physical disorder, and the quality of his or her evidence is likely to be diminished as a consequence.

18E.2   This process is governed by the Criminal Procedure Rules and careful attention should be paid to the court's case management powers and the obligations on the parties. Advocates should also refer to the annex of this practice direction which contains further detailed guidance on ground rules hearings.

18E.3   The Resident Judge may appoint a judicial lead from full time judges at the court centre who will be responsible for monitoring and supervision of the scheme. The Plea and Trial Preparation Hearing (PTPH) must be conducted by a full time judge authorised by the Resident Judge to sit on that class of case and who has been authorised to deal with s 28 YJCEA 1999 cases by the Resident Judge.

18E.4   Reference should be made to the joint protocol agreed between the police and the Crown Prosecution Service.

18E.5   Witnesses eligible for special measures under s 28 YJCEA 1999 should be identified by the police. The police and Crown Prosecution Service should discuss, with the witness or with the witness' parent or carer, special measures available and the witness' needs, such that the most appropriate package of special measures can be identified. This may include use of a Registered Intermediary. See Criminal Practice Directions of 2015 (CPD) General matters 3D: Vulnerable people in the courts and 3F: Intermediaries.

18E.6   For access to special measures under s 28 YJCEA 1999, the witness' interview must be recorded in accordance with the Achieving Best Evidence ('ABE') guidance which is available on the Ministry of Justice website.

18E.7   For timetabling of the case, it is imperative that the investigators and prosecutor commence the disclosure process at the start of the investigation. The Judicial Protocol on Disclosure of Unused Material in Criminal Proceedings (November 2013) must be followed, and if applicable, the 2013 Protocol and Good Practice Model on Disclosure of information in cases of alleged child abuse and linked criminal and care directions. Local Implementation Teams (LITs) should encourage all appropriate agencies to endorse and follow both the Protocol and the Good Practice Model. LITs should monitor compliance and issues should initially be raised at the LITs.

The first hearing in the magistrates' court

18E.8   Initial details of the prosecution case must be served in accordance with Part 8 of the Rules.

18E.9   The prosecutor must formally notify the court at the first hearing that the case is eligible for special measures under s 28 YJCEA 1999.

18E.10   At the hearing the court must follow part 9 of the Rules (Allocation) and refer to the Sentencing Council's guideline on Allocation. This practice direction applies only where the defendant indicates a not guilty plea or does not indicate a plea, and the case is sent for trial in the Crown Court, either with or without allocation.

18E.11   If the case is to be sent to the Crown Court, the prosecutor should inform the court and the defence if not already notified that the prosecution will seek special measures including under s 28 YJCEA 1999.

18E.12   In any case that is sent to the Crown Court for trial in which the prosecution has notified the court of its intention to make an application for special measures under s.28 of the YJCEA 1999 the timetable is that as established by the Better Case Management initiative. The Court must be mindful of its duties under Parts 1 and 3 of the Rules to manage the case effectively. Wherever the Crown Prosecution Service will seek a s.28 YJCEA 1999 special measures direction this should, where possible, be listed for PTPH within 28 days of the date of sending from the magistrates' court. Section 10.2 of *A protocol between the Association of Chief Police Officers, the Crown Prosecution Service and Her Majesty's Courts and Tribunals Service to expedite cases involving witnesses under 10 years* does not apply.

18E.13   From the point of grant of the s 28 YJCEA 1999 special measures application, timescales provided by section 8.6 of *A protocol between the Association of Chief Police Officers, the Crown Prosecution Service and Her Majesty's Courts and Tribunals Service to expedite cases involving witnesses under 10 years* will cease to apply and the case should be managed in accordance with the timescales established in this practice direction.

Before the PTPH hearing in the Crown Court

18E.14   On being notified of the sending of the case by the magistrates' court, the case should be flagged as a s 28 case and referred to the Resident Judge or the judicial lead at that Crown Court, according to instructions issued by the Resident Judge.

18E.15   A transcript of the ABE interview and the application for special measures, including under s 28 YJCEA 1999, must be served on the Court and defence at least 7 days prior to the PTPH. The report of any Registered Intermediary must be served with the application for special measures.

18E.16   Any defence representations about the application for special measures must be served before the PTPH, within 28 days from the first hearing at the magistrates' court, when notice was first given of the application.

Plea and Trial Preparation Hearing

18E.17 The s 28 YJCEA 1999 part of the PTPH form should, on enquiry of the parties, be completed by the judge during the hearing. Orders should be recorded on the form, and uploaded onto the Digital Case System (DCS) as the record of orders made by the court. Any unrepresented defendant should be served with a paper copy of the orders.

18E.18 A plea should be taken and recorded and the defence required to identify the issues. The detail of a defence statement is not required at this stage, but the defence should identify the core issues in dispute.

The application

18E.19 The judge may hear submissions from the advocates and will rule on the application. If it is refused (see the assumptions to be applied by the courts in s 21 and s 22 of the YJCEA 1999), this practice direction ceases to apply.

18E.20 If the application is granted, the judge should make orders and give directions for preparation for the recorded cross-examination and re-examination hearing and advance preparation for the trial, including for disclosure of unused material. The correct and timely application of the Criminal Procedure and Investigations Act 1996 ('CPIA 1996') will be vital and close attention should be paid to the *2013 Protocol and Good Practice Model on Disclosure (November 2013)*, above.

18E.21 The orders made are likely to include:

(i) Service of the prosecution evidence within 50 days of sending ;
(ii) Directions for service of defence witness requirements;
(iii) Service of initial disclosure; under the CPIA 1996, as soon as reasonably practical; in this context, this should be interpreted as being simultaneous with the service of the prosecution evidence, i.e. within 50 days of sending for both bail and custody cases. This will be within 3 weeks of the PTPH;
(iv) Orders on disclosure material held by a third party;
(v) Service of the defence statement; under the CPIA 1996, this must be served within 28 days of the prosecutor serving or purporting to serve initial disclosure;
(vi) Any editing of the ABE interview;
(vii) Fixing a date for a ground rules hearing, about one week prior to the recorded cross-examination and re-examination hearing, see CPD General matters 3E: Ground rules hearings to plan questioning of a vulnerable witness or defendant;
(viii) Service of the Ground Rules Hearing Form by the defence advocate;
(ix) Making arrangements for the witness to refresh his or her memory by viewing the recorded examination-in-chief ('ABE interview'), see CPD Evidence 18C: Visually recorded interviews: memory refreshing and watching at a different time from the jury;
(x) Making arrangements for the recorded cross-examination and re-examination hearing under s.28, including fixing a date, time and location;
(xi) Other special measures;
(xii) Directions for any further directions hearing whether at the conclusion of the recorded cross-examination and re-examination hearing or subsequently;
(xiii) Fixing a date for trial.

18E.22 The timetable should ensure the prosecution evidence and initial disclosure are served swiftly. The ground rules hearing will usually be soon after the deadline for service of the defence statement, the recorded cross-examination and re-examination hearing about one week later. However, there must be time afforded for any further disclosure of unused material following service of the defence statement and for determination of any application under s 8 of the CPIA 1996. Subject to judicial discretion applications for extensions of time for service of disclosure by either party should generally be refused.

18E.23 Where the defendant may be unfit to plead, a timetable for s 28 should usually still be set, taking into account extra time needed for the obtaining of medical reports, save in cases where it is indicated that it is unlikely that there would be a trial if the defendant is found fit.

18E.24 As far as possible, without diminishing the defendant's right to a fair trial, the timing and duration of the recorded cross-examination should take into account the needs of the witness. For a young child, the hearing should usually be in the morning and conclude before lunch time.

18E.25 An application for a witness summons to obtain material held by a third party, should be served in advance of the PTPH and determined at that hearing, or as soon as reasonably practicable thereafter. The timetable should accommodate any consequent hearings or applications, but it is imperative parties are prompt to obtain third party disclosure material. The prosecution must make the court and the defence aware of any difficulty as soon as it arises. As noted above, the *2013 Protocol and Good Practice Model on Disclosure of information in cases of alleged child abuse and linked criminal and care directions hearings* should be followed, if applicable. Engagement with the Protocol is to be overseen by LITs. A single point of contact in each relevant agency can facilitate speedy disclosure.

18E.26 The needs of other witnesses should not be neglected. Witness and intermediary availability dates should be available for the PTPH.

Prior to ground rules hearing and hearing under section 28

18E.27 It is imperative parties abide by orders made at the PTPH, including the completion and service of the Ground Rules Hearing Form by the defence advocate. Delays or failures must be reported to the judge as soon as they arise; this is the responsibility of each legal representative. If ordered, the lead lawyer for the prosecution and defence must provide a weekly update to the court Case Progression Officer, copied to the judge and parties, detailing the progress and any difficulties or delays in complying with orders. The court may order a further case management hearing if necessary.

18E.28 Any applications under s 100 of the Criminal Justice Act 2003 ('CJA 2003') (non-defendant's bad character) or under s 41 of the YJCEA 1999 (evidence or cross-examination about complainants sexual behaviour) or any other application which may affect the cross-examination must be made promptly, and responses submitted in time for the judge to rule on the application at the ground rules hearing. Parts 21 and 22 of the Rules apply to applications under s 100 and s 41 respectively.

18E.29 The witness' court familiarisation visit must take place, including an opportunity to practice on the live link/recording facilities, see the Code of Practice for Victims of Crime, October 2013, Chapter 3, paragraph 1.22. The witness must have the opportunity to view his or her ABE interview to refresh his or her memory. It may or may not be appropriate for this to take place on the day of the court visit: CPD Evidence 18C must be followed.

18E.30 When the court has deemed that the case is suitable for the witness to give evidence from a remote site then a familiarisation visit should take place at that site. At the ground rules hearing the judge and advocates should consider appropriate arrangements for them to talk to the witness before the cross examination hearing.

18E.31 Applications to vary or discharge a special measures declaration must comply with Rule 18.11. Although the need for prompt action will make case preparation tight.

Ground rules hearing

18E.32 Advocates should master the toolkits available through The Advocate's Gateway. These provide guidance on questioning a vulnerable witness, see CPD General matters 3D and the annex to this practice direction.

18E.33 Any appointed Registered Intermediary must attend the ground rules hearing, see CPD General matters 3E.2.

18E.34 The defence advocate at the ground rules hearing must be she or he who will conduct the recorded cross-examination. See listing and allocation below on continuity of counsel and release from other cases.

18E.35 Topics for discussion and agreement at the ground rules hearing will depend on the individual needs of the witness, and an intermediary may provide advance indications. CPD General matters 3E must be followed. Topics that will need discussion in every case will include:

(i)   the overall length of cross-examination;
(ii) cross-examination by a single advocate in a multi-handed case;
(iii) any restrictions on the advocate's usual duty to 'put the defence case'.

18E.36 It may be helpful to discuss at this stage how any limitations on questioning will be explained to the jury.

18E.37 At the ground rules hearing, the judge should:

(i)   rule on any application under s 100 of the CJA 2003 or s 41 of the YJCEA 1999, or other applications that may affect the cross-examination;
(ii) decide how the witness may view exhibits or documents;
(iii) review progress in complying with orders made at the preliminary hearing and make any necessary orders.

Recording of cross-examination and re-examination: hearing under s 28

18E.38 At the hearing, the witness will be cross-examined and re-examined, if required, via the live link from the court room to the witness suite (unless provision has been made for the use of a remote link) and the examination will be recorded. It is the responsibility of the designated court clerk to ensure in advance that all of the equipment is working and to contact the provider's Service Desk if support is required. Any other special measures must be in place and any intermediary or supporter should sit in the live link room with the witness. The intermediary's role is transparent and therefore must be visible and audible to the judge and advocates at the cross-examination and in the subsequent replaying.

18E.39 The judge, advocates and parties, including the defendant will usually assemble in the court room for the hearing. In some cases the judge and advocates may be in the witness suite with the witness, for example when questioning a very young child or where the witness has a particular communication need. The court will decide this on a case-by-case basis. The defendant should be able to communicate with his or her representatives and should be able to hear the witness via the live link and see the proceedings: s 28(2). Whether the witness is screened or not will depend on the other special measures ordered, for example screens may have been ordered under s 23 YJCEA 1999.

18E.40 On the admission of the public or media to the hearing, please see below.

18E.41 At the conclusion of the hearing, the judge will issue further orders, such as for the editing of the recorded cross-examination and may set a timetable for progress.

18E.42 Under s 28(4) YJCEA 1999, the judge, on application of any parties or on the court's own motion may direct that the recorded examination is not admitted into evidence, despite any previous direction. Such direction must be given promptly, preferably immediately after the conclusion of the examination.

18E.43 Without exception, editing of the ABE interview/examination-in-chief or recorded cross-examination is precluded without an order of the court.

18E.44 The ability to record simultaneously from a court and a witness room and to play back the recording at trial will be provided in all Crown Courts as an additional facility within the existing Justice Video Service (JVS). Courts will book recording slots with the Service Desk who will launch the recording at the scheduled time when the court is ready. Recordings will be stored in a secure data centre with backup and resiliency, for authorised access.

After the recording

18E.45 Following the recording the judge should review compliance with orders and progress towards preparation for trial, make any further orders necessary and confirm the date of the trial. Any further orders made by the judge should be recorded and uploaded onto the relevant section of the DCS.

18E.46 If the defendant enters a guilty plea, the judge should proceed towards sentence, making any appropriate orders, such as for a Pre-Sentence Report and setting a date for sentencing.

Any reduction for a guilty plea shall reflect the day of the recorded cross-examination as the first day of trial; the Sentencing Council guideline on guilty plea reductions should be applied.

Preparation for trial

18E.47   Parties must notify the court promptly if any difficulties arise or any orders are not complied with. The court may order a further case management hearing (FCMH).

18E.48   In accordance with orders, either after recorded cross-examination or at the FCMH, necessary editing of the ABE interview/examination-in-chief and/or the recorded cross-examination must be done only on the order of the court. Any editing must be done promptly.

18E.49   Recorded cross-examinations and re-examinations will be stored securely by the service provider so as to be accessible to the advocates and the court. It will not usually be necessary to obtain a transcript of the recorded cross-examination, but if it is difficult to comprehend, a transcript should be obtained and served. The ground rules hearing form outlines questions to the witness that might be completed electronically by the judge during cross-examination forming a contemporaneous note of the hearing, served on the parties as an agreed record.

18E.50   Editing, authorised by the judge, is to be submitted by the court to the Service Desk, who produce an edited copy. The master and all edited copy versions are retained in the secure data centre from where they can be accessed. Courts book playback timeslots with the Service Desk for the trial date. The court may authorise parties to view playback at JVS endpoints, by submitting a request form to the Service Desk. Access for those so authorised is via the Quickcode (recording ID) and a security PIN (password) on the courtroom touch panel or remote control.

18E.51   No further cross-examination or re-examination of the witness may take place unless the criteria in section 28(6) are satisfied and the judge makes a further special measures direction under section 28(5). Any such further examination must be recorded via live link as described above.

18E.52   Section 28(6) of the YJCEA 1999 provides as follows:

(6)   The court may only give such a further direction if it appears to the court—

    (a)   that the proposed cross-examination is sought by a party to the proceedings as a result of that party having become aware, since the time when the original recording was made in pursuance of subsection (1), of a matter which that party could not with reasonable diligence have ascertained by then, or

    (b)   that for any other reason it is in the interests of justice to give the further direction.

18E.53   Any application under section 28(5) must be in writing and be served on the court and the prosecution at least 28 days before the date of trial. The application must specify:

i.   the topics on which further cross-examination is sought;

ii.   the material or matter of which the defence has become aware since the original recording;

iii.   why it was not possible for the defence to have obtained the material or ascertained the matter earlier; and

iv.   the expected impact on the issues before the court at trial.

18E.54   The prosecution should respond in writing within 7 days of the application. The judge may determine the application on the papers or order a hearing. Any further cross-examination ordered must be recorded via live link in advance of the trial and served on the court and the parties.

Trial

18E.55   In accordance with the judge's directions, the ABE interview/examination-in-chief and the recorded cross-examination and re-examination, edited as directed, should be played to the jury at the appropriate point within the trial.

18E.56   The jury should not usually receive transcripts of the recordings, and if they do these should be removed from the jury as soon as the recording has been played, see CPD Trial 26L.2.

18E.57   If the matter was not addressed at the ground rules hearing, the judge should discuss with the advocates how any limitations on questioning should be explained to the jury before summing-up.

After conclusion of trial

18E.58   Immediately after the trial, the ABE interview/examination-in-chief and the recorded cross-examination and re-examination should be stored securely on the cloud.

Listing and allocation

18E.59   **Advocates**: It is the responsibility of the defence advocate, on accepting the brief, to ensure that he or she is available for both the ground rules hearing and the hearing under section 28; continuity at trial is obligatory except in exceptional circumstances. The judge and list office will make whatever reasonable arrangements are possible to achieve this, assisted by the Resident Judge where necessary.

18E.60   When the timetable for the case is being set, advocates must have their up to date availability with them (in so far as is possible). When an advocate who is part-heard in another trial at a different Crown Court centre finds themselves in difficulties in attending either the ground rules hearing, s 28 hearing itself or the trial where s 28 has been utilised, they must inform the Resident Judges of both courts as soon as practicable. The Resident Judges must resolve any conflict with the advocate's availability. The starting point should be that the case involving s 28 hearing takes priority. However, due consideration should also be given to custody time limits, other issues which make either case particularly complex or sensitive, high profile cases and anything else that the judges should take into consideration in the interests of justice.

18E.61   **Judicial**: All PTPHs must be listed before judges who have been authorised to deal with s 28 cases by the Resident Judge at the relevant court centre. The nominated lead judge (if there is one) or Resident Judge may allocate individual cases to one of the judges in the court centre identified to deal with the case if necessary. The Resident Judge, lead judge or allocated judge may make directions in the case if required.

18E.62   It is essential that the ground rules hearing and the s 28 YJCEA 1999 hearing are before the same judge. Once the s 28 hearing has taken place, any judge, in accordance with CPD XIII Listing E, including recorders, can deal with the trial.

18E.63 LITs should be established with all relevant agencies represented by someone of sufficient seniority. Their task will be to monitor the operation of the scheme and compliance with this practice direction and other relevant protocols.

18E.64 **Listing**: Due to the limited availability of recording facilities, the hearing held under section 28 must take precedence over other hearings. Section 28 hearings should be listed as the first matter in the morning and will usually conclude before lunch time. Ground rules hearings may be held at any time, including towards the end of the court day, to accommodate the advocates and intermediary (if there is one) and to minimise disruption to other trials.

Public, including media access, and reporting restrictions

18E.65 Open justice is an essential principle of the common law. However, certain automatic statutory restrictions may apply, and the judge may consider it appropriate in the specific circumstances of a case to make an order applying discretionary restrictions. CPD Preliminary proceedings 16B must be followed and the templates published by the Judicial College (available on LMS) should be used. The parties to the proceedings, and interested parties such as the media, should have the opportunity to make representations before an order is made.

18E.66 The statutory powers most likely to be available to the judge are listed below. The judge should consider the specific statutory requirements necessary for the making of the particular order carefully, and the order made must be in writing.

a)   Provisions to exclude the public from hearings:
    i.   Section 37 of the Children and Young Persons Act 1933, applicable to witnesses under 18;
    ii.   Section 25 of the YJCEA 1999, applicable to the evidence of a child or vulnerable adult in sexual offences cases.

b)   Automatic reporting restrictions:
    i.   Section 1 of the Sexual Offences (Amendment) Act 1992, applicable to the complainant in any sex offence case.

c)   Discretionary reporting restrictions:
    i.   Section 45 of the YJCEA 1999, applicable to under 18s concerned in criminal proceedings;
    ii.   Section 46 of the YJCEA 1999, applicable to an adult witness whose evidence would be diminished by fear or distress.

d)   Postponement of fair and accurate reports under section 4(2) of the Contempt of Court Act 1981.

18E.67 Note that public access to information held by the court is now the subject of Rule 5.8 and CPD General matters 5B that must be followed.

ANNEX FOR SECTION 28 GROUND RULES HEARINGS AT THE CROWN COURT WHEN DEALING WITH WITNESSES UNDER S 16 YJCEA 1999

Introduction

1. This annex is designed to assist all advocates in their preparation for cross-examination of vulnerable witnesses.

2. Adherence to the principles below will avoid interruption during the pre-recorded cross-examination and reduce any ordered editing.

3. Issues concerning the vulnerable witness and the nature of the cross-examination will be addressed by the judge at the Ground Rules Hearing (GRH).

4. In appropriate cases and in particular where the witness is of very young years or suffers from a disability or disorder it is expected that the advocate will have prepared his or her cross-examination in writing for consideration by the court.

5. It is thus incumbent on the Defence to ensure that full instructions have been taken prior to the GRH.

Required preparation prior to the GRH

6. All advocates should be familiar with the relevant toolkits, available through The Advocates Gateway www.theadvocatesgateway.org/toolkits which provide guidance on questioning a vulnerable witness. A synopsis of this guidance, which advocates should have read prior to any GRH, is included in this annex.

Attendance at, and procedure during, the GRH

7. In preparation for trial, courts must take every reasonable step to facilitate the participation of witnesses and defendants CPR 3.8(4) (d). The court should order that the defendant attends the GRH.

8. The defence advocate must complete and submit the Ground Rules Hearing form by the time and date ordered at the PTPH.

9. The hearing facilitates the judge's duty to control questioning if and when necessary.

10. The hearing enables the court to ensure its process is adapted to enable the witness to give his or her best evidence whilst ensuring the defendant's right to a fair trial is not diminished. Accordingly the ground rules and the nature of the questioning of the witness by the advocate (and limitations imposed if necessary in accordance with principles above) will be discussed.

11. Prior to the hearing it is necessary for both advocates and the judge to have viewed the ABE evidence.

12. The judge will state what ground rules will apply. The advocates must comply with them.

13. Any intermediary must attend the GRH. It is the responsibility of those instructing the intermediary to ensure this.

14. The defendant's advocate attending the hearing must be the same advocate who will be conducting the recorded cross-examination (and the subsequent trial, if any).

15. Any intermediary for the witness should only be warned for the GRH and the section 28 hearing they are assisting with. An Intermediary should not be instructed unless available to attend the GRH and the section 28 hearings ordered by the court.

16. Topics for discussion and agreement at the GRH will depend on the individual needs of the witness. CPD I General Matters 3E must be followed.

17. Topics of discussion at the hearing will include the length of cross-examination and any restrictions on the advocate's usual duty to "put the defence case". As was made plain by the Vice President of the Court of Appeal Criminal Division in *Regina v Lubemba and Pooley* 2014 EWCA Crim 2064, advocates cannot insist upon any supposed right "to put one's case" or previous inconsistent statements to a vulnerable witness. If there is a right to "put one's case" it must be modified for young or vulnerable witnesses. It is perfectly possible to ensure the jury are made aware of the defence case and of significant inconsistencies without intimidation or distressing a witness. It is expected that all advocates will be familiar with and have read this case.

18. At the GRH counsel need to agree with the judge how and when the matters referred to in paragraph 11 will be explained to the jury. This explanation will normally be done by the judge, but may exceptionally, and only with the permission of the judge, be explained by counsel. If there is no agreement the judge will rule on it.

19. A Section 28 Defence GRH form should be completed as far as possible prior to attendance at the GRH before the judge.

20. Rulings will be made on any application under section 100 of the CJA 2003 or section 41 of the YCEA 1999, and on any other application that may affect the conduct of the cross examination. Any ruling will be included in the trial practice note.

21. A review will take place of the progress made by the parties in complying with the orders made at the PTPH and the court will make any other necessary orders.

22. Additional information can be found in the Inns of Court College of Advocacy training document "Advocacy and the vulnerable: 20 principles of questioning" at the following link: www.icca.ac.uk/images/download/advocacy-and-the-vulnerable/20-principles-of-questioning.pdf

This document is part of a suite of training materials available to assist advocates in dealing with questioning vulnerable victims in the criminal justice system.

Court of Appeal guidance

In a series of decisions the Court of Appeal has made it clear that there has to be a different and fresh approach to the cross-examination of, in particular, children of tender years, and witnesses who are vulnerable as a result of mental incapacity. The following propositions have support in decisions on appeal: (*R v B 2010 EWCA Crim 4; R v F 2013 EWCA Crim 424; Wills v R 2011 EWCA Crim 1938; R v Edwards 2011 EWCA Crim 3028; R v Watts 2010 EWCA Crim 1824; R v W and M 2010 EWCA Crim 1926*)

"The reality of questioning children of tender years is that direct challenge that he or she is wrong or lying could lead to confusion and, worse, to capitulation which the child does not, in reality, accept.

Capitulation is not a consequence of unreliability but a function of the youngster's age. Experience has shown that young children are scared of disagreeing with a mature adult whom they do not wish to confront.

It is common, in the trial of an adult, to hear, once the nursery slopes of cross-examination have been skied, the assertion 'you were never punched or kicked, as you have suggested, were you?'

It was precisely that approach which the Court is anxious to avoid. Such an approach risks confusion in the minds of the witness whose evidence was bound to take centre stage, and it is difficult to see how it can be helpful. We struggle to understand how the defendant's right to a fair trial was in any way compromised simply because Mr X was not allowed to ask the question 'Simon did not punch you in the way you suggest?'"

"The overriding objective. The Criminal Procedure Rules objective is that criminal cases be dealt with justly. Dealing with a criminal case justly includes dealing with the case efficiently and expeditiously in ways that take account of the gravity of the offence alleged and the complexity of what is in issue.

In our collective experience the age of a witness is not determinative of his or her ability to give truthful and accurate evidence. Like adults some children will provide truthful and accurate testimony, and some will not. However children are not miniature adults, but children, and to be treated for what they are, not what they will, in the years ahead, grow to be.

There is undoubtedly a danger of a child witness wishing simply to please.

There is undoubtedly a danger of a child witness assenting to what is put rather than disagreeing during the questioning process in an endeavour to bring that process to a speedier conclusion.

It is particularly important in the case of a child witness to keep a question short and simple, and even more important than it is with an adult witness to avoid questions which are rolled up and contain, inadvertently two or three questions at once. It is generally recognised that, particularly with child witnesses, short and untagged questions are best at eliciting the evidence. By untagged we mean questions that do not contain a statement of the answer which is sought. That said, when it comes to directly contradicting a particular statement and inviting the witness to face a directly contradictory suggestion, it may often be difficult to examine otherwise.

No doubt if a way can be found of engaging the witness to tell the story, and the content then differs from what had been said before, that will be a yet better indication that the original account is wrong. But that is difficult to achieve and indeed may itself have the disadvantage of prolonging the child's time giving evidence. Even then there may be no guarantee as to which account is the more reliable.

Most of the questions which produced the answers which were chiefly relied upon, unlike many others, constituted the putting of direct suggestions with an indication of the answer ' this happened didn't it '? Or "this didn't happen, did it?" The consequence of that is that it can be very difficult to tell whether the child is truly changing her account or simply taking the line of least resistance.

At the same time the right of the defendant to a fair trial must be undiminished. When the issue is whether the child is lying or mistaken, when claiming that the defendant behaved indecently towards him or her, it should not be over problematic for the advocate to formulate short, simple questions, which put the essential elements of the defendant's case to the witness, and fully ventilate before the jury the areas of evidence which bear on the child's credibility.

Aspects of evidence which undermine or are believed to undermine the child's credibility must, of course, be revealed to the jury. However it is not necessarily appropriate for them to form the subject matter of detailed cross-examination of the child, and the advocate may have to forego much of the kind of contemporary cross-examination which consists of no more than comment on matters which will be before the jury, in any event, from different sources.

Notwithstanding some of the difficulties; when all is said and done, the witness whose cross-examination is in contemplation is a child, sometimes very young, and it should not take very lengthy cross examination to demonstrate, when it is the case, that the child may indeed be fabricating, or fantasising, or imagining, or reciting a well-rehearsed untruthful script, learned by rote; or simply just suggestible, or contaminated by or in collusion with others to make false allegations, or making assertions in language which is beyond his or her level of comprehension; and are therefore likely to be derived from another source. Comment on the evidence, including comment on evidence which may bear adversely on the credibility of the child, should be addressed after the child has finished giving evidence.

Clear limitations have to be imposed on the cross-examination of vulnerable young complainants."

CrimPR Part 19 Expert evidence

CPD V Evidence 19A: Expert evidence

19A.1   Expert opinion evidence is admissible in criminal proceedings at common law if, in summary, (i) it is relevant to a matter in issue in the proceedings; (ii) it is needed to provide the court with information likely to be outside the court's own knowledge and experience; and (iii) the witness is competent to give that opinion.

19A.2   Legislation relevant to the introduction and admissibility of such evidence includes section 30 of the Criminal Justice Act 1988, which provides that an expert report shall be admissible as evidence in criminal proceedings whether or not the person making it gives oral evidence, but that if he or she does not give oral evidence then the report is admissible only with the leave of the court; and CrimPR Part 19 , which in exercise of the powers conferred by section 81 of the Police and Criminal Evidence Act 1984 and section 20 of the Criminal Procedure and Investigations Act 1996 requires the service of expert evidence in advance of trial in the terms required by those rules.

19A.3   In the Law Commission report entitled 'Expert Evidence in Criminal Proceedings in England and Wales', report number 325, published in March, 2011, the Commission recommended a statutory test for the admissibility of expert evidence. However, in its response the government declined to legislate. The common law, therefore, remains the source of the criteria by reference to which the court must assess the admissibility and weight of such evidence; and CrimPR 19.4 lists those matters with which an expert's report must deal, so that the court can conduct an adequate such assessment.

19A.4   In its judgment in *R v Dlugosz and Others* [2013] EWCA Crim 2, the Court of Appeal observed (at paragraph 11): "It is essential to recall the principle which is applicable, namely in determining the issue of admissibility, the court must be satisfied that there is a sufficiently reliable scientific basis for the evidence to be admitted. If there is then the court leaves the opposing views to be tested before the jury." Nothing at common law precludes assessment by the court of the reliability of an expert opinion by reference to substantially similar factors to those the Law Commission recommended as conditions of admissibility, and courts are encouraged actively to enquire into such factors.

19A.5   Therefore factors which the court may take into account in determining the reliability of expert opinion, and especially of expert scientific opinion, include:

(a)   the extent and quality of the data on which the expert's opinion is based, and the validity of the methods by which they were obtained;

(b)   if the expert's opinion relies on an inference from any findings, whether the opinion properly explains how safe or unsafe the inference is (whether by reference to statistical significance or in other appropriate terms);

(c)   if the expert's opinion relies on the results of the use of any method (for instance, a test, measurement or survey), whether the opinion takes proper account of matters, such as the degree of precision or margin of uncertainty, affecting the accuracy or reliability of those results;

(d)   the extent to which any material upon which the expert's opinion is based has been reviewed by others with relevant expertise (for instance, in peer-reviewed publications), and the views of those others on that material;

(e)   the extent to which the expert's opinion is based on material falling outside the expert's own field of expertise;

(f)   the completeness of the information which was available to the expert, and whether the expert took account of all relevant information in arriving at the opinion (including information as to the context of any facts to which the opinion relates);

(g)   if there is a range of expert opinion on the matter in question, where in the range the expert's own opinion lies and whether the expert's preference has been properly explained; and

(h)   whether the expert's methods followed established practice in the field and, if they did not, whether the reason for the divergence has been properly explained.

19A.6   In addition, in considering reliability, and especially the reliability of expert scientific opinion, the court should be astute to identify potential flaws in such opinion which detract from its reliability, such as:

(a)   being based on a hypothesis which has not been subjected to sufficient scrutiny (including, where appropriate, experimental or other testing), or which has failed to stand up to scrutiny;

(b)   being based on an unjustifiable assumption;

(c)   being based on flawed data;

(d)   relying on an examination, technique, method or process which was not properly carried out or applied, or was not appropriate for use in the particular case; or

(e)   relying on an inference or conclusion which has not been properly reached.

CPD V Evidence 19B: Statements of understanding and declarations of truth in expert reports

19B.1   The statement and declaration required by CrimPR 19.4(j), (k) should be in the following terms, or in terms substantially the same as these:

'I (name) DECLARE THAT:

1.   I understand that my duty is to help the court to achieve the overriding objective by giving independent assistance by way of objective, unbiased opinion on matters within my expertise, both in preparing reports and giving oral evidence. I understand that this duty overrides any obligation to the party by whom I am engaged or the person who has paid or is liable to pay me. I confirm that I have complied with and will continue to comply with that duty.

2.   I confirm that I have not entered into any arrangement where the amount or payment of my fees is in any way dependent on the outcome of the case.

3.   I know of no conflict of interest of any kind, other than any which I have disclosed in my report.

4.   I do not consider that any interest which I have disclosed affects my suitability as an expert witness on any issues on which I have given evidence.

5.   I will advise the party by whom I am instructed if, between the date of my report and the trial, there is any change in circumstances which affect my answers to points 3 and 4 above.

6.   I have shown the sources of all information I have used.

7.   I have exercised reasonable care and skill in order to be accurate and complete in preparing this report.

8.   I have endeavoured to include in my report those matters, of which I have knowledge or of which I have been made aware, that might adversely affect the validity of my opinion. I have clearly stated any qualifications to my opinion.

9.   I have not, without forming an independent view, included or excluded anything which has been suggested to me by others including my instructing lawyers.

10.   I will notify those instructing me immediately and confirm in writing if for any reason my existing report requires any correction or qualification.

11.   I understand that:

    (a)   my report will form the evidence to be given under oath or affirmation;

    (b)   the court may at any stage direct a discussion to take place between experts;

    (c)   the court may direct that, following a discussion between the experts, a statement should be prepared showing those issues which are agreed and those issues which are not agreed, together with the reasons;

    (d)   I may be required to attend court to be cross-examined on my report by a cross-examiner assisted by an expert;

    (e)   I am likely to be the subject of public adverse criticism by the judge if the Court concludes that I have not taken reasonable care in trying to meet the standards set out above.

12.   I have read Part 19 of the Criminal Procedure Rules and I have complied with its requirements.

13.   I confirm that I have acted in accordance with the code of practice or conduct for experts of my discipline, namely [*identify the code*]

14.   14. [For Experts instructed by the Prosecution only] I confirm that I have read guidance contained in a booklet known as Disclosure: Experts' Evidence and Unused Material which details my role and documents my responsibilities, in relation to revelation as an expert witness. I have followed the guidance and recognise the continuing nature of my responsibilities of disclosure. In accordance with my duties of disclosure, as documented in the guidance booklet, I confirm that:

    (a)   I have complied with my duties to record, retain and reveal material in accordance with the Criminal Procedure and Investigations Act 1996, as amended;

    (b)   I have compiled an Index of all material. I will ensure that the Index is updated in the event I am provided with or generate additional material;

    (c)   in the event my opinion changes on any material issue, I will inform the investigating officer, as soon as reasonably practicable and give reasons.

I confirm that the contents of this report are true to the best of my knowledge and belief and that I make this report knowing that, if it is tendered in evidence, I would be liable to prosecution if I have wilfully stated anything which I know to be false or that I do not believe to be true.

CPD V Evidence 19C: Pre-hearing discussion of expert evidence

19C.1   To assist the court in the preparation of the case for trial, parties must consider, with their experts, at an early stage, whether there is likely to be any useful purpose in holding an experts' discussion and, if so, when. Under CrimPR 19.6 such pre-trial discussions are not compulsory unless directed by the court. However, such a direction is listed in the magistrates' courts Preparation for Effective Trial form and in the Crown Court Plea and Trial Preparation Hearing form as one to be given by default, and therefore the court can be expected to give such a direction in every case unless persuaded otherwise. Those standard directions include a timetable to which the parties must adhere unless it is varied. To assist the court in the preparation of the case for trial, parties must consider, with their experts, at an early stage, whether there is likely to be any useful purpose in holding an experts' discussion and, if so, when. Under CrimPR 19.6 such pre-trial discussions are not compulsory unless directed by the court. However, such a direction is listed in the magistrates' courts Preparation for Effective Trial form and in the Crown Court Plea and Trial Preparation Hearing form as one to be given by default, and therefore the court can be expected to give such a direction in every case unless persuaded otherwise. Those standard directions include a timetable to which the parties must adhere unless it is varied.

19C.2 The purpose of discussions between experts is to agree and narrow issues and in particular to identify:

(a) the extent of the agreement between them;
(b) the points of and short reasons for any disagreement;
(c) action, if any, which may be taken to resolve any outstanding points of disagreement; and
(d) any further material issues not raised and the extent to which these issues are agreed.

19C.3 Where the experts are to meet, that meeting conveniently may be conducted by telephone conference or live link; and experts' meetings always should be conducted by those means where that will avoid unnecessary delay and expense.

19C.4 Where the experts are to meet, the parties must discuss and if possible agree whether an agenda is necessary, and if so attempt to agree one that helps the experts to focus on the issues which need to be discussed. The agenda must not be in the form of leading questions or hostile in tone. The experts may not be required to avoid reaching agreement, or to defer reaching agreement, on any matter within the experts' competence.

19C.5 If the legal representatives do attend:

(a) they should not normally intervene in the discussion, except to answer questions put to them by the experts or to advise on the law; and
(b) the experts may if they so wish hold part of their discussions in the absence of the legal representatives.

19C.6 A statement must be prepared by the experts dealing with paragraphs 19C.2(a)-(d) above. Individual copies of the statements must be signed or otherwise authenticated by the experts, in manuscript or by electronic means, at the conclusion of the discussion, or as soon thereafter as practicable, and in any event within 5 business days. Copies of the statements must be provided to the parties no later than 10 business days after signing.

19C.7 Experts must give their own opinions to assist the court and do not require the authority of the parties to sign a joint statement. The joint statement should include a brief re-statement that the experts recognise their duties, which should be in the following terms, or in terms substantially the same as these:

'We each DECLARE THAT:

1. We individually here re-state the Expert's Declaration contained in our respective reports that we understand our overriding duties to the court, have complied with them and will continue to do so.
2. We have neither jointly nor individually been instructed to, nor has it been suggested that we should, avoid reaching agreement, or defer reaching agreement, on any matter within our competence.'

19C.8 If an expert significantly alters an Oopinion, the joint statement must include a note or addendum by that expert explaining the change of opinion.

CRIMPR PART 21 EVIDENCE OF BAD CHARACTER

CPD V Evidence 21A: Spent convictions

21A.1 The effect of section 4(1) of the Rehabilitation of Offenders Act 1974 is that a person who has become a rehabilitated person for the purpose of the Act in respect of a conviction (known as a 'spent' conviction) shall be treated for all purposes in law as a person who has not committed, or been charged with or prosecuted for, or convicted of or sentenced for, the offence or offences which were the subject of that conviction.

21A.2 Section 4(1) of the 1974 Act does not apply, however, to evidence given in criminal proceedings: section 7(2)(a). During the trial of a criminal charge, reference to previous convictions (and therefore to spent convictions) can arise in a number of ways. The most common is when a bad character application is made under the Criminal Justice Act 2003. When considering bad character applications under the 2003 Act, regard should always be had to the general principles of the Rehabilitation of Offenders Act 1974.

21A.3 On conviction, the court must be provided with a statement of the defendant's record for the purposes of sentence. The record supplied should contain all previous convictions, but those which are spent should, so far as practicable, be marked as such. No one should refer in open court to a spent conviction without the authority of the judge, which authority should not be given unless the interests of justice so require. When passing sentence the judge should make no reference to a spent conviction unless it is necessary to do so for the purpose of explaining the sentence to be passed.

CPD V Evidence 22A: Use of Ground Rules when Dealing with s 41 Youth Justice and Criminal Evidence Act 1999 (YJCEA 1999) Evidence of Complainant's Previous Sexual Behaviour

The application

22A.1 When a defendant wishes to introduce evidence, or cross-examine about the previous sexual behaviour of the complainant, then it is imperative that the timetable and procedure as laid down in the Criminal Procedure Rules Part 22 is followed. The application must be submitted in writing as soon as reasonably practicable and not more than 14 days after the prosecutor has disclosed material on which the application is based. Should the prosecution wish to make any representations then these should be served on the court and other parties not more than 14 days after receiving the application.

22A.2 The application must clearly state the issue to which the defendant says the complainant's sexual behaviour is relevant and the reasons why it should be admitted. It must outline the evidence which the defendant wants to introduce and articulate the questions which it is proposed should be asked. The application must identify the statutory exception to the prohibition in s.41 YJCEA 1999 on which the defendant relies and give the name and date of birth of any witness whose evidence about the complainant's sexual behaviour the defendant wants to introduce.

The hearing

22A.3 When determining the application, the judge should examine the questions with the usual level of scrutiny expected at a ground rules hearing. For each question that it is sought to put to a witness, or evidence it is sought to adduce, the defence should identify clearly for the judge the suggested relevance it has to an issue in the case. In order for the judge to rule on which evidence can be adduced or questions put, the defence must set out individual questions for the judge; merely identifying a topic is not sufficient for this type of application. The judge should make it clear that if the application is granted then no other questions on this topic will be allowed to be asked, unless with the express permission of the court.

22A.4 The application should be dealt with in private and in the absence of the complainant, but the judge must state in open court, without the jury or complainant present, the reasons for the decision, and if leave is granted, the extent of the questions or evidence that is allowed.

Late applications

22A.5 Late applications should be considered with particular scrutiny especially if there is a suggestion of tactical thinking behind the timing of the application and/ or when the application is based on material that has been available for some time. If consideration of a late application has the potential to disrupt the timetabling of witnesses, then the judge will need to take account of the potential impact of delay upon a witness who is due to give evidence. If necessary, the judge may defer consideration of any such application until later in the trial.

22A.6 By analogy, following the approach adopted by the Court of Appeal in *R v Musone* [2007] 1 WLR 2467, the trial judge is entitled to refuse the application where (s)he is satisfied that the applicant is seeking to manipulate the court process so as to prevent the respondent from being able to prepare an adequate response. This may be the only remedy available to the court to ensure that the fairness of the trial is upheld and will be particularly relevant when the application is made on the day of trial.

22A.7 Where the application has been granted in good time before the trial, the complainant is entitled to be made aware that such evidence is part of the defence case.

At the trial

22A.8 Advocates should be reminded that the questioning must be conducted in m appropriate manner. Any aggressive, repetitive and oppressive :questioning will be stopped by the judge. Judges should intervene and stop my attempts to refer to evidence that might have been adduced under s 41, but for which no leave has been given and/or should have formed the basis of a s 41 application, but did not do so. When evidence about the Complainant's previous sexual behaviour is referred to without an Ipplication, the judge may be required to consider whether the impact of that happening is so prejudicial to the overall fairness of the trial that the trial should be stopped and a re-trial should be ordered, should the impact Got be capable of being ameliorated by way of jury direction.

CPD V Evidence 23A: Cross-examination Advocates

Provisional appointment of advocate

23A.1 At the first hearing in the court in the case, and in a magistrates' court in particular, there may be occasions on which a defendant has engaged no legal representative, within the meaning of the Criminal Procedure Rules, for the purposes of the case generally, but still intends to do so - for example, where he or she has made an application for legal aid which has yet to be determined. Where the defendant nonetheless has identified a prospective legal representative who has a right of audience in the court; where the court is satisfied that that representative will be willing to cross-examine the relevant witness or witnesses in the interests of the defendant should it transpire that the defendant will not be represented for the purposes of the case generally; and if the court is in a position there and then to make, contingently, the decision required by section 38(3) of the Youth Justice and Criminal Evidence Act 1999 ('the court must consider whether it is necessary in the interests of justice for the witness to be cross-examined by a legal representative appointed to represent the interests of the accused'); then the court may appoint that representative under section 38(4) of the 1999 Act contingently, the appointment to come into effect only if, and when, it is established that the defendant will not be represented for the purposes of the case generally.

23A.2 Where such a provisional appointment is made it is essential that the role and status of the representative is clearly established at the earliest possible opportunity. The court's directions under CrimPR 23.2 (3) should require the defendant to notify the court officer, by the date set by the court. whether:

(i) the defendant will be represented by a legal representative for the purposes of the case generally, and if so by whom (in which event the court's provisional appointment has no effect);

(ii) the defendant will not be represented for the purposes of the case generally, but the defendant and the legal representative provisionally appointed by the court remain content with that provisional appointment (in which event the court's provisional appointment takes effect); or

(iii) the defendant will not be represented for the purposes of the case generally, but will arrange for a lawyer to cross-examine the relevant witness or witnesses on his or her behalf, giving that lawyer's name and contact details.

If in the event the defendant fails to give notice by the due date then, unless it is apparent that she or he will, in fact, be represented for the purposes of the case generally, the court may decide to confirm the provisional appointment and proceed accordingly.

Supply of case papers

23A.3 For the advocate to fulfil the duty imposed by the appointment, and to achieve a responsible, professional and appropriate treatment both of the defendant and of the witness, it is essential for the advocate to establish what is in issue. To that end, it is likewise essential for the advocate to have been supplied with the material listed in CrimPR 23.2(7).

23A.4 In the Crown Court, much of this this can be achieved most conveniently by giving the advocate access to the Crown Court Digital Case System. However, material disclosed by the prosecutor to the defendant under section 3 or section 7 A of the Criminal Procedure and Investigations Act 1996 is not stored in that system and therefore must be supplied to the advocate either by the defendant or by the prosecutor. In the latter case, the prosecutor reasonably may omit from the copies supplied to the advocate any material that can have no bearing on the cross-examination for which the advocate has been appointed - the medical or social services records of another witness, for example.

23A.5 In a magistrates' court, pending the introduction of comparable electronic arrangements:

(i)   in some instances the advocate may have received the relevant material at a point at which he or she was acting as the defendant's legal representative subject to a restriction on the purpose or duration of that appointment notified under CrimPR 46.2 (5) - for example, pending the outcome of an application for legal aid.

(ii)   in some instances the defendant may be able to provide spare copies of relevant material. Where that material has been disclosed by the prosecutor under section 3 or section 7 A of the Criminal Procedure and Investigations Act 1996 then its supply to the advocate by the defendant is permitted by section 17(2)(a) of the 1996 Act (exception to the prohibition against further disclosure where that further disclosure is 'in connection with the proceedings for whose purposes [the defendant] was given the object or allowed to inspect it'),

(iii)   in some instances the prosecutor may be able to supply the relevant material, or some of it, at no, or minimal, expense by electronic means.

(iv)   in the event that, unusually, none of those sources of supply is available, then the court's directions under CrimPR 23.2(3) should require the court officer to provide copies from the court's own records, as if the advocate were a party and had applied under CrimPR 5.7.

Obtaining information and observations from the defendant

23A.6 Advocates and courts should keep in mind section 38(5) of the 1999 Act, which provides 'A person so appointed shall not be responsible to the accused.' The advocate therefore cannot and should not take instructions from the defendant, in the usual sense; and to avoid any misapprehension in that respect, either by the defendant or by others, some advocates may prefer to avoid direct oral communication with the defendant before, and even perhaps during, the trial.

23A.7 However, as remarked above at paragraph 23A.3, for the advocate to fulfil the duty imposed by the appointment it is essential for him or her to establish what is in issue; which may require communication with the defendant both before and at the trial as well as a thorough examination of the case papers. CrimPR 23.2(7)(a) in effect requires the advocate to have identified the issues on which the cross-examination of the witness is expected to proceed before the court begins to receive prosecution evidence, and to have taken part in their discussion with the court. To that end, communication with the defendant may be necessary.

Extent of cross-examination advocate's appointment

23A.8 In *Abbas v Crown Prosecution Service* [2015] EWHC 579 (Admin); [2015] 2 Cr.App.R. 11 the Divisional Court observed:

> "The role of a section 38 advocate is, undoubtedly, limited to the proper performance of their duty as a cross examiner of a particular witness. Sections 36 and 38 are all about protecting vulnerable witnesses from cross examination by the accused. Therefore, it should not be thought that an advocate appointed under section 38 has a free ranging remit to conduct the trial on the accused's behalf. Their professional duty and their statutory duty would be to ensure that they are in a position properly to conduct the cross examination. Their duties might include therefore applications to admit bad character of the witness and or applications for disclosure of material relevant to the cross examination. That is as far as one can go. All these matters must be entirely fact specific. The important thing to note is that the section 38 advocate must ensure that s/he performs his/her duties in accordance with the words of the statute.
>
> It means also that their appointment comes to an end, under section 38, at the conclusion of the cross examination, save to the extent that the court otherwise determines. Technically the lawyer no longer has a role in the proceedings thereafter. However, if the lawyer is prepared to stay and assist the defendant on a pro bono basis, I see nothing in the Act and no logical reason why the court should oblige them to leave. The advocate may well prove beneficial to the efficient and fair resolution of the proceedings.
>
> The aim of the legislation as I have said is simply to stop the accused cross examining the witness. It is not to prevent the person appointed to cross examine from playing any other part in the trial."

23A.9 Advocates will be alert to, and courts should keep in mind, the extent of the remuneration available to a cross-examination advocate, in assessing the amount of which the court has only a limited role: see section 19(3) of the Prosecution of Offences Act 1985, which empowers the Lord Chancellor to make regulations authorising payments out of central funds 'to cover the proper fee or costs of a legal representative appointed under section 38(4) of the Youth Justice and Criminal Evidence Act 1999 and any expenses properly incurred in providing such a person with evidence or other material in connection with his appointment', and also sections 19(3ZA) and 20(IA)(d) of the 1985 Act and the Costs in Criminal Cases (General) Regulations 1986, as amended.

23A.10 Advocates and courts must be alert, too, to the possibility that were an ldvocate to agree to represent a defendant generally at trial, for no layment save that to which such regulations entitled him or her, then the :tatutory condition precedent for the appointment might be removed and he appointment in consequence withdrawn.

<h2 style="text-align:center">CRIMINAL PRACTICE DIRECTIONS 2015 DIVISION VI</h2>
Trial

CRIMPR PART 24 TRIAL AND SENTENCE IN A MAGISTRATES' COURT

CPD VI Trial 24A: Role of the justices' clerk/legal adviser

24A.1 The role of the justices' clerk/legal adviser is a unique one, which carries with it independence from direction when undertaking a judicial function and when advising magistrates. These functions must be carried out in accordance with the Bangalore Principles of Judicial Conduct (judicial independence, impartiality, integrity, propriety, ensuring fair treatment and competence and diligence). More specifically, duties must be discharged in accordance with the relevant professional Code of Conduct and the Legal Adviser Competence Framework.

24A.2 A justices' clerk is responsible for:

(a) the legal advice tendered to the justices within the area;
(b) the performance of any of the functions set out below by any member of his staff acting as justices' legal adviser;
(c) ensuring that competent advice is available to justices when the justices' clerk is not personally present in court; and
(d) ensuring that advice given at all stages of proceedings and powers exercised (including those delegated to justices' legal advisers) take into account the court's duty to deal with cases justly and actively to manage the case.

24A.3 Where a person other than the justices' clerk (a justices' legal adviser), who is authorised to do so, performs any of the functions referred to in this direction, he or she will have the same duties, powers and responsibilities as the justices' clerk. The justices' legal adviser may consult the justices' clerk, or other person authorised by the justices' clerk for that purpose, before tendering advice to the bench. If the justices' clerk or that person gives any advice directly to the bench, he or she should give the parties or their advocates an opportunity of repeating any relevant submissions, prior to the advice being given.

24A.4 When exercising judicial powers, a justices' clerk or legal adviser is acting in exactly the same capacity as a magistrate. The justices' clerk may delegate powers to a justices' legal adviser in accordance with the relevant statutory authority. The scheme of delegation must be clear and in writing, so that all justices' legal advisers are certain of the extent of their powers. Once a power is delegated, judicial discretion in an individual case lies with the justices' legal adviser exercising the power. When exercise of a power does not require the consent of the parties, a justices' clerk or legal adviser may deal with and decide a contested issue or may refer that issue to the court.

24A.5 It shall be the responsibility of the justices' clerk or legal adviser to provide the justices with any advice they require to perform their functions justly, whether or not the advice has been requested, on:

(a) questions of law;
(b) questions of mixed law and fact;
(c) matters of practice and procedure;
(d) the process to be followed at sentence and the matters to be taken into account, together with the range of penalties and ancillary orders available, in accordance with the relevant sentencing guidelines;
(e) any relevant decisions of the superior courts or other guidelines;
(f) the appropriate decision-making structure to be applied in any given case; and
(g) other issues relevant to the matter before the court.

24A.6 In addition to advising the justices, it shall be the justices' legal adviser's responsibility to assist the court, where appropriate, as to the formulation of reasons and the recording of those reasons.

24A.7 The justices' legal adviser has a duty to assist an unrepresented defendant, see CrimPR 9.4(3)(a), 14.3(2)(a) and 24.15(3)(a), in particular when the court is making a decision on allocation, bail, at trial and on sentence.

24A.8 Where the court must determine allocation, the legal adviser may deal with any aspect of the allocation hearing save for the decision on allocation, indication of sentence and sentence.

24A.9 When a defendant acting in person indicates a guilty plea, the legal adviser must explain the procedure and inform the defendant of their right to address the court on the facts and to provide details of their personal circumstances in order that the court can decide the appropriate sentence.

24A.10 When a defendant indicates a not guilty plea but has not completed the relevant sections of the Magistrates' Courts Trial Preparation Form, the legal adviser must either ensure that the Form is completed or, in appropriate cases, assist the court to obtain and record the essential information on the form.

24A.11 Immediately prior to the commencement of a trial, the legal adviser must summarise for the court the agreed and disputed issues, together with the way in which the parties propose to present their cases. If this is done by way of pre-court briefing, it should be confirmed in court or agreed with the parties.

24A.12 A justices' clerk or legal adviser must not play any part in making findings of fact, but may assist the bench by reminding them of the evidence, using any notes of the proceedings for this purpose, and clarifying the issues which are agreed and those which are to be determined.

24A.13 A justices' clerk or legal adviser may ask questions of witnesses and the parties in order to clarify the evidence and any issues in the case. A legal adviser has a duty to ensure that every case is conducted justly.

24A.14　When advising the justices, the justices' clerk or legal adviser, whether or not previously in court, should:

(a)　ensure that he is aware of the relevant facts; and

(b)　provide the parties with an opportunity to respond to any advice given.

24A.15　At any time, justices are entitled to receive advice to assist them in discharging their responsibilities. If they are in any doubt as to the evidence which has been given, they should seek the aid of their legal adviser, referring to his notes as appropriate. This should ordinarily be done in open court. Where the justices request their adviser to join them in the retiring room, this request should be made in the presence of the parties in court. Any legal advice given to the justices other than in open court should be clearly stated to be provisional; and the adviser should subsequently repeat the substance of the advice in open court and give the parties the opportunity to make any representations they wish on that provisional advice. The legal adviser should then state in open court whether the provisional advice is confirmed or, if it is varied, the nature of the variation.

24A.16　The legal adviser is under a duty to assist unrepresented parties, whether defendants or not, to present their case, but must do so without appearing to become an advocate for the party concerned. The legal adviser should also ensure that members of the court are aware of obligations under the Victims' Code.

24A.17　The role of legal advisers in fine default proceedings, or any other proceedings for the enforcement of financial orders, obligations or penalties, is to assist the court. They must not act in an adversarial or partisan manner, such as by attempting to establish wilful refusal or neglect or any other type of culpable behaviour, to offer an opinion on the facts, or to urge a particular course of action upon the justices. The expectation is that a legal adviser will ask questions of the defaulter to elicit information which the justices will require to make an adjudication, such as the explanation for the default. A legal adviser may also advise the justices as to the options open to them in dealing with the case.

24A.18　The performance of a legal adviser is subject to regular appraisal. For that purpose the appraiser may be present in the justices' retiring room. The content of the appraisal is confidential, but the fact that an appraisal has taken place, and the presence of the appraiser in the retiring room, should be briefly explained in open court.

CPD VI Trial 24B: Identification for the court of the issues in the case

24B.1　CrimPR 3.11(a) requires the court, with the active assistance of the parties, to establish what are the disputed issues in order to manage the trial. To that end, the purpose of the prosecutor's summary of the prosecution case is to explain briefly, in the prosecutor's own terms, what the case is about. It will not usually be necessary, or helpful, to present a detailed account of all the prosecution evidence due to be introduced.

24B.2　CrimPR 24.3(3)(b) provides for a defendant, or his or her advocate, immediately after the prosecution opening to set out the issues in the defendant's own terms, if invited to do so by the court. The purpose of any such identification of issues is to provide the court with focus as to what it is likely to be called upon to decide, so that the members of the court will be alert to those issues from the outset and can evaluate the prosecution evidence that they hear accordingly.

24B.3　The parties should keep in mind that, in most cases, the members of the court already will be aware of what has been declared to be in issue. The court will have access to any written admissions and to information supplied for the purposes of case management: CrimPR 24.13(2). The court's legal adviser will have drawn the court's attention to what is alleged and to what is understood to be in dispute: CrimPR 24.15(2). If a party has nothing of substance to add to that, then he or she should say so. The requirement to be concise will be enforced and the exchange with the court properly may be confined to enquiry and confirmation that the court's understanding of those allegations and issues is correct. Nevertheless, for the defendant to be offered an opportunity to identify issues at this stage may assist even if all he or she wishes to announce, or confirm, is that the prosecution is being put to proof.

24B.4　The identification of issues at the case management stage will have been made without the risk that they would be used at trial as statements of the defendant admissible in evidence against the defendant, provided the advocate follows the letter and the spirit of the Criminal Procedure Rules. The court may take the view that a party is not acting in the spirit of the Criminal Procedure Rules in seeking to ambush the other party or raising late and technical legal arguments that were not previously raised as issues. No party that seeks to ambush the other at trial should derive an advantage from such a course of action. The court may also take the view that a defendant is not acting in the spirit of the Criminal Procedure Rules if he or she refuses to identify the issues and puts the prosecutor to proof at the case management stage. In both such circumstances the court may limit the proceedings on the day of trial in accordance with CrimPR 3.11(d). In addition any significant divergence from the issues identified at case management at this late stage may well result in the exercise of the court's powers under CrimPR 3.5(6), the powers to impose sanctions.

CRIMPR PARTS 25 AND 26 TRIAL AND SENTENCE IN THE CROWN COURT; JURORS

CPD VI Trial 25A: Identification for the jury of the issues in the case
Part 25A is not reproduced

CPD VI Trial 26A: Juries: Introduction
Part 26A is not reproduced

CPD VI Trial 26B: Juries: Preliminary matters arising before jury service commences
Part 26B is not reproduced

CPD VI Trial 26C: Juries: Eligibility
Part 26C is not reproduced

CPD VI Trial 26D: Juries: Precautionary measures before swearing
Part 26D is not reproduced

CPD VI Trial 26E: Juries: Swearing in jurors
Part 26E is not reproduced

CPD VI Trial 26F: Juries: Ensuring an effective jury panel
Part 26F is not reproduced

CPD VI Trial 26G: Juries: Preliminary Instructions to jurors
Part 26G is not reproduced

CPD VI Trial 26H: Juries: Discharge of a juror for personal reasons
Part 26H is not reproduced

CPD VI Trial 26J: Juries: Views
Part 26J is not reproduced

CPD VI Trial 26K: Juries: Directions, written materials and summing up
Part 26K is not reproduced

CPD VI Trial 26L: Juries: Jury access to exhibits and evidence in retirement
Part 26L is not reproduced

CPD VI Trial 26M: Juries: Jury irregularities
Part 26M is not reproduced

CPD VI Trial 26N: Open justice
Part 26N is not reproduced

CPD VI Trial 26P: Defendant's right to give or not to give evidence

26P.1   At the conclusion of the evidence for the prosecution, section 35(2) of the Criminal Justice and Public Order Act 1994 requires the court to satisfy itself that the defendant is aware that the stage has been reached at which evidence can be given for the defence and that the defendant's failure to give evidence, or if he does so his failure to answer questions, without a good reason, may lead to inferences being drawn against him.

If the defendant is legally represented

26P.2   After the close of the prosecution case, if the defendant's representative requests a brief adjournment to advise his client on this issue the request should, ordinarily, be granted. When appropriate the judge should, in the presence of the jury, inquire of the representative in these terms:

'Have you advised your client that the stage has now been reached at which he may give evidence and, if he chooses not to do so or, having been sworn, without good cause refuses to answer any question, the jury may draw such inferences as appear proper from his failure to do so ?'

26P.3   If the representative replies to the judge that the defendant has been so advised, then the case shall proceed. If counsel replies that the defendant has not been so advised, then the judge shall direct the representative to advise his client of the consequences and should adjourn briefly for this purpose, before proceeding further.

If the defendant is not legally represented

26P.4   If the defendant is not represented, the judge shall, at the conclusion of the evidence for the prosecution, in the absence of the jury, indicate what he will say to him in the presence of the jury and ask if he understands and whether he would like a brief adjournment to consider his position.

26P.5   When appropriate, and in the presence of the jury, the judge should say to the defendant:

'You have heard the evidence against you. Now is the time for you to make your defence. You may give evidence on oath, and be cross-examined like any other witness. If you do not give evidence or, having been sworn, without good cause refuse to answer any question, the jury may draw such inferences as appear proper. That means they may hold it against you. You may also call any witness or witnesses whom you have arranged to attend court or lead any agreed evidence. Afterwards you may also, if you wish, address the jury. But you cannot at that stage give evidence. Do you now intend to give evidence?'

CPD VI Trial 26Q: Majority verdicts
Crown Court only

VII Sentencing

CPD Sentencing A: Pleas of guilty in the Crown Court
Crown Court only

CPD VII Sentencing B: Determining the factual basis of sentence
Crown Court only

CPD VII Sentencing C: Indications of sentence: R v Goodyear
Crown Court only

CPD VII Sentencing D: Facts to be stated on pleas of guilty

D.1   To enable the press and the public to know the circumstances of an offence of which an accused has been convicted and for which he is to be sentenced, in relation to each offence to which an accused has pleaded guilty the prosecution shall state those facts in open court, before sentence is imposed.

CPD VII Sentencing E: Concurrent and consecutive sentences

E.1   Where a court passes on a defendant more than one term of imprisonment, the court should state in the presence of the defendant whether the terms are to be concurrent or consecutive. Should this not be done, the court clerk should ask the court, before the defendant leaves court, to do so.

E.2   If a defendant is, at the time of sentence, already serving two or more consecutive terms of imprisonment and the court intends to increase the total period of imprisonment, it should use the expression 'consecutive to the total period of imprisonment to which you are already subject' rather than 'at the expiration of the term of imprisonment you are now serving', as the defendant may not then be serving the last of the terms to which he is already subject.

E.3   The Sentencing Council has issued a definitive guideline on Totality which should be consulted. Under section 125(1) of the Coroners and Justice Act 2009, for offences committed after 6 April 2010, the guideline must be followed unless it would be contrary to the interests of justice to do so.

CPD VII Sentencing F: Victim personal statements

F.1   Victims of crime are invited to make a statement, known as a Victim Personal Statement ('VPS'). The statement gives victims a formal opportunity to say how a crime has affected them. It may help to identify whether they have a particular need for information, support and protection. The court will take the statement into account when determining sentence. In some circumstances, it may be appropriate for relatives of a victim to make a VPS, for example where the victim has died as a result of the relevant criminal conduct. The revised Code of Practice for Victims of Crime, published on 29 October 2013 gives further information about victims' entitlements within the criminal justice system, and the duties placed on criminal justice agencies when dealing with victims of crime.

F.2   When a police officer takes a statement from a victim, the victim should be told about the scheme and given the chance to make a VPS. The decision about whether or not to make a VPS is entirely a matter for the victim; no pressure should be brought to bear on their decision, and no conclusion should be drawn if they choose not to make such a statement. A VPS or a further VPS may be made (in proper s.9 form, see below) at any time prior to the disposal of the case. It will not normally be appropriate for a VPS to be made after the disposal of the case; there may be rare occasions between sentence and appeal when a further VPS may be necessary, for example, when the victim was injured and the final prognosis was not available at the date of sentence. However, VPS after disposal should be confined to presenting up to date factual material, such as medical information, and should be used sparingly.

F.3   If the court is presented with a VPS the following approach, subject to the further guidance given by the Court of Appeal in *R v Perkins; Bennett; Hall* [2013] EWCA Crim 323, [2013] Crim L.R. 533, should be adopted:

(a)   The VPS and any evidence in support should be considered and taken into account by the court, prior to passing sentence.

(b)   Evidence of the effects of an offence on the victim contained in the VPS or other statement, must be in proper form, that is a witness statement made under section 9 of the Criminal Justice Act 1967 or an expert's report; and served in good time upon the defendant's solicitor or the defendant, if he or she is not represented. Except where inferences can properly be drawn from the nature of or circumstances surrounding the offence, a sentencing court must not make assumptions unsupported by evidence about the effects of an offence on the victim. The maker of a VPS may be cross-examined on its content.

(c)   At the discretion of the court, the VPS may also be read aloud or played in open court, in whole or in part, or it may be summarised. If the VPS is to be read aloud, the court should also determine who should do so. In making these decisions, the court should take account of the victim's preferences, and follow them unless there is good reason not to do so; examples of this include the inadmissibility of the content or the potentially harmful consequences for the victim or others. Court hearings should not be adjourned solely to allow the victim to attend court to read the VPS. For the purposes of CPD I General matters 5B: Access to information held by the court, a VPS that is read aloud or played in open court in whole or in part should be considered as such, and no longer treated as a confidential document.

(d)   In all cases it will be appropriate for a VPS to be referred to in the course of the sentencing hearing and/or in the sentencing remarks.

(e)   The court must pass what it judges to be the appropriate sentence having regard to the circumstances of the offence and of the offender, taking into account, so far as the court considers it appropriate, the impact on the victim. The opinions of the victim or the victim's close relatives as to what the sentence should be are therefore not relevant, unlike the consequences of the offence on them. Victims should be advised of this. If, despite the advice, opinions as to sentence are included in the statement, the court should pay no attention to them.

CPD VII Sentencing G: Families bereaved by homicide and other criminal conduct

G.1   In cases in which the victim has died as a result of the relevant criminal conduct, the victim's family is not a party to the proceedings, but does have an interest in the case. Bereaved families have particular entitlements under the Code of Practice for Victims of Crime. All parties should have regard to the needs of the victim's family and ensure that the trial process does not expose bereaved families to avoidable intimidation, humiliation or distress.

G.2 In so far as it is compatible with family members' roles as witnesses, the court should consider the following measures:

(a) Practical arrangements being discussed with the family and made in good time before the trial, such as seating for family members in the courtroom; if appropriate, in an alternative area, away from the public gallery.

(b) Warning being given to families if the evidence on a certain day is expected to be particularly distressing.

(c) Ensuring that appropriate use is made of the scheme for Victim Personal Statements, in accordance with the paragraphs above.

G.3 The sentencer should consider providing a written copy of the sentencing remarks to the family after sentence has been passed. Sentencers should tend in favour of providing such a copy, unless there is good reason not to do so, and the copy should be provided as soon as is reasonably practicable after the sentencing hearing.

CPD VII Sentencing H: Community impact statements

H.1 A community impact statement may be prepared by the police to make the court aware of particular crime trends in the local area and the impact of these on the local community.

H.2 Such statements must be in proper form, that is a witness statement made under section 9 of the Criminal Justice Act 1967 or an expert's report; and served in good time upon the defendant's solicitor or the defendant, if he is not represented.

H.3 The community impact statement and any evidence in support should be considered and taken into account by the court, prior to passing sentence. The statement should be referred to in the course of the sentencing hearing and/or in the sentencing remarks. Subject to the court's discretion, the contents of the statement may be summarised or read out in open court.

H.4 The court must pass what it judges to be the appropriate sentence having regard to the circumstances of the offence and of the offender, taking into account, so far as the court considers it appropriate, the impact on the local community. Opinions as to what the sentence should be are therefore not relevant. If, despite the advice, opinions as to sentence are included in the statement, the court should pay no attention to them.

H.5 Except where inferences can properly be drawn from the nature of or circumstances surrounding the offence, a sentencing court must not make assumptions unsupported by evidence about the effects of an offence on the local community.

H.6 It will not be appropriate for a Community Impact Statement to be made after disposal of the case but before an appeal.

CPD VII Sentencing I: Impact statements for businesses

I.1 Individual victims of crime are invited to make a statement, known as a Victim Personal Statement ('VPS', see CPD VII Sentencing F. If the victim, or one of the victims, is a business or enterprise (including charities but excluding public sector bodies), of any size, a nominated representative may make an Impact Statement for Business ('ISB'). The ISB gives a formal opportunity for the court to be informed how a crime has affected a business. The court will take the statement into account when determining sentence. This does not prevent individual employees from making a VPS about the impact of the same crime on them as individuals. Indeed the ISB should be about the impact on the business exclusively, and the impact on any individual included within a VPS.

I.2 When a police officer takes statements about the alleged offence, he or she should also inform the business about the scheme. An ISB may be made to the police at that time, or the ISB template may be downloaded from www.police.uk, completed and emailed or posted to the relevant police contact. Guidance on how to complete the form is available on www.police.uk and on the CPS website. There is no obligation on any business to make an ISB.

I.3 An ISB or an updated ISB may be made (in proper s.9 form, see below) at any time prior to the disposal of the case. It will not be appropriate for an ISB to be made after disposal of the case but before an appeal.

I.4 A business wishing to make an ISB should consider carefully who to nominate as the representative to make the statement on its behalf. A person making an ISB on behalf of a business, the nominated representative, must be authorised to do so on behalf of the business, either by nature of their position within the business, such as a director or owner, or by having been suitably authorised, such as by the owner or Board of Directors. The nominated representative must also be in a position to give admissible evidence about the impact of the crime on the business. This will usually be through first hand personal knowledge, or using business documents (as defined in section 117 of the Criminal Justice Act 2003). The most appropriate person will vary depending on the nature of the crime, and the size and structure of the business and may for example include a manager, director, chief executive or shop owner.

I.5 If the nominated representative leaves the business before the case comes to court, he or she will usually remain the representative, as the ISB made by him or her will still provide the best evidence of the impact of the crime, and he or she could still be asked to attend court. Nominated representatives should be made aware of the on-going nature of the role at the time of making the ISB.

I.6 If necessary a further ISB may be provided to the police if there is a change in circumstances. This could be made by an alternative nominated representative. However, the new ISB will usually supplement, not replace, the original ISB and again must contain admissible evidence. The prosecutor will decide which ISB to serve on the defence as evidence, and any ISB that is not served in evidence will be included in the unused material and considered for disclosure to the defence.

I.7 The ISB must be made in proper form, that is as a witness statement made under section 9 of the Criminal Justice Act 1967 or an expert's report; and served in good time upon the defendant's solicitor or the defendant, if he or she is not represented. The maker of an ISB can be cross-examined on its content.

I.8 The ISB and any evidence in support should be considered and taken into account by the court, prior to passing sentence. The statement should be referred to in the course of the sentencing hearing and/or in the sentencing remarks. Subject to the court's discretion, the contents of the statement may be summarised or read out in open court; the views of the business should be taken into account in reaching a decision.

I.9 The court must pass what it judges to be the appropriate sentence having regard to the circumstances of the offence and of the offender, taking into account, so far as the court considers it appropriate, the impact on the victims, including any business victim. Opinions as to what the sentence should be are therefore not relevant. If, despite the advice, opinions as to sentence are included in the statement, the court should pay no attention to them.

I.10 Except where inferences can properly be drawn from the nature of or circumstances surrounding the offence, a sentencing court must not make assumptions unsupported by evidence about the effects of an offence on a business.

CPD VII Sentencing J: Binding over orders and conditional discharges

J.1 This direction takes into account the judgments of the European Court of Human Rights in *Steel v United Kingdom* (1999) 28 EHRR 603, [1998] Crim. L.R. 893 and in *Hashman and Harrup v United Kingdom* (2000) 30 EHRR 241, [2000] Crim. L.R. 185. Its purpose is to give practical guidance, in the light of those two judgments, on the practice of imposing binding over orders. The direction applies to orders made under the court's common law powers, under the Justices of the Peace Act 1361, under section 1(7) of the Justices of the Peace Act 1968 and under section 115 of the Magistrates' Courts Act 1980. This direction also gives guidance concerning the court's power to bind over parents or guardians under section 150 of the Powers of Criminal Courts (Sentencing) Act 2000 and the Crown Court's power to bind over to come up for judgment. The court's power to impose a conditional discharge under section 12 of the Powers of Criminal Courts (Sentencing) Act 2000 is also covered by this direction.

Binding over to keep the peace

J.2 Before imposing a binding over order, the court must be satisfied so that it is sure that a breach of the peace involving violence, or an imminent threat of violence, has occurred or that there is a real risk of violence in the future. Such violence may be perpetrated by the individual who will be subject to the order or by a third party as a natural consequence of the individual's conduct.

J.3 In light of the judgment in *Hashman*, courts should no longer bind an individual over "to be of good behaviour". Rather than binding an individual over to "keep the peace" in general terms, the court should identify the specific conduct or activity from which the individual must refrain.

Written order

J.4 When making an order binding an individual over to refrain from specified types of conduct or activities, the details of that conduct or those activities should be specified by the court in a written order, served on all relevant parties. The court should state its reasons for the making of the order, its length and the amount of the recognisance. The length of the order should be proportionate to the harm sought to be avoided and should not generally exceed 12 months.

Evidence

J.5 Sections 51 to 57 of the Magistrates' Courts Act 1980 set out the jurisdiction of the magistrates' court to hear an application made on complaint and the procedure which is to be followed. This includes a requirement under section 53 to hear evidence and the parties, before making any order. This practice should be applied to all cases in the magistrates' court and the Crown Court where the court is considering imposing a binding over order. The court should give the individual who would be subject to the order and the prosecutor the opportunity to make representations, both as to the making of the order and as to its terms. The court should also hear any admissible evidence the parties wish to call and which has not already been heard in the proceedings. Particularly careful consideration may be required where the individual who would be subject to the order is a witness in the proceedings.

J.6 Where there is an admission which is sufficient to found the making of a binding over order and / or the individual consents to the making of the order, the court should nevertheless hear sufficient representations and, if appropriate, evidence, to satisfy itself that an order is appropriate in all the circumstances and to be clear about the terms of the order.

J.7 Where there is an allegation of breach of a binding over order and this is contested, the court should hear representations and evidence, including oral evidence, from the parties before making a finding. If unrepresented and no opportunity has been given previously the court should give a reasonable period for the person said to have breached the binding over order to find representation.

Burden and standard of proof

J.8 The court should be satisfied so that it is sure of the matters complained of before a binding over order may be imposed. Where the procedure has been commenced on complaint, the burden of proof rests on the complainant. In all other circumstances, the burden of proof rests upon the prosecution.

J.9 Where there is an allegation of breach of a binding over order, the court should be satisfied on the balance of probabilities that the defendant is in breach before making any order for forfeiture of a recognisance. The burden of proof shall rest on the prosecution.

Recognisance

J.10 The court must be satisfied on the merits of the case that an order for binding over is appropriate and should announce that decision before considering the amount of the recognisance. If unrepresented, the individual who is made subject to the binding over order should be told he has a right of appeal from the decision.

J.11 When fixing the amount of recognisance, courts should have regard to the individual's financial resources and should hear representations from the individual or his legal representatives regarding finances.

J.12   A recognisance is made in the form of a bond giving rise to a civil debt on breach of the order.

Refusal to enter into a recognizance

J.12   If there is any possibility that an individual will refuse to enter a recognizance, the court should consider whether there are any appropriate alternatives to a binding over order (for example, continuing with a prosecution). Where there are no appropriate alternatives and the individual continues to refuse to enter into the recognisance, the court may commit the individual to custody. In the magistrates' court, the power to do so will derive from section 1(7) of the Justices of the Peace Act 1968 or, more rarely, from section 115(3) of the Magistrates' Courts Act 1980, and the court should state which power it is acting under; in the Crown Court, this is a common law power.

J.14   Before the court exercises a power to commit the individual to custody, the individual should be given the opportunity to see a duty solicitor or another legal representative and be represented in proceedings if the individual so wishes. Public funding should generally be granted to cover representation. In the Crown Court this rests with the Judge who may grant a Representation Order.

J.15   In the event that the individual does not take the opportunity to seek legal advice, the court shall give the individual a final opportunity to comply with the request and shall explain the consequences of a failure to do so.

Antecedents

J.16   Courts are reminded of the provisions of section 7(5) of the Rehabilitation of Offenders Act 1974 which excludes from a person's antecedents any order of the court "with respect to any person otherwise than on a conviction".

Binding over to come up for judgment

J.17   If the Crown Court is considering binding over an individual to come up for judgment, the court should specify any conditions with which the individual is to comply in the meantime and not specify that the individual is to be of good behaviour.

J.18   The Crown Court should, if the individual is unrepresented, explain the consequences of a breach of the binding over order in these circumstances.

Binding over of parent or guardian

J.19   Where a court is considering binding over a parent or guardian under section 150 of the Powers of Criminal Courts (Sentencing) Act 2000 to enter into a recognisance to take proper care of and exercise proper control over a child or young person, the court should specify the actions which the parent or guardian is to take.

Security for good behaviour

J.20   Where a court is imposing a conditional discharge under section 12 of the Powers of Criminal Courts (Sentencing) Act 2000, it has the power, under section 12(6) to make an order that a person who consents to do so give security for the good behaviour of the offender. When making such an order, the court should specify the type of conduct from which the offender is to refrain.

CPD VII Sentencing K: Committal for sentence

K.1   CrimPR 28.10 applies when a case is committed to the Crown Court for sentence and specifies the information and documentation that must be provided by the magistrates' court. On a committal for sentence any reasons given by the magistrates for their decision should be included with the documents. All of these documents should be made available to the judge in the Crown Court if the judge requires them, in order to decide before the hearing questions of listing or representation or the like. They will also be available to the court during the hearing if it becomes necessary or desirable for the court to see what happened in the lower court.

CPD VII Sentencing L: Imposition of life sentences
Crown Court only

CPD VII Sentencing M: Mandatory life sentences
Crown Court only

CPD VII Sentencing N: Transitional arrangements for sentences where the offence was committed before 18 December 2003
Crown Court only

CPD VII Sentencing P: Procedure for announcing the minimum term in open court
[*Crown Court only*]

CPD VII Sentencing Q: Financial, etc. information required for sentencing

Q.1   These directions supplement CrimPR 24.11 and 25.16, which set out the procedure to be followed where a defendant pleads guilty, or is convicted, and is to be sentenced. They are not concerned exclusively with corporate defendants, or with offences of an environmental, public health, health and safety or other regulatory character, but the guidance which they contain is likely to be of particular significance in such cases.

Q.2   The rules set out the prosecutor's responsibilities in all cases. Where the offence is of a character, or is against a prohibition, with which the sentencing court is unlikely to be familiar, those responsibilities are commensurately more onerous. The court is entitled to the greatest possible assistance in identifying information relevant to sentencing.

Q.3   In such a case, save where the circumstances are very straightforward, it is likely that justice will best be served by the submission of the required information in writing: see *R v Friskies Petcare*

(UK) Ltd [2000] 2 Cr App R (S) 401. Though it is the prosecutor's responsibility to the court to prepare any such document, if the defendant pleads guilty, or indicates a guilty plea, then it is very highly desirable that such sentencing information should be agreed between the parties and jointly submitted. If agreement cannot be reached in all particulars, then the nature and extent of the disagreement should be indicated. If the court concludes that what is in issue is material to sentence, then it will give directions for resolution of the dispute, whether by hearing oral evidence or by other means. In every case, when passing sentence the sentencing court must make clear on what basis sentence is passed: in fairness to the defendant, and for the information of any other person, or court, who needs or wishes to understand the reasons for sentence.

Q.4 If so directed by or on behalf of the court, a defendant must supply accurate information about financial circumstances. In fixing the amount of any fine the court must take into account, amongst other considerations, the financial circumstances of the offender (whether an individual or other person) as they are known or as they appear to be. Before fixing the amount of fine when the defendant is an individual, the court must inquire into his financial circumstances. Where the defendant is an individual the court may make a financial circumstances order in respect of him. This means an order in which the court requires an individual to provide a statement as to his financial means, within a specified time. It is an offence, punishable with imprisonment, to fail to comply with such an order or for knowingly/recklessly furnishing a false statement or knowingly failing to disclose a material fact. The provisions of section 20A Criminal Justice Act 1991 apply to any person (thereby including a corporate organisation) and place the offender under a statutory duty to provide the court with a statement as to his financial means in response to an official request. There are offences for non-compliance, false statements or non-disclosure. It is for the court to decide how much information is required, having regard to relevant sentencing guidelines or guideline cases. However, by reference to those same guidelines and cases the parties should anticipate what the court will require, and prepare accordingly. In complex cases, and in cases involving a corporate defendant, the information required will be more extensive than in others. In the case of a corporate defendant, that information usually will include details of the defendant's corporate structure; annual profit and loss accounts, or extracts; annual balance sheets, or extracts; details of shareholders' receipts; and details of the remuneration of directors or other officers.

Q.5 In *R v F Howe and Son (Engineers) Ltd* [1999] 2 Cr App R (S) 37 the Court of Appeal observed:

"If a defendant company wishes to make any submission to the court about its ability to pay a fine it should supply copies of its accounts and any other financial information on which it intends to rely in good time before the hearing both to the court and to the prosecution. This will give the prosecution the opportunity to assist the court should the court wish it. Usually accounts need to be considered with some care to avoid reaching a superficial and perhaps erroneous conclusion. Where accounts or other financial information are deliberately not supplied the court will be entitled to conclude that the company is in a position to pay any financial penalty it is minded to impose. Where the relevant information is provided late it may be desirable for sentence to be adjourned, if necessary at the defendant's expense, so as to avoid the risk of the court taking what it is told at face value and imposing an inadequate penalty."

Q.6 In the case of an individual, the court is likewise entitled to conclude that the defendant is able to pay any fine imposed unless the defendant has supplied financial information to the contrary. It is the defendant's responsibility to disclose to the court such information relevant to his or her financial position as will enable it to assess what he or she reasonably can afford to pay. If necessary, the court may compel the disclosure of an individual defendant's financial circumstances. In the absence of such disclosure, or where the court is not satisfied that it has been given sufficient reliable information, the court will be entitled to draw reasonable inferences as to the offender's means from evidence it has heard and from all the circumstances of the case.

CPD VII R: MEDICAL REPORTS FOR SENTENCING PURPOSES

General observations

R.1 CrimPR 24.11 and 25.16 concern standard sentencing procedures in magistrates' courts and in the Crown Court respectively. CrimPR 28.8 deals with the obtaining of medical reports for sentencing purposes.

R.2 Rule 28.8 governs the procedure to be followed where a report is commissioned at the instigation of the court. It is not a substitute for the prompt commissioning of a report or reports by a defendant or defendant's representatives where expert medical opinion is material to the defence case. In particular, the defendant's representatives may wish to obtain a medical report or reports wholly independently of the court. Nothing in these directions, therefore, should be read as discouraging the commissioning of a medical report before the case comes before the court, where such a report is expected to be material and where it is possible promptly to commission it. However, where such a report has been commissioned then if that report has not been received in time for sentencing and if the court agrees that it seems likely to be material, then the court should set a timetable for the reception of that report and should give directions for progress to be reviewed at intervals, adopting the timetable set out in these directions with such adaptations as are needed.

R.3 In assessing the likely materiality of an expert medical report for sentencing purposes the court will be assisted by the parties' representations; by the views expressed in any pre-sentence report that may have been prepared; and by the views of practitioners in local criminal justice mental health services, whose assistance is available to the court under local liaison arrangements.

R.4 Where the court requires the assistance of such a report then it is essential that there should be (i) absolute clarity about who is expected to do what, by when, and at whose expense; and (ii) judicial directions for progress with that report to be monitored and reviewed at prescribed intervals, following a timetable set by the court which culminates in the consideration of the report at a hearing. This is especially important where the report in question is a psychiatric assessment of the defendant for the preparation of which specific expertise may be required which is not readily available and because in some circumstances a second such assessment, by another medical practitioner, may be required.

Timetable for the commissioning, preparation and consideration of a report or reports

R.5   CrimPR 28.8 requires the court to set a timetable appropriate to the case for the preparation and reception of a report. In doing so the court will take account of such representations and other information that it receives, including information about the anticipated availability and workload of practitioners with the appropriate expertise. However, the timetable ought not be a protracted one. It is essential to keep in mind the importance of maintaining progress: in recognition of the defendant's rights and with respect for the interests of victims and witnesses, as required by CrimPR Part 1 (the overriding objective). In a magistrates' court account must be taken, too, of section 11 of the Powers of Criminal Courts (Sentencing) Act 2000, which limits the duration of each remand pending the preparation of a report to 3 weeks, where the defendant is to be in custody, and to 4 weeks if the defendant is to be on bail.

R.6   Subject, therefore, to contrary judicial direction the timetable set by the court should require:

(a)   the convening of a hearing to consider the report no more than 6 – 8 weeks after the court makes its request;

(b)   the prompt identification of an appropriate medical practitioner or practitioners, if not already identified by the court, and the despatch of a commission or commissions accordingly, within 2 business days of the court's decision to request a report;

(c)   acknowledgement of a commission by its recipient, and acceptance or rejection of that commission, within 5 business days of its receipt;

(d)   enquiries by court staff to confirm that the commission has been received, and to ascertain the action being taken in response, in the event that no acknowledgement is received within 10 business days of its despatch;

(e)   delivery of the report within 5 weeks of the despatch of the commission;

(f)   enquiries into progress by court staff in the event that no report is received within 5 weeks of the despatch of the commission.

R.7   The hearing that is convened for the court to consider the report, at 6 – 8 weeks after the court requests that report, should not be adjourned before it takes place save in exceptional circumstances and then only by explicit judicial direction the reasons for which must be recorded. If by the time of that hearing the report is available, as usually should be the case, then at that hearing the court can be expected to determine the issue in respect of which the report was commissioned and pass sentence. If by that time, exceptionally, the report is not available then the court should take the opportunity provided by that hearing to enquire into the reasons, give such directions as are appropriate, and if necessary adjourn the hearing to a fixed date for further consideration then. Where it is known in advance of that hearing that the report will not be available in time, the hearing may be conducted by live link or telephone: subject, in the defendant's case, to the same considerations as are identified at paragraph I.3N.6 of these Practice Directions. However, it rarely will be appropriate to dispense altogether with that hearing, or to make enquiries and give further directions without any hearing at all, in view of the arrangements for monitoring and review that the court already will have directed and which, by definition therefore, thus far will have failed to secure the report's timely delivery.

R.8   Where a requirement of the timetable set by the court is not met, or where on enquiry by court staff it appears that the timetable is unlikely to be met, and in any instance in which a medical practitioner who accepts a commission asks for more time, then court staff should not themselves adjust the timetable or accede to such a request but instead should seek directions from an appropriate judicial authority. Subject to local judicial direction, that will be, in the Crown Court, the judge assigned to the case or the resident judge and, in a magistrates' court, a District Judge (Magistrates' Courts) or justice of the peace assigned to the case, or the Justices' Clerk, an assistant clerk or other senior legal adviser. Even if the timetable is adjusted in consequence:

(a)   the hearing convened to consider the report (that is, the hearing set for no more than 6 – 8 weeks after the court made its request) rarely should be adjourned before it takes place: see paragraph R.13 above;

(b)   directions should be given for court staff henceforth to make regular enquiries into progress, at intervals of not more than 2 weeks, and to report the outcome to an appropriate judicial authority who will decide what further directions, if any, to give.

R.9   Any adjournment of a hearing convened to consider the report should be to a specific date: the hearing should not be adjourned generally, or to a date to be set in due course. The adjournment of such a hearing should not be for more than a further 6 – 8 weeks save in the most exceptional circumstances; and no more than one adjournment of the hearing should be allowed without obtaining written or oral representations from the commissioned medical practitioner explaining the reasons for the delay.

Commissioning a report

R.10   Guidance entitled 'Good practice guidance: commissioning, administering and producing psychiatric reports for sentencing' prepared for and published by the Ministry of Justice and HM Courts and Tribunals Service in September 2010 contains material that will assist court staff and those who are asked to prepare such reports:

http://www.ohrn.nhs.uk/resource/policy/GoodPracticeGuidePsychRepo rts.pdf

That guidance includes standard forms of letters of instruction and other documents.

R.11   CrimPR 28.8 requires the commissioner of a report to explain why the court seeks the report and to include relevant information about the circumstances. The HMCTS Guidance contains forms for judicial use in the instruction of court staff, and guidance to court staff on the preparation of letters of instruction, where a report is required for sentencing purposes. Where a report is requested in a case involving manslaughter by reason of diminished responsibility, the report writer should have regard to the Sentencing Council's guideline on Manslaughter by reason of

Diminished Responsibility. This should assist the report writer in providing the most helpful assessment to enable the court to determine the level of diminution involved in the case.

R.12 The commission should invite a practitioner who is unable to accept it promptly to nominate a suitably qualified substitute, if possible, and to transfer the commission to that person, reporting the transfer when acknowledging the court officer's letter. It is entirely appropriate for the commission to draw the recipient's attention to CrimPR 1.2 (the duty of the participants in a criminal case) and to CrimPR 19.2(1)(b) (the obligation of an expert witness to comply with directions made by a court and at once to inform the court of any significant failure, by the expert or another, to take any step required by such a direction).

R.13 Where the relevant legislation requires a second psychiatric assessment by a second medical practitioner, and where no commission already has been addressed to a second such practitioner, the commission may invite the person to whom it is addressed to nominate a suitably qualified second person and to pass a copy of the commission to that person forthwith.

Funding arrangements

R.14 Where a medical report has been, or is to be, commissioned by a party then that party is responsible for arranging payment of the fees incurred, even though the report is intended for the court's use. That must be made clear in that party's commission.

R.15 Where a medical report is requested by the court and commissioned by a party or by court staff at the court's direction then the commission must include (i) confirmation that the fees will be paid by HMCTS, (ii) details of how, and to whom, to submit an invoice or claim for fees, and (iii) notice of the prescribed rates of fees and of any legislative or other criteria applicable to the calculation of the fees that may be paid.

Remand in custody

R.16 Where the defendant who is to be examined will be remanded in custody then notice that directions have been given for a medical report or reports to be prepared must be included in the information given to the defendant's custodian, to ensure that the preparation of the report or reports can be facilitated. This is especially important where bail is withheld on the ground that it would be otherwise impracticable to complete the required report, and in particular where that is the only ground for withholding bail.

CRIMINAL PRACTICE DIRECTIONS 2015 DIVISION IX
Appeal

CRIMPR PART 34 APPEAL TO THE CROWN COURT

CPD IX Appeal 34A: Appeals to the crown court

34A.1 On an appeal against conviction CrimPR 34.3 requires the appellant and respondent to supply information needed for the effective case management of the appeal, but allows the Crown Court to relieve the appellant – not the respondent – of that obligation, in whole or part.

34A.2 The court is most likely to exercise that discretion in an appellant's favour where he or she is not represented and is unable, without assistance, to provide reliable such information. The notes to the standard form of appeal notice invite the appellant to answer the relevant questions in that form to the extent that he or she is able, explaining that while the appellant may not be able to answer all those questions nevertheless any answers that can be given will assist in making arrangements for the hearing of the appeal. Where an appellant uses the prescribed form of easy read appeal notice the court usually should assume that the appellant will not be able to supply case management information, and that form contains no questions corresponding with those in the standard appeal notice. In such a case relevant information will be supplied by the respondent in the respondent's notice and may be gleaned from material obtained from magistrates' court records by Crown Court staff.

34A.3 On an appeal against sentence, the magistrates' court's reasons and factual finding leading to the finding of guilt should be included, but any reasons for the sentence imposed should be omitted as the Crown Court will be conducting a fresh sentencing exercise.

CPD IX Appeal 34B: Appeal to the crown court: Information from the Magistrates' Court

34B.1 CrimPR 34.4 applies when a defendant appeals to the Crown Court against conviction or sentence and specifies the information and documentation that must be made available by the magistrates' court.

34B.2 In all cases magistrates' court staff must ensure that Crown Court staff are notified of the appeal as soon as practicable: CrimPR 34.4(2)(b). In most cases Crown Court staff will be able to obtain the other information required by CrimPR 34.4(3) or (4) by direct access to the electronic records created by magistrates' court staff. However, if such access is not available then alternative arrangements must be made for the transfer of such information to Crown Court staff by electronic means. Paper copies of documents should be created and sent only as a last resort.

34B.3 On an appeal against conviction, the reasons given by the magistrates for their decision should not be included with the documents; the appeal hearing is not a review of the magistrates' court's decision but a re-hearing. There is no requirement for the Notice of Appeal form to be redacted in any way; the judge and magistrates presiding over the rehearing will base their decision on the evidence presented during the rehearing itself.

34B.4 On an appeal soley against sentence, the magistrates' court's reasons and factual finding leading to the finding of guilt should be included, but any reasons for the sentence imposed should be omitted as the Crown Court will be conducting a fresh sentencing exercise. Whilst reasons for the sentence imposed are not necessary for the rehearing, the Notice of Appeal form may include references to the sentence that is being appealed. There is no requirement to react this before the form is given to the judge and magistrates hearing the appeal.

CRIMPR PART 39 APPEAL TO THE COURT OF APPEAL ABOUT CONVICTION OR SENTENCE

CPD IX Appeal 39A: Appeals against conviction and sentence – The provision of notice to the prosecution
39A (Court of Appeal (Criminal Division))

CPD IX Appeal 39B: Listing of appeals against conviction and sentence in the court of appeal criminal division (CACD)
39B (Court of Appeal (Criminal Division))

CPD IX Appeal 39C: Appeal notices and grounds of appeal
39C (Court of Appeal (Criminal Division))

CPD IX Appeal 39D: Respondents' notices
39D (Court of Appeal (Criminal Division))

CPD IX Appeal 39E: Loss of time
39E (Court of Appeal (Criminal Division))

CPD IX Appeal 39F: Skeleton arguments
39F (Court of Appeal (Criminal Division))

CPD IX Appeal 39G: Criminal appeal office summaries
39G (Court of Appeal (Criminal Division))

CRIMPR PART 44 REQUEST TO THE EUROPEAN COURT FOR A PRELIMINARY RULING

CPD IX Appeal 44A: References to the European Court of Justice

44A.1 Further to CrimPR 44.3 of the Criminal Procedure Rules, the order containing the reference shall be filed with the Senior Master of the Queen's Bench Division of the High Court for onward transmission to the Court of Justice of the European Union. The order should be marked for the attention of Mrs Isaac and sent to the Senior Master:

c/o Queen's Bench Division Associates Dept
Room WG03
Royal Courts of Justice
Strand
London WC2A 2LL

44A.2 There is no longer a requirement that the relevant court file be sent to the Senior Master. The parties should ensure that all appropriate documentation is sent directly to the European Court at the following address:

The Registrar
Court of Justice of the European Union
Kirchberg L-2925 Luxemburg

44A.3 There is no prescribed form for use but the following details must be included in the back sheet to the order:

   (i)   Solicitor's full address;
   (ii) Solicitor's and Court references;
   (iii) Solicitor's e-mail address.

44A.4 The European Court of Justice regularly updates its Recommendation to national courts and tribunals in relation to the initiation of preliminary ruling proceedings. The current Recommendation is 2012/C 338/01: http://eurlex.europa.eu/LexUriServ/LexUriServ.do?uri=OJ:C:2012:338:0001:0006:EN:PDF

44A.5 The referring court may request the Court of Justice of the European Union to apply its urgent preliminary ruling procedure where the referring court's proceedings relate to a person in custody. For further information see Council Decision 2008/79/EC [2008] OJ L24/42: http://eurlex.europa.eu/LexUriServ/LexUriServ.do?uri=OJ:L:2008:024:0042:0043:EN:PDF

44A.6 Any such request must be made in a document separate from the order or in a covering letter and must set out:

   (iv) The matters of fact and law which establish the urgency;
   (v) The reasons why the urgent preliminary ruling procedure applies; and
   (vi) In so far as possible, the court's view on the answer to the question referred to the Court of Justice of the European Union for a preliminary ruling.

44A.7 Any request to apply the urgent preliminary ruling procedure should be filed with the Senior Master as described above.

CRIMINAL PRACTICE DIRECTIONS 2015 DIVISION X
Costs

CRIMPR PART 45 COSTS

[Costs Practice Direction]

CRIMINAL PRACTICE DIRECTIONS 2015 DIVISION XI
Other proceedings

CRIMPR PART 47 INVESTIGATION ORDERS AND WARRANTS

CPD XI Other proceedings 47A: Investigation orders and warrants

47A.1   Powers of entry, search and seizure, and powers to obtain banking and other confidential information, are among the most intrusive that investigators can exercise. Every application must be carefully scrutinised with close attention paid to what the relevant statutory provision requires of the applicant and to what it permits. CrimPR Part 47 must be followed, and the accompanying forms must be used. These are designed to prompt applicants, and the courts, to deal with all of the relevant criteria.

47A.2   The issuing of a warrant or the making of such an order is never to be treated as a formality and it is therefore essential that the judge or magistrate considering the application is given, and must take, sufficient time for the purpose. The prescribed forms require the applicant to provide a time estimate, and listing officers and justices' legal advisers should take account of these.

47A.3   Applicants for orders and warrants owe the court duties of candour and truthfulness. On any application made without notice to the respondent, and so on all applications for search warrants, the duty of frank and complete disclosure is especially onerous. The applicant must draw the court's attention to any information that is unfavourable to the application. The existence of unfavourable information will not necessarily lead to the application being refused; it will be a matter for the court what weight to place on each piece of information.

47A.4   Where an applicant supplements an application with additional oral or written information, on questioning by the court or otherwise, it is essential that the court keeps an adequate record. What is needed will depend upon the circumstances. The Rules require that a record of the 'gist' be retained. The purpose of such a record is to allow the sufficiency of the court's reasons for its decision subsequently to be assessed. The gravity of such decisions requires that their exercise should be susceptible to scrutiny and to explanation by reference to all of the information that was taken into account.

47A.5   The forms that accompany CrimPR Part 47 provide for the most frequently encountered applications. However, there are some hundreds of powers of entry, search and seizure, supplied by a corresponding number of legislative provisions. In any criminal matter, if there is no form designed for the particular warrant or order sought, the forms should still be used, as far as is practicable, and adapted as necessary. The applicant should pay particular attention to the specific legislative requirements for the granting of such an application to ensure that the court has all of the necessary information, and, if the court might be unfamiliar with the legislation, should provide a copy of the relevant provisions. Applicants must comply with the duties of candour and truthfulness, and include in their application the declarations required by the Rules and must make disclosure of any unfavourable information to the court.

CRIMPR PART 48 CONTEMPT OF COURT

CPD XI Other proceedings 48A: Contempt in the face of the magistrates' court

General

48A.1   The procedure to be followed in cases of contempt of court is given in CrimPR Part 48. The magistrates' courts' power to deal with contempt in the face of the court is contained within section 12 of the Contempt of Court Act 1981. Magistrates' courts also have the power to punish a witness who refuses to be sworn or give evidence under section 97(4) of the Magistrates' Courts Act 1980.

Contempt consisting of wilfully insulting anyone specified in section 12 or interrupting proceedings

48A.2   In the majority of cases, an apology and a promise as to future conduct should be sufficient for the court to order a person's release. However, there are likely to be certain cases where the nature and seriousness of the misconduct requires the court to consider using its powers, under section 12(2) of the Contempt of Court Act 1981, either to fine or to order the person's committal to custody.

Imposing a penalty for contempt

48A.3   The court should allow the person a further opportunity to apologise for his or her contempt, and should follow the procedure at CrimPR 48.8(4). The court should consider whether it is appropriate to release the person or whether it must exercise its powers to fine the person or to commit the person to custody under section 12 (2) of the 1981 Act. In deciding how to deal with the person, the court should have regard to the period for which he or she has been detained, whether the conduct was admitted and the seriousness of the contempt. Any period of committal to custody should be for the shortest period of time commensurate with the interests of preserving good order in the administration of justice.

CRIMPR PART 50 EXTRADITION: MANAGEMENT OF APPEAL TO THE HIGH COURT

CPD XI Other proceedings 50A: Extradition: General matters and case management

General matters: expedition at all times

50A.1   Compliance with these directions is essential to ensure that extradition proceedings are dealt with expeditiously, both in accordance with the spirit of the Council Framework Decision of 13 June 2002 on the European Arrest Warrant and surrender procedures between Member States and the United Kingdom's other treaty obligations. It is of the utmost importance that orders which provide directions for the proper management and progress of cases are obeyed so that the parties can fulfil their duty to assist the court in furthering the overriding objective and in making efficient use of judicial resources. To that end:

(i) the court may, and usually should, give case management directions, which may be based on a model, but adapted to the needs of the individual case, requiring the parties to supply case management information, consistently with the overriding objective of the Criminal Procedure Rules and compatibly with the parties' entitlement to legal professional and litigation privilege;

(ii) a defendant whose extradition is requested must expect to be required to identify what he or she intends to put in issue so that directions can be given to achieve a single, comprehensive and effective extradition hearing at the earliest possible date;

(iii) where the issues are such that further information from the requesting authority or state is needed then it is essential that the request is formulated clearly and in good time, in terms to which the parties can expect to contribute but which terms must be approved by the court, in order that those to whom the request is addressed will be able to understand what is sought, and why, and so can respond promptly;

(iv) where such a request or other document, including a formal notice to the defendant of a post-extradition consent request, requires transmission to an authority or other person in a requesting state or other place outside the UK, it is essential that clear and realistic directions for the transmission are given, identifying who is to be responsible and to what timetable, having regard to the capacity of the proposed courier. Once given, such directions must be promptly complied with and the court at once informed if difficulties are encountered..

General guidance under s 2(7A) Extradition Act 2003 (as amended by the Anti-Social Behaviour, Crime and Policing Act 2014)

50A.2 When proceeding under section 21A of the Act and considering under subsection (3)(a) of the Act the seriousness of the conduct alleged to constitute the extradition offence, the judge will determine the issue on the facts of each case as set out in the warrant, subject to the guidance in paragraph 50A.3 below.

50A.3 In any case where the conduct alleged to constitute the offence falls into one of the categories in the table at paragraph 50A.5 below, unless there are exceptional circumstances, the judge should generally determine that extradition would be disproportionate. It would follow under the terms of s 21A(4)(b) of the Act that the judge must order the person's discharge.

50A.4 The exceptional circumstances referred to above in paragraph 50A.3 will include:

(i) Vulnerable victim
(ii) Crime committed against someone because of their disability, gender-identity, race, religion or belief, or sexual orientation
(iii) Significant premeditation
(iv) Multiple counts
(v) Extradition also sought for another offence
(vi) Previous offending history

50A.5 The table is as follows:

Category of offence	Examples
Minor **theft** – (not robbery/ burglary or theft from the person)	Where the theft is of a low monetary value and **there is a low impact on the victim or indirect harm to others, for example**: (a) Theft of an item of food from a supermarket; (b) Theft of a small amount of scrap metal from company premises; (c) Theft of a very small sum of money.
Minor financial offences (**forgery, fraud** and **tax** offences)	Where the sums involved are small and there is a low impact on the victim and / or low indirect harm to others, for example: (a) Failure to file a tax return or invoices on time; (b) Making a false statement in a tax return; (c) Dishonestly applying for a tax refund; (d) Obtaining a bank loan using a forged or falsified document; (e) Non-payment of child maintenance.
Minor **road traffic, driving** and related offences	Where no injury, loss or damage was incurred to any person or property, for example: (a) Driving whilst using a mobile phone; (b) Use of a bicycle whilst intoxicated

Category of offence	Examples
Minor **public order** offences	Where there is no suggestion the person started the trouble, and the offending behaviour was for example: (a) Non-threatening verbal abuse of a law enforcement officer or government official; (b) Shouting or causing a disturbance, without threats; (c) Quarrelling in the street, without threats.
Minor **criminal damage**, (other than by fire)	For example, breaking a window
Possession of controlled substance (other than one with a high capacity for harm such as heroin, cocaine, LSD or crystal meth)	Where it was possession of a very small quantity and intended for personal use

CPD XI Other proceedings 50B: Management of appeal to the High Court

50B.1 Applications for permission to appeal to the High Court under theExtradition Act 2003 must be started in the Administrative Court of the Queen's Bench Division at the Royal Courts of Justice in London.

50B.2 A Lord Justice of Appeal appointed by the Lord Chief Justice will have responsibility to assist the President of the Queen's Bench Division with overall supervision of extradition appeals.

Definitions

50B.3 Where appropriate "appeal" includes "application for permission to appeal".

50B.4 "EAW" means European Arrest Warrant.

50B.5 A "nominated legal officer of the court" is a court officer assigned to the Administrative Court Office who is a barrister or solicitor and who has been nominated for the purpose by the Lord Chief Justice under CrimPR 50.18 and 50.30.

Forms

50B.6 The forms are to be used in the High Court, in accordance with CrimPR 50.19, 50.20, 50.21 and 50.22.

50B.7 The forms may be amended or withdrawn from time to time, or new forms added, under the authority of the Lord Chief Justice: see CrimPD I 5A.

Management of the Appeal

50B.8 Where it is not possible for the High Court to begin to hear the appeal in accordance with time limits contained in CrimPR 50.23(1) and (2), the Court may extend the time limit if it believes it to be in the interests of justice to do so and may do so even after the time limit has expired.

50B.9 The power to extend those time limits may be exercised by a Lord Justice of Appeal, a Single Judge of the High Court, a Master of the Administrative Court or a nominated legal officer of the court.

50B.10 Case Management directions setting down a timetable may be imposed upon the parties by a Lord Justice of Appeal, a Single Judge of the High Court, a Master of the Administrative Court or a nominated legal officer of the court. For the court's constitution and relevant powers and duties see section 4 of the Senior Courts Act 1981 and CrimPR 50.18 and 50.30.

Listing of Oral, Renewal and Substantive Hearings

50B.11 Arrangements for the fixing of dates for hearings will be made by a Listing Officer of the Administrative Court under the direction of the Judge with overall responsibility for supervision of extradition appeals.

50B.12 A Lord Justice of Appeal, a Single Judge of the High Court, a Master of the Administrative Court or a nominated legal officer of the court may give such directions to the Listing Officer as they deem necessary with regard to the fixing of dates, including as to whether cases in the same/related proceedings or raising the same or similar issues should be heard together or consecutively under the duty imposed by CrimPR 1.1 (2)(e). Parties must alert the nominated Court Officer for the need for such directions.

50B.13 Save in exceptional circumstances, regard will not be given to an advocate's existing commitments.This is in accordance with the spirit of the legislation that extradition matters should be dealt with expeditiously. Extradition matters are generally not so complex that an alternative advocate cannot be instructed.

50B.14 If a party disagrees with the time estimate given by the Court, they must inform the Listing Office within 5 business days of the notification of the listing and they must provide a time estimate of their own.

Expedited appeals

50B.15 The Court may direct that the hearing of an appeal be expedited.

50B.16 The Court will deal with requests for an expedited appeal without a hearing. Requests for expedition must be made in writing, either within the appeal notice, or by application notice, clearly marked with the Administrative Court reference number, which must be lodged with the Administrative Court Office or emailed to the appropriate email address: administrativecourtoffice.crimex@hmcts.x.gsi.gov.uk and notice must be given to the other parties.

50B.17 Any requests for an expedited appeal made to an out of hours Judge must be accompanied by:

(i)   A detailed chronology;
(ii) Reasons why the application could not be made within Court hours;
(iii) Any Orders or Judgments made in the proceedings

Amendment to Notices

50B.18   Amendment to Notice of Appeal requiring permission

(i)   subject to CrimPR 50.20(5), an appeal notice may not be amended without the permission of the court: CrimPR 50.17(6)(b);
(ii) an application for permission to amend made before permission to appeal has been considered will be determined without a hearing;
(iii) an application for permission to amend after permission to appeal has been granted and any submissions in opposition will normally be dealt with at the hearing unless there is any risk that the hearing may have to be adjourned. If there is any risk that the application to amend may lead the other party to seek time to answer the proposed amendment, the application must be made as soon as practicable and well in advance of the hearing. A failure to make immediate applications for such an amendment is likely to result in refusal;
(iv) legal representatives or the appellant, if acting in person, must
    (a) Inform the Court at the time they make the application if the existing time estimate is affected by the proposed amendment; and
    (b) Attempt to agree any revised time estimate no later than 5 business days after service of the application.
(v)   where the appellant wishes to restore grounds of appeal excluded on the grant of permission to appeal, the procedure is governed by CrimPR 50.22.

50B.19   Amendment to Respondent's Notice

(i)   a respondent's notice may not be amended without the permission of the court: CrimPR 50.17(6)(b);
(ii) an application for permission to amend made before permission to appeal has been considered will be determined without a hearing;
(iii) an application for permission to amend after permission to appeal has been granted and any submissions in opposition will normally be dealt with at the hearing unless there is any risk that the hearing may have to be adjourned. If there is any risk that the application to amend may lead the other party to seek time to answer the proposed amendment, the application must be made as soon as practicable and well in advance of the hearing. A failure to make immediate applications for such an amendment is likely to result in refusal;
(iv) legal representatives or the appellant, if acting in person, must
    (a) Inform the Court at the time they make the application if the existing time estimate is affected by the proposed amendment; and
    (b) Attempt to agree any revised time estimate no later than 5 business days after service of the application.

Use of Live-Links

50B.20   When a party acting in person is in custody, the Court office will request the institution to use live-link for attendance at any oral or renewal hearing or substantive appeal. The institution must give precedence to all such applications in the High Court over live-links to the lower courts, including the Crown Court.

Interpreters

50B.21   It is the responsibility of the Court Listing Officer to ensure the attendance of an accredited interpreter when an unrepresented party in extradition proceedings is acting in person and does not understand or speak English.

50B.22   Where a party who does not understand or speak English is legally represented it is the responsibility of his/her solicitors to instruct an interpreter if required for any hearing in extradition proceedings.

Disposing of applications and appeals by way of consent

50B.23   CrimPR 50.24 governs the submission of Consent Orders and lists the essential requirements for such orders. Any Consent Order, the effect of which will be to allow extradition to proceed, must specify the date on which the appeal proceedings are to be treated as discontinued, for the purposes of section 36 or 118, as the case may be, of the Extradition Act 2003: whether that is to be the date on which the order is made or some later date. A Consent Order may be approved by a Lord Justice of Appeal, a Single Judge of the High Court or, under CrimPR 50.30(2), a nominated legal officer of the court. The order may, but need not, be pronounced in open court: CrimPR 50.17(1)(c)(iii). Once approved, the order will be sent to the parties and to any other person as required by CrimPR 50.29(3)(b), (c).

50B.24   A consent order to allow an appeal brought under s 28 of the Extradition Act 2003 must provide –

(i)   for the quashing of the decision of the District Judge in Westminster Magistrates' Court discharging the Requested Person;
(ii) for the matter to be remitted to the District Judge to hold fresh extradition proceedings;
(iii) for any ancillary matter, such as bail or costs.

50B.25   A consent order to allow an appeal brought under s 110 of the Extradition Act 2003 must provide:

(i)   for the quashing of the decision of the Secretary of State for the Home Department not to order extradition;
(ii) for the matter to be remitted to the Secretary of State to make a fresh decision on whether or not to order extradition;
(iii) (iii) for any ancillary matter, such as bail or costs.

50B.26   Where:

(a) a Consent Order is intended to dispose of an application for permission to appeal which has not yet been considered by the court, the order must make clear by what means that will be achieved, bearing in mind that an application for permission which is refused without a hearing can be renewed under CrimPR 50.22(2). If the parties intend to exclude the possibility of renewal the order should declare either (i) that the time limit under rule 50.22(2) is reduced to nil, or (ii) permission to appeal is given and the appeal determined on the other terms of the order.

(b) one of the parties is a child or protected party, the documents served under CrimPR 50.24(5) must include an opinion from the advocate acting on behalf of the child or protected party and, in the case of a protected party, any relevant documents prepared for the Court of Protection.

Fees

50B.27 Applications to extend representation orders do not attract any fee.

50B.28 Fees are payable for all other applications in accordance with the current Fees Order.

CPD XI Other proceedings 50C: Extradition: representation orders

50C.1 Representation Orders may be granted by a Lord Justice of Appeal, a Single Judge of the High Court, a Master of the Administrative Court or a nominated legal officer of the court upon a properly completed CRM14 being lodged with the court. A Representation Order will cover junior advocate and solicitors for the preparation of the Notice of Appeal to determination of the appeal.

50C.2 Applications to extend Representation Orders may be granted by a Lord Justice of Appeal, a Single Judge of the High Court, a Master of the Administrative Court or a nominated court officer who may direct a case management hearing before a Lord Justice of Appeal, a Single Judge, or a Master of the Administrative Court. Since these applications do not attract a fee, parties may lodge them with the court by attaching them to an email addressed to the nominated legal officer of the court.

50C.3 Applications to extend Representation Orders to cover the instruction of Queen's Counsel to appear either alone or with a junior advocate must be made in writing, either by letter or application notice, clearly marked with the Administrative Court reference number, which must be lodged with the Administrative Court Office or emailed to the appropriate email address: administrativecourtoffice.crimex@hmcts.x.gsi.gov.uk.

The request must:

(i) identify the substantial novel or complex issues of law or fact in the case;
(ii) explain why these may only be adequately presented by a Queen's Counsel;
(iii) state whether a Queen's Counsel has been instructed on behalf of the respondent;
(iv) explain any delay in making the request;
(v) be supported by advice from junior advocate or Queen's Counsel

50C.4 Applications for prior authority to cover the cost of obtaining expert evidence must be made in writing, either by letter, clearly marked with the Administrative Court reference number, which must be sent or emailed to the Administrative Court Office.

The request must:

(i) confirm that the evidence sought has not been considered in any previous appeals determined by the appellate courts;
(ii) explain why the evidence was not called at the extradition hearing in Westminster Magistrates' Court and what evidence can be produced to support that;
(iii) explain why the new evidence would have resulted in the District Judge deciding a question at the extradition hearing differently and whether, if so, the District Judge would have been required to make a different order as to discharge of the requested person;
(iv) explain why the evidence was not raised when the case was being considered by the Secretary of State for the Home Department or information was available that was not available at that time;
(v) explain why the new evidence would have resulted in the Secretary of State deciding a question differently, and if the question had been decided differently, the Secretary of State would not have ordered the person's extradition;
(vi) state when the need for the new evidence first became known;
(vii) explain any delay in making the request;
(viii) explain what relevant factual, as opposed to expert evidence, is being given by whom to create the factual basis for the expert's opinion;
(ix) explain why this particular area of expertise is relevant: for example why a child psychologist should be appointed as opposed to a social worker;
(x) state whether the requested person has capacity;
(xi) set out a full breakdown of all costs involved including any VAT or other tax payable, including alternative quotes or explaining why none are available;
(xii) provide a list of all previous extensions of the representation order and the approval of expenditure to date;
(xiii) provide a timetable for the production of the evidence and its anticipated effect on the time estimate and hearing date;
(xiv) set out the level of compliance to date with any directions order.

50C.5 Experts must have direct personal experience of and proven expertise in the issue on which a report is sought; it is only if they do have such experience and it is relevant, that they can give evidence of what they have observed.

50C.6 Where an order is granted to extend a representation order to obtain further evidence it will still be necessary for the party seeking to rely on the new evidence to satisfy the Court hearing the application for permission or the substantive appeal that the evidence obtained should be admitted having regard to sections 27(4) and 29(4) of the Extradition Act 2003 and the judgment in *Szombathely City Court v Fenyvesi* [2009]EWHC 231 (Admin).

50C.7 Applications to extend representation for the translation of documents must be made in writing, either by letter, clearly marked with the Administrative Court reference number, which

must be sent or emailed to the appropriate email address: administrativecourtoffice.crimex@hmcts.x.gsi.gov.uk
The request should:

(i)   explain the importance of the document for which a translation is being sought and the justification for obtaining it.
(ii) explain what it is believed the contents of the document is and the issues it will assist the court to address in hearing the appeal;
(iii) confirm that the evidence sought has not been considered in any previous appeals determined by the appellate courts;
(iv) confirm that the evidence sought was not called at the extradition hearing in the Westminster Magistrates' Court;
(v)   explain why the evidence sought would have resulted in the District Judge deciding a question at the extradition hearing differently and whether, if so, the District Judge would have been required to make a different order as to discharge of the requested person;
(vi) confirm that the new evidence was not raised when the case was being considered by the Secretary of State for the Home Department;
(vii) explain why the new evidence sought would have resulted in the Secretary of State deciding a question differently, and if the question had been decided differently, the Secretary of State would not have ordered the person's extradition;
(viii) confirm when the need for the new evidence first became known;
(ix) explain any delay in making the request;
(x)   explain fully the evidential basis for incurring the expenditure;
(xi) explain why the appellant cannot produce the evidence himself or herself in the form of a statement of truth;
(xii) set out a full breakdown of all costs involved including any VAT or other tax payable and the Legal Aid Agency contractual rates;
(xiii) provide a list of all previous extensions of the representation order and the expenditure to date.

50C.8   Where an order is made to extend representation to cover the cost of the translation of documents it will still be necessary for the party seeking to rely on the documents as evidence to satisfy the Court that it should be admitted at the hearing of the appeal having regard to sections 27(4) and 29(4) of the Extradition Act 2003 and the judgment in *Szombathely City Court v Fenyvesi* [2009] EWHC 231 (Admin).

CPD XI Other proceedings 50D: Extradition: Applications, etc
50D.1   Extension or abridgement of time

(i)   Any party who seeks extension or abridgment of time for the service of documents, evidence or skeleton arguments must apply to the High Court on the appropriate form and pay the appropriate fee;
(ii) Applications for extension or abridgment of time may be determined by a Lord Justice of Appeal, a Single Judge of the High Court, a Master of the Administrative Court or a nominated legal officer of the court.
(iii) Applications for extension of time must include a witness statement setting out the reasons for non-compliance with any previous order and the proposed timetable for compliance.
(iv) Any application made to an out of hours Judge must be accompanied with:
    (a)   A detailed chronology;
    (b)   Reasons why the application could not be made within Court hours;
    (c)   Any Orders or Judgments made in the proceedings

Representatives
50D.2   CrimPR Part 46 applies.
50D.3   Where under CrimPR 46.2(1)(c) a legal representative withdraws from the case then that representative should satisfy him or herself that the defendant is aware of the time and date of the appeal hearing and of the need to attend, by live link if the court has so directed. If the legal representative has any reason to doubt that the defendant is so aware then he or she should promptly notify the Administrative Court Office.

Application to adjourn
50D.4   Where a hearing date has been fixed, any application to vacate the hearing must be made on the appropriate form. A fee is required for the application if it is made within 14 days of the hearing date. The application must:

(i)   explain the reasons why an application is being made to vacate the hearing;
(ii) detail the views of the other parties to the appeal;
(iii) include a draft order with the application notice.

50D.5   If the parties both seek an adjournment then the application must be submitted for consideration by a Lord Justice of Appeal, a single Judge of the High Court or a Master of the Administrative Court. Exceptional circumstances must be shown if a date for the hearing has been fixed or the adjournment will result in material delay to the determination of the appeal.
50D.6   An application to adjourn following a compromise agreement must be supported by evidence justifying exceptional circumstances and why it is in compliance with the overriding objective.

Variation of directions
50D.7   Where parties are unable to comply with any order of the court they must apply promptly to vary directions before deadlines for compliance have expired and seek further directions. An application to vary directions attracts a fee and the application notice, to be submitted on the appropriate form, must:

(i)   provide full and proper explanations for why the current and existing directions have not been complied with;

(ii) detail the views of the other parties to the appeal;
(iii) include a draft order setting out in full the timetable and directions as varied i.e. a superseding order which stands alone.

50D.8 A failure to make the application prior to the expiry of the date specified in the Order will generally result in the refusal of the application unless good reasons are shown.

Application to certify a point of law of general public importance

50D.9 Where an application is made under CrimPR 50.25(2)(b) the application must be made on the appropriate form accompanied by the relevant fee.

50D.10 Any response to the application must be made within 10 business days.

50D.11 Where an application to certify is granted but permission to appeal to the Supreme Court is refused, it shall be for those representing the Requested Person to apply for an extension of the Representation Order to cover proceedings in the Supreme Court, if so advised.

50D.12 The representation order may be extended by a Lord Justice of Appeal, a Single Judge of the High Court, a Master of the Administrative Court or a nominated legal officer of the court.

50D.13 The result of the application to certify a point of law of general public importance and permission to appeal to the Supreme Court may be notified in advance to the legal representatives but legal representatives must not communicate it to the Requested Person until 1 hour before the pronouncement is made in open court.

50D.14 There shall be no public announcement of the result until after it has been formally pronounced.

Application to reopen the determination of an appeal

50D.15 An application under CrimPR 50.27 to reopen an appeal must be referred to the court that determined the appeal, but may if circumstances require be considered by a Judge or Judges other than those who determined the original appeal.

Application to extend required period for removal pursuant to section 36 of the Extradition Act 2003

50D.16 Were an application is made for an extension of the required period within which to extradite a Requested Person it must be accompanied by:

(i) a witness statement explaining why it is not possible to remove the Requested Person within the required period and the proposed timetable for removal;
(ii) a draft order

50D.17 The application to extend time may be made before or after the expiry of the required period for extradition, but the court will scrutinise with particular care an application made after its expiry.

50D.18 Where extensions of time are sought for the same reason in respect of a number of Requested Persons who are due to be extradited at the same time, a single application may be made to the Court listing each of the Requested Persons for whom an extension is sought.

50D.19 The application may be determined by a Lord Justice of Appeal, a Single Judge of the High Court, a Master of the Administrative Court or a nominated legal officer of the court and a single order listing those persons may be granted.

Application for directions ancillary to a discharge pursuant to section 42 or 124 of the Extradition Act 2003

50D.20 Where the High Court is informed that the warrant or extradition request has been withdrawn then unless ancillary matters are dealt with by Consent Order an application notice must be issued seeking any such directions. The notice of discharge of a Requested Person must be accompanied by:

(i) the notification by the requesting state that the EAW has been withdrawn together with a translation of the same
(ii) a witness statement containing:
    (a) details of whether the withdrawn EAW is the only EAW outstanding in respect of the Requested Person;
    (b) details of other EAWs outstanding in respect of the Requested Person and the stage which the proceedings have reached;
    (c) whether only part of the EAW has been withdrawn;
    (d) details of any bail conditions
    (e) details of any institution in which the Requested Person is being detained, the Requested Person's prison number and date of birth.

50D.21 The decision to discharge may be made by a Lord Justice of Appeal, a Single Judge of the High Court, a Master of the Administrative Court or a nominated legal officer of the court.

50D.22 It is the responsibility of the High Court to serve the approved order on the appropriate institution and Westminster Magistrates' Court.

CPD XI Other proceedings 50E: Extradition: Court papers

Skeleton arguments

50E.1 The Court on granting permission to appeal or directing an oral hearing for permission to appeal will give directions as to the filing of skeleton arguments. Strict compliance is required with all time limits.

50E.2 A skeleton argument must:

(i) not normally exceed 25 pages (excluding front sheets and back sheets) and be concise;
(ii) be printed on A4 paper in not less than 12 point font and 1.5 line spacing;
(iii) define the issues in the appeal;
(iv) be set out in numbered paragraphs;
(v) be cross-referenced to any relevant document in the bundle;

(vi) be self-contained and not incorporate by reference material from previous skeleton arguments;

(vii) not include extensive quotations from documents or authorities.

50E.3 Where it is necessary to refer to an authority, the skeleton argument must:

(i) state the proposition of law the authority demonstrates; and

(ii) identify but not quote the parts of the authority that support the proposition.

50E.4 If more than one authority is cited in support of a given proposition, the skeleton argument must briefly state why.

50E.5 A chronology of relevant events will be necessary in most appeals.

50E.6 Where a skeleton argument has been prepared in respect of an application for permission to appeal, the same skeleton argument may be relied upon in the appeal upon notice being given to the Court or a replacement skeleton may be lodged not less than 10 business days before the hearing of the appeal.

50E.7 At the hearing the Court may refuse to hear argument on a point not included in a skeleton argument filed within the prescribed time.

Bundles

50E.8 The bundle for the hearing should be agreed by the parties save where the Requested Person is acting in person. In those circumstances the Court expects the Requesting State to prepare the bundle.

50E.9 The bundle must be paginated and indexed.

50E.10 Subject to any order made by the Court, the following documents must be included in the appeal bundle:

(i) a copy of the appellant's notice;

(ii) a copy of any respondent's notice;

(iii) a copy of any appellant's or respondent's skeleton argument;

(iv) a copy of the order under appeal;

(v) a copy of any order made by the Court in the exercise of its case management powers;

(vi) any judgment of the Court made in a previous appeal involving the party or parties which is relevant to the present proceedings.

(vii) where the bundle of papers reaches more than 200 pages, the parties should agree a core appeal bundle which must contain (i)-(vi) above.

50E.11 The Bundle should only contain relevant documents and must not include duplicate documents.

50E.12 Bundles lodged with the Court will not be returned to the parties but will be destroyed in the confidential waste system at the conclusion of the proceedings and without further notification.

CPD XI Other proceedings 50F: Extradition: Consequences of non compliance with directions

50F.1 Failure to comply with these directions will lead to applications for permission and appeals being dealt with on the material available to the Court at the time when the decision is made.

50F.2 Judges dealing with extradition appeals will seek full and proper explanations for any breaches of the rules and the provisions of this Practice Direction.

50F.3 If no good explanation can be given immediately by counsel or solicitors, the senior partner or the departmental head responsible is likely to be called to court to explain any failure to comply with a court order. Where counsel or solicitors fail to obey orders of the Court and are unable to provide proper and sufficient reasons for their disobedience they may anticipate the matter being formally referred to the President of the Queen's Bench Division with a recommendation that the counsel or solicitors involved be reported to their professional bodies.

50F.4 The court may also refuse to admit any material or any evidence not filed in compliance with the order for Directions or outside a time limit specified by the court

50F.5 A failure to comply with the time limits or other requirements for skeleton arguments will have the consequences specified in 50E.7.

CRIMINAL PRACTICE DIRECTIONS 2015 DIVISION XII
General application

CPD XII GENERAL APPLICATION A: COURT DRESS

A.1 In magistrates' courts, advocates appear without robes or wigs. In all other courts, Queen's Counsel wear a short wig and a silk (or stuff) gown over a court coat with bands, junior counsel wear a short wig and stuff gown with bands. Solicitors and other advocates authorised under the Courts and Legal Services Act 1990 wear a black solicitor's gown with bands; they may wear short wigs in circumstances where they would be worn by Queen's Counsel or junior counsel.

A.2 High Court Judges hearing criminal cases may wear the winter criminal robe year-round. However, scarlet summer robes may be worn.

CPD XII GENERAL APPLICATION B: MODES OF ADDRESS AND TITLES OF JUDGES AND MAGISTRATES

Modes of Address

B.1 The following judges, when sitting in court, should be addressed as 'My Lord' or 'My Lady', as the case may be, whatever their personal status:

(a) Judges of the Court of Appeal and of the High Court;

(b) any Circuit Judge sitting as a judge of the Court of Appeal (Criminal Division) or the High Court under section 9(1) of the Senior Courts Act 1981;

(c) any judge sitting at the Central Criminal Court;

(d) any Senior Circuit Judge who is an Honorary Recorder.

B.2 Subject to the paragraph above, Circuit Judges, qualifying judge advocates, Recorders and Deputy Circuit Judges should be addressed as 'Your Honour' when sitting in court.

District Judges (Magistrates' Courts) should be addressed as "Sir [or Madam]" or "Judge" when sitting in Court.

Magistrates in court should be addressed through the Chairperson as "Sir[or Madam]" or collectively as "Your Worships".

Description

B.3 In cause lists, forms and orders members of the judiciary should be described as follows:

(a) Circuit Judges, as 'His [or Her] Honour Judge A'.
(b) When the judge is sitting as a judge of the High Court under section 9(1) of the Senior Courts Act 1981, the words 'sitting as a judge of the High Court' should be added;
(c) Recorders, as 'Mr [or Mrs, Ms or Miss] Recorder B'.
(d) This style is appropriate irrespective of any honour or title which the recorder might possess, but if in any case it is desired to include an honour or title, the alternative description, 'Sir CD, Recorder' or 'The Lord D, Recorder' may be used;
(e) Deputy Circuit Judges, as 'His [or Her] Honour EF, sitting as a Deputy Circuit Judge'.
(f) qualifying judges advocates, as 'His [or Her] Honour GH, sitting as a qualifying judge advocate.'
(g) District Judges (Magistrates' Courts), as "District Judge (Magistrates' Courts) J"

CPD XII General application C: Availability of judgments given in the Court of Appeal and the High Court

Not reproduced

CPD XII General Application D: Citation of authority and provision of copies of judgments to the court

D.1 This Practice Direction applies to all criminal matters before the Court of Appeal (Criminal Division), the Crown Court and the magistrates' courts. In relation to those matters only, Practice Direction (Citation of Authorities) [2012] 1 WLR 780 is hereby revoked.

Citation of authority

D.2 In *R v Erskine; R v Williams* [2009] EWCA Crim 1425, [2010] 1 W.L.R. 183, (2009) 2 Cr. App. R. 29 the Lord Chief Justice stated:

75. The essential starting point, relevant to any appeal against conviction or sentence, is that, adapting the well known aphorism of Viscount Falkland in 1641: if it is not *necessary* to refer to a previous decision of the court, it is *necessary* not to refer to it. Similarly, if it is not *necessary* to include a previous decision in the bundle of authorities, it is *necessary* to exclude it. That approach will be rigidly enforced.

76. It follows that when the advocate is considering what authority, if any, to cite for a proposition, only an authority which establishes the principle should be cited. Reference should not be made to authorities which do no more than either (a) illustrate the principle or (b) restate it.

78. Advocates must expect to be required to justify the citation of each authority relied on or included in the bundle. The court is most unlikely to be prepared to look at an authority which does no more than illustrate or restate an established proposition.

80. . . . In particular, in sentencing appeals, where a definitive Sentencing Guidelines Council guideline is available there will rarely be any advantage in citing an authority reached before the issue of the guideline, and authorities after its issue which do not refer to it will rarely be of assistance. In any event, where the authority does no more than uphold a sentence imposed at the Crown Court, the advocate must be ready to explain how it can assist the court to decide that a sentence is manifestly excessive or wrong in principle.

D.3 Advocates should only cite cases when it is necessary to do so; when the case identifies or represents a principle or the development of a principle. In sentencing appeals, other cases are rarely helpful, providing only an illustration, and this is especially true if there is a sentencing guideline. Unreported cases should only be cited in exceptional circumstances, and the advocate must expect to explain why such a case has been cited.

D.4 Advocates should not assume that because a case cited to the court is not referred to in the judgment the court has not considered it; it is more likely that the court was not assisted by it.

D.5 When an authority is to be cited, whether in written or oral submissions, the advocate should always provide the neutral citation followed by the law report reference.

D.6 The following practice should be followed:

(i) Where a judgment is reported in the Official Law Reports (A.C., Q.B., Ch., Fam.) published by the Incorporated Council of Law Reporting for England and Wales or the Criminal Appeal Reports or the Criminal Appeal Reports (Sentencing) one of those two series of reports must be cited; either is equally acceptable. However, where a judgment is reported in the Criminal Appeal Reports or the Criminal Appeal Reports (Sentencing) that reference must be given in addition to any other reference. Other series of reports and official transcripts of judgment may only be used when a case is not reported, or not yet reported, in the Official Law Reports or the Criminal Appeal Reports or the Criminal Appeal Reports (Sentencing).

(ii) If a judgment is not reported in the Official Law Reports, the Criminal Appeal Reports or the Criminal Appeal Reports (Sentencing), but it is reported in an authoritative series of reports which contains a headnote and is made by individuals holding a Senior Courts qualification (for the purposes of section 115 of the Courts and Legal Services Act 1990), that report should be cited.

(iii) Where a judgment is not reported in any of the reports referred to above, but is reported in other reports, they may be cited.

(iv) Where a judgment has not been reported, reference may be made to the official transcript if that is available, not the handed-down text of the judgment, as this may have been subject to late revision after the text was handed down. Official transcripts may be obtained from, for instance, BAILLI (http://www.bailii.org/).

D.7 In the majority of cases, it is expected that all references will be to the Official Law Reports and the Criminal Appeal Reports or the Criminal Appeal Reports (Sentencing); it will be rare for there to be a need to refer to any other reports. An unreported case should not be cited unless it contains a relevant statement of legal principle not found in reported authority, and it is expected that this will only occur in exceptional circumstances.

Provision of copies of judgments to the Court

D.8 The paragraphs below specify whether or not copies should be provided to the court. Authorities should not be included for propositions not in dispute. If more than one authority is to be provided, the copies should be presented in paginated and tagged bundles.

D.9 If required, copies of judgments should be provided either by way of a photocopy of the published report or by way of a copy of a reproduction of the judgment in electronic form that has been authorised by the publisher of the relevant series, but in any event-

(i) the report must be presented to the court in an easily legible form (a 12-point font is preferred but a 10 or 11-point font is acceptable), and

(ii) the advocate presenting the report must be satisfied that it has not been reproduced in a garbled form from the data source.

In any case of doubt the court will rely on the printed text of the report (unless the editor of the report has certified that an electronic version is more accurate because it corrects an error contained in an earlier printed text of the report).

D.10 If such a copy is unavailable, a printed transcript such as from BAILLI may be included.

Provision of copies to the Court of Appeal (Criminal Division)

D.11 Advocates must provide to the Registrar of Criminal Appeals, with their appeal notice, respondent's notice or skeleton argument, a list of authorities upon which they wish to rely in their written or oral submissions. The list of authorities should contain the name of the applicant, appellant or respondent and the Criminal Appeal Office number where known. The list should include reference to the relevant paragraph numbers in each authority. An updated list can be provided if a new authority is issued, or in response to a respondent's notice or skeleton argument. From time to time, the Registrar may issue guidance as to the style or content of lists of authorities, including a suggested format; this guidance should be followed by all parties. The latest guidance is available from the Criminal Appeal Office.

D.12 If the case cited is reported in the Official Law Reports, the Criminal Appeal Reports or the Criminal Appeal Reports (Sentencing), the law report reference must be given after the neutral citation, and the relevant paragraphs listed, but copies should not be provided to the court.

D.13 If, exceptionally, reference is made to a case that is not reported in the Official Law Reports, the Criminal Appeal Reports or the Criminal Appeal Reports (Sentencing), three copies must be provided to the Registrar with the list of authorities and the relevant appeal notice or respondent's notice (or skeleton argument, if provided). The relevant passages of the authorities should be marked or sidelined.

Provision of copies to the Crown Court and the magistrates' courts

D.14 When the court is considering routine applications, it may be sufficient for the court to be referred to the applicable legislation or to one of the practitioner texts. However, it is the responsibility of the advocate to ensure that the court is provided with the material that it needs properly to consider any matter.

D.15 If it would assist the court to consider any authority, the directions at paragraphs D.2 to D.7 above relating to citation will apply and a list of authorities should be provided.

D.16 Copies should be provided by the party seeking to rely upon the authority in accordance with CrimPR 24.13. This Rule is applicable in the magistrates' courts, and in relation to the provision of authorities, should also be followed in the Crown Court since courts often do not hold library stock (see CrimPR 25.17). Advocates should comply with paragraphs D.8 to D.10 relating to the provision of copies to the court.

D.17 The court may give directions for the preparation of skeleton arguments. Such directions will provide for the time within which skeleton arguments must be served and for the issues which they must address. Such directions may provide for the number of pages, or the number of words, to which a skeleton argument is to be confined. Any such directions displace the following to the extent of any inconsistency. Subject to that, however, a skeleton argument must:

(i) not normally exceed 15 pages (excluding front sheets and back sheets) and be concise;

(ii) be presented in A4 page size and portrait orientation, in not less than 12 point font and in 1.5 line spacing;

(iii) define the issues;

(iv) be set out in numbered paragraphs;

(v) be cross-referenced to any relevant document in any bundle prepared for the court;

(vi) be self-contained and not incorporate by reference material from previous skeleton arguments;

(vii) not include extensive quotations from documents or authorities.

D.18 Where it is necessary to refer to an authority, the skeleton argument must:

(i) state the proposition of law the authority demonstrates; and

(ii) identify but not quote the parts of the authority that support the proposition.

D.19 If more than one authority is cited in support of a given proposition, the skeleton argument must briefly state why.

D.20 A chronology of relevant events will be necessary in most cases.

D.21 There are directions at paragraphs I 3C.3 and 3C.4 of these Practice Directions that apply to the service of skeleton arguments in support of, and in opposition to, an application to stay an indictment on the grounds of abuse of process; and directions at paragraphs IX 39F.I to 39F.3 that apply to the service of skeleton arguments in the Court of Appeal. Where a skeleton argument has been prepared in respect of an application for permission to appeal, the same skeleton argument may be relied upon in the appeal upon notice being given to the court, or a replacement skeleton may be served to the timetable set out in those paragraphs.

D.22 At the hearing the court may refuse to hear argument on a point not included in a skeleton argument served within the prescribed time.

D.23 In *R v James, R v Selby* [2016] EWCA Crim 1639; [2017] Crim.L.R. 228 the Court of Appeal observed (at paragraphs 52 to 54):

"Legal documents of unnecessary and too often of excessive length offer very little assistance to the court. In *Tombstone Ltd v Raja* [2008] EWCA Civ 1441, [2009] 1 WLR 1143 Mummery LJ said:

"Practitioners ... are well advised to note the risk of the court's negative reaction to unnecessarily long written submissions. The skeleton argument procedure was introduced to assist the court, as well as the parties, by improving preparations for, and the efficiency of, adversarial oral hearings, which remain central to this court's public role... An unintended and unfortunate side effect of the growth in written advocacy ... has been that too many practitioners, at increased cost to their clients and diminishing assistance to the court, burden their opponents and the court with written briefs."

He might have penned those remarks had he been sitting in these two cases, and many more, in this Division.

In *Standard Bank PLC v Via Mat International* [2013] EWCA Civ 490, [2013] 2 All ER (Comm) 1222 the excessive length of court documents prompted:

"It is important that both practitioners and their clients understand that skeleton arguments are not intended to serve as vehicles for extended advocacy and that in general a short, concise skeleton is both more helpful to the court and more likely to be persuasive than a longer document which seeks to develop every point which the advocate would wish to make in oral argument."

No area of law is exempt from the requirement to produce careful and concise documents: *Tchenquiz v Director of the Serious Fraud Office* [2014] EWCA Civ 1333, [2015] 1 WLR 838, paragraph 10,"

CPD XII GENERAL APPLICATION E: PREPARATION OF JUDGMENTS: NEUTRAL CITATION

E.1 Since 11 January 2001 every judgment of the Court of Appeal, and of the Administrative Court, and since 14 January 2002 every judgment of the High Court, has been prepared and issued as approved with single spacing, paragraph numbering (in the margins) and no page numbers. In courts with more than one judge, the paragraph numbering continues sequentially through each judgment and does not start again at the beginning of each judgment. Indented paragraphs are not numbered. A unique reference number is given to each judgment. For judgments of the Court of Appeal, this number is given by the official shorthand writers, Merrill Legal Solutions (Tel: 020 7421 4000 ext.4036). For judgments of the High Court, it is provided by the Courts Recording and Transcription Unit at the Royal Courts of Justice. Such a number will also be furnished, on request to the Courts Recording and Transcription Unit, Royal Courts of Justice, Strand, London WC2A 2LL (Tel: 020 7947 7820), (e-mail: rcj.cratu@hmcts.gsi.gov.uk) for High Court judgments delivered outside London.

E.2 Each Court of Appeal judgment starts with the year, followed by EW (for England and Wales), then CA (for Court of Appeal), followed by Civ or Crim and finally the sequential number. For example, 'Smith v Jones [2001] EWCA Civ 10'.

E.3 In the High Court, represented by HC, the number comes before the divisional abbreviation and, unlike Court of Appeal judgments, the latter is bracketed: (Ch), (Pat), (QB), (Admin), (Comm), (Admlty), (TCC) or (Fam), as appropriate. For example, '[2002] EWHC 123 (Fam)', or '[2002] EWHC 124 (QB)', or '[2002] EWHC 125 (Ch)'.

E.4 This 'neutral citation', as it is called, is the official number attributed to the judgment and must always be used at least once when the judgment is cited in a later judgment. Once the judgment is reported, this neutral citation appears in front of the familiar citation from the law reports series. Thus: 'Smith v Jones [2001] EWCA Civ 10; [2001] QB 124; [2001] 2 All ER 364', etc.

E.5 Paragraph numbers are referred to in square brackets. When citing a paragraph from a High Court judgment, it is unnecessary to include the descriptive word in brackets: (Admin), (QB), or whatever. When citing a paragraph from a Court of Appeal judgment, however, 'Civ' or 'Crim' is included. If it is desired to cite more than one paragraph of a judgment, each numbered paragraph should be enclosed with a square bracket. Thus paragraph 59 in Green v White [2002] EWHC 124 (QB) would be cited: 'Green v White [2002] EWHC 124 at [59]'; paragraphs 30 – 35 in Smith v Jones would be 'Smith v Jones [2001] EWCA Civ 10 at [30] – [35]'; similarly, where a number of paragraphs are cited: 'Smith v Jones [2001] EWCA Civ 10 at [30], [35] and [40 – 43]'.

E.6 If a judgment is cited more than once in a later judgment, it is helpful if only one abbreviation is used, e.g., 'Smith v Jones' or 'Smith's case', but preferably not both (in the same judgment).

CPD XII General application F: Citation of hansard

F.1   Where any party intends to refer to the reports of Parliamentary proceedings as reported in the Official Reports of either House of Parliament ("Hansard") in support of any such argument as is permitted by the decisions in *Pepper v Hart* [1993] AC 593 and *Pickstone v Freemans PLC* [1989] AC 66, or otherwise, he must, unless the court otherwise directs, serve upon all other parties and the court copies of any such extract, together with a brief summary of the argument intended to be based upon such extract. No other report of Parliamentary proceedings may be cited.

F.2   Unless the court otherwise directs, service of the extract and summary of the argument shall be effected not less than 5 clear working days before the first day of the hearing, whether or not it has a fixed date. Advocates must keep themselves informed as to the state of the lists where no fixed date has been given. Service on the court shall be effected by sending three copies to the Registrar of Criminal Appeals, Royal Courts of Justice, Strand, London, WC2A 2LL or to the court manager of the relevant Crown Court centre, as appropriate. If any party fails to do so, the court may make such order (relating to costs or otherwise) as is, in all the circumstances, appropriate.

Criminal practice directions 2015 division XIII
Listing

CPD XIII Listing A: Judicial responsibility for listing and key principles
Listing as a judicial responsibility and function

A.1   Listing is a judicial responsibility and function. The purpose is to ensure that all cases are brought to a hearing or trial in accordance with the interests of justice, that the resources available for criminal justice are deployed as effectively as possible, and that cases are heard by an appropriate judge or bench with the minimum of delay.

A.2   The agreement reached between the Lord Chief Justice and the Secretary of State for Constitutional Affairs and Lord Chancellor set out in a statement to the House of Lords on 26 January 2004 ('the Concordat'), states that judges, working with HMCTS, are responsible for deciding on the assignment of cases to particular courts and the listing of those cases before particular judges. Therefore:

    (a)   The Presiding Judges of each circuit have the overall responsibility for listing at all courts, Crown and magistrates', on their circuit;

    (b)   Subject to the supervision of the Presiding Judges, the Resident Judge at each Crown Court has the general responsibility within his or her court centre for the allocation of criminal judicial work, to ensure the just and efficient despatch of the business of the court or group of courts. This includes overseeing the deployment of allocated judges at the court or group, including the distribution of work between all the judges allocated to that court. A Resident Judge must appoint a deputy or deputies to exercise his or her functions when he or she is absent from his or her court centre. See also paragraph A.5: Discharge of judicial responsibilities.

    (c)   The listing officer in the Crown Court is responsible for carrying out the day-to-day operation of listing practice under the direction of the Resident Judge. The listing officer at each Crown Court centre has one of the most important functions at that Crown Court and makes a vital contribution to the efficient running of that Crown Court and to the efficient operation of the administration of criminal justice;

    (d)   In the magistrates' courts, the Judicial Business Group, subject to the supervision of the Presiding Judges of the circuit, is responsible for determining the listing practice in that area. The day-to-day operation of that listing practice is the responsibility of the justices' clerk with the assistance of the listing officer.

Key principles of listing

A.3   When setting the listing practice, the Resident Judge or the Judicial Business Group should take into account principles a-j:

    (a)   Ensure the timely trial of cases and resolution of other issues (such as confiscation) so that justice is not delayed. The following factors are relevant:
        (i)   In general, each case should be tried within as short a time of its arrival in the court as is consistent with the interests of justice, the needs of victims and witnesses, and with the proper and timely preparation by the prosecution and defence of their cases in accordance with the directions and timetable set;
        (ii)   Priority should be accorded to the trial of young defendants, and cases where there are vulnerable or young witnesses. In *R v Barker* [2010] EWCA Crim 4, the Lord Chief Justice highlighted "the importance to the trial and investigative process of keeping any delay in a case involving a child complainant to an irreducible minimum";
        (iii)   Custody time limits (CTLs) should be observed, see CPD XIII Listing F;
        (iv)   Every effort must be made to avoid delay in cases in which the defendant is on bail;

    (b)   Ensure that in the magistrates' court unless impracticable, non-custody anticipated guilty plea cases are listed 14 days after charge, and non-custody anticipated not guilty pleas are listed 28 days after charge;

    (c)   Provide, when possible, for certainty and/or as much advance notice as possible, of the trial date; and take all reasonable steps to ensure that the trial date remains fixed;

    (d)   Ensure that a judge or bench with any necessary authorisation and of appropriate experience is available to try each case and, wherever desirable and practicable, there is judicial continuity, including in relation to post-trial hearings;

    (e)   Strike an appropriate balance in the use of resources, by taking account of:
        (i)   The efficient deployment of the judiciary in the Crown Court and the magistrates' courts taking into account relevant sitting requirements for magistrates. See CPD XIII Annex 1 for information to support judicial deployment in the magistrates' courts;
        (ii)   The proper use of the courtrooms available at the court;

(iii) The provision in long and/or complex cases for adequate reading time for the judiciary;
(iv) The facilities in the available courtrooms, including the security needs (such as a secure dock), size and equipment, such as video and live link facilities;
(v) The proper use of those who attend the Crown Court as jurors;
(vi) The availability of legal advisers in the magistrates' courts;
(vii) The need to return those sentenced to custody as soon as possible after the sentence is passed, and to facilitate the efficient operation of the prison escort contract;
(f) Provide where practicable:
   (i) the defendant and the prosecution with the advocate of their choice where this does not result in any delay to the trial of the case; and,
   (ii) for the efficient deployment of advocates, lawyers and associate prosecutors of the Crown Prosecution Service, and other prosecuting authorities, and of the resources available to the independent legal profession, for example by trying to group certain cases together;
(g) Meet the need for special security measures for category A and other high-risk defendants;
(h) Ensure that proper time (including judicial reading time) is afforded to hearings in which the court is exercising powers that impact on the rights of individuals, such as applications for investigative orders or warrants;
(i) Consider the significance of ancillary proceedings, such as confiscation hearings, and the need to deal with such hearings promptly and, where possible, for such hearings to be conducted by the trial judge;
(j) Provide for government initiatives or projects approved by the Lord Chief Justice.

A.4 Although the listing practice at each Crown Court centre and magistrates' court will take these principles into account, the listing practice adopted will vary from court to court depending particularly on the number of courtrooms and the facilities available, the location and the workload, its volume and type.

Discharge of judicial responsibilities

A.5 The Resident Judge of each court is responsible for:

(i) ensuring that good practice is implemented throughout the court, such that all hearings commence on time;
(ii) ensuring that the causes of trials that do not proceed on the date originally fixed are examined to see if there is any systemic issue;
(iii) monitoring the general performance of the court and the listing practices;
(iv) monitoring the timeliness of cases and reporting any cases of serious concern to the Presiding Judge;
(v) maintaining and reviewing annually a list of Recorders, qualifying judge advocates and Deputy Circuit Judges authorised to hear appeals from the magistrates' courts unless such a list is maintained by the Presiding Judge.

A.6 The Judicial Business Group for each clerkship subject to the overall jurisdiction of the Presiding Judge is responsible for:

(i) monitoring the workload and anticipated changes which may impact on listing policies;
(ii) ensuring that any listing practice meets the needs of the system as a whole.

CPD XIII Listing B: Classification

B.1 The classification structure outlined below is solely for the purposes of trial in the Crown Court. The structure has been devised to accommodate practical administrative functions and is not intended to reflect a hierarchy of the offences therein.
Offences are classified as follows:
Class 1: A:

(i) Murder;
(ii) Attempted Murder;
(iii) Manslaughter;
(iv) Infanticide;
(v) Child destruction (section 1(1) of the Infant Life (Preservation) Act 1929;
(vi) Abortion (section 58 of the Offences Against the Person Act 1861);
(vii) Assisting a suicide;
(viii) Cases including section 5 of the Domestic Violence, Crime and Victims Act 2004, as amended (if a fatality has resulted);
(ix) Soliciting, inciting, encouraging or assisting, attempting or conspiring to commit any of the above offences or assisting an offender having committed such an offence.

Class 1: B:

(i) Genocide;
(ii) Torture, hostage-taking and offences under the War Crimes Act 1991;
(iii) Offences under ss.51 and 52 International Criminal Courts Act 2001;
(iv) An offence under section 1 of the Geneva Conventions Act 1957;
(v) Terrorism offences (where offence charged is indictable only and took place during an act of terrorism or for the purposes of terrorism as defined in s.1 of the Terrorism Act 2000);
(vi) Piracy, under the Merchant Shipping and Maritime Security Act 1997;
(vii) Treason;
(viii) An offence under the Official Secrets Acts;
(ix) Incitement to disaffection;
(x) Soliciting, inciting, encouraging or assisting, attempting or conspiring to commit any of the above offences or assisting an offender having committed such an offence.

Class 1: C:

(i) Prison mutiny, under the Prison Security Act 1992;

(ii) Riot in the course of serious civil disturbance;

(iii) Serious gang related crime resulting in the possession or discharge of firearms, particularly including a campaign of firebombing or extortion, especially when accompanied by allegations of drug trafficking on a commercial scale;

(iv) Complex sexual offence cases in which there are many complainants (often under age, in care or otherwise particularly vulnerable) and/or many defendants who are alleged to have systematically groomed and abused them, often over a long period of time;

(v) Cases involving people trafficking for sexual, labour or other exploitation and cases of human servitude;

(vi) Soliciting, inciting, encouraging or assisting, attempting or conspiring to commit any of the above offences or assisting an offender having committed such an offence.

Class 1: D:

(i) Causing death by dangerous driving;

(ii) Causing death by careless driving;

(iii) Causing death by unlicensed, disqualified or uninsured driving;

(iv) Any Health and Safety case resulting in a fatality or permanent serious disability;

(v) Any other case resulting in a fatality or permanent serious disability;

(vi) Soliciting, inciting, encouraging or assisting, attempting or conspiring to commit any of the above offences or assisting an offender having committed such an offence.

Class 2: A

(i) Arson with intent to endanger life or reckless as to whether life was endangered;

(ii) Cases in which explosives, firearms or imitation firearms are used or carried or possessed;

(iii) Kidnapping or false imprisonment (without intention to commit a sexual offence but charged on the same indictment as a serious offence of violence such as under section 18 or section 20 of the Offences Against the Person Act 1861);

(iv) Cases in which the defendant is a police officer, member of the legal profession or a high profile or public figure;

(v) Cases in which the complainant or an important witness is a high profile or public figure;

(vi) Riot otherwise than in the course of serious civil disturbance;

(vii) Child cruelty;

(viii) Cases including section 5 of the Domestic Violence, Crime and Victims Act 2004, as amended (if no fatality has resulted);

(ix) Soliciting, inciting, encouraging or assisting, attempting or conspiring to commit any of the above offences or assisting an offender having committed such an offence.

Class 2: B

(i) Any sexual offence, with the exception of those included in Class 1C;

(ii) Kidnapping or false imprisonment (with intention to commit a sexual offence or charged on the same indictment as a sexual offence);

(iii) Soliciting, inciting, encouraging or assisting, attempting or conspiring to commit any of the above offences or assisting an offender having committed such an offence.

Class 2: C:

(i) Serious, complex fraud;

(ii) Serious and/or complex money laundering;

(iii) Serious and/or complex bribery;

(iv) Corruption;

(v) Complex cases in which the defendant is a corporation (including cases for sentence as well as for trial);

(vi) Any case in which the defendant is a corporation with a turnover in excess of £1bn (including cases for sentence as well as for trial);

(vii) Soliciting, inciting, encouraging or assisting, attempting or conspiring to commit any of the above offences or assisting an offender having committed such an offence.

Class 3: All other offences not listed in the classes above.

Deferred Prosecution Agreements

B.2 Cases coming before the court under section 45 and Schedule 17 of the Crime and Courts Act 2013 must be referred to the President of the Queen's Bench Division who will allocate the matter to a judge from a list of judges approved by the Lord Chief Justice. Only the allocated judge may thereafter hear any matter or make any decision in relation to that case.

Criminal Cases Review Commission

B.3 Where the CCRC refers a case upon conviction from the magistrates' courts to the Crown Court, this shall be dealt with at a Crown Court centre designated by the Senior Presiding Judge.

CPD XIII LISTING C: REFERRAL OF CASES IN THE CROWN COURT TO THE RESIDENT JUDGE AND TO THE PRESIDING JUDGES

C.1 This Practice Direction specifies:

(a) cases which must be referred to a Presiding Judge for release; and

(b) cases which must be referred to the Resident Judge before being assigned to a judge, Recorder or qualifying judge advocate to hear.

It is applicable to all Crown Courts, but its application may be modified by the Senior Presiding Judge or the Presiding Judges, with the approval of the Senior Presiding Judge, through the provision of further specific guidance to Resident Judges in relation to the allocation and management of the work at their court.

C.2 This Practice Direction does not prescribe the way in which the Resident Judge gives directions as to listing policy to the listing officer; its purpose is to ensure that there is appropriate judicial control over the listing of cases. However, the Resident Judge must arrange with the listing officers a satisfactory means of ensuring that all cases listed at their court are listed before judges, Recorders or qualifying judge advocates of suitable seniority and experience, subject to the requirements of this Practice Direction. The Resident Judge should ensure that listing officers are made aware of the contents and importance of this Practice Direction, and that listing officers develop satisfactory procedures for referral of cases to him or her.

C.3   In order to assist the Resident Judge and the listing officer, all cases sent to the Crown Court should where possible include a brief case summary prepared by the prosecution. The prosecutor should ensure that any factors that make the case complex, or would lead it to be referred to the Resident Judge or a Presiding Judge are highlighted. The defence may also send submissions to the court, again highlighting any areas of complexity or any other factors that might assist in the case being allocated to an appropriate judge.

Cases in the Crown Court to be referred to the Resident Judge

C.4   All cases in Class 1A, 1B, 1C, 1D, 2A and 2C must be referred to the Resident Judge as must any case which appears to raise particularly complex, sensitive or serious issues.

C.5   Resident Judges should give guidance to the judges and staff of their respective courts as to which Class 2B cases should be referred to them following consultation with the Senior Presiding Judge. This will include any cases that may be referred to the Presiding Judge, see below. Class 2B cases to be referred to the Resident Judge are likely to be identified by the list officer, or by the judge at the first hearing in the Crown Court.

C.6   Once a case has been referred to the Resident Judge, the Resident Judge should refer the case to the Presiding Judge, following the guidance below, or allocate the case to an appropriate category of judge, and if possible to a named judge.

Cases in the Crown Court to be referred to a Presiding Judge

C.7   All cases in Class 1A, 1B and 1C must be referred by the Resident Judge to a Presiding Judge, as must a case in any class which is:

(i)   An usually grave or complex case or one in which a novel and important point of law is to be raised;
(ii)   A case where it is alleged that the defendant caused more than one fatality;
(iii) A non-fatal case of baby shaking where serious injury resulted;
(iv)   A case where the defendant is a police officer, or a member of the legal profession or a high profile figure;
(v)   A case which for any reason is likely to attract exceptional media attention;
(vi)   A case where a large organisation or corporation may, if convicted, be ordered to pay a very large fine;
(vii) Any case likely to last more than three months.

C.8   Resident Judges are encouraged to refer any other case if they think it is appropriate to do so.

C.9   Presiding Judges and Resident Judges should agree a system for the referral of cases to the Presiding Judge, ideally by electronic means. The system agreed should include provision for the Resident Judge to provide the Presiding Judge with a brief summary of the case, a clear recommendation by the Resident Judge about the judges available to try the case and any other comments. A written record of the decision and brief reasons for it must be made and retained.

C.10   Once a case has been referred to the Presiding Judge, the Presiding Judge may retain the case for trial by a High Court Judge, or release the case back to the Resident Judge, either for trial by a named judge, or for trial by an identified category of judges, to be allocated by the Resident Judge.

CPD XIII Listing D: Authorisation of judges

D.1   Judges must be authorised by the Lord Chief Justice before they may hear certain types of case.

D.2   Judges (other than High Court Judges) to hear Class 1A cases must be authorised to hear such cases. Any judge previously granted a 'Class 1' or 'murder' authorisation is authorised to hear Class 1A cases. Judges previously granted an 'attempted murder' (including soliciting, incitement or conspiracy thereof) authorisation can only deal with these cases within Class 1A.

D.3   Judges (other than High Court Judges) to hear sexual offences cases in Class 1C or any case within Class 2B must be authorised to hear such cases. Any judge previously granted a 'Class 2' or 'serious sex offences' authorisation is authorised to hear sexual offences cases in Class 1C or 2B. It is a condition of the authorisation that it does not take effect until the judge has attended the relevant Judicial College course; the Resident Judge should check in the case of newly authorised judges that they have attended the course. Judges who have been previously authorised to try such cases should make every effort to ensure their training is up-to-date and maintained by attending the Serious Sexual Offences Seminar at least once every three years. See CPD XIII Annex 2 for guidance in dealing with sexual offences in the youth court.

D.4   **Cases in the magistrates' courts involving the imposition of very large fines**

(i)   Where a defendant appears before a magistrates' court for an either way offence, to which CPD XIII Annex 3 applies the case must be dealt with by a DJ (MC) who has been authorised to deal with such cases by the Chief Magistrate.
(ii)   The authorised DJ (MC) must first consider whether such cases should be allocated to the Crown Court or, where the defendant pleads guilty, committed for sentence under s.3 Powers of Courts (Sentence) Act 2000, and must do so when the DJ (MC) considers the offence or combination of offences so serious that the Crown Court should deal with the defendant had they been convicted on indictment.
(iii) If an authorised DJ (MC) decides not to commit such a case the reasons must be recorded in writing to be entered onto the court register.

CPD XIII Listing E: Allocation of business within the Crown Court

E.1 Cases in Class 1A may only be tried by:

(i) a High Court Judge, or

(ii) a Circuit Judge or a Deputy High Court Judge authorised to try such cases and provided that the Presiding Judge has released the case for trial by such a judge; or

(iii) a Deputy Circuit Judge to whom the case has been specifically released by the Presiding Judge.

E.2 Cases in Class 1B may only be tried by:

(i) a High Court Judge, or

(ii) a Circuit Judge, or a Deputy High Court Judge, provided that the Presiding Judge has released the case for trial by such a judge.

(iii) a Deputy Circuit Judge to whom the case has been specifically released by the Presiding Judge

E.3 Cases in Class 1C may only be tried by:

(i) a High Court Judge, or

(ii) a Circuit Judge, or a Deputy High Court Judge, or Deputy Circuit Judge, authorised to try such cases (if the case requires the judge to be authorised to hear sexual offences cases), provided that the Presiding Judge has released the case for trial by such a judge, or, if the case is a sexual offence, the Presiding Judge has assigned the case to that named judge.

See also CPD XIII Listing C.10

E.4 Cases in Class 1D and 2A may be tried by:

(i) a High Court Judge, or

(ii) a Circuit Judge, or Deputy High Court Judge, or Deputy Circuit Judge, or a Recorder or a qualifying judge advocate, provided that either the Presiding Judge has released the case or the Resident Judge has allocated the case for trial by such a judge; with the exception that Class 2A i) cases may not be tried by a Recorder or qualifying judge advocate.

E.5 Cases in Class 2B may be tried by:

(i) a High Court Judge, or

(ii) a Circuit Judge, or Deputy High Court Judge, or Deputy Circuit Judge, or a Recorder or a qualifying judge advocate, authorised to try such cases and provided that either the Presiding Judge has released the case or the Resident Judge has allocated the case for trial by such a judge.

E.6 Cases in Class 2C may be tried by:

(i) a High Court Judge, or

(ii) a Circuit Judge, or Deputy High Court Judge, or Deputy Circuit Judge, or a Recorder or a qualifying judge advocate, with suitable experience (for example, with company accounts or other financial information) and provided that either the Presiding Judge has released the case or the Resident Judge has allocated the case for trial by such a judge.

E.7 Cases in Classes 1D, 2A and 2C will usually be tried by a Circuit Judge.

E.8 Cases in Class 3 may be tried by a High Court Judge, or a Circuit Judge, a Deputy Circuit Judge, a Recorder or a qualifying judge advocate. A case in Class 3 shall not be listed for trial by a High Court Judge except with the consent of a Presiding Judge.

E.9 If a case has been allocated to a judge, Recorder or qualifying judge advocate, the preliminary hearing should be conducted by the allocated judge if practicable, and if not, if possible by a judge of at least equivalent standing. PCMHs should only be heard by Recorders or qualifying judge advocates with the approval of the Resident Judge.

E.10 For cases in Class 1A, 1B or 1C, or any case that has been referred to the Presiding Judge, the preliminary hearing and PCMH must be conducted by a High Court Judge; by a Circuit Judge; or by a judge authorised by the Presiding Judges to conduct such hearings. In the event of a guilty plea before such an authorised judge, the case will be adjourned for sentencing and will immediately be referred to the Presiding Judge who may retain the case for sentence by a High Court Judge, or release the case back to the Resident Judge, either for sentence by a named judge, or for sentence by an identified category of judges, to be allocated by the Resident Judge.

E.11 Appeals from decisions of magistrates' courts shall be heard by:

(i) a Resident Judge, or

(ii) a Circuit Judge, nominated by the Resident Judge, who regularly sits at the Crown Court centre, or

(iii) a Recorder or qualifying judge advocate or a Deputy Circuit Judge listed by the Presiding Judge to hear such appeals; or, if there is no such list nominated by the Resident Judge to hear such appeals;

(iv) and, no less than two and no more than four justices of the peace, none of whom took part in the decision under appeal;

(v) where no Circuit Judge or Recorder or qualifying judge advocate satisfying the requirements above is available, by a Circuit Judge, Recorder, qualifying judge advocate or Deputy Circuit Judge selected by the Resident Judge to hear a specific case or cases listed on a specific day.

E.12 Allocation or committal for sentence following breach (such as a matter in which a community order has been made, or a suspended sentence passed), should, where possible, be listed before the judge who originally dealt with the matter or, if not, before a judge of the same or higher level.

E.13 Applications for removal of a driving disqualification should be made to the location of the Crown Court where the order of disqualification was made. Where possible, the matter should be listed before the judge who originally dealt with the matter or, if not, before a judge of the same or higher level.

CPD XIII Listing F: Listing of trials, custody time limits and transfer of cases

Estimates of trial length

F.1   Under the regime set out in the Criminal Procedure Rules, the parties will be expected to provide an accurate estimate of the length of trial at the hearing where the case is to be managed based on a detailed estimate of the time to be taken with each witness to be called, and accurate information about the availability of witnesses.

F.2   At the hearing the judge will ask the prosecution to clarify any custody time limit ('CTL') dates. The court clerk must ensure the CTL date is marked clearly on the court file or electronic file. When a case is subject to a CTL all efforts must be made at the first hearing to list the case within the CTL and the judge should seek to ensure this. Further guidance on listing CTL cases can be found below.

Cases that should usually have fixed trial dates

F.3   The cases where fixtures should be given will be set out in the listing practice applicable at the court, but should usually include the following:

(i)   Cases in classes 1A, 1B, 1C, 2B and 2C;
(ii)   Cases involving vulnerable and intimidated witnesses (including domestic violence cases), whether or not special measures have been ordered by the court;
(iii)   Cases where the witnesses are under 18 or have to come from overseas;
(iv)   Cases estimated to last more than a certain time – the period chosen will depend on the size of the centre and the available judges;
(v)   Cases where a previous fixed hearing has not been effective;
(vi)   Re-trials; and,
(vii)   Cases involving expert witnesses.

Custody Time Limits

F.4   Every effort must be made to list cases for trial within the CTL limits set by Parliament. The guiding principles are:

(i)   At the first hearing in the Crown Court, prosecution will inform the court when the CTL lapses.
(ii)   All efforts must be made to list the case within the CTL. The CTL may only be extended in accordance with *s.22 Prosecution of Offences Act 1985* and the *Prosecution of Offences (Custody Time Limits) Regulations 1987.*
(iii)   If suitable, given priority and listed on a date not less than 2 weeks before the CTL expires, the case may be placed in a warned list.
(iv)   The CTL must be kept under continual review by the parties, HMCTS and the Resident Judge.
(v)   If the CTL is at risk of being exceeded, an additional hearing should take place and should be listed before the Resident Judge or trial judge or other judge nominated by the Resident Judge.
(vi)   An application to extend the CTL in any case listed outside the CTL must be considered by the court whether or not it was listed with the express consent of the defence.
(vii)   Any application to extend CTLs must be considered as a matter of urgency. The reasons for needing the extension must be ascertained and fully explained to the court.
(viii)   Where courtroom or judge availability is an issue, the court must itself list the case to consider the extension of any CTL. The Delivery Director of the circuit must provide a statement setting out in detail what has been done to try to accommodate the case within the CTL.
(ix)   Where courtroom or judge availability is not in issue, but all parties and the court agree that the case will not be ready for trial before the expiration of the CTL, a date may be fixed outside the CTL. This may be done without prejudice to any application to extend the CTLs or with the express consent of the defence; this must be noted on the papers.

F.5   As legal argument may delay the swearing in of a jury, it is desirable to extend the CTL to a date later than the first day of the trial.

Re-trials ordered by the Court of Appeal

F.6   The Crown Court must comply with the directions of the Court of Appeal and cannot vary those directions without reference to the Court of Appeal.

F.7   In cases where a retrial is ordered by the Court of Appeal the CTL is 112 days starting from the date that the new indictment is preferred i.e. from the date that the indictment is delivered to the Crown Court. Court centres should check that CREST has calculated the dates correctly and that it has not used 182 days on cases that have previously been 'sent'.

Changes to the date of fixed cases

F.8   Once a trial date or window is fixed, it should not be vacated or moved without good reason. Under the Criminal Procedure Rules, parties are expected to be ready by the trial date.

F.9   The listing officer may, in circumstances determined by the Resident Judge, agree to the movement of the trial to a date to which the defence and prosecution both consent, provided the timely hearing of the case is not delayed. The prosecution will be expected to have consulted the witnesses before agreeing to any change.

F.10   In all other circumstances, requests to adjourn or vacate fixtures or trial windows must be referred to the Resident Judge for his or her personal attention; the Resident Judge may delegate the decision to a named deputy.

Transferring cases to another court

F.11   Transfer between courts on the same circuit must be agreed by the Resident Judges of each court, subject to guidance from the Presiding Judges of the circuit.

F.12   Transfer of trials between circuits must be agreed between the Presiding Judges and Delivery Directors of the respective circuits.

F.13 Transfers may be agreed either in specific cases or in accordance with general principles agreed between those cited above.

CPD XIII LISTING G: LISTING OF HEARINGS OTHER THAN TRIALS

G.1 In addition to trials, the court's listing practice will have to provide court time for shorter matters, such as those listed below. These hearings are important, often either for setting the necessary case management framework for the proper and efficient preparation of cases for trial, or for determining matters that affect the rights of individuals. They must be afforded the appropriate level of resource that they require to be considered properly, and this may include judicial reading time as well as an appropriate length of hearing.

G.2 The applicant is responsible for notifying the court, and the other party if appropriate, and ensuring that the papers are served in good time, including a time estimate for judicial reading time and for the hearing. The applicant must endeavour to complete the application within the time estimate provided unless there are exceptional circumstances.

G.3 Hearings other than trials include the following:

(i)   Applications for search warrants and Production Orders, sufficient reading time must be provided, see G.8 below;
(ii)   Bail applications;
(iii) Applications to vacate or adjourn hearings;
(iv) Applications for dismissal of charges;
(v)   Preliminary hearings;
(vi) Preparatory hearings;
(vii) Plea and case management hearings;
(viii) Applications for disclosure of further unused material under section 8 of CPIA 1996;
(ix) Case progression or case management hearings;
(x)   Applications in respect of sentence indications not sought at the PCMH;
(xi) Sentences;
(xii) Civil applications under the Anti-Social Behaviour, Crime and Policing Act 2014;
(xiii) Appeals from the magistrates' court: it is essential in all cases where witnesses are likely to be needed on the appeal to check availability before a date is fixed.

G.4 Short hearings should not generally be listed before a judge such that they may delay the start or continuation of a trial at the Crown Court. It is envisaged that any such short hearing will be completed by 10.30am or start after 4.30pm.

G.5 Each Crown Court equipped with a video link with a prison must have in place arrangements for the conduct of PCMHs, other pre-trial hearings and sentencing hearings by video link.

Notifying sureties of hearing dates

G.6 Where a surety has entered into a recognizance in the magistrates' court in respect of a case allocated or sent to the Crown Court and where the bail order or recognizance refers to attendance at the first hearing in the Crown Court, the defendant should be reminded by the listing officer that the surety should attend the first hearing in the Crown Court in order to provide further recognizance. If attendance is not arranged, the defendant may be remanded in custody pending the recognisance being provided.

G.7 The Court should also notify sureties of the dates of the hearing at the Crown Court at which the defendant is ordered to appear in as far in advance as possible: see the observations of Parker LJ in *R v Crown Court at Reading ex p. Bello* [1992] 3 All ER 353.

Applications for Production Orders and Search Warrants

G.8 The use of production orders and search warrants involve the use of intrusive state powers that affect the rights and liberties of individuals. It is the responsibility of the court to ensure that those powers are not abused. To do so, the court must be presented with a properly completed application, on the appropriate form, which includes a summary of the investigation to provide the context for the order, a clear explanation of how the statutory requirements are fulfilled, and full and frank disclosure of anything that might undermine the basis for the application. Further directions on the proper making and consideration of such applications will be provided by Practice Direction. However, the complexity of the application must be taken into account in listing it such that the judge is afforded appropriate reading time and the hearing is given sufficient time for the issues to be considered thoroughly, and a short judgment given.

Confiscation and Related Hearings

G.9 Applications for restraint orders should be determined by the Resident Judge, or a judge nominated by the Resident Judge, at the Crown Court location at which they are lodged.

G.10 In order to prevent possible dissipation of assets of significant value, applications under the Proceeds of Crime Act 2002 should be considered urgent when lists are being fixed. In order to prevent potential prejudice, applications for the variation and discharge of orders, for the appointment of receivers, and applications to punish alleged breaches of orders as a contempt of court should similarly be treated as urgent and listed expeditiously.

Confiscation Hearings

G.11 It is important that confiscation hearings take place in good time after the defendant is convicted or sentenced.

CPD XIII ANNEX 1:

GENERAL PRINCIPLES FOR THE DEPLOYMENT OF THE JUDICIARY IN THE MAGISTRATES' COURT

This distils the full deployment guidance issued in November 2012. The relevant sections dealing specifically with the allocation of work within the magistrates' court have been incorporated into this Practice Direction. It does not seek to replace the guidance in its entirety.

PRESUMPTIONS

1. The presumptions which follow are intended to provide an acceptable and flexible frame-work establishing the deployment of the DJ (MC)s and magistrates. The system must be capable of adaptation to meet particular needs, whether of locality or caseload. In any event, the presumptions which follow are illustrative not exhaustive.

2. DJ(MC)s should generally (not invariably) be deployed in accordance with the following presumptions ("the Presumptions"):

(a) Cases involving complex points of law and evidence.
(b) Cases involving complex procedural issues.
(c) Long cases (included on grounds of practicality).
(d) Interlinked cases (given the need for consistency, together with their likely complexity and novelty).
(e) Cases for which armed police officers are required in court, such as high end firearms cases.
(f) A share of the more routine business of the Court, including case management and pre-trial reviews, (for a variety of reasons, including the need for DJ(MC)s to have competence in all areas of work and the desirability of an equitable division of work between magistrates and DJ(MC)s, subject always to the interests of the administration of justice).
(g) Where appropriate, in supporting the training of magistrates.
(h) Occasionally, in mixed benches of DJ(MC)s and magistrates (with a particular view both to improving the case management skills of magistrates and to improving the culture of collegiality).
(i) In the short term tackling of particular local backlogs ("backlog busting"), some times in combination with magistrates from the local or (with the SPJ's approval) adjoining benches.

3. In accordance with current arrangements certain classes of cases necessarily require DJ(MC)s and have therefore been excluded from the above presumptions; these are as follows:

(a) Extradition;
(b) Terrorism;
(c) Prison Adjudications;
(d) Sex cases in the Youth Court as per Annex 2;
(e) Cases where the defendant is likely to be sentenced to a very large fine, see Annex 3;
(f) The Special Jurisdiction of the Chief Magistrate.

4. In formulating the Presumptions, the following considerations have been taken into account:

(a) The listing of cases is here, as elsewhere, a judicial function, see CPD XIII A.1. In the magistrates' courts the Judicial Business Group, subject to the supervision of the Presiding Judges of the circuit, is responsible for determining the day to day listing practice in that area. The day-to-day operation of that listing practice is the responsibility of the justices' clerk with the assistance of the listing officer.
(b) Equally, providing the training of magistrates is a responsibility of justices' clerks.
(c) It is best not to treat "high profile" cases as a separate category but to consider their listing in the light of the principles and presumptions. The circumstances surrounding high profile cases do not permit ready generalisation, save that they are likely to require especially sensitive handling. Listing decisions involving such cases will often benefit from good communication at a local level between the justices' clerk, the DJ (MC) and the Bench Chairman.
(d) Account must be taken of the need to maintain the competences of all members of the judiciary sitting in the magistrates' court.

5. The Special Jurisdiction of the Senior District Judge (Chief Magistrate) concerns cases which fall into the following categories:

(i) cases with a terrorism connection;
(ii) cases involving war crimes and crimes against humanity;
(iii) matters affecting state security;
(iv) cases brought under the Official Secrets Act;
(v) offences involving royalty or parliament;
(vi) offences involving diplomats;
(vii) corruption of public officials;
(viii) police officers charged with serious offences;
(ix) cases of unusual sensitivity.

6. Where cases fall within the category of the Special Jurisdiction they must be heard bv:

(i) the Senior District Judge (or if not available);
(ii) the Deputy Senior District Judge (or if not available);
(iii) a District Judge approved by the Senior District Judge or his/her deputy for the particular case.

7. Where a doubt may exist as to whether or not a case falls within the Special jurisdiction, reference should always be made to the Senior District judge or to the Deputy Senior District judge for clarification.

CPD XIII ANNEX 2

SEXUAL OFFENCES IN THE YOUTH COURT

1. This annex sets out the procedure to be applied in the Youth Court in all cases involving allegations of sexual offences which are capable of being sent for trial at the Crown Court under the grave crime provisions.

2. This applies to all cases involving such charges, irrespective of the gravity of the allegation, the age of the defendant and / or the antecedent history of the defendant[1].

3. This does not alter the test[2] that the Youth Court must apply when determining whether a case is a "grave crime".

4. In the Crown Court, cases involving allegations of sexual offences frequently involve complex and sensitive issues and only those Circuit Judges and Recorders who have been specifically authorised and who have attended the appropriate Judicial College course may try this type of work.

5. A number of District Judges (Magistrates' Courts) have now undertaken training in dealing with these difficult cases and have been specifically authorised to hear cases involving serious sexual offences which fall short of requiring to be sent to the Crown Court ("an authorised DJ (MC)"). As such, a procedure similar to that of the Crown Court will now apply to allegations of sexual offences in the Youth Court.

PROCEDURE

6. The determination of venue in the Youth Court is governed by section 51 Crime and Disorder Act 1998, which provides that the youth must be tried summarily unless charged with such a grave crime that long term detention is a realistic possibility[3], or that one of the other exceptions to this presumption arises.

7. Wherever possible such cases should be listed before an authorised DJ (MC), to decide whether the case falls within the grave crime provisions and should therefore be sent for trial. If jurisdiction is retained and the allegation involves actual, or attempted, penetrative activity, the case must be tried by an authorised DJ (MC). In all other cases, the authorised DJ (MC) must consider whether the case is so serious and / or complex that it must be tried by an authorised DJ (MC), or whether the case can be heard by any DJ (MC) or any Youth Court Bench.

8. If it is not practicable for an authorised DJ(MC) to determine venue, any DJ(MC) or any Youth Court Bench may consider that issue. If jurisdiction is retained, appropriate directions may be given but the case papers, including a detailed case summary and a note of any representations made by the parties, must be sent to an authorised DJ(MC) to consider. As soon as possible the authorised DJ(MC) must decide whether the case must be tried by an authorised DJ(MC) or whether the case is suitable to be heard by any DJ(MC) or any Youth Court Bench; however, if the case involves actual, or alleged, penetrative activity, the trial must be heard by an authorised DJ(MC).

9. Once an authorised DJ(MC) has decided that the case is one which must be tried by an authorised DJ(MC), and in all cases involving actual or alleged penetrative activity, all further procedural hearings should, so far as practicable, be heard by an authorised DJ(MC).

CASES REMITTED FOR SENTENCE

10. All cases which are remitted for sentence from the Crown Court to the Youth Court should be listed for sentence before an authorised DJ(MC).

ARRANGEMENTS FOR AN AUTHORISED DJ(MC) TO BE APPOINTED

11. Where a case is to be tried by an authorised DJ(MC) but no such Judge is available, the Bench Legal Adviser should contact the Chief Magistrates Office for an authorised DJ(MC) to be assigned.

---

[1] So, for example, every allegation of sexual touching, under s3 of the Sexual Offences Act 2003, is covered by this protocol.

[2] Set out in the Sentencing Guidelines Council's definitive guideline, entitled "Overarching Principles – Sentencing Youths" Published by the Sentencing Guidelines Council in November 2009.

[3] Section 24(1) of the Magistrates Court Act 1980

CPD XIII Annex 3

CASES INVOLVING VERY LARGE FINES IN THE MAGISTRATES' COURT

1. This Annex applies when s.85 Legal Aid, Sentencing and Punishment of Offenders Act 2012 comes into force and the magistrates' court has the power to impose a maximum fine of any amount.

2. An authorised DJ (MC) must deal with any allocation decision, trial and sentencing hearing in the following types of cases which are triable either way:

(a) Cases involving death or significant, life changing injury or a high risk of death or significant, life-changing injury;

(b) Cases involving substantial environmental damage or polluting material of a dangerous nature;

(c) Cases where major adverse effect on human health or quality of life, animal health or flora has resulted;

(d) Cases where major costs through clean up, site restoration or animal rehabilitation have been incurred;

(e) Cases where the defendant corporation has a turnover in excess of £10 million but does not exceed £250 million, and has acted in a deliberate, reckless or negligent manner;

(f) Cases where the defendant corporation has a turnover in excess of £250 million;

(g) Cases where the court will be expected to analyse complex company accounts;

(h) High profile cases or ones of an exceptionally sensitive nature.

3. The prosecution agency must notify the justices' clerk where practicable of any case of the type mentioned in paragraph 2 of this Annex, no less than 7 days before the first hearing to ensure that an authorised DJ (MC) is available at the first hearing.

4. The justices' clerk shall contact the Office of the Chief Magistrate to ensure that an authorised DJ (MC) can be assigned to deal with such a case if there is not such a person available in the courthouse. The justices' clerk shall also notify a Presiding Judge of the Circuit that such a case has been listed.

5. Where an authorised DJ (MC) is not appointed at the first hearing the court shall adjourn the case. The court shall ask the accused for an indication of his plea, but shall not allocate the case nor, if the accused indicates a guilty plea, sentence him, commit him for sentence, ask for a pre sentence report or give any indication as to likely sentence that will be imposed. The justices' clerk shall ensure an authorised DJ (MC) is appointed for the following hearing and notify the Presiding Judge of the Circuit that the case has been listed.

6. When dealing with sentence, section 3 of the Powers of Criminal Courts (Sentence) Act 2000 can be invoked where, despite the magistrates' court having maximum fine powers available to it, the offence or combination of offences make it so serious that the Crown Court should deal with it as though the person had been convicted on indictment.

7. An authorised DJ (MC) should consider allocating the case to the Crown Court or committing the accused for sentence.

CPD XIII Annex 4

This annex replaces the Protocol on the case management of Terrorism Cases issued in December 2006 by the President of the Queen's Bench Division.

Application

1. This annex applies to 'terrorism cases'. For the purposes of this annex a case is a 'terrorism case' where:

- (a) one of the offences charged against any of the defendants is indictable only and it is alleged by the prosecution that there is evidence that it took place during an act of terrorism or for the purposes of terrorism as defined in s1 of the Terrorism Act 2000. This may include, but is not limited to:
  - (i) murder;
  - (ii) manslaughter;
  - (iii) an offence under section 18 of the Offences against the Person Act 1861 (wounding with intent);
  - (iv) an offence under section 23 or 24 of that Act (administering poison etc);
  - (v) an offence under section 28 or 29 of that Act (explosives);
  - (vi) an offence under section 2, 3 or 5 of the Explosive Substances Act 1883 (causing explosions);
  - (vii) an offence under section 1(2) of the Criminal Damage Act 1971 (endangering life by damaging property);
  - (viii) an offence under section 1 of the Biological Weapons Act 1974 (biological weapons);
  - (ix) an offence under section 2 of the Chemical Weapons Act 1996 (chemical weapons);
  - (x) an offence under section 56 of the Terrorism Act 2000 (directing a terrorist organisation);
  - (xi) an offence under section 59 of that Act (inciting terrorism overseas);
  - (xii) offences under (v), (vii) and (viii) above given jurisdiction by virtue of section 62 of that Act (terrorist bombing overseas); and
  - (xiii) an offence under section 5 of the Terrorism Act 2006 (preparation of terrorism acts).
- (b) one of the offences charged is indictable only and includes an allegation by the prosecution of serious fraud that took place during an act of terrorism or for the purposes of terrorism as defined in s1 of the Terrorism Act 2000, and the prosecutor gives a notice under section 51B of the Crime and Disorder Act 1998 (Notices in serious or complex fraud cases);
- (c) one of the offences charged is indictable only, which includes an allegation that a defendant conspired, incited or attempted to commit an offence under sub paragraphs (1)(a) or (b) above; or
- (d) it is a case (which can be indictable only or triable either way) that a judge of the terrorism cases list (see paragraph 2(a) below) considers should be a terrorism case. In deciding whether a case not covered by subparagraphs (1)(a), (b) or (c) above should be a terrorism case, the judge may hear representations from the Crown Prosecution Service.

The terrorism cases list

2(a) All terrorism cases, wherever they originate in England and Wales, will be managed in a list known as the 'terrorism cases list' by such judges of the High Court as are nominated by the President of the Queen's Bench Division.

2(b) Such cases will be tried, unless otherwise directed by the President of the Queen's Bench Division, by a judge of the High Court as nominated by the President of the Queen's Bench Division.

3. The judges managing the terrorism cases referred to in paragraph 2(a) will be supported by the London and South Eastern Regional Co-ordinator's Office (the 'Regional Co-ordinator's Office'). An official of that office or an individual nominated by that office will act as the case progression officer for cases in that list for the purposes of CrimPR 3.4.

Procedure after charge

4. Immediately after a person has been charged in a terrorism case, anywhere in England and Wales, a representative of the Crown Prosecution Service will notify the person on the 24 hour rota for special jurisdiction matters at Westminster Magistrates' Court of the following information:

- (a) the full name of each defendant and the name of his solicitor of other legal representative, if known;
- (b) the charges laid;
- (c) the name and contact details of the Crown Prosecutor with responsibility for the case, if known; and
- (d) confirmation that the case is a terrorism case.

5. The person on the 24-hour rota will then ensure that all terrorism cases wherever they are charged in England and Wales are listed before the Chief Magistrate or other District Judge designated under the Terrorism Act 2000. Unless the Chief Magistrate or other District Judge designated under the Terrorism Act 2000 directs otherwise, the first appearance of all defendants accused of terrorism offences will be listed at Westminster Magistrates' Court.

6. In order to comply with section 46 of the Police and Criminal Evidence Act 1984, if a defendant in a terrorism case is charged at a police station within the local justice area in which Westminster

Magistrates' Court is situated, the defendant must be brought before Westminster Magistrates' Court as soon as is practicable and in any event not later than the first sitting after he is charged with the offence. If a defendant in a terrorism case is charged in a police station outside the local justice area in which Westminster Magistrates' Court is situated, unless the Chief Magistrate or other designated judge directs otherwise, the defendant must be removed to that area as soon as is practicable. He must then be brought before Westminster Magistrates' Court as soon as is practicable after his arrival in the area and in any event not later than the first sitting of Westminster Magistrates' Court after his arrival in that area.

7. As soon as is practicable after charge a representative of the Crown Prosecution Service will also provide the Regional Listing Co-ordinator's Office with the information listed in paragraph 4 above.

8. The Regional Co-ordinator's Office will then ensure that the Chief Magistrate and the Legal Aid Agency have the same information.

Cases to be sent to the Crown Court under section 51 of the Crime and Disorder Act 1998

9. The court should ordinarily direct that the plea and trial preparation hearing should take place about 14 days after charge.

10. The sending magistrates' court should contact the Regional Listing Co-ordinator's Office who will be responsible for notifying the magistrates' court as to the relevant Crown Court to which to send the case.

11. In all terrorism cases, the magistrates' court case progression form for cases sent to the Crown Court under section 51 of the Crime and Disorder Act 1998 should not be used. Instead of the automatic directions set out in that form, the magistrates' court shall make the following directions to facilitate the preliminary hearing at the Crown Court:

(a) three days prior to the preliminary hearing in the terrorism cases list, the prosecution must serve upon each defendant and the Regional Listing co-ordinator:
  (i) a preliminary summary of the case;
  (ii) the names of those who are to represent the prosecution, if known;
  (iii) an estimate of the length of the trial;
  (iv) a suggested provisional timetable which should generally include:
  - the general nature of further enquiries being made by the prosecution,
  - the time needed for the completion of such enquiries,
  - the time required by the prosecution to review the case,
  - a timetable for the phased service of the evidence,
  - the time for the provision by the Attorney General for his consent if necessary,
  - the time for service of the detailed defence case statement,
  - the date for the case management hearing, and
  - the estimated trial date;
  (v) a preliminary statement of the possible disclosure issues setting out the nature and scale of the problem, including the amount of unused material, the manner in which the prosecution seeks to deal with these matters and a suggested timetable for discharging their statutory duty; and
  (vi) any information relating to bail and custody time limits.
(b) one day prior to the preliminary hearing in the terrorist cases list, each defendant must serve in writing on the Regional Listing Co-ordinator and the prosecution:
  (i) the proposed representation;
  (ii) observations on the timetable; and
  (iii) an indication of plea and the general nature of the defence.

Cases to be sent to the Crown Court after the prosecutor gives notice under section 51B of the Crime and Disorder Act 1998

12. If a terrorism case is to be sent to the Crown Court after the prosecutor gives a notice under section 51B of the Crime and Disorder Act 1998 the magistrates' court should proceed as in paragraphs 9 – 11 above.

13. When a terrorism case is so sent the case will go into the terrorism list and be managed by a judge as described in paragraph 2(a) above.

The plea and trial preparation hearing at the Crown Court

14. At the plea and trial preparation hearing, the judge will determine whether the case is one to remain in the terrorism list and if so, give directions setting the provisional timetable.

15. The Legal Aid Agency must attend the hearing by an authorised officer to assist the court.

Use of video links

16. Unless a judge otherwise directs, all Crown Court hearings prior to the trial will be conducted by video link for all defendants in custody.

Security

17. The police service and the prison service will provide the Regional Listing Co-ordinator's Office with an initial joint assessment of the security risks associated with any court appearance by the defendants within 14 days of charge. Any subsequent changes in circumstances or the assessment of risk which have the potential to impact upon the choice of trial venue will be notified to the Regional Listing Co-ordinator's Office immediately.

CPD XIII ANNEX 5

MANAGEMENT OF CASES FROM THE ORGANISED CRIME DIVISION OF THE CROWN PROSECUTION SERVICE

This annex replaces the guidance issued by the Senior Presiding Judge in January 2014.

1. The Organised Crime Division (OCD) of the CPS is responsible for prosecution of cases from the National Crime Agency (NCA). Typically, these cases involve more than one defendant, are

voluminous and raise complex and specialised issues of law. It is recognised that if not closely managed, such cases have the potential to cost vast amounts of public money and take longer than necessary.

2.   This annex applies to all cases handled by the OCD.

Designated court centres

3.   Subject to the overriding discretion of the Presiding Judges of the circuit, OCD cases should normally be heard at Designated Court Centres (DCC). The process of designating court centres for this purpose has taken into account geographical factors and the size, security and facilities of those court centres. The designated court centres are:

(a)   Northern Circuit: Manchester, Liverpool and Preston.
(b)   North Eastern Circuit: Leeds, Newcastle and Sheffield.
(c)   Western Circuit: Bristol and Winchester.
(d)   South Eastern Circuit (not including London): Reading, Luton, Chelmsford, Ipswich, Maidstone, Lewes and Hove.
(e)   South Eastern Circuit (London only): Southwark, Blackfriars, Kingston, Woolwich, Croydon and the Central Criminal Court.
(f)   Midland Circuit: Birmingham, Leicester and Nottingham.
(g)   Wales Circuit: Cardiff, Swansea and Mold.

Selection of designated court centres

4.   If arrests are made in different parts of the country and the OCD seeks to have all defendants tried by one Crown Court, the OCD will, at the earliest opportunity, write to the relevant court cluster manager with a recommendation as to the appropriate designated court centre, requesting that the decision be made by the relevant Presiding Judges. In the event that the designated court centre within one region is unable to accommodate a case, for example, as a result of a custody time limit expiry date, consideration may be given to transferring the case to a DCC in another region with the consent of the relevant Presiding Judges.

5.   There will be a single point of contact person at the OCD for each HMCTS region, to assist listing co-ordinators.

6.   The single contact person for each HMCTS region will be the relevant cluster manager, with the exception of the South Eastern Circuit where the appropriate person will be the Regional Listing Co-ordinator.

Designation of the trial judge

7.   The trial judge will be assigned by the Presiding Judge at the earliest opportunity, and in accordance with CPD XIII Listing E: Allocation of Business within the Crown Court. Where the trial judge is unable to continue with the case, all further pre-trial hearings should be by a single judge until a replacement has been assigned.

Procedure after charge

8.   Within 24 hours of the laying of a charge, a representative of the OCD will notify the relevant cluster manager of the following information to enable an agreement to be reached between that cluster manager and the reviewing CPS lawyer before the first appearance as to the DCC to which the case should be sent :

(a)   the full name of each defendant and the name of his legal representatives, if known;
(b)   the charges laid; and
(c)   the name and contact details of the Crown Prosecutor with responsibility for the case.

Exceptions

9.   Where it is not possible to have a case dealt with at a DCC, the OCD should liaise closely with the relevant cluster manager and the Presiding Judges to ensure that the cases are sent to the most appropriate court centre. This will, among other things, take into account the location of the likely source of the case, convenience of the witnesses, travelling distance for OCD staff and facilities at the court centres.

10.   In the event that it is allocated to a non-designated court centre, the OCD should be permitted to make representations in writing to the Presiding Judges within 14 days as to why the venue is not suitable. The Presiding Judges will consider the reasons and, if necessary, hold a hearing. The CPS may renew their request at any stage where further reasons come to light that may affect the original decision on venue.

11.   Nothing in this annex should be taken to remove the right of the defence to make representations as to the venue.

CRIMINAL PROCEDURE RULES 2015

Made by the Criminal Procedure Rule Committee in accordance with s 69 of the Courts Act 2003.

CrimPR 2015

(SI 2015/1490 as amended by SI 2016/120 and 705, SI 2017/144, 282, 755 and 915 and SI 2018/132 and 847)

Arrangement of Rules

PART 1 THE OVERRIDING OBJECTIVE

Contents of this Part

B.1 *1.1. The overriding objective* (1) The overriding objective of this procedural code is that criminal cases be dealt with justly.
(2) Dealing with a criminal case justly includes—
(a) acquitting the innocent and convicting the guilty;
(b) dealing with the prosecution and the defence fairly;
(c) recognising the rights of a defendant, particularly those under Article 6 of the European Convention on Human Rights;
(d) respecting the interests of witnesses, victims and jurors and keeping them informed of the progress of the case;
(e) dealing with the case efficiently and expeditiously;
(f) ensuring that appropriate information is available to the court when bail and sentence are considered; and
(g) dealing with the case in ways that take into account—
(i) the gravity of the offence alleged,
(ii) the complexity of what is in issue,
(iii) the severity of the consequences for the defendant and others affected, and
(iv) the needs of other cases.

1.2. The duty of the participants in a criminal case (1) Each participant, in the conduct of each case, must—
(a) prepare and conduct the case in accordance with the overriding objective;
(b) comply with these Rules, practice directions and directions made by the court; and
(c) at once inform the court and all parties of any significant failure (whether or not that participant is responsible for that failure) to take any procedural step required by these Rules, any practice direction or any direction of the court. A failure is significant if it might hinder the court in furthering the overriding objective.
(2) Anyone involved in any way with a criminal case is a participant in its conduct for the purposes of this rule.

1.3. The application by the court of the overriding objective The court must further the overriding objective in particular when—
(a) exercising any power given to it by legislation (including these Rules);
(b) applying any practice direction; or
(c) interpreting any rule or practice direction.

PART 2   UNDERSTANDING AND APPLYING THE RULES

Contents of this Part

B.2 *2.1. When the Rules apply* (1) In general, Criminal Procedure Rules apply—
(a) in all criminal cases in magistrates' courts and in the Crown Court;
(b) in extradition cases in the High Court; and
(c) in all cases in the criminal division of the Court of Appeal.
(2) If a rule applies only in one or some of those courts, the rule makes that clear.
(3) These Rules apply on and after 5th October, 2015, but—
(a) unless the court otherwise directs, they do not affect a right or duty existing under the Criminal Procedure Rules 2014; and
(b) unless the High Court otherwise directs, Section 3 of Part 50 (Extradition – appeal to the High Court) does not apply to a case in which notice of an appeal was given before 6th October, 2014.
(4) In a case in which a request for extradition was received by a relevant authority in the United Kingdom on or before 31st December, 2003—
(a) the rules in Part 50 (Extradition) do not apply; and
(b) the rules in Part 17 of the Criminal Procedure Rules 2012 (Extradition) continue to apply as if those rules had not been revoked.
[Note. The rules replaced by the first Criminal Procedure Rules (the Criminal Procedure Rules 2005) were revoked when those Rules came into force by provisions of the Courts Act 2003, the Courts Act 2003 (Consequential Amendments) Order 2004 and the Courts Act 2003 (Commencement No 6 and Savings) Order 2004. The first Criminal Procedure Rules reproduced the substance of all the

rules they replaced.
The rules in Part 17 of the Criminal Procedure Rules 2012 applied to extradition proceedings under the Backing of Warrants (Republic of Ireland) Act 1965 or under the Extradition Act 1989. By section 218 of the Extradition Act 2003, the 1965 and 1989 Acts ceased to have effect when the 2003 Act came into force. By article 2 of the Extradition Act 2003 (Commencement and Savings) Order 2003, the 2003 Act came into force on 1st January, 2004. However, article 3 of that Order provided that the coming into force of the Act did not apply for the purposes of any request for extradition, whether made under any of the provisions of the Extradition Act 1989 or of the Backing of Warrants (Republic of Ireland) Act 1965 or otherwise, which was received by the relevant authority in the United Kingdom on or before 31st December, 2003.]

2.2.   *Definitions*   (1)   In these Rules, unless the context makes it clear that something different is meant:

'advocate' means a person who is entitled to exercise a right of audience in the court under section 13 of the Legal Services Act 2007;

'business day' means any day except Saturday, Sunday, Christmas Day, Boxing Day, Good Friday, Easter Monday or a bank holiday;

'court' means a tribunal with jurisdiction over criminal cases. It includes a judge, recorder, District Judge (Magistrates' Court), lay justice and, when exercising their judicial powers, the Registrar of Criminal Appeals, a justices' clerk or assistant clerk;

'court officer' means the appropriate member of the staff of a court;

'justices' legal adviser' means a justices' clerk or an assistant to a justices' clerk;

'legal representative' means:

 (i) the person for the time being named as a party's representative in any legal aid representation order made under section 16 of the Legal Aid, Sentencing and Punishment of Offenders Act 2012, or

 (ii) subject to that, the person named as a party's representative in any notice for the time being given under rule 46.2 (Notice of appointment, etc of legal representative: general rules), provided that person is entitled to conduct litigation in the court under section 13 of the Legal Services Act 2007;

'live link' means an arrangement by which a person can see and hear, and be seen and heard by, the court when that person is not in the courtroom;

'Practice Direction' means the Lord Chief Justice's Criminal Practice Directions, as amended, and 'Criminal Costs Practice Direction' means the Lord Chief Justice's Practice Direction (Costs in Criminal Proceedings), as amended;

'public interest ruling' means a ruling about whether it is in the public interest to disclose prosecution material under sections 3(6), 7A(8) or 8(5) of the Criminal Procedure and Investigations Act 1996; and

'Registrar' means the Registrar of Criminal Appeals or a court officer acting with the Registrar's authority.

(2)   Definitions of some other expressions are in the rules in which they apply.

[Note. The glossary at the end of the Rules is a guide to the meaning of certain legal expressions used in them.]

2.3.   *References to legislation, including these Rules*   (1)   In these Rules, where a rule refers to an Act of Parliament or to subordinate legislation by title and year, subsequent references to that Act or to that legislation in the rule are shortened: so, for example, after a reference to the Criminal Procedure and Investigations Act 1996 that Act is called 'the 1996 Act'; and after a reference to the Criminal Procedure and Investigations Act 1996 (Defence Disclosure Time Limits) Regulations 2011 those Regulations are called 'the 2011 Regulations'.

(2)   In the courts to which these Rules apply —

(a) unless the context makes it clear that something different is meant, a reference to the Criminal Procedure Rules, without reference to a year, is a reference to the Criminal Procedure Rules in force at the date on which the event concerned occurs or occurred;

(b) a reference to the Criminal Procedure Rules may be abbreviated to 'CrimPR'; and

(c) a reference to a Part or rule in the Criminal Procedure Rules may be abbreviated to, for example, 'CrimPR Part 3' or 'CrimPR 3.5'.

PART 3   CASE MANAGEMENT

Contents of this Part

General rules

GENERAL RULES

B.3 *3.1. When this Part applies* (1) Rules 3.1 to 3.12 apply to the management of each case in a magistrates' court and in the Crown Court (including an appeal to the Crown Court) until the conclusion of that case.
(2) Rules 3.13 to 3.26 apply where—
(a)   the defendant is sent to the Crown Court for trial;
(b)   a High Court or Crown Court judge gives permission to serve a draft indictment; or
(c)   the Court of Appeal orders a retrial.
(3) Rule 3.27 applies in a magistrates' court unless—
(a)   the court sends the defendant for trial in the Crown Court; or
(b)   the case is one to which rule 24.8 or rule 24.9 applies (Written guilty plea: special rules; Single justice procedure: special rules).
(4) Rule 3.28 applies in a magistrates' court and in the Crown Court (including on an appeal to the Crown Court).
[Note. *Rules that apply to procedure in the Court of Appeal are in Parts 36 to 42 of these Rules.*
A magistrates' court may send a defendant for trial in the Crown Court under section 51 or 51A of the Crime and Disorder Act 1998. See Part 9 for the procedure on allocation and sending for trial. Under paragraph 2(1) of Schedule 17 to the Crime and Courts Act 2013 and section 2 of the Administration of Justice (Miscellaneous Provisions) Act 1933,the Crown Court may give permission to serve a draft indictment where it approves a deferred prosecution agreement. See Part 11 for the rules about that procedure and Part 10 for the rules about indictments.
The procedure for applying for the permission of a High Court judge to serve a draft indictment is in rules 6 to 10 of the Indictments (Procedure) Rules 1971. See also the Practice Direction.
The Court of Appeal may order a retrial under section 8 of the Criminal Appeal Act 1968 (on a defendant's appeal against conviction) or under section 77 of the Criminal Justice Act 2003 (on a prosecutor's application for the retrial of a serious offence after acquittal). Section 8 of the 1968 Act, section 84 of the 2003 Act and rules 27.6 and 39.14 require the arraignment of a defendant within 2 months.
The circumstances in which the court may commission a medical examination of a defendant and a report, other than for sentencing purposes, are listed in rule 3.28.]

3.2. The duty of the court (1) The court must further the overriding objective by actively managing the case.
(2) Active case management includes—
(a)   the early identification of the real issues;
(b)   the early identification of the needs of witnesses;
(c)   achieving certainty as to what must be done, by whom, and when, in particular by the early setting of a timetable for the progress of the case;
(d)   monitoring the progress of the case and compliance with directions;

(e)   ensuring that evidence, whether disputed or not, is presented in the shortest and clearest way;

(f)   discouraging delay, dealing with as many aspects of the case as possible on the same occasion, and avoiding unnecessary hearings;

(g)   encouraging the participants to co-operate in the progression of the case; and

(h)   making use of technology.

(3)   The court must actively manage the case by giving any direction appropriate to the needs of that case as early as possible.

(4)   Where appropriate live links are available, making use of technology for the purposes of this rule includes directing the use of such facilities, whether an application for such a direction is made or not—

(a)   for the conduct of a pre-trial hearing, including a pre-trial case management hearing;

(b)   for the defendant's attendance at such a hearing—

    (i)   where the defendant is in custody, or where the defendant is not in custody and wants to attend by live link, but

    (ii)   only if the court is satisfied that the defendant can participate effectively by such means, having regard to all the circumstances including whether the defendant is represented or not; and

(c)   for receiving evidence under one of the powers to which the rules in Part 18 apply (Measures to assist a witness or defendant to give evidence).

(5)   Where appropriate telephone facilities are available, making use of technology for the purposes of this rule includes directing the use of such facilities, whether an application for such a direction is made or not, for the conduct of a pre-trial case management hearing—

(a)   if telephone facilities are more convenient for that purpose than live links;

(b)   unless at that hearing the court expects to take the defendant's plea; and

(c)   only if—

    (i)   the defendant is represented, or

    (ii)   exceptionally, the court is satisfied that the defendant can participate effectively by such means without a representative.

[Note. In relation to the defendant's attendance by live link at a pre-trial hearing, see sections 46ZA and 47 of the Police and Criminal Evidence Act 1984 and sections 57A to 57D and 57F of the Crime and Disorder Act 1998.

In relation to the giving of evidence by a witness and the giving of evidence by the defendant, see section 32 of the Criminal Justice Act 1988, sections 19, 24 and 33A of the Youth Justice and Criminal Evidence Act 1999 and section 51 of the Criminal Justice Act 2003. Part 18 (Measures to assist a witness or defendant to give evidence) contains relevant rules.]

3.3.   The duty of the parties   (1)   Each party must—

(a)   actively assist the court in fulfilling its duty under rule 3.2, without or if necessary with a direction; and

(b)   apply for a direction if needed to further the overriding objective.

(2)   Active assistance for the purposes of this rule includes—

(a)   at the beginning of the case, communication between the prosecutor and the defendant at the first available opportunity and in any event no later than the beginning of the day of the first hearing;

(b)   after that, communication between the parties and with the court officer until the conclusion of the case;

(c)   by such communication establishing, among other things—

    (i)   whether the defendant is likely to plead guilty or not guilty,

    (ii)   what is agreed and what is likely to be disputed,

    (iii)   what information, or other material, is required by one party of another, and why, and

    (iv)   what is to be done, by whom, and when (without or if necessary with a direction);

(d)   reporting on that communication to the court—

    (i)   at the first hearing, and

    (ii)   after that, as directed by the court; and

(e)   alerting the court to any reason why—

    (i)   a direction should not be made in any of the circumstances listed in rule 3.2(4) or (5) (The duty of the court: use of live link or telephone facilities), or

    (ii)   such a direction should be varied or revoked.

3.4.   Case progression officers and their duties   (1)   At the beginning of the case each party must, unless the court otherwise directs—

(a)   nominate someone responsible for progressing that case; and

(b)   tell other parties and the court who that is and how to contact that person.

(2)   In fulfilling its duty under rule 3.2, the court must where appropriate—

(a)   nominate a court officer responsible for progressing the case; and

(b)   make sure the parties know who that is and how to contact that court officer.

(3)   In this Part a person nominated under this rule is called a case progression officer.

(4)   A case progression officer must—

(a)   monitor compliance with directions;

(b)   make sure that the court is kept informed of events that may affect the progress of that case;

(c)   make sure that he or she can be contacted promptly about the case during ordinary business hours;

(d)   act promptly and reasonably in response to communications about the case; and

(e)   if he or she will be unavailable, appoint a substitute to fulfil his or her duties and inform the other case progression officers.

3.5.   The court's case management powers   (1)   In fulfilling its duty under rule 3.2 the court may give any direction and take any step actively to manage a case unless that direction or step would be inconsistent with legislation, including these Rules.

(2)   In particular, the court may—

(a)   nominate a judge, magistrate or justices' legal adviser to manage the case;

(b)   give a direction on its own initiative or on application by a party;

(c)   ask or allow a party to propose a direction;

(d)   receive applications, notices, representations and information by letter, by telephone, by live link, by email or by any other means of electronic communication, and conduct a hearing by live link, telephone or other such electronic means;

(e)   give a direction—

      (i)   at a hearing, in public or in private, or

      (ii)   without a hearing;

(f)   fix, postpone, bring forward, extend, cancel or adjourn a hearing;

(g)   shorten or extend (even after it has expired) a time limit fixed by a direction;

(h)   require that issues in the case should be—

      (i)   identified in writing,

      (ii)   determined separately, and decide in what order they will be determined; and

(i)   specify the consequences of failing to comply with a direction.

(3)   A magistrates' court may give a direction that will apply in the Crown Court if the case is to continue there.

(4)   The Crown Court may give a direction that will apply in a magistrates' court if the case is to continue there.

(5)   Any power to give a direction under this Part includes a power to vary or revoke that direction.

(6)   If a party fails to comply with a rule or a direction, the court may—

(a)   fix, postpone, bring forward, extend, cancel or adjourn a hearing;

(b)   exercise its powers to make a costs order; and

(c)   impose such other sanction as may be appropriate.

[Note. Depending upon the nature of a case and the stage that it has reached, its progress may be affected by other Criminal Procedure Rules and by other legislation. The note at the end of this Part lists other rules and legislation that may apply.

See also rule 3.9 (Case preparation and progression).

The court may make a costs order under—

(a)   *section 19 of the Prosecution of Offences Act 1985, where the court decides that one party to criminal proceedings has incurred costs as a result of an unnecessary or improper act or omission by, or on behalf of, another party;*

(b)   *section 19A of that Act, where the court decides that a party has incurred costs as a result of an improper, unreasonable or negligent act or omission on the part of a legal representative;*

(c)   *section 19B of that Act, where the court decides that there has been serious misconduct by a person who is not a party.*

Under some other legislation, including Parts 19, 20 and 21 of these Rules, if a party fails to comply with a rule or a direction then in some circumstances—

(a)   *the court may refuse to allow that party to introduce evidence;*

(b)   *evidence that that party wants to introduce may not be admissible;*

(c)   *the court may draw adverse inferences from the late introduction of an issue or evidence.*

See also—

(a)   *section 81(1) of the Police and Criminal Evidence Act 1984 and section 20(3) of the Criminal Procedure and Investigations Act 1996 (advance disclosure of expert evidence);*

(b)   *section 11(5) of the Criminal Procedure and Investigations Act 1996 (faults in disclosure by accused);*

(c)   *section 132(5) of the Criminal Justice Act 2003 (failure to give notice of hearsay evidence).]*

3.6.   Application to vary a direction   (1)   A party may apply to vary a direction if—

(a)   the court gave it without a hearing;

(b)   the court gave it at a hearing in that party's absence; or

(c)   circumstances have changed.

(2)   A party who applies to vary a direction must—

(a)   apply as soon as practicable after becoming aware of the grounds for doing so; and

(b)   give as much notice to the other parties as the nature and urgency of the application permits.

3.7.   Agreement to vary a time limit fixed by a direction   (1)   The parties may agree to vary a time limit fixed by a direction, but only if—

(a)   the variation will not—

      (i)   affect the date of any hearing that has been fixed, or

      (ii)   significantly affect the progress of the case in any other way;

(b)   the court has not prohibited variation by agreement; and

(c)   the court's case progression officer is promptly informed.

(2)   The court's case progression officer must refer the agreement to the court if in doubt that the condition in paragraph (1)(a) is satisfied.

3.8.   *Court's power to vary requirements under this Part*   (1)   The court may—

(a)   shorten or extend (even after it has expired) a time limit set by this Part; and

(b)   allow an application or representations to be made orally.

(2)   A person who wants an extension of time must—

(a)   apply when serving the application or representations for which it is needed; and

(b)   explain the delay.

3.9.   *Case preparation and progression*   (1)   At every hearing, if a case cannot be concluded there and then the court must give directions so that it can be concluded at the next hearing or as soon as possible after that.

(2)   At every hearing the court must, where relevant—

(a)   if the defendant is absent, decide whether to proceed nonetheless;

(b)   take the defendant's plea (unless already done) or if no plea can be taken then find out whether the defendant is likely to plead guilty or not guilty;

(c)   set, follow or revise a timetable for the progress of the case, which may include a timetable for any hearing including the trial or (in the Crown Court) the appeal;

(d)   in giving directions, ensure continuity in relation to the court and to the parties' representatives where that is appropriate and practicable; and

(e)   where a direction has not been complied with, find out why, identify who was responsible, and take appropriate action.

(3)   In order to prepare for the trial, the court must take every reasonable step—

(a)   to encourage and to facilitate the attendance of witnesses when they are needed; and

(b)   to facilitate the participation of any person, including the defendant.

(4)   Facilitating the participation of the defendant includes finding out whether the defendant needs interpretation because—

(a)   the defendant does not speak or understand English; or

(b)   the defendant has a hearing or speech impediment.

(5)   Where the defendant needs interpretation—

(a)   the court officer must arrange for interpretation to be provided at every hearing which the defendant is due to attend;

(b)   interpretation may be by an intermediary where the defendant has a speech impediment, without the need for a defendant's evidence direction;

(c)   on application or on its own initiative, the court may require a written translation to be provided for the defendant of any document or part of a document, unless—

      (i)   translation of that document, or part, is not needed to explain the case against the defendant, or

      (ii)   the defendant agrees to do without and the court is satisfied that the agreement is clear and voluntary and that the defendant has had legal advice or otherwise understands the consequences;

(d)   on application by the defendant, the court must give any direction which the court thinks appropriate, including a direction for interpretation by a different interpreter, where—

      (i)   no interpretation is provided,

      (ii)   no translation is ordered or provided in response to a previous application by the defendant, or

      (iii)   the defendant complains about the quality of interpretation or of any translation.

(6)   Facilitating the participation of any person includes giving directions for the appropriate treatment and questioning of a witness or the defendant, especially where the court directs that such questioning is to be conducted through an intermediary.

(7)   Where directions for appropriate treatment and questioning are required[ED], the court must—

(a)   invite representations by the parties and by any intermediary; and

(b)   set ground rules for the conduct of the questioning, which rules may include—

      (i)   a direction relieving a party of any duty to put that party's case to a witness or a defendant in its entirety,

      (ii)   directions about the manner of questioning,

      (iii)   directions about the duration of questioning,

      (iv)   if necessary, directions about the questions that may or may not be asked,

      (v)   where there is more than one defendant, the allocation among them of the topics about which a witness may be asked, and

      (vi)   directions about the use of models, plans, body maps or similar aids to help communicate a question or an answer.

[Note. Part 18 (Measures to assist a witness or defendant to give evidence) contains rules about an application for a defendant's evidence direction under (among other provisions) sections 33BA and 33BB of the Youth Justice and Criminal Evidence Act 1999.

See also Directive 2010/64/EU of the European Parliament and of the Council of 20th October, 2010,

on the right to interpretation and translation in criminal proceedings.
Where a trial in the Crown Court will take place in Wales and a participant wishes to use the Welsh
language, see rule 3.26. Where a trial in a magistrates' court will take place in Wales, a participant
may use the Welsh language: see rule 24.14.]

ᴱᴰ Where a witness was vulnerable and the subject of special measures and was likely to suffer distress in giving
evidence owing to her own circumstances and the circumstances of the case, the judge was bound to ensure that the
questioning was controlled: *R v Jonas (Sandor)* [2015] EWCA Crim 562, [2015] Crim LR 742.

3.10. Readiness for trial or appeal (1) This rule applies to a party's preparation for trial or
appeal, and in this rule and rule 3.11 'trial' includes any hearing at which evidence will be
introduced.
(2)   In fulfilling the duty under rule 3.3, each party must—
(a)   comply with directions given by the court;
(b)   take every reasonable step to make sure that party's witnesses will attend when they are
       needed;
(c)   make appropriate arrangements to present any written or other material; and
(d)   promptly inform the court and the other parties of anything that may—
       (i)   affect the date or duration of the trial or appeal, or
       (ii)   significantly affect the progress of the case in any other way.
(3)   The court may require a party to give a certificate of readiness.

3.11. Conduct of a trial or an appeal In order to manage a trial or an appeal, the court—
(a)   must establish, with the active assistance of the parties, what are the disputed issues;
(b)   must consider setting a timetable that—
       (i)   takes account of those issues and of any timetable proposed by a party, and
       (ii)   may limit the duration of any stage of the hearing;
(c)   may require a party to identify—
       (i)   which witnesses that party wants to give evidence in person,
       (ii)   the order in which that party wants those witnesses to give their evidence,
       (iii) whether that party requires an order compelling the attendance of a witness,
       (iv)   what arrangements are desirable to facilitate the giving of evidence by a witness,
       (v)   what arrangements are desirable to facilitate the participation of any other person,
              including the defendant,
       (vi)   what written evidence that party intends to introduce,
       (vii) what other material, if any, that person intends to make available to the court in the
              presentation of the case, and
       (viii) whether that party intends to raise any point of law that could affect the conduct of
              the trial or appeal; and
(d)   may limit—
       (i)   the examination, cross-examination or re-examination of a witness, and
       (ii)   the duration of any stage of the hearing.
[Note. See also rules 3.5 (The court's case management powers) and 3.9 (Case preparation and
progression).]

3.12. Duty of court officer The court officer must—
(a)   where a person is entitled or required to attend a hearing, give as much notice as
       reasonably practicable to—
       (i)   that person, and
       (ii)   that person's custodian (if any);
(b)   where the court gives directions, promptly make a record available to the parties.
[Note. See also rule 5.7 (Supply to a party of information or documents from records or case
materials).]

PREPARATION FOR TRIAL IN THE CROWN COURT

3.13. Pre-trial hearings in the Crown Court: general rules (1)   The Crown Court—
(a)   may, and in some cases must, conduct a preparatory hearing where rule 3.14 applies;
(b)   must conduct a plea and trial preparation hearing;
(c)   may conduct a further pre-trial case management hearing (and if necessary more than
       one such hearing) only where—
       (i)   the court anticipates a guilty plea,
       (ii)   it is necessary to conduct such a hearing in order to give directions for an effective
              trial, or
       (iii) such a hearing is required to set ground rules for the conduct of the questioning of
              a witness or defendant.
(2)   At the plea and trial preparation hearing the court must⁻
(a)   satisfy itself that there has been explained to the defendant, in terms the defendant can
       understand (with help, if necessary), that the defendant will receive credit for a guilty plea;
(b)   take the defendant's plea or if no plea can be taken then find out whether the defendant is
       likely to plead guilty or not guilty;
(c)   unless the defendant pleads guilty, satisfy itself that there has been explained to the
       defendant, in terms the defendant can understand (with help, if necessary), that at the
       trial⁻

     (i)   the defendant will have the right to give evidence after the court has heard the prosecution case,

     (ii)   if the defendant does not attend, the trial may take place in the defendant's absence,

     (iii)   if the trial takes place in the defendant's absence, the judge may inform the jury of the reason for that absence, and

     (iv)   where the defendant is released on bail, failure to attend court when required is an offence for which the defendant may be arrested and punished and bail may be withdrawn; and

(d)   give directions for an effective trial.

(3)   A pre-trial case management hearing—

(a)   must be in public, as a general rule, but all or part of the hearing may be in private if the court so directs; and

(b)   must be recorded, in accordance with rule 5.5 (Recording and transcription of proceedings in the Crown Court).

(4)   Where the court determines a pre-trial application in private, it must announce its decision in public.

(5)   The court—

(a)   at the first hearing in the Crown Court must require a defendant who is present—

     (i)   to provide, in writing or orally, his or her name, date of birth and nationality, or

     (ii)   to confirm that information by those means, where the information was given to the magistrates' court which sent the defendant for trial; and

(b)   at any subsequent hearing may require such a defendant to provide or confirm that information by those means.

[Note. See also the general rules in the first section of this Part (rules 3.1 to 3.12) and the other rules in this section.

The Practice Direction lists the circumstances in which a further pre-trial case management hearing is likely to be needed in order to give directions for an effective trial.

There are rules relevant to applications which may be made at a pre-trial hearing in Part 6 (Reporting, etc restrictions), Part 14 (Bail and custody time limits), Part 15 (Disclosure), Part 17 (Witness summonses, warrants and orders), Part 18 (Measures to assist a witness or defendant to give evidence), Part 19 (Expert evidence), Part 20 (Hearsay evidence), Part 21 (Evidence of bad character), Part 22 (Evidence of a complainant's previous sexual behaviour) and Part 23 (Restriction on cross-examination by a defendant).

On an application to which Part 14 (Bail and custody time limits) applies, rule 14.2 (exercise of court's powers under that Part) may require the defendant's presence, which may be by live link. Where rule 14.10 applies (Consideration of bail in a murder case), the court officer must arrange for the Crown Court to consider bail within 2 business days of the first hearing in the magistrates' court.

Under section 40 of the Criminal Procedure and Investigations Act 1996, a pre-trial ruling about the admissibility of evidence or any other question of law is binding unless it later appears to the court in the interests of justice to discharge or vary that ruling.]

Under section 86A of the Courts Act 2003, Criminal Procedure Rules must specify stages of proceedings at which the court must require the information listed in rule 3.13(5). A person commits an offence if, without reasonable excuse, that person fails to comply with such a requirement, whether by providing false or incomplete information or by providing no information.

3.14. *Preparatory hearing* (1) This rule applies where the Crown Court—

(a)   can order a preparatory hearing, under—

     (i)   section 7 of the Criminal Justice Act 1987 (cases of serious or complex fraud), or

     (ii)   section 29 of the Criminal Procedure and Investigations Act 1996 (other complex, serious or lengthy cases);

(b)   must order such a hearing, to determine an application for a trial without a jury, under—

     (i)   section 44 of the Criminal Justice Act 2003 (danger of jury tampering), or

     (ii)   section 17 of the Domestic Violence, Crime and Victims Act 2004 (trial of sample counts by jury, and others by judge alone);

(c)   must order such a hearing, under section 29 of the 1996 Act, where section 29(1B) or (1C) applies (cases in which a terrorism offence is charged, or other serious cases with a terrorist connection).

(2)   The court may decide whether to order a preparatory hearing—

(a)   on an application or on its own initiative;

(b)   at a hearing (in public or in private), or without a hearing;

(c)   in a party's absence, if that party—

     (i)   applied for the order, or

     (ii)   has had at least 14 days in which to make representations.

[Note. See also section 45(2) of the Criminal Justice Act 2003 and section 18(1) of the Domestic Violence, Crime and Victims Act 2004.

At a preparatory hearing, the court may—

(a)   *require the prosecution to set out its case in a written statement, to arrange its evidence in a form that will be easiest for the jury (if there is one) to understand, to prepare a list of agreed facts, and to amend the case statement following representations from the defence (section 9(4) of the 1987 Act, section 31(4) of the 1996 Act); and*

(b)   require the defence to give notice of any objection to the prosecution case statement, and to give notice stating the extent of agreement with the prosecution as to documents and other matters and the reason for any disagreement *(section 9(5) of the 1987 Act, section 31(6), (7), (9) of the 1996 Act).*

Under section 10 of the 1987 Act, and under section 34 of the 1996 Act, if either party later departs from the case or objections disclosed by that party, then the court, or another party, may comment on that, and the court may draw such inferences as appear proper.]

3.15. *Application for preparatory hearing* (1) A party who wants the court to order a preparatory hearing must—

(a)   apply in writing—
     (i)   as soon as reasonably practicable, and in any event
     (ii)   not more than 14 days after the defendant pleads not guilty;
(b)   serve the application on—
     (i)   the court officer, and
     (ii)   each other party.
(2) The applicant must—
(a)   if relevant, explain what legislation requires the court to order a preparatory hearing;
(b)   otherwise, explain—
     (i)   what makes the case complex or serious, or makes the trial likely to be long,
     (ii)   why a substantial benefit will accrue from a preparatory hearing, and
     (iii) why the court's ordinary powers of case management are not adequate.
(3) A prosecutor who wants the court to order a trial without a jury must explain—
(a)   where the prosecutor alleges a danger of jury tampering—
     (i)   what evidence there is of a real and present danger that jury tampering would take place,
     (ii)   what steps, if any, reasonably might be taken to prevent jury tampering, and
     (iii) why, notwithstanding such steps, the likelihood of jury tampering is so substantial as to make it necessary in the interests of justice to order such a trial; or
(b)   where the prosecutor proposes trial without a jury on some counts on the indictment—
     (i)   why a trial by jury involving all the counts would be impracticable,
     (ii)   how the counts proposed for jury trial can be regarded as samples of the others, and
     (iii) why it would be in the interests of justice to order such a trial.

3.16. *Application for non-jury trial containing information withheld from a defendant* (1) This rule applies where—

(a)   the prosecutor applies for an order for a trial without a jury because of a danger of jury tampering; and
(b)   the application includes information that the prosecutor thinks ought not be revealed to a defendant.
(2) The prosecutor must—
(a)   omit that information from the part of the application that is served on that defendant;
(b)   mark the other part to show that, unless the court otherwise directs, it is only for the court; and
(c)   in that other part, explain why the prosecutor has withheld that information from that defendant.
(3) The hearing of an application to which this rule applies—
(a)   must be in private, unless the court otherwise directs; and
(b)   if the court so directs, may be, wholly or in part, in the absence of a defendant from whom information has been withheld.
(4) At the hearing of an application to which this rule applies—
(a)   the general rule is that the court will receive, in the following sequence—
     (i)   representations first by the prosecutor and then by each defendant, in all the parties' presence, and then
     (ii)   further representations by the prosecutor, in the absence of a defendant from whom information has been withheld; but
(b)   the court may direct other arrangements for the hearing.
(5) Where, on an application to which this rule applies, the court orders a trial without a jury—
(a)   the general rule is that the trial will be before a judge other than the judge who made the order; but
(b)   the court may direct other arrangements.

3.17. *Representations in response to application for preparatory hearing* (1) This rule applies where a party wants to make representations about—

(a)   an application for a preparatory hearing;
(b)   an application for a trial without a jury.
(2) Such a party must—
(a)   serve the representations on—
     (i)   the court officer, and
     (ii)   each other party;
(b)   do so not more than 14 days after service of the application;

(c)   ask for a hearing, if that party wants one, and explain why it is needed.

(3)   Where representations include information that the person making them thinks ought not be revealed to another party, that person must—

(a)   omit that information from the representations served on that other party;

(b)   mark the information to show that, unless the court otherwise directs, it is only for the court; and

(c)   with that information include an explanation of why it has been withheld from that other party.

(4)   Representations against an application for an order must explain why the conditions for making it are not met.

3.18. *Commencement of preparatory hearing* At the beginning of a preparatory hearing, the court must—

(a)   announce that it is such a hearing; and

(b)   take the defendant's plea under rule 3.24 (Arraigning the defendant on the indictment), unless already done.

[Note. See section 8 of the Criminal Justice Act 1987 and section 30 of the Criminal Procedure and Investigations Act 1996.]

3.19. *Defence trial advocate* (1) The defendant must notify the court officer of the identity of the intended defence trial advocate—

(a)   as soon as practicable, and in any event no later than the day of the plea and trial preparation hearing;

(b)   in writing, or orally at that hearing.

(2)   The defendant must notify the court officer in writing of any change in the identity of the intended defence trial advocate as soon as practicable, and in any event not more than 5 business days after that change.

3.20. *Application to stay case for abuse of process* (1) This rule applies where a defendant wants the Crown Court to stay the case on the grounds that the proceedings are an abuse of the court, or otherwise unfair.

(2)   Such a defendant must—

(a)   apply in writing—

      (i)   as soon as practicable after becoming aware of the grounds for doing so,

      (ii)   at a pre-trial hearing, unless the grounds for the application do not arise until trial, and

      (iii)   in any event, before the defendant pleads guilty or the jury (if there is one) retires to consider its verdict at trial;

(b)   serve the application on—

      (i)   the court officer, and

      (ii)   each other party; and

(c)   in the application—

      (i)   explain the grounds on which it is made,

      (ii)   include, attach or identify all supporting material,

      (iii)   specify relevant events, dates and propositions of law, and

      (iv)   identify any witness the applicant wants to call to give evidence in person.

(3)   A party who wants to make representations in response to the application must serve the representations on—

(a)   the court officer; and

(b)   each other party,

not more than 14 days after service of the application.

3.21. *Application for joint or separate trials, etc* (1) This rule applies where a party wants the Crown Court to order—

(a)   the joint trial of—

      (i)   offences charged by separate indictments, or

      (ii)   defendants charged in separate indictments;

(b)   separate trials of offences charged by the same indictment;

(c)   separate trials of defendants charged in the same indictment; or

(d)   the deletion of a count from an indictment.

(2)   Such a party must—

(a)   apply in writing—

      (i)   as soon as practicable after becoming aware of the grounds for doing so, and

      (ii)   before the trial begins, unless the grounds for the application do not arise until trial;

(b)   serve the application on—

      (i)   the court officer, and

      (ii)   each other party; and

(c)   in the application—

      (i)   specify the order proposed, and

      (ii)   explain why it should be made.

(3)   A party who wants to make representations in response to the application must serve the representations on—

(a)   the court officer; and

(b)   each other party,

not more than 14 days after service of the application.

(4)   Where the same indictment charges more than one offence, the court may exercise its power to order separate trials of those offences if of the opinion that—

(a)   the defendant otherwise may be prejudiced or embarrassed in his or her defence (for example, where the offences to be tried together are neither founded on the same facts nor form or are part of a series of offences of the same or a similar character); or

(b)   for any other reason it is desirable that the defendant should be tried separately for any one or more of those offences.

[Note. See section 5 of the Indictments Act 1915. Rule 10.2 governs the form and content of an indictment.]

Any issue arising from a decision under this rule may be subject to appeal to the Court of Appeal. Part 37 (Appeal to the Court of Appeal against ruling at preparatory hearing), Part 38 (Appeal to the Court of Appeal against ruling adverse to prosecution) and Part 39 (Appeal to the Court of Appeal about conviction or sentence) each contains relevant rules. The powers of the Court of Appeal on an appeal to which Part 39 applies are set out in sections 2, 3 and 7 of the Criminal Appeal Act 1968.

3.22.   *Order for joint or separate trials, or amendment of the indictment*   (1)   This rule applies where the Crown Court makes an order—

(a)   on an application under rule 3.21 applies (Application for joint or separate trials, etc); or

(b)   amending an indictment in any other respect.

(2)   Unless the court otherwise directs, the court officer must endorse any paper copy of each affected indictment made for the court with—

(a)   a note of the court's order; and

(b)   the date of that order.

3.23.   *Application for indication of sentence*   (1)   This rule applies where a defendant wants the Crown Court to give an indication of the maximum sentence that would be passed if a guilty plea were entered when the indication is sought.

(2)   Such a defendant must—

(a)   apply in writing as soon as practicable; and

(b)   serve the application on—

(i)   the court officer, and

(ii)   the prosecutor.

(3)   The application must—

(a)   specify—

(i)   the offence or offences to which it would be a guilty plea, and

(ii)   the facts on the basis of which that plea would be entered; and

(b)   include the prosecutor's agreement to, or representations on, that proposed basis of plea.

(4)   The prosecutor must—

(a)   provide information relevant to sentence, including—

(i)   any previous conviction of the defendant, and the circumstances where relevant,

(ii)   any statement of the effect of the offence on the victim, the victim's family or others; and

(b)   identify any other matter relevant to sentence, including—

(i)   the legislation applicable,

(ii)   any sentencing guidelines, or guideline cases, and

(iii)   aggravating and mitigating factors.

(5)   The hearing of the application—

(a)   may take place in the absence of any other defendant;

(b)   must be attended by—

(i)   the applicant defendant's legal representatives (if any), and

(ii)   the prosecution advocate.

3.24.   *Arraigning the defendant on the indictment*   (1)   In order to take the defendant's plea, the Crown Court must—

(a)   obtain the prosecutor's confirmation, in writing or orally—

(i)   that the indictment (or draft indictment, as the case may be) sets out a statement of each offence that the prosecutor wants the court to try and such particulars of the conduct constituting the commission of each such offence as the prosecutor relies upon to make clear what is alleged, and

(ii)   of the order in which the prosecutor wants the defendants' names to be listed in the indictment, if the prosecutor proposes that more than one defendant should be tried at the same time;

(b)   ensure that the defendant is correctly identified by the indictment or draft indictment;

(c)   in respect of each count—

(i)   read the count aloud to the defendant, or arrange for it to be read aloud or placed before the defendant in writing,

(ii)   ask whether the defendant pleads guilty or not guilty to the offence charged by that count, and

(iii)   take the defendant's plea.

(2)   Where a count is read which is substantially the same as one already read aloud, then only

the materially different details need be read aloud.

(3)   Where a count is placed before the defendant in writing, the court must summarise its gist aloud.

(4)   In respect of each count in the indictment—

(a)   if the defendant declines to enter a plea, the court must treat that as a not guilty plea unless rule 25.10 applies (Defendant unfit to plead);

(b)   if the defendant pleads not guilty to the offence charged by that count but guilty to another offence of which the court could convict on that count—

(i)   if the prosecutor and the court accept that plea, the court must treat the plea as one of guilty of that other offence, but

(ii)   otherwise, the court must treat the plea as one of not guilty;

(c)   if the defendant pleads a previous acquittal or conviction of the offence charged by that count—

(i)   the defendant must identify that acquittal or conviction in writing, explaining the basis of that plea, and

(ii)   the court must exercise its power to decide whether that plea disposes of that count.

(5)   In a case in which a magistrates' court sends the defendant for trial, the Crown Court must take the defendant's plea—

(a)   not less than 2 weeks after the date on which that sending takes place, unless the parties otherwise agree; and

(b)   not more than 16 weeks after that date, unless the court otherwise directs (either before or after that period expires).

[Note. See section 6 of the Criminal Law Act 1967, section 77 of the Senior Courts Act 1981 and section 122 of the Criminal Justice Act 1988. Part 10 contains rules about indictments: see in particular rule 10.2 (The indictment: general rules)

Under section 6(2) of the 1967 Act, on an indictment for murder a defendant may instead be convicted of manslaughter or another offence specified by that provision. Under section 6(3) of that Act, on an indictment for an offence other than murder or treason a defendant may instead be convicted of another offence if—

(a)   *the allegation in the indictment amounts to or includes an allegation of that other offence; and*

(b)   *the Crown Court has power to convict and sentence for that other offence.]*

3.25.   Place of trial   (1)   Unless the court otherwise directs, the court officer must arrange for the trial to take place in a courtroom provided by the Lord Chancellor.

(2)   The court officer must arrange for the court and the jury (if there is one) to view any place required by the court.

[Note. See section 3 of the Courts Act 2003 and section 14 of the Juries Act 1974.

In some circumstances the court may conduct all or part of the hearing outside a courtroom.]

3.26.   Use of Welsh language at trial   Where the trial will take place in Wales and a participant wishes to use the Welsh language—

(a)   that participant must serve notice on the court officer, or arrange for such a notice to be served on that participant's behalf—

(i)   at or before the plea and trial preparation hearing, or

(ii)   in accordance with any direction given by the court; and

(b)   if such a notice is served, the court officer must arrange for an interpreter to attend.

[Note. See section 22 of the Welsh Language Act 1993.]

Other provisions affecting case management

Case management may be affected by the following other rules and legislation:

Criminal Procedure Rules

Part 8 Initial details of the prosecution case

Part 9 Allocation and sending for trial

Part 10 The indictment

Part 15 Disclosure

Parts 16–23: the rules that deal with evidence

Part 24 Trial and sentence in a magistrates' court

Part 25 Trial and sentence in the Crown Court

Regulations

The Prosecution of Offences (Custody Time Limits) Regulations 1987

The Crime and Disorder Act 1998 (Service of Prosecution Evidence) Regulations 2005

The Criminal Procedure and Investigations Act 1996 (Defence Disclosure Time Limits) Regulations 2011

Acts of Parliament

Sections 10 and 18, Magistrates' Courts Act 1980: powers to adjourn hearings

Sections 128 and 129, Magistrates' Courts Act 1980: remand in custody by magistrates' courts

Sections 19 and 24A, Magistrates' Courts Act 1980 and sections 51 and 51A, Crime and Disorder Act 1998: allocation and sending for trial

Section 2, Administration of Justice (Miscellaneous Provisions) Act 1933: procedural conditions for trial in the Crown Court

Sections 8A and 8B, Magistrates' Courts Act 1980: pre-trial hearings in magistrates' courts

Section 7, Criminal Justice Act 1987; Parts III and IV, Criminal Procedure and Investigations Act 1996: pre-trial and preparatory hearings in the Crown Court

Section 9, Criminal Justice Act 1967: proof by written witness statement
Part 1, Criminal Procedure and Investigations Act 1996: disclosure.]

PREPARATION FOR TRIAL IN A MAGISTRATES' COURT

3.27. **Pre-trial hearings in a magistrates' court: general rules** (1) A magistrates' court—

(a) must conduct a preparation for trial hearing unless—

    (i) the court sends the defendant for trial in the Crown Court, or

    (ii) the case is one to which rule 24.8 or rule 24.9 applies (Written guilty plea: special rules; Single justice procedure: special rules);

(b) may conduct a further pre-trial case management hearing (and if necessary more than one such hearing) only where—

    (i) the court anticipates a guilty plea,

    (ii) it is necessary to conduct such a hearing in order to give directions for an effective trial, or

    (iii) such a hearing is required to set ground rules for the conduct of the questioning of a witness or defendant.

(2) At a preparation for trial hearing the court must give directions for an effective trial.

(3) At a preparation for trial hearing, if the defendant is present the court must—

(a) satisfy itself that there has been explained to the defendant, in terms the defendant can understand (with help, if necessary), that the defendant will receive credit for a guilty plea;

(b) take the defendant's plea or if no plea can be taken then find out whether the defendant is likely to plead guilty or not guilty; and

(c) unless the defendant pleads guilty, satisfy itself that there has been explained to the defendant, in terms the defendant can understand (with help, if necessary), that at the trial—

    (i) the defendant will have the right to give evidence after the court has heard the prosecution case,

    (ii) if the defendant does not attend, the trial is likely to take place in the defendant's absence, and

    (iii) where the defendant is released on bail, failure to attend court when required is an offence for which the defendant may be arrested and punished and bail may be withdrawn.

(4) A pre-trial case management hearing must be in public, as a general rule, but all or part of the hearing may be in private if the court so directs.

(5) The court—

(a) at the first hearing in the case must require a defendant who is present to provide, in writing or orally, his or her name, date of birth and nationality; and

(b) at any subsequent hearing may require such a defendant to provide that information by those means.

[Note. At the first hearing in a magistrates' court the court may, and in some cases must, send the defendant to the Crown Court for trial, depending upon (i) the classification of the offence, (ii) the defendant's age, (iii) whether the defendant is awaiting Crown Court trial for another offence, (iv) whether another defendant charged with the same offence is awaiting Crown Court trial, and (v) in some cases, the value of property involved. See also Part 9 (Allocation and sending for trial).

Under section 11 of the Magistrates' Courts Act 1980, where the defendant does not attend the trial, where the defendant is at least 18 years old, and subject to some exceptions, then the court must proceed in his or her absence unless it appears to the court to be contrary to the interests of justice to do so. Where the defendant does not attend the trial and he or she is under 18 then, again subject to some exceptions, the court may proceed in his or her absence.

Under sections 8A and 8B of the Magistrates' Courts Act 1980, a pre-trial ruling about the admissibility of evidence or any other question of law is binding unless it later appears to the court in the interests of justice to discharge or vary that ruling.

Under section 86A of the Courts Act 2003, Criminal Procedure Rules must specify stages of proceedings at which the court must require the information listed in rule 3.27(5) and may specify other stages of proceedings when such requirements may be imposed. A person commits an offence if, without reasonable excuse, that person fails to comply with such a requirement, whether by providing false or incomplete information or by providing no information.]

MEDICAL REPORTS

3.28. **Directions for commissioning medical reports, other than for sentencing purposes**

(1) This rule applies where, because of a defendant's suspected mental ill-health—

(a) a magistrates' court requires expert medical opinion about the potential suitability of a hospital order under section 37(3) of the Mental Health Act 1983 (hospital order without convicting the defendant);

(b) the Crown Court requires expert medical opinion about the defendant's fitness to participate at trial, under section 4 of the Criminal Procedure (Insanity) Act 1964; or

(c) a magistrates' court or the Crown Court requires expert medical opinion to help the court determine a question of intent or insanity,

other than such opinion introduced by a party.

(2) A court may exercise the power to which this rule applies on its own initiative having regard to—

(a) an assessment of the defendant's health by a mental health practitioner acting independently of the parties to assist the court;

(b)	representations by a party; or
(c)	observations by the court.
(3)	A court that requires expert medical opinion to which this rule applies must—
(a)	identify each issue in respect of which the court requires such opinion and any legislation applicable;
(b)	specify the nature of the expertise likely to be required for giving such opinion;
(c)	identify each party or participant by whom a commission for such opinion must be prepared, who may be—

     (i)   a party (or party's representative) acting on that party's own behalf,

     (ii)   a party (or party's representative) acting on behalf of the court, or

     (iii)   the court officer acting on behalf of the court;

(d)   where there are available to the court arrangements with the National Health Service under which an assessment of a defendant's mental health may be prepared, give such directions as are needed under those arrangements for obtaining the expert report or reports required;

(e)   where no such arrangements are available to the court, or they will not be used, give directions for the commissioning of an expert report or expert reports, including—

     (i)   such directions as can be made about supplying the expert or experts with the defendant's medical records,

     (ii)   directions about the other information, about the defendant and about the offence or offences alleged to have been committed by the defendant, which is to be supplied to each expert, and

     (iii)   directions about the arrangements that will apply for the payment of each expert;

(f)   set a timetable providing for—

     (i)   the date by which a commission is to be delivered to each expert,

     (ii)   the date by which any failure to accept a commission is to be reported to the court,

     (iii)   the date or dates by which progress in the preparation of a report or reports is to be reviewed by the court officer, and

     (iv)   the date by which each report commissioned is to be received by the court; and

(g)   identify the person (each person, if more than one) to whom a copy of a report is to be supplied, and by whom.

(4)   A commission addressed to an expert must—

(a)   identify each issue in respect of which the court requires expert medical opinion and any legislation applicable;

(b)   include—

     (i)   the information required by the court to be supplied to the expert,

     (ii)   details of the timetable set by the court, and

     (iii)   details of the arrangements that will apply for the payment of the expert;

(c)   identify the person (each person, if more than one) to whom a copy of the expert's report is to be supplied; and

(d)   request confirmation that the expert from whom the opinion is sought—

     (i)   accepts the commission, and

     (ii)   will adhere to the timetable.

[Note. See also rule 28.8 (Directions for commissioning medical reports for sentencing purposes). The court may request a medical examination of the defendant and a report under—

(a)   section 4 of the Criminal Procedure (Insanity) Act 1964, under which the Crown Court may determine a defendant's fitness to plead;

(b)   section 35 of the Mental Health Act 1983, under which the court may order the defendant's detention in hospital to obtain a medical report;

(c)   section 36 of the 1983 Act, under which the Crown Court may order the defendant's detention in hospital instead of in custody pending trial;

(d)   section 37 of the 1983 Act, under which the court may order the defendant's detention and treatment in hospital, or make a guardianship order, instead of disposing of the case in another way (section 37(3) allows a magistrates' court to make such an order without convicting the defendant if satisfied that the defendant did the act or made the omission charged);

(e)   section 38 of the 1983 Act, under which the court may order the defendant's temporary detention and treatment in hospital instead of disposing of the case in another way;

(f)   section 157 of the Criminal Justice Act 2003, under which the court must usually obtain and consider a medical report before passing a custodial sentence if the defendant is, or appears to be, mentally disordered;

(g)   section 207 of the 2003 Act (in the case of a defendant aged 18 or over), or section 1(1)(k) of the Criminal Justice and Immigration Act 2008 (in the case of a defendant who is under 18), under which the court may impose a mental health treatment requirement.

For the purposes of the legislation listed in (a), (c), (d) and (e) above, the court requires the written or oral evidence of at least two registered medical practitioners, at least one of whom is approved as having special experience in the diagnosis or treatment of mental disorder. For the purposes of (b), (f) and (g), the court requires the evidence of one medical practitioner so approved.

Under section 11 of the Powers of Criminal Courts (Sentencing) Act 2000, a magistrates' court may adjourn a trial to obtain medical reports.

Part 19 (Expert evidence) contains rules about the content of expert medical reports.
For the authorities from whom the court may require information about hospital treatment or guardianship, see sections 39 and 39A of the 1983 Act.
The Practice Direction includes a timetable for the commissioning and preparation of a report or reports which the court may adopt with such adjustments as the court directs.
Payments to medical practitioners for reports and for giving evidence are governed by section 19(3) of the Prosecution of Offences Act 1985 and by the Costs in Criminal Cases (General) Regulations 1986, regulation 17 (Determination of rates or scales of allowances payable out of central funds), regulation 20 (Expert witnesses, etc) and regulation 25 (Written medical reports). The rates and scales of allowances payable under those Regulations are determined by the Lord Chancellor.]

Part 4   Service of Documents

Contents of this Part

B.4   *4.1. When this Part applies*   (1)   The rules in this Part apply—
(a)   to the service of every document in a case to which these Rules apply; and
(b)   for the purposes of section 12 of the Road Traffic Offenders Act 1988, to the service of a requirement to which that section applies.
(2)   The rules apply subject to any special rules in other legislation (including other Parts of these Rules) or in the Practice Direction.
[Note. Section 12 of the Road Traffic Offenders Act 1988 allows the court to accept the documents to which it refers as evidence of a driver's identity where a requirement to state that identity has been served under section 172 of the Road Traffic Act 1988 or under section 112 of the Road Traffic Regulation Act 1984.]

4.2. Methods of service   (1)   A document may be served by any of the methods described in rules 4.3 to 4.6 (subject to rules 4.7 and 4.10), or in rule 4.8.
(2)   Where a document may be served by electronic means under rule 4.6, the general rule is that the person serving it must use that method.

4.3. Service by handing over a document   (1)   A document may be served on—
(a)   an individual by handing it to him or her;
(b)   a corporation by handing it to a person holding a senior position in that corporation;
(c)   an individual or corporation who is legally represented in the case by handing it to that legal representative;
(d)   the prosecution by handing it to the prosecutor or to the prosecution representative;
(e)   the court officer by handing it to a court officer with authority to accept it at the relevant court office; and
(f)   the Registrar of Criminal Appeals by handing it to a court officer with authority to accept it at the Criminal Appeal Office.
(2)   If an individual is under 18, a copy of a document served under paragraph (1)(a) must be handed to his or her parent, or another appropriate adult, unless no such person is readily available.
(3)   Unless the court otherwise directs, for the purposes of paragraph (1)(c) or (d) (service by handing a document to a party's representative) 'representative' includes an advocate appearing for that party at a hearing.
(4)   In this rule, 'the relevant court office' means—
(a)   in relation to a case in a magistrates' court or in the Crown Court, the office at which that court's business is administered by court staff;
(b)   in relation to an application to a High Court judge for permission to serve a draft indictment—
    (i)   in London, the Listing Office of the Queen's Bench Division of the High Court, and
    (ii)   elsewhere, the office at which court staff administer the business of any court then constituted of a High Court judge;

(c)   in relation to an extradition appeal case in the High Court, the Administrative Court Office of the Queen's Bench Division of the High Court.

[Note. Some legislation treats a body that is not a corporation as if it were one for the purposes of rules about service of documents. See for example section 143 of the Adoption and Children Act 2002.]

4.4. Service by leaving or posting a document   (1)   A document may be served by addressing it to the person to be served and leaving it at the appropriate address for service under this rule, or by sending it to that address by first class post or by the equivalent of first class post.

(2)   The address for service under this rule on—

(a)   an individual is an address where it is reasonably believed that he or she will receive it;

(b)   a corporation is its principal office, and if there is no readily identifiable principal office then any place where it carries on its activities or business;

(c)   an individual or corporation who is legally represented in the case is that legal representative's office;

(d)   the prosecution is the prosecutor's office;

(e)   the court officer is the relevant court office; and

(f)   the Registrar of Criminal Appeals is the Criminal Appeal Office, Royal Courts of Justice, Strand, London WC2A 2LL.

(3)   In this rule, 'the relevant court office' means—

(a)   in relation to a case in a magistrates' court or in the Crown Court, the office at which that court's business is administered by court staff;

(b)   in relation to an application to a High Court judge for permission to serve a draft indictment—

     (i)   in London, the Queen's Bench Listing Office, Royal Courts of Justice, Strand, London WC2A 2LL, and

     (ii)   elsewhere, the office at which court staff administer the business of any court then constituted of a High Court judge;

(c)   in relation to an extradition appeal case in the High Court, the Administrative Court Office, Royal Courts of Justice, Strand, London WC2A 2LL.

[Note. In addition to service in England and Wales for which these rules provide, service outside England and Wales may be allowed under other legislation. See—

(a)   section 39 of the Criminal Law Act 1977 (service of summons, etc in Scotland and Northern Ireland);

(b)   section 1139(4) of the Companies Act 2006 (service of copy summons, etc on company's registered office in Scotland and Northern Ireland);

(c)   sections 3, 4, 4A and 4B of the Crime (International Co-operation) Act 2003 (service of summons, etc outside the United Kingdom) and rules 49.1 and 49.2; and

(d)   section 1139(2) of the Companies Act 2006 (service on overseas company).]

4.5. Service by document exchange   (1)   This rule applies where—

(a)   the person to be served—

     (i)   has given a document exchange (DX) box number, and

     (ii)   has not refused to accept service by DX; or

(b)   the person to be served is legally represented in the case and the legal representative has given a DX box number.

(2)   A document may be served by—

(a)   addressing it to that person or legal representative, as appropriate, at that DX box number; and

(b)   leaving it at—

     (i)   the document exchange at which the addressee has that DX box number, or

     (ii)   a document exchange at which the person serving it has a DX box number.

4.6. Service by electronic means   (1)   This rule applies where—

(a)   the person to be served—

     (i)   has given an electronic address and has not refused to accept service at that address, or

     (ii)   is given access to an electronic address at which a document may be deposited and has not refused to accept service by the deposit of a document at that address; or

(b)   the person to be served is legally represented in the case and the legal representative—

     (i)   has given an electronic address, or

     (ii)   is given access to an electronic address at which a document may be deposited.

(2)   A document may be served—

(a)   by sending it by electronic means to the address which the recipient has given; or

(b)   by depositing it at an address to which the recipient has been given access and—

     (i)   in every case, making it possible for the recipient to read the document, or view or listen to its content, as the case may be,

     (ii)   unless the court otherwise directs, making it possible for the recipient to make and keep an electronic copy of the document, and

     (iii)   notifying the recipient of the deposit of the document (which notice may be given by electronic means).

(3)   Where a document is served under this rule the person serving it need not provide a paper copy as well.

4.7. Documents that must be served by specified methods (1)   An application or written statement, and notice, under rule 48.9 alleging contempt of court may be served—
(a)   on an individual, only under rule 4.3(1)(a) (by handing it to him or her);
(b)   on a corporation, only under rule 4.3(1)(b) (by handing it to a person holding a senior position in that corporation).
(2)   For the purposes of section 12 of the Road Traffic Offenders Act 1988, a notice of a requirement under section 172 of the Road Traffic Act 1988 or under section 112 of the Road Traffic Regulation Act 1984 to identify the driver of a vehicle may be served—
(a)   on an individual, only by post under rule 4.4(1) and (2)(a);
(b)   on a corporation, only by post under rule 4.4(1) and (2)(b).

4.8. Service by person in custody (1)   A person in custody may serve a document by handing it to the custodian addressed to the person to be served.
(2)   The custodian must—
(a)   endorse it with the time and date of receipt;
(b)   record its receipt; and
(c)   forward it promptly to the addressee.

4.9. Service by another method (1)   The court may allow service of a document by a method—
(a)   other than those described in rules 4.3 to 4.6 and in rule 4.8;
(b)   other than one specified by rule 4.7, where that rule applies.
(2)   An order allowing service by another method must specify—
(a)   the method to be used; and
(b)   the date on which the document will be served.

4.10. Documents that may not be served on a legal representative Unless the court otherwise directs, service on a party's legal representative of any of the following documents is not service of that document on that party—
(a)   a summons, requisition, single justice procedure notice or witness summons;
(b)   notice of an order under section 25 of the Road Traffic Offenders Act 1988;
(c)   a notice of registration under section 71(6) of that Act;
(d)   notice of a hearing to review the postponement of the issue of a warrant of detention or imprisonment under section 77(6) of the Magistrates' Courts Act 1980;
(e)   notice under section 86 of that Act of a revised date to attend a means inquiry;
(f)   any notice or document served under Part 14 (Bail and custody time limits);
(g)   notice under rule 24.16(a) of when and where an adjourned hearing will resume;
(h)   notice under rule 28.5(3) of an application to vary or discharge a compensation order;
(i)   notice under rule 28.10(2)(c) of the location of the sentencing or enforcing court;
(j)   a collection order, or notice requiring payment, served under rule 30.2(a); or
(k)   an application or written statement, and notice, under rule 48.9 alleging contempt of court.

4.11. Date of service (1)   A document served under rule 4.3 or rule 4.8 is served on the day it is handed over.
(2)   Unless something different is shown, a document served on a person by any other method is served—
(a)   in the case of a document left at an address, on the next business day after the day on which it was left;
(b)   in the case of a document sent by first class post or by the equivalent of first class post, on the second business day after the day on which it was posted or despatched;
(c)   in the case of a document served by document exchange, on the second business day after the day on which it was left at a document exchange allowed by rule 4.5;
(d)   in the case of a document served by electronic means—
    (i)   on the day on which it is sent under rule 4.6(2)(a), if that day is a business day and if it is sent by no later than 2.30pm that day (4.30pm that day, in an extradition appeal case in the High Court),
    (ii)   on the day on which notice of its deposit is given under rule 4.6(2)(b), if that day is a business day and if that notice is given by no later than 2.30pm that day (4.30pm that day, in an extradition appeal case in the High Court), or
    (iii)   otherwise, on the next business day after it was sent or such notice was given; and
(e)   in any case, on the day on which the addressee responds to it, if that is earlier.
(3)   Unless something different is shown, a document produced by a computer system for dispatch by post is to be taken as having been sent by first class post, or by the equivalent of first class post, to the addressee on the business day after the day on which it was produced.
(4)   Where a document is served on or by the court officer, 'business day' does not include a day on which the court office is closed.

4.12. Proof of service The person who serves a document may prove that by signing a certificate explaining how and when it was served.

4.13. Court's power to give directions about service (1)   The court may specify the time as well as the date by which a document must be—
(a)   served under rule 4.3 (Service by handing over a document) or rule 4.8 (Service by person in custody); or

(b)   sent or deposited by electronic means, if it is served under rule 4.6.   (2)   The court may treat a document as served if the addressee responds to it even if it was not served in accordance with the rules in this Part.

PART 5   FORMS AND COURT RECORDS

FORMS

B.5   *5.1.   Applications, etc by forms or electronic means*   (1)   This rule applies where a rule, a practice direction or the court requires a person to—

(a)   make an application or give a notice;

(b)   supply information for the purposes of case management by the court; or

(c)   supply information needed for other purposes by the court.

(2)   Unless the court otherwise directs, such a person must—

(a)   use such electronic arrangements as the court officer may make for that purpose, in accordance with those arrangements; or

(b)   if no such arrangements have been made, use the appropriate form set out in the Practice Direction or the Criminal Costs Practice Direction, in accordance with those Directions.

5.2.   Forms in Welsh   (1)   Any Welsh language form set out in the Practice Direction, or in the Criminal Costs Practice Direction, is for use in connection with proceedings in courts in Wales.

(2)   Both a Welsh form and an English form may be contained in the same document.

(3)   Where only a Welsh form, or only the corresponding English form, is served—

(a)   the following words in Welsh and English must be added:

"Darperir y ddogfen hon yn Gymraeg / Saesneg os bydd arnoch ei heisiau. Dylech wneud cais yn ddi-oed i (swyddog y llys) (rhodder yma'r cyfeiriad)

This document will be provided in Welsh / English if you require it. You should apply immediately to (the court officer) (address)"; and

(b)   the court officer, or the person who served the form, must, on request, supply the corresponding form in the other language to the person served.

5.3.   Signature of forms   (1)   This rule applies where a form provides for its signature.

(2)   Unless other legislation otherwise requires, or the court otherwise directs, signature may be by any written or electronic authentication of the form by, or with the authority of, the signatory.

[Note. Section 7 of the Electronic Communications Act 2000 provides for the use of an electronic signature in an electronic communication.]

COURT RECORDS

5.4.   Duty to make records   (1)   For each case, as appropriate, the court officer must record, by such means as the Lord Chancellor directs—

(a)   each charge or indictment against the defendant;

(b)   the defendant's plea to each charge or count;

(c)   each acquittal, conviction, sentence, determination, direction or order;

(d)   each decision about bail;

(e)   the power exercised where the court commits or adjourns the case to another court—

(i)   for sentence, or

(ii)   for the defendant to be dealt with for breach of a community order, a deferred sentence, a conditional discharge, or a suspended sentence of imprisonment, imposed by that other court;

(f)   the court's reasons for a decision, where legislation requires those reasons to be recorded;

(g)   any appeal;

(h)   each party's presence or absence at each hearing;

(i)   any consent that legislation requires before the court can proceed with the case, or proceed to a decision;

(j)   in a magistrates' court—

    (i)   any indication of sentence given in connection with the allocation of a case for trial, and

    (ii)   the registration of a fixed penalty notice for enforcement as a fine, and any related endorsement on a driving record;

(k)   in the Crown Court, any request for assistance or other communication about the case received from a juror;

(l)   the identity of—

    (i)   the prosecutor,

    (ii)   the defendant,

    (iii)   any other applicant to whom these Rules apply,

    (iv)   any interpreter or intermediary,

    (v)   the parties' legal representatives, if any, and

    (vi)   the judge, magistrate or magistrates, justices' legal adviser or other person who made each recorded decision;

(m)   where a defendant is entitled to attend a hearing, any agreement by the defendant to waive that right; and

(n)   where interpretation is required for a defendant, any agreement by that defendant to do without the written translation of a document.

(2)   Such records must include—

(a)   each party's and representative's address, including any electronic address and telephone number available;

(b)   the defendant's date of birth, if available; and

(c)   the date of each event and decision recorded.

[Note. For the duty to keep court records, see sections 5 and 8 of the Public Records Act 1958.

Requirements to record the court's reasons for its decision are contained in: section 5 of the Bail Act 1976; section 47(1) of the Road Traffic Offenders Act 1988; sections 20, 33A and 33BB of the Youth Justice and Criminal Evidence Act 1999; section 174 of the Criminal Justice Act 2003; and rule 16.8.

The prosecution of some offences requires the consent of a specified authority. Requirements for the defendant's consent to proceedings in his or her absence are contained in sections 23 and 128 of the Magistrates' Courts Act 1980.

In the circumstances for which it provides, section 20 of the Magistrates' Courts Act 1980 allows the court to give an indication of whether a custodial or non-custodial sentence is more likely in the event of a guilty plea at trial in that court.

Requirements to register fixed penalty notices and to record any related endorsement of a driving record are contained in sections 57, 57A and 71 of the Road Traffic Offenders Act 1988.

For agreement to do without a written translation in a case in which the defendant requires interpretation, see rule 3.9(5).]

5.5.   *Recording and transcription of proceedings in the Crown Court*   (1)   Where someone may appeal to the Court of Appeal, the court officer must—

(a)   arrange for the recording of the proceedings in the Crown Court, unless the court otherwise directs; and

(b)   arrange for the transcription of such a recording if—

    (i)   the Registrar wants such a transcript, or

    (ii)   anyone else wants such a transcript (but that is subject to the restrictions in paragraph (2)).

(2)   Unless the court otherwise directs, a person who transcribes a recording of proceedings under such arrangements—

(a)   may only supply a transcript of a recording of a hearing in private to—

    (i)   the Registrar, or

    (ii)   an individual who was present at that hearing;

(b)   if the recording of a hearing in public contains information to which reporting restrictions apply, may only supply a transcript containing that information to—

    (i)   the Registrar, or

    (ii)   a recipient to whom that supply will not contravene those reporting restrictions;

(c)   subject to paragraph (2)(a) and (b), must supply any person with any transcript for which that person asks—

    (i)   in accordance with the transcription arrangements made by the court officer, and

    (ii)   on payment by that person of any fee prescribed.

(3)   A party who wants to hear a recording of proceedings must—

(a)   apply—

    (i)   in writing to the Registrar, if an appeal notice has been served where Part 36 applies (Appeal to the Court of Appeal: general rules), or

    (ii)   orally or in writing to the Crown Court officer;

(b)   explain the reasons for the request; and

(c)   pay any fee prescribed.

(4)   If the Crown Court or the Registrar so directs, the Crown Court officer must allow that party to hear a recording of—

(a)   a hearing in public;

(b)   a hearing in private, if the applicant was present at that hearing.

[Note. See also section 32 of the Criminal Appeal Act 1968.]

[For the circumstances in which reporting restrictions may apply, see the provisions listed in the note to rule 6.1. In summary, reporting restrictions prohibit the publication of the information to which they apply where that publication is likely to lead members of the public to acquire the information concerned.]

5.6. *Custody of case materials*   Unless the court otherwise directs, in respect of each case the court officer may—

(a)   keep any evidence, application, representation or other material served by the parties; or

(b)   arrange for the whole or any part to be kept by some other appropriate person, subject to—

    (i)   any condition imposed by the court, and

    (ii)   the rules in Part 34 (Appeal to the Crown Court) and Part 36 (Appeal to the Court of Appeal: general rules) about keeping exhibits pending any appeal.

5.7. *Supply to a party of information or documents from records or case materials*   (1)   This rule

(a)   applies where—

    (i)   a party wants information, or a copy of a document, from records or case materials kept by the court officer (for example, in case of loss, or to establish what is retained), or

    (ii)   a person affected by an order made, or warrant issued, by the court wants such information or such a copy; but

(b)   does not apply to—

    (i)   a recording arranged under rule 5.5 (Recording and transcription of proceedings in the Crown Court),

    (ii)   a copy of such a recording, or

    (iii)   a transcript of such a recording.

(2)   Such a party or person must—

(a)   apply to the court officer;

(b)   specify the information or document required; and

(c)   pay any fee prescribed.

(3)   The application—

(a)   may be made orally, giving no reasons, if paragraph (4) requires the court officer to supply the information or document requested;

(b)   must be in writing, unless the court otherwise permits, and must explain for what purpose the information is required, in any other case.

(4)   The court officer must supply to the applicant party or person—

(a)   a copy of any document served by, or on, that party or person (but not of any document not so served);

(b)   by word of mouth, or in writing, as requested—

    (i)   information that was received from that party or person in the first place,

    (ii)   information about the terms of any direction or order directed to that party or person, or made on an application by that party or person, or at a hearing in public,

    (iii)   information about the outcome of the case.

(5)   If the court so directs, the court officer must supply to the applicant party or person, by word of mouth or in writing, as requested, information that paragraph (4) does not require the court officer to supply.

(6)   Where the information requested is about the grounds on which an order was made, or a warrant was issued, in the absence of the party or person applying for that information—

(a)   that party or person must also serve the request on the person who applied for the order or warrant;

(b)   if the person who applied for the order or warrant objects to the supply of the information requested, that objector must—

    (i)   give notice of the objection not more than 14 days after service of the request (or within any longer period allowed by the court),

    (ii)   serve that notice on the court officer and on the party or person requesting the information, and

    (iii)   if the objector wants a hearing, explain why one is needed;

(c)   the court may determine the application for information at a hearing (which must be in private unless the court otherwise directs), or without a hearing;

(d)   the court must not permit the information requested to be supplied unless the person who applied for the order or warrant has had at least 14 days (or any longer period allowed by the court) in which to make representations.

(7)   A notice of objection under paragraph (6) must explain—

(a)   whether the objection is to the supply of any part of the information requested, or only to the supply of a specified part, or parts, of it;

(b)   whether the objection is to the supply of the information at any time, or only to its supply before a date or event specified by the objector; and

(c)   the grounds of the objection.

(8)   Where a notice of objection under paragraph (6) includes material that the objector thinks ought not be revealed to the party or person applying for information, the objector must—

(a)   omit that material from the notice served on that party or person;

(b)   mark the material to show that it is only for the court; and

(c)   with that material include an explanation of why it has been withheld.

(9)   Where paragraph (8) applies—

(a)   a hearing of the application may take place, wholly or in part, in the absence of the party or person applying for information;

(b)   at any such hearing, the general rule is that the court must consider, in the following sequence—

      (i)   representations first by the party or person applying for information and then by the objector, in the presence of both, and then

      (ii)   further representations by the objector, in the absence of that party or person

but the court may direct other arrangements for the hearing.

5.8.   Supply to the public, including reporters, of information about cases (1) This rule—

(a)   applies where a member of the public, including a reporter, wants information about a case from the court officer;

(b)   requires the court officer to publish information about cases due to be heard.

(c)   does not apply to—

      (i)   a recording arranged under rule 5.5 (Recording and transcription of proceedings in the Crown Court)

      (ii)   a copy of such a recording, or

      (iii)   a transcript of such a recording.

(2)   A person who wants information about a case from the court officer must—

(a)   apply to the court officer;

(b)   specify the information requested; and

(c)   pay any fee prescribed.

(3)   The application—

(a)   may be made orally, giving no reasons, if paragraph (4) requires the court officer to supply the information requested;

(b)   must be in writing, unless the court otherwise permits, and must explain for what purpose the information is required, in any other case.

(4)   The court officer must supply to the applicant—

(a)   any information listed in paragraph (6), if—

      (i)   the information is available to the court officer,

      (ii)   the supply of the information is not prohibited by a reporting restriction, and

      (iii)   the trial has not yet concluded, or the verdict was not more than 6 months ago; and

(b)   details of any reporting or access restriction ordered by the court.

(5)   The court officer must supply that information—

(a)   by word of mouth; or

(b)   by such other arrangements as the Lord Chancellor directs.

(6)   The information that paragraph (4) requires the court officer to supply is—

(a)   the date of any hearing in public, unless any party has yet to be notified of that date;

(b)   each alleged offence and any plea entered;

(c)   the court's decision at any hearing in public, including any decision about—

      (i)   bail, or

      (ii)   the committal, sending or transfer of the case to another court;

(d)   whether the case is under appeal;

(e)   the outcome of any trial and any appeal; and

(f)   the identity of—

      (i)   the prosecutor,

      (ii)   the defendant,

      (iii)   the parties' representatives, including their addresses, and

      (iv)   the judge, magistrate or magistrates, or justices' legal adviser by whom a decision at a hearing in public was made.

(7)   If the court so directs, the court officer must—

(a)   supply to the applicant, by word of mouth, other information about the case; or

(b)   allow the applicant to inspect or copy a document, or part of a document, containing information about the case.

(8)   The court may determine an application to which paragraph (7) applies—

(a)   at a hearing, in public or in private; or

(b)   without a hearing.

(9)   The court officer must publish the information listed in paragraph (11) if—

(a)   the information is available to the court officer;

(b)   the hearing to which the information relates is due to take place in public; and

(c)   the publication of the information is not prohibited by a reporting restriction.

(10)   The court officer must publish that information—

(a)   by notice displayed somewhere prominent in the vicinity of the court room in which the hearing is due to take place;

(b)   by such other arrangements as the Lord Chancellor directs, including arrangements for publication by electronic means; and

(c)   for no longer than 2 business days.

(11)   The information that paragraph (9) requires the court officer to publish is—

(a)   the date, time and place of the hearing;

(b)   the identity of the defendant; and

(c)   such other information as it may be practicable to publish concerning—

    (i)   the type of hearing,

    (ii)   the identity of the court,

    (iii) the offence or offences alleged, and

    (iv) whether any reporting restriction applies.

[Note. Rule 5.8(4) requires the court officer to supply on request the information to which that paragraph refers. On an application for other information about a case, rule 5.8(3)(b), (7) and (8) apply and the court's decision on such an application may be affected by—

(a)   any reporting restriction imposed by legislation or by the court (Part 6 lists the reporting restrictions that might apply);

(b)   Articles 6, 8 and 10 of the European Convention on Human Rights, and the court's duty to have regard to the importance of—

*   (i)   dealing with criminal cases in public, and*

*   (ii)   allowing a public hearing to be reported to the public;*

(c)   the Rehabilitation of Offenders Act 1974 (section 5 of the Act lists sentences and rehabilitation periods);

(d)   section 18 of the Criminal Procedure and Investigations Act 1996, which affects the supply of information about material, other than evidence, disclosed by the prosecutor;

(e)   the Data Protection Act 1998 (sections 34 and 35 of the Act contain relevant exemptions from prohibitions against disclosure that usually apply) and Part 3 of the Data Protection Act 2018 (sections 43(3) and 117 of which make exceptions for criminal proceedings from some other provisions of that Act);

(f)   sections 33, 34 and 35 of the Legal Aid, Sentencing and Punishment of Offenders Act 2012, which affect the supply of information about applications for legal aid.]

5.9. Supply of written certificate or extract from records (1) This rule applies where legislation—

(a)   allows a certificate of conviction or acquittal, or an extract from records kept by the court officer, to be introduced in evidence in criminal proceedings; or

(b)   requires such a certificate or extract to be supplied by the court officer to a specified person for a specified purpose.

(2)   A person who wants such a certificate or extract must—

(a)   apply in writing to the court officer;

(b)   specify the certificate or extract required;

(c)   explain under what legislation and for what purpose it is required; and

(d)   pay any fee prescribed.

(3)   If the application satisfies the requirements of that legislation, the court officer must supply the certificate or extract requested—

(a)   to a party;

(b)   unless the court otherwise directs, to any other applicant.

[Note. Under sections 73 to 75 of the Police and Criminal Evidence Act 1984, a certificate of conviction or acquittal, and certain other details from records to which this Part applies, may be admitted in evidence in criminal proceedings.

Under section 115 of the Crime and Disorder Act 1998, information from records to which this Part applies may be obtained by specified authorities for the purposes of that Act.

Under section 92 of the Sexual Offences Act 2003, a certificate which records a conviction for an offence and a statement by the convicting court that that offence is listed in Schedule 3 to the Act is evidence of those facts for certain purposes of that Act.

A certificate of conviction or acquittal, and certain other information, required for other purposes, may be obtained from the Secretary of State under sections 112, 113A and 113B of the Police Act 1997.]

Part 6   Reporting, etc Restrictions

Contents of this Part

General rules

GENERAL RULES

B.6 *6.1. When this Part applies* (1) This Part applies where the court can—
(a) impose a restriction on—
    (i) reporting what takes place at a public hearing, or
    (ii) public access to what otherwise would be a public hearing;
(b) vary or remove a reporting or access restriction that is imposed by legislation;
(c) withhold information from the public during a public hearing;
(d) order a trial in private;
(e) allow there to take place during a hearing—
    (i) sound recording, or
    (ii) communication by electronic means.
(2) This Part does not apply to arrangements required by legislation, or directed by the court, in connection with—
(a) sound recording during a hearing, or the transcription of such a recording; or
(b) measures to assist a witness or defendant to give evidence.
[Note. The court can impose reporting restrictions under—
(a) section 4(2) of the Contempt of Court Act 1981 (postponed report of public hearing);
(b) section 11 of the Contempt of Court Act 1981 (matter withheld from the public during a public hearing);
(c) section 58 of the Criminal Procedure and Investigations Act 1996 (postponed report of derogatory assertion in mitigation);
(d) section 45 of the Youth Justice and Criminal Evidence Act 1999 (identity of a person under 18);
(e) section 45A of the Youth Justice and Criminal Evidence Act 1999 (identity of a witness or victim under 18);
(f) section 46 of the Youth Justice and Criminal Evidence Act 1999 (identity of a vulnerable adult witness);
(g) section 82 of the Criminal Justice Act 2003 (order for retrial after acquittal); or
(h) section 75 of the Serious Organised Crime and Police Act 2005 (identity of a defendant who assisted the police).
There are reporting restrictions imposed by legislation that the court can vary or remove, under—
(a) section 49 of the Children and Young Persons Act 1933 (youth court proceedings);
(b) section 8C of the Magistrates' Courts Act 1980 (pre-trial ruling in magistrates' courts);
(c) section 11 of the Criminal Justice Act 1987 (preparatory hearing in the Crown Court);
(d) section 1 of the Sexual Offences (Amendment) Act 1992 (identity of complainant of sexual offence);
(e) section 37 of the Criminal Procedure and Investigations Act 1996 (preparatory hearing in the Crown Court);
(f) section 41 of the Criminal Procedure and Investigations Act 1996 (pre-trial ruling in the Crown Court);
(g) section 52A of, and paragraph 3 of Schedule 3 to, the Crime and Disorder Act 1998 (allocation and sending for trial proceedings);
(h) section 47 of the Youth Justice and Criminal Evidence Act 1999 (special measures direction);
(i) section 141F of the Education Act 2002 (restrictions on reporting alleged offences by teachers);
(j) section 71 of the Criminal Justice Act 2003 (prosecution appeal against Crown Court ruling); and
(k) section 4A of, and paragraph 1 of Schedule 1 to, the Female Genital Mutilation Act 2003 (identity of person against whom a female genital mutilation offence is alleged to have been committed).
There are reporting restrictions imposed by legislation that the court has no power to vary or remove, under—
(a) section 1 of the Judicial Proceedings (Regulation of Reports) Act 1926 (indecent or medical matter);
(b) section 2 of the Contempt of Court Act 1981 (risk of impeding or prejudicing active proceedings).
Access to a youth court is restricted under section 47 of the Children and Young Persons Act 1933. See also rule 24.2 (Trial and sentence in a magistrates' court – general rules).
Under section 36 of the Children and Young Persons Act 1933, no-one under 14 may be present in court when someone else is on trial, or during proceedings preliminary to a trial, unless that person is required as a witness, or for the purposes of justice, or the court permits. The court can restrict access to the courtroom under—

(a)   *section 8(4) of the Official Secrets Act 1920, during proceedings for an offence under the Official Secrets Acts 1911 and 1920;*

(b)   *section 37 of the Children and Young Persons Act 1933, where the court receives evidence from a person under 18;*

(c)   *section 75 of the Serious Organised Crime and Police Act 2005, where the court reviews a sentence passed on a defendant who assisted an investigation.*

The court has an inherent power, in exceptional circumstances—

(a)   *to allow information, for example a name or address, to be withheld from the public at a public hearing;*

(b)   *to restrict public access to what otherwise would be a public hearing, for example to control disorder;*

(c)   *to hear a trial in private, for example for reasons of national security.*

Under section 9(1) of the Contempt of Court Act 1981, it is a contempt of court without the court's permission to—

(a)   *use in court, or bring into court for use, a device for recording sound;*

(b)   *publish a recording of legal proceedings made by means of such a device; or*

(c)   *use any such recording in contravention of any condition on which permission was granted.*

Under section 41 of the Criminal Justice Act 1925, it is an offence to take or attempt to take a photograph, or with a view to publication to make or attempt to make a portrait or sketch, of any judge, juror, witness or party, in the courtroom, or in the building or in the precincts of the building in which the court is held, or while that person is entering or leaving the courtroom, building or precincts; or to publish such a photograph, portrait or sketch.

Section 32 of the Crime and Courts Act 2013 (Enabling the making, and use, of films and other recordings of proceedings) allows for exceptions to be made to the prohibitions imposed by section 9 of the 1981 Act and section 41 of the 1925 Act.

By reason of sections 15 and 45 of the Senior Courts Act 1981, the Court of Appeal and the Crown Court each has an inherent power to deal with a person for contempt of court for disrupting the proceedings. Under section 12 of the Contempt of Court Act 1981, a magistrates' court has a similar power.

See also—

(a)   *rule 5.5, under which the court officer must make arrangements for recording proceedings in the Crown Court;*

(b)   *Part 18, which applies to live links and other measures to assist a witness or defendant to give evidence;*

(c)   *rule 45.10, which applies to costs orders against a non-party for serious misconduct; and*

(d)   *Part 48, which contains rules about contempt of court.]*

6.2. Exercise of court's powers to which this Part applies (1) When exercising a power to which this Part applies, as well as furthering the overriding objective, in accordance with rule 1.3, the court must have regard to the importance of—

(a)   dealing with criminal cases in public; and

(b)   allowing a public hearing to be reported to the public.

(2) The court may determine an application or appeal under this Part—

(a)   at a hearing, in public or in private; or

(b)   without a hearing.

(3) But the court must not exercise a power to which this Part applies unless each party and any other person directly affected—

(a)   is present; or

(b)   has had an opportunity—

      (i)   to attend, or

      (ii)   to make representations.

[Note. See also section 121 of the Magistrates' Courts Act 1980 and rule 24.2 (general rules about trial and sentence in a magistrates' court).]

6.3. Court's power to vary requirements under this Part (1) The court may—

(a)   shorten or extend (even after it has expired) a time limit under this Part;

(b)   require an application to be made in writing instead of orally;

(c)   consider an application or representations made orally instead of in writing;

(d)   dispense with a requirement to—

      (i)   give notice, or

      (ii)   serve an application.

(2) Someone who wants an extension of time must—

(a)   apply when making the application or representations for which it is needed; and

(b)   explain the delay.

REPORTING AND ACCESS RESTRICTIONS

6.4. Reporting and access restrictions (1) This rule applies where the court can—

(a)   impose a restriction on—

      (i)   reporting what takes place at a public hearing, or

      (ii)   public access to what otherwise would be a public hearing;

(b)   withhold information from the public during a public hearing.

(2)   Unless other legislation otherwise provides, the court may do so—

(a)   on application by a party; or

(b)   on its own initiative.

(3)   A party who wants the court to do so must—

(a)   apply as soon as reasonably practicable;

(b)   notify—

      (i)   each other party, and

      (ii)   such other person (if any) as the court directs;

(c)   specify the proposed terms of the order, and for how long it should last;

(d)   explain—

      (i)   what power the court has to make the order, and

      (ii)   why an order in the terms proposed is necessary;

(e)   where the application is for a reporting direction under section 45A of the Youth Justice and Criminal Evidence Act 1999 (Power to restrict reporting of criminal proceedings for lifetime of witnesses and victims under 18), explain—

      (i)   how the circumstances of the person whose identity is concerned meet the conditions prescribed by that section, having regard to the factors which that section lists; and

      (ii)   why such a reporting direction would be likely to improve the quality of any evidence given by that person, or the level of co-operation given by that person to any party in connection with the preparation of that party's case, taking into account the factors listed in that section;

(f)   where the application is for a reporting direction under section 46 of the Youth Justice and Criminal Evidence Act 1999 (Power to restrict reports about certain adult witnesses in criminal proceedings), explain—

      (i)   how the witness is eligible for assistance, having regard to the factors listed in that section, and

      (ii)   why such a reporting direction would be likely to improve the quality of the witness' evidence, or the level of co-operation given by the witness to the applicant in connection with the preparation of the applicant's case, taking into account the factors that section lists.

[Note. Under section 45A(10) or section 46(9) of the Youth Justice and Criminal Evidence Act 1999, if the conditions prescribed by those sections are met the court may make an excepting direction dispensing, to any extent specified, with the restrictions imposed by a reporting direction made under those sections.]

6.5. *Varying or removing restrictions* (1) This rule applies where the court can vary or remove a reporting or access restriction.

(2)   Unless other legislation otherwise provides, the court may do so—

(a)   on application by a party or person directly affected; or

(b)   on its own initiative.

(3)   A party or person who wants the court to do so must—

(a)   apply as soon as reasonably practicable;

(b)   notify—

      (i)   each other party, and

      (ii)   such other person (if any) as the court directs;

(c)   specify the restriction;

(d)   explain, as appropriate, why it should be varied or removed.

(4)   A person who wants to appeal to the Crown Court under section 141F of the Education Act 2002 must—

(a)   serve an appeal notice on—

      (i)   the Crown Court officer, and

      (ii)   each other party;

(b)   serve on the Crown Court officer, with the appeal notice, a copy of the application to the magistrates' court;

(c)   serve the appeal notice not more than 21 days after the magistrates' court's decision against which the appellant wants to appeal; and

(d)   in the appeal notice, explain, as appropriate, why the restriction should be maintained, varied or removed.

(5)   Rule 34.11 (Constitution of the Crown Court) applies on such an appeal.

[Note. Under section 141F(7) of the Education Act 2002, a party to an application to a magistrates' court to remove the statutory restriction on reporting an alleged offence by a teacher may appeal to the Crown Court against the decision of the magistrates' court. With the Crown Court's permission, any other person may appeal against such a decision.]

6.6. *Trial in private* (1) This rule applies where the court can order a trial in private.

(2)   A party who wants the court to do so must—

(a)   apply in writing not less than 5 business days before the trial is due to begin; and

(b)   serve the application on—

      (i)   the court officer, and

      (ii)   each other party.

(3)   The applicant must explain—

(a)   the reasons for the application;
(b)   how much of the trial the applicant proposes should be in private; and
(c)   why no measures other than trial in private will suffice, such as—
        (i)   reporting restrictions,
        (ii)   an admission of facts,
        (iii)   the introduction of hearsay evidence,
        (iv)   a direction for a special measure under section 19 of the Youth Justice and Criminal Evidence Act 1999,
        (v)   a witness anonymity order under section 86 of the Coroners and Justice Act 2009, or
        (vi)   arrangements for the protection of a witness.
(4)   Where the application includes information that the applicant thinks ought not be revealed to another party, the applicant must—
(a)   omit that information from the part of the application that is served on that other party;
(b)   mark the other part to show that, unless the court otherwise directs, it is only for the court; and
(c)   in that other part, explain why the applicant has withheld that information from that other party.
(5)   The court officer must at once—
(a)   display notice of the application somewhere prominent in the vicinity of the courtroom; and
(b)   give notice of the application to reporters by such other arrangements as the Lord Chancellor directs.
(6)   The application must be determined at a hearing which—
(a)   must be in private, unless the court otherwise directs;
(b)   if the court so directs, may be, wholly or in part, in the absence of a party from whom information has been withheld; and
(c)   in the Crown Court, must be after the defendant is arraigned but before the jury is sworn.
(7)   At the hearing of the application—
(a)   the general rule is that the court must consider, in the following sequence—
        (i)   representations first by the applicant and then by each other party, in all the parties' presence, and then
        (ii)   further representations by the applicant, in the absence of a party from whom information has been withheld; but
(b)   the court may direct other arrangements for the hearing.
(8)   The court must not hear a trial in private until—
(a)   the business day after the day on which it orders such a trial, or
(b)   the disposal of any appeal against, or review of, any such order, if later.

6.7. *Representations in response* (1)   This rule applies where a party, or person directly affected, wants to make representations about an application or appeal.
(2)   Such a party or person must—
(a)   serve the representations on—
        (i)   the court officer,
        (ii)   the applicant,
        (iii)   each other party, and
        (iv)   such other person (if any) as the court directs;
(b)   do so as soon as reasonably practicable after notice of the application; and
(c)   ask for a hearing, if that party or person wants one, and explain why it is needed.
(3)   Representations must—
(a)   explain the reasons for any objection;
(b)   specify any alternative terms proposed.

6.8. *Order about restriction or trial in private* (1)   This rule applies where the court—
(a)   orders, varies or removes a reporting or access restriction; or
(b)   orders a trial in private.
(2)   The court officer must—
(a)   record the court's reasons for the decision; and
(b)   as soon as reasonably practicable, arrange for notice of the decision to be—
        (i)   displayed somewhere prominent in the vicinity of the courtroom, and
        (ii)   communicated to reporters by such other arrangements as the Lord Chancellor directs.

SOUND RECORDING AND ELECTRONIC COMMUNICATION

6.9. *Sound recording and electronic communication* (1)   This rule applies where the court can give permission to—
(a)   bring into a hearing for use, or use during a hearing, a device for—
        (i)   recording sound, or
        (ii)   communicating by electronic means; or
(b)   publish a sound recording made during a hearing.
(2)   The court may give such permission—

(a)   on application; or
(b)   on its own initiative.
(3)   A person who wants the court to give such permission must—
(a)   apply as soon as reasonably practicable;
(b)   notify—
         (i)   each party, and
         (ii)   such other person (if any) as the court directs; and
(c)   explain why the court should permit the use or publication proposed.
(4)   As a condition of the applicant using such a device, the court may direct arrangements to minimise the risk of its use—
(a)   contravening a reporting restriction;
(b)   disrupting the hearing; or
(c)   compromising the fairness of the hearing, for example by affecting—
         (i)   the evidence to be given by a witness, or
         (ii)   the verdict of a jury.
(5)   Such a direction may require that the device is used only—
(a)   in a specified part of the courtroom;
(b)   for a specified purpose;
(c)   for a purpose connected with the applicant's activity as a member of a specified group, for example representatives of news-gathering or reporting organisations;
(d)   at a specified time, or in a specified way.

6.10. Forfeiture of unauthorised sound recording (1) This rule applies where someone without the court's permission—
(a)   uses a device for recording sound during a hearing; or
(b)   publishes a sound recording made during a hearing.
(2)   The court may exercise its power to forfeit the device or recording—
(a)   on application by a party, or on its own initiative;
(b)   provisionally, despite rule 6.2(3), to allow time for representations.
(3)   A party who wants the court to forfeit a device or recording must—
(a)   apply as soon as reasonably practicable;
(b)   notify—
         (i)   as appropriate, the person who used the device, or who published the recording, and
         (ii)   each other party; and
(c)   explain why the court should exercise that power.
[Note. Under section 9(3) of the Contempt of Court Act 1981, the court can forfeit any device or recording used or made in contravention of section 9(1) of the Act.]

PART 7   STARTING A PROSECUTION IN A MAGISTRATES' COURT

Contents of this Part

B.7 *7.1. When this Part applies* (1) This Part applies in a magistrates' court where—
(a)   a prosecutor wants the court to issue a summons or warrant under section 1 of the Magistrates' Courts Act 1980;
(b)   a prosecutor with the power to do so issues—
         (i)   a written charge and requisition, or
         (ii)   a written charge and single justice procedure notice
    under section 29 of the Criminal Justice Act 2003;
(c)   a person who is in custody is charged with an offence.
(2)   In this Part, 'authorised prosecutor' means a prosecutor authorised under section 29 of the Criminal Justice Act 2003 to issue a written charge and requisition or single justice procedure notice.
[Note. Under section 1 of the Magistrates' Courts Act 1980, on receiving a formal statement (described in that section as an 'information') alleging that someone has committed an offence, the court may issue—
(a)   *a summons requiring that person to attend court; or*
(b)   *a warrant for that person's arrest, if—*
         (i)   *the alleged offence must or may be tried in the Crown Court,*
         (ii)   *the alleged offence is punishable with imprisonment, or*
         (iii)   *the person's address cannot be established sufficiently clearly to serve a summons or requisition.*
The powers of the court to which this Part applies may be exercised by a single justice of the peace. Under section 29 of the Criminal Justice Act 2003, a prosecutor authorised under that section may issue a written charge alleging that someone has committed an offence, and either—

(a)   a *requisition requiring that person to attend court; or*
(b)   a *notice that the single justice procedure under section 16A of the Magistrates' Courts Act 1980 and rule 24.9 of these Rules applies.*
Section 30 of the 2003 Act contains other provisions about written charges, requisitions and single justice procedure notices.
A person detained under a power of arrest may be charged if the custody officer decides that there is sufficient evidence to do so. See sections 37 and 38 of the Police and Criminal Evidence Act 1984.]

7.2.   *Application for summons, etc*

7.2 Application for summons, etc   (1)   A prosecutor who wants the court to issue a summons must—
(a)   serve on the court officer a written application; or
(b)   unless other legislation prohibits this, present an application orally to the court, with a written statement of the allegation or allegations made by the prosecutor.
(2)   A prosecutor who wants the court to issue a warrant must—
(a)   serve on the court officer—
           (i)   a written application, or
           (ii)   a copy of a written charge that has been issued; or
(b)   present to the court either of those documents.
(3)   An application for the issue of a summons or warrant must—
(a)   set out the allegation or allegations made by the applicant in terms that comply with rule 7.3 (Allegation of offence in application or charge); and
(b)   demonstrate—
           (i)   that the application is made in time, if legislation imposes a time limit, and
           (ii)   that the applicant has the necessary consent, if legislation requires it.
(4)   As well as complying with paragraph (3), an application for the issue of a warrant must—
(a)   demonstrate that the offence or offences alleged can be tried in the Crown Court;
(b)   demonstrate that the offence or offences alleged can be punished with imprisonment; or
(c)   concisely outline the applicant's grounds for asserting that the defendant's address is not sufficiently established for a summons to be served.
(5)   Paragraph (6) applies unless the prosecutor is—
(a)   represented by a legal representative for the purposes of the application under this rule;
(b)   a public authority within the meaning of section 17 of the Prosecution of Offences Act 1985; or
(c)   a person acting—
           (i)   on behalf of such an authority, or
           (ii)   in that person's capacity as an official appointed by such an authority.
(6)   Where this paragraph applies, as well as complying with paragraph (3), and with paragraph (4) if applicable, an application for the issue of a summons or warrant must—
(a)   concisely outline the grounds for asserting that the defendant has committed the alleged offence or offences;
(b)   disclose—
           (i)   details of any previous such application by the same applicant in respect of any allegation now made, and
           (ii)   details of any current or previous proceedings brought by another prosecutor in respect of any allegation now made; and
(c)   include a statement that to the best of the applicant's knowledge, information and belief—
           (i)   the allegations contained in the application are substantially true,
           (ii)   the evidence on which the applicant relies will be available at the trial,
           (iii)   the details given by the applicant under paragraph (6)(b) are true, and
           (iv)   the application discloses all the information that is material to what the court must decide.
(7)   Where the statement required by paragraph (6)(c) is made orally—
(a)   the statement must be on oath or affirmation, unless the court otherwise directs; and
(b)   the court must arrange for a record of the making of the statement.
(8)   An authorised prosecutor who issues a written charge must notify the court officer immediately.
(9)   A single document may contain—
(a)   more than one application; or
(b)   more than one written charge.
(10)   Where an offence can be tried only in a magistrates' court, then unless other legislation otherwise provides—
(a)   a prosecutor must serve an application for the issue of a summons or warrant on the court officer or present it to the court; or
(b)   an authorised prosecutor must issue a written charge,
not more than 6 months after the offence alleged.
(11)   Where an offence can be tried in the Crown Court then—
(a)   a prosecutor must serve an application for the issue of a summons or warrant on the court officer or present it to the court; or
(b)   an authorised prosecutor must issue a written charge,

within any time limit that applies to that offence.

(12)   The court may determine an application to issue or withdraw a summons or warrant—

(a)   without a hearing, as a general rule, or at a hearing (which must be in private unless the court otherwise directs);

(b)   in the absence of—

(i)   the prosecutor,

(ii)   the defendant;

(c)   with or without representations by the defendant.

(13)   If the court so directs, a party to an application to issue or withdraw a summons or warrant may attend a hearing by live link or telephone.

[Note In some legislation, including the Magistrates' Courts Act 1980, an application for the issue of a summons or warrant is described as an 'information' and serving an application on the court officer or presenting it to the court is described as 'laying' that information.

The time limits for serving or presenting an application and for issuing a written charge are prescribed by section 127 of the Magistrates' Courts Act 1980 and section 30(5) of the Criminal Justice Act 2003.

In section 17 of the Prosecution of Offences Act 1985 'public authority' means (a) a police force as defined by that Act, (b) the Crown Prosecution Service or any other government department, (c) a local authority or other authority or body constituted for purposes of the public service or of local government, or carrying on under national ownership any industry or undertaking or part of an industry or undertaking, or (d) any other authority or body whose members are appointed by Her Majesty or by any Minister of the Crown or government department or whose revenues consist wholly or mainly of money provided by Parliament.

Part 46 (Representatives) contains rules allowing a member, officer or employee of a prosecutor, on the prosecutor's behalf, to—

(a)   serve on the court officer or present to the court an application for the issue of a summons or warrant; or

(b)   issue a written charge and requisition.

See Part 3 for the court's general powers of case management, including power to consider applications and give directions for (among other things) the amendment of an allegation or charge and for separate trials.

See also Part 32 (Breach, revocation and amendment of community and other orders). Rule 32.2(2) (Application by responsible officer) applies rules 7.2 to 7.4 to the procedure with which that rule deals.

The Practice Direction sets out a form of application for use in connection with rule 7.2(6).]

7.3.   *Allegation of offence in application for summons, etc or charge*   (1)   An allegation of an offence in an application for the issue of a summons or warrant or in a charge must contain—

(a)   a statement of the offence that—

(i)   describes the offence in ordinary language, and

(ii)   identifies any legislation that creates it; and

(b)   such particulars of the conduct constituting the commission of the offence as to make clear what the prosecutor alleges against the defendant.

(2)   More than one incident of the commission of the offence may be included in the allegation if those incidents taken together amount to a course of conduct having regard to the time, place or purpose of commission.

7.4.   *Summons, warrant and requisition*   (1)   A summons, warrant or requisition may be issued in respect of more than one offence.

(2)   A summons or requisition must—

(a)   contain notice of when and where the defendant is required to attend the court;

(b)   specify each offence in respect of which it is issued;

(c)   in the case of a summons, identify—

(i)   the court that issued it, unless that is otherwise recorded by the court officer, and

(ii)   the court office for the court that issued it; and

(d)   in the case of a requisition, identify the person under whose authority it is issued.

(3)   A summons may be contained in the same document as an application for the issue of that summons.

(4)   A requisition may be contained in the same document as a written charge.

(5)   Where the court issues a summons—

(a)   the prosecutor must—

(i)   serve it on the defendant, and

(ii)   notify the court officer; or

(b)   the court officer must—

(i)   serve it on the defendant, and

(ii)   notify the prosecutor.

(6)   Where an authorised prosecutor issues a requisition that prosecutor must—

(a)   serve on the defendant—

(i)   the requisition, and

(ii)   the written charge; and

(b)   serve a copy of each on the court officer.

(7)   Unless it would be inconsistent with other legislation, a replacement summons or requisition may be issued without a fresh application or written charge where the one replaced—

(a)   was served by leaving or posting it under rule 4.7 (documents that must be served only by handing them over, leaving or posting them); but

(b)   is shown not to have been received by the addressee.   (8)   A summons or requisition issued to a defendant under 18 may require that defendant's parent or guardian to attend the court with the defendant, or a separate summons or requisition may be issued for that purpose.

[Note. Part 13 contains other rules about warrants.

Section 47 of the Magistrates' Courts Act 1980 and section 30(5) of the Criminal Justice Act 2003 make special provision about time limits under other legislation for the issue and service of a summons or requisition, where service by post is not successful.

Section 34A of the Children and Young Persons Act 1933 allows, and in some cases requires, the court to summon the parent or guardian of a defendant under 18.]

PART 8   INITIAL DETAILS OF THE PROSECUTION CASE

Contents of this Part

When this Part applies	rule 8.1
Providing initial details of the prosecution case	rule 8.2
Content of initial details	rule 8.3
Use of initial details	rule 8.4

B.8   *8.1.   When this Part applies*   This Part applies in a magistrates' court.

8.2.   Providing initial details of the prosecution case   (1)   The prosecutor must serve initial details of the prosecution case on the court officer—

(a)   as soon as practicable; and

(b)   in any event, no later than the beginning of the day of the first hearing.

(2)   Where a defendant requests those details, the prosecutor must serve them on the defendant—

(a)   as soon as practicable; and

(b)   in any event, no later than the beginning of the day of the first hearing.

(3)   Where a defendant does not request those details, the prosecutor must make them available to the defendant at, or before, the beginning of the day of the first hearing.

8.3.   Content of initial details   Initial details of the prosecution case must include—

(a)   where, immediately before the first hearing in the magistrates' court, the defendant was in police custody for the offence charged—

    (i)   a summary of the circumstances of the offence, and

    (ii)   the defendant's criminal record, if any;

(b)   where paragraph (a) does not apply—

    (i)   a summary of the circumstances of the offence,

    (ii)   any account given by the defendant in interview, whether contained in that summary or in another document,

    (iii)   any written witness statement or exhibit that the prosecutor then has available and considers material to plea, or to the allocation of the case for trial, or to sentence,

    (iv)   the defendant's criminal record, if any, and

    (v)   any available statement of the effect of the offence on a victim, a victim's family or others.

*8.4.   **Use of initial details**   (1)   This rule applies where—

(a)   the prosecutor wants to introduce information contained in a document listed in rule 8.3; and

(b)   the prosecutor has not—

    (i)   served that document on the defendant, or

    (ii)   made that information available to the defendant.

(2)   The court must not allow the prosecutor to introduce that information unless the court first allows the defendant sufficient time to consider it."; and

PART 9   ALLOCATION AND SENDING FOR TRIAL

B.9   *Contents of this Part*

General rules

When this Part applies	rule 9.1
Exercise of magistrates' court's powers	rule 9.2
Matters to be specified on sending for trial	rule 9.3
Duty of justices' legal adviser	rule 9.4
Duty of magistrates' court officer	rule 9.5

Sending without allocation for Crown Court trial

Prosecutor's notice requiring Crown Court trial	rule 9.6

GENERAL RULES

9.1. *When this Part applies* (1) This Part applies to the allocation and sending of cases for trial under—

(a)   sections 17A to 26 of the Magistrates' Courts Act 1980; and

(b)   sections 50A to 52 of the Crime and Disorder Act 1998.

(2)   Rules 9.6 and 9.7 apply in a magistrates' court where the court must, or can, send a defendant to the Crown Court for trial, without allocating the case for trial there.

(3)   Rules 9.8 to 9.14 apply in a magistrates' court where the court must allocate the case to a magistrates' court or to the Crown Court for trial.

(4)   Rules 9.15 and 9.16 apply in the Crown Court, where a defendant is sent for trial there.

[Note. A magistrates' court's powers to send a defendant to the Crown Court for trial are contained in section 51 of the Crime and Disorder Act 1998.

The exercise of the court's powers is affected by—

(a)   the classification of the offence (and the general rule, subject to exceptions, is that an offence classified as triable on indictment exclusively must be sent for Crown Court trial; an offence classified as triable only summarily must be tried in a magistrates' court; an offence classified as triable either on indictment or summarily must be allocated to one or the other court for trial: see in particular sections 50A, 51 and 51A of the 1998 Act and section 19 of the Magistrates' Courts Act 1980;

(b)   the defendant's age (and the general rule, subject to exceptions, is that an offence alleged against a defendant under 18 must be tried in a magistrates' court sitting as a youth court: see in particular sections 24 and 24A of the 1980 Act;

(c)   whether the defendant is awaiting Crown Court trial for another offence;

(d)   whether another defendant, charged with the same offence, is awaiting Crown Court trial for that offence; and

(e)   in some cases (destroying or damaging property; aggravated vehicle taking), whether the value involved is more or less than £5,000.

The court's powers of sending and allocation, including its powers (i) to receive a defendant's indication of an intention to plead guilty (see rules 9.7, 9.8 and 9.13) and (ii) to give an indication of likely sentence (see rule 9.11), may be exercised by a single justice: see sections 51 and 51A(11) of the 1998 Act, and sections 17E, 18(5) and 24D of the 1980 Act.]

9.2. *Exercise of magistrates' court's powers* (1) This rule applies to the exercise of the powers to which rules 9.6 to 9.14 apply.

(2)   The general rule is that the court must exercise its powers at a hearing in public, but it may exercise any power it has to—

(a)   withhold information from the public; or

(b)   order a hearing in private.

(3)   The general rule is that the court must exercise its powers in the defendant's presence, but it may exercise the powers to which the following rules apply in the defendant's absence on the conditions specified—

(a)   where rule 9.8 (Adult defendant: request for plea), rule 9.9 (Adult defendant: guilty plea) or rule 9.13 (Young defendant) applies, if—

       (i)   the defendant is represented, and

       (ii)   the defendant's disorderly conduct makes his or her presence in the courtroom impracticable;

(b)   where rule 9.10 (Adult defendant: not guilty plea) or rule 9.11 (Adult defendant: allocation for magistrates' court trial) applies, if—

       (i)   the defendant is represented and waives the right to be present, or

       (ii)   the defendant's disorderly conduct makes his or her presence in the courtroom impracticable.

(4)   The court may exercise its power to adjourn—

(a)   if either party asks; or

(b)   on its own initiative.

(5)   Where the court on the same occasion deals with two or more offences alleged against the same defendant, the court must deal with those offences in the following sequence—

(a)   any to which rule 9.6 applies (Prosecutor's notice requiring Crown Court trial);

(b)   any to which rule 9.7 applies (sending for Crown Court trial, without allocation there), in this sequence—

       (i)   any the court must send for trial, then

       (ii)   any the court can send for trial; and

(c)   any to which rule 9.14 applies (Allocation and sending for Crown Court trial).

(6)   Where the court on the same occasion deals with two or more defendants charged jointly with an offence that can be tried in the Crown Court then in the following sequence—

(a)   the court must explain, in terms each defendant can understand (with help, if necessary), that if the court sends one of them to the Crown Court for trial then the court must send for trial in the Crown Court, too, any other of them—

       (i)   who is charged with the same offence as the defendant sent for trial, or with an offence which the court decides is related to that offence,

       (ii)   who does not wish to plead guilty to each offence with which he or she is charged, and

       (iii)   (if that other defendant is under 18, and the court would not otherwise have sent him or her for Crown Court trial) where the court decides that sending is necessary in the interests of justice

   even if the court by then has decided to allocate that other defendant for magistrates' court trial; and

(b)   the court may ask the defendants questions to help it decide in what order to deal with them.

(7)   After following paragraph (5), if it applies, where the court on the same occasion—

(a)   deals with two or more defendants charged jointly with an offence that can be tried in the Crown Court;

(b)   allocates any of them to a magistrates' court for trial; and

(c)   then sends another one of them to the Crown Court for trial,

the court must deal again with each one whom, on that occasion, it has allocated for magistrates' court trial.

[Note. See sections 50A, 51, 51A and 52 of the Crime and Disorder Act 1998 and sections 17A, 17B, 17C, 18, 23, 24A, 24B and 24C of the Magistrates' Courts Act 1980.

Under sections 57A to 57E of the 1998 Act, the court may require a defendant to attend by live link a hearing to which this Part applies.

Where a defendant waives the right to be present then the court may nonetheless require his or her attendance by summons or warrant: see section 26 of the 1980 Act.

Under section 52A of the 1998 Act, reporting restrictions apply to the proceedings to which rules 9.6 to 9.14 apply.

Part 46 contains rules allowing a representative to act on a defendant's behalf for the purposes of these Rules.

Part 3 contains rules about the court's powers of case management.]

9.3.   *Matters to be specified on sending for trial*   (1)   Where the court sends a defendant to the Crown Court for trial, it must specify—

(a)   each offence to be tried;

(b)   in respect of each, the power exercised to send the defendant for trial for that offence; and

(c)   the Crown Court centre at which the trial will take place.

(2)   In a case in which the prosecutor serves a notice to which rule 9.6(1)(a) applies (notice requiring Crown Court trial in a case of serious or complex fraud), the court must specify the Crown Court centre identified by that notice.

(3)   In any other case, in deciding the Crown Court centre at which the trial will take place, the court must take into account—

(a)   the convenience of the parties and witnesses;

(b)   how soon a suitable courtroom will be available; and

(c)   the directions on the allocation of Crown Court business contained in the Practice Direction.

[Note. See sections 51 and 51D of the Crime and Disorder Act 1998.]

9.4.   *Duty of justices' legal adviser*   (1)   This rule applies—

(a)   only in a magistrates' court; and

(b)   unless the court—

       (i)   includes a District Judge (Magistrates' Courts), and

       (ii)   otherwise directs.

(2)   On the court's behalf, a justices' legal adviser may—

(a)   read the allegation of the offence to the defendant;

(b)   give any explanation and ask any question required by the rules in this Part;

(c)   make any announcement required by the rules in this Part, other than an announcement of—
- (i)   the court's decisions about allocation and sending,
- (ii)   any indication by the court of likely sentence, or
- (iii) sentence.

(3) A justices' legal adviser must—

(a)   assist an unrepresented defendant;

(b)   give the court such advice as is required to enable it to exercise its powers;

(c)   if required, attend the members of the court outside the courtroom to give such advice, but inform the parties of any advice so given.

[Note. For the functions of a justices' legal adviser, see sections 28 and 29 of the Courts Act 2003.]

9.5. *Duty of magistrates' court officer* (1) The magistrates' court officer must—

(a)   serve notice of a sending for Crown Court trial on—
- (i)   the Crown Court officer, and
- (ii)   the parties;

(b)   in that notice record—
- (i)   the matters specified by the court under rule 9.3 (Matters to be specified on sending for trial),
- (ii)   any indication of intended guilty plea given by the defendant under rule 9.7 (Sending for Crown Court trial),
- (iii) any decision by the defendant to decline magistrates' court trial under rule 9.11 (Adult defendant: allocation to magistrates' court for trial), and
- (iv) the date on which any custody time limit will expire;

(c)   record any indication of likely sentence to which rule 9.11 applies; and

(d)   give the court such other assistance as it requires.

(2) The magistrates' court officer must include with the notice served on the Crown Court officer—

(a)   the initial details of the prosecution case served by the prosecutor under rule 8.2;

(b)   a record of any—
- (i)   listing or case management direction affecting the Crown Court,
- (ii)   direction about reporting restrictions,
- (iii) decision about bail, for the purposes of section 5 of the Bail Act 1976,
- (iv) recognizance given by a surety, or
- (v) representation order; and

(c)   if relevant, any available details of any—
- (i)   interpreter,
- (ii)   intermediary, or
- (iii) other supporting adult, where the defendant is assisted by such a person.

[Note. See sections 51 and 51D of the Crime and Disorder Act 1998, and section 20A of the Magistrates' Courts Act 1980.]

SENDING WITHOUT ALLOCATION FOR CROWN COURT TRIAL

9.6. *Prosecutor's notice requiring Crown Court trial* (1) This rule applies where a prosecutor with power to do so requires a magistrates' court to send for trial in the Crown Court—

(a)   a case of serious or complex fraud; or

(b)   a case which will involve a child witness.

(2) The prosecutor must serve notice of that requirement—

(a)   on the magistrates' court officer and on the defendant; and

(b)   before trial in a magistrates' court begins under Part 24 (Trial and sentence in a magistrates' court).

(3) The notice must identify—

(a)   the power on which the prosecutor relies; and

(b)   the Crown Court centre at which the prosecutor wants the trial to take place.

(4) The prosecutor—

(a)   must, when choosing a Crown Court centre, take into account the matters listed in rule 9.3(3) (court deciding to which Crown Court centre to send a case); and

(b)   may change the centre identified before the case is sent for trial.

[Note. Under section 51B of the Crime and Disorder Act 1998, the Director of Public Prosecutions or a Secretary of State may require the court to send a case for trial in the Crown Court if, in that prosecutor's opinion, the evidence of the offence charged—

(a)   is sufficient for the person charged to be put on trial for the offence; and

(b)   reveals a case of fraud of such seriousness or complexity that it is appropriate that the management of the case should without delay be taken over by the Crown Court.

Under section 51C of the Crime and Disorder Act 1998, the Director of Public Prosecutions may require the court to send for trial in the Crown Court a case involving one of certain specified violent or sexual offences if, in the Director's opinion—

(a)   the evidence of the offence would be sufficient for the person charged to be put on trial for that offence;

(b)   a child would be called as a witness at the trial; and

(c)   for the purpose of avoiding any prejudice to the welfare of the child, the case should be

taken over and proceeded with without delay by the Crown Court.
'Child' for these purposes is defined by section 51C(7) of the 1998 Act.]

9.7. Sending for Crown Court trial (1) This rule applies where a magistrates' court must, or can, send a defendant to the Crown Court for trial without first allocating the case for trial there.
(2) The court must read the allegation of the offence to the defendant.
(3) The court must explain, in terms the defendant can understand (with help, if necessary)—
(a) the allegation, unless it is self-explanatory;
(b) that the offence is one for which the court, as appropriate—
   (i) must send the defendant to the Crown Court for trial because the offence is one which can only be tried there or because the court for some other reason is required to send that offence for trial,
   (ii) may send the defendant to the Crown Court for trial if the magistrates' court decides that the offence is related to one already sent for trial there, or
   (iii) (where the offence is low-value shoplifting and the defendant is 18 or over) must send the defendant to the Crown Court for trial if the defendant wants to be tried there;
(c) that reporting restrictions apply, which the defendant may ask the court to vary or remove.
(4) In the following sequence, the court must then—
(a) invite the prosecutor to—
   (i) identify the court's power to send the defendant to the Crown Court for trial for the offence, and
   (ii) make representations about any ancillary matters, including bail and directions for the management of the case in the Crown Court;
(b) invite the defendant to make representations about—
   (i) the court's power to send the defendant to the Crown Court, and
   (ii) any ancillary matters;
(c) (where the offence is low-value shoplifting and the defendant is 18 or over) offer the defendant the opportunity to require trial in the Crown Court; and
(d) decide whether or not to send the defendant to the Crown Court for trial.
(5) If the court sends the defendant to the Crown Court for trial, it must—
(a) ask whether the defendant intends to plead guilty in the Crown Court and—
   (i) if the answer is 'yes', make arrangements for the Crown Court to take the defendant's plea as soon as possible, or
   (ii) if the defendant does not answer, or the answer is 'no', make arrangements for a case management hearing in the Crown Court; and
(b) give any other ancillary directions.
[Note. See sections 51, 51A and 51E of the Crime and Disorder Act 1998, and sections 22A and 24A of the Magistrates' Courts Act 1980.
See also Part 6 (Reporting, etc restrictions).]

ALLOCATION FOR MAGISTRATES' COURT OR CROWN COURT TRIAL

9.8. Adult defendant: request for plea (1) This rule applies where—
(a) the defendant is 18 or over; and
(b) the court must decide whether a case is more suitable for trial in a magistrates' court or in the Crown Court.
(2) The court must read the allegation of the offence to the defendant.
(3) The court must explain, in terms the defendant can understand (with help, if necessary)—
(a) the allegation, unless it is self-explanatory;
(b) that the offence is one which can be tried in a magistrates' court or in the Crown Court;
(c) that the court is about to ask whether the defendant intends to plead guilty;
(d) that if the answer is 'yes', then the court must treat that as a guilty plea and must sentence the defendant, or commit the defendant to the Crown Court for sentence;
(e) that if the defendant does not answer, or the answer is 'no', then—
   (i) the court must decide whether to allocate the case to a magistrates' court or to the Crown Court for trial,
   (ii) the value involved may require the court to order trial in a magistrates' court (where the offence is one to which section 22 of the Magistrates' Courts Act 1980 applies), and
   (iii) if the court allocates the case to a magistrates' court for trial, the defendant can nonetheless require trial in the Crown Court (unless the offence is one to which section 22 of the Magistrates' Courts Act 1980 applies and the value involved requires magistrates' court trial); and
(f) that reporting restrictions apply, which the defendant may ask the court to vary or remove.
(4) The court must then ask whether the defendant intends to plead guilty.
[Note. See section 17A of the Magistrates' Courts Act 1980.
For the circumstances in which a magistrates' court may (and in some cases must) commit a defendant to the Crown Court for sentence after that defendant has indicated an intention to plead guilty where this rule applies, see sections 4 and 6 of the Powers of Criminal Courts (Sentencing) Act 2000.
See also Part 6 (Reporting, etc restrictions).]

9.9. Adult defendant: guilty plea (1) This rule applies where—

(a)   rule 9.8 applies; and

(b)   the defendant indicates an intention to plead guilty.

(2)   The court must exercise its power to deal with the case—

(a)   as if the defendant had just pleaded guilty at a trial in a magistrates' court; and

(b)   in accordance with rule 24.11 (Procedure if the court convicts).

[Note. See section 17A of the Magistrates' Courts Act 1980.]

9.10.   Adult defendant: not guilty plea   (1)   This rule applies where—

(a)   rule 9.8 applies; and

(b)   the defendant—

      (i)   indicates an intention to plead not guilty, or

      (ii)   gives no indication of intended plea.

(2)   In the following sequence, the court must then—

(a)   where the offence is one to which section 22 of the Magistrates' Courts Act 1980 applies, explain in terms the defendant can understand (with help, if necessary) that—

      (i)   if the court decides that the value involved clearly is less than £5,000, the court must order trial in a magistrates' court,

      (ii)   if the court decides that it is not clear whether that value is more or less than £5,000, then the court will ask whether the defendant agrees to be tried in a magistrates' court, and

      (iii)   if the answer to that question is 'yes', then the court must order such a trial and if the defendant is convicted then the maximum sentence is limited;

(b)   invite the prosecutor to—

      (i)   identify any previous convictions of which it can take account, and

      (ii)   make representations about how the court should allocate the case for trial, including representations about the value involved, if relevant;

(c)   invite the defendant to make such representations;

(d)   where the offence is one to which section 22 of the Magistrates' Courts Act 1980 applies—

      (i)   if it is not clear whether the value involved is more or less than £5,000, ask whether the defendant agrees to be tried in a magistrates' court,

      (ii)   if the defendant's answer to that question is 'yes', or if that value clearly is less than £5,000, order a trial in a magistrates' court,

      (iii)   if the defendant does not answer that question, or the answer is 'no', or if that value clearly is more than £5,000, apply paragraph (2)(e);

(e)   exercise its power to allocate the case for trial, taking into account—

      (i)   the adequacy of a magistrates' court's sentencing powers,

      (ii)   any representations by the parties, and

      (iii)   any allocation guidelines issued by the Sentencing Council.

[Note. See sections 17A, 18, 19, 22 and 24A of the Magistrates' Courts Act 1980.

Under section 22 of the 1980 Act, some offences, which otherwise could be tried in a magistrates' court or in the Crown Court, must be tried in a magistrates' court in the circumstances described in this rule.

The convictions of which the court may take account are those specified by section 19 of the 1980 Act.

The Sentencing Council may issue allocation guidelines under section 122 of the Coroners and Justice Act 2009. The definitive allocation guideline which took effect on 1st March, 2016 provides:

(1)   In general, either way offences should be tried summarily unless—

(a)   the outcome would clearly be a sentence in excess of the court's powers for the offence(s) concerned after taking into account personal mitigation and any potential reduction for a guilty plea; or

(b)   for reasons of unusual legal, procedural or factual complexity, the case should be tried in the Crown Court. This exception may apply in cases where a very substantial fine is the likely sentence. Other circumstances where this exception will apply are likely to be rare and case specific; the court will rely on the submissions of the parties to identify relevant cases.

(2)   In cases with no factual or legal complications the court should bear in mind its power to commit for sentence after a trial and may retain jurisdiction notwithstanding that the likely sentence might exceed its powers.

(3)   Cases may be tried summarily even where the defendant is subject to a Crown Court Suspended Sentence Order or Community Order.

(4)   All parties should be asked by the court to make representations as to whether the case is suitable for summary trial. The court should refer to definitive guidelines (if any) to assess the likely sentence for the offence in the light of the facts alleged by the prosecution case, taking into account all aspects of the case including those advanced by the defence, including any personal mitigation to which the defence wish to refer.

Where the court decides that the case is suitable to be dealt with in the magistrates' court, it must warn the defendant that all sentencing options remain open and, if the defendant consents to summary trial and is convicted by the court or pleads guilty, the defendant may be committed to the Crown Court for sentence.]

9.11.   Adult defendant: allocation for magistrates' court trial   (1)   This rule applies where—

(a)   rule 9.10 applies; and

(b)   the court allocates the case to a magistrates' court for trial.

(2)   The court must explain, in terms the defendant can understand (with help, if necessary) that—

(a)   the court considers the case more suitable for trial in a magistrates' court than in the Crown Court;

(b)   if the defendant is convicted at a magistrates' court trial, then in some circumstances the court may commit the defendant to the Crown Court for sentence;

(c)   if the defendant does not agree to a magistrates' court trial, then the court must send the defendant to the Crown Court for trial; and

(d)   before deciding whether to accept magistrates' court trial, the defendant may ask the court for an indication of whether a custodial or non-custodial sentence is more likely in the event of a guilty plea at such a trial, but the court need not give such an indication.

(3)   If the defendant asks for such an indication of sentence and the court gives such an indication—

(a)   the court must then ask again whether the defendant intends to plead guilty;

(b)   if, in answer to that question, the defendant indicates an intention to plead guilty, then the court must exercise its power to deal with the case—

    (i)   as if the defendant had just pleaded guilty to an offence that can be tried only in a magistrates' court, and

    (ii)   in accordance with rule 24.11 (Procedure if the court convicts);

(c)   if, in answer to that question, the defendant indicates an intention to plead not guilty, or gives no indication of intended plea, in the following sequence the court must then—

    (i)   ask whether the defendant agrees to trial in a magistrates' court,

    (ii)   if the defendant's answer to that question is 'yes', order such a trial,

    (iii)   if the defendant does not answer that question, or the answer is 'no', apply rule 9.14.

(4)   If the defendant asks for an indication of sentence but the court gives none, or if the defendant does not ask for such an indication, in the following sequence the court must then—

(a)   ask whether the defendant agrees to trial in a magistrates' court;

(b)   if the defendant's answer to that question is 'yes', order such a trial;

(c)   if the defendant does not answer that question, or the answer is 'no', apply rule 9.14.

[Note. See section 20 of the Magistrates' Courts Act 1980.

For the circumstances in which a magistrates' court may (and in some cases must) commit a defendant to the Crown Court for sentence after that defendant has been convicted at a magistrates' court trial, see sections 3, 3A, 3C, and 6 of the Powers of Criminal Courts (Sentencing) Act 2000.

For the circumstances in which an indication of sentence to which this rule applies restricts the sentencing powers of a court, see section 20A of the 1980 Act.]

9.12. Adult defendant: prosecutor's application for Crown Court trial (1) This rule applies where—

(a)   rule 9.11 applies;

(b)   the defendant agrees to trial in a magistrates' court; but

(c)   the prosecutor wants the court to exercise its power to send the defendant to the Crown Court for trial instead.

(2)   The prosecutor must—

(a)   apply before trial in a magistrates' court begins under Part 24 (Trial and sentence in a magistrates' court); and

(b)   notify—

    (i)   the defendant, and

    (ii)   the magistrates' court officer.

(3)   The court must determine an application to which this rule applies before it deals with any other pre-trial application.

[Note. See sections 8A and 25 of the Magistrates' Courts Act 1980. Under section 25(2B), the court may grant an application to which this rule applies only if it is satisfied that the sentence which a magistrates' court would have power to impose would be inadequate.]

9.13. Young defendant (1) This rule applies where—

(a)   the defendant is under 18; and

(b)   the court must decide whether to send the defendant for Crown Court trial instead of ordering trial in a youth court.

(2)   The court must read the allegation of the offence to the defendant.

(3)   The court must explain, in terms the defendant can understand (with help, if necessary)—

(a)   the allegation, unless it is self-explanatory;

(b)   that the offence is one which can be tried in the Crown Court instead of in a youth court;

(c)   that the court is about to ask whether the defendant intends to plead guilty;

(d)   that if the answer is 'yes', then the court must treat that as a guilty plea and must sentence the defendant, or commit the defendant to the Crown Court for sentence;

(e)   that if the defendant does not answer, or the answer is 'no', then the court must decide whether to send the defendant for Crown Court trial instead of ordering trial in a youth court; and

(f)   that reporting restrictions apply, which the defendant may ask the court to vary or remove.

(4)   The court must then ask whether the defendant intends to plead guilty.

(5)   If the defendant's answer to that question is 'yes', the court must exercise its power to deal with the case—

(a)   as if the defendant had just pleaded guilty at a trial in a youth court; and

(b)   in accordance with rule 24.11 (Procedure if the court convicts).

(6)   If the defendant does not answer that question, or the answer is 'no', in the following sequence the court must then—

(a)   invite the prosecutor to make representations about whether Crown Court or youth court trial is more appropriate;

(b)   invite the defendant to make such representations;

(c)   exercise its power to allocate the case for trial, taking into account—

(i)   the offence and the circumstances of the offence,

(ii)   the suitability of a youth court's sentencing powers,

(iii)   where the defendant is jointly charged with an adult, whether it is necessary in the interests of justice for them to be tried together in the Crown Court, and

(iv)   any representations by the parties.

[Note. See section 24A of the Magistrates' Courts Act 1980.

For the circumstances in which a magistrates' court may (and in some cases must) commit a defendant who is under 18 to the Crown Court for sentence after that defendant has indicated a guilty plea, see sections 3B, 3C, 4A and 6 of the Powers of Criminal Courts (Sentencing) Act 2000.]

9.14.   Allocation and sending for Crown Court trial   (1)   This rule applies where—

(a)   under rule 9.10 or rule 9.13, the court allocates the case to the Crown Court for trial;

(b)   under rule 9.11, the defendant does not agree to trial in a magistrates' court; or

(c)   under rule 9.12, the court grants the prosecutor's application for Crown Court trial.

(2)   In the following sequence, the court must—

(a)   invite the prosecutor to make representations about any ancillary matters, including bail and directions for the management of the case in the Crown Court;

(b)   invite the defendant to make any such representations; and

(c)   exercise its powers to—

(i)   send the defendant to the Crown Court for trial, and

(ii)   give any ancillary directions.

[Note. See sections 21 and 24A of the Magistrates' Courts Act 1980 and section 51 of the Crime and Disorder 1998. See also rule 9.3 (matters to be specified on sending for trial).]

CROWN COURT INITIAL PROCEDURE AFTER SENDING FOR TRIAL

9.15.   Service of prosecution evidence   (1)   This rule applies where—

(a)   a magistrates' court sends the defendant to the Crown Court for trial; and

(b)   the prosecutor serves on the defendant copies of the documents containing the evidence on which the prosecution case relies.

(2)   The prosecutor must at the same time serve copies of those documents on the Crown Court officer.

[Note. See the Crime and Disorder Act 1998 (Service of Prosecution Evidence) Regulations 2005. The time for service of the prosecution evidence is prescribed by regulation 2. It is—

(a)   n*ot more than 50 days after sending for trial, where the defendant is in custody; and*

(b)   n*ot more than 70 days after sending for trial, where the defendant is on bail.]*

9.16.   Application to dismiss offence sent for Crown Court trial   (1)   This rule applies where a defendant wants the Crown Court to dismiss an offence sent for trial there.

(2)   The defendant must—

(a)   apply in writing—

(i)   not more than 28 days after service of the prosecution evidence, and

(ii)   before the defendant's arraignment;

(b)   serve the application on—

(i)   the Crown Court officer, and

(ii)   each other party;

(c)   in the application—

(i)   explain why the prosecution evidence would not be sufficient for the defendant to be properly convicted,

(ii)   ask for a hearing, if the defendant wants one, and explain why it is needed,

(iii)   identify any witness whom the defendant wants to call to give evidence in person, with an indication of what evidence the witness can give,

(iv)   identify any material already served that the defendant thinks the court will need to determine the application, and

(v)   include any material not already served on which the defendant relies.

(3)   A prosecutor who opposes the application must—

(a)   serve notice of opposition, not more than 14 days after service of the defendant's notice, on—

(i)   the Crown Court officer, and

(ii)   each other party;

(b)   in the notice of opposition—

(i)   explain the grounds of opposition,

    (ii)   ask for a hearing, if the prosecutor wants one, and explain why it is needed,

    (iii)   identify any witness whom the prosecutor wants to call to give evidence in person, with an indication of what evidence the witness can give,

    (iv)   identify any material already served that the prosecutor thinks the court will need to determine the application, and

    (v)   include any material not already served on which the prosecutor relies.   (4)   The court may determine an application under this rule—

(a)   at a hearing, in public or in private, or without a hearing;

(b)   in the absence of—

    (i)   the defendant who made the application,

    (ii)   the prosecutor, if the prosecutor has had at least 14 days in which to serve notice opposing the application.

(5)   The court may—

(a)   shorten or extend (even after it has expired) a time limit under this rule;

(b)   allow a witness to give evidence in person even if that witness was not identified in the defendant's application or in the prosecutor's notice.

[Note. Under paragraph 2 of Schedule 3 to the Crime and Disorder Act 1998, on an application by the defendant the Crown Court must dismiss an offence charged if it appears to the court that the evidence would not be sufficient for the applicant to be properly convicted.]

PART 10   THE INDICTMENT

Contents of this Part

10.1.   **When this Part applies**   This Part applies where—

(a)   a magistrates' court sends a defendant to the Crown Court for trial under section 51 or section 51A of the Crime and Disorder Act 1998;

(b)   a prosecutor wants a High Court judge's permission to serve a draft indictment;

(c)   the Crown Court approves a proposed indictment under paragraph 2 of Schedule 17 to the Crime and Courts Act 2013 and rule 11.4 (Deferred prosecution agreements: Application to approve the terms of an agreement);

(d)   a prosecutor wants to re-institute proceedings in the Crown Court under section 22B of the Prosecution of Offences Act 1985;

(e)   the Court of Appeal orders a retrial, under section 8 of the Criminal Appeal Act 1968 or under section 77 of the Criminal Justice Act 2003.

[Note. See also sections 3, 4 and 5 of the Indictments Act 1915 and section 2 of the Administration of Justice (Miscellaneous Provisions) Act 1933. Under section 2(1) of the 1933 Act, a draft indictment (in the Act, a 'bill of indictment') becomes an indictment when it is 'preferred' in accordance with these rules. See rule 10.2.

Part 3 contains rules about the court's general powers of case management, including power to consider applications and give directions for (among other things) the amendment of an indictment and for separate trials under section 5 of the Indictments Act 1915. See in particular rule 3.21 (Application for joint or separate trials, etc).

Under section 51D of the Crime and Disorder Act 1998, the magistrates' court must notify the Crown Court of the offence or offences for which the defendant is sent for trial. Part 9 (Allocation and sending for trial) contains relevant rules.

A Crown Court judge may approve a proposed indictment on approving a deferred prosecution agreement. Part 11 (Deferred prosecution agreements) contains relevant rules.

A prosecutor may apply to a High Court judge for permission to serve a draft indictment under rule 10.9.

Under section 22B of the Prosecution of Offences Act 1985, one of the prosecutors listed in that section may re-institute proceedings that have been stayed under section 22(4) of that Act on the expiry of an overall time limit (where such a time limit has been prescribed). Section 22B(2) requires the service of a draft indictment within 3 months of the date on which the Crown Court

ordered the stay, or within such longer period as the court allows.
The Court of Appeal may order a retrial under section 8 of the Criminal Appeal Act 1968 (on a defendant's appeal against conviction) or under section 77 of the Criminal Justice Act 2003 (on a prosecutor's application for the retrial of a serious offence after acquittal). Section 8 of the 1968 Act and section 84 of the 2003 Act require the arraignment of a defendant within 2 months. See also rules 27.7 and 39.14.
With effect from 30tth August 2013, Schedule 3 to the Criminal Justice Act 2003 abolished committal for trial under section 6 of the Magistrates' Courts Act 1980, and transfer for trial under section 4 of the Criminal Justice Act 1987 (serious fraud cases) or under section 53 of the Criminal Justice Act 1991 (certain cases involving children).
Where a magistrates' court sends a defendant to the Crown Court for trial under section 51 or 51A of the Crime and Disorder Act 1998, in some circumstances the Crown Court may try the defendant for other offences: see section 2(2) of the Administration of Justice (Miscellaneous Provisions) Act 1933 (indictable offences founded on the prosecution evidence), section 40 of the Criminal Justice Act 1988 (specified summary offences founded on that evidence) and paragraph 6 of Schedule 3 to the Crime and Disorder Act 1998 (power of Crown Court to deal with related summary offence sent to that court).]

10.2. The indictment: general rules (1) The indictment on which the defendant is arraigned under rule 3.24 (Arraigning the defendant on the indictment) must be in writing and must contain, in a paragraph called a 'count'—
(a) a statement of the offence charged that—
(i) describes the offence in ordinary language, and
(ii) identifies any legislation that creates it; and
(b) such particulars of the conduct constituting the commission of the offence as to make clear what the prosecutor alleges against the defendant.
(2) More than one incident of the commission of the offence may be included in a count if those incidents taken together amount to a course of conduct having regard to the time, place or purpose of commission.
(3) The counts must be numbered consecutively.
(4) An indictment may contain—
(a) any count charging substantially the same offence as one for which the defendant was sent for trial;
(b) any count contained in a draft indictment served with the permission of a High Court judge or at the direction of the Court of Appeal; and
(c) any other count charging an offence that the Crown Court can try and which is based on the prosecution evidence that has been served.
(5) For the purposes of section 2 of the Administration of Justice (Miscellaneous Provisions) Act 1933—
(a) a draft indictment constitutes a bill of indictment;
(b) the draft, or bill, is preferred before the Crown Court and becomes the indictment—
(i) where rule 10.3 applies (Draft indictment generated electronically on sending for trial), immediately before the first count (or the only count, if there is only one) is read to or placed before the defendant to take the defendant's plea under rule 3.24(1)(c),
(ii) when the prosecutor serves the draft indictment on the Crown Court officer, where rule 10.4 (Draft indictment served by the prosecutor after sending for trial), rule 10.5 (Draft indictment served by the prosecutor with a High Court judge's permission), rule 10.7 (Draft indictment served by the prosecutor on re-instituting proceedings) or rule 10.8 (Draft indictment served by the prosecutor at the direction of the Court of Appeal) applies,
(iii) when the Crown Court approves the proposed indictment, where rule 10.6 applies (Draft indictment approved by the Crown Court with deferred prosecution agreement).
(6) An indictment must be in one of the forms set out in the Practice Direction unless—
(a) rule 10.3 applies; or
(b) the Crown Court otherwise directs.
(7) Unless the Crown Court otherwise directs, the court officer must—
(a) endorse any paper copy of the indictment made for the court with—
(i) a note to identify it as a copy of the indictment, and
(ii) the date on which the draft indictment became the indictment under paragraph (5); and
(b) where rule 10.4, 10.5, 10.7 or 10.8 applies, serve a copy of the indictment on all parties.
(8) The Crown Court may extend the time limit under rule 10.4, 10.5, 10.7 or 10.8, even after it has expired.
[Note. Under section 2(6) of the Administration of Justice (Miscellaneous Provisions) Act 1933, Criminal Procedure Rules may provide for the manner in which and the time at which 'bills of indictment' are to be 'preferred'.
Under rule 3.21 (Application for joint or separate trials, etc), the court may order separate trials of counts in the circumstances listed in that rule.]

10.3. Draft indictment generated electronically on sending for trial (1) Unless the Crown Court otherwise directs before the defendant is arraigned, this rule applies where—
(a) a magistrates' court sends a defendant to the Crown Court for trial;

(b)   the magistrates' court officer serves on the Crown Court officer the notice required by rule 9.5 (Duty of magistrates' court officer); and

(c)   by means of such electronic arrangements as the court officer may make for the purpose, there is presented to the Crown Court as a count—

    (i)   each allegation of an indictable offence specified in the notice, and

    (ii)   each allegation specified in the notice to which section 40 of the Criminal Justice Act 1988 applies (specified summary offences founded on the prosecution evidence).

(2)   Where this rule applies—

(a)   each such allegation constitutes a count;

(b)   the allegation or allegations so specified together constitute a draft indictment;

(c)   before the draft indictment so constituted is preferred before the Crown Court under rule 10.2(5)(b)(i) the prosecutor may substitute for any count an amended count to the same effect and charging the same offence;

(d)   if under rule 9.15 (Service of prosecution evidence) the prosecutor has served copies of the documents containing the evidence on which the prosecution case relies then, before the draft indictment is preferred before the Crown Court under rule 10.2(5)(b)(i), the prosecutor may substitute or add—

    (i)   any count charging substantially the same offence as one specified in the notice, and

    (ii)   any other count charging an offence which the Crown Court can try and which is based on the prosecution evidence so served; and

(e)   a prosecutor who substitutes or adds a count under paragraph (2)(c) or (d) must serve that count on the Crown Court officer and the defendant.

[Note. An 'indictable offence' is (i) an offence classified as triable on indictment exclusively, or (ii) an offence classified as triable either on indictment or summarily. See also the note to rule 9.1 (Allocation and sending for trial: When this Part applies).

Section 40 of the Criminal Justice Act 1988 lists summary offences which may be included in an indictment if the charge—

(a)   is founded on the same facts or evidence as a count charging an indictable offence; or

(b)   is part of a series of offences of the same or similar character as an indictable offence which is also charged.]

10.4.   Draft indictment served by the prosecutor after sending for trial   (1)   This rule applies where—

(a)   a magistrates' court sends a defendant to the Crown Court for trial; and

(b)   rule 10.3 (Draft indictment generated electronically on sending for trial) does not apply.

(2)   The prosecutor must serve a draft indictment on the Crown Court officer not more than 28 days after serving under rule 9.15 (Service of prosecution evidence) copies of the documents containing the evidence on which the prosecution case relies.

[10.5.   Draft indictment served by the prosecutor with a High Court judge's permission]

    [(1)   This rule applies where—

(a)   the prosecutor applies to a High Court judge under rule 10.9 (Application to a High Court judge for permission to serve a draft indictment); and

(b)   the judge gives permission to serve a proposed indictment.

(2)   Where this rule applies—

(a)   that proposed indictment constitutes the draft indictment; and

(b)   the prosecutor must serve the draft indictment on the Crown Court officer not more than 28 days after the High Court judge's decision.]

10.6.   Draft indictment approved with deferred prosecution agreement   (1)   This rule applies where—

(a)   the prosecutor applies to the Crown Court under rule 11.4 (Deferred prosecution agreements: Application to approve the terms of an agreement); and

(b)   the Crown Court approves the proposed indictment served with that application.

(2)   Where this rule applies, that proposed indictment constitutes the draft indictment.

10.7.   Draft indictment served by the prosecutor on re-instituting proceedings]   [(1)   This rule applies where the prosecutor wants to re-institute proceedings in the Crown Court under section 22B of the Prosecution of Offences Act 1985.

(2)   The prosecutor must serve a draft indictment on the Crown Court officer not more than 3 months after the proceedings were stayed under section 22(4) of that Act.

10.8.   Draft indictment served by the prosecutor at the direction of the Court of Appeal]   [(1)   This rule applies where the Court of Appeal orders a retrial.

(2)   The prosecutor must serve a draft indictment on the Crown Court officer not more than 28 days after that order.

10.9.   Application to a High Court judge for permission to serve a draft indictment]   [(1)   This rule applies where a prosecutor wants a High Court judge's permission to serve a draft indictment.

(2)   Such a prosecutor must—

(a)   apply in writing;

(b)   serve the application on—

    (i)   the court officer, and

    (ii)   the proposed defendant, unless the judge otherwise directs; and

(c)   ask for a hearing, if the prosecutor wants one, and explain why it is needed.

(3)   The application must—

(a)   attach—

         (i)   the proposed indictment,

         (ii)   copies of the documents containing the evidence on which the prosecutor relies, including any written witness statement or statements complying with rule 16.2 (Content of written witness statement) and any documentary exhibit to any such statement,

         (iii)   a copy of any indictment on which the defendant already has been arraigned, and

         (iv)   if not contained in such an indictment, a list of any offence or offences for which the defendant already has been sent for trial;

(b)   include—

         (i)   a concise statement of the circumstances in which, and the reasons why, the application is made, and

         (ii)   a concise summary of the evidence contained in the documents accompanying the application, identifying each passage in those documents said to evidence each offence alleged by the prosecutor and relating that evidence to each count in the proposed indictment; and

(c)   contain a statement that, to the best of the prosecutor's knowledge, information and belief—

         (i)   the evidence on which the prosecutor relies will be available at the trial, and

         (ii)   the allegations contained in the application are substantially true

    unless the application is made by or on behalf of the Director of Public Prosecutions or the Director of the Serious Fraud Office.

(4)   A proposed defendant served with an application who wants to make representations to the judge must—

(a)   serve the representations on the court officer and on the prosecutor;

(b)   do so as soon as practicable, and in any event within such period as the judge directs; and

(c)   ask for a hearing, if the proposed defendant wants one, and explain why it is needed.

(5)   The judge may determine the application—

(a)   without a hearing, or at a hearing in public or in private;

(b)   with or without receiving the oral evidence of any proposed witness.

(6)   At any hearing, if the judge so directs a statement required by paragraph (3)(c) must be repeated on oath or affirmation.

(7)   If the judge gives permission to serve a draft indictment, the decision must be recorded in writing and endorsed on, or annexed to, the proposed indictment.

[Note. See section 2(6) of the Administration of Justice (Miscellaneous Provisions) Act 1933.]

PART 11   DEFERRED PROSECUTION AGREEMENTS

Note

     [Part 11 is not reproduced.]

PART 12   DISCONTINUING A PROSECUTION

B.11   *12.1. When this Part applies*   (1)   This Part applies where—

(a)   the Director of Public Prosecutions can discontinue a case in a magistrates' court, under section 23 of the Prosecution of Offences Act 1985;

(b)   the Director of Public Prosecutions, or another public prosecutor, can discontinue a case sent for trial in the Crown Court, under section 23A of the Prosecution of Offences Act 1985.

(2)   In this Part, 'prosecutor' means one of those authorities.

[Note. Under section 23 of the Prosecution of Offences Act 1985, the Director of Public Prosecutions may discontinue proceedings in a magistrates' court, before the court—

(a)   sends the defendant for trial in the Crown Court; or

(b)   begins to hear the prosecution evidence, at a trial in the magistrates' court.

Under section 23(4) of the 1985 Act, the Director may discontinue proceedings where a person charged is in custody but has not yet been brought to court.

Under section 23 of the 1985 Act, the defendant has a right to require the proceedings to continue. See rule 12.3.

Under section 23A of the 1985 Act, the Director of Public Prosecutions, or a public authority within the meaning of section 17 of that Act, may discontinue proceedings where the defendant was sent for trial in the Crown Court under section 51 of the Crime and Disorder Act 1998. In such a case—

(a)   the prosecutor must discontinue before a draft indictment becomes an indictment under rule 10.2(5); and

(b)   the defendant has no right to require the proceedings to continue.

Where a prosecution does not proceed, the court has power to order the payment of the defendant's costs out of central funds. See rule 45.4.]

12.2. Discontinuing a case (1) A prosecutor exercising a power to which this Part applies must serve notice on—
(a)   the court officer;
(b)   the defendant; and
(c)   any custodian of the defendant.
(2)   Such a notice must—
(a)   identify—
    (i)   the defendant and each offence to which the notice relates,
    (ii)   the person serving the notice, and
    (iii) the power that that person is exercising;
(b)   explain—
    (i)   in the copy of the notice served on the court officer, the reasons for discontinuing the case,
    (ii)   that the notice brings the case to an end,
    (iii) if the defendant is in custody for any offence to which the notice relates, that the defendant must be released from that custody, and
    (iv) if the notice is under section 23 of the 1985 Act, that the defendant has a right to require the case to continue.
(3)   Where the defendant is on bail, the court officer must notify—
(a)   any surety; and
(b)   any person responsible for monitoring or securing the defendant's compliance with a condition of bail.

12.3. Defendant's notice to continue (1) This rule applies where a prosecutor serves a notice to discontinue under section 23 of the 1985 Act.
(2)   A defendant who wants the case to continue must serve notice—
(a)   on the court officer; and
(b)   not more than 35 days after service of the notice to discontinue.
(3)   If the defendant serves such a notice, the court officer must—
(a)   notify the prosecutor; and
(b)   refer the case to the court.

PART 13   WARRANTS FOR ARREST, DETENTION OR IMPRISONMENT

Contents of this Part

Note
    [Note. Part 30 contains rules about warrants to take goods to pay fines, etc]
B.12 *13.1. When this Part applies* (1) This Part applies where the court can issue a warrant for arrest, detention or imprisonment.
(2)   In this Part, 'defendant' means anyone against whom such a warrant is issued.

13.2. Terms of a warrant for arrest A warrant for arrest must require each person to whom it is directed to arrest the defendant and—
(a)   bring the defendant to a court—
    (i)   specified in the warrant, or
    (ii)   required or allowed by law; or
(b)   release the defendant on bail (with conditions or without) to attend court at a date, time and place—
    (i)   specified in the warrant, or
    (ii)   to be notified by the court.
[Note. The principal provisions under which the court can issue a warrant for arrest are—
(a)   section 4 of the Criminal Procedure (Attendance of Witnesses) Act 1965;
(b)   section 7 of the Bail Act 1976;
(c)   sections 1 and 97 of the Magistrates' Courts Act 1980; and
(d)   sections 79, 80 and 81(4), (5) of the Senior Courts Act 1981.
See also section 27A of the Magistrates' Courts Act 1980 (power to transfer criminal proceedings) and section 78(2) of the Senior Courts Act 1981 (adjournment of Crown Court case to another place).]

13.3. Terms of a warrant for detention or imprisonment (1)   A warrant for detention or imprisonment must—

(a)   require each person to whom it is directed to detain the defendant and—

 (i)   take the defendant to any place specified in the warrant or required or allowed by law, and

 (ii)   deliver the defendant to the custodian of that place; and

(b)   require that custodian to detain the defendant, as ordered by the court, until in accordance with the law—

 (i)   the defendant is delivered to the appropriate court or place, or

 (ii)   the defendant is released.

(2)   Where a magistrates' court remands a defendant to police detention under section 128(7) or section 136 of the Magistrates' Courts Act 1980, or to customs detention under section 152 of the Criminal Justice Act 1988, the warrant it issues must—

(a)   be directed, as appropriate, to—

 (i)   a constable, or

 (ii)   an officer of Her Majesty's Revenue and Customs; and

(b)   require that constable or officer to detain the defendant—

 (i)   for a period (not exceeding the maximum permissible) specified in the warrant, or

 (ii)   until in accordance with the law the defendant is delivered to the appropriate court or place.

(3)   Where a magistrates' court sentences a defendant to imprisonment or detention and section 11(3) of the Magistrates' Courts Act 1980 applies (custodial sentence imposed in the defendant's absence), the warrant it issues must—

(a)   require each person to whom the warrant is directed—

 (i)   to arrest the defendant and bring him or her to a court specified in the warrant, and

 (ii)   unless the court then otherwise directs, after that to act as required by paragraph (1)(a) of this rule; and

(b)   require the custodian to whom the defendant is delivered in accordance with that paragraph to act as required by paragraph (1)(b) of this rule.

[Note. Under section 128(7) of the Magistrates' Courts Act 1980, a magistrates' court can remand a defendant to police detention for not more than 3 clear days, if the defendant is an adult, or for not more than 24 hours if the defendant is under 18.

Under section 136 of the 1980 Act, a magistrates' court can order a defendant's detention in police custody until the following 8am for non-payment of a fine, etc

Under section 152 of the Criminal Justice Act 1988, a magistrates' court can remand a defendant to customs detention for not more than 192 hours if the defendant is charged with a drug trafficking offence.]

13.4. Information to be included in a warrant (1)   A warrant must identify—

(a)   each person to whom it is directed;

(b)   the defendant against whom it was issued;

(c)   the reason for its issue;

(d)   the court that issued it, unless that is otherwise recorded by the court officer; and

(e)   the court office for the court that issued it.

(2)   A warrant for detention or imprisonment must contain a record of any decision by the court under—

(a)   section 91 of the Legal Aid, Sentencing and Punishment of Offenders Act 2012 (remands of children otherwise than on bail), including in particular—

 (i)   whether the defendant must be detained in local authority accommodation or youth detention accommodation,

 (ii)   the local authority designated by the court,

 (iii)   any requirement imposed by the court on that authority,

 (iv)   any condition imposed by the court on the defendant, and

 (v)   the reason for any such requirement or condition;

(b)   section 80 of the Magistrates' Courts Act 1980 (application of money found on defaulter to satisfy sum adjudged); or

(c)   section 82(1) or (4) of the 1980 Act (conditions for issue of a warrant).

(3)   A warrant that contains an error is not invalid, as long as—

(a)   it was issued in respect of a lawful decision by the court; and

(b)   it contains enough information to identify that decision.

[Note. See sections 93(7) and 102(5) of the Legal Aid, Sentencing and Punishment of Offenders Act 2012. Under section 91 of the Act, instead of granting bail to a defendant under 18 the court may—

(a)   *remand him or her to local authority accommodation and, after consulting with that authority, impose on the defendant a condition that the court could impose if granting bail; or*

(b)   *remand him or her to youth detention accommodation, if the defendant is at least 12 years old and the other conditions, about the offence and the defendant, prescribed by the Act are met.*

Under section 80 of the Magistrates' Courts Act 1980, the court may decide that any money found on the defendant must not be applied towards payment of the sum for which a warrant is issued

under section 76 of that Act (enforcement of sums adjudged to be paid).
See section 82(6) of the 1980 Act. Under section 82(1) and (4), the court may only issue a warrant for the defendant's imprisonment for non-payment of a sum due where it finds that the prescribed conditions are met.
Under section 123 of the 1980 Act, "no objection shall be allowed to any . . . warrant to procure the presence of the defendant, for any defect in it in substance or in form . . . ".]

13.5.   *Execution of a warrant*   (1)   A warrant may be executed—
(a)   by any person to whom it is directed; or
(b)   if the warrant was issued by a magistrates' court, by anyone authorised to do so by section 125 (warrants), 125A (civilian enforcement officers) or 125B (execution by approved enforcement agency) of the Magistrates' Courts Act 1980.
(2)   The person who executes a warrant must—
(a)   explain, in terms the defendant can understand, what the warrant requires, and why;
(b)   show the defendant the warrant, if that person has it; and
(c)   if the defendant asks—
         (i)   arrange for the defendant to see the warrant, if that person does not have it, and
         (ii)   show the defendant any written statement of that person's authority required by section 125A or 125B of the 1980 Act.
(3)   The person who executes a warrant of arrest that requires the defendant to be released on bail must—
(a)   make a record of—
         (i)   the defendant's name,
         (ii)   the reason for the arrest,
         (iii)   the defendant's release on bail, and
         (iv)   when and where the warrant requires the defendant to attend court; and
(b)   serve the record on—
         (i)   the defendant, and
         (ii)   the court officer.
(4)   The person who executes a warrant of detention or imprisonment must—
(a)   take the defendant—
         (i)   to any place specified in the warrant, or
         (ii)   if that is not immediately practicable, to any other place at which the defendant may be lawfully detained (and the warrant then has effect as if it specified that place);
(b)   obtain a receipt from the custodian; and
(c)   notify the court officer that the defendant has been taken to that place.
[Note. Under section 125 of the Magistrates' Courts Act 1980, a warrant issued by a magistrates' court may be executed by any person to whom it is directed or by any constable acting within that constable's police area.
Certain warrants issued by a magistrates' court may be executed anywhere in England and Wales by a civilian enforcement officer, under section 125A of the 1980 Act; or by an approved enforcement agency, under section 125B of the Act. In either case, the person executing the warrant must, if the defendant asks, show a written statement indicating: that person's name; the authority or agency by which that person is employed, or in which that person is a director or partner; that that person is authorised to execute warrants; and, where section 125B applies, that the agency is registered as one approved by the Lord Chancellor.
See also section 125D of the 1980 Act, under which—
(a)   *a warrant to which section 125A applies may be executed by any person entitled to execute it even though it is not in that person's possession at the time; and*
(b)   *certain other warrants, including any warrant to arrest a person in connection with an offence, may be executed by a constable even though it is not in that constable's possession at the time.]*

13.6.   *Warrants that cease to have effect on payment*   (1)   This rule applies to a warrant issued by a magistrates' court under any of the following provisions of the Magistrates' Courts Act 1980—
(a)   section 76 (enforcement of sums adjudged to be paid);
(b)   section 83 (process for securing attendance of offender);
(c)   section 86 (power of magistrates' court to fix day for appearance of offender at means inquiry, etc);
(d)   section 136 (committal to custody overnight at police station for non-payment of sum adjudged by conviction).
(2)   The warrant no longer has effect if—
(a)   the sum in respect of which the warrant was issued is paid to the person executing it;
(b)   that sum is offered to, but refused by, that person; or
(c)   that person is shown a receipt for that sum given by—
         (i)   the court officer, or
         (ii)   the authority to which that sum is due.
[Note. See sections 79 and 125(1) of the Magistrates' Courts Act 1980.]

13.7.   *Warrant issued when the court office is closed*   (1)   This rule applies where the court issues a warrant when the court office is closed.
(2)   The applicant for the warrant must, not more than 72 hours later, serve on the court officer—
(a)   a copy of the warrant; and

(b)   any written material that was submitted to the court.

PART 14   BAIL AND CUSTODY TIME LIMITS

GENERAL RULES

B.13   *14.1.   When this Part applies*   (1)   This Part applies where—
(a)   a magistrates' court or the Crown Court can—
    (i)   grant or withhold bail, or impose or vary a condition of bail, and
    (ii)   where bail has been withheld, extend a custody time limit;
(b)   a magistrates' court can monitor and enforce compliance with a supervision measure imposed in another European Union member State.
(2)   Rules 14.20, 14.21 and 14.22 apply where a magistrates' court can authorise an extension of the period for which a defendant is released on bail before being charged with an offence.
(3)   In this Part, 'defendant' includes a person who has been granted bail by a police officer.
[Note. See in particular—
(a)   *the Bail Act 1976;*
(b)   *section 128 of the Magistrates' Courts Act 1980 (general powers of magistrates' courts in relation to bail);*
(c)   *section 81 of the Senior Courts Act 1981 (general powers of the Crown Court in relation to bail);*
(d)   *section 115 of the Coroners and Justice Act 2009 (exclusive power of the Crown Court to grant bail to a defendant charged with murder);*
(e)   *Part 7 of the Criminal Justice and Data Protection (Protocol No 36) Regulations 2014, which gives effect to Council Framework Decision 2009/829/JHA of 23rd October, 2009, on the application, between member States of the European Union, of the principle of mutual recognition to decisions on supervision measures as an alternative to provisional detention (bail conditions pending trial);*
(f)   *section 22 of the Prosecution of Offences Act 1985 (provision for custody time limits);*
(g)   *the Prosecution of Offences (Custody Time Limits) Regulations 1987 (maximum periods during which a defendant may be kept in custody pending trial); and*
(h)   *sections 47ZF and 47ZG of the Police and Criminal Evidence Act 1984(extensions by court of pre-charge bail time limit).;*
At the end of this Part there is—
(a)   *a summary of the general entitlement to bail, and of the exceptions to that entitlement; and*

(b)   a list of the types of supervision measure to which Part 7 of the Criminal Justice and Data Protection (Protocol No 36) Regulations 2014 applies, and a list of the grounds for refusing to monitor and enforce such a measure.]

14.2.   *Exercise of court's powers: general*   (1)   The court must not make a decision to which this Part applies unless—
(a)   each party to the decision and any surety directly affected by the decision—
            (i)   is present, in person or by live link, or
            (ii)   has had an opportunity to make representations;
(b)   on an application for bail by a defendant who is absent and in custody, the court is satisfied that the defendant—
            (i)   has waived the right to attend, or
            (ii)   was present when a court withheld bail in the case on a previous occasion and has been in custody continuously since then;
(c)   on a prosecutor's appeal against a grant of bail, application to extend a custody time limit or appeal against a refusal to extend such a time limit—
            (i)   the court is satisfied that a defendant who is absent has waived the right to attend, or
            (ii)   the court is satisfied that it would be just to proceed even though the defendant is absent.
(d)   the court is satisfied that sufficient time has been allowed—
            (i)   for the defendant to consider the information provided by the prosecutor under rule 14.5(2), and
            (ii)   for the court to consider the parties' representations and make the decision required.
(2)   The court may make a decision to which this Part applies at a hearing, in public or in private.
(3)   The court may determine without a hearing an application to vary a condition of bail if—
(a)   the parties to the application have agreed the terms of the variation proposed; or
(b)   on an application by a defendant, the court determines the application no sooner than the fifth business day after the application was served.
(4)   The court may adjourn a determination to which this Part applies, if that is necessary to obtain information sufficient to allow the court to make the decision required.
(5)   At any hearing at which the court makes one of the following decisions, the court must announce in terms the defendant can understand (with help, if necessary), and by reference to the circumstances of the defendant and the case, its reasons for—
(a)   withholding bail, or imposing or varying a bail condition;
(b)   granting bail, where the prosecutor opposed the grant; or
(c)   where the defendant is under 18—
            (i)   imposing or varying a bail condition when ordering the defendant to be detained in local authority accommodation, or
            (ii)   ordering the defendant to be detained in youth detention accommodation.
(6)   At any hearing at which the court grants bail, the court must—
(a)   tell the defendant where and when to surrender to custody; or
(b)   arrange for the court officer to give the defendant, as soon as practicable, notice of where and when to surrender to custody.
(7)   This rule does not apply on an application to a magistrates' court to authorise an extension of pre-charge bail.
[Note. See section 5 of the Bail Act 1976 and sections 93(7) and 102(4) of the Legal Aid, Sentencing and Punishment of Offenders Act 2012.
Under sections 57A and 57B of the Crime and Disorder Act 1998 and under regulation 79(3) of the Criminal Justice and Data Protection (Protocol No 36) Regulations 2014, a defendant is to be treated as present in court when, by virtue of a live link direction within the meaning of those provisions, he or she attends a hearing through a live link.
Under section 91 of the 2012 Act, instead of granting bail to a defendant under 18 the court may—
(a)   remand him or her to local authority accommodation and, after consulting with that authority, impose on the defendant a condition that the court could impose if granting bail; or
(b)   remand him or her to youth detention accommodation, if the defendant is at least 12 years old and the other conditions, about the offence and the defendant, prescribed by the Act are met.]
See also rule 14.20 (Exercise of court's powers: extension of pre-charge bail).

14.3.   *Duty of justices' legal adviser*   (1)   This rule applies—
(a)   only in a magistrates' court; and
(b)   unless the court—
            (i)   includes a District Judge (Magistrates' Courts), and
            (ii)   otherwise directs.
(2)   A justices' legal adviser must—
(a)   assist an unrepresented defendant;
(b)   give the court such advice as is required to enable it to exercise its powers;
(c)   if required, attend the members of the court outside the courtroom to give such advice, but inform the parties of any advice so given.
[Note. For the functions of a justices' legal adviser, see sections 28 and 29 of the Courts Act 2003.]

14.4. *General duties of court officer* (1) The court officer must arrange for a note or other record to be made of—

(a) the parties' representations about bail; and

(b) the court's reasons for a decision—
- (i) to withhold bail, or to impose or vary a bail condition,
- (ii) to grant bail, where the prosecutor opposed the grant, or.
- (iii) on an application to which rule 14.21 applies (Application to authorise extension of pre-charge bail).

(2) The court officer must serve notice of a decision about bail on—

(a) the defendant (but, in the Crown Court, only where the defendant's legal representative asks for such a notice, or where the defendant has no legal representative);

(b) the prosecutor (but only where the court granted bail, the prosecutor opposed the grant, and the prosecutor asks for such a notice);

(c) a party to the decision who was absent when it was made;

(d) a surety who is directly affected by the decision;

(e) the defendant's custodian, where the defendant is in custody and the decision requires the custodian—
- (i) to release the defendant (or will do so, if a requirement ordered by the court is met), or
- (ii) to transfer the defendant to the custody of another custodian;

(f) the court officer for any other court at which the defendant is required by that decision to surrender to custody.

(3) Where the court postpones the date on which a defendant who is on bail must surrender to custody, the court officer must serve notice of the postponed date on—

(a) the defendant; and

(b) any surety.

(4) Where a magistrates' court withholds bail in a case to which section 5(6A) of the Bail Act 1976 applies (remand in custody after hearing full argument on an application for bail), the court officer must serve on the defendant a certificate that the court heard full argument.

(5) Where the court determines without a hearing an application to which rule 14.21 applies (Application to authorise extension of pre-charge bail), the court officer must—

(a) if the court allows the application, notify the applicant;

(b) if the court refuses the application, notify the applicant and the defendant.

[Note. See section 5 of the Bail Act 1976; section 43 of the Magistrates' Courts Act 1980; and section 52 of the Mental Health Act 1983.]

BAIL

14.5. *Prosecutor's representations about bail* (1) This rule applies whenever the court can grant or withhold bail.

(2) The prosecutor must as soon as practicable—

(a) provide the defendant with all the information in the prosecutor's possession which is material to what the court must decide; and

(b) provide the court with the same information.

(3) A prosecutor who opposes the grant of bail must specify—

(a) each exception to the general right to bail on which the prosecutor relies; and

(b) each consideration that the prosecutor thinks relevant.

(4) A prosecutor who wants the court to impose a condition on any grant of bail must—

(a) specify each condition proposed; and

(b) explain what purpose would be served by such a condition.

[Note. A summary of the general entitlement to bail and of the exceptions to that entitlement is at the end of this Part.]

14.6. *Reconsideration of police bail by magistrates' court* (1) This rule applies where—

(a) a party wants a magistrates' court to reconsider a bail decision by a police officer after the defendant is charged with an offence;

(b) a defendant wants a magistrates' court to reconsider a bail condition imposed by a police officer before the defendant is charged with an offence.

(2) An application under this rule must be made to—

(a) the magistrates' court to whose custody the defendant is under a duty to surrender, if any; or

(b) any magistrates' court acting for the police officer's local justice area, in any other case.

(3) The applicant party must—

(a) apply in writing; and

(b) serve the application on—
- (i) the court officer,
- (ii) the other party, and
- (iii) any surety affected or proposed.

(4) The application must—

(a) specify—
- (i) the decision that the applicant wants the court to make,
- (ii) each offence charged, or for which the defendant was arrested, and

           (iii)   the police bail decision to be reconsidered and the reasons given for it;

(b)   explain, as appropriate—

           (i)   why the court should grant bail itself, or withdraw it, or impose or vary a condition, and

           (ii)   if the applicant is the prosecutor, what material information has become available since the police bail decision was made;

(c)   propose the terms of any suggested condition of bail; and

(d)   if the applicant wants an earlier hearing than paragraph (7) requires, ask for that, and explain why it is needed.

(5)   A prosecutor who applies under this rule must serve on the defendant, with the application, notice that the court has power to withdraw bail and, if the defendant is absent when the court makes its decision, order the defendant's arrest.

(6)   A party who opposes an application must—

(a)   so notify the court officer and the applicant at once; and

(b)   serve on each notice of the reasons for opposition.

(7)   Unless the court otherwise directs, the court officer must arrange for the court to hear the application as soon as practicable and in any event—

(a)   if it is an application to withdraw bail, no later than the second business day after it was served;

(b)   in any any other case, no later than the fifth business day after it was served.

(8)   The court may—

(a)   vary or waive a time limit under this rule;

(b)   allow an application to be in a different form to one set out in the Practice Direction;

(c)   if rule 14.2 allows, determine without a hearing an application to vary a condition.

[Note. The Practice Direction sets out a form of application for use in connection with this rule.
Under section 5B of the Bail Act 1976—

(a)   *where a defendant has been charged with an offence which can be tried in the Crown Court; or*

(b)   *in an extradition case,*

on application by the prosecutor a magistrates' court may withdraw bail granted by a constable, impose conditions of bail, or vary conditions of bail. See also sections 37, 37C(2)(b), 37CA(2)(b), 46A and 47(1B) of the Police and Criminal Evidence Act 1984.
Under section 43B of the Magistrates' Courts Act 1980, where a defendant has been charged with an offence, on application by the defendant a magistrates' court may grant bail itself, in substitution for bail granted by a custody officer, or vary the conditions of bail granted by a custody officer. See also sections 37, 37C(2)(b), 37CA(2)(b), 46A and 47(1C), (1D) of the Police and Criminal Evidence Act 1984.
Under section 47(1E) of the Police and Criminal Evidence Act 1984, where a defendant has been released on bail by a custody officer without being charged with an offence, on application by the defendant a magistrates' court may vary any conditions of that bail. See also sections 37, 37C(2)(b), 37CA(2)(b), 46A and 47(1C) of the Act.]

14.7.   *Notice of application to consider bail*   (1)   This rule applies where—

(a)   in a magistrates' court—

           (i)   a prosecutor wants the court to withdraw bail granted by the court, or to impose or vary a condition of such bail, or

           (ii)   a defendant wants the court to reconsider such bail before the next hearing in the case;

(b)   in the Crown Court—

           (i)   a party wants the court to grant bail that has been withheld, or to withdraw bail that has been granted, or to impose a new bail condition or to vary a present one, or

           (ii)   a prosecutor wants the court to consider whether to grant or withhold bail, or impose or vary a condition of bail, under section 88 or section 89 of the Criminal Justice Act 2003 (bail and custody in connection with an intended application to the Court of Appeal to which Part 27 (Retrial after acquittal) applies).

(2)   Such a party must—

(a)   apply in writing;

(b)   serve the application on—

           (i)   the court officer,

           (ii)   the other party, and

           (iii)   any surety affected or proposed; and

(c)   serve the application not less than 2 business days before any hearing in the case at which the applicant wants the court to consider it, if such a hearing is already due.

(3)   The application must—

(a)   specify—

           (i)   the decision that the applicant wants the court to make,

           (ii)   each offence charged, and

           (iii)   each relevant previous bail decision and the reasons given for each;

(b)   if the applicant is a defendant, explain—

           (i)   as appropriate, why the court should not withhold bail, or why it should vary a condition, and

      (ii)   what further information or legal argument, if any, has become available since the most recent previous bail decision was made;

(c)   if the applicant is the prosecutor, explain—

      (i)   as appropriate, why the court should withdraw bail, or impose or vary a condition, and

      (ii)   what material information has become available since the most recent previous bail decision was made;

(d)   propose the terms of any suggested condition of bail; and

(e)   if the applicant wants an earlier hearing than paragraph (6) requires, ask for that, and explain why it is needed.

(4)   A prosecutor who applies under this rule must serve on the defendant, with the application, notice that the court has power to withdraw bail and, if the defendant is absent when the court makes its decision, order the defendant's arrest.

(5)   A party who opposes an application must—

(a)   so notify the court officer and the applicant at once; and

(b)   serve on each notice of the reasons for opposition.

(6)   Unless the court otherwise directs, the court officer must arrange for the court to hear the application as soon as practicable and in any event—

(a)   if it is an application to grant or withdraw bail, no later than the second business day after it was served;

(b)   if it is an application to impose or vary a condition, no later than the fifth business day after it was served.

(7)   The court may—

(a)   vary or waive a time limit under this rule;

(b)   allow an application to be in a different form to one set out in the Practice Direction, or to be made orally;

(c)   if rule 14.2 allows, determine without a hearing an application to vary a condition.

[*Note. The Practice Direction sets out a form of application for use in connection with this rule, and forms of application, draft order and certificate for use where an applicant wants the court to exercise the powers to which rule 14.16 applies (Bail condition to be enforced in another European Union member State).*

In addition to the court's general powers in relation to bail—

(a)   *under section 3(8) of the Bail Act 1976, on application by either party the court may impose a bail condition or vary a condition it has imposed. Until the Crown Court makes its first bail decision in the case, a magistrates' court may vary a condition which it imposed on committing or sending a defendant for Crown Court trial.*

(b)   *under section 5B of the Bail Act 1976, where the defendant is on bail and the offence is one which can be tried in the Crown Court, or in an extradition case, on application by the prosecutor a magistrates' court may withdraw bail, impose conditions of bail or vary the conditions of bail.*

(c)   *under sections 88 and 89 of the Criminal Justice Act 2003, the Crown Court may remand in custody, or grant bail to, a defendant pending an application to the Court of Appeal for an order for retrial under section 77 of that Act.*

Under Part IIA of Schedule 1 to the Bail Act 1976, if the court withholds bail then at the first hearing after that the defendant may support an application for bail with any argument as to fact or law, whether or not that argument has been advanced before. At subsequent hearings, the court need not hear arguments which it has heard previously.]

14.8.   Defendant's application or appeal to the Crown Court after magistrates' court bail decision

   (1)   This rule applies where a defendant wants to—

(a)   apply to the Crown Court for bail after a magistrates' court has withheld bail; or

(b)   appeal to the Crown Court after a magistrates' court has refused to vary a bail condition as the defendant wants.

(2)   The defendant must—

(a)   apply to the Crown Court in writing as soon as practicable after the magistrates' court's decision; and

(b)   serve the application on—

      (i)   the Crown Court officer,

      (ii)   the magistrates' court officer,

      (iii)   the prosecutor, and

      (iv)   any surety affected or proposed.

(3)   The application must—

(a)   specify—

      (i)   the decision that the applicant wants the Crown Court to make, and

      (ii)   each offence charged;

(b)   explain—

      (i)   as appropriate, why the Crown Court should not withhold bail, or why it should vary the condition under appeal, and

      (ii)   what further information or legal argument, if any, has become available since the magistrates' court's decision;

(c)   propose the terms of any suggested condition of bail;

(d)   if the applicant wants an earlier hearing than paragraph (6) requires, ask for that, and explain why it is needed; and

(e)   on an application for bail, attach a copy of the certificate of full argument served on the defendant under rule 14.4(4).

(4)   The magistrates' court officer must as soon as practicable serve on the Crown Court officer—

(a)   a copy of the note or record made under rule 14.4(1) in connection with the magistrates' court's decision; and

(b)   the date of the next hearing, if any, in the magistrates' court.

(5)   A prosecutor who opposes the application must—

(a)   so notify the Crown Court officer and the defendant at once; and

(b)   serve on each notice of the reasons for opposition.

(6)   Unless the Crown Court otherwise directs, the court officer must arrange for the court to hear the application or appeal as soon as practicable and in any event no later than the business day after it was served.

(7)   The Crown Court may vary a time limit under this rule.

[Note. The Practice Direction sets out a form of application for use in connection with this rule.
Under section 81 of the Senior Courts Act 1981, the Crown Court may grant bail in a magistrates'
court case in which the magistrates' court has withheld bail.
Under section 16 of the Criminal Justice Act 2003, a defendant may appeal to the Crown Court
against a bail condition imposed by a magistrates' court only where—

(a)   *the condition is one that the defendant must—*

        (i)   *live and sleep at a specified place, or away from a specified place,*

        (ii)   *give a surety or a security,*

        (iii)   *stay indoors between specified hours,*

        (iv)   *comply with electronic monitoring requirements, or*

        (v)   *make no contact with a specified person; and*

(b)   *the magistrates' court has determined an application by either party to vary that condition.*

In an extradition case, where a magistrates' court withholds bail or imposes bail conditions, on application by the defendant the High Court may grant bail, or vary the conditions, under section 22 of the Criminal Justice Act 1967. For the procedure in the High Court, see Schedule 1 to the Civil Procedure Rules 1998 (RSC Order 79).]

14.9. Prosecutor's appeal against grant of bail (1)   This rule applies where a prosecutor wants to appeal—

(a)   to the Crown Court against a grant of bail by a magistrates' court, in a case in which the defendant has been charged with, or convicted of, an offence punishable with imprisonment; or

(b)   to the High Court against a grant of bail—

        (i)   by a magistrates' court, in an extradition case, or

        (ii)   by the Crown Court, in a case in which the defendant has been charged with, or convicted of, an offence punishable with imprisonment (but not in a case in which the Crown Court granted bail on an appeal to which paragraph (1)(a) applies).

(2)   The prosecutor must tell the court which has granted bail of the decision to appeal—

(a)   at the end of the hearing during which the court granted bail; and

(b)   before the defendant is released on bail.

(3)   The court which has granted bail must exercise its power to remand the defendant in custody pending determination of the appeal.

(4)   The prosecutor must serve an appeal notice—

(a)   on the court officer for the court which has granted bail and on the defendant;

(b)   not more than 2 hours after telling that court of the decision to appeal.

(5)   The appeal notice must specify—

(a)   each offence with which the defendant is charged;

(b)   the decision under appeal;

(c)   the reasons given for the grant of bail; and

(d)   the grounds of appeal.

(6)   On an appeal to the Crown Court, the magistrates' court officer must, as soon as practicable, serve on the Crown Court officer—

(a)   the appeal notice;

(b)   a copy of the note or record made under rule 14.4(1) (record of bail decision); and

(c)   notice of the date of the next hearing in the court which has granted bail.

(7)   If the Crown Court so directs, the Crown Court officer must arrange for the defendant to be assisted by the Official Solicitor in a case in which the defendant—

(a)   has no legal representative; and

(b)   asks for such assistance.

(8)   On an appeal to the Crown Court, the Crown Court officer must arrange for the court to hear the appeal as soon as practicable and in any event no later than the second business day after the appeal notice was served.

(9)   The prosecutor—

(a)   may abandon an appeal to the Crown Court without the court's permission, by serving a notice of abandonment, signed by or on behalf of the prosecutor, on—

        (i)   the defendant,

      (ii)   the Crown Court officer, and

      (iii)   the magistrates' court officer

before the hearing of the appeal begins; but

(b)   after the hearing of the appeal begins, may only abandon the appeal with the Crown Court's permission.

(10)   The court officer for the court which has granted bail must instruct^{Ed} the defendant's custodian to release the defendant on the bail granted by that court, subject to any condition or conditions of bail imposed, if—

(a)   the prosecutor fails to serve an appeal notice within the time to which paragraph (4) refers; or

(b)   the prosecutor serves a notice of abandonment under paragraph (9).

[Note. See section 1 of the Bail (Amendment) Act 1993. The time limit for serving an appeal notice is prescribed by section 1(5) of the Act. It may be neither extended nor shortened.

For the procedure in the High Court, see Schedule 1 to the Civil Procedure Rules 1998 (RSC Order 79, rule 9) and the Practice Direction which supplements that Order. Under those provisions, the prosecutor must file in the High Court, among other things—

(a)   *a copy of the appeal notice served by the prosecutor under rule 14.9(4);*

(b)   *notice of the Crown Court decision to grant bail served on the prosecutor under rule 14.4(2); and*

(c)   *notice of the date of the next hearing in the Crown Court.]*

---

   ^{Ed} This does not imply a duty on the magistrates' court to ensure that service of the appeal notice by the prosecutor has taken place. The obligation is to effect the defendant's release when it becomes clear that those obligations have not been met. If there is a dispute about that which could not be resolved prior to the matter coming before the Crown Court, then, once the Crown Court has ruled it has jurisdiction to hear the appeal and decides the defendant should remain in custody, r 14.9(1)) has no relevance: *R (on the Application of Cardin) v Birmingham Crown Court and another* [2017] EWHC 2101 (Admin), (2017) 181 JP 421, [2018] 1 Cr App R 3, [2017] Crim L R 969.

14.10. Consideration of bail in a murder case (1) This rule applies in a case in which—

(a)   the defendant is charged with murder; and

(b)   the Crown Court has not yet considered bail.

(2)   The magistrates' court officer must arrange with the Crown Court officer for the Crown Court to consider bail as soon as practicable and in any event no later than the second business day after—

(a)   a magistrates' court sends the defendant to the Crown Court for trial; or

(b)   the first hearing in the magistrates' court, if the defendant is not at once sent for trial.

[Note. See section 115 of the Coroners and Justice Act 2009.]

14.11. Condition of residence (1) The defendant must notify the prosecutor of the address at which the defendant will live and sleep if released on bail with a condition of residence—

(a)   as soon as practicable after the institution of proceedings, unless already done; and

(b)   as soon as practicable after any change of that address.

(2)   The prosecutor must help the court to assess the suitability of an address proposed as a condition of residence.

14.12. Electronic monitoring requirements (1) This rule applies where the court imposes electronic monitoring requirements, where available, as a condition of bail.

(2)   The court officer must—

(a)   inform the person responsible for the monitoring ('the monitor') of—

      (i)   the defendant's name, and telephone number if available,

      (ii)   each offence with which the defendant is charged,

      (iii)   details of the place at which the defendant's presence must be monitored,

      (iv)   the period or periods during which the defendant's presence at that place must be monitored, and

      (v)   if fixed, the date on which the defendant must surrender to custody;

(b)   inform the defendant and, where the defendant is under 16, an appropriate adult, of the monitor's identity and the means by which the monitor may be contacted; and

(c)   notify the monitor of any subsequent—

      (i)   variation or termination of the electronic monitoring requirements, or

      (ii)   fixing or variation of the date on which the defendant must surrender to custody.

[Note. Under section 3(6ZAA) of the Bail Act 1976, the conditions of bail that the court may impose include requirements for the electronic monitoring of a defendant's compliance with other bail conditions, for example a curfew. Sections 3AA and 3AB of the 1976 Act set out conditions for imposing such requirements.

Under section 3AC of the 1976 Act, where the court imposes electronic monitoring requirements they must provide for the appointment of a monitor.]

14.13. Accommodation or support requirements (1) This rule applies where the court imposes as a condition of bail a requirement, where available, that the defendant must—

(a)   reside in accommodation provided for that purpose by, or on behalf of, a public authority;

(b)   receive bail support provided by, or on behalf of, a public authority.

(2)   The court officer must—

(a)   inform the person responsible for the provision of any such accommodation or support ('the service provider') of—

      (i)   the defendant's name, and telephone number if available,

   (ii) each offence with which the defendant is charged,

   (iii) details of the requirement,

   (iv) any other bail condition, and

   (v) if fixed, the date on which the defendant must surrender to custody;

(b) inform the defendant and, where the defendant is under 16, an appropriate adult, of—

   (i) the service provider's identity and the means by which the service provider may be contacted, and

   (ii) the address of any accommodation in which the defendant must live and sleep; and

(c) notify the service provider of any subsequent—

   (i) variation or termination of the requirement,

   (ii) variation or termination of any other bail condition, and

   (iii) fixing or variation of the date on which the defendant must surrender to custody.

14.14. Requirement for a surety or payment, etc (1) This rule applies where the court imposes as a condition of bail a requirement for—

(a) a surety;

(b) a payment;

(c) the surrender of a document or thing.

(2) The court may direct how such a condition must be met.

(3) Unless the court otherwise directs, if any such condition or direction requires a surety to enter into a recognizance—

(a) the recognizance must specify—

   (i) the amount that the surety will be required to pay if the purpose for which the recognizance is entered is not fulfilled, and

   (ii) the date, or the event, upon which the recognizance will expire;

(b) the surety must enter into the recognizance in the presence of—

   (i) the court officer,

   (ii) the defendant's custodian, where the defendant is in custody, or

   (iii) someone acting with the authority of either; and

(c) the person before whom the surety enters into the recognizance must at once serve a copy on—

   (i) the surety, and

   (ii) as appropriate, the court officer and the defendant's custodian.

(4) Unless the court otherwise directs, if any such condition or direction requires someone to make a payment, or surrender a document or thing—

(a) that payment, document or thing must be made or surrendered to—

   (i) the court officer,

   (ii) the defendant's custodian, where the defendant is in custody, or

   (iii) someone acting with the authority of either; and

(b) the court officer or the custodian, as appropriate, must serve immediately on the other a statement that the payment, document or thing has been made or surrendered.

(5) The custodian must release the defendant when each requirement ordered by the court has been met.

[Note. See also section 119 of the Magistrates' Courts Act 1980.]

14.15. Forfeiture of a recognizance given by a surety (1) This rule applies where the court imposes as a condition of bail a requirement that a surety enter into a recognizance and, after the defendant is released on bail,—

(a) the defendant fails to surrender to custody as required, or

(b) it appears to the court that the surety has failed to comply with a condition or direction.

(2) The court officer must serve notice on—

(a) the surety; and

(b) each party to the decision to grant bail,

of the hearing at which the court will consider the forfeiture of the recognizance.

(3) The court must not forfeit the recognizance less than 5 business days after service of notice under paragraph (2).

[Note. If the purpose for which a recognizance is entered is not fulfilled, that recognizance may be forfeited by the court. If the court forfeits a surety's recognizance, the sum promised by that person is then payable to the Crown. See also section 120 of the Magistrates' Courts Act 1980.]

14.16. Bail condition to be enforced in another European Union member State (1) This rule applies where the court can impose as a condition of bail pending trial a requirement—

(a) with which the defendant must comply while in another European Union member State; and

(b) which that other member State can monitor and enforce.

(2) The court—

(a) must not exercise its power to impose such a requirement until the court has decided what, if any, condition or conditions of bail to impose while the defendant is in England and Wales;

(b) subject to that, may exercise its power to make a request for the other member State to monitor and enforce that requirement.

(3) Where the court makes such a request, the court officer must—

(a)   issue a certificate requesting the monitoring and enforcement of the defendant's compliance with that requirement, in the form required by EU Council Framework Decision 2009/829/JHA;

(b)   serve on the relevant authority of the other member State—

     (i)   the court's decision or a certified copy of that decision,

     (ii)   the certificate, and

     (iii)   a copy of the certificate translated into an official language of the other member State, unless English is such a language or the other member State has declared that it will accept a certificate in English; and

(c)   report to the court—

     (i)   any request for further information returned by the competent authority in the other member State, and

     (ii)   that authority's decision.

(4)   Where the competent authority in the other member State agrees to monitor and enforce the requirement—

(a)   the court—

     (i)   may exercise its power to withdraw the request (where it can), but

     (ii)   whether or not it does so, must continue to exercise the powers to which this Part applies in accordance with the rules in this Part;

(b)   the court officer must immediately serve notice on that authority if—

     (i)   legal proceedings are brought in relation to the requirement being monitored and enforced, or

     (ii)   the court decides to vary or revoke that requirement, or to issue a warrant for the defendant's arrest; and

(c)   the court officer must promptly report to the court any information and any request received from that authority.

(5)   A party who wants the court to exercise the power to which this rule applies must serve with an application under rule 14.7 (Notice of application to consider bail)—

(a)   a draft order; and

(b)   a draft certificate in the form required by EU Council Framework Decision 2009/829/JHA.

[*Note. The Practice Direction sets out a form of application under rule 14.7 and forms of draft order and certificate for use in connection with this rule.*

See regulations 77 to 84 of the Criminal Justice and Data Protection (Protocol No 36) Regulations 2014.

Where a defendant is to live or stay in another European Union member State pending trial in England and Wales, the court may grant bail subject to a requirement to be monitored and enforced by the competent authority in that other state. The types of requirement that can be monitored and enforced are set out in Article 8 of EU Council Framework Decision 2009/829/JHA. A list of those requirements is at the end of this Part.

Under regulation 80 of the 2014 Regulations, where the conditions listed in that regulation are met the court may withdraw a request for the competent authority in another member State to monitor and enforce the defendant's compliance with a requirement.]

14.17. *Enforcement of measure imposed in another European Union member State* (1) This rule applies where the Lord Chancellor serves on the court officer a certificate requesting the monitoring and enforcement of a defendant's compliance with a supervision measure imposed by an authority in another European Union member State.

(2)   The court officer must arrange for the court to consider the request—

(a)   as a general rule—

     (i)   within 20 business days of the date on which the Lord Chancellor received it from the requesting authority, or

     (ii)   within 40 business days of that date, if legal proceedings in relation to the supervision measure are brought within the first 20 business days;

(b)   exceptionally, later than that, but in such a case the court officer must immediately serve on the requesting authority—

     (i)   an explanation for the delay, and

     (ii)   an indication of when the court's decision is expected.

(3)   On consideration of the request by the court, the court officer must—

(a)   without delay serve on the requesting authority—

     (i)   notice of any further information required by the court, and

     (ii)   subject to any such requirement and any response, notice of the court's decision; and

(b)   where the court agrees to monitor the supervision measure, serve notice of the court's decision on any supervisor specified by the court.

(4)   Where the court agrees to monitor the supervision measure—

(a)   the court officer must immediately serve notice on the requesting authority if there is reported to the court—

     (i)   a breach of the measure, or

     (ii)   any other event that might cause the requesting authority to review its decision;

(b)   the court officer must without delay serve notice on the requesting authority if—

     (i)   legal proceedings are brought in relation to the decision to monitor compliance with the bail condition,

    (ii)   there is reported to the court a change of the defendant's residence, or
    (iii)   the court decides (where it can) to stop monitoring the defendant's compliance with the measure.

[Note. See regulations 85 to 94 of the Criminal Justice and Data Protection (Protocol No 36) Regulations 2014.

Where the Lord Chancellor receives a request for the monitoring and enforcement in England and Wales of a supervision measure ordered in another European Union member State, a magistrates' court to which the request is given must monitor and enforce that measure unless one of the specified grounds for refusal applies. The grounds for refusal are listed at the end of this Part.

Under regulation 91 of the 2014 Regulations, the defendant may be arrested for breach of the measure and subsequently detained by the court for up to 28 days (or 21 days, in the case of a defendant who is under 18).

Under regulation 90 of the 2014 Regulations, the magistrates' court may cease the monitoring and enforcement where the requesting authority takes no further decision in response to notice of a breach of the measure. Under regulation 93, the court ceases to be responsible for the monitoring and enforcement of the measure where regulation 90 applies and in the other cases listed in regulation 93.]

CUSTODY TIME LIMITS

14.18. *Application to extend a custody time limit*   (1) This rule applies where the prosecutor gives notice of application to extend a custody time limit.

(2)   The court officer must arrange for the court to hear that application as soon as practicable after the expiry of—

(a)   5 days from the giving of notice, in the Crown Court; or

(b)   2 days from the giving of notice, in a magistrates' court.

(3)   The court may shorten a time limit under this rule.

[Note. See regulation 7 of the Prosecution of Offences (Custody Time Limits) Regulations 1987.

Under regulations 4 and 5 of the 1987 Regulations, unless the court extends the time limit the maximum period during which the defendant may be in pre-trial custody is—

(a)   *in a case which can be tried only in a magistrates' court, 56 days pending the beginning of the trial;*

(b)   *in a magistrates' court, in a case which can be tried either in that court or in the Crown Court—*

    (i)   *70 days, pending the beginning of a trial in the magistrates' court, or*

    (ii)   *56 days, pending the beginning of a trial in the magistrates' court, if the court decides on such a trial during that period;*

(c)   *in the Crown Court, pending the beginning of the trial, 182 days from the sending of the defendant for trial, less any period or periods during which the defendant was in custody in the magistrates' court.*

Under section 22(3) of the Prosecution of Offences Act 1985, the court cannot extend a custody time limit which has expired, and must not extend such a time limit unless satisfied—

(a)   *that the need for the extension is due to—*

    (i)   *the illness or absence of the accused, a necessary witness, a judge or a magistrate,*

    (ii)   *a postponement which is occasioned by the ordering by the court of separate trials in the case of two or more defendants or two or more offences, or*

    (iii)   *some other good and sufficient cause; and*

(b)   *that the prosecution has acted with all due diligence and expedition.]*

14.19. *Appeal against custody time limit decision*   (1) This rule applies where—

(a)   a defendant wants to appeal to the Crown Court against a decision by a magistrates' court to extend a custody time limit;

(b)   a prosecutor wants to appeal to the Crown Court against a decision by a magistrates' court to refuse to extend a custody time limit.

(2)   The appellant must serve an appeal notice—

(a)   on—

    (i)   the other party to the decision,

    (ii)   the Crown Court officer, and

    (iii)   the magistrates' court officer;

(b)   in a defendant's appeal, as soon as practicable after the decision under appeal;

(c)   in a prosecutor's appeal—

    (i)   as soon as practicable after the decision under appeal, and

    (ii)   before the relevant custody time limit expires.

(3)   The appeal notice must specify—

(a)   each offence with which the defendant is charged;

(b)   the decision under appeal;

(c)   the date on which the relevant custody time limit will expire;

(d)   on a defendant's appeal, the date on which the relevant custody time limit would have expired but for the decision under appeal; and

(e)   the grounds of appeal.

(4)   The Crown Court officer must arrange for the Crown Court to hear the appeal as soon as practicable and in any event no later than the second business day after the appeal notice was

served.

(5)   The appellant—

(a)   may abandon an appeal without the Crown Court's permission, by serving a notice of abandonment, signed by or on behalf of the appellant, on—

(i)   the other party,

(ii)   the Crown Court officer, and

(iii)   the magistrates' court officer

before the hearing of the appeal begins; but

(b)   after the hearing of the appeal begins, may only abandon the appeal with the Crown Court's permission.

[Note. See section 22(7), (8), (9) of the Prosecution of Offences Act 1985.]

Summary of the general entitlement to bail and of the exceptions

The court must consider bail whenever it can order the defendant's detention pending trial or sentencing, or in an extradition case, and whether an application is made or not. Under section 4 of the Bail Act 1976, the general rule, subject to exceptions, is that a defendant must be granted bail. Under Part IIA of Schedule 1 to the Act, if the court decides not to grant the defendant bail then at each subsequent hearing the court must consider whether to grant bail.

Section 3 of the Bail Act 1976 allows the court, before granting bail, to require a surety or security to secure the defendant's surrender to custody; and allows the court, on granting bail, to impose such requirements as appear to the court to be necessary—

(a)   to secure that the defendant surrenders to custody;

(b)   to secure that the defendant does not commit an offence while on bail;

(c)   to secure that the defendant does not interfere with witnesses or otherwise obstruct the course of justice whether in relation to the defendant or any other person;

(d)   for the defendant's own protection or, if a child or young person, for the defendant's welfare or in the defendant's own interests;

(e)   to secure the defendant's availability for the purpose of enabling enquiries or a report to be made to assist the court in dealing with the defendant for the offence;

(f)   to secure that before the time appointed for surrender to custody the defendant attends an interview with a legal representative.

Under section 3 of the Bail Act 1976, a person granted bail in criminal proceedings is under a duty to surrender to custody as required by that bail. Under section 6 of the Act, such a person who fails without reasonable cause so to surrender commits an offence and, under section 7, may be arrested.

Exceptions to the general right to bail are listed in Schedule 1 to the Bail Act 1976. They differ according to the category of offence concerned. Under section 4(2B) of the 1976 Act, in an extradition case there is no general right to bail where the defendant is alleged to have been convicted in the territory requesting extradition.

Under Part I of Schedule 1 to the 1976 Act, where the offence is punishable with imprisonment, and is not one that can be tried only in a magistrates' court, or in an extradition case—

(a)   the defendant need not be granted bail if the court is satisfied that—

(i)   there are substantial grounds for believing that, if released on bail (with or without conditions), the defendant would fail to surrender to custody, would commit an offence, or would interfere with witnesses or otherwise obstruct the course of justice,

(ii)   there are substantial grounds for believing that, if released on bail (with or without conditions), the defendant would commit an offence by engaging in conduct that would, or would be likely to, cause physical or mental injury to an associated person (within the meaning of section 33 of the Family Law Act 1996), or cause that person to fear injury,

(iii)   the defendant should be kept in custody for his or her own protection or welfare, or

(iv)   it has not been practicable, for want of time since the institution of the proceedings, to obtain sufficient information for the court to take the decisions required;

(b)   the defendant need not be granted bail if it appears to the court that the defendant was on bail at the time of the offence (this exception does not apply in an extradition case);

(c)   the defendant need not be granted bail if, having been released on bail in the case on a previous occasion, the defendant since has been arrested for breach of bail;

(d)   the defendant need not be granted bail if in custody pursuant to a sentence;

(e)   the defendant need not be granted bail if it appears to the court that it would be impracticable to complete enquiries or a report for which the case is to be adjourned without keeping the defendant in custody;

(f)   the defendant may not be granted bail if charged with murder, unless the court is of the opinion that there is no significant risk of the defendant committing an offence while on bail that would, or would be likely to, cause physical or mental injury to some other person;

(g)   the defendant in an extradition case need not be granted bail if he or she was on bail on the date of the alleged offence and that offence is not one that could be tried only in a magistrates' court if it were committed in England or Wales.

Exceptions (a)(i), (b) and (c) do not apply where—

(a)   the defendant is 18 or over;

(b)   the defendant has not been convicted of an offence in those proceedings; and

(c)   it appears to the court that there is no real prospect that the defendant will be sentenced *to a custodial sentence in those proceedings.*

In deciding whether an exception to the right to bail applies the court must have regard to any relevant consideration, including—

(a) *the nature and seriousness of the offence, and the probable method of dealing with the defendant for it;*

(b) *the character, antecedents, associations and community ties of the defendant;*

(c) *the defendant's record of fulfilling obligations imposed under previous grants of bail; and*

(d) *except where the case is adjourned for enquires or a report, the strength of the evidence of the defendant having committed the offence.*

Under Part IA of Schedule 1 to the 1976 Act, where the offence is punishable with imprisonment, and is one that can be tried only in a magistrates' court—

(a) *the defendant need not be granted bail if it appears to the court that—*

    (i) *having previously been granted bail in criminal proceedings, the defendant has failed to surrender as required and, in view of that failure, the court believes that, if released on bail (with or without conditions), the defendant would fail to surrender to custody, or*

    (ii) *the defendant was on bail on the date of the offence and the court is satisfied that there are substantial grounds for believing that, if released on bail (with or without conditions), the defendant would commit an offence while on bail;*

(b) *the defendant need not be granted bail if the court is satisfied that—*

    (i) *there are substantial grounds for believing that, if released on bail (with or without conditions), the defendant would commit an offence while on bail by engaging in conduct that would, or would be likely to, cause physical or mental injury to some other person, or cause some other person to fear such injury,*

    (ii) *the defendant should be kept in custody for his or her own protection or welfare, or*

    (iii) *it has not been practicable, for want of time since the institution of the proceedings, to obtain sufficient information for the court to take the decisions required;*

(c) *the defendant need not be granted bail if in custody pursuant to a sentence;*

(d) *the defendant need not be granted bail if, having been released on bail in the case on a previous occasion, the defendant since has been arrested for breach of bail, and the court is satisfied that there are substantial grounds for believing that, if released on bail (with or without conditions), the defendant would fail to surrender to custody, would commit an offence, or would interfere with witnesses or otherwise obstruct the course of justice.*

Exceptions (a) and (d) do not apply where—

(a) *the defendant is 18 or over;*

(b) *the defendant has not been convicted of an offence in those proceedings; and*

(c) *it appears to the court that there is no real prospect that the defendant will be sentenced to a custodial sentence in those proceedings.*

Under Part II of Schedule 1 to the 1976 Act, where the offence is not punishable with imprisonment—

(a) *the defendant need not be granted bail if it appears to the court that having previously been granted bail in criminal proceedings, the defendant has failed to surrender as required and, in view of that failure, the court believes that, if released on bail (with or without conditions), the defendant would fail to surrender to custody;*

(b) *the defendant need not be granted bail if the court is satisfied that the defendant should be kept in custody for his or her own protection or welfare;*

(c) *the defendant need not be granted bail if in custody pursuant to a sentence;*

(d) *the defendant need not be granted bail if, having been released on bail in the case on a previous occasion, the defendant since has been arrested for breach of bail, and the court is satisfied that there are substantial grounds for believing that, if released on bail (with or without conditions), the defendant would fail to surrender to custody, would commit an offence, or would interfere with witnesses or otherwise obstruct the course of justice;*

(e) *the defendant need not be granted bail if, having been released on bail in the case on a previous occasion, the defendant since has been arrested for breach of bail, and the court is satisfied that there are substantial grounds for believing that, if released on bail (with or without conditions), the defendant would commit an offence while on bail by engaging in conduct that would, or would be likely to, cause physical or mental injury to an associated person (within the meaning of section 33 of the Family Law Act 1996), or to cause that person to fear such injury.*

Exceptions (a) and (d) apply only where—

(a) *the defendant is under 18; and*

(b) *the defendant has been convicted in those proceedings.*

Further exceptions to the general right to bail are set out in section 25 of the Criminal Justice and Public Order Act 1994, under which a defendant charged with murder, attempted murder, manslaughter, rape or another sexual offence specified in that section, and who has been previously convicted of such an offence, may be granted bail only if there are exceptional circumstances which justify it.

Requirements that may be monitored and enforced in another European Union member State

Under Article 8(1) of EU Council Framework Decision 2009/829/JHA of 23rd October, 2009, on the application of the principle of mutual recognition to decisions on supervision measures as an alternative to provisional detention, the following are the requirements that may be monitored and enforced in a European Union member State ('the monitoring State') other than the state in which they were imposed as a condition of bail—

(a)   an obligation for the person to inform the competent authority in the monitoring State of any change of residence, in particular for the purpose of receiving a summons to attend a hearing or a trial in the course of criminal proceedings;

(b)   an obligation not to enter certain localities, places or defined areas in the issuing or monitoring State;

(c)   an obligation to remain at a specified place, where applicable during specified times;

(d)   an obligation containing limitations on leaving the territory of the monitoring State;

(e)   an obligation to report at specified times to a specific authority;

(f)   an obligation to avoid contact with specific persons in relation to the offence or offences allegedly committed.

Under Article 8(2) of the Framework Decision, other measures that a monitoring State may be prepared to monitor may include—

(a)   an obligation not to engage in specified activities in relation to the offence or offences allegedly committed, which may include involvement in a specified profession or field of employment;

(b)   an obligation not to drive a vehicle;

(c)   an obligation to deposit a certain sum of money or to give another type of guarantee, which may either be provided through a specified number of instalments or entirely at once;

(d)   an obligation to undergo therapeutic treatment or treatment for addiction; or

(e)   an obligation to avoid contact with specific objects in relation to the offence or offences allegedly committed.

Grounds for refusing to monitor and enforce a supervision measure imposed in another European Union member State

Under Schedule 6 to the Criminal Justice and Data Protection (Protocol No 36) Regulations 2014, the grounds for refusal are—

(a)   the certificate requesting monitoring under the Framework Decision—

(i)   is incomplete or obviously does not correspond to the decision on supervision measures, and

(ii)   is not completed or corrected within a period specified by the court;

(b)   where the defendant subject to the decision on supervision measures is lawfully and ordinarily resident in England and Wales, the defendant has not consented to return there with a view to the supervision measures being monitored there under the Framework Decision;

(c)   where the defendant subject to the decision on supervision measures is not lawfully and ordinarily resident in England and Wales, the defendant—

(i)   has not asked for a request to be made for monitoring of the supervision measures under the Framework Decision by a competent authority in in England and Wales, or

(ii)   has asked for such a request to be made but has not given adequate reasons as to why it should be made;

(d)   the certificate includes measures other than those referred to in Article 8 of the Framework Decision (see the list above);

(e)   recognition of the decision on supervision measures would contravene the principle of ne bis in idem;

(f)   the decision on supervision measures was based on conduct that would not constitute an offence under the law of England and Wales if it occurred there (with the exception of some specified categories of offence);

(g)   the decision was based on conduct where, under the law of England and Wales—

(i)   the criminal prosecution of the conduct would be statute-barred, and

(ii)   the conduct falls within the jurisdiction of England and Wales;

(h)   the decision on supervision measures was based on conduct by a defendant who was under the age of 10 when the conduct took place;

(i)   the conduct on which the decision on supervision measures was based is such that—

(i)   if there was a breach of the supervision measures, and

(ii)   a warrant was issued by the issuing State for the arrest of the defendant subject to the decision

the defendant would have to be discharged at an extradition hearing under the Extradition Act 2003;

(j)   it appears that the decision on supervision measures was in fact made for the purpose of punishing the defendant on account of the defendant's race, ethnic origin, religion, nationality, language, gender, sexual orientation or political opinions.

EXTENSION OF BAIL BEFORE CHARGE

14.20.   Exercise of court's powers: extension of pre-charge bail   (1)   The court must determine an application to which rule 14.21 (Application to authorise extension of pre-charge bail) applies—

(a)   without a hearing, subject to paragraph (2); and

(b)   as soon as practicable, but as a general rule no sooner than the fifth business day after the application was served.

(2)   The court must determine an application at a hearing where—

(a)   if the application succeeds, its effect will be to extend the period for which the defendant is on bail to less than 12 months from the day after the defendant's arrest for the offence and the court considers that the interests of justice require a hearing;

(b)   if the application succeeds, its effect will be to extend that period to more than 12 months from that day and the applicant or the defendant asks for a hearing;

(c)   it is an application to withhold information from the defendant and the court considers that the interests of justice require a hearing.

(3)   Any hearing must be in private.

(4)   Subject to rule 14.22 (Application to withhold information from the defendant), at a hearing the court may determine an application in the absence of—

(a)   the applicant;

(b)   the defendant, if the defendant has had at least 5 business days in which to make representations.

(5)   If the court so directs, a party to an application may attend a hearing by live link or telephone.

(6)   The court must not authorise an extension of the period for which a defendant is on bail before being charged unless—

(a)   the applicant states, in writing or orally, that to the best of the applicant's knowledge and belief—

(i)   the application discloses all the information that is material to what the court must decide, and

(ii)   the content of the application is true; or

(b)   the application includes a statement by an investigator of the suspected offence that to the best of that investigator's knowledge and belief those requirements are met.

(7)   Where the statement required by paragraph (6) is made orally—

(a)   the statement must be on oath or affirmation, unless the court otherwise directs; and

(b)   the court must arrange for a record of the making of the statement.

(8)   The court may shorten or extend (even after it has expired) a time limit imposed by this rule or by rule 14.21 (Application to authorise extension of pre-charge bail).

[Note. For the definition of 'defendant' for the purposes of this rule and rules 14.21 and 14.22, see rule 14.1(3).

Sections 47ZA and 47ZB of the Police and Criminal Evidence Act 1984 limit the period during which a defendant who has been arrested for an offence may be on bail after being released without being charged. That period ('the applicable bail period') is—

(a)   3 months from the day after the day on which the defendant was arrested (the defendant's 'bail start date') in 'an SFO case' (that is, a case investigated by the Serious Fraud Office);

(b)   28 days from the defendant's bail start date in 'a standard case' (that is, 'an FCA case', meaning a case investigated by the Financial Conduct Authority, or any other non-SFO case).

Under sections 47ZC and 47ZD of the 1984 Act, in a standard case the applicable bail period may be extended on the authority of a police officer of the rank of superintendent or above until the end of 3 months from the bail start date.

Under sections 47ZC and 47ZE of the Act, if the case is designated by a qualifying prosecutor as exceptionally complex (a 'designated case') the applicable bail period may be extended, in an SFO case, or further extended, in a standard case, on the authority of one of the senior officers listed in section 47ZE, until the end of 6 months from the bail start date.

Under section 47ZF of the Act, on an application made before the date on which the applicable bail period ends by a member of the Serious Fraud Office, a member of staff of the Financial Conduct Authority, a constable or a Crown Prosecutor, a magistrates' court may authorise an extension of that period—

(a)   from a previous total of 3 months to a new total of 6 months or, if the investigation is unlikely to be completed or a police charging decision made within a lesser period, a new total of 9 months;

(b)   from a previous total of 6 months to a new total of 9 months or, if the investigation is unlikely to be completed or a police charging decision made within a lesser period, a new total of 12 months,

where the conditions listed in that section are met.

Under section 47ZG of the Act, on a further such application (of which there may be more than one) a magistrates' court may authorise a further extension of the applicable bail period, on each occasion by a further 3 months or, if the investigation is unlikely to be completed or a police charging decision made within a lesser period, a further 6 months, where the conditions listed in that section are met.

Under section 47ZL of the Act, the running of the applicable bail period does not begin (in the case of a first release on bail) or is suspended (in any other case) where—

(a)   the defendant is released on bail to await a charging decision by the Director of Public Prosecutions under section 37B of the Act; or

(b)   following arrest for breach of such bail the defendant is again released on bail.

The court's authority therefore is not required for an extension of an applicable bail period the running of which is postponed or suspended pending a Director's charging decision. However—

(a)   time runs in any period during which information requested by the Director is being obtained; and

(b)   if the Director requests information less than 7 days before the applicable bail period otherwise would end then the running of that period is further suspended until the end of

7 days beginning with the day on which the Director's request is made.
See alsosection 47ZI of the Police and Criminal Evidence Act 1984(Sections 47ZF to 47ZH: proceedings in magistrates' courts). The requirement for the court except in specified circumstances to determine an application without a hearing is prescribed by that section. Under that section the court must comprise a single justice of the peace unless a hearing is convened, when it must comprise two or more justices.]

14.21. Application to authorise extension of pre-charge bail (1) This rule applies where an applicant wants the court to authorise an extension of the period for which a defendant is released on bail before being charged with an offence.

(2) The applicant must—

(a) apply in writing before the date on which the defendant's pre-charge bail is due to end;

(b) demonstrate that the applicant is entitled to apply as a constable, a member of staff of the Financial Conduct Authority, a member of the Serious Fraud Office or a Crown Prosecutor;

(c) serve the application on—

(i) the court officer, and

(ii) the defendant; and

(d) serve on the defendant, with the application, a form of response notice for the defendant's use.

(3) The application must specify—

(a) the offence or offences for which the defendant was arrested;

(b) the date on which the defendant's pre-charge bail began;

(c) the date and period of any previous extension of that bail;

(d) the date on which that bail is due to end;

(e) the conditions of that bail; and

(f) if different, the bail conditions which are to be imposed if the court authorises an extension, or further extension, of the period for which the defendant is released on pre-charge bail.

(4) The application must explain—

(a) the grounds for believing that, as applicable—

(i) further investigation is needed of any matter in connection with the offence or offences for which the defendant was released on bail, or

(ii) further time is needed for making a decision as to whether to charge the defendant with that offence or those offences;

(b) the grounds for believing that, as applicable—

(i) the investigation into the offence or offences for which the defendant was released on bail is being conducted diligently and expeditiously, or

(ii) the decision as to whether to charge the defendant with that offence or those offences is being made diligently and expeditiously; and

(c) the grounds for believing that the defendant's further release on bail is necessary and proportionate in all the circumstances having regard, in particular, to any conditions of bail imposed.

(5) The application must—

(a) indicate whether the applicant wants the court to authorise an extension of the defendant's bail for 3 months or for 6 months; and

(b) if for 6 months, explain why the investigation is unlikely to be completed or the charging decision made, as the case may be, within 3 months.

(6) The application must explain why it was not made earlier where—

(a) the application is made before the date on which the defendant's bail is due to end; but

(b) it is not likely to be practicable for the court to determine the application before that date.

(7) A defendant who objects to the application must—

(a) serve notice on—

(i) the court officer, and

(ii) the applicant,

not more than 5 business days after service of the application; and

(b) in the notice explain the grounds of the objection.

[Note. The Practice Direction sets out forms of application and response notice for use in connection with this rule.
See sections 47ZF (Applicable bail period: first extension of limit by the court), 47ZG (Applicable bail period: subsequent extensions of limit by the court) and 47ZJ (Sections 47ZF and 47ZG: late applications to magistrates' court) of the Police and Criminal Evidence Act 1984.
The time limit for making an application is prescribed by section 47ZF(2) and by section 47ZG(2) of the 1984 Act. It may be neither extended nor shortened. Under section 47ZJ(2) of the Act, if it is not practicable for the court to determine the application before the applicable bail period ends then the court must determine the application as soon as practicable. Under section 47ZJ(3), the applicable bail period is treated as extended until the application is determined. Under section 47ZJ(4), if it appears to the court that it would have been reasonable for the application to have been made in time for it to be determined by the court before the end of the applicable bail period then the court may refuse the application.]

14.22. Application to withhold information from the defendant (1) This rule applies where an application to authorise an extension of pre-charge bail includes an application to withhold information from the defendant.

(2)   The applicant must—

(a)   omit that information from the part of the application that is served on the defendant;

(b)   mark the other part to show that, unless the court otherwise directs, it is only for the court; and

(c)   in that other part, explain the grounds for believing that the disclosure of that information would have one or more of the following results—

(i)   evidence connected with an indictable offence would be interfered with or harmed,

(ii)   a person would be interfered with or physically injured,

(iii)   a person suspected of having committed an indictable offence but not yet arrested for the offence would be alerted, or

(iv)   the recovery of property obtained as a result of an indictable offence would be hindered.

(3)   At any hearing of an application to which this rule applies—

(a)   the court must first determine the application to withhold information, in the defendant's absence and that of any legal representative of the defendant;

(b)   if the court allows the application to withhold information, then in the following sequence—

(i)   the court must consider representations first by the applicant and then by the defendant, in the presence of both, and

(ii)   the court may consider further representations by the applicant in the defendant's absence and that of any legal representative of the defendant, if satisfied that there are reasonable grounds for believing that information withheld from the defendant would be disclosed during those further representations.

(4)   If the court refuses an application to withhold information from the defendant, the applicant may withdraw the application to authorise an extension of pre-charge bail.

[Note. See sections 47ZH and 47ZI(5), (6), (8) of the Police and Criminal Evidence Act 1984(withholding sensitive information; proceedings in magistrates' courts: determination of applications to withhold sensitive information).]

PART 15   DISCLOSURE

Contents of this Part

B.14   *15.1.   When this Part applies*   This Part applies—

(a)   in a magistrates' court and in the Crown Court;

(b)   where Parts I and II of the Criminal Procedure and Investigations Act 1996 apply.

[Note. A summary of the disclosure requirements of the Criminal Procedure and Investigations Act 1996 is at the end of this Part.]

15.2.   Prosecution disclosure   (1)   This rule applies where, under section 3 of the Criminal Procedure and Investigations Act 1996, the prosecutor—

(a)   discloses prosecution material to the defendant; or

(b)   serves on the defendant a written statement that there is no such material to disclose.

(2)   The prosecutor must at the same time so inform the court officer.

[Note. See section 3 of the Criminal Procedure and Investigations Act 1996 and paragraph 10 of the Code of Practice accompanying the Criminal Procedure and Investigations Act 1996 (Code of Practice) Order 2015.]

15.3.   Prosecutor's application for public interest ruling   (1)   This rule applies where—

(a)   without a court order, the prosecutor would have to disclose material; and

(b)   the prosecutor wants the court to decide whether it would be in the public interest to disclose it.

(2)   The prosecutor must—

(a)   apply in writing for such a decision; and

(b)   serve the application on—

(i)   the court officer,

(ii)   any person who the prosecutor thinks would be directly affected by disclosure of the material, and

(iii)   the defendant, but only to the extent that serving it on the defendant would not disclose what the prosecutor thinks ought not be disclosed.

(3)   The application must—

(a)   describe the material, and explain why the prosecutor thinks that—
    (i)   it is material that the prosecutor would have to disclose,
    (ii)   it would not be in the public interest to disclose that material, and
    (iii) no measure such as the prosecutor's admission of any fact, or disclosure by summary, extract or edited copy, adequately would protect both the public interest and the defendant's right to a fair trial;
(b)   omit from any part of the application that is served on the defendant anything that would disclose what the prosecutor thinks ought not be disclosed (in which case, paragraph (4) of this rule applies); and
(c)   explain why, if no part of the application is served on the defendant.
(4)   Where the prosecutor serves only part of the application on the defendant, the prosecutor must—
(a)   mark the other part, to show that it is only for the court; and
(b)   in that other part, explain why the prosecutor has withheld it from the defendant.
(5)   Unless already done, the court may direct the prosecutor to serve an application on—
(a)   the defendant;
(b)   any other person who the court considers would be directly affected by the disclosure of the material.
(6)   The court must determine the application at a hearing which—
(a)   must be in private, unless the court otherwise directs; and
(b)   if the court so directs, may take place, wholly or in part, in the defendant's absence.
(7)   At a hearing at which the defendant is present—
(a)   the general rule is that the court must consider, in the following sequence—
    (i)   representations first by the prosecutor and any other person served with the application, and then by the defendant, in the presence of them all, and then
    (ii)   further representations by the prosecutor and any such other person in the defendant's absence; but
(b)   the court may direct other arrangements for the hearing.
(8)   The court may only determine the application if satisfied that it has been able to take adequate account of—
(a)   such rights of confidentiality as apply to the material; and
(b)   the defendant's right to a fair trial.
(9)   Unless the court otherwise directs, the court officer—
(a)   must not give notice to anyone other than the prosecutor—
    (i)   of the hearing of an application under this rule, unless the prosecutor served the application on that person, or
    (ii)   of the court's decision on the application;
(b)   may—
    (i)   keep a written application or representations, or
    (ii)   arrange for the whole or any part to be kept by some other appropriate person, subject to any conditions that the court may impose.
[Note. The court's power to order that it is not in the public interest to disclose material is provided for by sections 3(6), 7(6) (where the investigation began between 1st April, 1997 and 3rd April, 2005) and 7A(8) (where the investigation began on or after 4th April, 2005) of the Criminal Procedure and Investigations Act 1996.
See also sections 16 and 19 of the 1996 Act.]

15.4.   *Defence disclosure*   (1)   This rule applies where—
(a)   under section 5 or 6 of the Criminal Procedure and Investigations Act 1996, the defendant gives a defence statement;
(b)   under section 6C of the 1996 Act, the defendant gives a defence witness notice.
(2)   The defendant must serve such a statement or notice on—
(a)   the court officer; and
(b)   the prosecutor.
[Note. The Practice Direction sets out forms of—
(a)   defence statement; and
(b)   defence witness notice.
Under section 5 of the 1996 Act, in the Crown Court the defendant must give a defence statement. Under section 6 of the Act, in a magistrates' court the defendant may give such a statement but need not do so.
Under section 6C of the 1996 Act, in the Crown Court and in magistrates' courts the defendant must give a defence witness notice indicating whether he or she intends to call any witnesses (other than him or herself) and, if so, identifying them.]

15.5.   *Defendant's application for prosecution disclosure*   (1)   This rule applies where the defendant—
(a)   has served a defence statement given under the Criminal Procedure and Investigations Act 1996; and
(b)   wants the court to require the prosecutor to disclose material.
(2)   The defendant must serve an application on—
(a)   the court officer; and
(b)   the prosecutor.
(3)   The application must—

(a)   describe the material that the defendant wants the prosecutor to disclose;
(b)   explain why the defendant thinks there is reasonable cause to believe that—
    (i)   the prosecutor has that material, and
    (ii)   it is material that the Criminal Procedure and Investigations Act 1996 requires the prosecutor to disclose; and
(c)   ask for a hearing, if the defendant wants one, and explain why it is needed.
(4)   The court may determine an application under this rule—
(a)   at a hearing, in public or in private; or
(b)   without a hearing.
(5)   The court must not require the prosecutor to disclose material unless the prosecutor—
(a)   is present; or
(b)   has had at least 14 days in which to make representations.
[Note. The Practice Direction sets out a form of application for use in connection with this rule.
Under section 8 of the Criminal Procedure and Investigations Act 1996, a defendant may apply for prosecution disclosure only if the defendant has given a defence statement.]

15.6. *Review of public interest ruling* (1) This rule applies where the court has ordered that it is not in the public interest to disclose material that the prosecutor otherwise would have to disclose, and—
(a)   the defendant wants the court to review that decision; or
(b)   the Crown Court reviews that decision on its own initiative.
(2)   Where the defendant wants the court to review that decision, the defendant must—
(a)   serve an application on—
    (i)   the court officer, and
    (ii)   the prosecutor; and
(b)   in the application—
    (i)   describe the material that the defendant wants the prosecutor to disclose, and
    (ii)   explain why the defendant thinks it is no longer in the public interest for the prosecutor not to disclose it.
(3)   The prosecutor must serve any such application on any person who the prosecutor thinks would be directly affected if that material were disclosed.
(4)   The prosecutor, and any such person, must serve any representations on—
(a)   the court officer; and
(b)   the defendant, unless to do so would in effect reveal something that either thinks ought not be disclosed.
(5)   The court may direct—
(a)   the prosecutor to serve any such application on any person who the court considers would be directly affected if that material were disclosed;
(b)   the prosecutor and any such person to serve any representations on the defendant.
(6)   The court must review a decision to which this rule applies at a hearing which—
(a)   must be in private, unless the court otherwise directs; and
(b)   if the court so directs, may take place, wholly or in part, in the defendant's absence.
(7)   At a hearing at which the defendant is present—
(a)   the general rule is that the court must consider, in the following sequence—
    (i)   representations first by the defendant, and then by the prosecutor and any other person served with the application, in the presence of them all, and then
    (ii)   further representations by the prosecutor and any such other person in the defendant's absence; but
(b)   the court may direct other arrangements for the hearing.
(8)   The court may only conclude a review if satisfied that it has been able to take adequate account of—
(a)   such rights of confidentiality as apply to the material; and
(b)   the defendant's right to a fair trial.
[Note. The court's power to review a public interest ruling is provided for by sections 14 and 15 of the Criminal Procedure and Investigations Act 1996. Under section 14 of the Act, a magistrates' court may reconsider an order for non-disclosure only if a defendant applies. Under section 15, the Crown Court may do so on an application, or on its own initiative.
See also sections 16 and 19 of the 1996 Act.]

15.7. *Defendant's application to use disclosed material* (1) This rule applies where a defendant wants the court's permission to use disclosed prosecution material—
(a)   otherwise than in connection with the case in which it was disclosed; or
(b)   beyond the extent to which it was displayed or communicated publicly at a hearing.
(2)   The defendant must serve an application on—
(a)   the court officer; and
(b)   the prosecutor.
(3)   The application must—
(a)   specify what the defendant wants to use or disclose; and
(b)   explain why.
(4)   The court may determine an application under this rule—
(a)   at a hearing, in public or in private; or

(b)   without a hearing.

(5)   The court must not permit the use of such material unless—

(a)   the prosecutor has had at least 28 days in which to make representations; and

(b)   the court is satisfied that it has been able to take adequate account of any rights of confidentiality that may apply to the material.

[Note. The court's power to allow a defendant to use disclosed material is provided for by section 17 of the Criminal Procedure and Investigations Act 1996.
See also section 19 of the 1996 Act.]

15.8.   *Unauthorised use of disclosed material* (1)   This rule applies where a person is accused of using disclosed prosecution material in contravention of section 17 of the Criminal Procedure and Investigations Act 1996.

(2)   A party who wants the court to exercise its power to punish that person for contempt of court must comply with the rules in Part 48 (Contempt of court).

(3)   The court must not exercise its power to forfeit material used in contempt of court unless—

(a)   the prosecutor; and

(b)   any other person directly affected by the disclosure of the material,

is present, or has had at least 14 days in which to make representations.

[Note. Under section 17 of the Criminal Procedure and Investigations Act 1996, a defendant may use disclosed prosecution material—

(a)   in connection with the case in which it was disclosed, including on an appeal;

(b)   to the extent to which it was displayed or communicated publicly at a hearing in public; or

(c)   with the court's permission.

Under section 18 of the 1996 Act, the court can punish for contempt of court any other use of disclosed prosecution material. See also section 19 of the 1996 Act.]

15.9.   *Court's power to vary requirements under this Part* The court may—

(a)   shorten or extend (even after it has expired) a time limit under this Part;

(b)   allow a defence statement, or a defence witness notice, to be in a different written form to one set out in the Practice Direction, as long as it contains what the Criminal Procedure and Investigations Act 1996 requires;

(c)   allow an application under this Part to be in a different form to one set out in the Practice Direction, or to be presented orally; and

(d)   specify the period within which—

      (i)   any application under this Part must be made, or

      (ii)   any material must be disclosed, on an application to which rule 15.5 applies (Defendant's application for prosecution disclosure).

Summary of disclosure requirements of Criminal Procedure and Investigations Act 1996

The Criminal Procedure and Investigations Act 1996 came into force on 1st April, 1997. It does not apply where the investigation began before that date. With effect from 4th April, 2005, the Criminal Justice Act 2003 made changes to the 1996 Act that do not apply where the investigation began before that date.

In some circumstances, the prosecutor may be required to disclose material to which the 1996 Act does not apply: see sections 1 and 21.

Part I of the 1996 Act contains sections 1 to 21A. Part II, which contains sections 22 to 27, requires an investigator to record information relevant to an investigation that is obtained during its course. See also the Criminal Procedure and Investigations Act 1996 (Code of Practice) (No 2) Order 1997, the Criminal Procedure and Investigations Act 1996 (Code of Practice) Order 2005 and the Criminal Procedure and Investigations Act 1996 (Code of Practice) Order 2015 issued under sections 23 to 25 of the 1996 Act.

Prosecution disclosure

Where the investigation began between 1st April, 1997, and 3rd April, 2005, sections 3 and 7 of the 1996 Act require the prosecutor—

(a)   to disclose material not previously disclosed that in the prosecutor's opinion might undermine the case for the prosecution against the defendant—

      (i)   in a magistrates' court, as soon as is reasonably practicable after the defendant pleads not guilty, and

      (ii)   in the Crown Court, as soon as is reasonably practicable after the case is committed or transferred for trial, or after the evidence is served where the case is sent for trial; and

(b)   as soon as is reasonably practicable after service of the defence statement, to disclose material not previously disclosed that might be reasonably expected to assist the defendant's case as disclosed by that defence statement; or in either event

(c)   if there is no such material, then to give the defendant a written statement to that effect.

Where the investigation began on or after 4th April, 2005, sections 3 and 7A of the 1996 Act require the prosecutor—

(a)   to disclose prosecution material not previously disclosed that might reasonably be considered capable of undermining the case for the prosecution against the defendant or of assisting the case for the defendant—

      (i)   in a magistrates' court, as soon as is reasonably practicable after the defendant pleads not guilty, or

      (ii)   in the Crown Court, as soon as is reasonably practicable after the case is committed or transferred for trial, or after the evidence is served where the case is sent for trial, or after a count is added to the indictment; and in either case

(b)   if there is no such material, then to give the defendant a written statement to that effect; and after that

(c)   in either court, to disclose any such material—
   (i)   whenever there is any, until the court reaches its verdict or the prosecutor decides not to proceed with the case, and
   (ii)   in particular, after the service of the defence statement.

Sections 2 and 3 of the 1996 Act define material, and prescribe how it must be disclosed.
In some circumstances, disclosure is prohibited by section 17 of the Regulation of Investigatory Powers Act 2000.
The prosecutor must not disclose material that the court orders it would not be in the public interest to disclose: see sections 3(6), 7(6) and 7A(8) of the 1996 Act.
Sections 12 and 13 of the 1996 Act prescribe the time for prosecution disclosure. Under paragraph 10 of the Code of Practice accompanying the Criminal Procedure and Investigations Act 1996 (Code of Practice) Order 2015, in a magistrates' court the prosecutor must disclose any material due to be disclosed at the hearing where a not guilty plea is entered, or as soon as possible following a formal indication from the accused or representative that a not guilty plea will be entered at that hearing.
See also sections 1, 4 and 10 of the 1996 Act.

Defence disclosure
Under section 5 of the 1996 Act, in the Crown Court the defendant must give a defence statement.
Under section 6 of the Act, in a magistrates' court the defendant may give such a statement but need not do so.
Under section 6C of the 1996 Act, in the Crown Court and in magistrates' courts the defendant must give a defence witness notice indicating whether he or she intends to call any witnesses (other than him or herself) and, if so, identifying them.
The time for service of a defence statement is prescribed by section 12 of the 1996 Act and by the Criminal Procedure and Investigations Act 1996 (Defence Disclosure Time Limits) Regulations 2011. It is—

(a)   in a magistrates' court, not more than 14 days after the prosecutor—
   (i)   discloses material under section 3 of the 1996 Act, or
   (ii)   serves notice that there is no such material to disclose;

(b)   in the Crown Court, not more than 28 days after either of those events, if the prosecution evidence has been served on the defendant.

The requirements for the content of a defence statement are set out in—

(a)   section 5 of the 1996 Act, where the investigation began between 1st April, 1997 and 3rd April, 2005;

(b)   section 6A of the 1996 Act, where the investigation began on or after 4th April, 2005. See also section 6E of the Act.

Where the investigation began between 1st April, 1997 and 3rd April, 2005, the defence statement must—

(a)   set out in general terms the nature of the defence;

(b)   indicate the matters on which the defendant takes issue with the prosecutor, and, in respect of each, explain why;

(c)   if the defence statement discloses an alibi, give particulars, including—
   (i)   the name and address of any witness whom the defendant believes can give evidence in support (that is, evidence that the defendant was in a place, at a time, inconsistent with having committed the offence),
   (ii)   where the defendant does not know the name or address, any information that might help identify or find that witness.

Where the investigation began on or after 4th April, 2005, the defence statement must—

(a)   set out the nature of the defence, including any particular defences on which the defendant intends to rely;

(b)   indicate the matters of fact on which the defendant takes issue with the prosecutor, and, in respect of each, explain why;

(c)   set out particulars of the matters of fact on which the defendant intends to rely for the purposes of the defence;

(d)   indicate any point of law that the defendant wants to raise, including any point about the admissibility of evidence or about abuse of process, and any authority relied on; and

(e)   if the defence statement discloses an alibi, give particulars, including—
   (i)   the name, address and date of birth of any witness whom the defendant believes can give evidence in support (that is, evidence that the defendant was in a place, at a time, inconsistent with having committed the offence),
   (ii)   where the defendant does not know any of those details, any information that might help identify or find that witness.

The time for service of a defence witness notice is prescribed by section 12 of the 1996 Act and by the Criminal Procedure and Investigations Act 1996 (Defence Disclosure Time Limits) Regulations 2011. The time limits are the same as those for a defence statement.
A defence witness notice that identifies any proposed defence witness (other than the defendant) must—

(a)   give the name, address and date of birth of each such witness, or as many of those details as are known to the defendant when the notice is given;

(b)   provide any information in the defendant's possession which might be of material assistance in identifying or finding any such witness in whose case any of the details mentioned in paragraph (a) are not known to the defendant when the notice is given; and

(c)   amend any earlier such notice, if the defendant—

    (i)   decides to call a person not included in an earlier notice as a proposed witness,

    (ii)   decides not to call a person so included, or

    (iii) discovers any information which the defendant would have had to include in an earlier notice, if then aware of it.   Under section 11 of the 1996 Act, if a defendant—

(a)   fails to disclose what the Act requires;

(b)   fails to do so within the time prescribed;

(c)   at trial, relies on a defence, or facts, not mentioned in the defence statement;

(d)   at trial, introduces alibi evidence without having given in the defence statement—

    (i)   particulars of the alibi, or

    (ii)   the details of the alibi witness, or witnesses, required by the Act; or

(e)   at trial, calls a witness not identified in a defence witness notice,

then the court or another party at trial may comment on that, and the court may draw such inferences as appear proper in deciding whether the defendant is guilty.

Under section 6E(2) of the 1996 Act, if before trial in the Crown Court it seems to the court that section 11 may apply, then the court must warn the defendant.

PART 16   WRITTEN WITNESS STATEMENTS

Contents of this Part

B.15 *16.1. When this Part applies* This Part applies where a party wants to introduce a written witness statement in evidence under section 9 of the Criminal Justice Act 1967.

[Note. Under section 9 of the Criminal Justice Act 1967, if the conditions specified in that section are met, the written statement of a witness is admissible in evidence to the same extent as if that witness gave evidence in person.]

16.2. Content of written witness statement The statement must contain—

(a)   at the beginning—

    (i)   the witness' name, and

    (ii)   the witness' age, if under 18;

(b)   a declaration by the witness that—

    (i)   it is true to the best of the witness' knowledge and belief, and

    (ii)   the witness knows that if it is introduced in evidence, then it would be an offence wilfully to have stated in it anything that the witness knew to be false or did not believe to be true;

(c)   if the witness cannot read the statement, a signed declaration by someone else that that person read it to the witness; and

(d)   the witness' signature.

[Note. The Practice Direction sets out a form of written statement for use in connection with this rule.]

16.3. Reference to exhibit Where the statement refers to a document or object as an exhibit, it must identify that document or object clearly.

[Note. See section 9(7) of the Criminal Justice Act 1967.]

16.4. Written witness statement in evidence (1) A party who wants to introduce in evidence a written witness statement must—

(a)   before the hearing at which that party wants to introduce it, serve a copy of the statement on—

    (i)   the court officer, and

    (ii)   each other party; and

(b)   at or before that hearing, serve on the court officer the statement or an authenticated copy.

(2) If that party relies on only part of the statement, that party must mark the copy in such a way as to make that clear.

(3) A prosecutor must serve on a defendant, with the copy of the statement, a notice—

(a)   of the right to object to the introduction of the statement in evidence instead of the witness giving evidence in person;

(b)   of the time limit for objecting under this rule; and

(c)   that if the defendant does not object in time, the court—

    (i)   can nonetheless require the witness to give evidence in person, but

    (ii)   may decide not to do so.

(4) A party served with a written witness statement who objects to its introduction in evidence must—

(a)   serve notice of the objection on—
    (i)   the party who served it, and
    (ii)   the court officer; and
(b)   serve the notice of objection not more than 7 days after service of the statement unless—
    (i)   the court extends that time limit, before or after the statement was served,
    (ii)   rule 24.8 (Written guilty plea: special rules) applies, in which case the time limit is the later of 7 days after service of the statement or 7 days before the hearing date, or
    (iii)   rule 24.9 (Single justice procedure: special rules) applies, in which case the time limit is 21 days after service of the statement.
(5)   The court may exercise its power to require the witness to give evidence in person—
(a)   on application by any party; or
(b)   on its own initiative.
(6)   A party entitled to receive a copy of a statement may waive that entitlement by so informing—
(a)   the party who would have served it; and
(b)   the court.
[Note. The Practice Direction sets out a form of written witness statement and a form of notice for use in connection with this rule.
Under section 9(2A) of the Criminal Justice Act 1967, Criminal Procedure Rules may prescribe the period within which a party served with a written witness statement must object to its introduction in evidence, subject to a minimum period of 7 days from its service.
Under section 133 of the Criminal Justice Act 2003, where a statement in a document is admissible as evidence in criminal proceedings, the statement may be proved by producing either (a) the document, or (b) (whether or not the document exists) a copy of the document or of the material part of it, authenticated in whatever way the court may approve. By section 134 of the 2003 Act, 'document' means anything in which information of any description is recorded.]

PART 17   WITNESS SUMMONSES, WARRANTS AND ORDERS

Contents of this Part

B.16 *17.1.   When this Part applies* (1)   This Part applies in magistrates' courts and in the Crown Court where—
(a)   a party wants the court to issue a witness summons, warrant or order under—
    (i)   section 97 of the Magistrates' Courts Act 1980,
    (ii)   paragraph 4 of Schedule 3 to the Crime and Disorder Act 1998,
    (iii)   section 2 of the Criminal Procedure (Attendance of Witnesses) Act 1965, or
    (iv)   section 7 of the Bankers' Books Evidence Act 1879;
(b)   the court considers the issue of such a summons, warrant or order on its own initiative as if a party had applied; or
(c)   one of those listed in rule 17.7 wants the court to withdraw such a summons, warrant or order.
(2)   A reference to a 'witness' in this Part is a reference to a person to whom such a summons, warrant or order is directed.
[Note. A magistrates' court may require the attendance of a witness to give evidence or to produce in evidence a document or thing by a summons, or in some circumstances a warrant for the witness' arrest, under section 97 of the Magistrates' Courts Act 1980 or under paragraph 4 of Schedule 3 to the Crime and Disorder Act 1998. The Crown Court may do so under sections 2, 2D, 3 and 4 of the Criminal Procedure (Attendance of Witnesses) Act 1965. Either court may order the production in evidence of a copy of an entry in a banker's book without the attendance of an officer of the bank, under sections 6 and 7 of the Bankers' Books Evidence Act 1879. See section 2D of the Criminal Procedure (Attendance of Witnesses) Act 1965 for the Crown Court's power to issue a witness summons on the court's own initiative.
See Part 3 for the court's general powers to consider an application and to give directions.]

17.2. Issue etc of summons, warrant or order with or without a hearing (1) The court may issue or withdraw a witness summons, warrant or order with or without a hearing.

(2) A hearing under this Part must be in private unless the court otherwise directs.

[Note. If rule 17.5 applies, a person served with an application for a witness summons will have an opportunity to make representations about whether there should be a hearing of that application before the witness summons is issued.]

17.3. Application for summons, warrant or order: general rules (1) A party who wants the court to issue a witness summons, warrant or order must apply as soon as practicable after becoming aware of the grounds for doing so.

(2) A party applying for a witness summons or order must—

(a) identify the proposed witness;

(b) explain—

(i) what evidence the proposed witness can give or produce,

(ii) why it is likely to be material evidence, and

(iii) why it would be in the interests of justice to issue a summons, order or warrant as appropriate.

(3) A party applying for an order to be allowed to inspect and copy an entry in bank records must—

(a) identify the entry;

(b) explain the purpose for which the entry is required; and

(c) propose—

(i) the terms of the order, and

(ii) the period within which the order should take effect, if 3 days from the date of service of the order would not be appropriate.

(4) The application may be made orally unless—

(a) rule 17.5 applies; or

(b) the court otherwise directs.

(5) The applicant must serve any order made on the witness to whom, or the bank to which, it is directed.

[Note. The court may issue a warrant for a witness' arrest if that witness fails to obey a witness summons directed to him: see section 97(3) of the Magistrates' Courts Act 1980, paragraph 4(5) of Schedule 3 to the Crime and Disorder Act 1998 and section 4 of the Criminal Procedure (Attendance of Witnesses) Act 1965. Before a magistrates' court may issue a warrant under section 97(3) of the 1980 Act, the witness must first be paid or offered a reasonable amount for costs and expenses.]

17.4. Written application: form and service (1) An application in writing under rule 17.3 must be in the form set out in the Practice Direction, containing the same declaration of truth as a witness statement.

(2) The party applying must serve the application—

(a) in every case, on the court officer and as directed by the court; and

(b) as required by rule 17.5, if that rule applies.

[Note. Declarations of truth in witness statements are required by section 9 of the Criminal Justice Act 1967. Section 89 of the 1967 Act makes it an offence to make a written statement under section 9 of that Act which the person making it knows to be false or does not believe to be true.]

17.5. Application for summons to produce a document, etc: special rules (1) This rule applies to an application under rule 17.3 for a witness summons requiring the proposed witness—

(a) to produce in evidence a document or thing; or

(b) to give evidence about information apparently held in confidence,

that relates to another person.

(2) The application must be in writing in the form required by rule 17.4.

(3) The party applying must serve the application—

(a) on the proposed witness, unless the court otherwise directs; and

(b) on one or more of the following, if the court so directs—

(i) a person to whom the proposed evidence relates,

(ii) another party.

(4) The court must not issue a witness summons where this rule applies unless—

(a) everyone served with the application has had at least 14 days in which to make representations, including representations about whether there should be a hearing of the application before the summons is issued; and

(b) the court is satisfied that it has been able to take adequate account of the duties and rights, including rights of confidentiality, of the proposed witness and of any person to whom the proposed evidence relates.

(5) This rule does not apply to an application for an order to produce in evidence a copy of an entry in a banker's book.

[Note. Under section 2A of the Criminal Procedure (Attendance of Witnesses) Act 1965, a witness summons to produce a document or thing issued by the Crown Court may require the witness to produce it for inspection by the applicant before producing it in evidence.]

17.6. Application for summons to produce a document, etc: court's assessment of relevance and confidentiality (1) This rule applies where a person served with an application for a witness summons requiring the proposed witness to produce in evidence a document or thing objects to its production on the ground that—

(a) it is not likely to be material evidence; or

(b)   even if it is likely to be material evidence, the duties or rights, including rights of confidentiality, of the proposed witness or of any person to whom the document or thing relates, outweigh the reasons for issuing a summons.

(2)   The court may require the proposed witness to make the document or thing available for the objection to be assessed.

(3)   The court may invite—

(a)   the proposed witness or any representative of the proposed witness; or

(b)   a person to whom the document or thing relates or any representative of such a person, to help the court assess the objection.

17.7. Application to withdraw a summons, warrant or order   (1)   The court may withdraw a witness summons, warrant or order if one of the following applies for it to be withdrawn—

(a)   the party who applied for it, on the ground that it no longer is needed;

(b)   the witness, on the grounds that—

        (i)   he was not aware of any application for it, and

        (ii)   he cannot give or produce evidence likely to be material evidence, or

        (iii)   even if he can, his duties or rights, including rights of confidentiality, or those of any person to whom the evidence relates, outweigh the reasons for the issue of the summons, warrant or order; or

(c)   any person to whom the proposed evidence relates, on the grounds that—

        (i)   he was not aware of any application for it, and

        (ii)   that evidence is not likely to be material evidence, or

        (iii)   even if it is, his duties or rights, including rights of confidentiality, or those of the witness, outweigh the reasons for the issue of the summons, warrant or order.

(2)   A person applying under the rule must—

(a)   apply in writing as soon as practicable after becoming aware of the grounds for doing so, explaining why he wants the summons, warrant or order to be withdrawn; and

(b)   serve the application on the court officer and as appropriate on—

        (i)   the witness,

        (ii)   the party who applied for the summons, warrant or order, and

        (iii)   any other person who he knows was served with the application for the summons, warrant or order.

(3)   Rule 17.6 applies to an application under this rule that concerns a document or thing to be produced in evidence.

[Note. See sections 2B, 2C and 2E of the Criminal Procedure (Attendance of Witnesses) Act 1965 for the Crown Court's powers to withdraw a witness summons, including the power to order costs.]

17.8. Court's power to vary requirements under this Part   (1)   The court may—

(a)   shorten or extend (even after it has expired) a time limit under this Part; and

(b)   where a rule or direction requires an application under this Part to be in writing, allow that application to be made orally instead.

(2)   Someone who wants the court to allow an application to be made orally under paragraph (1)(b) of this rule must—

(a)   give as much notice as the urgency of his application permits to those on whom he would otherwise have served an application in writing; and

(b)   in doing so explain the reasons for the application and for wanting the court to consider it orally.

Part 18   Measures to Assist a Witness or Defendant to Give Evidence

Contents of this Part

General rules

GENERAL RULES

B.17   *18.1. When this Part applies*   This Part applies—

(a)   where the court can give a direction (a 'special measures direction'), under section 19 of the Youth Justice and Criminal Evidence Act 1999, on an application or on its own initiative, for any of the following measures—

         (i)   preventing a witness from seeing the defendant (section 23 of the 1999 Act),

         (ii)   allowing a witness to give evidence by live link (section 24 of the 1999 Act),

         (iii)   hearing a witness' evidence in private (section 25 of the 1999 Act),

         (iv)   dispensing with the wearing of wigs and gowns (section 26 of the 1999 Act),

         (v)   admitting video recorded evidence (sections 27 and 28 of the 1999 Act),

         (vi)   questioning a witness through an intermediary (section 29 of the 1999 Act),

         (vii)   using a device to help a witness communicate (section 30 of the 1999 Act);

(b)   where the court can vary or discharge such a direction, under section 20 of the 1999 Act;

(c)   where the court can give, vary or discharge a direction (a 'defendant's evidence direction') for a defendant to give evidence—

         (i)   by live link, under section 33A of the 1999 Act, or

         (ii)   through an intermediary, under sections 33BA and 33BB of the 1999 Act;

(d)   where the court can—

         (i)   make a witness anonymity order, under section 86 of the Coroners and Justice Act 2009, or

         (ii)   vary or discharge such an order, under section 91, 92 or 93 of the 2009 Act;

(e)   where the court can give or discharge a direction (a 'live link direction'), on an application or on its own initiative, for a witness to give evidence by live link under—

         (i)   section 32 of the Criminal Justice Act 1988, or

         (ii)   sections 51 and 52 of the Criminal Justice Act 2003;

(f)   where the court can exercise any other power it has to give, vary or discharge a direction for a measure to help a witness give evidence.

18.2. Meaning of 'witness'   In this Part, 'witness' means anyone (other than a defendant) for whose benefit an application, direction or order is made.

[Note. At the end of this Part is a summary of the circumstances in which a witness or defendant may be eligible for the assistance of one of the measures to which this Part applies.]

18.3. Making an application for a direction or order   A party who wants the court to exercise its power to give or make a direction or order must—

(a)   apply in writing as soon as reasonably practicable, and in any event not more than—

         (i)   28 days after the defendant pleads not guilty, in a magistrates' court, or

         (ii)   14 days after the defendant pleads not guilty, in the Crown Court; and

(b)   serve the application on—

         (i)   the court officer, and

         (ii)   each other party.

[Note. See also rule 18.10 (Content of application for a special measures direction), rule 18.15 (Content of application for a defendant's evidence direction), rule 18.19 (Content and conduct of application for a witness anonymity order) and rule 18.24 (Content of application for a live link

direction).
The Practice Direction sets out forms for use in connection with—
(a)   *an application under rule 18.10 for a special measures direction;*
(b)   *an application under rule 18.24 for a live link direction (otherwise than as a special measures direction).]*

18.4.   *Decisions and reasons*   (1)   A party who wants to introduce the evidence of a witness who is the subject of an application, direction or order must—
(a)   inform the witness of the court's decision as soon as reasonably practicable; and
(b)   explain to the witness the arrangements that as a result will be made for him or her to give evidence.
(2)   The court must—
(a)   promptly determine an application; and
(b)   allow a party sufficient time to comply with the requirements of—
        (i)   paragraph (1), and
        (ii)   the code of practice issued under section 32 of the Domestic Violence, Crime and Victims Act 2004.
(3)   The court must announce, at a hearing in public before the witness gives evidence, the reasons for a decision—
(a)   to give, make, vary or discharge a direction or order; or
(b)   to refuse to do so.
[Note. See sections 20(5), 33A(8) and 33BB(4) of the Youth Justice and Criminal Evidence Act 1999 and sections 51(8) and 52(7) of the Criminal Justice Act 2003.
Under section 32 of the Domestic Violence, Crime and Victims Act 2004, the Secretary of State for Justice must issue a code of practice as to the services to be provided by specified persons to a victim of criminal conduct.]]

18.5.   *Court's power to vary requirements under this Part*   (1)   The court may—
(a)   shorten or extend (even after it has expired) a time limit under this Part; and
(b)   allow an application or representations to be made in a different form to one set out in the Practice Direction, or to be made orally.
(2)   A person who wants an extension of time must—
(a)   apply when serving the application or representations for which it is needed; and
(b)   explain the delay.

18.6.   *Custody of documents*   Unless the court otherwise directs, the court officer may—
(a)   keep a written application or representations; or
(b)   arrange for the whole or any part to be kept by some other appropriate person, subject to any conditions that the court may impose.

18.7.   *Declaration by intermediary*   (1)   This rule applies where—
(a)   a video recorded interview with a witness is conducted through an intermediary;
(b)   the court directs the examination of a witness or defendant through an intermediary.
(2)   An intermediary must make a declaration—
(a)   before such an interview begins;
(b)   before the examination begins (even if such an interview with the witness was conducted through the same intermediary).
(3)   The declaration must be in these terms—
    "I solemnly, sincerely and truly declare [*or* I swear by Almighty God that I will well and faithfully communicate questions and answers and make true explanation of all matters and things as shall be required of me according to the best of my skill and understanding."

SPECIAL MEASURES DIRECTIONS

18.8.   *Exercise of court's powers*   The court may decide whether to give, vary or discharge a special measures direction—
(a)   at a hearing, in public or in private, or without a hearing;
(b)   in a party's absence, if that party—
        (i)   applied for the direction, variation or discharge, or
        (ii)   has had at least 14 days in which to make representations.

18.9.   *Special measures direction for a young witness*   (1)   This rule applies where, under section 21 or section 22 of the Youth Justice and Criminal Evidence Act 1999, the primary rule requires the court to give a direction for a special measure to assist a child witness or a qualifying witness—
(a)   on an application, if one is made; or
(b)   on the court's own initiative, in any other case.
(2)   A party who wants to introduce the evidence of such a witness must as soon as reasonably practicable—
(a)   notify the court that the witness is eligible for assistance;
(b)   provide the court with any information that the court may need to assess the witness' views, if the witness does not want the primary rule to apply; and
(c)   serve any video recorded evidence on—
        (i)   the court officer, and

(ii)   each other party.

[Note. Under sections 21 and 22 of the Youth Justice and Criminal Evidence Act 1999, a 'child witness' is one who is under 18, and a 'qualifying witness' is one who was a child witness when interviewed.

Under those sections, the 'primary rule' requires the court to give a direction—

(a)   for the evidence of a child witness or of a qualifying witness to be admitted—
   (i)   by means of a video recording of an interview with the witness, in the place of examination-in-chief, and
   (ii)   after that, by live link; or
(b)   if one or both of those measures is not taken, for the witness while giving evidence to be screened from seeing the defendant.

The primary rule always applies unless—

(a)   the witness does not want it to apply, and the court is satisfied that to omit a measure usually required by that rule would not diminish the quality of the witness' evidence; or
(b)   the court is satisfied that to direct one of the measures usually required by that rule would not be likely to maximise, so far as practicable, the quality of the witness' evidence.]

18.10.   Content of application for a special measures direction   An applicant for a special measures direction must—

(a)   explain how the witness is eligible for assistance;
(b)   explain why special measures would be likely to improve the quality of the witness' evidence;
(c)   propose the measure or measures that in the applicant's opinion would be likely to maximise, so far as practicable, the quality of that evidence;
(d)   report any views that the witness has expressed about—
   (i)   his or her eligibility for assistance,
   (ii)   the likelihood that special measures would improve the quality of his or her evidence, and
   (iii)   the measure or measures proposed by the applicant;
(e)   in a case in which a child witness or a qualifying witness does not want the primary rule to apply, provide any information that the court may need to assess the witness' views;
(f)   in a case in which the applicant proposes that the witness should give evidence by live link—
   (i)   identify someone to accompany the witness while the witness gives evidence,
   (ii)   name that person, if possible, and
   (iii)   explain why that person would be an appropriate companion for the witness, including the witness' own views;
(g)   in a case in which the applicant proposes the admission of video recorded evidence, identify—
   (i)   the date and duration of the recording,
   (ii)   which part the applicant wants the court to admit as evidence, if the applicant does not want the court to admit all of it;
(h)   attach any other material on which the applicant relies; and
(i)   if the applicant wants a hearing, ask for one, and explain why it is needed.

[Note. The Practice Direction sets out a form of application for use in connection with this rule.]

18.11.   Application to vary or discharge a special measures direction   (1)   A party who wants the court to vary or discharge a special measures direction must—

(a)   apply in writing, as soon as reasonably practicable after becoming aware of the grounds for doing so; and
(b)   serve the application on—
   (i)   the court officer, and
   (ii)   each other party.

(2)   The applicant must—

(a)   explain what material circumstances have changed since the direction was given (or last varied, if applicable);
(b)   explain why the direction should be varied or discharged; and
(c)   ask for a hearing, if the applicant wants one, and explain why it is needed.

[Note. Under section 20 of the Youth Justice and Criminal Evidence Act 1999, the court can vary or discharge a special measures direction—

(a)   on application, if there has been a material change of circumstances; or
(b)   on the court's own initiative.]

18.12.   Application containing information withheld from another party   (1)   This rule applies where—

(a)   an applicant serves an application for a special measures direction, or for its variation or discharge; and
(b)   the application includes information that the applicant thinks ought not be revealed to another party.

(2)   The applicant must—

(a)   omit that information from the part of the application that is served on that other party;
(b)   mark the other part to show that, unless the court otherwise directs, it is only for the court; and

(c)   in that other part, explain why the applicant has withheld that information from that other party.
(3)   Any hearing of an application to which this rule applies—
(a)   must be in private, unless the court otherwise directs; and
(b)   if the court so directs, may be, wholly or in part, in the absence of a party from whom information has been withheld.
(4)   At any hearing of an application to which this rule applies—
(a)   the general rule is that the court must consider, in the following sequence—
      (i)   representations first by the applicant and then by each other party, in all the parties' presence, and then
      (ii)   further representations by the applicant, in the absence of a party from whom information has been withheld; but
(b)   the court may direct other arrangements for the hearing.
[Note. See section 20 of the Youth Justice and Criminal Evidence Act 1999.]

18.13. Representations in response (1)   This rule applies where a party wants to make representations about—
(a)   an application for a special measures direction;
(b)   an application for the variation or discharge of such a direction; or
(c)   a direction, variation or discharge that the court proposes on its own initiative.
(2)   Such a party must—
(a)   serve the representations on—
      (i)   the court officer, and
      (ii)   each other party;
(b)   do so not more than 14 days after, as applicable—
      (i)   service of the application, or
      (ii)   notice of the direction, variation or discharge that the court proposes; and
(c)   ask for a hearing, if that party wants one, and explain why it is needed.
(3)   Where representations include information that the person making them thinks ought not be revealed to another party, that person must—
(a)   omit that information from the representations served on that other party;
(b)   mark the information to show that, unless the court otherwise directs, it is only for the court; and
(c)   with that information include an explanation of why it has been withheld from that other party.
(4)   Representations against a special measures direction must explain, as appropriate—
(a)   why the witness is not eligible for assistance;
(b)   if the witness is eligible for assistance, why—
      (i)   no special measure would be likely to improve the quality of the witness' evidence,
      (ii)   the proposed measure or measures would not be likely to maximise, so far as practicable, the quality of the witness' evidence, or
      (iii)   the proposed measure or measures might tend to inhibit the effective testing of that evidence;
(c)   in a case in which the admission of video recorded evidence is proposed, why it would not be in the interests of justice for the recording, or part of it, to be admitted as evidence.
(5)   Representations against the variation or discharge of a special measures direction must explain why it should not be varied or discharged.
[Note. Under sections 21 and 22 of the Youth Justice and Criminal Evidence Act 1999, where the witness is a child witness or a qualifying witness the special measures that the court usually must direct must be treated as likely to maximise, so far as practicable, the quality of the witness' evidence, irrespective of representations to the contrary.]

DEFENDANT'S EVIDENCE DIRECTIONS

18.14. Exercise of court's powers   The court may decide whether to give, vary or discharge a defendant's evidence direction—
(a)   at a hearing, in public or in private, or without a hearing;
(b)   in a party's absence, if that party—
      (i)   applied for the direction, variation or discharge, or
      (ii)   has had at least 14 days in which to make representations.

18.15. Content of application for a defendant's evidence direction   An applicant for a defendant's evidence direction must—
(a)   explain how the proposed direction meets the conditions prescribed by the Youth Justice and Criminal Evidence Act 1999;
(b)   in a case in which the applicant proposes that the defendant give evidence by live link—
      (i)   identify a person to accompany the defendant while the defendant gives evidence, and
      (ii)   explain why that person is appropriate;
(c)   ask for a hearing, if the applicant wants one, and explain why it is needed.
[Note. See sections 33A and 33BA of the Youth Justice and Criminal Evidence Act 1999.]

18.16. Application to vary or discharge a defendant's evidence direction (1)   A party who wants the court to vary or discharge a defendant's evidence direction must—

(a)   apply in writing, as soon as reasonably practicable after becoming aware of the grounds for doing so; and

(b)   serve the application on—
          (i)   the court officer, and
          (ii)   each other party.

(2)   The applicant must—

(a)   on an application to discharge a live link direction, explain why it is in the interests of justice to do so;

(b)   on an application to discharge a direction for an intermediary, explain why it is no longer necessary in order to ensure that the defendant receives a fair trial;

(c)   on an application to vary a direction for an intermediary, explain why it is necessary for the direction to be varied in order to ensure that the defendant receives a fair trial; and

(d)   ask for a hearing, if the applicant wants one, and explain why it is needed.

[Note. See sections 33A(7) and 33BB of the Youth Justice and Criminal Evidence Act 1999.]

18.17. Representations in response (1)   This rule applies where a party wants to make representations about—

(a)   an application for a defendant's evidence direction;

(b)   an application for the variation or discharge of such a direction; or

(c)   a direction, variation or discharge that the court proposes on its own initiative.

(2)   Such a party must—

(a)   serve the representations on—
          (i)   the court officer, and
          (ii)   each other party;

(b)   do so not more than 14 days after, as applicable—
          (i)   service of the application, or
          (ii)   notice of the direction, variation or discharge that the court proposes; and

(c)   ask for a hearing, if that party wants one, and explain why it is needed.

(3)   Representations against a direction, variation or discharge must explain why the conditions prescribed by the Youth Justice and Criminal Evidence Act 1999 are not met.

WITNESS ANONYMITY ORDERS

18.18. Exercise of court's powers (1)   The court may decide whether to make, vary or discharge a witness anonymity order—

(a)   at a hearing (which must be in private, unless the court otherwise directs), or without a hearing (unless any party asks for one);

(b)   in the absence of a defendant.

(2)   The court must not exercise its power to make, vary or discharge a witness anonymity order, or to refuse to do so—

(a)   before or during the trial, unless each party has had an opportunity to make representations;

(b)   on an appeal by the defendant to which applies Part 34 (Appeal to the Crown Court) or Part 39 (Appeal to the Court of Appeal about conviction or sentence), unless in each party's case—
          (i)   that party has had an opportunity to make representations, or
          (ii)   the appeal court is satisfied that it is not reasonably practicable to communicate with that party;

(c)   after the trial and any such appeal are over, unless in the case of each party and the witness—
          (i)   each has had an opportunity to make representations, or
          (ii)   the court is satisfied that it is not reasonably practicable to communicate with that party or witness.

18.19. Content and conduct of application for a witness anonymity order (1)   An applicant for a witness anonymity order must—

(a)   include in the application nothing that might reveal the witness' identity;

(b)   describe the measures proposed by the applicant;

(c)   explain how the proposed order meets the conditions prescribed by section 88 of the Coroners and Justice Act 2009;

(d)   explain why no measures other than those proposed will suffice, such as—
          (i)   an admission of the facts that would be proved by the witness,
          (ii)   an order restricting public access to the trial,
          (iii)   reporting restrictions, in particular under sections 45, 45A or 46 of the Youth Justice and Criminal Evidence Act 1999,
          (iv)   a direction for a special measure under section 19 of the Youth Justice and Criminal Evidence Act 1999,
          (v)   introduction of the witness' written statement as hearsay evidence, under section 116 of the Criminal Justice Act 2003, or
          (vi)   arrangements for the protection of the witness;

(e)   attach to the application—
          (i)   a witness statement setting out the proposed evidence, edited in such a way as not to reveal the witness' identity,

      (ii)   where the prosecutor is the applicant, any further prosecution evidence to be served, and any further prosecution material to be disclosed under the Criminal Procedure and Investigations Act 1996, similarly edited, and

      (iii)   any defence statement that has been served, or as much information as may be available to the applicant that gives particulars of the defence; and

(f)   ask for a hearing, if the applicant wants one.

(2)   At any hearing of the application, the applicant must—

(a)   identify the witness to the court, unless at the prosecutor's request the court otherwise directs; and

(b)   present to the court, unless it otherwise directs—

      (i)   the unedited witness statement from which the edited version has been prepared,

      (ii)   where the prosecutor is the applicant, the unedited version of any further prosecution evidence or material from which an edited version has been prepared, and

      (iii)   such further material as the applicant relies on to establish that the proposed order meets the conditions prescribed by section 88 of the 2009 Act.

(3)   At any such hearing—

(a)   the general rule is that the court must consider, in the following sequence—

      (i)   representations first by the applicant and then by each other party, in all the parties' presence, and then

      (ii)   information withheld from a defendant, and further representations by the applicant, in the absence of any (or any other) defendant; but

(b)   the court may direct other arrangements for the hearing.

(4)   Before the witness gives evidence, the applicant must identify the witness to the court—

(a)   if not already done;

(b)   without revealing the witness' identity to any other party or person; and

(c)   unless at the prosecutor's request the court otherwise directs.

18.20.   Duty of court officer to notify the Director of Public Prosecutions   The court officer must notify the Director of Public Prosecutions of an application, unless the prosecutor is, or acts on behalf of, a public authority.

18.21.   Application to vary or discharge a witness anonymity order   (1)   A party who wants the court to vary or discharge a witness anonymity order, or a witness who wants the court to do so when the case is over, must—

(a)   apply in writing, as soon as reasonably practicable after becoming aware of the grounds for doing so; and

(b)   serve the application on—

      (i)   the court officer, and

      (ii)   each other party.

(2)   The applicant must—

(a)   explain what material circumstances have changed since the order was made (or last varied, if applicable);

(b)   explain why the order should be varied or discharged, taking account of the conditions for making an order; and

(c)   ask for a hearing, if the applicant wants one.

(3)   Where an application includes information that the applicant thinks might reveal the witness' identity, the applicant must—

(a)   omit that information from the application that is served on a defendant;

(b)   mark the information to show that it is only for the court and the prosecutor (if the prosecutor is not the applicant); and

(c)   with that information include an explanation of why it has been withheld.

(4)   Where a party applies to vary or discharge a witness anonymity order after the trial and any appeal are over, the party who introduced the witness' evidence must serve the application on the witness.

[Note. Under sections 91, 92 and 93 of the Coroners and Justice Act 2009, the court can vary or discharge a witness anonymity order—

(a)   *on an application, if there has been a material change of circumstances since it was made or previously varied; or*

(b)   *on the court's own initiative, unless the trial and any appeal are over.]*

18.22.   Representations in response   (1)   This rule applies where a party or, where the case is over, a witness, wants to make representations about—

(a)   an application for a witness anonymity order;

(b)   an application for the variation or discharge of such an order; or

(c)   a variation or discharge that the court proposes on its own initiative.

(2)   Such a party or witness must—

(a)   serve the representations on—

      (i)   the court officer, and

      (ii)   each other party;

(b)   do so not more than 14 days after, as applicable—

      (i)   service of the application, or

      (ii)   notice of the variation or discharge that the court proposes; and

(c)   ask for a hearing, if that party or witness wants one.

(3)   Where representations include information that the person making them thinks might reveal the witness' identity, that person must—

(a)   omit that information from the representations served on a defendant;

(b)   mark the information to show that it is only for the court (and for the prosecutor, if relevant); and

(c)   with that information include an explanation of why it has been withheld.

(4)   Representations against a witness anonymity order must explain why the conditions for making the order are not met.

(5)   Representations against the variation or discharge of such an order must explain why it would not be appropriate to vary or discharge it, taking account of the conditions for making an order.

(6)   A prosecutor's representations in response to an application by a defendant must include all information available to the prosecutor that is relevant to the conditions and considerations specified by sections 88 and 89 of the Coroners and Justice Act 2009.

LIVE LINK DIRECTIONS

Note

[Note. The rules in this Section do not apply to an application for a special measures direction allowing a witness to give evidence by live link: as to which, see rules 18.8 to 18.13.]

18.23.   *Exercise of court's powers*   The court may decide whether to give or discharge a live link direction—

(a)   at a hearing, in public or in private, or without a hearing;

(b)   in a party's absence, if that party—

   (i)   applied for the direction or discharge, or

   (ii)   has had at least 14 days in which to make representations in response to an application by another party.

18.24.   *Content of application for a live link direction*   (1)   An applicant for a live link direction must—

(a)   unless the court otherwise directs, identify the place from which the witness will give evidence;

(b)   if that place is in the United Kingdom, explain why it would be in the interests of the efficient or effective administration of justice for the witness to give evidence by live link;

(c)   if the applicant wants the witness to be accompanied by another person while giving evidence—

   (i)   name that person, if possible, and

   (ii)   explain why it is appropriate for the witness to be accompanied;

(d)   ask for a hearing, if the applicant wants one, and explain why it is needed.

(2)   An applicant for a live link direction under section 32 of the Criminal Justice Act 1988 who wants the court also to make a European investigation order must—

(a)   identify the participating State in which, and the place in that State from which, the witness will give evidence;

(b)   explain why it is necessary and proportionate to make a European investigation order;

(c)   if applicable, explain how the requirements of regulation 14 of the Criminal Justice (European Investigation Order) Regulations 2017 are met (Hearing a person by videoconference or telephone); and

(d)   attach a draft order in the form required by regulation 8 of the 2017 Regulations (Form and content of a European investigation order) and Directive 2014/41/EU.

(3)   Where the court makes a European investigation order, the court officer must promptly—

(a)   issue an order in the form required by regulation 8 of the 2017 Regulations (Form and content of a European investigation order) and Directive 2014/41/EU;

(b)   where the applicant is a constable or a prosecuting authority, serve that order on the applicant;

(c)   in any other case, serve that order on the appropriate authority in the participating State in which the measure or measures are to be carried out.

[Note. See section 32 of the Criminal Justice Act 1988, section 51 of the Criminal Justice Act 2003 and regulation 6 of the Criminal Justice (European Investigation Order) Regulations 2017.
The Practice Direction sets out a form of application for use in connection with this rule.]

18.25.   *Application to discharge a live link direction, etc*   (1)   A party who wants the court to discharge a live link direction must—

(a)   apply in writing, as soon as reasonably practicable after becoming aware of the grounds for doing so; and

(b)   serve the application on—

   (i)   the court officer, and

   (ii)   each other party.

(2)   The applicant must—

(a)   explain what material circumstances have changed since the direction was given;

(b)   explain why it is in the interests of justice to discharge the direction; and

(c)   ask for a hearing, if the applicant wants one, and explain why it is needed.

(3)   An applicant for the variation or revocation of a European investigation order made on an application under rule 18.24 must demonstrate that the applicant is, as the case may be—

(a)   the person who applied for the order;
(b)   a prosecuting authority; or
(c)   any other person affected by the order.
(4)   Where the court varies or revokes such an order, the court officer must promptly notify the appropriate authority in the participating State in which the measure or measures are to be carried out.
[Note. See section 32(4) of the Criminal Justice Act 1988, section 52(3) of the Criminal Justice Act 2003 and regulation 10 of the Criminal Justice (European Investigation Order) Regulations 2017.]

18.26.   Representations in response (1) This rule applies where a party wants to make representations about an application for a live link direction or for the discharge of such a direction.
(2)   Such a party must—
(a)   serve the representations on—
          (i)   the court officer, and
          (ii)   each other party;
(b)   do so not more than 14 days after service of the application; and—
(c)   ask for a hearing, if that party wants one, and explain why it is needed.
(3)   Representations against a direction or discharge must explain, as applicable, why the conditions prescribed by the Criminal Justice Act 1988 or the Criminal Justice Act 2003 are not met.
Summary of eligibility for measures to which this Part applies
Special measures direction
Under section 16 of the Youth Justice and Criminal Evidence Act 1999, a witness is eligible for the assistance of a special measures direction given under section 19 of that Act if—
(a)   *the witness is under 18; or*
(b)   *the witness has—*
          (i)   *a mental disorder, or a significant impairment of intelligence and social functioning, or*
          (ii)   *a physical disability or disorder*
     and the court considers that the completeness, coherence and accuracy (the 'quality') of evidence given by the witness is likely to be diminished by reason of those circumstances.
Under section 17 of the 1999 Act, a witness is eligible for such assistance if—
(a)   *the court is satisfied that the quality of evidence given by the witness is likely to be diminished because of his or her fear or distress in connection with giving evidence, taking account particularly of—*
          (i)   *the circumstances of the offence,*
          (ii)   *the witness' age, social and cultural background, ethnic origins, domestic and employment circumstances, religious beliefs or political opinions,*
          (iii)   *any behaviour towards the witness on the part of the defendant, the defendant's family or associates, or any other potential defendant or witness, and*
          (iv)   *the witness' own views;*
(b)   *the witness is the complainant in respect of a sexual offence, and has not declined such assistance; or*
(c)   *the offence is one of a list of offences involving weapons, and the witness has not declined such assistance.*
Section 28 of the 1999 Act (video recorded cross-examination or re-examination) is not yet in force. With that exception, all the special measures listed in rule 18.1 potentially are available where the witness is eligible for assistance under section 16 of the Act. Those numbered (i) to (v) are available where the witness is eligible for assistance under section 17.
As a general rule, but with exceptions, the court must give a special measures direction—
(a)   *under section 21 or 22 of the 1999 Act, where the witness—*
          (i)   *is under 18, or*
          (ii)   *was under that age when interviewed*
     whether or not an application for a direction is made;
(b)   *under section 22A of the 1999 Act, where an application is made in the Crown Court for the evidence of a witness who is the complainant of a sexual offence to be admitted by means of a video recording of an interview with the witness in the place of examination-in-chief.*
Defendant's evidence direction
Under section 33A of the 1999 Act, the court can allow a defendant to give evidence by live link, or (when the Coroners and Justice Act 2009 comes into force) under section 33BA can allow a defendant to give evidence through an intermediary, if—
(a)   *the defendant—*
          (i)   *is under 18, and the defendant's ability to participate effectively as a witness giving oral evidence is compromised by his or her level of intellectual ability or social functioning; or*
          (ii)   *suffers from a mental disorder or some other significant impairment of intelligence and social functioning and cannot participate effectively as a witness giving oral evidence for that reason;*
(b)   *the use of a live link—*
          (i)   *would enable the defendant to participate more effectively, and*
          (ii)   *is in the interests of justice;*
(c)   *the examination of the defendant through an intermediary is necessary to ensure that the*

defendant receives a fair trial.

Witness anonymity order

Under section 86 of the Coroners and Justice Act 2009, a witness anonymity order is an order that specifies measures to be taken to ensure that the identity of a witness is not disclosed, such as withholding the witness' name from materials disclosed to a party to the proceedings, the use of a pseudonym, the screening of the witness from view, the modulation of the witness' voice, and the prohibition of questions that might reveal his or her identity. Before making such an order, the court must—

(a)   *be satisfied that three conditions prescribed by the Act are met (section 88 of the 2009 Act); and*

(b)   *have regard to considerations specified by the Act (section 89 of the 2009 Act).*

Live link direction

Under section 32 of the Criminal Justice Act 1988, the court can allow a witness who is outside the United Kingdom to give evidence by live link—

(a)   in proceedings in a youth court, or on appeal from such proceedings; or

(b)   at a trial in the Crown Court, or on appeal from such a trial.

Under section 51 of the Criminal Justice Act 2003, on an application or on its own initiative, the court can allow a witness who is in the United Kingdom, but outside the building in which the proceedings are held, to give evidence by live link. The court must be satisfied that that is in the interests of the efficient or effective administration of justice.

The Criminal Justice (European Investigation Order) Regulations 2017 give effect in the United Kingdom to Directive 2014/41/EU of the European Parliament and of the Council regarding the European Investigation Order in criminal matters. Under regulation 6 of the 2017 Regulations the court can make an order specifying one or more 'investigative measures' that are to be carried out in a State listed in Schedule 2 to those Regulations (a 'participating State'). One such measure is hearing in proceedings in England and Wales, by live video or, potentially, audio link (described in the Regulations as 'videoconference or other audio visual transmission' and as 'telephone conference' respectively), a witness who is in a participating State. See also regulations 6(4)(c) and 14 of the 2017 Regulations, and regulation 9 which governs the transmission of an order to the participating State.

Under regulations 6(4)(b) and 11 of the 2017 Regulations any such measure must be one that could have been ordered or undertaken under the same conditions in a similar domestic case; but under regulation 11(5) that does not require the court to take into account any provision of domestic law imposing a procedural requirement which the court considers cannot effectively be applied when making a European investigation order for the measure concerned.".

If a witness is eligible for the assistance of a special measures direction (as to which, see the note above), the court can allow the witness to give evidence by live link under sections 19 and 24 of the 1999 Act. See rules 18.8 to 18.13.

PART 19   EXPERT EVIDENCE

B.18   *19.1.*   *When this Part applies*   (1)   This Part applies where a party wants to introduce expert opinion evidence.

(2)   A reference to an 'expert' in this Part is a reference to a person who is required to give or prepare expert evidence for the purpose of criminal proceedings, including evidence required to determine fitness to plead or for the purpose of sentencing.

[Note. Expert medical evidence may be required to determine fitness to plead under section 4 of the Criminal Procedure (Insanity) Act 1964. It may be required also under section 11 of the Powers of Criminal Courts (Sentencing) Act 2000, under Part III of the Mental Health Act 1983 or under Part 12 of the Criminal Justice Act 2003. Those Acts contain requirements about the qualification of medical experts.]

19.2.   Expert's duty to the court   (1)   An expert must help the court to achieve the overriding objective—

(a)   by giving opinion which is—

        (i)   objective and unbiased, and

        (ii)   within the expert's area or areas of expertise; and

(b)   by actively assisting the court in fulfilling its duty of case management under rule 3.2, in particular by—

       (i)   complying with directions made by the court, and

       (ii)   at once informing the court of any significant failure (by the expert or another) to take any step required by such a direction.

(2)   This duty overrides any obligation to the person from whom the expert receives instructions or by whom the expert is paid.

(3)   This duty includes obligations—

(a)   to define the expert's area or areas of expertise—

       (i)   in the expert's report, and

       (ii)   when giving evidence in person;

(b)   when giving evidence in person, to draw the court's attention to any question to which the answer would be outside the expert's area or areas of expertise; and

(c)   to inform all parties and the court if the expert's opinion changes from that contained in a report served as evidence or given in a statement.

19.3. Introduction of expert evidence (1) A party who wants another party to admit as fact a summary of an expert's conclusions must serve that summary—

(a)   on the court officer and on each party from whom that admission is sought;

(b)   as soon as practicable after the defendant whom it affects pleads not guilty.

(2)   A party on whom such a summary is served must—

(a)   serve a response stating—

       (i)   which, if any, of the expert's conclusions are admitted as fact, and

       (ii)   where a conclusion is not admitted, what are the disputed issues concerning that conclusion; and

(b)   serve the response—

       (i)   on the court officer and on the party who served the summary,

       (ii)   as soon as practicable, and in any event not more than 14 days after service of the summary.

(3)   A party who wants to introduce expert evidence otherwise than as admitted fact must—

(a)   serve a report by the expert which complies with rule 19.4 (Content of expert's report) on—

       (i)   the court officer, and

       (ii)   each other party;

(b)   serve the report as soon as practicable, and in any event with any application in support of which that party relies on that evidence;

(c)   serve with the report notice of anything of which the party serving it is aware which might reasonably be thought capable of detracting substantially from the credibility of that expert;

(d)   if another party so requires, give that party a copy of, or a reasonable opportunity to inspect—

       (i)   a record of any examination, measurement, test or experiment on which the expert's findings and opinion are based, or that were carried out in the course of reaching those findings and opinion, and

       (ii)   anything on which any such examination, measurement, test or experiment was carried out.

(4)   Unless the parties otherwise agree or the court directs, a party may not—

(a)   introduce expert evidence if that party has not complied with paragraph (3);

(b)   introduce in evidence an expert report if the expert does not give evidence in person.

[Note. A party who accepts another party's expert's conclusions may admit them as fact under section 10 of the Criminal Justice Act 1967.

Under section 81 of the Police and Criminal Evidence Act 1984, and under section 20(3) of the Criminal Procedure and Investigations Act 1996, Criminal Procedure Rules may require the disclosure of expert evidence before it is introduced as part of a party's case and prohibit its introduction without the court's permission, if it was not disclosed as required.

Under section 30 of the Criminal Justice Act 1988, an expert report is admissible in evidence whether or not the person who made it gives oral evidence, but if that person does not give oral evidence then the report is admissible only with the court's permission.]

19.4. Content of expert's report^{Ed} Where rule 19.3(3) applies, an expert's report must—

(a)   give details of the expert's qualifications, relevant experience and accreditation;

(b)   give details of any literature or other information which the expert has relied on in making the report;

(c)   contain a statement setting out the substance of all facts given to the expert which are material to the opinions expressed in the report, or upon which those opinions are based;

(d)   make clear which of the facts stated in the report are within the expert's own knowledge;

(e)   where the expert has based an opinion or inference on a representation of fact or opinion made by another person for the purposes of criminal proceedings (for example, as to the outcome of an examination, measurement, test or experiment)—

       (i)   identify the person who made that representation to the expert,

       (ii)   give the qualifications, relevant experience and any accreditation of that person, and

       (iii) certify that that person had personal knowledge of the matters stated in that representation;

(f)   where there is a range of opinion on the matters dealt with in the report—

       (i)   summarise the range of opinion, and

(ii)   give reasons for the expert's own opinion;
(g)   if the expert is not able to give an opinion without qualification, state the qualification;
(h)   include such information as the court may need to decide whether the expert's opinion is sufficiently reliable to be admissible as evidence;
(i)   contain a summary of the conclusions reached;
(j)   contain a statement that the expert understands an expert's duty to the court, and has complied and will continue to comply with that duty; and
(k)   contain the same declaration of truth as a witness statement.
[Note. Part 16 contains rules about written witness statements. Declarations of truth in witness statements are required by section 9 of the Criminal Justice Act 1967. Evidence of examinations etc on which an expert relies may be admissible under section 127 of the Criminal Justice Act 2003.]

Ed For an example of a case where non compliance with the requirements of the predecessor to r 19.4 was such as to justify exclusion of the report, see *R v Berberi and others* [2014] EWCA Crim 2961, [2015] 2 Cr App R 2.

19.5.   *Expert to be informed of service of report*   A party who serves on another party or on the court a report by an expert must, at once, inform that expert of that fact.

19.6.   *Pre-hearing discussion of expert evidence*   (1)   This rule applies where more than one party wants to introduce expert evidence.
(2)   The court may direct the experts to—
(a)   discuss the expert issues in the proceedings; and
(b)   prepare a statement for the court of the matters on which they agree and disagree, giving their reasons.
(3)   Except for that statement, the content of that discussion must not be referred to without the court's permission.
(4)   A party may not introduce expert evidence without the court's permission if the expert has not complied with a direction under this rule.
[Note. At a pre-trial hearing, a court may make binding rulings about the admissibility of evidence and about questions of law under section 9 of the Criminal Justice Act 1987; sections 31 and 40 of the Criminal Procedure and Investigations Act 1996; and section 8A of the Magistrates' Courts Act 1980.]

19.7.   *Court's power to direct that evidence is to be given by a single joint expert*   (1)   Where more than one defendant wants to introduce expert evidence on an issue at trial, the court may direct that the evidence on that issue is to be given by one expert only.
(2)   Where the co-defendants cannot agree who should be the expert, the court may—
(a)   select the expert from a list prepared or identified by them; or
(b)   direct that the expert be selected in another way.

19.8.   *Instructions to a single joint expert*   (1)   Where the court gives a direction under rule 19.7 for a single joint expert to be used, each of the co-defendants may give instructions to the expert.
(2)   A co-defendant who gives instructions to the expert must, at the same time, send a copy of the instructions to each other co-defendant.
(3)   The court may give directions about—
(a)   the payment of the expert's fees and expenses; and
(b)   any examination, measurement, test or experiment which the expert wishes to carry out.
(4)   The court may, before an expert is instructed, limit the amount that can be paid by way of fees and expenses to the expert.
(5)   Unless the court otherwise directs, the instructing co-defendants are jointly and severally liable for the payment of the expert's fees and expenses.

19.9.   *Court's power to vary requirements under this Part*   (1)   The court may extend (even after it has expired) a time limit under this Part.
(2)   A party who wants an extension of time must—
(a)   apply when serving the report, summary or notice for which it is required; and
(b)   explain the delay.

PART 20   HEARSAY EVIDENCE

Contents of this Part

B.19 **20.1.   *When this Part applies***   This Part applies—
(a)   in a magistrates' court and in the Crown Court;
(b)   where a party wants to introduce hearsay evidence, within the meaning of section 114 of the Criminal Justice Act 2003.
[Note. Under section 114 of the Criminal Justice Act 2003, a statement not made in oral evidence is admissible as evidence of any matter stated if—

(a)   a *statutory provision makes it admissible;*
(b)   a *rule of law preserved by section 118 makes it admissible;*
(c)   the *parties agree to it being admissible; or*
(d)   it *is in the interests of justice for it to be admissible.*
Under section 115 of the Act—
(a)   a *"statement" means any representation of fact or opinion, by any means, and includes a representation in pictorial form; and*
(b)   a *"matter stated" is something stated by someone with the apparent purpose of—*
        (i)   *causing another person to believe it, or*
        (ii)   *causing another person, or a machine, to act or operate on the basis that the matter is as stated.]*

20.2.   *Notice to introduce hearsay evidence* (1)   This rule applies where a party wants to introduce hearsay evidence for admission under any of the following sections of the Criminal Justice Act 2003—
(a)   section 114(1)(d) (evidence admissible in the interests of justice);
(b)   section 116 (evidence where a witness is unavailable);
(c)   section 117(1)(c) (evidence in a statement prepared for the purposes of criminal proceedings);
(d)   section 121 (multiple hearsay).
(2)   That party must—
(a)   serve notice on—
        (i)   the court officer, and
        (ii)   each other party;
(b)   in the notice—
        (i)   identify the evidence that is hearsay,
        (ii)   set out any facts on which that party relies to make the evidence admissible,
        (iii)   explain how that party will prove those facts if another party disputes them, and
        (iv)   explain why the evidence is admissible; and
(c)   attach to the notice any statement or other document containing the evidence that has not already been served.
(3)   A prosecutor who wants to introduce such evidence must serve the notice not more than—
(a)   28 days after the defendant pleads not guilty, in a magistrates' court; or
(b)   14 days after the defendant pleads not guilty, in the Crown Court.
(4)   A defendant who wants to introduce such evidence must serve the notice as soon as reasonably practicable.
(5)   A party entitled to receive a notice under this rule may waive that entitlement by so informing—
(a)   the party who would have served it; and
(b)   the court.
[Note. The Practice Direction sets out a form of notice for use in connection with this rule.
The sections of the Criminal Justice Act 2003 listed in this rule set out the conditions on which hearsay evidence may be admitted under them.
If notice is not given as this rule requires, then under section 132(5) of the 2003 Act—
(a)   *the evidence is not admissible without the court's permission;*
(b)   *if the court gives permission, it may draw such inferences as appear proper from the failure to give notice; and*
(c)   *the court may take the failure into account in exercising its powers to order costs.*
This rule does not require notice of hearsay evidence that is admissible under any of the following sections of the 2003 Act—
(a)   *section 117 (business and other documents), otherwise than as required by rule 20.2(1)(c);*
(b)   *section 118 (preservation of certain common law categories of admissibility);*
(c)   *section 119 (inconsistent statements);*
(d)   *section 120 (other previous statements of witness); or*
(e)   *section 127 (expert evidence: preparatory work): but see Part 19 for the procedure where a party wants to introduce such evidence.]*

20.3.   *Opposing the introduction of hearsay evidence* (1)   This rule applies where a party objects to the introduction of hearsay evidence.
(2)   That party must—
(a)   apply to the court to determine the objection;
(b)   serve the application on—
        (i)   the court officer, and
        (ii)   each other party;
(c)   serve the application as soon as reasonably practicable, and in any event not more than 14 days after—
        (i)   service of notice to introduce the evidence under rule 20.2,
        (ii)   service of the evidence to which that party objects, if no notice is required by that rule, or
        (iii)   the defendant pleads not guilty
   whichever of those events happens last; and
(d)   in the application, explain—

(i) which, if any, facts set out in a notice under rule 20.2 that party disputes,

(ii) why the evidence is not admissible, and

(iii) any other objection to the evidence.

(3) The court—

(a) may determine an application—

   (i) at a hearing, in public or in private, or

   (ii) without a hearing;

(b) must not determine the application unless the party who served the notice—

   (i) is present, or

   (ii) has had a reasonable opportunity to respond;

(c) may adjourn the application; and

(d) may discharge or vary a determination where it can do so under—

   (i) section 8B of the Magistrates' Courts Act 1980 (ruling at pre-trial hearing in a magistrates' court), or

   (ii) section 9 of the Criminal Justice Act 1987, or section 31 or 40 of the Criminal Procedure and Investigations Act 1996 (ruling at preparatory or other pre-trial hearing in the Crown Court).

20.4. *Unopposed hearsay evidence* (1) This rule applies where—

(a) a party has served notice to introduce hearsay evidence under rule 20.2; and

(b) no other party has applied to the court to determine an objection to the introduction of the evidence.

(2) The court must treat the evidence as if it were admissible by agreement.

[Note. Under section 132(4) of the Criminal Justice Act 2003, rules may provide that evidence is to be treated as admissible by agreement of the parties if notice to introduce that evidence has not been opposed.]

20.5. *Court's power to vary requirements under this Part* (1) The court may—

(a) shorten or extend (even after it has expired) a time limit under this Part;

(b) allow an application or notice to be in a different form to one set out in the Practice Direction, or to be made or given orally;

(c) dispense with the requirement for notice to introduce hearsay evidence.

(2) A party who wants an extension of time must—

(a) apply when serving the application or notice for which it is needed; and

(b) explain the delay.

PART 21 EVIDENCE OF BAD CHARACTER

Contents of this Part

B.20 21.1. *When this Part applies* This Part applies—

(a) in a magistrates' court and in the Crown Court;

(b) where a party wants to introduce evidence of bad character, within the meaning of section 98 of the Criminal Justice Act 2003.

[Note. Under section 98 of the Criminal Justice Act 2003, evidence of a person's bad character means evidence of, or of a disposition towards, misconduct on that person's part, other than evidence that—

(a) has to do with the alleged facts of the offence; or

(b) is evidence of misconduct in connection with the investigation or prosecution.

Under section 100(1) of the Criminal Justice Act 2003, evidence of a non-defendant's bad character is admissible if—

(a) it is important explanatory evidence;

(b) it has substantial probative value in relation to a matter which—

   (i) is a matter in issue in the proceedings, and

   (ii) is of substantial importance in the context of the case as a whole; or

(c) all parties to the proceedings agree to the evidence being admissible.

The section explains requirements (a) and (b). Unless the parties agree to the evidence being admissible, it may not be introduced without the court's permission.

Under section 101(1) of the Criminal Justice Act 2003, evidence of a defendant's bad character is admissible if—

(a) all parties to the proceedings agree to the evidence being admissible;

(b)   the evidence is introduced by the defendant, or is given in answer to a question asked by the defendant in cross-examination which was intended to elicit that evidence;

(c)   it is important explanatory evidence;

(d)   it is relevant to an important matter in issue between the defendant and the prosecution;

(e)   it has substantial probative value in relation to an important matter in issue between the defendant and a co-defendant;

(f)   it is evidence to correct a false impression given by the defendant; or

(g)   the defendant has made an attack on another person's character.

Sections 102 to 106 of the Act supplement those requirements. The court must not admit evidence under (d) or (g) if, on an application by the defendant, the court concludes that to do so would be unfair.]

21.2. *Content of application or notice* (1) A party who wants to introduce evidence of bad character must—

(a)   make an application under rule 21.3, where it is evidence of a non-defendant's bad character;

(b)   give notice under rule 21.4, where it is evidence of a defendant's bad character.

(2)   An application or notice must—

(a)   set out the facts of the misconduct on which that party relies,

(b)   explain how that party will prove those facts (whether by certificate of conviction, other official record, or other evidence), if another party disputes them, and

(c)   explain why the evidence is admissible.

[Note. The Practice Direction sets out forms of application and notice for use in connection with rules 21.3 and 21.4.

The fact that a person was convicted of an offence may be proved under—

(a)   *section 73 of the Police and Criminal Evidence Act 1984 (conviction in the United Kingdom or European Union); or*

(b)   *section 7 of the Evidence Act 1851 (conviction outside the United Kingdom).*

See also sections 117 and 118 of the Criminal Justice Act 2003 (admissibility of evidence contained in business and other documents).

Under section 10 of the Criminal Justice Act 1967, a party may admit a matter of fact.]

21.3. *Application to introduce evidence of a non-defendant's bad character* (1) This rule applies where a party wants to introduce evidence of the bad character of a person other than the defendant.

(2)   That party must serve an application to do so on—

(a)   the court officer; and

(b)   each other party.

(3)   The applicant must serve the application—

(a)   as soon as reasonably practicable; and in any event

(b)   not more than 14 days after the prosecutor discloses material on which the application is based (if the prosecutor is not the applicant).

(4)   A party who objects to the introduction of the evidence must—

(a)   serve notice on—

         (i)   the court officer, and

         (ii)   each other party

   not more than 14 days after service of the application; and

(b)   in the notice explain, as applicable—

         (i)   which, if any, facts of the misconduct set out in the application that party disputes,

         (ii)   what, if any, facts of the misconduct that party admits instead,

         (iii)   why the evidence is not admissible, and

         (iv)   any other objection to the application.

(5)   The court—

(a)   may determine an application—

         (i)   at a hearing, in public or in private, or

         (ii)   without a hearing;

(b)   must not determine the application unless each party other than the applicant—

         (i)   is present, or

         (ii)   has had at least 14 days in which to serve a notice of objection;

(c)   may adjourn the application; and

(d)   may discharge or vary a determination where it can do so under—

         (i)   section 8B of the Magistrates' Courts Act 1980 (ruling at pre-trial hearing in a magistrates' court), or

         (ii)   section 9 of the Criminal Justice Act 1987, or section 31 or 40 of the Criminal Procedure and Investigations Act 1996 (ruling at preparatory or other pre-trial hearing in the Crown Court).

[Note. The Practice Direction sets out a form of application for use in connection with this rule. See also rule 21.5 (reasons for decisions must be given in public).]

21.4. *Notice to introduce evidence of a defendant's bad character* (1) This rule applies where a party wants to introduce evidence of a defendant's bad character.

(2)   A prosecutor or co-defendant who wants to introduce such evidence must serve notice on—

(a)   the court officer; and

(b)   each other party.
(3)   A prosecutor must serve any such notice not more than—
(a)   28 days after the defendant pleads not guilty, in a magistrates' court; or
(b)   14 days after the defendant pleads not guilty, in the Crown Court.
(4)   A co-defendant must serve any such notice—
(a)   as soon as reasonably practicable; and in any event
(b)   not more than 14 days after the prosecutor discloses material on which the notice is based.
(5)   A party who objects to the introduction of the evidence identified by such a notice must—
(a)   apply to the court to determine the objection;
(b)   serve the application on—
           (i)   the court officer, and
           (ii)   each other party
    not more than 14 days after service of the notice; and
(c)   in the application explain, as applicable—
           (i)   which, if any, facts of the misconduct set out in the notice that party disputes,
           (ii)   what, if any, facts of the misconduct that party admits instead,
           (iii)   why the evidence is not admissible,
           (iv)   why it would be unfair to admit the evidence, and
           (v)   any other objection to the notice.
(6)   The court—
(a)   may determine such an application—
           (i)   at a hearing, in public or in private, or
           (ii)   without a hearing;
(b)   must not determine the application unless the party who served the notice—
           (i)   is present, or
           (ii)   has had a reasonable opportunity to respond;
(c)   may adjourn the application; and
(d)   may discharge or vary a determination where it can do so under—
           (i)   section 8B of the Magistrates' Courts Act 1980 (ruling at pre-trial hearing in a magistrates' court), or
           (ii)   section 9 of the Criminal Justice Act 1987, or section 31 or 40 of the Criminal Procedure and Investigations Act 1996 (ruling at preparatory or other pre-trial hearing in the Crown Court).
(7)   A party entitled to receive such a notice may waive that entitlement by so informing—
(a)   the party who would have served it; and
(b)   the court.
(8)   A defendant who wants to introduce evidence of his or her own bad character must—
(a)   give notice, in writing or orally—
           (i)   as soon as reasonably practicable, and in any event
           (ii)   before the evidence is introduced, either by the defendant or in reply to a question asked by the defendant of another party's witness in order to obtain that evidence; and
(b)   in the Crown Court, at the same time give notice (in writing, or orally) of any direction about the defendant's character that the defendant wants the court to give the jury under rule 25.14 (Directions to the jury and taking the verdict).
[Note. The Practice Direction sets out a form of notice for use in connection with this rule.
See also rule 21.5 (reasons for decisions must be given in public).
If notice is not given as this rule requires, then under section 111(4) of the Criminal Justice Act 2003 the court may take the failure into account in exercising its powers to order costs.]

21.5.   Reasons for decisions   The court must announce at a hearing in public (but in the absence of the jury, if there is one) the reasons for a decision—
(a)   to admit evidence as evidence of bad character, or to refuse to do so; or
(b)   to direct an acquittal or a retrial under section 107 of the Criminal Justice Act 2003.
[Note. See section 110 of the Criminal Justice Act 2003.]

21.6.   Court's power to vary requirements under this Part   (1)   The court may—
(a)   shorten or extend (even after it has expired) a time limit under this Part;
(b)   allow an application or notice to be in a different form to one set out in the Practice Direction, or to be made or given orally;
(c)   dispense with a requirement for notice to introduce evidence of a defendant's bad character.
(2)   A party who wants an extension of time must—
(a)   apply when serving the application or notice for which it is needed; and
(b)   explain the delay.

PART 22   EVIDENCE OF A COMPLAINANT'S PREVIOUS SEXUAL BEHAVIOUR

Contents of this Part

B.21 22.1. *When this Part applies* This Part applies—
(a)   in a magistrates' court and in the Crown Court;
(b)   where—
    (i)   section 41 of the Youth Justice and Criminal Evidence Act 1999 prohibits the introduction of evidence or cross-examination about any sexual behaviour of the complainant of a sexual offence, and
    (ii)   despite that prohibition, a defendant wants to introduce such evidence or to cross-examine a witness about such behaviour.
[Note Section 41 of the Youth Justice and Criminal Evidence Act 1999 prohibits evidence or cross-examination about the sexual behaviour of a complainant of a sexual offence, subject to exceptions.
See also—
(a)   section 42 of the 1999 Act, which among other things defines 'sexual behaviour' and 'sexual offence';
(b)   section 34, which prohibits cross-examination by a defendant in person of the complainant of a sexual offence (Part 23 contains relevant rules).]

22.2. *Exercise of court's powers* The court—
(a)   must determine an application under rule 22.4 (Application for permission to introduce evidence or cross-examine)—
    (i)   at a hearing in private, and
    (ii)   in the absence of the complainant;
(b)   must not determine the application unless—
    (i)   each party other than the applicant is present, or has had at least 14 days in which to make representations, and
    (ii)   the court is satisfied that it has been able to take adequate account of the complainant's rights;
(c)   may adjourn the application; and
(d)   may discharge or vary a determination where it can do so under—
    (i)   section 8B of the Magistrates' Courts Act 1980 (ruling at pre-trial hearing in a magistrates' court), or
    (ii)   section 9 of the Criminal Justice Act 1987, or section 31 or 40 of the Criminal Procedure and Investigations Act 1996 (ruling at preparatory or other pre-trial hearing in the Crown Court).
[Note See also section 43 of the Youth Justice and Criminal Evidence Act 1999, which among other things requires an application under section 41 of the Act to be heard in private and in the absence of the complainant.
At a pre-trial hearing a court may make binding rulings about the admissibility of evidence and about questions of law under sections 31 and 40 of the Criminal Procedure and Investigations Act 1996 and section 8A of the Magistrates' Courts Act 1980.]

22.3. *Decisions and reasons* (1) A prosecutor who wants to introduce the evidence of a complainant in respect of whom the court allows the introduction of evidence or cross-examination about any sexual behaviour must—
(a)   inform the complainant of the court's decision as soon as reasonably practicable; and
(b)   explain to the complainant any arrangements that as a result will be made for him or her to give evidence.
(2)   The court must—
(a)   promptly determine an application; and
(b)   allow the prosecutor sufficient time to comply with the requirements of—
    (i)   paragraph (1), and
    (ii)   the code of practice issued under section 32 of the Domestic Violence, Crime and Victims Act 2004.
(3)   The court must announce at a hearing in public—
(a)   the reasons for a decision to allow or refuse an application under rule 22.4; and
(b)   if it allows such an application, the extent to which evidence may be introduced or questions asked.
[Note Under section 43 of the Youth Justice and Criminal Evidence Act 1999—
(a)   the reasons for the court's decision on an application must be given in open court; and
(b)   the court must state in open court the extent to which evidence may be introduced or questions asked.]

22.4. Application for permission to introduce evidence or cross-examine (1)   A defendant who wants to introduce evidence or cross-examine a witness about any sexual behaviour of the complainant must—

(a)   serve an application for permission to do so on—
     (i)   the court officer, and
     (ii)   each other party;
(b)   serve the application—
     (i)   as soon as reasonably practicable after becoming aware of the grounds for doing so, and in any event
     (ii)   not more than 14 days after the prosecutor discloses material on which the application is based.

(2)   The application must—
(a)   identify the issue to which the defendant says the complainant's sexual behaviour is relevant;
(b)   give particulars of—
     (i)   any evidence that the defendant wants to introduce, and
     (ii)   any questions that the defendant wants to ask;
(c)   identify the exception to the prohibition in section 41 of the Youth Justice and Criminal Evidence Act 1999 on which the defendant relies; and
(d)   give the name and date of birth of any witness whose evidence about the complainant's sexual behaviour the defendant wants to introduce.

22.5. Application containing information withheld from another party (1)   This rule applies where—

(a)   an applicant serves an application under rule 22.4 (Application for permission to introduce evidence or cross-examine); and
(b)   the application includes information that the applicant thinks ought not be revealed to another party.

(2)   The applicant must—
(a)   omit that information from the part of the application that is served on that other party;
(b)   mark the other part to show that, unless the court otherwise directs, it is only for the court; and
(c)   in that other part, explain why the applicant has withheld that information from that other party.

(3)   If the court so directs, the hearing of an application to which this rule applies may be, wholly or in part, in the absence of a party from whom information has been withheld.

(4)   At the hearing of an application to which this rule applies—
(a)   the general rule is that the court must consider, in the following sequence—
     (i)   representations first by the applicant and then by each other party, in all the parties' presence, and then
     (ii)   further representations by the applicant, in the absence of a party from whom information has been withheld; but
(b)   the court may direct other arrangements for the hearing.

[Note See section 43(3)(c) of the Youth Justice and Criminal Evidence Act 1999.]

22.6. Representations in response (1)   This rule applies where a party wants to make representations about—

(a)   an application under rule 22.4 (Application for permission to introduce evidence or cross-examine); or
(b)   a proposed variation or discharge of a decision allowing such an application.

(2)   Such a party must—
(a)   serve the representations on—
     (i)   the court officer, and
     (ii)   each other party; and
(b)   do so not more than 14 days after, as applicable—
     (i)   service of the application, or
     (ii)   notice of the proposal to vary or discharge.

(3)   Where representations include information that the person making them thinks ought not be revealed to another party, that person must—
(a)   omit that information from the representations served on that other party;
(b)   mark the information to show that, unless the court otherwise directs, it is only for the court; and
(c)   with that information include an explanation of why it has been withheld from that other party.

(4)   Representations against an application under rule 22.4 must explain the grounds of objection.

(5)   Representations against the variation or discharge of a decision must explain why it should not be varied or discharged.

22.7. Special measures, etc for a witness (1)   This rule applies where the court allows an application under rule 22.4 (Application for permission to introduce evidence or cross-examine).

(2)   Despite the time limits in rule 18.3 (Making an application for a direction or order)—

(a)   a party may apply not more than 14 days after the court's decision for a special measures direction or for the variation of an existing special measures direction; and

(b)   the court may shorten the time for opposing that application.   (3)   Where the court allows the cross-examination of a witness, the court must give directions for the appropriate treatment and questioning of that witness in accordance with rule 3.9(6) and (7) (setting ground rules for the conduct of questioning).

[Note Special measures to improve the quality of evidence given by certain witnesses may be directed by the court under section 19 of the Youth Justice and Criminal Evidence Act 1999 and varied under section 20. An application for a special measures direction may be made by a party under Part 18 or the court may make a direction on its own initiative. Rule 18.13(2) sets the usual time limit (14 days) for opposing a special measures application.]

22.8.   Court's power to vary requirements under this Part   The court may shorten or extend (even after it has expired) a time limit under this Part.

PART 23   RESTRICTION ON CROSS-EXAMINATION BY A DEFENDANT

Contents of this Part

General rules

GENERAL RULES

B.22   *23.1.   When this Part applies*   This Part applies where—

(a)   a defendant may not cross-examine in person a witness because of section 34 or section 35 of the Youth Justice and Criminal Evidence Act 1999 (Complainants in proceedings for sexual offences; Child complainants and other child witnesses);

(b)   the court can prohibit a defendant from cross-examining in person a witness under section 36 of that Act (Direction prohibiting accused from cross-examining particular witness).

[Note. Under section 34 of the Youth Justice and Criminal Evidence Act 1999, no defendant charged with a sexual offence may cross-examine in person a witness who is the complainant, either—

(a)   *in connection with that offence; or*

(b)   *in connection with any other offence (of whatever nature) with which that defendant is charged in the proceedings.*

Under section 35 of the 1999 Act, no defendant charged with an offence listed in that section may cross-examine in person a protected witness, either—

(a)   *in connection with that offence; or*

(b)   *in connection with any other offence (of whatever nature) with which that defendant is charged in the proceedings.*

A 'protected witness' is one who—

(a)   *either is the complainant or is alleged to have been a witness to the commission of the offence;*

(b)   *either is a child, within the meaning of section 35, or is due to be cross-examined after giving evidence in chief—*

(i)   *by means of a video recording made when the witness was a child, or*

(ii)   *in any other way when the witness was a child.*

Under section 36 of the 1999 Act, where neither section 34 nor section 35 applies the court may give a direction prohibiting the defendant from cross-examining, or further cross-examining, in person a witness, on application by the prosecutor or on the court's own initiative. See also rules 23.3 to 23.7.]

23.2.   Appointment of advocate to cross-examine witness   (1)   This rule applies where a defendant may not cross-examine in person a witness in consequence of—

(a)   the prohibition imposed by section 34 or section 35 of the Youth Justice and Criminal Evidence Act 1999; or

(b)   a prohibition imposed by the court under section 36 of the 1999 Act.

(2)   The court must, as soon as practicable, explain in terms the defendant can understand (with help, if necessary)—

(a)   the prohibition and its effect;

(b)   that if the defendant will not be represented by a lawyer with a right of audience in the court for the purposes of the case then the defendant is entitled to arrange for such a lawyer to cross-examine the witness on his or her behalf;

(c)   that the defendant must notify the court officer of the identity of any such lawyer, with details of how to contact that person, by no later than a date set by the court;

(d)   that if the defendant does not want to make such arrangements, or if the defendant gives no such notice by that date, then—

     (i)   the court must decide whether it is necessary in the interests of justice to appoint such a lawyer to cross-examine the witness in the defendant's interests, and

     (ii)   if the court decides that that is necessary, the court will appoint a lawyer chosen by the court who will not be responsible to the defendant.

(3)   Having given those explanations, the court must—

(a)   ask whether the defendant wants to arrange for a lawyer to cross-examine the witness, and set a date by when the defendant must notify the court officer of the identity of that lawyer if the answer to that question is 'yes';

(b)   if the answer to that question is 'no', or if by the date set the defendant has given no such notice—

     (i)   decide whether it is necessary in the interests of justice for the witness to be cross-examined by an advocate appointed to represent the defendant's interests, and

     (ii)   if the court decides that that is necessary, give directions for the appointment of such an advocate.

(4)   The court may give the explanations and ask the questions required by this rule—

(a)   at a hearing, in public or in private; or

(b)   without a hearing, by written notice to the defendant.

(5)   The court may extend (even after it has expired) the time limit that it sets under paragraph (3)(a)—

(a)   on application by the defendant; or

(b)   on its own initiative.

(6)   Paragraphs (7), (8), (9) and (10) apply where the court appoints an advocate.

(7)   The directions that the court gives under paragraph (3)(b)(ii) must provide for the supply to the advocate of a copy of—

(a)   all material served by one party on the other, whether before or after the advocate's appointment, to which applies—

     (i)   Part 8 (Initial details of the prosecution case),

     (ii)   in the Crown Court, rule 9.15 (service of prosecution evidence in a case sent for trial),

     (iii) Part 16 (Written witness statements),

     (iv) Part 19 (Expert evidence),

     (v)   Part 20 (Hearsay evidence),

     (vi)   Part 21 (Evidence of bad character),

     (vii) Part 22 (Evidence of a complainant's previous sexual behaviour);

(b)   any material disclosed, given or served, whether before or after the advocate's appointment, which is—

     (i)   prosecution material disclosed to the defendant under section 3 (Initial duty of prosecutor to disclose) or section 7A (Continuing duty of prosecutor to disclose) of the Criminal Procedure and Investigations Act 1996,

     (ii)   a defence statement given by the defendant under section 5 (Compulsory disclosure by accused) or section 6 (Voluntary disclosure by accused) of the 1996 Act,

     (iii) a defence witness notice given by the defendant under section 6C of that Act (Notification of intention to call defence witnesses), or

     (iv) an application by the defendant under section 8 of that Act (Application by accused for disclosure);

(c)   any case management questionnaire prepared for the purposes of the trial or, as the case may be, the appeal; and

(d)   all case management directions given by the court for the purposes of the trial or the appeal.

(8)   Where the defendant has given a defence statement—

(a)   section 8(2) of the Criminal Procedure and Investigations Act 1996 is modified to allow the advocate, as well as the defendant, to apply for an order for prosecution disclosure under that subsection if the advocate has reasonable cause to believe that there is prosecution material concerning the witness which is required by section 7A of the Act to be disclosed to the defendant and has not been; and

(b)   rule 15.5 (Defendant's application for prosecution disclosure) applies to an application by the advocate as it does to an application by the defendant.

(9)   Before receiving evidence the court must establish, with the active assistance of the parties and of the advocate, and in the absence of any jury in the Crown Court—

(a)   what issues will be the subject of the advocate's cross-examination; and

(b)   whether the court's permission is required for any proposed question, for example where Part 21 or Part 22 applies.

(10)   The appointment terminates at the conclusion of the cross-examination of the witness.
[Note. See section 38 of the Youth Justice and Criminal Evidence Act 1999. Under section 38(8) the references in that section to a 'legal representative' are to a representative who is an advocate within the meaning of rule 2.2.]
"Under section 38(7) of the 1999 Act, where the court appoints an advocate Criminal Procedure Rules may apply with modifications any of the provisions of Part I of the Criminal Procedure and Investigations Act 1996. A summary of the disclosure requirements of the 1996 Act is at the end of Part 15 (Disclosure). Under section 5 of that Act, in the Crown Court the defendant must give a defence statement. Under section 6, in a magistrates' court the defendant may give such a statement but need not do so. Under section 6C, in the Crown Court and in magistrates' courts the defendant must give a defence witness notice indicating whether he or she intends to call any witnesses (other than him or herself) and, if so, identifying them. Under section 8 a defendant may apply for prosecution disclosure only if the defendant has given a defence statement."; and

APPLICATION TO PROHIBIT CROSS-EXAMINATION

23.3.   *Exercise of court's powers*   (1)   The court may decide whether to impose or discharge a prohibition against cross-examination under section 36 of the Youth Justice and Criminal Evidence Act 1999—
(a)   at a hearing, in public or in private, or without a hearing;
(b)   in a party's absence, if that party—
　　(i)   applied for the prohibition or discharge, or
　　(ii)   has had at least 14 days in which to make representations.
(2)   The court must announce, at a hearing in public before the witness gives evidence, the reasons for a decision—
(a)   to impose or discharge such a prohibition; or
(b)   to refuse to do so.
[Note. See section 37 of the Youth Justice and Criminal Evidence Act 1999.]

23.4.   *Application to prohibit cross-examination*   (1)   This rule applies where under section 36 of the Youth Justice and Criminal Evidence Act 1999 the prosecutor wants the court to prohibit the cross-examination of a witness by a defendant in person.
(2)   The prosecutor must—
(a)   apply in writing, as soon as reasonably practicable after becoming aware of the grounds for doing so; and
(b)   serve the application on—
　　(i)   the court officer,
　　(ii)   the defendant who is the subject of the application, and
　　(iii)   any other defendant, unless the court otherwise directs.
(3)   The application must—
(a)   report any views that the witness has expressed about whether he or she is content to be cross-examined by the defendant in person;
(b)   identify—
　　(i)   the nature of the questions likely to be asked, having regard to the issues in the case,
　　(ii)   any relevant behaviour of the defendant at any stage of the case, generally and in relation to the witness,
　　(iii)   any relationship, of any nature, between the witness and the defendant,
　　(iv)   any other defendant in the case who is subject to such a prohibition in respect of the witness, and
　　(v)   any special measures direction made in respect of the witness, or for which an application has been made;
(c)   explain why the quality of evidence given by the witness on cross-examination—
　　(i)   is likely to be diminished if no such prohibition is imposed, and
　　(ii)   would be likely to be improved if it were imposed; and
(d)   explain why it would not be contrary to the interests of justice to impose the prohibition.
[Note. The Practice Direction sets out a form of application for use in connection with this rule.]

23.5.   *Application to discharge prohibition imposed by the court*   (1)   A party who wants the court to discharge a prohibition against cross-examination which the court imposed under section 36 of the Youth Justice and Criminal Evidence Act 1999 must—
(a)   apply in writing, as soon as reasonably practicable after becoming aware of the grounds for doing so; and
(b)   serve the application on—
　　(i)   the court officer, and
　　(ii)   each other party.
(2)   The applicant must—
(a)   explain what material circumstances have changed since the prohibition was imposed; and
(b)   ask for a hearing, if the applicant wants one, and explain why it is needed.
[Note. Under section 37 of the Youth Justice and Criminal Evidence Act 1999, the court can discharge a prohibition against cross-examination which it has imposed—
(a)   on application, if there has been a material change of circumstances; or
(b)   on its own initiative.]

23.6. Application containing information withheld from another party (1) This rule applies where—

(a) an applicant serves an application for the court to impose a prohibition against cross-examination, or for the discharge of such a prohibition; and

(b) the application includes information that the applicant thinks ought not be revealed to another party.

(2) The applicant must—

(a) omit that information from the part of the application that is served on that other party;

(b) mark the other part to show that, unless the court otherwise directs, it is only for the court; and

(c) in that other part, explain why the applicant has withheld that information from that other party.

(3) Any hearing of an application to which this rule applies—

(a) must be in private, unless the court otherwise directs; and

(b) if the court so directs, may be, wholly or in part, in the absence of a party from whom information has been withheld.

(4) At any hearing of an application to which this rule applies—

(a) the general rule is that the court must consider, in the following sequence—

   (i) representations first by the applicant and then by each other party, in all the parties' presence, and then

   (ii) further representations by the applicant, in the absence of a party from whom information has been withheld; but

(b) the court may direct other arrangements for the hearing.

[Note. See section 37 of the Youth Justice and Criminal Evidence Act 1999.]

23.7. Representations in response (1) This rule applies where a party wants to make representations about—

(a) an application under rule 23.4 for a prohibition against cross-examination;

(b) an application under rule 23.5 for the discharge of such a prohibition; or

(c) a prohibition or discharge that the court proposes on its own initiative.

(2) Such a party must—

(a) serve the representations on—

   (i) the court officer, and

   (ii) each other party;

(b) do so not more than 14 days after, as applicable—

   (i) service of the application, or

   (ii) notice of the prohibition or discharge that the court proposes; and

(c) ask for a hearing, if that party wants one, and explain why it is needed.

(3) Representations against a prohibition must explain in what respect the conditions for imposing it are not met.

(4) Representations against the discharge of a prohibition must explain why it should not be discharged.

(5) Where representations include information that the person making them thinks ought not be revealed to another party, that person must—

(a) omit that information from the representations served on that other party;

(b) mark the information to show that, unless the court otherwise directs, it is only for the court; and

(c) with that information include an explanation of why it has been withheld from that other party.

23.8. Court's power to vary requirements (1) The court may—

(a) shorten or extend (even after it has expired) a time limit under rule 23.4 (Application to prohibit cross-examination), rule 23.5 (Application to discharge prohibition imposed by the court) or rule 23.7 (Representations in response); and

(b) allow an application or representations required by any of those rules to be made in a different form to one set out in the Practice Direction, or to be made orally.

(2) A person who wants an extension of time must—

(a) apply when serving the application or representations for which it is needed; and

(b) explain the delay.

Part 24   Trial and Sentence in a Magistrates' Court

Contents of this Part

Note

[Note. Part 3 contains rules about case management that apply at trial as well as during preparation for trial. The rules in this Part must be read in conjunction with those rules.]

B.23 24.1. *When this Part applies* (1) This Part applies in a magistrates' court where—
- (a)   the court tries a case;
- (b)   the defendant pleads guilty;
- (c)   under section 14 or section 16E of the Magistrates' Courts Act 1980, the defendant makes a statutory declaration of not having found out about the case until after the trial began;
- (d)   under section 142 of the 1980 Act, the court can—
    - (i)   set aside a conviction, or
    - (ii)   vary or rescind a costs order, or an order to which Part 31 applies (Behaviour orders).
- (2)   Where the defendant is under 18, in this Part—
- (a)   a reference to convicting the defendant includes a reference to finding the defendant guilty of an offence; and
- (b)   a reference to sentence includes a reference to an order made on a finding of guilt.

[Note. A magistrates' court's powers to try an allegation of an offence are contained in section 2 of the Magistrates' Courts Act 1980. In relation to a defendant under 18, they are contained in sections 45, 46 and 48 of the Children and Young Persons Act 1933.

See also section 18 of the Children and Young Persons Act 1963, section 47 of the Crime and Disorder Act 1998 and section 9 of the Powers of Criminal Courts (Sentencing) Act 2000.

The exercise of the court's powers is affected by—
- (a)   the classification of the offence (and the general rule, subject to exceptions, is that a magistrates' court must try—
    - (i)   an offence classified as one that can be tried only in a magistrates' court (in other legislation, described as triable only summarily), and
    - (ii)   an offence classified as one that can be tried either in a magistrates' court or in the Crown Court (in other legislation, described as triable either way) that has been allocated for trial in a magistrates' court); and
- (b)   the defendant's age (and the general rule, subject to exceptions, is that an allegation of an offence against a defendant under 18 must be tried in a magistrates' court sitting as a youth court, irrespective of the classification of the offence and without allocation for trial there).

Under sections 10, 14, 27A, 121 and 148 of the Magistrates' Courts Act 1980 and the Justices of the Peace Rules 2016, the court—
- (a)   must comprise at least two but not more than three justices, or a District Judge (Magistrates' Courts) (but a single member can adjourn the hearing);
- (b)   must not include any member who adjudicated at a hearing to which rule 24.17 applies (defendant's declaration of no knowledge of hearing);
- (c)   when reaching a verdict, must not include any member who was absent from any part of the hearing;
- (d)   when passing sentence, need not include any of the members who reached the verdict (but may do so).

Under section 16A of the Magistrates' Courts Act 1980, the court may comprise a single justice where—
- (a)   the offence charged is a summary offence not punishable with imprisonment;
- (b)   the defendant was at least 18 years old when charged;
- (c)   the court is satisfied that specified documents giving notice of the procedure under that section and containing other specified information have been served on the defendant; and
- (d)   the defendant has not served notice of an intention to plead not guilty, or of a desire not to be tried in accordance with that section.

Under the Youth Courts (Constitution of Committees and Right to Preside) Rules 2007, where the court is a youth court comprising justices—
- (a)   each member must be qualified to sit as a member of that youth court; and
- (b)   the members must include at least one man and one woman, unless—

(i)   *either is unavailable, and*

(ii)   *the members present decide that the hearing will be delayed unreasonably if they do not proceed.*

Under section 45 of the Children and Young Persons Act 1933 and under the Justices of the Peace Rules 2016, where the court is a youth court comprising justices each member must be authorised to sit as a member of that youth court..

Under section 150 of the Magistrates' Courts Act 1980, where two or more justices are present one may act on behalf of all.

Section 59 of the Children and Young Persons Act 1933 requires that—

(a)   *the expressions 'conviction' and 'sentence' must not be used by a magistrates' court dealing with a defendant under 18; and*

(b)   *a reference in legislation to a defendant who is convicted, to a conviction, or to a sentence, must be read as including a reference to a defendant who is found guilty of an offence, a finding of guilt, or an order made on a finding of guilt, respectively.*

Under section 14 of the Magistrates' Courts Act 1980, proceedings which begin with a summons or requisition will become void if the defendant, at any time during or after the trial, makes a statutory declaration that he or she did not know of them until a date after the trial began. See rule 24.17.

Under section 142 of the Magistrates' Courts Act 1980—

(a)   *where a defendant is convicted by a magistrates' court, the court may order that the case should be heard again by different justices; and*

(b)   *the court may vary or rescind an order which it has made when dealing with a convicted defendant,*

if in either case it appears to the court to be in the interests of justice to do so. See rule 24.18.

See also Part 32 (Breach, revocation and amendment of community and other orders). Rule 32.4 (Procedure on application by responsible officer) applies rules in this Part to the procedure with which that rule deals.]

24.2.   *General rules*   (1)   Where this Part applies—

(a)   the general rule is that the hearing must be in public; but

(b)   the court may exercise any power it has to—

    (i)   impose reporting restrictions,

    (ii)   withhold information from the public, or

    (iii)   order a hearing in private; and

(c)   unless the court otherwise directs, only the following may attend a hearing in a youth court—

    (i)   the parties and their legal representatives,

    (ii)   a defendant's parents, guardian or other supporting adult,

    (iii)   a witness,

    (iv)   anyone else directly concerned in the case, and

    (v)   a representative of a news-gathering or reporting organisation.

(2)   Unless already done, the justices' legal adviser or the court must—

(a)   read the allegation of the offence to the defendant;

(b)   explain, in terms the defendant can understand (with help, if necessary)—

    (i)   the allegation, and

    (ii)   what the procedure at the hearing will be;

(c)   ask whether the defendant has been advised about the potential effect on sentence of a guilty plea;

(d)   ask whether the defendant pleads guilty or not guilty; and

(e)   take the defendant's plea.

(3)   The court may adjourn the hearing—

(a)   at any stage, to the same or to another magistrates' court; or

(b)   to a youth court, where the court is not itself a youth court and the defendant is under 18.

(4)   Paragraphs (1) and (2) of this rule do not apply where the court tries a case under rule 24.9 (Single justice procedure: special rules).

[Note. See sections 10, 16A, 27A, 29 and 121 of the Magistrates' Courts Act 1980 and sections 46 and 47 of the Children and Young Persons Act 1933.

Where the case has been allocated for trial in a magistrates' court, part of the procedure under rule 24.2(2) will have taken place.

Part 6 contains rules about reporting, etc restrictions. For a list of the court's powers to impose reporting and access restrictions, see the note to rule 6.1.

Under section 34A of the Children and Young Persons Act 1933, the court—

(a)   *may require the defendant's parents or guardian to attend court with the defendant, where the defendant is under 18; and*

(b)   *must do so, where the defendant is under 16,*

unless satisfied that that would be unreasonable.

Part 7 contains rules about (among other things) the issue of a summons to a parent or guardian. Part 46 (Representatives) contains rules allowing a parent, guardian or other supporting adult to help a defendant under 18.]

24.3.   *Procedure on plea of not guilty*   (1)   This rule applies—

(a)   if the defendant has—

    (i)   entered a plea of not guilty, or

    (ii)   not entered a plea; or

(b)   if, in either case, it appears to the court that there may be grounds for making a hospital order without convicting the defendant.

(2)   If a not guilty plea was taken on a previous occasion, the justices' legal adviser or the court must ask the defendant to confirm that plea.

(3)   In the following sequence—

(a)   the prosecutor may summarise the prosecution case, concisely identifying the relevant law, outlining the facts and indicating the matters likely to be in dispute;

(b)   to help the members of the court to understand the case and resolve any issue in it, the court may invite the defendant concisely to identify what is in issue;

(c)   the prosecutor must introduce the evidence on which the prosecution case relies;

(d)   at the conclusion of the prosecution case, on the defendant's application or on its own initiative, the court—

(i)   may acquit on the ground that the prosecution evidence is insufficient for any reasonable court properly to convict, but

(ii)   must not do so unless the prosecutor has had an opportunity to make representations;

(e)   the justices' legal adviser or the court must explain, in terms the defendant can understand (with help, if necessary)—

(i)   the right to give evidence, and

(ii)   the potential effect of not doing so at all, or of refusing to answer a question while doing so;

(f)   the defendant may introduce evidence;

(g)   a party may introduce further evidence if it is then admissible (for example, because it is in rebuttal of evidence already introduced);

(h)   the prosecutor may make final representations in support of the prosecution case, where—

(i)   the defendant is represented by a legal representative, or

(ii)   whether represented or not, the defendant has introduced evidence other than his or her own; and

(i)   the defendant may make final representations in support of the defence case.

(4)   Where a party wants to introduce evidence or make representations after that party's opportunity to do so under paragraph (3), the court—

(a)   may refuse to receive any such evidence or representations; and

(b)   must not receive any such evidence or representations after it has announced its verdict.

(5)   If the court—

(a)   convicts the defendant; or

(b)   makes a hospital order instead of doing so,

it must give sufficient reasons to explain its decision.

(6)   If the court acquits the defendant, it may—

(a)   give an explanation of its decision; and

(b)   exercise any power it has to make—

(i)   a behaviour order,

(ii)   a costs order.

[Note. See section 9 of the Magistrates' Courts Act 1980.

Under section 37(3) of the Mental Health Act 1983, if the court is satisfied that the defendant did the act or made the omission alleged, then it may make a hospital order without convicting the defendant.

Under section 35 of the Criminal Justice and Public Order Act 1994, the court may draw such inferences as appear proper from a defendant's failure to give evidence, or refusal without good cause to answer a question while doing so. The procedure set out in rule 24.3(3)(e) is prescribed by that section.

The admissibility of evidence that a party introduces is governed by rules of evidence.

Section 2 of the Criminal Procedure Act 1865 and section 3 of the Criminal Evidence Act 1898 restrict the circumstances in which the prosecutor may make final representations without the court's permission.

See rule 24.11 for the procedure if the court convicts the defendant.

Part 31 contains rules about behaviour orders.]

24.4. Evidence of a witness in person (1)   This rule applies where a party wants to introduce evidence by calling a witness to give that evidence in person.

(2)   Unless the court otherwise directs—

(a)   a witness waiting to give evidence must not wait inside the courtroom, unless that witness is—

(i)   a party, or

(ii)   an expert witness;

(b)   a witness who gives evidence in the courtroom must do so from the place provided for that purpose; and

(c)   a witness' address must not be announced unless it is relevant to an issue in the case.

(3)   Unless other legislation otherwise provides, before giving evidence a witness must take an oath or affirm.

(4)   In the following sequence—

(a)   the party who calls a witness must ask questions in examination-in-chief;

(b) every other party may ask questions in cross-examination;

(c) the party who called the witness may ask questions in re-examination.

(5) If other legislation so permits, at any time while giving evidence a witness may refer to a record of that witness' recollection of events.

(6) The justices' legal adviser or the court may—

(a) ask a witness questions; and in particular

(b) where the defendant is not represented, ask any question necessary in the defendant's interests.

[Note. Section 53 of the Youth Justice and Criminal Evidence Act 1999 provides that everyone is competent to give evidence in criminal proceedings unless unable to understand questions put or give intelligible answers. See also section 1 of the Criminal Evidence Act 1898.

Sections 1, 3, 5 and 6 of the Oaths Act 1978 provide for the taking of oaths and the making of affirmations, and for the words that must be used. Section 28 of the Children and Young Persons Act 1963 provides that in a youth court, and where a witness in any court is under 18, an oath must include the words 'I promise' in place of the words 'I swear'. Under sections 55 and 56 of the Youth Justice and Criminal Evidence Act 1999, a person may give evidence without taking an oath, or making an affirmation, where that person (i) is under 14 or (ii) has an insufficient appreciation of the solemnity of the occasion and of the particular responsibility to tell the truth which is involved in taking an oath.

The questions that may be put to a witness—

(a) *by a party are governed by rules of evidence, for example—*

    (i) *the rule that a question must be relevant to what is in issue,*

    (ii) *the rule that the party who calls a witness must not ask that witness a leading question about what is in dispute, and*

    (iii) *the rule that a party who calls a witness may contradict that witness only in limited circumstances (see section 3 of the Criminal Procedure Act 1865);*

(b) *by the justices' legal adviser or the court are in their discretion, but that is subject to—*

    (i) *rules of evidence, and*

    (ii) *rule 1.3 (the application by the court of the overriding objective).*

Under sections 34, 35 and 36 of the Youth Justice and Criminal Evidence Act 1999, a defendant who is not represented may not cross-examine a witness where—

(a) *the defendant is charged with a sexual offence against the witness;*

(b) *the defendant is charged with a sexual offence, or one of certain other offences, and the witness is a child; or*

(c) *the court prohibits the defendant from cross-examining the witness.*

Part 23 contains rules relevant to restrictions on cross-examination.

Under section 139 of the Criminal Justice Act 2003, a witness may refresh his or her memory by referring to a record made before the hearing, either contained in a document made or verified by the witness, or in the transcript of a sound recording, if—

(a) *the witness states that it records his or her recollection of events at that earlier time; and*

(b) *that recollection is likely to have been significantly better when the record was made than at the time of the hearing.*

In some circumstances, a witness may give evidence in accordance with special measures directed by the court under section 19 of the Youth Justice and Criminal Evidence Act 1999, or by live link under section 32 of the Criminal Justice Act 1988 or section 51 of the Criminal Justice Act 2003. Part 18 contains relevant rules.]

24.5. *Evidence of a witness in writing* (1) This rule applies where a party wants to introduce in evidence the written statement of a witness to which applies—

(a) Part 16 (Written witness statements);

(b) Part 19 (Expert evidence); or

(c) Part 20 (Hearsay evidence).

(2) If the court admits such evidence—

(a) the court must read the statement; and

(b) unless the court otherwise directs, if any member of the public, including any reporter, is present, each relevant part of the statement must be read or summarised aloud.

[Note. See Parts 16, 19 and 20, and the other legislation to which those Parts apply. The admissibility of evidence that a party introduces is governed by rules of evidence.]

24.6. *Evidence by admission* (1) This rule applies where—

(a) a party introduces in evidence a fact admitted by another party; or

(b) parties jointly admit a fact.

(2) Unless the court otherwise directs, a written record must be made of the admission.

[Note. See section 10 of the Criminal Justice Act 1967. The admissibility of evidence that a party introduces is governed by rules of evidence.]

24.7. *Procedure on plea of guilty* (1) This rule applies if—

(a) the defendant pleads guilty; and

(b) the court is satisfied that the plea represents a clear acknowledgement of guilt.

(2) The court may convict the defendant without receiving evidence.

[Note. See section 9 of the Magistrates' Courts Act 1980.]

24.8. *Written guilty plea: special rules* (1) This rule applies where—

(a) the offence alleged—

    (i) can be tried only in a magistrates' court, and

(ii)   is not one specified under section 12(1)(a) of the Magistrates' Courts Act 1980;

(b)   the defendant is at least 16 years old;

(c)   the prosecutor has served on the defendant—

    (i)   the summons or requisition,

    (ii)   the material listed in paragraph (2) on which the prosecutor relies to set out the facts of the offence,

    (iii)   the material listed in paragraph (3) on which the prosecutor relies to provide the court with information relevant to sentence,

    (iv)   a notice that the procedure set out in this rule applies, and

    (v)   a notice for the defendant's use if the defendant wants to plead guilty without attending court; and

(d)   the prosecutor has served on the court officer—

    (i)   copies of those documents, and

    (ii)   a certificate of service of those documents on the defendant.

(2)   The material that the prosecutor must serve to set out the facts of the offence is—

(a)   a summary of the evidence on which the prosecution case is based;

(b)   any—

    (i)   written witness statement to which Part 16 (Written witness statements) applies, or

    (ii)   document or extract setting out facts; or

(c)   any combination of such a summary, statement, document or extract.

(3)   The material that the prosecutor must serve to provide information relevant to sentence is—

(a)   details of any previous conviction of the defendant which the prosecutor considers relevant, other than any conviction listed in the defendant's driving record;

(b)   if applicable, a notice that the defendant's driving record will be made available to the court;

(c)   a notice containing or describing any other information about the defendant, relevant to sentence, which will be made available to the court.

(4)   A defendant who wants to plead guilty without attending court must, before the hearing date specified in the summons or requisition—

(a)   serve a notice of guilty plea on the court officer; and

(b)   include with that notice—

    (i)   any representations that the defendant wants the court to consider, and

    (ii)   a statement of the defendant's assets and other financial circumstances.

(5)   A defendant who wants to withdraw such a notice must notify the court officer in writing before the hearing date.

(6)   If the defendant does not withdraw the notice before the hearing date, then on or after that date—

(a)   to establish the facts of the offence and other information about the defendant relevant to sentence, the court may take account only of—

    (i)   information contained in a document served by the prosecutor under paragraph (1),

    (ii)   any previous conviction listed in the defendant's driving record, where the offence is under the Road Traffic Regulation Act 1984, the Road Traffic Act 1988, the Road Traffic (Consequential Provisions) Act 1988 or the Road Traffic (Driver Licensing and Information Systems) Act 1989,

    (iii)   any other information about the defendant, relevant to sentence, of which the prosecutor served notice under paragraph (1), and

    (iv)   any representations and any other information served by the defendant under paragraph (4)

    and rule 24.11(3) to (9) inclusive must be read accordingly;

(b)   unless the court otherwise directs, the prosecutor need not attend; and

(c)   the court may accept such a guilty plea and pass sentence in the defendant's absence.

(7)   With the defendant's agreement, the court may deal with the case in the same way as under paragraph (6) where the defendant is present and—

(a)   has served a notice of guilty plea under paragraph (4); or

(b)   pleads guilty there and then.

[Note. The procedure set out in this rule is prescribed by sections 12 and 12A of the Magistrates' Courts Act 1980. Under section 12(1)(a), the Secretary of State can specify offences to which the procedure will not apply. None has been specified.

Under section 1 of the Magistrates' Courts Act 1980 a justice of the peace may issue a summons requiring a defendant to attend court to answer an allegation of an offence. Under section 29 of the Criminal Justice Act 2003 a prosecutor authorised under that section may issue a written charge alleging an offence and a requisition requiring a defendant to attend court. Part 7 contains relevant rules.

For the court's power, where this rule applies, to take account of a previous conviction listed in a defendant's driving record, see section 13(3A) of the Road Traffic Offenders Act 1988.

The Practice Direction sets out forms of notice for use in connection with this rule.]

24.9.   *Single justice procedure: special rules*   (1)   This rule applies where—

(a)   the offence alleged—

    (i)   can be tried only in a magistrates' court, and

    (ii)   is not one punishable with imprisonment;

(b)   the defendant is at least 18 years old;

(c)   the prosecutor has served on the defendant—

    (i)   a written charge,

    (ii)   the material listed in paragraph (2) on which the prosecutor relies to set out the facts of the offence,

    (iii)   the material listed in paragraph (3) on which the prosecutor relies to provide the court with information relevant to sentence,

    (iv)   a notice that the procedure set out in this rule applies,

    (v)   a notice for the defendant's use if the defendant wants to plead guilty,

    (vi)   a notice for the defendant's use if the defendant wants to plead guilty but wants the case dealt with at a hearing by a court comprising more than one justice, and

    (vii) a notice for the defendant's use if the defendant wants to plead not guilty; and

(d)   the prosecutor has served on the court officer—

    (i)   copies of those documents, and

    (ii)   a certificate of service of those documents on the defendant.

(2)   The material that the prosecutor must serve to set out the facts of the offence is—

(a)   a summary of the evidence on which the prosecution case is based;

(b)   any—

    (i)   written witness statement to which Part 16 (Written witness statements) applies, or

    (ii)   document or extract setting out facts; or

(c)   any combination of such a summary, statement, document or extract.

(3)   The material that the prosecutor must serve to provide information relevant to sentence is—

(a)   details of any previous conviction of the defendant which the prosecutor considers relevant, other than any conviction listed in the defendant's driving record;

(b)   if applicable, a notice that the defendant's driving record will be made available to the court;

(c)   a notice containing or describing any other information about the defendant, relevant to sentence, which will be made available to the court.

(4)   Not more than 21 days after service on the defendant of the documents listed in paragraph (1)(c)—

(a)   a defendant who wants to plead guilty must serve a notice to that effect on the court officer and include with that notice—

    (i)   any representations that the defendant wants the court to consider, and

    (ii)   a statement of the defendant's assets and other financial circumstances;

(b)   a defendant who wants to plead guilty but wants the case dealt with at a hearing by a court comprising more than one justice must serve a notice to that effect on the court officer;

(c)   a defendant who wants to plead not guilty must serve a notice to that effect on the court officer.

(5)   If within 21 days of service on the defendant of the documents listed in paragraph (1)(c) the defendant serves a notice to plead guilty under paragraph (4)(a)—

(a)   the court officer must arrange for the court to deal with the case in accordance with that notice; and

(b)   the time for service of any other notice under paragraph (4) expires at once.

(6)   If within 21 days of service on the defendant of the documents listed in paragraph (1)(c) the defendant wants to withdraw a notice which he or she has served under paragraph (4)(b) (notice to plead guilty at a hearing) or under paragraph (4)(c) (notice to plead not guilty), the defendant must—

(a)   serve notice of that withdrawal on the court officer; and

(b)   serve any substitute notice under paragraph (4).

(7)   Paragraph (8) applies where by the date of trial the defendant has not—

(a)   served notice under paragraph (4)(b) or (c) of wanting to plead guilty at a hearing, or wanting to plead not guilty; or

(b)   given notice to that effect under section 16B(2) of the Magistrates' Courts Act 1980.

(8)   Where this paragraph applies—

(a)   the court may try the case in the parties' absence and without a hearing;

(b)   the court may accept any guilty plea of which the defendant has given notice under paragraph (4)(a);

(c)   to establish the facts of the offence and other information about the defendant relevant to sentence, the court may take account only of—

    (i)   information contained in a document served by the prosecutor under paragraph (1),

    (ii)   any previous conviction listed in the defendant's driving record, where the offence is under the Road Traffic Regulation Act 1984, the Road Traffic Act 1988, the Road Traffic (Consequential Provisions) Act 1988 or the Road Traffic (Driver Licensing and Information Systems) Act 1989,

    (iii)   any other information about the defendant, relevant to sentence, of which the prosecutor served notice under paragraph (1), and

    (iv)   any representations and any other information served by the defendant under paragraph (4)(a)

and rule 24.11(3) to (9) inclusive must be read accordingly.
(9)   Paragraph (10) applies where—
(a)   the defendant serves on the court officer a notice under paragraph (4)(b) or (c); or
(b)   the court which tries the defendant under paragraph (8) adjourns the trial for the defendant to attend a hearing by a court comprising more than one justice.
(10)   Where this paragraph applies, the court must exercise its power to issue a summons and—
(a)   the rules in Part 7 apply (Starting a prosecution in a magistrates' court) as if the prosecutor had just served an information in the same terms as the written charge;
(b)   the rules in Part 8 (Initial details of the prosecution case) apply as if the documents served by the prosecutor under paragraph (1) had been served under that Part;
(c)   except for rule 24.8 (Written guilty plea: special rules) and this rule, the rules in this Part apply.
[Note. The procedure set out in this rule is prescribed by sections 16A to 16D of the Magistrates' Courts Act 1980 and section 29 of the Criminal Justice Act 2003. Under section 16A of the 1980 Act, the court may comprise a single justice. Under section 29 of the 2003 Act, a prosecutor authorised under that section may issue a written charge alleging an offence and a single justice procedure notice. Part 7 contains relevant rules.
Under section 1 of the Magistrates' Courts Act 1980 a justice of the peace may issue a summons requiring a defendant to attend court to answer an allegation of an offence. Under sections 16C and 16D of the 1980 Act, a justice may issue a summons requiring a defendant to attend court in the circumstances listed in rule 24.9(9).
For the court's power, where this rule applies, to take account of—
(a)   *information contained or described in a document served by the prosecutor under rule 24.9(1), see section 16F of the Magistrates' Courts Act 1980;*
(b)   *a previous conviction listed in a defendant's driving record, see section 13(3A) of the Road Traffic Offenders Act 1988.*
The Practice Direction sets out forms of notice for use in connection with this rule.]

24.10. *Application to withdraw a guilty plea* (1)   This rule applies where the defendant wants to withdraw a guilty plea.
(2)   The defendant must apply to do so—
(a)   as soon as practicable after becoming aware of the reasons for doing so; and
(b)   before sentence.
(3)   Unless the court otherwise directs, the application must be in writing and the defendant must serve it on—
(a)   the court officer; and
(b)   the prosecutor.
(4)   The application must—
(a)   explain why it would be unjust not to allow the defendant to withdraw the guilty plea;
(b)   identify—
      (i)   any witness that the defendant wants to call, and
      (ii)   any other proposed evidence; and
(c)   say whether the defendant waives legal professional privilege, giving any relevant name and date.

24.11. *Procedure if the court convicts* (1)   This rule applies if the court convicts the defendant.
(2)   The court—
(a)   may exercise its power to require—
      (i)   a statement of the defendant's assets and other financial circumstances,
      (ii)   a pre-sentence report; and
(b)   may (and in some circumstances must) remit the defendant to a youth court for sentence where—
      (i)   the defendant is under 18, and
      (ii)   the convicting court is not itself a youth court.
(3)   The prosecutor must—
(a)   summarise the prosecution case, if the sentencing court has not heard evidence;
(b)   identify any offence to be taken into consideration in sentencing;
(c)   provide information relevant to sentence, including any statement of the effect of the offence on the victim, the victim's family or others; and
(d)   where it is likely to assist the court, identify any other matter relevant to sentence, including—
      (i)   the legislation applicable,
      (ii)   any sentencing guidelines, or guideline cases,
      (iii)   aggravating and mitigating features affecting the defendant's culpability and the harm which the offence caused, was intended to cause or might forseeably have caused, and
      (iv)   the effect of such of the information listed in paragraph (2)(a) as the court may need to take into account.
(4)   The defendant must provide details of financial circumstances—
(a)   in any form required by the court officer;
(b)   by any date directed by the court or by the court officer.
(5)   Where the defendant pleads guilty but wants to be sentenced on a different basis to that disclosed by the prosecution case—

(a) the defendant must set out that basis in writing, identifying what is in dispute;

(b) the court may invite the parties to make representations about whether the dispute is material to sentence; and

(c) if the court decides that it is a material dispute, the court must—

  (i) invite such further representations or evidence as it may require, and

  (ii) decide the dispute.

(6) Where the court has power to order the endorsement of the defendant's driving record, or power to order the defendant to be disqualified from driving—

(a) if other legislation so permits, a defendant who wants the court not to exercise that power must introduce the evidence or information on which the defendant relies;

(b) the prosecutor may introduce evidence; and

(c) the parties may make representations about that evidence or information.

(7) Before the court passes sentence—

(a) the court must—

  (i) give the defendant an opportunity to make representations and introduce evidence relevant to sentence, and

  (ii) where the defendant is under 18, give the defendant's parents, guardian or other supporting adult, if present, such an opportunity as well; and

(b) the justices' legal adviser or the court must elicit any further information relevant to sentence that the court may require.

(8) If the court requires more information, it may exercise its power to adjourn the hearing for not more than—

(a) 3 weeks at a time, if the defendant will be in custody; or

(b) 4 weeks at a time.

(9) When the court has taken into account all the evidence, information and any report available, the court must—

(a) as a general rule, pass sentence there and then;

(b) when passing sentence, explain the reasons for deciding on that sentence, unless neither the defendant nor any member of the public, including any reporter, is present;

(c) when passing sentence, explain to the defendant its effect, the consequences of failing to comply with any order or pay any fine, and any power that the court has to vary or review the sentence, unless—

  (i) the defendant is absent, or

  (ii) the defendant's ill-health or disorderly conduct makes such an explanation impracticable;

(d) give any such explanation in terms the defendant, if present, can understand (with help, if necessary); and

(e) consider exercising any power it has to make a costs or other order.

(10) Despite the general rule—

(a) the court must adjourn the hearing if the defendant is absent, the case started with a summons, requisition or single justice procedure notice, and either—

  (i) the court considers passing a custodial sentence (where it can do so), or

  (ii) the court considers imposing a disqualification (unless it has already adjourned the hearing to give the defendant an opportunity to attend);

(b) the court may exercise any power it has to—

  (i) commit the defendant to the Crown Court for sentence (and in some cases it must do so), or

  (ii) defer sentence for up to 6 months.

[Note. See sections 9, 10 and 11 of the Magistrates' Courts Act 1980, and sections 143, 158, 164, 172 and 174 of the Criminal Justice Act 2003.

Under section 11(3A) of the 1980 Act, a custodial sentence passed in the defendant's absence does not take effect until the defendant is brought before the court.

Under sections 57D and 57E of the Crime and Disorder Act 1998, the court may require a defendant to attend a sentencing hearing by live link.

Under section 162 of the Criminal Justice Act 2003, the court may require a defendant who is an individual to provide a statement of assets and other financial circumstances if the defendant—

(a) serves notice of guilty plea, where rule 24.8 (Written guilty plea: special rules) applies; or

(b) is convicted.

Under section 20A of the Criminal Justice Act 1991, it is an offence for a defendant knowingly or recklessly to make a false or incomplete statement of assets or other financial circumstances, or to fail to provide such a statement, in response to a request by a court officer on behalf of the court.

Under section 156 of the Criminal Justice Act 2003, the general rule (subject to exceptions) is that the court must obtain and consider a pre-sentence report—

(a) where it is considering a custodial sentence or a community sentence;

(b) where it thinks the defendant may pose a significant risk of causing serious harm to the public by further offending.

Under section 159 of the Criminal Justice Act 2003, where the court obtains a written pre-sentence report about a defendant who is under 18, it may direct that information in it must be withheld, if it would be likely to create a risk of significant harm to the defendant.

For the circumstances in which a magistrates' court may (and in some cases must) remit the defendant to a youth court for sentence, see section 8 of the Powers of Criminal Courts

(Sentencing) Act 2000.
The Sentencing Council may issue sentencing guidelines under section 120 of the Coroners and Justice Act 2009.
For the circumstances in which a court may (and in some cases must) order the endorsement of a defendant's driving record, or the disqualification of a defendant from driving, see sections 34, 35 and 44 of the Road Traffic Offenders Act 1988. Under that legislation, in some circumstances the court has discretion not to make such an order. See also rule 29.1.
The evidence that may be introduced is subject to rules of evidence.
In addition to the specific powers to which this rule applies, the court has a general power to adjourn a trial: see rule 24.2.
Under section 174(4) of the Criminal Justice Act 2003, Criminal Procedure Rules may prescribe cases in which there do not apply the court's usual duties to give reasons and explanations. Written notice of the effect of some sentences is required by rule 28.2 (Notice of requirements of suspended sentence or community, etc order), rule 28.3 (Notification requirements) and rule 30.2 (notice of fine or other financial order).
For the circumstances in which a magistrates' court may (and in some cases must) commit a defendant to the Crown Court for sentence, see sections 3, 3A, 3B, 3C, 4, 4A and 6 of the Powers of Criminal Courts (Sentencing) Act 2000.
Under section 1 of the 2000 Act, if (among other things) the defendant consents, the court may defer sentence for up to 6 months, for the purpose of allowing it to take account of the defendant's conduct after conviction, or any change in the defendant's circumstances.]

24.12. *Procedure where a party is absent* (1)   This rule—
(a)   applies where a party is absent; but
(b)   does not apply where—
  (i)   the defendant has served a notice of guilty plea under rule 24.8 (Written guilty plea: special rules), or
  (ii)   the court tries a case under rule 24.9 (Single justice procedure: special rules).
(2)   Where the prosecutor is absent, the court may—
(a)   if it has received evidence, deal with the case as if the prosecutor were present; and
(b)   in any other case—
  (i)   enquire into the reasons for the prosecutor's absence, and
  (ii)   if satisfied there is no good reason, exercise its power to dismiss the allegation.
(3)   Where the defendant is absent—
(a)   the general rule is that the court must proceed as if the defendant—
  (i)   were present, and
  (ii)   had pleaded not guilty (unless a plea already has been taken)
    and the court must give reasons if it does not do so; but
(b)   the general rule does not apply if the defendant is under 18;
(c)   the general rule is subject to the court being satisfied that—
  (i)   any summons or requisition was served on the defendant a reasonable time before the hearing, or
  (ii)   in a case in which the hearing has been adjourned, the defendant had reasonable notice of where and when it would resume;
(d)   the general rule is subject also to rule 24.11(10)(a) (restrictions on passing sentence in the defendant's absence).
(4)   Where the defendant is absent, the court—
(a)   must exercise its power to issue a warrant for the defendant's arrest and detention in the terms required by rule 13.3(3) (Terms of a warrant for detention or imprisonment), if it passes a custodial sentence; and
(b)   may exercise its power to issue a warrant for the defendant's arrest in any other case, if it does not apply the general rule in paragraph (3)(a) of this rule about proceeding in the defendant's absence.
[Note. See sections 11, 15 and 16 of the Magistrates' Courts Act 1980.
Under section 27 of the 1980 Act, where a magistrates' court dismisses an allegation of an offence classified as one that can be tried either in a magistrates' court or in the Crown Court (in other legislation, described as triable either way), that dismissal has the same effect as an acquittal in the Crown Court.
Under section 11 of the 1980 Act, the court may pass a custodial sentence: see also rule 13.3 in the defendant's absence if the case started with the defendant's arrest and charge (and not with a summons or requisition). Section 11(3A) requires that, in that event, the defendant must be brought before the court before being taken to a prison or other institution to begin serving that sentence. Under section 7(1) of the Bail Act 1976, the court has power to issue a warrant for the arrest of a defendant released on bail who has failed to attend court when due to do so.
Under section 13 of the 1980 Act, the court has power to issue a warrant for the arrest of an absent defendant, instead of proceeding, where—
(1)   the case started with—
(a)   the defendant's arrest and charge, or
(b)   a summons or requisition, if—
  (i)   the court is satisfied that that summons or requisition was served on the defendant a reasonable time before the hearing, or
  (ii)   the defendant was present when the hearing was arranged; and

(2)   the offence is punishable with imprisonment; or
(3)   the defendant has been convicted and the court considers imposing a disqualification.]

24.13. Provision of documents for the court (1)   A party who introduces a document in evidence, or who otherwise uses a document in presenting that party's case, must provide a copy for—
(a)   each other party;
(b)   any witness that party wants to refer to that document;
(c)   the court; and
(d)   the justices' legal adviser.
(2)   Unless the court otherwise directs, on application or on its own initiative, the court officer must provide for the court—
(a)   any copy received under paragraph (1) before the hearing begins; and
(b)   a copy of the court officer's record of—
         (i)   information supplied by each party for the purposes of case management, including any revision of information previously supplied,
         (ii)   each pre-trial direction for the management of the case,
         (iii)   any pre-trial decision to admit evidence,
         (iv)   any pre-trial direction about the giving of evidence, and
         (v)   any admission to which rule 24.6 applies.
(3)   Where rule 24.8 (Written guilty plea: special rules) applies, the court officer must provide for the court—
(a)   each document served by the prosecutor under rule 24.8(1)(d);
(b)   the defendant's driving record, where the offence is under the Road Traffic Regulation Act 1984, the Road Traffic Act 1988, the Road Traffic (Consequential Provisions) Act 1988 or the Road Traffic (Driver Licensing and Information Systems) Act 1989;
(c)   any other information about the defendant, relevant to sentence, of which the prosecutor served notice under rule 24.8(1); and
(d)   the notice of guilty plea and any representations and other information served by the defendant under rule 24.8(4).
(4)   Where the court tries a case under rule 24.9 (Single justice procedure: special rules), the court officer must provide for the court—
(a)   each document served by the prosecutor under rule 24.9(1)(d);
(b)   the defendant's driving record, where the offence is under the Road Traffic Regulation Act 1984, the Road Traffic Act 1988, the Road Traffic (Consequential Provisions) Act 1988 or the Road Traffic (Driver Licensing and Information Systems) Act 1989;
(c)   any other information about the defendant, relevant to sentence, of which the prosecutor served notice under rule 24.9(1); and
(d)   any notice, representations and other information served by the defendant under rule 24.9(4)(a).
[Note. A written witness statement to which Part 16 applies may only be introduced in evidence if there has been no objection within the time limit to which rule 16.4 refers.
An expert report to which Part 19 applies may only be introduced in evidence if it has been served in accordance with rule 19.3.
See also rule 20.3 for the procedure where a party objects to the introduction of hearsay evidence, including such evidence in a document, and rules 21.3 and 21.4 for the procedure where a party objects to the introduction of evidence of bad character.
A direction about the giving of evidence may be made on an application to which Part 18 applies (Measures to assist a witness or defendant to give evidence).]

24.14. Place of trial (1)   The hearing must take place in a courtroom provided by the Lord Chancellor, unless—
(a)   the court otherwise directs; or
(b)   the court tries a case under rule 24.9 (Single justice procedure: special rules).
(2)   Where the hearing takes place in Wales—
(a)   any party or witness may use the Welsh language; and
(b)   if practicable, at least one member of the court must be Welsh-speaking.
[Note. See section 3 of the Courts Act 2003, section 16A of the Magistrates' Courts Act 1980 and section 22 of the Welsh Language Act 1993.
In some circumstances the court may conduct all or part of the hearing outside a courtroom. The members of the court may discuss the verdict and sentence outside the courtroom.]

24.15. Duty of justices' legal adviser (1)   A justices' legal adviser must attend the court and carry out the duties listed in this rule, as applicable, unless the court—
(a)   includes a District Judge (Magistrates' Courts); and
(b)   otherwise directs.
(2)   A justices' legal adviser must—
(a)   before the hearing begins, by reference to what is provided for the court under rule 24.13 (Provision of documents for the court) draw the court's attention to—
         (i)   what the prosecutor alleges,
         (ii)   what the parties say is agreed,
         (iii)   what the parties say is in dispute, and
         (iv)   what the parties say about how each expects to present the case, especially where that may affect its duration and timetabling;

(b)   whenever necessary, give the court legal advice and—
        (i)   if necessary, attend the members of the court outside the courtroom to give such advice, but
        (ii)   inform the parties (if present) of any such advice given outside the courtroom; and
(c)   assist the court, where appropriate, in the formulation of its reasons and the recording of those reasons.
(3)   A justices' legal adviser must—
(a)   assist an unrepresented defendant;
(b)   assist the court by—
        (i)   making a note of the substance of any oral evidence or representations, to help the court recall that information,
        (ii)   if the court rules inadmissible part of a written statement introduced in evidence, marking that statement in such a way as to make that clear,
        (iii)   ensuring that an adequate record is kept of the court's decisions and the reasons for them, and
        (iv)   making any announcement, other than of the verdict or sentence.
(4)   Where the defendant has served a notice of guilty plea to which rule 24.8 (Written guilty plea: special rules) applies, a justices' legal adviser must—
(a)   unless the court otherwise directs, if any member of the public, including any reporter, is present, read aloud to the court—
        (i)   the material on which the prosecutor relies to set out the facts of the offence and to provide information relevant to sentence (or summarise any written statement included in that material, if the court so directs), and
        (ii)   any written representations by the defendant;
(b)   otherwise, draw the court's attention to—
        (i)   what the prosecutor alleges, and any significant features of the material listed in paragraph (4)(a)(i), and
        (ii)   any written representations by the defendant.
(5)   Where the court tries a case under rule 24.9 (Single justice procedure: special rules), a justices' legal adviser must draw the court's attention to—
(a)   what the prosecutor alleges, and any significant features of the material on which the prosecutor relies to prove the alleged offence and to provide information relevant to sentence; and
(b)   any representations served by the defendant.
[Note. Section 28 of the Courts Act 2003 provides for the functions of a justices' legal adviser. See also sections 12 and 16A of the Magistrates' Courts Act 1980.
Under section 12(7ZA) of the 1980 Act, Criminal Procedure Rules may specify which of the documents listed in section 12(7) of that Act, if any, must be read aloud, and may require them to be read aloud only in circumstances specified in the rules.]

24.16. *Duty of court officer*   The court officer must—
(a)   serve on each party notice of where and when an adjourned hearing will resume, unless—
        (i)   the party was present when that was arranged,
        (ii)   the defendant has served a notice of guilty plea to which rule 24.8 (Written guilty plea: special rules) applies, and the adjournment is for not more than 4 weeks, or
        (iii)   the court tries a case under rule 24.9 (Single justice procedure: special rules), and the adjourned trial will resume under that rule;
(b)   if the reason for the adjournment was to postpone sentence, include that reason in any such notice to the defendant;
(c)   unless the court otherwise directs, make available to the parties any written report to which rule 24.11 (Procedure if the court convicts) applies;
(d)   where the court has ordered a defendant to provide information under section 25 of the Road Traffic Offenders Act 1988, serve on the defendant notice of that order unless the defendant was present when it was made;
(e)   serve on the prosecutor—
        (i)   any notice of guilty plea to which rule 24.8 (Written guilty plea: special rules) applies,
        (ii)   any declaration served under rule 24.17 (Statutory declaration of ignorance of proceedings) that the defendant did not know about the case;
(f)   serve on the prosecutor notice of any hearing date arranged in consequence of such a declaration, unless—
        (i)   the prosecutor was present when that was arranged, or
        (ii)   the court otherwise directs;
(g)   serve on the prosecutor—
        (i)   notice of any hearing date arranged in consequence of the issue of a summons under rule 37.9 (Single justice procedure: special rules), and in that event
        (ii)   any notice served by the defendant under rule 37.9(2)(b) or (c);
(h)   record the court's reasons for not proceeding in the defendant's absence where rule 24.12(3)(a) applies; and
(i)   give the court such other assistance as it requires.

[Note. See sections 10, 11 and 12 of the Magistrates' Courts Act 1980.
Under section 25 of the Road Traffic Offenders Act 1988, where the court does not know a defendant's sex or date of birth, then on convicting the defendant of an offence involving obligatory or discretionary disqualification, the court must order the defendant to provide that information.
Under Part 5, the magistrates' court officer must record details of a case and of the court's decisions.]

24.17. *Statutory declaration of ignorance of proceedings* (1) This rule applies where —

(a)   the case started with —

    (i)   an application for a summons,

    (ii)   a written charge and requisition, or

    (iii)   a written charge and single justice procedure notice; and

(b)   under section 14 or section 16E of the Magistrates' Courts Act 1980, the defendant makes a statutory declaration of not having found out about the case until after the trial began.

(2)   The defendant must —

(a)   serve such a declaration on the court officer —

    (i)   not more than 21 days after the date of finding out about the case, or

    (ii)   with an explanation for the delay, if serving it more than 21 days after that date;

(b)   serve with the declaration one of the following, as appropriate, if the case began with a written charge and single justice procedure notice —

    (i)   a notice under rule 24.9(4)(a) (notice of guilty plea), with any representations that the defendant wants the court to consider and a statement of the defendant's assets and other financial circumstances, as required by that rule,

    (ii)   a notice under rule 24.9(4)(b) (notice of intention to plead guilty at a hearing before a court comprising more than one justice), or

    (iii)   a notice under rule 24.9(4)(c) (notice of intention to plead not guilty).

(3)   The court may extend that time limit, even after it has expired —

(a)   at a hearing, in public or in private; or

(b)   without a hearing.

(4)   Where the defendant serves such a declaration, in time or with an extension of time in which to do so, and the case began with a summons or requisition —

(a)   the court must treat the summons or requisition and all subsequent proceedings as void (but not the application for the summons or the written charge with which the case began);

(b)   if the defendant is present when the declaration is served, the rules in this Part apply as if the defendant had been required to attend the court on that occasion;

(c)   if the defendant is absent when the declaration is served —

    (i)   the rules in Part 7 apply (Starting a prosecution in a magistrates' court) as if the prosecutor had just served an application for a summons in the same terms as the original application;

    (ii)   the court may exercise its power to issue a summons in accordance with those rules; and

    (iii)   except for rule 24.8 (Written guilty plea: special rules), the rules in this Part then apply.

(5)   Where the defendant serves such a declaration, in time or with an extension of time in which to do so, and the case began with a single justice procedure notice —

(a)   the court must treat the single justice procedure notice and all subsequent proceedings as void (but not the written charge with which the case began);

(b)   rule 24.9 (Single justice procedure: special rules) applies as if the defendant had served the notice required by paragraph (2)(b) of this rule within the time allowed by rule 24.9(4); and

(c)   where that notice is under rule 24.9(4)(b) (notice of intention to plead guilty at a hearing before a court comprising more than one justice) or under rule 24.9(4)(c) (notice of intention to plead not guilty), then —

    (i)   if the defendant is present when the declaration is served, the rules in this Part apply as if the defendant had been required to attend the court on that occasion,

    (ii)   if the defendant is absent when the declaration is served, paragraph (6) of this rule applies.

(6)   Where this paragraph applies, the court must exercise its power to issue a summons and —

(a)   the rules in Part 7 apply (Starting a prosecution in a magistrates' court) as if the prosecutor had just served an application for a summons in the same terms as the written charge;

(b)   except for rule 24.8 (Written guilty plea: special rules) and rule 24.9 (Single justice procedure: special rules), the rules in this Part apply.

[Note. Under sections 14 and 16E of the Magistrates' Courts Act 1980, proceedings which begin with a summons, requisition or single justice procedure notice will become void if the defendant, at any time during or after the trial, makes a statutory declaration that he or she did not know of them until a date after the trial began.
Under section 14(3) or section 16E(9) of the 1980 Act, the court which decides whether or not to extend the time limit for serving a declaration under this rule may comprise a single justice.
The Practice Direction sets out a form of declaration for use in connection with this rule.]

24.18. Setting aside a conviction or varying a costs etc order (1)   This rule applies where under section 142 of the Magistrates' Courts Act 1980, the court can—

(a)   set aside a conviction, or

(b)   vary or rescind—

    (i)   a costs order, or

    (ii)   an order to which Part 31 applies (Behaviour orders).

(2)   The court may exercise its power—

(a)   on application by a party, or on its own initiative;

(b)   at a hearing, in public or in private, or without a hearing.

(3)   The court must not exercise its power in a party's absence unless—

(a)   the court makes a decision proposed by that party;

(b)   the court makes a decision to which that party has agreed in writing; or

(c)   that party has had an opportunity to make representations at a hearing (whether or not that party in fact attends).

(4)   A party who wants the court to exercise its power must—

(a)   apply in writing as soon as reasonably practicable after the conviction or order that that party wants the court to set aside, vary or rescind;

(b)   serve the application on—

    (i)   the court officer, and

    (ii)   each other party; and

(c)   in the application—

    (i)   explain why, as appropriate, the conviction should be set aside, or the order varied or rescinded,

    (ii)   specify any variation of the order that the applicant proposes,

    (iii)   identify any witness that the defendant wants to call, and any other proposed evidence,

    (iv)   say whether the defendant waives legal professional privilege, giving any relevant name and date, and

    (v)   if the application is late, explain why.

(5)   The court may—

(a)   extend (even after it has expired) the time limit under paragraph (4), unless the court's power to set aside the conviction, or vary the order, can no longer be exercised;

(b)   allow an application to be made orally.

[Note. Under section 142 of the Magistrates' Courts Act 1980—

(a)   *where a defendant is convicted by a magistrates' court, the court may order that the case should be heard again by different justices; and*

(b)   *the court may vary or rescind an order which it has made when dealing with a convicted defendant,*

if in either case it appears to the court to be in the interests of justice to do so.

The power cannot be exercised if the Crown Court or the High Court has determined an appeal about that conviction or order.

See also rule 28.4 (Variation of sentence), which applies to an application under section 142 of the 1980 Act to vary or rescind a sentence.]

PART 25   TRIAL AND SENTENCE IN THE CROWN COURT

Note

[Part 25 is not reproduced.]

PART 26   JURORS

Note

[Part 26 is not reproduced.]

PART 27   RETRIAL AFTER ACQUITTAL

Contents of this Part

General

Application of other rules about procedure   rule 27.7
in the Court of Appeal

GENERAL

B.24 *27.1. When this Part applies* (1) Rule 27.2 applies where, under section 54 of the Criminal Procedure and Investigations Act 1996, the Crown Court or a magistrates' court can certify for the High Court that interference or intimidation has been involved in proceedings leading to an acquittal.

(2) Rules 27.3 to 27.7 apply where, under section 77 of the Criminal Justice Act 2003, the Court of Appeal can—

(a)   quash an acquittal for a serious offence and order a defendant to be retried; or

(b)   order that an acquittal outside the United Kingdom is no bar to the defendant being tried in England and Wales,

if there is new and compelling evidence and it is in the interests of justice to make the order.

APPLICATION FOR CERTIFICATE TO ALLOW ORDER FOR RETRIAL

27.2. Application for certificate (1) This rule applies where—

(a)   a defendant has been acquitted of an offence;

(b)   a person has been convicted of one of the following offences involving interference with or intimidation of a juror or a witness (or potential witness) in any proceedings which led to the defendant's acquittal—

    (i)   perverting the course of justice,

    (ii)   intimidation etc of witnesses, jurors and others under section 51(1) of the Criminal Justice and Public Order Act 1994, or

    (iii)   aiding, abetting, counselling, procuring, suborning or inciting another person to commit an offence under section 1 of the Perjury Act 1911; and

(c)   the prosecutor wants the court by which that person was convicted to certify for the High Court that there is a real possibility that, but for the interference or intimidation, the defendant would not have been acquitted.

(2) The prosecutor must—

(a)   apply in writing as soon as practicable after that person's conviction; and

(b)   serve the application on—

    (i)   the court officer, and

    (ii)   the defendant who was acquitted, if the court so directs.

(3) The application must—

(a)   give details, with relevant facts and dates, of—

    (i)   the conviction for interference or intimidation, and

    (ii)   the defendant's acquittal; and

(b)   explain—

    (i)   why there is a real possibility that, but for the interference or intimidation, the defendant would not have been acquitted, and

    (ii)   why it would not be contrary to the interests of justice to prosecute the defendant again for the offence of which he or she was acquitted, despite any lapse of time or other reason.

(4) The court may—

(a)   extend the time limit under paragraph (2);

(b)   allow an application to be in a different form to one set out in the Practice Direction, or to be made orally;

(c)   determine an application under this rule—

    (i)   at a hearing, in private or in public; or

    (ii)   without a hearing.

(5) If the court gives a certificate, the court officer must serve it on—

(a)   the prosecutor; and

(b)   the defendant who was acquitted.

[Note: See Section 54 of the Criminal Procedure and Investigations Act 1996 (Acquittals tainted by intimidation, etc).

For the procedure on application to the High Court, see rules 77.6 to 77.15 of the Civil Procedure Rules 1998.]

APPLICATION TO COURT OF APPEAL TO QUASH ACQUITTAL AND ORDER RETRIAL

27.3. Application for reporting restriction pending application for order for retrial (1) This rule applies where—

(a)   no application has been made under rule 27.4 (Application for order for retrial);

(b)   an investigation by officers has begun into an offence with a view to an application under that rule; and

(c)   the Director of Public Prosecutions wants the Court of Appeal to make, vary or remove an order for a reporting restriction under section 82 of the Criminal Justice Act 2003 (Restrictions on publication in the interests of justice).

(2) The Director must—

(a)   apply in writing;

(b)   serve the application on—
    (i)   the Registrar, and
    (ii)   the defendant, unless the court otherwise directs.
(3)   The application must, as appropriate—
(a)   explain why the Director wants the court to direct that it need not be served on the defendant until the application under rule 27.4 is served;
(b)   specify the proposed terms of the order, and for how long it should last;
(c)   explain why an order in the terms proposed is necessary;
(d)   explain why an order should be varied or removed.
[Note: For other rules about reporting restrictions, see Part 6.]

27.4.   *Application for order for retrial*   (1)   This rule applies where—
(a)   a defendant has been acquitted—
    (i)   in the Crown Court, or on appeal from the Crown Court, of an offence listed in Part 1 of Schedule 5 to the Criminal Justice Act 2003 (qualifying offences),
    (ii)   in proceedings elsewhere than in the United Kingdom of an offence under the law of that place, if what was alleged would have amounted to or included one of those listed offences;
(b)   with the Director of Public Prosecutions' written consent, a prosecutor wants the Court of Appeal to make an order, as the case may be—
    (i)   quashing the acquittal in the Crown Court and ordering the defendant to be retried for the offence, or
    (ii)   declaring whether the acquittal outside the United Kingdom is a bar to the defendant's trial in England and Wales and, if it is, whether that acquittal shall not be such a bar.
(2)   Such a prosecutor must—
(a)   apply in writing;
(b)   serve the application on the Registrar;
(c)   not more than 2 business days later serve on the defendant who was acquitted—
    (i)   the application, and
    (ii)   a notice charging the defendant with the offence, unless the defendant has already been arrested and charged under section 87 of the Criminal Justice Act 2003 (arrest, under warrant or otherwise, and charge).
(3)   The application must—
(a)   give details, with relevant facts and dates, of the defendant's acquittal;
(b)   explain—
    (i)   what new and compelling evidence there is against the defendant, and
    (ii)   why in all the circumstances it would be in the interests of justice for the court to make the order sought;
(c)   include or attach any application for the following, with reasons—
    (i)   an order under section 80(6) of the Criminal Justice Act 2003 (Procedure and evidence) for the production of any document, exhibit or other thing which in the prosecutor's opinion is necessary for the determination of the application,
    (ii)   an order under that section for the attendance before the court of any witness who would be a compellable witness at the trial the prosecutor wants the court to order,
    (iii)   an order for a reporting restriction under section 82 of the Criminal Justice Act 2003 (Restrictions on publication in the interests of justice); and
(d)   attach—
    (i)   written witness statements of the evidence on which the prosecutor relies as new and compelling evidence against the defendant,
    (ii)   relevant documents from the trial at which the defendant was acquitted, including a record of the offence or offences charged and of the evidence given, and
    (iii)   any other document or thing that the prosecutor thinks the court will need to decide the application.
[Note. See sections 75, 76, 77, 80 and 82 of the Criminal Justice Act 2003. Under Part 1 of Schedule 5 to that Act, the qualifying offences include murder and other serious offences against the person, offences of importation and exportation of Class A drugs, offences of causing explosions and other serious damage, terrorism offences and war crimes and other international offences.
The time limit for serving an application on the defendant is prescribed by section 80(2) of the 2003 Act. It may be extended but not shortened.]

27.5.   *Respondent's notice*   (1)   A defendant on whom a prosecutor serves an application may serve a respondent's notice, and must do so if the defendant wants to make representations to the court.
(2)   Such a defendant must serve the respondent's notice on—
(a)   the Registrar; and
(b)   the prosecutor,
not more than 28 days after service of the application.
(3)   The respondent's notice must—
(a)   give the date on which the respondent was served with the prosecutor's application;
(b)   summarise any relevant facts not contained in that application;
(c)   explain the defendant's grounds for opposing that application;

(d)   include or attach any application for the following, with reasons—
  (i)   an extension of time within which to serve the respondent's notice,
  (ii)   bail pending the hearing of the prosecutor's application, if the defendant is in custody,
  (iii)   a direction to attend in person any hearing that the defendant could attend by live link, if the defendant is in custody,
  (iv)   an order under section 80(6) of the Criminal Justice Act 2003 (Procedure and evidence) for the production of any document, exhibit or other thing which in the defendant's opinion is necessary for the determination of the prosecutor's application,
  (v)   an order under that section for the attendance before the court of any witness who would be a compellable witness at the trial the prosecutor wants the court to order; and
(e)   attach or identify any other document or thing that the defendant thinks the court will need to decide the application.

27.6. Application to Crown Court for summons or warrant (1) This rule applies where—
(a)   the prosecutor has served on the Registrar an application under rule 27.4 (Application for order for retrial);
(b)   the defendant is not in custody as a result of arrest under section 88 of the Criminal Justice Act 2003 (Bail and custody before application); and
(c)   the prosecutor wants the Crown Court to issue—
  (i)   a summons requiring the defendant to appear before the Court of Appeal at the hearing of the prosecutor's application, or
  (ii)   a warrant for the defendant's arrest
    under section 89 of the 2003 Act (Bail and custody before hearing).
(2)   The prosecutor must—
(a)   apply in writing; and
(b)   serve the application on the Crown Court officer.
(3)   The application must—
(a)   explain what the case is about, including a brief description of the defendant's acquittal, the new evidence and the stage that the application to the Court of Appeal has reached;
(b)   specify—
  (i)   the decision that the prosecutor wants the Crown Court to make,
  (ii)   each offence charged, and
  (iii)   any relevant previous bail decision and the reasons given for it;
(c)   propose the terms of any suggested condition of bail.
[Note. Under section 87 of the Criminal Justice Act 2003, in the circumstances prescribed by that section a justice of the peace may issue a warrant for the arrest of the defendant who was acquitted and that defendant may be charged with an offence that is to be the subject of an application to the Court of Appeal under rule 27.4.
Under section 88 of the 2003 Act, in the circumstances prescribed by that section a defendant who has been arrested and charged must be brought before the Crown Court and that court must either grant bail for that defendant to attend the Court of Appeal on the hearing of an application under rule 27.4, or remand the defendant in custody.
Under section 89 of the 2003 Act, where the prosecutor has made an application to the Court of Appeal under rule 27.4—
(a)   if the defendant is in custody, the Crown Court must decide whether to remand him or her in custody to be brought before the Court of Appeal or to grant bail for that purpose; or
(b)   if the defendant is not in custody, and if the prosecutor so applies, the Crown Court may either issue a summons for the defendant to attend the Court of Appeal or issue a warrant for the defendant's arrest.]

27.7. Application of other rules about procedure in the Court of Appeal On an application under rule 27.4 (Application for order for retrial)—
(a)   the rules in Part 36 (Appeal to the Court of Appeal: general rules) apply with the necessary modifications;
(b)   rules 39.8, 39.9 and 39.10 (bail and bail conditions in the Court of Appeal) apply as if the references in those rules to appeal included references to an application under rule 27.4; and
(c)   rule 39.14 (Renewal or setting aside of order for retrial) applies as if the reference to section 7 of the Criminal Appeal Act 1968 were a reference to section 84 of the Criminal Justice Act 2003 (Retrial).
[Note. See also the notes to the rules listed in this rule.
For the powers of the Court of Appeal that may be exercised by one judge of that court or by the Registrar, and for the right to renew an application for directions to a judge or to the Court of Appeal, see the Criminal Justice Act 2003 (Retrial for Serious Offences) Order 2005 and rule 36.5 (Renewing an application refused by a judge or the Registrar).
For rules governing applications for reporting restrictions, see Part 6. For rules governing proceedings in the Crown Court about bail, see Part 14.]

PART 28   SENTENCING PROCEDURES IN SPECIAL CASES

Contents of this Part

Note

[Note. See also—
(a) Part 24, which contains rules about the general procedure on sentencing in a magistrates court;
(b) Part 25, which contains rules about the general procedure on sentencing in the Crown Court;
(c) Part 29 (Road traffic penalties);
(d) Part 30 (Enforcement of fines and other orders for payment); and
(e) Part 32 (Breach, revocation and amendment of community and other orders).]

B.25   28.1. *Reasons for not following usual sentencing requirements* (1) This rule applies where the court decides—

(a)   not to follow a relevant sentencing guideline;

(b)   not to make, where it could—
    (i)   a reparation order (unless it passes a custodial or community sentence),
    (ii)   a compensation order,
    (iii)   a slavery and trafficking reparation order, or
    (iv)   a travel restriction order;

(c)   not to order, where it could—
    (i)   that a suspended sentence of imprisonment is to take effect,
    (ii)   the endorsement of the defendant's driving record, or
    (iii)   the defendant's disqualification from driving, for the usual minimum period or at all;

(d)   to pass a lesser sentence than it otherwise would have passed because the defendant has assisted, or has agreed to assist, an investigator or prosecutor in relation to an offence.

(2)   The court must explain why it has so decided, when it explains the sentence that it has passed.

(3)   Where paragraph (1)(d) applies, the court must arrange for such an explanation to be given to the defendant and to the prosecutor in writing, if the court thinks that it would not be in the public interest to explain in public.

[Note. See section 174 of the Criminal Justice Act 2003; section 73(8) of the Powers of Criminal Courts (Sentencing) Act 2000; section 130(3) of the 2000 Act; section 8(7) of the Modern Slavery Act 2015; section 33(2) of the Criminal Justice and Police Act 2001; paragraph 8(3) of Schedule 12 to the 2003 Act; section 47(1) of the Road Traffic Offenders Act 1988; and section 73 of the Serious Organised Crime and Police Act 2005.

For the duty to explain the sentence the court has passed, see section 174(1) of the 2003 Act and rules 24.11(9) (procedure where a magistrates' court convicts) and 25.16(7) (procedure where the Crown Court convicts).

Under section 125 of the Coroners and Justice Act 2009, the court when sentencing must follow any relevant sentencing guideline unless satisfied that to do so would be contrary to the interests of justice.

For the circumstances in which the court may make—

(a)   a reparation or compensation order, see sections 73 and 130 of the 2000 Act;

(b)   a slavery and trafficking reparation order, see section 8 of the 2015 Act;

(c)   a travel restriction order against a defendant convicted of drug trafficking, see sections 33 and 34 of the 2001 Act.]

28.2. *Notice of requirements of suspended sentence and community, etc orders* (1) This rule applies where the court—

(a)   makes a suspended sentence order;

(b)   imposes a requirement under—
    (i)   a community order,
    (ii)   a youth rehabilitation order, or
    (iii)   a suspended sentence order; or
(c)   orders the defendant to attend meetings with a supervisor.
(2)   The court officer must notify—
(a)   the defendant of—
    (i)   the length of the sentence suspended by a suspended sentence order, and
    (ii)   the period of the suspension;
(b)   the defendant and, where the defendant is under 14, an appropriate adult, of—
    (i)   any requirement or requirements imposed, and
    (ii)   the identity of any responsible officer or supervisor, and the means by which that person may be contacted.
(c)   any responsible officer or supervisor, and, where the defendant is under 14, the appropriate qualifying officer (if that is not the responsible officer), of—
    (i)   the defendant's name, address and telephone number (if available),
    (ii)   the offence or offences of which the defendant was convicted, and
    (iii)   the requirement or requirements imposed; and
(d)   the person affected, where the court imposes a requirement—
    (i)   for the protection of that person from the defendant, or
    (ii)   requiring the defendant to reside with that person.
(3)   If the court imposes an electronic monitoring requirement, the monitor of which is not the responsible officer, the court officer must—
(a)   notify the defendant and, where the defendant is under 16, an appropriate adult, of the monitor's identity, and the means by which the monitor may be contacted; and
(b)   notify the monitor of—
    (i)   the defendant's name, address and telephone number (if available),
    (ii)   the offence or offences of which the defendant was convicted,
    (iii)   the place or places at which the defendant's presence must be monitored,
    (iv)   the period or periods during which the defendant's presence there must be monitored, and
    (v)   the identity of the responsible officer, and the means by which that officer may be contacted.

[Note. See section 219(1) of the Criminal Justice Act 2003; paragraph 34(1) of Schedule 1 to the Criminal Justice and Immigration Act 2008; and section 1A(7) of the Street Offences Act 1959. For the circumstances in which the court may—
(a)   make a suspended sentence order, see section 189 of the 2003 Act;
(b)   make a community order (defined by section 177 of the Criminal Justice Act 2003), or a youth rehabilitation order (defined by section 7 of the Criminal Justice and Immigration Act 2008), and for the identity and duties of responsible officers and qualifying officers, see generally—
*   (i)   Part 12 of the 2003 Act, and*
*   (ii)   Part 1 of the 2008 Act;*
(c)   order the defendant to attend meetings with a supervisor, see section 1(2A) of the Street Offences Act 1959.
Under sections 190 or 215 of the 2003 Act, or section 1(2) of the 2008 Act, the court may impose an electronic monitoring requirement to secure the monitoring of the defendant's compliance with certain other requirements (for example, a curfew or an exclusion).]

28.3.   *Notification requirements*   (1)   This rule applies where, on a conviction, sentence or order, legislation requires the defendant—
(a)   to notify information to the police; or
(b)   to be included in a barred list.
(2)   The court must tell the defendant that such requirements apply, and under what legislation.
[Note. For the circumstances in which a defendant is required to notify information to the police, see—
(a)   Part 2 of, and Schedule 3 to, the Sexual Offences Act 2003 (notification for the period specified by section 82 of the Act after conviction, etc of an offence listed in Schedule 3 and committed in the circumstances specified in that Schedule);
(b)   Part 4 of the Counter Terrorism Act 2008 (notification after conviction of a specified offence of, or connected with, terrorism, for which a specified sentence is imposed).
For the circumstances in which a defendant will be included in a barred list, see paragraphs 1, 2, 7, 8 and 24 of Schedule 3 to the Safeguarding Vulnerable Groups Act 2006. See also paragraph 25 of that Schedule.
These requirements are not part of the court's sentence.]

28.4.   *Variation of sentence*   (1)   This rule—
(a)   applies where a magistrates' court or the Crown Court can vary or rescind a sentence or order, other than an order to which rule 24.18 applies (Setting aside a conviction or varying a costs etc order); and
(b)   authorises the Crown Court, in addition to its other powers, to do so within the period of 56 days beginning with another defendant's acquittal or sentencing where—

(i)   defendants are tried separately in the Crown Court on the same or related facts alleged in one or more indictments, and

(ii)   one is sentenced before another is acquitted or sentenced.

(2)   The court may exercise its power—

(a)   on application by a party, or on its own initiative;

(b)   at a hearing, in public or in private, or without a hearing.

(3)   A party who wants the court to exercise that power must—

(a)   apply in writing as soon as reasonably practicable after—

    (i)   the sentence or order that that party wants the court to vary or rescind, or

    (ii)   where paragraph (1)(b) applies, the other defendant's acquittal or sentencing;

(b)   serve the application on—

    (i)   the court officer, and

    (ii)   each other party; and

(c)   in the application—

    (i)   explain why the sentence should be varied or rescinded,

    (ii)   specify the variation that the applicant proposes, and

    (iii)   if the application is late, explain why.

(4)   The court must not exercise its power in the defendant's absence unless—

(a)   the court makes a variation—

    (i)   which is proposed by the defendant, or

    (ii)   the effect of which is that the defendant is no more severely dealt with under the sentence as varied than before; or

(b)   the defendant has had an opportunity to make representations at a hearing (whether or not the defendant in fact attends).

(5)   The court may—

(a)   extend (even after it has expired) the time limit under paragraph (3), unless the court's power to vary or rescind the sentence cannot be exercised;

(b)   allow an application to be made orally.

[Note. Under section 142 of the Magistrates' Courts Act 1980, in some cases a magistrates' court can vary or rescind a sentence or other order that it has imposed or made, if that appears to be in the interests of justice. The power cannot be exercised if the Crown Court or the High Court has determined an appeal about that sentence or order. See also rule 24.18 (Setting aside a conviction or varying a costs etc order), which governs the exercise by a magistrates' court of the power conferred by section 142 of the 1980 Act in the circumstances to which that rule applies.

Under section 155 of the Powers of Criminal Courts (Sentencing) Act 2000, the Crown Court can vary or rescind a sentence or other order that it has imposed or made. The power cannot be exercised—

(a)   after the period of 56 days beginning with the sentence or order (but see the note below); or

(b)   if an appeal or application for permission to appeal against that sentence or order has been determined.

Under section 155(7), Criminal Procedure Rules can extend that period of 56 days where another defendant is tried separately in the Crown Court on the same or related facts alleged in one or more indictments.]

28.5.   *Application to vary or discharge a compensation, etc order*   (1)   This rule applies where on application by the defendant a magistrates' court can vary or discharge—

(a)   a compensation order; or

(b)   a slavery and trafficking reparation order.

(2)   A defendant who wants the court to exercise that power must—

(a)   apply in writing as soon as practicable after becoming aware of the grounds for doing so;

(b)   serve the application on the magistrates' court officer;

(c)   where the order was made in the Crown Court, serve a copy of the application on the Crown Court officer; and

(d)   in the application, specify the order that the defendant wants the court to vary or discharge and explain (as applicable)—

    (i)   what civil court finding shows that the injury, loss or damage was less than it had appeared to be when the order was made,

    (ii)   in what circumstances the person for whose benefit the order was made has recovered the property for the loss of which it was made,

    (iii)   why a confiscation order, unlawful profit order or slavery and trafficking reparation order makes the defendant now unable to pay compensation or reparation in full, or

    (iv)   in what circumstances the defendant's means have been reduced substantially and unexpectedly, and why they seem unlikely to increase for a considerable period.

(3)   The court officer must serve a copy of the application on the person for whose benefit the order was made.

(4)   The court must not vary or discharge the order unless—

(a)   the defendant, and the person for whose benefit it was made, each has had an opportunity to make representations at a hearing (whether or not either in fact attends); and

(b)   where the order was made in the Crown Court, the Crown Court has notified its consent.
[Note. For the circumstances in which—
(a)   the court may make a compensation order, see section 130 of the Powers of Criminal Courts (Sentencing) Act 2000;
(b)   the court may make a slavery and trafficking reparation order, see section 8 of the Modern Slavery Act 2015;
(c)   a magistrates' court with power to enforce such an order may vary or discharge it under the 2000 Act, see section 133. (Under section 133(4), where the order was made in the Crown Court, the magistrates' court must first obtain the Crown Court's consent.)]

28.6. *Application to remove, revoke or suspend a disqualification or restriction* (1)   This rule applies where, on application by the defendant, the court can remove, revoke or suspend a disqualification or restriction included in a sentence (except a disqualification from driving).
(2)   A defendant who wants the court to exercise such a power must—
(a)   apply in writing, no earlier than the date on which the court can exercise the power;
(b)   serve the application on the court officer; and
(c)   in the application—
    (i)   specify the disqualification or restriction, and
    (ii)   explain why the defendant wants the court to remove, revoke or suspend it.
(3)   The court officer must serve a copy of the application on the chief officer of police for the local justice area.
[Note. Part 29 contains rules about disqualification from driving. See in particular rule 29.2.
Part 34 (Appeal to the Crown Court) and Part 35 (Appeal to the High Court by case stated) contain rules about applications to suspend disqualifications pending appeal.
For the circumstances in which the court may—
(a)   remove a disqualification from keeping a dog, see section 4(6) of the Dangerous Dogs Act 1991. The court may not consider an application made within 1 year of the disqualification; or, after that, within 1 year of any previous application that was refused.
(b)   revoke or suspend a travel restriction order against a defendant convicted of drug trafficking, see section 35 of the Criminal Justice and Police Act 2001. The court may not consider an application made within 2 years of the disqualification, in any case; or, after that, before a specified period has expired.]

28.7. *Application for a restitution order by the victim of a theft* (1)   This rule applies where, on application by the victim of a theft, the court can order a defendant to give that person goods obtained with the proceeds of goods stolen in that theft.
(2)   A person who wants the court to exercise that power if the defendant is convicted must—
(a)   apply in writing as soon as practicable (without waiting for the verdict);
(b)   serve the application on the court officer; and
(c)   in the application—
    (i)   identify the goods, and
    (ii)   explain why the applicant is entitled to them.
(3)   The court officer must serve a copy of the application on each party.
(4)   The court must not determine the application unless the applicant and each party has had an opportunity to make representations at a hearing (whether or not each in fact attends).
(5)   The court may—
(a)   extend (even after it has expired) the time limit under paragraph (2); and
(b)   allow an application to be made orally.
[Note. For the circumstances in which the court may order—
(a)   the return of stolen goods, see section 148 of the Powers of Criminal Courts (Sentencing) Act 2000;
(b)   the defendant to give the victim of the theft goods that are not themselves the stolen goods but which represent their proceeds, see section 148(2)(b) of the 2000 Act.]

28.8. *Directions for commissioning medical reports for sentencing purposes* (1)   This rule applies where for sentencing purposes the court requires—
(a)   a medical examination of the defendant and a report; or
(b)   information about the arrangements that could be made for the defendant where the court is considering—
    (i)   a hospital order, or
    (ii)   a guardianship order.
(2)   The court must—
(a)   identify each issue in respect of which the court requires expert medical opinion and the legislation applicable;
(b)   specify the nature of the expertise likely to be required for giving such opinion;
(c)   identify each party or participant by whom a commission for such opinion must be prepared, who may be—
    (i)   a party (or party's representative) acting on that party's own behalf,
    (ii)   a party (or party's representative) acting on behalf of the court, or
    (iii)   the court officer acting on behalf of the court;
(d)   where there are available to the court arrangements with the National Health Service under which an assessment of a defendant's mental health may be prepared, give such directions as are needed under those arrangements for obtaining the expert report or reports required;

(e)   where no such arrangements are available to the court, or they will not be used, give directions for the commissioning of an expert report or expert reports, including—

    (i)   such directions as can be made about supplying the expert or experts with the defendant's medical records,

    (ii)   directions about the other information, about the defendant and about the offence or offences alleged to have been committed by the defendant, which is to be supplied to each expert, and

    (iii)   directions about the arrangements that will apply for the payment of each expert;

(f)   set a timetable providing for—

    (i)   the date by which a commission is to be delivered to each expert,

    (ii)   the date by which any failure to accept a commission is to be reported to the court,

    (iii)   the date or dates by which progress in the preparation of a report or reports is to be reviewed by the court officer, and

    (iv)   the date by which each report commissioned is to be received by the court; and

(g)   identify the person (each person, if more than one) to whom a copy of a report is to be supplied, and by whom.

(3)   A commission addressed to an expert must—

(a)   identify each issue in respect of which the court requires expert medical opinion and the legislation applicable;

(b)   include—

    (i)   the information required by the court to be supplied to the expert,

    (ii)   details of the timetable set by the court, and

    (iii)   details of the arrangements that will apply for the payment of the expert;

(c)   identify the person (each person, if more than one) to whom a copy of the expert's report is to be supplied; and

(d)   request confirmation that the expert from whom the opinion is sought—

    (i)   accepts the commission, and

    (ii)   will adhere to the timetable.

[Note. See also rule 3.28 (directions for commissioning medical reports in connection with fitness to participate in the trial, etc).

For sentencing purposes the court may request a medical examination of the defendant and a report under—

(a)   *section 35 of the Mental Health Act 1983, under which the court may order the defendant's detention in hospital to obtain a medical report;*

(b)   *section 36 of the 1983 Act, under which the Crown Court may order the defendant's detention in hospital instead of in custody pending trial;*

(c)   *section 37 of the 1983 Act, under which the court may order the defendant's detention and treatment in hospital, or make a guardianship order, instead of disposing of the case in another way (section 37(3) allows a magistrates' court to make such an order without convicting the defendant if satisfied that the defendant did the act or made the omission charged);*

(d)   *section 38 of the 1983 Act, under which the court may order the defendant's temporary detention and treatment in hospital instead of disposing of the case in another way;*

(e)   *section 157 of the Criminal Justice Act 2003, under which the court must usually obtain and consider a medical report before passing a custodial sentence if the defendant is, or appears to be, mentally disordered;*

(f)   *section 207 of the 2003 Act (in the case of a defendant aged 18 or over), or section 1(1)(k) of the Criminal Justice and Immigration Act 2008 (in the case of a defendant who is under 18), under which the court may impose a mental health treatment requirement.*

For the purposes of the legislation listed in (b), (c) and (d) above, the court requires the written or oral evidence of at least two registered medical practitioners, at least one of whom is approved as having special experience in the diagnosis or treatment of mental disorder. For the purposes of (a), (e) and (f) the court requires the evidence of one medical practitioner so approved.

Under section 11 of the Powers of Criminal Courts (Sentencing) Act 2000, a magistrates' court may adjourn a trial to obtain medical reports.

Part 19 (Expert evidence) contains rules about the content of expert medical reports.

For the authorities from whom the court may require information about hospital treatment or guardianship, see sections 39 and 39A of the 1983 Act.

The Practice Direction includes a timetable for the commissioning and preparation of a report or reports which the court may adopt with such adjustments as the court directs.

Payments to medical practitioners for reports and for giving evidence are governed by section 19(3) of the Prosecution of Offences Act 1985 and by the Costs in Criminal Cases (General) Regulations 1986, regulation 17 (Determination of rates or scales of allowances payable out of central funds), regulation 20 (Expert witnesses, etc) and regulation 25 (Written medical reports). The rates and scales of allowances payable under those Regulations are determined by the Lord Chancellor.]

28.9. Information to be supplied on admission to hospital or guardianship (1) This rule applies where the court—

(a)   orders the defendant's detention and treatment in hospital; or

(b)   makes a guardianship order.

(2)   Unless the court otherwise directs, the court officer must, as soon as practicable, serve on (as applicable) the hospital or the guardian—

(a)   a record of the court's order;
(b)   such information as the court has received that appears likely to assist in treating or otherwise dealing with the defendant, including information about—
    (i)   the defendant's mental condition,
    (ii)   the defendant's other circumstances, and
    (iii)   the circumstances of the offence.
[Note. For the circumstances in which the court may order the defendant's detention and treatment in hospital, see sections 35, 36, 37, 38 and 44 of the Mental Health Act 1983. For the circumstances in which the court may make a guardianship order, see the same section 37.]

28.10. *Information to be supplied on committal for sentence, etc* (1) This rule applies where a magistrates' court or the Crown Court convicts the defendant and—
(a)   commits or adjourns the case to another court—
    (i)   for sentence, or
    (ii)   for the defendant to be dealt with for breach of a deferred sentence, a conditional discharge, or a suspended sentence of imprisonment, imposed by that other court;
(b)   deals with a deferred sentence, a conditional discharge, or a suspended sentence of imprisonment, imposed by another court; or
(c)   makes an order that another court is, or may be, required to enforce.
(2)   Unless the convicting court otherwise directs, the court officer must, as soon as practicable—
(a)   where paragraph (1)(a) applies, arrange the transmission from the convicting to the other court of a record of any relevant—
    (i)   certificate of conviction,
    (ii)   magistrates' court register entry,
    (iii)   decision about bail, for the purposes of section 5 of the Bail Act 1976,
    (iv)   note of evidence,
    (v)   statement or other document introduced in evidence,
    (vi)   medical or other report,
    (vii)   representation order or application for such order, and
    (viii) interim driving disqualification;
(b)   where paragraph (1)(b) or (c) applies, arrange—
    (i)   the transmission from the convicting to the other court of notice of the convicting court's order, and
    (ii)   the recording of that order at the other court;
(c)   in every case, notify the defendant and, where the defendant is under 14, an appropriate adult, of the location of the other court.
[Note. For the circumstances in which—
(a)   *a magistrates' court may (and in some cases must) commit the defendant to the Crown Court for sentence, see sections 3, 3A, 3B, 3C, 4, 4A and 6 of the Powers of Criminal Courts (Sentencing) Act 2000 and section 43 of the Mental Health Act 1983;*
(b)   *a magistrates' court may adjourn the case to another magistrates' court for sentence, see section 10 of the Magistrates' Courts Act 1980 and section 10 of the 2000 Act;*
(c)   *a magistrates' court or the Crown Court may (and in some cases must) adjourn the case to a youth court for sentence, see section 8 of the 2000 Act;*
(d)   *a youth court may adjourn the case to a magistrates' court for sentence, see section 9 of the 2000 Act;*
(e)   *a magistrates' court may transfer a fine to be enforced to another court, see sections 89 and 90 of the 1980 Act.*
For the court's powers where it convicts a defendant who is subject to a deferred sentence, a conditional discharge, or a suspended sentence of imprisonment, imposed by another court, see sections 1C and 13 of the 2000 Act and section 189 of, and Schedule 12 to, the Criminal Justice Act 2003.
Under section 140 of the 2000 Act, a fine imposed or other sum ordered to be paid in the Crown Court is enforceable by a magistrates' court specified in the order, or from which the case was committed or sent to the Crown Court.
See also section 219(3) of the 2003 Act; paragraph 34(3) of Schedule 1 to the Criminal Justice and Immigration Act 2008; and section 1A(9) of the Street Offences Act 1959.]

28.11. *Application to review sentence because of assistance given or withheld* (1) This rule applies where the Crown Court can reduce or increase a sentence on application by a prosecutor in a case in which—
(a)   since being sentenced, the defendant has assisted, or has agreed to assist, an investigator or prosecutor in relation to an offence; or
(b)   since receiving a reduced sentence for agreeing to give such assistance, the defendant has failed to do so.
(2)   A prosecutor who wants the court to exercise that power must—
(a)   apply in writing as soon as practicable after becoming aware of the grounds for doing so;
(b)   serve the application on—
    (i)   the court officer, and
    (ii)   the defendant; and
(c)   in the application—
    (i)   explain why the sentence should be reduced, or increased, as appropriate, and

(ii)   identify any other matter relevant to the court's decision, including any sentencing guideline or guideline case.   (3)   The general rule is that the application must be determined by the judge who passed the sentence, unless that judge is unavailable.

(4)   The court must not determine the application in the defendant's absence unless the defendant has had an opportunity to make representations at a hearing (whether or not the defendant in fact attends).

[Note. Under section 73 of the Serious Organised Crime and Police Act 2005, the Crown Court may pass a lesser sentence than it otherwise would have passed because the defendant has assisted, or has agreed to assist, an investigator or prosecutor in relation to an offence.

Under section 74 of the 2005 Act, where the Crown Court has sentenced a defendant a prosecutor may apply to the court—

(a)   *to reduce the sentence, if the defendant subsequently assists, or agrees to assist, in the investigation or prosecution of an offence; or*

(b)   *to increase a reduced sentence to that which the court otherwise would have passed, if the defendant agreed to give such assistance but subsequently has knowingly failed to do so.*

Such an application may be made only where the defendant is still serving the sentence and the prosecutor thinks it is in the interests of justice to apply.]

PART 29   ROAD TRAFFIC PENALTIES

Contents of this Part

Note

[Note. Part 24 contains rules about the general procedure on sentencing in a magistrates' court. Part 25 contains corresponding rules for the Crown Court.]

B.26   **29.1.** *Representations about obligatory disqualification or endorsement* (1)   This rule applies—

(a)   where the court—
  (i)   convicts the defendant of an offence involving obligatory disqualification from driving and section 34(1) of the Road Traffic Offenders Act 1988 (Disqualification for certain offences) applies,
  (ii)   convicts the defendant of an offence where section 35 of the 1988 Act (Disqualification for repeated offences) applies, or
  (iii)   convicts the defendant of an offence involving obligatory endorsement of the defendant's driving record and section 44 of the 1988 Act (Orders for endorsement) applies;

(b)   unless the defendant is absent.

(2)   The court must explain, in terms the defendant can understand (with help, if necessary)—

(a)   where paragraph (1)(a)(i) applies (obligatory disqualification under section 34)—
  (i)   that the court must order the defendant to be disqualified from driving for a minimum of 12 months (or 2 or 3 years, as the case may be, according to the offence and the defendant's driving record), unless the court decides that there are special reasons to order disqualification for a shorter period, or not to order disqualification at all, and
  (ii)   if applicable, that the period of disqualification will be reduced by at least 3 months if, by no later than 2 months before the end of the reduced period, the defendant completes an approved driving course;

(b)   where paragraph (1)(a)(ii) applies (disqualification under section 35)—
  (i)   that the court must order the defendant to be disqualified from driving for a minimum of 6 months (or 1 or 2 years, as the case may be, according to the defendant's driving record), unless, having regard to all the circumstances, the court decides to order disqualification for a shorter period, or not to order disqualification at all, and
  (ii)   that circumstances of which the court cannot take account in making its decision are any that make the offence not a serious one; hardship (other than exceptional hardship); and any that during the last 3 years already have been taken into account by a court when ordering disqualification for less than the usual minimum period, or not at all, for repeated driving offences;

(c) where paragraph (1)(a)(iii) applies (obligatory endorsement), that the court must order the endorsement of the defendant's driving record unless the court decides that there are special reasons not to do so;

(d) in every case, as applicable—

  (i) that the court already has received representations from the defendant about whether any such special reasons or mitigating circumstances apply and will take account of them, or

  (ii) that the defendant may make such representations now, on oath or affirmation.

(3) Unless the court already has received such representations from the defendant, before it applies rule 24.11 (magistrates' court procedure if the court convicts) or rule 25.16 (Crown Court procedure if the court convicts), as the case may be, the court must—

(a) ask whether the defendant wants to make any such representations; and

(b) if the answer to that question is 'yes', require the defendant to take an oath or affirm and make them.

[Note. For the circumstances in which the court—

(a) may, and in some cases must, order disqualification from driving under the Road Traffic Offenders Act 1988, see sections 26, 34, 35 and 36 of that Act;

(b) may, for some reasons or in some circumstances, abbreviate or dispense with a period of disqualification otherwise required by the 1988 Act, see sections 34(1) and 35(1), (4) of that Act;

(c) must usually order endorsement, see sections 9, 44 and 96 of, and Schedule 2 to, the 1988 Act.

For the circumstances in which the period of a disqualification from driving will be reduced if the defendant completes an approved driving course, see section 34A of the 1988 Act.]

29.2. *Application to remove a disqualification from driving* (1) This rule applies where, on application by the defendant, the court can remove a disqualification from driving.

(2) A defendant who wants the court to exercise that power must—

(a) apply in writing, no earlier than the date on which the court can exercise the power;

(b) serve the application on the court officer; and

(c) in the application—

  (i) specify the disqualification, and

  (ii) explain why the defendant wants the court to remove it.

(3) The court officer must serve a copy of the application on the chief officer of police for the local justice area.

[Note. For the circumstances in which the court may remove a disqualification from driving imposed under section 34 or 35 of the Road Traffic Offenders Act 1988, see section 42 of the Act. The court may not consider an application made within 2 years of the disqualification, in any case; or, after that, before a specified period has expired.]

29.3. *Information to be supplied on order for endorsement of driving record, etc* (1) This rule applies where the court—

(a) convicts the defendant of an offence involving obligatory endorsement, and orders there to be endorsed on the defendant's driving record (and on any counterpart licence, if other legislation requires)—

  (i) particulars of the conviction,

  (ii) particulars of any disqualification from driving that the court imposes, and

  (iii) the penalty points to be attributed to the offence;

(b) disqualifies the defendant from driving for any other offence; or

(c) suspends or removes a disqualification from driving.

(2) The court officer must, as soon as practicable, serve on the Secretary of State notice that includes details of—

(a) where paragraph (1)(a) applies—

  (i) the local justice area in which the court is acting,

  (ii) the dates of conviction and sentence,

  (iii) the offence, and the date on which it was committed,

  (iv) the sentence, and

  (v) the date of birth, and sex, of the defendant, where those details are available;

(b) where paragraph (1)(b) applies—

  (i) the date and period of the disqualification,

  (ii) the power exercised by the court;

(c) where paragraph (1)(c) applies—

  (i) the date and period of the disqualification,

  (ii) the date and terms of the order for its suspension or removal,

  (iii) the power exercised by the court, and

  (iv) where the court suspends the disqualification pending appeal, the court to which the defendant has appealed.

[Note. See sections 39(3), 42(5), 44A, 47 and 97A of the Road Traffic Offenders Act 1988.

Under section 25 of the 1988 Act, the court may order a defendant to disclose his or her date of birth, and sex, where that is not apparent (for example, where the defendant is convicted in his or her absence). Under section 27 of the 1988 Act, and under sections 146(4) and 147(5) of the Powers of Criminal Courts (Sentencing) Act 2000, the court may order a defendant to produce his or her

driving licence, if not already produced.
For the circumstances in which the court—
(a) must usually order endorsement, see sections 9, 44 and 96 of, and Schedule 2 to, the 1988 Act;
(b) may, and in some cases must, order disqualification from driving under the 1988 Act, see sections 26, 34, 35 and 36 of that Act;
(c) may order disqualification from driving under the 2000 Act, see sections 146 and 147 of that Act;
(d) may suspend a disqualification from driving pending appeal, see sections 39 and 40 of the 1988 Act (Part 34 (Appeal to the Crown Court) and Part 35 (Appeal to the High Court by case stated) contain relevant rules);
(e) may remove a disqualification from driving imposed under section 34 or 35 of the 1988 Act, see section 42 of that Act (rule 29.2 applies).]

29.4. Statutory declaration to avoid fine after fixed penalty notice (1) This rule applies where—
(a) a chief officer of police, or the Secretary of State, serves on the magistrates' court officer a certificate registering, for enforcement as a fine, a sum payable by a defendant after failure to comply with a fixed penalty notice;
(b) the court officer notifies the defendant of the registration; and
(c) the defendant makes a statutory declaration with the effect that there become void—
 (i) the fixed penalty notice, or any associated notice sent to the defendant as owner of the vehicle concerned, and
 (ii) the registration and any enforcement proceedings.
(2) The defendant must serve that statutory declaration not more than 21 days after service of notice of the registration, unless the court extends that time limit.
(3) The court officer must—
(a) serve a copy of the statutory declaration on the person by whom the certificate was registered;
(b) cancel any endorsement on the defendant's driving record (and on any counterpart licence, if other legislation requires); and
(c) notify the Secretary of State of any such cancellation.
[Note. See sections 72(1), (6), (6A), 73(1) and 74(2) of the Road Traffic Offenders Act 1988.
For the circumstances in which—
(a) a sum may be registered for enforcement as a fine after failure to comply with a fixed penalty notice, see sections 54, 55, 62, 63, 64, 70 and 71 of the 1988 Act;
(b) the registration may become void on the making of a statutory declaration by the defendant, see sections 72 and 73 of the 1988 Act.]

29.5. Application for declaration about a course or programme certificate decision (1) This rule applies where the court can declare unjustified—
(a) a course provider's failure or refusal to give a certificate of the defendant's satisfactory completion of an approved course; or
(b) a programme provider's giving of a certificate of the defendant's failure fully to participate in an approved programme.
(2) A defendant who wants the court to exercise that power must—
(a) apply in writing, not more than 28 days after—
 (i) the date by which the defendant was required to complete the course, or
 (ii) the giving of the certificate of failure fully to participate in the programme;
(b) serve the application on the court officer; and
(c) in the application, specify the course or programme and explain (as applicable)—
 (i) that the course provider has failed to give a certificate,
 (ii) where the course provider has refused to give a certificate, why the defendant disagrees with the reasons for that decision, or
 (iii) where the programme provider has given a certificate, why the defendant disagrees with the reasons for that decision.
(3) The court officer must serve a copy of the application on the course or programme provider.
(4) The court must not determine the application unless the defendant, and the course or programme provider, each has had an opportunity to make representations at a hearing (whether or not either in fact attends).
[Note. For the circumstances in which the court may reduce a road traffic penalty on condition that the defendant attend an approved course, or take part in an approved programme, see sections 30A, 34A and 34D of the Road Traffic Offenders Act 1988.
Under sections 30B, 34B and 34E of the 1988 Act, the court that made the order, or the defendant's local magistrates' court, on application by the defendant may review a course or programme provider's decision that the defendant has not completed the course satisfactorily, or has not participated fully in the programme.]

29.6. Appeal against recognition of foreign driving disqualification (1) This rule applies where—
(a) a Minister gives a disqualification notice under section 57 of the Crime (International Co-operation) Act 2003; and
(b) the person to whom it is given wants to appeal under section 59 of the Act to a

magistrates' court.

(2) That person ('the appellant') must serve an appeal notice on—

(a) the court officer, at a magistrates' court in the local justice area in which the appellant lives; and

(b) the Minister, at the address given in the disqualification notice.

(3) The appellant must serve the appeal notice within the period for which section 59 of the 2003 Act provides.

(4) The appeal notice must—

(a) attach a copy of the disqualification notice;

(b) explain which of the conditions in section 56 of the 2003 Act is not met, and why section 57 of the Act therefore does not apply; and

(c) include any application to suspend the disqualification, under section 60 of the Act.

(5) The Minister may serve a respondent's notice, and must do so if—

(a) the Minister wants to make representations to the court; or

(b) the court so directs.

(6) The Minister must—

(a) unless the court otherwise directs, serve any such respondent's notice not more than 14 days after—

(i) the appellant serves the appeal notice, or

(ii) a direction to do so;

(b) in any such respondent's notice—

(i) identify the grounds of opposition on which the Minister relies,

(ii) summarise any relevant facts not already included in the disqualification and appeal notices, and

(iii) identify any other document that the Minister thinks the court will need to decide the appeal (and serve any such document with the notice).

(7) Where the court determines an appeal, the general rule is that it must do so at a hearing (which must be in public, unless the court otherwise directs).

(8) The court officer must serve on the Minister—

(a) notice of the outcome of the appeal;

(b) notice of any suspension of the disqualification; and

(c) the appellant's driving licence, if surrendered to the court officer.

[Note. Section 56 of the Crime (International Co-operation) Act 2003 sets out the conditions for recognition in the United Kingdom of a foreign driving disqualification, and provides that section 57 of the Act applies where they are met. Under section 57, the appropriate Minister may, and in some cases must, give the person concerned notice that he or she is disqualified in the UK, too, and for what period.

Under section 59 of the 2003 Act, that person may appeal to a magistrates' court. If the court is satisfied that section 57 of the Act does not apply in that person's case, the court must allow the appeal and notify the Minister. Otherwise, it must dismiss the appeal.

The time limit for appeal under section 59 of the 2003 Act is the end of the period of 21 days beginning with the day on which the Minister gives the notice under section 57. That period may be neither extended nor shortened.

Under section 60 of the 2003 Act, court may suspend the disqualification, on such terms as it thinks fit.

Under section 63 of the 2003 Act, it is an offence for a person to whom the Minister gives a notice under section 57 not to surrender any licence that he or she holds, within the same period as for an appeal.]

PART 30   ENFORCEMENT OF FINES AND OTHER ORDERS FOR PAYMENT

Contents of this Part

Note

[Note. Part 13 contains rules about warrants for arrest, detention or imprisonment, including such warrants issued for failure to pay fines, etc

Part 24 contains rules about the procedure on sentencing in a magistrates' court
Part 28 contains rules about the exercise of a magistrates' court's powers to enforce an order made by another court.]

B.27   *30.1.   When this Part applies*   (1)   This Part applies where a magistrates' court can enforce payment of—
(a)   a fine, or a sum that legislation requires the court to treat as a fine; or
(b)   any other sum that a court has ordered to be paid—
           (i)   on a conviction, or
           (ii)   on the forfeiture of a surety.
(2)   Rules 30.7 to 30.9 apply where the court, or a fines officer, issues a warrant for an enforcement agent to take control of a defendant's goods and sell them, using the procedure in Schedule 12 to the Tribunals, Courts and Enforcement Act 2007.
(3)   In this Part—
(a)   'defendant' means anyone liable to pay a sum to which this Part applies;
(b)   'payment terms' means by when, and by what (if any) instalments, such a sum must be paid.
[Note. For the means by which a magistrates' court may enforce payment, see—
(a)   Part 3 of the Magistrates' Courts Act 1980; and
(b)   Schedule 5 to the Courts Act 2003 and the Fines Collection Regulations 2006.
Under that Schedule and those Regulations, some enforcement powers may be exercised by a fines officer.
See also section 62 of, and Schedule 12 to, the Tribunals, Courts and Enforcement Act 2007. In that Act, a warrant to which this Part applies is described as 'a warrant of control'.]

30.2.   Exercise of court's powers   The court must not exercise its enforcement powers unless—
(a)   the court officer has served on the defendant any collection order or other notice of—
           (i)   the obligation to pay,
           (ii)   the payment terms, and
           (iii)   how and where the defendant must pay; and
(b)   the defendant has failed to comply with the payment terms.
[Note. See section 76 of the Magistrates' Courts Act 1980; and paragraphs 12 and 13 of Schedule 5 to the Courts Act 2003.]

30.3.   Duty to give receipt   (1)   This rule applies where the defendant makes a payment to—
(a)   the court officer specified in an order or notice served under rule 30.2;
(b)   another court officer;
(c)   any—
           (i)   custodian of the defendant,
           (ii)   supervisor appointed to encourage the defendant to pay, or
           (iii)   responsible officer appointed under a community sentence or a suspended sentence of imprisonment; or
(d)   a person executing a warrant to which rule 13.6 (warrants for arrest, detention or imprisonment that cease to have effect on payment) or this Part applies.
(2)   The person receiving the payment must—
(a)   give the defendant a receipt, unless the method of payment generates an independent record (for example, a bank record); and
(b)   as soon as practicable transmit the payment to the court officer specified in an order or notice served under rule 30.2, if the recipient is not that court officer.
[Note. For the effect of payment to a person executing a warrant to which rule 13.6 applies, see that rule and sections 79 and 125(1) of the Magistrates' Courts Act 1980.
For the circumstances in which the court may appoint a person to supervise payment, see section 88 of the 1980 Act.]

30.4.   Appeal against decision of fines officer   (1)   This rule applies where—
(a)   a collection order is in force;
(b)   a fines officer makes a decision under one of these paragraphs of Schedule 5 to the Courts Act 2003—
           (i)   paragraph 22 (Application to fines officer for variation of order or attachment of earnings order, etc),
           (ii)   paragraph 31 (Application to fines officer for variation of reserve terms), or
           (iii)   paragraph 37 (Functions of fines officer in relation to defaulters: referral or further steps notice); and
(c)   the defendant wants to appeal against that decision.
(2)   Unless the court otherwise directs, the defendant must—
(a)   appeal in writing not more than 10 business days after the decision;
(b)   serve the appeal on the court officer; and
(c)   in the appeal—
           (i)   explain why a different decision should be made, and
           (ii)   specify the decision that the defendant proposes.
(3)   Where the court determines an appeal, the general rule is that it must do so at a hearing.
[Note. Under paragraph 12 of Schedule 5 to the Courts Act 2003, where a collection order is in force the court's powers to deal with the defendant's liability to pay the sum for which that order was made are subject to the provisions of that Schedule and to fines collection regulations.
For the circumstances in which a defendant may appeal against a decision to which this

rule applies, see paragraphs 23, 32 and 37(9) of Schedule 5 to the 2003 Act. The time limit for appeal is prescribed by those paragraphs. It may be neither extended nor shortened.]

30.5. *Application to reduce a fine, vary payment terms or remit a courts charge* (1) This rule applies where—

(a)   no collection order is in force and the defendant wants the court to—

    (i)   reduce the amount of a fine, or

    (ii)   vary payment terms;

(b)   the defendant, a fines officer or an enforcement agent wants the court to remit a criminal courts charge.

(2)   Unless the court otherwise directs, such a defendant, fines officer or enforcement agent must—

(a)   apply in writing;

(b)   serve the application on the court officer;

(c)   if the application is to reduce a fine or vary payment terms, explain—

    (i)   what relevant circumstances have not yet been considered by the court, and

    (ii)   why the fine should be reduced, or the payment terms varied;

(d)   if the application is to remit a criminal courts charge, explain—

    (i)   how the circumstances meet the time limits and other conditions in section 21E of the Prosecution of Offences Act 1985, and

    (ii)   why the charge should be remitted.

(3)   The court may determine an application—

(a)   at a hearing, which may be in public or in private; or

(b)   without a hearing.

[Note. See sections 75, 85 and 85A of the Magistrates' Courts Act 1980, section 165 of the Criminal Justice Act 2003 and section 21E of the Prosecution of Offences Act 1985.

Under section 21A of the 1985 Act, a court must, at the times listed in section 21B, order a defendant convicted of an offence to pay a charge in respect of relevant court costs. Under section 21E of the Act, a magistrates' court may remit the whole or part of such a charge, but—

(a)   *the court may do so only if it is satisfied that—*

    (i)   *the defendant has taken all reasonable steps to pay the charge, having regard to his or her personal circumstances, or*

    (ii)   *collection and enforcement of the charge is impracticable;*

(b)   *the court may not do so at a time when the defendant is in prison; and*

(c)   *the court may not do so unless the periods specified by regulations under section 21E all have expired.]*

30.6. *Claim to avoid fine after penalty notice* (1)   This rule applies where—

(a)   a chief officer of police serves on the magistrates' court officer a certificate registering, for enforcement as a fine, a sum payable by a defendant after failure to comply with a penalty notice; and

(b)   the court or a fines officer enforces the fine.

(2)   A defendant who claims not to be the person to whom the penalty notice was issued must, unless the court otherwise directs—

(a)   make that claim in writing; and

(b)   serve it on the court officer.

(3)   The court officer must—

(a)   notify the chief officer of police by whom the certificate was registered; and

(b)   refer the case to the court.

(4)   Where such a claim is made—

(a)   the general rule is that the court must adjourn the enforcement for 28 days and fix a hearing; but

(b)   the court may make a different order.

(5)   At any such hearing, the chief officer of police must introduce any evidence to contradict the defendant's claim.

[Note. See section 10 of the Criminal Justice and Police Act 2001.

For the circumstances in which a sum may be registered for enforcement as a fine after failure to comply with a penalty notice, see sections 8 and 9 of the 2001 Act.]

30.7. *Information to be included in a warrant of control* (1)   A warrant must identify—

(a)   each person to whom it is directed;

(b)   the defendant against whom it was issued;

(c)   the sum for which it was issued and the reason that sum is owed;

(d)   the court or fines officer who issued it, unless that is otherwise recorded by the court officer; and

(e)   the court office for the court or fines officer who issued it.

(2)   A person to whom a warrant is directed must record on it the date and time at which it is received.

(3)   A warrant that contains an error is not invalid, as long as—

(a)   it was issued in respect of a lawful decision by the court or fines officer; and

(b)   it contains enough information to identify that decision.

[Note. See sections 78 and 125ZA of the Magistrates' Courts Act 1980.]

30.8.   *Warrant of control: application by enforcement agent for extension of time, etc*   (1)   This rule applies where an enforcement agent wants the court to exercise a power under Schedule 12 to the Tribunals, Courts and Enforcement Act 2007, or under regulations made under that Schedule, to—

(a)   shorten or extend a time limit;

(b)   give the agent authority to—

    (i)   enter premises which the agent would not otherwise have authority to enter,

    (ii)   enter or remain on premises at a time at which the agent would not otherwise have authority to be there,

    (iii)   use reasonable force, in circumstances in which the agent would not otherwise have authority to use such force,

    (iv)   sell goods by a method which the agent would not otherwise have authority to use, or

    (v)   recover disbursements which the agent would not otherwise have authority to recover;

(c)   specify the manner in which goods which have not been sold must be disposed of.

(2)   Such an enforcement agent must—

(a)   apply in writing;

(b)   serve the application on the court officer; and

(c)   pay any fee prescribed.

(3)   The application must—

(a)   identify the power that the agent wants the court to exercise;

(b)   explain how the conditions for the exercise of that power are satisfied, including any condition that requires the agent to give another person notice of the application;

(c)   specify those persons, if any, to whom the agent has given notice in accordance with such a condition; and

(d)   propose the terms of the order that the agent wants the court to make;

(4)   A person to whom the enforcement agent has given notice of an application and who wants to make representations to the court must—

(a)   serve the representations on—

    (i)   the court officer,

    (ii)   the enforcement agent, and

    (iii)   any other person to whom the enforcement agent gave notice;

(b)   do so as soon as reasonably practicable and in any event within such period as the court directs; and

(c)   in the representations, propose the terms of the order that that person wants the court to make, and explain why.

(5)   The court—

(a)   must not determine an application unless any person to whom the enforcement agent gave notice—

    (i)   is present, or

    (ii)   has had a reasonable opportunity to respond;

(b)   subject to that, may determine an application—

    (i)   at a hearing, which must be in private unless the court otherwise directs, or

    (ii)   without a hearing.

[Note. See paragraphs 8, 15, 20, 21, 25, 31, 32 and 41 of Schedule 12 to the Tribunals, Courts and Enforcement Act 2007, regulations 6, 9, 13, 22, 25, 28, 29, 41 and 47 of the Taking Control of Goods Regulations 2013 and regulation 10 of the Taking Control of Goods (Fees) Regulations 2014. Under paragraph 41 of that Schedule and regulation 41 of the 2013 Regulations, on an application for authority to sell goods otherwise than by public auction the enforcement agent must give notice to a creditor of the defendant in the circumstances described in those provisions.]

30.9.   *Warrant of control: application to resolve dispute*   (1)   This rule applies where a defendant's goods are sold using the procedure in Schedule 12 to the Tribunals, Courts and Enforcement Act 2007 and there is a dispute about—

(a)   what share of the proceeds of those goods should be paid by the enforcement agent to a co-owner; or

(b)   the fees or disbursements sought or recovered by the enforcement agent out of the proceeds.

(2)   An enforcement agent, a defendant or a co-owner who wants the court to resolve the dispute must—

(a)   apply in writing as soon as practicable after becoming aware of the grounds for doing so;

(b)   serve the application on

    (i)   the court officer,

    (ii)   each other party to the dispute, and

    (iii)   any other co-owner; and

(c)   pay any fee prescribed.

(3)   The application must—

(a)   identify the warrant of control;

(b)   specify the goods sold, the proceeds, and the fees and disbursements sought or recovered by the enforcement agent;

(c)   identify the power that the applicant wants the court to exercise;

(d)   specify the persons served with the application;

(e)   explain the circumstances of the dispute; and

(f)   propose the terms of the order that the applicant wants the court to make.

(4)   A person served with an application who wants to make representations to the court must—

(a)   serve the representations on—

  (i)   the court officer,

  (ii)   the applicant, and

  (iii)   any other person on whom the application was served;

(b)   do so as soon as reasonably practicable and in any event within such period as the court directs; and

(c)   in the representations, propose the terms of the order that that person wants the court to make, and explain why.

(5)   The court—

(a)   must determine an application at a hearing, which must be in private unless the court otherwise directs;

(b)   must not determine an application unless each party—

  (i)   is present, or

  (ii)   has had a reasonable opportunity to attend.

[Note. See paragraph 50 of Schedule 12 to the Tribunals, Courts and Enforcement Act 2007, and regulations 15 and 16 of the Taking Control of Goods (Fees) Regulations 2014.]

30.10. *Financial penalties imposed in other European Union member States* (1) This rule applies where the Lord Chancellor gives the court officer a request to enforce a financial penalty imposed in another European Union member State.

(2)   The court officer must serve on the defendant—

(a)   notice of the request for enforcement, and of its effect;

(b)   a copy of—

  (i)   the certificate requesting enforcement, and

  (ii)   the decision requiring payment to which that certificate relates; and

(c)   notice that the procedure set out in this rule applies.

(3)   A defendant who wants the court to refuse enforcement must—

(a)   serve notice of objection on the court officer;

(b)   unless the court otherwise directs, serve that notice not more than 14 days after service of notice of the request; and

(c)   in the notice of objection—

  (i)   identify each ground for refusal on which the defendant relies,

  (ii)   summarise any relevant facts not already included in the certificate and decision served with the notice of the request, and

  (iii)   identify any other document that the defendant thinks the court will need to determine the request (and serve any such document with the notice).

(4)   The court—

(a)   may determine a request for enforcement—

  (i)   at a hearing, which must be in public unless the court otherwise directs, or

  (ii)   without a hearing; but

(b)   must not allow enforcement unless the defendant has had at least 14 days in which to serve notice of objection.

(5)   Paragraphs (2) and (3) do not apply if, on receipt of the request, the court decides that a ground for refusal applies.

(6)   The court officer must serve on the Lord Chancellor notice of the court's decision.

[Note. Under section 84 of the Criminal Justice and Immigration Act 2008—

(a)   the Lord Chancellor may receive—

  (i)   a certificate issued in another European Union member State, requesting enforcement of a financial penalty to which applies the Framework Decision of the Council of the European Union 2005/214/JHA, as amended by Council Framework Decision 2009/299/JHA, on the application of the principle of mutual recognition to financial penalties; and

  (ii)   the decision requiring payment of the penalty to which that certificate relates; and

(b)   the Lord Chancellor must then give the court officer—

  (i)   that certificate and that decision, and

  (ii)   a notice stating whether the Lord Chancellor thinks that any of the grounds for refusal of the request apply, and giving reasons for that opinion.

Under section 85 of the 2008 Act—

(a)   the court must then decide whether it is satisfied that any of the grounds for refusal of the request apply; and

(b)   if the court is not so satisfied, then the decision requiring payment may be enforced as if the penalty concerned were a sum that the court itself had ordered to be paid on convicting the defendant.

The grounds for refusal are listed in Schedule 19 to the 2008 Act, paraphrasing the grounds set out in the Framework Decision.

See also sections 91 and 92 of the 2008 Act.]

PART 31 BEHAVIOUR ORDERS

Note

[Note. See Part 3 for the court's general powers to consider an application and to give directions].

B.28 31.1. *When this Part applies* (1) This Part applies where—
(a) a magistrates' court or the Crown Court can make, vary or revoke a civil order—
  (i) as well as, or instead of, passing a sentence, or in any other circumstances in which other legislation allows the court to make such an order, and
  (ii) that requires someone to do, or not do, something;
(b) a magistrates' court or the Crown Court can make a European protection order;
(c) a magistrates' court can give effect to a European protection order made in another European Union member State.
(2) A reference to a 'behaviour order' in this Part is a reference to any such order.
(3) A reference to 'hearsay evidence' in this Part is a reference to evidence consisting of hearsay within the meaning of section 1(2) of the Civil Evidence Act 1995.
[Note. In the circumstances set out in the Acts listed, the court can make a behaviour order—
(a) on conviction, under—
  (i) section 14A of the Football Spectators Act 1989 (football banning orders),
  (ii) section 5 of the Protection from Harassment Act 1997 (restraining orders),
  (iii) sections 1C and 1D of the Crime and Disorder Act 1998 (anti-social behaviour orders and interim anti-social behaviour orders),
  (iv) sections 8 and 9 of the Crime and Disorder Act 1998 (parenting orders),
  (v) section 103A of the Sexual Offences Act 2003 (sexual harm prevention orders),
  (vi) section 19 or 21 of the Serious Crime Act 2007 (serious crime prevention orders),
  (vii) section 22 of the Anti-social Behaviour, Crime and Policing Act 2014 (criminal behaviour orders),
  (viii) section 14 of the Modern Slavery Act 2015 (slavery and trafficking prevention orders);
  (ix) section 19 of the Psychoactive Substances Act 2016 (prohibition orders);
  (x) section 20 of the Immigration Act 2016 (labour market enforcement orders);;
(b) on acquittal, under section 5A of the Protection from Harassment Act 1997 (restraining orders on acquittal);
(c) on the making of a finding of not guilty by reason of insanity, or a finding of disability, under section 14 of the Modern Slavery Act 2015 (slavery and trafficking prevention orders); and
(d) in proceedings for a genital mutilation offence, under paragraph 3 of Schedule 2 to the Female Genital Mutilation Act 2003 (female genital mutilation protection orders).
In the circumstances set out in the Criminal Justice (European Protection Order) Regulations 2014, which give effect to Directive 2011/99/EU of the European Parliament and of the Council of 13th December, 2011, on the European protection order—
(a) a magistrates' court, and in some cases the Crown Court, may make a European protection order to supplement a protection measure ordered by a court in England and Wales, where the protected person has decided to reside or stay in another European Union member State or is already residing or staying there (see also rule 31.9); and
(b) a magistrates' court may make a restraining order to give effect in England and Wales to a European protection order made by a competent authority in another European Union member State (see also rule 31.10).
Section 1(2) of the Civil Evidence Act 1995 defines hearsay as meaning "a statement made otherwise than by a person while giving oral evidence in the proceedings which is tendered as

evidence of the matters stated". Section 13 of that Act defines a statement as meaning "any representation of fact or opinion, however made".]

31.2. *Behaviour orders: general rules* (1) The court must not make a behaviour order unless the person to whom it is directed has had an opportunity—

(a)   to consider—

(i)   what order is proposed and why, and

(ii)   the evidence in support; and

(b)   to make representations at a hearing (whether or not that person in fact attends).

(2) That restriction does not apply to making—

(a)   an interim behaviour order, but unless other legislation otherwise provides such an order has no effect unless the person to whom it is directed—

(i)   is present when it is made, or

(ii)   is handed a document recording the order not more than 7 days after it is made;

(b)   a restraining order that gives effect to a European protection order, where rule 31.10 applies (Giving effect to a European protection order made in another EU member State).

(3) Where the court decides not to make, where it could—

(a)   a football banning order; or

(b)   a parenting order, after a person under 16 is convicted of an offence,

the court must announce, at a hearing in public, the reasons for its decision.

(4) Where the court makes an order which imposes one or more of the prohibitions or restrictions listed in rule 31.9(1), the court must arrange for someone to explain to the person who benefits from that protection—

(a)   that that person may apply for a European protection order, if he or she decides to reside or stay in another European Union member State;

(b)   the basic conditions for making such an application; and

(c)   that it is advisable to make any such application before leaving the United Kingdom.

[Note. The Acts listed in the note to rule 31.1 impose requirements specific to each different type of behaviour order. Not all allow the court to make an interim behaviour order.

See section 14A(3) of the Football Spectators Act 1989, section 9(1) of the Crime and Disorder Act 1998 and regulation 7 of the Criminal Justice (European Protection Order) Regulations 2014.]

31.3. *Application for behaviour order and notice of terms of proposed order: special rules*
(1) This rule applies where—

(a)   a prosecutor wants the court to make one of the following orders if the defendant is convicted—

(i)   an anti-social behaviour order (but this rule does not apply to an application for an interim anti-social behaviour order),

(ii)   a serious crime prevention order,

(iii)   a criminal behaviour order, or

(iv)   a prohibition order;

(b)   a prosecutor proposes, on the prosecutor's initiative or at the court's request, a sexual harm prevention order if the defendant is convicted;

(c)   a prosecutor proposes a restraining order whether the defendant is convicted or acquitted.

(2) Where paragraph (1)(a) applies (order on application), the prosecutor must serve a notice of intention to apply for such an order on—

(a)   the court officer;

(b)   the defendant against whom the prosecutor wants the court to make the order; and

(c)   any person on whom the order would be likely to have a significant adverse effect,

as soon as practicable (without waiting for the verdict).

(3) A notice under paragraph (2) must—

(a)   summarise the relevant facts;

(b)   identify the evidence on which the prosecutor relies in support;

(c)   attach any written statement that the prosecutor has not already served; and

(d)   specify the order that the prosecutor wants the court to make.

(4) A defendant served with a notice under paragraph (2) must—

(a)   serve notice of any evidence on which the defendant relies on—

(i)   the court officer, and

(ii)   the prosecutor,

as soon as practicable (without waiting for the verdict); and

(b)   in the notice, identify that evidence and attach any written statement that has not already been served.

(5) Where paragraph (1)(b) applies (sexual harm prevention order proposed), the prosecutor must—

(a)   serve a draft order on the court officer and on the defendant not less than 2 business days before the hearing at which the order may be made;

(b)   in the draft order specify those prohibitions which the prosecutor proposes as necessary for the purpose of—

(i)   protecting the public or any particular members of the public from sexual harm from the defendant, or

   (ii) protecting children or vulnerable adults generally, or any particular children or vulnerable adults, from sexual harm from the defendant outside the United Kingdom.

(6) Where paragraph (1)(c) applies (restraining order proposed), the prosecutor must—

(a) serve a draft order on the court officer and on the defendant as soon as practicable (without waiting for the verdict);

(b) in the draft order specify—

   (i) those prohibitions which, if the defendant is convicted, the prosecutor proposes for the purpose of protecting a person from conduct which amounts to harassment or will cause fear of violence, or

   (ii) those prohibitions which, if the defendant is acquitted, the prosecutor proposes as necessary to protect a person from harassment by the defendant.

(7) Where the prosecutor wants the court to make an anti-social behaviour order, a criminal behaviour order or a prohibition order, the rules about special measures directions in Part 18 (Measures to assist a witness or defendant to give evidence) apply, but—

(a) the prosecutor must apply when serving a notice under paragraph (2); and

(b) the time limits in rule 18.3(a) do not apply.

[Note. The Practice Direction sets out a form of notice for use in connection with this rule.

The orders listed in rule 31.3(1)(a) may be made on application by the prosecutor. The orders to which rule 31.3(1)(b) and (c) apply require no application and may be made on the court's own initiative. Under section 8 of the Serious Crime Act 2007 a serious crime prevention order may be made only on an application by the Director of Public Prosecutions or the Director of the Serious Fraud Office. See also paragraphs 2, 7 and 13 of Schedule 2 to the 2007 Act.

Under section 1I of the Crime and Disorder Act 1998, on an application for an anti-social behaviour order the court may give a special measures direction under the Youth Justice and Criminal Evidence Act 1999. Under section 31 of the Anti-social Behaviour, Crime and Policing Act 2014 the court may give such a direction on an application for a criminal behaviour order.

If a party relies on hearsay evidence, see also rules 31.6, 31.7, and 31.8.]

31.4. *Evidence to assist the court: special rules* (1) This rule applies where the court can make on its own initiative—

(a) a football banning order;

(b) a restraining order; or

(c) an anti-social behaviour order.

(2) A party who wants the court to take account of evidence not already introduced must—

(a) serve notice on—

   (i) the court officer, and

   (ii) every other party,

 as soon as practicable (without waiting for the verdict); and

(b) in the notice, identify that evidence; and

(c) attach any written statement containing such evidence.

[Note. If a party relies on hearsay evidence, see also rules 31.6, 31.7, and 31.8.]

31.5. *Application to vary or revoke behaviour order* (1) The court may vary or revoke a behaviour order if—

(a) the legislation under which it is made allows the court to do so; and

(b) one of the following applies—

   (i) the prosecutor[Ed 1],

   (ii) the person to whom the order is directed,

   (iii) any other person protected or affected by the order,

   (iv) the relevant authority or responsible officer,

   (v) the relevant Chief Officer of Police,

   (vi) the Director of Public Prosecutions, or

   (vii) the Director of the Serious Fraud Office.

(2) A person applying under this rule must—

(a) apply in writing as soon as practicable after becoming aware of the grounds for doing so, explaining—

   (i) what material circumstances have changed since the order was made, and

   (ii) why the order should be varied or revoked as a result; and

(b) serve the application on—

   (i) the court officer,

   (ii) as appropriate, the prosecutor or defendant, and

   (iii) any other person listed in paragraph (1)(b), if the court so directs.

(3) A party who wants the court to take account of any particular evidence before making its decision must, as soon as practicable—

(a) serve notice on—

   (i) the court officer,

   (ii) as appropriate, the prosecutor or defendant, and

   (iii) any other person listed in paragraph (1)(b) on whom the court directed the application to be served; and

(b) in that notice identify the evidence and attach any written statement that has not already been served.

(4)   The court may decide an application under this rule with or without a hearing.

(5)   But the court must not—

(a)   dismiss an application under this rule unless the applicant has had an opportunity to make representations at a hearing (whether or not the applicant in fact attends); or

(b)   allow an application under this rule unless everyone required to be served, by this rule or by the court, has had at least 14 days in which to make representations, including representations about whether there should be a hearing.

(6)   The court officer must—

(a)   serve the application on any person, if the court so directs; and

(b)   give notice of any hearing to—

(i)   the applicant, and

(ii)   any person required to be served, by this rule or by the court.

[Note. The legislation that gives the court power to make a behaviour order may limit the circumstances in which it may be varied or revoked and may require a hearing. Under section 22E of the Serious Crime Act 2007, where a person already subject to a serious crime prevention order is charged with a serious offence or with an offence of failing to comply with the order, the court may vary the order so that it continues in effect until that prosecution concludes.

If a party relies on hearsay evidence, see also rules 31.6, 31.7 and 31.8.]

Ed 1   Only the defendant or a "Chief Officer of Police" can apply pursuant to s 108(2) of the Sexual Offences Act 2003 to vary a SOPO: the Crim PR cannot enlarge the exhaustive list of applicants prescribed by s 108(2): *R v Hamer (Robert)* [2017] EWCA Crim 192, [2017] 2 Cr App R (S) 13.

31.6.   *Notice of hearsay evidence*   (1)   A party who wants to introduce hearsay evidence must—

(a)   serve notice on—

(i)   the court officer, and

(ii)   every other party directly affected; and

(b)   in that notice—

(i)   explain that it is a notice of hearsay evidence,

(ii)   identify that evidence,

(iii)   identify the person who made the statement which is hearsay, or explain why if that person is not identified, and

(iv)   explain why that person will not be called to give oral evidence.

(2)   A party may serve one notice under this rule in respect of more than one notice and more than one witness.

[Note. For the time within which to serve a notice of hearsay evidence, see rule 31.3(2) to (4), rule 31.4(2) and rule 31.5(3). See also the requirement in section 2 of the Civil Evidence Act 1995 for reasonable and practicable notice of a proposal to introduce hearsay evidence.

Rules 31.6, 31.7 and 31.8 broadly correspond with rules 3, 4 and 5 of the Magistrates' Courts (Hearsay Evidence in Civil Proceedings) Rules 1999, which apply in civil proceedings in magistrates' courts. Rule 3 of the 1999 Rules however includes a time limit, which may be varied by the court, or a justices' clerk, of 21 days before the date fixed for the hearing, for service of a hearsay notice.]

31.7.   *Cross-examination of maker of hearsay statement*   (1)   This rule applies where a party wants the court's permission to cross-examine a person who made a statement which another party wants to introduce as hearsay.

(2)   The party who wants to cross-examine that person must—

(a)   apply in writing, with reasons, not more than 7 days after service of the notice of hearsay evidence; and

(b)   serve the application on—

(i)   the court officer,

(ii)   the party who served the hearsay evidence notice, and

(iii)   every party on whom the hearsay evidence notice was served.

(3)   The court may decide an application under this rule with or without a hearing.

(4)   But the court must not—

(a)   dismiss an application under this rule unless the applicant has had an opportunity to make representations at a hearing (whether or not the applicant in fact attends); or

(b)   allow an application under this rule unless everyone served with the application has had at least 7 days in which to make representations, including representations about whether there should be a hearing.

[Note. See also section 3 of the Civil Evidence Act 1995.]

31.8.   *Credibility and consistency of maker of hearsay statement*   (1)   This rule applies where a party wants to challenge the credibility or consistency of a person who made a statement which another party wants to introduce as hearsay.

(2)   The party who wants to challenge the credibility or consistency of that person must—

(a)   serve notice of intention to do so on—

(i)   the court officer, and

(ii)   the party who served the notice of hearsay evidence

not more than 7 days after service of that hearsay evidence notice; and

(b)   in the notice, identify any statement or other material on which that party relies.

(3)   The party who served the hearsay notice—

(a)   may call that person to give oral evidence instead; and

(b)   if so, must serve notice of intention to do so on—

     (i)   the court officer, and

     (ii)   every party on whom the hearsay notice was served

not more than 7 days after service of the notice under paragraph (2).

[Note. Section 5(2) of the Civil Evidence Act 1995 describes the procedure for challenging the credibility of the maker of a statement of which hearsay evidence is introduced. See also section 6 of that Act. The 1995 Act does not allow the introduction of evidence of a previous inconsistent statement otherwise than in accordance with sections 5, 6 and 7 of the Criminal Procedure Act 1865.]

31.9. *European protection order to be given effect in another EU member State* (1) This rule applies where—

(a)   a person benefits from the protection of one or more of the following prohibitions or restrictions imposed on another person by an order of a court in England and Wales when dealing with a criminal cause or matter—

     (i)   a prohibition from entering certain localities, places or defined areas where the protected person resides or visits,

     (ii)   a prohibition or restriction of contact with the protected person by any means (including by telephone, post, facsimile transmission or electronic mail),

     (iii)   a prohibition or restriction preventing the other person from approaching the protected person whether at all or to within a particular distance; and either

(b)   that protected person wants the Crown Court or a magistrates' court to make a European protection order to supplement such an order; or

(c)   the court varies or revokes such a prohibition or restriction in such an order and correspondingly amends or revokes a European protection order already made.

(2)   Such a protected person—

(a)   may apply orally or in writing to the Crown Court at the hearing at which the order imposing the prohibition or restriction is made by that court; or

(b)   in any other case, must apply in writing to a magistrates' court and serve the application on the court officer.

(3)   The application must—

(a)   identify the prohibition or restriction that the European protection order would supplement;

(b)   identify the date, if any, on which that prohibition or restriction will expire;

(c)   specify the European Union member State in which the applicant has decided to reside or stay, or in which he or she already is residing or staying;

(d)   indicate the length of the period for which the applicant intends to reside or stay in that member State;

(e)   explain why the applicant needs the protection of that measure while residing or staying in that member State; and

(f)   include any other information of which the applicant wants the court to take account.

(4)   Where the court makes or amends a European protection order, the court officer must—

(a)   issue an order in the form required by Directive 2011/99/EU;

(b)   serve on the competent authority of the European Union member State in which the protected person has decided to reside or stay—

     (i)   a copy of that form, and

     (ii)   a copy of the form translated into an official language of that member State, or into an official language of the European Union if that member State has declared that it will accept a translation in that language.

(5)   Where the court revokes a European protection order, the court officer must without delay so inform that authority.

(6)   Where the court refuses to make a European protection order, the court officer must arrange for the protected person to be informed of any available avenue of appeal or review against the court's decision.

[Note. See regulations 3 to 10 of the Criminal Justice (European Protection Order) Regulations 2014. Under regulation 5, an application by a protected person to which this rule applies may be made to an authority in another European Union member State and transferred to the Lord Chancellor for submission to a magistrates' court.

The Practice Direction sets out a form of application for use in connection with this rule.]

31.10. *Giving effect to a European protection order made in another EU member State* (1) This rule applies where the Lord Chancellor serves on the court officer—

(a)   a request by an authority in another European Union member State to give effect to a European protection order;

(b)   a request by such an authority to give effect to a variation of such an order; or

(c)   notice by such an authority of the revocation or withdrawal of such an order.

(2)   In the case of a request to which paragraph (1) refers, the court officer must, without undue delay—

(a)   arrange for the court to consider the request;

(b)   serve on the requesting authority—

     (i)   notice of any further information required by the court, and

     (ii)   subject to any such requirement and any response, notice of the court's decision;

(c)   where the court gives effect to the European protection order—

(i)   include in the notice served on the requesting authority the terms of the restraining order made by the court,

(ii)   serve notice of those terms, and of the potential legal consequences of breaching them, on the person restrained by the order made by the court and on the person protected by that order, and

(iii)   serve notice on the Lord Chancellor of any breach of the restraining order which is reported to the court;

(d)   where the court refuses to give effect to the European protection order—

(i)   include in the notice served on the requesting authority the grounds for the refusal,

(ii)   where appropriate, inform the protected person, or any representative or guardian of that person, of the possibility of applying for a comparable order under the law of England and Wales, and

(iii)   arrange for that person, representative or guardian to be informed of any available avenue of appeal or review against the court's decision.

(3)   In the case of a notice to which paragraph (1) refers, the court officer must, as soon as possible, arrange for the court to act on that notice.

(4)   Unless the court otherwise directs, the court officer must omit from any notice served on a person against whom a restraining order may be, or has been, made the address or contact details of the person who is the object of the European protection order.

[Note. See regulations 11 to 19 of the Criminal Justice (European Protection Order) Regulations 2014.

Where the Lord Chancellor receives a request to give effect in England and Wales to a European protection order, a magistrates' court to which the request is given must give effect to that order by making a restraining order under section 5 of the Protection from Harassment Act 1997, as adapted by regulation 13 of the 2014 Regulations, unless one of the specified grounds for refusal applies. The grounds for refusal are—

(a)   the European protection order—

(i)   is incomplete, and

(ii)   is not completed within a period specified by the court;

(b)   the requirements set out in Article 5 of Directive 2011/99/EU of the European Parliament and of the Council of 13th December, 2011, on the European protection order have not been met;

(c)   the protection measure on the basis of which the European protection order was issued was based on conduct that would not constitute an offence under the law of England and Wales if it occurred there;

(d)   the person causing danger (within the meaning of the 2014 Regulations and the Directive) benefits from an immunity under the law of England and Wales which makes it impossible to give effect to the European protection order under the Regulations;

(e)   the protection measure on the basis of which the European protection order was issued was based on conduct where, under the law of England and Wales—

(i)   the criminal prosecution of the conduct would be statute-barred, and

(ii)   the conduct falls within the jurisdiction of England and Wales;

(f)   giving effect to the European protection order would contravene the principle of ne bis in idem;

(g)   the protection measure on the basis of which the European protection order was issued was based on conduct by a defendant who was under the age of 10 when the conduct took place;

(h)   the protection measure on the basis of which the European protection order was issued relates to a criminal offence which, under the law of England and Wales, is regarded as having been committed wholly, or for a major or essential part, within its territory.

Under regulation 17 of the 2014 Regulations, the magistrates' court may vary a restraining order which gives effect to a European protection order if that protection order is modified. Under regulation 18 of those Regulations, the magistrates' court must discharge such a restraining order on notice that the European protection order to which it gives effect has been revoked or withdrawn.]

31.11.   *Court's power to vary requirements under this Part*   Unless other legislation otherwise provides, the court may—

(a)   shorten a time limit or extend it (even after it has expired);

(b)   allow a notice or application to be given in a different form, or presented orally.

PART 32   BREACH, REVOCATION AND AMENDMENT OF COMMUNITY AND OTHER ORDERS

Contents of this Part

B.29   **32.1.**   *When this Part applies*   This Part applies where—

(a)   the person responsible for a defendant's compliance with an order to which applies—

(i)   Schedule 3, 5, 7 or 8 to the Powers of Criminal Courts (Sentencing) Act 2000,

(ii)   Schedule 8 or 12 to the Criminal Justice Act 2003,

(iii)   Schedule 2 to the Criminal Justice and Immigration Act 2008, or

(iv)   the Schedule to the Street Offences Act 1959

wants the court to deal with that defendant for failure to comply;

(b)   one of the following wants the court to exercise any power it has to revoke or amend such an order—

(i)   the responsible officer or supervisor,

(ii)   the defendant, or

(iii)   where the legislation allows, a person affected by the order; or

(c)   the court considers exercising on its own initiative any power it has to revoke or amend such an order.

[Note. In the Powers of Criminal Courts (Sentencing) Act 2000—

(a)   Schedule 3 deals with the breach, revocation and amendment of curfew orders and exclusion orders;

(b)   Schedule 5 deals with the breach, revocation and amendment of attendance centre orders;

(c)   Schedule 7 deals with the breach, revocation and amendment of supervision orders;

(d)   Schedule 8 deals with the breach, revocation and amendment of action plan orders and reparation orders; and

(e)   Schedules 3, 5 and 7 are repealed, with savings for existing orders, by the relevant provisions of the Criminal Justice and Immigration Act 2008; and, with savings for existing orders, Schedule 8 no longer refers to action plan orders.

In the Criminal Justice Act 2003—

(a)   Schedule 8 deals with the breach, revocation and amendment of community orders; and

(b)   Schedule 12 deals with the breach and amendment of suspended sentence orders.

Schedule 2 to the Criminal Justice and Immigration Act 2008 deals with the breach, revocation and amendment of youth rehabilitation orders.

Under Schedule 8 to the 2000 Act, Schedule 8 to the 2003 Act and Schedule 2 to the 2008 Act, a single member of the court can adjourn a hearing to which this Part applies.]

32.2.   *Application by responsible officer or supervisor*   (1)   This rule applies where—

(a)   the responsible officer or supervisor wants the court to—

(i)   deal with a defendant for failure to comply with an order to which this Part applies, or

(ii)   revoke or amend such an order; or

(b)   the court considers exercising on its own initiative any power it has to—

(i)   revoke or amend such an order, and

(ii)   summon the defendant to attend for that purpose.

(2)   Rules 7.2 to 7.4, which deal, among other things, with starting a prosecution in a magistrates', apply—

(a)   as if—

(i)   a reference in those rules to an allegation of an offence included a reference to an allegation of failure to comply with an order to which this Part applies, and

(ii)   a reference to the prosecutor included a reference to the responsible officer or supervisor; and

(b)   with the necessary consequential modifications.

32.3.   *Application by defendant or person affected*   (1)   This rule applies where—

(a)   the defendant wants the court to exercise any power it has to revoke or amend an order to which this Part applies; or

(b)   where the legislation allows, a person affected by such an order wants the court to exercise any such power.

(2)   That defendant, or person affected, must—

(a)   apply in writing, explaining why the order should be revoked or amended; and

(b)   serve the application on—

(i)   the court officer,

(ii)   the responsible officer or supervisor, and

(iii)   as appropriate, the defendant or the person affected.

32.4.   *Procedure on application by responsible officer or supervisor*   (1)   Except for rules 24.8 (Written guilty plea: special rules) and 24.9 (Single justice procedure: special rules), the rules in Part 24, which deal with the procedure at a trial in a magistrates' court, apply—

(a)   as if—

(i)   a reference in those rules to an allegation of an offence included a reference to an allegation of failure to comply with an order to which this Part applies,

(ii)   a reference to the court's verdict included a reference to the court's decision to revoke or amend such an order, or to exercise any other power it has to deal with the defendant, and

(iii)   a reference to the court's sentence included a reference to the exercise of any such power; and

(b)   with the necessary consequential modifications.   (2)   The court officer must serve on each party any order revoking or amending an order to which this Part applies.

PART 33   CONFISCATION AND RELATED PROCEEDINGS

Contents of this Part

GENERAL RULES

B.30 *33.1.* *Interpretation*   In this Part:
'document' means anything in which information of any description is recorded;
'hearsay evidence' means evidence consisting of hearsay within the meaning of section 1(2) of the Civil Evidence Act 1995;

'restraint proceedings' means proceedings under sections 42 and 58(2) and (3) of the Proceeds of Crime Act 2002;

'receivership proceedings' means proceedings under sections 48, 49, 50, 51, 54(4), 59(2) and (3), 62 and 63 of the 2002 Act;

'witness statement' means a written statement signed by a person which contains the evidence, and only that evidence, which that person would be allowed to give orally; and

words and expressions used have the same meaning as in Part 2 of the 2002 Act.

33.2. Calculation of time   (1) This rule shows how to calculate any period of time for doing any act which is specified by this Part for the purposes of any proceedings under Part 2 of the Proceeds of Crime Act 2002 or by an order of the Crown Court in restraint proceedings or receivership proceedings.

(2) A period of time expressed as a number of days shall be computed as clear days.

(3) In this rule 'clear days' means that in computing the number of days—

(a)   the day on which the period begins; and

(b)   if the end of the period is defined by reference to an event, the day on which that event occurs,

are not included.

(4) Where the specified period is 5 days or less and includes a day which is not a business day that day does not count.

33.3. Court office closed   When the period specified by this Part, or by an order of the Crown Court under Part 2 of the Proceeds of Crime Act 2002, for doing any act at the court office falls on a day on which the office is closed, that act shall be in time if done on the next day on which the court office is open.

33.4. Application for registration of Scottish or Northern Ireland order   (1) This rule applies to an application for registration of an order under article 6 of the Proceeds of Crime Act 2002 (Enforcement in different parts of the United Kingdom) Order 2002.

(2) The application may be made without notice.

(3) The application must be in writing and may be supported by a witness statement which must—

(a)   exhibit the order or a certified copy of the order; and

(b)   to the best of the witness's ability, give full details of the realisable property located in England and Wales in respect of which the order was made and specify the person holding that realisable property.

(4) If the court registers the order, the applicant must serve notice of the registration on—

(a)   any person who holds realisable property to which the order applies; and

(b)   any other person whom the applicant knows to be affected by the order.

(5) The permission of the Crown Court under rule 33.10 (Service outside the jurisdiction) is not required to serve the notice outside England and Wales.

33.5. Application to vary or set aside registration   (1) An application to vary or set aside registration of an order under article 6 of the Proceeds of Crime Act 2002 (Enforcement in different parts of the United Kingdom) Order 2002 may be made to the Crown Court by—

(a)   any person who holds realisable property to which the order applies; and

(b)   any other person affected by the order.

(2) The application must be in writing and may be supported by a witness statement.

(3) The application and any witness statement must be lodged with the Crown Court.

(4) The application must be served on the person who applied for registration at least 7 days before the date fixed by the court for hearing the application, unless the Crown Court specifies a shorter period.

(5) No property in England and Wales may be realised in pursuance of the order before the Crown Court has decided the application.

33.6. Register of orders   (1) The Crown Court must keep, under the direction of the Lord Chancellor, a register of the orders registered under article 6 of the Proceeds of Crime Act 2002 (Enforcement in different parts of the United Kingdom) Order 2002.

(2) The register must include details of any variation or setting aside of a registration under rule 33.5 and of any execution issued on a registered order.

(3) If the person who applied for registration of an order which is subsequently registered notifies the Crown Court that the court which made the order has varied or discharged the order, details of the variation or discharge, as the case may be, must be entered in the register.

33.7. Statements of truth   (1) Any witness statement required to be served by this Part must be verified by a statement of truth contained in the witness statement.

(2) A statement of truth is a declaration by the person making the witness statement to the effect that the witness statement is true to the best of his knowledge and belief and that he made the statement knowing that, if it were tendered in evidence, he would be liable to prosecution if he wilfully stated in it anything which he knew to be false or did not believe to be true.

(3) The statement of truth must be signed by the person making the witness statement.

(4) If the person making the witness statement fails to verify the witness statement by a statement of truth, the Crown Court may direct that it shall not be admissible as evidence.

33.8. Use of witness statements for other purposes   (1) Except as provided by this rule, a witness statement served in proceedings under Part 2 of the Proceeds of Crime Act 2002 may be used only for the purpose of the proceedings in which it is served.

(2) Paragraph (1) does not apply if and to the extent that—

(a)   the witness gives consent in writing to some other use of it;
(b)   the Crown Court gives permission for some other use; or
(c)   the witness statement has been put in evidence at a hearing held in public.

33.9. Service of documents (1)   Rule 49.1 (Notice required to accompany process served outside the United Kingdom and translations) shall not apply in restraint proceedings and receivership proceedings.
(2)   An order made in restraint proceedings or receivership proceedings may be enforced against the defendant or any other person affected by it notwithstanding that service of a copy of the order has not been effected in accordance with Part 4 if the Crown Court is satisfied that the person had notice of the order by being present when the order was made.

33.10. Service outside the jurisdiction (1)   Where this Part requires a document to be served on someone who is outside England and Wales, it may be served outside England and Wales with the permission of the Crown Court.
(2)   Where a document is to be served outside England and Wales it may be served by any method permitted by the law of the country in which it is to be served.
(3)   Nothing in this rule or in any court order shall authorise or require any person to do anything in the country where the document is to be served which is against the law of that country.
(4)   Where this Part requires a document to be served a certain period of time before the date of a hearing and the recipient does not appear at the hearing, the hearing must not take place unless the Crown Court is satisfied that the document has been duly served.

33.11. Certificates of service (1)   Where this Part requires that the applicant for an order in restraint proceedings or receivership proceedings serve a document on another person, the applicant must lodge a certificate of service with the Crown Court within 7 days of service of the document.
(2)   The certificate must state—
(a)   the method of service;
(b)   the date of service; and
(c)   if the document is served under rule 4.9 (Service by another method), such other information as the court may require when making the order permitting service by that method.
(3)   Where a document is to be served by the Crown Court in restraint proceedings and receivership proceedings and the court is unable to serve it, the court must send a notice of non-service stating the method attempted to the party who requested service.

33.12. External requests and orders (1)   The rules in this Part and in Part 42 (Appeal to the Court of Appeal in confiscation and related proceedings) apply with the necessary modifications to proceedings under the Proceeds of Crime Act 2002 (External Requests and Orders) Order 2005 in the same way that they apply to corresponding proceedings under Part 2 of the Proceeds of Crime Act 2002.
(2)   This table shows how provisions of the 2005 Order correspond with provisions of the 2002 Act.

Article of the Proceeds of Crime Act 2002 (External Requests and Orders) Order 2005	Section of the Proceeds of Crime Act 2002
8	41
9	42
10	43
11	44
15	48
16	49
17	58
23	31
27	50
28	51
41	62
42	63
44	65
45	66

CONFISCATION PROCEEDINGS

33.13. Statements in connection with confiscation orders (1)   This rule applies where—
(a)   the court can make a confiscation order; and
(b)   the prosecutor asks the court to make such an order, or the court decides to make such an order on its own initiative.
(2)   Within such periods as the court directs—
(a)   if the court so orders, the defendant must give such information, in such manner, as the court directs;

(b)   the prosecutor must serve a statement of information relevant to confiscation on the court officer and the defendant;

(c)   if the court so directs—

    (i)   the defendant must serve a response notice on the court officer and the prosecutor, and

    (ii)   the parties must identify what is in dispute.

(3)   Where it appears to the court that a person other than the defendant holds, or may hold, an interest in property held by the defendant which property is likely to be realised or otherwise used to satisfy a confiscation order—

(a)   the court must not determine the extent of the defendant's interest in that property unless that other person has had a reasonable opportunity to make representations; and

(b)   the court may order that other person to give such information, in such manner and within such a period, as the court directs.

(4)   The court may—

(a)   shorten or extend a time limit which it has set;

(b)   vary, discharge or supplement an order which it has made;

(c)   postpone confiscation proceedings without a hearing.

(5)   A prosecutor's statement of information must—

(a)   identify the maker of the statement and show its date;

(b)   identify the defendant in respect of whom it is served;

(c)   specify the conviction which gives the court power to make the confiscation order, or each conviction if more than one;

(d)   if the prosecutor believes the defendant to have a criminal lifestyle, include such matters as the prosecutor believes to be relevant in connection with deciding—

    (i)   whether the defendant has such a lifestyle,

    (ii)   whether the defendant has benefited from his or her general criminal conduct,

    (iii)   the defendant's benefit from that conduct, and

    (iv)   whether the court should or should not make such assumptions about the defendant's property as legislation permits;

(e)   if the prosecutor does not believe the defendant to have a criminal lifestyle, include such matters as the prosecutor believes to be relevant in connection with deciding—

    (i)   whether the defendant has benefited from his or her particular criminal conduct, and

    (ii)   the defendant's benefit from that conduct;

(f)   in any case, include such matters as the prosecutor believes to be relevant in connection with deciding—

    (i)   whether to make a determination about the extent of the defendant's interest in property in which another person holds, or may hold, an interest, and

    (ii)   what determination to make, if the court decides to make one.

(6)   A defendant's response notice must—

(a)   indicate the extent to which the defendant accepts the allegations made in the prosecutor's statement of information; and

(b)   so far as the defendant does not accept an allegation, give particulars of any matters on which the defendant relies,

in any manner directed by the court.

(7)   The court must satisfy itself that there has been explained to the defendant, in terms the defendant can understand (with help, if necessary)—

(a)   that if the defendant accepts to any extent an allegation in a prosecutor's statement of information, then the court may treat that as conclusive for the purposes of deciding whether the defendant has benefited from general or particular criminal conduct, and if so by how much;

(b)   that if the defendant fails in any respect to comply with a direction to serve a response notice, then the court may treat that as acceptance of each allegation to which the defendant has not replied, except the allegation that the defendant has benefited from general or particular criminal conduct; and

(c)   that if the defendant fails without reasonable excuse to comply with an order to give information, then the court may draw such inference as it believes is appropriate.

[*Note. Under section 6 of the Proceeds of Crime Act 2002, where a defendant is convicted of an offence the Crown Court must (with some exceptions)—*

(a)   *decide whether the defendant has 'a criminal lifestyle', within the meaning of the Act, or has benefited from particular criminal conduct;*

(b)   *decide the 'recoverable amount', within the meaning of the Act; and*

(c)   *make a confiscation order requiring the defendant to pay that amount.*

Under section 14 of the 2002 Act, unless exceptional circumstances apply the court may postpone confiscation proceedings for a maximum of 2 years from the date of conviction, or until the end of a period of 3 months following the determination of an appeal by the defendant against conviction, if that is later.

Under section 16 of the 2002 Act, where the Crown Court is considering confiscation the prosecutor must give the court a statement of information which the prosecutor believes to be relevant to what the court must decide, within such period as the court directs. Under section 17 of the Act, where the prosecutor gives such a statement the court may order the defendant to respond and, if the defendant does not do so, then the court may treat the defendant as accepting the prosecutor's allegations. Under section 18, for the purpose of obtaining information to help it in carrying out its functions the court may at any time order the defendant to give it information specified in the order and, if the defendant does not do so, then the court may draw such inference as it believes appropriate. Under section 18A, for the purpose of obtaining information to help it to determine the extent of the defendant's interest in property the court may at any time order a person who the court thinks may hold an interest in that property to give it information specified in the order and, if that person does not do so, then the court may draw such inference as it believes appropriate.

Under section 27 of the 2002 Act, special provisions apply where the defendant absconds.

Under section 97 of the Serious Organised Crime and Police Act 2005, the Secretary of State may by order provide for confiscation orders to be made by magistrates' courts.]

33.14.   *Application for compliance order*   (1)   This rule applies where—
(a)   the prosecutor wants the court to make a compliance order after a confiscation order has been made;
(b)   the prosecutor or a person affected by a compliance order wants the court to vary or discharge the order.
(2)   Such a prosecutor or person must—
(a)   apply in writing; and
(b)   serve the application on—
           (i)   the court officer, and
           (ii)   as appropriate, the prosecutor and any person who is affected by the compliance order (or who would be affected if it were made), unless the court otherwise directs.
(3)   The application must—
(a)   specify—
           (i)   the confiscation order,
           (ii)   the compliance order, if it is an application to vary or discharge that order;
(b)   if it is an application for a compliance order—
           (i)   specify each measure that the prosecutor proposes to ensure that the confiscation order is effective, including in particular any restriction or prohibition on the defendant's travel outside the United Kingdom, and
           (ii)   explain why each such measure is appropriate;
(c)   if it is an application to vary or discharge a compliance order, as appropriate—
           (i)   specify any proposed variation, and
           (ii)   explain why it is appropriate for the order to be varied or discharged;
(d)   attach any material on which the applicant relies;
(e)   propose the terms of the order; and
(f)   ask for a hearing, if the applicant wants one, and explain why it is needed.
(4)   A person who wants to make representations about the application must—
(a)   serve the representations on—
           (i)   the court officer, and
           (ii)   the applicant;
(b)   do so as soon as reasonably practicable after service of the application;
(c)   attach any material on which that person relies; and
(d)   ask for a hearing, if that person wants one, and explain why it is needed.
(5)   The court—
(a)   may determine the application at a hearing (which must be in private unless the court otherwise directs), or without a hearing;
(b)   may dispense with service on any person of a prosecutor's application for a compliance order if, in particular—
           (i)   the application is urgent, or
           (ii)   there are reasonable grounds for believing that to give notice of the application would cause the dissipation of property that otherwise would be available to satisfy the confiscation order.

[Note. See section 13A of the Proceeds of Crime Act 2002.]

33.15.   *Application for reconsideration*   (1)   This rule applies where the prosecutor wants the court, in view of fresh evidence—
(a)   to consider making a confiscation order where the defendant was convicted but no such order was considered;
(b)   to reconsider a decision that the defendant had not benefited from criminal conduct;
(c)   to reconsider a decision about the amount of the defendant's benefit.
(2)   The application must—
(a)   be in writing and give—
           (i)   the name of the defendant,
           (ii)   the date on which and the place where any relevant conviction occurred,
           (iii)   the date on which and the place where any relevant confiscation order was made or varied,
           (iv)   details of any slavery and trafficking reparation order made by virtue of any relevant confiscation order,
           (v)   the grounds for the application, and
           (vi)   an indication of the evidence available to support the application; and

(b) where the parties are agreed on the terms of the proposed order include, in one or more documents—

  (i) a draft order in the terms proposed, and

  (ii) evidence of the parties' agreement.

(3) The application must be served on—

(a) the court officer; and

(b) the defendant.

(4) The court—

(a) may determine the application without a hearing where the parties are agreed on the terms of the proposed order;

(b) must determine the application at a hearing in any other case.

(5) Where this rule or the court requires the application to be heard, the court officer must arrange for the court to hear it no sooner than the eighth day after it was served unless the court otherwise directs.

[Note. See sections 19, 20 and 21 of the Proceeds of Crime Act 2002 and section 10 of the Modern Slavery Act 2015.]

33.16. Application for new calculation of available amount (1) This rule applies where the prosecutor or a receiver wants the court to make a new calculation of the amount available for confiscation.

(2) The application—

(a) must be in writing and may be supported by a witness statement;

(b) must identify any slavery and trafficking reparation order made by virtue of the confiscation order and

(c) where the parties are agreed on the terms of the proposed order, must include in one or more documents—

  (i) a draft order in the terms proposed, and

  (ii) evidence of the parties' agreement.

(3) The application and any witness statement must be served on the court officer.

(4) The application and any witness statement must be served on—

(a) the defendant;

(b) the receiver, if the prosecutor is making the application and a receiver has been appointed; and

(c) the prosecutor, if the receiver is making the application.

(5) The court—

(a) may determine the application without a hearing where the parties are agreed on the terms of the proposed order;

(b) must determine the application at a hearing in any other case.

(6) Where this rule or the court requires the application to be heard, the court officer must arrange for the court to hear it no sooner than the eighth day after it was served unless the court otherwise directs.

[Note. See section 22 of the Proceeds of Crime Act 2002 and section 10 of the Modern Slavery Act 2015.]

33.17. Variation of confiscation order due to inadequacy of available amount (1) This rule applies where the defendant, the prosecutor or a receiver wants the court to vary a confiscation order because the amount available is inadequate.

(2) The application—

(a) must be in writing and may be supported by a witness statement;

(b) must identify any slavery and trafficking reparation order made by virtue of the confiscation order and

(c) where the parties are agreed on the terms of the proposed order, must include in one or more documents—

  (i) a draft order in the terms proposed, and

  (ii) evidence of the parties' agreement.

(3) The application and any witness statement must be served on the court officer.

(4) The application and any witness statement must be served on—

(a) the prosecutor;

(b) the defendant, if the receiver is making the application; and

(c) the receiver, if the defendant is making the application and a receiver has been appointed,

(5) The court—

(a) may determine the application without a hearing where the parties are agreed on the terms of the proposed order;

(b) must determine the application at a hearing in any other case.

(6) Where this rule or the court requires the application to be heard, the court officer must arrange for the court to hear it no sooner than the eighth day after it was served unless the court otherwise directs.

[Note. See section 23 of the Proceeds of Crime Act 2002 and section 10 of the Modern Slavery Act 2015.]

33.18. Application by magistrates' court officer to discharge confiscation order (1) This rule applies where a magistrates' court officer wants the court to discharge a confiscation order because the amount available is inadequate or the sum outstanding is very small.

(2) The application must be in writing and give details of—

(a)   the confiscation order;
(b)   any slavery and trafficking reparation order made by virtue of the confiscation order;
(c)   the amount outstanding under the order; and
(d)   the grounds for the application.
(3)   The application must be served on—
(a)   the defendant;
(b)   the prosecutor; and
(c)   any receiver.
(4)   The court may determine the application without a hearing unless a person listed in paragraph (3) indicates, within 7 days after the application was served, that he or she would like to make representations.
(5)   If the court makes an order discharging the confiscation order, the court officer must, at once, send a copy of the order to—
(a)   the magistrates' court officer who applied for the order;
(b)   the defendant;
(c)   the prosecutor; and
(d)   any receiver.
[Note. See sections 24 and 25 of the Proceeds of Crime Act 2002 and section 10 of the Modern Slavery Act 2015.]

33.19.   *Application for variation of confiscation order made against an absconder* (1)   This rule applies where the defendant wants the court to vary a confiscation order made while the defendant was an absconder.
(2)   The application must be in writing and supported by a witness statement which must give details of—
(a)   the confiscation order;
(b)   any slavery and trafficking reparation order made by virtue of the confiscation order;
(c)   the circumstances in which the defendant ceased to be an absconder;
(d)   the defendant's conviction of the offence or offences concerned; and
(e)   the reason why the defendant believes the amount required to be paid under the confiscation order was too large.
(3)   The application and witness statement must be served on the court officer.
(4)   The application and witness statement must be served on the prosecutor at least 7 days before the date fixed by the court for hearing the application, unless the court specifies a shorter period.
[Note. See section 29 of the Proceeds of Crime Act 2002 and section 10 of the Modern Slavery Act 2015.]

33.20.   *Application for discharge of confiscation order made against an absconder* (1)   This rule applies where the defendant wants the court to discharge a confiscation order made while the defendant was an absconder and—
(a)   the defendant since has been tried and acquitted of each offence concerned; or
(b)   the prosecution has not concluded or is not to proceed.
(2)   The application must be in writing and supported by a witness statement which must give details of—
(a)   the confiscation order;
(b)   the date on which the defendant ceased to be an absconder;
(c)   the acquittal of the defendant if he or she has been acquitted of the offence concerned; and
(d)   if the defendant has not been acquitted of the offence concerned—
         (i)   the date on which the defendant ceased to be an absconder,
         (ii)   the date on which the proceedings taken against the defendant were instituted and a summary of steps taken in the proceedings since then, and
         (iii)   any indication that the prosecutor does not intend to proceed against the defendant.
(3)   The application and witness statement must be served on the court officer.
(4)   The application and witness statement must be served on the prosecutor at least 7 days before the date fixed by the court for hearing the application, unless the court specifies a shorter period.
(5)   If the court orders the discharge of the confiscation order, the court officer must serve notice on any other court responsible for enforcing the order.
[Note. See section 30 of the Proceeds of Crime Act 2002.]

33.21.   *Application for increase in term of imprisonment in default* (1)   This rule applies where—
(a)   a court varies a confiscation order; and
(b)   the prosecutor wants the court in consequence to increase the term of imprisonment to be served in default of payment.
(2)   The application must be made in writing and give details of—
(a)   the name and address of the defendant;
(b)   the confiscation order;
(c)   the grounds for the application; and
(d)   the enforcement measures taken, if any.
(3)   On receipt of the application, the court officer must—

(a) at once, send to the defendant and any other court responsible for enforcing the order, a copy of the application; and

(b) fix a time, date and place for the hearing and notify the applicant and the defendant of that time, date and place.

(4) If the court makes an order increasing the term of imprisonment in default, the court officer must, at once, send a copy of the order to—

(a) the applicant;

(b) the defendant;

(c) where the defendant is in custody at the time of the making of the order, the person having custody of the defendant; and

(d) any other court responsible for enforcing the order.

[Note. See section 39(5) of the Proceeds of Crime Act 2002.]

33.22. Compensation—general (1) This rule applies where a person who held realisable property wants the court to award compensation for loss suffered in consequence of anything done in relation to that property in connection with confiscation proceedings.

(2) The application must be in writing and may be supported by a witness statement.

(3) The application and any witness statement must be served on the court officer.

(4) The application and any witness statement must be served on—

(a) the person alleged to be in default; and

(b) the person or authority by whom the compensation would be payable,

at least 7 days before the date fixed by the court for hearing the application, unless the court directs otherwise.

[Note. See section 72 of the Proceeds of Crime Act 2002.]

33.23. Compensation—confiscation order made against absconder (1) This rule applies where—

(a) the court varies or discharges a confiscation order made against an absconder;

(b) a person who held realisable property suffered loss as a result of the making of that confiscation order; and

(c) that person wants the court to award compensation for that loss.

(2) The application must be in writing and supported by a witness statement which must give details of—

(a) the confiscation order;

(b) the variation or discharge of the confiscation order;

(c) the realisable property to which the application relates; and

(d) the loss suffered by the applicant as a result of the confiscation order.

(3) The application and witness statement must be served on the court officer.

(4) The application and witness statement must be served on the prosecutor at least 7 days before the date fixed by the court for hearing the application, unless the court specifies a shorter period.

[Note. See section 73 of the Proceeds of Crime Act 2002.]

33.24. Payment of money held or detained in satisfaction of confiscation order (1) An order under section 67 of the Proceeds of Crime Act 2002 requiring the payment of money to a magistrates' court officer ('a payment order') shall—

(a) be directed to—

    (i) the bank or building society concerned, where the money is held in an account maintained with that bank or building society, or

    (ii) the person on whose authority the money is detained, in any other case;

(b) name the person against whom the confiscation order has been made;

(c) state the amount which remains to be paid under the confiscation order;

(d) state the name and address of the branch at which the account in which the money ordered to be paid is held and the sort code of that branch, if the sort code is known;

(e) state the name in which the account in which the money ordered to be paid is held and the account number of that account, if the account number is known;

(f) state the amount which the bank or building society is required to pay to the court officer under the payment order;

(g) give the name and address of the court officer to whom payment is to be made; and

(h) require the bank or building society to make payment within a period of 7 days beginning on the day on which the payment order is made, unless it appears to the court that a longer or shorter period would be appropriate in the particular circumstances.

(2) In this rule 'confiscation order' has the meaning given to it by section 88(6) of the Proceeds of Crime Act 2002.

33.25. Application to realise seized property (1) This rule applies where—

(a) property is held by a defendant against whom a confiscation order has been made;

(b) the property has been seized by or produced to an officer; and

(c) an officer who is entitled to apply wants a magistrates' court—

    (i) to make an order under section 67A of the Proceeds of Crime Act 2002 authorising the realisation of the property towards satisfaction of the confiscation order, or

    (ii) to determine any storage, insurance or realisation costs in respect of the property which may be recovered under section 67B of the 2002 Act.

(2) Such an officer must—

(a)   apply in writing; and
(b)   serve the application on—
      (i)   the court officer, and
      (ii)   any person whom the applicant believes would be affected by an order.
(3)   The application must—
(a)   specify the property;
(b)   explain—
      (i)   the applicant's entitlement to apply,
      (ii)   how the proposed realisation meets the conditions prescribed by section 67A of the 2002 Act, and
      (iii)   how any storage, etc costs have been calculated;
(c)   attach any material on which the applicant relies; and
(d)   propose the terms of the order.
(4)   The court may—
(a)   determine the application at a hearing, or without a hearing;
(b)   consider an application made orally instead of in writing;
(c)   consider an application which has not been served on a person likely to be affected by an order.
(5)   If the court authorises the realisation of the property, the applicant must—
(a)   notify any person affected by the order who was absent when it was made; and
(b)   serve on the court officer a list of those so notified.
[Note. Under section 67A of the Proceeds of Crime Act 2002, one of the officers listed in section 41A of the Act may apply to a magistrates' court for authority to realise property seized by such an officer if—
(a)   a confiscation order has been made against the owner of the property;
(b)   no receiver has been appointed in relation to that property; and
(c)   any period allowed for payment of the confiscation order has expired.
Under section 67B of the 2002 Act, if a magistrates' court makes an order under section 67A then on the same or a subsequent occasion the court may determine an amount which may be recovered by the applicant in respect of reasonable costs incurred in storing or insuring the property, or realising it.]

33.26. *Appeal about decision on application to realise seized property* (1) This rule applies where on an application under rule 33.25 for an order authorising the realisation of property—
(a)   a magistrates' court decides not to make such an order and an officer who is entitled to apply wants to appeal against that decision to the Crown Court, under section 67C(1) of the Proceeds of Crime Act 2002;
(b)   a magistrates' court makes such an order and a person who is affected by that decision, other than the defendant against whom the confiscation order was made, wants to appeal against it to the Crown Court, under section 67C(2) of the 2002 Act;
(c)   a magistrates' court makes a decision about storage, etc costs and an officer who is entitled to apply wants to appeal against that decision to the Crown Court, under section 67C(4) of the 2002 Act.
(2)   The appellant must serve an appeal notice—
(a)   on the Crown Court officer and on any other party;
(b)   not more than 21 days after the magistrates' court's decision, or, if applicable, service of notice under rule 33.25(5).
(3)   The appeal notice must—
(a)   specify the decision under appeal;
(b)   where paragraph (1)(a) applies, explain why the property should be realised;
(c)   in any other case, propose the order that the appellant wants the court to make, and explain why.
(4)   Rule 34.11 (Constitution of the Crown Court) applies on such an appeal.
[Note. Under section 67C of the Proceeds of Crime Act 2002, an officer entitled to apply for an order under section 67A or 67B of that Act (authority to realise seized property towards satisfaction of a confiscation order; determination of storage, etc costs) may appeal against a refusal to make an order, or against a costs determination; and a person affected by an order, other than the owner, may appeal against the order.]

33.27. *Application for direction about surplus proceeds* (1) This rule applies where—
(a)   on an application under rule 33.25, a magistrates' court has made an order authorising an officer to realise property;
(b)   an officer so authorised holds proceeds of that realisation;
(c)   the confiscation order has been fully paid; and
(d)   the officer, or a person who had or has an interest in the property represented by the proceeds, wants a magistrates' court or the Crown Court to determine under section 67D of the Proceeds of Crime Act 2002—
      (i)   to whom the remaining proceeds should be paid, and
      (ii)   in what amount or amounts.
(2)   Such a person must—
(a)   apply in writing; and
(b)   serve the application on—

      (i)   the court officer, and

      (ii)   as appropriate, the officer holding the proceeds, or any person to whom such proceeds might be paid.

(3)   The application must—

(a)   specify the property which was realised;

(b)   explain the applicant's entitlement to apply;

(c)   describe the distribution proposed by the applicant and explain why that is proposed;

(d)   attach any material on which the applicant relies; and

(e)   ask for a hearing, if the applicant wants one, and explain why it is needed.

(4)   A person who wants to make representations about the application must—

(a)   serve the representations on—

      (i)   the court officer,

      (ii)   the applicant, and

      (iii)   any other person to whom proceeds might be paid;

(b)   do so as soon as reasonably practicable after service of the application;

(c)   attach any material on which that person relies; and

(d)   ask for a hearing, if that person wants one, and explain why it is needed.

(5)   The court—

(a)   must not determine the application unless the applicant and each person on whom it was served—

      (i)   is present, or

      (ii)   has had an opportunity to attend or to make representations;

(b)   subject to that, may determine the application—

      (i)   at a hearing (which must be in private unless the court otherwise directs), or without a hearing,

      (ii)   in the absence of any party to the application.

[Note. Under section 67D of the Proceeds of Crime Act 2002, a magistrates' court or the Crown Court may determine to whom, and in what proportions, any surplus proceeds of realisation must be distributed. Once a magistrates' court has made such a determination, the Crown Court may not do so, and vice versa.]

SEIZURE AND DETENTION PROCEEDINGS

33.28. Application for approval to seize property or to search (1)   This rule applies where an officer who is entitled to apply wants the approval of a magistrates' court, under section 47G of the Proceeds of Crime Act 2002—

(a)   to seize property, under section 47C of that Act;

(b)   to search premises or a person or vehicle for property to be seized, under section 47D, 47E or 47F of that Act.

(2)   Such an officer must—

(a)   apply in writing; and

(b)   serve the application on the court officer.

(3)   The application must—

(a)   explain—

      (i)   the applicant's entitlement to apply, and

      (ii)   how the proposed seizure meets the conditions prescribed by sections 47B, 47C and, if applicable, 47D, 47E or 47F of the 2002 Act;

(b)   if applicable, specify any premises, person or vehicle to be searched;

(c)   attach any material on which the applicant relies; and

(d)   propose the terms in which the applicant wants the court to give its approval.

(4)   The court—

(a)   must determine the application—

      (i)   at a hearing, which must be in private unless the court otherwise directs, and

      (ii)   in the applicant's presence;

(b)   may consider an application made orally instead of in writing.

[Note. Under section 47C of the Proceeds of Crime Act 2002, if any of the conditions listed in section 47B of the Act are met then one of the officers listed in section 47A may seize property other than cash or exempt property, as defined in the section, if that officer has reasonable grounds for suspecting that—

(a)   the property may otherwise be made unavailable for satisfying any confiscation order that has been or may be made against a defendant; or

(b)   the value of the property may otherwise be diminished as a result of conduct by the defendant or any other person.

Under sections 47D, 47E and 47F of the 2002 Act, such an officer may search premises, a person or a vehicle, respectively, for such property, on the conditions listed in those sections.

By sections 47C(6), 47D(2), 47E(4), 47F(6) and 47G of the 2002 Act, such an officer may seize property, and may search for it, only with the approval of a magistrates' court or, if that is impracticable, the approval of a senior officer (as defined by section 47G), unless in the circumstances it is not practicable to obtain the approval of either.]

33.29. Application to extend detention period (1)   This rule applies where an officer who is entitled to apply, or the prosecutor, wants a magistrates' court to make an order, under section 47M of the Proceeds of Crime Act 2002, extending the period for which seized property

may be detained.
(2)   Such an officer or prosecutor must—
(a)   apply in writing; and
(b)   serve the application on—
             (i)   the court officer, and
             (ii)   any person whom the applicant believes would be affected by an order.
(3)   The application must—
(a)   specify—
             (i)   the property to be detained, and
             (ii)   whether the applicant wants it to be detained for a specified period or indefinitely;
(b)   explain—
             (i)   the applicant's entitlement to apply, and
             (ii)   how the proposed detention meets the conditions prescribed by section 47M of the
                        2002 Act;
(c)   attach any material on which the applicant relies; and
(d)   propose the terms of the order.
(4)   The court—
(a)   must determine the application—
             (i)   at a hearing, which must be in private unless the court otherwise directs, and
             (ii)   in the applicant's presence;
(b)   may—
             (i)   consider an application made orally instead of in writing,
             (ii)   require service of the application on the court officer after it has been heard, instead
                        of before.
(5)   If the court extends the period for which the property may be detained, the applicant must—
(a)   notify any person affected by the order who was absent when it was made; and
(b)   serve on the court officer a list of those so notified.
[*Note. Under section 47M of the Proceeds of Crime Act 2002, one of the officers listed in that
section, or the prosecutor, may apply to a magistrates' court for an order extending the period of
48 hours for which, under section 47J of the Act, property seized under section 47C may be
detained.*
*On an application to which this rule applies, hearsay evidence within the meaning of section 1(2) of
the Civil Evidence Act 1995 is admissible: see section 47Q of the 2002 Act.*]

33.30.   *Application to vary or discharge order for extended detention*   (1)   This rule applies
where an officer who is entitled to apply, the prosecutor, or a person affected by an order to which
rule 33.29 applies, wants a magistrates' court to vary or discharge that order, under section 47N of
the Proceeds of Crime Act 2002.
(2)   Such a person must—
(a)   apply in writing; and
(b)   serve the application on—
             (i)   the court officer, and
             (ii)   as appropriate, the applicant for the order, or any person affected by the order.
(3)   The application must—
(a)   specify the order and the property detained;
(b)   explain—
             (i)   the applicant's entitlement to apply,
             (ii)   why it is appropriate for the order to be varied or discharged,
             (iii)   if applicable, on what grounds the court must discharge the order;
(c)   attach any material on which the applicant relies;
(d)   if applicable, propose the terms of any variation; and
(e)   ask for a hearing, if the applicant wants one, and explain why it is needed.
(4)   A person who wants to make representations about the application must—
(a)   serve the representations on—
             (i)   the court officer, and
             (ii)   the applicant;
(b)   do so as soon as reasonably practicable after service of the application;
(c)   attach any material on which that person relies; and
(d)   ask for a hearing, if that person wants one, and explain why it is needed.
(5)   The court—
(a)   must not determine the application unless the applicant and each person on whom it was
           served—
             (i)   is present, or
             (ii)   has had an opportunity to attend or to make representations;
(b)   subject to that, may determine the application—
             (i)   at a hearing (which must be in private unless the court otherwise directs), or
                        without a hearing,
             (ii)   in the absence of any party to the application.
[*Note. Under section 47N of the Proceeds of Crime Act 2002, one of the officers listed in
section 47M of the Act, the prosecutor, or a person affected by an order under section 47M, may
apply to a magistrates' court for the order to be varied or discharged. Section 47N(3) lists the*

circumstances in which the court must discharge such an order.
On an application to which this rule applies, hearsay evidence within the meaning of section 1(2) of the Civil Evidence Act 1995 is admissible: see section 47Q of the 2002 Act.]

33.31.   *Appeal about property detention decision*   (1)   This rule applies where—

(a)   on an application under rule 33.29 for an order extending the period for which property may be detained—

       (i)   a magistrates' court decides not to make such an order, and

      (ii)   an officer who is entitled to apply for such an order, or the prosecutor, wants to appeal against that decision to the Crown Court under section 47O(1) of the Proceeds of Crime Act 2002;

(b)   on an application under rule 33.30 to vary or discharge an order under rule 33.29—

       (i)   a magistrates' court determines the application, and

      (ii)   a person who is entitled to apply under that rule wants to appeal against that decision to the Crown Court under section 47O(2) of the 2002 Act.

(2)   The appellant must serve an appeal notice—

(a)   on the Crown Court officer and on any other party;

(b)   not more than 21 days after the magistrates' court's decision, or, if applicable, service of notice under rule 33.29(5).

(3)   The appeal notice must—

(a)   specify the decision under appeal;

(b)   where paragraph (1)(a) applies, explain why the detention period should be extended;

(c)   where paragraph (1)(b) applies, propose the order that the appellant wants the court to make, and explain why.

(4)   Rule 34.11 (Constitution of the Crown Court) applies on such an appeal.

[Note. Under section 47O of the Proceeds of Crime Act 2002, one of those entitled to apply for an order under section 47M of that Act (extension of detention of property) may appeal against a refusal to make an order, and one of those entitled to apply for the variation or discharge of such an order, under section 47N of that Act, may appeal against the decision on such an application.
On an appeal to which this rule applies, hearsay evidence within the meaning of section 1(2) of the Civil Evidence Act 1995 is admissible: see section 47Q of the 2002 Act.]

RESTRAINT AND RECEIVERSHIP PROCEEDINGS: RULE THAT APPLY GENERALY

33.32.   *Taking control of goods and forfeiture*
  [Omitted]

33.33.   *Joining of applications*
  [Omitted]

33.34.   *Applications to be dealt with in writing*
  [Omitted]

33.35.   *Business in chambers*
  [Omitted]

33.36.   *Power of court to control evidence*
  [Omitted]

33.37.   *Evidence of witnesses*
  [Omitted]

33.38.   *Witness summons*
  [Omitted]

33.39.   *Hearsay evidence*
  [Omitted]

33.40.   *Disclosure and inspection of documents*
  [Omitted]

33.41.   *Court documents*
  [Omitted]

33.42.   *Consent orders*
  [Omitted]

33.43.   *Slips and omissions*
  [Omitted]

33.44.   *Supply of documents from court records*
  [Omitted]

33.45.   *Discolsure of documents in criminal proceedings*
  [Omitted]

33.46.   *Preparation of documents*
  [Omitted]

33.47.   *Order for costs*
  [Omitted]

33.48.   *Assesment of costs*
  [Omitted]

RESTRAINT PROCEEDINGS

RECEIVERSHIP PROCEEDINGS

PROCEEDINGS UNDER THE CRIMINAL JUSTICE ACT 1988 AND THE DRUG TRAFFICKING ACT 1994

[Note. The relevant provisions of the 1988 and 1994 Acts were repealed on 24th March 2003, but they continue to have effect in respect of proceedings for offences committed before that date.]

33.64.   Statements, etc relevant to making confiscation orders   (1)   Where a prosecutor or defendant—
(a)   serves on the magistrates' court officer any statement or other document under section 73 of the Criminal Justice Act 1988 in any proceedings in respect of an offence listed in Schedule 4 to that Act; or
(b)   serves on the Crown Court officer any statement or other document under section 11 of the Drug Trafficking Act 1994 or section 73 of the 1988 Act in any proceedings in respect of a drug trafficking offence or in respect of an offence to which Part VI of the 1988 Act applies,
that party must serve a copy as soon as practicable on the defendant or the prosecutor, as the case may be.
(2)   Any statement tendered by the prosecutor to the magistrates' court under section 73 of the 1988 Act or to the Crown Court under section 11(1) of the 1994 Act or section 73(1A) of the 1988 Act must include the following particulars—
(a)   the name of the defendant;
(b)   the name of the person by whom the statement is made and the date on which it was made;
(c)   where the statement is not tendered immediately after the defendant has been convicted, the date on which and the place where the relevant conviction occurred; and
(d)   such information known to the prosecutor as is relevant to the determination as to whether or not the defendant has benefited from drug trafficking or relevant criminal conduct and to the assessment of the value of any proceeds of drug trafficking or, as the case may be, benefit from relevant criminal conduct.
(3)   Where, in accordance with section 11(7) of the 1994 Act or section 73(1C) of the 1988 Act, the defendant indicates in writing the extent to which he or she accepts any allegation contained within the prosecutor's statement, the defendant must serve a copy of that reply on the court

officer.
(4) Expressions used in this rule have the same meanings as in the 1994 Act or, where appropriate, the 1988 Act.

33.65. Postponed determinations (1) Where an application is made by the defendant or the prosecutor—

(a) to a magistrates' court under section 72A(5)(a) of the Criminal Justice Act 1988 asking the court to exercise its powers under section 72A(4) of that Act; or

(b) to the Crown Court under section 3(5)(a) of the Drug Trafficking Act 1994 asking the court to exercise its powers under section 3(4) of that Act, or under section 72A(5)(a) of the 1988 Act asking the court to exercise its powers under section 72A(4) of the 1988 Act,

the application must be in writing and the applicant must serve a copy on the prosecutor or the defendant, as the case may be.
(2) A party served with a copy of an application under paragraph (1) must, within 28 days of the date of service, notify the applicant and the court officer, in writing, whether or not that party opposes the application, giving reasons for any opposition.
(3) After the expiry of the period referred to in paragraph (2), the court may determine an application under paragraph (1)—

(a) without a hearing; or

(b) at a hearing at which the parties may be represented.

33.66. Confiscation orders—revised assessments (1) Where the prosecutor makes an application under section 13, 14 or 15 of the Drug Trafficking Act 1994 or section 74A, 74B or 74C of the Criminal Justice Act 1988, the application must be in writing and a copy must be served on the defendant.
(2) The application must include the following particulars—

(a) the name of the defendant;

(b) the date on which and the place where any relevant conviction occurred;

(c) the date on which and the place where any relevant confiscation order was made or, as the case may be, varied;

(d) the grounds on which the application is made; and

(e) an indication of the evidence available to support the application.

33.67. Application to the Crown Court to discharge or vary order to make material available
(1) Where an order under section 93H of the Criminal Justice Act 1988 (order to make material available) or section 55 of the Drug Trafficking Act 1994 (order to make material available) has been made by the Crown Court, any person affected by it may apply in writing to the court officer for the order to be discharged or varied, and on hearing such an application the court may discharge the order or make such variations to it as the court thinks fit.
(2) Subject to paragraph (3), where a person proposes to make an application under paragraph (1) for the discharge or variation of an order, that person must give a copy of the application, not later than 48 hours before the making of the application—

(a) to a constable at the police station specified in the order; or

(b) to the office of the appropriate officer who made the application, as specified in the order,

in either case together with a notice indicating the time and place at which the application for discharge or variation is to be made.
(3) The court may direct that paragraph (2) need not be complied with if satisfied that the person making the application has good reason to seek a discharge or variation of the order as soon as possible and it is not practicable to comply with that paragraph.
(4) In this rule:

'constable' includes a person commissioned by the Commissioners for Her Majesty's Revenue and Customs;

'police station' includes a place for the time being occupied by Her Majesty's Revenue and Customs.

33.68. Application to the Crown Court for increase in term of imprisonment in default of payment
(1) This rule applies to applications made, or that have effect as made, to the Crown Court under section 10 of the Drug Trafficking Act 1994 and section 75A of the Criminal Justice Act 1988 (interest on sums unpaid under confiscation orders).
(2) Notice of an application to which this rule applies to increase the term of imprisonment or detention fixed in default of payment of a confiscation order by a person ('the defendant') must be made by the prosecutor in writing to the court officer.
(3) A notice under paragraph (2) shall—

(a) state the name and address of the defendant;

(b) specify the grounds for the application;

(c) give details of the enforcement measures taken, if any; and

(d) include a copy of the confiscation order.

(4) On receiving a notice under paragraph (2), the court officer must—

(a) forthwith send to the defendant and the magistrates' court required to enforce payment of the confiscation order under section 140(1) of the Powers of Criminal Courts (Sentencing) Act 2000, a copy of the said notice; and

(b) notify in writing the applicant and the defendant of the date, time and place appointed for the hearing of the application.

(5) Where the Crown Court makes an order pursuant to an application mentioned in paragraph (1) above, the court officer must send forthwith a copy of the order—

(a)   to the applicant;
(b)   to the defendant;
(c)   where the defendant is at the time of the making of the order in custody, to the person having custody of him or her; and
(d)   to the magistrates' court mentioned in paragraph (4)(a).

33.69. Drug trafficking – compensation on acquittal in the Crown Court   Where the Crown Court cancels a confiscation order under section 22(2) of the Drug Trafficking Act 1994, the Crown Court officer must serve notice to that effect on the High Court officer and on the court officer of the magistrates' court which has responsibility for enforcing the order.

CONTEMPT PROCEEDINGS

33.70. Application to punish for contempt of court
   [Omitted]

PART 34   APPEAL TO THE CROWN COURT

Contents of this Part

B.31 *34.1. When this Part applies*   (1)   This Part applies where—
(a)   a defendant wants to appeal under—
        (i)   section 108 of the Magistrates' Courts Act 1980,
        (ii)   section 45 of the Mental Health Act 1983,
        (iii)   paragraph 10 of Schedule 3 to the Powers of Criminal Courts (Sentencing) Act 2000, or paragraphs 9(8) or 13(5) of Schedule 8 to the Criminal Justice Act 2003,
        (iv)   section 42 of the Counter Terrorism Act 2008;
(b)   the Criminal Cases Review Commission refers a defendant's case to the Crown Court under section 11 of the Criminal Appeal Act 1995;
(c)   a prosecutor wants to appeal under—
        (i)   section 14A(5A) of the Football Spectators Act 1989, or
        (ii)   section 147(3) of the Customs and Excise Management Act 1979; or
(d)   a person wants to appeal under—
        (i)   section 1 of the Magistrates' Courts (Appeals from Binding Over Orders) Act 1956,
        (ii)   section 12(5) of the Contempt of Court Act 1981,
        (iii)   regulation 3C or 3H of the Costs in Criminal Cases (General) Regulations 1986,
        (iv)   section 22 of the Football Spectators Act 1989, or
        (v)   section 10(4) or (5) of the Crime and Disorder Act 1998.
(2)   A reference to an 'appellant' in this Part is a reference to such a party or person.
[Note. An appeal to the Crown Court is by way of re-hearing: see section 79(3) of the Senior Courts Act 1981. For the powers of the Crown Court on an appeal, see section 48 of that Act.
A defendant may appeal from a magistrates' court to the Crown Court—
(a)   under section 108 of the Magistrates' Courts Act 1980, against sentence after a guilty plea and after a not guilty plea against conviction, against a finding of guilt or against sentence;
(b)   under section 45 of the Mental Health Act 1983, where the magistrates' court makes a hospital order or guardianship order without convicting the defendant;
(c)   under paragraph 10 of Schedule 3 to the Powers of Criminal Courts (Sentencing) Act 2000, or under paragraphs 9(8) or 13(5) of Schedule 8 to the Criminal Justice Act 2003, where the magistrates' court revokes a community order and deals with the defendant in another way;
(d)   under section 42 of the Counter Terrorism Act 2008, where the magistrates' court decides that an offence has a terrorist connection.
See section 13 of the Criminal Appeal Act 1995 for the circumstances in which the Criminal Cases Review Commission may refer a conviction or sentence to the Crown Court.
Under section 14A(5A) of the Football Spectators Act 1989, a prosecutor may appeal to the Crown Court against a failure by a magistrates' court to make a football banning order.
Under section 147(3) of the Customs and Excise Management Act 1979, a prosecutor may appeal to the Crown Court against any decision of a magistrates' court in proceedings for an offence

under any Act relating to customs or excise.

Under section 1 of the Magistrates' Courts (Appeals from Binding Over Orders) Act 1956, a person bound over to keep the peace or be of good behaviour by a magistrates' court may appeal to the Crown Court.

Under section 12(5) of the Contempt of Court Act 1981, a person detained, committed to custody or fined by a magistrates' court for insulting a member of the court or another participant in the case, or for interrupting the proceedings, may appeal to the Crown Court.

Under regulation 3C of the Costs in Criminal Cases (General) Regulations 1986, a legal representative against whom a magistrates' court makes a wasted costs order under section 19A of the Prosecution of Offences Act 1985 and regulation 3B may appeal against that order to the Crown Court.

Under regulation 3H of the Costs in Criminal Cases (General) Regulations 1986, a third party against whom a magistrates' court makes a costs order under section 19B of the Prosecution of Offences Act 1985 and regulation 3F may appeal against that order to the Crown Court.

Under section 22 of the Football Spectators Act 1989, any person aggrieved by the decision of a magistrates' court making a football banning order may appeal to the Crown Court.

Under section 10(4) or (5) of the Crime and Disorder Act 1998, a person in respect of whom a magistrates' court makes a parenting order may appeal against that order to the Crown Court.]

34.2. Service of appeal and respondent's notices (1) An appellant must serve an appeal notice on—

(a) the magistrates' court officer; and

(b) every other party.

(2) The appellant must serve the appeal notice—

(a) as soon after the decision appealed against as the appellant wants; but

(b) not more than 21 days after—

(i) sentence or the date sentence is deferred, whichever is earlier, if the appeal is against conviction or against a finding of guilt,

(ii) sentence, if the appeal is against sentence, or

(iii) the order or failure to make an order about which the appellant wants to appeal, in any other case.

(3) The appellant must serve with the appeal notice any application for the following, with reasons—

(a) an extension of the time limit under this rule, if the appeal notice is late;

(b) bail pending appeal, if the appellant is in custody;

(c) the suspension of any disqualification imposed in the case, where the magistrates' court or the Crown Court can order such a suspension pending appeal.

(4) Where both the magistrates' court and the Crown Court can grant bail or suspend a disqualification pending appeal, an application must indicate by which court the appellant wants the application determined.

(5) Where the appeal is against conviction or against a finding of guilt, unless the respondent agrees that the court should allow the appeal—

(a) the respondent must serve a respondent's notice on—

(i) the Crown Court officer; and

(ii) the appellant; and

(b) the respondent must serve that notice not more than 21 days after service of the appeal notice.

[Note. Under section 1(1) of the Powers of Criminal Courts (Sentencing) Act 2000, a magistrates' court may defer passing sentence for up to 6 months.

[Under section 113 of the Magistrates' Courts Act 1980, the magistrates' court may grant an appellant bail pending appeal. Under section 81(1)(b) of the Senior Courts Act 1981, the Crown Court also may do so. See also rule 14.7.

Under section 39 of the Road Traffic Offenders Act 1988, a court which has made an order disqualifying a person from driving may suspend the disqualification pending appeal. Under section 40 of the 1988 Act, the appeal court may do so. See also rule 29.2.]

34.3. Form of appeal and respondent's notices (1) The appeal notice must—

(a) specify—

(i) the conviction or finding of guilt,

(ii) the sentence, or

(iii) the order, or the failure to make an order,

about which the appellant wants to appeal;

(b) summarise the issues;

(c) in an appeal against conviction or against a finding of guilt, to the best of the appellant's ability and to assist the court in fulfilling its duty under rule 3.2 (the court's duty of case management)—

(i) identify the witnesses who gave oral evidence in the magistrates' court,

(ii) identify the witnesses who gave written evidence in the magistrates' court,

(iii) identify the prosecution witnesses whom the appellant will want to question if they are called to give oral evidence in the Crown Court,

(iv) identify the likely defence witnesses,

(v) give notice of any special arrangements or other measures that the appellant thinks are needed for witnesses,

(vi) explain whether the issues in the Crown Court differ from the issues in the magistrates' court, and if so how, and

(vii) say how long the trial lasted in the magistrates' court and how long the appeal is likely to last in the Crown Court;

(d) in an appeal against a sentence, order or failure to make an order—

(i) identify any circumstances, report or other information of which the appellant wants the court to take account, and

(ii) explain the significance of those circumstances or that information to what is in issue;

(e) in an appeal against a finding that the appellant insulted someone or interrupted proceedings in the magistrates' court, attach—

(i) the magistrates' court's written findings of fact, and

(ii) the appellant's response to those findings;

(f) say whether the appellant has asked the magistrates' court to reconsider the case; and

(g) include a list of those on whom the appellant has served the appeal notice.

(2) A respondent's notice must—

(a) give the date on which the respondent was served with the appeal notice; and

(b) to assist the court in fulfilling its duty under rule 3.2—

(i) identify the witnesses who gave oral evidence in the magistrates' court,

(ii) identify the witnesses who gave written evidence in the magistrates' court,

(iii) identify the prosecution witnesses whom the respondent intends to call to give oral evidence in the Crown Court,

(iv) give notice of any special arrangements or other measures that the respondent thinks are needed for witnesses,

(v) explain whether the issues in the Crown Court differ from the issues in the magistrates' court, and if so how, and

(vi) say how long the trial lasted in the magistrates' court and how long the appeal is likely to last in the Crown Court.

(3) Paragraph (4) applies in an appeal against conviction or against a finding of guilt where in the magistrates' court a party to the appeal—

(a) introduced in evidence material to which applies—

(i) Part 16 (Written witness statements),

(ii) Part 19 (Expert evidence),

(iii) Part 20 (Hearsay evidence),

(iv) Part 21 (Evidence of bad character), or

(v) Part 22 (Evidence of a complainant's previous sexual behaviour); or

(b) made an application to which applies—

(i) Part 17 (Witness summonses, warrants and orders),

(ii) Part 18 (Measures to assist a witness or defendant to give evidence), or

(iii) Part 23 (Restriction on cross-examination by a defendant).

(4) If such a party wants to reintroduce that material or to renew that application in the Crown Court that party must include a notice to that effect in the appeal or respondent's notice, as the case may be.

[Note. The Practice Direction sets out forms of appeal and respondent's notices for use in connection with this rule.

In some cases, a magistrates' court can reconsider a conviction, sentence or other order and make a fresh decision. See section 142 of the Magistrates' Courts Act 1980.

See also rule 3.11 (Conduct of a trial or an appeal).]

34.4. Duty of magistrates' court officer (1) The magistrates' court officer must—

(a) arrange for the magistrates' court to hear as soon as practicable any application to that court under rule 34.2(3)(c) (suspension of disqualification pending appeal); and

(b) as soon as practicable notify the Crown Court officer of the service of the appeal notice and make available to that officer—

(i) the appeal notice and any accompanying application served by the appellant,

(ii) details of the parties including their addresses, and

(iii) a copy of each magistrates' court register entry relating to the decision under appeal and to any application for bail pending appeal.

(2) Where the appeal is against conviction or against a finding of guilt, the magistrates' court officer must make available to the Crown Court officer as soon as practicable—

(a) all material served on the magistrate's court officer to which applies—

(i) Part 8 (Initial details of the prosecution case),

(ii) Part 16 (Written witness statements),

(iii) Part 17 (Witness summonses, warrants and orders),

(iv) Part 18 (Measures to assist a witness or defendant to give evidence),

(v) Part 19 (Expert evidence),

(vi) Part 20 (Hearsay evidence),

(vii) Part 21 (Evidence of bad character),

(viii) Part 22 (Evidence of a complainant's previous sexual behaviour),

(ix) Part 23 (Restriction on cross-examination by a defendant);

(b) any case management questionnaire prepared for the purposes of the trial;

(c)   all case management directions given by the magistrates' court for the purposes of the trial; and

(d)   any other document, object or information for which the Crown Court officer asks.

(3)   Where the appeal is against sentence, the magistrates' court officer must make available to the Crown Court officer as soon as practicable any report received for the purposes of sentencing.

(4)   Unless the magistrates' court otherwise directs, the magistrates' court officer—

(a)   must keep any document or object exhibited in the proceedings in the magistrates' court, or arrange for it to be kept by some other appropriate person, until at least—

    (i)   6 weeks after the conclusion of those proceedings, or

    (ii)   the conclusion of any proceedings in the Crown Court that begin within that 6 weeks; but

(b)   need not keep such a document if—

    (i)   the document that was exhibited is a copy of a document retained by the party who produced it, and

    (ii)   what was in evidence in the magistrates' court was the content of that document.

[Note. See also section 133 of the Criminal Justice Act 2003 (Proof of statements in documents).]

34.5.   *Duty of person keeping exhibit*   A person who, under arrangements made by the magistrates' court officer, keeps a document or object exhibited in the proceedings in the magistrates' court must—

(a)   keep that exhibit until—

    (i)   6 weeks after the conclusion of those proceedings, or

    (ii)   the conclusion of any proceedings in the Crown Court that begin within that 6 weeks,

  unless the magistrates' court or the Crown Court otherwise directs; and

(b)   provide the Crown Court with any such document or object for which the Crown Court officer asks, within such period as the Crown Court officer may require.

34.6.   *Reference by the Criminal Cases Review Commission*   (1)   The Crown Court officer must, as soon as practicable, serve a reference by the Criminal Cases Review Commission on—

(a)   the appellant;

(b)   every other party; and

(c)   the magistrates' court officer.

(2)   The appellant may serve an appeal notice on—

(a)   the Crown Court officer; and

(b)   every other party,

not more than 21 days later.

(3)   The Crown Court must treat the reference as the appeal notice if the appellant does not serve an appeal notice.

34.7.   *Preparation for appeal*   (1)   The Crown Court may conduct a preparation for appeal hearing (and if necessary more than one such hearing) where—

(a)   it is necessary to conduct such a hearing in order to give directions for the effective determination of the appeal; or

(b)   such a hearing is required to set ground rules for the conduct of the questioning of a witness or appellant.

(2)   Where under rule 34.3(4) a party gives notice to reintroduce material or to renew an application first introduced or made in the magistrates' court—

(a)   no other notice or application to the same effect otherwise required by these Rules need be served; and

(b)   any objection served by the other party in the magistrates' court is treated as renewed unless within 14 days that party serves notice withdrawing it.

(3)   Paragraphs (4) and (5) apply where—

(a)   the appeal is against conviction or against a finding of guilt;

(b)   a party wants to introduce material or make an application under a Part of these Rules listed in rule 34.3(3); and

(c)   that party gives no notice of reintroduction or renewal under rule 34.3(4) (whether because the conditions for giving such a notice are not met or for any other reason).

(4)   Such a party must serve the material, notice or application required by that Part not more than 14 days after service of the appeal notice.

(5)   Subject to paragraph (4), the requirements of that Part apply (for example, as to the form in which a notice must be given or an application made and as to the time and form in which such a notice or application may be opposed).

34.8.   *Hearings and decisions*   (1)   The Crown Court as a general rule must hear in public an appeal or reference to which this Part applies, but—

(a)   may order any hearing to be in private; and

(b)   where a hearing is about a public interest ruling, must hold that hearing in private.

(2)   The Crown Court officer must give as much notice as reasonably practicable of every hearing to—

(a)   the parties;

(b)   any party's custodian; and

(c)   any other person whom the Crown Court requires to be notified.

(3)   The Crown Court officer must serve every decision on—

(a)   the parties;

(b)   any other person whom the Crown Court requires to be served; and

(c)   the magistrates' court officer and any party's custodian, where the decision determines an appeal.

(4)   But where a hearing or decision is about a public interest ruling, the Crown Court officer must not—

(a)   give notice of that hearing to; or

(b)   serve that decision on,

anyone other than the prosecutor who applied for that ruling, unless the court otherwise directs.
[Note. See also Part 15 (Disclosure).]

34.9. *Abandoning an appeal* (1)   The appellant—

(a)   may abandon an appeal without the Crown Court's permission, by serving a notice of abandonment on—

       (i)   the magistrates' court officer,

       (ii)   the Crown Court officer, and

       (iii)   every other party

    before the hearing of the appeal begins; but

(b)   after the hearing of the appeal begins, may only abandon the appeal with the Crown Court's permission.

(2)   A notice of abandonment must be signed by or on behalf of the appellant.

(3)   Where an appellant who is on bail pending appeal abandons an appeal—

(a)   the appellant must surrender to custody as directed by the magistrates' court officer; and

(b)   any conditions of bail apply until then.

[Note. The Practice Direction sets out a form of notice of abandonment for use in connection with this rule.

Where an appellant abandons an appeal to the Crown Court, both the Crown Court and the magistrates' court have power to make a costs order against that appellant in favour of the respondent: see section 52 of the Senior Courts Act 1981 and section 109 of the Magistrates' Courts Act 1980. Part 45 contains rules about costs on abandoning an appeal.]

34.10. *Court's power to vary requirements under this Part* The Crown Court may—

(a)   shorten or extend (even after it has expired) a time limit under this Part;

(b)   allow an appellant to vary an appeal notice that that appellant has served;

(c)   direct that an appeal notice be served on any person;

(d)   allow an appeal notice or a notice of abandonment to be in a different form to one set out in the Practice Direction, or to be presented orally.

34.11. *Constitution of the Crown Court* [(1)   On the hearing of an appeal the general rule is that—

(a)   the Crown Court must comprise—

       (i)   a judge of the High Court, a Circuit judge, a Recorder or a qualifying judge advocate, and

       (ii)   no less than two and no more than four justices of the peace, none of whom took part in the decision under appeal; and

(b)   if the appeal is from a youth court, each justice of the peace must be qualified to sit as a member of a youth court.

(2)   Despite the general rule—

(a)   the Crown Court may include only one justice of the peace if—

       (i)   the presiding judge decides that otherwise the start of the appeal hearing will be delayed unreasonably, or

       (ii)   one or more of the justices of the peace who started hearing the appeal is absent; and

(b)   the Crown Court may comprise only a judge of the High Court, a Circuit judge, a Recorder or a qualifying judge advocate if—

       (i)   the appeal is against conviction, under section 108 of the Magistrates' Courts Act 1980, and

       (ii)   the respondent agrees that the court should allow the appeal, under section 48(2) of the Senior Courts Act 1981.

(3)   Before the hearing of an appeal begins and after that hearing ends—

(a)   the Crown Court may comprise only a judge of the High Court, a Circuit judge, a Recorder or a qualifying judge advocate; and

(b)   so constituted, the court may, among other things, exercise the powers to which apply—

       (i)   the rules in this Part and in Part 3 (Case management), and

       (ii)   rule 35.2 (stating a case for the opinion of the High Court, or refusing to do so).

[Note. See sections 73 and 74 of the Senior Courts Act 1981(which allow rules of court to provide for the constitution of the Crown Court in proceedings on appeal), section 45 of the Children and Young Persons Act 1933 and section 9 of the Courts Act 2003. Under section 8(1A) of the Senior Courts Act 1981, a qualifying judge advocate may not exercise the jurisdiction of the Crown Court on an appeal from a youth court.]]

PART 35   APPEAL TO THE HIGH COURT BY CASE STATED

Contents of this Part

B.32   *35.1.*   *When this Part applies*   This Part applies where a person wants to appeal to the High Court by case stated—

(a)   under section 111 of the Magistrates' Courts Act 1980, against a decision of a magistrates' court; or

(b)   under section 28 of the Senior Courts Act 1981, against a decision of the Crown Court.

[*Note. Under section 111 of the Magistrates' Courts Act 1980, 'any person who was a party to any proceeding before a magistrates' court or is aggrieved by the conviction, order, determination or other proceeding of the court may question the proceeding on the ground that it is wrong in law or is in excess of jurisdiction by applying to the justices composing the court to state a case for the opinion of the High Court on the question of law or jurisdiction involved'.*

Under section 28 of the Senior Courts Act 1981, 'any order, judgment or other decision of the Crown Court may be questioned by any party to the proceedings, on the ground that it is wrong in law or is in excess of jurisdiction, by applying to the Crown Court to have a case stated by that court for the opinion of the High Court.'

Under section 28A of the 1981 Act, the High Court may 'reverse, affirm or amend the determination in respect of which the case has been stated; or remit the matter to the magistrates' court, or the Crown Court, with the opinion of the High Court, and may make such other order . . . as it thinks fit.' Under that section, the High Court also may send the case back for amendment, if it thinks fit.]

35.2.   *Application to state a case*   (1)   A party who wants the court to state a case for the opinion of the High Court must—

(a)   apply in writing, not more than 21 days after the decision against which the applicant wants to appeal; and

(b)   serve the application on—

         (i)   the court officer, and

         (ii)   each other party.

(2)   The application must—

(a)   specify the decision in issue;

(b)   specify the proposed question or questions of law or jurisdiction on which the opinion of the High Court will be asked;

(c)   indicate the proposed grounds of appeal; and

(d)   include or attach any application for the following, with reasons—

         (i)   if the application is to the Crown Court, an extension of time within which to apply to state a case,

         (ii)   bail pending appeal,

         (iii)   the suspension of any disqualification imposed in the case, where the court can order such a suspension pending appeal.

(3)   A party who wants to make representations about the application must—

(a)   serve the representations on—

         (i)   the court officer, and

         (ii)   each other party; and

(b)   do so not more than 14 days after service of the application.

(4)   The court may determine the application without a hearing.

(5)   If the court decides not to state a case, the court officer must serve on each party—

(a)   notice of that decision; and

(b)   the court's written reasons for that decision, if not more than 21 days later the applicant asks for those reasons.

[*Note. The time limit for applying to a magistrates' court to state a case is prescribed by section 111(2) of the Magistrates' Courts Act 1980. It may be neither extended nor shortened.*

Under section 113 of the Magistrates' Courts Act 1980, the magistrates' court may grant an appellant bail pending appeal. Under section 81(1)(d) of the Senior Courts Act 1981, the Crown Court may do so. See also rule 14.7.

Where Part 34 (Appeal to the Crown Court) applies, an application to which this rule applies may be determined by a judge of the High Court, a Circuit judge, a Recorder or a qualifying judge advocate without justices of the peace: see rule 34.11 (Constitution of the Crown Court).

Under section 39 of the Road Traffic Offenders Act 1988, a court which has made an order disqualifying a person from driving may suspend the disqualification pending appeal. See also rule 29.2.

The Practice Direction sets out a form of application for use in connection with this rule.]

35.3.   *Preparation of case stated*   (1)   This rule applies where the court decides to state a case for the opinion of the High Court.

(2)   The court officer must serve on each party notice of—

(a)   the decision to state a case, and
(b)   any recognizance ordered by the court.
(3)   Unless the court otherwise directs, not more than 21 days after the court's decision to state a case—
(a)   in a magistrates court, the court officer must serve a draft case on each party;
(b)   in the Crown Court, the applicant must serve a draft case on the court officer and each other party.
(4)   The draft case must—
(a)   specify the decision in issue;
(b)   specify the question(s) of law or jurisdiction on which the opinion of the High Court will be asked;
(c)   include a succinct summary of—
    (i)   the nature and history of the proceedings,
    (ii)   the court's relevant findings of fact, and
    (iii)   the relevant contentions of the parties;
(d)   if a question is whether there was sufficient evidence on which the court reasonably could reach a finding of fact—
    (i)   specify that finding, and
    (ii)   include a summary of the evidence on which the court reached that finding.
(5)   Except to the extent that paragraph (4)(d) requires, the draft case must not include an account of the evidence received by the court.
(6)   A party who wants to make representations about the content of the draft case, or to propose a revised draft, must—
(a)   serve the representations, or revised draft, on—
    (i)   the court officer, and
    (ii)   each other party; and
(b)   do so not more than 21 days after service of the draft case.
(7)   The court must state the case not more than 21 days after the time for service of representations under paragraph (6) has expired.
(8)   A case stated for the opinion of the High Court must—
(a)   comply with paragraphs (4) and (5); and
(b)   identify—
    (i)   the court that stated it, and
    (ii)   the court office for that court.
(9)   The court officer must serve the case stated on each party.
[Note. Under section 114 of the Magistrates' Courts Act 1980, a magistrates' court need not state a case until the person who applied for it has entered into a recognizance to appeal promptly to the High Court. The Crown Court has a corresponding inherent power.
Under section 121(6) of the 1980 Act, the magistrates' court which states a case need not include all the members of the court which took the decision questioned.
For the procedure on appeal to the High Court, see Part 52 of the Civil Procedure Rules 1998 and the associated Practice Direction.]

35.4.   Duty of justices' legal adviser   (1)   This rule applies—
(a)   only in a magistrates' court; and
(b)   unless the court—
    (i)   includes a District Judge (Magistrates' Courts), and
    (ii)   otherwise directs.
(2)   A justices' legal adviser must—
(a)   give the court legal advice; and
(b)   if the court so requires, assist it by—
    (i)   preparing and amending the draft case, and
    (ii)   completing the case stated.

35.5.   Court's power to vary requirements under this Part   (1)   The court may shorten or extend (even after it has expired) a time limit under this Part.
(2)   A person who wants an extension of time must—
(a)   apply when serving the application, representations or draft case for which it is needed; and
(b)   explain the delay.
[Note. See also rule 35.2(2)(d)(i) and the note to rule 35.2.]

PART 36   APPEAL TO THE COURT OF APPEAL: GENERAL RULES

Note
    [Part 36 is not reproduced.]

PART 37   APPEAL TO THE COURT OF APPEAL AGAINST RULING AT PREPARATORY HEARING

Note
    [Part 37 is not reproduced.]

Part 38   Appeal to the Court of Appeal against Ruling Adverse to Prosecution

Note
> [Part 38 is not reproduced.]

Part 39   Appeal to the Court of Appeal about Conviction or Sentence

Note
> [Part 39 is not reproduced.]

Part 40   Appeal to the Court of Appeal about Reporting or Public Access Restriction

Note
> [Part 40 is not reproduced.]

Part 41   Reference to the Court of Appeal of Point of Law or Unduly Lenient Sentencing

Note
> [Part 41 is not reproduced.]

Part 42   Appeal to the Court of Appeal in Confiscation and Related Proceedings

Note
> [Part 42 is not reproduced.]

Part 43   Appeal or reference to the Supreme Court

Note
> [Part 43 is not reproduced.]

Part 44   Request to the European Court for a Preliminary Ruling

Contents of this Part

B.33   *44.1. When this Part applies*   This Part applies where the court can request the Court of Justice of the European Union ('the European Court') to give a preliminary ruling, under Article 267 of the Treaty on the Functioning of the European Union.
[Note. Under Article 267, if a court of a Member State considers that a decision on the question is necessary to enable it to give judgment, it may request the European Court to give a preliminary ruling concerning—

(a)   *the interpretation of the Treaty on European Union, or of the Treaty on the Functioning of the European Union;*

(b)   *the validity and interpretation of acts of the institutions, bodies, offices or agencies of the Union.]*

44.2. Preparation of request   (1)   The court may—

(a)   make an order for the submission of a request—

       (i)   on application by a party, or

       (ii)   on its own initiative;

(b)   give directions for the preparation of the terms of such a request.

(2)   The court must—

(a)   include in such a request—

       (i)   the identity of the court making the request,

       (ii)   the parties' identities,

       (iii)   a statement of whether a party is in custody,

       (iv)   a succinct statement of the question on which the court seeks the ruling of the European Court,

       (v)   a succinct statement of any opinion on the answer that the court may have expressed in any judgment that it has delivered,

       (vi)   a summary of the nature and history of the proceedings, including the salient facts and an indication of whether those facts are proved, admitted or assumed,

       (vii)   the relevant rules of national law,

       (viii)   a summary of the relevant contentions of the parties,

       (ix)   an indication of the provisions of European Union law that the European Court is asked to interpret, and

       (x)   an explanation of why a ruling of the European Court is requested;

(b)   express the request in terms that can be translated readily into other languages; and

(c)   set out the request in a schedule to the order.

44.3. Submission of request   (1)   The court officer must serve the order for the submission of the request on the Senior Master of the Queen's Bench Division of the High Court.

(2)   The Senior Master must—

(a)   submit the request to the European Court; but
(b)   unless the court otherwise directs, postpone the submission of the request until—
    (i)   the time for any appeal against the order has expired, and
    (ii)   any appeal against the order has been determined.

PART 45   COSTS

Contents of this Part

General rules

Costs out of central funds

Payment of costs by one party to another

Other costs orders

Assessment of costs

GENERAL RULES

B.34   *45.1.   When this Part applies* (1)   This Part applies where the court can make an order about costs under—
(a)   Part II of the Prosecution of Offences Act 1985 and Part II, IIA or IIB of The Costs in Criminal Cases (General) Regulations 1986;
(b)   section 109 of the Magistrates' Courts Act 1980;
(c)   section 52 of the Senior Courts Act 1981 and rule 45.6 or rule 45.7;
(d)   section 8 of the Bankers Books Evidence Act 1879;
(e)   section 2C(8) of the Criminal Procedure (Attendance of Witnesses) Act 1965;
(f)   section 36(5) of the Criminal Justice Act 1972;
(g)   section 159(5) and Schedule 3, paragraph 11, of the Criminal Justice Act 1988;
(h)   section 14H(5) of the Football Spectators Act 1989;
(i)   section 4(7) of the Dangerous Dogs Act 1991;
(j)   Part 3 of the Serious Crime Act 2007 (Appeals under Section 24) Order 2008; or
(k)   Part 1 or 2 of the Extradition Act 2003.
(2)   In this Part, 'costs' means—
(a)   the fees payable to a legal representative;
(b)   the disbursements paid by a legal representative; and
(c)   any other expenses incurred in connection with the case.
[Note. A costs order can be made under—
(a)   section 16 of the Prosecution of Offences Act 1985 (defence costs), for the payment out of central funds of a defendant's costs (see rule 45.4);
(b)   section 17 of the Prosecution of Offences Act 1985 (prosecution costs), for the payment out of central funds of a private prosecutor's costs (see rule 45.4);
(c)   section 18 of the Prosecution of Offences Act 1985 (award of costs against accused), for the payment by a defendant of another person's costs (see rules 45.5 and 45.6);
(d)   section 19(1) of the Prosecution of Offences Act 1985 and regulation 3 of the Costs in Criminal Cases (General) Regulations 1986, for the payment by a party of another party's costs incurred as a result of an unnecessary or improper act or omission by or on behalf of the first party (see rule 45.8);
(e)   section 19A of the Prosecution of Offences Act 1985 (costs against legal representatives, etc)—
(i)   for the payment by a legal representative of a party's costs incurred as a result of an improper, unreasonable or negligent act or omission by or on behalf of the representative, or
(ii)   disallowing the payment to that representative of such costs
(see rule 45.9);

(f)   section 19B of the Prosecution of Offences Act 1985 (provision for award of costs against third parties) and regulation 3F of the Costs in Criminal Cases (General) Regulations 1986, for the payment by a person who is not a party of a party's costs where there has been serious misconduct by the non-party (see rule 45.10);

(g)   section 109 of the Magistrates' Courts Act 1980, section 52 of the Senior Courts Act 1981 and rule 45.6, for the payment by an appellant of a respondent's costs on abandoning an appeal to the Crown Court (see rule 45.6);

(h)   section 52 of the Senior Courts Act 1981 and—

     (i)   rule 45.6, for the payment by a party of another party's costs on an appeal to the Crown Court in any case not covered by (c) or (g);

     (ii)   rule 45.7, for the payment by a party of another party's costs on an application to the Crown Court about the breach or variation of a deferred prosecution agreement, or on an application to lift the suspension of a prosecution after breach of such an agreement;

(i)   section 8 of the Bankers Books Evidence Act 1879, for the payment of costs by a party or by the bank against which an application for an order is made (see rule 45.7);

(j)   section 2C(8) of the Criminal Procedure (Attendance of Witnesses) Act 1965, for the payment by the applicant for a witness summons of the costs of a party who applies successfully under rule 17.7 to have it withdrawn (see rule 45.7);

(k)   section 36(5) of the Criminal Justice Act 1972 or Schedule 3, paragraph 11, of the Criminal Justice Act 1988, for the payment out of central funds of a defendant's costs on a reference by the Attorney General of—

     (i)   a point of law, or

     (ii)   an unduly lenient sentence

  (see rule 45.4);

(l)   section 159(5) of the Criminal Justice Act 1988, for the payment by a person of another person's costs on an appeal about a reporting or public access restriction (see rule 45.6);

(m)   section 14H(5) of the Football Spectators Act 1989, for the payment by a defendant of another person's costs on an application to terminate a football banning order (see rule 45.7);

(n)   section 4(7) of the Dangerous Dogs Act 1991, for the payment by a defendant of another person's costs on an application to terminate a disqualification for having custody of a dog (see rule 45.7);

(o)   article 14 of the Serious Crime Act 2007 (Appeals under Section 24) Order 2008, corresponding with section 16 of the Prosecution of Offences Act 1985 (see rule 45.4);

(p)   article 15 of the Serious Crime Act 2007 (Appeals under Section 24) Order 2008, corresponding with section 18 of the Prosecution of Offences Act 1985 (see rule 45.6);

(q)   article 16 of the Serious Crime Act 2007 (Appeals under Section 24) Order 2008, corresponding with an order under section 19(1) of the 1985 Act (see rule 45.8);

(r)   article 17 of the Serious Crime Act 2007 (Appeals under Section 24) Order 2008, corresponding with an order under section 19A of the 1985 Act (see rule 45.9);

(s)   article 18 of the Serious Crime Act 2007 (Appeals under Section 24) Order 2008, corresponding with an order under section 19B of the 1985 Act (see rule 45.10);

(t)   section 60 or 133 of the Extradition Act 2003 (costs where extradition ordered) for the payment by a defendant of another person's costs (see rule 45.4); or

(u)   section 61 or 134 of the Extradition Act 2003 (costs where discharge ordered) for the payment out of central funds of a defendant's costs (see rule 45.4).

See also the Criminal Costs Practice Direction.

Part 39 (Appeal to the Court of Appeal about conviction or sentence) contains rules about appeals against costs orders made in the Crown Court under the legislation listed in (c) above.

Part 34 (Appeal to the Crown Court) and Part 39 (Appeal to the Court of Appeal about conviction or sentence) contain rules about appeals against costs orders made under the legislation listed in (e) and (f) above.

As to costs in restraint or receivership proceedings under Part 2 of the Proceeds of Crime Act 2002, see rules 33.47 to 33.50.

A costs order can be enforced—

(a)   against a defendant, under section 41(1) or (3) of the Administration of Justice Act 1970;

(b)   against a prosecutor, under section 41(2) or (3) of the Administration of Justice Act 1970;

(c)   against a representative, under regulation 3D of the Costs in Criminal Cases (General) Regulations 1986 or article 18 of the Serious Crime Act 2007 (Appeals under Section 24) Order 2008;

(d)   against a non-party, under regulation 3I of the Costs in Criminal Cases (General) Regulations 1986 or article 31 of the Serious Crime Act 2007 (Appeals under Section 24) Order 2008.

See also section 58, section 150(1) and Part III of the Magistrates' Courts Act 1980 and Schedule 5 to the Courts Act 2003.]

45.2. *Costs orders: general rules* (1) The court must not make an order about costs unless each party and any other person directly affected—

(a)   is present; or

(b)   has had an opportunity—

     (i)   to attend, or

(ii)   to make representations.
(2)   The court may make an order about costs—
(a)   at a hearing in public or in private; or
(b)   without a hearing.
(3)   In deciding what order, if any, to make about costs, the court must have regard to all the circumstances, including—
(a)   the conduct of all the parties; and
(b)   any costs order already made.
(4)   If the court makes an order about costs, it must—
(a)   specify who must, or must not, pay what, to whom; and
(b)   identify the legislation under which the order is made, where there is a choice of powers.
(5)   The court must give reasons if it—
(a)   refuses an application for a costs order; or
(b)   rejects representations opposing a costs order.
(6)   If the court makes an order for the payment of costs—
(a)   the general rule is that it must be for an amount that is sufficient reasonably to compensate the recipient for costs—
        (i)   actually, reasonably and properly incurred, and
        (ii)   reasonable in amount; but
(b)   the court may order the payment of—
        (i)   a proportion of that amount,
        (ii)   a stated amount less than that amount,
        (iii)   costs from or until a certain date only,
        (iv)   costs relating only to particular steps taken, or
        (v)   costs relating only to a distinct part of the case.
(7)   On an assessment of the amount of costs, relevant factors include—
(a)   the conduct of all the parties;
(b)   the particular complexity of the matter or the difficulty or novelty of the questions raised;
(c)   the skill, effort, specialised knowledge and responsibility involved;
(d)   the time spent on the case;
(e)   the place where and the circumstances in which work or any part of it was done; and
(f)   any direction or observations by the court that made the costs order.
(8)   If the court orders a party to pay costs to be assessed under rule 45.11, it may order that party to pay an amount on account.
(9)   An order for the payment of costs takes effect when the amount is assessed, unless the court exercises any power it has to order otherwise.
[Note. Under the powers to which apply rule 45.8 (Costs resulting from unnecessary or improper act, etc) and rule 45.9 (Costs against a legal representative), specified conduct must be established for such orders to be made.
The amount recoverable under a costs order may be affected by the legislation under which the order is made. See, for example, section 16A of the Prosecution of Offences Act 1985.
Under section 141 of the Powers of Criminal Courts (Sentencing) Act 2000 and section 75 of the Magistrates' Courts Act 1980, the Crown Court and magistrates' court respectively can allow time for payment, or payment by instalments.]

45.3.   *Court's power to vary requirements*   (1)   Unless other legislation otherwise provides, the court may
(a)   extend a time limit for serving an application or representations under rules 45.4 to 45.10, even after it has expired; and
(b)   consider an application or representations—
        (i)   made in a different form to one set out in the Practice Direction, or
        (ii)   made orally instead of in writing.
(2)   A person who wants an extension of time must—
(a)   apply when serving the application or representations for which it is needed; and
(b)   explain the delay.
[Note. The time limit for applying for a costs order may be affected by the legislation under which the order is made. See, for example, sections 19(1), (2) and 19A of the Prosecution of Offences Act 1985, regulation 3 of the Costs in Criminal Cases (General) Regulations 1986 and rules 45.8(4)(a) and 45.9(4)(a).]

COSTS OUT OF CENTRAL FUNDS

45.4.   *Costs out of central funds*   (1)   This rule applies where the court can order the payment of costs out of central funds.
(2)   In this rule, costs—
(a)   include—
        (i)   on an appeal, costs incurred in the court that made the decision under appeal, and
        (ii)   at a retrial, costs incurred at the initial trial and on any appeal; but
(b)   do not include costs met by legal aid.
(3)   The court may make an order—
(a)   on application by the person who incurred the costs; or
(b)   on its own initiative.
(4)   Where a person wants the court to make an order that person must—

(a)   apply as soon as practicable; and

(b)   outline the type of costs and the amount claimed, if that person wants the court to direct an assessment; or

(c)   specify the amount claimed, if that person wants the court to assess the amount itself.

(5)   The general rule is that the court must make an order, but—

(a)   the court may decline to make a defendant's costs order if, for example—

    (i)   the defendant is convicted of at least one offence, or

    (ii)   the defendant's conduct led the prosecutor reasonably to think the prosecution case stronger than it was; and

(b)   the court may decline to make a prosecutor's costs order if, for example, the prosecution was started or continued unreasonably.

(6)   If the court makes an order—

(a)   the court may direct an assessment under, as applicable—

    (i)   Part III of the Costs in Criminal Cases (General) Regulations 1986, or

    (ii)   Part 3 of the Serious Crime Act 2007 (Appeals under Section 24) Order 2008;

(b)   the court may assess the amount itself in a case in which either—

    (i)   the recipient agrees the amount, or

    (ii)   the court decides to allow a lesser sum than that which is reasonably sufficient to compensate the recipient for expenses properly incurred in the proceedings;

(c)   an order for the payment of a defendant's costs which includes an amount in respect of fees payable to a legal representative, or disbursements paid by a legal representative, must include a statement to that effect.

(7)   If the court directs an assessment, the order must specify any restriction on the amount to be paid that the court considers appropriate.

(8)   If the court assesses the amount itself, it must do so subject to any restriction on the amount to be paid that is imposed by regulations made by the Lord Chancellor.

[Note. See also rule 45.2.

An order for the payment of costs out of central funds can be made—

(a)   for a defendant—

    (i)   on acquittal,

    (ii)   where a prosecution does not proceed,

    (iii)   where the Crown Court allows any part of a defendant's appeal from a magistrates' court,

    (iv)   where the Court of Appeal allows any part of a defendant's appeal from the Crown Court,

    (v)   where the Court of Appeal decides a prosecutor's appeal under Part 37 (Appeal to the Court of Appeal against ruling at preparatory hearing) or Part 38 (Appeal to the Court of Appeal against ruling adverse to prosecution),

    (vi)   where the Court of Appeal decides a reference by the Attorney General under Part 41 (Reference to the Court of Appeal of point of law or unduly lenient sentence),

    (vii)   where the Court of Appeal decides an appeal by someone other than the defendant about a serious crime prevention order, or

    (viii) where the defendant is discharged under Part 1 or 2 of the Extradition Act 2003;

(See section 16 of the Prosecution of Offences Act 1985 and regulation 14 of the Costs in Criminal Cases (General) Regulations 1986; section 36(5) of the Criminal Justice Act 1972 and paragraph 11 of Schedule 3 to the Criminal Justice Act 1988; article 14 of the Serious Crime Act 2007 (Appeals under Section 24) Order 2008; and sections 61 and 134 of the Extradition Act 2003.)

(b)   for a private prosecutor, in proceedings in respect of an offence that must or may be tried in the Crown Court;

(See section 17 of the Prosecution of Offences Act 1985 and regulation 14 of the Costs in Criminal Cases (General) Regulations 1986.)

(c)   for a person adversely affected by a serious crime prevention order, where the Court of Appeal—

    (i)   allows an appeal by that person about that order, or

    (ii)   decides an appeal about that order by someone else.

(See article 14 of the Serious Crime Act 2007 (Appeals under Section 24) Order 2008.)

Where the court makes an order for the payment of a defendant's costs out of central funds—

(a)   the general rule is that the order may not require the payment of any amount in respect of fees payable to a legal representative, or disbursements paid by a legal representative (including expert witness costs), but if the defendant is an individual then an order may require payment of such an amount in a case—

    (i)   in a magistrates' court, including in an extradition case,

    (ii)   in the Crown Court, on appeal from a magistrates' court,

    (iii)   in the Crown Court, where the defendant has been sent for trial, the High Court gives permission to serve a draft indictment or the Court of Appeal orders a retrial and the defendant has been found financially ineligible for legal aid, or

    (iv)   in the Court of Appeal, on an appeal against a verdict of not guilty by reason of insanity, or against a finding under the Criminal Procedure (Insanity) Act 1964, or on an appeal under section 16A of the Criminal Appeal Act 1968 (appeal against order made in cases of insanity or unfitness to plead); and

(b)   any such amount may not exceed an amount specified by regulations made by the Lord
        Chancellor.
        *(See section 16A of the Prosecution of Offences Act 1985, sections 62A, 62B, 135A and 135B of
        the Extradition Act 2003 and regulations 4A and 7 of the Costs in Criminal Cases (General)
        Regulations 1986.)]*

PAYMENT OF COSTS BY ONE PARTY TO ANOTHER

45.5.   *Costs on conviction and sentence, etc*   (1)   This rule applies where the court can order a
defendant to pay the prosecutor's costs if the defendant is—
(a)   convicted or found guilty;
(b)   dealt with in the Crown Court after committal for sentence there;
(c)   dealt with for breach of a sentence; or
(d)   in an extradition case—
        (i)   ordered to be extradited, under Part 1 of the Extradition Act 2003,
        (ii)   sent for extradition to the Secretary of State, under Part 2 of that Act, or
        (iii)   unsuccessful on an appeal by the defendant to the High Court, or on an application
                by the defendant for permission to appeal from the High Court to the
                Supreme Court.
(2)   The court may make an order—
(a)   on application by the prosecutor; or
(b)   on its own initiative.
(3)   Where the prosecutor wants the court to make an order—
(a)   the prosecutor must—
        (i)   apply as soon as practicable, and
        (ii)   specify the amount claimed; and
(b)   the general rule is that the court must make an order if it is satisfied that the defendant can
        pay.
(4)   A defendant who wants to oppose an order must make representations as soon as
practicable.
(5)   If the court makes an order, it must assess the amount itself.
[Note. See—
(a)   rule 45.2;
*(b)   section 18 of the Prosecution of Offences Act 1985 and regulation 14 of the Costs in
        Criminal Cases (General) Regulations 1986; and*
(c)   sections 60 and 133 of the Extradition Act 2003.
Under section 18(4) and (5) of the 1985 Act, if a magistrates' court—
(a)   imposes a fine, a penalty, forfeiture or compensation that does not exceed £5—
        *(i)   the general rule is that the court will not make a costs order against the defendant,
                but*
        (ii)   the court may do so;
*(b)   fines a defendant under 18, no costs order against the defendant may be for more than
        the fine.*
*Part 39 (Appeal to the Court of Appeal about conviction or sentence) contains rules about appeal
against a Crown Court costs order to which this rule applies.]*

45.6.   *Costs on appeal*   (1)   This rule—
(a)   applies where a magistrates' court, the Crown Court or the Court of Appeal can order a
        party to pay another person's costs on an appeal, or an application for permission to
        appeal;
(b)   authorises the Crown Court, in addition to its other powers, to order a party to pay
        another party's costs on an appeal to that court, except on an appeal under—
        (i)   section 108 of the Magistrates' Courts Act 1980, or
        (ii)   section 45 of the Mental Health Act 1983.
(2)   In this rule, costs include—
(a)   costs incurred in the court that made the decision under appeal; and
(b)   costs met by legal aid.
(3)   The court may make an order—
(a)   on application by the person who incurred the costs; or
(b)   on its own initiative.
(4)   A person who wants the court to make an order must—
(a)   apply as soon as practicable;
(b)   notify each other party;
(c)   specify—
        (i)   the amount claimed, and
        (ii)   against whom; and
(d)   where an appellant abandons an appeal to the Crown Court by serving a notice of
        abandonment—
        (i)   apply in writing not more than 14 days later, and
        (ii)   serve the application on the appellant and on the Crown Court officer.
(5)   A party who wants to oppose an order must—
(a)   make representations as soon as practicable; and

(b) where the application was under paragraph (4)(d), serve representations on the applicant, and on the Crown Court officer, not more than 7 days after it was served.

(6) Where the application was under paragraph (4)(d), the Crown Court officer may—

(a) submit it to the Crown Court; or

(b) serve it on the magistrates' court officer, for submission to the magistrates' court.

(7) If the court makes an order, it may direct an assessment under rule 45.11, or assess the amount itself where—

(a) the appellant abandons an appeal to the Crown Court;

(b) the Crown Court decides an appeal, except an appeal under—

(i) section 108 of the Magistrates' Courts Act 1980, or

(ii) section 45 of the Mental Health Act 1983; or

(c) the Court of Appeal decides an appeal to which Part 40 applies (Appeal to the Court of Appeal about reporting or public access restriction).

(8) If the court makes an order in any other case, it must assess the amount itself.

[Note. See also rule 45.2.

A magistrates' court can order an appellant to pay a respondent's costs on abandoning an appeal to the Crown Court.

The Crown Court can order—

(a) the defendant to pay the prosecutor's costs on dismissing a defendant's appeal—

(i) against conviction or sentence, under section 108 of the Magistrates' Courts Act 1980, or

(ii) where the magistrates' court makes a hospital order or guardianship order without convicting the defendant, under section 45 of the Mental Health Act 1983; and

(b) one party to pay another party's costs on deciding any other appeal to which Part 34 (Appeal to the Crown Court) applies.

The Court of Appeal can order—

(a) the defendant to pay another person's costs on dismissing a defendant's appeal or application to which Part 37 (Appeal to the Court of Appeal against ruling at preparatory hearing), Part 39 (Appeal to the Court of Appeal about conviction or sentence) or Part 43 (Appeal or reference to the Supreme Court) applies;

(b) the defendant to pay another person's costs on allowing a prosecutor's appeal to which Part 38 (Appeal to the Court of Appeal against ruling adverse to the prosecution) applies;

(c) the appellant to pay another person's costs on dismissing an appeal or application by a person affected by a serious crime prevention order;

(d) one party to pay another party's costs on deciding an appeal to which Part 40 (Appeal to the Court of Appeal about reporting or public access restriction) applies.

See section 109 of the Magistrates' Courts Act 1980; section 52 of the Senior Courts Act 1981 (which allows rules of court to authorise the Crown Court to order costs); section 18 of the Prosecution of Offences Act 1985; section 159(5) of the Criminal Justice Act 1988; and article 15 of the Serious Crime Act 2007 (Appeals under Section 24) Order 2008.]

45.7. *Costs on an application* (1) This rule—

(a) applies where the court can order a party to pay another person's costs in a case in which—

(i) the court decides an application for the production in evidence of a copy of a bank record,

(ii) a magistrates' court or the Crown Court decides an application to terminate a football banning order,

(iii) a magistrates' court or the Crown Court decides an application to terminate a disqualification for having custody of a dog,

(iv) the Crown Court allows an application to withdraw a witness summons, or

(v) the Crown Court decides an application relating to a deferred prosecution agreement under rule 11.5 (breach), rule 11.6 (variation) or rule 11.7 (lifting suspension of prosecution);

(b) authorises the Crown Court, in addition to its other powers, to order a party to pay another party's costs on an application to that court under rule 11.5, 11.6 or 11.7.

(2) The court may make an order—

(a) on application by the person who incurred the costs; or

(b) on its own initiative.

(3) A person who wants the court to make an order must—

(a) apply as soon as practicable;

(b) notify each other party; and

(c) specify—

(i) the amount claimed, and

(ii) against whom.

(4) A party who wants to oppose an order must make representations as soon as practicable.

(5) If the court makes an order, it may direct an assessment under rule 45.11, or assess the amount itself.

[Note. See—

(a) rule 45.2;

(b) section 8 of the Bankers Books Evidence Act 1879;

(c) section 14H(5) of the Football Spectators Act 1989;

(d)   section 2C(8) of the Criminal Procedure (Attendance of Witnesses) Act 1965; and
(e)   section 4(7) of the Dangerous Dogs Act 1991.
Section 52 of the Senior Courts Act 1981 allows rules of court to authorise the Crown Court to order costs.]

45.8. *Costs resulting from unnecessary or improper act, etc*   (1)   This rule applies where the court can order a party to pay another party's costs incurred as a result of an unnecessary or improper act or omission by or on behalf of the first party.
(2)   In this rule, costs include costs met by legal aid.
(3)   The court may make an order—
(a)   on application by the party who incurred such costs; or
(b)   on its own initiative.
(4)   A party who wants the court to make an order must—
(a)   apply in writing as soon as practicable after becoming aware of the grounds for doing so, and in any event no later than the end of the case;
(b)   serve the application on—
       (i)   the court officer (or, in the Court of Appeal, the Registrar), and
       (ii)   each other party;
(c)   in that application specify—
       (i)   the party by whom costs should be paid,
       (ii)   the relevant act or omission,
       (iii)   the reasons why that act or omission meets the criteria for making an order,
       (iv)   the amount claimed, and
       (v)   those on whom the application has been served.
(5)   Where the court considers making an order on its own initiative, it must—
(a)   identify the party against whom it proposes making the order; and
(b)   specify—
       (i)   the relevant act or omission,
       (ii)   the reasons why that act or omission meets the criteria for making an order, and
       (iii)   with the assistance of the party who incurred the costs, the amount involved.
(6)   A party who wants to oppose an order must—
(a)   make representations as soon as practicable; and
(b)   in reply to an application, serve representations on the applicant and on the court officer (or Registrar) not more than 7 days after it was served.
(7)   If the court makes an order, it must assess the amount itself.
(8)   To help assess the amount, the court may direct an enquiry by—
(a)   the Lord Chancellor, where the assessment is by a magistrates' court or by the Crown Court; or
(b)   the Registrar, where the assessment is by the Court of Appeal.
(9)   In deciding whether to direct such an enquiry, the court must have regard to all the circumstances including—
(a)   any agreement between the parties about the amount to be paid;
(b)   the amount likely to be allowed;
(c)   the delay and expense that may be incurred in the conduct of the enquiry; and
(d)   the particular complexity of the assessment, or the difficulty or novelty of any aspect of the assessment.
(10)   If the court directs such an enquiry—
(a)   paragraphs (3) to (8) inclusive of rule 45.11 (Assessment and re-assessment) apply as if that enquiry were an assessment under that rule (but rules 45.12 (Appeal to a costs judge) and 45.13 (Appeal to a High Court judge) do not apply);
(b)   the authority that carries out the enquiry must serve its conclusions on the court officer as soon as reasonably practicable after following that procedure; and
(c)   the court must then assess the amount to be paid.
[Note. See—
(a)   rule 45.2;
(b)   section 19(1) of the Prosecution of Offences Act 1985 and regulation 3 of the Costs in Criminal Cases (General) Regulations 1986; and
(c)   article 16 of the Serious Crime Act 2007 (Appeals under Section 24) Order 2008.
Under section 19(1), (2) of the 1985 Act and regulation 3(1) of the 1986 Regulations, the court's power to make a costs order to which this rule applies can only be exercised during the proceedings.
Under regulation 3(5) of the 1986 Regulations, if a magistrates' court fines a defendant under 17, no costs order to which this rule applies may be for more than the fine.
The Criminal Costs Practice Direction sets out a form of application for use in connection with this rule.]

OTHER COSTS ORDERS

45.9. *Costs against a legal representative*   (1)   This rule applies where—
(a)   a party has incurred costs—
       (i)   as a result of an improper, unreasonable or negligent act or omission by a legal or other representative or representative's employee, or

    (ii)   which it has become unreasonable for that party to have to pay because of such an act or omission occurring after those costs were incurred; and

(b)   the court can—

    (i)   order the representative responsible to pay such costs, or

    (ii)   prohibit the payment of costs to that representative.

(2)   In this rule, costs include costs met by legal aid.

(3)   The court may make an order—

(a)   on application by the party who incurred such costs; or

(b)   on its own initiative.

(4)   A party who wants the court to make an order must—

(a)   apply in writing as soon as practicable after becoming aware of the grounds for doing so, and in any event no later than the end of the case;

(b)   serve the application on—

    (i)   the court officer (or, in the Court of Appeal, the Registrar),

    (ii)   the representative responsible,

    (iii)   each other party, and

    (iv)   any other person directly affected;

(c)   in that application specify—

    (i)   the representative responsible,

    (ii)   the relevant act or omission,

    (iii)   the reasons why that act or omission meets the criteria for making an order,

    (iv)   the amount claimed, and

    (v)   those on whom the application has been served.

(5)   Where the court considers making an order on its own initiative, it must—

(a)   identify the representative against whom it proposes making that order; and

(b)   specify—

    (i)   the relevant act or omission,

    (ii)   the reasons why that act or omission meets the criteria for making an order, and

    (iii)   with the assistance of the party who incurred the costs, the amount involved.

(6)   A representative who wants to oppose an order must—

(a)   make representations as soon as practicable; and

(b)   in reply to an application, serve representations on the applicant and on the court officer (or Registrar) not more than 7 days after it was served.

(7)   If the court makes an order—

(a)   the general rule is that it must do so without waiting until the end of the case, but it may postpone making the order; and

(b)   it must assess the amount itself.

(8)   To help assess the amount, the court may direct an enquiry by—

(a)   the Lord Chancellor, where the assessment is by a magistrates' court or by the Crown Court; or

(b)   the Registrar, where the assessment is by the Court of Appeal.

(9)   In deciding whether to direct such an enquiry, the court must have regard to all the circumstances including—

(a)   any agreement between the parties about the amount to be paid;

(b)   the amount likely to be allowed;

(c)   the delay and expense that may be incurred in the conduct of the enquiry; and

(d)   the particular complexity of the assessment, or the difficulty or novelty of any aspect of the assessment.

(10)   If the court directs such an enquiry—

(a)   paragraphs (3) to (8) inclusive of rule 45.11 (Assessment and re-assessment) apply as if that enquiry were an assessment under that rule (but rules 45.12 (Appeal to a costs judge) and 45.13 (Appeal to a High Court judge) do not apply);

(b)   the authority that carries out the enquiry must serve its conclusions on the court officer as soon as reasonably practicable after following that procedure; and

(c)   the court must then assess the amount to be paid.

(11)   Instead of making an order, the court may make adverse observations about the representative's conduct for use in an assessment where—

(a)   a party's costs are—

    (i)   to be met by legal aid, or

    (ii)   to be paid out of central funds; or

(b)   there is to be an assessment under rule 45.11.

[Note. See—

(a)   rule 45.2;

(b)   section 19A of the Prosecution of Offences Act 1985;

(c)   article 17 of the Serious Crime Act 2007 (Appeals under Section 24) Order 2008.

Under section 19A(1) of the 1985 Act, the court's power to make a costs order to which this rule applies can only be exercised during the proceedings.

The Criminal Costs Practice Direction sets out a form of application for use in connection with this

rule.
Part 34 (Appeal to the Crown Court) and Part 39 (Appeal to the Court of Appeal about conviction or sentence) contain rules about appeals against a costs order to which this rule applies.]

45.10. *Costs against a third party*   (1)   This rule applies where—
(a)   there has been serious misconduct by a person who is not a party; and
(b)   the court can order that person to pay a party's costs.
(2)   In this rule, costs include costs met by legal aid.
(3)   The court may make an order—
(a)   on application by the party who incurred the costs; or
(b)   on its own initiative.
(4)   A party who wants the court to make an order must—
(a)   apply in writing as soon as practicable after becoming aware of the grounds for doing so;
(b)   serve the application on—
          (i)   the court officer (or, in the Court of Appeal, the Registrar),
          (ii)   the person responsible,
          (iii)   each other party, and
          (iv)   any other person directly affected;
(c)   in that application specify—
          (i)   the person responsible,
          (ii)   the relevant misconduct,
          (iii)   the reasons why the criteria for making an order are met,
          (iv)   the amount claimed, and
          (v)   those on whom the application has been served.
(5)   Where the court considers making an order on its own initiative, it must—
(a)   identify the person against whom it proposes making that order; and
(b)   specify—
          (i)   the relevant misconduct,
          (ii)   the reasons why the criteria for making an order are met, and
          (iii)   with the assistance of the party who incurred the costs, the amount involved.
(6)   A person who wants to oppose an order must—
(a)   make representations as soon as practicable; and
(b)   in reply to an application, serve representations on the applicant and on the court officer (or Registrar) not more than 7 days after it was served.
(7)   If the court makes an order—
(a)   the general rule is that it must do so at the end of the case, but it may do so earlier; and
(b)   it must assess the amount itself.
[(8)   To help assess the amount, the court may direct an enquiry by—
(a)   the Lord Chancellor, where the assessment is by a magistrates' court or by the Crown Court; or
(b)   the Registrar, where the assessment is by the Court of Appeal.
(9)   In deciding whether to direct such an enquiry, the court must have regard to all the circumstances including—
(a)   any agreement between the parties about the amount to be paid;
(b)   the amount likely to be allowed;
(c)   the delay and expense that may be incurred in the conduct of the enquiry; and
(d)   the particular complexity of the assessment, or the difficulty or novelty of any aspect of the assessment.
(10)   If the court directs such an enquiry—
(a)   paragraphs (3) to (8) inclusive of rule 45.11 (Assessment and re-assessment) apply as if that enquiry were an assessment under that rule (but rules 45.12 (Appeal to a costs judge) and 45.13 (Appeal to a High Court judge) do not apply);
(b)   the authority that carries out the enquiry must serve its conclusions on the court officer as soon as reasonably practicable after following that procedure; and
(c)   the court must then assess the amount to be paid.]
[Note. See—
(a)   rule 45.2;
(b)   section 19B of the Prosecution of Offences Act 1985 and regulation 3F of the Costs in Criminal Cases (General) Regulations 1986; and
(c)   article 18 of the Serious Crime Act 2007 (Appeals under Section 24) Order 2008.
The Criminal Costs Practice Direction sets out a form of application for use in connection with this rule.
Part 34 (Appeal to the Crown Court) and Part 39 (Appeal to the Court of Appeal about conviction or sentence) contain rules about appeals against a costs order to which this rule applies.]
[Note. See—
(a)   rule 45.2;
(b)   section 19B of the Prosecution of Offences Act 1985 and regulation 3F of the Costs in Criminal Cases (General) Regulations 1986; and
(c)   article 18 of the Serious Crime Act 2007 (Appeals under Section 24) Order 2008.
The Criminal Costs Practice Direction sets out a form of application for use in connection with this

rule.
Part 34 (Appeal to the Crown Court) and Part 39 (Appeal to the Court of Appeal about conviction or sentence) contain rules about appeals against a costs order to which this rule applies.]

ASSESSMENT OF COSTS

45.11. *Assessment and re-assessment* (1) This rule applies where the court directs an assessment under—

(a) rule 33.48 (Confiscation and related proceedings—restraint and receivership proceedings: rules that apply generally—assessment of costs);

(b) rule 45.6 (Costs on appeal); or

(c) rule 45.7 (Costs on an application).

(2) The assessment must be carried out by the relevant assessing authority, namely—

(a) the Lord Chancellor, where the direction was given by a magistrates' court or by the Crown Court; or

(b) the Registrar, where the direction was given by the Court of Appeal.

(3) The party in whose favour the court made the costs order ('the applicant') must—

(a) apply for an assessment—

    (i) in writing, in any form required by the assessing authority, and

    (ii) not more than 3 months after the costs order; and

(b) serve the application on—

    (i) the assessing authority, and

    (ii) the party against whom the court made the costs order ('the respondent').

(4) The applicant must—

(a) summarise the work done;

(b) specify—

    (i) each item of work done, giving the date, time taken and amount claimed,

    (ii) any disbursements or expenses, including the fees of any advocate, and

    (iii) any circumstances of which the applicant wants the assessing authority to take particular account; and

(c) supply—

    (i) receipts or other evidence of the amount claimed, and

    (ii) any other information or document for which the assessing authority asks, within such period as that authority may require.

(5) A respondent who wants to make representations about the amount claimed must—

(a) do so in writing; and

(b) serve the representations on the assessing authority, and on the applicant, not more than 21 days after service of the application.

(6) The assessing authority must—

(a) if it seems likely to help with the assessment, obtain any other information or document;

(b) resolve in favour of the respondent any doubt about what should be allowed; and

(c) serve the assessment on the parties.

(7) Where either party wants the amount allowed re-assessed—

(a) that party must—

    (i) apply to the assessing authority, in writing and in any form required by that authority,

    (ii) serve the application on the assessing authority, and on the other party, not more than 21 days after service of the assessment,

    (iii) explain the objections to the assessment,

    (iv) supply any additional supporting information or document, and

    (v) ask for a hearing, if that party wants one; and

(b) a party who wants to make representations about an application for re-assessment must—

    (i) do so in writing,

    (ii) serve the representations on the assessing authority, and on the other party, not more than 21 days after service of the application, and

    (iii) ask for a hearing, if that party wants one;

(c) the assessing authority—

    (i) must arrange a hearing, in public or in private, if either party asks for one,

    (ii) subject to that, may re-assess the amount allowed with or without a hearing,

    (iii) must re-assess the amount allowed on the initial assessment, taking into account the reasons for disagreement with that amount and any other representations,

    (iv) may maintain, increase or decrease the amount allowed on the assessment,

    (v) must serve the re-assessment on the parties, and

    (vi) must serve reasons on the parties, if not more than 21 days later either party asks for such reasons.

(8) A time limit under this rule may be extended even after it has expired—

(a) by the assessing authority, or

(b) by the Senior Costs Judge, if the assessing authority declines to do so.

45.12. *Appeal to a costs judge* (1) This rule applies where—

(a)   the assessing authority has re-assessed the amount allowed under rule 45.11; and
(b)   either party wants to appeal against that amount.
(2)   That party must—
(a)   serve an appeal notice on—
    (i)   the Senior Costs Judge,
    (ii)   the other party, and
    (iii)   the assessing authority
not more than 21 days after service of the written reasons for the re-assessment;
(b)   explain the objections to the re-assessment;
(c)   serve on the Senior Costs Judge with the appeal notice—
    (i)   the applications for assessment and re-assessment,
    (ii)   any other information or document considered by the assessing authority,
    (iii)   the assessing authority's written reasons for the re-assessment, and
    (iv)   any other information or document for which a costs judge asks, within such period as the judge may require; and
(d)   ask for a hearing, if that party wants one.
(3)   A party who wants to make representations about an appeal must—
(a)   serve representations in writing on—
    (i)   the Senior Costs Judge, and
    (ii)   the applicant
not more than 21 days after service of the appeal notice; and
(b)   ask for a hearing, if that party wants one.
(4)   Unless a costs judge otherwise directs, the parties may rely only on—
(a)   the objections to the amount allowed on the initial assessment; and
(b)   any other representations and material considered by the assessing authority.
(5)   A costs judge—
(a)   must arrange a hearing, in public or in private, if either party asks for one;
(b)   subject to that, may determine an appeal with or without a hearing;
(c)   may—
    (i)   consult the assessing authority,
    (ii)   consult the court which made the costs order, and
    (iii)   obtain any other information or document;
(d)   must reconsider the amount allowed by the assessing authority, taking into account the objections to the re-assessment and any other representations;
(e)   may maintain, increase or decrease the amount allowed on the re-assessment;
(f)   may provide for the costs incurred by either party to the appeal; and
(g)   must serve reasons for the decision on—
    (i)   the parties, and
    (ii)   the assessing authority.
(6)   A costs judge may extend a time limit under this rule, even after it has expired.
[Note. The Criminal Costs Practice Direction sets out a form for use in connection with this rule.]

45.13. *Appeal to a High Court judge*   (1)   This rule applies where—
(a)   a costs judge has determined an appeal under rule 45.12; and
(b)   either party wants to appeal against the amount allowed.
(2)   A party who wants to appeal—
(a)   may do so only if a costs judge certifies that a point of principle of general importance was involved in the decision on the review; and
(b)   must apply in writing for such a certificate and serve the application on—
    (i)   the costs judge,
    (ii)   the other party
not more than 21 days after service of the decision on the review.
(3)   That party must—
(a)   appeal to a judge of the High Court attached to the Queen's Bench Division as if it were an appeal from the decision of a master under Part 52 of the Civil Procedure Rules 1998; and
(b)   serve the appeal not more than 21 days after service of the costs judge's certificate under paragraph (2).
(4)   A High Court judge—
(a)   may extend a time limit under this rule even after it has expired;
(b)   has the same powers and duties as a costs judge under rule 45.12; and
(c)   may hear the appeal with one or more assessors.
[Note. See also section 70 of the Senior Courts Act 1981.]

45.14. *Application for an extension of time*   A party who wants an extension of time under rule 45.11, 45.12 or 45.13 must—
(a)   apply in writing;
(b)   explain the delay; and
(c)   attach the application, representations or appeal for which the extension of time is needed.

PART 46 REPRESENTATIVES

Contents of this Part

B.35   *46.1.*   *Functions of representatives and supporters*   (1)   Under these Rules, anything that a party may or must do may be done—

(a)   by a legal representative on that party's behalf;

(b)   by a person with the corporation's written authority, where that corporation is a defendant;

(c)   with the help of a parent, guardian or other suitable supporting adult where that party is a defendant—

     (i)   who is under 18, or

     (ii)   whose understanding of what the case involves is limited

unless other legislation (including a rule) otherwise requires.

(2)   A member, officer or employee of a prosecutor may, on the prosecutor's behalf—

(a)   serve on the magistrates' court officer, or present to a magistrates' court, an application for a summons or warrant under section 1 of the Magistrates' Courts Act 1980; or

(b)   issue a written charge and requisition, or single justice procedure notice, under section 29 of the Criminal Justice Act 2003.

[Note. See also section 122 of the Magistrates' Courts Act 1980. A party's legal representative must be entitled to act as such under section 13 of the Legal Services Act 2007.

Section 33(6) of the Criminal Justice Act 1925, section 46 of the Magistrates' Courts Act 1980 and Schedule 3 to that Act provide for the representation of a corporation.

Sections 3 and 6 of the Prosecution of Offences Act 1985 make provision about the institution of prosecutions.

Section 223 of the Local Government Act 1972 allows a member or officer of a local authority on that authority's behalf to prosecute or defend a case before a magistrates' court, and to appear in and to conduct any proceedings before a magistrates' court.

Part 7 contains rules about starting a prosecution.]

46.2.   *Notice of appointment, etc of legal representative: general rules*   (1)   This rule applies—

(a)   in relation to—

     (i)   a party who does not have legal aid for the purposes of a case, and

     (ii)   a party to an extradition case in the High Court, whether that party has legal aid or not;

(b)   where such a party—

     (i)   appoints a legal representative for the purposes of the case, or

     (ii)   dismisses such a representative, with or without appointing another;

(c)   where a legal representative for such a party withdraws from the case.

(2)   Where paragraph (1)(b) applies, that party must give notice of the appointment or dismissal to—

(a)   the court officer;

(b)   each other party; and

(c)   where applicable, the legal representative who has been dismissed,

as soon as practicable and in any event within 5 business days.

(3)   Where paragraph (1)(c) applies, that legal representative must—

(a)   as soon as practicable give notice to—

     (i)   the court officer,

     (ii)   the party whom he or she has represented, and

     (iii)   each other party; and

(b)   where that legal representative has represented the defendant in an extradition case in the High Court, include with the notice—

     (i)   confirmation that the defendant has notice of when and where the appeal hearing will take place and of the need to attend, if the defendant is on bail,

     (ii)   details sufficient to locate the defendant, including details of the custodian and of the defendant's date of birth and custody reference, if the defendant is in custody, and

     (iii)   details of any arrangements likely to be required by the defendant to facilitate his or her participation in consequence of the representative's withdrawal, including arrangements for interpretation."; and

(4)   Any such notice—

(a)   may be given orally, but only if—

     (i)   it is given at a hearing, and

     (ii)   it specifies no restriction under paragraph (5)(b) (restricted scope of appointment);

(b)   otherwise, must be in writing.

(5)   A notice of the appointment of a legal representative—

(a)   must identify—
- (i)   the legal representative who has been appointed, with details of how to contact that representative, and
- (ii)   all those to whom the notice is given;

(b)   may specify a restriction, or restrictions, on the purpose or duration of the appointment; and

(c)   if it specifies any such restriction, may nonetheless provide that documents may continue to be served on the represented party at the representative's address until—
- (i)   further notice is given under this rule, or
- (ii)   that party obtains legal aid for the purposes of the case.

(6)   A legal representative who is dismissed by a party or who withdraws from representing a party must, as soon as practicable, make available to that party such documents in the representative's possession as have been served on that party.

46.3. *Application to change legal representative: legal aid* (1) This rule applies in a magistrates' court, the Crown Court and the Court of Appeal—

(a)   in relation to a party who has legal aid for the purposes of a case;

(b)   where such a party wants to select a legal representative in place of the representative named in the legal aid representation order.

(2)   Such a party must—

(a)   apply in writing as soon as practicable after becoming aware of the grounds for doing so; and

(b)   serve the application on—
- (i)   the court officer, and
- (ii)   the legal representative named in the legal aid representation order.

(3)   The application must—

(a)   explain what the case is about, including what offences are alleged, what stage it has reached and what is likely to be in issue at trial;

(b)   explain how and why the applicant chose the legal representative named in the legal aid representation order;

(c)   if an advocate other than that representative has been instructed for the applicant, explain whether the applicant wishes to replace that advocate;

(d)   explain, giving relevant facts and dates—
- (i)   in what way, in the applicant's opinion, there has been a breakdown in the relationship between the applicant and the current representative such that neither the individual representing the applicant nor any colleague of his or hers any longer can provide effective representation, or
- (ii)   what other compelling reason, in the applicant's opinion, means that neither the individual representing the applicant nor any colleague of his or hers any longer can provide effective representation;

(e)   give details of any previous application by the applicant to replace the legal representative named in the legal aid representation order;

(f)   state whether the applicant—
- (i)   waives the legal professional privilege attaching to the applicant's communications with the current representative, to the extent required to allow that representative to respond to the matters set out in the application, or
- (ii)   declines to waive that privilege and acknowledges that the court may draw such inferences as it thinks fit in consequence;

(g)   explain how and why the applicant has chosen the proposed new representative;

(h)   include or attach a statement by the proposed new representative which—
- (i)   confirms that that representative is eligible and willing to conduct the case for the applicant,
- (ii)   confirms that that representative can and will meet the current timetable for the case, including any hearing date or dates that have been set, if the application succeeds,
- (iii)   explains what, if any, dealings that representative has had with the applicant before the present case; and

(i)   ask for a hearing, if the applicant wants one, and explain why it is needed.

(4)   The legal representative named in the legal aid representation order must—

(a)   respond in writing no more than 5 business days after service of the application; and

(b)   serve the response on—
- (i)   the court officer,
- (ii)   the applicant, and
- (iii)   the proposed new representative.

(5)   The response must—

(a)   explain which, if any, of the matters set out in the application the current representative disputes;

(b)   explain, as appropriate, giving relevant facts and dates—
- (i)   whether, and if so in what way, in the current representative's opinion, there has been a breakdown in the relationship with the applicant such that neither the individual representing the applicant nor any colleague of his or hers any longer can provide effective representation,

(ii)　whether, in the current representative's opinion, there is some other compelling reason why neither the individual representing the applicant nor any colleague of his or hers any longer can provide effective representation, and if so what reason,

(iii)　whether the current representative considers there to be a duty to withdraw from the case in accordance with professional rules of conduct, and if so the nature of that duty, and

(iv)　whether the current representative no longer is able to represent the applicant through circumstances outside the representative's control, and if so the particular circumstances that render the representative unable to do so;

(c)　explain what, if any, dealings the current representative had had with the applicant before the present case; and

(d)　ask for a hearing, if the current representative wants one, and explain why it is needed.

(6)　The court may determine the application—

(a)　without a hearing, as a general rule; or

(b)　at a hearing, which must be in private unless the court otherwise directs.

(7)　Unless the court otherwise directs, any hearing must be in the absence of each other party and each other party's representative and advocate (if any).

(8)　If the court allows the application, as soon as practicable—

(a)　the current representative must make available to the new representative such documents in the current representative's possession as have been served on the applicant party; and

(b)　the new representative must serve notice of appointment on each other party.

(9)　Paragraph (10) applies where—

(a)　the court refuses the application;

(b)　in response to that decision—

(i)　the applicant declines further representation by the current representative or asks for legal aid to be withdrawn, or

(ii)　the current representative declines further to represent the applicant; and

(c)　the court in consequence withdraws the applicant's legal aid.

(10)　The court officer must serve notice of the withdrawal of legal aid on—

(a)　the applicant; and

(b)　the current representative.

[Note. Under sections 16 and 19 of the Legal Aid, Sentencing and Punishment of Offenders Act 2012 and Part 2 of the Criminal Legal Aid (Determinations by a Court and Choice of Representative) Regulations 2013, a court before which criminal proceedings take place may determine whether an individual qualifies for legal aid representation in accordance with the 2012 Act.

Under regulation 13 of the 2013 Regulations, in relation to any proceedings involving co-defendants a represented person must select a representative who is also instructed by a co-defendant unless there is, or there is likely to be, a conflict of interest between the two defendants. Under regulation 14 of the 2013 Regulations, once a representative has been selected the person who is represented has no right to select another in the place of the first unless the court so decides, in the circumstances set out in the regulation.

Under regulation 9 of the 2013 Regulations, if a represented person declines to accept representation on the terms offered or requests that legal aid representation is withdrawn, or if the current representative declines to continue to represent that person, the court may withdraw legal aid.

See also regulation 11 of the 2013 Regulations, which requires that an application under regulation 14 (among others) must be made by the represented person, must be in writing and must specify the grounds.

The Practice Direction sets out forms of application and response for use in connection with this rule.]

PART 47　INVESTIGATION ORDERS AND WARRANTS

Contents of this Part

Section 1: general rules

Section 2: investigation orders

Orders under the Police and Criminal Evidence Act 1984

SECTION 1: GENERAL RULES

B.36 *47.1. When this Part applies* [This Part applies to the exercise of the powers listed in each of rules 47.4, 47.24, 47.35, 47.42, 47.46, 47.51, 47.54 and 47.59 47.54, 47.59 and 47.62.

47.2. Meaning of 'court', 'applicant' and 'respondent' In this Part—
(a) a reference to the 'court' includes a reference to any justice of the peace or judge who can exercise a power to which this Part applies;
(b) 'applicant' means a person who, or an authority which, can apply for an order or warrant to which this Part applies; and
(c) 'respondent' means any person—
(i) against whom such an order is sought or made, or
(ii) on whom an application for such an order is served.

47.3. Documents served on the court officer (1) Unless the court otherwise directs, the court officer may—

(a) keep a written application; or

(b) arrange for the whole or any part to be kept by some other appropriate person, subject to any conditions that the court may impose.

(2) Where the court makes an order when the court office is closed, the applicant must, not more than 72 hours later, serve on the court officer—

(a) a copy of the order; and

(b) any written material that was submitted to the court.

(3) Where the court issues a warrant—

(a) the applicant must return it to the court officer as soon as practicable after it has been executed, and in any event not more than 3 months after it was issued (unless other legislation otherwise provides); and

(b) the court officer must—

(i) keep the warrant for 12 months after its return, and

(ii) during that period, make it available for inspection by the occupier of the premises to which it relates, if that occupier asks to inspect it.

[Note. See section 16(10) of the Police and Criminal Evidence Act 1984.]

SECTION 2: INVESTIGATION ORDERS

47.4 *When this Section applies* This Section applies where—

(a) a Circuit judge can make, vary or discharge an order for the production of, or for giving access to, material under paragraph 4 of Schedule 1 to the Police and Criminal Evidence Act 1984, other than material that consists of or includes journalistic material;

(b) for the purposes of a terrorist investigation, a Circuit judge can make, vary or discharge—

(i) an order for the production of, or for giving access to, material, or for a statement of its location, under paragraphs 5 and 10 of Schedule 5 to the Terrorism Act 2000,

(ii) an explanation order, under paragraphs 10 and 13 of Schedule 5 to the 2000 Act,

(iii) a customer information order, under paragraphs 1 and 4 of Schedule 6 to the 2000 Act;

(c) for the purposes of—

(i) a terrorist investigation, a Circuit judge can make, and the Crown Court can vary or discharge, an account monitoring order, under paragraphs 2 and 4 of Schedule 6A to the 2000 Act,

(ii) a terrorist financing investigation, a judge entitled to exercise the jurisdiction of the Crown Court can make, and the Crown Court can vary or discharge, a disclosure order, under paragraphs 9 and 14 of Schedule 5A to the 2000 Act;

(d) for the purposes of an investigation to which Part 8 of the Proceeds of Crime Act 2002 or the Proceeds of Crime Act 2002 (External Investigations) Order 2014 applies, a Crown Court judge can make, and the Crown Court can vary or discharge—

(i) a production order, under sections 345 and 351 of the 2002 Act or under articles 6 and 12 of the 2014 Order,

(ii) an order to grant entry, under sections 347 and 351 of the 2002 Act or under articles 8 and 12 of the 2014 Order,

(iii) a disclosure order, under sections 357 and 362 of the 2002 Act or under articles 16 and 21 of the 2014 Order,

(iv) a customer information order, under sections 363 and 369 of the 2002 Act or under articles 22 and 28 of the 2014 Order,

(v) an account monitoring order, under sections 370, 373 and 375 of the 2002 Act or under articles 29, 32 and 34 of the 2014 Order;

(e) in connection with an extradition request, a Circuit judge can make an order for the production of, or for giving access to, material under section 157 of the Extradition Act 2003.

(f) a magistrates' court can make a further information order under section 22B of the Terrorism Act 2000 in connection with—

(i) an investigation into whether a person is involved in the commission of an offence under any of sections 15 to 18 of the 2000 Act,

(ii) determining whether such an investigation should be started, or

(iii) identifying terrorist property or its movement or use;

(g) a magistrates' court can make a further information order under section 339ZH of the Proceeds of Crime Act 2002 in connection with—

(i) an investigation into whether a person is engaged in money laundering,

(ii) determining whether such an investigation should be started, or

(iii) an investigation into money laundering by an authority in a country outside the United Kingdom."

[Note. In outline, the orders to which these rules apply are—

(a) under the Police and Criminal Evidence Act 1984, a production order requiring a person to produce or give access to material, other than material that consists of or includes journalistic material;

(b) for the purposes of a terrorist investigation under the Terrorism Act 2000—

(i) an order requiring a person to produce, give access to, or state the location of material,

(ii)   an *explanation order*, requiring a person to explain material obtained under a production, etc order,

(iii)   a *customer information order*, requiring a financial institution to provide information about an account holder,

(iv)   an *account monitoring order*, requiring a financial institution to provide specified information, for a specified period, about an account held at that institution;

(c)   for the purposes of a terrorist financing investigation under the Terrorism Act 2000, a *disclosure order*, requiring a person to provide information or documents, or to answer questions;

(d)   for the purposes of an investigation to which Part 8 of the Proceeds of Crime Act 2002 or the Proceeds of Crime Act 2002 (External Investigations) Order 2014 applies—

(i)   a *production order*, requiring a person to produce or give access to material,

(ii)   an *order to grant entry*, requiring a person to allow entry to premises so that a production order can be enforced,

(iii)   a *disclosure order*, requiring a person to provide information or documents, or to answer questions,

(iv)   a *customer information order*, requiring a financial institution to provide information about an account holder,

(v)   an *account monitoring order*, requiring a financial institution to provide specified information, for a specified period, about an account held at that institution;

(e)   in connection with extradition proceedings, a *production order* requiring a person to produce or give access to material.

(f)   under the Terrorism Act 2000, a *further information order* requiring a person to provide information related to a matter arising from a disclosure under section 21A of that Act (Failure to disclose: regulated sector) or under the law of a country outside the United Kingdom which corresponds with Part III of that Act (Terrorist property);

(g)   under the Proceeds of Crime Act 2002, a *further information order* requiring a person to provide information related to a matter arising from a disclosure under Part 7 of that Act (Money laundering) or under the law of a country outside the United Kingdom which corresponds with that Part of that Act.

These rules do not apply to an application for a production order under the Police and Criminal Evidence Act 1984 requiring a person to produce or give access to journalistic material: see paragraph 15A of Schedule 1 to the Act.

For all the relevant terms under which these orders can be made, see the provisions listed in rule 47.4.

Under section 8 of the Senior Courts Act 1981, a High Court judge, a Circuit judge, a Recorder, a qualifying judge advocate and a District Judge (Magistrates' Courts) each may act as a Crown Court judge.

When the relevant provisions of the Courts Act 2003 come into force, a District Judge (Magistrates' Courts) will have the same powers as a Circuit judge under the Police and Criminal Evidence Act 1984 and under the Terrorism Act 2000.

Under section 66 of the Courts Act 2003, in criminal cases a High Court judge, a Circuit judge, a Recorder and a qualifying judge advocate each has the powers of a justice of the peace who is a District Judge (Magistrates' Courts).

By section 341 of the Proceeds of Crime Act 2002, an investigation under Part 8 of the Act may be—

(a)   an investigation into (i) whether a person has benefited from criminal conduct, (ii) the extent or whereabouts of such benefit, (iii) the available amount in respect of that person, or (iv) the extent or whereabouts of realisable property available for satisfying a confiscation order made in respect of that person ('a confiscation investigation');

(b)   an investigation into whether a person has committed a money laundering offence ('a money laundering investigation');

(c)   an investigation into whether property is recoverable property or associated property (as defined by section 316 of the 2002 Act), or into who holds the property or its extent or whereabouts ('a civil recovery investigation');

(d)   an investigation into the derivation of cash detained under the 2002 Act, or into whether such cash is intended to be used in unlawful conduct ('a detained cash investigation');

(e)   an investigation into the derivation of property detained under the 2002 Act, or into whether such property is intended to be used in unlawful conduct ('a detained property investigation');

(f)   an investigation into the derivation of money held in an account in relation to which an account freezing order made under the 2002 Act has effect, or into whether such money is intended to be used in unlawful conduct ('a frozen funds investigation');",

(g)   an investigation for the purposes of Part 7 of the Coroners and Justice Act 2009 (criminal memoirs, etc) into whether a person is a qualifying offender or has obtained exploitation proceeds from a relevant offence, or into the value of any benefits derived by such a person from such an offence or the amount available ('an exploitation proceeds investigation').

Under section 343 of the Proceeds of Crime Act 2002—

(a)   any Crown Court judge may make an order to which this Section applies for the purposes of a confiscation investigation, a money launderinginvestigation, a detained cash investigation, a detained property investigation or a frozen funds investigation;

(b)   only a High Court judge may make such an order for the purposes of a civil recovery investigation or an exploitation proceeds investigation (and these rules do not apply to an

application to such a judge in such a case).
As well as governing procedure on an application to the Crown Court, under the following provisions rules may govern the procedure on an application to an individual judge—
(a)   *paragraph 15A of Schedule 1 to the Police and Criminal Evidence Act 1984;*
(b)   *paragraph 10 of Schedule 5, paragraph 14 of Schedule 5A, paragraph 4 of Schedule 6 and paragraph 5 of Schedule 6A to the Terrorism Act 2000; and*
(c)   *sections 351, 362, 369, 375 and 446 of the Proceeds of Crime Act 2002.]*

47.5 *Exercise of court's powers* (1)   Subject to paragraphs (2), (3) and (4), the court may determine an application for an order, or to vary or discharge an order—
(a)   at a hearing (which must be in private unless the court otherwise directs), or without a hearing; and
(b)   in the absence of—
    (i)   the applicant,
    (ii)   the respondent (if any),
    (iii)   any other person affected by the order.
(2)   The court must not determine such an application in the applicant's absence if—
(a)   the applicant asks for a hearing; or
(b)   it appears to the court that—
    (i)   the proposed order may infringe legal privilege, within the meaning of section 10 of the Police and Criminal Evidence Act 1984, section 348 or 361 of the Proceeds of Crime Act 2002 or article 9 of the Proceeds of Crime Act 2002 (External Investigations) Order 2014,
    (ii)   the proposed order may require the production of excluded material, within the meaning of section 11 of the 1984 Act, or
    (iii)   for any other reason the application is so complex or serious as to require the court to hear the applicant.
(3)   The court must not determine such an application in the absence of any respondent or other person affected, unless—
(a)   the absentee has had at least 2 business days in which to make representations; or
(b)   the court is satisfied that—
    (i)   the applicant cannot identify or contact the absentee,
    (ii)   it would prejudice the investigation if the absentee were present,
    (iii)   it would prejudice the investigation to adjourn or postpone the application so as to allow the absentee to attend, or
    (iv)   the absentee has waived the opportunity to attend.
(4)   The court must not determine such an application in the absence of any respondent who, if the order sought by the applicant were made, would be required to produce or give access to journalistic material, unless that respondent has waived the opportunity to attend.
(5)   The court officer must arrange for the court to hear such an application no sooner than 2 business days after it was served, unless—
(a)   the court directs that no hearing need be arranged; or
(b)   the court gives other directions for the hearing.
(6)   The court must not determine an application unless satisfied that sufficient time has been allowed for it.
(7)   If the court so directs, the parties to an application may attend a hearing by live link or telephone.
(8)   The court must not make, vary or discharge an order unless the applicant states, in writing or orally, that to the best of the applicant's knowledge and belief—
(a)   the application discloses all the information that is material to what the court must decide; and
(b)   the content of the application is true.
(9)   Where the statement required by paragraph (8) is made orally—
(a)   the statement must be on oath or affirmation, unless the court otherwise directs; and
(b)   the court must arrange for a record of the making of the statement.
(10)   The court may—
(a)   shorten or extend (even after it has expired) a time limit under this Section;
(b)   dispense with a requirement for service under this Section (even after service was required); and
(c)   consider an application made orally instead of in writing.
(10)   A person who wants an extension of time must—
(a)   apply when serving the application for which it is needed; and
(b)   explain the delay.

47.6 *Application for order: general rules* (1)   This rule applies to each application for an order to which this Section applies.
(2)   The applicant must—
(a)   apply in writing and serve the application on the court officer;
(b)   demonstrate that the applicant is entitled to apply, for example as a constable or under legislation that applies to other officers;
(c)   give the court an estimate of how long the court should allow—
    (i)   to read the application and prepare for any hearing, and

      (ii)   for any hearing of the application;
(d)   attach a draft order in the terms proposed by the applicant;
(e)   serve notice of the application on the respondent, unless the court otherwise directs;
(f)   serve the application on the respondent to such extent, if any, as the court directs.
(3)   A notice served on the respondent must—
(a)   specify the material or information in respect of which the application is made; and
(b)   identify—
      (i)   the power that the applicant invites the court to exercise, and
      (ii)   the conditions for the exercise of that power which the applicant asks the court to find are met.
(4)   The applicant must serve any order made on the respondent.

47.7 *Application containing information withheld from a respondent or other person*   (1)   This rule applies where an application includes information that the applicant thinks ought to be revealed only to the court.
(2)   The application must—
(a)   identify that information; and
(b)   explain why that information ought not to be served on the respondent or another person.
(3)   At a hearing of an application to which this rule applies—
(a)   the general rule is that the court must consider, in the following sequence—
      (i)   representations first by the applicant and then by the respondent and any other person, in the presence of them all, and then
      (ii)   further representations by the applicant, in the others' absence; but
(b)   the court may direct other arrangements for the hearing.

47.8 *Application to vary or discharge an order*   (1)   This rule applies where one of the following wants the court to vary or discharge an order to which a rule in this Section refers—
(a)   an applicant;
(b)   the respondent; or
(c)   a person affected by the order.
(2)   That applicant, respondent or person affected must—
(a)   apply in writing as soon as practicable after becoming aware of the grounds for doing so;
(b)   serve the application on—
      (i)   the court officer, and
      (ii)   the respondent, applicant, or any person known to be affected, as applicable;
(c)   explain why it is appropriate for the order to be varied or discharged;
(d)   propose the terms of any variation; and
(e)   ask for a hearing, if one is wanted, and explain why it is needed.

47.9 *Application to punish for contempt of court*   (1)   This rule applies where a person is accused of disobeying—
(a)   a production order made under paragraph 4 of Schedule 1 to the Police and Criminal Evidence Act 1984;
(b)   a production etc order made under paragraph 5 of Schedule 5 to the Terrorism Act 2000;
(c)   an explanation order made under paragraph 13 of that Schedule;
(d)   an account monitoring order made under paragraph 2 of Schedule 6A to that Act;
(e)   a production order made under section 345 of the Proceeds of Crime Act 2002 or article 6 of the Proceeds of Crime Act 2002 (External Investigations) Order 2014;
(f)   an account monitoring order made under section 370 of the 2002 Act or article 29 of the 2014 Order; or
(g)   a production order made under section 157 of the Extradition Act 2003.
(2)   An applicant who wants the court to exercise its power to punish that person for contempt of court must comply with the rules in Part 48 (Contempt of court).
[Note. The Crown Court has power to punish for contempt of court a person who disobeys its order. See paragraphs 10(1) and 13(5) of Schedule 5, and paragraph 6(1) of Schedule 6A, to the Terrorism Act 2000; sections 351(7) and 375(6) of the Proceeds of Crime Act 2002 and articles 12(6) and 34(5) of the Proceeds of Crime Act 2002 (External Investigations) Order 2014; and section 45 of the Senior Courts Act 1981.
A Circuit judge has power to punish a person who disobeys a production order under the Police and Criminal Evidence Act 1984 as if that were a contempt of the Crown Court: see paragraph 15 of Schedule 1 to the Act.
Disobedience to an explanation order, to a disclosure order or to a customer information order under the Terrorism Act 2000 is an offence: see paragraph 14 of Schedule 5, paragraph 11 of Schedule 5A, and paragraph1(3) of Schedule 6, to the Act.
Disobedience to a disclosure order or to a customer information order under the Proceeds of Crime Act 2002 or under the Proceeds of Crime Act 2002 (External Investigations) Order 2014 is an offence: see sections 359 and 366 of the Act and articles 18 and 25 of the Order. Under section 342 of the Act and under article 5 of the Order, subject to the exceptions for which those provide it is an offence to make a disclosure likely to prejudice an investigation or to interfere with documents relevant to it.]
If a person fails to comply with a further information order under the Terrorism Act 2000 or under the Proceeds of Crime Act 2002 the magistrates' court may order that person to pay an amount not

exceeding £5,000, which order may be enforced as if the sum due had been adjudged to be paid by a conviction: see section 22B(8), (9) of the Terrorism Act 2000 and section 339ZH((8), (9) of the Proceeds of Crime Act 2002.

ORDERS UNDER THE POLICE AND CRIMINAL EVIDENCE ACT 1984

47.10 *Application for a production order under the Police and Criminal Evidence Act 1984*
(1)   This rule applies where an applicant wants the court to make an order to which rule 47.4(a) refers.
(2)   As well as complying with rule 47.6 (Application for order: general rules), the application must, in every case—
(a)   specify the offence under investigation (and see paragraph (3)(a));
(b)   describe the material sought;
(c)   identify the respondent;
(d)   specify the premises on which the material is believed to be, or explain why it is not reasonably practicable to do so;
(e)   explain the grounds for believing that the material is on the premises specified, or (if applicable) on unspecified premises of the respondent;
(f)   specify the set of access conditions on which the applicant relies (and see paragraphs (3) and (4)); and
(g)   propose—
      (i)   the terms of the order, and
      (ii)   the period within which it should take effect.
(3)   Where the applicant relies on paragraph 2 of Schedule 1 to the Police and Criminal Evidence Act 1984 ('the first set of access conditions': general power to gain access to special procedure material), the application must—
(a)   specify the indictable offence under investigation;
(b)   explain the grounds for believing that the offence has been committed;
(c)   explain the grounds for believing that the material sought—
      (i)   is likely to be of substantial value to the investigation (whether by itself, or together with other material),
      (ii)   is likely to be admissible evidence at trial for the offence under investigation, and
      (iii)   does not consist of or include items subject to legal privilege or excluded material;
(d)   explain what other methods of obtaining the material—
      (i)   have been tried without success, or
      (ii)   have not been tried because they appeared bound to fail; and
(e)   explain why it is in the public interest for the respondent to produce the material, having regard to—
      (i)   the benefit likely to accrue to the investigation if the material is obtained, and
      (ii)   the circumstances under which the respondent holds the material.
(4)   Where the applicant relies on paragraph 3 of Schedule 1 to the Police and Criminal Evidence Act 1984 ('the second set of access conditions': use of search warrant power to gain access to excluded or special procedure material), the application must—
(a)   state the legislation under which a search warrant could have been issued, had the material sought not been excluded or special procedure material (in this paragraph, described as 'the main search power');
(b)   include or attach the terms of the main search power;
(c)   explain how the circumstances would have satisfied any criteria prescribed by the main search power for the issue of a search warrant; and
(d)   explain why the issue of such a search warrant would have been appropriate.
[Note. See paragraphs 1 to 4 of Schedule 1 to the Police and Criminal Evidence Act 1984. The applicant for an order must be a constable. Sections 10, 11 and 14 of the 1984 Act define 'items subject to legal privilege', 'excluded material' and 'special procedure material'. The period within which an order takes effect must be specified in the order and, unless the court considers a longer period appropriate, must be 7 days from the date of the order.
See also the code of practice for searches of premises by police officers and the seizure of property found by police officers on persons or premises issued under section 66 of the Police and Criminal Evidence Act 1984.
The Practice Direction sets out forms of application, notice and order for use in connection with this rule.]

ORDERS UNDER THE TERRORISM ACT 2000

47.11 *Application for an order under the Terrorism Act 2000* (1)   This rule applies where an applicant wants the court to make one of the orders to which rule 47.4(b) and (c) refers.
(2)   As well as complying with rule 47.6 (Application for order: general rules), the application must—
(a)   specify the offence under investigation;
(b)   explain how the investigation constitutes a terrorist investigation or terrorist financing investigation, as appropriate, within the meaning of the Terrorism Act 2000;
(c)   identify the respondent; and
(d)   give the information required by whichever of rules 47.12 to 47.16 applies.

47.12 *Content of application for a production etc order under the Terrorism Act 2000* (1) As well as complying with rules 47.6 and 47.11, an applicant who wants the court to make an order for the production of, or for giving access to, material, or for a statement of its location, must—

(a)   describe that material;

(b)   explain why the applicant thinks the material is—

      (i)   in the respondent's possession, custody or power, or

      (ii)   expected to come into existence and then to be in the respondent's possession, custody or power within 28 days of the order;

(c)   explain how the material constitutes or contains excluded material or special procedure material;

(d)   confirm that none of the material is expected to be subject to legal privilege;

(e)   explain why the material is likely to be of substantial value to the investigation;

(f)   explain why it is in the public interest for the material to be produced, or for the applicant to be given access to it, having regard to—

      (i)   the benefit likely to accrue to the investigation if it is obtained, and

      (ii)   the circumstances in which the respondent has the material, or is expected to have it; and

(g)   propose—

      (i)   the terms of the order, and

      (ii)   the period within which it should take effect.

(2) An applicant who wants the court to make an order to grant entry in aid of a production order must—

(a)   specify the premises to which entry is sought;

(b)   explain why the order is needed; and

(c)   propose the terms of the order.

Note. See paragraphs 5 to 9 of Schedule 5 to the Terrorism Act 2000. The applicant for a production, etc order must be an 'appropriate officer' as defined by paragraph 5(6) of that Schedule. Where the applicant is a counter-terrorism financial investigator the application must be for the purposes of an investigation relating to 'terrorist property'as defined by section 14 of the 2000 Act. Under paragraphs 5 and 7 of Schedule 5 to that Act a production order may require a specified person—

(a)   *to produce to a an appropriate officer within a specified period for seizure and retention any material which that person has in his or her possession, custody or power and to which the application relates; to give a constable access to any such material within a specified period; and to state to the best of that person's knowledge and belief the location of material to which the application relates if it is not in, and it will not come into, his or her possession, custody or power within the period specified; or*

(b)   *where such material is expected to come into existence within the period of 28 days beginning with the date of the order, to notify a named appropriate officer as soon as is reasonably practicable after any material to which the application relates comes into that person's possession, custody or power, and then to produce that material to a constable; to give a constable access to it; and to state to the best of that person's knowledge and belief the location of material to which the application relates if it is not in, and it will not come into, his or her possession, custody or power within that period of 28 days.*

Under paragraph 4 of Schedule 5 to the 2000 Act, 'legal privilege', 'excluded material' and 'special procedure material' mean the same as under sections 10, 11 and 14 of the Police and Criminal Evidence Act 1984.

The period within which an order takes effect must be specified in the order and, unless the court otherwise directs, must be—

(a)   *where the respondent already has the material, 7 days from the date of the order; or*

(b)   *where the respondent is expected to have the material within 28 days, 7 days from the date the respondent notifies the applicant of its receipt.*

The Practice Direction sets out forms of application, notice and order for use in connection with this rule.]

47.13 *Content of application for a disclosure order or further information order under the Terrorism Act 2000* (1) As well as complying with rules 47.6 and 47.11, an applicant who wants the court to make a disclosure order must—

(a)   explain why the applicant thinks that—

      (i)   a person has committed an offence under any of sections 15 to 18 of the Terrorism Act 2000, or

      (ii)   property described in the application is terrorist property within the meaning of section 14 of the 2000 Act;

(b)   describe in general terms the information that the applicant wants the respondent to provide;

(c)   confirm that none of the information is—

      (i)   expected to be subject to legal privilege, or

      (ii)   excluded material;

(d)   explain why the information is likely to be of substantial value to the investigation;

(e)   explain why it is in the public interest for the information to be provided, having regard to the benefit likely to accrue to the investigation if it is obtained; and

(f)   propose the terms of the order.

"(2)   As well as complying with rule 47.6, an applicant who wants the court to make a further information order must—

(a)   identify the respondent from whom the information is sought and explain—

   (i)   whether the respondent is the person who made the disclosure to which the information relates or is otherwise carrying on a business in the regulated sector within the meaning of Part 1 of Schedule 3A to the 2000 Act, and

   (ii)   why the applicant thinks that the information is in the possession, or under the control, of the respondent;

(b)   specify or describe the information that the applicant wants the respondent to provide;

(c)   where the information sought relates to a disclosure of information by someone under section 21A of the 2000 Act (Failure to disclose: regulated sector), explain—

   (i)   how the information sought relates to a matter arising from that disclosure,

   (ii)   how the information would assist in investigating whether a person is involved in the commission of an offence under any of sections 15 to 18 of that Act, or in determining whether an investigation of that kind should be started, or in identifying terrorist property or its movement or use, and

   (iii)   why it is reasonable in all the circumstances for the information to be provided;

(d)   where the information sought relates to a disclosure made under a requirement of the law of a country outside the United Kingdom which corresponds with Part III of the 2000 Act (Terrorist property), and an authority in that country which investigates offences corresponding with sections 15 to 18 of that Act has asked the National Crime Agency for information in connection with that disclosure, explain—

   (i)   how the information sought relates to a matter arising from that disclosure,

   (ii)   why the information is likely to be of substantial value to the authority that made the request in determining any matter in connection with the disclosure, and

   (iii)   why it is reasonable in all the circumstances for the information to be provided;

(e)   confirm that none of the information is expected to be subject to legal privilege; and

(f)   propose the terms of the order, including—

   (i)   how the respondent must provide the information required, and

   (ii)   the date by which the information must be provided.

(3)   Rule 47.8 (Application to vary or discharge an order) does not apply to a further information order.

(4)   Paragraph (5) applies where a party to an application for a further information order wants to appeal to the Crown Court from the decision of the magistrates' court.

(5)   The appellant must—

(a)   serve an appeal notice—

   (i)   on the Crown Court officer and on the other party,

   (ii)   not more than 21 days after the magistrates' court's decision; and

(b)   in the appeal notice, explain, as appropriate, why the Crown Court should (as the case may be) make, discharge or vary a further information order.

(6)   Rule 34.11 (Constitution of the Crown Court) applies on such an appeal.", and

[Note *See sections 22B, 22D and 22E of, and Schedule 5A to, the Terrorism Act 2000.*

Under paragraph 9(6) of Schedule 5A to the 2000 Act the applicant for a disclosure order must be an 'appropriate officer', as defined by paragraph 5, who is, or who is authorised to apply by, a police officer of at least the rank of superintendent.

Under section 22B(12) of the 2000 Act the applicant for a further information order must be 'a law enforcement officer', as defined by section 22B(14), who is, or who is authorised to apply by, a 'senior law enforcement officer', defined by section 22B(14) as a police officer of at least the rank of superintendent, the Director General of the National Crime Agency or an officer of that Agency authorised by the Director General for that purpose.

Section 14 of the 2000 Act defines terrorist property as money or other property which is likely to be used for the purposes of terrorism; proceeds of the commission of terrorism; and proceeds of acts carried out for the purposes of terrorism. Sections 15 to 18 of the Act create offences of fund raising for the purposes of terrorism; use or possession of property for the purposes of terrorism; funding terrorism; making an insurance payment in response to a terrorist demand; and facilitating the retention or control of terrorist property.

A disclosure order can require a lawyer to provide a client's name and address.

Under section 21A of the 2000 Act a person engaged in a business in the regulated sector commits an offence where the conditions listed in that section are met and that person does not disclose, in the manner required by that section, knowledge or a suspicion that another person has committed or attempted to commit an offence under any of sections 15 to 18 in Part III of the Act. Part III of the Act also contains other disclosure provisions.

The Practice Direction sets out forms of application, notice and order for use in connection with this rule.]

47.14 *Content of application for an explanation order under the Terrorism Act 2000* As well as complying with rules 47.6 and 47.11, an applicant who wants the court to make an explanation order must—

(a)   identify the material that the applicant wants the respondent to explain;

(b)   confirm that the explanation is not expected to infringe legal privilege; and

(c)   propose the terms of the order.

[Note. See paragraph 13 of Schedule 5 to the Terrorism Act 2000. The applicant for an explanation order may be a constable or, where the application concerns material produced to a counter-terrorism financial investigator, such an investigator.

An explanation order can require a lawyer to provide a client's name and address.

The Practice Direction sets out forms of application, notice and order for use in connection with this rule.]

47.15 *Content of application for a customer information order under the Terrorism Act 2000*   As well as complying with rules 47.6 and 47.11, an applicant who wants the court to make a customer information order must—

(a)   explain why it is desirable for the purposes of the investigation to trace property said to be terrorist property within the meaning of the Terrorism Act 2000;

(b)   explain why the order will enhance the effectiveness of the investigation; and

(c)   propose the terms of the order.

[Note. See Schedule 6 to the Terrorism Act 2000. The applicant for a customer information order must be a police officer of at least the rank of superintendent.

'Customer information' is defined by paragraph 7 of Schedule 6 to the 2000 Act. 'Terrorist property' is defined by section 14 of the Act.

The Practice Direction sets out forms of application, notice and order for use in connection with this rule.]

47.16 *Content of application for an account monitoring order under the Terrorism Act 2000*   As well as complying with rules 47.6 and 47.11, an applicant who wants the court to make an account monitoring order must—

(a)   specify—

    (i)   the information sought,

    (ii)   the period during which the applicant wants the respondent to provide that information (to a maximum of 90 days), and

    (iii)   where, when and in what manner the applicant wants the respondent to provide that information;

(b)   explain why it is desirable for the purposes of the investigation to trace property said to be terrorist property within the meaning of the Terrorism Act 2000;

(c)   explain why the order will enhance the effectiveness of the investigation; and

(d)   propose the terms of the order.

[Note. See Schedule 6A to the Terrorism Act 2000. The applicant for an account monitoring order may be a police officer or a counter-terrorism financial investigator.

'Terrorist property' is defined by section 14 of the Act.

The Practice Direction sets out forms of application, notice and order for use in connection with this rule.]

ORDERS UNDER THE PROCEEDS OF CRIME ACT 2002

47.17 *Application for an order under the Proceeds of Crime Act 2002*   (1)   This rule applies where an applicant wants the court to make one of the orders to which rule 47.4(d) refers.

(2)   As well as complying with rule 47.6 (Application for order: general rules), the application must—

(a)   identify—

    (i)   the respondent, and

    (ii)   the person or property the subject of the investigation;

(b)   in the case of an investigation in the United Kingdom, explain why the applicant thinks that—

    (i)   the person under investigation has benefited from criminal conduct, in the case of a confiscation investigation, or committed a money laundering offence, in the case of a money laundering investigation, or

    (ii)   in the case of a detained cash investigation, a detained property investigation or a frozen funds investigation, the cash or property involved, or the money held in the frozen account, was obtained through unlawful conduct or is intended to be used in unlawful conduct;

(c)   in the case of an investigation outside the United Kingdom, explain why the applicant thinks that—

    (i)   there is an investigation by an overseas authority which relates to a criminal investigation or to criminal proceedings (including proceedings to remove the benefit of a person's criminal conduct following that person's conviction), and

    (ii)   the investigation is into whether property has been obtained as a result of or in connection with criminal conduct, or into the extent or whereabouts of such property;

(d)   give the additional information required by whichever of rules 47.18 to 47.22 applies.

[Note. See also the code of practice for those exercising functions as officers and investigators issued under section 377 of the 2002 Act, and the code of practice for prosecutors and others issued under section 377A of that Act.]

47.18 *Content of application for a production order under the Proceeds of Crime Act 2002*   As well as complying with rules 47.6 and 47.17, an applicant who wants the court to make an order for the production of, or for giving access to, material, must—

(a)   describe that material;

(b)   explain why the applicant thinks the material is in the respondent's possession or control;

(c)   confirm that none of the material is—

     (i)   expected to be subject to legal privilege, or

     (ii)   excluded material;

(d)   explain why the material is likely to be of substantial value to the investigation;

(e)   explain why it is in the public interest for the material to be produced, or for the applicant to be given access to it, having regard to—

     (i)   the benefit likely to accrue to the investigation if it is obtained, and

     (ii)   the circumstances in which the respondent has the material; and

(f)   propose—

     (i)   the terms of the order, and

     (ii)   the period within which it should take effect, if 7 days from the date of the order would not be appropriate.

[Note. See sections 345 to 350 of the Proceeds of Crime Act 2002 and articles 6 to 11 of the Proceeds of Crime Act 2002 (External Investigations) Order 2014. Under those provisions—

(a)   *'excluded material' means the same as under section 11 of the Police and Criminal Evidence Act 1984; and*

(b)   *'legal privilege' is defined by section 348 of the 2002 Act.*

A Crown Court judge may make a production order for the purposes of a confiscation investigation, a money laundering investigation, a detained cash investigation, a detained property investigation or a frozen funds investigation.

The applicant for a production order must be an 'appropriate officer' as defined by section 378(1), (4) and (5) of the 2002 Act and article 2(1) of the 2014 Order.

The Practice Direction sets out forms of application, notice and order for use in connection with this rule.]

47.19 *Content of application for an order to grant entry under the Proceeds of Crime Act 2002*
An applicant who wants the court to make an order to grant entry in aid of a production order must—

(a)   specify the premises to which entry is sought;

(b)   explain why the order is needed; and

(c)   propose the terms of the order.

[Note. See section 347 of the Proceeds of Crime Act 2002 and article 8 of the Proceeds of Crime Act 2002 (External Investigations) Order 2014. The applicant for an order to grant entry must be an 'appropriate officer' as defined by section 378(1), (4) and (5) of the Act and article 2(1) of the 2014 Order.]

47.20 *Content of application for a disclosure order or further information order under the Proceeds of Crime Act 2002* (1) As well as complying with rules 47.6 and 47.17, an applicant who wants the court to make a disclosure order must—

(a)   describe in general terms the information that the applicant wants the respondent to provide;

(b)   confirm that none of the information is—

     (i)   expected to be subject to legal privilege, or

     (ii)   excluded material;

(c)   explain why the information is likely to be of substantial value to the investigation;

(d)   explain why it is in the public interest for the information to be provided, having regard to the benefit likely to accrue to the investigation if it is obtained; and

(e)   propose the terms of the order.

(2) As well as complying with rule 47.6, an applicant who wants the court to make a further information order must—

(a)   identify the respondent from whom the information is sought and explain—

     (i)   whether the respondent is the person who made the disclosure to which the information relates or is otherwise carrying on a business in the regulated sector within the meaning of Part 1 of Schedule 9 to the Proceeds of Crime Act 2002, and

     (ii)   why the applicant thinks that the information is in the possession, or under the control, of the respondent;

(b)   specify or describe the information that the applicant wants the respondent to provide;

(c)   where the information sought relates to a disclosure of information under Part 7 of the Proceeds of Crime Act 2002 (Money laundering), explain—

     (i)   how the information sought relates to a matter arising from that disclosure,

     (ii)   how the information would assist in investigating whether a person is engaged in money laundering or in determining whether an investigation of that kind should be started, and

     (iii)   why it is reasonable in all the circumstances for the information to be provided;

(d)   where the information sought relates to a disclosure made under a requirement of the law of a country outside the United Kingdom which corresponds with Part 7 of the 2002 Act, and an authority in that country which investigates money laundering has asked the National Crime Agency for information in connection with that disclosure, explain—

     (i)   how the information sought relates to a matter arising from that disclosure,

(ii)   why the information is likely to be of substantial value to the authority that made the request in determining any matter in connection with the disclosure, and

(iii)   why it is reasonable in all the circumstances for the information to be provided;

(e)   confirm that none of the information is expected to be subject to legal privilege; and

(f)   propose the terms of the order, including—

(i)   how the respondent must provide the information required, and

(ii)   the date by which the information must be provided.

(3)   Rule 47.8 (Application to vary or discharge an order) does not apply to a further information order.

(4)   Paragraph (5) applies where a party to an application for a further information order wants to appeal to the Crown Court from the decision of the magistrates' court.

(5)   The appellant must—

(a)   serve an appeal notice—

(i)   on the Crown Court officer and on the other party,

(ii)   not more than 21 days after the magistrates' court's decision; and

(b)   in the appeal notice, explain, as appropriate, why the Crown Court should (as the case may be) make, discharge or vary a further information order.

(6)   Rule 34.11 (Constitution of the Crown Court) applies on such an appeal.

[Note See sections 339ZH, 339ZJ, 339ZK, 357, 358 and 361 of the Proceeds of Crime Act 2002and articles 16, 17 and 20 of the Proceeds of Crime Act 2002 (External Investigations) Order 2014.

Where the 2002 Act applies, a Crown Court judge may make a disclosure order for the purposes of a confiscation investigation or a money laundering investigation.

The applicant for a disclosure order must be a 'relevant authority' as defined by section 357(7) of the 2002 Act, or an 'appropriate officer' as defined by article 2(1) of the 2014 Order where the Order applies. Under section 362(6) of the Act, a relevant authority who under section 357(7) is an 'appropriate officer' (as defined by section 378(1), (4) and (5)) may apply only if that person is, or is authorised to do so by, a 'senior appropriate officer' (as defined by section 378(2)).

Under section 339ZH(1), (12) the applicant for a further information order must be the Director General of the National Crime Agency or an officer of that Agency authorised by the Director General for that purpose.

A disclosure order can require a lawyer to provide a client's name and address.

Under sections 330, 331 and 332 in Part 7 of the 2002 Act a person engaged in a business in the regulated sector commits an offence where the conditions listed in any of those sections are met and that person does not disclose, in the manner required by the relevant section, knowledge or a suspicion that another person is engaged in money laundering.

The Practice Direction sets out forms of application, notice and order for use in connection with this rule.]

47.21 *Content of application for a customer information order under the Proceeds of Crime Act 2002*   As well as complying with rules 47.6 and 47.17, an applicant who wants the court to make a customer information order must—

(a)   explain why customer information about the person under investigation is likely to be of substantial value to that investigation;

(b)   explain why it is in the public interest for the information to be provided, having regard to the benefit likely to accrue to the investigation if it is obtained; and

(c)   propose the terms of the order.

[Note. See sections 363, 364, 365 and 368 of the Proceeds of Crime Act 2002and articles 22, 23, 24 and 27 of the Proceeds of Crime Act 2002 (External Investigations) Order 2014.

A Crown Court judge may make a customer information order for the purposes of a confiscation investigation or a money laundering investigation.

The applicant for a customer information order must be an 'appropriate officer' as defined by section 378(1), (4) and (5) of the 2002 Act and article 2(1) of the 2014 Order.

'Customer information' is defined by section 364 of the 2002 Act and article 2(1) of the 2014 Order.

The Practice Direction sets out forms of application, notice and order for use in connection with this rule.]

47.22 *Content of application for an account monitoring order under the Proceeds of Crime Act 2002*   As well as complying with rules 47.6 and 47.17, an applicant who wants the court to make an account monitoring order for the provision of account information must—

(a)   specify—

(i)   the information sought,

(ii)   the period during which the applicant wants the respondent to provide that information (to a maximum of 90 days), and

(iii)   when and in what manner the applicant wants the respondent to provide that information;

(b)   explain why the information is likely to be of substantial value to the investigation;

(c)   explain why it is in the public interest for the information to be provided, having regard to the benefit likely to accrue to the investigation if it is obtained; and

(d)   propose the terms of the order.

[Note. See sections 370, 371 and 374 of the Proceeds of Crime Act 2002and articles 29, 30 and 33 of the Proceeds of Crime Act 2002 (External Investigations) Order 2014.

Where the 2002 Act applies, a Crown Court judge may make an account monitoring order for the purposes of a confiscation investigation, a money laundering investigation, a detained cash

investigation, a detained property investigation or a frozen funds investigation
The applicant for an account monitoring order must be an 'appropriate officer' as defined by
section 378(1), (4) and (5) of the 2002 Act and article 2(1) of the 2014 Order.
'Account information' is defined by section 370 of the 2002 Act and article 29(3) of the 2014 Order.
The Practice Direction sets out forms of application, notice and order for use in connection with
this rule.]

ORDERS UNDER THE EXTRADITION ACT 2003

47.23 *Application for a production order under the Extradition Act 2003* (1)   This rule applies
where an applicant wants the court to make an order to which rule 47.4(e) refers.
(2)   As well as complying with rule 47.6 (Application for order: general rules), the application
must—
(a)   identify the person whose extradition is sought;
(b)   specify the extradition offence of which that person is accused;
(c)   identify the respondent; and
(d)   describe the special procedure or excluded material sought.
(3)   In relation to the person whose extradition is sought, the application must explain the
grounds for believing that—
(a)   that person has committed the offence for which extradition is sought;
(b)   that offence is an extradition offence; and
(c)   that person is in the United Kingdom or is on the way to the United Kingdom.
(4)   In relation to the material sought, the application must—
(a)   specify the premises on which the material is believed to be;
(b)   explain the grounds for believing that—
    (i)   the material is on those premises,
    (ii)   the material consists of or includes special procedure or excluded material, and
    (iii)   the material would be likely to be admissible evidence at a trial in England and
    Wales for the offence for which extradition is sought;
(c)   explain what other methods of obtaining the material—
    (i)   have been tried without success, or
    (ii)   have not been tried because they appeared bound to fail; and
(d)   explain why it is in the public interest for the respondent to produce or give access to the
material.
(5)   The application must propose—
(a)   the terms of the order, and
(b)   the period within which it should take effect.
[Note. See sections 157 and 158 of the Extradition Act 2003. Under those provisions—
(a)   *'special procedure material' means the same as under section 14 of the Police and*
Criminal Evidence Act 1984; and
(b)   *'excluded material' means the same as under section 11 of the 1984 Act.*
The applicant for a production order must be a constable.
The period within which an order takes effect must be specified in the order and, unless the court
considers a longer period appropriate, must be 7 days from the date of the order.]

SECTION 3: INVESTIGATION WARRANTS

47.24 *When this Section applies*   This Section applies where—
(a)   a justice of the peace can issue a warrant under—
    (i)   section 8 of the Police and Criminal Evidence Act 1984,
    (ii)   section 2 of the Criminal Justice Act 1987;
(b)   a Circuit judge can issue a warrant under—
    (i)   paragraph 12 of Schedule 1 to the Police and Criminal Evidence Act 1984,
    (ii)   paragraph 11 of Schedule 5 to the Terrorism Act 2000,
    (iii)   section 160 of the Extradition Act 2003;
(c)   a Crown Court judge can issue a warrant under—
    (i)   section 352 of the Proceeds of Crime Act 2002, or
    (ii)   article 13 of the Proceeds of Crime Act 2002 (External Investigations) Order 2014;
(d)   a court to which these Rules apply can issue a warrant to search for and seize articles or
persons under a power not listed in paragraphs (a), (b) or (c).
[Note. In outline, the warrants to which these rules apply are—
(a)   *under the Police and Criminal Evidence Act 1984, a warrant authorising entry to, and the*
search of, premises for material, articles or persons;
(b)   *under the Criminal Justice Act 1987, a warrant authorising entry to, and the search of,*
premises for documents sought by the Director of the Serious Fraud Office;
(c)   *under the Terrorism Act 2000, a warrant authorising entry to, and the search of, premises*
for material sought for the purposes of a terrorist investigation;
(d)   *under the Proceeds of Crime Act 2002 or under the Proceeds of Crime Act 2002 (External*
Investigations) Order 2014, a warrant authorising entry to, and the search of, premises for
material sought for the purposes of a confiscation investigation, a money laundering
investigation, a detained cash investigation or an external investigation;

(e) under the Extradition Act 2003, a warrant authorising entry to, and the search of, premises for material sought in connection with the prosecution of a person whose extradition has been requested;
(f) under other Acts, comparable warrants.
For all the relevant terms under which such warrants can be issued, see the provisions listed in this rule.
Under section 8 of the Senior Courts Act 1981, a High Court judge, a Circuit judge, a Recorder, a qualifying judge advocate and a District Judge (Magistrates' Courts) each may act as a Crown Court judge.
When the relevant provisions of the Courts Act 2003 come into force, a District Judge (Magistrates' Courts) will have the same powers as a Circuit judge under the Police and Criminal Evidence Act 1984 and under the Terrorism Act 2000.
Under section 66 of the Courts Act 2003, in criminal cases a High Court judge, a Circuit judge, a Recorder and a qualifying judge advocate each has the powers of a justice of the peace who is a District Judge (Magistrates' Courts).
As well as governing procedure on an application to a magistrates' court or the Crown Court, under the following provisions rules may govern the procedure on an application to an individual Circuit or Crown Court judge—
(a) paragraph 15A of Schedule 1 to the Police and Criminal Evidence Act 1984;
(b) paragraph 11 of Schedule 5 to the Terrorism Act 2000;
(c) section 352 of the Proceeds of Crime Act 2002; and
(d) section 160 of the Extradition Act 2003.]

47.25 *Exercise of court's powers* (1) The court must determine an application for a warrant—
(a) at a hearing, which must be in private unless the court otherwise directs;
(b) in the presence of the applicant; and
(c) in the absence of any person affected by the warrant, including any person in occupation or control of premises which the applicant wants to search.
(2) If the court so directs, the applicant may attend the hearing by live link or telephone.
(3) The court must not determine an application unless satisfied that sufficient time has been allowed for it.
(4) The court must not determine an application unless the applicant confirms, on oath or affirmation, that to the best of the applicant's knowledge and belief—
(a) the application discloses all the information that is material to what the court must decide, including any circumstances that might reasonably be considered capable of undermining any of the grounds of the application; and
(b) the content of the application is true.
(5) If the court requires the applicant to answer a question about an application—
(a) the applicant's answer must be on oath or affirmation;
(b) the court must arrange for a record of the gist of the question and reply; and
(c) if the applicant cannot answer to the court's satisfaction, the court may—
　　(i) specify the information the court requires, and
　　(ii) give directions for the presentation of any renewed application.
(6) Unless to do so would be inconsistent with other legislation, on an application the court may issue—
(a) a warrant in respect of specified premises;
(b) a warrant in respect of all premises occupied or controlled by a specified person;
(c) a warrant in respect of all premises occupied or controlled by a specified person which specifies some of those premises; or
(d) more than one warrant—
　　(i) each one in respect of premises specified in the warrant,
　　(ii) each one in respect of all premises occupied or controlled by a person specified in the warrant (whether or not such a warrant also specifies any of those premises), or
　　(iii) at least one in respect of specified premises and at least one in respect of all premises occupied or controlled by a specified person (whether or not such a warrant also specifies any of those premises).
[Note. See section 15 of the Police and Criminal Evidence Act 1984 and section 2(4) of the Criminal Justice Act 1987. Not all the powers to which the rules in this Section apply permit the issue of a warrant in respect of all premises occupied or controlled by a specified person: see, for example, rule 47.32 (Application for warrant under section 352 of the Proceeds of Crime Act 2002).]

47.26 *Application for warrant: general rules* (1) This rule applies to each application to which this Section applies.
(2) The applicant must—
(a) apply in writing;
(b) serve the application on—
　　(i) the court officer, or
　　(ii) if the court office is closed, the court;
(c) demonstrate that the applicant is entitled to apply, for example as a constable or under legislation that applies to other officers;
(d) give the court an estimate of how long the court should allow—
　　(i) to read and prepare for the application, and
　　(ii) for the hearing of the application; and

(e)   tell the court when the applicant expects any warrant issued to be executed.
(3)   The application must disclose anything known or reported to the applicant that might reasonably be considered capable of undermining any of the grounds of the application.
(4)   Where the application includes information that the applicant thinks should not be supplied under rule 5.7 (Supply to a party of information or documents from records or case materials) to a person affected by a warrant, the applicant may—
(a)   set out that information in a separate document, marked accordingly; and
(b)   in that document, explain why the applicant thinks that that information ought not to be supplied to anyone other than the court.
(5)   The application must include—
(a)   a declaration by the applicant that to the best of the applicant's knowledge and belief—
(i)   the application discloses all the information that is material to what the court must decide, including anything that might reasonably be considered capable of undermining any of the grounds of the application, and
(ii)   the content of the application is true; and
(b)   a declaration by an officer senior to the applicant that the senior officer has reviewed and authorised the application.
(6)   The application must attach a draft warrant or warrants in the terms proposed by the applicant.

47.27 *Information to be included in a warrant*   (1)   A warrant must identify—
(a)   the person or description of persons by whom it may be executed;
(b)   any person who may accompany a person executing the warrant;
(c)   so far as practicable, the material, documents, articles or persons to be sought;
(d)   the legislation under which it was issued;
(e)   the name of the applicant;
(f)   the court that issued it, unless that is otherwise recorded by the court officer;
(g)   the court office for the court that issued it; and
(h)   the date on which it was issued.
(2)   A warrant must specify—
(a)   either—
(i)   the premises to be searched, where the application was for authority to search specified premises, or
(ii)   the person in occupation or control of premises to be searched, where the application was for authority to search any premises occupied or controlled by that person; and
(b)   the number of occasions on which specified premises may be searched, if more than one.
(3)   A warrant must include, by signature, initial, or otherwise, an indication that it has been approved by the court that issued it.
(4)   Where a warrant comprises more than a single page, each page must include such an indication.
(5)   A copy of a warrant must include a prominent certificate that it is such a copy.
[Note. See sections 15 and 16 of the Police and Criminal Evidence Act 1984. Not all the powers to which the rules in this Section apply permit the issue of a warrant in respect of all premises occupied or controlled by a specified person: see, for example, rule 47.32 (Application for warrant under section 352 of the Proceeds of Crime Act 2002).]

47.28 *Application for warrant under section 8 of the Police and Criminal Evidence Act 1984*
(1)   This rule applies where an applicant wants a magistrates' court to issue a warrant or warrants under section 8 of the Police and Criminal Evidence Act 1984.
(2)   As well as complying with rule 47.26, the application must—
(a)   specify the offence under investigation (and see paragraph (3));
(b)   so far as practicable, identify the material sought (and see paragraph (4));
(c)   specify the premises to be searched (and see paragraphs (5) and (6));
(d)   state whether the applicant wants the premises to be searched on more than one occasion (and see paragraph (7)); and
(e)   state whether the applicant wants other persons to accompany the officers executing the warrant or warrants (and see paragraph (8)).
(3)   In relation to the offence under investigation, the application must—
(a)   state whether that offence is—
(i)   an indictable offence, or
(ii)   a relevant offence as defined in section 28D of the Immigration Act 1971; and
(b)   explain the grounds for believing that the offence has been committed.
(4)   In relation to the material sought, the application must explain the grounds for believing that that material—
(a)   is likely to be of substantial value to the investigation (whether by itself, or together with other material);
(b)   is likely to be admissible evidence at trial for the offence under investigation; and
(c)   does not consist of or include items subject to legal privilege, excluded material or special procedure material.
(5)   In relation to premises which the applicant wants to be searched and can specify, the application must—
(a)   specify each set of premises;

(b)   in respect of each set of premises, explain the grounds for believing that material sought is on those premises; and

(c)   in respect of each set of premises, explain the grounds for believing that—

   (i)   it is not practicable to communicate with any person entitled to grant entry to the premises,

   (ii)   it is practicable to communicate with such a person but it is not practicable to communicate with any person entitled to grant access to the material sought,

   (iii)   entry to the premises will not be granted unless a warrant is produced, or

   (iv)   the purpose of a search may be frustrated or seriously prejudiced unless a constable arriving at the premises can secure immediate entry to them.

(6)   In relation to premises which the applicant wants to be searched but at least some of which the applicant cannot specify, the application must—

(a)   explain the grounds for believing that—

   (i)   because of the particulars of the offence under investigation it is necessary to search any premises occupied or controlled by a specified person, and

   (ii)   it is not reasonably practicable to specify all the premises which that person occupies or controls which might need to be searched;

(b)   specify as many sets of premises as is reasonably practicable;

(c)   in respect of each set of premises, whether specified or not, explain the grounds for believing that material sought is on those premises; and

(d)   in respect of each specified set of premises, explain the grounds for believing that—

   (i)   it is not practicable to communicate with any person entitled to grant entry to the premises,

   (ii)   it is practicable to communicate with such a person but it is not practicable to communicate with any person entitled to grant access to the material sought,

   (iii)   entry to the premises will not be granted unless a warrant is produced, or

   (iv)   the purpose of a search may be frustrated or seriously prejudiced unless a constable arriving at the premises can secure immediate entry to them.

(7)   In relation to any set of premises which the applicant wants to be searched on more than one occasion, the application must—

(a)   explain why it is necessary to search on more than one occasion in order to achieve the purpose for which the applicant wants the court to issue the warrant; and

(b)   specify any proposed maximum number of occasions.

(8)   In relation to any set of premises which the applicant wants to be searched by the officers executing the warrant with other persons authorised by the court, the application must—

(a)   identify those other persons, by function or description; and

(b)   explain why those persons are required.

[Note. Under section 8 of the Police and Criminal Evidence Act 1984, where there are reasonable grounds for believing that an indictable offence has been committed a constable may apply to a justice of the peace for a warrant authorising a search for evidence on specified premises, or on the premises of a specified person. Under section 8(6) of the 1984 Act, section 8 applies also in relation to relevant offences as defined in section 28D(4) of the Immigration Act 1971 (some of which are not indictable offences).

Under section 23 of the 1984 Act, 'premises' includes any place, and in particular any vehicle, vessel, aircraft or hovercraft, any offshore installation, any renewable energy installation and any tent or moveable structure.

Under section 16(3) of the 1984 Act, entry and search under a warrant must be within 3 months from the date of its issue.

See also the code of practice for the search of premises issued under section 66 of the 1984 Act.

The Practice Direction sets out forms of application and warrant for use in connection with this rule.]

47.29 *Application for warrant under section 2 of the Criminal Justice Act 1987* (1)   This rule applies where an applicant wants a magistrates' court to issue a warrant or warrants under section 2 of the Criminal Justice Act 1987.

(2)   As well as complying with rule 47.26, the application must—

(a)   describe the investigation being conducted by the Director of the Serious Fraud Office and include—

   (i)   an explanation of what is alleged and why, and

   (ii)   a chronology of relevant events;

(b)   specify the document, documents or description of documents sought by the applicant (and see paragraphs (3) and (4)); and

(c)   specify the premises which the applicant wants to be searched (and see paragraph (5)).

(3)   In relation to each document or description of documents sought, the application must—

(a)   explain the grounds for believing that each such document—

   (i)   relates to a matter relevant to the investigation, and

   (ii)   could not be withheld from disclosure or production on grounds of legal professional privilege; and

(b)   explain the grounds for believing that—

   (i)   a person has failed to comply with a notice by the Director to produce the document or documents,

   (ii)   it is not practicable to serve such a notice, or

(iii)   the service of such a notice might seriously impede the investigation.   (4)   In relation to any document or description of documents which the applicant wants to be preserved but not seized under a warrant, the application must—

(a)   specify the steps for which the applicant wants the court's authority in order to preserve and prevent interference with the document or documents; and

(b)   explain why such steps are necessary.

(5)   In respect of each set of premises which the applicant wants to be searched, the application must explain the grounds for believing that a document or description of documents sought by the applicant is on those premises.

(6)   If the court so directs, the applicant must make available to the court material on which is based the information given under paragraph (2).

[Note. Under section 2 of the Criminal Justice Act 1987, where the Director of the Serious Fraud Office is investigating a case of serious or complex fraud a member of that Office may apply to a justice of the peace for a warrant authorising a search of specified premises for documents relating to any matter relevant to the investigation. Under section 66 of the Courts Act 2003, a Circuit judge can exercise the power to issue a warrant.

Under section 16(3) of the Police and Criminal Evidence Act 1984, entry and search under a warrant must be within 3 months from the date of its issue.

The Practice Direction sets out forms of application and warrant for use in connection with this rule.]

47.30 *Application for warrant under paragraph 12 of Schedule 1 to the Police and Criminal Evidence Act 1984*   (1)   This rule applies where an applicant wants a Circuit judge to issue a warrant or warrants under paragraph 12 of Schedule 1 to the Police and Criminal Evidence Act 1984.

(2)   As well as complying with rule 47.26, the application must—

(a)   specify the offence under investigation (and see paragraph (3)(a));

(b)   specify the set of access conditions on which the applicant relies (and see paragraphs (3) and (4));

(c)   so far as practicable, identify the material sought;

(d)   specify the premises to be searched (and see paragraphs (6) and (7)); and

(e)   state whether the applicant wants other persons to accompany the officers executing the warrant or warrants (and see paragraph (8)).

(3)   Where the applicant relies on paragraph 2 of Schedule 1 to the Police and Criminal Evidence Act 1984 ('the first set of access conditions': general power to gain access to special procedure material), the application must—

(a)   specify the indictable offence under investigation;

(b)   explain the grounds for believing that the offence has been committed;

(c)   explain the grounds for believing that the material sought—

(i)   is likely to be of substantial value to the investigation (whether by itself, or together with other material),

(ii)   is likely to be admissible evidence at trial for the offence under investigation, and

(iii)   does not consist of or include items subject to legal privilege or excluded material;

(d)   explain what other methods of obtaining the material—

(i)   have been tried without success, or

(ii)   have not been tried because they appeared bound to fail; and

(e)   explain why it is in the public interest to obtain the material, having regard to—

(i)   the benefit likely to accrue to the investigation if the material is obtained, and

(ii)   the circumstances under which the material is held.

(4)   Where the applicant relies on paragraph 3 of Schedule 1 to the Police and Criminal Evidence Act 1984 ('the second set of access conditions': use of search warrant power to gain access to excluded or special procedure material), the application must—

(a)   state the legislation under which a search warrant could have been issued, had the material sought not been excluded or special procedure material (in this paragraph, described as 'the main search power');

(b)   include or attach the terms of the main search power;

(c)   explain how the circumstances would have satisfied any criteria prescribed by the main search power for the issue of a search warrant;

(d)   explain why the issue of such a search warrant would have been appropriate.

(5)   Where the applicant relies on the second set of access conditions and on an assertion that a production order made under paragraph 4 of Schedule 1 to the 1984 Act in respect of the material sought has not been complied with—

(a)   the application must—

(i)   identify that order and describe its terms, and

(ii)   specify the date on which it was served; but

(b)   the application need not comply with paragraphs (6) or (7).

(6)   In relation to premises which the applicant wants to be searched and can specify, the application must (unless paragraph (5) applies)—

(a)   specify each set of premises;

(b)   in respect of each set of premises, explain the grounds for believing that material sought is on those premises; and

(c)   in respect of each set of premises, explain the grounds for believing that—

    (i)   it is not practicable to communicate with any person entitled to grant entry to the premises,

    (ii)   it is practicable to communicate with such a person but it is not practicable to communicate with any person entitled to grant access to the material sought,

    (iii)   the material sought contains information which is subject to a restriction on disclosure or an obligation of secrecy contained in an enactment and is likely to be disclosed in breach of the restriction or obligation if a warrant is not issued, or

    (iv)   service of notice of an application for a production order under paragraph 4 of Schedule 1 to the 1984 Act may seriously prejudice the investigation.

(7)   In relation to premises which the applicant wants to be searched but at least some of which the applicant cannot specify, the application must (unless paragraph (5) applies)—

(a)   explain the grounds for believing that—

    (i)   because of the particulars of the offence under investigation it is necessary to search any premises occupied or controlled by a specified person, and

    (ii)   it is not reasonably practicable to specify all the premises which that person occupies or controls which might need to be searched;

(b)   specify as many sets of premises as is reasonably practicable;

(c)   in respect of each set of premises, whether specified or not, explain the grounds for believing that material sought is on those premises; and

(d)   in respect of each specified set of premises, explain the grounds for believing that—

    (i)   it is not practicable to communicate with any person entitled to grant entry to the premises,

    (ii)   it is practicable to communicate with such a person but it is not practicable to communicate with any person entitled to grant access to the material sought,

    (iii)   the material sought contains information which is subject to a restriction on disclosure or an obligation of secrecy contained in an enactment and is likely to be disclosed in breach of the restriction or obligation if a warrant is not issued, or

    (iv)   service of notice of an application for a production order under paragraph 4 of Schedule 1 to the 1984 Act may seriously prejudice the investigation.

(8)   In relation to any set of premises which the applicant wants to be searched by the officers executing the warrant with other persons authorised by the court, the application must—

(a)   identify those other persons, by function or description; and

(b)   explain why those persons are required.

[Note. Under paragraph 12 of Schedule 1 to the Police and Criminal Evidenced Act 1984, where the conditions listed in that paragraph and, if applicable, in paragraphs 12A and 14 of that Schedule are fulfilled a constable may apply to a Circuit judge for a warrant authorising a search for evidence consisting of special procedure material or, in some cases, excluded material on specified premises or on the premises of a specified person.

Under section 16(3) of the 1984 Act, entry and search under a warrant must be within 3 months from the date of its issue.

See also the code of practice for the search of premises issued under section 66 of the 1984 Act.

The Practice Direction sets out forms of application and warrant for use in connection with this rule.]

47.31 *Application for warrant under paragraph 11 of Schedule 5 to the Terrorism Act 2000*

(1)   This rule applies where an applicant wants a Circuit judge to issue a warrant or warrants under paragraph 11 of Schedule 5 to the Terrorism Act 2000.

(2)   As well as complying with rule 47.26, the application must—

(a)   specify the offence under investigation;

(b)   explain how the investigation constitutes a terrorist investigation within the meaning of the Terrorism Act 2000;

(c)   so far as practicable, identify the material sought (and see paragraph (4));

(d)   specify the premises to be searched (and see paragraph (5)); and

(e)   state whether the applicant wants other persons to accompany the officers executing the warrant or warrants (and see paragraph (6)).

(3)   Where the applicant relies on an assertion that a production order made under paragraph 5 of Schedule 5 to the 2000 Act in respect of material on the premises has not been complied with—

(a)   the application must—

    (i)   identify that order and describe its terms, and

    (ii)   specify the date on which it was served; but

(b)   the application need not comply with paragraphs (4) or (5)(b).

(4)   In relation to the material sought, unless paragraph (3) applies the application must explain the grounds for believing that—

(a)   the material consists of or includes excluded material or special procedure material but does not include items subject to legal privilege;

(b)   the material is likely to be of substantial value to a terrorist investigation (whether by itself, or together with other material); and

(c)   it is not appropriate to make an order under paragraph 5 of Schedule 11 to the 2000 Act in relation to the material because—

    (i)   it is not practicable to communicate with any person entitled to produce the material,

(ii)   it is not practicable to communicate with any person entitled to grant access to the material or entitled to grant entry to premises to which the application for the warrant relates, or

(iii)   a terrorist investigation may be seriously prejudiced unless a constable can secure immediate access to the material.

(5)   In relation to the premises which the applicant wants to be searched, the application must—

(a)   specify—

    (i)   where paragraph (3) applies, the respondent and any premises to which the production order referred, or

    (ii)   in any other case, one or more sets of premises, or any premises occupied or controlled by a specified person (which may include one or more specified sets of premises); and

(b)   unless paragraph (3) applies, in relation to premises which the applicant wants to be searched but cannot specify, explain why—

    (i)   it is necessary to search any premises occupied or controlled by the specified person, and

    (ii)   it is not reasonably practicable to specify all the premises which that person occupies or controls which might need to be searched;

(c)   explain the grounds for believing that material sought is on those premises.

(6)   In relation to any set of premises which the applicant wants to be searched by the officers executing the warrant with other persons authorised by the court, the application must—

(a)   identify those other persons, by function or description; and

(b)   explain why those persons are required.

[Note. Under paragraph 11 of Schedule 5 to the Terrorism Act 2000, where the conditions listed in that paragraph and in paragraph 12 of that Schedule are fulfilled a constable may apply to a Circuit judge for a warrant authorising a search for material consisting of excluded material or special procedure material on specified premises or on the premises of a specified person.

Under section 16(3) of the 1984 Act, entry and search under a warrant must be within 3 months from the date of its issue.

See also the code of practice for the search of premises issued under section 66 of the 1984 Act.

The Practice Direction sets out forms of application and warrant for use in connection with this rule.]

47.32   *Application for warrant under section 352 of the Proceeds of Crime Act 2002*   (1)   This rule applies where an applicant wants a Crown Court judge to issue a warrant or warrants under—

(a)   section 352 of the Proceeds of Crime Act 2002; or

(b)   article 13 of the Proceeds of Crime Act 2002 (External Investigations) Order 2014.

(2)   As well as complying with rule 47.26, the application must—

(a)   explain whether the investigation is a confiscation investigation, a money laundering investigation, a detained cash investigation, a detained property investigation, a frozen funds investigation or an external investigation;

(b)   in the case of an investigation in the United Kingdom, explain why the applicant suspects that—

    (i)   the person under investigation has benefited from criminal conduct, in the case of a confiscation investigation, or committed a money laundering offence, in the case of a money laundering investigation, or

    (ii)   in the case of a detained cash investigation, a detained property investigation or a frozen funds investigation, the cash or property involved, or the money held in the frozen account, was obtained through unlawful conduct or is intended to be used in unlawful conduct;

(c)   in the case of an investigation outside the United Kingdom, explain why the applicant believes that—

    (i)   there is an investigation by an overseas authority which relates to a criminal investigation or to criminal proceedings (including proceedings to remove the benefit of a person's criminal conduct following that person's conviction), and

    (ii)   the investigation is into whether property has been obtained as a result of or in connection with criminal conduct, or into the extent or whereabouts of such property;

(d)   indicate what material is sought (and see paragraphs (4) and (5));

(e)   specify the premises to be searched (and see paragraph (6)); and

(f)   state whether the applicant wants other persons to accompany the officers executing the warrant or warrants (and see paragraph (7)).

(3)   Where the applicant relies on an assertion that a production order made under sections 345 and 351 of the 2002 Act or under articles 6 and 12 of the 2014 Order has not been complied with—

(a)   the application must—

    (i)   identify that order and describe its terms,

    (ii)   specify the date on which it was served, and

    (iii)   explain the grounds for believing that the material in respect of which the order was made is on the premises specified in the application for the warrant; but

(b)   the application need not comply with paragraphs (4) or (5).

(4)   Unless paragraph (3) applies, in relation to the material sought the application must—

(a)   specify the material; or

(b)   give a general description of the material and explain the grounds for believing that it relates to the person under investigation and—

(i)   in the case of a confiscation investigation, relates to the question whether that person has benefited from criminal conduct, or to any question about the extent or whereabouts of that benefit,

(ii)   in the case of a money laundering investigation, relates to the question whether that person has committed a money laundering offence,

(iii)   in the case of a detained cash investigation into the derivation of cash, relates to the question whether that cash is recoverable property,

(iv)   in the case of a detained cash investigation, a detained property investigation or a frozen funds investigation into the intended use of cash, property or money, relates to the question whether that cash, property or money is intended by any person to be used in unlawful conduct,

(v)   in the case of an investigation outside the United Kingdom, relates to that investigation.

(5)   Unless paragraph (3) applies, in relation to the material sought the application must explain also the grounds for believing that—

(a)   the material consists of or includes special procedure material but does not include excluded material or privileged material;

(b)   the material is likely to be of substantial value to the investigation (whether by itself, or together with other material); and

(c)   it is in the public interest for the material to be obtained, having regard to—

(i)   other potential sources of information,

(ii)   the benefit likely to accrue to the investigation if the material is obtained.

(6)   In relation to the premises which the applicant wants to be searched, unless paragraph (3) applies the application must—

(a)   explain the grounds for believing that material sought is on those premises;

(b)   if the application specifies the material sought, explain the grounds for believing that it is not appropriate to make a production order under sections 345 and 351 of the 2002 Act or under articles 6 and 12 of the 2014 Order because—

(i)   it is not practicable to communicate with any person against whom the production order could be made,

(ii)   it is not practicable to communicate with any person who would be required to comply with an order to grant entry to the premises, or

(iii)   the investigation might be seriously prejudiced unless an appropriate person is able to secure immediate access to the material;

(c)   if the application gives a general description of the material sought, explain the grounds for believing that—

(i)   it is not practicable to communicate with any person entitled to grant entry to the premises,

(ii)   entry to the premises will not be granted unless a warrant is produced, or

(iii)   the investigation might be seriously prejudiced unless an appropriate person arriving at the premises is able to secure immediate access to them;

(7)   In relation to any set of premises which the applicant wants to be searched by those executing the warrant with other persons authorised by the court, the application must—

(a)   identify those other persons, by function or description; and

(b)   explain why those persons are required.

[Note. Under section 352 of the Proceeds of Crime Act 2002 where there is a confiscation investigation, a money laundering investigation or, a detained cash investigation, a detained property investigation or a frozen funds investigation"an 'appropriate officer' within the meaning of that section may apply to a Crown Court judge for a warrant authorising a search for special procedure material on specified premises, on the conditions listed in that section and in section 353 of the Act.

Under article 13 of the Proceeds of Crime Act 2002 (External Investigations) Order 2014, where there is an external investigation an 'appropriate officer' within the meaning of that article may apply to a Crown Court judge for a warrant authorising a search for special procedure material on specified premises, on the conditions listed in that article and in article 14 of the Order.

Under section 16(3) of the 1984 Act, as applied by article 3 of the Proceeds of Crime Act 2002 (Application of Police and Criminal Evidence Act 1984) Order 2015, entry and search under a warrant must be within 3 months from the date of its issue.

See also the code of practice for the search of premises issued under section 66 of the 1984 Act. The Practice Direction sets out forms of application and warrant for use in connection with this rule.]

47.33 *Application for warrant under section 160 of the Extradition Act 2003* (1) This rule applies where an applicant wants a Circuit judge to issue a warrant or warrants under section 160 of the Extradition Act 2003.

(2)   As well as complying with rule 47.26, the application must—

(a)   identify the person whose extradition is sought (and see paragraph (3));

(b)   specify the extradition offence of which that person is accused;

(c)   specify the material, or description of material, sought (and see paragraph (4)); and

(d)   specify the premises to be searched (and see paragraph (5)).

(3)   In relation to the person whose extradition is sought, the application must explain the grounds for believing that—

(a)   that person has committed the offence for which extradition is sought;

(b)   that offence is an extradition offence; and

(c)   that person is in the United Kingdom or is on the way to the United Kingdom.

(4)   In relation to the material sought, the application must explain the grounds for believing that—

(a)   the material consists of or includes special procedure or excluded material; and

(b)   the material would be likely to be admissible evidence at a trial in England and Wales for the offence for which extradition is sought.

(5)   In relation to the premises which the applicant wants to search, the application must explain the grounds for believing that—

(a)   material sought is on those premises;

(b)   one or more of the following conditions is satisfied, namely—

    (i)   it is not practicable to communicate with any person entitled to grant entry to the premises,

    (ii)   it is practicable to communicate with such a person but it is not practicable to communicate with any person entitled to grant access to the material sought, or

    (iii)   the material contains information which is subject to a restriction on disclosure or an obligation of secrecy contained in an enactment and is likely to be disclosed in breach of the restriction or obligation if a warrant is not issued.

(6)   In relation to any set of premises which the applicant wants to be searched by the officers executing the warrant with other persons authorised by the court, the application must—

(a)   identify those other persons, by function or description; and

(b)   explain why those persons are required.

[Note. Under section 160 of the Extradition Act 2003, where a person's extradition is sought a constable may apply to a Circuit judge for a warrant authorising a search for special procedure material or excluded material on specified premises, on the conditions listed in that section.

Under section 16(3) of the 1984 Act, entry and search under a warrant must be within 3 months from the date of its issue.

See also the code of practice for the search of premises issued under section 66 of the 1984 Act.

47.34 *Application for warrant under any other power*   (1)   This rule applies—

(a)   where an applicant wants a court to issue a warrant or warrants under a power (in this rule, 'the relevant search power') to which rule 47.24(d) (other powers) refers; but

(b)   subject to any inconsistent provision in legislation that applies to the relevant search power.

(2)   As well as complying with rule 47.26, the application must—

(a)   demonstrate the applicant's entitlement to apply;

(b)   identify the relevant search power (and see paragraph (3));

(c)   so far as practicable, identify the articles or persons sought (and see paragraph (4));

(d)   specify the premises to be searched (and see paragraphs (5) and (6));

(e)   state whether the applicant wants the premises to be searched on more than one occasion, if the relevant search power allows (and see paragraph (7)); and

(f)   state whether the applicant wants other persons to accompany the officers executing the warrant or warrants, if the relevant search power allows (and see paragraph (8)).

(3)   The application must—

(a)   include or attach the terms of the relevant search power; and

(b)   explain how the circumstances satisfy the criteria prescribed by that power for making the application.

(4)   In relation to the articles or persons sought, the application must explain how they satisfy the criteria prescribed by the relevant search power about such articles or persons.

(5)   In relation to premises which the applicant wants to be searched and can specify, the application must—

(a)   specify each set of premises; and

(b)   in respect of each, explain how the circumstances satisfy any criteria prescribed by the relevant search power—

    (i)   for asserting that the articles or persons sought are on those premises, and

    (ii)   for asserting that the court can exercise its power to authorise the search of those particular premises.

(6)   In relation to premises which the applicant wants to be searched but at least some of which the applicant cannot specify, the application must—

(a)   explain how the relevant search power allows the court to authorise such searching;

(b)   specify the person who occupies or controls such premises;

(c)   specify as many sets of such premises as is reasonably practicable;

(d)   explain why—

    (i)   it is necessary to search more premises than those specified, and

    (ii)   it is not reasonably practicable to specify all the premises which the applicant wants to be searched;

(e) in respect of each set of premises, whether specified or not, explain how the circumstances satisfy any criteria prescribed by the relevant search power for asserting that the articles or persons sought are on those premises; and

(f) in respect of each specified set of premises, explain how the circumstances satisfy any criteria prescribed by the relevant search power for asserting that the court can exercise its power to authorise the search of those premises.

(7) In relation to any set of premises which the applicant wants to be searched on more than one occasion, the application must—

(a) explain how the relevant search power allows the court to authorise such searching;

(b) explain why the applicant wants the premises to be searched more than once; and

(c) specify any proposed maximum number of occasions.

(8) In relation to any set of premises which the applicant wants to be searched by the officers executing the warrant with other persons authorised by the court, the application must—

(a) identify those other persons, by function or description; and

(b) explain why those persons are required.

[Note. See, among other provisions, sections 15 and 16 of the Police and Criminal Evidence Act 1984, which apply to an application by a constable under any Act for a warrant authorising the search of specified premises, or the search of premises of a specified person, and to the execution of such a warrant. Unless other legislation otherwise provides, under section 16(3) of the 1984 Act entry and search under a warrant must be within 3 months from the date of its issue.

The Practice Direction sets out forms of application and warrant for use in connection with this rule.]

SECTION 4: ORDERS FOR THE RETENTION OR RETURN OF PROPERTY

47.35 *When this Section applies* (1) This Section applies where—

(a) under section 1 of the Police (Property) Act 1897, a magistrates' court can—

    (i) order the return to the owner of property which has come into the possession of the police or the National Crime Agency in connection with an investigation of a suspected offence, or

    (ii) make such order with respect to such property as the court thinks just, where the owner cannot be ascertained;

(b) a Crown Court judge can—

    (i) order the return of seized property under section 59(4) of the Criminal Justice and Police Act 2001, or

    (ii) order the examination, retention, separation or return of seized property under section 59(5) of the Act.

(2) In this Section, a reference to a person with 'a relevant interest' in seized property means someone from whom the property was seized, or someone with a proprietary interest in the property, or someone who had custody or control of it immediately before it was seized.

47.36 *Exercise of court's powers* (1) The court may determine an application for an order—

(a) at a hearing (which must be in private unless the court otherwise directs), or without a hearing;

(b) in a party's absence, if that party—

    (i) applied for the order, or

    (ii) has had at least 14 days in which to make representations.

(2) The court officer must arrange for the court to hear such an application no sooner than 14 days after it was served, unless—

(a) the court directs that no hearing need be arranged; or

(b) the court gives other directions for the hearing.

(3) If the court so directs, the parties to an application may attend a hearing by live link or telephone.

(4) The court may—

(a) shorten or extend (even after it has expired) a time limit under this Section;

(b) dispense with a requirement for service under this Section (even after service was required); and

(c) consider an application made orally instead of in writing.

(5) A person who wants an extension of time must—

(a) apply when serving the application or representations for which it is needed; and

(b) explain the delay.

47.37 *Application for an order under section 1 of the Police (Property) Act 1897* (1) This rule applies where an applicant wants the court to make an order to which rule 47.35(1)(a) refers.

(2) The applicant must apply in writing and serve the application on—

(a) the court officer; and

(b) as appropriate—

    (i) the officer who has the property,

    (ii) any person who appears to be its owner.

(3) The application must—

(a) explain the applicant's interest in the property (either as a person who claims to be its owner or as an officer into whose possession the property has come);

(b) specify the direction that the applicant wants the court to make, and explain why; and

(c)   include or attach a list of those on whom the applicant has served the application.

[Note. Under section 1 of the Police (Property) Act 1897, the owner of property which has come into the possession of the police or the National Crime Agency in connection with the investigation of a suspected offence can apply to a magistrates' court for an order for its delivery to the claimant.]

47.38 *Application for an order under section 59 of the Criminal Justice and Police Act 2001*
(1)   This rule applies where an applicant wants the court to make an order to which rule 47.35(1)(b) refers.
(2)   The applicant must apply in writing and serve the application on—
(a)   the court officer; and
(b)   as appropriate—
     (i)   the person who for the time being has the seized property,
     (ii)   each person whom the applicant knows or believes to have a relevant interest in the property.
(3)   In each case, the application must—
(a)   explain the applicant's interest in the property (either as a person with a relevant interest, or as possessor of the property in consequence of its seizure, as appropriate);
(b)   explain the circumstances of the seizure of the property and identify the power that was exercised to seize it (or which the person seizing it purported to exercise, as appropriate); and
(c)   include or attach a list of those on whom the applicant has served the application.
(4)   On an application for an order for the return of property under section 59(4) of the Criminal Justice and Police Act 2001, the application must explain why any one or more of these applies—
(a)   there was no power to make the seizure;
(b)   the property seized is, or contains, an item subject to legal privilege which is not an item that can be retained lawfully in the circumstances listed in section 54(2) of the Act;
(c)   the property seized is, or contains, excluded or special procedure material which is not material that can be retained lawfully in the circumstances listed in sections 55 and 56 of the Act;
(d)   the property seized is, or contains, something taken from premises under section 50 of the Act, or from a person under section 51 of the Act, in the circumstances listed in those sections and which cannot lawfully be retained on the conditions listed in the Act.
(5)   On an application for an order for the examination, retention, separation or return of property under section 59(5) of the 2001 Act, the application must—
(a)   specify the direction that the applicant wants the court to make, and explain why;
(b)   if applicable, specify each requirement of section 53(2) of the Act (examination and return of property) which is not being complied with;
(c)   if applicable, explain why the retention of the property by the person who now has it would be justified on the grounds that, even if it were returned, it would immediately become appropriate for that person to get it back under—
     (i)   a warrant for its seizure, or
     (ii)   a production order made under paragraph 4 of Schedule 1 to the Police and Criminal Evidence Act 1984, section 20BA of the Taxes Management Act 1970 or paragraph 5 of Schedule 5 to the Terrorism Act 2000.

[Note. Under section 59 of the Criminal Justice and Police Act 2001, a person with a 'relevant interest' (see rule 47.35(2)) in seized property can apply in the circumstances listed in the Act to a Crown Court judge for an order for its return. A person who has the property in consequence of its seizure can apply for an order authorising its retention. Either can apply for an order relating to the examination of the property.]

47.39 *Application containing information withheld from another party* (1) This rule applies where—
(a)   an applicant serves an application to which rule 47.37 (Application for an order under section 1 of the Police (Property) Act 1897) or rule 47.38 (Application for an order under section 59 of the Criminal Justice and Police Act 2001) applies; and
(b)   the application includes information that the applicant thinks ought not be revealed to another party.
(2)   The applicant must—
(a)   omit that information from the part of the application that is served on that other party;
(b)   mark the other part to show that, unless the court otherwise directs, it is only for the court; and
(c)   in that other part, explain why the applicant has withheld that information from that other party.
(3)   If the court so directs, any hearing of an application to which this rule applies may be, wholly or in part, in the absence of a party from whom information has been withheld.
(4)   At any hearing of an application to which this rule applies—
(a)   the general rule is that the court must consider, in the following sequence—
     (i)   representations first by the applicant and then by each other party, in all the parties' presence, and then
     (ii)   further representations by the applicant, in the absence of a party from whom information has been withheld; but
(b)   the court may direct other arrangements for the hearing.

47.40 *Representations in response* (1) This rule applies where a person wants to make

representations about an application under rule 47.37 or rule 47.38.
(2)   Such a person must—
(a)   serve the representations on—
    (i)   the court officer, and
    (ii)   the applicant and any other party to the application;
(b)   do so not more than 14 days after service of the application; and
(c)   ask for a hearing, if that person wants one.
(3)   Representations in opposition to an application must explain why the grounds on which the applicant relies are not met.
(4)   Where representations include information that the person making them thinks ought not be revealed to another party, that person must—
(a)   omit that information from the representations served on that other party;
(b)   mark the information to show that, unless the court otherwise directs, it is only for the court; and
(c)   with that information include an explanation of why it has been withheld from that other party.

47.41 *Application to punish for contempt of court*   (1)   This rule applies where a person is accused of disobeying an order under section 59 of the Criminal Justice and Police Act 2001.
(2)   A person who wants the court to exercise its power to punish that person for contempt of court must comply with the rules in Part 48 (Contempt of court).
[Note. A Crown Court judge has power to punish a person who disobeys an order under section 59 of the 2001 Act as if that were a contempt of the Crown Court: see section 59(9) of the Act.]

SECTION 5: ORDERS FOR THE RETENTION OF FINGERPRINTS, ETC

47.42 *When this Section applies*   This Section applies where—
(a)   a District Judge (Magistrates' Court) can make an order under—
    (i)   section 63F(7) or 63R(6) of the Police and Criminal Evidence Act 1984, or
    (ii)   paragraph 20B(5) or 20G(6) of Schedule 8 to the Terrorism Act 2000;
(b)   the Crown Court can determine an appeal under—
    (i)   section 63F(10) of the Police and Criminal Evidence Act 1984, or
    (ii)   paragraph 20B(8) of Schedule 8 to the Terrorism Act 2000.
[Note. Under the Police and Criminal Evidence Act 1984 or under the Terrorism Act 2000, an order may be made extending the period during which fingerprints, DNA profiles or samples may be retained by the police.]

47.43 *Exercise of court's powers*   (1)   The court must determine an application under rule 47.44, and an appeal under rule 47.45—
(a)   at a hearing, which must be in private unless the court otherwise directs; and
(b)   in the presence of the applicant or appellant.
(2)   The court must not determine such an application or appeal unless any person served under those rules—
(a)   is present; or
(b)   has had an opportunity—
    (i)   to attend, or
    (ii)   to make representations.

47.44 *Application to extend retention period*   (1)   This rule applies where a magistrates' court can make an order extending the period for which there may be retained material consisting of—
(a)   fingerprints taken from a person—
    (i)   under a power conferred by Part V of the Police and Criminal Evidence Act 1984,
    (ii)   with that person's consent, in connection with the investigation of an offence by the police, or
    (iii)   under a power conferred by Schedule 8 to the Terrorism Act 2000 in relation to a person detained under section 41 of that Act;
(b)   a DNA profile derived from a DNA sample so taken; or
(c)   a sample so taken.
(2)   A chief officer of police who wants the court to make such an order must—
(a)   apply in writing—
    (i)   within the period of 3 months ending on the last day of the retention period, where the application relates to fingerprints or a DNA profile, or
    (ii)   before the expiry of the retention period, where the application relates to a sample;
(b)   in the application—
    (i)   identify the material,
    (ii)   state when the retention period expires,
    (iii)   give details of any previous such application relating to the material, and
    (iv)   outline the circumstances in which the material was acquired;
(c)   serve the application on the court officer, in every case; and
(d)   serve the application on the person from whom the material was taken, where—
    (i)   the application relates to fingerprints or a DNA profile, or
    (ii)   the application is for the renewal of an order extending the retention period for a

sample.

(3) An application to extend the retention period for fingerprints or a DNA profile must explain why that period should be extended.

(4) An application to extend the retention period for a sample must explain why, having regard to the nature and complexity of other material that is evidence in relation to the offence, the sample is likely to be needed in any proceedings for the offence for the purposes of—

(a) disclosure to, or use by, a defendant; or

(b) responding to any challenge by a defendant in respect of the admissibility of material that is evidence on which the prosecution proposes to rely.

(5) On an application to extend the retention period for fingerprints or a DNA profile, the applicant must serve notice of the court's decision on any respondent where—

(a) the court makes the order sought; and

(b) the respondent was absent when it was made.

[Note. See rule 47.42(a). The powers to which rule 47.44 applies may be exercised only by a District Judge (Magistrates' Courts).

The time limits for making an application under this rule are prescribed by sections 63F(8) and 63R(8) of the Police and Criminal Evidence Act 1984, and by paragraphs 20B(6) and 20G(8) of Schedule 8 to the Terrorism Act 2000. They may be neither extended nor shortened.

Sections 63D and 63R of the 1984 Act, and paragraphs 20A and 20G of Schedule 8 to the 2000 Act, provide for the circumstances in which there must be destroyed the material to which this rule applies.

Section 63F of the 1984 Act, and paragraph 20B of Schedule 8 to the 2000 Act, provide for the circumstances in which fingerprints and DNA profiles may be retained instead of being destroyed. Under section 63F(7) and paragraph 20B(5), a chief officer of police to whom those provisions apply may apply for an order extending the statutory retention period of 3 years by up to another 2 years.

Section 63R of the 1984 Act and paragraph 20G of Schedule 8 to the 2000 Act provide for the circumstances in which samples taken from a person may be retained instead of being destroyed. Under section 63R(6) of the 1984 Act and paragraph 20G(6) of Schedule 8 to the 2000 Act, a chief officer of police to whom those provisions apply may apply for an order to retain a sample for up to 12 months after the date on which it would otherwise have to be destroyed. Under section 63R(9) and paragraph 20G(9), such an order may be renewed, on one or more occasions, for a further period of not more than 12 months from the end of the period when the order would otherwise cease to have effect.]

47.45 *Appeal* (1) This rule applies where, under rule 47.44, a magistrates' court determines an application relating to fingerprints or a DNA profile and—

(a) the person from whom the material was taken wants to appeal to the Crown Court against an order extending the retention period; or

(b) a chief officer of police wants to appeal to the Crown Court against a refusal to make such an order.

(2) The appellant must—

(a) serve an appeal notice—

(i) on the Crown Court officer and on the other party, and

(ii) not more than 21 days after the magistrates' court's decision, or, if applicable, service of notice under rule 47.44(5); and

(b) in the appeal notice, explain, as appropriate, why the retention period should, or should not, be extended.

(3) Rule 34.11 (Constitution of the Crown Court) applies on such an appeal.

[Note. Under section 63F(10) of the Police and Criminal Evidence Act 1984, and under paragraph 20B(8) of Schedule 8 to the Terrorism Act 2000, the person from whom fingerprints were taken, or from whom a DNA profile derives, may appeal to the Crown Court against an order extending the retention period; and a chief officer of police may appeal to the Crown Court against the refusal of such an order.]

SECTION 6: INVESTIGATION ANONYMITY ORDERS UNDER THE CORONERS AND JUSTICE ACT 2009

47.46 *When this Section applies* This Section applies where—

(a) a justice of the peace can make or discharge an investigation anonymity order, under sections 76 and 80(1) of the Coroners and Justice Act 2009;

(b) a Crown Court judge can determine an appeal against—

(i) a refusal of such an order, under section 79 of the 2009 Act,

(ii) a decision on an application to discharge such an order, under section 80(6) of the 2009 Act.

[Note. Under the Coroners and Justice Act 2009, an investigation anonymity order may be made prohibiting the disclosure of information that identifies, or might identify, a specified person as someone who is, or was, willing to assist the investigation of an offence of murder or manslaughter caused by a gun or knife.]

47.47 *Exercise of court's powers* (1) The court may determine an application for an investigation anonymity order, and any appeal against the refusal of such an order—

(a) at a hearing (which must be in private unless the court otherwise directs); or

(b)   without a hearing.

(2)   The court must determine an application to discharge an investigation anonymity order, and any appeal against the decision on such an application—

(a)   at a hearing (which must be in private unless the court otherwise directs); and

(b)   in the presence of the person specified in the order, unless—

      (i)   that person applied for the discharge of the order,

      (ii)   that person has had an opportunity to make representations, or

      (iii)   the court is satisfied that it is not reasonably practicable to communicate with that person.

(3)   The court may consider an application or an appeal made orally instead of in writing.

47.48 *Application for an investigation anonymity order* (1)   This rule applies where an applicant wants a magistrates' court to make an investigation anonymity order.

(2)   The applicant must—

(a)   apply in writing;

(b)   serve the application on the court officer;

(c)   identify the person to be specified in the order, unless—

      (i)   the applicant wants the court to determine the application at a hearing, or

      (ii)   the court otherwise directs;

(d)   explain how the proposed order meets the conditions prescribed by section 78 of the Coroners and Justice Act 2009;

(e)   say if the applicant intends to appeal should the court refuse the order;

(f)   attach any material on which the applicant relies; and

(g)   propose the terms of the order.

(3)   At any hearing of the application, the applicant must—

(a)   identify to the court the person to be specified in the order, unless—

      (i)   the applicant has done so already, or

      (ii)   the court otherwise directs; and

(b)   unless the applicant has done so already, inform the court if the applicant intends to appeal should the court refuse the order.

[Note. See section 77 of the Coroners and Justice Act 2009.]

47.49 *Application to discharge an investigation anonymity order* (1)   This rule applies where one of the following wants a magistrates' court to discharge an investigation anonymity order—

(a)   an applicant; or

(b)   the person specified in the order.

(2)   That applicant or the specified person must—

(a)   apply in writing as soon as practicable after becoming aware of the grounds for doing so;

(b)   serve the application on—

      (i)   the court officer, and as applicable

      (ii)   the applicant for the order, and

      (iii)   the specified person;

(c)   explain—

      (i)   what material circumstances have changed since the order was made, or since any previous application was made to discharge it, and

      (ii)   why it is appropriate for the order to be discharged; and

(d)   attach—

      (i)   a copy of the order, and

      (ii)   any material on which the applicant relies.

(3)   A party must inform the court if that party intends to appeal should the court discharge the order.

[Note. See section 80 of the Coroners and Justice Act 2009.]

47.50 *Appeal* (1)   This rule applies where one of the following ('the appellant') wants to appeal to the Crown Court—

(a)   the applicant for an investigation anonymity order, where a magistrates' court has refused to make the order;

(b)   a party to an application to discharge such an order, where a magistrates' court has decided that application.

(2)   The appellant must—

(a)   serve on the Crown Court officer a copy of the application to the magistrates' court; and

(b)   where the appeal concerns a discharge decision, notify each other party,

not more than 21 days after the decision against which the appellant wants to appeal.

(3)   The Crown Court must hear the appeal without justices of the peace.

[Note. See sections 79 and 80(6) of the Coroners and Justice Act 2009, and section 74 of the Senior Courts Act 1981.]

SECTION 7: INVESTIGATION APPROVAL ORDERS UNDER THE REGULATION OF INVESTIGATORY POWERS ACT 2000

47.51 *When this Section applies* This Section applies where a justice of the peace can make an order approving—

(a) the grant or renewal of an authorisation, or the giving or renewal of a notice, under section 23A of the Regulation of Investigatory Powers Act 2000;

(b) the grant or renewal of an authorisation under section 32A of the 2000 Act.

[Note. Under the Regulation of Investigatory Powers Act 2000, an order may be made approving a local authority officer's authorisation for the obtaining of information about the use of postal or telecommunications services, or for the use of surveillance or of a 'covert human intelligence source'.]

47.52 *Exercise of court's powers* (1) Rule 47.5 (Investigation orders; Exercise of court's powers) applies, subject to sections 23B(2) and 32B(2) of the Regulation of Investigatory Powers Act 2000.

(2) Where a magistrates' court refuses to approve the grant, giving or renewal of an authorisation or notice, the court must not exercise its power to quash that authorisation or notice unless the applicant has had at least 2 business days from the date of the refusal in which to make representations.

[Note. Under sections 23B(2) and 32B(2) of the Regulation of Investigatory Powers Act 2000, the applicant is not required to give notice of an application to any person to whom the authorisation or notice relates, or to such a person's legal representatives. See also sections 23B(3) and 32B(3) of the 2000 Act.];

47.53 *Application for approval for authorisation or notice* (1) This rule applies where an applicant wants a magistrates' court to make an order approving—

(a) under sections 23A and 23B of the Regulation of Investigatory Powers Act 2000—

    (i) an authorisation to obtain or disclose communications data, under section 22(3) of the 2000 Act, or

    (ii) a notice that requires a postal or telecommunications operator if need be to obtain, and in any case to disclose, communications data, under section 22(4) of the 2000 Act;

(b) under sections 32A and 32B of the Regulation of Investigatory Powers Act 2000, an authorisation for—

    (i) the carrying out of directed surveillance, under section 28 of the 2000 Act, or

    (ii) the conduct or use of a covert human intelligence source, under section 29 of the 2000 Act.

(2) The applicant must—

(a) apply in writing and serve the application on the court officer;

(b) attach the authorisation or notice which the applicant wants the court to approve;

(c) attach such other material (if any) on which the applicant relies to satisfy the court—

    (i) as required by section 23A(3) and (4) of the 2000 Act, in relation to communications data,

    (ii) as required by section 32A(3) and (4) of the 2000 Act, in relation to directed surveillance, or

    (iii) as required by section 32A(5) and (6), and, if relevant, section 43(6A), of the 2000 Act, in relation to a covert human intelligence source; and

(d) propose the terms of the order.

[Note. See also rule 47.5, under which the court may—

(a) exercise its powers in the parties' absence; and

(b) consider an application made orally.

Under section 23A(3) to (5) of the Regulation of Investigatory Powers Act 2000, on an application for an order approving an authorisation or notice concerning communications data (as defined in section 21 of the Act), the court must be satisfied that—

(a) the person who granted or renewed the authorisation, or who gave or renewed the notice, was entitled to do so;

(b) the grant, giving or renewal met any prescribed restrictions or conditions;

(c) at the time the authorisation or notice was granted, given or renewed, as the case may be, there were reasonable grounds for believing that to obtain or disclose the data described in the authorisation or notice was—

    (i) necessary, for the purpose of preventing or detecting crime or preventing disorder, and

    (ii) proportionate to what was sought to be achieved by doing so; and

(d) there remain reasonable grounds for believing those things, at the time the court considers the application.

The Regulation of Investigatory Powers (Communications Data) Order 2010 specifies the persons who are entitled to grant, give or renew an authorisation or notice concerning such data, and for what purpose each may do so.

Under section 32A(3) and (4) of the Regulation of Investigatory Powers Act 2000, on an application for an order approving an authorisation concerning directed surveillance (as defined in section 26 of the Act), the court must be satisfied that—

(a) the person who granted the authorisation was entitled to do so;

(b) the grant met any prescribed restrictions or conditions;

(c) at the time the authorisation was granted there were reasonable grounds for believing that the surveillance described in the authorisation was—

    (i) necessary, for the purpose of preventing or detecting crime or preventing disorder, and

(ii)   proportionate to what was sought to be achieved by it; and

(d)   there remain reasonable grounds for believing those things, at the time the court considers the application.

Under section 32A(5) and (6) of the Regulation of Investigatory Powers Act 2000, on an application for an order approving an authorisation of the conduct or use of a covert human intelligence source (as defined in section 26 of the Act), the court must be satisfied that—

(a)   the person who granted the authorisation was entitled to do so;

(b)   the grant met any prescribed restrictions or conditions;

(c)   at the time the authorisation was granted there were reasonable grounds for believing that the conduct or use of a covert human intelligence source described in the authorisation was—

(i)   necessary, for the purpose of preventing or detecting crime or preventing disorder, and

(ii)   proportionate to what was sought to be achieved by it; and

(d)   there remain reasonable grounds for believing those things, at the time the court considers the application.

Under section 43(6A) of the 2000 Act, on an application to approve the renewal of such an authorisation the court in addition must—

(a)   be satisfied that, since the grant or latest renewal of the authorisation, a review has been carried out of the use made of the source, of the tasks given to him or her and of the information obtained; and

(b)   consider the results of that review.

The Regulation of Investigatory Powers (Directed Surveillance and Covert Human Intelligence Sources) Order 2010 specifies the persons who are entitled to grant an authorisation concerning such surveillance or such a source, and for what purpose each may do so.

Under sections 23B(2) and 32B(2) of the 2000 Act, the applicant is not required to give notice of an application to any person to whom the authorisation or notice relates, or to such a person's legal representatives.]

SECTION 8: ORDERS FOR ACCESS TO DOCUMENTS, ETC UNDER THE CRIMINAL APPEAL ACT 1995

47.54 When this Section applies This Section applies where the Crown Court can order a person to give the Criminal Cases Review Commission access to a document or other material under section 18A of the Criminal Appeal Act 1995.

[Note. Under section 18A of the Criminal Appeal Act 1995, on an application by the Criminal Cases Review Commission the court may order that the Commission be given access to a document or material in a person's possession or control if the court thinks that that document or material may assist the Commission in the exercise of any of their functions.]

47.55 *Exercise of court's powers* (1) Subject to paragraphs (2), (3) and (4), the court may determine an application by the Criminal Cases Review Commission for an order—

(a)   at a hearing (which must be in private unless the court otherwise directs), or without a hearing; and

(b)   in the absence of—

(i)   the Commission,

(ii)   the respondent,

(iii)   any other person affected by the order.

(2)   The court must not determine such an application in the Commission's absence if—

(a)   the Commission asks for a hearing; or

(b)   it appears to the court that the application is so complex or serious as to require the court to hear the Commission.

(3)   The court must not determine such an application in the absence of any respondent or other person affected, unless—

(a)   the absentee has had at least 2 business days in which to make representations; or

(b)   the court is satisfied that—

(i)   the Commission cannot identify or contact the absentee,

(ii)   it would prejudice the exercise of the Commission's functions to adjourn or postpone the application so as to allow the absentee to attend, or

(iii)   the absentee has waived the opportunity to attend.

(4)   The court must not determine such an application in the absence of any respondent who, if the order sought by the Commission were made, would be required to produce or give access to journalistic material, unless that respondent has waived the opportunity to attend.

(5)   The court officer must arrange for the court to hear such an application no sooner than 2 business days after it was served, unless—

(a)   the court directs that no hearing need be arranged; or

(b)   the court gives other directions for the hearing.

(6)   The court must not determine an application unless satisfied that sufficient time has been allowed for it.

(7)   If the court so directs, the parties to an application may attend a hearing by live link or telephone.

(8)   The court must not make an order unless an officer of the Commission states, in writing or orally, that to the best of that officer's knowledge and belief—

(a)   the application discloses all the information that is material to what the court must decide; and

(b)   the content of the application is true.

(9)   Where the statement required by paragraph (8) is made orally—

(a)   the statement must be on oath or affirmation, unless the court otherwise directs; and

(b)   the court must arrange for a record of the making of the statement.

(10)   The court may shorten or extend (even after it has expired) a time limit under this Section.

47.56 *Application for an order for access* (1)   Where the Criminal Cases Review Commission wants the court to make an order for access to a document or other material, the Commission must—

(a)   apply in writing and serve the application on the court officer;

(b)   give the court an estimate of how long the court should allow—

(i)   to read the application and prepare for any hearing, and

(ii)   for any hearing of the application;

(c)   attach a draft order in the terms proposed by the Commission; and

(d)   serve the application and draft order on the respondent.

(2)   The application must—

(a)   identify the respondent;

(b)   describe the document, or documents, or other material sought;

(c)   explain the reasons for thinking that—

(i)   what is sought is in the respondent's possession or control, and

(ii)   access to what is sought may assist the Commission in the exercise of any of its functions; and

(d)   explain the Commission's proposals for—

(i)   the manner in which the respondent should give access, and

(ii)   the period within which the order should take effect.

(3)   The Commission must serve any order made on the respondent.

[Note. Under section 18A(3) of the Criminal Appeal Act 1995, the court may give directions for the manner in which access to a document or other material must be given, and may direct that the Commission must be allowed to take away such a document or material, or to make copies. Under section 18A(4) of the Act, the court may direct that the respondent must not destroy, damage or alter a document or other material before the direction is withdrawn by the court.]

47.57 *Application containing information withheld from a respondent or other person* (1)   This rule applies where—

(a)   the Criminal Cases Review Commission serves an application under rule 47.56 (Application for an order for access); and

(b)   the application includes information that the Commission thinks ought not be revealed to a recipient.

(2)   The Commission must—

(a)   omit that information from the part of the application that is served on that recipient;

(b)   mark the other part, to show that it is only for the court; and

(c)   in that other part, explain why the Commission has withheld it from that recipient.

(3)   A hearing of an application to which this rule applies may take place, wholly or in part, in the absence of that recipient and any other person.

(4)   At a hearing of an application to which this rule applies—

(a)   the general rule is that the court must consider, in the following sequence—

(i)   representations first by the Commission and then by the other parties, in the presence of them all, and then

(ii)   further representations by the Commission, in the others' absence; but

(b)   the court may direct other arrangements for the hearing.]

47.58 *Application to punish for contempt of court* (1)   This rule applies where a person is accused of disobeying an order for access made under section 18A of the Criminal Appeal Act 1995.

(2)   An applicant who wants the court to exercise its power to punish that person for contempt of court must comply with the rules in Part 48 (Contempt of court).

[Note. The Crown Court has power to punish for contempt of court a person who disobeys its order. See section 45 of the Senior Courts Act 1981.]

SECTION 9: EUROPEAN INVESTIGATION ORDERS

47.59. *When this Section applies* This Section—

(a)   applies where the court can—

(i)   make a European investigation order under regulation 6 of the Criminal Justice (European Investigation Order) Regulations 2017,

(ii)   vary or revoke such an order under regulation 10 of the 2017 Regulations;

(b)   does not apply where rule 18.24 or rule 18.25 applies (application to make or discharge, etc a live link direction supplemented by a European investigation order).

[Note. The Criminal Justice (European Investigation Order) Regulations 2017 give effect in the United Kingdom to Directive 2014/41/EU of the European Parliament and of the Council regarding the European Investigation Order in criminal matters. See also the note to rule 47.61.

Part 18 (Measures to assist a witness or defendant to give evidence) contains rules about applications to make, vary or revoke a live link direction which is supplemented by a European investigation order. Part 49 (International co-operation) contains rules about giving effect to a European investigation order made in another participating State.]

47.60. Exercise of court's powers (1) Subject to paragraphs (2) and (3), the court may determine an application under rule 47.61 to make, vary or revoke a European investigation order—

(a)   at a hearing (which must be in private unless the court otherwise directs), or without a hearing; and

(b)   in the absence of—

     (i)   the applicant,

     (ii)   the respondent (if any),

     (iii)   any other person affected by the order.

(2)   The court must not determine such an application in the applicant's absence if—

(a)   under the same conditions in a similar domestic case the investigative measure to be specified in the order would be a search warrant;

(b)   the applicant asks for a hearing;

(c)   it appears to the court that the investigative measure which the applicant wants the court to specify in the European investigation order—

     (i)   may infringe legal privilege, within the meaning of section 10 of the Police and Criminal Evidence Act 1984, section 348 or 361 of the Proceeds of Crime Act 2002 or article 9 of the Proceeds of Crime Act 2002 (External Investigations) Order 2014, or

     (ii)   may require the production of excluded material, within the meaning of section 11 of the 1984 Act; or

(d)   it appears to the court that for any other reason the application is so complex or serious as to require the court to hear the applicant.

(3)   The court—

(a)   must determine such an application in the absence of any respondent or other person affected if under the same conditions in a similar domestic case—

     (i)   an investigative measure to be specified in the European investigation order would be a search warrant, or

     (ii)   each investigative measure to be specified in the European investigation order would be one to an application for which no Criminal Procedure Rule would apply other than the rules in Section 1 and this Section of this Part;

(b)   may determine such an application in the absence of any respondent or other person affected where the court considers that—

     (i)   no requirement for the absentee's participation could be applied effectively because the application is for a European investigation order and not for a warrant, order, notice or summons to be given effect in England and Wales,

     (ii)   the applicant cannot identify or contact the absentee,

     (iii)   it would prejudice the investigation if the absentee were present,

     (iv)   it would prejudice the investigation to adjourn or postpone the application so as to allow the absentee to attend, or

     (v)   the absentee has waived the opportunity to attend.

(4)   The court must not determine an application unless satisfied that sufficient time has been allowed for it.

(5)   If the court so directs, a party to an application may attend a hearing by live link or telephone.

(6)   The court must not make, vary or discharge an order unless the applicant states, in writing or orally, that to the best of the applicant's knowledge and belief—

(a)   the application discloses all the information that is material to what the court must decide; and

(b)   the content of the application is true.

(7)   Where the statement required by paragraph (6) is made orally—

(a)   the statement must be on oath or affirmation, unless the court otherwise directs; and

(b)   the court must arrange for a record of the making of the statement.

(8)   The court may—

(a)   dispense with a requirement for service under this Section (even after service was required); and

(b)   consider an application made orally instead of in writing.

47.61. Application to make, vary or revoke a European investigation order (1) This rule applies where—

(a)   one of the following wants the court to make a European investigation order—

     (i)   a constable, acting with the consent of a prosecuting authority,

     (ii)   a prosecuting authority, or

     (iii)   a party to a prosecution;

(b)   one of the following wants the court to vary or revoke a European investigation order made by the court—

     (i)   the person who applied for the order,

     (ii)   a prosecuting authority, or

     (iii)   any other person affected by the order.

(2)   The applicant must—

(a)   apply in writing and serve the application on the court officer;

(b)   demonstrate that the applicant is entitled to apply;

(c)   if, and only if, the court cannot determine an application for a European investigation order in the absence of a respondent or other person affected (see rule 47.60(3)), serve on that respondent or other person such notice of the application as the court may direct;

(d)   serve notice of an application to vary or revoke a European investigation order on, as appropriate, the person who applied for the order and any other person affected by the order.

(3)   An application for the court to make a European investigation order must—

(a)   specify the offence under prosecution or investigation;

(b)   explain why it is suspected that the offence has been committed;

(c)   describe, as appropriate—

    (i)   the proceedings for the offence, or

    (ii)   the investigation;

(d)   specify the investigative measure or measures sought for the purpose of obtaining evidence for use in the proceedings or investigation, as the case may be;

(e)   specify the participating State in which the measure or measures are to be carried out;

(f)   explain why it is necessary and proportionate to make a European investigation order for the purposes of the proceedings or investigation;

(g)   where a measure is one which would require the issue of a warrant, order, notice or witness summons before it could be lawfully carried out in England and Wales, explain how such an instrument could have been issued taking into account—

    (i)   the nature of the evidence to be obtained,

    (ii)   the purpose for which that evidence is sought (including its relevance to the investigation or proceedings in respect of which the European investigation order is sought),

    (iii)   the circumstances in which the evidence is held,

    (iv)   the nature and seriousness of the offence to which the investigation or proceedings relates, and

    (v)   any provision or rule of domestic law applicable to the issuing of such an instrument;

(h)   where a measure is one which would require authorisation under any enactment relating to the acquisition and disclosure of data relating to communications, or the carrying out of surveillance, before it could be lawfully carried out in England and Wales, explain whether such authorisation has in fact been granted, or could have been granted, taking into account—

    (i)   the factors listed in paragraph (3)(g)(i) to (iv), and

    (ii)   the provisions of the legislation applicable to the granting of such authorisation;

(i)   where a measure is in connection with, or in the form of, the interception of communications, explain whether any additional requirements imposed by legislation relating to the making of such a request have been complied with;

(j)   where the application is for an order specifying one of the measures listed in any of regulations 15 to 19 of the Criminal Justice (European Investigation Order) Regulations 2017 (banking and other financial information; gathering of evidence in real time; covert investigations; provisional measures; interception of telecommunications where technical assistance is needed), explain how the requirements of that regulation are met;

(k)   attach a draft order in the form required by regulation 8 of the 2017 Regulations (Form and content of a European investigation order) and Directive 2014/41/EU.

(4)   An application for the court to vary or revoke a European investigation order must—

(a)   explain why it is appropriate for the order to be varied or revoked;

(b)   propose the terms of any variation; and

(c)   ask for a hearing, if one is wanted, and explain why it is needed.

(5)   Where the court—

(a)   makes a European investigation order the court officer must promptly—

    (i)   issue an order in the form required by regulation 8 of the 2017 Regulations (Form and content of a European investigation order) and Directive 2014/41/EU,

    (ii)   where the applicant is a constable or a prosecuting authority, serve that order on the applicant,

    (iii)   in any other case, serve that order on the appropriate authority in the participating State in which the measure or measures are to be carried out;

(b)   varies or revokes a European investigation order the court officer must promptly notify the appropriate authority in the participating State in which the measure or measures are to be carried out.

[Note. Under regulation 6 of the Criminal Justice (European Investigation Order) Regulations 2017 the court may make an order specifying one or more 'investigative measures' that are to be carried out in a State listed in Schedule 2 to those Regulations (a 'participating State') for the purpose of obtaining evidence for use in a criminal investigation or criminal proceedings. Under regulation 10 of the 2017 Regulations the court may vary or revoke such an order.

Under regulations 6(4)(b) and 11 of the 2017 Regulations any such measure must be one that could have been ordered or undertaken under the same conditions in a similar domestic case; but under regulation 11(5) that does not require the court to take into account any provision of domestic law imposing a procedural requirement which the court considers cannot effectively be applied when

making a European investigation order for the measure concerned. See also regulations 9 and 10(5), (6) of the 2017 Regulations, which govern the transmission of an order or varied order and the giving of notice of revocation of an order.
The Practice Direction sets out a form of application for use in connection with this rule.;

SECTION 10: ORDERS FOR THE EXTENSION OF A MORATORIUM PERIOD UNDER THE PROCEEDS OF CRIME ACT 2002

47.62. *(Crown Court only)*

PART 48   CONTEMPT OF COURT

Contents of this Part

General rules

GENERAL RULES

B.37 *48.1.   When this Part applies*   (1)   This Part applies where the court can deal with a person for conduct—
(a)   in contempt of court; or
(b)   in contravention of the legislation to which rules 48.5 and 48.9 refer.
(2)   In this Part, 'respondent' means any such person.
[Note. For the court's powers to punish for contempt of court, see the notes to rules 48.5 and 48.9.]

48.2.   Exercise of court's power to deal with contempt of court   (1)   The court must determine at a hearing—
(a)   an enquiry under rule 48.8;
(b)   an allegation under rule 48.9.
(2)   The court must not proceed in the respondent's absence unless—
(a)   the respondent's behaviour makes it impracticable to proceed otherwise; or
(b)   the respondent has had at least 14 days' notice of the hearing, or was present when it was arranged.
(3)   If the court hears part of an enquiry or allegation in private, it must announce at a hearing in public—
(a)   the respondent's name;
(b)   in general terms, the nature of any conduct that the respondent admits, or the court finds proved; and
(c)   any punishment imposed.

48.3. Notice of suspension of imprisonment by Court of Appeal or Crown Court (1)   This rule applies where—

(a)   the Court of Appeal or the Crown Court suspends an order of imprisonment for contempt of court; and

(b)   the respondent is absent when the court does so.

(2)   The respondent must be served with notice of the terms of the court's order—

(a)   by any applicant under rule 48.9; or

(b)   by the court officer, in any other case.

[Note. By reason of sections 15 and 45 of the Senior Courts Act 1981, the Court of Appeal and the Crown Court each has an inherent power to suspend imprisonment for contempt of court, on conditions, or for a period, or both.]

48.4. Application to discharge an order for imprisonment   (1)   This rule applies where the court can discharge an order for a respondent's imprisonment for contempt of court.

(2)   A respondent who wants the court to discharge such an order must—

(a)   apply in writing, unless the court otherwise directs, and serve any written application on—

(i)   the court officer, and

(ii)   any applicant under rule 48.9 on whose application the respondent was imprisoned;

(b)   in the application—

(i)   explain why it is appropriate for the order for imprisonment to be discharged, and

(ii)   give details of any appeal, and its outcome; and

(c)   ask for a hearing, if the respondent wants one.

[Note. By reason of sections 15 and 45 of the Senior Courts Act 1981, the Court of Appeal and the Crown Court each has an inherent power to discharge an order for a respondent's imprisonment for contempt of court in failing to comply with a court order.

Under section 97(4) of the Magistrates' Courts Act 1980, a magistrates' court can discharge an order for imprisonment if the respondent gives evidence.

Under section 12(4) of the Contempt of Court Act 1981, a magistrates' court can discharge an order for imprisonment made under that section.]

CONTEMPT OF COURT BY OBSTRUCTION, DISRUPTION, ETC

48.5. Initial procedure on obstruction, disruption, etc (1)   This rule applies where the court observes, or someone reports to the court—

(a)   in the Court of Appeal or the Crown Court, obstructive, disruptive, insulting or intimidating conduct, in the courtroom or in its vicinity, or otherwise immediately affecting the proceedings;

(b)   in the Crown Court, a contravention of—

(i)   section 3 of the Criminal Procedure (Attendance of Witnesses) Act 1965 (disobeying a witness summons);

(ii)   section 20 of the Juries Act 1974 (disobeying a jury summons);

(c)   in a magistrates' court, a contravention of—

(i)   section 97(4) of the Magistrates' Courts Act 1980 (refusing to give evidence), or

(ii)   section 12 of the Contempt of Court Act 1981 (insulting or interrupting the court, etc);

(d)   a contravention of section 9 of the Contempt of Court Act 1981 (without the court's permission, recording the proceedings, etc);

(e)   any other conduct with which the court can deal as, or as if it were, a criminal contempt of court, except failure to surrender to bail under section 6 of the Bail Act 1976.

(2)   Unless the respondent's behaviour makes it impracticable to do so, the court must—

(a)   explain, in terms the respondent can understand (with help, if necessary)—

(i)   the conduct that is in question,

(ii)   that the court can impose imprisonment, or a fine, or both, for such conduct,

(iii)   (where relevant) that the court has power to order the respondent's immediate temporary detention, if in the court's opinion that is required,

(iv)   that the respondent may explain the conduct,

(v)   that the respondent may apologise, if he or she so wishes, and that this may persuade the court to take no further action, and

(vi)   that the respondent may take legal advice; and

(b)   allow the respondent a reasonable opportunity to reflect, take advice, explain and, if he or she so wishes, apologise.

(3)   The court may then—

(a)   take no further action in respect of that conduct;

(b)   enquire into the conduct there and then; or

(c)   postpone that enquiry (if a magistrates' court, only until later the same day).

[Note. The conduct to which this rule applies is sometimes described as 'criminal' contempt of court.

By reason of sections 15 and 45 of the Senior Courts Act 1981, the Court of Appeal and the Crown Court each has an inherent power to imprison (for a maximum of 2 years), or fine (to an unlimited amount), or both, a respondent for contempt of court for the conduct listed in

paragraph (1)(a), (b), (d) or (e). See also section 14 of the Contempt of Court Act 1981.
Under section 97(4) of the Magistrates' Courts Act 1980, and under sections 12 and 14 of the Contempt of Court Act 1981, a magistrates' court can imprison (for a maximum of 1 month), or fine (to a maximum of £2,500), or both, a respondent who contravenes a provision listed in paragraph (1)(c) or (d). Section 12(1) of the 1981 Act allows the court to deal with any person who—

(a)   wilfully insults the justice or justices, any witness before or officer of the court or any solicitor or counsel having business in the court, during his or their sitting or attendance in court or in going to or returning from the court; or

(b)   wilfully interrupts the proceedings of the court or otherwise misbehaves in court.

Under section 89 of the Powers of Criminal Courts (Sentencing) Act 2000, no respondent who is under 21 may be imprisoned for contempt of court. Under section 108 of that Act, a respondent who is at least 18 but under 21 may be detained if the court is of the opinion that no other method of dealing with him or her is appropriate. Under section 14(2A) of the Contempt of Court Act 1981, a respondent who is under 17 may not be ordered to attend an attendance centre.
Under section 258 of the Criminal Justice Act 2003, a respondent who is imprisoned for contempt of court must be released unconditionally after serving half the term.
Under sections 14, 15 and 16 of the Legal Aid, Sentencing and Punishment of Offenders Act 2012, the respondent may receive advice and representation in "proceedings for contempt committed, or alleged to have been committed, by an individual in the face of the court".
By reason of sections 15 and 45 of the Senior Courts Act 1981, the Court of Appeal and the Crown Court each has an inherent power temporarily to detain a respondent, for example to restore order, when dealing with obstructive, disruptive, insulting or intimidating conduct. Under section 12(2) of the Contempt of Court Act 1981, a magistrates' court can temporarily detain a respondent until later the same day on a contravention of that section.
Part 14 contains rules about bail.]

48.6. *Review after temporary detention* (1) This rule applies in a case in which the court has ordered the respondent's immediate temporary detention for conduct to which rule 48.5 applies.
(2)   The court must review the case—
(a)   if a magistrates' court, later the same day;
(b)   if the Court of Appeal or the Crown Court, no later than the next business day.
(3)   On the review, the court must—
(a)   unless the respondent is absent, repeat the explanations required by rule 48.5(2)(a); and
(b)   allow the respondent a reasonable opportunity to reflect, take advice, explain and, if he or she so wishes, apologise.
(4)   The court may then—
(a)   take no further action in respect of the conduct;
(b)   if a magistrates' court, enquire into the conduct there and then; or
(c)   if the Court of Appeal or the Crown Court—
(i)   enquire into the conduct there and then, or
(ii)   postpone the enquiry, and order the respondent's release from such detention in the meantime.

48.7. *Postponement of enquiry* (1) This rule applies where the Court of Appeal or the Crown Court postpones the enquiry.
(2)   The court must arrange for the preparation of a written statement containing such particulars of the conduct in question as to make clear what the respondent appears to have done.
(3)   The court officer must serve on the respondent—
(a)   that written statement;
(b)   notice of where and when the postponed enquiry will take place; and
(c)   a notice that—
(i)   reminds the respondent that the court can impose imprisonment, or a fine, or both, for contempt of court, and
(ii)   warns the respondent that the court may pursue the postponed enquiry in the respondent's absence, if the respondent does not attend.

48.8. *Procedure on enquiry* (1) At an enquiry, the court must—
(a)   ensure that the respondent understands (with help, if necessary) what is alleged, if the enquiry has been postponed from a previous occasion;
(b)   explain what the procedure at the enquiry will be; and
(c)   ask whether the respondent admits the conduct in question.
(2)   If the respondent admits the conduct, the court need not receive evidence.
(3)   If the respondent does not admit the conduct, the court must consider—
(a)   any statement served under rule 48.7;
(b)   any other evidence of the conduct;
(c)   any evidence introduced by the respondent; and
(d)   any representations by the respondent about the conduct.
(4)   If the respondent admits the conduct, or the court finds it proved, the court must—
(a)   before imposing any punishment for contempt of court, give the respondent an opportunity to make representations relevant to punishment;
(b)   explain, in terms the respondent can understand (with help, if necessary)—
(i)   the reasons for its decision, including its findings of fact, and
(ii)   the punishment it imposes, and its effect; and

(c)   if a magistrates' court, arrange for the preparation of a written record of those findings.

(5)   The court that conducts an enquiry—

(a)   need not include the same member or members as the court that observed the conduct; but

(b)   may do so, unless that would be unfair to the respondent.

CONTEMPT OF COURT BY FAILURE TO COMPLY WITH COURT ORDER, ETC

48.9. *Initial procedure on failure to comply with court order, etc* (1) This rule applies where—

(a)   a party, or other person directly affected, alleges—

     (i)   in the Crown Court, a failure to comply with an order to which applies rule 33.70 (compliance order, restraint order or ancillary order), rule 47.9 (certain investigation orders under the Police and Criminal Evidence Act 1984, the Terrorism Act 2000, the Proceeds of Crime Act 2002, the Proceeds of Crime Act 2002 (External Investigations) Order 2014 and the Extradition Act 2003), rule 47.41 (order for retention or return of property under section 59 of the Criminal Justice and Police Act 2001) or rule 47.58 (order for access under section 18A of the Criminal Appeal Act 1995),

     (ii)   in the Court of Appeal or the Crown Court, any other conduct with which that court can deal as a civil contempt of court, or

     (iii)   in the Crown Court or a magistrates' court, unauthorised use of disclosed prosecution material under section 17 of the Criminal Procedure and Investigations Act 1996;

(b)   the court deals on its own initiative with conduct to which paragraph (1)(a) applies.

(2)   Such a party or person must—

(a)   apply in writing and serve the application on the court officer; and

(b)   serve on the respondent—

     (i)   the application, and

     (ii)   notice of where and when the court will consider the allegation (not less than 14 days after service).

(3)   The application must—

(a)   identify the respondent;

(b)   explain that it is an application for the respondent to be dealt with for contempt of court;

(c)   contain such particulars of the conduct in question as to make clear what is alleged against the respondent; and

(d)   include a notice warning the respondent that the court—

     (i)   can impose imprisonment, or a fine, or both, for contempt of court, and

     (ii)   may deal with the application in the respondent's absence, if the respondent does not attend the hearing.

(4)   A court which acts on its own initiative under paragraph (1)(b) must—

(a)   arrange for the preparation of a written statement containing the same information as an application; and

(b)   arrange for the service on the respondent of—

     (i)   that written statement, and

     (ii)   notice of where and when the court will consider the allegation (not less than 14 days after service).

[Note. The conduct to which this rule applies is sometimes described as 'civil' contempt of court. By reason of section 45 of the Senior Courts Act 1981, the Crown Court has an inherent power to imprison (for a maximum of 2 years), or fine (to an unlimited amount), or both, a respondent for conduct in contempt of court by failing to comply with a court order or an undertaking given to the court.

Under section 18 of the Criminal Procedure and Investigations Act 1996—

(a)   the Crown Court can imprison (for a maximum of 2 years), or fine (to an unlimited amount), or both;

(b)   a magistrates' court can imprison (for a maximum of 6 months), or fine (to a maximum of £5,000), or both,

a person who uses disclosed prosecution material in contravention of section 17 of that Act. See also rule 15.8.

Under section 89 of the Powers of Criminal Courts (Sentencing) Act 2000, no respondent who is under 21 may be imprisoned for contempt of court. Under section 108 of that Act, a respondent who is at least 18 but under 21 may be detained if the court is of the opinion that no other method of dealing with him or her is appropriate. Under section 14(2A) of the Contempt of Court Act 1981, a respondent who is under 17 may not be ordered to attend an attendance centre.

Under section 258 of the Criminal Justice Act 2003, a respondent who is imprisoned for contempt of court must be released unconditionally after serving half the term.

The Practice Direction sets out a form of application for use in connection with this rule.

The rules in Part 4 require that an application under this rule must be served by handing it to the person accused of contempt of court unless the court otherwise directs.]

48.10. *Procedure on hearing* (1) At the hearing of an allegation under rule 48.9, the court must—

(a)   ensure that the respondent understands (with help, if necessary) what is alleged;

(b)   explain what the procedure at the hearing will be; and

(c)   ask whether the respondent admits the conduct in question.

(2)   If the respondent admits the conduct, the court need not receive evidence.
(3)   If the respondent does not admit the conduct, the court must consider—
(a)   the application or written statement served under rule 48.9;
(b)   any other evidence of the conduct;
(c)   any evidence introduced by the respondent; and
(d)   any representations by the respondent about the conduct.
(4)   If the respondent admits the conduct, or the court finds it proved, the court must—
(a)   before imposing any punishment for contempt of court, give the respondent an opportunity to make representations relevant to punishment;
(b)   explain, in terms the respondent can understand (with help, if necessary)—
    (i)   the reasons for its decision, including its findings of fact, and
    (ii)   the punishment it imposes, and its effect; and
(c)   in a magistrates' court, arrange for the preparation of a written record of those findings.

48.11.   Introduction of written witness statement or other hearsay   (1)   Where rule 48.9 applies, an applicant or respondent who wants to introduce in evidence the written statement of a witness, or other hearsay, must—
(a)   serve a copy of the statement, or notice of other hearsay, on—
    (i)   the court officer, and
    (ii)   the other party; and
(b)   serve the copy or notice—
    (i)   when serving the application under rule 48.9, in the case of an applicant, or
    (ii)   not more than 7 days after service of that application or of the court's written statement, in the case of the respondent.
(2)   Such service is notice of that party's intention to introduce in evidence that written witness statement, or other hearsay, unless that party otherwise indicates when serving it.
(3)   A party entitled to receive such notice may waive that entitlement.
[Note. On an application under rule 48.9, hearsay evidence is admissible under the Civil Evidence Act 1995. Section 1(2) of the 1995 Act defines hearsay as meaning 'a statement made otherwise than by a person while giving oral evidence in the proceedings which is tendered as evidence of the matters stated'. Section 13 of the Act defines a statement as meaning 'any representation of fact or opinion, however made'.
Under section 2 of the 1995 Act, a party who wants to introduce hearsay in evidence must give reasonable and practicable notice, in accordance with procedure rules, unless the recipient waives that requirement.]

48.12.   Content of written witness statement   (1)   This rule applies to a written witness statement served under rule 48.11.
(2)   Such a written witness statement must contain a declaration by the person making it that it is true to the best of that person's knowledge and belief.
[Note. By reason of sections 15 and 45 of the Senior Courts Act 1981, the Court of Appeal and the Crown Court each has an inherent power to imprison (for a maximum of 2 years), or fine (to an unlimited amount), or both, for contempt of court a person who, in a written witness statement to which this rule applies, makes, or causes to be made, a false statement without an honest belief in its truth. See also section 14 of the Contempt of Court Act 1981.]

48.13.   Content of notice of other hearsay   (1)   This rule applies to a notice of hearsay, other than a written witness statement, served under rule 48.11.
(2)   Such a notice must—
(a)   set out the evidence, or attach the document that contains it; and
(b)   identify the person who made the statement that is hearsay.

48.14.   Cross-examination of maker of written witness statement or other hearsay   (1)   This rule applies where a party wants the court's permission to cross-examine a person who made a statement which another party wants to introduce as hearsay.
(2)   The party who wants to cross-examine that person must—
(a)   apply in writing, with reasons; and
(b)   serve the application on—
    (i)   the court officer, and
    (ii)   the party who served the hearsay.
(3)   A respondent who wants to cross-examine such a person must apply to do so not more than 7 days after service of the hearsay by the applicant.
(4)   An applicant who wants to cross-examine such a person must apply to do so not more than 3 days after service of the hearsay by the respondent.
(5)   The court—
(a)   may decide an application under this rule without a hearing; but
(b)   must not dismiss such an application unless the person making it has had an opportunity to make representations at a hearing.
[Note. See also section 3 of the Civil Evidence Act 1995.]

48.15.   Credibility and consistency of maker of written witness statement or other hearsay   (1)   This rule applies where a party wants to challenge the credibility or consistency of a person who made a statement which another party wants to introduce as hearsay.
(2)   The party who wants to challenge the credibility or consistency of that person must—
(a)   serve notice of intention to do so on—

        (i)   the court officer, and

        (ii)   the party who served the hearsay; and

(b)   in it, identify any statement or other material on which that party relies.

(3)   A respondent who wants to challenge such a person's credibility or consistency must serve such a notice not more than 7 days after service of the hearsay by the applicant.

(4)   An applicant who wants to challenge such a person's credibility or consistency must serve such a notice not more than 3 days after service of the hearsay by the respondent.

(5)   The party who served the hearsay—

(a)   may call that person to give oral evidence instead; and

(b)   if so, must serve notice of intention to do so on—

        (i)   the court officer, and

        (ii)   the other party

   as soon as practicable after service of the notice under paragraph (2).

[Note. Section 5(2) of the Civil Evidence Act 1995 describes the procedure for challenging the credibility of the maker of a statement of which hearsay evidence is introduced. See also section 6 of that Act.

The 1995 Act does not allow the introduction of evidence of a previous inconsistent statement otherwise than in accordance with sections 5, 6 and 7 of the Criminal Procedure Act 1865.]

48.16. *Magistrates' courts' powers to adjourn, etc*   (1)   This rule applies where a magistrates' court deals with unauthorised disclosure of prosecution material under sections 17 and 18 of the Criminal Procedure and Investigations Act 1996.

(2)   The sections of the Magistrates' Courts Act 1980 listed in paragraph (3) apply as if in those sections—

(a)   'complaint' and 'summons' each referred to an application or written statement under rule 48.9;

(b)   'complainant' meant an applicant; and

(c)   'defendant' meant the respondent.

(3)   Those sections are—

(a)   section 51 (issue of summons on complaint);

(b)   section 54 (adjournment);

(c)   section 55 (non-appearance of defendant);

(d)   section 97(1) (summons to witness);

(e)   section 121(1) (constitution and place of sitting of court);

(f)   section 123 (defect in process).

(4)   Section 127 of the 1980 Act (limitation of time) does not apply.

[Note. Under section 19(3) of the Criminal Procedure and Investigations Act 1996, Criminal Procedure Rules may contain provisions equivalent to those contained in Schedule 3 to the Contempt of Court Act 1981 (which allows magistrates' courts in cases of contempt of court to use certain powers such courts possess in other cases).]

48.17. *Court's power to vary requirements*   (1)   The court may shorten or extend (even after it has expired) a time limit under rule 48.11, 48.14 or 48.15.

(2)   A person who wants an extension of time must—

(a)   apply when serving the statement, notice or application for which it is needed; and

(b)   explain the delay.

PART 49   INTERNATIONAL CO-OPERATION

B.38 *49.1. Notice required to accompany process served outside the United Kingdom and translations* (1)   The notice which by virtue of section 3(4)(b) of the Crime (International Co-operation) Act 2003 (general requirements for service of process) must accompany any process served outside the United Kingdom must give the information specified in paragraphs (2) and (4) below.

(2)   The notice must—

(a)   state that the person required by the process to appear as a party or attend as a witness can obtain information about his rights in connection therewith from the relevant authority; and

(b)   give the particulars specified in paragraph (4) about that authority.

(3)   The relevant authority where the process is served—

(a)   at the request of the prosecuting authority, is that authority; or

(b)   at the request of the defendant or the prosecutor in the case of a private prosecution, is the court by which the process is served.

(4)   The particulars referred to in paragraph (2) are—

(a)   the name and address of the relevant authority, together with its telephone and fax numbers and e-mail address; and

(b)   the name of a person at the relevant authority who can provide the information referred to in paragraph (2)(a), together with his telephone and fax numbers and e-mail address.

(5)   The justices' clerk or Crown Court officer must send, together with any process served outside the United Kingdom—

(a)   any translation which is provided under section 3(3)(b) of the 2003 Act; and

(b)   any translation of the information required to be given by this rule which is provided to him.

(6)   In this rule, 'process' has the same meaning as in section 51(3) of the 2003 Act.

49.2. Proof of service outside the United Kingdom (1)   A statement in a certificate given by or on behalf of the Secretary of State—

(a)   that process has been served on any person under section 4(1) of the Crime (International Co-operation) Act 2003(service of process otherwise than by post);

(b)   of the manner in which service was effected; and

(c)   of the date on which process was served;

shall be admissible as evidence of any facts so stated.

(2)   In this rule, 'process' has the same meaning as in section 51(3) of the 2003 Act.

49.3. Supply of copy of notice of request for assistance abroad   Where a request for assistance under section 7 of the Crime (International Co-operation) Act 2003 is made by a justice of the peace or a judge exercising the jurisdiction of the Crown Court and is sent in accordance with section 8(1) of the 2003 Act, the justices' clerk or the Crown Court officer shall send a copy of the letter of request to the Secretary of State as soon as practicable after the request has been made.

49.4. Persons entitled to appear and take part in proceedings before a nominated court, and exclusion of the public   A court nominated under section 15(1) of the Crime (International Co-operation) Act 2003 (nominating a court to receive evidence) may—

(a)   determine who may appear or take part in the proceedings under Schedule 1 to the 2003 Act before the court and whether a party to the proceedings is entitled to be legally represented; and

(b)   direct that the public be excluded from those proceedings if it thinks it necessary to do so in the interests of justice.

49.5. Record of proceedings to receive evidence before a nominated court (1)   Where a court is nominated under section 15(1) of the Crime (International Co-operation) Act 2003 the justices' clerk or Crown Court officer shall enter in an overseas record—

(a)   details of the request in respect of which the notice under section 15(1) of the 2003 Act was given;

(b)   the date on which, and place at which, the proceedings under Schedule 1 to the 2003 Act in respect of that request took place;

(c)   the name of any witness who gave evidence at the proceedings in question;

(d)   the name of any person who took part in the proceedings as a legal representative or an interpreter;

(e)   whether a witness was required to give evidence on oath or (by virtue of section 5 of the Oaths Act 1978) after making a solemn affirmation; and

(f)　　　whether the opportunity to cross-examine any witness was refused.
(2)　　When the court gives the evidence received by it under paragraph 6(1) of Schedule 1 to the 2003 Act to the court or authority that made the request or to the territorial authority for forwarding to the court or authority that made the request, the justices' clerk or Crown Court officer shall send to the court, authority or territorial authority (as the case may be) a copy of an extract of so much of the overseas record as relates to the proceedings in respect of that request.
[Note. As to the keeping of an overseas record, see rule 49.9.]

49.6.　Interpreter for the purposes of proceedings involving a television or telephone link
(1)　　This rule applies where a court is nominated under section 30(3) (hearing witnesses in the UK through television links) or section 31(4) (hearing witnesses in the UK by telephone) of the Crime (International Co-operation) Act 2003.
(2)　　Where it appears to the justices' clerk or the Crown Court officer that the witness to be heard in the proceedings under Part 1 or 2 of Schedule 2 to the 2003 Act ('the relevant proceedings') is likely to give evidence in a language other than English, he shall make arrangements for an interpreter to be present at the proceedings to translate what is said into English.
(3)　　Where it appears to the justices' clerk or the Crown Court officer that the witness to be heard in the relevant proceedings is likely to give evidence in a language other than that in which the proceedings of the court referred to in section 30(1) or, as the case may be, 31(1) of the 2003 Act ('the external court') will be conducted, he shall make arrangements for an interpreter to be present at the relevant proceedings to translate what is said into the language in which the proceedings of the external court will be conducted.
(4)　　Where the evidence in the relevant proceedings is either given in a language other than English or is not translated into English by an interpreter, the court shall adjourn the proceedings until such time as an interpreter can be present to provide a translation into English.
(5)　　Where a court in Wales understands Welsh—
(a)　　　paragraph (2) does not apply where it appears to the justices' clerk or Crown Court officer that the witness in question is likely to give evidence in Welsh;
(b)　　　paragraph (4) does not apply where the evidence is given in Welsh; and
(c)　　　any translation which is provided pursuant to paragraph (2) or (4) may be into Welsh instead of English.

49.7.　Record of television link hearing before a nominated court　(1)　This rule applies where a court is nominated under section 30(3) of the Crime (International Co-operation) Act 2003.
(2)　　The justices' clerk or Crown Court officer shall enter in an overseas record—
(a)　　　details of the request in respect of which the notice under section 30(3) of the 2003 Act was given;
(b)　　　the date on which, and place at which, the proceedings under Part 1 of Schedule 2 to that Act in respect of that request took place;
(c)　　　the technical conditions, such as the type of equipment used, under which the proceedings took place;
(d)　　　the name of the witness who gave evidence;
(e)　　　the name of any person who took part in the proceedings as a legal representative or an interpreter; and
(f)　　　the language in which the evidence was given.
(3)　　As soon as practicable after the proceedings under Part 1 of Schedule 2 to the 2003 Act took place, the justices' clerk or Crown Court officer shall send to the external authority that made the request a copy of an extract of so much of the overseas record as relates to the proceedings in respect of that request.
[Note. As to the keeping of an overseas record, see rule 49.9.]

49.8.　Record of telephone link hearing before a nominated court　(1)　This rule applies where a court is nominated under section 31(4) of the Crime (International Co-operation) Act 2003.
(2)　　The justices' clerk or Crown Court officer shall enter in an overseas record—
(a)　　　details of the request in respect of which the notice under section 31(4) of the 2003 Act was given;
(b)　　　the date, time and place at which the proceedings under Part 2 of Schedule 2 to the 2003 Act took place;
(c)　　　the name of the witness who gave evidence;
(d)　　　the name of any interpreter who acted at the proceedings; and
(e)　　　the language in which the evidence was given.
[Note. As to the keeping of an overseas record, see rule 49.9.]

49.9.　Overseas record　(1)　The overseas records of a magistrates' court shall be part of the register (within the meaning of section 150(1) of the Magistrates' Courts Act 1980).
(2)　　The overseas records of any court shall not be open to inspection by any person except—
(a)　　　as authorised by the Secretary of State; or
(b)　　　with the leave of the court.
[Note. As to the making of court records, see rule 5.4.]

49.10.　Overseas freezing orders　(1)　This rule applies where a court is nominated under section 21(1) of the Crime (International Co-operation) Act 2003 to give effect to an overseas freezing order.
(2)　　Where the Secretary of State serves a copy of such an order on the court officer—
(a)　　　the general rule is that the court must consider the order no later than the next business day;

(b) exceptionally, the court may consider the order later than that, but not more than 5 business days after service.

(3) The court must not consider the order unless—

(a) it is satisfied that the chief officer of police for the area in which the evidence is situated has had notice of the order; and

(b) that chief officer of police has had an opportunity to make representations, at a hearing if that officer wants.

(4) The court may consider the order—

(a) without a hearing; or

(b) at a hearing, in public or in private.

[Note. Under sections 20, 21 and 22 of the Crime (International Co-operation) Act 2003, a court nominated by the Secretary of State must consider an order, made by a court or other authority in a country outside the United Kingdom, the purpose of which is to protect evidence in the United Kingdom which may be used in proceedings or an investigation in that other country pending the transfer of that evidence to that country. The court may decide not to give effect to such an order only if—

(a) were the person whose conduct is in question to be charged with the offence to which the order relates, a previous conviction or acquittal would entitle that person to be discharged; or

(b) giving effect to the order would be incompatible with a Convention right, within the meaning of the Human Rights Act 1998.]

49.11. Overseas forfeiture orders (1) This rule applies where—

(a) the Crown Court can—

    (i) make a restraint order under article 5 of the Criminal Justice (International Co-operation) Act 1990 (Enforcement of Overseas Forfeiture Orders) Order 2005, or

    (ii) give effect to an external forfeiture order under article 19 of that Order;

(b) the Director of Public Prosecutions or the Director of the Serious Fraud Office receives—

    (i) a request for the restraint of property to which article 3 of the 2005 Order applies, or

    (ii) a request to give effect to an external forfeiture order to which article 15 of the Order applies; and

(c) the Director wants the Crown Court to—

    (i) make such a restraint order, or

    (ii) give effect to such a forfeiture order.

(2) The Director must—

(a) apply in writing;

(b) serve the application on the court officer; and

(c) serve the application on the defendant and on any other person affected by the order, unless the court is satisfied that—

    (i) the application is urgent, or

    (ii) there are reasonable grounds for believing that to give notice of the application would cause the dissipation of the property which is the subject of the application.

(3) The application must—

(a) identify the property the subject of the application;

(b) identify the person who is or who may become the subject of such a forfeiture order;

(c) explain how the requirements of the 2005 Order are satisfied, as the case may be—

    (i) for making a restraint order, or

    (ii) for giving effect to a forfeiture order;

(d) where the application is to give effect to a forfeiture order, include an application to appoint the Director as the enforcement authority; and

(e) propose the terms of the Crown Court order.

(4) If the court allows the application, it must—

(a) where it decides to make a restraint order—

    (i) specify the property the subject of the order,

    (ii) specify the person or persons who are prohibited from dealing with that property,

    (iii) specify any exception to that prohibition, and

    (iv) include any ancillary order that the court believes is appropriate to ensure that the restraint order is effective;

(b) where it decides to give effect to a forfeiture order, exercise its power to—

    (i) direct the registration of the order as an order of the Crown Court,

    (ii) give directions for notice of the order to be given to any person affected by it, and

    (iii) appoint the applicant Director as the enforcement authority.

(5) Paragraph (6) applies where a person affected by an order, or the Director, wants the court to vary or discharge a restraint order or cancel the registration of a forfeiture order.

(6) Such a person must—

(a) apply in writing as soon as practicable after becoming aware of the grounds for doing so;

(b) serve the application on the court officer and, as applicable—

    (i) the other party, and

    (ii) any other person who will or may be affected;

(c) explain why it is appropriate, as the case may be—

    (i) for the restraint order to be varied or discharged, or

       (ii)   for the registration of the forfeiture order to be cancelled;

(d)   propose the terms of any variation; and

(e)   ask for a hearing, if one is wanted, and explain why it is needed.

(7)   The court may—

(a)   consider an application

       (i)   at a hearing, which must be in private unless the court otherwise directs, or

       (ii)   without a hearing;

(b)   allow an application to be made orally.

[Note. Under article 19 of the Criminal Justice (International Co-operation) Act 1990 (Enforcement of Overseas Forfeiture Orders) Order 2005, on the application of the Director of Public Prosecutions or the Director of the Serious Fraud Office the Crown Court may give effect to an order made by a court in a country outside the United Kingdom for the forfeiture and destruction, or other disposal, of any property in respect of which an offence has been committed in that country, or which was used or intended for use in connection with the commission of such an offence (described in the Order as an 'external forfeiture order').

Under article 5 of the 2005 Order, on the application of the Director of Public Prosecutions or the Director of the Serious Fraud Office the Crown Court may make a restraint order prohibiting any specified person from dealing with property, for the purpose of facilitating the enforcement of such a forfeiture order which has yet to be made.]

49.12.   *Overseas restraint orders*   (1)   This rule applies where—

(a)   the Crown Court can give effect to an overseas restraint order under regulation 10 of the Criminal Justice and Data Protection (Protocol No 36) Regulations 2014;

(b)   the Director of Public Prosecutions or the Director of the Serious Fraud Office receives a request from a court or authority in another European Union member State to give effect to such an order; and

(c)   the Director serves on the Crown Court officer—

       (i)   the certificate which accompanied the request for enforcement of the order,

       (ii)   a copy of the order restraining the property to which that certificate relates, and

       (iii)   a copy of an order confiscating the property in respect of which the restraint order was made, or an indication of when such a confiscation order is expected.

(2)   On service of those documents on the court officer—

(a)   the general rule is that the Crown Court must consider the order, with a view to its registration, no later than the next business day;

(b)   exceptionally, the court may consider the order later than that, but not more than 5 business days after service.

(3)   The court—

(a)   must not consider the order unless the Director—

       (i)   is present, or

       (ii)   has had a reasonable opportunity to make representations;

(b)   subject to that, may consider the order—

       (i)   at a hearing, which must be in private unless the court otherwise directs, or

       (ii)   without a hearing.

(4)   If the court decides to give effect to the order, the court must—

(a)   direct its registration as an order of the Crown Court; and

(b)   give directions for notice of the order to be given to any person affected by it.

(5)   Paragraph (6) applies where a person affected by the order, or the Director, wants the court to cancel the registration or vary the property to which the order applies.

(6)   Such a person must—

(a)   apply in writing as soon as practicable after becoming aware of the grounds for doing so;

(b)   serve the application on the court officer and, as applicable—

       (i)   the other party, and

       (ii)   any other person who will or may be affected;

(c)   explain, as applicable—

       (i)   when the overseas restraint order ceased to have effect in the European Union member State in which it was made,

       (ii)   why continuing to give effect to that order would be impossible as a consequence of an immunity under the law of England and Wales,

       (iii)   why continuing to give effect to that order would be incompatible with a Convention right within the meaning of the Human Rights Act 1998,

       (iv)   why therefore it is appropriate for the registration to be cancelled or varied;

(d)   include with the application any evidence in support;

(e)   propose the terms of any variation; and

(f)   ask for a hearing, if one is wanted, and explain why it is needed.

[Note. See regulations 8, 9 and 10 of the Criminal Justice and Data Protection (Protocol No 36) Regulations 2014.

An overseas restraint order is an order made by a court or authority in a European Union member State which—

(a)   relates to—

       (i)   criminal proceedings instituted in that state, or

       (ii)   a criminal investigation being carried on there; and

(b)   prohibits dealing with property in England and Wales which the court or authority considers to be property that—

(i)   has been or is likely to be used for the purposes of criminal conduct, or

(ii)   is the proceeds of criminal conduct.

Where this rule applies, the Crown Court—

(a)   may decide not to give effect to an overseas restraint order only if that would be—

(i)   impossible as a consequence of an immunity under the law of England and Wales, or

(ii)   incompatible with a Convention right within the meaning of the Human Rights Act 1998;

(b)   may postpone giving effect to an overseas restraint order in respect of any property—

(i)   in order to avoid prejudicing a criminal investigation which is taking place in the United Kingdom, or

(ii)   if, under an order made by a court in criminal proceedings in the UK, the property may not be dealt with;

(c)   may cancel a registration, or vary the property to which an order applies, if or to the extent that—

(i)   any of the circumstances listed in paragraph (a) of this note applies, or

(ii)   the order has ceased to have effect in the member State in which it was made.

Under regulation 10(6) of the 2014 Regulations, no challenge to the substantive reasons in relation to which an overseas restraint order has been made by an appropriate court or authority in a European Union member State may be considered by the court.

Under regulation 3 of the 2014 Regulations, a reference to the proceeds of criminal conduct includes a reference to—

(a)   any property which wholly or partly, and directly or indirectly, represents the proceeds of an offence (including payments or other rewards in connection with the commission of an offence); and

(b)   any property which is the equivalent to the full value or part of the value of such property.]

49.13.   Overseas confiscation orders   (1)   This rule applies where—

(a)   the Crown Court can give effect to an overseas confiscation order under regulation 15 of the Criminal Justice and Data Protection (Protocol No 36) Regulations 2014;

(b)   the Director of Public Prosecutions or the Director of the Serious Fraud Office receives a request from a court or authority in another European Union member State to give effect to such an order; and

(c)   the Director serves on the Crown Court officer—

(i)   the certificate which accompanied the request for enforcement of the order, and

(ii)   a copy of the confiscation order to which that certificate relates.

(2)   The court—

(a)   must not consider the order unless the Director—

(i)   is present, or

(ii)   has had a reasonable opportunity to make representations;

(b)   subject to that, may consider the order—

(i)   at a hearing, which must be in private unless the court otherwise directs, or

(ii)   without a hearing.

(3)   If the court decides to give effect to the order, the court must—

(a)   direct its registration as an order of the Crown Court; and

(b)   give directions for notice of the order to be given to any person affected by it.

(4)   Paragraph (5) applies where a person affected by the order, or the Director, wants the court to cancel the registration or vary the property to which the order applies.

(5)   Such a person must—

(a)   apply in writing as soon as practicable after becoming aware of the grounds for doing so;

(b)   serve the application on the court officer and, as applicable—

(i)   the other party, and

(ii)   any other person who will or may be affected;

(c)   explain, as applicable—

(i)   when the overseas confiscation order ceased to have effect in the European Union member State in which it was made,

(ii)   why continuing to give effect to that order would be statute-barred, provided that the criminal conduct that gave rise to the order falls within the jurisdiction of England and Wales,

(iii)   why continuing to give effect to that order would be impossible as a consequence of an immunity under the law of England and Wales,

(iv)   why continuing to give effect to that order would be incompatible with a Convention right within the meaning of the Human Rights Act 1998,

(v)   why therefore it is appropriate for the registration to be cancelled or varied;

(d)   include with the application any evidence in support;

(e)   propose the terms of any variation; and

(f)   ask for a hearing, if one is wanted, and explain why it is needed.

[Note. See regulations 13, 14 and 15 of the Criminal Justice and Data Protection (Protocol No 36)

Regulations 2014.
An overseas confiscation order is an order made by a court or authority in a European Union member State for the confiscation of property which is in England and Wales, or is the property of a resident of England and Wales, and which the court or authority considers—
(a)   was used or intended to be used for the purposes of criminal conduct; or
(b)   is the proceeds of criminal conduct.
Where this rule applies, the Crown Court—
(a)   may decide not to give effect to an overseas confiscation order only if that would be—
    (i)   statute-barred, provided that the criminal conduct that gave rise to the order falls within the jurisdiction of England and Wales,
    (ii)   impossible as a consequence of an immunity under the law of England and Wales, or
    (iii)   incompatible with a Convention right within the meaning of the Human Rights Act 1998;
(b)   may postpone giving effect to an overseas confiscation order in respect of any property—
    (i)   in order to avoid prejudicing a criminal investigation which is taking place in the United Kingdom,
    (ii)   where the court considers that there is a risk that the amount recovered through the execution of the order in England and Wales may exceed the amount specified in the order because of the simultaneous execution of the order in more than one member State,
    (iii)   if, under an order made by a court in criminal proceedings in the UK, the property may not be dealt with, or the property is subject to proceedings for such an order, or
    (iv)   if a person affected by the order has applied to cancel the registration, or vary the property to which it applies;
(c)   may cancel a registration, or vary the property to which an order applies, if or to the extent that—
    (i)   any of the circumstances listed in paragraph (a) of this note applies, or
    (ii)   the order has ceased to have effect in the member State in which it was made.]
Under regulation 15(7) of the 2014 Regulations, no challenge to the substantive reasons in relation to which an overseas restraint order has been made by an appropriate court or authority in a European Union member State may be considered by the court.
Regulation 3 of the 2014 Regulations applies also where this rule applies. See the note to rule 49.12.]

49.14.   Giving effect to a European investigation order for the receipt of oral evidence   (1)   This rule applies where a court is nominated under regulation 35 of the Criminal Justice (European Investigation Order) Regulations 2017 to give effect to a European investigation order by—
(a)   examining a witness; and
(b)   transmitting the product to the participating State in which the order was made.
(2)   The court—
(a)   must give effect to the order within 90 days beginning with the day after the day on which the court is nominated, unless a different period is agreed between the court, the Secretary of State and the issuing authority in the participating State in which the order was made;
(b)   must conduct the examination in accordance with Schedule 5 to the 2017 Regulations;
(c)   subject to that, may conduct the examination—
    (i)   in public or in private,
    (ii)   in the presence of such other persons as the court allows.
(3)   Subject to paragraph (2) and to such adaptations as the court directs, the court must receive the witness' evidence as if it were given at trial and to that extent—
(a)   Part 17 (Witness summonses, warrants and orders) applies to the exercise of the power to secure a witness' attendance under paragraph 2 of Schedule 5 to the 2017 Regulations as if that power were one of those listed in rule 17.1(a) (When this Part applies);
(b)   rule 24.4 (Evidence of a witness in person) applies where the evidence is received in a magistrates' court;
(c)   rule 25.11 (Evidence of a witness in person) applies where the evidence is received in the Crown Court.
[Note. The Criminal Justice (European Investigation Order) Regulations 2017 give effect in the United Kingdom to Directive 2014/41/EU of the European Parliament and of the Council regarding the European Investigation Order in criminal matters. Schedule 2 to the Regulations lists participating States.
Under regulation 35 of the 2017 Regulations (Nominating a court to receive evidence from a person) the Secretary of State may nominate a court to give effect to a European investigation order by receiving the evidence to which the order relates.]

49.15.   Giving effect to a European investigation order for hearing a person by live link   (1)   This rule applies where a court is nominated under regulation 36 or 37 of the Criminal Justice (European Investigation Order) Regulations 2017 to give effect to a European investigation order by—
(a)   facilitating the giving of oral evidence by live video or audio link by a person who is in England and Wales in proceedings in the participating State in which the order was made; and

(b)   superintending the giving of evidence by that person by those means.

(2)   The court—

(a)   must give effect to the order within 90 days beginning with the day after the day on which the court is nominated, unless a different period is agreed between the court, the Secretary of State and the issuing authority in the participating State in which the order was made;

(b)   must conduct the proceedings—

     (i)   in accordance with Schedule 6 to the 2017 Regulations,

     (ii)   subject to that, under the supervision of the court which receives the evidence in the participating State in which the order was made;

(c)   subject to paragraph (2)(b), may conduct the proceedings—

     (i)   in public or in private,

     (ii)   in the presence of such other persons as the court allows.

(3)   Subject to paragraph (2) and to such adaptations as the court directs, the court must conduct the proceedings as if the witness were giving evidence at a trial in England and Wales and to that extent—

(a)   Part 17 (Witness summonses, warrants and orders) applies to the exercise of the power to secure a witness' attendance under paragraph 2 of Schedule 6 to the 2017 Regulations as if that power were one of those listed in rule 17.1a (When this Part applies);

(b)   rule 24.4 (Evidence of a witness in person) applies where the proceedings take place in a magistrates' court;

(c)   rule 25.11 (Evidence of a witness in person) applies where the proceedings take place in the Crown Court.

[Note. *Under regulation 36 or regulation 37 of the Criminal Justice (European Investigation Order) Regulations 2017 (respectively, Hearing a person through videoconference or other audio visual transmission and Hearing a person by telephone conference) the Secretary of State may nominate a court to give effect to a European investigation order by requiring a person to give evidence, under the court's superintendence, by live video or audio link (described in the Regulations as 'videoconference or other audio visual transmission' and as 'telephone conference' respectively) in proceedings before a court in a participating State.]*

49.16. **Giving effect to a European investigation order by issuing a search warrant or production,**
etc order (1)   This rule applies where—

(a)   a court is nominated under regulation 38 of the Criminal Justice (European Investigation Order) Regulations 2017 (Search warrants and production orders: nominating a court) to give effect to a European investigation order by issuing—

     (i)   a search warrant under regulation 39(1) (Search warrants and production orders: giving effect to the European investigation order),

     (ii)   a production order in respect of excluded material or special procedure material under regulation 39(2), or

     (iii)   a search warrant in respect of excluded material or special procedure material under regulation 39(8);

(b)   a court is nominated under regulation 43 of the 2017 Regulations (Nominating a court to make a customer information order or an account monitoring order) to give effect to a European investigation order by making—

     (i)   a customer information order under regulation 44 (Court's power to make a customer information order), or

     (ii)   an account monitoring order under regulation 45 (Court's power to make an account monitoring order).

(2)   The Secretary of State must serve on the court officer a draft warrant or order in terms that give effect to the European investigation order.

(3)   The court must consider the European investigation order—

(a)   without a hearing, as a general rule; and

(b)   within 5 business days beginning with the day after the day on which the court is nominated, unless a different period is agreed between the court and the Secretary of State.

(4)   The court must not give effect to the European investigation order unless it is satisfied that each of the following authorities has had notice of that order and has had an opportunity to make representations, at a hearing if that authority wants—

(a)   the relevant chief officer of police; and

(b)   any other authority that will be responsible for the execution of the warrant or order.

[Note. *Under regulations 38, 39, 43, 44 and 45 of the Criminal Justice (European Investigation Order) Regulations 2017 the Secretary of State may nominate a court to give effect to a European investigation order by means of one of the warrants or orders listed in rule 49.16 and must send that court the order. Under regulations 38(5) and 43(5) the Secretary of State must send a copy of the European investigation order to the chief officer of police for the police area in which the evidence is situated, in the case of a search warrant or production order or, in the case of a customer information order or account monitoring order, to the chief officer of police for a police area appearing to the Secretary of State to be the appropriate chief officer to receive it.*

Under regulation 39(5), (6) or 46 the court may refuse to give effect to the European investigation order only if the court is of the opinion that—

(a)   *the execution of the European investigation order would be contrary to the principle of ne bis in idem;*

(b)   there are substantial grounds for believing that executing the European investigation order would be incompatible with any of the Convention rights (within the meaning of the Human Rights Act 1998);

(c)   there are substantial grounds for believing that the European investigation order has been issued for the purpose of prosecuting or punishing a person on account of that person's sex, racial or ethnic origin, religion, sexual orientation, nationality, language or political opinions;

(d)   there are substantial grounds for believing that a person's position in relation to the investigation or proceedings to which the European investigation order relates might be prejudiced by reason of that person's sex, racial or ethnic origin, religion, sexual orientation, nationality, language or political opinions.

Under regulation 39(7) or 47 the court may postpone giving effect to the European investigation order if—

(a)   to do so might prejudice a criminal investigation or proceedings taking place in the United Kingdom; or

(b)   if, under an order made by a court in criminal proceedings in the United Kingdom, the evidence may not be removed from the United Kingdom.]

49.17. **Application to vary or revoke a search warrant or production etc order issued to give effect to a European investigation order** (1) This rule applies where—

(a)   under regulation 41 of the Criminal Justice (European Investigation Order) Regulations 2017 (Power to revoke or vary a search warrant or production order or to authorise the release of evidence seized or produced) the court can vary or revoke—

    (i)   a search warrant issued under regulation 39(1) of the 2017 Regulations,

    (ii)   a production order issued in respect of excluded material or special procedure material under regulation 39(2),

    (iii)   a search warrant issued in respect of excluded material or special procedure material under regulation 39(8);

(b)   under regulation 41 of the 2017 Regulations the court can authorise the release of evidence seized by or produced to a constable on the execution of a search warrant or production order issued on an application under rule 49.16;

(c)   under regulation 48 of the 2017 Regulations (Power to vary or revoke customer information and account monitoring orders) the court can vary or revoke—

    (i)   a customer information order issued under regulation 44,

    (ii)   an account monitoring order issued under regulation 45.

(2)   The applicant must—

(a)   apply in writing and serve the application on—

    (i)   the court officer, and as appropriate

    (ii)   the chief officer of police to whom the European investigation order was sent by the Secretary of State,

    (iii)   any other person affected by the warrant or order;

(b)   demonstrate that the applicant is, as the case may be—

    (i)   the chief officer of police to whom the European investigation order was sent by the Secretary of State, or

    (ii)   any other person affected by the warrant or order.

(3)   An application to vary a warrant or order must propose the terms of the variation.

(4)   An application to revoke a warrant or order or to authorise the release of evidence seized or produced must indicate, as the case may be, that—

(a)   the European investigation order has been withdrawn or no longer has effect in the participating State in which it was issued; or

(b)   one of the grounds for refusing to give effect to the order obtains.

(5)   Where the court—

(a)   varies a warrant or order to which this rule applies the court officer must promptly serve a copy of that warrant or order, as varied, on the Secretary of State;

(b)   revokes such a warrant or order the court officer must promptly notify the Secretary of State.

PART 50   EXTRADITION

Contents of this Part

SECTION 1: GENERAL RULES

B.39 *50.1. When this Part applies* (1) This Part applies to extradition under Part 1 or Part 2 of the Extradition Act 2003.

(2) Section 2 of this Part applies to proceedings in a magistrates' court, and in that Section—

(a) rules 50.3 to 50.7, 50.15 and 50.16 apply to extradition under Part 1 of the Act;

(b) rules 50.3, 50.4 and 50.8 to 50.16 apply to extradition under Part 2 of the Act.

(3) Section 3 of this Part applies where—

(a) a party wants to appeal to the High Court against an order by the magistrates' court or by the Secretary of State;

(b) a party to an appeal to the High Court wants to appeal further to the Supreme Court under—

(i) section 32 of the Act (appeal under Part 1 of the Act), or

(ii) section 114 of the Act (appeal under Part 2 of the Act).

(4) Section 4 of this Part applies to proceedings in a magistrates' court under—

(a) sections 54 and 55 of the Act (Request for consent to other offence being dealt with; Questions for decision at consent hearing);

(b) sections 56 and 57 of the Act (Request for consent to further extradition to category 1 territory; Questions for decision at consent hearing).

(5) In this Part, and for the purposes of this Part in other rules—

(a)   'magistrates' court' means a District Judge (Magistrates' Courts) exercising the powers to which Section 2 of this Part applies;

(b)   'presenting officer' means an officer of the National Crime Agency, a police officer, a prosecutor or other person representing an authority or territory seeking the extradition of a defendant;

(c)   'defendant' means a person arrested under Part 1 or Part 2 of the Extradition Act 2003.

[Note. The Extradition Act 2003 provides for the extradition of a person accused or convicted of a crime to the territory within which that person is accused was convicted or is to serve a sentence.
Under Part 1 of the Act (sections 1 to 68), the magistrates' court may give effect to a warrant for arrest issued by an authority in a territory designated for the purposes of that Part, including a Member State of the European Union.
Under Part 2 of the Act (sections 69 to 141), the magistrates' court and the Secretary of State may give effect to a request for extradition made under a treaty between the United Kingdom and the requesting territory.
There are rights of appeal to the High Court from decisions of the magistrates' court and of the Secretary of State: see Section 3 of this Part.
Under sections 67 and 139 of the Extradition Act 2003, a District Judge (Magistrates' Courts) must be designated for the purposes of the Act to exercise the powers to which Section 2 of this Part applies.]

50.2.   ***Further objective in extradition proceedings***   When exercising a power to which this Part applies, in furthering the overriding objective, in accordance with rule 1.3, the court must have regard to the importance of—

(a)   mutual confidence and recognition between judicial authorities in the United Kingdom and in requesting territories; and

(b)   the conduct of extradition proceedings in accordance with international obligations, including obligations to deal swiftly with extradition requests.

[Note. Under sections 67 and 139 of the Extradition Act 2003, a District Judge (Magistrates' Courts) must be designated for the purposes of the Act to exercise the powers to which Section 2 of this Part applies.]

SECTION 2: EXTRADITION PROCEEDINGS IN A MAGISTRATES' COURT

50.3.   *Exercise of magistrates' court's powers*   (1)   The general rule is that the magistrates' court must exercise its powers at a hearing in public, but—

(a)   that is subject to any power the court has to—
   (i)   impose reporting restrictions,
   (ii)   withhold information from the public, or
   (iii)   order a hearing in private; and

(b)   despite the general rule the court may, without a hearing—
   (i)   give any directions to which rule 50.4 applies (Case management in the magistrates' court and duty of court officer), or
   (ii)   determine an application which these Rules allow to be determined by a magistrates' court without a hearing in a case to which this Part does not apply.

(2)   If the court so directs, a party may attend by live link any hearing except an extradition hearing under rule 50.6 or 50.13.

(3)   Where the defendant is absent from a hearing—

(a)   the general rule is that the court must proceed as if the defendant—
   (i)   were present, and
   (ii)   opposed extradition on any ground of which the court has been made aware;

(b)   the general rule does not apply if the defendant is under 18;

(c)   the general rule is subject to the court being satisfied that—
   (i)   the defendant had reasonable notice of where and when the hearing would take place,
   (ii)   the defendant has been made aware that the hearing might proceed in his or her absence, and
   (iii)   there is no good reason for the defendant's absence; and

(d)   the general rule does not apply but the court may exercise its powers in the defendant's absence where—
   (i)   the court discharges the defendant,
   (ii)   the defendant is represented and the defendant's presence is impracticable by reason of his or her ill health or disorderly conduct, or
   (iii)   on an application under rule 50.32 (Application for consent to deal with another offence or for consent to further extradition), the defendant is represented or the defendant's presence is impracticable by reason of his or her detention in the territory to which he or she has been extradited.

(4)   The court may exercise its power to adjourn—

(a)   if either party asks, or on its own initiative; and

(b)   in particular—
   (i)   to allow there to be obtained information that the court requires,
   (ii)   following a provisional arrest under Part 1 of the Extradition Act 2003, pending receipt of the warrant,

(iii)   following a provisional arrest under Part 2 of the Act, pending receipt of the extradition request,

(iv)   if the court is informed that the defendant is serving a custodial sentence in the United Kingdom,

(v)   if it appears to the court that the defendant is not fit to be extradited, unless the court discharges the defendant for that reason,

(vi)   where a court dealing with a warrant to which Part 1 of the Act applies is informed that another such warrant has been received in the United Kingdom,

(vii)   where a court dealing with a warrant to which Part 1 of the Act applies is informed of a request for the temporary transfer of the defendant to the territory to which the defendant's extradition is sought, or a request for the defendant to speak to the authorities of that territory, or

(viii)   during a hearing to which rule 50.32 applies (Application for consent to deal with another offence or for consent to further extradition).

(5)   The court must exercise its power to adjourn if informed that the defendant has been charged with an offence in the United Kingdom.

(6)   The general rule is that, before exercising a power to which this Part applies, the court must give each party an opportunity to make representations, unless that party is absent without good reason.

(7)   The court may—

(a)   shorten a time limit or extend it (even after it has expired), unless that is inconsistent with other legislation;

(b)   direct that a notice or application be served on any person;

(c)   allow a notice or application to be in a different form to one set out in the Practice Direction, or to be presented orally.

(8)   A party who wants an extension of time within which to serve a notice or make an application must—

(a)   apply for that extension of time when serving that notice or making that application; and

(b)   give the reasons for the application for an extension of time.

[Note. See sections 8A, 8B, 9, 21B, 22, 23, 25 and 44 of the Extradition Act 2003 (powers in relation to extradition under Part 1 of the Act) and sections 76A, 76B, 77, 88, 89 and 91 of the Act (powers in relation to extradition under Part 2 of the Act). Under sections 9 and 77 of the Act, at the extradition hearing the court has the same powers (as nearly as may be) as a magistrates' court would have if the proceedings were the summary trial of an allegation against the defendant: see also rule 24.12(3) (Trial and sentence in a magistrates' court; procedure where the defendant is absent). Under sections 206A to 206C of the 2003 Act, the court may require a defendant to attend by live link a preliminary hearing to which rule 50.5, 50.9 or 50.11 applies, any hearing for the purposes of rule 50.12 and the hearing to which rule 50.32 applies.

Part 6 contains rules about reporting and access restrictions.

Part 14 contains rules about bail. Rules 14.2(3) and 14.7(7)(c) allow an application to be determined without a hearing in the circumstances to which those rules apply.

The principal time limits are prescribed by the Extradition Act 2003: see rule 50.16.]

50.4. Case management in the magistrates' court and duty of court officer (1) The magistrates' court and the parties have the same duties and powers as under Part 3 (Case management), subject to—

(a)   rule 50.2 (Further objective in extradition proceedings); and

(b)   paragraph (2) of this rule.

(2)   Rule 3.6 (Application to vary a direction) does not apply to a decision to extradite or discharge.

(3)   Where this rule applies, active case management by the court includes—

(a)   if the court requires information from the authorities in the requesting territory—

      (i)   nominating a court officer, the designated authority which certified the arrest warrant where Part 1 of the Extradition Act 2003 Act applies, a party or other person to convey that request to those authorities, and

      (ii)   in a case in which the terms of that request need to be prepared in accordance with directions by the court, giving such directions accordingly;

(b)   giving such directions as are required where, under section 21B of the Extradition Act 2003, the parties agree—

      (i)   to the temporary transfer of the defendant to the requesting territory, or

      (ii)   that the defendant should speak with representatives of an authority in that territory.

(4)   Where this rule applies, active assistance by the parties includes—

(a)   applying for any direction needed as soon as reasonably practicable;

(b)   concisely explaining the reasons for any application for the court to direct—

      (i)   the preparation of a request to which paragraph (3)(a) applies,

      (ii)   the making of arrangements to which paragraph (3)(b) applies.

(5)   The court officer must—

(a)   as soon as practicable, serve notice of the court's decision to extradite or discharge—

      (i)   on the defendant,

      (ii)   on the designated authority which certified the arrest warrant, where Part 1 of the 2003 Act applies,

      (iii)   on the Secretary of State, where Part 2 of the Act applies; and

(b)   give the court such assistance as it requires.

[Note. Part 3 contains rules about case management which apply at an extradition hearing and during preparation for that hearing. This rule must be read in conjunction with those rules.

Under section 21B of the Extradition Act 2003 (Request for temporary transfer etc), where Part 1 of the Act applies, and in the circumstances described in that section, the parties may agree to the defendant's temporary transfer to the requesting territory, or may agree that the defendant will speak to representatives of an investigating, prosecuting or judicial authority in that territory. On the making by a party of a request to such effect the court must if necessary adjourn the proceedings for 7 days while the other party considers it. If the parties then agree to proceed with the proposed transfer or discussion the court must adjourn the proceedings for however long seems necessary.]

EXTRADITION UNDER PART 1 OF THE EXTRADITION ACT 2003

50.5. *Preliminary hearing after arrest*   (1)   This rule applies where the defendant is first brought before the court after—

(a)   arrest under a warrant to which Part 1 of the Extradition Act 2003 applies; or

(b)   provisional arrest under Part 1 of the Act.

(2)   The presenting officer must—

(a)   serve on the court officer—

   (i)   the arrest warrant, and

   (ii)   a certificate, given by the authority designated by the Secretary of State, that the warrant was issued by an authority having the function of issuing such warrants in the territory to which the defendant's extradition is sought; or

(b)   apply at once for an extension of time within which to serve that warrant and that certificate.

(3)   An application under paragraph (2)(b) must—

(a)   explain why the requirement to serve the warrant and certificate at once could not reasonably be complied with; and

(b)   include—

   (i)   any written material in support of that explanation, and

   (ii)   representations about bail pending service of those documents.

(4)   When the presenting officer serves the warrant and certificate, in the following sequence the court must—

(a)   decide whether the defendant is the person in respect of whom the warrant was issued;

(b)   explain, in terms the defendant can understand (with help, if necessary)—

   (i)   the allegation made in the warrant, and

   (ii)   that the defendant may consent to extradition, and how that may be done and with what effect;

(c)   give directions for an extradition hearing to begin—

   (i)   no more than 21 days after the defendant's arrest, or

   (ii)   if either party so applies, at such a later date as the court decides is in the interests of justice;

(d)   consider any ancillary application, including an application about bail pending the extradition hearing; and

(e)   give such directions as are required for the preparation and conduct of the extradition hearing.

[Note. See sections 4, 6, 7 and 8 of the Extradition Act 2003.

Under section 6 of the Act, following a provisional arrest pending receipt of a warrant the defendant must be brought before the court within 48 hours, and the warrant and certificate must be served within that same period. If they are not so served, the court may extend the time for service by a further 48 hours.

Under section 45 of the Act, a defendant's consent to extradition must be given before the court, must be recorded in writing, and is irrevocable. Consent may not be given unless the defendant has a legal representative with him or her when giving consent, or the defendant has failed or refused to apply for legal aid, or legal aid has been refused or withdrawn.

Part 14 contains rules about bail.]

50.6. *Extradition hearing*   (1)   This rule applies at the extradition hearing directed by the court under rule 50.5.

(2)   In the following sequence, the court must decide—

(a)   whether the offence specified in the warrant is an extradition offence;

(b)   whether a bar to extradition applies, namely—

   (i)   the rule against double jeopardy,

   (ii)   absence of prosecution decision,

   (iii)   extraneous considerations,

   (iv)   the passage of time,

   (v)   the defendant's age,

   (vi)   speciality,

   (vii)   earlier extradition or transfer to the United Kingdom, or

   (viii) forum;

(c)   where the warrant alleges that the defendant is unlawfully at large after conviction, whether conviction was in the defendant's presence and if not—

(i)   whether the defendant was absent deliberately,

(ii)   if the defendant was not absent deliberately, whether the defendant would be entitled to a retrial (or to a review of the conviction, amounting to a retrial);

(d)   whether extradition would be—

       (i)   compatible with the defendant's human rights, and

       (ii)   proportionate;

(e)   whether it would be unjust or oppressive to extradite the defendant because of his or her physical or mental condition;

(f)   after deciding each of (a) to (e) above, before progressing to the next, whether to order the defendant's discharge;

(g)   whether to order the temporary transfer of the defendant to the territory to which the defendant's extradition is sought.

(3)   If the court discharges the defendant, the court must consider any ancillary application, including an application about—

(a)   reporting restrictions; or

(b)   costs.

(4)   If the court does not discharge the defendant, the court must—

(a)   exercise its power to order the defendant's extradition;

(b)   explain, in terms the defendant can understand (with help, if necessary), that the defendant may appeal to the High Court within the next 7 days; and

(c)   consider any ancillary application, including an application about—

       (i)   bail pending extradition,

       (ii)   reporting restrictions, or

       (iii)   costs.

(5)   If the court orders the defendant's extradition, the court must order its postponement where—

(a)   the defendant has been charged with an offence in the United Kingdom; or

(b)   the defendant has been sentenced to imprisonment or detention in the United Kingdom.

[Note. See sections 10, 11, 20, 21, 21B, 25, 26, 36A, 36B, 64 and 65 of the Extradition Act 2003. Part 6 contains rules about reporting restrictions. Part 45 contains rules about costs.]

50.7. Discharge where warrant withdrawn (1)   This rule applies where the authority that certified the warrant gives the court officer notice that the warrant has been withdrawn—

(a)   after the start of the hearing under rule 50.5; and

(b)   before the court orders the defendant's extradition or discharge.

(2)   The court must exercise its power to discharge the defendant.

[Note. See section 41 of the Extradition Act 2003.]

EXTRADITION UNDER PART 2 OF THE EXTRADITION ACT 2003

50.8. Issue of arrest warrant (1)   This rule applies where the Secretary of State serves on the court officer—

(a)   an extradition request to which Part 2 of the Extradition Act 2003 applies;

(b)   a certificate given by the Secretary of State that the request was received in the way approved for the request; and

(c)   a copy of any Order in Council which applies to the request.

(2)   In the following sequence, the court must decide—

(a)   whether the offence in respect of which extradition is requested is an extradition offence; and

(b)   whether there is sufficient evidence, or (where the Secretary of State has so ordered, for this purpose) information, to justify the issue of a warrant of arrest.

(3)   The court may issue an arrest warrant—

(a)   without giving the parties an opportunity to make representations; and

(b)   without a hearing, or at a hearing in public or in private.

[Note. See sections 70, 71, 137 and 138 of the Extradition Act 2003.]

50.9. Preliminary hearing after arrest (1)   This rule applies where a defendant is first brought before the court after arrest under a warrant to which rule 50.8 applies.

(2)   In the following sequence, the court must—

(a)   explain, in terms the defendant can understand (with help, if necessary)—

       (i)   the content of the extradition request, and

       (ii)   that the defendant may consent to extradition, and how that may be done and with what effect;

(b)   give directions for an extradition hearing to begin—

       (i)   no more than 2 months later, or

       (ii)   if either party so applies, at such a later date as the court decides is in the interests of justice;

(c)   consider any ancillary application, including an application about bail pending the extradition hearing; and

(d)   give such directions as are required for the preparation and conduct of the extradition hearing.

[Note. See sections 72 and 75 of the Extradition Act 2003.

Under section 127 of the 2003 Act a defendant's consent to extradition must be given before the

court, must be recorded in writing, and is irrevocable. Consent may not be given unless the defendant has a legal representative with him or her when giving consent, or the defendant has failed or refused to apply for legal aid, or legal aid has been refused or withdrawn.
Part 14 contains rules about bail.]

50.10. *Issue of provisional arrest warrant* (1) This rule applies where a presenting officer wants a justice of the peace to issue a provisional arrest warrant under Part 2 of the Extradition Act 2003, pending receipt of an extradition request.
(2) The presenting officer must—
(a) serve an application for a warrant on the court officer; and
(b) verify that application on oath or affirmation.
(3) In the following sequence, the justice must decide—
(a) whether the alleged offence is an extradition offence; and
(b) whether there is sufficient evidence, or (where the Secretary of State has so ordered, for this purpose) information, to justify the issue of a warrant of arrest.
[Note. See sections 73, 137 and 138 of the Extradition Act 2003.]

50.11. *Preliminary hearing after provisional arrest* (1) This rule applies where a defendant is first brought before the court after arrest under a provisional arrest warrant to which rule 50.10 applies.
(2) The court must—
(a) explain, in terms the defendant can understand (with help, if necessary)—
   (i) the allegation in respect of which the warrant was issued, and
   (ii) that the defendant may consent to extradition, and how that may be done and with what effect; and
(b) consider any ancillary application, including an application about bail pending receipt of the extradition request.
[Note. See section 74 of the Extradition Act 2003. Under section 127 of the Act, a defendant's consent to extradition must be given before the court, must be recorded in writing, and is irrevocable. Consent may not be given unless the defendant has a legal representative with him or her when giving consent, or the defendant has failed or refused to apply for legal aid, or legal aid has been refused or withdrawn.]

50.12. *Arrangement of extradition hearing after provisional arrest* (1) This rule applies when the Secretary of State serves on the court officer—
(a) a request for extradition in respect of which a defendant has been arrested under a provisional arrest warrant to which rule 50.10 applies;
(b) a certificate given by the Secretary of State that the request was received in the way approved for the request; and
(c) a copy of any Order in Council which applies to the request.
(2) Unless a time limit for service of the request has expired, the court must—
(a) give directions for an extradition hearing to begin—
   (i) no more than 2 months after service of the request, or
   (ii) if either party so applies, at such a later date as the court decides is in the interests of justice;
(b) consider any ancillary application, including an application about bail pending the extradition hearing; and
(c) give such directions as are required for the preparation and conduct of the extradition hearing.
[Note. See section 76 of the Extradition Act 2003.]

50.13. *Extradition hearing* (1) This rule applies at the extradition hearing directed by the court under rule 50.9 or rule 50.12.
(2) In the following sequence, the court must decide—
(a) whether the documents served on the court officer by the Secretary of State include—
   (i) those listed in rule 50.8(1) or rule 50.12(1), as the case may be,
   (ii) particulars of the person whose extradition is requested,
   (iii) particulars of the offence specified in the request, and
   (iv) as the case may be, a warrant for the defendant's arrest, or a certificate of the defendant's conviction and (if applicable) sentence, issued in the requesting territory;
(b) whether the defendant is the person whose extradition is requested;
(c) whether the offence specified in the request is an extradition offence;
(d) whether the documents served on the court officer by the Secretary of State have been served also on the defendant;
(e) whether a bar to extradition applies, namely—
   (i) the rule against double jeopardy,
   (ii) extraneous considerations,
   (iii) the passage of time,
   (iv) hostage-taking considerations, or
   (v) forum;

(f)   where the request accuses the defendant of an offence, whether there is evidence which would be sufficient to make a case requiring an answer by the defendant if the extradition proceedings were a trial (unless the Secretary of State has otherwise ordered, for this purpose);

(g)   where the request accuses the defendant of being unlawfully at large after conviction, whether the defendant was—

    (i)   convicted in his or her presence, or

    (ii)   absent deliberately;

(h)   where the request accuses the defendant of being unlawfully at large after conviction, and the defendant was absent but not deliberately—

    (i)   whether the defendant would be entitled to a retrial (or to a review of the conviction amounting to a retrial), and

    (ii)   if so, whether there is evidence which would be sufficient to make a case requiring an answer by the defendant if the extradition proceedings were a trial (unless the Secretary of State has otherwise ordered, for this purpose);

(i)   whether extradition would be compatible with the defendant's human rights;

(j)   whether it would be unjust or oppressive to extradite the defendant because of his or her physical or mental condition;

(k)   after deciding each of (a) to (j) above, before progressing to the next, whether to order the defendant's discharge.

(3)   If the court discharges the defendant, the court must consider any ancillary application, including an application about—

(a)   reporting restrictions; or

(b)   costs.

(4)   If the court does not discharge the defendant, the court must—

(a)   exercise its power to send the case to the Secretary of State to decide whether to extradite the defendant;

(b)   explain, in terms the defendant can understand (with help, if necessary), that—

    (i)   the defendant may appeal to the High Court not more than 14 days after being informed of the Secretary of State's decision, and

    (ii)   any such appeal brought before the Secretary of State's decision has been made will not be heard until after that decision; and

(c)   consider any ancillary application, including an application about—

    (i)   bail pending extradition,

    (ii)   reporting restrictions, or

    (iii)   costs.

(5)   If the Secretary of State orders the defendant's extradition, the court must order its postponement where—

(a)   the defendant has been charged with an offence in the United Kingdom; or

(b)   the defendant has been sentenced to imprisonment or detention in the United Kingdom.

[Note. See sections 78, 79, 84, 85, 86, 87, 91, 92, 137 and 138 of the Extradition Act 2003.
Part 6 contains rules about reporting restrictions. Part 45 contains rules about costs.]

50.14. Discharge where extradition request withdrawn (1) This rule applies where the Secretary of State gives the court officer notice that the extradition request has been withdrawn—

(a)   after the start of the hearing under rule 50.9 or 50.11; and

(b)   before the court—

    (i)   sends the case to the Secretary of State to decide whether to extradite the defendant, or

    (ii)   discharges the defendant.

(2)   The court must exercise its power to discharge the defendant.

[Note. See section 122 of the Extradition Act 2003.]

EVIDENCE AT EXTRADITION HEARING

50.15. Introduction of additional evidence (1) Where a party wants to introduce evidence at an extradition hearing under the law that would apply if that hearing were a trial, the relevant Part of these Rules applies with such adaptations as the court directs.

(2)   If the court admits as evidence the written statement of a witness—

(a)   each relevant part of the statement must be read or summarised aloud; or

(b)   the court must read the statement and its gist must be summarised aloud.

(3)   If a party introduces in evidence a fact admitted by another party, or the parties jointly admit a fact, a written record must be made of the admission.

[Note. The admissibility of evidence that a party introduces is governed by rules of evidence.
Under section 202 of the Extradition Act 2003, the court may receive in evidence—

(a)   a warrant to which Part 1 of the Act applies;

(b)   any other document issued in a territory to which Part 1 of the Act applies, if the document is authenticated as required by the Act;

(c)   a document issued in a territory to which Part 2 of the Act applies, if the document is authenticated as required by the Act.

Under sections 84 and 86 of the Act, which apply to evidence, if required, at an extradition hearing to which Part 2 of the Act applies, the court may accept as evidence of a fact a statement by a

person in a document if oral evidence by that person of that fact would be admissible, and the statement was made to a police officer, or to someone else responsible for investigating offences or charging offenders.
Under section 205 of the Act, section 9 (proof by written witness statement) and section 10 (proof by formal admission) of the Criminal Justice Act 1967 apply to extradition proceedings as they apply in relation to proceedings for an offence.]

DISCHARGE AFTER FAILURE TO COMPLY WITH A TIME LIMIT

50.16. *Defendant's application to be discharged* (1)   This rule applies where a defendant wants to be discharged—
(a)   because of a failure—
    (i)   to give the defendant a copy of any warrant under which the defendant is arrested as soon as practicable after arrest,
    (ii)   to bring the defendant before the court as soon as practicable after arrest under a warrant,
    (iii)   to bring the defendant before the court no more than 48 hours after provisional arrest under Part 1 of the Extradition Act 2003;
(b)   following the expiry of a time limit for—
    (i)   service of a warrant to which Part 1 of the 2003 Act applies, after provisional arrest under that Part of the Act (48 hours, under section 6 of the Act, unless the court otherwise directs),
    (ii)   service of an extradition request to which Part 2 of the Act applies, after provisional arrest under that Part of the Act (45 days, under section 74 of the Act, unless the Secretary of State has otherwise ordered for this purpose),
    (iii)   receipt of an undertaking that the defendant will be returned to complete a sentence in the United Kingdom, where the court required such an undertaking (21 days, under section 37 of the Act),
    (iv)   making an extradition order, after the defendant has consented to extradition under Part 1 of the Act (10 days, under section 46 of the Act),
    (v)   extradition, where an extradition order has been made under Part 1 of the Act and any appeal by the defendant has failed (10 days, under sections 35, 36 and 47 of the Act, unless the court otherwise directs),
    (vi)   extradition, where an extradition order has been made under Part 2 of the Act and any appeal by the defendant has failed (28 days, under sections 117 and 118 of the Act),
    (vii)   the resumption of extradition proceedings, where those proceedings were adjourned pending disposal of another extradition claim which has concluded (21 days, under section 180 of the Act),
    (viii)   extradition, where extradition has been deferred pending the disposal of another extradition claim which has concluded (21 days, under section 181 of the Act), or
    (ix)   re-extradition, where the defendant has been returned to the United Kingdom to serve a sentence before serving a sentence overseas (as soon as practicable, under section 187 of the Act); or
(c)   because an extradition hearing does not begin on the date arranged by the court.
(2)   Unless the court otherwise directs—
(a)   such a defendant must apply in writing and serve the application on—
    (i)   the magistrates' court officer,
    (ii)   the High Court officer, where paragraph (1)(b)(v) applies, and
    (iii)   the prosecutor;
(b)   the application must explain the grounds on which it is made; and
(c)   the court officer must arrange a hearing as soon as practicable, and in any event no later than the second business day after an application is served.
[Note. See sections 4(4) & (5), 6(6) & (7), 8(7) & (8), 35(5), 36(8), 37(7), 46(8), 47(4), 72(5) & (6), 74(5), (6) & (10), 75(4), 76(5), 117(3), 118(7), 180(4) & (5), 181(4) & (5) and 187(3) of the Extradition Act 2003.]

SECTION 3: APPEAL TO THE HIGH COURT

[Note. Under Part 1 of the Extradition Act 2003—

    (a)   a defendant may appeal to the High Court against an order for extradition made by the magistrates' court; and
    (b)   the authority requesting the defendant's extradition may appeal to the High Court against an order for the defendant's discharge,
(see sections 26 and 28 of the Act).
Under Part 2 of the 2003 Act—

    (a)   a defendant may appeal to the High Court against an order by the magistrates' court sending a case to the Secretary of State for a decision whether to extradite the defendant;
    (b)   a defendant may appeal to the High Court against an order for extradition made by the Secretary of State; and
    (c)   the territory requesting the defendant's extradition may appeal to the High Court against an order for the defendant's discharge by the magistrates court or by the Secretary of State,
(see sections 103, 105, 108 and 110 of the Act).
In each case the appellant needs the High Court's permission to appeal (in the 2003 Act, described as 'leave to appeal').]

50.17. *Exercise of the High Court's powers* (1)   The general rule is that the High Court must exercise its powers at a hearing in public, but—
(a)   that is subject to any power the court has to—
    (i)   impose reporting restrictions,
    (ii)   withhold information from the public, or

        (iii)   order a hearing in private;

(b)   despite the general rule, the court may determine without a hearing—

        (i)   an application for the court to consider out of time an application for permission to appeal to the High Court,

        (ii)   an application for permission to appeal to the High Court (but a renewed such application must be determined at a hearing),

        (iii)   an application for permission to appeal from the High Court to the Supreme Court,

        (iv)   an application for permission to reopen a decision under rule 50.27 (Reopening the determination of an appeal), or

        (v)   an application concerning bail; and

(c)   despite the general rule the court may, without a hearing—

        (i)   give case management directions,

        (ii)   reject a notice or application and, if applicable, dismiss an application for permission to appeal, where rule 50.31 (Payment of High Court fees) applies and the party who served the notice or application fails to comply with that rule, or

        (iii)   make a determination to which the parties have agreed in writing.

(2)   If the High Court so directs, a party may attend a hearing by live link.

(3)   The general rule is that where the High Court exercises its powers at a hearing it may do so only if the defendant attends, in person or by live link, but, despite the general rule, the court may exercise its powers in the defendant's absence if—

(a)   the defendant waives the right to attend;

(b)   subject to any appeal to the Supreme Court, the result of the court's order would be the discharge of the defendant; or

(c)   the defendant is represented and—

        (i)   the defendant is in custody, or

        (ii)   the defendant's presence is impracticable by reason of his or her ill health or disorderly conduct.

(4)   If the High Court gives permission to appeal to the High Court—

(a)   unless the court otherwise directs, the decision indicates that the appellant has permission to appeal on every ground identified by the appeal notice;

(b)   unless the court otherwise directs, the decision indicates that the court finds reasonably arguable each ground on which the appellant has permission to appeal; and

(c)   the court must give such directions as are required for the preparation and conduct of the appeal, including a direction as to whether the appeal must be heard by a single judge of the High Court or by a divisional court.

(5)   If the High Court decides without a hearing an application for permission to appeal from the High Court to the Supreme Court, the High Court must announce its decision at a hearing in public.

(6)   The High Court may—

(a)   shorten a time limit or extend it (even after it has expired), unless that is inconsistent with other legislation;

(b)   allow or require a party to vary or supplement a notice that that party has served;

(c)   direct that a notice or application be served on any person;

(d)   allow a notice or application to be in a different form to one set out in the Practice Direction, or to be presented orally.

(7)   A party who wants an extension of time within which to serve a notice or make an application must—

(a)   apply for that extension of time when serving that notice or making that application; and

(b)   give the reasons for the application for an extension of time.

[Note. The time limits for serving an appeal notice are prescribed by the Extradition Act 2003: see rule 50.19.]

50.18. Case management in the High Court   (1)   The High Court and the parties have the same duties and powers as under Part 3 (Case management), subject to—

(a)   rule 50.2 (Further objective in extradition proceedings); and

(b)   paragraph (3) of this rule.

(2)   A master of the High Court, a deputy master, or a court officer nominated for the purpose by the Lord Chief Justice—

(a)   must fulfil the duty of active case management under rule 3.2, and in fulfilling that duty may exercise any of the powers of case management under—

        (i)   rule 3.5 (the court's general powers of case management),

        (ii)   rule 3.10(3) (requiring a certificate of readiness), and

        (iii)   rule 3.11 (requiring a party to identify intentions and anticipated requirements)

   subject to the directions of a judge of the High Court; and

(b)   must nominate a case progression officer under rule 3.4.

(3)   Rule 3.6 (Application to vary a direction) does not apply to a decision to give or to refuse—

(a)   permission to appeal; or

(b)   permission to reopen a decision under rule 50.27 (Reopening the determination of an appeal).

50.19. Service of appeal notice   (1)   A party who wants to appeal to the High Court must serve an appeal notice on—

(a)   in every case—

        (i)   the High Court officer,

        (ii)   the other party, and

        (iii)   the Director of Public Prosecutions, unless the Director already has the conduct of the proceedings;

(b)   the designated authority which certified the arrest warrant, where Part 1 of the Extradition Act 2003 applies; and

(c)   the Secretary of State, where the appeal is against—

        (i)   an order by the Secretary of State, or

        (ii)   an order by the magistrates' court sending a case to the Secretary of State.

(2)   A defendant who wants to appeal must serve the appeal notice—

(a)   not more than 7 days after the day on which the magistrates' court makes an order for the defendant's extradition, starting with that day, where that order is under Part 1 of the Extradition Act 2003;

(b)   not more than 14 days after the day on which the Secretary of State informs the defendant of the Secretary of State's decision, starting with that day, where under Part 2 of the Act—

        (i)   the magistrates' court sends the case to the Secretary of State for a decision whether to extradite the defendant, or

        (ii)   the Secretary of State orders the defendant's extradition.

(3)   An authority or territory seeking the defendant's extradition which wants to appeal against an order for the defendant's discharge must serve the appeal notice—

(a)   not more than 7 days after the day on which the magistrates' court makes that order, starting with that day, if the order is under Part 1 of the Extradition Act 2003;

(b)   not more than 14 days after the day on which the magistrates' court makes that order, starting with that day, if the order is under Part 2 of the Act;

(c)   not more than 14 days after the day on which the Secretary of State informs the territory's representative of the Secretary of State's order, starting with that day, where the order is under Part 2 of the Act.

[Note. See sections 26, 28, 103, 105, 108 and 110 of the Extradition Act 2003. The time limits for serving an appeal notice are prescribed by those sections. They may be neither shortened nor extended, but—

(a)   if a defendant applies out of time for permission to appeal to the High Court the court must not for that reason refuse to consider the application if the defendant did everything reasonably possible to ensure that the notice was given as soon as it could be; and

(b)   a defendant may apply out of time for permission to appeal to the High Court on human rights grounds against an order for extradition made by the Secretary of State.

Under section 3 of the Prosecution of Offences Act 1985, the Director of Public Prosecutions may conduct extradition proceedings (but need not do so).]

50.20.   *Form of appeal notice*   (1)   An appeal notice constitutes—

(a)   an application to the High Court for permission to appeal to that court; and

(b)   an appeal to that court, if the court gives permission.

(2)   An appeal notice must be in writing.

(3)   In every case, the appeal notice must—

(a)   specify—

        (i)   the date of the defendant's arrest under Part 1 or Part 2 of the Extradition Act 2003, and

        (ii)   the decision about which the appellant wants to appeal, including the date of that decision;

(b)   identify each ground of appeal on which the appellant relies;

(c)   summarise the relevant facts;

(d)   identify any document or other material that the appellant thinks the court will need to decide the appeal; and

(e)   include or attach a list of those on whom the appellant has served the appeal notice.

(4)   If a defendant serves an appeal notice after the expiry of the time limit specified in rule 50.19 (Service of appeal notice)—

(a)   the notice must—

        (i)   explain what the defendant did to ensure that it was served as soon as it could be, and

        (ii)   include or attach such evidence as the defendant relies upon to support that explanation; and

(b)   where the appeal is on human rights grounds against an order for extradition made by the Secretary of State, the notice must explain why—

        (i)   the appeal is necessary to avoid real injustice, and

        (ii)   the circumstances are exceptional and make it appropriate to consider the appeal.

(5)   Unless the High Court otherwise directs, the appellant may amend the appeal notice—

(a)   by serving on those listed in rule 50.19(1) the appeal notice as so amended;

(b)   not more than 10 business days after service of the appeal notice.

(6)   Where the appeal is against an order by the magistrates' court—

(a)   if the grounds of appeal are that the magistrates' court ought to have decided differently a question of fact or law at the extradition hearing, the appeal notice must—

        (i)   identify that question,

        (ii)   explain what decision the magistrates' court should have made, and why, and

      (iii)   explain why the magistrates' court would have been required not to make the order under appeal, if that question had been decided differently;

(b)   if the grounds of appeal are that there is an issue which was not raised at the extradition hearing, or that evidence is available which was not available at the extradition hearing, the appeal notice must—

      (i)   identify that issue or evidence,

      (ii)   explain why it was not then raised or available,

      (iii)   explain why that issue or evidence would have resulted in the magistrates' court deciding a question differently at the extradition hearing, and

      (iv)   explain why, if the court had decided that question differently, the court would have been required not to make the order it made.

(7)   Where the appeal is against an order by the Secretary of State—

(a)   if the grounds of appeal are that the Secretary of State ought to have decided differently a question of fact or law, the appeal notice must—

      (i)   identify that question,

      (ii)   explain what decision the Secretary of State should have made, and why, and

      (iii)   explain why the Secretary of State would have been required not to make the order under appeal, if that question had been decided differently;

(b)   if the grounds of appeal are that there is an issue which was not raised when the case was being considered by the Secretary of State, or that information is available which was not then available, the appeal notice must—

      (i)   identify that issue or information,

      (ii)   explain why it was not then raised or available,

      (iii)   explain why that issue or information would have resulted in the Secretary of State deciding a question differently, and

      (iv)   explain why, if the Secretary of State had decided that question differently, the order under appeal would not have been made.

[Note. The Practice Direction sets out a form of appeal notice for use in connection with this rule.]

50.21. *Respondent's notice* (1) A party on whom an appellant serves an appeal notice under rule 50.19 may serve a respondent's notice, and must do so if—

(a)   that party wants to make representations to the High Court; or

(b)   the court so directs.

(2)   Such a party must serve any such notice on—

(a)   the High Court officer;

(b)   the appellant;

(c)   the Director of Public Prosecutions, unless the Director already has the conduct of the proceedings; and

(d)   any other person on whom the appellant served the appeal notice.

(3)   Such a party must serve any such notice, as appropriate—

(a)   not more than 10 business days after—

      (i)   service on that party of an amended appeal notice under rule 50.20(5) (Form of appeal notice), or

      (ii)   the expiry of the time for service of any such amended appeal notice

   whichever of those events happens first;

(b)   not more than 5 business days after service on that party of—

      (i)   an appellant's notice renewing an application for permission to appeal,

      (ii)   a direction to serve a respondent's notice.

(4)   A respondent's notice must—

(a)   give the date or dates on which the respondent was served with, as appropriate—

      (i)   the appeal notice,

      (ii)   the appellant's notice renewing the application for permission to appeal,

      (iii)   the direction to serve a respondent's notice;

(b)   identify each ground of opposition on which the respondent relies and the ground of appeal to which each such ground of opposition relates;

(c)   summarise any relevant facts not already summarised in the appeal notice; and

(d)   identify any document or other material that the respondent thinks the court will need to decide the appeal.

[Note. Under rule 50.17, the High Court may extend or shorten the time limit under this rule.]

50.22. *Renewing an application for permission to appeal, restoring excluded grounds, etc*
  (1)   This rule—

(a)   applies where the High Court—

      (i)   refuses permission to appeal to the High Court, or

      (ii)   gives permission to appeal to the High Court but not on every ground identified by the appeal notice;

(b)   does not apply where—

      (i)   a defendant applies out of time for permission to appeal to the High Court, and

      (ii)   the court for that reason refuses to consider that application.

(2)   Unless the court refuses permission to appeal at a hearing, the appellant may renew the application for permission by serving notice on—

(a)   the High Court officer;

(b)   the respondent; and
(c)   any other person on whom the appellant served the appeal notice,
not more than 5 business days after service of notice of the court's decision on the appellant.
(3)   If the court refuses permission to appeal, the renewal notice must explain the grounds for the renewal.
(4)   If the court gives permission to appeal but not on every ground identified by the appeal notice the decision indicates that—
(a)   at the hearing of the appeal the court will not consider representations that address any ground thus excluded from argument; and
(b)   an appellant who wants to rely on such an excluded ground needs the court's permission to do so.
(5)   An appellant who wants to rely at the hearing of an appeal on a ground of appeal excluded from argument must—
(a)   apply in writing, with reasons, and identify each such ground;
(b)   serve the application on—
           (i)   the High Court officer, and
           (ii)   the respondent;
(c)   serve the application not more than 5 business days after—
           (i)   the giving of permission to appeal, or
           (ii)   the High Court officer serves notice of that decision on the applicant, if the applicant was not present in person or by live link when permission to appeal was given.
(6)   Paragraph (7) applies where a party wants to abandon—
(a)   a ground of appeal on which that party has permission to appeal; or
(b)   a ground of opposition identified in a respondent's notice.
(7)   Such a party must serve notice on—
(a)   the High Court officer; and
(b)   each other party,
before any hearing at which that ground will be considered by the court.
[Note. Under rule 50.17 (Exercise of the High Court's powers), the High Court may extend or shorten the time limits under this rule.
Rule 50.19 (Service of appeal notice) and the note to that rule set out the time limits for appeal.]

50.23.   Appeal hearing   (1)   Unless the High Court otherwise directs, where the appeal to the High Court is under Part 1 of the Extradition Act 2003 the hearing of the appeal must begin no more than 40 days after the defendant's arrest.
(2)   Unless the High Court otherwise directs, where the appeal to the High Court is under Part 2 of the 2003 Act the hearing of the appeal must begin no more than 76 days after the later of—
(a)   service of the appeal notice; or
(b)   the day on which the Secretary of State informs the defendant of the Secretary of State's order, in a case in which—
           (i)   the appeal is by the defendant against an order by the magistrates' court sending the case to the Secretary of State, and
           (ii)   the appeal notice is served before the Secretary of State decides whether the defendant should be extradited.
(3)   If the effect of the decision of the High Court on the appeal is that the defendant is to be extradited—
(a)   the High Court must consider any ancillary application, including an application about—
           (i)   bail pending extradition,
           (ii)   reporting restrictions,
           (iii)   costs;
(b)   the High Court is the appropriate court to order a postponement of the defendant's extradition where—
           (i)   the defendant has been charged with an offence in the United Kingdom, or
           (ii)   the defendant has been sentenced to imprisonment or detention in the United Kingdom.
(4)   If the effect of the decision of the High Court on the appeal is that the defendant is discharged, the High Court must consider any ancillary application, including an application about—
(a)   reporting restrictions;
(b)   costs.
[Note. Under sections 31 and 113 of the Extradition Act 2003, if the appeal hearing does not begin within the period prescribed by this rule or ordered by the High Court the appeal must be taken to have been dismissed by decision of the High Court.
Under section 103 of the Extradition Act 2003, a defendant's appeal against an order by the magistrates' court sending the case to the Secretary of State must not be heard until after the Secretary of State has decided whether to order the defendant's extradition.
Part 6 contains rules about reporting restrictions. Part 45 contains rules about costs.
See sections 36A, 36B, 118A and 118B Extradition Act 2003. Where there is an appeal against an order for extradition, rules may provide that the appeal court may exercise the power under those sections to postpone the extradition.]

50.24.   Early termination of appeal: order by consent, etc   (1)   This rule applies where—
(a)   an appellant has served an appeal notice under rule 50.19; and
(b)   the High Court—

(i)   has not determined the application for permission to appeal, or

(ii)   where the court has given permission to appeal, has not determined the appeal.

(2)   Where the warrant or extradition request with which the appeal is concerned is withdrawn—

(a)   the party or person so informing the court must serve on the High Court officer—

(i)   notice to that effect by the authority or territory requesting the defendant's extradition,

(ii)   details of how much of the warrant or extradition request remains outstanding, if any, and of any other warrant or extradition request outstanding in respect of the defendant,

(iii)   details of any bail condition to which the defendant is subject, if the defendant is on bail, and

(iv)   details sufficient to locate the defendant, including details of the custodian and of the defendant's date of birth and custody reference, if the defendant is in custody; and

(b)   paragraph (5) applies but only to the extent that the parties want the court to deal with an ancillary matter.

(3)   Where a defendant with whose discharge the appeal is concerned consents to extradition, paragraph (5) applies but only to the extent that the parties want the court to—

(a)   give directions for that consent to be given to the magistrates' court or to the Secretary of State, as the case may be;

(b)   deal with an ancillary matter.

(4)   Paragraph (5) applies where the parties want the court to make a decision on which they are agreed—

(a)   determining the application for permission to appeal or the appeal, as the case may be;

(b)   specifying the date on which that application or appeal is to be treated as discontinued; and

(c)   determining an ancillary matter, including costs, if applicable.

(5)   The parties must serve on the High Court officer, in one or more documents—

(a)   a draft order in the terms proposed;

(b)   evidence of each party's agreement to those terms; and

(c)   concise reasons for the request that the court make the proposed order.

[Note. Under sections 42 and 124 of the Extradition Act 2003, where an appeal is pending in the High Court and the court is informed that the relevant warrant or extradition request has been withdrawn the court must—

(a)   *order the defendant's discharge and quash the extradition order or decision, where the defendant has appealed against extradition;*

(b)   *dismiss the application for permission to appeal or the appeal, as the case may be, where the authority or territory requesting the defendant's extradition has appealed against the defendant's discharge.*

Under sections 45 and 127 of the 2003 Act, a defendant in respect of whom no extradition order or decision has been made may give consent to extradition in the magistrates' court, or may give such consent to the Secretary of State if the case has been sent there.

Where the effect of the High Court's decision is that the defendant is to be extradited, sections 36 and 118 of the Act set time limits for extradition after the end of the case.

Part 45 contains rules about costs.]

50.25. *Application for permission to appeal to the Supreme Court* (1)   This rule applies where a party to an appeal to the High Court wants to appeal to the Supreme Court.

(2)   Such a party must—

(a)   apply orally to the High Court for permission to appeal immediately after the court's decision; or

(b)   apply in writing and serve the application on the High Court officer and every other party not more than 14 days after that decision.

(3)   Such a party must—

(a)   identify the point of law of general public importance that the appellant wants the High Court to certify is involved in the decision;

(b)   serve on the High Court officer a statement of that point of law; and

(c)   give reasons why—

(i)   that point of law ought to be considered by the Supreme Court, and

(ii)   the High Court ought to give permission to appeal.

(4)   As well as complying with paragraph (3), a defendant's application for permission to appeal to the Supreme Court must include or attach any application for the following, with reasons—

(a)   bail pending appeal;

(b)   permission to attend any hearing in the Supreme Court, if the appellant is in custody.

[Note. See sections 32 and 114 of the Extradition Act 2003. Those sections prescribe the time limit for serving an application for permission to appeal to the Supreme Court. It may be neither shortened nor extended.]

50.26. *Determination of detention pending appeal to the Supreme Court against discharge* On an application for permission to appeal to the Supreme Court against a decision of the High Court which, but for that appeal, would have resulted in the defendant's discharge, the High Court must—

(a)   decide whether to order the detention of the defendant; and

(b)   determine any application for—
        (i)   bail pending appeal,
        (ii)   permission to attend any hearing in the Supreme Court,
        (iii)   a representation order.
[Note. See sections 33A and 115A of the Extradition Act 2003.
For the grant of legal aid for proceedings in the Supreme Court, see sections 14, 16 and 19 of the
Legal Aid, Sentencing and Punishment of Offenders Act 2012.]

50.27.   Reopening the determination of an appeal   (1)   This rule applies where a party wants the
High Court to reopen a decision of that court which determines an appeal or an application for
permission to appeal.
(2)   Such a party must—
(a)   apply in writing for permission to reopen that decision, as soon as practicable after
        becoming aware of the grounds for doing so; and
(b)   serve the application on the High Court officer and every other party.
(3)   The application must—
(a)   specify the decision which the applicant wants the court to reopen; and
(b)   give reasons why—
        (i)   it is necessary for the court to reopen that decision in order to avoid real injustice,
        (ii)   the circumstances are exceptional and make it appropriate to reopen the decision,
                and
        (iii)   there is no alternative effective remedy.
(4)   The court must not give permission to reopen a decision unless each other party has had an
opportunity to make representations.

50.28.   Declaration of incompatibility with a Convention right   (1)   This rule applies where a
party—
(a)   wants the High Court to make a declaration of incompatibility with a Convention right
        under section 4 of the Human Rights Act 1998; or
(b)   raises an issue that appears to the High Court may lead to the court making such a
        declaration.
(2)   If the High Court so directs, the High Court officer must serve notice on—
(a)   the relevant person named in the list published under section 17(1) of the Crown
        Proceedings Act 1947; or
(b)   the Treasury Solicitor, if it is not clear who is the relevant person.
(3)   That notice must include or attach details of—
(a)   the legislation affected and the Convention right concerned;
(b)   the parties to the appeal; and
(c)   any other information or document that the High Court thinks relevant.
(4)   A person who has a right under the 1998 Act to become a party to the appeal must—
(a)   serve notice on—
        (i)   the High Court officer, and
        (ii)   the other parties,
    if that person wants to exercise that right; and
(b)   in that notice—
        (i)   indicate the conclusion that that person invites the High Court to reach on the
                question of incompatibility, and
        (ii)   identify each ground for that invitation, concisely outlining the arguments in
                support.
(5)   The High Court must not make a declaration of incompatibility—
(a)   less than 21 days after the High Court officer serves notice under paragraph (2); and
(b)   without giving any person who serves a notice under paragraph (4) an opportunity to
        make representations at a hearing.

50.29.   Duties of court officers   (1)   The magistrates' court officer must—
(a)   keep any document or object exhibited in the proceedings in the magistrates' court, or
        arrange for it to be kept by some other appropriate person, until—
        (i)   6 weeks after the conclusion of those proceedings, or
        (ii)   the conclusion of any proceedings in the High Court that begin within that 6 weeks;
(b)   provide the High Court with any document, object or information for which the High Court
        officer asks, within such period as the High Court officer may require; and
(c)   arrange for the magistrates' court to hear as soon as practicable any application to that
        court for bail pending appeal.
(2)   A person who, under arrangements made by the magistrates' court officer, keeps a document
or object exhibited in the proceedings in the magistrates' court must—
(a)   keep that exhibit until—
        (i)   6 weeks after the conclusion of those proceedings, or
        (ii)   the conclusion of any proceedings in the High Court that begin within that 6 weeks,
    unless the magistrates' court or the High Court otherwise directs; and
(b)   provide the High Court with any such document or object for which the High Court officer
        asks, within such period as the High Court officer may require.
(3)   The High Court officer must—
(a)   give as much notice as reasonably practicable of each hearing to—

(i)   the parties,

(ii)   the defendant's custodian, if any, and

(iii)   any other person whom the High Court requires to be notified;

(b)   serve a record of each order or direction of the High Court on—

(i)   the parties,

(ii)   any other person whom the High Court requires to be notified;

(c)   if the High Court's decision determines an appeal or application for permission to appeal, serve a record of that decision on—

(i)   the defendant's custodian, if any,

(ii)   the magistrates' court officer, and

(iii)   the designated authority which certified the arrest warrant, where Part 1 of the Extradition Act 2003 applies;

(d)   where rule 50.24 applies (Early termination of appeal: order by consent, etc), arrange for the High Court to consider the document or documents served under that rule;

(e)   treat the appeal as if it had been dismissed by the High Court where—

(i)   the hearing of the appeal does not begin within the period required by rule 50.23 (Appeal hearing) or ordered by the High Court, or

(ii)   on an appeal by a requesting territory under section 105 of the Extradition Act 2003, the High Court directs the magistrates' court to decide a question again and the magistrates' court comes to the same conclusion as it had done before.

[Note. See section 106 of the Extradition Act 2003.]

50.30.   *Constitution of the High Court*   (1)   A master of the High Court, a deputy master, or a court officer nominated for the purpose by the Lord Chief Justice, may exercise any power of the High Court to which the rules in this Section apply, except the power to—

(a)   give or refuse permission to appeal;

(b)   determine an appeal;

(c)   reopen a decision which determines an appeal or an application for permission to appeal;

(d)   grant or withhold bail; or

(e)   impose or vary a condition of bail.

(2)   Despite paragraph (1), such a master, deputy master or court officer may exercise one of the powers listed in paragraph (1)(a), (b), (d) or (e) if making a decision to which the parties have agreed in writing.

(3)   A renewed application for permission to appeal to the High Court may be determined by—

(a)   a single judge of the High Court other than the judge who first refused permission, or

(b)   a divisional court.

(4)   An appeal may be determined by—

(a)   a single judge of the High Court; or

(b)   a divisional court.

[Note. See sections 19 and 66 of the Senior Courts Act 1981.]

50.31.   *Payment of High Court fees*   (1)   This rule applies where a party serves on the High Court officer a notice or application in respect of which a court fee is payable under legislation that requires the payment of such a fee.

(2)   Such a party must pay the fee, or satisfy the conditions for any remission of the fee, when so serving the notice or application.

(3)   If such a party fails to comply with paragraph (2), then unless the High Court otherwise directs—

(a)   the High Court officer must serve on that party a notice requiring payment of the fee due, or satisfaction of the conditions for any remission of that fee, within a period specified in the notice;

(b)   that party must comply with such a requirement; and

(c)   until the expiry of the period specified in the notice, the High Court must not exercise its power—

(i)   to reject the notice or application in respect of which the fee is payable, or

(ii)   to dismiss an application for permission to appeal, in consequence of rejecting an appeal notice.

[Note. Section 92 of the Courts Act 2003 and the Civil Proceedings Fees Order 2008 require the payment of High Court fees in cases to which this Section of this Part applies. Article 5 and Schedule 2 to the 2008 Order provide for the remission of such fees in some cases.]

SECTION 4: POST-EXTRADITION PROCEEDINGS

50.32.   ***Application for consent to deal with another offence or for consent to further extradition***

(1)   This rule applies where—

(a)   a defendant has been extradited to a territory under Part 1 of the Extradition Act 2003; and

(b)   the court officer receives from the authority designated by the Secretary of State a request for the court's consent to—

(i)   the defendant being dealt with in that territory for an offence other than one in respect of which the extradition there took place, or

(ii)   the defendant's further extradition from there to another such territory for an offence.

(2)   The presenting officer must serve on the court officer—

(a)   the request; and

(b)   a certificate given by the designated authority that the request was made by a judicial authority with the function of making such requests in the territory to which the defendant was extradited.

(3)   The court must—

(a)   give directions for service by a party or other person on the defendant of notice that the request for consent has been received, unless satisfied that it would not be practicable for such notice to be served;

(b)   give directions for a hearing to consider the request to begin—

    (i)   no more than 21 days after the request was received by the designated authority, or

    (ii)   at such a later date as the court decides is in the interests of justice; and

(c)   give such directions as are required for the preparation and conduct of that hearing.

(4)   At the hearing directed under paragraph (3), in the following sequence the court must decide—

(a)   whether the consent requested is required, having regard to—

    (i)   any opportunity given for the defendant to leave the requesting territory after extradition which the defendant did not take within 45 days of arrival there,

    (ii)   if the defendant did not take such an opportunity, any requirements for consent imposed by the law of the requesting territory or by arrangements between that territory and the United Kingdom where the request is for consent to deal with the defendant in that territory for another offence,

    (iii) if the defendant did not take such an opportunity, any requirements for consent imposed by arrangements between the requesting territory and the United Kingdom where the request is for consent to extradite the defendant to another territory for an offence;

(b)   if such consent is required, then—

    (i)   whether the offence in respect of which consent is requested is an extradition offence, and

    (ii)   if it is, whether the court would order the defendant's extradition under sections 11 to 25 of the Extradition Act 2003 (bars to extradition and other considerations) were the defendant in the United Kingdom and the court was considering extradition for that offence.

(5)   The court must give directions for notice of its decision to be conveyed to the authority which made the request.

(6)   Rules 50.3 (Exercise of magistrates' court's powers) and 50.4 (Case management in the magistrates' court and duty of court officer) apply on an application under this rule.

[Note. See sections 54, 55, 56 and 57 of the Extradition Act 2003.]

Glossary   This glossary is a guide to the meaning of certain legal expressions used in these rules.

Expression	**Meaning**
account monitoring order	*an order requiring certain types of financial institution to provide certain information held by them relating to a customer for the purposes of an investigation;*
action plan order	*a type of community sentence requiring a child or young person to comply with a three month plan relating to his actions and whereabouts and to comply with the directions of a responsible officer (eg probation officer);*
admissible evidence	*evidence allowed in proceedings (not all evidence introduced by the parties may be allowable in court);*
adjourn	*to suspend or delay the hearing of a case;*
affidavit	*a written, sworn statement of evidence;*
affirmation	*a non-religious alternative to the oath sworn by someone about to give evidence in court or swearing a statement;*
appellant	*person who is appealing against a decision of the court;*
arraign	*to put charges to the defendant in open court in the Crown Court;*
arraignment	*the formal process of putting charges to the defendant in the Crown Court which consists of three parts: (1) calling him to the bar by name, (2) putting the charges to him by reading from the indictment and (3) asking him whether he pleads guilty or not guilty;*
authorities	*judicial decisions or opinions of authors of repute used as grounds of statements of law;*

bill of indictment	a written accusation of a crime against one or more persons – a criminal trial in the Crown Court cannot start without a valid indictment;
case stated	an appeal to the High Court against the decision of a magistrates court on the basis that the decision was wrong in law or in excess of the magistrates' jurisdiction;
in chambers	non-trial hearing in private;
committal	sending someone to another court (for example, from a magistrates' court to the Crown Court to be sentenced), or sending someone to be detained (for example, in prison);
compellable witness	a witness who can be forced to give evidence against an accused (not all witnesses are compellable);
compensation order	an order that a convicted person must pay compensation for loss or damage caused by the convicted person;
complainant	a person who makes a formal complaint. In relation to an offence of rape or other sexual offences the complainant is the person against whom the offence is alleged to have been committed;
conditional discharge	an order which does not impose any immediate punishment on a person convicted of an offence, subject to the condition that he does not commit an offence in a specified period;
confiscation order	an order that private property be taken into possession by the state;
Convention right	a right under the European Convention on Human Rights;
costs	the expenses involved in a court case, including the fees of the lawyers and of the court;
counsel	a barrister;
cross examination	questioning of a witness by a party other than the party who called the witness;
custody time limit	the maximum period, as set down in statute, for which a person may be kept in custody before being brought to trial – these maximum periods may only be extended by an order of the judge;
customer information order	an order requiring a financial institution to provide certain information held by them relating to a customer for the purposes of an investigation into the proceeds of crime;
declaration of incompatibility	a declaration by a court that a piece of UK legislation is incompatible with the provisions of the European Convention on Human Rights;
deferred sentence	a sentence which is determined after a delay to allow the court to assess any change in the person's conduct or circumstances after his or her conviction;
exhibit	a document or thing presented as evidence in court;
forfeiture by peaceable re-entry	the re-possession by a landlord of premises occupied by tenants;
guardianship order	an order appointing someone to take charge of a child's affairs and property;

hearsay evidence	oral or written statements made by someone who is not a witness in the case but which the court is asked to accept as proving what they say. This expression is defined further by rule 34.1 for the purposes of Part 34, and by rule 57.1 for the purposes of Parts 57 - 61 This expression is defined further by rule 20.1 for the purposes of Part 20 and by rule 33.1 for the purposes of Part 33;
hospital order	an order that an offender be admitted to and detained in a specified hospital;
indictment	the document containing the formal charges against a defendant – a trial in the Crown Court cannot start without this;
information	statement by which a magistrate is informed of the offence for which a summons or warrant is required – the procedure by which this statement is brought to the magistrates' attention is known as laying an information;
intermediary	a person who asks a witness (particularly a child) questions posed by the cross-examining legal representative;
justice of the peace	a magistrate, either a lay justice or a District Judge (Magistrates' Courts);
justices' clerk	post in the magistrates' court of person who has various powers and duties, including giving advice to the magistrates on law and procedure;
leave of the court	permission granted by the court;
leave to appeal	permission to appeal the decision of a court;
letter of request	letter issued to a foreign court asking a judge to take the evidence of some person within that court's jurisdiction;
to levy distress	to seize property from a debtor or a wrong-doer;
local justice area	an area established for the purposes of the administration of magistrates' courts;
nominated court	a court nominated to take evidence pursuant to a request by a foreign court;
offence triable either way	an offence which may be tried either in the magistrates' court or in the Crown Court;
in open court	in a courtroom which is open to the public;
parenting order	an order which can be made in certain circumstances where a child has been convicted of an offence which may require parents of the offender to comply with certain requirements including attendance of counselling or guidance sessions;
party	a person or organisation directly involved in a criminal case, usually as prosecutor or defendant
prefer, preferment	to bring or lay a charge or indictment;
preparatory hearing	a hearing forming part of the trial sometimes used in long and complex cases to settle various issues without requiring the jury to attend;
realisable property	property which can be sold for money.
receiver	a person appointed with certain powers in respect of the property and affairs of a person who has obtained such property in the course of criminal conduct and who has been convicted of an offence – there are various types or receiver (management receiver, director's receiver, enforcement receiver);
receivership order	an order that a person's assets be put into the hands of an official with certain powers and duties to deal with that property;

recognizance	formal undertaking to pay the crown a specified sum if an accused fails to surrender to custody;
register	the formal records kept by a magistrates' court;
to remand	to send a person away when a case is adjourned until another date – the person may be remanded on bail (when he can leave, subject to conditions) or in custody;
reparation order	an order made against a child or young person who has been convicted of an offence, requiring him or her to make specific reparations to the victim or to the community at large;
representation order	an order authorising payment of legal aid for a defendant;
requisition	a document issued by a prosecutor requiring a person to attend a magistrates' court to answer a written charge;
respondent	the other party (to the appellant) in a case which is the subject of an appeal;
restraint order	an order prohibiting a person from dealing with any realisable property held by him;
seal	a formal mark which the court puts on a document to indicate that the document has been issued by the court;
security	money deposited to ensure that the defendant attends court;
sending for trial	procedure by which some cases are transferred from a magistrates' court to the Crown Court for trial;
skeleton argument	a document prepared by a party or their legal representative, setting out the basis of the party's argument, including any arguments based on law – the court may require such documents to be served on the court and on the other party prior to a trial;
special measures	measures which can be put in place to provide protection and/or anonymity to a witness (eg a screen separating witness from the accused);
statutory declaration	a declaration made before a Commissioner for Oaths in a prescribed form;
to stay	to halt proceedings, apart from taking any steps allowed by the Rules or the terms of the stay - proceedings may be continued if a stay is lifted;
summons	a document signed by a magistrate after an information is laid which sets out the basis of the accusation against the defendant and the time and place he or she must attend court;
surety	a person who guarantees that a defendant will attend court;
suspended sentence	sentence which takes effect only if the offender commits another offence punishable with imprisonment within the specified period;
supervision order	an order placing a person who has been given a suspended sentence under the supervision of a local officer;
taxing authority	a body which assesses costs;
territorial authority	the UK authority which has power to do certain things in connection with co-operation with other countries and international organisations in relation to the collection of or hearing of evidence etc;
warrant of arrest	court order to arrest a person;
warrant of detention	a court order authorising someone's detention;

wasted costs order	an order that a barrister or solicitor is not to be paid fees that they would normally be paid;
witness	a person who gives evidence, either by way of a written statement or orally in court;
witness summons	a document served on a witness requiring him or her to attend court to give evidence;
written charge	a document, issued by a prosecutor under section 29 of the Criminal Justice Act 2003, which institutes criminal proceedings by charging a person with an offence;
youth court	a magistrates' court exercising jurisdiction over offences committed by, and other matters related to, children and young persons.

MAGISTRATES' COURT SENTENCING GUIDELINES

These Sentencing Guidelines were issued by the Sentencing Guidelines Council on 12 May 2008 and regular updates are issued. They are reproduced with the permission of the Council.

Following these guidelines

C.1   When sentencing offences committed after 6 April 2010, every court is under a statutory obligation to follow any relevant Sentencing Council guideline unless it would be contrary to the interests of justice to do so (Coroners and Justice Act 2009, s 125(1)). If a court imposes a sentence outside the range indicated in an offence specific guideline, it is obliged to state its reasons for doing so (Criminal Justice Act 2003, s 174(2)(a)).

WHEN TO USE THESE GUIDELINES

C.2
- These guidelines apply to sentencing in a magistrates' court whatever the composition of the court. They cover offences for which sentences are frequently imposed in a magistrates' court when dealing with adult offenders.
- They also apply to allocation (mode of trial) decisions. When dealing with an either way offence for which there is no plea or an indication of a not guilty plea, these guidelines will be relevant to the allocation decision and should be consulted at this stage to assess the likely sentence. Reference should be made to the allocation guideline.
- These guidelines apply also to the Crown Court when dealing with appeals against sentences imposed in a magistrates' court and when sentencing for summary only offences.

USING PRE-SENTENCING COUNCIL GUIDELINES

C.3   The offence guidelines include two structures: pre-Sentencing Council guidelines (issued by the Sentencing Guidelines Council) before 2010 and Sentencing Council guidelines issued from 2011 onwards.

Using pre-Sentencing Council guidelines (guidelines issued before 2010)
This section explains the key decisions involved in the sentencing process for SGC guidelines.

1. ASSESS OFFENCE SERIOUSNESS (CULPABILITY AND HARM)

Offence seriousness is the starting point for sentencing under the Criminal Justice Act 2003. The court's assessment of offence seriousness will:
- determine which of the sentencing thresholds has been crossed;
- indicate whether a custodial, community or other sentence is the most appropriate;
- be the key factor in deciding the length of a custodial sentence, the onerousness of requirements to be incorporated in a community sentence and the amount of any fine imposed.

When considering the seriousness of any offence, the court must consider the offender's **culpability** in committing the offence and any **harm** which the offence caused, was intended to cause, or might forseeably have caused.[3] In using these guidelines, this assessment should be approached in two stages:

---

[3]   Criminal Justice Act 2003, s.143(1)

2. OFFENCE SERIOUSNESS (CULPABILITY AND HARM)

A. Identify the appropriate starting point

The guidelines set out **examples** of the nature of activity which may constitute the offence, progressing from less to more serious conduct, and provide a **starting point** based on a **first time offender pleading not guilty.** The guidelines also specify a sentencing **range** for each example of activity. Refer to pages 145-146 for further guidance on the meaning of the terms 'starting point', 'range' and 'first time offender'.

Sentencers should begin by considering which of the examples of offence activity corresponds most closely to the circumstances of the particular case in order to identify the appropriate **starting point:**
- where the starting point is a fine, this is indicated as band A, B or C. The approach to assessing fines is set out on pages 148-155;
- where the community sentence threshold is passed, the guideline sets out whether the starting point should be a low, medium or high level community order. Refer to pages 160-162 for further guidance;
- where the starting point is a custodial sentence, refer to pages 163-164 for further guidance.

The Council's definitive guideline *Overarching Principles: Seriousness*, published 16 December 2004, identifies four levels of culpability for sentencing purposes (intention, recklessness, knowledge and negligence). The starting points in the individual offence guidelines assume that culpability is at the highest level applicable to the offence (often, but not always, intention). **Where a lower level of culpability is present, this should be taken into account.**

B. Consider the effect of aggravating and mitigating factors

Once the starting point has been identified, the court can add to or reduce this to reflect any aggravating or mitigating factors that impact on the **culpability** of the offender and/or **harm** caused by the offence to reach a provisional sentence. Any factors contained in the description of the activity used to reach the starting point must not be counted again.

The **range** is the bracket into which the provisional sentence will normally fall after having regard to factors which aggravate or mitigate the seriousness of the offence.

However:

- the court is not precluded from going outside the range where the facts justify it;
- previous convictions which aggravate the seriousness of the current offence may take the provisional sentence beyond the range, especially where there are significant other aggravating factors present.

In addition, where an offender is being sentenced for multiple offences, the court's assessment of the totality of the offending may result in a sentence above the range indicated for the individual offences, including a sentence of a different type. Refer to [page 18g] for further guidance.

The guidelines identify aggravating and mitigating factors which may be particularly relevant to each individual offence. These include some factors drawn from the general list of aggravating and mitigating factors in the Council's definitive guideline *Overarching Principles: Seriousness* published 16 December 2004, (reproduced on the pullout card). In each case, sentencers should have regard to the full list, which includes the factors that, by statute, make an offence more serious:

- offence committed while on bail for other offences;
- offence was racially or religiously aggravated;
- offence was motivated by, or demonstrates, hostility based on the victim's sexual orientation (or presumed sexual orientation);
- offence was motivated by, or demonstrates, hostility based on the victim's disability (or presumed disability);
- offender has previous convictions that the court considers can reasonably be treated as aggravating factors having regard to their relevance to the current offence and the time that has elapsed since conviction.

While the lists in the offence guidelines and pullout card aim to identify the most common aggravating and mitigating factors, **they are not intended to be exhaustive**. Sentencers should always consider whether there are any other factors that make the offence more or less serious.

3. FORM A PRELIMINARY VIEW OF THE APPROPRIATE SENTENCE, THEN CONSIDER OFFENDER MITIGATION

When the court has reached a provisional sentence based on its assessment of offence seriousness, it should take into account matters of offender mitigation. The Council guideline *Overarching Principles: Seriousness* states that the issue of remorse should be taken into account at this point along with other mitigating features such as admissions to the police in interview.

4. CONSIDER A REDUCTION FOR A GUILTY PLEA

For cases where the first hearing is before 1 June 2017

The Council guideline Reduction in Sentence for a Guilty Plea, revised 2007, states that the punitive elements of the sentence should be reduced to recognise an offender's guilty plea. The reduction has no impact on sentencing decisions in relation to ancillary orders, including disqualification. The level of the reduction should reflect the stage at which the offender indicated a willingness to admit guilt and will be gauged on a sliding scale, ranging from a recommended one third (where the guilty plea was entered at the first reasonable opportunity), reducing to a recommended one quarter (where a trial date has been set) and to a recommended one tenth (for a guilty plea entered at the 'door of the court' or after the trial has begun). There is a presumption that the recommended reduction will be given unless there are good reasons for a lower amount. The application of the reduction may affect the type, as well as the severity, of the sentence. It may also take the sentence below the range in some cases. The court must state that it has reduced a sentence to reflect a guilty plea (Criminal Justice Act 2003, s 174(2)(d)). It should usually indicate what the sentence would have been if there had been no reduction as a result of the plea.

For cases where the first hearing is on or after 1 June 2017

Refer to the new Sentencing Council Reduction in Sentence for a Guilty Plea guideline.

5. CONSIDER ANCILLARY ORDERS, INCLUDING COMPENSATION

Ancillary orders of particular relevance to individual offences are identified in the relevant guidelines. The court must always consider making a compensation order where the offending has resulted in personal injury, loss or damage (Powers of Criminal Courts (Sentencing) Act 2000, s 130(1)). The court is required to give reasons if it decides not to make such an order (Powers of Criminal Courts (Sentencing) Act 2000, s 130(3)).

6. DECIDE SENTENCE

Review the total sentence to ensure that it is proportional to the offending behaviour and properly balanced. Sentencers must state reasons for the sentence passed in every case, including for any ancillary orders imposed (Criminal Justice Act 2003, s 174(1)). It is particularly important to identify any aggravating or mitigating factors, or matters of offender mitigation, that have resulted in a sentence more or less severe than the suggested starting point. If a court imposes a sentence of a different kind or outside the range indicated in the guidelines, it must state its reasons for doing so (Criminal Justice Act 2003, s 174(2)(a)). The court should also give its reasons for not making an order that has been canvassed before it or that it might have been expected to make.

Where there is no guideline for an offence, it may assist in determining sentence to consider the starting points and ranges indicated for offences that are of a similar level of seriousness.

Using Sentencing Council Guidelines

C.4 The offence guidelines include two structures: pre-Sentencing Council guidelines (issued by the Sentencing Guidelines Council) before 2010 and Sentencing Council guidelines issued from 2011 onwards.

Using Sentencing Council guidelines (guidelines effective from 2011 onwards)
This section of the user guide explains the key decisions involved in the sentencing process for Sentencing Council guidelines.
Using Parts 3 and 4
The first section of the user guide explains the key decisions involved in the sentencing process for guidelines in **Parts 3 and 4**. A step-by-step summary is provided on the pullout card.

Step one
Determining the offence category
The decision making process includes a two step approach to assessing seriousness. The first step is to determine the offence category by means of an assessment of the offender's culpability and the harm caused, or intended, by reference **only** to the factors set out at step one in each guideline. The contents are tailored for each offence and comprise the principal factual elements of the offence.

Step two
Starting point and category range
The guidelines provide a **starting point** which applies to all offenders irrespective of plea or previous convictions. The guidelines also specify a **category range** for each offence category.

The guidelines provide non-exhaustive lists of aggravating and mitigating factors relating to the context of the offence and to the offender. Sentencers should identify whether any combination of these, or other relevant factors, should result in an upward or downward adjustment from the starting point.

In some cases, it may be appropriate to move outside the identified category range when reaching a provisional sentence.

Further steps
Having reached a provisional sentence, there are a number of further steps within the guidelines. These steps are clearly set out within each guideline and are tailored specifically for each offence in order to ensure that only the most appropriate guidance is included within each offence specific guideline.

The further steps include:

- reduction for assistance to the prosecution;
- reduction for guilty pleas (courts should refer to the *Guilty Plea* guideline);
- where an offender is being sentenced for multiple offences — the court's assessment of the totality of the offending may result in a sentence above the range indicated for the individual offences, including a sentence of a different type (refer to page 18g for further guidance);
- compensation orders and/or ancillary orders appropriate to the case; and
- give reasons for, and explain the effect of, the sentence.

Where there is no guideline for an offence, it may assist in determining sentence to consider the starting points and ranges indicated for offences that are of a similar level of seriousness.

List of aggravating and mitigating factors

Taken from Sentencing Guidelines Council Guideline *Overarching Principles: Seriousness*

Aggravating factors

C.5 Factors indicating higher culpability:

- Offence committed whilst on bail for other offences
- Failure to respond to previous sentences
- Offence was racially or religiously aggravated
- Offence motivated by, or demonstrating, hostility to the victim based on his or her sexual orientation (or presumed sexual orientation)
- Offence motivated by, or demonstrating, hostility based on the victim's disability (or presumed disability)
- Previous conviction(s), particularly where a pattern of repeat offending is disclosed
- Planning of an offence
- An intention to commit more serious harm than actually resulted from the offence
- Offenders operating in groups or gangs
- 'Professional' offending
- Commission of the offence for financial gain (where this is not inherent in the offence itself)
- High level of profit from the offence
- An attempt to conceal or dispose of evidence
- Failure to respond to warnings or concerns expressed by others about the offender's behaviour
- Offence committed whilst on licence
- Offence motivated by hostility towards a minority group, or a member or members of it
- Deliberate targeting of vulnerable victim(s)

- Commission of an offence while under the influence of alcohol or drugs
- Use of a weapon to frighten or injure victim
- Deliberate and gratuitous violence or damage to property, over and above what is needed to carry out the offence
- Abuse of power
- Abuse of a position of trust

Factors indicating a more than usually serious degree of harm:

- Multiple victims
- An especially serious physical or psychological effect on the victim, even if unintended
- A sustained assault or repeated assaults on the same victim
- Victim is particularly vulnerable
- Location of the offence (for example, in an isolated place)
- Offence is committed against those working in the public sector or providing a service to the public
- Presence of others eg relatives, especially children or partner of the victim
- Additional degradation of the victim (eg taking photographs of a victim as part of a sexual offence)
- In property offences, high value (including sentimental value) of property to the victim, or substantial consequential loss (eg where the theft of equipment causes serious disruption to a victim's life or business)

Mitigating factors

Factors indicating lower culpability:

- A greater degree of provocation than normally expected
- Mental illness or disability
- Youth or age, where it affects the responsibility of the individual defendant
- The fact that the offender played only a minor role in the offence

Offender mitigation

- Genuine remorse
- Admissions to police in interview
- Ready co-operation with authorities

SENTENCING GUIDELINES FOR SPECIFIC OFFENCES

ALCOHOL SALE OFFENCES (REVISED **2017**)

C.6   Licensing Act 2003, s.141 (sale of alcohol to drunk person); s.146 (sale of alcohol to children); s.147 (allowing sale of alcohol to children)

Effective from: 24 April 2017

Triable only summarily:

Maximum: Level 3 fine (s.141); Unlimited fine (ss.146 and 147)

Offence range: Conditional Discharge — Band C fine

Note

This guideline may also be relevant when sentencing offences under s147A of the Licensing Act 2003, persistently selling alcohol to children, which is committed if, on three or more different occasions within a period of three consecutive months, alcohol is unlawfully sold on the same premises to a person under 18. The offence is summary only and the maximum penalty is an unlimited fine. The court should refer to the sentencing approach in this guideline, adjusting the starting points and ranges bearing in mind the increased seriousness of this offence.

STEP 1 — DETERMINING THE OFFENCE CATEGORY

The Court should determine the offence category using the table below.

Category 1	Higher culpability **and** greater harm
Category 2	Higher culpability **and** lesser harm **or** lower culpability **and** greater harm
Category 3	Lower culpability **and** lesser harm

The court should determine the offender's culpability and the harm caused with reference **only** to the factors below. Where an offence does not fall squarely into a category, individual factors may require a degree of weighting before making an overall assessment and determining the appropriate offence category.

CULPABILITY demonstrated by one or more of the following:

Factors indicating higher culpability

- No attempt made to establish age
- Sale for consumption by group of intoxicated persons
- Sale intended for consumption by a child or young person
- Offender in management position (or equivalent)
- Evidence of failure to police the sale of alcohol

Factors indicating lower culpability

- Offender deceived by false identification
- Evidence of substantial effort to police the sale of alcohol
- Offender acting under direction

HARM demonstrated by one or more of the following:

Factors indicating greater harm

- Supply to younger child/children
- Supply causes or contributes to antisocial behaviour
- Large quantity of alcohol supplied

Factors indicating lesser harm

- All other cases

STEP 2 — STARTING POINT AND CATEGORY RANGE

Having determined the category at step one, the court should use the starting point to reach a sentence within the appropriate category range in the table below. The starting point applies to all offenders irrespective of plea or previous convictions.

Offence Category	Starting Point	Range
Category 1	Band C fine	Band B fine — Band C fine
Category 2	Band B fine	Band A fine — Band C fine
Category 3	Band A fine	Conditional discharge — Band B fine

Note: refer to fines for offence committed for 'commercial' purposes

The court should then consider adjustment for any aggravating or mitigating factors. The following is a **non-exhaustive** list of additional factual elements providing the context of the offence and factors relating to the offender. Identify whether any combination of these, or other relevant factors, should result in an upward or downward adjustment from the sentence arrived at so far.

Factors increasing seriousness

Statutory aggravating factors:

- Previous convictions, having regard to a) the **nature** of the offence to which the conviction relates and its **relevance** to the current offence; and b) the **time** that has elapsed since the conviction

- Offence committed whilst on bail
- Offence motivated by, or demonstrating hostility based on any of the following character-istics or presumed characteristics of the victim: religion, race, disability, sexual orientation or transgender identity

Other aggravating factors:

- Failure to comply with current court orders
- Offence committed on licence or post sentence supervision

Factors reducing seriousness or reflecting personal mitigation

- No previous convictions **or** no relevant/recent convictions
- Offence committed as the result of substantial intimidation

STEP 3 — CONSIDER ANY FACTORS WHICH INDICATE A REDUCTION, SUCH AS ASSISTANCE TO THE PROSECUTION

The court should take into account sections 73 and 74 of the Serious Organised Crime and Police Act 2005 (assistance by defendants: reduction or review of sentence) and any other rule of law by virtue of which an offender may receive a discounted sentence in consequence of assistance given (or offered) to the prosecutor or investigator.

STEP 4 — REDUCTION FOR GUILTY PLEAS

The court should take account of any potential reduction for a guilty plea in accordance with section 144 of the Criminal Justice Act 2003 and the *Guilty Plea* guideline.

STEP 5 — TOTALITY PRINCIPLE

If sentencing an offender for more than one offence, or where the offender is already serving a sentence, consider whether the total sentence is just and proportionate to the overall offending behaviour in accordance with the *Offences Taken into Consideration and Totality* guideline.

STEP 6 — COMPENSATION AND ANCILLARY ORDERS

In all cases, the court should consider whether to make compensation and/or other ancillary orders including deprivation and/or forfeiture or suspension of personal liquor licence.

STEP 7 — REASONS

Section 174 of the Criminal Justice Act 2003 imposes a duty to give reasons for, and explain the effect of, the sentence.

ANIMAL CRUELTY (REVISED 2017)

Animal Welfare Act 2006, s.4 (unnecessary suffering), s.8 (fighting etc), s.9 (breach of duty of person responsible for animal to ensure welfare)
Effective from: 24 April 2017
Triable only summarily:
Maximum: Unlimited fine and/or 6 months
Offence range: Band A fine — 26 weeks' custody
Step 1 — Determining the offence category   The court should determine culpability and harm caused with reference **only** to the factors below. Where an offence does not fall squarely into a category, individual factors may require a degree of weighting before making an overall assessment and determining the appropriate offence category.
CULPABILITY demonstrated by one or more of the following: Factors indicating high culpability

- Deliberate or gratuitous attempt to cause suffering
- Prolonged or deliberate ill treatment or neglect
- Ill treatment in a commercial context
- A leading role in illegal activity

Factors indicating medium culpability

- All cases not falling into high or low culpability

Factors indicating low culpability

- Well intentioned but incompetent care
- Mental disorder or learning disability, where linked to the commission of the offence

HARM demonstrated by one or more of the following: Factors indicating greater harm

- Death or serious injury/harm to animal
- High level of suffering caused

Factors indicating lesser harm

- All other cases

Step 2 — Starting point and category range   Having determined the category at step one, the court should use the corresponding starting point to reach a sentence within the category range below. The starting point applies to all offenders irrespective of plea or previous convictions.

A case of particular gravity, reflected by multiple features of culpability in step one, could merit upward adjustment from the starting point before further adjustment for aggravating or mitigating features, set out below.

	High culpability	Medium culpability	Low culpability
Greater harm	**Starting point** 18 weeks' custody	**Starting point** Medium level community order	**Starting point** Band C fine
	Category range 12 – 26 weeks' custody	**Category range** Low level community order — High level community order	**Category range** Band B fine — Low level community order
Lesser harm	**Starting point** High level community order	**Starting point** Low level community order	**Starting point** Band B fine
	Category range Low level community order — 12 weeks' custody	**Category range** Band C fine — Medium level community order	**Category range** Band A fine — Band C fine

The court should then consider further adjustment for any aggravating or mitigating factors. The following is a **non-exhaustive** list of additional factual elements providing the context of the offence and factors relating to the offender. Identify whether any combination of these, or other relevant factors, should result in an upward or downward adjustment from the sentence arrived at so far.
Factors increasing seriousness   *Statutory aggravating factors:*

- Previous convictions, having regard to a) the **nature** of the offence to which the conviction relates and its **relevance** to the current offence; and b) the **time** that has elapsed since the conviction
- Offence committed whilst on bail
- Offence motivated by, or demonstrating hostility based on any of the following characteristics or presumed characteristics of the owner/keeper of the animal: religion, race, disability, sexual orientation or transgender identity

Other aggravating factors:

- Distress caused to owner where not responsible for the offence
- Failure to comply with current court orders
- Offence committed on licence or post sentence supervision
- Use of weapon
- Allowing person of insufficient experience or training to have care of animal(s)
- Use of technology to publicise or promote cruelty
- Ignores warning/professional advice/declines to obtain professional advice
- Use of another animal to inflict death or injury
- Offender in position of responsibility

- Animal requires significant intervention to recover
- Animal being used in public service or as an assistance dog

- No previous convictions **or** no relevant/recent convictions
- Remorse
- Good character and/or exemplary conduct
- Serious medical condition requiring urgent, intensive or long-term treatment
- Age and/or lack of maturity where it affects the responsibility of the offender
- Mental disorder or learning disability, where not linked to the commission of the offence
- Sole or primary carer for dependent relatives
- Offender has been given an inappropriate level of trust or responsibility
- Voluntary surrender of animals to authorities
- Cooperation with the investigation
- Isolated incident

Factors reducing seriousness or reflecting personal mitigation

Step 3 — Consider any factors which indicate a reduction, such as assistance to the prosecution
The court should take into account sections 73 and 74 of the Serious Organised Crime and Police Act 2005 (assistance by defendants: reduction or review of sentence) and any other rule of law by virtue of which an offender may receive a discounted sentence in consequence of assistance given (or offered) to the prosecutor or investigator.

Step 4 — Reduction for guilty pleas The court should take account of any potential reduction for a guilty plea in accordance with section 144 of the Criminal Justice Act 2003 and the *Guilty Plea* guideline.

Step 5 — Totality principle If sentencing an offender for more than one offence, or where the offender is already serving a sentence, consider whether the total sentence is just and proportionate to the overall offending behaviour in accordance with the *Offences Taken into Consideration and Totality* guideline.

Step 6 — Compensation and ancillary orders In all cases, the court should consider whether to make compensation and/or other ancillary orders including deprivation of ownership and disqualification of ownership of animals.

Step 7 — Reasons Section 174 of the Criminal Justice Act 2003 imposes a duty to give reasons for, and explain the effect of, the sentence.

Step 8 — Consideration for time spent on bail The court must consider whether to give credit for time spent on bail in accordance with section 240A of the Criminal Justice Act 2003.

ARSON (CRIMINAL DAMAGE BY FIRE)

Arson (criminal damage by fire)

Criminal Damage Act 1971, s.1

Triable either way:
Maximum when tried summarily: Level 5 fine and/or 6 months
Maximum when tried on indictment: Life

Where offence committed in domestic context, refer to page 177 for guidance

Identify dangerous offenders
This is a serious offence for the purposes of the public protection provisions in the Criminal Justice Act 2003 – refer to page 187 and consult legal adviser for guidance

Offence seriousness (culpability and harm)
A. Identify the appropriate starting point
Starting points based on first time offender pleading not guilty

Examples of nature of activity	Starting point	Range
Minor damage by fire	High level community order	Medium level community order to 12 weeks custody
Moderate damage by fire	12 weeks custody	6 to 26 weeks custody
Significant damage by fire	Crown Court	Crown Court

Offence seriousness (culpability and harm)
B. Consider the effect of aggravating and mitigating factors
(other than those within examples above)
Common aggravating and mitigating factors are identified in the pullout card – the following may be particularly relevant but **these lists are not exhaustive**

Factor indicating higher culpability	Factor indicating lower culpability
1. Revenge attack	1. Damage caused recklessly
Factors indicating greater degree of harm	
1. Damage to emergency equipment	
2. Damage to public amenity	
3. Significant public or private fear caused e.g. in domestic context	

Form a preliminary view of the appropriate sentence, then consider offender mitigation
Common factors are identified in the pullout card

Consider a reduction for a guilty plea

Consider ancillary orders, including compensation
Refer to pages 168-174 for guidance on available ancillary orders

Decide sentence
Give reasons

Bladed Articles and Offensive Weapons *Definitive Guideline*

Applicability of guideline   The Sentencing Council issues this definitive guideline in accordance with section 120 of the Coroners and Justice Act 2009.

The guidelines on pages 3 to 14 apply to all offenders aged 18 and older, who are sentenced on or after 1 June 2018, regardless of the date of the offence.

The guideline on pages 15 to 21 applies to all children or young people, who are sentenced on or after 1 June 2018, regardless of the date of the offence.

Section 125(1) of the Coroners and Justice Act 2009 provides that when sentencing offences committed after 6 April 2010:

"Every court –

(a) must, in sentencing an offender, follow any sentencing guidelines which are relevant to the offender's case, and

(b) ,must, in exercising any other function relating to the sentencing of offenders, follow any sentencing guidelines which are relevant to the exercise of the function,

unless the court is satisfied that it would be contrary to the interests of justice to do so."

Bladed Articles and Offensive Weapons – Possession

Possession of an Offensive Weapon in a Public Place
Prevention of Crime Act 1953 (section 1(1))

Possession of an Article with Blade/Point in a Public Place
Criminal Justice Act 1988 (section 139(1))

Possession of an Offensive Weapon on School Premises
Criminal Justice Act 1988 (section 139A(2))

Possession of an Article with Blade/Point on School Premises
Criminal Justice Act 1988 (section 139A(1))

Unauthorised possession in prison of a knife or offensive weapon
Prison Act 1952 (section 40CA)

Triable either way

Maximum: 4 years' custody

Offence range: Fine – 2 years 6 months' custody

This guideline applies only to offenders aged 18 and older

This offence is subject to **statutory minimum** sentencing provisions.

See STEP THREE for further details.

STEP ONE Determing the offence category   The court should determine the offence category with reference **only** to the factors listed in the tables below. In order to determine the category, the court should assess **culpability** and **harm**.

The court should weigh all the factors set out below in determining the offender's culpability.

Where there are characteristics present which fall under different levels of culpability, the court should balance these characteristics to reach a fair assessment of the offender's culpability.

Culpability demonstrated by one or more of the following:	
A	• Possession of a bladed article • Possession of a highly dangerous weapon* • Offence motivated by, or demonstrating hostility based on any of the following characteristics or presumed characteristics of the victim: religion, race, disability, sexual orientation or transgender identity
B	• Possession of weapon (other than a bladed article or a highly dangerous weapon) – used to threaten or cause fear
C	• Possession of weapon (other than a bladed article or a highly dangerous weapon) – not used to threaten or cause fear
D	• Possession of weapon falls just short of reasonable excuse

* NB an offensive weapon is defined in legislation as 'any article made or adapted for use for causing injury, or is intended by the person having it with him for such use'. A highly dangerous weapon is, therefore, a weapon, including a corrosive substance (such as acid), whose dangerous nature must be substantially above and beyond this. The court must determine whether the weapon is highly dangerous on the facts and circumstances of the case.

Harm

The court should consider the factors set out below to determine the level of harm that has been caused or was risked

Category 1	• Offence committed at a school or other place where vulnerable people are likely to be present • Offence committed in prison • Offence committed in circumstances where there is a risk of serious disorder • Serious alarm/distress
Category 2	• All other cases

STEP TWO Starting point and category range Having determined the category at step one, the court should use the corresponding starting point to reach a sentence within the category range below. The starting point applies to all offenders irrespective of plea or previous convictions. A case of particular gravity, reflected by multiple features of culpability or harm in step one, could merit upward adjustment from the starting point before further adjustment for aggravating or mitigating features, set out on the next page.

	Culpability			
Harm	**A**	**B**	**C**	**D**
Category 1	**Starting point** 1 year 6 months' custody	**Starting point** 9 months' custody	**Starting point** 3 months' custody	**Starting point** High level community order
	Category range 1–2 years' 6 months' custody	**Category range** 6 months' – 1 year 6 months' custody	**Category range** High level community order – 6 months' custody	**Category range** Medium level community order – 3 months' custody
Category 2	**Starting point** 6 months' custody	**Starting point** High level community order	**Starting point** Medium level community order	**Starting point** Low level community order
	Category range 3 months' – 1 year's custody	**Category range** Medium level community order – months' custody	**Category range** Low level community order – High level community order	**Category range** Band C fine – Medium level community order

The table below contains a non-exhaustive list of additional factual elements providing the context of the offence and factors relating to the offender. Identify whether any combination of these, or other relevant factors, should result in an upward or downward adjustment from the sentence arrived at so far. In particular, relevant recent convictions are likely to result in an upward adjustment. In some cases, having considered these factors, it may be appropriate to move outside the identified category range.

Aggravating factors

Statutory aggravating factors:

- Previous convictions, having regard to a) the **nature** of the offence to which the conviction relates and its **relevance** to the current offence; and b) the **time** that has elapsed since the conviction (unless the convictions will be relevant for the purposes of the statutory minimum sentencing provisions – see step three)
- Offence committed whilst on bail

Other aggravating factors (nan-exhaustive):

- Offence was committed as part of a group or gang
- Attempts to conceal identity
- Commission of offence whilst under the influence of alcohol or drugs
- Attempts to conceal/dispose of evidence
- Failure to comply with current court orders
- Offence committed on licence or post sentence supervision
- Offences taken into consideration
- Failure to respond to warnings about behaviour

Factors reducing seriousness or reflecting personal mitigation

- No previous convictions or **no** relevant/recent convictions
- Good character and/or exemplary conduct
- Serious medical condition requiring urgent, intensive or long-term treatment
- Age and/or lack of maturity where it affects the responsibility of the offender
- Mental disorder or learning disability
- Sole or primary carer for dependent relatives
- Co-operation with the police

STEP THREE Minimum Terms – second or further relevant offence When sentencing the offences of:

- possession of an offensive weapon in a public place;
- possession of an article with a blade/point in a public place;

- possession of an offensive weapon on school premises; and
- possession of an article with blade/point on school premises

a court must impose a sentence of at least 6 months' imprisonment where this is a second or further relevant offence **unless the court is of the opinion that there are particular circumstances relating to the offence, the previous offence or the offender which make it unjust to do so in all the circumstances.**

A 'relevant offence' includes those offences listed above and the following offences:

- threatening with an offensive weapon in a public place;
- threatening with an article with a blade/point in a public place;
- threatening with an article with a blade/point on school premises; and
- threatening with an offensive weapon on school premises.

Unjust in all of the circumstances   In considering whether a statutory minimum sentence would be 'unjust in all of the circumstances' the court must have regard to the particular circumstances of the offence and the offender. If the circumstances of the offence, the previous offence or the offender make it unjust to impose the statutory minimum sentence then the court **must impose either a shorter custodial sentence than the statutory minimum provides or an alternative sentence.**

The offence: Having reached this stage of the guideline the court should have made a provisional assessment of the seriousness of the current offence. In addition, the court must consider the seriousness of the previous offence(s) and the period of time that has elapsed between offences. Where the seriousness of the combined offences is such that it falls far below the custody threshold, or where there has been a significant period of time between the offences, the court may consider it unjust to impose the statutory minimum sentence.

The offender: The court should consider the following factors to determine whether it would be unjust to impose the statutory minimum sentence;

- any strong personal mitigation;
- whether there is a realistic prospect of rehabilitation;
- whether custody will result in significant impact on others.

STEP FOUR Consider any factors which indicate a reduction for assistance to the prosecution   The court should take into account sections 73 and 74 of the Serious Organised Crime and Police Act 2005 (assistance by defendants: reduction or review of sentence) and any other rule of law by virtue of which an offender may receive a discounted sentence in consequence of assistance given (or offered) to the prosecutor or investigator.

STEP FIVE Reduction for guilty pleas   The court should take account of any potential reduction for a guilty plea in accordance with section 144 of the Criminal Justice Act 2003 and the *Guilty Plea* guideline.

Where a **statutory minimum sentence** has been imposed, the court must ensure that any reduction for a guilty plea does not reduce the sentence to less than 80 per cent of the statutory minimum.

STEP SIX Totality principle   If sentencing an offender for more than one offence, or where the offender is already serving a sentence, consider whether the total sentence is just and proportionate to the overall offending behaviour in accordance with the *Offences Taken into Consideration and Totality* guideline.

STEP SEVEN Ancillary orders   In all cases the court should consider whether to make ancillary orders.

STEP EIGHT Reasons   Section 174 of the Criminal Justice Act 2003 imposes a duty to give reasons for, and explain the effect of, the sentence.

STEP NINE Consideration for time spent on bail   The court must consider whether to give credit for time spent on bail in accordance with section 240A of the Criminal Justice Act 2003.

BLADED ARTICLES AND OFFENSIVE WEAPONS – THREATS

THREATENING WITH AN OFFENSIVE WEAPON IN A PUBLIC PLACE
Prevention of Crime Act 1953 (section 1A)

THREATENING WITH AN ARTICLE WITH BLADE/POINT IN A PUBLIC PLACE
Criminal Justice Act 1988 (section 139AA(1))

THREATENING WITH AN ARTICLE WITH BLADE/POINT OR OFFENSIVE WEAPON ON SCHOOL PREMISES
Criminal Justice Act 1988 (section 139AA(1))

Triable either way
Maximum: 4 years' custody
Offence range: 6 months' custody – 3 years' custody
This guideline applies only to offenders aged 18 and older
This offence is subject to **statutory minimum** sentencing provisions.
See STEP THREE for further details.

STEP ONE Determing the offence category The court should determine the offence category with reference **only** to the factors listed in the tables below. In order to determine the category, the court should assess **culpability** and **harm**.

The court should weigh all the factors set out below in determining the offender's culpability.

Where there are characteristics present which fall under different levels of culpability, the court should balance these characteristics to reach a fair assessment of the offender's culpability.

Culpability demonstrated by one or more of the following:

A – Higher culpability	• Offence committed using a bladed article • Offence committed using a highly dangerous weapon* • Offence motivated by, or demonstrating hostility based on any of the following characteristics or presumed characteristics of the victim: religion, race, disability, sexual orientation or transgender identity • Significant degree of planning or premeditation
B – Lower culpability	• All other cases

* NB an offensive weapon is defined in legislation as 'any article made or adapted for use for causing injury, or is intended by the person having it with him for such use'. A highly dangerous weapon is, therefore, a weapon, including a corrosive substance (such as acid), whose dangerous nature must be substantially above and beyond this. The court must determine whether the weapon is highly dangerous on the facts and circumstances of the case.

Harm
The court should consider the factors set out below to determine the level of harm that has been caused intended to cause to the victim.

Category 1	• Offence committed at a school or other place where vulnerable people are likely to be present • Offence committed in prison • Offence committed in circumstances where there is a risk of serious disorder • Serious alarm/distress caused to the victim • Prolonged incident
Category 2	• All other cases

STEP TWO Starting point and category range Having determined the category at step one, the court should use the corresponding starting point to reach a sentence within the category range below. The starting point applies to all offenders irrespective of plea or previous convictions. A case of particular gravity, reflected by multiple features of culpability or harm in step one, could merit upward adjustment from the starting point before further adjustment for aggravating or mitigating features, set out on the next page.

	Culpability	
Harm	**A**	**B**
Category 1	**Starting point** 2 years' custody	**Starting point** 1 year 6 months' custody
	Category range 1 year 6 months' – 3 years' custody	**Category range** 1 – 2 years' custody
Category 2	**Starting point** 15 months' custody	**Starting point** 6 months' custody

	Culpability	
Harm	A	B
	Category range 9 months' – 2 year's custody	Category range 6 months' – 1 year 6 months' custody

The table below contains a non-exhaustive list of additional factual elements providing the context of the offence and factors relating to the offender. Identify whether any combination of these, or other relevant factors, should result in an upward or downward adjustment from the sentence arrived at so far. In particular, relevant recent convictions are likely to result in an upward adjustment. In some cases, having considered these factors, it may be appropriate to move outside the identified category range.

Factors increasing seriousness
Statutory aggravating factors:

- Previous convictions, having regard to a) the nature of the offence to which the conviction relates and its relevance to the current offence; and b) the time that has elapsed since the conviction
- Offence committed whilst on bail

Other aggravating factors:

- Victim is targeted due to a vulnerability (or a perceived vulnerability)
- Offence was committed as part of a group or gang
- Attempts to conceal identity
- Commission of offence whilst under the influence of alcohol or drugs
- Attempts to conceal/dispose of evidence
- Offence committed against those working in the public sector or providing a service to the public
- Offence committed against those working in the public sector or providing a service to the public
- Steps taken to prevent the victim reporting or obtaining assistance and/or from assisting or supporting the prosecution
- Failure to comply with current court orders
- Offence committed on licence or post sentence supervision
- Offences taken into consideration
- Failure to respond to warnings about behaviour

Factors reducing seriousness or reflecting personal mitigation

- No previous convictions or no relevant/recent convictions
- Good character and/or exemplary conduct
- Serious medical condition requiring urgent, intensive or long-term treatment
- Age and/or lack of maturity where it affects the responsibility of the offender
- Mental disorder or learning disability (where not linked to the commission of the offence)
- Little or no planning
- Sole or primary carer for dependent relatives
- Co-operation with the police

STEP THREE Minimum Terms   When sentencing these offences a court must impose a sentence of at least 6 months imprisonment **unless the court is of the opinion that there are particular circumstances relating to the offence or the offender which make it unjust to do so in all the circumstances.**

Unjust in all of the circumstances   In considering whether a statutory minimum sentence would be 'unjust in all of the circumstances' the court must have regard to the particular circumstances of the offence and the offender. If the circumstances of the offence, the previous offence or the offender make it unjust to impose the statutory minimum sentence then the court **must impose either a shorter custodial sentence than the statutory minimum provides or an alternative sentence.**

The offence: Having reached this stage of the guideline the court should have made a provisional assessment of the seriousness of the offence. Where the court has determ ined that the offence seriousness falls far below the custodial threshold the court may consider it unjust to impose the statutory minimum sentence.

The offender: The court should consider the following factors to determine whether it would be unjust to impose the statutory minimum sentence;

- any strong personal mitigation;
- whether there is a realistic prospect of rehabilitation;
- whether custody will result in significant impact on others.

STEP FOUR Consider any factors which indicate a reduction for assistance to the prosecution
Consider any factors which indicate a reduction for assistance to the prosecution The court should take into account sections 73 and 74 of the Serious Organised Crime and Police Act 2005 (assistance by defendants: reduction or review of sentence) and any other rule of law by virtue of which an offender may receive a discounted sentence in consequence of assistance given (or offered) to the prosecutor or investigator.

STEP FIVE Reduction for guilty pleas   The court should take account of any potential reduction for a guilty plea in accordance with section 144 of the Criminal Justice Act 2003 and the *Guilty Plea* guideline.

Where a **statutory minimum sentence** has been imposed, the court must ensure that any reduction for a guilty plea does not reduce the sentence to less than 80 per cent of the statutory minimum.

STEP SIX Totality principle If sentencing an offender for more than one offence, or where the offender is already serving a sentence, consider whether the total sentence is just and proportionate to the overall offending behaviour in accordance with the *Offences Taken into Consideration and Totality* guideline.

STEP SEVEN Ancillary orders In all cases the court should consider whether to make ancillary orders.

STEP EIGHT Reasons Section 174 of the Criminal Justice Act 2003 imposes a duty to give reasons for, and explain the effect of, the sentence.

STEP NINE Consideration for time spent on bail The court must consider whether to give credit for time spent on bail in accordance with section 240A of the Criminal Justice Act 2003.

BLADED ARTICLES AND OFFENSIVE WEAPONS (POSSESSION AND THREATS) – CHILDREN AND YOUNG PEOPLE

This guideline should be read alongside the *Overarching Principles – Sentencing Children and Young People* definitive guideline which provides comprehensive guidance on the sentencing principles and welfare considerations that the court should have in mind when sentencing children and young people.

This offence is subject to statutory minimum sentencing provisions. See STEP FIVE for further details.

The first step in determining the sentence is to assess the seriousness of the offence. This assessment is made by considering the nature of the offence and any aggravating and mitigating factors relating to the offence itself. The fact that a sentence threshold is crossed does not necessarily mean that that sentence should be imposed.

STEP ONE Offence Seriousness – Nature of the offence   The boxes below give **examples** of the type of culpability and harm factors that may indicate that a particular threshold of sentence has been crossed.

A non-custodial sentence* may be the most suitable disposal where one or more of the following factors apply:

- Possession of weapon falls just short of reasonable excuse
- No/minimal risk of weapon being used to threaten or cause harm
- Fleeting incident and no/minimal distress

A custodial sentence or youth rehabilitation order with intensive supervision and surveillance* or fostering* may be justified where one or more of the following factors apply:

- Possession of a bladed article whether produced or not
- Possession of a highly dangerous weapon+ whether produced or not
- Offence motivated by, or demonstrating hostility based on any of the following characteristics or presumed characteristics of the victim: religion, race, disability, sexual orientation or transgender identity
- Prolonged incident and serious alarm/distress
- Offence committed at a school or other place where vulnerable people may be present

---

* Where the child or young person appears in the magistrates' court, and the conditions for a compulsory referral order apply, a referral order must be imposed unless the court is considering imposing a discharge, hospital order or custody.

+ NB an offensive weapon is defined in legislation as 'any article made or adapted for use for causing injury, or is intended by the person having it with him for such use'. A highly dangerous weapon is, therefore, a weapon, including a corrosive substance (such as acid), whose dangerous nature must be substantially above and beyond this. The court must determine whether the weapon is highly dangerous on the facts and circumstances of the case.

STEP TWO Offence Seriousness – Aggravating and mitigating factors   To complete the assessment of seriousness the court should consider the aggravating and mitigating factors relevant to the offence.

Aggravating factors

Statutory aggravating factors:

- Previous findings of guilt, having regard to a) the **nature** of the offence to which the finding of guilt relates and its **relevance** to the current offence; and b) the **time** that has elapsed since the finding of guilt (unless the convictions will be relevant for the purposes of the statutory minimum sentencing provisions – see step five)
- Offence committed whilst on bail

Other aggravating factors (nan-exhaustive):

- Significant degree of planning/premeditation
- Deliberate humiliation of victim, including but not limited to filming of the offence, deliberately committing the offence before a group of peers with the intent of causing additional distress or circulating details/photos/videos etc of the offence on social media or within peer groups
- Victim is particularly vulnerable due to factors including but not limited to age, mental or physical disability
- Offence was committed as part of a group or gang
- Attempts to conceal identity
- Steps taken to prevent reporting the incident/seeking assistance
- Commission of offence whilst under the influence of alcohol or drugs
- Offence committed against those working in the public sector or providing a service to the public

Mitigating factors (non-exhaustive)

- No findings of guilt or no relevant/recent findings of guilt
- Good character and/or exemplary conduct
- Participated in offence due to bullying, peer pressure, coercion or manipulation
- Little or no planning
- Co-operation with the police

STEP THREE Personal Mitigation   Having assessed the offence seriousness the court should then consider the mitigation personal to the child or young person to determine whether a custodial sentence or a community sentence is necessary. The effect of personal mitigation may reduce what would otherwise be a custodial sentence to a non-custodial one or a community sentence to a different means of disposal.

Personal mitigating factors (non-exhaustive)

Particularly young or immature child or young person (where it affects their responsibility)

Communication or learning disabilities or mental health concerns

Unstable upbringing including but not limited to:-
- time spent looked after
- lack of familial presence or support
- disrupted experiences in accommodation or education
- exposure to drug/alcohol abuse, familial criminal behaviour or domestic abuse
- victim of neglect or abuse, or exposure to neglect or abuse of others
- experiences of trauma or loss

Determination and/or demonstration of steps taken to address offending behaviour

Child or young person in education, training or employment

STEP FOUR Reduction for guilty pleas   The court should take account of any potential reduction for a guilty plea in accordance with section 144 of the Criminal Justice Act 2003 and part one, section five of the *Overarching Principles Sentencing Children and Young People* definitive guideline.

The reduction in sentence for a guilty plea can be taken into account by imposing one type of sentence rather than another; for example:
- by reducing a custodial sentence to a community sentence, or
- by reducing a community sentence to a different means of disposal.

Alternatively the court could reduce the length or severity of any punitive requirements attached to a community sentence.

See the *Overarching Principles – Sentencing Children and Young People* definitive guideline for details of other available sentences including Referral Orders and Reparation Orders.

STEP FIVE Statutory minimum sentencing provisions   The following provisions apply to those young people who were aged 16 or over on the date of the offence[1]

Threatening with Bladed Articles or Offensive Weapons

When sentencing these offences a court must impose a sentence of at least 4 months Detention and Training Order **unless the court is of the opinion that there are particular circumstances relating to the offence, the previous offence or the young person which make it unjust to do so in all the circumstances.**

Possession of Bladed Articles or Offensive Weapons

When sentencing the offences of:
- possession of an offensive weapon in a public place;
- possession of an article with a blade/point in a public place;
- possession of an offensive weapon on school premises; and
- possession of an article with blade/point on school premises

a court must impose a sentence of at least 4 months' Detention and Training Order where this is **a second or further** relevant offence **unless the court is of the opinion that there are particular circumstances relating to the offence, any previous relevant offence or the young person which make it unjust to do so in all the circumstances.**

A 'relevant offence' includes those offences listed above and the following offences:
- threatening with an offensive weapon in a public place;
- threatening with an article with a blade/point in a public place;
- threatening with an article with a blade/point on school premises; and
- threatening with an offensive weapon on school premises.

Unjust in all of the circumstances

In considering whether a statutory minimum sentence would be 'unjust in all of the circumstances' the court must have regard to the particular circumstances of the offence, any relevant previous offence and the young person. If the circumstances make it unjust to impose the statutory minimum sentence then the court **must impose an alternative sentence**.

The offence:

Having reached this stage of the guideline the court should have made a provisional assessment of the seriousness of the offence. Where the court has determined that the offence seriousness falls far below the custody threshold the court may consider it unjust to impose the statutory minimum sentence.

Where the court is considering a statutory minimum sentence as a result of a second or further relevant offence, consideration should be given to the seriousness of the previous offence(s) and the period of time that has elapsed between offending. Where the seriousness of the combined offences is such that it falls far below the custody threshold, or where there has been a significant period of time between the offences, the court may consider it unjust to impose the statutory minimum sentence.

The young person:

The statutory obligation to have regard to the welfare of a young person includes the obligation to secure proper provision for education and training, to remove the young person from undesirable surroundings where appropriate, and the need to choose the best option for the young person taking account of the circumstances of the offence.

In having regard to the welfare of the young person, a court should ensure that it considers:
- any mental health problems or learning difficulties/disabilities;
- any experiences of brain injury or traumatic life experience (including exposure to drug and alcohol abuse) and the developmental impact this mav have had;
- any speech and language difficulties and the effect this may have on the ability of the young person (or any accompanying adult) to communicate with the court, to understand the sanction imposed or to fulfil the obligations resulting from that sanction;
- the vulnerability of young people to self harm, particularly within a custodial environment; and
- the effect on young people of experiences of loss and neglect and/or abuse.

In certain cases the concerns about the welfare of the young person may be so significant that the court considers it unjust to impose the statutory minimum sentence.

[1] The age of the young person at the date of the earlier offence(s) is irrelevant.

STEP SIX Review the sentence The court must now review the sentence to ensure it is the most appropriate one for the child or young person. This will include an assessment of the likelihood of reoffending and the risk of causing serious harm. A report from the Youth Offending Team may assist.

See the *Overarching Principles – Sentencing Children and Young People* definitive guideline for comprehensive guidance on the sentencing principles and welfare considerations that the court should have in mind when sentencing children and young people, and for the full range of sentences available to the court.

Referral Orders In cases where children or young people have offended for the first time and have pleaded guilty to committing an offence which is on the cusp of the custody threshold, youth offending teams (YOT) should be encouraged to convene a Youth Offender Panel prior to sentence (sometimes referred to as a "pseudo-panel" or "pre-panel") where the child or young person is asked to attend before a panel and agree an intensive contract. If that contract is placed before the sentencing youth court, the court can then decide whether it is sufficient to move below custody on this occasion. The proposed contract is not something the court can alter in any way; the court will still have to make a decision between referral order and custody but can do so on the basis that if it makes a referral order it can have confidence in what that will entail in the particular case.

The court determines the length of the order but a Referral Order Panel determines the requirements of the order.

Offence seriousness	Suggested length of referral order
Low	3–5 months
Medium	5–7 months
High	7–9 months
Very high	10–12 months

The YOT may propose certain requirements and the length of these requirements may not correspond to the above table; if the court feels these requirements will best achieve the aims of the youth justice system then they may still be imposed.

Youth Rehabilitation Order (YRO)

REQUIREMENTS OF ORDER

Standard	Low likelihood of re-offending and a low risk of serious harm.	Primarily seek to repair harm caused through, for example: • reparation; • unpaid work; • supervision; and/or • Attendance centre.
Enhanced	Medium likelihood of re-offending **or** a medium risk of serious harm	Seek to repair harm caused and to enable help or change through, for example: • supervision; • reparation; • requirement to address behaviour e.g. drug treatment, offending behaviour programme, education programme; and/or • a combination of the above.
Intensive	High likelihood of re-offending **or** a very high risk of serious harm	Seek to ensure the control of and enable help or change for the child or young person through, for example: • supervision; • reparation; • requirement to address behaviour • requirement to monitor or restrict movement, e.g. prohibited activity, curfew, exclusion or electronic monitoring; and/or • a combination of the above.

YRO with Intensive Supervision and Surveillance (ISS) or YRO with fostering A YRO with an ISS or fostering requirement can only be imposed where the court is of the opinion that the offence has crossed the custody threshold and custody is merited.

The YRO with ISS includes an extended activity requirement, a supervision requirement and curfew. The YRO with fostering requires the child or young person to reside with a local authority foster parent for a specified period of up to 12 months.

Custodial Sentences If a custodial sentence is imposed, the court must state its reasons for being satisfied that the offence is so serious that no other sanction would be appropriate and, in particular, why a YRO with ISS or fostering could not be justified.

Where a custodial sentence is **unavoidable** the length of custody imposed must be the shortest commensurate with the seriousness of the offence. The court may want to consider the equivalent adult guideline in order to determine the appropriate length of the sentence.

If considering the adult guideline, the court may feel it appropriate to apply a sentence broadly within the region of half to two thirds of the appropriate adult sentence for those aged 15–17 and allow a greater reduction for those aged under 15. This is only a rough guide and must not be applied mechanistically. The individual factors relating to the offence and the child or young person are of the greatest importance and may present good reason to impose a sentence outside of this range.

Annex: Fine bands and community orders

Fine Bands

In this guideline, fines are expressed as one of three fine bands (A, B, C).

Fine Band	Starting point *(applicable to all offenders)*	Category range *(applicable to all offenders)*
Band A	50% of relevant weekly income	25–75% of relevant weekly income
Band B	100% of relevant weekly income	75–125% of relevant weekly income
Band C	150% of relevant weekly income	125–175% of relevant weekly income

Community Orders

In this guideline, community sentences are expressed as one of three levels (low, medium or high).

An illustrative description of examples of requirements that might be appropriate for each level is provided below. Where two or more requirements are ordered, they must be compatible with each other. Save in exceptional circumstances, the court must impose at least one requirement for the purpose of punishment, or combine the community order with a fine, or both (see section 177 Criminal Justice Act 2003).

LOW	MEDIUM	HIGH
Offences only just cross community order threshold, where the seriousness of the offence or the nature of the offender's record means that a discharge or fine is inappropriate	Offences that obviously fall within the community order band	Offences only just fall below the custody threshold or the custody threshold is crossed but a community order is more appropriate in the circumstances
In general, only one requirement will be appropriate and the length may be curtailed if additional requirements are necessary		More intensive sentences which combine two or more requirements may be appropriate
Suitable requirements might include:	Suitable requirements might include:	Suitable requirements might include:
• Any appropriate rehabilitative requirement(s)	• Any appropriate rehabilitative requirement(s)	• Any appropriate rehabilitative requirement(s)
• 40–80 hours unpaid work;	• greater number of hours of unpaid work (for example, 80–150 hours);	• 150–300 hours unpaid work;
• Curfew requirement within the lowest range (for example up to 16 hours per day for a few weeks)	• Curfew requirement within the middle range (for example up to 16 hours for 2–3 months)	• Curfew requirement up to 16 hours per day for 4–12 months
• Exclusion requirement, for a few months	• Exclusion requirement lasting in the region of 6 months	• Exclusion order lasting in the region of 12 months
• prohibited activity requirement;	• prohibited activity requirement.	
• Attendance centre requirement (where available)		
If order does not contain a punitive requirement, suggested fine levels are indicated below:		
Band A fine	Band B fine	Band C fine

The *Magistrates' Court Sentencing Guidelines* includes further guidance on fines. The table above is also set out in the *Imposition of Community and Custodial Sentences Guideline* which includes further guidance on community orders.

BREACH OF A COMMUNITY ORDER

Criminal Justice Act 2003 (Schedule 8)

BREACH OF COMMUNITY ORDER BY FAILING TO COMPLY WITH REQUIREMENTS

The court must take into account the extent to which the offender has complied with the requirements of the community order when imposing a penalty.

In assessing the level of compliance with the order the court should consider:

(i) the overall attitude and engagement with the order as well as the proportion of elements completed;
(ii) the impact of any completed or partially completed requirements on the offender's behaviour;
(iii) the proximity of breach to imposition of order; and
(iv) evidence of circumstances or offender characteristics, such as disability, mental health issues or learning difficulties which have impeded offender's compliance with the order.

Overall Compliance with order	Penalty
Wilful and persistent non-compliance	Revoke the order and re-sentence imposing custodial sentence (even where the offence seriousness did not originally merit custody)
Low level of compliance	Revoke the order and re-sentence original offence **OR** Add curfew requirement 20 – 30 days* **OR** 30 – 50 hours additional unpaid work/extend length of order/add additional requirement(s) **OR** Band C fine
Medium level of compliance	Revoke the order and resentence original offence **OR** Add curfew requirement 10 – 20 days* **OR** 20 – 30 hours additional unpaid work/extend length of order/add additional requirement(s) **OR** Band B fine
High level of compliance	Add curfew requirement 6 – 10 days* **OR** 10 – 20 hours additional unpaid work/extend length of order/add additional requirement(s) **OR** Band A fine

* curfew days do not have to be consecutive and may be distributed over particular periods, for example at weekends, as the court deems appropriate. The period of the curfew should not exceed the duration of the community order and cannot be for longer than 12 months.

TECHNICAL GUIDANCE

(a) If imposing more onerous requirements the length of the order may be extended up to 3 years or six months longer than the previous length, which ever is longer (but only once).
(b) If imposing unpaid work as a more onerous requirement and an unpaid work requirement was not previously included, the minimum number of hours that can be imposed is 20.
(c) The maximum fine that can be imposed is £2,500.
(d) If re-sentencing, a suspended sentence **MUST NOT** be imposed as a more severe alternative to a community order. A suspended sentence may only be imposed if it is fully intended that the offender serve a custodial sentence in accordance with the *Imposition of Community and Custodial Sentences* guideline.
(e) Where the order was imposed by the Crown Court, magistrates should consider their sentencing powers in dealing with a breach. Where the judge imposing the order reserved any breach proceedings commit the breach for sentence.

Powers of the court following a subsequent conviction

A conviction for a further offence does not constitute a breach of a community order. However, in such a situation, the court should consider the following guidance from the *Offences Taken into Consideration and Totality guideline*:[1]

---

[1] https://wwwsentencingcouncil.org.uk/wp-content/uploads/ Definitive_guideline_TICs_totality_Final_web.pdf P.14

Offender convicted of an offence while serving a community order

The power to deal with the offender depends on his being convicted whilst the order is still in force; it does not arise where the order has expired, even if the additional offence was committed whilst it was still current.

If an offender, in respect of whom a community order made by a magistrates' court is in force, is convicted by a magistrates' court of an additional offence, the magistrates' court should ordinarily revoke the previous community order and sentence afresh for both the original and the additional offence.

Where an offender, in respect of whom a community order made by a Crown Court is in force, is convicted by a magistrates' court, the magistrates' court may, and ordinarily should, commit the offender to the Crown Court, in order to allow the Crown Court to re-sentence for the original offence and the additional offence.

The sentencing court should consider the overall seriousness of the offending behaviour taking into account the additional offence and the original offence. The court should consider whether the combination of associated offences is sufficiently serious to justify a custodial sentence.

If the court does not consider that custody is necessary, it should impose a single community order that reflects the overall totality of criminality. The court must take into account the extent to which the offender complied with the requirements of the previous order.

BREACH OF A CRIMINAL BEHAVIOUR ORDER (ALSO APPLICABLE TO BREACH OF AN ANTI-SOCIAL BEHAVIOUR ORDER)

Anti-Social Behaviour, Crime and Policing Act 2014, s 30
Effective from: 01 October 2018
Triable either way
Maximum: 5 years' custody
Offence range: Fine – 4 years' custody

STEP 1 — DETERMINING THE OFFENCE CATEGORY

The court should determine the offence category with reference only to the factors listed in the tables below. In order to determine the category the court should assess **culpability** and **harm**.

Culpability

A	Very serious or persistent breach
B	Deliberate breach falling between A and C
C	Minor breach Breach just short of reasonable excuse

Harm

The level of **harm** is determined by weighing up all the factors of the case to determine the harm that has been caused or was at risk of being caused.

In assessing any risk of harm posed by the breach, consideration should be given to the original offence(s) or activity for which the order was imposed and the circumstances in which the breach arose.

Category 1	Breach causes very serious harm or distress Breach demonstrates a continuing risk of serious criminal and/or anti-social behaviour
Category 2	Cases falling between categories 1 and 3
Category 3	Breach causes little or no harm or distress Breach demonstrates a continuing risk of minor criminal and/or anti-social behaviour

STEP 2 — STARTING POINT AND CATEGORY RANGE

Having determined the category at step one, the court should use the corresponding starting point to reach a sentence within the category range in the table below. The starting point applies to all offenders irrespective of plea or previous convictions.

Harm	Culpability		
	A	**B**	**C**
Category 1	**Starting point** 2 years' custody **Category range** 1–4 years' custody	**Starting point** 1 years' custody **Category range** High level community order – 2 years' custody	**Starting point** 12 weeks' custody **Category range** Medium level community order – 1 year's custody
Category 2	**Starting point** 1 years' custody **Category range** High level community order – 2 years' custody	**Starting point** 12 weeks' custody **Category range** Medium level community order – 1 year's custody	**Starting point** High level community order **Category range** Low level community order – 26 weeks' custody
Category 3	**Starting point** 12 weeks' custody **Category range** Medium level community order – 1 year's custody	**Starting point** High level community order **Category range** Low level community order – 26 weeks' custody	**Starting point** Medium level community order **Category range** Band B fine – High level community order

NOTE: A Conditional Discharge **MAY NOT** be imposed for breach of a criminal behaviour order.

The table below contains a **non-exhaustive** list of additional factual elements providing the context of the offence and factors relating to the offender. Identify whether any combination of these, or other relevant factors, should result in an upward or downward adjustment from the starting point. In some cases, having considered these factors, it may be appropriate to move outside the identified category range.

Factors increasing seriousness

Statutory aggravating factors:

- Previous convictions, having regard to a) the **nature** of the offence to which the conviction relates and its **relevance** to the current offence; and b) the **time** that has elapsed since the conviction
- Offence committed whilst on bail

Other aggravating factors:
- Offence is a further breach, following earlier breach proceedings
- Breach committed shortly after order made
- History of disobedience of court orders or orders imposed by local authorities
- Breach constitutes a further offence (where not separately prosecuted)
- Targeting of a person the order was made to protect or a witness in the original proceedings
- Victim or protected subject of order breached is particularly vulnerable due to age, disability, culture, religion, language, or other factors
- •Offence committed on licence or while subject to post sentence supervision

Factors reducing seriousness or reflecting personal mitigation
- Genuine misunderstanding of terms of order
- Breach committed after long period of compliance
- Prompt voluntary surrender/admission of breach or failure
- Age and/or lack of maturity where it affects the responsibility of the offender
- Mental disorder or learning disability
- Sole or primary carer for dependent relatives
- Offence committed on licence or while subject to post sentence supervision

STEP 3 — CONSIDER ANY FACTORS WHICH INDICATE A REDUCTION, SUCH AS ASSISTANCE TO THE PROSECUTION

The court should take into account sections 73 and 74 of the Serious Organised Crime and Police Act 2005 (assistance by defendants: reduction or review of sentence) and any other rule of law by virtue of which an offender may receive a discounted sentence in consequence of assistance given (or offered) to the prosecutor or investigator.

STEP 4 — REDUCTION FOR GUILTY PLEAS

The court should take account of any potential reduction for a guilty plea in accordance with section 144 of the Criminal Justice Act 2003 and the *Guilty Plea* guideline.

STEP 5 — TOTALITY PRINCIPLE

If sentencing an offender for more than one offence, or where the offender is already serving a sentence, consider whether the total sentence is just and proportionate to the overall offending behaviour in accordance with the *Offences Taken into Consideration and Totality* guideline.

STEP 6 — ANCILLARY ORDERS

In all cases, the court should consider whether to make compensation and/or ancillary orders.

STEP 7 — REASONS

Section 174 of the Criminal Justice Act 2003 imposes a duty to give reasons for, and explain the effect of, the sentence.

Step 8 — Consideration for time spent on bail The court must consider whether to give credit for time spent on bail in accordance with section 240A of the Criminal Justice Act 2003.

BREACH OF A SEXUAL HARM PREVENTION ORDER (ALSO APPLICABLE TO BREACH OF A SEXUAL OFFENCES PREVENTION ORDER AND TO BREACH OF A FOREIGN TRAVEL ORDER)

Sexual Offences Act 2003 (Section 103I)
Effective from: 1 October 2018
Triable either way
Maximum: 5 years' custody
Offence range: Fine – 4 years and 6 months' custody

STEP 1 — DETERMINING THE OFFENCE CATEGORY

The court should determine the offence category with reference only to the factors listed in the tables below. In order to determine the category the court should assess **culpability** and **harm**.

Culpability

In assessing culpability, the court should consider the intention and motivation of the offender in committing any breach.

A	Very serious or persistent breach
B	Deliberate breach falling between A and C
C	Minor breach Breach just short of reasonable excuse

Harm

The level of **harm** is determined by weighing up all the factors of the case to determine the harm that has been caused or was at risk of being caused.

In assessing any risk of harm posed by the breach, consideration should be given to the original offence(s) or activity for which the order was imposed and the circumstances in which the breach arose.

Category 1	Breach causes very serious harm or distress
Category 2	Cases falling between categories 1 and 3
Category 3	Breach causes little or no harm or distress

STEP 2 — STARTING POINT AND CATEGORY RANGE

Having determined the category at step one, the court should use the corresponding starting point to reach a sentence within the category range in the table below. The starting point applies to all offenders irrespective of plea or previous convictions.

Harm	Culpability		
	A	**B**	**C**
Category 1	**Starting point** 3 years' custody **Category range** 2–4 years 6 months' custody	**Starting point** 2 years' custody **Category range** 36 week – 3 years' custody	**Starting point** 1 years' custody **Category range** High level community order – 2 year's custody
Category 2	**Starting point** 2 years' custody **Category range** 36 weeks – 3 years' custody	**Starting point** 1 years' custody **Category range** High level community order – 2 year's custody	**Starting point** High level community order **Category range** Medium level community order – 26 weeks' custody
Category 3	**Starting point** 1 years' custody **Category range** High level community order – 2 year's custody	**Starting point** 26 weeks' custody **Category range** Medium level community order – 36 weeks' custody	**Starting point** Medium level community order **Category range** Band B fine – High level community order

The table below contains a **non-exhaustive** list of additional factual elements providing the context of the offence and factors relating to the offender. Identify whether any combination of these, or other relevant factors, should result in an upward or downward adjustment from the starting point. In some cases, having considered these factors, it may be appropriate to move outside the identified category range.

Factors increasing seriousness

Statutory aggravating factors:

- Previous convictions, having regard to a) the **nature** of the offence to which the conviction relates and its **relevance** to the current offence; and b) the **time** that has elapsed since the conviction
- Offence committed whilst on bail

Other aggravating factors:

- Breach committed immediately or shortly after order made

- History of disobedience of court orders (where not already taken into account as a previous conviction)
- Breach involves a further offence (where not separately prosecuted)
- Targeting of particular individual the order was made to protect
- Victim or protected subject of order is particularly vulnerable
- Offender takes steps to prevent victim or subject harmed by breach from reporting an incident or seeking assistance
- Offence committed on licence or while subject to post sentence supervision

Factors reducing seriousness or reflecting personal mitigation

- Breach committed after long period of compliance
- Prompt voluntary surrender/admission of breach or failure
- Age and/or lack of maturity where it affects the responsibility of the offender
- Mental disorder or learning disability where linked to the commission of the offence
- Sole or primary carer for dependent relatives

STEP 3 — CONSIDER ANY FACTORS WHICH INDICATE A REDUCTION, SUCH AS ASSISTANCE TO THE PROSECUTION
The court should take into account sections 73 and 74 of the Serious Organised Crime and Police Act 2005 (assistance by defendants: reduction or review of sentence) and any other rule of law by virtue of which an offender may receive a discounted sentence in consequence of assistance given (or offered) to the prosecutor or investigator.

STEP 4 — REDUCTION FOR GUILTY PLEAS
The court should take account of any potential reduction for a guilty plea in accordance with section 144 of the Criminal Justice Act 2003 and the *Guilty Plea* guideline.

STEP 5 — TOTALITY PRINCIPLE
If sentencing an offender for more than one offence, or where the offender is already serving a sentence, consider whether the total sentence is just and proportionate to the overall offending behaviour in accordance with the *Offences Taken into Consideration and Totality* guideline.

STEP 6 — ANCILLARY ORDERS
In all cases, the court should consider whether to make compensation and/or ancillary orders.

STEP 7 — REASONS
Section 174 of the Criminal Justice Act 2003 imposes a duty to give reasons for, and explain the effect of, the sentence.

STEP 8 — CONSIDERATION FOR TIME SPENT ON BAIL
The court must consider whether to give credit for time spent on bail in accordance with section 240A of the Criminal Justice Act 2003.

BREACH OF A PROTECTIVE ORDER (RESTRAINING AND NON-MOLESTATION ORDERS)
Restraining orders: Protection from Harassment Act 1997 (section 5(5) and (5A))
Non-molestation orders: Family Law Act 1996, s 42A,
Effective from: 1 October 2018
Triable either way
Maximum: 5 years' custody
Offence range: Fine – 4 years' custody

STEP 1 — DETERMINING THE OFFENCE CATEGORY

The court should determine the offence category with reference only to the factors listed in the tables below. In order to determine the category the court should assess **culpability** and **harm**.

Culpability

In assessing culpability, the court should consider the **intention** and **motivation** of the offender in committing any breach.

A	Very serious or persistent breach
B	Deliberate breach falling between A and C
C	Minor breach Breach just short of reasonable excuse

Harm

The level of **harm** is determined by weighing up all the factors of the case to determine the harm that has been caused or was at risk of being caused.

In assessing any risk of harm posed by the breach, consideration should be given to the original offence(s) or activity for which the order was imposed and the circumstances in which the breach arose.

Category 1	Breach causes **very** serious harm or distress
Category 2	Cases falling between categories 1 and 3
Category 3	Breach causes little or no harm or distress*

* where a breach is committed in the context of a background of domestic abuse, the sentencer should take care not to underestimate the harm which may be present in a breach

STEP 2 — STARTING POINT AND CATEGORY RANGE

Having determined the category at step one, the court should use the corresponding starting point to reach a sentence within the category range in the table below. The starting point applies to all offenders irrespective of plea or previous convictions.

	Culpability		
Harm	**A**	**B**	**C**
Category 1	**Starting point** 2 years' custody **Category range** 1–4 years' custody	**Starting point** 1 years' custody **Category range** High level community order – 2 years' custody	**Starting point** 12 weeks' custody **Category range** Medium level community order – 1 year's custody
Category 2	**Starting point** 1 years' custody **Category range** High level community order – 2 years' custody	**Starting point** 12 weeks' custody **Category range** Medium level community order – 1 year's custody	**Starting point** High level community order **Category range** Low level community order – 26 weeks' custody
Category 3	**Starting point** 12 weeks' custody **Category range** Medium level community order – 1 year's custody	**Starting point** High level community order **Category range** Low level community order – 26 weeks' custody	**Starting point** Low level community order **Category range** Band B fine – High level community order

The table below contains a **non-exhaustive** list of additional factual elements providing the context of the offence and factors relating to the offender. Identify whether any combination of these, or other relevant factors, should result in an upward or downward adjustment from the starting point. In some cases, having considered these factors, it may be appropriate to move outside the identified category range.

Factors increasing seriousness

Statutory aggravating factors:

* Previous convictions, having regard to a) the **nature** of the offence to which the conviction relates and its **relevance** to the current offence; and b) the **time** that has elapsed since the conviction

- Offence committed whilst on bail

Other aggravating factors:

- Breach committed shortly after order made
- History of disobedience of court orders (where not already taken into account as a previous conviction)
- Breach involves a further offence (where not separately prosecuted)
- Using contact arrangements with a child/children to instigate offence and/or proven history of violence or threats by offender
- Breach results in victim or protected person being forced to leave their home
- Impact upon children or family members
- Victim or protected subject of order breached is particularly vulnerable
- Offender takes steps to prevent victim or subject harmed by breach from reporting an incident or seeking assistance
- Offence committed on licence or while subject to post sentence supervision

Factors reducing seriousness or reflecting personal mitigation

- Breach committed after long period of compliance
- Prompt voluntary surrender/admission of breach or failure
- Age and/or lack of maturity where it affects the responsibility of the offender
- Mental disorder or learning disability where linked to the commission of the offence
- Contact not initiated by offender – a careful examination of all the circumstances is required before weight is given to this factor

STEP 3 — CONSIDER ANY FACTORS WHICH INDICATE A REDUCTION, SUCH AS ASSISTANCE TO THE PROSECUTION
The court should take into account sections 73 and 74 of the Serious Organised Crime and Police Act 2005 (assistance by defendants: reduction or review of sentence) and any other rule of law by virtue of which an offender may receive a discounted sentence in consequence of assistance given (or offered) to the prosecutor or investigator.

STEP 4 — REDUCTION FOR GUILTY PLEAS
The court should take account of any reduction for a guilty plea in accordance with section 144 of the Criminal Justice Act 2003 and the guideline for Reduction in Sentence for a Guilty Plea (where first hearing is on or after 1 June 2017, or first hearing before 1 June 2017).

STEP 5 — TOTALITY PRINCIPLE
If sentencing an offender for more than one offence, or where the offender is already serving a sentence, consider whether the total sentence is just and proportionate to the overall offending behaviour in accordance with the *Offences Taken into Consideration and Totality* guideline.

STEP 6 — ANCILLARY ORDERS
In all cases, the court should consider whether to make compensation and/or ancillary orders.

STEP 7 — REASONS
Section 174 of the Criminal Justice Act 2003 imposes a duty to give reasons for, and explain the effect of, the sentence.

STEP 8 — CONSIDERATION FOR TIME SPENT ON BAIL
The court must consider whether to give credit for time spent on bail in accordance with section 240A of the Criminal Justice Act 2003.

BREACH OF A SUSPENDED SENTENCE ORDER

Criminal Justice Act 2003, Sch 12
Effective from: 01 October 2018

1) CONVICTION FOR FURTHER OFFENCE COMMITTED DURING OPERATIONAL PERIOD OF ORDER

The court **must activate the custodial sentence** unless it would be unjust in all the circumstances to do so. The predominant factor in determining whether activation is unjust relates to the level of compliance with the suspended sentence order and the facts/nature of any new offence. **These factors are already provided for in the penalties below which are determined by the nature of the new offence and level of compliance, but permit a reduction to the custodial term for relevant completed or partially completed requirements where appropriate.**

The facts/nature of the new offence is the primary consideration in assessing the action to be taken on the breach.

Where the breach is in the second or third category below, the prior level of compliance is also relevant. In assessing the level of compliance with the order the court should consider:

(i)   the overall attitude and engagement with the order as well as the proportion of elements completed;

(ii)   the impact of any completed or partially completed requirements on the offender's behaviour;

(iii)   the proximity of breach to imposition of order; and

(iv)   evidence of circumstances or offender characteristics, such as disability, mental health issues or learning difficulties which have impeded offender's compliance with the order.

Breach involves	Penalty
Multiple and/or more serious new offence(s) committed	Full activation of original custodial term
New offence similar in type and gravity to offence for which suspended sentence order imposed and:	
a) No/low level of compliance with suspended sentence order	Full activation of original custodial term
OR	
b) Medium or high level of compliance with suspended sentence order	Activate sentence but apply appropriate reduction* to original custodial term taking into consideration any unpaid work or curfew requirements completed
New offence less serious than original offence but requires a custodial sentence and:	
a) No/low level of compliance with suspended sentence order	Full activation of original custodial term
OR	
b) Medium or high level of compliance with suspended sentence order	Activate sentence but apply appropriate reduction* to original custodial term taking into consideration any unpaid work or curfew requirements completed
New offence less serious than original offence but requires a custodial sentence and:	Activate sentence but apply appropriate reduction* to original custodial term taking into consideration any unpaid work or curfew requirements completed **OR** Impose more onerous requirement(s) and/or extend supervision period and/or extend operational period and/or impose fine

* It is for the court dealing with the breach to identify the appropriate proportionate reduction depending on the extent of any compliance with the requirements specified.

Unjust in all the circumstances

The court dealing with the breach should remember that the court imposing the original sentence determined that a custodial sentence was appropriate in the original case.

In determining if there are other factors which would cause activation to be unjust, the court may consider all factors including:

•   any strong personal mitigation;

•   whether there is a realistic prospect of rehabilitation;

•   whether immediate custody will result in significant impact on others.

Only new and exceptional factors/circumstances not present at the time the suspended sentence order was imposed should be taken into account.

In cases where the court considers that it would be unjust to order the custodial sentence to take effect, it **must** state its reasons and it must deal with the offender in one of the following ways:

(a)   impose a fine not exceeding £2,500; **OR**

(b) extend the operational period (to a maximum of two years from date of original sentence);
OR
(c) if the SSO imposes community requirements, do one or more of:
(i) impose more onerous community requirements;
(ii) extend the supervision period (to a maximum of two years from date of original sentence);
(iii) extend the operational period (to a maximum of two years from date of original sentence).

2) FAILURE TO COMPLY WITH A COMMUNITY REQUIREMENT DURING THE SUPERVISION PERIOD OF THE ORDER

The court **must activate the custodial sentence** unless it would be unjust in all the circumstances to do so. The predominant factor in determining whether activation is unjust relates to the level of compliance with the suspended sentence order. **This factor is already provided for in the penalties below which are determined by the level of compliance, but permit a reduction to the custodial term for relevant completed or partially completed requirements where appropriate.**

The court must take into account the extent to which the offender has complied with the suspended sentence order when imposing a sentence.

In assessing the level of compliance with the order the court should consider:

(i) the overall attitude and engagement with the order as well as the proportion of elements completed;
(ii) the impact of any completed or partially completed requirements on the offender's behaviour; and
(iii) the proximity of breach to imposition of order; and
(iv) evidence of circumstances or offender characteristics, such as disability, mental health issues or learning difficulties which have impeded offender's compliance with the order.

Breach involves	Penalty
No/low level of compliance	Full activation of original custodial term
Medium level of compliance	Activate sentence but apply appropriate reduction* to original custodial term taking into consideration any unpaid work or curfew requirements completed
High level of compliance	Activate sentence but apply appropriate reduction* to original custodial term taking into consideration any unpaid work or curfew requirements completed **OR** Impose more onerous requirement(s) and/or extend supervision period and/or extend operational period and/or impose fine

* It is for the court dealing with the breach to identify the appropriate proportionate reduction depending on the extent of any compliance with the requirements specified.

Unjust in all the circumstances

The court dealing with the breach should remember that the court imposing the original sentence determined that a custodial sentence was appropriate in the original case.

In determining if there are other factors which would cause activation to be unjust, the court may consider all factors including:

- any strong personal mitigation;
- whether there is a realistic prospect of rehabilitation;
- whether immediate custody will result in significant impact on others.

Only new and exceptional factors/circumstances not present at the time the suspended sentence order was imposed should be taken into account.

In cases where the court considers that it would be unjust to order the custodial sentence to take effect, it must state its reasons and it **must** deal with the offender in one of the following ways:

(a) impose a fine not exceeding £2,500; **OR**
(b) extend the operational period (to a maximum of two years from date of original sentence); **OR**
(c) if the SSO imposes community requirements, do one or more of:
(i) impose more onerous community requirements;
(ii) extend the supervision period (to a maximum of two years from date of original sentence);
(iii) extend the operational period (to a maximum of two years from date of original sentence).

BREACH OF DISQUALIFICATION FROM ACTING AS A DIRECTOR

Company Directors Disqualification Act 1986, s 13
Effective from: 1 October 2018
Triable either way
Maximum: 2 years' custody
Offence range: Discharge – 1 year and 6 months' custody

STEP 1 — DETERMINING THE OFFENCE CATEGORY

The court should determine the offence category with reference only to the factors listed in the tables below. In order to determine the category the court should assess **culpability** and **harm**.

Culpability

A	Breach involves deceit/dishonesty in relation to actual role within company Breach involves deliberate concealment of disqualified status
B	All other cases

Harm

The level of **harm** is determined by weighing up all the factors of the case to determine the harm that has been caused or was at risk of being caused.

In assessing any risk of harm posed by the breach, consideration should be given to the original offence(s) or activity for which the order was imposed and the circumstances in which the breach arose.

Category 1	Breach results in significant risk of or actual serious financial loss **OR** Breach results in significant risk of or actual serious non-financial harm to company/ organisation or others
Category 2	Cases falling between categories 1 and 3
Category 3	Breach results in very low risk of or little or no harm (financial or non-financial) to company/ organisation or others

STEP 2 — STARTING POINT AND CATEGORY RANGE

Having determined the category at step one, the court should use the corresponding starting point to reach a sentence within the category range from the appropriate sentence table below. The starting point applies to all offenders irrespective of plea or previous convictions. The court should then consider further adjustment within the category range for aggravating or mitigating features.

	Culpability	
Harm	**A**	**B**
Category 1	**Starting point** 1 years' custody **Category range** 26 weeks – 1 year 6 months' custody	**Starting point** 12 weeks' custody **Category range** High level community order – 36 weeks' custody
Category 2	**Starting point** 26 weeks' custody **Category range** 12 weeks – 36 weeks' custody	**Starting point** High level community order **Category range** Medium level community order – 26 weeks' custody
Category 3	**Starting point** 12 weeks' custody **Category range** Medium level community order – 26 weeks' custody	**Starting point** Medium level community order **Category range** Band C Fine – High level community order

The table below contains a **non-exhaustive** list of additional factual elements providing the context of the offence and factors relating to the offender. Identify whether any combination of these, or other relevant factors, should result in an upward or downward adjustment from the starting point. In some cases, having considered these factors, it may be appropriate to move outside the identified category range.

Factors increasing seriousness
Statutory aggravating factors:

•   Previous convictions, having regard to a) the **nature** of the offence to which the conviction

relates and its **relevance** to the current offence; and b) the **time** that has elapsed since the conviction
* Offence committed whilst on bail

Other aggravating factors:

* Breach committed shortly after order made
* Breach continued after warnings received
* Breach is continued over a sustained period of time
* Breach motivated by personal gain
* Offence committed on licence or while subject to post sentence supervision

Factors reducing seriousness or reflecting personal mitigation

* Breach not motivated by personal gain
* Breach committed after long period of compliance
* Genuine misunderstanding of terms of disqualification
* Evidence of voluntary reparation/compensation made to those suffering loss
* Breach activity minimal or committed for short duration
* Age and/or lack of maturity where it affects the responsibility of the offender
* Mental disorder or learning disability where linked to the commission of the offence
* Sole or primary carer for dependent relatives

STEP 3 — CONSIDER ANY FACTORS WHICH INDICATE A REDUCTION, SUCH AS ASSISTANCE TO THE PROSECUTION

The court should take into account sections 73 and 74 of the Serious Organised Crime and Police Act 2005 (assistance by defendants: reduction or review of sentence) and any other rule of law by virtue of which an offender may receive a discounted sentence in consequence of assistance given (or offered) to the prosecutor or investigator.

STEP 4 — REDUCTION FOR GUILTY PLEAS

The court should take account of any potential reduction for a guilty plea in accordance with section 144 of the Criminal Justice Act 2003 and the *Guilty Plea* guideline.

STEP 5 — TOTALITY PRINCIPLE

If sentencing an offender for more than one offence, or where the offender is already serving a sentence, consider whether the total sentence is just and proportionate to the overall offending behaviour in accordance with the *Offences Taken into Consideration and Totality* guideline.

STEP 6 — ANCILLARY ORDERS

In all cases, the court should consider whether to make compensation and/or ancillary orders.

STEP 7 — REASONS

Section 174 of the Criminal Justice Act 2003 imposes a duty to give reasons for, and explain the effect of, the sentence.

STEP 8 — CONSIDERATION FOR TIME SPENT ON BAIL

The court must consider whether to give credit for time spent on bail in accordance with section 240A of the Criminal Justice Act 2003.

Breach of Post-Sentence Supervision

Criminal Justice Act 2003, s 256AC and Sch.19A
Effective from: 1 October 2018

Breach of Post-Sentence Supervision

Where the court determines a penalty is appropriate for a breach of a post sentence supervision requirement it must take into account the extent to which the offender has complied with all of the requirements of the post-sentence supervision or supervision default order when imposing a penalty.

In assessing the level of compliance with the order the court should consider:

(i) the offender's overall attitude and engagement with the order as well as the proportion of elements completed;

(ii) the impact of any completed or partially completed requirements on the offender's behaviour;

(iii) the proximity of the breach to the imposition of the order; and

(iv) evidence of circumstances or offender characteristics, such as disability, mental health issues or learning difficulties which have impeded offender's compliance with the order.

Level of Compliance	Penalty
Low	Up to 7 days' committal to custody **OR** Supervision default order in range of 30 – 40 hours unpaid work **OR** 8 – 12 hour curfew for minimum of 20 days
Medium	Supervision default order in range of 20 – 30 hours unpaid work **OR** 4 – 8 hour curfew for minimum of 20 days **OR** Band B fine
High	Band A fine

Breach of Supervision Order

Level of Compliance	Penalty
Low	Revoke supervision default order and order up to 14 days' committal to custody
Medium	Revoke supervision default order and impose new order in range of 40 – 60 hours unpaid work **OR** 8 – 16 hour curfew for minimum of 20 days
High	Band B fine

(i) A supervision default order must include either:
an unpaid work requirement of between 20 hours – 60 hours
OR
a curfew requirement for between 2 – 16 hours for a minimum of 20 days and no longer than the end of the post sentence supervision period.

(ii) The maximum fine which can be imposed is £1,000.

COMMUNICATION NETWORK OFFENCES (REVISED 2017)

Communications Act 2003, ss. 127(1) and 127(2)
Effective from: 24 April 2017
Triable only summarily:
Maximum: Unlimited fine and/or 6 months
Offence range: Band A fine — 15 weeks' custody
Step 1 — Determining the offence category The Court should determine the offence category using the table below.

Category 1	Higher culpability **and** greater harm
Category 2	Higher culpability **and** lesser harm **or** lower culpability **and** greater harm
Category 3	Lower culpability **and** lesser harm

The court should determine the offender's culpability and the harm caused with reference **only** to the factors below. Where an offence does not fall squarely into a category, individual factors may require a degree of weighting before making an overall assessment and determining the appropriate offence category.
CULPABILITY demonstrated by one or more of the following: Factors indicating higher culpability

- Targeting of a vulnerable victim
- Targeting offending (in terms of timing or location) to maximise effect
- Use of threats (including blackmail)
- Threat to disclose intimate material or sexually explicit images
- Campaign demonstrated by multiple calls and/or wide distribution
- False calls to emergency services
- Offence motivated by, or demonstrating, hostility based on any of the following characteristics or presumed characteristics of the victim(s): religion, race, disability, sexual orientation or transgender identity

Factors indicating lower culpability

- All other cases

HARM demonstrated by one or more of the following: Factors indicating greater harm

- Substantial distress or fear to victim(s) **or** moderate impact on several victims
- Major disruption

Factors indicating lesser harm

- All other cases

Step 2 — Starting point and category range Having determined the category at step one, the court should use the corresponding starting point to reach a sentence within the category range in the table below. The starting point applies to all offenders irrespective of plea or previous convictions.

Offence Category	Starting Point	Range
Category 1	9 weeks' custody	High level community order — 15 weeks' custody
Category 2	Medium level community order	Low level community order — High level community order
Category 3	Band B fine	Band A fine — Band C fine

The court should then consider adjustment for any aggravating or mitigating factors. The following is a **non-exhaustive** list of additional factual elements providing the context of the offence and factors relating to the offender. Identify whether any combination of these, or other relevant factors, should result in an upward or downward adjustment from the sentence arrived at so far.
Factors increasing seriousness *Statutory aggravating factors:*

- Previous convictions, having regard to a) the **nature** of the offence to which the conviction relates and its **relevance** to the current offence; and b) the **time** that has elapsed since the conviction
- Offence committed whilst on bail

Other aggravating factors:

- Failure to comply with current court orders including restraining order
- Offence committed on licence or post sentence supervision
- Offence committed whilst subject to sex offender notification requirements
- Offence linked to domestic abuse
- Abuse of trust
- Targeting emergency services (where not taken into account at step one)

- No previous convictions **or** no relevant/recent convictions
- Remorse
- Good character and/or exemplary conduct
- Isolated incident
- Age and/or lack of maturity where it affects the responsibility of the offender
- Mental disorder or learning disability
- Sole or primary carer for dependent relatives

- Limited awareness or understanding of the offence

Step 3 — Consider any factors which indicate a reduction, such as assistance to the prosecution
The court should take into account sections 73 and 74 of the Serious Organised Crime and Police Act 2005 (assistance by defendants: reduction or review of sentence) and any other rule of law by virtue of which an offender may receive a discounted sentence in consequence of assistance given (or offered) to the prosecutor or investigator.

Step 4 — Reduction for guilty pleas   The court should take account of any potential reduction for a guilty plea in accordance with section 144 of the Criminal Justice Act 2003 and the *Guilty Plea* guideline.

Step 5 — Totality principle   If sentencing an offender for more than one offence, or where the offender is already serving a sentence, consider whether the total sentence is just and proportionate to the overall offending behaviour in accordance with the *Offences Taken into Consideration and Totality* guideline.

Step 6 — Compensation and ancillary orders   In all cases, the court should consider whether to make compensation and/or other ancillary orders including restraining orders.

Step 7 — Reasons   Section 174 of the Criminal Justice Act 2003 imposes a duty to give reasons for, and explain the effect of, the sentence.

Step 8 — Consideration for time spent on bail   The court must consider whether to give credit for time spent on bail in accordance with section 240A of the Criminal Justice Act 2003.

CONTROLLING OR COERCIVE BEHAVIOUR IN AN INTIMATE OR FAMILY RELATIONSHIP

Serious Crime Act 2015, s 76
Effective from: 1 October 2018
Triable either way
Maximum: 5 years' custody
Offence range: Community order – 4 years' custody
Also refer to the Overarching principles: Domestic abuse guideline
Where offence committed in a domestic context, also refer to the *Overarching principles: Domestic abuse guideline*

STEP 1 — DETERMINING THE OFFENCE CATEGORY

The court should determine the offence category with reference only to the factors in the tables below. In order to determine the category the court should assess culpability and harm.
The level of **culpability** is determined by weighing up all the factors of the case. **Where there are characteristics present which fall under different levels of culpability, the court should balance these characteristics to reach a fair assessment of the offender's culpability.**

A – Higher culpability	Conduct intended to maximise fear or distress Persistent action over a prolonged period Use of multiple methods of controlling or coercive behaviour Sophisticated offence Conduct intended to humiliate and degrade the victim
B – Medium culpability	Conduct intended to cause some fear or distress Scope and duration of offence that falls between categories A and C All other cases that fall between categories A and C
C – Lesser culpability	Offender's responsibility substantially reduced by mental disorder or learning disability Offence was limited in scope and duration

Harm The level of harm is assessed by weighing up all the factors of the case.

Category 1	Fear of violence on many occasions Very serious alarm or distress which has a substantial adverse effect on the victim Significant psychological harm
Category 2	Fear of violence on at least two occasions Serious alarm or distress which has a substantial adverse effect on the victim

STEP 2 — STARTING POINT AND CATEGORY RANGE

Having determined the category at step one, the court should use the corresponding starting point to reach a sentence within the category range in the table below. The starting point applies to all offenders irrespective of plea or previous convictions.

Harm	Culpability		
	A	**B**	**C**
Category 1	**Starting point** 2 years 6 months' custody **Category range** 1–4 years 6 months' custody	**Starting point** 1 years' custody **Category range** 26 weeks' – 2 years 6 months' custody	**Starting point** 26 weeks' custody **Category range** High level community order – 1year's custody
Category 2	**Starting point** 1 years' custody **Category range** 26 weeks – 2 years 6 months' custody	**Starting point** 26 weeks' custody **Category range** High level community order – 1year's custody	**Starting point** High level community order **Category range** Low level community order – 26 weeks' custody

The court should then consider any adjustment for any aggravating or mitigating factors. Below is a **non-exhaustive** list of additional factual elements providing the context of the offence and factors relating to the offender.
Identify whether any combination of these, or other relevant factors, should result in an upward or downward adjustment from the starting point.

Factors increasing seriousness
Statutory aggravating factors:

- Previous convictions, having regard to a) the **nature** of the offence to which the conviction relates and its **relevance** to the current offence; and b) the **time** that has elapsed since the conviction

- Offence committed whilst on bail
- Offence motivated by, or demonstrating hostility based on any of the following character-istics or presumed characteristics of the victim: religion, race, disability, sexual orientation, or transgender identity

Other aggravating factors:

- Steps taken to prevent the victim reporting an incident
- Steps taken to prevent the victim obtaining assistance
- A proven history of violence or threats by the offender in a domestic context
- Impact of offence on others particularly children
- Exploiting contact arrangements with a child to commit the offence
- Victim is particularly vulnerable (not all vulnerabilities are immediately apparent)
- Victim left in debt, destitute or homeless
- Failure to comply with current court orders
- Offence committed on licence or post sentence supervision
- Offences taken into consideration

Factors reducing seriousness or reflecting personal mitigation

- No previous convictions **or** no relevant/recent convictions
- Remorse
- Good character and/or exemplary conduct
- Serious medical condition requiring urgent, intensive or long-term treatment
- Age and/or lack of maturity
- Mental disorder or learning disability (where not taken into account at step one)
- Sole or primary carer for dependent relatives
- Limited awareness or understanding of the offence
- Determination and/or demonstration of steps having been taken to address offending behaviour

STEP 3 — CONSIDER ANY FACTORS WHICH INDICATE A REDUCTION, SUCH AS ASSISTANCE TO THE PROSECUTION

The court should take into account sections 73 and 74 of the Serious Organised Crime and Police Act 2005 (assistance by defendants: reduction or review of sentence) and any other rule of law by virtue of which an offender may receive a discounted sentence in consequence of assistance given (or offered) to the prosecutor or investigator.

STEP 4 — REDUCTION FOR GUILTY PLEAS

The court should take account of any potential reduction for a guilty plea in accordance with section 144 of the Criminal Justice Act 2003 and the *Guilty Plea* guideline.

STEP 5 — TOTALITY PRINCIPLE

If sentencing an offender for more than one offence, or where the offender is already serving a sentence, consider whether the total sentence is just and proportionate to the overall offending behaviour in accordance with the *Offences Taken into Consideration and Totality* guideline.

STEP 6 — COMPENSATION AND ANCILLARY ORDERS

The court should consider compensation orders in all cases where personal injury, loss or damage has resulted from the offence. The court must give reasons if it decides not to award compensation in such cases.

Other ancillary orders available include: Restraining order Where an offender is convicted of any offence, the court may make a restraining order (section 5 of the Protection from Harassment Act 1997).

The order may prohibit the offender from doing anything for the purpose of protecting the victim of the offence, or any other person mentioned in the order, from further conduct which amounts to harassment or will cause a fear of violence.

The order may have effect for a specified period or until further order.

STEP 7 — REASONS

Section 174 of the Criminal Justice Act 2003 imposes a duty to give reasons for, and explain the effect of, the sentence.

STEP 8 — CONSIDERATION FOR TIME SPENT ON BAIL

The court must consider whether to give credit for time spent on bail in accordance with section 240A of the Criminal Justice Act 2003.

CRIMINAL DAMAGE (OTHER THAN BY FIRE)
RACIALLY OR RELIGIOUSLY AGGRAVATED CRIMINAL DAMAGE

Criminal damage (other than by fire)
Criminal Damage Act 1971, s.1(1)

Racially or religiously aggravated criminal damage
Crime and Disorder Act 1998, s.30

Criminal damage: triable only summarily if value involved does not exceed £5,000:
Maximum: Level 4 fine and/or 3 months

Triable either way if value involved exceeds £5,000:
Maximum when tried summarily: Level 5 fine and/or 6 months
Maximum when tried on indictment: 10 years

Racially or religiously aggravated criminal damage: triable either way
Maximum when tried summarily: Level 5 fine and/or 6 months
Maximum when tried on indictment: 14 years

Where offence committed in domestic context, refer to page 177 for guidance

Offence seriousness (culpability and harm)
A. Identify the appropriate starting point
Starting points based on first time offender pleading not guilty

Examples of nature of activity	Starting point	Range
Minor damage e.g. breaking small window; small amount of graffiti	Band B fine	Conditional discharge to band C fine
Moderate damage e.g. breaking large plate-glass or shop window; widespread graffiti	Low level community order	Band C fine to medium level community order
Significant damage up to £5,000 e.g. damage caused as part of a spree	High level community order	Medium level community order to 12 weeks custody
Damage between £5,000 and £10,000	12 weeks custody	6 to 26 weeks custody
Damage over £10,000	Crown Court	Crown Court

Offence seriousness (culpability and harm)
B. Consider the effect of aggravating and mitigating factors
(other than those within examples above)
Common aggravating and mitigating factors are identified in the pullout card –
the following may be particularly relevant but **these lists are not exhaustive**

Factors indicating higher culpability	Factors indicating lower culpability
1. Revenge attack 2. Targeting vulnerable victim **Factors indicating greater degree of harm** 1. Damage to emergency equipment 2. Damage to public amenity 3. Significant public or private fear caused e.g. in domestic context	1. Damage caused recklessly 2. Provocation

Form a preliminary view of the appropriate sentence
If offender charged and convicted of the racially or religiously aggravated offence, increase the sentence to reflect this element
Refer to pages 178-179 for guidance

Consider offender mitigation
Common factors are identified in the pullout card

Consider a reduction for a guilty plea

Consider ancillary orders, including compensation
Refer to pages 168-174 for guidance on available ancillary orders

Decide sentence
Give reasons

CRUELTY TO A CHILD – ASSAULT AND ILL TREATMENT, ABANDONMENT, NEGLECT, AND FAILURE TO PROTECT

Children and Young Persons Act 1933 (section 1(1))

Effective from: 1 January 2019

Triable either way

Maximum: 10 years' custody

Offence range: Community Order– 8 years' custody

This is a specified offence for the purposes of section 226A (extended sentence for certain violent or sexual offences) of the Criminal Justice Act 2003

STEP 1 — DETERMINING THE OFFENCE CATEGORY

The court should determine the offence category with reference **only** to the factors in the tables below. In order to determine the category the court should assess **culpability** and **harm**.

The court should weigh all the factors set out below in determining the offender's culpability.

Where there are characteristics present which fall under different levels of culpability, the court should balance these characteristics to reach a fair assessment of the offender's culpability.

Culpability demonstrated by one or more of the following:

A – Higher culpability	Prolonged and/or multiple incidents of serious cruelty, including serious neglect Gratuitous degradation of victim and/or sadistic behaviour Use of very significant force Use of a weapon Deliberate disregard for the welfare of the victim Failure to take any steps to protect the victim from offences in which the above factors are present Offender with professional responsibility for the victim (where linked to the commission of the offence)
B – Medium culpability	Use of significant force Prolonged and/or multiple incidents of cruelty, including neglect Limited steps taken to protect victim in cases with category A factors present Other cases falling between A and C because: • Factors in both high and lesser categories are present which balance each other out; and/or •The offender's culpability falls between the factors as described in high and lesser culpability
C – Lesser culpability	Offender's responsibility substantially reduced by mental disorder or learning disability or lack of maturity Offender is victim of domestic abuse, including coercion and/or intimidation (where linked to the commission of the offence) Steps taken to protect victim but fell just short of what could reasonably be expected Momentary or brief lapse in judgement including in cases of neglect Use of some force or failure to protect the victim from an incident involving some force Low level of neglect

Harm

The court should consider the factors set out below to determine the level of harm that has been caused or was intended to be caused to the victim.

Psychological, developmental or emotional harm

A finding that the psychological, developmental or emotional harm is serious may be based on a clinical diagnosis but the court may make such a finding based on other evidence from or on behalf of the victim that serious psychological, developmental or emotional harm exists. It is important to be clear that the absence of such a finding does **not** imply that the psychological, developmental or emotional harm suffered by the victim is minor or trivial.

Category 1	Serious psychological, developmental, and/or emotional harm Serious physical harm (including illnesses contracted due to neglect)
Category 2	Cases falling between categories 1 and 3 A high likelihood of category 1 harm being caused
Category 3	Little or no psychological, developmental, and/or emotional harm Little or no physical harm

Step 2 — Starting point and category range

Having determined the category at step one, the court should use the corresponding starting point to reach a sentence within the category range in the table below. The starting point applies to all offenders irrespective of plea or previous convictions.

Where a case does not fall squarely within a category, adjustment from the starting point may be required before adjustment for aggravating or mitigating features.

Harm	Culpability		
	A	**B**	**C**
Category 1	**Starting point** 6 year's custody **Category range** 4–8 years' custody	**Starting point** 3 years' custody **Category range** 2–6 years' custody	**Starting point** 1 years' custody **Category range** High level community order – 2 years 6 months' custody
Category 2	**Starting point** 3 years' custody **Category range** 2– 6 years' custody	**Starting point** 1 years' custody **Category range** High level community order – 2 years 6 months' custody	**Starting point** High level community order **Category range** Medium level community order – 1 years' custody
Category 3	**Starting point** 1 years' custody **Category range** High level community order – 2 years 6 months' custody	**Starting point** High level community order **Category range** medium level community order – 1 years' custody	**Starting point** Medium level community order **Category range** low level community order – 6 months' custody

The table below contains a **non-exhaustive** list of additional factual elements providing the context of the offence and factors relating to the offender. Identify whether any combination of these, or other relevant factors, should result in an upward or downward adjustment from the sentence arrived at so far. In particular, relevant recent convictions are likely to result in an upward adjustment. In some cases, having considered these factors, it may be appropriate to move outside the identified category range.

Factors increasing seriousness

Statutory aggravating factors:

- Previous convictions, having regard to a) the **nature** of the offence to which the conviction relates and its **relevance** to the current offence; and b) the **time** that has elapsed since the conviction
- Offence committed whilst on bail

Other aggravating factors:

- Failure to seek medical help (where not taken into account at step one)
- Commission of offence whilst under the influence of alcohol or drugs
- Deliberate concealment and/or covering up of the offence
- Blame wrongly placed on others
- Failure to respond to interventions or warnings about behaviour
- Failure to comply with current court orders
- Offence committed on licence or post sentence supervision
- Offences taken into consideration
- Offence committed in the presence of another child

Factors reducing seriousness or reflecting personal mitigation

- No previous convictions **or** no relevant/recent convictions
- Remorse
- Determination and demonstration of steps having been taken to address addiction or offending behaviour, including co-operation with agencies working for the welfare of the victim
- Sole or primary carer for dependent relatives (**see step five for further guidance on parental responsibilities**)
- Good character and/or exemplary conduct (where previous good character/exemplary conduct has been used to facilitate or conceal the offence, this should not normally constitute mitigation and such conduct may constitute aggravation)
- Serious medical condition requiring urgent, intensive or long-term treatment
- Mental disorder, learning disability or lack of maturity (where not taken into account at step one)
- Co-operation with the investigation

Step 3 — Consider any factors which indicate a reduction, such as assistance to the prosecution

The court should take into account sections 73 and 74 of the Serious Organised Crime and Police Act 2005 (assistance by defendants: reduction or review of sentence) and any other rule of law by virtue of which an offender may receive a discounted sentence in consequence of assistance given (or offered) to the prosecutor or investigator.

Step 4 — Reduction for guilty pleas

The court should take account of any potential reduction for a guilty plea in accordance with section 144 of the Criminal Justice Act 2003 and the *Guilty Plea* guideline.

Step 5 — Parental responsibilities of sole or primary carers

In the majority of child cruelty cases the offender will have parental responsibility for the victim.

When considering whether to impose custody the court should step back and review whether this sentence will be in the best interests of the victim (as well as other children in the offender's care). This must be balanced with the seriousness of the offence and all sentencing options remain open to the court but careful consideration should be given to the effect that a custodial sentence could have on the family life of the victim and whether this is proportionate to the seriousness of the offence. This may be of particular relevance in lower culpability cases or where the offender has otherwise been a loving and capable parent/carer.

Where custody is unavoidable consideration of the impact on the offender's children may be relevant to the length of the sentence imposed. For more serious offences where a substantial period of custody is appropriate, this consideration will carry less weight.

Step 6 — Dangerousness

The court should consider whether having regard to the criteria contained in Chapter 5 of Part 12 of the Criminal Justice Act 2003 it would be appropriate to impose an extended sentence (section 226A).

Step 7 — Totality principle

If sentencing an offender for more than one offence, or where the offender is already serving a sentence, consider whether the total sentence is just and proportionate to the overall offending behaviour in accordance with the *Offences Taken into Consideration and Totality* guideline.

Step 8 — Ancillary orders

TIn all cases the court should consider whether to make ancillary orders.

Step 9 — Reasons

Section 174 of the Criminal Justice Act 2003 imposes a duty to give reasons for, and explain the effect of, the sentence.

Step 10 — Consideration for time spent on bail (tagged curfew)

The court must consider whether to give credit for time spent on bail in accordance with section 240A of the Criminal Justice Act 2003.

Disclosing private sexual images

Criminal Justice and Courts Act 2015, s 33

Effective from: 1 October 2018

Triable either way

Maximum: 2 years' custody

Offence range: Discharge – 1 year 6 months' custody

Where offence committed in a domestic context, also refer to the *Overarching principles: Domestic abuse guideline*

Step 1 — Determining the offence category

The court should determine the offence category with reference only to the factors in the tables below. In order to determine the category the court should assess **culpability** and **harm**.

The level of **culpability** is determined by weighing up all the factors of the case. **Where there are characteristics present which fall under different levels of culpability, the court should balance these characteristics to reach a fair assessment of the offender's culpability.**

A – Higher culpability	Conduct intended to maximise distress and/or humiliation Images circulated widely/publically Significant planning and/or sophisticated offence Repeated efforts to keep images available for viewing
B – Medium culpability	Some planning Scope and duration of offence that falls between categories A and C All other cases that fall between categories A and C
C – Lesser culpability	Offender's responsibility substantially reduced by mental disorder or learning disability Little or no planning Conduct intended to cause limited distress and/or humiliation Offence was limited in scope and duration

Harm The level of harm is assessed by weighing up all the factors of the case.

Category 1	Very serious distress caused to the victim Significant psychological harm caused to the victim Offence has a considerable practical impact on the victim
Category 2	Harm that falls between categories 1 and 3, and in particular: Some distress caused to the victim Some psychological harm caused to the victim Offence has some practical impact on the victim
Category 3	Limited distress or harm caused to the victim

Step 2 — Starting point and category range

Having determined the category at step one, the court should use the corresponding starting point to reach a sentence within the category range in the table below. The starting point applies to all offenders irrespective of plea or previous convictions.

Harm	Culpability		
	A	**B**	**C**
Category 1	**Starting point** 1 year's custody **Category range** 26 weeks' custody	**Starting point** 26 weeks' custody **Category range** 12 weeks' – 1 year's custody	**Starting point** 12 weeks' custody **Category range** High level community order – 26 weeks' custody
Category 2	**Starting point** 26 weeks' custody **Category range** 12 weeks – 1 years' custody	**Starting point** 12 weeks' custody **Category range** High level community order – 26 weeks' custody	**Starting point** High level community order **Category range** Low level community order – 12 weeks' custody
Category 3	**Starting point** 12 weeks' custody **Category range** High level community order – 26 weeks' custody	**Starting point** High level community order **Category range** Low level community order – 12 weeks' custody	**Starting point** Low level community order **Category range** Discharge – High level community order

The court should then consider any adjustment for any aggravating or mitigating factors. Below is a **non-exhaustive** list of additional factual elements providing the context of the offence and factors relating to the offender.

Identify whether any combination of these, or other relevant factors, should result in an upward or downward adjustment from the starting point.

Factors increasing seriousness

Statutory aggravating factors:

- Previous convictions, having regard to a) the **nature** of the offence to which the conviction relates and its **relevance** to the current offence; and b) the **time** that has elapsed since the conviction
- Offence committed whilst on bail
- Offence motivated by, or demonstrating hostility based on any of the following characteristics or presumed characteristics of the victim: religion, race, disability, sexual orientation, or transgender identity

Other aggravating factors:

- Impact of offence on others particularly children
- Victim is particularly vulnerable (not all vulnerabilities are immediately apparent)
- Failure to comply with current court orders
- Offence committed on licence or post sentence supervision
- Offences taken into consideration

Factors reducing seriousness or reflecting personal mitigation

- No previous convictions **or** no relevant/recent convictions
- Offender took steps to limit circulation of images
- Remorse
- Good character and/or exemplary conduct
- Serious medical condition requiring urgent, intensive or long-term treatment
- Age and/or lack of maturity
- Mental disorder or learning disability (where not taken into account at step one)
- Sole or primary carer for dependent relatives
- Determination and/or demonstration of steps having been taken to address offending behaviour

STEP 3 — CONSIDER ANY FACTORS WHICH INDICATE A REDUCTION, SUCH AS ASSISTANCE TO THE PROSECUTION

The court should take into account sections 73 and 74 of the Serious Organised Crime and Police Act 2005 (assistance by defendants: reduction or review of sentence) and any other rule of law by virtue of which an offender may receive a discounted sentence in consequence of assistance given (or offered) to the prosecutor or investigator.

STEP 4 — REDUCTION FOR GUILTY PLEAS

The court should take account of any potential reduction for a guilty plea in accordance with section 144 of the Criminal Justice Act 2003 and the *Guilty Plea* guideline.

STEP 5 — TOTALITY PRINCIPLE

If sentencing an offender for more than one offence, or where the offender is already serving a sentence, consider whether the total sentence is just and proportionate to the overall offending behaviour in accordance with the *Offences Taken into Consideration and Totality* guideline.

STEP 6 — COMPENSATION AND ANCILLARY ORDERS

In all cases, the court must consider whether to make a compensation order and/or other ancillary orders.

Compensation order

The court should consider compensation orders in all cases where personal injury, loss or damage has resulted from the offence. The court must give reasons if it decides not to award compensation in such cases.

Other ancillary orders available include: Restraining order Where an offender is convicted of any offence, the court may make a restraining order (section 5 of the Protection from Harassment Act 1997).

The order may prohibit the offender from doing anything for the purpose of protecting the victim of the offence, or any other person mentioned in the order, from further conduct which amounts to harassment or will cause a fear of violence.

The order may have effect for a specified period or until further order.

STEP 7 — REASONS

Section 174 of the Criminal Justice Act 2003 imposes a duty to give reasons for, and explain the effect of, the sentence.

STEP 8 — CONSIDERATION FOR TIME SPENT ON BAIL

The court must consider whether to give credit for time spent on bail in accordance with section 240A of the Criminal Justice Act 2003.

D<small>RUGS</small> — <small>CLASS</small> A — <small>FAIL TO ATTEND/REMAIN FOR</small>
<small>INITIAL ASSESSMENT</small> (R<small>EVISED</small> 2017)

Drugs Act 2005, s.12
Effective from: 24 April 2017
Triable only summarily:
Maximum: Level 4 fine and/or 3 months
Offence range: Band A fine — High level community order
Step 1 — Determining the offence category   The Court should determine the offence category using the table below.

Category 1	Higher culpability **and** greater harm
Category 2	Higher culpability **and** lesser harm **or** lower culpability **and** greater harm
Category 3	Lower culpability **and** lesser harm

The court should determine the offender's culpability and the harm caused with reference **only** to the factors below. Where an offence does not fall squarely into a category, individual factors may require a degree of weighting before making an overall assessment and determining the appropriate offence category.

CULPABILITY demonstrated by one or more of the following: Factor indicating higher culpability

- Deliberate failure to attend/remain

Factor indicating lower culpability

- All other cases

HARM demonstrated by one or more of the following: Factor indicating greater harm

- Aggressive, abusive or disruptive behaviour

Factor indicating lesser harm

- All other cases

Step 2 — Starting point and category range   Having determined the category at step one, the court should use the corresponding starting point to reach a sentence within the category range in the table below. The starting point applies to all offenders irrespective of plea or previous convictions.

Offence Category	Starting Point	Range
Category 1	Medium level community order	Low level community order — High level community order
Category 2	Band C fine	Band B fine — Low level community order
Category 3	Band B fine	Band A fine — Band C fine

The court should then consider further adjustment for any aggravating or mitigating factors. The following is a **non-exhaustive** list of additional factual elements providing the context of the offence and factors relating to the offender. Identify whether any combination of these, or other relevant factors, should result in an upward or downward adjustment from the sentence arrived at so far.

Factors increasing seriousness   *Statutory aggravating factors:*

- Previous convictions, having regard to a) the **nature** of the offence to which the conviction relates and its **relevance** to the current offence; and b) the **time** that has elapsed since the conviction
- Offence committed whilst on bail
- Offence motivated by, or demonstrating hostility based on any of the following characteristics or presumed characteristics of the victim: religion, race, disability, sexual orientation or transgender identity

Other aggravating factors:

- Failure to comply with current court orders
- Offence committed on licence or post sentence supervision
- Offender's actions result in a waste of resources

- No previous convictions **or** no relevant/recent convictions
- Remorse
- Good character and/or exemplary conduct
- Serious medical condition requiring urgent, intensive or long-term treatment
- Age and/or lack of maturity where it affects the responsibility of the offender
- Mental disorder or learning disability
- Sole or primary carer for dependent relatives
- Determination and/or demonstration of steps having been taken to address addiction or offending behaviour
- Attempts made to re-arrange appointments

Factors reducing seriousness or reflecting personal mitigation
Step 3 — Consider any factors which indicate a reduction, such as assistance to the prosecution
    The court should take into account sections 73 and 74 of the Serious Organised Crime and Police Act 2005 (assistance by defendants: reduction or review of sentence) and any other rule of law by virtue of which an offender may receive a discounted sentence in consequence of assistance given (or offered) to the prosecutor or investigator.

Step 4 — Reduction for guilty pleas   The court should take account of any potential reduction for a guilty plea in accordance with section 144 of the Criminal Justice Act 2003 and the *Guilty Plea* guideline.

Step 5 — Totality principle   If sentencing an offender for more than one offence, or where the offender is already serving a sentence, consider whether the total sentence is just and proportionate to the overall offending behaviour in accordance with the *Offences Taken into Consideration and Totality* guideline.

Step 6 — Consider ancillary orders   In all cases, the court should consider whether to make compensation and/or other ancillary orders.

Step 7 — Reasons   Section 174 of the Criminal Justice Act 2003 imposes a duty to give reasons for, and explain the effect of, the sentence.

DRUGS — CLASS A — FAIL/REFUSE TO PROVIDE A
SAMPLE (REVISED 2017)

Police and Criminal Evidence Act 1984, s.63B
Effective from: 24 April 2017
Triable only summarily:
Maximum: Level 4 fine and/or 3 months
Offence range: Band A fine — High level community order
Step 1 — Determining the offence category The Court should determine the offence category using the table below.

Category 1	Higher culpability **and** greater harm
Category 2	Higher culpability **and** lesser harm **or** lower culpability **and** greater harm
Category 3	Lower culpability **and** lesser harm

The court should determine the offender's culpability and the harm caused with reference **only** to the factors below. Where an offence does not fall squarely into a category, individual factors may require a degree of weighting before making an overall assessment and determining the appropriate offence category.
CULPABILITY demonstrated by one or more of the following: Factors indicating higher culpability

- Deliberate refusal

Factors indicating lower culpability

- All other cases

HARM demonstrated by one or more of the following: Factors indicating greater harm

- Aggressive, abusive or disruptive behaviour

Factors indicating lesser harm

- All other cases

Step 2 — Starting point and category range Having determined the category at step one, the court should use the starting point to reach a sentence within the appropriate category range in the table below. The starting point applies to all offenders irrespective of plea or previous convictions.

Offence Category	Starting Point	Range
Category 1	Medium level community order	Low level community order — High level community order
Category 2	Band C fine	Band B fine — Low level community order
Category 3	Band B fine	Band A fine — Band C fine

The court should then consider adjustment for any aggravating or mitigating factors. The following is a **non-exhaustive** list of additional factual elements providing the context of the offence and factors relating to the offender. Identify whether any combination of these, or other relevant factors, should result in an upward or downward adjustment from the sentence arrived at so far.
Factors increasing seriousness *Statutory aggravating factors:*

- Previous convictions, having regard to a) the **nature** of the offence to which the conviction relates and its **relevance** to the current offence; and b) the **time** that has elapsed since the conviction
- Offence committed whilst on bail
- Offence motivated by, or demonstrating hostility based on any of the following characteristics or presumed characteristics of the victim: religion, race, disability, sexual orientation or transgender identity

Other aggravating factors:

- Failure to comply with current court orders
- Offence committed on licence or post sentence supervision
- Offender's actions result in a waste of resources

- No previous convictions **or** no relevant/recent convictions
- Remorse
- Good character and/or exemplary conduct
- Serious medical condition requiring urgent, intensive or long-term treatment
- Age and/or lack of maturity where it affects the responsibility of the offender
- Mental disorder or learning disability
- Sole or primary carer for dependent relatives
- Determination and/or demonstration of steps having been taken to address addiction or offending behaviour

Factors reducing seriousness or reflecting personal mitigation
Step 3 — Consider any factors which indicate a reduction, such as assistance to the prosecution
The court should take into account sections 73 and 74 of the Serious Organised Crime and Police Act 2005 (assistance by defendants: reduction or review of sentence) and any other rule of law by virtue of which an offender may receive a discounted sentence in consequence of assistance given (or offered) to the prosecutor or investigator.

Step 4 — Reduction for guilty pleas   The court should take account of any potential reduction for a guilty plea in accordance with section 144 of the Criminal Justice Act 2003 and the *Guilty Plea* guideline.

Step 5 — Totality principle   If sentencing an offender for more than one offence, or where the offender is already serving a sentence, consider whether the total sentence is just and proportionate to the overall offending behaviour in accordance with the *Offences Taken into Consideration and Totality* guideline.

Step 6 — Consider ancillary orders   In all cases, the court should consider whether to make compensation and/or other ancillary orders.

Step 7 — Reasons   Section 174 of the Criminal Justice Act 2003 imposes a duty to give reasons for, and explain the effect of, the sentence.

DRUNK AND DISORDERLY IN A PUBLIC PLACE (REVISED 2017)

Criminal Justice Act 1967, s.91
Effective from: 24 April 2017
Triable only summarily:
Maximum: Level 3 fine
Offence range: Conditional discharge — Band C fine
Steps 1 and 2 — Determining the offence seriousness The starting point applies to all offenders irrespective of plea or previous convictions.

Starting Point	Range
Band A fine	Conditional discharge — Band C fine

The court should then consider adjustment for any aggravating or mitigating factors. The following is a **non-exhaustive** list of additional factual elements providing the context of the offence and factors relating to the offender. Identify whether any combination of these, or other relevant factors, should result in an upward or downward adjustment from the sentence arrived at so far.
Factors increasing seriousness *Statutory aggravating factors:*

- Previous convictions, having regard to a) the **nature** of the offence to which the conviction relates and its **relevance** to the current offence; and b) the **time** that has elapsed since the conviction
- Offence committed whilst on bail
- Offence motivated by, or demonstrating hostility based on any of the following characteristics or presumed characteristics of the victim: religion, race, disability, sexual orientation or transgender identity

Other aggravating factors:

- Substantial disturbance caused
- Offence ties up disproportionate police resource
- Disregard of earlier warning regarding conduct
- Failure to comply with current court orders
- Offence committed on licence or post sentence supervision
- Location of the offence
- Timing of the offence
- Offence committed against those working in the public sector or providing a service to the public
- Presence of others including, especially children or vulnerable people

- Minimal disturbance caused
- No previous convictions **or** no relevant/recent convictions
- Remorse
- Good character and/or exemplary conduct
- Age and/or lack of maturity where it affects the responsibility of the offender
- Mental disorder or learning disability

Factors reducing seriousness or reflecting personal mitigation
Step 3 — Consider any factors which indicate a reduction, such as assistance to the prosecution The court should take into account sections 73 and 74 of the Serious Organised Crime and Police Act 2005 (assistance by defendants: reduction or review of sentence) and any other rule of law by virtue of which an offender may receive a discounted sentence in consequence of assistance given (or offered) to the prosecutor or investigator.

Step 4 — Reduction for guilty pleas The court should take account of any potential reduction for a guilty plea in accordance with section 144 of the Criminal Justice Act 2003 and the *Guilty Plea* guideline.

Step 5 — Totality principle If sentencing an offender for more than one offence, or where the offender is already serving a sentence, consider whether the total sentence is just and proportionate to the overall offending behaviour in accordance with the *Offences Taken into Consideration and Totality* guideline.

Step 6 — Compensation and ancillary orders In all cases, the court should consider whether to make compensation and/or other ancillary orders, including a football banning order (where appropriate).

Step 7 — Reasons Section 174 of the Criminal Justice Act 2003 imposes a duty to give reasons for, and explain the effect of, the sentence.

FIREARM, CARRYING IN PUBLIC PLACE

| Firearms Act 1968, s.19 | **Firearm, carrying in public place** |

Triable either way (but triable only summarily if the firearm is an air weapon):
Maximum when tried summarily: Level 5 fine and/or 6 months
Maximum when tried on indictment: 7 years (12 months for imitation firearms)

Offence seriousness (culpability and harm)
A. Identify the appropriate starting point
Starting points based on first time offender pleading not guilty

Examples of nature of activity	Starting point	Range
Carrying an unloaded air weapon	Low level community order	Band B fine to medium level community order
Carrying loaded air weapon/imitation firearm/unloaded shot gun without ammunition	High level community order	Medium level community order to 26 weeks custody (air weapon)
		Medium level community order to Crown Court (imitation firearm, unloaded shot gun)
Carrying loaded shot gun/carrying shot gun or any other firearm together with ammunition for it	Crown Court	Crown Court

Offence seriousness (culpability and harm)
B. Consider the effect of aggravating and mitigating factors
(other than those within examples above)
Common aggravating and mitigating factors are identified in the pullout card – the following may be particularly relevant but **these lists are not exhaustive**

Factors indicating higher culpability	Factors indicating lower culpability
1. Brandishing the firearm 2. Carrying firearm in a busy place 3. Planned illegal use **Factors indicating greater degree of harm** 1. Person or people put in fear 2. Offender participating in violent incident	1. Firearm not in sight 2. No intention to use firearm 3. Firearm to be used for lawful purpose (not amounting to a defence)

Form a preliminary view of the appropriate sentence, then consider offender mitigation
Common factors are identified in the pullout card

Consider a reduction for a guilty plea

Consider ancillary orders, including compensation, forfeiture or suspension of personal liquor licence and football banning order (where appropriate)
Refer to pages 168-174 for guidance on available ancillary orders

Decide sentence
Give reasons

FOOTBALL RELATED OFFENCES (REVISED 2017)

Criminal Justice and Public Order Act 1994: s.166 (unauthorised sale or attempted sale of tickets);, Football Offences Act 1991: s.2 (throwing missile); s.3 (indecent or racist chanting); s.4 (going onto prohibited areas)., Sporting Events (Control of Alcohol etc.) Act 1985: s.2(1) (possession of alcohol whilst entering or trying to enter ground); s.2(2) (being drunk in, or whilst trying to enter, ground).

Effective from: 24 April 2017
Triable only summarily:
Maximum:
Level 2 fine (being drunk in ground)
Level 3 fine (throwing missile; indecent or racist chanting; going onto prohibited areas)
Unlimited fine (unauthorised sale of tickets)
Level 3 fine and/or 3 months (possession of alcohol)
Offence range:
Conditional discharge — High level community order (possession of alcohol) Conditional discharge — Band C fine (all other offences)
Step 1 — Determining the offence category The Court should determine the offence category using the table below.

Category 1	Higher culpability **and** greater harm
Category 2	Higher culpability **and** lesser harm **or** lower culpability **and** greater harm
Category 3	Lower culpability **and** lesser harm

The court should determine the offender's culpability and the harm caused with reference **only** to the factors below. Where an offence does not fall squarely into a category, individual factors may require a degree of weighting before making an overall assessment and determining the appropriate offence category.

CULPABILITY demonstrated by one or more of the following: **Factors indicating higher culpability**

- Deliberate or flagrant action
- Disregard of warnings
- Commercial operation
- Inciting others
- (Possession of) Large quantity of alcohol
- Targeted abuse

Factors indicating lower culpability

- All other cases

HARM demonstrated by one or more of the following: **Factor indicating greater harm**

- Distress or alarm caused
- Actual injury or risk of injury
- Significant financial loss to others

Factors indicating lesser harm

- All other cases

Step 2 — Starting point and category range Having determined the category at step one, the court should use the starting point to reach a sentence within the appropriate category range in the table below. The starting point applies to all offenders irrespective of plea or previous convictions.

Offence Category	Starting Point	Range
Category 1	Band C fine	Band C fine
Category 2	Band B fine	Band A fine — Band C fine
Category 3	Band A fine	Conditional discharge — Band B fine

Possession of alcohol only

Offence Category	Starting Point	Range
Category 1	Band C fine	Band C fine — High level community order
Category 2	Band B fine	Band A fine — Band C fine
Category 3	Band A fine	Conditional discharge — Band B fine

The court should then consider adjustment for any aggravating or mitigating factors. The following is a **non-exhaustive** list of additional factual elements providing the context of the offence and factors relating to the offender. Identify whether any combination of these, or other relevant factors, should result in an upward or downward adjustment from the sentence arrived at so far.

Factors increasing seriousness *Statutory aggravating factors:*

- Previous convictions, having regard to a) the **nature** of the offence to which the conviction relates and its **relevance** to the current offence; and b) the **time** that has elapsed since the conviction
- Offence committed whilst on bail

- Offence motivated by, or demonstrating hostility based on any of the following character-istics or presumed characteristics of the owner/keeper of the animal: religion, race, disabil-ity, sexual orientation or transgender identity

Other aggravating factors:

- Presence of children
- Offence committed on licence or post sentence supervision

- Remorse
- Admissions to police in interview
- Ready co-operation with authorities
- Minimal disturbance caused
- No previous convictions **or** no relevant/recent convictions
- Good character and/or exemplary conduct
- Age and/or lack of maturity where it affects the responsibility of the offender
- Mental disorder or learning disability

Factors reducing seriousness or reflecting personal mitigation

Step 3 — Consider any factors which indicate a reduction, such as assistance to the prosecution
The court should take into account sections 73 and 74 of the Serious Organised Crime and Police Act 2005 (assistance by defendants: reduction or review of sentence) and any other rule of law by virtue of which an offender may receive a discounted sentence in consequence of assistance given (or offered) to the prosecutor or investigator.

Step 4 — Reduction for guilty pleas   The court should take account of any potential reduction for a guilty plea in accordance with section 144 of the Criminal Justice Act 2003 and the *Guilty Plea* guideline.

Step 5 — Totality principle   If sentencing an offender for more than one offence, or where the offender is already serving a sentence, consider whether the total sentence is just and proportion-ate to the overall offending behaviour in accordance with the *Offences Taken into Consideration and Totality* guideline.

Step 6 — Compensation and ancillary orders   In all cases, the court should consider whether to make compensation and/or other ancillary orders, including a football banning order.

Step 7 — Reasons   Section 174 of the Criminal Justice Act 2003 imposes a duty to give reasons for, and explain the effect of, the sentence.

HARASSMENT (PUTTING PEOPLE IN FEAR OF VIOLENCE) / STALKING (INVOLVING FEAR OF VIOLENCE OR SERIOUS ALARM OR DISTRESS) / RACIALLY OR RELIGIOUSLY AGGRAVATED HARASSMENT (PUTTING PEOPLE IN FEAR OF VIOLENCE) / RACIALLY OR RELIGIOUSLY AGGRAVATED STALKING (INVOLVING FEAR OF VIOLENCE OR SERIOUS ALARM OR DISTRESS)

Crime and Disorder Act 1998, s 32(1)(b), Protection from Harassment Act 1997, s 4, Protection from Harassment Act 1997, s 4A

Effective from: 1 October 2018

HARASSMENT (PUTTING PEOPLE IN FEAR OF VIOLENCE)
Protection from Harassment Act 1997 (section 4)

STALKING (INVOLVING FEAR OF VIOLENCE OR SERIOUS ALARM OR DISTRESS)
Protection from Harassment Act 1997 (section 4A)

Triable either way
Maximum: 14 years' custody
Offence range: Fine – 8 years' custody

RACIALLY OR RELIGIOUSLY AGGRAVATED HARASSMENT (PUTTING PEOPLE IN FEAR OF VIOLENCE)
Crime and Disorder Act 1998 (section 32(1)(b))

RACIALLY OR RELIGIOUSLY AGGRAVATED STALKING (INVOLVING FEAR OF VIOLENCE OR SERIOUS ALARM OR DISTRESS)
Crime and Disorder Act 1998 (section 32(1)(b))

Triable either way
Maximum: 10 years' custody

The racially or religiously aggravated offence is a specified offence for the purposes of section 226A (extended sentence for certain violent or sexual offences) of the Criminal Justice Act 2003

Where offence committed in a domestic context, also refer to the *Overarching principles: Domestic abuse guideline*

STEP 1 — DETERMINING THE OFFENCE CATEGORY

The court should determine the offence category with reference only to the factors in the tables below. In order to determine the category the court should assess **culpability** and **harm**.

The level of **culpability** is determined by weighing up all the factors of the case. **Where there are characteristics present which fall under different levels of culpability, the court should balance these characteristics to reach a fair assessment of the offender's culpability.**

Culpability demonstrated by one or more of the following:

A	Very high culpability – the extreme nature of one or more culpability B factors or the extreme culpability indicated by a combination of culpability B factors may elevate to category A.
B	High culpability: Conduct intended to maximise fear or distress High degree of planning and/or sophisticated offence Persistent action over a prolonged period Offence motivated by, or demonstrating, hostility based on any of the following characteristics or presumed characteristics of the victim: age, sex, disability, sexual orientation or transgender identity
C	Medium culpability: Cases that fall between categories B and D, and in particular: Some planning Scope and duration of offence that falls between categories B and D
D	Lesser culpability: Offender's responsibility substantially reduced by mental disorder or learning disability Conduct unlikely to cause significant fear or distress Little or no planning Offence was limited in scope and duration

Harm The level of harm is assessed by weighing up all the factors of the case.

Category 1	Very serious distress caused to the victim Significant psychological harm caused to the victim Victim caused to make considerable changes to lifestyle to avoid contact

Category 2	Harm that falls between categories 1 and 3, and in particular: Some distress caused to the victim Some psychological harm caused to the victim Victim caused to make some changes to lifestyle to avoid contact
Category 3	Limited distress or harm caused to the victim

STEP 2 — STARTING POINT AND CATEGORY RANGE

Having determined the category at step one, the court should use the corresponding starting point to reach a sentence within the category range in the table below. The starting point applies to all offenders irrespective of plea or previous convictions.

Sentencers should consider whether to ask for psychiatric reports in order to assist in the appropriate sentencing (hospital orders, or mental health treatment requirements) of certain offenders to whom this consideration may be relevant.

Maximum: 10 years' custody (basic offence)

Harm	Culpability			
	A	**B**	**C**	**D**
Category 1	**Starting point** 5 year's custody **Category range** 3 years 6 months' – 8 years' custody	**Starting point** 2 years 6 months' custody **Category range** 1 – 4 year's custody	**Starting point** 36 weeks' custody **Category range** 12 weeks – 1 year 6 months' custody	**Starting point** 12 weeks' custody **Category range** High level community order – 36 weeks' custody
Category 2	**Starting point** 2 years 6 months' custody **Category range** 1 – 4 years' custody	**Starting point** 36 weeks' custody **Category range** 12 weeks' – 1 year 6 months' custody	**Starting point** 12 weeks' custody **Category range** High level community order – 36 weeks' custody	**Starting point** High level community order **Category range** Low level community order – 12 weeks' custody
Category 3	**Starting point** 36 weeks' custody **Category range** 12 weeks' – 1 year 6 months' custody	**Starting point** 12 weeks' custody **Category range** High level community order – 36 weeks' custody	**Starting point** High level community order **Category range** Low level community order – 12 weeks' custody	**Starting point** Band C fine – High level community order

The court should then consider any adjustment for any aggravating or mitigating factors. Below is a **non-exhaustive** list of additional factual elements providing the context of the offence and factors relating to the offender.

Identify whether any combination of these, or other relevant factors, should result in an upward or downward adjustment from the starting point.

Factors increasing seriousness

Statutory aggravating factors:

- Previous convictions, having regard to a) the **nature** of the offence to which the conviction relates and its **relevance** to the current offence; and b) the **time** that has elapsed since the conviction
- Offence committed whilst on bail

Other aggravating factors:

- Using a position of trust to facilitate the offence
- Victim is particularly vulnerable (not all vulnerabilities are immediately apparent)
- Grossly violent or offensive material sent
- Impact of offence on others, particularly children
- Exploiting contact arrangements with a child to commit the offence
- Offence committed against those working in the public sector or providing a service to the public
- Failure to comply with current court orders
- Offence committed on licence or post sentence supervision
- Offences taken into consideration

Factors reducing seriousness or reflecting personal mitigation

- No previous convictions **or** no relevant/recent convictions
- Offender took steps to limit circulation of images
- Remorse
- Good character and/or exemplary conduct
- Serious medical condition requiring urgent, intensive or long-term treatment
- Age and/or lack of maturity
- Mental disorder or learning disability (where not taken into account at step one)
- Sole or primary carer for dependent relatives
- Determination and/or demonstration of steps having been taken to address offending behaviour

Racially or religiously aggravated harassment/stalking offences only

Having determined the category of the basic offence to identify the sentence of a non-aggravated offence, the court should now consider the level of racial or religious aggravation involved and apply an appropriate uplift to the sentence in accordance with the guidance below. The following is a list of factors which the court should consider to determine the level of aggravation. Where there are characteristics present which fall under different levels of aggravation, the court should balance these to reach a fair assessment of the level of aggravation present in the offence.

Maximum sentence for the aggravated offence on indictment is 14 years' custody (maximum for the basic offence is 10 years' custody)

HIGH LEVEL OF RACIAL OR RELIGIOUS AGGRAVATION	SENTENCE UPLIFT.
Racial or religious aggravation was the predominant motivation for the offence. Offender was a member of, or was associated with, a group promoting hostility based on race or religion (where linked to the commission of the offence). Aggravated nature of the offence caused severe distress to the victim or the victim's family (over and above the distress already considered at step one).	Increase the length of custodial sentence if already considered for the basic offence or consider a custodial sentence, if not already considered for the basic offence.
MEDIUM LEVEL OF RACIAL OR RELIGIOUS AGGRAVATION	SENTENCE UPLIFT
Racial or religious aggravation formed a significant proportion of the offence as a whole. Aggravated nature of the offence caused some distress to the victim or the victim's family (over and above the distress already considered at step one). Aggravated nature of the offence caused some fear and distress throughout local community or more widely.	Consider a significantly more onerous penalty of the same type or consider a more severe type of sentence than for the basic offence.
LOW LEVEL OF RACIAL OR RELIGIOUS AGGRAVATION	SENTENCE UPLIFT
Aggravated element formed a minimal part of the offence as a whole. Aggravated nature of the offence caused minimal or no distress to the victim or the victim's family (over and above the distress already considered at step one).	Consider a more onerous penalty of the same type identified for the basic offence.

Magistrates may find that, although the appropriate sentence for the basic offence would be within their powers, the appropriate increase for the aggravated offence would result in a sentence in excess of their powers. If so, they must commit for sentence to the Crown Court.

The sentencer should state in open court that the offence was aggravated by reason of race or religion, and should also state what the sentence would have been without that element of aggravation.

STEP 3 — CONSIDER ANY FACTORS WHICH INDICATE A REDUCTION, SUCH AS ASSISTANCE TO THE PROSECUTION

The court should take into account sections 73 and 74 of the Serious Organised Crime and Police Act 2005 (assistance by defendants: reduction or review of sentence) and any other rule of law by virtue of which an offender may receive a discounted sentence in consequence of assistance given (or offered) to the prosecutor or investigator.

STEP 4 — REDUCTION FOR GUILTY PLEAS

The court should take account of any potential reduction for a guilty plea in accordance with section 144 of the Criminal Justice Act 2003 and the *Guilty Plea* guideline.

STEP 5 — DANGEROUSNESS

The court should consider whether having regard to the criteria contained in Chapter 5 of Part 12 of the Criminal Justice Act 2003 it would be appropriate to impose an extended sentence (section 226A).

STEP 6 — TOTALITY PRINCIPLE

If sentencing an offender for more than one offence, or where the offender is already serving a sentence, consider whether the total sentence is just and proportionate to the overall offending behaviour in accordance with the *Offences Taken into Consideration and Totality* guideline.

Step 7 — Compensation and ancillary orders

In all cases, the court must consider whether to make a compensation order and/or other ancillary orders.

Compensation order

The court should consider compensation orders in all cases where personal injury, loss or damage has resulted from the offence. The court must give reasons if it decides not to award compensation in such cases.

Other ancillary orders available include: Restraining order Where an offender is convicted of any offence, the court may make a restraining order (section 5 of the Protection from Harassment Act 1997).

The order may prohibit the offender from doing anything for the purpose of protecting the victim of the offence, or any other person mentioned in the order, from further conduct which amounts to harassment or will cause a fear of violence.

The order may have effect for a specified period or until further order.

Step 8 — Reasons

Section 174 of the Criminal Justice Act 2003 imposes a duty to give reasons for, and explain the effect of, the sentence.

Step 9 — Consideration for time spent on bail (tagged curfew)

The court must consider whether to give credit for time spent on bail in accordance with section 240A of the Criminal Justice Act 2003.

Harassment / Stalking / Racially or religiously aggravated harassment / Racially or religiously aggravated stalking

Crime and Disorder Act 1998, s 32(1)(a), Protection from Harassment Act 1997, s 2, Protection from Harassment Act 1997, s 2A
Effective from: 1 October 2018

Harassment
Protection from Harassment Act 1997 (section 2)

Stalking
Protection from Harassment Act 1997 (section 2A)
Triable only summarily
Maximum: 6 months' custody
Offence range: Discharge – 26 weeks' custody

Racially or religiously aggravated harassment
Crime and Disorder Act 1998 (section 32(1)(a))

Racially or religiously aggravated stalking
Crime and Disorder Act 1998 (section 32(1)(a))
Triable either way
Maximum: 2 years' custody

Where offence committed in a domestic context, also refer to the *Overarching principles: Domestic abuse guideline*

Step 1 — Determining the offence category

The court should determine the offence category with reference only to the factors in the tables below. In order to determine the category the court should assess **culpability** and **harm**.

The level of culpability is determined by weighing up all the factors of the case. **Where there are characteristics present which fall under different levels of culpability, the court should balance these characteristics to reach a fair assessment of the offender's culpability.**

Culpability demonstrated by one or more of the following:

A	Very high culpability: Conduct intended to maximise fear or distress High degree of planning and/or sophisticated offence Persistent action over a prolonged period Threat of serious violence Offence motivated by, or demonstrating, hostility based on any of the following characteristics or presumed characteristics of the victim: age, sex, disability, sexual orientation or transgender identity
B	Medium Culpability Cases that fall between categories A and C, in particular: Conduct intended to cause some fear or distress Some planning Threat of some violence Scope and duration of offence that falls between categories A and C
C	Lesser culpability: Offender's responsibility substantially reduced by mental disorder or learning disability Little or no planning Offence was limited in scope and duration

Harm The level of harm is assessed by weighing up all the factors of the case.

Category 1	Very serious distress caused to the victim Significant psychological harm caused to the victim Victim caused to make considerable changes to lifestyle to avoid contact
Category 2	Harm that falls between categories 1 and 3, and in particular: Some distress caused to the victim Some psychological harm caused to the victim Victim caused to make some changes to lifestyle to avoid contact
Category 3	Limited distress or harm caused to the victim

Step 2 — Starting point and category range

Having determined the category at step one, the court should use the corresponding starting point to reach a sentence within the category range below. The starting point applies to all offenders irrespective of plea or previous convictions.

Maximum: months' custody (basic offence)

Culpability			
Harm	**A**	**B**	**C**
Category 1	**Starting point** 12 weeks' custody **Category range** High level community order – 26 weeks' custody	**Starting point** High level community order **Category range** Medium level community order – 16 weeks' custody	**Starting point** Medium level community order **Category range** Low level community order – 12 weeks' custody
Category 2	**Starting point** High level community order **Category range** Medium level community order – 16 weeks' custody	**Starting point** Medium level community order **Category range** Low level community order – 12 weeks' custody	**Starting point** Low level community order **Category range** Band B fine – Medium level community order
Category 3	**Starting point** Medium level community order 12 weeks' custody **Category range** Medium level community order 12 weeks' custody	**Starting point** Low level community order **Category range** Band B fine – Medium level community order	**Starting point** Band B fine **Category range** Discharge – Low level community order

The court should then consider any adjustment for any aggravating or mitigating factors. Below is a **non-exhaustive** list of additional factual elements providing the context of the offence and factors relating to the offender.

Identify whether any combination of these, or other relevant factors, should result in an upward or downward adjustment from the starting point.

Factors increasing seriousness

Statutory aggravating factors:

- Previous convictions, having regard to a) the **nature** of the offence to which the conviction relates and its **relevance** to the current offence; and b) the **time** that has elapsed since the conviction
- Offence committed whilst on bail

Other aggravating factors:

- Using a position of trust to facilitate the offence
- Victim is particularly vulnerable (not all vulnerabilities are immediately apparent)
- Grossly violent or offensive material sent
- Impact of offence on others, particularly children
- Exploiting contact arrangements with a child to commit the offence
- Offence committed against those working in the public sector or providing a service to the public
- Failure to comply with current court orders
- Offence committed on licence or post sentence supervision
- Offences taken into consideration

Factors reducing seriousness or reflecting personal mitigation

- No previous convictions **or** no relevant/recent convictions
- Offender took steps to limit circulation of images
- Remorse
- Good character and/or exemplary conduct
- Serious medical condition requiring urgent, intensive or long-term treatment
- Age and/or lack of maturity
- Mental disorder or learning disability (where not taken into account at step one)
- Sole or primary carer for dependent relatives
- Determination and/or demonstration of steps having been taken to address offending behaviour

Racially or religiously aggravated harassment/stalking offences only

Having determined the category of the basic offence to identify the sentence of a non-aggravated offence, the court should now consider the level of racial or religious aggravation involved and apply an appropriate uplift to the sentence in accordance with the guidance below. The following is a list of factors which the court should consider to determine the level of aggravation. Where there are characteristics present which fall under different levels of aggravation, the court should balance these to reach a fair assessment of the level of aggravation present in the offence.

Maximum sentence for the aggravated offence on indictment is 2 years' custody (maximum for the basic offence is 6 months' custody)

HIGH LEVEL OF RACIAL OR RELIGIOUS AGGRAVATION	SENTENCE UPLIFT.
Racial or religious aggravation was the predominant motivation for the offence. Offender was a member of, or was associated with, a group promoting hostility based on race or religion (where linked to the commission of the offence). Aggravated nature of the offence caused severe distress to the victim or the victim's family (over and above the distress already considered at step one). Aggravated nature of the offence caused serious fear and distress throughout local community or more widely.	Increase the length of custodial sentence if already considered for the basic offence or consider a custodial sentence, if not already considered for the basic offence.
MEDIUM LEVEL OF RACIAL OR RELIGIOUS AGGRAVATION	SENTENCE UPLIFT
Racial or religious aggravation formed a significant proportion of the offence as a whole. Aggravated nature of the offence caused some distress to the victim or the victim's family (over and above the distress already considered at step one). Aggravated nature of the offence caused some fear and distress throughout local community or more widely.	Consider a significantly more onerous penalty of the same type or consider a more severe type of sentence than for the basic offence.
LOW LEVEL OF RACIAL OR RELIGIOUS AGGRAVATION	SENTENCE UPLIFT
Aggravated element formed a minimal part of the offence as a whole. Aggravated nature of the offence caused minimal or no distress to the victim or the victim's family (over and above the distress already considered at step one).	Consider a more onerous penalty of the same type identified for the basic offence.

Magistrates may find that, although the appropriate sentence for the basic offence would be within their powers, the appropriate increase for the aggravated offence would result in a sentence in excess of their powers. If so, they must commit for sentence to the Crown Court.

The sentencer should state in open court that the offence was aggravated by reason of race or religion, and should also state what the sentence would have been without that element of aggravation.

STEP 3 — CONSIDER ANY FACTORS WHICH INDICATE A REDUCTION, SUCH AS ASSISTANCE TO THE PROSECUTION

The court should take into account sections 73 and 74 of the Serious Organised Crime and Police Act 2005 (assistance by defendants: reduction or review of sentence) and any other rule of law by virtue of which an offender may receive a discounted sentence in consequence of assistance given (or offered) to the prosecutor or investigator.

STEP 4 — REDUCTION FOR GUILTY PLEAS

The court should take account of any potential reduction for a guilty plea in accordance with section 144 of the Criminal Justice Act 2003 and the *Guilty Plea* guideline.

STEP 5— TOTALITY PRINCIPLE

If sentencing an offender for more than one offence, or where the offender is already serving a sentence, consider whether the total sentence is just and proportionate to the overall offending behaviour in accordance with the *Offences Taken into Consideration and Totality* guideline.

STEP 6— COMPENSATION AND ANCILLARY ORDERS

In all cases, the court must consider whether to make a compensation order and/or other ancillary orders.

Compensation order

The court should consider compensation orders in all cases where personal injury, loss or damage has resulted from the offence. The court must give reasons if it decides not to award compensation in such cases.

Other ancillary orders available include: Restraining order Where an offender is convicted of any offence, the court may make a restraining order (section 5 of the Protection from Harassment Act 1997).

The order may prohibit the offender from doing anything for the purpose of protecting the victim of the offence, or any other person mentioned in the order, from further conduct which amounts to harassment or will cause a fear of violence.

The order may have effect for a specified period or until further order.

Step 7— Reasons

Section 174 of the Criminal Justice Act 2003 imposes a duty to give reasons for, and explain the effect of, the sentence.

Step 8— Consideration for time spent on bail (tagged curfew)

The court must consider whether to give credit for time spent on bail in accordance with section 240A of the Criminal Justice Act 2003.

IDENTITY DOCUMENTS – POSSESS FALSE/ANOTHER'S/IMPROPERLY OBTAINED

Identity Cards Act 2006, s.25(5) (possession of a false identity document (as defined in s.26 – includes a passport))

Identity documents – possess false/another's/improperly obtained

Triable either way:
Maximum when tried summarily: Level 5 fine and/or 6 months
Maximum when tried on indictment: 2 years (s.25(5))

Note: possession of a false identity document with the intention of using it is an indictable-only offence (Identity Cards Act 2006, s.25(1)). The maximum penalty is 10 years imprisonment.

Offence seriousness (culpability and harm)
A. Identify the appropriate starting point
Starting points based on first time offender pleading not guilty

Examples of nature of activity	Starting point	Range
Single document possessed	Medium level community order	Band C fine to high level community order
Small number of documents, no evidence of dealing	12 weeks custody	6 weeks custody to Crown Court
Considerable number of documents possessed, evidence of involvement in larger operation	Crown Court	Crown Court

Offence seriousness (culpability and harm)
B. Consider the effect of aggravating and mitigating factors
(other than those within examples above)
Common aggravating and mitigating factors are identified in the pullout card – the following may be particularly relevant but **these lists are not exhaustive**

Factors indicating higher culpability 1. Clear knowledge that documents false 2. Number of documents possessed (where not in offence descriptions above) **Factors indicating greater degree of harm** 1. Group activity 2. Potential impact of use (where not in offence descriptions above)	**Factor indicating lower culpability** 1. Genuine mistake or ignorance

Form a preliminary view of the appropriate sentence, then consider offender mitigation
Common factors are identified in the pullout card

Consider a reduction for a guilty plea

Decide sentence
Give reasons

OBSTRUCT/RESIST A POLICE CONSTABLE IN
EXECUTION OF DUTY (REVISED 2017)

Police Act 1996, s.89(2)
Effective from: 24 April 2017
Triable only summarily:
Maximum: Level 3 fine and/or one month
Offence range: Conditional Discharge — Medium level community order
Step 1 — Determining the offence category The Court should determine the offence category using the table below.

Category 1	Higher culpability **and** greater harm
Category 2	Higher culpability **and** lesser harm **or** lower culpability **and** greater harm
Category 3	Lower culpability **and** lesser harm

The court should determine the offender's culpability and the harm caused with reference **only** to the factors below. Where an offence does not fall squarely into a category, individual factors may require a degree of weighting before making an overall assessment and determining the appropriate offence category.

CULPABILITY demonstrated by one or more of the following: Factors indicating higher culpability

- Deliberate obstruction or interference
- Use of force, aggression or intimidation
- Group action

Factors indicating lower culpability

- All other cases

HARM demonstrated by one or more of the following: Factors indicating greater harm

- Offender's actions significantly increase risk to officer or other(s)
- Offender's actions result in a suspect avoiding arrest
- Offender's actions result in a significant waste of resources

Factors indicating lesser harm

- All other cases

Step 2 — Starting point and category range Having determined the category at step one, the court should use the corresponding starting point to reach a sentence within the category range below. The starting point applies to all offenders irrespective of plea or previous convictions.

Offence Category	Starting Point	Range
Category 1	Low level community order	Band C fine — Medium level community order
Category 2	Band B fine	Band A fine — Band C fine
Category 3	Band A fine	Conditional discharge — Band B fine

The court should then consider adjustment for any aggravating or mitigating factors. The following is a **non-exhaustive** list of additional factual elements providing the context of the offence and factors relating to the offender. Identify whether any combination of these, or other relevant factors, should result in an upward or downward adjustment from the sentence arrived at so far.

Factors increasing seriousness *Statutory aggravating factors:*

- Previous convictions, having regard to a) the **nature** of the offence to which the conviction relates and its **relevance** to the current offence; and b) the **time** that has elapsed since the conviction
- Offence committed whilst on bail
- Offence motivated by, or demonstrating hostility based on any of the following characteristics or presumed characteristics of the victim: religion, race, disability, sexual orientation or transgender identity

Other aggravating factors:

- Failure to comply with current court orders
- Offence committed on licence or post sentence supervision
- Blame wrongly placed on others
- Injury caused to an officer/another
- Giving false details

- No previous convictions **or** no relevant/recent convictions
- Remorse
- Brief incident
- Acting under direction or coercion of another
- Genuinely held belief if coming to the aid of another, that the other was suffering severe medical difficulty
- Good character and/or exemplary conduct
- Serious medical condition requiring urgent, intensive or long-term treatment
- Age and/or lack of maturity where it affects the responsibility of the offender
- Mental disorder or learning disability

- Sole or primary carer for dependent relatives

Step 3 — Consider any factors which indicate a reduction, such as assistance to the prosecution
The court should take into account sections 73 and 74 of the Serious Organised Crime and Police Act 2005 (assistance by defendants: reduction or review of sentence) and any other rule of law by virtue of which an offender may receive a discounted sentence in consequence of assistance given (or offered) to the prosecutor or investigator.

Step 4 — Reduction for guilty pleas   The court should take account of any potential reduction for a guilty plea in accordance with section 144 of the Criminal Justice Act 2003 and the *Guilty Plea* guideline.

Step 5 — Totality principle   If sentencing an offender for more than one offence, or where the offender is already serving a sentence, consider whether the total sentence is just and proportionate to the overall offending behaviour in accordance with the *Offences Taken into Consideration and Totality* guideline.

Step 6 — Compensation and ancillary orders   In all cases, the court should consider whether to make compensation and/or other ancillary orders.

Step 7 — Reasons   Section 174 of the Criminal Justice Act 2003 imposes a duty to give reasons for, and explain the effect of, the sentence.

PUBLIC ORDER ACT, S 2 — VIOLENT OFFENDER

Public Order Act, s.2 – violent disorder

Public Order Act 1986, s.2

Triable either way:
Maximum when tried summarily: Level 5 fine and/or 6 months
Maximum when tried on indictment: 5 years

Identify dangerous offenders

This is a specified offence for the purposes of the public protection provisions in the Criminal Justice Act 2003 – refer to page 187 and consult legal adviser for guidance

Offence seriousness (culpability and harm)
A. Identify the appropriate starting point
Starting points based on first time offender pleading not guilty

These offences should normally be dealt with in the Crown Court. However, there may be rare cases involving minor violence or threats of violence leading to no or minor injury, with few people involved and no weapon or missiles, in which a custodial sentence within the jurisdiction of a magistrates' court may be appropriate.

PUBLIC ORDER ACT, S 3 — AFFRAY

Public Order Act 1986, s.3

Public Order Act, s.3 – affray

Triable either way:
Maximum when tried summarily: Level 5 fine and/or 6 months
Maximum when tried on indictment: 3 years

Identify dangerous offenders
This is a specified offence for the purposes of the public protection provisions in the Criminal Justice Act 2003 – refer to page 187 and consult legal adviser for guidance

Offence seriousness (culpability and harm)
A. Identify the appropriate starting point
Starting points based on first time offender pleading not guilty

Examples of nature of activity	Starting point	Range
Brief offence involving low-level violence, no substantial fear created	Low level community order	Band C fine to medium level community order
Degree of fighting or violence that causes substantial fear	High level community order	Medium level community order to 12 weeks custody
Fight involving a weapon/throwing objects, or conduct causing risk of serious injury	18 weeks custody	12 weeks custody to Crown Court

Offence seriousness (culpability and harm)
B. Consider the effect of aggravating and mitigating factors
(other than those within examples above)
Common aggravating and mitigating factors are identified in the pullout card – the following may be particularly relevant but **these lists are not exhaustive**

Factors indicating higher culpability	Factors indicating lower culpability
1. Group action	1. Did not start the trouble
2. Threats	2. Provocation
3. Lengthy incident	3. Stopped as soon as police arrived
Factors indicating greater degree of harm	
1. Vulnerable person(s) present	
2. Injuries caused	
3. Damage to property	

Form a preliminary view of the appropriate sentence, then consider offender mitigation
Common factors are identified in the pullout card

Consider a reduction for a guilty plea

Consider ancillary orders, including compensation and football banning order (where appropriate)
Refer to pages 168-174 for guidance on available ancillary orders

Decide sentence
Give reasons

PUBLIC ORDER ACT, S 4 — THREATENING BEHAVIOUR — FEAR OR PROVOCATION OF VIOLENCE
RACIALLY OR RELIGIOUSLY AGGRAVATED THREATENING BEHAVIOUR

Public Order Act, s.4 – threatening behaviour – fear or provocation of violence	Public Order Act 1986, s.4
Racially or religiously aggravated threatening behaviour	Crime and Disorder Act 1998, s.31

Threatening behaviour: triable only summarily
Maximum: Level 5 fine and/or 6 months
Racially or religiously aggravated threatening behaviour: triable either way
Maximum when tried summarily: Level 5 fine and/or 6 months
Maximum when tried on indictment: 2 years
Where offence committed in domestic context, refer to page 177 for guidance

Offence seriousness (culpability and harm)
A. Identify the appropriate starting point
Starting points based on first time offender pleading not guilty

Examples of nature of activity	Starting point	Range
Fear or threat of low level immediate unlawful violence such as push, shove or spit	Low level community order	Band B fine to medium level community order
Fear or threat of medium level immediate unlawful violence such as punch	High level community order	Low level community order to 12 weeks custody
Fear or threat of high level immediate unlawful violence such as use of weapon; missile thrown; gang involvement	12 weeks custody	6 to 26 weeks custody

Offence seriousness (culpability and harm)
B. Consider the effect of aggravating and mitigating factors
(other than those within examples above)
Common aggravating and mitigating factors are identified in the pullout card –
the following may be particularly relevant but **these lists are not exhaustive**

Factors indicating higher culpability	Factors indicating lower culpability
1. Planning 2. Offender deliberately isolates victim 3. Group action 4. Threat directed at victim because of job 5. History of antagonism towards victim	1. Impulsive action 2. Short duration 3. Provocation
Factors indicating greater degree of harm 1. Offence committed at school, hospital or other place where vulnerable persons may be present 2. Offence committed on enclosed premises such as public transport 3. Vulnerable victim(s) 4. Victim needs medical help/counselling	

Form a preliminary view of the appropriate sentence
If offender charged and convicted of the racially or religiously
aggravated offence, increase the sentence to reflect this element
Refer to pages 178-179 for guidance

Consider offender mitigation
Common factors are identified in the pullout card

Consider a reduction for a guilty plea

Consider ancillary orders, including compensation and
football banning order (where appropriate)
Refer to pages 168-174 for guidance on available ancillary orders

Decide sentence
Give reasons

PUBLIC ORDER ACT, S 4A — DISORDERLY BEHAVIOUR WITH INTENT TO CAUSE HARASSMENT, ALARM OR DISTRESS
RACIALLY OR RELIGIOUSLY AGGRAVATED DISORDERLY BEHAVIOUR WITH INTENT TO CAUSE HARASSMENT, ALARM
OR DISTRESS

Public Order Act 1986, s.4A	**Public Order Act, s.4A – disorderly behaviour with intent to cause harassment, alarm or distress**
Crime and Disorder Act 1998, s.31	**Racially or religiously aggravated disorderly behaviour with intent to cause harassment, alarm or distress**

Disorderly behaviour with intent to cause harassment, alarm or distress: triable only summarily
Maximum: Level 5 fine and/or 6 months

Racially or religiously aggravated disorderly behaviour with intent to cause harassment etc.: triable either way
Maximum when tried summarily: Level 5 fine and/or 6 months
Maximum when tried on indictment: 2 years

Offence seriousness (culpability and harm)
A. Identify the appropriate starting point
Starting points based on first time offender pleading not guilty

Examples of nature of activity	Starting point	Range
Threats, abuse or insults made more than once but on same occasion against the same person e.g. while following down the street	Band C fine	Band B fine to low level community order
Group action or deliberately planned action against targeted victim	Medium level community order	Low level community order to 12 weeks custody
Weapon brandished or used or threats against vulnerable victim – course of conduct over longer period	12 weeks custody	High level community order to 26 weeks custody

Offence seriousness (culpability and harm)
B. Consider the effect of aggravating and mitigating factors
(other than those within examples above)
Common aggravating and mitigating factors are identified in the pullout card –
the following may be particularly relevant but **these lists are not exhaustive**

Factors indicating higher culpability 1. High degree of planning 2. Offender deliberately isolates victim **Factors indicating greater degree of harm** 1. Offence committed in vicinity of victim's home 2. Large number of people in vicinity 3. Actual or potential escalation into violence 4. Particularly serious impact on victim	**Factors indicating lower culpability** 1. Very short period 2. Provocation

Form a preliminary view of the appropriate sentence
If offender charged and convicted of the racially or religiously
aggravated offence, increase the sentence to reflect this element
Refer to pages 178-179 for guidance

Consider offender mitigation
Common factors are identified in the pullout card

Consider a reduction for a guilty plea

Consider ancillary orders, including compensation and
football banning order (where appropriate)
Refer to pages 168-174 for guidance on available ancillary orders

Decide sentence
Give reasons

Public Order Act, s.5 – disorderly behaviour (harassment, alarm or distress)	Public Order Act 1986, s.5
Racially or religiously aggravated disorderly behaviour	Crime and Disorder Act 1998, s.31

Disorderly behaviour: triable only summarily
Maximum: Level 3 fine

Racially or religiously aggravated disorderly behaviour: triable only summarily
Maximum: Level 4 fine

Offence seriousness (culpability and harm)		
A. Identify the appropriate starting point		
Starting points based on first time offender pleading not guilty		
Examples of nature of activity	**Starting point**	**Range**
Shouting, causing disturbance for some minutes	Band A fine	Conditional discharge to band B fine
Substantial disturbance caused	Band B fine	Band A fine to band C fine

Offence seriousness (culpability and harm)
B. Consider the effect of aggravating and mitigating factors
(other than those within examples above)
Common aggravating and mitigating factors are identified in the pullout card –
the following may be particularly relevant but **these lists are not exhaustive**

Factors indicating higher culpability	Factors indicating lower culpability
1. Group action	1. Stopped as soon as police arrived
2. Lengthy incident	2. Brief/minor incident
	3. Provocation
Factors indicating greater degree of harm	
1. Vulnerable person(s) present	
2. Offence committed at school, hospital or other place where vulnerable persons may be present	
3. Victim providing public service	

Form a preliminary view of the appropriate sentence
If offender charged and convicted of the racially or religiously
aggravated offence, increase the sentence to reflect this element
Refer to pages 178-179 for guidance

Consider offender mitigation
Common factors are identified in the pullout card

Consider a reduction for a guilty plea

Consider ancillary orders, including compensation and
football banning order (where appropriate)
Refer to pages 168-174 for guidance on available ancillary orders

Decide sentence
Give reasons

RAILWAY FARE EVASION (REVISED 2017)

Regulation of Railways Act 1889, s.5(3) (travelling on railway without paying fare, with intent to avoid payment); s.5(1) (failing to produce ticket)

Effective from: 24 April 2017

Triable only summarily:

Maximum:

Level 2 fine (s.5(1) failing to produce ticket)

Level 3 fine and/or 3 months (s.5(3) travelling on railway with intent to avoid payment)

Offence range:

Conditional Discharge — Band C fine (s.5(1))

Conditional Discharge — Low level community order (s.5(3))

Step 1 — Determining the offence category   The Court should determine the offence category using the table below.

Category 1	Higher culpability **and** greater harm
Category 2	Higher culpability **and** lesser harm **or** lower culpability **and** greater harm
Category 3	Lower culpability **and** lesser harm

The court should determine the offender's culpability and the harm caused with reference **only** to the factors below. Where an offence does not fall squarely into a category, individual factors may require a degree of weighting before making an overall assessment and determining the appropriate offence category.

CULPABILITY demonstrated by one or more of the following: Factors indicating higher culpability

- Aggressive, abusive or disruptive behaviour

Factors indicating lower culpability

- All other cases

HARM demonstrated by one or more of the following: Factors indicating greater harm

- High revenue loss

Factors indicating lesser harm

- All other cases

Step 2 — Starting point and category range

Having determined the category at step one, the court should use the corresponding starting point to reach a sentence within the category range below. The starting point applies to all offenders irrespective of plea or previous convictions.

Travelling on railway without paying fare, with intent

Offence Category	Starting Point	Range
Category 1	Band C fine	Band B fine — Low level community order
Category 2	Band B fine	Band A fine — Band C fine
Category 3	Band A fine	Conditional discharge — Band B fine

Failing to Produce a ticket

Offence Category	Starting Point	Range
Category 1	Band B fine	Band B fine — Band C fine
Category 2	Band A fine	Band A fine — Band B fine
Category 3	Band A fine	Conditional discharge — Band B fine

The court should then consider adjustment for any aggravating or mitigating factors. The following is a **non-exhaustive** list of additional factual elements providing the context of the offence and factors relating to the offender. Identify whether any combination of these, or other relevant factors, should result in an upward or downward adjustment from the sentence arrived at so far.

Factors increasing seriousness   *Statutory aggravating factors:*

- Previous convictions, having regard to a) the **nature** of the offence to which the conviction relates and its **relevance** to the current offence; and b) the **time** that has elapsed since the conviction
- Offence committed whilst on bail
- Offence motivated by, or demonstrating hostility based on any of the following characteristics or presumed characteristics of the victim: religion, race, disability, sexual orientation or transgender identity

Other aggravating factors:

- Offender has avoided paying any of the fare
- Offender produces incorrect ticket or document to pass as legitimate fare payer

- Failure to comply with current court orders
- Abuse to staff
- Offence committed on licence or post sentence supervision

- No previous convictions **or** no relevant/recent convictions
- Remorse
- Good character and/or exemplary conduct
- Serious medical condition requiring urgent, intensive or long-term treatment
- Age and/or lack of maturity where it affects the responsibility of the offender
- Mental disorder or learning disability
- Sole or primary carer for dependent relatives

Factors reducing seriousness or reflecting personal mitigation

Step 3 — Consider any factors which indicate a reduction, such as assistance to the prosecution
The court should take into account sections 73 and 74 of the Serious Organised Crime and Police Act 2005 (assistance by defendants: reduction or review of sentence) and any other rule of law by virtue of which an offender may receive a discounted sentence in consequence of assistance given (or offered) to the prosecutor or investigator.

Step 4 — Reduction for guilty pleas The court should take account of any potential reduction for a guilty plea in accordance with section 144 of the Criminal Justice Act 2003 and the *Guilty Plea* guideline.

Step 5 — Totality principle If sentencing an offender for more than one offence, or where the offender is already serving a sentence, consider whether the total sentence is just and proportionate to the overall offending behaviour in accordance with the *Offences Taken into Consideration and Totality* guideline.

Step 6 — Compensation and ancillary orders In all cases, the court should consider whether to make compensation and/or other ancillary orders.

Step 7 — Reasons Section 174 of the Criminal Justice Act 2003 imposes a duty to give reasons for, and explain the effect of, the sentence.

SCHOOL NON-ATTENDANCE (REVISED 2017)

Education Act 1996, s.444(1) (parent fails to secure regular attendance at school of registered pupil); s.444(1A) (Parent knowingly fails to secure regular attendance at school of registered pupil)
Effective from: 24 April 2017
Triable only summarily:
Maximum:
Level 3 fine (s.444(1) parent fails to secure regular attendance at school);
Level 4 fine and/or 3 months (s.444(1A) parent knowingly fails to secure regular attendance at school)
Offence range:
Conditional discharge - Band C fine (s.444(1))
Band A fine - High level community order (s.444(1A))
Step 1 — Determining the offence seriousness The Court should determine the offence category using the table below.

Category 1	Higher culpability **and** greater harm
Category 2	Higher culpability **and** lesser harm **or** lower culpability **and** greater harm
Category3	Lower culpability **and** lesser harm

The court should determine the offender's culpability and the harm caused with reference only to the factors below. Where an offence does not fall squarely into a category, individual factors may require a degree of weighting before making an overall assessment and determining the appropriate offence category.
CULPABILITY demonstrated by one or more of the following: Factors indicating higher culpability

- Refusal/failure to engage with guidance and support offered
- Threats to teachers and/or officials
- Parent encouraging non attendance

Factors indicating lower culpability

- Genuine efforts to ensure attendance
- Parent concerned by child's allegations of bullying
- Parent put in fear of violence and/or threats from the child

HARM demonstrated by one or more of the following: Factors indicating greater harm

- Significant and lengthy period of education missed
- Adverse influence on other children of the family

Factors indicating lesser harm

- All other cases

Step 2 — Starting point and category range Having determined the category at step one, the court should use the corresponding starting point to reach a sentence within the category range below. The starting point applies to all offenders irrespective of plea or previous convictions.
s 444(1A) (Parent knowingly fails to secure regular attendance at school of registered pupil)

Offence Category	Starting Point	Range
Category 1	Medium level community order	Low level community order — High level community order
Category 2	Band C fine	Band B fine — Low level community order
Category 3	Band B fine	Band A fine — Band C fine

s.444(1) (parent fails to secure regular attendance at school of registered pupil)

Offence Category	Starting Point	Range
Category 1	Band C fine	Band B fine — Band C fine
Category 2	Band B fine	Band A fine — Band B fine
Category 3	Band A fine	Conditional Discharge — Band B fine

The court should then consider adjustment for any aggravating or mitigating factors. The following is a **non-exhaustive** list of additional factual elements providing the context of the offence and factors relating to the offender. Identify whether any combination of these, or other relevant factors, should result in an upward or downward adjustment from the sentence arrived at so far.
Factors increasing seriousness *Statutory aggravating factors:*

- Previous convictions, having regard to a) the **nature** of the offence to which the conviction relates and its **relevance** to the current offence; and b) the **time** that has elapsed since the conviction
- Offence committed whilst on bail

Other aggravating factors:
- Failure to comply with current court orders
- Offence committed on licence or post sentence supervision

- No previous convictions **or** no relevant/recent convictions
- Remorse
- Good character and/or exemplary conduct
- Serious medical condition requiring urgent, intensive or long-term treatment
- Age and/or lack of maturity where it affects the responsibility of the offender
- Mental disorder or learning disability (of offender)
- Parent unaware of child's whereabouts
- Previously good attendance

Factors reducing seriousness or reflecting personal mitigation

Step 3 — Consider any factors which indicate a reduction, such as assistance to the prosecution
The court should take into account sections 73 and 74 of the Serious Organised Crime and Police Act 2005 (assistance by defendants: reduction or review of sentence) and any other rule of law by virtue of which an offender may receive a discounted sentence in consequence of assistance given (or offered) to the prosecutor or investigator.

Step 4 — Reduction for guilty pleas The court should take account of any potential reduction for a guilty plea in accordance with section 144 of the Criminal Justice Act 2003 and the *Guilty Plea* guideline.

Step 5 — Totality principle If sentencing an offender for more than one offence, or where the offender is already serving a sentence, consider whether the total sentence is just and proportionate to the overall offending behaviour in accordance with the *Offences Taken into Consideration and Totality* guideline.

Step 6 — Compensation and ancillary orders In all cases, the court should consider whether to make compensation and/or other ancillary orders including parenting orders.

Step 7 — Reasons Section 174 of the Criminal Justice Act 2003 imposes a duty to give reasons for, and explain the effect of, the sentence.

SEXUAL ACTIVITY IN A PUBLIC LAVATORY
(REVISED 2017)

Sexual Offences Act 2003, s.71
Effective from: 24 April 2017
Triable only summarily:
Maximum: Unlimited fine and/or 6 months
Offence range: Band A fine — High level community order
Step 1 — Determining the offence category The Court should determine the offence category using the table below.

Category 1	Higher culpability **and** greater harm
Category 2	Higher culpability **and** lesser harm **or** lower culpability **and** greater harm
Category 3	Lower culpability **and** lesser harm

The court should determine the offender's culpability and the harm caused with reference **only** to the factors below. Where an offence does not fall squarely into a category, individual factors may require a degree of weighting before making an overall assessment and determining the appropriate offence category.

CULPABILITY demonstrated by one or more of the following: **Factors indicating higher culpability**

- Intimidating behaviour/threats of violence to member(s) of the public
- Blatant behaviour

Factors indicating lower culpability

- All other cases

HARM demonstrated by one or more of the following: **Factors indicating greater harm**

- Distress suffered by members of the public
- Children or young persons present

Factors indicating lesser harm

- All other cases

Step 2 — Starting point and category range Having determined the category at step one, the court should use the starting point to reach a sentence within the appropriate category range in the table below. The starting point applies to all offenders irrespective of plea or previous convictions.

Offence Category	Starting Point	Range
Category 1	Low level community order	Band C fine — High level community order
Category 2	Band C fine	Band B fine — Low level community order
Category 3	Band B fine	Band A fine — Band C fine

Persistent offending of this nature may justify an upward adjustment outside the category range and may cross the community threshold even though the offence otherwise warrants a lesser sentence.

The court should then consider adjustment for any aggravating or mitigating factors. The following is a **non-exhaustive** list of additional factual elements providing the context of the offence and factors relating to the offender. Identify whether any combination of these, or other relevant factors, should result in an upward or downward adjustment from the sentence arrived at so far.

Factors increasing seriousness *Statutory aggravating factors:*

- Previous convictions, having regard to a) the **nature** of the offence to which the conviction relates and its **relevance** to the current offence; and b) the **time** that has elapsed since the conviction
- Offence committed whilst on bail

Other aggravating factors:

- Failure to comply with current court orders
- Offence committed on licence or post sentence supervision
- Offences taken into consideration
- Location
- Presence of children
- Established evidence of community/wider impact

- No previous convictions **or** no relevant/recent convictions
- Remorse
- Good character and/or exemplary conduct
- Serious medical condition requiring urgent, intensive or long-term treatment
- Age and/or lack of maturity where it affects the responsibility of the offender
- Mental disorder or learning disability

Factors reducing seriousness or reflecting personal mitigation
Step 3 — Consider any factors which indicate a reduction, such as assistance to the prosecution
The court should take into account sections 73 and 74 of the Serious Organised Crime and

Police Act 2005 (assistance by defendants: reduction or review of sentence) and any other rule of law by virtue of which an offender may receive a discounted sentence in consequence of assistance given (or offered) to the prosecutor or investigator.

Step 4 — Reduction for guilty pleas   The court should take account of any potential reduction for a guilty plea in accordance with section 144 of the Criminal Justice Act 2003 and the *Guilty Plea* guideline.

Step 5 — Totality principle   If sentencing an offender for more than one offence, or where the offender is already serving a sentence, consider whether the total sentence is just and proportionate to the overall offending behaviour in accordance with the *Offences Taken into Consideration and Totality* guideline.

Step 6 — Compensation and ancillary orders   In all cases, the court should consider whether to make compensation and/or other ancillary orders.

Step 7 — Reasons   Section 174 of the Criminal Justice Act 2003 imposes a duty to give reasons for, and explain the effect of, the sentence.

TAXI TOUTING/SOLICITING FOR HIRE (REVISED
2017)

Criminal Justice and Public Order Act 1994, s.167
Effective from: 24 April 2017
Triable only summarily: Maximum: Level 4 fine
Offence range: Conditional Discharge — Band C fine
Step 1 — Determining the offence category   The Court should determine the offence category using the table below.

Category 1	Higher culpability **and** greater harm
Category 2	Higher culpability **and** lesser harm **or** lower culpability **and** greater harm
Category 3	Lower culpability **and** lesser harm

The court should determine the offender's culpability and the harm caused with reference **only** to the factors below. Where an offence does not fall squarely into a category, individual factors may require a degree of weighting before making an overall assessment and determining the appropriate offence category.
CULPABILITY demonstrated by one or more of the following: Factors indicating higher culpability

- Targeting of vulnerable/unsuspecting victim(s) (including tourists)
- Commercial business/large scale operation
- Offender not licensed to drive
- Positive step(s) taken to deceive

Factors indicating lower culpability

- All other cases

HARM demonstrated by one or more of the following: Factors indicating greater harm

- Passenger safety compromised by vehicle condition
- Passenger(s) overcharged

Factors indicating lesser harm

- All other cases

Step 2 — Starting point and category range   Having determined the category at step one, the court should use the starting point to reach a sentence within the appropriate category range in the table below. The starting point applies to all offenders irrespective of plea or previous convictions.

Offence Category	Starting Point	Range
Category 1	Band C fine	Band B fine — Band C fine and disqualification 6–12 months
Category 2	Band B fine	Band A fine — Band B fine and consider disqualification 3–6 months
Category 3	Band A fine	Conditional discharge — Band A fine and consider disqualification 1–3 months

Note: refer to fines for offence committed for 'commercial' purposes
The court should then consider adjustment for any aggravating or mitigating factors. The following is a **non-exhaustive** list of additional factual elements providing the context of the offence and factors relating to the offender. Identify whether any combination of these, or other relevant factors, should result in an upward or downward adjustment from the sentence arrived at so far.
Factors increasing seriousness   *Statutory aggravating factors:*

- Previous convictions, having regard to a) the **nature** of the offence to which the conviction relates and its **relevance** to the current offence; and b) the **time** that has elapsed since the conviction
- Offence committed whilst on bail

Other aggravating factors:

- Failure to comply with current court orders
- Offence committed on licence or post sentence supervision
- PHV licence refused/ ineligible

- No previous convictions **or** no relevant/recent convictions
- Remorse
- Good character and/or exemplary conduct
- Mental disorder or learning disability
- Sole or primary carer for dependent relatives

Factors reducing seriousness or reflecting personal mitigation
Step 3 — Consider any factors which indicate a reduction, such as assistance to the prosecution
The court should take into account sections 73 and 74 of the Serious Organised Crime and

Police Act 2005 (assistance by defendants: reduction or review of sentence) and any other rule of law by virtue of which an offender may receive a discounted sentence in consequence of assistance given (or offered) to the prosecutor or investigator.

Step 4 — Reduction for guilty pleas   The court should take account of any potential reduction for a guilty plea in accordance with section 144 of the Criminal Justice Act 2003 and the *Guilty Plea* guideline.

Step 5 — Totality principle   If sentencing an offender for more than one offence, or where the offender is already serving a sentence, consider whether the total sentence is just and proportionate to the overall offending behaviour in accordance with the *Offences Taken into Consideration and Totality* guideline.

Step 6 — Compensation and ancillary orders   In all cases, the court should consider whether to make compensation and/or other ancillary orders, including disqualification from driving and the deprivation of a vehicle.

Step 7 — Reasons   Section 174 of the Criminal Justice Act 2003 imposes a duty to give reasons for, and explain the effect of, the sentence.

THREATS TO KILL

Offences against the Person Act 1861, s 16
Effective from: 1 October 2018
Triable either way
Maximum: 10 years' custody
Offence range: Community order – 7 years' custody
This is a specified offence for the purposes of section 226A (extended sentence for certain violent or sexual offences) of the Criminal Justice Act 2003
Where offence committed in a domestic context, also refer to the *Overarching principles: Domestic abuse guideline*

STEP 1 — DETERMINING THE OFFENCE CATEGORY

The court should determine the offence category with reference only to the factors in the tables below. In order to determine the category the court should assess **culpability** and **harm**.

The level of **culpability** is determined by weighing up all the factors of the case. **Where there are characteristics present which fall under different levels of culpability, the court should balance these characteristics to reach a fair assessment of the offender's culpability.**

A – Higher culpability	• Significant planning and/or sophisticated offence • Visible weapon • Threat(s) made in the presence of children • History of and/or campaign of violence towards the victim • Threat(s) with significant violence
B – Medium culpability	Cases that fall between categories A and C because: • Factors are present in A and C which balance each other out and/or • The offender's culpability falls between the factors described in A and C
C – Lesser culpability	• Offender's responsibility substantially reduced by mental disorder or learning disability • Offence was limited in scope and duration

Harm
The level of harm is assessed by weighing up all the factors of the case.

Category 1	• Very serious distress caused to the victim • Significant psychological harm caused to the victim • Offence has a considerable practical impact on the victim
Category 2	Harm that falls between categories 1 and 3, and in particular: • Some distress caused to the victim • Some psychological harm caused to the victim • Offence has some practical impact on the victim
Category 3	• Little or no distress or harm caused to the victim

STEP 2 — STARTING POINT AND CATEGORY RANGE

Having determined the category at step one, the court should use the corresponding starting point to reach a sentence within the category range in the table below. The starting point applies to all offenders irrespective of plea or previous convictions.

Harm	Culpability		
	A	**B**	**C**
Category 1	**Starting point** 4 years' custody **Category range** 2–7 years' custody	**Starting point** 2 years' custody **Category range** 1 – 4 years' custody	**Starting point** 1 years' custody **Category range** 26 weeks' custody
Category 2	**Starting point** 2 years' custody **Category range** 1–4 years' custody	**Starting point** 1 years' custody **Category range** 26 weeks' – 2 years 6 months' custody	**Starting point** 26 weeks' **Category range** High level community order – 1 years' custody
Category 3	**Starting point** 1 years' custody **Category range** 1–4 years' custody	**Starting point** 1 years' custody **Category range** 26 weeks' – 2 years 6 months' custody	**Starting point** 26 weeks' **Category range** High level community order – 1 years' custody

The court should then consider any adjustment for any aggravating or mitigating factors. Below is a **non-exhaustive** list of additional factual elements providing the context of the offence and factors relating to the offender.

Identify whether any combination of these, or other relevant factors, should result in an upward or downward adjustment from the starting point.

Factors increasing seriousness

Statutory aggravating factors:

- Previous convictions, having regard to a) the **nature** of the offence to which the conviction relates and its **relevance** to the current offence; and b) the **time** that has elapsed since the conviction
- Offence committed whilst on bail
- •Offence motivated by, or demonstrating hostility based on any of the following character- istics or presumed characteristics of the victim: religion, race, disability, sexual orientation, or transgender identity

Other aggravating factors:

- Offence committed against those working in the public sector or providing a service to the public
- Impact of offence on others, particularly children
- Victim is particularly vulnerable (not all vulnerabilities are immediately apparent)
- Failure to comply with current court orders
- Offence committed on licence or post sentence supervision
- Offences taken into consideration

Factors reducing seriousness or reflecting personal mitigation

- No previous convictions **or** no relevant/recent convictions
- Remorse
- Good character and/or exemplary conduct
- Serious medical condition requiring urgent, intensive or long-term treatment
- Age and/or lack of maturity
- Mental disorder or learning disability (where not taken into account at step one)
- Sole or primary carer for dependent relatives
- Determination and/or demonstration of steps having been taken to address offending behaviour

STEP 3 — CONSIDER ANY FACTORS WHICH INDICATE A REDUCTION, SUCH AS ASSISTANCE TO THE PROSECUTION

The court should take into account sections 73 and 74 of the Serious Organised Crime and Police Act 2005 (assistance by defendants: reduction or review of sentence) and any other rule of law by virtue of which an offender may receive a discounted sentence in consequence of assistance given (or offered) to the prosecutor or investigator.

STEP 4 — REDUCTION FOR GUILTY PLEAS

The court should take account of any potential reduction for a guilty plea in accordance with section 144 of the Criminal Justice Act 2003 and the *Guilty Plea* guideline.

STEP 5 — DANGEROUSNESS

The court should consider whether having regard to the criteria contained in Chapter 5 of Part 12 of the Criminal Justice Act 2003 it would be appropriate to impose an extended sentence (section 226A).

STEP 6— TOTALITY PRINCIPLE

If sentencing an offender for more than one offence, or where the offender is already serving a sentence, consider whether the total sentence is just and proportionate to the overall offending behaviour in accordance with the *Offences Taken into Consideration and Totality* guideline.

STEP 7 — COMPENSATION AND ANCILLARY ORDERS

In all cases, the court must consider whether to make a compensation order and/or other ancillary orders.

Compensation order

The court should consider compensation orders in all cases where personal injury, loss or damage has resulted from the offence. The court must give reasons if it decides not to award compensation in such cases.

Other ancillary orders available include: Restraining order Where an offender is convicted of any offence, the court may make a restraining order (section 5 of the Protection from Harassment Act 1997).

The order may prohibit the offender from doing anything for the purpose of protecting the victim of the offence, or any other person mentioned in the order, from further conduct which amounts to harassment or will cause a fear of violence.

The order may have effect for a specified period or until further order.

STEP 8— REASONS

Section 174 of the Criminal Justice Act 2003 imposes a duty to give reasons for, and explain the effect of, the sentence.

STEP 9— CONSIDERATION FOR TIME SPENT ON BAIL (TAGGED CURFEW)

The court must consider whether to give credit for time spent on bail in accordance with section 240A of the Criminal Justice Act 2003.

TRADE MARK, UNAUTHORISED USE OF ETC

Trade Marks Act 1994, s.92

Trade mark, unauthorised use of etc.

Triable either way:
Maximum when tried summarily: Level 5 fine and/or 6 months
Maximum when tried on indictment: 10 years

Offence seriousness (culpability and harm)
A. Identify the appropriate starting point
Starting points based on first time offender pleading not guilty

Examples of nature of activity	Starting point	Range
Small number of counterfeit items	Band C fine	Band B fine to low level community order
Larger number of counterfeit items but no involvement in wider operation	Medium level community order, plus fine*	Low level community order to 12 weeks custody, plus fine*
High number of counterfeit items or involvement in wider operation e.g. manufacture or distribution	12 weeks custody	6 weeks custody to Crown Court
Central role in large-scale operation	Crown Court	Crown Court

* This may be an offence for which it is appropriate to combine a fine with a community order. Consult your legal adviser for further guidance.

Offence seriousness (culpability and harm)
B. Consider the effect of aggravating and mitigating factors
(other than those within examples above)
Common aggravating and mitigating factors are identified in the pullout card –
the following may be particularly relevant but **these lists are not exhaustive**

Factors indicating higher culpability	Factor indicating lower culpability
1. High degree of professionalism 2. High level of profit **Factor indicating greater degree of harm** 1. Purchasers at risk of harm e.g. from counterfeit drugs	1. Mistake or ignorance about provenance of goods

Form a preliminary view of the appropriate sentence,
then consider offender mitigation
Common factors are identified in the pullout card

Consider a reduction for a guilty plea

Consider ancillary orders
Refer to pages 168-174 for guidance on available ancillary orders
Consider ordering forfeiture and destruction of the goods

Decide sentence
Give reasons

TV LICENCE PAYMENT EVASION (REVISED 2017)

Communications act 2003, s.363
Effective from: 24 April 2017
Triable only summarily:
Maximum: Level 3 fine
Offence range: Band A fine — Band B fine
Step 1 — Determining the offence category   The Court should determine the offence category using the table below.

Category 1	Higher culpability **and** greater harm
Category 2	Higher culpability **and** lesser harm **or** lower culpability **and** greater harm
Category 3	Lower culpability **and** lesser harm

The court should determine the offender's culpability and the harm caused with reference **only** to the factors below. Where an offence does not fall squarely into a category, individual factors may require a degree of weighting before making an overall assessment and determining the appropriate offence category.

CULPABILITY demonstrated by one or more of the following: **Factors indicating higher culpability**

- No attempt to obtain TV Licence
- Had additional subscription television service
- Attempts made to evade detection

Factors indicating lower culpability

- Accidental oversight or belief licence held (eg failure of financial arrangement)
- Confusion of responsibility
- Licence immediately obtained
- Significant efforts made to be licensed

HARM demonstrated by one or more of the following: **Factor indicating greater harm**

- Prolonged period without TV licence (over 6 months unlicensed use)

Factors indicating lesser harm

- Short period without television licence (under 6 months unlicensed use)

Step 2 — Starting point and category range   Having determined the category at step one, the court should use the starting point to reach a sentence within the appropriate category range in the table below. The starting point applies to all offenders irrespective of plea or previous convictions.

Offence Category	Starting Point	Range
Category 1	Band B fine	Band B fine
Category 2	Band B fine	Band A fine — Band B fine
Category 3	Band A fine	Conditional discharge — Band A fine

The court should then consider adjustment for any aggravating or mitigating factors. The following is a **non-exhaustive** list of additional factual elements providing the context of the offence and factors relating to the offender. Identify whether any combination of these, or other relevant factors, should result in an upward or downward adjustment from the sentence arrived at so far.

Factors increasing seriousness   *Statutory aggravating factors:*

- Previous convictions, having regard to a) the **nature** of the offence to which the conviction relates and its **relevance** to the current offence; and b) the **time** that has elapsed since the conviction
- Offence committed whilst on bail

Other aggravating factors:

- Failure to comply with current court orders
- Offence committed on licence or post sentence supervision

- No previous convictions **or** no relevant/recent convictions
- Remorse, especially if evidenced by immediate purchase of television licence
- Good character and/or exemplary conduct
- Age and/or lack of maturity where it affects the responsibility of the offender
- Mental disorder or learning disability
- Offender experiencing significant financial hardship at time of offence due to **exceptional** circumstances

Factors reducing seriousness or reflecting personal mitigation
Step 3 — Consider any factors which indicate a reduction, such as assistance to the prosecution
The court should take into account sections 73 and 74 of the Serious Organised Crime and Police Act 2005 (assistance by defendants: reduction or review of sentence) and any other rule of law by virtue of which an offender may receive a discounted sentence in consequence of assistance given (or offered) to the prosecutor or investigator.

Step 4 — Reduction for guilty pleas   The court should take account of any potential reduction for a guilty plea in accordance with section 144 of the Criminal Justice Act 2003 and the *Guilty Plea* guideline.

Step 5 — Totality principle   If sentencing an offender for more than one offence, or where the offender is already serving a sentence, consider whether the total sentence is just and proportionate to the overall offending behaviour in accordance with the *Offences Taken into Consideration and Totality* guideline.

Step 6 — Compensation and ancillary orders   In all cases, the court should consider whether to make compensation and/or other ancillary orders.

Step 7 — Reasons   Section 174 of the Criminal Justice Act 2003 imposes a duty to give reasons for, and explain the effect of, the sentence.

VEHICLE INTERFERENCE (REVISED 2017)

Criminal Attempts Act 1981, s.9
Effective from: 24 April 2017
Triable only summarily:
Maximum: Level 4 fine and/or 3 months
Offence range: Band A fine — 12 weeks' custody

Step 1 — Determining the offence category The Court should determine the offence category using the table below.

Category 1	Higher culpability **and** greater harm
Category 2	Higher culpability **and** lesser harm **or** lower culpability **and** greater harm
Category 3	Lower culpability **and** lesser harm

The court should determine the offender's culpability and the harm caused with reference **only** to the factors below. Where an offence does not fall squarely into a category, individual factors may require a degree of weighting before making an overall assessment and determining the appropriate offence category.

CULPABILITY demonstrated by one or more of the following: **Factors indicating higher culpability**

- Leading role where offending is part of a group activity
- Targeting of particular vehicles and/or contents
- Planning

Factors indicating lower culpability

- All other cases

HARM demonstrated by one or more of the following: **Factors indicating greater harm**

- Damage caused significant financial loss, inconvenience or distress to victim
- Vehicle left in a dangerous condition

Factors indicating lesser harm

- All other cases

Step 2 — Starting point and category range Having determined the category at step one, the court should use the corresponding starting point to reach a sentence within the category range in the table below. The starting point applies to all offenders irrespective of plea or previous convictions.

Offence Category	Starting Point	Range
Category 1	High level community order	Medium level community order — 12 weeks' custody
Category 2	Medium level community order	Band C fine — High level community order
Category 3	Band C fine	Band A fine — Low level community order

The court should then consider adjustment for any aggravating or mitigating factors. The following is a **non-exhaustive** list of additional factual elements providing the context of the offence and factors relating to the offender. Identify whether any combination of these, or other relevant factors, should result in an upward or downward adjustment from the sentence arrived at so far.

Factors increasing seriousness *Statutory aggravating factors:*

- Previous convictions, having regard to a) the **nature** of the offence to which the conviction relates and its **relevance** to the current offence; and b) the **time** that has elapsed since the conviction
- Offence committed whilst on bail

Other aggravating factors:

- Failure to comply with current court orders
- Offence committed on licence or post sentence supervision
- Part of a spree
- Offence against emergency services vehicle

- No previous convictions **or** no relevant/recent convictions
- Good character and/or exemplary conduct
- Age and/or lack of maturity where it affects the responsibility of the offender
- Mental disorder or learning disability
- Sole or primary carer for dependent relatives

Factors reducing seriousness or reflecting personal mitigation

Step 3 — Consider any factors which indicate a reduction, such as assistance to the prosecution
The court should take into account sections 73 and 74 of the Serious Organised Crime and Police Act 2005 (assistance by defendants: reduction or review of sentence) and any other rule of law by virtue of which an offender may receive a discounted sentence in consequence of assistance given (or offered) to the prosecutor or investigator.

Step 4 — Reduction for guilty pleas   The court should take account of any potential reduction for a guilty plea in accordance with section 144 of the Criminal Justice Act 2003 and the *Guilty Plea* guideline.

Step 5 — Totality principle   If sentencing an offender for more than one offence, or where the offender is already serving a sentence, consider whether the total sentence is just and proportionate to the overall offending behaviour in accordance with the *Offences Taken into Consideration and Totality* guideline.

Step 6 — Compensation and ancillary orders   In all cases, the court should consider whether to make compensation and/or other ancillary orders, including disqualification from driving.

Step 7 — Reasons   Section 174 of the Criminal Justice Act 2003 imposes a duty to give reasons for, and explain the effect of, the sentence.

Step 8 — Consideration for time spent on bail   The court must consider whether to give credit for time spent on bail in accordance with section 240A of the Criminal Justice Act 2003.

VEHICLE LICENCE/REGISTRATION FRAUD

Vehicle Excise and Registration Act 1994, s.44

Vehicle licence/registration fraud

Triable either way:
Maximum when tried summarily: Level 5 fine
Maximum when tried on indictment: 2 years

Offence seriousness (culpability and harm)
A. Identify the appropriate starting point
Starting points based on first time offender pleading not guilty

Examples of nature of activity	Starting point	Range
Use of unaltered licence from another vehicle	Band B fine	Band B fine
Forged licence bought for own use, or forged/ altered for own use	Band C fine	Band C fine
Use of number plates from another vehicle; or Licence/number plates forged or altered for sale to another	High level community order (in Crown Court)	Medium level community order to Crown Court (Note: community order and custody available only in Crown Court)

Offence seriousness (culpability and harm)
B. Consider the effect of aggravating and mitigating factors
(other than those within examples above)
Common aggravating and mitigating factors are identified in the pullout card –
the following may be particularly relevant but **these lists are not exhaustive**

Factors indicating higher culpability	Factors indicating lower culpability
1. LGV, PSV, taxi etc. 2. Long-term fraudulent use **Factors indicating greater degree of harm** 1. High financial gain 2. Innocent victim deceived 3. Legitimate owner inconvenienced	1. Licence/registration mark from another vehicle owned by defendant 2. Short-term use

Form a preliminary view of the appropriate sentence, then consider offender mitigation
Common factors are identified in the pullout card

Consider a reduction for a guilty plea

Consider ancillary orders
Refer to pages 168-174 for guidance on available ancillary orders
Consider disqualification from driving and deprivation of property (including vehicle)

Decide sentence
Give reasons

Vehicle taking, without consent (Revised 2017)

Theft Act 1968, s.12
Effective from: 24 April 2017
Triable only summarily:
Maximum: Unlimited fine and/or 6 months
Offence range: Band B fine — 26 weeks' custody
Step 1 — Determining the offence category   The Court should determine the offence category using the table below.

Category 1	Higher culpability **and** greater harm
Category 2	Higher culpability **and** lesser harm **or** lower culpability **and** greater harm
Category 3	Lower culpability **and** lesser harm

The court should determine the offender's culpability and the harm caused with reference **only** to the factors below. Where an offence does not fall squarely into a category, individual factors may require a degree of weighting before making an overall assessment and determining the appropriate offence category.
CULPABILITY demonstrated by one or more of the following: Factors indicating higher culpability

- A leading role where offending is part of a group activity
- Involvement of others through coercion, intimidation or exploitation
- Sophisticated nature of offence/significant planning
- Abuse of position of power or trust or responsibility
- Commission of offence in association with or to further other criminal activity

Factors indicating lower culpability

- Performed limited function under direction
- Involved through coercion, intimidation or exploitation
- Limited awareness or understanding of offence
- Exceeding authorised use of e.g. employer's or relative's vehicle
- Retention of hire car for short period beyond return date

HARM demonstrated by one or more of the following: Factors indicating greater harm

- Vehicle later burnt
- Vehicle belonging to elderly/disabled person
- Emergency services vehicle
- Medium to large goods vehicle
- Passengers carried
- Damage to lock/ignition
- Vehicle taken from private premises

Factors indicating lesser harm

- All other cases

Step 2 — Starting point and category range   Having determined the category at step one, the court should use the appropriate starting point to reach a sentence within the category range in the table below. The starting point applies to all offenders irrespective of plea or previous convictions.

Level of seriousness	Starting Point	Range	Disqualification
Category 1	High level community order	Medium level community order — 26 weeks' custody	Consider disqualification 9 to 12 months (Extend if imposing immediate custody)
Category 2	Medium level community order	Low level community order — High level community order	Consider disqualification 5 to 8 months
Category 3	Low level community order	Band B fine — Medium level community order	Consider disqualification

- **Extend any disqualification if imposing immediate custody**
The court should then consider further adjustment for any aggravating or mitigating factors. The following is a **non-exhaustive** list of additional factual elements providing the context of the offence and factors relating to the offender. Identify whether any combination of these, or other relevant factors, should result in an upward or downward adjustment from the sentence arrived at so far.
Factors increasing seriousness   *Statutory aggravating factors:*

- Previous convictions, having regard to a) the **nature** of the offence to which the conviction relates and its **relevance** to the current offence; and b) the **time** that has elapsed since the conviction
- Offence committed whilst on bail

Other aggravating factors:

- Failure to comply with current court orders
- Offence committed on licence or post sentence supervision

- No previous convictions **or** no relevant/recent convictions
- Remorse
- Good character and/or exemplary conduct
- Age and/ or lack of maturity where it affects the responsibility of the offender
- Mental disorder or learning disability
- Sole or primary carer for dependent relatives
- Co-operation with the investigation

Factors reducing seriousness or reflecting personal mitigation

Step 3 — Consider any factors which indicate a reduction, such as assistance to the prosecution
The court should take into account sections 73 and 74 of the Serious Organised Crime and Police Act 2005 (assistance by defendants: reduction or review of sentence) and any other rule of law by virtue of which an offender may receive a discounted sentence in consequence of assistance given (or offered) to the prosecutor or investigator.

Step 4 — Reduction for guilty pleas   The court should take account of any potential reduction for a guilty plea in accordance with section 144 of the Criminal Justice Act 2003 and the *Guilty Plea* guideline.

Step 5 — Totality principle   If sentencing an offender for more than one offence, or where the offender is already serving a sentence, consider whether the total sentence is just and proportionate to the overall offending behaviour in accordance with the *Offences Taken into Consideration and Totality* guideline.

Step 6 — Compensation and ancillary orders   In all cases, the court should consider whether to make compensation and/or other ancillary orders, including disqualification from driving.

Step 7 — Reasons   Section 174 of the Criminal Justice Act 2003 imposes a duty to give reasons for, and explain the effect of, the sentence.

Step 8 — Consideration for time spent on bail   The court must consider whether to give credit for time spent on bail in accordance with section 240A of the Criminal Justice Act 2003.

VEHICLE TAKING (AGGRAVATED)

DAMAGE CAUSED TO PROPERTY OTHER THAN THE VEHICLE IN ACCIDENT OR DAMAGE CAUSED TO THE VEHICLE

Theft Act 1968, ss.12A(2)(c) and (d)

Vehicle taking (aggravated)

Damage caused to property other than the vehicle in accident or damage caused to the vehicle

Triable either way (triable only summarily if damage under £5,000):
Maximum when tried summarily: Level 5 fine and/or 6 months
Maximum when tried on indictment: 2 years

- Must endorse and disqualify for at least 12 months
- Must disqualify for **at least** 2 years if offender has had two or more disqualifications for periods of 56 days or more in preceding 3 years – **refer to page 184 and consult your legal adviser for further guidance**

If there is a delay in sentencing after conviction, consider interim disqualification

Offence seriousness (culpability and harm)
A. Identify the appropriate starting point
Starting points based on first time offender pleading not guilty

Examples of nature of activity	Starting point	Range
Exceeding authorised use of e.g. employer's or relative's vehicle; retention of hire car beyond return date; minor damage to taken vehicle	Medium level community order	Low level community order to high level community order
Greater damage to taken vehicle and/or moderate damage to another vehicle and/or property	High level community order	Medium level community order to 12 weeks custody
Vehicle taken as part of burglary or from private premises; severe damage	18 weeks custody	12 to 26 weeks custody (Crown Court if damage over £5,000)

Offence seriousness (culpability and harm)
B. Consider the effect of aggravating and mitigating factors
(other than those within examples above)
Common aggravating and mitigating factors are identified in the pullout card –
the following may be particularly relevant but **these lists are not exhaustive**

Factors indicating higher culpability	Factors indicating lower culpability
1. Vehicle deliberately damaged/destroyed 2. Offender under influence of alcohol/drugs **Factors indicating greater degree of harm** 1. Passenger(s) carried 2. Vehicle belonging to elderly or disabled person 3. Emergency services vehicle 4. Medium to large goods vehicle 5. Damage caused in moving traffic accident	1. Misunderstanding with owner 2. Damage resulting from actions of another (where this does not provide a defence)

Form a preliminary view of the appropriate sentence,
then consider offender mitigation
Common factors are identified in the pullout card

Consider a reduction for a guilty plea

Consider ancillary orders, including compensation
Refer to pages 168-174 for guidance on available ancillary orders

Decide sentence
Give reasons

Vehicle taking (aggravated)
Dangerous driving or accident causing injury

Theft Act 1968, ss.12A(2)(a) and (b)

Triable either way:
Maximum when tried summarily: Level 5 fine and/or 6 months
Maximum when tried on indictment: 2 years; 14 years if accident caused death

- Must endorse and disqualify for at least 12 months
- Must disqualify for **at least** 2 years if offender has had two or more disqualifications for periods of 56 days or more in preceding 3 years – **refer to page 184 and consult your legal adviser for further guidance**

If there is a delay in sentencing after conviction, consider interim disqualification

Offence seriousness (culpability and harm)
A. Identify the appropriate starting point
Starting points based on first time offender pleading not guilty

Examples of nature of activity	Starting point	Range
Taken vehicle involved in single incident of bad driving where little or no damage or risk of personal injury	High level community order	Medium level community order to 12 weeks custody
Taken vehicle involved in incident(s) involving excessive speed or showing off, especially on busy roads or in built-up area	18 weeks custody	12 to 26 weeks custody
Taken vehicle involved in prolonged bad driving involving deliberate disregard for safety of others	Crown Court	Crown Court

Offence seriousness (culpability and harm)
B. Consider the effect of aggravating and mitigating factors
(other than those within examples above)
Common aggravating and mitigating factors are identified in the pullout card –
the following may be particularly relevant but **these lists are not exhaustive**

Factors indicating higher culpability 1. Disregarding warnings of others 2. Evidence of alcohol or drugs 3. Carrying out other tasks while driving 4. Carrying passengers or heavy load 5. Tiredness 6. Trying to avoid arrest 7. Aggressive driving, such as driving much too close to vehicle in front, inappropriate attempts to overtake, or cutting in after overtaking **Factors indicating greater degree of harm** 1. Injury to others 2. Damage to other vehicles or property	

Form a preliminary view of the appropriate sentence, then consider offender mitigation
Common factors are identified in the pullout card

Consider a reduction for a guilty plea

Consider ordering disqualification until appropriate driving test passed
Consider ancillary orders, including compensation
Refer to pages 168-174 for guidance on available ancillary orders

Decide sentence
Give reasons

Witness intimidation

Criminal Justice and Public Order Act 1994, s.51

Triable either way:
Maximum when tried summarily: 6 months or level 5 fine
Maximum when tried on indictment: 5 years

Where offence committed in domestic context, refer to page 177 for guidance

Offence seriousness (culpability and harm)
A. Identify the appropriate starting point
Starting points based on first time offender pleading not guilty

Examples of nature of activity	Starting point	Range
Sudden outburst in chance encounter	6 weeks custody	Medium level community order to 18 weeks custody
Conduct amounting to a threat; staring at, approaching or following witnesses; talking about the case; trying to alter or stop evidence	18 weeks custody	12 weeks custody to Crown Court
Threats of violence to witnesses and/or their families; deliberately seeking out witnesses	Crown Court	Crown Court

Offence seriousness (culpability and harm)
B. Consider the effect of aggravating and mitigating factors
(other than those within examples above)
Common aggravating and mitigating factors are identified in the pullout card –
the following may be particularly relevant but **these lists are not exhaustive**

Factors indicating higher culpability 1. Breach of bail conditions 2. Offender involves others **Factors indicating greater degree of harm** 1. Detrimental impact on administration of justice 2. Contact made at or in vicinity of victim's home	

Form a preliminary view of the appropriate sentence,
then consider offender mitigation
Common factors are identified in the pullout card

Consider a reduction for a guilty plea

Consider ancillary orders, including compensation
Refer to pages 168-174 for guidance on available ancillary orders

Decide sentence
Give reasons

CARELESS DRIVING (DRIVE WITHOUT DUE CARE AND ATTENTION) (REVISED 2017)
Road Traffic Act 1988, s.3
Effective from: 24 April 2017
Triable only summarily:
Maximum: Unlimited fine
Offence range: Band A fine — Band C fine
Step 1 — Determining the offence category The Court should determine the offence category using the table below.

Category 1	Higher culpability **and** greater harm
Category 2	Higher culpability **and** lesser harm **or** lower culpability **and** greater harm
Category3	Lower culpability **and** lesser harm

The court should determine the offender's culpability and the harm caused with reference only to the factors below. Where an offence does not fall squarely into a category, individual factors may require a degree of weighting before making an overall assessment and determining the appropriate offence category.
CULPABILITY demonstrated by one or more of the following: Factors indicating higher culpability

- Excessive speed or aggressive driving
- Carrying out other tasks while driving
- Vehicle used for the carriage of heavy goods or for the carriage of passengers for reward
- Tiredness or driving whilst unwell
- Driving contrary to medical advice (including written advice from the drug manufacturer not to drive when taking any medicine)

Factors indicating lower culpability

- All other cases

HARM demonstrated by one or more of the following: Factors indicating greater harm

- Injury to others
- Damage to other vehicles or property
- High level of traffic or pedestrians in vicinity

Factors indicating lesser harm

- All other cases

Step 2 — Starting point and category range Having determined the category at step one, the court should use the appropriate starting point to reach a sentence within the category range in the table below. The starting point applies to all offenders irrespective of plea or previous convictions.

Level of serious-ness	Starting Point	Range	Disqualification/points
Category 1	Band C fine	Band C fine	Consider disqualification **OR** 7 – 9 points
Category 2	Band B fine	Band B fine	5 – 6 points
Category 3	Band A fine	Band A fine	3 – 4 points

• Must endorse and may disqualify. If no disqualification impose 3 – 9 points
The court should then consider further adjustment for any aggravating or mitigating factors. The following is a **non-exhaustive** list of additional factual elements providing the context of the offence and factors relating to the offender. Identify whether any combination of these, or other relevant factors, should result in an upward or downward adjustment from the sentence arrived at so far.
Factors increasing seriousness *Statutory aggravating factors:*

- Previous convictions, having regard to a) the **nature** of the offence to which the conviction relates and its **relevance** to the current offence; and b) the **time** that has elapsed since the conviction
- Offence committed whilst on bail

Other aggravating factors:

- Failure to comply with current court orders
- Offence committed on licence or post sentence supervision
- Contravening a red signal at a level crossing

- No previous convictions **or** no relevant/recent convictions
- Remorse
- Good character and/or exemplary conduct

Factors reducing seriousness or reflecting personal mitigation
Step 3 — Consider any factors which indicate a reduction, such as assistance to the prosecution
The court should take into account sections 73 and 74 of the Serious Organised Crime and Police Act 2005 (assistance by defendants: reduction or review of sentence) and any other rule of law by virtue of which an offender may receive a discounted sentence in consequence of assistance given (or offered) to the prosecutor or investigator.

Step 4 — Reduction for guilty pleas The court should take account of any potential reduction for a guilty plea in accordance with section 144 of the Criminal Justice Act 2003 and the *Guilty Plea* guideline.

Step 5 — Totality principle If sentencing an offender for more than one offence, or where the offender is already serving a sentence, consider whether the total sentence is just and proportionate to the overall offending behaviour in accordance with the *Offences Taken into Consideration and Totality* guideline.

Step 6 — Compensation and ancillary orders In all cases, the court should consider whether to make compensation and/or other ancillary orders, including disqualification from driving.

Step 7 — Reasons Section 174 of the Criminal Justice Act 2003 imposes a duty to give reasons for, and explain the effect of, the sentence.

CAUSING DEATH BY CARELESS OR INCONSIDERATE DRIVING – FACTORS TO TAKE INTO CONSIDERATION

This guideline and accompanying notes are taken from the Sentencing Guidelines Council's definitive guideline *Causing Death by Driving*, published 15 July 2008

Key factors

(a) It is unavoidable that some cases will be on the borderline between *dangerous* and *careless* driving, or may involve a number of factors that significantly increase the seriousness of an offence. As a result, the guideline for this offence identifies three levels of seriousness, the range for the highest of which overlaps with ranges for the lower levels of seriousness for *causing death by dangerous driving*.

(b) The three levels of seriousness are defined by the degree of carelessness involved in the standard of driving:

- the most serious level for this offence is where the offender's driving fell not that far short of dangerous;
- the least serious group of offences relates to those cases where the level of culpability is low – for example in a case involving an offender who misjudges the speed of another vehicle, or turns without seeing an oncoming vehicle because of restricted visibility;
- other cases will fall into the intermediate level.

(c) Where the level of carelessness is low and there are no aggravating factors, even the fact that death was caused is not sufficient to justify a prison sentence.

(d) A fine is unlikely to be an appropriate sentence for this offence; where a non-custodial sentence is considered appropriate, this should be a community order. The nature of the requirements will be determined by the purpose[1] identified by the court as of primary importance. Requirements most likely to be relevant include unpaid work requirement, activity requirement, programme requirement and curfew requirement.

(e) Offender mitigation particularly relevant to this offence includes conduct after the offence such as where the offender gave direct, positive, assistance at the scene of a collision to victim(s). It may also include remorse – whilst it can be expected that anyone who has caused a death by driving would be remorseful, this cannot undermine its importance for sentencing purposes. It is for the court to determine whether an expression of remorse is genuine.

(f) Where an offender has a good driving record, this is not a factor that automatically should be treated as mitigation, especially now that the presence of previous convictions is a statutory aggravating factor. However, any evidence to show that an offender has previously been an exemplary driver, for example having driven an ambulance, police vehicle, bus, taxi or similar vehicle conscientiously and without incident for many years, is a fact that the courts may well wish to take into account by way of offender mitigation. This is likely to have even greater effect where the driver is driving on public duty (for example, on ambulance, fire services or police duties) and was responding to an emergency.

(g) Disqualification of the offender from driving and endorsement of the offender's driving licence are mandatory, and the offence carries between 3 and 11 penalty points when the court finds special reasons for not imposing disqualification. There is a discretionary power[2] to order an extended driving test/re-test where a person is convicted of this offence.

---

[1] Criminal Justice Act 2003, s 142(1).
[2] Road Traffic Offenders Act 1988, s 36(4).

CAUSING DEATH BY CARELESS OR INCONSIDERATE DRIVING

Road Traffic Act 1988, s.2B	**Causing death by careless or inconsiderate driving**

Triable either way:
Maximum when tried summarily: Level 5 fine and/or 6 months
Maximum when tried on indictment: 5 years

Offence seriousness (culpability and harm)
A. Identify the appropriate starting point
Starting points based on first time offender pleading not guilty

Examples of nature of activity	Starting point	Range
Careless or inconsiderate driving arising from momentary inattention with no aggravating factors	Medium level community order	Low level community order to high level community order
Other cases of careless or inconsiderate driving	Crown Court	High level community order to Crown Court
Careless or inconsiderate driving falling not far short of dangerous driving	Crown Court	Crown Court

Offence seriousness (culpability and harm)
B. Consider the effect of aggravating and mitigating factors
(other than those within examples above)
Common aggravating and mitigating factors are identified in the pullout card – the following may be particularly relevant but **these lists are not exhaustive**

Factors indicating higher culpability	Factors indicating lower culpability
1. Other offences committed at the same time, such as driving other than in accordance with the terms of a valid licence; driving while disqualified; driving without insurance; taking a vehicle without consent; driving a stolen vehicle 2. Previous convictions for motoring offences, particularly offences that involve bad driving 3. Irresponsible behaviour, such as failing to stop or falsely claiming that one of the victims was responsible for the collision **Factors indicating greater degree of harm** 1. More than one person was killed as a result of the offence 2. Serious injury to one or more persons in addition to the death(s)	1. Offender seriously injured in the collision 2. The victim was a close friend or relative 3. The actions of the victim or a third party contributed to the commission of the offence 4. The offender's lack of driving experience contributed significantly to the likelihood of a collision occurring and/or death resulting 5. The driving was in response to a proven and genuine emergency falling short of a defence

Form a preliminary view of the appropriate sentence,
then consider offender mitigation
Common factors are identified in the pullout card

Consider a reduction for a guilty plea

Consider ancillary orders, including disqualification and deprivation of property
Refer to pages 168-174 for guidance on available ancillary orders

Decide sentence
Give reasons

CAUSING DEATH BY DRIVING: UNLICENSED, DISQUALIFIED OR UNINSURED DRIVERS – FACTORS TO TAKE INTO CONSIDERATION

This guideline and accompanying notes are taken from the Sentencing Guidelines Council's definitive guideline *Causing Death by Driving* , published 15 July 2008

Key factors

(a) Culpability arises from the offender driving a vehicle on a road or other public place when, by law, not allowed to do so; the offence does not involve any fault in the standard of driving.

(b) Since driving whilst disqualified is more culpable than driving whilst unlicensed or uninsured, a higher starting point is proposed when the offender was disqualified from driving at the time of the offence.

(c) Being uninsured, unlicensed or disqualified are the only determinants of seriousness for this offence, as there are no factors relating to the standard of driving. The list of aggravating factors identified is slightly different as the emphasis is on the decision to drive by an offender who is not permitted by law to do so.

(d) A fine is unlikely to be an appropriate sentence for this offence; where a non-custodial sentence is considered appropriate, this should be a community order.

(e) Where the *decision to drive was brought about by a genuine and proven emergency*, that may mitigate offence seriousness and so it is included as an additional mitigating factor.

(f) An additional mitigating factor covers those situations where an offender genuinely believed that there was valid insurance or a valid licence.

(g) Offender mitigation particularly relevant to this offence includes conduct after the offence such as where the offender gave direct, positive, assistance at the scene of a collision to victim(s). It may also include remorse – whilst it can be expected that anyone who has caused a death by driving would be remorseful, this cannot undermine its importance for sentencing purposes. It is for the court to determine whether an expression of remorse is genuine.

(h) Where an offender has a good driving record, this is not a factor that automatically should be treated as mitigation, especially now that the presence of previous convictions is a statutory aggravating factor. However, any evidence to show that an offender has previously been an exemplary driver, for example having driven an ambulance, police vehicle, bus, taxi or similar vehicle conscientiously and without incident for many years, is a fact that the courts may well wish to take into account by way of offender mitigation. This is likely to have even greater effect where the driver is driving on public duty (for example, on ambulance, fire services or police duties) and was responding to an emergency.

(i) Disqualification of the offender from driving and endorsement of the offender's driving licence are mandatory, and the offence carries between 3 and 11 penalty points when the court finds special reasons for not imposing disqualification. There is a discretionary power[1] to order an extended driving test/re-test where a person is convicted of this offence.

---

[1] Road Traffic Offenders Act 1988, s 36(4).

CAUSING DEATH BY DRIVING: UNLICENSED, DISQUALIFIED[Ed 1] OR UNINSURED DRIVERS

Road Traffic Act 1988, s.3ZB

Causing death by driving: unlicensed, disqualified or uninsured drivers

Triable either way:
Maximum when tried summarily: Level 5 fine and/or 6 months
Maximum when tried on indictment: 2 years

Offence seriousness (culpability and harm)
A. Identify the appropriate starting point
Starting points based on first time offender pleading not guilty

Examples of nature of activity	Starting point	Range
The offender was unlicensed or uninsured – no aggravating factors	Medium level community order	Low level community order to high level community order
The offender was unlicensed or uninsured plus at least 1 aggravating factor from the list below	26 weeks custody	High level community order to Crown Court
The offender was disqualified from driving OR The offender was unlicensed or uninsured plus 2 or more aggravating factors from the list below	Crown Court	Crown Court

Offence seriousness (culpability and harm)
B. Consider the effect of aggravating and mitigating factors
(other than those within examples above)
Common aggravating and mitigating factors are identified in the pullout card – the following may be particularly relevant but **these lists are not exhaustive**

Factors indicating higher culpability	Factors indicating lower culpability
1. Previous convictions for motoring offences, whether involving bad driving or involving an offence of the same kind that forms part of the present conviction (i.e. unlicensed, disqualified or uninsured driving) 2. Irresponsible behaviour such as failing to stop or falsely claiming that someone else was driving **Factors indicating greater degree of harm** 1. More than one person was killed as a result of the offence 2. Serious injury to one or more persons in addition to the death(s)	1. The decision to drive was brought about by a proven and genuine emergency falling short of a defence 2. The offender genuinely believed that he or she was insured or licensed to drive 3. The offender was seriously injured as a result of the collision 4. The victim was a close friend or relative

Form a preliminary view of the appropriate sentence, then consider offender mitigation
Common factors are identified in the pullout card

Consider a reduction for a guilty plea

Consider ancillary orders, including disqualification and deprivation of property
refer to pages 168-174 for guidance on available ancillary orders

Decide sentence
Give reasons

Ed 1 Causing death by driving while disqualified is now triable only on indictment, and there is a new either way offence of causing serious injury by driving while disqualified. These changes, which were made by the Criminal Justice and Courts Act 2015, have yet to included with the sentencing guidelines.

Dangerous driving

Road Traffic Act 1988, s.2

Triable either way:
Maximum when tried summarily: Level 5 fine and/or 6 months
Maximum when tried on indictment: 2 years

- Must endorse and disqualify for at least 12 months. Must order extended re-test
- Must disqualify for **at least** 2 years if offender has had two or more disqualifications for periods of 56 days or more in preceding 3 years – **refer to page 184 and consult your legal adviser for further guidance**

If there is a delay in sentencing after conviction, consider interim disqualification

Offence seriousness (culpability and harm) **A. Identify the appropriate starting point** Starting points based on first time offender pleading not guilty		
Examples of nature of activity	**Starting point**	**Range**
Single incident where little or no damage or risk of personal injury	Medium level community order	Low level community order to high level community order Disqualify 12 – 15 months
Incident(s) involving excessive speed or showing off, especially on busy roads or in built-up area; OR Single incident where little or no damage or risk of personal injury but offender was disqualified driver	12 weeks custody	High level community order to 26 weeks custody Disqualify 15 – 24 months
Prolonged bad driving involving deliberate disregard for safety of others; OR Incident(s) involving excessive speed or showing off, especially on busy roads or in built-up area, by disqualified driver; OR Driving as described in box above while being pursued by police	Crown Court	Crown Court

Offence seriousness (culpability and harm) **B. Consider the effect of aggravating and mitigating factors** **(other than those within examples above)** Common aggravating and mitigating factors are identified in the pullout card – the following may be particularly relevant but **these lists are not exhaustive**	
Factors indicating higher culpability 1. Disregarding warnings of others 2. Evidence of alcohol or drugs 3. Carrying out other tasks while driving 4. Carrying passengers or heavy load 5. Tiredness 6. Aggressive driving, such as driving much too close to vehicle in front, racing, inappropriate attempts to overtake, or cutting in after overtaking 7. Driving when knowingly suffering from a medical condition which significantly impairs the offender's driving skills 8. Driving a poorly maintained or dangerously loaded vehicle, especially where motivated by commercial concerns **Factors indicating greater degree of harm** 1. Injury to others 2. Damage to other vehicles or property	**Factors indicating lower culpability** 1. Genuine emergency 2. Speed not excessive 3. Offence due to inexperience rather than irresponsibility of driver

**Form a preliminary view of the appropriate sentence,
then consider offender mitigation**
Common factors are identified in the pullout card

Consider a reduction for guilty plea

Consider ancillary orders, including compensation and deprivation of property
Refer to pages 168-174 for guidance on available ancillary orders

**Decide sentence
Give reasons**

DRIVE WHILST DISQUALIFIED (REVISED 2017)

Road Traffic Act 1988, s.103
Effective from: 24 April 2017
Triable only summarily:
Maximum: Unlimited fine and/or 6 months
Offence range: Band C fine — 26 weeks' custody

Step 1 — Determining the offence category The Court should determine the offence category using the table below.

Category 1	Higher culpability **and** greater harm
Category 2	Higher culpability **and** lesser harm **or** lower culpability **and** greater harm
Category 3	Lower culpability **and** lesser harm

The court should determine the offender's culpability and the harm caused with reference **only** to the factors below. Where an offence does not fall squarely into a category, individual factors may require a degree of weighting before making an overall assessment and determining the appropriate offence category.

CULPABILITY demonstrated by one or more of the following: **Factors indicating higher culpability**

- Driving shortly after disqualification imposed
- Vehicle obtained during disqualification period
- Driving for reward

Factors indicating lower culpability

- All other cases

HARM demonstrated by one or more of the following: **Factors indicating greater harm**

- Significant distance driven
- Evidence of associated bad driving

Factors indicating lesser harm

- All other cases

Step 2 — Starting point and category range Having determined the category at step one, the court should use the appropriate starting point to reach a sentence within the category range in the table below. The starting point applies to all offenders irrespective of plea or previous convictions.

Level of seriousness	Starting Point	Range	Penalty points/disqualification
Category 1	12 weeks' custody	High Level community order — 26 weeks' custody	Disqualify for 12 – 18 months beyond expiry of current ban (Extend if imposing immediate custody)
Category 2	High level community order	Medium level community order -12 weeks' custody	Disqualify for 6 – 12 months beyond expiry of current ban (Extend if imposing immediate custody)
Category 3	Low level community order	Band C fine — Medium level community order	Disqualify for 3 – 6 months beyond expiry of current ban **OR** 6 points

- **Must endorse and may disqualify. If no disqualification impose 6 points**
- **Extend disqualification if imposing immediate custody**

The court should then consider further adjustment for any aggravating or mitigating factors. The following is a **non-exhaustive** list of additional factual elements providing the context of the offence and factors relating to the offender. Identify whether any combination of these, or other relevant factors, should result in an upward or downward adjustment from the sentence arrived at so far.

Factors increasing seriousness *Statutory aggravating factors:*

- Previous convictions, having regard to a) the **nature** of the offence to which the conviction relates and its **relevance** to the current offence; and b) the **time** that has elapsed since the conviction

Note An offender convicted of this offence will always have at least one relevant previous conviction for the offence that resulted in disqualification. The starting points and ranges take this into account; any other previous convictions should be considered in the usual way.

- Offence committed whilst on bail

Other aggravating factors:

- Failure to comply with current court orders (not including the current order for disqualification)
- Offence committed on licence or post sentence supervision
- Carrying passengers
- Giving false details

- No previous convictions **or** no relevant/recent convictions
- Good character and/or exemplary conduct
- Remorse
- Genuine emergency established
- Age and/or lack of maturity where it affects the responsibility of the offender
- Serious medical condition requiring urgent, intensive or long-term treatment
- Sole or primary carer for dependent relatives

Factors reducing seriousness or reflecting personal mitigation

Step 3 — Consider any factors which indicate a reduction, such as assistance to the prosecution
The court should take into account sections 73 and 74 of the Serious Organised Crime and Police Act 2005 (assistance by defendants: reduction or review of sentence) and any other rule of law by virtue of which an offender may receive a discounted sentence in consequence of assistance given (or offered) to the prosecutor or investigator.

Step 4 — Reduction for guilty pleas   The court should take account of any potential reduction for a guilty plea in accordance with section 144 of the Criminal Justice Act 2003 and the *Guilty Plea* guideline.

Step 5 — Totality principle   If sentencing an offender for more than one offence, or where the offender is already serving a sentence, consider whether the total sentence is just and proportionate to the overall offending behaviour in accordance with the *Offences Taken into Consideration and Totality* guideline.

Step 6 — Compensation and ancillary orders   In all cases, the court should consider whether to make compensation and/or other ancillary orders including disqualification from driving.

Step 7 — Reasons   Section 174 of the Criminal Justice Act 2003 imposes a duty to give reasons for, and explain the effect of, the sentence.

Step 8 — Consideration for time spent on bail   The court must consider whether to give credit for time spent on bail in accordance with section 240A of the Criminal Justice Act 2003.

EXCESS ALCOHOL (DRIVE/ATTEMPT TO DRIVE)
(REVISED 2017)

Road Traffic Act 1988, s.5(1)(a)
Effective from: 24 April 2017
Triable only summarily:
Maximum: Unlimited fine and/or 6 months
Offence range: Band B fine — 26 weeks' custody

- **Must endorse and disqualify for at least 12 months**
- **Must disqualify for at least 2 years if offender has had two or more disqualifications for periods of 56 days or more in preceding 3 years — refer to disqualification guidance and consult your legal adviser for further guidance**
- **Must disqualify for at least 3 years if offender has been convicted of a relevant offence in preceding 10 years — consult your legal adviser for further guidance**
- **Extend disqualification if imposing immediate custody**

Steps 1 and 2 — Determining the offence seriousness If there is a delay in sentencing after conviction, consider interim disqualification

The starting point applies to all offenders irrespective of plea or previous convictions.

Level of alcohol			Starting point	Range	Disqualification	Disqual. 2nd offence in 10 years — see note above
Breath (ug)	Blood (mg)	Urine (mg)				
120–150 and above	276–345 and above	367–459 and above	12 weeks' custody	High level community order — 26 weeks' custody	29 – 36 months (Extend if imposing immediate custody)	**36 – 60 months**
90–119	207–275	275–366	Medium level community order	Low level community order — High level community order	23–28 months	**36 – 52 months**
60–89	138–206	184–274	Band C Fine	Band C Fine — Low level community order	17 – 22 months	**36–46 months**
36–59	81–137	108–183	Band C Fine	Band B Fine — Band C fine	12–16 months	**36–40 months**

Note: when considering the guidance regarding the length of disqualification in the case of a second offence, the period to be imposed in any individual case will depend on an assessment of all the relevant circumstances, including the length of time since the earlier ban was imposed and the gravity of the current offence but disqualification must be for at least three years.

The court should then consider further adjustment for any aggravating or mitigating factors. The following is a **non-exhaustive** list of additional factual elements providing the context of the offence and factors relating to the offender. Identify whether any combination of these, or other relevant factors, should result in an upward or downward adjustment from the sentence arrived at so far.

Factors increasing seriousness *Statutory aggravating factors:*

- Previous convictions, having regard to a) the **nature** of the offence to which the conviction relates and its **relevance** to the current offence; and b) the **time** that has elapsed since the conviction
- Offence committed whilst on bail

Other aggravating factors:

- Failure to comply with current court orders
- Offence committed on licence or post sentence supervision
- LGV, HGV, PSV etc
- Poor road or weather conditions
- Carrying passengers
- Driving for hire or reward
- Evidence of unacceptable standard of driving
- Involved in accident
- High level of traffic or pedestrians in the vicinity

- No previous convictions **or** no relevant/recent convictions
- Genuine emergency established*
- Spiked drinks *
- Very short distance driven*

- Remorse
- Good character and/or exemplary conduct
- Serious medical condition requiring urgent, intensive or long-term treatment
- Age and/or lack of maturity where it affects the responsibility of the offender
- Mental disorder or learning disability
- Sole or primary carer for dependent relatives

---

* even where not amounting to special reasons

Step 3 — Consider any factors which indicate a reduction, such as assistance to the prosecution   The court should take into account sections 73 and 74 of the Serious Organised Crime and Police Act 2005 (assistance by defendants: reduction or review of sentence) and any other rule of law by virtue of which an offender may receive a discounted sentence in consequence of assistance given (or offered) to the prosecutor or investigator.

Step 4 — Reduction for guilty pleas   The court should take account of any potential reduction for a guilty plea in accordance with section 144 of the Criminal Justice Act 2003 and the *Guilty Plea* guideline.

Step 5 — Totality principle   If sentencing an offender for more than one offence, or where the offender is already serving a sentence, consider whether the total sentence is just and proportionate to the overall offending behaviour in accordance with the *Offences Taken into Consideration and Totality* guideline.

Step 6 — Compensation and ancillary orders   In all cases, the court should consider whether to make compensation and/or other ancillary orders including offering a drink/drive rehabilitation course, deprivation, and /or forfeiture or suspension of personal liquor licence.

Step 7 — Reasons   Section 174 of the Criminal Justice Act 2003 imposes a duty to give reasons for, and explain the effect of, the sentence.

Step 8 — Consideration for time spent on bail   The court must consider whether to give credit for time spent on bail in accordance with section 240A of the Criminal Justice Act 2003.

Excess Alcohol (in charge) (Revised 2017)

Road Traffic Act 1988, s.5(1)(b)
Effective from: 24 April 2017
Triable only summarily:
Maximum: Level 4 fine and/ or 3 months
Offence range: Band A fine — 6 weeks' custody

- **Must endorse and may disqualify. If no disqualification impose 10 points**
- **Extend any disqualification if imposing immediate custody**

Steps 1 and 2 — Determining the offence seriousness The starting point applies to all offenders irrespective of plea or previous convictions.

Level of alcohol			Starting point	Range	Disqualification/Points
Breath (Ug)	Blood (mg)	Urine (mg)			
120–150 and above	276–345 and above	367–459 and above	Medium level community order	Low level community order — 6 weeks' custody	Disqualify 6 – 12 months (Extend if imposing immediate custody)
90–119	207–275	275–366	Band C fine	Band C Fine — Medium level community order	Consider disqualification up to 6 months **OR** 10 points
60–89	138–206	184–274	Band B fine	Band B fine — Band C fine	Consider disqualification **OR** 10 points
36–59	81–137	108–183	Band B fine	Band A fine — Band B fine	10 points

The court should then consider further adjustment for any aggravating or mitigating factors. The following is a **non-exhaustive** list of additional factual elements providing the context of the offence and factors relating to the offender. Identify whether any combination of these, or other relevant factors, should result in an upward or downward adjustment from the sentence arrived at so far.

Factors increasing seriousness *Statutory aggravating factors:*

- Previous convictions, having regard to a) the **nature** of the offence to which the conviction relates and its **relevance** to the current offence; and b) the **time** that has elapsed since the conviction
- Offence committed whilst on bail

Other aggravating factors:

- Failure to comply with current court orders
- Offence committed on licence or post sentence supervision
- In charge of LGV, HGV, PSV etc
- High likelihood of driving
- Offering to drive for hire or reward

- No previous convictions **or** no relevant/recent convictions
- Low likelihood of driving
- Spiked drinks*
- Remorse
- Good character and/or exemplary conduct
- Serious medical condition requiring urgent, intensive or long-term treatment
- Age and/or lack of maturity where it affects the responsibility of the offender
- Mental disorder or learning disability
- Sole or primary carer for dependent relatives

Factors reducing seriousness or reflecting personal mitigation

Step 3 — Consider any factors which indicate a reduction, such as assistance to the prosecution The court should take into account sections 73 and 74 of the Serious Organised Crime and Police Act 2005 (assistance by defendants: reduction or review of sentence) and any other rule of law by virtue of which an offender may receive a discounted sentence in consequence of assistance given (or offered) to the prosecutor or investigator.

Step 4 — Reduction for guilty pleas The court should take account of any potential reduction for a guilty plea in accordance with section 144 of the Criminal Justice Act 2003 and the *Guilty Plea* guideline.

Step 5 — Totality principle If sentencing an offender for more than one offence, or where the offender is already serving a sentence, consider whether the total sentence is just and proportionate to the overall offending behaviour in accordance with the *Offences Taken into Consideration and Totality* guideline.

Step 6 — Compensation and ancillary orders In all cases, the court should consider whether to make compensation and/or other ancillary orders including offering a drink/drive rehabilitation course, deprivation, and /or forfeiture or suspension of personal liquor licence.

Step 7 — Reasons Section 174 of the Criminal Justice Act 2003 imposes a duty to give reasons for, and explain the effect of, the sentence.

Step 8 — Consideration for time spent on bail   The court must consider whether to give credit for time spent on bail in accordance with section 240A of the Criminal Justice Act 2003.

---

* even where not amounting to special reasons

FAIL TO STOP/REPORT ROAD ACCIDENT (REVISED 2017)

Road Traffic Act 1988, s.170(4)
Effective from: 24 April 2017
Triable only summarily:
Maximum: Unlimited fine and/or 6 months
Offence range: Band A fine — 26 weeks' custody
Step 1 — Determining the offence category The Court should determine the offence category using the table below.

Category 1	Higher culpability **and** greater harm
Category 2	Higher culpability **and** lesser harm **or** lower culpability **and** greater harm
Category 3	Lower culpability **and** lesser harm

The court should determine the offender's culpability and the harm caused with reference **only** to the factors below. Where an offence does not fall squarely into a category, individual factors may require a degree of weighting before making an overall assessment and determining the appropriate offence category.

CULPABILITY demonstrated by one or more of the following: Factors indicating higher culpability

- Offence committed in circumstances where a request for a sample of breath, blood or urine would have been made had the offender stopped
- Offence committed by offender seeking to avoid arrest for another offence
- Offender knew or suspected that personal injury caused and/or left injured party at scene
- Giving false details

Factors indicating lower culpability

- All other cases

HARM demonstrated by one or more of the following: Factors indicating greater harm

- Injury caused
- Significant damage

Factors indicating lesser harm

- All other cases

Step 2 — Starting point and category range Having determined the category at step one, the court should use the appropriate starting point to reach a sentence within the category range in the table below. The starting point applies to all offenders irrespective of plea or previous convictions.

Level of seriousness	Starting Point	Range	Disqualification/points
Category 1	High level community order	Low level community order — 26 weeks' custody	Disqualify 6 – 12 months **OR** 9 – 10 points (Extend if imposing immediate custody)
Category 2	Band C fine	Band B fine — Medium level community order	Disqualify up to 6 months **OR** 7 – 8 points
Category 3	Band B fine	Band A fine — Band C fine	5 – 6 points

• **Must endorse and may disqualify. If no disqualification impose 5 – 10 points**
• **Extend disqualification if imposing immediate custody**

The court should then consider further adjustment for any aggravating or mitigating factors. The following is a **non-exhaustive** list of additional factual elements providing the context of the offence and factors relating to the offender. Identify whether any combination of these, or other relevant factors, should result in an upward or downward adjustment from the sentence arrived at so far.

Factors increasing seriousness *Statutory aggravating factors:*

- Previous convictions, having regard to a) the **nature** of the offence to which the conviction relates and its **relevance** to the current offence; and b) the **time** that has elapsed since the conviction
- Offence committed whilst on bail

Other aggravating factors:

- Little or no attempt made to comply with duty
- Evidence of bad driving
- Failure to comply with current court orders
- Offence committed on licence or post sentence supervision

- No previous convictions **or** no relevant/recent convictions
- Remorse
- Good character and/or exemplary conduct
- Reasonably believed identity known
- Genuine fear of retribution

- Significant attempt made to comply with duty
- Serious medical condition requiring urgent, intensive or long-term treatment
- Age and/or lack of maturity where it affects the responsibility of the offender
- Mental disorder or learning disability
- Sole or primary carer for dependent relatives

Step 3 — Consider any factors which indicate a reduction, such as assistance to the prosecution
The court should take into account sections 73 and 74 of the Serious Organised Crime and Police Act 2005 (assistance by defendants: reduction or review of sentence) and any other rule of law by virtue of which an offender may receive a discounted sentence in consequence of assistance given (or offered) to the prosecutor or investigator.

Step 4 — Reduction for guilty pleas   The court should take account of any potential reduction for a guilty plea in accordance with section 144 of the Criminal Justice Act 2003 and the *Guilty Plea* guideline.

Step 5 — Totality principle   If sentencing an offender for more than one offence, or where the offender is already serving a sentence, consider whether the total sentence is just and proportionate to the overall offending behaviour in accordance with the *Offences Taken into Consideration and Totality* guideline.

Step 6 — Compensation and ancillary orders   In all cases, the court should consider whether to make compensation and/or other ancillary orders, including disqualification from driving and deprivation of a vehicle.

Step 7 — Reasons   Section 174 of the Criminal Justice Act 2003 imposes a duty to give reasons for, and explain the effect of, the sentence.

Step 8 — Consideration for time spent on bail   The court must consider whether to give credit for time spent on bail in accordance with section 240A of the Criminal Justice Act 2003.

FAIL TO PROVIDE SPECIMEN FOR ANALYSIS

(DRIVE/ATTEMPT TO DRIVE) (REVISED 2017)

Road Traffic Act 1988, s.7(6)
Effective from: 24 April 2017
Triable only summarily:
Maximum: Unlimited fine and/ or 6 months
Offence range: Band B fine — 26 weeks' custody
Step 1 — Determining the offence category   The Court should determine the offence category using the table below.

Category 1	Higher culpability **and** greater harm
Category 2	Higher culpability **and** lesser harm **or** lower culpability **and** greater harm
Category 3	Lower culpability **and** lesser harm

The court should determine the offender's culpability and the harm caused with reference **only** to the factors below. Where an offence does not fall squarely into a category, individual factors may require a degree of weighting before making an overall assessment and determining the appropriate offence category.
CULPABILITY demonstrated by one or more of the following: **Factors indicating higher culpability**

* Deliberate refusal/ failure

Factors indicating lower culpability

* All other cases

HARM demonstrated by one or more of the following: **Factors indicating greater harm**

* High level of impairment

Factors indicating lesser harm

* All other cases

Step 2 — Starting point and category range   Having determined the category at step one, the court should use the appropriate starting point to reach a sentence within the category range in the table below.

* **Must endorse and disqualify for at least 12 months**
* **Must disqualify for at least 2 years if offender has had two or more disqualifications for periods of 56 days or more in preceding 3 years — refer to the disqualification guidance and consult your legal adviser for further guidance**
* **Must disqualify for at least 3 years if offender has been convicted of a relevant offence in preceding 10 years -consult your legal adviser for further guidance**
* **Extend disqualification if imposing immediate custody**

If there is a delay in sentencing after conviction, consider interim disqualification.
The starting point applies to all offenders irrespective of plea or previous convictions.

Level of seriousness	Starting point	Range	Disqualification	Disqual. 2nd offence in 10 years
Category 1	12 weeks' custody	High level community order — 26 weeks' custody	29 – 36 months (Extend if imposing immediate custody)	36 – 60 months (Extend if imposing immediate custody
Category 2	Medium level community order	Low level community order — High level community order	17 – 28 months	36 – 52 months
Category 3	Band C fine	Band B fine — Low level community order	12 – 16 months	36 – 40 months

Note: when considering the guidance regarding the length of disqualification in the case of a second offence, the period to be imposed in any individual case will depend on an assessment of all the relevant circumstances, including the length of time since the earlier ban was imposed and the gravity of the current offence but disqualification must be for at least three years.

The court should then consider further adjustment for any aggravating or mitigating factors. The following is a **non-exhaustive** list of additional factual elements providing the context of the offence and factors relating to the offender. Identify whether any combination of these, or other relevant factors, should result in an upward or downward adjustment from the sentence arrived at so far.
Factors increasing seriousness
Statutory aggravating factors:

* Previous convictions, having regard to a) the **nature** of the offence to which the conviction relates and its **relevance** to the current offence; and b) the **time** that has elapsed since the conviction
* Offence committed whilst on bail

Other aggravating factors:
- Failure to comply with current court orders
- Offence committed on licence or post sentence supervision
- LGV, HGV PSV etc.
- Poor road or weather conditions
- Carrying passengers
- Driving for hire or reward
- Evidence of unacceptable standard of driving
- Involved in accident
- High level of traffic or pedestrians in the vicinity

Factors reducing seriousness or reflecting personal mitigation

- No previous convictions **or** no relevant/recent convictions
- Remorse
- Good character and/or exemplary conduct
- Serious medical condition requiring urgent, intensive or long-term treatment
- Age and/or lack of maturity where it affects the responsibility of the offender
- Mental disorder or learning disability
- Sole or primary carer for dependent relatives

Step 3 — Consider any factors which indicate a reduction, such as assistance to the prosecution
The court should take into account sections 73 and 74 of the Serious Organised Crime and Police Act 2005 (assistance by defendants: reduction or review of sentence) and any other rule of law by virtue of which an offender may receive a discounted sentence in consequence of assistance given (or offered) to the prosecutor or investigator.

Step 4 — Reduction for guilty pleas The court should take account of any potential reduction for a guilty plea in accordance with section 144 of the Criminal Justice Act 2003 and the *Guilty Plea* guideline.

Step 5 — Totality principle If sentencing an offender for more than one offence, or where the offender is already serving a sentence, consider whether the total sentence is just and proportionate to the overall offending behaviour in accordance with the *Offences Taken into Consideration and Totality* guideline.

Step 6 — Consider ancillary orders In all cases, the court should consider whether to make compensation and/or other ancillary orders including offering a drink/drive rehabilitation course.

Step 7 — Reasons Section 174 of the Criminal Justice Act 2003 imposes a duty to give reasons for, and explain the effect of, the sentence.

Step 8 — Consideration for time spent on bail The court must consider whether to give credit for time spent on bail in accordance with section 240A of the Criminal Justice Act 2003.

Fᴀɪʟ ᴛᴏ ᴘʀᴏᴠɪᴅᴇ ꜱᴘᴇᴄɪᴍᴇɴ ꜰᴏʀ ᴀɴᴀʟʏꜱɪꜱ (ɪɴ
ᴄʜᴀʀɢᴇ) (Rᴇᴠɪꜱᴇᴅ 2017)

Road Traffic Act 1988, s.7(6)
Effective from: 24 April 2017
Triable only summarily:
Maximum: Level 4 fine and/ or 3 months
Offence range: Band B fine — 6 weeks' custody
Step 1 — Determining the offence category   The Court should determine the offence category using the table below.

Category 1	Higher culpability **and** greater harm
Category 2	Higher culpability **and** lesser harm **or** lower culpability **and** greater harm
Category 3	Lower culpability **and** lesser harm

The court should determine the offender's culpability and the harm caused with reference **only** to the factors below. Where an offence does not fall squarely into a category, individual factors may require a degree of weighting before making an overall assessment and determining the appropriate offence category.
CULPABILITY demonstrated by one or more of the following: Factors indicating higher culpability

- Deliberate refusal/ failure

Factors indicating lower culpability

- Honestly held belief but unreasonable excuse
- Genuine attempt to comply
- All other cases

HARM demonstrated by one or more of the following: Factors indicating greater harm

- High level of impairment

Factors indicating lesser harm

- All other cases

Step 2 — Starting point and category range   Having determined the category at step one, the court should use the corresponding starting point to reach a sentence within the category range below.

- **Must endorse and may disqualify. If no disqualification impose 10 points**
- **Extend any disqualification if imposing immediate custody**

The starting point applies to all offenders irrespective of plea or previous convictions.

Level of seriousness	Starting Point	Range	Disqualification/points
Category 1	Medium level community order	Low level community order — 6 weeks' custody	Disqualify 6 – 12 months (Extend if imposing immediate custody)
Category 2	Band C fine	Band C fine — Medium level community order	Disqualify up to 6 months **OR** 10 points
Category 3	Band B fine	Band B fine	10 points

The court should then consider further adjustment for any aggravating or mitigating factors. The following is a **non-exhaustive** list of additional factual elements providing the context of the offence and factors relating to the offender. Identify whether any combination of these, or other relevant factors, should result in an upward or downward adjustment from the sentence arrived at so far.
Factors increasing seriousness   *Statutory aggravating factors:*

- Previous convictions, having regard to a) the **nature** of the offence to which the conviction relates and its **relevance** to the current offence; and b) the **time** that has elapsed since the conviction
- Offence committed whilst on bail

Other aggravating factors:

- High likelihood of driving
- Failure to comply with current court orders
- Offence committed on licence or post sentence supervision
- In charge of LGV, HGV, PSV etc.
- Offering to drive for hire or reward

- No previous convictions **or** no relevant/recent convictions
- Remorse
- Good character and/or exemplary conduct
- Serious medical condition requiring urgent, intensive or long-term treatment
- Age and/or lack of maturity where it affects the responsibility of the offender
- Mental disorder or learning disability
- Sole or primary carer for dependent relatives

Factors reducing seriousness or reflecting personal mitigation

Step 3 — Consider any factors which indicate a reduction, such as assistance to the prosecution
The court should take into account sections 73 and 74 of the Serious Organised Crime and Police Act 2005 (assistance by defendants: reduction or review of sentence) and any other rule of law by virtue of which an offender may receive a discounted sentence in consequence of assistance given (or offered) to the prosecutor or investigator.

Step 4 — Reduction for guilty pleas The court should take account of any potential reduction for a guilty plea in accordance with section 144 of the Criminal Justice Act 2003 and the *Guilty Plea* guideline.

Step 5 — Totality principle If sentencing an offender for more than one offence, or where the offender is already serving a sentence, consider whether the total sentence is just and proportionate to the overall offending behaviour in accordance with the *Offences Taken into Consideration and Totality* guideline.

Step 6 — Compensation and ancillary orders In all cases, the court should consider whether to make compensation and/or other ancillary orders including offering a drink/drive rehabilitation course, deprivation, and /or forfeiture or suspension of personal liquor licence.

Step 7 — Reasons Section 174 of the Criminal Justice Act 2003 imposes a duty to give reasons for, and explain the effect of, the sentence.

Step 8 — Consideration for time spent on bail The court must consider whether to give credit for time spent on bail in accordance with section 240A of the Criminal Justice Act 2003.

No insurance (Revised 2017)

Road Traffic Act 1988, s.143
Effective from: 24 April 2017
Triable only summarily:
Maximum: Unlimited fine
Offence range: Band B — Band C fine
Step 1 — Determining the offence category   The Court should determine the offence category using the table below.

Category 1	Higher culpability **and** greater harm
Category 2	Higher culpability **and** lesser harm **or** lower culpability **and** greater harm
Category 3	Lower culpability **and** lesser harm

The court should determine the offender's culpability and the harm caused with reference **only** to the factors below. Where an offence does not fall squarely into a category, individual factors may require a degree of weighting before making an overall assessment and determining the appropriate offence category.
CULPABILITY demonstrated by one or more of the following: Factors indicating higher culpability

- Never passed test
- Gave false details
- Driving LGV, HGV, PSV etc
- Driving for hire or reward
- Evidence of sustained uninsured use

Factors indicating lower culpability

- All other cases

HARM demonstrated by one or more of the following: Factors indicating greater harm

- Involved in accident where injury caused
- Involved in accident where damage caused

Factors indicating lesser harm

- All other cases

Step 2 — Starting point and category range   Having determined the category at step one, the court should use the appropriate starting point to reach a sentence within the category range in the table below. The starting point applies to all offenders irrespective of plea or previous convictions.

Level of seriousness	Starting Point	Range	Disqualification/points
Category 1	Band C fine	Band C fine	Disqualify 6 — 12 months
Category 2	Band C fine	Band C fine	Consider disqualification for up to 6 months **OR** 8 points
Category 3	Band C fine	Band B fine — Band C fine	6 – 8 points

• Must endorse and may disqualify. If no disqualification impose 6–8 points
The court should then consider further adjustment for any aggravating or mitigating factors. The following is a **non-exhaustive** list of additional factual elements providing the context of the offence and factors relating to the offender. Identify whether any combination of these, or other relevant factors, should result in an upward or downward adjustment from the sentence arrived at so far.
Factors increasing seriousness   *Statutory aggravating factors:*

- Previous convictions, having regard to a) the **nature** of the offence to which the conviction relates and its **relevance** to the current offence; and b) the **time** that has elapsed since the conviction
- Offence committed whilst on bail

Other aggravating factors:

- Failure to comply with current court orders
- Offence committed on licence or post sentence supervision

- No previous convictions **or** no relevant/recent convictions
- Remorse
- Good character and/or exemplary conduct
- Responsibility for providing insurance rests with another (where not amounting to a defence)
- Genuine misunderstanding
- Recent failure to renew or failure to transfer vehicle details where insurance was in existence
- Vehicle not being driven

Factors reducing seriousness or reflecting personal mitigation
Step 3 — Consider any factors which indicate a reduction, such as assistance to the prosecution
The court should take into account sections 73 and 74 of the Serious Organised Crime and Police Act 2005 (assistance by defendants: reduction or review of sentence) and any other rule of

law by virtue of which an offender may receive a discounted sentence in consequence of assistance given (or offered) to the prosecutor or investigator.

Step 4 — Reduction for guilty pleas   The court should take account of any potential reduction for a guilty plea in accordance with section 144 of the Criminal Justice Act 2003 and the *Guilty Plea* guideline.

Step 5 — Totality principle   If sentencing an offender for more than one offence, or where the offender is already serving a sentence, consider whether the total sentence is just and proportionate to the overall offending behaviour in accordance with the *Offences Taken into Consideration and Totality* guideline.

Step 6 — Compensation and ancillary orders   In all cases, the court should consider whether to make compensation and/or other ancillary orders.

Step 7 — Reasons   Section 174 of the Criminal Justice Act 2003 imposes a duty to give reasons for, and explain the effect of, the sentence.

SPEEDING (REVISED 2017)

Road Traffic Regulation Act 1984, s.89(1)
Effective from: 24 April 2017
Triable only summarily:
Maximum: Level 3 fine (level 4 if motorway)
Offence range: Band A fine — Band C fine
Steps 1 and 2 — Determining the offence seriousness   The starting point applies to all offenders irrespective of plea or previous convictions.

Speed limit (mph)	Recorded speed (mph)		
20	41 and above	31 – 40	21 – 30
30	51 and above	41 – 50	31 – 40
40	66 and above	56 – 65	41 – 55
50	76 and above	66 – 75	51 – 65
60	91 and above	81 – 90	61 – 80
70	101 and above	91 – 100	71 – 90
Sentencing range	**Band C fine**	**Band B fine**	**Band A fine**
Points/disqualification	Disqualify 7 – 56 days **OR** 6 points	Disqualify 7 – 28 days **OR** 4 – 6 points	3 points

• **Must endorse and may disqualify. If no disqualification impose 3 – 6 points**
• **Where an offender is driving grossly in excess of the speed limit the court should consider a disqualification in excess of 56 days.**
The court should then consider further adjustment for any aggravating or mitigating factors. The following is a **non-exhaustive** list of additional factual elements providing the context of the offence and factors relating to the offender. Identify whether any combination of these, or other relevant factors, should result in an upward or downward adjustment from the sentence arrived at so far.
Factors increasing seriousness   *Statutory aggravating factors:*

- Previous convictions, having regard to a) the **nature** of the offence to which the conviction relates and its **relevance** to the current offence; and b) the **time** that has elapsed since the conviction
- Offence committed whilst on bail

Other aggravating factors:

- Offence committed on licence or post sentence supervision
- Poor road or weather conditions
- Driving LGV, HGV, PSV etc.
- Towing caravan/trailer
- Carrying passengers or heavy load
- Driving for hire or reward
- Evidence of unacceptable standard of driving over and above speed
- Location e.g. near school
- High level of traffic or pedestrians in the vicinity

- No previous convictions **or** no relevant/recent convictions
- Good character and/or exemplary conduct
- Genuine emergency established

Factors reducing seriousness or reflecting personal mitigation
Step 3 — Consider any factors which indicate a reduction, such as assistance to the prosecution
   The court should take into account sections 73 and 74 of the Serious Organised Crime and Police Act 2005 (assistance by defendants: reduction or review of sentence) and any other rule of law by virtue of which an offender may receive a discounted sentence in consequence of assistance given (or offered) to the prosecutor or investigator.

Step 4 — Reduction for guilty pleas   The court should take account of any potential reduction for a guilty plea in accordance with section 144 of the Criminal Justice Act 2003 and the *Guilty Plea* guideline.

Step 5 — Totality principle   If sentencing an offender for more than one offence, or where the offender is already serving a sentence, consider whether the total sentence is just and proportionate to the overall offending behaviour in accordance with the *Offences Taken into Consideration and Totality* guideline.

Step 6 — Compensation and ancillary orders   In all cases, the court should consider whether to make compensation and/or other ancillary orders.

Step 7 — Reasons   Section 174 of the Criminal Justice Act 2003 imposes a duty to give reasons for, and explain the effect of, the sentence.

Unfit through drink or drugs (drive/attempt to drive) (Revised 2017)

RoadTraffic Act 1988, s.4(1)
Effective from: 24 April 2017
Triable only summarily:
Maximum: Unlimited fine and/or 6 months
Offence range: Band B fine — 26 weeks' custody
Step 1 — Determining the offence category The Court should determine the offence category using the table below.

Category 1	Higher culpability **and** greater harm
Category 2	Higher culpability **and** lesser harm **or** lower culpability **and** greater harm
Category 3	Lower culpability **and** lesser harm

The court should determine the offender's culpability and the harm caused with reference **only** to the factors below. Where an offence does not fall squarely into a category, individual factors may require a degree of weighting before making an overall assessment and determining the appropriate offence category.

CULPABILITY demonstrated by one or more of the following: Factors indicating higher culpability

- Driving LGV, HGV or PSV etc.
- Driving for hire or reward

Factors indicating lower culpability

- All other cases

HARM demonstrated by one or more of the following: Factors indicating greater harm

- High level of impairment

Factors indicating lesser harm

- All other cases

Step 2 — Starting point and category range Having determined the category at step one, the court should use the appropriate starting point to reach a sentence within the category range in the table below.

- **Must endorse and disqualify for at least 12 months**
- **Must disqualify for at least 2 years if offender has had two or more disqualifications for periods of 56 days or more in preceding 3 years — refer to the disqualification guidance and consult your legal adviser for further guidance**
- **Must disqualify for at least 3 years if offender has been convicted of a relevant offence in preceding 10 years -consult your legal adviser for further guidance**
- **Extend disqualification if imposing immediate custody**

If there is a delay in sentencing after conviction, consider interim disqualification.
The starting point applies to all offenders irrespective of plea or previous convictions.

Level of seriousness	Starting point	Range	Disqualification	Disqual. 2nd offence in 10 years
Category 1	12 weeks' custody	High level community order — 26 weeks' custody	29 – 36 months (Extend if imposing immediate custody)	36 – 60 months (Extend if imposing immediate custody
Category 2	Medium level community order	Low level community order — High level community order	17 – 28 months	36 – 52 months
Category 3	Band C fine	Band B fine — Low level community order	12 – 16 months	36 – 40 months

Note: when considering the guidance regarding the length of disqualification in the case of a second offence, the period to be imposed in any individual case will depend on an assessment of all the relevant circumstances, including the length of time since the earlier ban was imposed and the gravity of the current offence but disqualification must be for at least three years.

The court should then consider further adjustment for any aggravating or mitigating factors.The following is a **non-exhaustive** list of additional factual elements providing the context of the offence and factors relating to the offender. Identify whether any combination of these, or other relevant factors, should result in an upward or downward adjustment from the sentence arrived at so far.

Factors increasing seriousness *Statutory aggravating factors:*

- Previous convictions, having regard to a) the **nature** of the offence to which the conviction relates and its **relevance** to the current offence; and b) the **time** that has elapsed since the conviction
- Offence committed whilst on bail

Other aggravating factors:

- Failure to comply with current court orders
- Offence committed on licence or post sentence supervision
- Poor road or weather conditions
- Evidence of unacceptable standard of driving
- Involved in accident
- Carrying passengers
- High level of traffic or pedestrians in the vicinity

- No previous convictions **or** no relevant/recent convictions
- Remorse
- Good character and/or exemplary conduct
- Serious medical condition requiring urgent, intensive or long-term treatment
- Age and/or lack of maturity where it affects the responsibility of the offender
- Mental disorder or learning disability
- Sole or primary carer for dependent relatives

Factors reducing seriousness or reflecting personal mitigation

Step 3 — Consider any factors which indicate a reduction, such as assistance to the prosecution
The court should take into account sections 73 and 74 of the Serious Organised Crime and Police Act 2005 (assistance by defendants: reduction or review of sentence) and any other rule of law by virtue of which an offender may receive a discounted sentence in consequence of assistance given (or offered) to the prosecutor or investigator.

Step 4 — Reduction for guilty pleas   The court should take account of any potential reduction for a guilty plea in accordance with section 144 of the Criminal Justice Act 2003 and the *Guilty Plea* guideline.

Step 5 — Totality principle   If sentencing an offender for more than one offence, or where the offender is already serving a sentence, consider whether the total sentence is just and proportionate to the overall offending behaviour in accordance with the *Offences Taken into Consideration and Totality* guideline.

Step 6 — Compensation and ancillary orders   In all cases, the court should consider whether to make compensation and/or other ancillary orders including offering a drink/drive rehabilitation course, deprivation, and /or forfeiture or suspension of personal liquor licence.

Step 7 — Reasons   Section 174 of the Criminal Justice Act 2003 imposes a duty to give reasons for, and explain the effect of, the sentence.

Step 8 — Consideration for time spent on bail   The court must consider whether to give credit for time spent on bail in accordance with section 240A of the Criminal Justice Act 2003.

UNFIT THROUGH DRINK OR DRUGS (IN CHARGE)
(REVISED 2017)

Road Traffic Act, 1988, s.4(2)
Effective from: 24 April 2017
Triable only summarily:
Maximum: Level 4 fine and/ or 3 months
Offence range: Band B fine — 12 weeks' custody
Step 1 — Determining the offence category The Court should determine the offence category using the table below.

Category 1	Higher culpability **and** greater harm
Category 2	Higher culpability **and** lesser harm **or** lower culpability **and** greater harm
Category 3	Lower culpability **and** lesser harm

The court should determine the offender's culpability and the harm caused with reference **only** to the factors below. Where an offence does not fall squarely into a category, individual factors may require a degree of weighting before making an overall assessment and determining the appropriate offence category.
CULPABILITY demonstrated by one or more of the following: Factors indicating higher culpability

- High likelihood of driving
- In charge of LGV, HGV or PSV etc.
- Offering to drive for hire or reward

Factors indicating lower culpability

- All other cases

HARM demonstrated by one or more of the following: Factors indicating greater harm

- High level of impairment

Factors indicating lesser harm

- All other cases

Step 2 — Starting point and category range Having determined the category at step one, the court should use the appropriate starting point to reach a sentence within the category range in the table below.

- **Must endorse and may disqualify. If no disqualification impose 10 points**
- **Extend disqualification if imposing immediate custody**

The starting point applies to all offenders irrespective of plea or previous convictions.

Level of seriousness	Starting Point	Range	Disqualification/points
Category 1	High level community order	Medium level community order — 12 weeks' custody	Consider disqualification (extend if imposing immediate custody) **OR** 10 points
Category 2	Band C fine	Band B fine — Medium level community order	Consider disqualification **OR** 10 points
Category 3	Band B fine	Band B fine	10 points

The court should then consider further adjustment for any aggravating or mitigating factors. The following is a **non-exhaustive** list of additional factual elements providing the context of the offence and factors relating to the offender. Identify whether any combination of these, or other relevant factors, should result in an upward or downward adjustment from the sentence arrived at so far.
Factors increasing seriousness *Statutory aggravating factors:*

- Previous convictions, having regard to a) the **nature** of the offence to which the conviction relates and its **relevance** to the current offence; and b) the **time** that has elapsed since the conviction
- Offence committed whilst on bail

Other aggravating factors:

- Failure to comply with current court orders
- Offence committed on licence or post sentence supervision

- No previous convictions **or** no relevant/recent convictions
- Remorse
- Good character and/or exemplary conduct
- Serious medical condition requiring urgent, intensive or long-term treatment
- Age and/or lack of maturity where it affects the responsibility of the offender
- Mental disorder or learning disability
- Sole or primary carer for dependent relatives

Factors reducing seriousness or reflecting personal mitigation

Step 3 — Consider any factors which indicate a reduction, such as assistance to the prosecution   The court should take into account sections 73 and 74 of the Serious Organised Crime and Police Act 2005 (assistance by defendants: reduction or review of sentence) and any other rule of law by virtue of which an offender may receive a discounted sentence in consequence of assistance given (or offered) to the prosecutor or investigator.

Step 4 — Reduction for guilty pleas   The court should take account of any potential reduction for a guilty plea in accordance with section 144 of the Criminal Justice Act 2003 and the *Guilty Plea* guideline.

Step 5 — Totality principle   If sentencing an offender for more than one offence, or where the offender is already serving a sentence, consider whether the total sentence is just and proportionate to the overall offending behaviour in accordance with the *Offences Taken into Consideration and Totality* guideline.

Step 6 — Compensation and ancillary orders   In all cases, the court should consider whether to make compensation and/or other ancillary orders including offering a drink/drive rehabilitation course, deprivation, and /or forfeiture or suspension of personal liquor licence.

Step 7 — Reasons   Section 174 of the Criminal Justice Act 2003 imposes a duty to give reasons for, and explain the effect of, the sentence.

Step 8 — Consideration for time spent on bail   The court must consider whether to give credit for time spent on bail in accordance with section 240A of the Criminal Justice Act 2003.

OFFENCES APPROPRIATE FOR IMPOSITION OF FINE OR DISCHARGE

PART 1: OFFENCES CONCERNING THE DRIVER

Offence	Maximum	Points	Starting point	Special considerations
Fail to co-operate with preliminary (roadside) breath test	L3	4	B	
Fail to give information of driver's identity as required	L3	6	C	For limited companies, endorsement is not available; a fine is the only available penalty
Fail to produce insurance certificate	L4	–	A	Fine per offence, not per document
Fail to produce test certificate	L3	–	A	
Drive otherwise than in accordance with licence (where could be covered)	L3	–	A	
Drive otherwise than in accordance with licence	L3	3–6	A	Aggravating factor if no licence ever held

PART 2: OFFENCES CONCERNING THE VEHICLE

* The guidelines for some of the offences below differentiate between three types of offender when the offence is committed in the course of business: driver, owner-driver and owner-company. **For owner-driver, the starting point is the same as for driver; however, the court should consider an uplift of at least 25%.**

Offence	Maximum	Points	Starting point	Special considerations
No excise licence	L3 or 5 times annual duty, whichever is greater	–	A (1–3 months unpaid) B (4–6 months unpaid) C (7–12 months unpaid)	Add duty lost
Fail to notify change of ownership to DVLA	L3	–	A	If offence committed in course of business: A (driver) A* (owner-driver) B (owner-company)
No test certificate	L3	–	A	If offence committed in course of business: A (driver) A* (owner-driver) B (owner-company)
Brakes defective	L4	3	B	If offence committed in course of business: B (driver) B* (owner-driver) C (owner-company) L5 if goods vehicle – see Part 5 below
Steering defective	L4	3	B	If offence committed in course of business: B (driver) B* (owner-driver)

Offence	Maximum	Points	Starting point	Special considerations
				B (owner-company)
				L5 if goods vehicle – see Part 5 below
Tyres defective	L4	3	B	If offence committed in course of business:
				B (driver)
				B* (owner-driver)
				C (owner-company)
				L5 if goods vehicle – see Part 5 below Penalty per tyre
Condition of vehicle/accessories/equipment involving danger of injury	L4	3	B	If offence committed in course of business:
				B (driver)
				B* (owner-driver)
(Road Traffic Act 1988, s 40A)				C (owner-company)
				L5 if goods vehicle – see Part 5 below
Exhaust defective	L3	–	A	If offence committed in course of business:
				A (driver)
				A* (owner-driver)
				B (owner-company)
Lights defective	L3	–	A	If offence committed in course of business:
				A (driver)
				A* (owner-driver)
				B (owner-company)

PART 3: OFFENCES CONCERNING USE OF VEHICLE

* The guidelines for some of the offences below differentiate between three types of offender when the offence is committed in the course of business: driver, owner-driver and owner-company. **For owner-driver, the starting point is the same as for driver; however, the court should consider an uplift of at least 25%.**

Offence	Maximum	Points	Starting point	Special considerations
Weight, position or distribution of load or manner in which load secured involving danger of injury	L4	3	B	Must disqualify for at least 6 months if offender has one or more previous convictions for same offence within three years
(Road Traffic Act 1988, s 40A)				If offence committed in course of business:
				A (driver)
				A* (owner-driver)
				B (owner-company)
				L5 if goods vehicle – see Part 5 below
Number of passengers or way carried involving danger of injury	L4	3	B	If offence committed in course of business:
				A (driver)
(Road Traffic Act 1988, s 40A)				A* (owner-driver)
				B (owner-company)
				L5 if goods vehicle – see Part 5 below

Offence	Maximum	Points	Starting point	Special considerations
Position or manner in which load secured (not involving danger)	L3	–	A	L4 if goods vehicle – see Part 5 below
(Road Traffic Act 1988, s 42)				
Overloading/exceeding axle weight	L5	–	A	Starting point caters for cases where the over-load is up to and including 10%. Thereafter, 10% should be added to the penalty for each additional 1% of overload
				Penalty per axle
				If offence committed in course of business:
				A (driver)
				A* (owner-driver)
				B (owner-company)
				if goods vehicle – see Part 5 below
Dangerous parking	L3	3	A	
Pelican/zebra crossing contravention	L3	3	A	
Fail to comply with traffic sign (eg red traffic light, stop sign, double white lines, no entry sign)	L3	3	A	
Fail to comply with traffic sign (eg give way sign, keep left sign,	L3	–	A	
Fail to comply with police constable directing traffic	L3	3	A	
Fail to stop when required by police constable	L5	–	B	
	(mechanically propelled vehicle)			
	L3 (cycle)			
Use of mobile telephone	L3	3	A	
Seat belt offences	L2 (adult or child in front)	–	A	
	L2 (child in rear)	–	A	
Fail to use appropriate child car seat	L2	–	A	

PART 4: MOTORWAY OFFENCES

Offence	Maximum	Points	Starting point	Special considerations
Drive in reverse or wrong way on slip road	L4	3	B	
Drive in reverse or wrong way on motorway	L4	3	C	
Drive off carriageway (central reservation or hard shoulder)	L4	3	B	
Make U turn	L4	3	C	
learner driver or excluded vehicle	L4	3	B	

Offence	Maximum	Points	Starting point	Special considerations
Stop on hard shoulder	L4	–	A	
Vehicle in prohibited lane	L4	3	A	
Walk on motorway, slip road or hard shoulder	L4	–	A	

PART 5: OFFENCES RE BUSES/GOODS VEHICLES OVER 3.5 TONNES (GVW)

*The guidelines for these offences differentiate between three types of offender: driver; owner-driver; and owner-company. **For owner-driver, the starting point is the same as for driver; however, the court should consider an uplift of at least 25%.**

** In all cases, take safety, damage to roads and commercial gain into account. Refer to [page 150] for approach to fines for 'commercially motivated' offences.

Offence	Maximum	Points	Starting point	Special considerations
No goods vehicle plating certificate	L3	–	A (driver)	
			A* (owner-driver)	
			B (owner-company)	
No goods vehicle test certificate	L4	–	B (driver)	
			B* (owner-driver)	
			C (owner-company)	
Brakes defective	L5	3	B (driver)	
			B* (owner-driver)	
			C (owner-company)	
Steering defective	L5	3	B (driver)	
			B* (owner-driver)	
			C (owner-company)	
Tyres defective	L5	3	B (driver)	Penalty per tyre
			B* (owner-driver)	
			C (owner-company)	
Exhaust emission	L4	–	B (driver)	
			B* (owner-driver)	
			C (owner-company)	
Condition of vehicle/accessories/equipment involving danger of injury (Road Traffic Act 1988, s 40A)	L5	3	B (driver)	Must disqualify for at least 6 months if offender has one or more previous convictions for same offence within three years
			B* (owner-driver)	
			C (owner-company)	
Number of passengers or way carried involving danger of injury (Road Traffic Act 1988, s 40A)	L5	3	B (driver)	Must disqualify for at least 6 months if offender has one or more previous convictions for same offence within three years
			B* (owner-driver)	

Offence	Maximum	Points	Starting point	Special considerations
			C (owner-company)	
Weight, position or distribution of load or manner in which load secured involving danger of injury	L5	3	B (driver)	Must disqualify for at least 6 months if offender has one or more previous convictions for same offence within three years
			B* (owner-driver)	
(Road Traffic Act 1988, s 40A)			C (owner-company)	
Position or manner in which load secured (not involving danger)	L4	–	B (driver)	
			B* (owner-driver)	
(Road Traffic Act 1988, s 42)			C (owner-company)	
Overloading/exceeding axle weight	L5	–	B (driver)	Starting points cater for cases where the overload is up to and including 10%. Thereafter, 10% should be added to the penalty for each additional 1% of overload Penalty per axle
			B* (owner-driver)	
			C (owner-company)	
No operators licence	L4 (PSV)	–	B (driver)	
	L5 (Goods)		B* (owner-driver)	
			C (owner-company)	
Speed limiter not used or incorrectly calibrated	L4	–	B (driver)	
			B* (owner-driver)	
			C (owner-company)	
Tachograph not used/not working	L5	–	B (driver)	
			B* (owner-driver)	
			C (owner-company)	
Exceed permitted driving time/periods of duty	L4	–	B (driver)	
			B* (owner-driver)	
			C (owner-company)	
Fail to keep/return written record sheets	L4	–	B (driver)	
			B* (owner-driver)	
			C (owner-company)	
Falsity or alter records with intent to deceive	L5/2 years	–	B (driver)	Either way offence
			B* (owner-driver)	
			C (owner-company)	

Drug Driving

Introduction

Since the new offence came into force in March 2015 the Sentencing Council has received a large number of requests for a sentencing guideline. It has been brought to our attention that there are concerns with sentencing in this area and a risk of inconsistent practices developing.

The new offence is a strict liability offence, which is committed once the specified limit for any of 17 specified controlled drugs is exceeded. The 17 drugs include both illegal drugs and drugs that may be medically prescribed.

The limits for illegal drugs are set in line with a zero tolerance approach but ruling out accidental exposure. The limits for drugs that may be medically prescribed are set in line with a road safety risk-based approach, at levels above the normal concentrations found with therapeutic use. This is different from the approach taken when setting the limit for alcohol, where the limit was set at a level where the effect of the alcohol would be expected to have impaired a person's driving ability. **For these reasons it would be wrong to rely on the Driving with Excess Alcohol guideline when sentencing an offence under this legislation.**

Guidance Only

At present there is insufficient reliable data available from the Department for Transport upon which the Sentencing Council can devise a full guideline. For that reason, and given the number of requests for guidance that have been received, the Sentencing Council has devised the attached *guidance* to assist sentencers.

It is important to note that this guidance does not carry the same authority as a sentencing guideline, and sentencers are not obliged to follow it. However, it is hoped that the majority of sentencers will find it useful in assisting them to deal with these cases.

The Sentencing Council will, in due course produce a guideline with the assistance of evidence and data gathered by the Department for Transport. Any new guideline will be made subject to public consultation before it is finalised.

Drug Driving Guidance

Background

The Crime and Courts Act 2013 inserted a new section 5A into the Road Traffic Act 1988 (RTA), which makes it an offence to drive, attempt to drive, or be in charge of a motor vehicle with a concentration of a specified controlled drug in the body above the specified limit. The offence came into force on 2 March 2015.

Driving or Attempting to Drive

Triable only summarily:
Maximum: Unlimited fine and/or 6 months

- Must endorse and disqualify for at least 12 months
- Must disqualify for at least 2 years if offender has had two or more disqualifications for periods of 56 days or more in preceding 3 years refer to disqualification guidance and consult your legal adviser for further guidance
- Must disqualify for at least 3 years if offender has been convicted of a relevant offence in preceding 10 years – consult your legal adviser for further guidance

If there is a delay In sentencing after conviction, consider interim disqualification

- As a guide, where an offence of driving or attempting to drive has been committed and there are no factors that increase seriousness the Court should consider a starting point of a **Band C fine**, and a disqualification in the region of 12 - 22 months. The list of factors that increase seriousness appears at page 170. Please note this is an exhaustive list and only factors that appear in the list should be considered.
- Where there are factors that increase seriousness the Court should consider increasing the sentence on the basis of the level of seriousness.
- The community order threshold is likely to be crossed where there is evidence of one or more factors that increase seriousness. The Court should also consider imposing a disqualification in the region of 23–28 months.
- The custody threshold is likely to be crossed where there is evidence of one or more factors that increase seriousness and one or more aggravating factors (see below). The Court should also consider imposing a disqualification in the region of 29–36 months.
- Where the prosecutor wishes to substitute or add counts to a draft indictment, or to invite the court to allow an indictment to be amended, so that the draft indictment, or indictment, will charge offences which differ from those with which the defendant first was charged, the defendant should be given as much notice as possible of what is proposed. It is likely that the defendant will need time to consider his or her position and advance notice will help to avoid delaying the proceedings.

Factors that increase seriousness (this is an exhaustive list)

- Evidence of another specified drug[1] or of alcohol in the body
- Evidence of an unacceptable standard of driving
- Driving (or in charge of) an LGV, HGV or PSV
- Driving (or in charge of) a vehicle driven for hire or reward

AGGRAVATING AND MITIGATING FACTORS (THESE ARE NON-EXHAUSTIVE LISTS)

Aggravating Factors

- Previous convictions having regard to a) the nature of the offence to which the conviction relates and its relevance to the current offence; and b) the time that has elapsed since the conviction
  - Location eg near school
- Carrying passengers
- High level of traffic or pedestrians in the vicinity
- Poor road or weather conditions

Mitigating Factors

- No previous convictions or no relevant/recent convictions
- Remorse
- Good character and/or exemplary conduct
- Age and/or lack of maturity where it affects the responsibility of the offender
- Mental disorder or learning disability
- Sole or primary carer for dependent relatives
- Very short distance driven
- Genuine emergency established

---

[1] For these purposes, cocaine and benzoylecgonine (BZE) shall be treated as one drug as they both occur in the body as a result of cocaine use rather than poly-drug use. Similarly 6-Monoacteylmorphine and Morphine shall be treated as one drug as they both occur in the body as a result of heroin use. Finally, Diazepam and Temazepam shall be treated as one drug as they also both occur in the body as a result of Temazepam use.

IN CHARGE

Triable only summarily:
Maximum: Level 4 fine and/or 3 months
Must endorse and may disqualify. If no disqualification, impose 10 points

- As a guide, where an offence of being in charge has been committed but there are no factors that increase seriousness the Court should consider a starting point of a Band B fine, and endorsing the licence with 10 penalty points. The list of factors that increase seriousness appears below. Please note this is an exhaustive list and only factors that appear in the list should be considered.
- Where there are factors that increase seriousness the Court should consider increasing the sentence on the basis of the level of seriousness.
- Where there is evidence of one or more factors that increase seriousness and a greater number of aggravating factors (see below) the Court may consider it appropriate to impose a short custodial sentence of up to 12 weeks. The Court should also consider imposing a disqualification.
- Having determined a starting point the Court should consider additional factors that may make the offence more or less serious. A non-exhaustive list of aggravating and mitigating factors is set out below.

FACTORS THAT INCREASE SERIOUSNESS – (THIS IS AN EXHAUSTIVE LIST)

- Evidence of another specified drug[2] or of alcohol in the body
- Evidence of an unacceptable standard of driving
- Driving (or in charge of) an LGV, HGV or PSV
- Driving (or in charge of) a vehicle driven for hire or reward

AGGRAVATING AND MITIGATING FACTORS (THESE ARE NON-EXHAUSTIVE LISTS)

Aggravating Factors

- Previous convictions having regard to a) the nature of the offence to which the conviction relates and its relevance to the current offence; and b) the time that has elapsed since the conviction
  - Location eg near school
- Carrying passengers
- High level of traffic or pedestrians in the vicinity
- Poor road or weather conditions

Mitigating Factors

- No previous convictions or no relevant/recent convictions
- Remorse
- Good character and/or exemplary conduct
- Age and/or lack of maturity where it affects the responsibility of the offender
- Mental disorder or learning disability
- Sole or primary carer for dependent relatives
- Very short distance driven
- Genuine emergency established

---

[2] For these purposes, cocaine and benzoylecgonine (BZE) shall be treated as one drug as they both occur in the body as a result of cocaine use rather than poly-drug use. Similarly 6-Monoacteylmorphine and Morphine shall be treated as one drug as they both occur in the body as a result of heroin use. Finally, Diazepam and Temazepam shall be treated as one drug as they also both occur in the body as a result of Temazepam use.

INFLICTING GRIEVOUS BODILY HARM/UNLAWFUL WOUNDING
Offences against the Person Act 1861 (section 20)

RACIALLY/RELIGIOUSLY AGGRAVATED GBH/UNLAWFUL WOUNDING
Crime and Disorder Act 1998 (section 29)

These are specified offences for the purposes of section 224 of the Criminal Justice Act 2003
Triable either way
Section 20
Maximum when tried summarily: Level 5 fine and/or 26 weeks' custody
Maximum when tried on indictment: 5 years' custody
Section 29
Maximum when tried summarily: Level 5 fine and/or 26 weeks' custody
Maximum when tried on indictment: 7 years' custody
Offence range: Community order — 4 years' custody
This guideline applies to all offenders aged 18 and older, who are sentenced on or after 13 June 2011. The definitions at [page 145] of 'starting point' and 'first time offender' do not apply for this guideline. Starting point and category ranges apply to all offenders in all cases, irrespective of plea or previous convictions.
STEP ONE Determining the offence category   The court should determine the offence category using the table below.

Category 1	Greater harm[Ed 1] (serious injury must normally be present) **and** higher culpability
Category 2	Greater harm (serious injury must normally be present) **and** lower culpability;
	or lesser harm **and** higher culpability
Category 3	Lesser harm **and** lower culpability

The court should determine the offender's culpability and the harm caused, or intended, by reference **only** to the factors below (as demonstrated by the presence of one or more). These factors comprise the principal factual elements of the offence and should determine the category.
Factors indicating greater harm   Injury (which includes disease transmission and/or psychological harm) which is serious in the context of the offence (must normally be present)
Victim is particularly vulnerable[Ed 2] because of personal circumstances
Sustained or repeated assault on the same victim
Factors indicating lesser harm   Injury which is less serious in the context of the offence
Factors indicating higher culpability   *Statutory aggravating factors:*
Offence motivated by, or demonstrating, hostility to the victim based on his or her sexual orientation (or presumed sexual orientation)
Offence motivated by, or demonstrating, hostility to the victim based on the victim's disability (or presumed disability)
Other aggravating factors:
A significant degree of premeditation
Use of weapon or weapon equivalent (for example, shod foot, headbutting, use of acid, use of animal)[Ed 3]
Intention to commit more serious harm than actually resulted from the offence
Deliberately causes more harm than is necessary for commission of offence
Deliberate targeting of vulnerable victim
Leading role in group or gang
Offence motivated by, or demonstrating, hostility based on the victim's age, sex, gender identity (or presumed gender identity)
Factors indicating lower culpability   Subordinate role in a group or gang
A greater degree of provocation than normally expected
Lack of premeditation
Mental disorder or learning disability, where linked to commission of the offence
Excessive self defence

STEP TWO Starting point and category range   Having determined the category, the court should use the corresponding starting points to reach a sentence within the category range below. The starting point applies to all offenders irrespective of plea or previous convictions. A case of particular gravity, reflected by multiple features of culpability in step one, could merit upward adjustment from the starting point before further adjustment for aggravating or mitigating features, set out below.

Offence Category	Starting Point *(Applicable to all offenders)*	Category Range *(Applicable to all offenders)*
Category 1	Crown Court	Crown Court
Category 2	Crown Court	Crown Court
Category 3	High level community order	Low level community order – Crown Court (51 weeks' custody)

The table below contains a **non-exhaustive** list of additional factual elements providing the context of the offence and factors relating to the offender. Identify whether any combination of these, or other relevant factors, should result in an upward or downward adjustment from the starting point. In some cases, having considered these factors, it may be appropriate to move outside the identified category range.

When sentencing **category 3** offences, the court should also consider the custody threshold as follows:

- has the custody threshold been passed?
- if so, is it unavoidable that a custodial sentence be imposed?
- if so, can that sentence be suspended?

Factors increasing seriousness *Statutory aggravating factors:*
Previous convictions, having regard to a) the nature of the offence to which the conviction relates and its relevance to the current offence; and b) the time that has elapsed since the conviction
Offence committed whilst on bail
Other aggravating factors include:
Location of the offence
Timing of the offence
Ongoing effect upon the victim
Offence committed against those working in the public sector or providing a service to the public
Presence of others including relatives, especially children or partner of the victim
Gratuitous degradation of victim
In domestic violence cases, victim forced to leave their home
Failure to comply with current court orders
Offence committed whilst on licence
An attempt to conceal or dispose of evidence
Failure to respond to warnings or concerns expressed by others about the offender's behaviour
Commission of offence whilst under the influence of alcohol or drugs
Abuse of power and/or position of trust
Exploiting contact arrangements with a child to commit an offence
Established evidence of community impact
Any steps taken to prevent the victim reporting an incident, obtaining assistance and/or from assisting or supporting the prosecution
Offences taken into consideration (TICs)
Factors reducing seriousness or reflecting personal mitigation No previous convictions **or** no relevant/recent convictions
Single blow
Remorse
Good character and/or exemplary conduct
Determination and/or demonstration of steps taken to address addiction or offending behaviour
Serious medical conditions requiring urgent, intensive or long-term treatment
Isolated incident
Age and/or lack of maturity where it affects the responsibility of the offender
Lapse of time since the offence where this is not the fault of the offender
Mental disorder or learning disability, where **not** linked to the commission of the offence
Sole or primary carer for dependent relatives
Section 29 offences only: The court should determine the appropriate sentence for the offence without taking account of the element of aggravation and then make an addition to the sentence, considering the level of aggravation involved. It may be appropriate to move outside the identified category range, taking into account the increased statutory maximum.

STEP THREE Consider any other factors which indicate a reduction, such as assistance to the prosecution The court should take into account any rule of law by virtue of which an offender may receive a discounted sentence in consequence of assistance given (or offered) to the prosecutor or investigator.

STEP FOUR Reduction for guilty pleas The court should take account of any potential reduction for a guilty plea in accordance with section 144 of the Criminal Justice Act 2003 and the *Guilty Plea* guideline.

STEP FIVE Dangerousness Inflicting grievous bodily harm/Unlawful wounding and racially/religiously aggravated GBH/Unlawful wounding are specified offences within the meaning of Chapter 5 of the Criminal Justice Act 2003 and at this stage the court should consider whether having regard to the criteria contained in that Chapter it would be appropriate to award an extended sentence.

STEP SIX Totality principle If sentencing an offender for more than one offence, or where the offender is already serving a sentence, consider whether the total sentence is just and proportionate to the offending behaviour.

STEP SEVEN Compensation and ancillary orders In all cases, the court should consider whether to make compensation and/or other ancillary orders.

STEP EIGHT Reasons Section 174 of the Criminal Justice Act 2003 imposes a duty to give reasons for, and explain the effect of, the sentence.

STEP NINE Consideration for remand time   Sentencers should take into consideration any remand time served in relation to the final sentence. The court should consider whether to give credit for time spent on remand in custody or on bail in accordance with sections 240 and 240A of the Criminal Justice Act 2003.

[Ed 1] Where the defendant had ridden a stolen moped into a uniformed police officer who was standing in the road, instructing him to stop, and the officer had suffered a fractured ankle and torn ligaments in his knee, those injuries were of the normal level which constituted grievous bodily harm and not of the level of severity to bring the case within category 1: *R v McIntosh* [2014] EWCA Crim 1003, [2014] 2 Cr App R (S) 64.

[Ed 2] Not every victim of domestic violence is 'particularly vulnerable': see *R v Thomas* [2014] EWCA Crim 1715, [2015] 1 Cr App R (S) 3. See also *R v Maloney* [2015] EWCA Crim 798, [2015] 2 Cr App R (S) 32, [2015] Crim LR 831 where the victim of the assault, the defendant's girlfriend, was seven months pregnant; this constituted 'greater harm' but not 'higher culpability' since the defendant had not deliberately targeted the offender because she was vulnerable.

[Ed 3] Causing injury by biting falls within use of 'weapon equivalent': *R v Thompson* [2015] EWCA Crim 1575, [2016] Cr App R (S) 26.

ASSAULT OCCASIONING ACTUAL BODILY HARM
Offences against the Person Act 1861 (section 47)

RACIALLY/RELIGIOUSLY AGGRAVATED ABH
Crime and Disorder Act 1998 (section 29)

These are specified offences for the purposes of section 224 of the Criminal Justice Act 2003
Triable either way
Section 47
Maximum when tried summarily: Level 5 fine and/or 26 weeks' custody
Maximum when tried on indictment: 5 years' custody
Section 29
Maximum when tried summarily: Level 5 fine and/or 26 weeks' custody
Maximum when tried on indictment: 7 years' custody
Offence range: Fine — 3 years' custody
This guideline applies to all offenders aged 18 and older, who are sentenced on or after 13 June 2011. The definitions at [page 145] of 'starting point' and 'first time offender' do not apply for this guideline. Starting point and category ranges apply to all offenders in all cases, irrespective of plea or previous convictions.
STEP ONE Determining the offence category   The court should determine the offence category using the table below.

Category 1	Greater harm (serious injury must normally be present) **and** higher culpability
Category 2	Greater harm (serious injury must normally be present) **and** lower culpability;
	or lesser harm **and** higher culpability
Category 3	Lesser harm **and** lower culpability

The court should determine the offender's culpability and the harm caused, or intended, by reference **only** to the factors identified in the table below (as demonstrated by the presence of one or more). These factors comprise the principal factual elements of the offence and should determine the category.

Factors indicating greater harm   Injury (which includes disease transmission and/or psychological harm) which is serious in the context of the offence (must normally be present)
   Victim is particularly vulnerable[Ed 1] because of personal circumstances
   Sustained or repeated assault on the same victim
Factors indicating lesser harm   Injury which is less serious in the context of the offence
Factors indicating higher culpability   *Statutory aggravating factors:*
   Offence motivated by, or demonstrating, hostility to the victim based on his or her sexual orientation (or presumed sexual orientation)
   Offence motivated by, or demonstrating, hostility to the victim based on the victim's disability (or presumed disability)
   Other aggravating factors:
   A significant degree of premeditation
   Use of weapon or weapon equivalent (for example, shod foot, headbutting, use of acid, use of animal)
   Intention to commit more serious harm than actually resulted from the offence
   Deliberately causes more harm than is necessary for commission of offence
   Deliberate targeting of vulnerable victim
   Leading role in group or gang
   Offence motivated by, or demonstrating, hostility based on the victim's age, sex, gender identity (or presumed gender identity)
Factors indicating lower culpability   Subordinate role in group or gang
   A greater degree of provocation than normally expected
   Lack of premeditation
   Mental disorder or learning disability, where linked to commission of the offence
   Excessive self defence
STEP TWO Starting point and category range   Having determined the category, the court should use the corresponding starting points to reach a sentence within the category range below. The starting point applies to all offenders irrespective of plea or previous convictions. A case of particular gravity, reflected by multiple features of culpability in step one, could merit upward adjustment from the starting point before further adjustment for aggravating or mitigating features, set out below.

Offence Category	Starting Point *(Applicable to all offenders)*	Category Range *(Applicable to all offenders)*
Category 1	Crown Court	Crown Court
Category 2	26 weeks' custody	Low level community order – Crown Court (51 weeks' custody)

Offence Category	Starting Point *(Applicable to all offenders)*	Category Range *(Applicable to all offenders)*
Category 3	Medium level community order	Band A fine – High level community order

The table below contains a **non-exhaustive** list of additional factual elements providing the context of the offence and factors relating to the offender. Identify whether any combination of these, or other relevant factors, should result in an upward or downward adjustment from the starting point. In some cases, having considered these factors, it may be appropriate to move outside the identified category range.

When sentencing **category 2** offences, the court should also consider the custody threshold as follows:

- has the custody threshold been passed?
- if so, is it unavoidable that a custodial sentence be imposed?
- if so, can that sentence be suspended?

When sentencing **category 3** offences, the court should also consider the community order threshold as follows:

- has the community order threshold been passed?

Factors increasing seriousness *Statutory aggravating factors:*
Previous convictions, having regard to a) the nature of the offence to which the conviction relates and its relevance to the current offence; and b) the time that has elapsed since the conviction
Offence committed whilst on bail
Other aggravating factors include:
Location of the offence
Timing of the offence
Ongoing effect upon the victim
Offence committed against those working in the public sector or providing a service to the public
Presence of others including relatives, especially children or partner of the victim
Gratuitous degradation of victim
In domestic violence cases, victim forced to leave their home
Failure to comply with current court orders
Offence committed whilst on licence
An attempt to conceal or dispose of evidence
Failure to respond to warnings or concerns expressed by others about the offender's behaviour
Commission of offence whilst under the influence of alcohol or drugs
Abuse of power and/or position of trust
Exploiting contact arrangements with a child to commit an offence
Established evidence of community impact
Any steps taken to prevent the victim reporting an incident, obtaining assistance and/or from assisting or supporting the prosecution
Offences taken into consideration (TICs)
Factors reducing seriousness or reflecting personal mitigation No previous convictions **or** no relevant/recent convictions
Single blow
Remorse
Good character and/or exemplary conduct
Determination and/or demonstration of steps taken to address addiction or offending behaviour
Serious medical conditions requiring urgent, intensive or long-term treatment
Isolated incident
Age and/or lack of maturity where it affects the responsibility of the offender
Lapse of time since the offence where this is not the fault of the offender
Mental disorder or learning disability, where **not** linked to the commission of the offence
Sole or primary carer for dependent relatives
Section 29 offences only: The court should determine the appropriate sentence for the offence without taking account of the element of aggravation and then make an addition to the sentence, considering the level of aggravation involved. It may be appropriate to move outside the identified category range, taking into account the increased statutory maximum.
STEP THREE Consider any other factors which indicate a reduction, such as assistance to the prosecution The court should take into account any rule of law by virtue of which an offender may receive a discounted sentence in consequence of assistance given (or offered) to the prosecutor or investigator.
STEP FOUR Reduction for guilty pleas The court should take account of any potential reduction for a guilty plea in accordance with section 144 of the Criminal Justice Act 2003 and the *Guilty Plea* guideline.
STEP FIVE Dangerousness Assault occasioning actual bodily harm and racially/religiously aggravated ABH are specified offences within the meaning of Chapter 5 of the Criminal Justice Act 2003 and at this stage the court should consider whether having regard to the criteria contained in that Chapter it would be appropriate to award an extended sentence.
STEP SIX Totality principle If sentencing an offender for more than one offence, or where the offender is already serving a sentence, consider whether the total sentence is just and proportionate to the offending behaviour.
STEP SEVEN Compensation and ancillary orders In all cases, the court should consider whether to make compensation and/or other ancillary orders.

STEP EIGHT Reasons Section 174 of the Criminal Justice Act 2003 imposes a duty to give reasons for, and explain the effect of, the sentence.

STEP NINE Consideration for remand time Sentencers should take into consideration any remand time served in relation to the final sentence. The court should consider whether to give credit for time spent on remand in custody or on bail in accordance with sections 240 and 240A of the Criminal Justice Act 2003.

Ed 1 The fact that the victim struck the first blow does not mean that he ceased to be vulnerable: *R v Halane* [2014] EWCA Crim 477, [2014] 2 Cr App R (S) 46. Not every victim of domestic violence is 'particularly vulnerable': see *R v Thomas* [2014] EWCA Crim 1715, [2015] 1 Cr App R (S) 3.

ASSAULT WITH INTENT TO RESIST ARREST
Offences against the Person Act 1861 (section 38)
This is a specified offence for the purposes of section 224 of the Criminal Justice Act 2003
Triable either way
Maximum when tried summarily: Level 5 fine and/or 26 weeks' custody
Maximum when tried on indictment: 2 years' custody
Offence range: Fine — 51 weeks' custody
This guideline applies to all offenders aged 18 and older, who are sentenced on or after 13 June 2011. The definitions at [page 145] of 'starting point' and 'first time offender' do not apply for this guideline. Starting point and category ranges apply to all offenders in all cases, irrespective of plea or previous convictions.

STEP ONE Determining the offence category   The court should determine the offence category using the table below.

Category 1	Greater harm **and** higher culpability
Category 2	Greater harm **and** lower culpability; **or** lesser harm **and** higher culpability
Category 3	Lesser harm **and** lower culpability

The court should determine the offender's culpability and the harm caused, or intended, by reference **only** to the factors identified in the table below (as demonstrated by the presence of one or more). These factors comprise the principal factual elements of the offence and should determine the category.

Factors indicating greater harm   Sustained or repeated assault on the same victim
Factors indicating lesser harm   Injury which is less serious in the context of the offence
Factors indicating higher culpability   *Statutory aggravating factors:*
     Offence racially or religiously aggravated
     Offence motivated by, or demonstrating, hostility to the victim based on his or her sexual orientation (or presumed sexual orientation)
     Offence motivated by, or demonstrating, hostility to the victim based on the victim's disability (or presumed disability)
     Other aggravating factors:
     A significant degree of premeditation
     Use of weapon or weapon equivalent (for example, shod foot, headbutting, use of acid, use of animal)
     Intention to commit more serious harm than actually resulted from the offence
     Deliberately causes more harm than is necessary for commission of offence
     Leading role in group or gang
     Offence motivated by, or demonstrating, hostility based on the victim's age, sex, gender identity (or presumed gender identity)
Factors indicating lower culpability   Subordinate role in group or gang
     Lack of premeditation
     Mental disorder or learning disability, where linked to commission of the offence

STEP TWO Starting point and category range   Having determined the category, the court should use the corresponding starting points to reach a sentence within the category range below. The starting point applies to all offenders irrespective of plea or previous convictions. A case of particular gravity, reflected by multiple features of culpability in step one, could merit upward adjustment from the starting point before further adjustment for aggravating or mitigating features, set out below.

Offence Category	Starting Point *(Applicable to all offenders)*	Category Range *(Applicable to all offenders)*
Category 1	26 weeks' custody	12 weeks' custody - Crown Court (51 weeks' custody)
Category 2	Medium level community order	Low level community order — High level community order
Category 3	Band B fine	Band A fine — Band C fine

The table below contains a **non-exhaustive** list of additional factual elements providing the context of the offence and factors relating to the offender. Identify whether any combination of these, or other relevant factors, should result in an upward or downward adjustment from the starting point. In some cases, having considered these factors, it may be appropriate to move outside the identified category range.

When sentencing **category 1** offences, the court should consider whether the sentence can be suspended.

Factors increasing seriousness   *Statutory aggravating factors:*
     Previous convictions, having regard to a) the nature of the offence to which the conviction relates and its relevance to the current offence; and b) the time that has elapsed since the conviction
     Offence committed whilst on bail
     Other aggravating factors include:

Location of the offence
Timing of the offence
Ongoing effect upon the victim
Gratuitous degradation of victim
Failure to comply with current court orders
Offence committed whilst on licence
An attempt to conceal or dispose of evidence
Failure to respond to warnings or concerns expressed by others about the offender's behaviour
Commission of offence whilst under the influence of alcohol or drugs
Established evidence of community impact
Any steps taken to prevent the victim reporting an incident, obtaining assistance and/or from assisting or supporting the prosecution
Offences taken into consideration (TICs)

Factors reducing seriousness or reflecting personal mitigation   No previous convictions **or** no relevant/recent convictions
Single blow
Remorse
Good character and/or exemplary conduct
Determination and/or demonstration of steps taken to address addiction or offending behaviour
Serious medical conditions requiring urgent, intensive or long-term treatment
Isolated incident
Age and/or lack of maturity where it affects the responsibility of the defendant
Mental disorder or learning disability, where **not** linked to the commission of the offence
Sole or primary carer for dependent relatives

STEP THREE Consider any other factors which indicate a reduction, such as assistance to the prosecution   The court should take into account any rule of law by virtue of which an offender may receive a discounted sentence in consequence of assistance given (or offered) to the prosecutor or investigator.

STEP FOUR Reduction for guilty pleas   The court should take account of any potential reduction for a guilty plea in accordance with section 144 of the Criminal Justice Act 2003 and the *Guilty Plea* guideline.

STEP FIVE Dangerousness   Assault with intent to resist arrest is a specified offence within the meaning of Chapter 5 of the Criminal Justice Act 2003 and at this stage the court should consider whether having regard to the criteria contained in that Chapter it would be appropriate to award an extended sentence.

STEP SIX Totality principle   If sentencing an offender for more than one offence or where the offender is already serving a sentence, consider whether the total sentence is just and proportionate to the offending behaviour.

STEP SEVEN Compensation and ancillary orders   In all cases, the court should consider whether to make compensation and/or other ancillary orders.

STEP EIGHT Reasons   Section 174 of the Criminal Justice Act 2003 imposes a duty to give reasons for, and explain the effect of, the sentence.

STEP NINE Consideration for remand time   Sentencers should take into consideration any remand time served in relation to the final sentence. The court should consider whether to give credit for time spent on remand in custody or on bail in accordance with sections 240 and 240A of the Criminal Justice Act 2003.

ASSAULT ON A POLICE CONSTABLE IN EXECUTION OF HIS DUTY
Police Act 1996 (section 89)

Triable only summarily
Maximum: Level 5 fine and/or 26 weeks' custody
Offence range: Fine — 26 weeks' custody
This guideline applies to all offenders aged 18 and older, who are sentenced on or after 13 June 2011. The definitions at [page 145] of 'starting point' and 'first time offender' do not apply for this guideline. Starting point and category ranges apply to all offenders in all cases, irrespective of plea or previous convictions.

STEP ONE Determining the offence category   The court should determine the offence category using the table below.

Category 1	Greater harm **and** higher culpability
Category 2	Greater harm **and** lower culpability; **or** lesser harm **and** higher culpability
Category 3	Lesser harm **and** lower culpability

The court should determine the offender's culpability and the harm caused, or intended, by reference **only** to the factors below (as demonstrated by the presence of one or more). These factors comprise the principal factual elements of the offence and should determine the category.
Factors indicating greater harm   Sustained or repeated assault on the same victim
Factors indicating lesser harm   Injury which is less serious in the context of the offence
Factors indicating higher culpability   *Statutory aggravating factors:*
   Offence racially or religiously aggravated
   Offence motivated by, or demonstrating, hostility to the victim based on his or her sexual orientation (or presumed sexual orientation)
   Offence motivated by, or demonstrating, hostility to the victim based on the victim's disability (or presumed disability)
   Other aggravating factors:
   A significant degree of premeditation
   Use of weapon or weapon equivalent (for example, shod foot, headbutting, use of acid, use of animal)
   Intention to commit more serious harm than actually resulted from the offence
   Deliberately causes more harm than is necessary for commission of offence
   Leading role in group or gang
   Offence motivated by, or demonstrating, hostility based on the victim's age, sex, gender identity (or presumed gender identity)
Factors indicating lower culpability   Subordinate role in group or gang
   Lack of premeditation
   Mental disorder or learning disability, where linked to commission of the offence

STEP TWO Starting point and category range   Having determined the category, the court should use the corresponding starting points to reach a sentence within the category range below. The starting point applies to all offenders irrespective of plea or previous convictions. A case of particular gravity, reflected by multiple features of culpability in step one, could merit upward adjustment from the starting point before further adjustment for aggravating or mitigating features, set out below.

Offence Category	**Starting Point** *(Applicable to all offenders)*	**Category Range** *(Applicable to all offenders)*
Category 1	12 weeks' custody	Low level community order – 26 weeks' custody
Category 2	Medium level community order	Low level community order – High level community order
Category 3	Band B fine	Band A fine – Band C fine

The table below contains a **non-exhaustive** list of additional factual elements providing the context of the offence and factors relating to the offender. Identify whether any combination of these, or other relevant factors, should result in an upward or downward adjustment from the starting point. In some cases, having considered these factors, it may be appropriate to move outside the identified category range.

When sentencing **category 1** offences, the court should also consider the custody threshold as follows:

- has the custody threshold been passed?
- if so, is it unavoidable that a custodial sentence be imposed?
- if so, can that sentence be suspended?

Factors increasing seriousness   *Statutory aggravating factors:*
Previous convictions, having regard to a) the nature of the offence to which the conviction relates and its relevance to the current offence; and b) the time that has elapsed since the conviction
Offence committed whilst on bail

Other aggravating factors include:
Location of the offence
Timing of the offence
Ongoing effect upon the victim
Gratuitous degradation of victim
Failure to comply with current court orders
Offence committed whilst on licence
An attempt to conceal or dispose of evidence
Failure to respond to warnings or concerns expressed by others about the offender's behaviour
Commission of offence whilst under the influence of alcohol or drugs
Established evidence of community impact
Any steps taken to prevent the victim reporting an incident, obtaining assistance and/or from assisting or supporting the prosecution
Offences taken into consideration (TICs)

Factors reducing seriousness or reflecting personal mitigation No previous convictions **or** no relevant/recent convictions
Single blow
Remorse
Good character and/or exemplary conduct
Determination and/or demonstration of steps taken to address addiction or offending behaviour
Serious medical conditions requiring urgent, intensive or long-term treatment
Isolated incident
Age and/or lack of maturity where it affects the responsibility of the offender
Lapse of time since the offence where this is not the fault of the offender
Mental disorder or learning disability, where **not** linked to the commission of the offence
Sole or primary carer for dependent relatives

STEP THREE Consider any other factors which indicate a reduction, such as assistance to the prosecution The court should take into account any rule of law by virtue of which an offender may receive a discounted sentence in consequence of assistance given (or offered) to the prosecutor or investigator.

STEP FOUR Reduction for guilty pleas The court should take account of any potential reduction for a guilty plea in accordance with section 144 of the Criminal Justice Act 2003 and the *Guilty Plea* guideline.

STEP FIVE Totality principle If sentencing an offender for more than one offence, or where the offender is already serving a sentence, consider whether the total sentence is just and proportionate to the offending behaviour.

STEP SIX Compensation and ancillary orders In all cases, courts should consider whether to make compensation and/or other ancillary orders.

STEP SEVEN Reasons Section 174 of the Criminal Justice Act 2003 imposes a duty to give reasons for, and explain the effect of, the sentence.

STEP EIGHT Consideration for remand time Sentencers should take into consideration any remand time served in relation to the final sentence. The court should consider whether to give credit for time spent on remand in custody or on bail in accordance with sections 240 and 240A of the Criminal Justice Act 2003.

COMMON ASSAULT
Criminal Justice Act 1988 (section 39)

RACIALLY/RELIGIOUSLY AGGRAVATED COMMON ASSAULT
Crime and Disorder Act 1998 (section 29)

Racially/religiously aggravated assault is a specified offence for the purposes of section 224 of the Criminal Justice Act 2003
Section 39
Triable only summarily
Maximum when tried summarily: Level 5 fine and/or 26 weeks' custody
Section 29 Triable either way
Maximum when tried summarily: Level 5 fine and/or 26 weeks' custody
Maximum when tried on indictment: 2 years' custody
Offence range: Discharge — 26 weeks' custody
This guideline applies to all offenders aged 18 and older, who are sentenced on or after 13 June 2011. The definitions at [page 145] of 'starting point' and 'first time offender' do not apply for this guideline. Starting point and category ranges apply to all offenders in all cases, irrespective of plea or previous convictions.

STEP ONE Determining the offence category   The court should determine the offence category using the table below.

Category 1	Greater harm (injury or fear of injury must normally be present) **and** higher culpability
Category 2	Greater harm (injury or fear of injury must normally be present) **and** lower culpability;
	or lesser harm and higher culpability
Category 3	Lesser harm **and** lower culpability

The court should determine the offender's culpability and the harm caused, or intended, by reference **only** to the factors below (as demonstrated by the presence of one or more). These factors comprise the principal factual elements of the offence and should determine the category.
Factors indicating greater harm   Injury or fear of injury which is serious in the context of the offence (must normally be present)
   Victim is particularly vulnerable because of personal circumstances
   Sustained or repeated assault on the same victim
Factors indicating lesser harm   Injury which is less serious in the context of the offence
Factors indicating higher culpability   *Statutory aggravating factors:*
   Offence motivated by, or demonstrating, hostility to the victim based on his or her sexual orientation (or presumed sexual orientation)
   Offence motivated by, or demonstrating, hostility to the victim based on the victim's disability (or presumed disability)
   Other aggravating factors:
   A significant degree of premeditation
   Threatened or actual use of weapon or weapon equivalent (for example, shod foot, headbutting, use of acid, use of animal)
   Intention to commit more serious harm than actually resulted from the offence
   Deliberately causes more harm than is necessary for commission of offence
   Deliberate targeting of vulnerable victim
   Leading role in group or gang
   Offence motivated by, or demonstrating, hostility based on the victim's age, sex, gender identity (or presumed gender identity)
Factors indicating lower culpability   Subordinate role in group or gang
   A greater degree of provocation than normally expected
   Lack of premeditation
   Mental disorder or learning disability, where linked to commission of the offence
   Excessive self defence

STEP TWO Starting point and category range   Having determined the category, the court should use the corresponding starting points to reach a sentence within the category range below. The starting point applies to all offenders irrespective of plea or previous convictions. A case of particular gravity, reflected by multiple features of culpability in step one, could merit upward adjustment from the starting point before further adjustment for aggravating or mitigating features, set out below.

Offence Category	**Starting Point** (Applicable to all offenders)	**Category Range** (Applicable to all offenders)
Category 1	High level community order	Low level community order – 26 weeks' custody
Category 2	Medium level community order	Band A fine – High level community order

Offence Category	Starting Point *(Applicable to all offenders)*	Category Range *(Applicable to all offenders)*
Category 3	Band A fine	Discharge – Band C fine

The table below contains a **non-exhaustive** list of additional factual elements providing the context of the offence and factors relating to the offender. Identify whether any combination of these, or other relevant factors, should result in an upward or downward adjustment from the starting point. In some cases, having considered these factors, it may be appropriate to move outside the identified category range.

When sentencing **category 1** offences, the court should also consider the custody threshold as follows:

- has the custody threshold been passed?
- if so, is it unavoidable that a custodial sentence be imposed?
- if so, can that sentence be suspended?

When sentencing **category 2** offences, the court should also consider the community order threshold as follows:

- has the community order threshold been passed?

Factors increasing seriousness *Statutory aggravating factors:*
Previous convictions, having regard to a) the nature of the offence to which the conviction relates and its relevance to the current offence; and b) the time that has elapsed since the conviction
Offence committed whilst on bail
Other aggravating factors include:
Location of the offence
Timing of the offence
Ongoing effect upon the victim
Offence committed against those working in the public sector or providing a service to the public
Presence of others including relatives, especially children or partner of the victim
Gratuitous degradation of victim
In domestic violence cases, victim forced to leave their home
Failure to comply with current court orders
Offence committed whilst on licence
An attempt to conceal or dispose of evidence
Failure to respond to warnings or concerns expressed by others about the offender's behaviour
Commission of offence whilst under the influence of alcohol or drugs
Abuse of power and/or position of trust
Exploiting contact arrangements with a child to commit an offence
Established evidence of community impact
Any steps taken to prevent the victim reporting an incident, obtaining assistance and/or from assisting or supporting the prosecution
Offences taken into consideration (TICs)
Factors reducing seriousness or reflecting personal mitigation No previous convictions **or** no relevant/recent convictions
Single blow
Remorse
Good character and/or exemplary conduct
Determination and/or demonstration of steps taken to address addiction or offending behaviour
Serious medical conditions requiring urgent, intensive or long-term treatment
Isolated incident
Age and/or lack of maturity where it affects the responsibility of the offender
Lapse of time since the offence where this is not the fault of the offender
Mental disorder or learning disability, where **not** linked to the commission of the offence
Sole or primary carer for dependent relatives
Section 29 offences only: The court should determine the appropriate sentence for the offence without taking account of the element of aggravation and then make an addition to the sentence, considering the level of aggravation involved. It may be appropriate to move outside the identified category range, taking into account the increased statutory maximum.

STEP THREE Consider any other factors which indicate a reduction, such as assistance to the prosecution The court should take into account any rule of law by virtue of which an offender may receive a discounted sentence in consequence of assistance given (or offered) to the prosecutor or investigator.

STEP FOUR Reduction for guilty pleas The court should take account of any potential reduction for a guilty plea in accordance with section 144 of the Criminal Justice Act 2003 and the *Guilty Plea* guideline.

STEP FIVE Dangerousness Racially/religiously aggravated common assault is a specified offence within the meaning of Chapter 5 of the Criminal Justice Act 2003 and at this stage the court should consider whether having regard to the criteria contained in that Chapter it would be appropriate to award an extended sentence.

STEP SIX Totality principle   If sentencing an offender for more than one offence, or where the offender is already serving a sentence, consider whether the total sentence is just and proportionate to the offending behaviour.

STEP SEVEN Compensation and ancillary orders   In all cases, the court should consider whether to make compensation and/or other ancillary orders.

STEP EIGHT Reasons   Section 174 of the Criminal Justice Act 2003 imposes a duty to give reasons for, and explain the effect of, the sentence.

STEP NINE Consideration for remand time   Sentencers should take into consideration any remand time served in relation to the final sentence. The court should consider whether to give credit for time spent on remand in custody or on bail in accordance with sections 240 and 240A of the Criminal Justice Act 2003.

DOMESTIC BURGLARY
Theft Act 1968 (section 9)

This is a serious specified offence for the purposes of section 224 Criminal Justice Act 2003 if it was committed with intent to:

(a) **inflict grievous bodily harm on a person, or**
(b) **do unlawful damage to a building or anything in it.**

Triable either way
Maximum when tried summarily: Level 5 fine and/or 26 weeks' custody
Maximum when tried on indictment: 14 years' custody
Offence range: Community order — 6 years' custody

Where sentencing an offender for a qualifying **third domestic burglary**, the Court must apply Section 111 of the Powers of the Criminal Courts (Sentencing) Act 2000 and impose a custodial term of at least three years, unless it is satisfied that there are particular circumstances which relate to any of the offences or to the offender which would make it unjust to do so.

This guideline applies to all offenders aged 18 and older, who are sentenced on or after 16 January 2012. The definitions at [page 145] of 'starting point' and 'first time offender' do not apply for this guideline. Starting point and category ranges apply to all offenders in all cases, irrespective of plea or previous convictions.

STEP ONE Determining the offence category   The court should determine the offence category using the table below.

Category 1	Greater harm **and** higher culpability
Category 2	Greater harm **and** lower culpability **or** lesser harm **and** higher culpability
Category 3	Lesser harm **and** lower culpability

The court should determine culpability and harm caused or intended, by reference **only** to the factors below, which comprise the principal factual elements of the offence. Where an offence does not fall squarely into a category, individual factors may require a degree of weighting before making an overall assessment and determining the appropriate offence category.

Factors indicating greater harm   Theft of/damage to property causing a significant degree of loss to the victim (whether economic, sentimental or personal value)
   Soiling, ransacking or vandalism of property
   Occupier at home (or returns home) while offender present
   Trauma to the victim, beyond the normal inevitable consequence of intrusion and theft
   Violence used or threatened against victim
   Context of general public disorder

Factors indicating lesser harm   Nothing stolen or only property of very low value to the victim (whether economic, sentimental or personal)
   Limited damage or disturbance to property

Factors indicating higher culpability   Victim or premises deliberately targeted (for example, due to vulnerability or hostility based on disability, race, sexual orientation)
   A significant degree of planning or organisation
   Knife or other weapon carried (where not charged separately)
   Equipped for burglary (for example, implements carried and/or use of vehicle)
   Member of a group or gang

Factors indicating lower culpability   Offence committed on impulse, with limited intrusion into property
   Offender exploited by others
   Mental disorder or learning disability, where linked to the commission of the offence

STEP TWO Starting point and category range   Having determined the category, the court should use the corresponding starting points to reach a sentence within the category range below. The starting point applies to all offenders irrespective of plea or previous convictions.

Where the defendant is dependant on or has a propensity to misuse drugs and there is sufficient prospect of success, a community order with a drug rehabilitation requirement under section 209 of the Criminal Justice Act 2003 may be a proper alternative to a short or moderate custodial sentence.

A case of particular gravity, reflected by multiple features of culpability or harm in step 1, could merit upward adjustment from the starting point before further adjustment for aggravating or mitigating features, set out on the next page.

Offence Category	Starting Point *(Applicable to all offenders)*	Category Range *(Applicable to all offenders)*
Category 1	Crown Court	Crown Court
Category 2	1 year's custody	High level community order – Crown Court (2 years' custody)
Category 3	High Level Community Order	Low level community order – 26 weeks' custody

The table below contains a **non-exhaustive** list of additional factual elements providing the context of the offence and factors relating to the offender. Identify whether any combination of these, or other relevant factors, should result in an upward or downward adjustment from the starting point. **In particular, relevant recent convictions are likely to result in an upward adjustment.** In some cases, having considered these factors, it may be appropriate to move outside the identified category range.

When sentencing **category 2 or 3** offences, the court should also consider the custody threshold as follows:

- has the custody threshold been passed?
- if so, is it unavoidable that a custodial sentence be imposed?
- if so, can that sentence be suspended?

Factors increasing seriousness   *Statutory aggravating factors:*
Previous convictions, having regard to a) the nature of the offence to which the conviction relates and its relevance to the current offence; and b) the time that has elapsed since the conviction[*]
Offence committed whilst on bail
Other aggravating factors include:
Child at home (or returns home) when offence committed
Offence committed at night
Gratuitous degradation of the victim
Any steps taken to prevent the victim reporting the incident or obtaining assistance and/or from assisting or supporting the prosecution
Victim compelled to leave their home (in particular victims of domestic violence)
Established evidence of community impact
Commission of offence whilst under the influence of alcohol or drugs
Failure to comply with current court orders
Offence committed whilst on licence
Offences Taken Into Consideration (TICs)

Factors reducing seriousness or reflecting personal mitigation   Offender has made voluntary reparation to the victim
Subordinate role in a group or gang
No previous convictions **or** no relevant/recent convictions
Remorse
Good character and/or exemplary conduct
Determination, and/or demonstration of steps taken to address addiction or offending behaviour
Serious medical conditions requiring urgent, intensive or long-term treatment
Age and/or lack of maturity where it affects the responsibility of the offender
Lapse of time since the offence where this is not the fault of the offender
Mental disorder or learning disability, where not linked to the commission of the offence
Sole or primary carer for dependent relatives

---

[*] Where sentencing an offender for a qualifying **third domestic burglary**, the Court must apply Section 111 of the Powers of the Criminal Courts (Sentencing) Act 2000 and impose a custodial term of at least three years, unless it is satisfied that there are particular circumstances which relate to any of the offences or to the offender which would make it unjust to do so.

STEP THREE Consider any factors which indicate a reduction, such as assistance to the prosecution
The court should take into account any rule of law by virtue of which an offender may receive a discounted sentence in consequence of assistance given (or offered) to the prosecutor or investigator.

STEP FOUR Reduction for guilty pleas   The court should take account of any potential reduction for a guilty plea in accordance with section 144 of the Criminal Justice Act 2003 and the *Guilty Plea* guideline.
Where a minimum mandatory sentence is imposed under section 111 Powers of Criminal Courts (Sentencing) Act, the discount for an early guilty plea must not exceed 20 per cent.

STEP FIVE Dangerousness   A burglary offence under section 9 Theft Act 1986 is a serious specified offence within the meaning of chapter 5 of the Criminal Justice Act 2003 if it was committed with the intent to (a) inflict grievous bodily harm on a person, or (b) do unlawful damage to a building or anything in it. The court should consider whether having regard to the criteria contained in that chapter it would be appropriate to award imprisonment for public protection or an extended sentence. Where offenders meet the dangerousness criteria, the notional determinate sentence should be used as the basis for the setting of a minimum term.

STEP SIX Totality principle   If sentencing an offender for more than one offence, or where the offender is already serving a sentence, consider whether the total sentence is just and proportionate to the offending behaviour.

STEP SEVEN Compensation and ancillary orders   In all cases, courts should consider whether to make compensation and/or other ancillary orders.

STEP EIGHT Reasons   Section 174 of the Criminal Justice Act 2003 imposes a duty to give reasons for, and explain the effect of, the sentence.

Consideration for remand time

STEP NINE   Sentencers should take into consideration any remand time served in relation to the final sentence at this final step. The court should consider whether to give credit for time spent on remand in custody or on bail in accordance with sections 240 and 240A of the Criminal Justice Act 2003.

NON-DOMESTIC BURGLARY
Theft Act 1968 (section 9)

This is a serious specified offence for the purposes of section 224 Criminal Justice Act 2003 if it was committed with intent to:

(a)   **inflict grievous bodily harm on a person, or**
(b)   **do unlawful damage to a building or anything in it.**

Triable either way
Maximum when tried summarily: Level 5 fine and/or 26 weeks' custody
Maximum when tried on indictment: 10 years' custody
Offence range: Fine — 5 years' custody

This guideline applies to all offenders aged 18 and older, who are sentenced on or after 16 January 2012. The definitions at [page 145] of 'starting point' and 'first time offender' do not apply for this guideline. Starting point and category ranges apply to all offenders in all cases, irrespective of plea or previous convictions.

STEP ONE Determining the offence category   The court should determine the offence category using the table below.

Category 1	Greater harm **and** higher culpability
Category 2	Greater harm **and** lower culpability **or** lesser harm **and** higher culpability
Category 3	Lesser harm **and** lower culpability

The court should determine culpability and harm caused or intended, by reference **only** to the factors below, which comprise the principal factual elements of the offence. Where an offence does not fall squarely into a category, individual factors may require a degree of weighting before making an overall assessment and determining the appropriate offence category.

Factors indicating greater harm   Theft of/damage to property causing a significant degree of loss to the victim (whether economic, commercial or personal value)

Soiling, ransacking or vandalism of property
Victim on the premises (or returns) while offender present
Trauma to the victim, beyond the normal inevitable consequence of intrusion and theft
Violence used or threatened against victim
Context of general public disorder

Factors indicating lesser harm   Nothing stolen or only property of very low value to the victim (whether economic, commercial or personal)

Limited damage or disturbance to property

Factors indicating higher culpability   Premises or victim deliberately targeted (to include pharmacy or doctor's surgery and targeting due to vulnerability of victim or hostility based on disability, race, sexual orientation and so forth)

A significant degree of planning or organisation
Knife or other weapon carried (where not charged separately)
Equipped for burglary (for example, implements carried and/or use of vehicle)
Member of a group or gang

Factors indicating lower culpability   Offence committed on impulse, with limited intrusion into property

Offender exploited by others
Mental disorder or learning disability, where linked to the commission of the offence

STEP TWO Starting point and category range   Having determined the category, the court should use the corresponding starting points to reach a sentence within the category range below. The starting point applies to all offenders irrespective of plea or previous convictions.

Where the defendant is dependant on or has a propensity to misuse drugs and there is sufficient prospect of success, a community order with a drug rehabilitation requirement under section 209 of the Criminal Justice Act 2003 may be a proper alternative to a short or moderate custodial sentence.

A case of particular gravity, reflected by multiple features of culpability or harm in step 1, could merit upward adjustment from the starting point before further adjustment for aggravating or mitigating features, set out on the next page.

Offence Category	Starting Point *(Applicable to all offenders)*	Category Range *(Applicable to all offenders)*
Category 1	Crown Court	Crown Court
Category 2	18 weeks' custody	Low level community order – Crown Court (51 weeks' custody)
Category 3	Medium level community order	Band B fine – 18 weeks' custody

The table below contains a **non-exhaustive** list of additional factual elements providing the context of the offence and factors relating to the offender. Identify whether any combination of these, or other relevant factors, should result in an upward or downward adjustment from the starting point. **In particular, relevant recent convictions are likely to result in an upward adjustment.** In some cases, having considered these factors, it may be appropriate to move outside the identified category range.

When sentencing **category 2 or 3** offences, the court should also consider the custody threshold as follows:

- has the custody threshold been passed?
- if so, is it unavoidable that a custodial sentence be imposed?
- if so, can that sentence be suspended?

When sentencing **category 3** offences, the court should also consider the community order threshold as follows:

- has the community order threshold been passed?

Factors increasing seriousness *Statutory aggravating factors:*
Previous convictions, having regard to a) the nature of the offence to which the conviction relates and its relevance to the current offence; and b) the time that has elapsed since the conviction
Offence committed whilst on bail
Other aggravating factors include:
Offence committed at night, particularly where staff present or likely to be present
Abuse of a position of trust
Gratuitous degradation of the victim
Any steps taken to prevent the victim reporting the incident or obtaining assistance and/or from assisting or supporting the prosecution
Established evidence of community impact
Commission of offence whilst under the influence of alcohol or drugs
Failure to comply with current court orders
Offence committed whilst on licence
Offences Taken Into Consideration (TICs)
Factors reducing seriousness or reflecting personal mitigation Offender has made voluntary reparation to the victim
Subordinate role in a group or gang
No previous convictions **or** no relevant/recent convictions
Remorse
Good character and/or exemplary conduct
Determination, and/or demonstration of steps taken to address addiction or offending behaviour
Serious medical conditions requiring urgent, intensive or long-term treatment
Age and/or lack of maturity where it affects the responsibility of the offender
Lapse of time since the offence where this is not the fault of the offender
Mental disorder or learning disability, where not linked to the commission of the offence
Sole or primary carer for dependent relatives

STEP THREE Consider any factors which indicate a reduction, such as assistance to the prosecution
The court should take into account any rule of law by virtue of which an offender may receive a discounted sentence in consequence of assistance given (or offered) to the prosecutor or investigator.

STEP FOUR Reduction for guilty pleas The court should take account of any potential reduction for a guilty plea in accordance with section 144 of the Criminal Justice Act 2003 and the *Guilty Plea* guideline.

STEP FIVE Dangerousness A burglary offence under section 9 of the Theft Act 1986 is a serious specified offence within the meaning of chapter5 of the Criminal Justice Act 2003 if it was committed with the intent to (a) inflict grievous bodily harm on a person, or (b) do unlawful damage to a building or anything in it. The court should consider whether having regard to the criteria contained in that chapter it would be appropriate to award imprisonment for public protection or an extended sentence. Where offenders meet the dangerousness criteria, the notional determinate sentence should be used as the basis for the setting of a minimum term.

STEP SIX Totality principle If sentencing an offender for more than one offence, or where the offender is already serving a sentence, consider whether the total sentence is just and proportionate to the offending behaviour.

STEP SEVEN Compensation and ancillary orders In all cases, courts should consider whether to make compensation and/or other ancillary orders.

STEP EIGHT Reasons Section 174 of the Criminal Justice Act 2003 imposes a duty to give reasons for, and explain the effect of, the sentence.

STEP NINE Consideration for remand time Sentencers should take into consideration any remand time served in relation to the final sentence at this final step. The court should consider whether to give credit for time spent on remand in custody or on bail in accordance with sections 240 and 240A of the Criminal Justice Act 2003.

FRAUDULENT EVASION OF A PROHIBITION BY BRINGING INTO OR TAKING OUT OF THE UK A CONTROLLED DRUG

Misuse of Drugs Act 1971 (section 3)
Customs and Excise Management Act 1979
(section 170(2))

Triable either way unless the defendant could receive the minimum sentence of seven years for a third drug trafficking offence under section 110 Powers of Criminal Courts (Sentencing) Act 2000 in which case the offence is triable only on indictment.

Class A

Maximum: Life imprisonment

Offence range: 3 years 6 months' – 16 years' custody

A class A offence is a drug trafficking offence for the purpose of imposing a minimum sentence under section 110 Powers of Criminal Courts (Sentencing) Act 2000

Class B

Maximum: 14 years' custody and/or unlimited fine

Offence range: 12 weeks' – 10 years' custody

Class C

Maximum: 14 years' custody and/or unlimited fine

Offence range: Community order – 8 years' custody

STEP ONE Determining the offence category   The court should determine the offender's culpability (role) and the harm caused (quantity) with reference to the tables below.

In assessing culpability, the sentencer should weigh up all the factors of the case to determine role. Where there are characteristics present which fall under different role categories, the court should balance these characteristics to reach a fair assessment of the offender's culpability.

In assessing harm, quantity is determined by the weight of the product. Purity is not taken into account at step 1 but is dealt with at step 2.

Where the operation is on the most serious and commercial scale, involving a quantity of drugs significantly higher than category 1, sentences of 20 years and above may be appropriate, depending on the role of the offender.

Culpability demonstrated by offender's role

One or more of these characteristics may demonstrate the offender's role. These lists are not exhaustive.

LEADING role:

- directing or organising buying and selling on a commercial scale;
- substantial links to, and influence on, others in a chain;
- close links to original source;
- expectation of substantial financial gain;
- uses business as cover;
- abuses a position of trust or responsibility.

SIGNIFICANT role:

- operational or management function within a chain;
- involves others in the operation whether by pressure, influence, intimidation or reward;
- motivated by financial or other advantage, whether or not operating alone;
- some awareness and understanding of scale of operation.

LESSER role:

- performs a limited function under direction;
- engaged by pressure, coercion, intimidation;
- involvement through naivety/exploitation;
- no influence on those above in a chain;
- very little, if any, awareness or understanding of the scale of operation;
- if own operation, solely for own use (considering reasonableness of account in all the circumstances).

Category of harm

Indicative quantity of drug concerned (upon which the starting point is based):

Category 1

- heroin, cocaine – 5kg;
- ecstasy – 10,000 tablets;
- LSD – 250,000 squares;
- amphetamine – 20kg;
- cannabis – 200kg;
- ketamine – 5kg.

Category 2

- heroin, cocaine – 1kg;
- ecstasy – 2,000 tablets;
- LSD – 25,000 squares;
- amphetamine – 4kg;
- cannabis – 40kg;
- ketamine – 1kg.

Category 3

- heroin, cocaine – 150g;
- ecstasy – 300 tablets;

- LSD – 2,500 squares;
- amphetamine – 750g;
- cannabis – 6kg;
- ketamine – 150g.

Category 4

- heroin, cocaine – 5g;
- ecstasy – 20 tablets;
- LSD – 170 squares;
- amphetamine – 20g;
- cannabis – 100g;
- ketamine – 5g.

STEP TWO Starting point and category range   Having determined the category, the court should use the corresponding starting point to reach a sentence within the category range below. The starting point applies to all offenders irrespective of plea or previous convictions. The court should then consider further adjustment within the category range for aggravating or mitigating features, set out over the page. In cases where the offender is regarded as being at the very top of the 'leading' role it may be justifiable for the court to depart from the guideline.

Where the defendant is dependent on or has a propensity to misuse drugs and there is sufficient prospect of success, a community order with a drug rehabilitation requirement under section 209 of the Criminal Justice Act 2003 can be a proper alternative to a short or moderate length custodial sentence.

For **class A** cases, section 110 of the Powers of Criminal Courts (Sentencing) Act 2000 provides that a court should impose a minimum sentence of at least seven years' imprisonment for a third class A trafficking offence except where the court is of the opinion that there are particular circumstances which (a) relate to any of the offences or to the offender; and (b) would make it unjust to do so in all the circumstances.

CLASS A	Leading role	Significant role	Lesser role
Category 1	**Starting point**	**Starting point**	**Starting point**
	14 years' custody	10 years' custody	8 years' custody
	Category range	**Category range**	**Category range**
	12 – 16 years' custody	9 – 12 years' custody	6 – 9 years' custody
Category 2	**Starting point**	**Starting point**	**Starting point**
	11 years' custody	8 years' custody	6 years' custody
	Category range	**Category range**	**Category range**
	9 – 13 years' custody	6 years 6 months' – 10 years' custody	5 – 7 years' custody
Category 3	**Starting point**	**Starting point**	**Starting point**
	8 years 6 months' custody	6 years 6 months' – 10 years' custody	4 years 6 months' custody
	Category range	**Category range**	**Category range**
	6 years' custody	5 – 7 years' custody	3 years 6 months' – 5 years' custody
Category 4	Where the quantity falls below the indicative amount set out for category 4 on the previous page, first identify the role for the importation offence, then refer to the starting point and ranges for possession or supply offences, depending on intent.		
	Where the quantity is significantly larger than the indicative amounts for category 4 but below category 3 amounts, refer to the category 3 ranges above.		

CLASS B	Leading role	Significant role	Lesser role
Category 1	**Starting point**	**Starting point**	**Starting point**
	8 years' custody	5 years 6 months' custody	4 years' custody
	Category range	**Category range**	**Category range**
	7 – 10 years' custody	5 – 7 years' custody	2 years 6 months' – 5 years' custody
Category 2	**Starting point**	**Starting point**	**Starting point**
	6 years' custody	4 years' custody	2 years' custody
	Category range	**Category range**	**Category range**
	4 years 6 months' – 8 years' custody	2 years 6 months' – 5 years' custody	18 months' – 3 years' custody
Category 3	**Starting point**	**Starting point**	**Starting point**

CLASS B	Leading role	Significant role	Lesser role
	4 years' custody	2 years' custody	1 year's custody
	Category range	**Category range**	**Category range**
	2 years 6 months' – 5 years' custody	18 months' – 3 years' custody	12 weeks' – 18 months' custody
Category 4	Where the quantity falls below the indicative amount set out for category 4 on the previous page, first identify the role for the importation offence, then refer to the starting point and ranges for possession or supply offences, depending on intent.		
	Where the quantity is significantly larger than the indicative amounts for category 4 but below category 3 amounts, refer to the category 3 ranges above.		

CLASS C	Leading role	Significant role	Lesser role
Category 1	**Starting point**	**Starting point**	**Starting point**
	5 years' custody	3 years' custody	18 months' custody
	Category range	**Category range**	**Category range**
	4 – 8 years' custody	2 – 5 years' custody	1 – 3 years' custody
Category 2	**Starting point**	**Starting point**	**Starting point**
	3 years 6 months' custody	18 months' custody	26 weeks' custody
	Category range	**Category range**	**Category range**
	2 – 5 years' custody	1 – 3 years' custody	12 weeks' – 18 months' custody
Category 3	**Starting point**	**Starting point**	**Starting point**
	18 months' custody	26 weeks' custody	High level community order
	Category range	**Category range**	**Category range**
	1 – 3 years' custody	12 weeks' – 18 months' custody	Medium level community order – 12 weeks' custody
Category 4	Where the quantity falls below the indicative amount set out for category 4 on the previous page, first identify the role for the importation offence, then refer to the starting point and ranges for possession or supply offences, depending on intent.		
	Where the quantity is significantly larger than the indicative amounts for category 4 but below category 3 amounts, refer to the category 3 ranges above.		

The table below contains a **non-exhaustive** list of additional factual elements providing the context of the offence and factors relating to the offender. Identify whether any combination of these, or other relevant factors, should result in an upward or downward adjustment from the starting point. In some cases, having considered these factors, it may be appropriate to move outside the identified category range.

For appropriate **class C** ranges, consider the custody threshold as follows:

- has the custody threshold been passed?
- if so, is it unavoidable that a custodial sentence be imposed?
- if so, can that sentence be suspended?

Factors increasing seriousness   *Statutory aggravating factors:*

Previous convictions, having regard to a) nature of the offence to which conviction relates and relevance to current offence; and b) time elapsed since conviction (see box at [page 227] if third drug trafficking conviction)

Offender used or permitted a person under 18 to deliver a controlled drug to a third person

Offence committed on bail

Other aggravating factors include:

Sophisticated nature of concealment and/or attempts to avoid detection

Attempts to conceal or dispose of evidence, where not charged separately

Exposure of others to more than usual danger, for example drugs cut with harmful substances

Presence of weapon, where not charged separately

High purity

Failure to comply with current court orders

Offence committed on licence

Factors reducing seriousness or reflecting personal mitigation   Lack of sophistication as to nature of concealment

Involvement due to pressure, intimidation or coercion falling short of duress, except where already taken into account at step 1

Mistaken belief of the offender regarding the type of drug, taking into account the reasonableness of such belief in all the circumstances

Isolated incident

Low purity
No previous convictions **or** no relevant or recent convictions
Offender's vulnerability was exploited
Remorse
Good character and/or exemplary conduct
Determination and/or demonstration of steps having been taken to address addiction or offending behaviour
Serious medical conditions requiring urgent, intensive or long-term treatment
Age and/or lack of maturity where it affects the responsibility of the offender
Mental disorder or learning disability
Sole or primary carer for dependent relatives

STEP THREE Consider any factors which indicate a reduction, such as assistance to the prosecution
The court should take into account sections 73 and 74 of the Serious Organised Crime and Police Act 2005 (assistance by defendants: reduction or review of sentence) and any other rule of law by virtue of which an offender may receive a discounted sentence in consequence of assistance given (or offered) to the prosecutor or investigator.

STEP FOUR Reduction for guilty pleas The court should take account of any potential reduction for a guilty plea in accordance with section 144 of the Criminal Justice Act 2003 and the *Guilty Plea* guideline.
For class A offences, where a minimum mandatory sentence is imposed under section 110 Powers of Criminal Courts (Sentencing) Act, the discount for an early guilty plea must not exceed 20 per cent.

STEP FIVE Totality principle If sentencing an offender for more than one offence, or where the offender is already serving a sentence, consider whether the total sentence is just and proportionate to the offending behaviour.

STEP SIX Confiscation and ancillary orders In all cases, the court is required to consider confiscation where the Crown invokes the process or where the court considers it appropriate. It should also consider whether to make ancillary orders.

STEP SEVEN Reasons Section 174 of the Criminal Justice Act 2003 imposes a duty to give reasons for, and explain the effect of, the sentence.

STEP EIGHT Consideration for remand time Sentencers should take into consideration any remand time served in relation to the final sentence at this final step. The court should consider whether to give credit for time spent on remand in custody or on bail in accordance with sections 240 and 240A of the Criminal Justice Act 2003.

SUPPLYING OR OFFERING TO SUPPLY A CONTROLLED DRUG

MISUSE OF DRUGS ACT 1971 (SECTION 4(3))

POSSESSION OF A CONTROLLED DRUG WITH INTENT TO SUPPLY IT TO ANOTHER

MISUSE OF DRUGS ACT 1971 (SECTION 5(3))

Triable either way unless the defendant could receive the minimum sentence of seven years for a third drug trafficking offence under section 110 Powers of Criminal Courts (Sentencing) Act 2000 in which case the offence is triable only on indictment.

Class A

Maximum: Life imprisonment

Offence range: Community order – 16 years' custody

A class A offence is a drug trafficking offence for the purpose of imposing a minimum sentence under section 110 Powers of Criminal Courts (Sentencing) Act 2000

Class B

Maximum: 14 years' custody and/or unlimited fine

Offence range: Fine – 10 years' custody

Class C

Maximum: 14 years' custody and/or unlimited fine

Offence range: Fine – 8 years' custody

STEP ONE Determining the offence category The court should determine the offender's culpability (role) and the harm caused (quantity/type of offender) with reference to the tables below.

In assessing culpability, the sentencer should weigh up all the factors of the case to determine role. Where there are characteristics present which fall under different role categories, the court should balance these characteristics to reach a fair assessment of the offender's culpability.

In assessing harm, quantity is determined by the weight of the product. Purity is not taken into account at step 1 but is dealt with at step 2. Where the offence is **street dealing**[Ed 1] or **supply of drugs in prison by a prison employee**, the quantity of the product is less indicative of the harm caused and therefore the **starting point is not based on quantity**.

Where the operation is on the most serious and commercial scale, involving a quantity of drugs significantly higher than category 1, sentences of 20 years and above may be appropriate, depending on the role of the offender.

[See page 233.]

Culpability demonstrated by offender's role

One or more of these characteristics may demonstrate the offender's role. These lists are not exhaustive.

LEADING role:

- directing or organising buying and selling on a commercial scale;
- substantial links to, and influence on, others in a chain;
- close links to original source;
- expectation of substantial financial gain;
- uses business as cover;
- abuses a position of trust or responsibility, for example prison employee, medical professional.

SIGNIFICANT role:

- operational or management function within a chain;
- involves others in the operation whether by pressure, influence, intimidation or reward;
- motivated by financial or other advantage, whether or not operating alone;
- some awareness and understanding of scale of operation;
- supply, other than by a person in a position of responsibility, to a prisoner for gain without coercion.

LESSER role:

- performs a limited function under direction;
- engaged by pressure, coercion, intimidation;
- involvement through naivety/exploitation;
- no influence on those above in a chain;
- very little, if any, awareness or understanding of the scale of operation;
- if own operation, absence of any financial gain, for example joint purchase for no profit, or sharing minimal quantity between peers on non-commercial basis.

Category of harm

Indicative quantity of drug concerned (upon which the starting point is based):

Category 1

- heroin, cocaine – 5kg;
- ecstasy – 10,000 tablets;
- LSD – 250,000 squares;
- amphetamine – 20kg;
- cannabis – 200kg;
- ketamine – 5kg.

Category 2

- heroin, cocaine – 1kg;
- ecstasy – 2,000 tablets;
- LSD – 25,000 squares;
- amphetamine – 4kg;

- cannabis – 40kg;
- ketamine – 1kg.

Category 3

Where the offence is selling directly to users[1] ('street dealing'), the starting point is not based on a quantity,

OR

where the offence is supply of drugs in prison by a prison employee, the starting point is not based on a quantity – see shaded box on [page 232],

OR

- heroin, cocaine – 150g;
- ecstasy – 300 tablets;
- LSD – 2,500 squares;
- amphetamine – 750g;
- cannabis – 6kg;
- ketamine – 150g.

Category 4

- heroin, cocaine – 5g;
- ecstasy – 20 tablets;
- LSD – 170 squares;
- amphetamine – 20g;
- cannabis – 100g;
- ketamine – 5g;

OR

where the offence is selling directly to users[1] ('street dealing') the starting point is not based on quantity – go to category 3.

Ed 1 *R v Leigh (Nedeme Jamie)* [2015] EWCA Crim 1045; [2015] 2 Cr App R (S) 42, [2015] Crim LR 910 the defendant secreted in his anus a plastic object containing a vessel in which there was 14.97g of cocaine. He claimed he was couriering the drugs to some dealers and that because of the secreting of the drugs there was no possibility of street dealing. This claim was dismissed as 'nonsense'. The drugs were clearly intended in due course to be dealt on the street and the whole course of events was related to street dealing.

Ed 1 "Street dealing" is a term of art. The supply does not have to take place on a 'street'; the essence of street dealing is that it involves selling directly to users: *R v Shahadat* [2017] EWCA Crim 822, [2017] ALL ER (D) 153 (Jun).

1 Including test purchase officers

STEP TWO Starting point and category range Having determined the category, the court should use the corresponding starting point to reach a sentence within the category range below. The starting point applies to all offenders irrespective of plea or previous convictions. The court should then consider further adjustment within the category range for aggravating or mitigating features, set out on [page 236]. In cases where the offender is regarded as being at the very top of the 'leading' role it may be justifiable for the court to depart from the guideline.

Where the defendant is dependent on or has a propensity to misuse drugs and there is sufficient prospect of success, a community order with a drug rehabilitation requirement under section 209 of the Criminal Justice Act 2003 can be a proper alternative to a short or moderate length custodial sentence.

For **class A** cases, section 110 of the Powers of Criminal Courts (Sentencing) Act 2000 provides that a court should impose a minimum sentence of at least seven years' imprisonment for a third class A trafficking offence except where the court is of the opinion that there are particular circumstances which (a) relate to any of the offences or to the offender; and (b) would make it unjust to do so in all the circumstances.

CLASS A	Leading role	Significant role	Lesser role
Category 1	**Starting point**	**Starting point**	**Starting point**
	14 years' custody	10 years' custody	7 years' custody
	Category range	**Category range**	**Category range**
	12 – 16 years' custody	9 – 12 years' custody	6 – 9 years' custody
Category 2	**Starting point**	**Starting point**	**Starting point**
	11 years' custody	8 years' custody	5 years' custody
	Category range	**Category range**	**Category range**
	9 – 13 years' custody	6 years 6 months' – 10 years' custody	3 years 6 months' – 7 years' custody
Category 3	**Starting point**	**Starting point**	**Starting point**
	8 years 6 months' custody	4 years 6 months' custody	3 years' custody
	Category range	**Category range**	**Category range**
	6 years 6 months' – 10 years' custody	3 years 6 months' – 7 years' custody	2 – 4 years 6 months' custody

CLASS A **Category 4**	**Leading role**	**Significant role**	**Lesser role**
	Starting point	**Starting point**	**Starting point**
	5 years 6 months' custody	3 years 6 months' custody	18 months' custody
	Category range	**Category range**	**Category range**
	4 years 6 months' – 7 years 6 months' custody	2 – 5 years' custody	High level community order – 3 years' custody

CLASS B **Category 1**	**Leading role**	**Significant role**	**Lesser role**
	Starting point	**Starting point**	**Starting point**
	8 years' custody	5 years 6 months' custody	3 years' custody
	Category range	**Category range**	**Category range**
	7 – 10 years' custody	5 – 7 years' custody	2 years 6 months' – 5 years' custody
Category 2	**Starting point**	**Starting point**	**Starting point**
	6 years' custody	4 years' custody	1 year's custody
	Category range	**Category range**	**Category range**
	4 years 6 months' – 8 years' custody	2 years 6 months' – 5 years' custody	26 weeks' – 3 years' custody
Category 3	**Starting point**	**Starting point**	**Starting point**
	4 years' custody	1 year's custody	High level community order
	Category range	**Category range**	**Category range**
	2 years 6 months' – 5 years' custody	26 weeks' – 3 years' custody	Low level community order – 26 weeks' custody
Category 4	**Starting point**	**Starting point**	**Starting point**
	18 months' custody	High level community order	Low level community order
	Category range	**Category range**	**Category range**
	26 weeks' – 3 years' custody	Medium level community order – 26 weeks' custody	Band B fine – medium level community order

CLASS C **Category 1**	**Leading role**	**Significant role**	**Lesser role**
	Starting point	**Starting point**	**Starting point**
	5 years' custody	3 years' custody	18 months' custody
	Category range	**Category range**	**Category range**
	4 – 8 years' custody	2 – 5 years' custody	1 – 3 years' custody
Category 2	**Starting point**	**Starting point**	**Starting point**
	3 years 6 months' custody	18 months' custody	26 weeks' custody
	Category range	**Category range**	**Category range**
	2 – 5 years' custody	1 – 3 years' custody	12 weeks' – 18 months' custody
Category 3	**Starting point**	**Starting point**	**Starting point**
	18 months' custody	26 weeks' custody	High level community order
	Category range	**Category range**	**Category range**
	1 – 3 years' custody	12 weeks' – 18 months' custody	Low level community order – 12 weeks' custody
Category 4	**Starting point**	**Starting point**	**Starting point**
	26 weeks' custody	High level community order	Low level community order
	Category range	**Category range**	**Category range**
	High level community order – 18 months' custody	Low level community order – 12 weeks' custody	Band A fine – medium level community order

The table below contains a **non-exhaustive** list of additional factual elements providing the context of the offence and factors relating to the offender. Identify whether any combination of these, or other relevant factors, should result in an upward or downward adjustment from the starting point. In some cases, having considered these factors, it may be appropriate to move outside the identified category range.

For appropriate **class B** and **C** ranges, consider the custody threshold as follows:

- has the custody threshold been passed?
- if so, is it unavoidable that a custodial sentence be imposed?
- if so, can that sentence be suspended?

For appropriate **class B** and **C** ranges, the court should also consider the community threshold as follows:

- has the community threshold been passed?

Factors increasing seriousness *Statutory aggravating factors:*

Previous convictions, having regard to a) nature of the offence to which conviction relates and relevance to current offence; and b) time elapsed since conviction (see shaded box at [page 234] if third drug trafficking conviction)

Offender used or permitted a person under 18 to deliver a controlled drug to a third person

Offender 18 or over supplies or offers to supply a drug on, or in the vicinity of, school premises either when school in use as such or at a time between one hour before and one hour after they are to be used

Offence committed on bail

Other aggravating factors include:

Targeting of any premises intended to locate vulnerable individuals or supply to such individuals and/or supply to those under 18

Exposure of others to more than usual danger, for example drugs cut with harmful substances

Attempts to conceal or dispose of evidence, where not charged separately

Presence of others, especially children and/or non-users

Presence of weapon, where not charged separately

Charged as importation of a very small amount

High purity

Failure to comply with current court orders

Offence committed on licence

Established evidence of community impact

Factors reducing seriousness or reflecting personal mitigation Involvement due to pressure, intimidation or coercion falling short of duress, except where already taken into account at step 1

Supply only of drug to which offender addicted

Mistaken belief of the offender regarding the type of drug, taking into account the reasonableness of such belief in all the circumstances

Isolated incident

Low purity

No previous convictions **or** no relevant or recent convictions

Offender's vulnerability was exploited

Remorse

Good character and/or exemplary conduct

Determination and/or demonstration of steps having been taken to address addiction or offending behaviour

Serious medical conditions requiring urgent, intensive or long-term treatment

Age and/or lack of maturity where it affects the responsibility of the offender

Mental disorder or learning disability

Sole or primary carer for dependent relatives

STEP THREE Consider any factors which indicate a reduction, such as assistance to the prosecution

The court should take into account sections 73 and 74 of the Serious Organised Crime and Police Act 2005 (assistance by defendants: reduction or review of sentence) and any other rule of law by virtue of which an offender may receive a discounted sentence in consequence of assistance given (or offered) to the prosecutor or investigator.

STEP FOUR Reduction for guilty pleas The court should take account of any potential reduction for a guilty plea in accordance with section 144 of the Criminal Justice Act 2003 and the *Guilty Plea* guideline.

For class A offences, where a minimum mandatory sentence is imposed under section 110 Powers of Criminal Courts (Sentencing) Act, the discount for an early guilty plea must not exceed 20 per cent.

STEP FIVE Totality principle If sentencing an offender for more than one offence, or where the offender is already serving a sentence, consider whether the total sentence is just and proportionate to the offending behaviour.

STEP SIX Confiscation and ancillary orders In all cases, the court is required to consider confiscation where the Crown invokes the process or where the court considers it appropriate. It should also consider whether to make ancillary orders.

STEP SEVEN Reasons Section 174 of the Criminal Justice Act 2003 imposes a duty to give reasons for, and explain the effect of, the sentence.

STEP EIGHT Consideration for remand time   Sentencers should take into consideration any remand time served in relation to the final sentence at this final step. The court should consider whether to give credit for time spent on remand in custody or on bail in accordance with sections 240 and 240A of the Criminal Justice Act 2003.

PRODUCTION OF A CONTROLLED DRUG

Misuse of Drugs Act 1971 (section 4(2)(a) or (b))

Triable either way unless the defendant could receive the minimum sentence of seven years for a third drug trafficking offence under section 110 Powers of Criminal Courts (Sentencing) Act 2000 in which case the offence is triable only on indictment.

Class A

Maximum: Life imprisonment

Offence range: Community order – 16 years' custody

A class A offence is a drug trafficking offence for the purpose of imposing a minimum sentence under section 110 Powers of Criminal Courts (Sentencing) Act 2000

Class B

Maximum: 14 years' custody

Offence range: Discharge – 10 years' custody

Class C

Maximum: 14 years' custody

Offence range: Discharge – 8 years' custody

CULTIVATION OF CANNABIS PLANT

Misuse of Drugs Act 1971 (section 6(2))

Maximum: 14 years' custody

Offence range: Discharge – 10 years' custody

STEP ONE Determining the offence category   The court should determine the offender's culpability (role) and the harm caused (output or potential output) with reference to the tables below.

In assessing culpability, the sentencer should weigh up all of the factors of the case to determine role. Where there are characteristics present which fall under different role categories, the court should balance these characteristics to reach a fair assessment of the offender's culpability.

In assessing harm, output or potential output is determined by the weight of the product or number of plants/scale of operation. For production offences, purity is not taken into account at step 1 but is dealt with at step 2.

Where the operation is on the most serious and commercial scale, involving a quantity of drugs significantly higher than category 1, sentences of 20 years and above may be appropriate, depending on the role of the offender.

Culpability demonstrated by offender's role

One or more of these characteristics may demonstrate the offender's role. These lists are not exhaustive.

LEADING role:

- directing or organising production on a commercial scale;
- substantial links to, and influence on, others in a chain;
- expectation of substantial financial gain;
- uses business as cover;
- abuses a position of trust or responsibility.

SIGNIFICANT role:

- operational or management function within a chain;
- involves others in the operation whether by pressure, influence, intimidation or reward;
- motivated by financial or other advantage, whether or not operating alone;
- some awareness and understanding of scale of operation.

LESSER role:

- performs a limited function under direction;
- engaged by pressure, coercion, intimidation;
- involvement through naivety/exploitation;
- no influence on those above in a chain;
- very little, if any, awareness or understanding of the scale of operation;
- if own operation, solely for own use (considering reasonableness of account in all the circumstances).

Category of harm

Indicative output or potential output (upon which the starting point is based):

Category 1

- heroin, cocaine – 5kg;
- ecstasy – 10,000 tablets;
- LSD – 250,000 tablets;
- amphetamine – 20kg;
- cannabis – operation capable of producing industrial quantities for commercial use;[Ed]
- ketamine – 5kg.

Category 2

- heroin, cocaine – 1kg;
- ecstasy – 2,000 tablets;
- LSD – 25,000 squares;
- amphetamine – 4kg;
- cannabis – operation capable of producing significant quantities for commercial use;[Ed]

- ketamine – 1kg.

Category 3

- heroin, cocaine – 150g;
- ecstasy – 300 tablets;
- LSD – 2,500 squares;
- amphetamine – 750g;
- cannabis – 28 plants;[1]
- ketamine – 150g.

Category 4

- heroin, cocaine – 5g;
- ecstasy – 20 tablets;
- LSD – 170 squares;
- amphetamine – 20g;
- cannabis – 9 plants (domestic operation);[1]
- ketamine – 5g.

---

[1] With assumed yield of 40g per plant

STEP TWO Starting point and category range Having determined the category, the court should use the corresponding starting point to reach a sentence within the category range below. The starting point applies to all offenders irrespective of plea or previous convictions. The court should then consider further adjustment within the category range for aggravating or mitigating features, set out on [page 243]. In cases where the offender is regarded as being at the very top of the 'leading' role it may be justifiable for the court to depart from the guideline.

Where the defendant is dependent on or has a propensity to misuse drugs and there is sufficient prospect of success, a community order with a drug rehabilitation requirement under section 209 of the Criminal Justice Act 2003 can be a proper alternative to a short or moderate length custodial sentence.

For **class A** cases, section 110 of the Powers of Criminal Courts (Sentencing) Act 2000 provides that a court should impose a minimum sentence of at least seven years' imprisonment for a third class A trafficking offence except where the court is of the opinion that there are particular circumstances which (a) relate to any of the offences or to the offender; and (b) would make it unjust to do so in all the circumstances.

CLASS A	Leading role	Significant role	Lesser role
	Starting point	Starting point	Starting point
	14 years' custody	10 years' custody	7 years' custody
	Category range	Category range	Category range
	12 – 16 years' custody	9 – 12 years' custody	6 – 9 years' custody
Category 2	Starting point	Starting point	Starting point
	11 years' custody	8 years' custody	5 years' custody
	Category range	Category range	Category range
	9 – 13 years' custody	6 years 6 months' – 10 years' custody	3 years 6 months' – 7 years' custody
Category 3	Starting point	Starting point	Starting point
	8 years 6 months' custody	5 years' custody	3 years 6 months' custody
	Category range	Category range	Category range
	6 years 6 months' – 10 years' custody	3 years 6 months' – 7 years' custody	2 – 5 years' custody
Category 4	Starting point	Starting point	Starting point
	5 years 6 months' custody	3 years 6 months' custody	18 months' custody
	Category range	Category range	Category range
	4 years 6 months' – 7 years 6 months' custody	2 – 5 years' custody	High level community order – 3 years' custody

CLASS B	Leading role	Significant role	Lesser role
Category 1	Starting point	Starting point	Starting point
	8 years' custody	5 years 6 months' custody	3 years' custody
	Category range	Category range	Category range
	7 – 10 years' custody	5 – 7 years' custody	2 years 6 months' – 5 years' custody
Category 2	Starting point	Starting point	Starting point

CLASS B	**Leading role**	**Significant role**	**Lesser role**
	6 years' custody	4 years' custody	1 year's custody
	Category range	**Category range**	**Category range**
	4 years 6 months' – 8 years' custody	2 years 6 months' – 5 years' custody	26 weeks' – 3 years' custody
Category 3	**Starting point**	**Starting point**	**Starting point**
	4 years' custody	1 year's custody	High level community order
	Category range	**Category range**	**Category range**
	2 years 6 months' – 5 years' custody	26 weeks' – 3 years' custody	Low level community order – 26 weeks' custody
Category 4	**Starting point**	**Starting point**	**Starting point**
	1 year's custody	High level community order	Band C fine
	Category range	**Category range**	**Category range**
	High level community order – 3 years' custody	Medium level community order – 26 weeks' custody	Discharge – medium level community order

CLASS C	**Leading role**	**Significant role**	**Lesser role**
Category 1	**Starting point**	**Starting point**	**Starting point**
	5 years' custody	3 years' custody	18 months' custody
	Category range	**Category range**	**Category range**
	4 – 8 years' custody	2 – 5 years' custody	1 – 3 years' custody
Category 2	**Starting point**	**Starting point**	**Starting point**
	3 years 6 months' custody	18 months' custody	26 weeks' custody
	Category range	**Category range**	**Category range**
	2 – 5 years' custody	1 – 3 years' custody	High level community order – 18 months' custody
Category 3	**Starting point**	**Starting point**	**Starting point**
	18 months' custody	26 weeks' custody	High level community order
	Category range	**Category range**	**Category range**
	1 – 3 years' custody	High level community order – 18 months' custody	Low level community order – 12 weeks' custody
Category 4	**Starting point**	**Starting point**	**Starting point**
	26 weeks' custody	High level community order	Band C fine
	Category range	**Category range**	**Category range**
	High level community order – 18 months' custody	Low level community order – 12 weeks' custody	Discharge – medium level community order

The table below contains a **non-exhaustive** list of additional factual elements providing the context of the offence and factors relating to the offender. Identify whether any combination of these, or other relevant factors, should result in an upward or downward adjustment from the starting point. In some cases, having considered these factors, it may be appropriate to move outside the identified category range.

Where appropriate, consider the custody threshold as follows:

- has the custody threshold been passed?
- if so, is it unavoidable that a custodial sentence be imposed?
- if so, can that sentence be suspended?

Where appropriate, the court should also consider the community threshold as follows:

- has the community threshold been passed?

Factors increasing seriousness   *Statutory aggravating factors:*

Previous convictions, having regard to a) nature of the offence to which conviction relates and relevance to current offence; and b) time elapsed since conviction (see shaded box at [page 241] if third drug trafficking conviction)

Offence committed on bail

Other aggravating factors include:

Nature of any likely supply Level of any profit element
Use of premises accompanied by unlawful access to electricity/other utility supply of others
Ongoing/large scale operation as evidenced by presence and nature of specialist equipment
Exposure of others to more than usual danger, for example drugs cut with harmful substances
Attempts to conceal or dispose of evidence, where not charged separately
Presence of others, especially children and/or non-users
Presence of weapon, where not charged separately
High purity or high potential yield
Failure to comply with current court orders
Offence committed on licence
Established evidence of community impact
Factors reducing seriousness or reflecting personal mitigation
Involvement due to pressure, intimidation or coercion falling short of duress, except where already taken into account at step 1
Isolated incident
Low purity
No previous convictions **or** no relevant or recent convictions
Offender's vulnerability was exploited
Remorse
Good character and/or exemplary conduct
Determination and/or demonstration of steps having been taken to address addiction or offending behaviour
Serious medical conditions requiring urgent, intensive or long-term treatment
Age and/or lack of maturity where it affects the responsibility of the offender
Mental disorder or learning disability
Sole or primary carer for dependent relatives

STEP THREE Consider any factors which indicate a reduction, such as assistance to the prosecution
The court should take into account sections 73 and 74 of the Serious Organised Crime and Police Act 2005 (assistance by defendants: reduction or review of sentence) and any other rule of law by virtue of which an offender may receive a discounted sentence in consequence of assistance given (or offered) to the prosecutor or investigator.

STEP FOUR Reduction for guilty pleas The court should take account of any potential reduction for a guilty plea in accordance with section 144 of the Criminal Justice Act 2003 and the *Guilty Plea* guideline.
For class A offences, where a minimum mandatory sentence is imposed under section 110 Powers of Criminal Courts (Sentencing) Act, the discount for an early guilty plea must not exceed 20 per cent.

STEP FIVE Totality principle If sentencing an offender for more than one offence, or where the offender is already serving a sentence, consider whether the total sentence is just and proportionate to the offending behaviour.

STEP SIX Confiscation and ancillary orders In all cases, the court is required to consider confiscation where the Crown invokes the process or where the court considers it appropriate. It should also consider whether to make ancillary orders.

STEP SEVEN Reasons Section 174 of the Criminal Justice Act 2003 imposes a duty to give reasons for, and explain the effect of, the sentence.

STEP EIGHT Consideration for remand time Sentencers should take into consideration any remand time served in relation to the final sentence at this final step. The court should consider whether to give credit for time spent on remand in custody or on bail in accordance with sections 240 and 240A of the Criminal Justice Act 2003.

[Ed] No indicative weight to quantity is stated because comparison with cases of supply or importation is inapt; the latter cases relate to an identified quantity.

Misuse of Drugs Act 1971 (section 8)
Triable either way unless the defendant could receive the minimum sentence of seven years for a third drug trafficking offence under section 110 Powers of Criminal Courts (Sentencing) Act 2000 in which case the offence is triable only on indictment.

Class A
Maximum: 14 years' custody
Offence range: Community order – 4 years' custody
A class A offence is a drug trafficking offence for the purpose of imposing a minimum sentence under section 110 Powers of Criminal Courts (Sentencing) Act 2000

Class B
Maximum: 14 years' custody
Offence range: Fine – 18 months' custody

Class C
Maximum: 14 years' custody
Offence range: Discharge – 26 weeks' custody

STEP ONE Determining the offence category   The court should determine the offender's culpability and the harm caused (extent of the activity and/or the quantity of drugs) with reference to the table below.

In assessing harm, quantity is determined by the weight of the product. Purity is not taken into account at step 1 but is dealt with at step 2.

Category 1	Higher culpability **and** greater harm
Category 2	Lower culpability **and** greater harm; **or** higher culpability **and** lesser harm
Category 3	Lower culpability **and** lesser harm

Factors indicating culpability (non-exhaustive)   *Higher culpability:*
Permits premises to be used primarily for drug activity, for example crack house
Permits use in expectation of substantial financial gain
Uses legitimate business premises to aid and/or conceal illegal activity, for example public house or club
Lower culpability:
Permits use for limited or no financial gain
No active role in any supply taking place
Involvement through naivety

Factors indicating harm (non-exhaustive)   *Greater harm:*
Regular drug-related activity
Higher quantity of drugs, for example:

- heroin, cocaine – more than 5g;
- cannabis – more than 50g.

Lesser harm:
Infrequent drug-related activity
Lower quantity of drugs, for example:

- heroin, cocaine – up to 5g;
- cannabis – up to 50g.

STEP TWO Starting point and category range   Having determined the category, the court should use the table below to identify the corresponding starting point to reach a sentence within the category range. The starting point applies to all offenders irrespective of plea or previous convictions. The court should then consider further adjustment within the category range for aggravating or mitigating features, set out over the page.

Where the defendant is dependent on or has a propensity to misuse drugs and there is sufficient prospect of success, a community order with a drug rehabilitation requirement under section 209 of the Criminal Justice Act 2003 can be a proper alternative to a short or moderate length custodial sentence.

For **class A** cases, section 110 of the Powers of Criminal Courts (Sentencing) Act 2000 provides that a court should impose a minimum sentence of at least seven years' imprisonment for a third class A trafficking offence except where the court is of the opinion that there are particular circumstances which (a) relate to any of the offences or to the offender; and (b) would make it unjust to do so in all the circumstances.

Class A

Offence category	Starting point (applicable to all offenders)	Category range (applicable to all offenders)
Category 1	2 years 6 months' custody	18 months' – 4 years' custody
Category 2	36 weeks' custody	High level community order – 18 months' custody
Category 3	Medium level community order	Low level community order – high level community order

Class B

Offence category	Starting point (applicable to all offenders)	Category range (applicable to all offenders)
Category 1	1 year's custody	26 weeks' – 18 months' custody
Category 2	High level community order	Low level community order – 26 weeks' custody
Category 3	Band C fine	Band A fine – low level community order

Class C

Offence category	Starting point (applicable to all offenders)	Category range (applicable to all offenders)
Category 1	12 weeks' custody	High level community order – 26 weeks' custody*
Category 2	Low level community order	Band C fine – high level community order
Category 3	Band A fine	Discharge – band C fine

* When tried summarily, the maximum penalty is 12 weeks' custody.

The table below contains a **non-exhaustive** list of additional factual elements providing the context of the offence and factors relating to the offender. Identify whether any combination of these, or other relevant factors, should result in an upward or downward adjustment from the starting point. In some cases, having considered these factors, it may be appropriate to move outside the identified category range.

Where appropriate, consider the custody threshold as follows:

- has the custody threshold been passed?
- if so, is it unavoidable that a custodial sentence be imposed?
- if so, can that sentence be suspended?

Where appropriate, the court should also consider the community threshold as follows:

- has the community threshold been passed?

Factors increasing seriousness   *Statutory aggravating factors:*
Previous convictions, having regard to a) nature of the offence to which conviction relates and relevance to current offence; and b) time elapsed since conviction (see shaded box at [page 247] if third drug trafficking conviction)
Offence committed on bail
Other aggravating factors include:
Length of time over which premises used for drug activity
Volume of drug activity permitted
Premises adapted to facilitate drug activity
Location of premises, for example proximity to school
Attempts to conceal or dispose of evidence, where not charged separately
Presence of others, especially children and/or non-users
High purity
Presence of weapons, where not charged separately
Failure to comply with current court orders
Offence committed on licence
Established evidence of community impact
Factors reducing seriousness or reflecting personal mitigation   Involvement due to pressure, intimidation or coercion falling short of duress
Isolated incident Low purity
No previous convictions **or** no relevant or recent convictions
Offender's vulnerability was exploited
Remorse
Good character and/or exemplary conduct
Determination and/or demonstration of steps having been taken to address addiction or offending behaviour
Serious medical conditions requiring urgent, intensive or long-term treatment
Age and/or lack of maturity where it affects the responsibility of the offender

Mental disorder or learning disability
Sole or primary carer for dependent relatives

STEP THREE Consider any factors which indicate a reduction, such as assistance to the prosecution
The court should take into account sections 73 and 74 of the Serious Organised Crime and Police Act 2005 (assistance by defendants: reduction or review of sentence) and any other rule of law by virtue of which an offender may receive a discounted sentence in consequence of assistance given (or offered) to the prosecutor or investigator.

STEP FOUR Reduction for guilty pleas   The court should take account of any potential reduction for a guilty plea in accordance with section 144 of the Criminal Justice Act 2003 and the *Guilty Plea* guideline.
For class A offences, where a minimum mandatory sentence is imposed under section 110 Powers of Criminal Courts (Sentencing) Act, the discount for an early guilty plea must not exceed 20 per cent.

STEP FIVE Totality principle   If sentencing an offender for more than one offence or where the offender is already serving a sentence, consider whether the total sentence is just and proportionate to the offending behaviour.

STEP SIX Confiscation and ancillary orders   In all cases, the court is required to consider confiscation where the Crown invokes the process or where the court considers it appropriate. It should also consider whether to make ancillary orders.

STEP SEVEN Reasons   Section 174 of the Criminal Justice Act 2003 imposes a duty to give reasons for, and explain the effect of, the sentence.

STEP EIGHT Consideration for remand time   Sentencers should take into consideration any remand time served in relation to the final sentence at this final step. The court should consider whether to give credit for time spent on remand in custody or on bail in accordance with sections 240 and 240A of the Criminal Justice Act 2003.

POSSESSION OF A CONTROLLED DRUG

Misuse of Drugs Act 1971 (section 5(2))

Triable either way
Class A
Maximum: 7 years' custody
Offence range: Fine – 51 weeks' custody
Class B
Maximum: 5 years' custody
Offence range: Discharge – 26 weeks' custody
Class C
Maximum: 2 years' custody
Offence range: Discharge – Community order

STEP ONE Determining the offence category   The court should identify the offence category based on the class of drug involved.

Category 1	Class A drug
Category 2	Class B drug
Category 3	Class C drug

STEP TWO Starting point and category range   The court should use the table below to identify the corresponding starting point. The starting point applies to all offenders irrespective of plea or previous convictions. The court should then consider further adjustment within the category range for aggravating or mitigating features, set out on the opposite page.

Where the defendant is dependent on or has a propensity to misuse drugs and there is sufficient prospect of success, a community order with a drug rehabilitation requirement under section 209 of the Criminal Justice Act 2003 can be a proper alternative to a short or moderate length custodial sentence.

Offence category	Starting point (applicable to all offenders)	Category range (applicable to all offenders)
Category 1 (class A)	Band C fine	Band A fine – 51 weeks' custody
Category 2 (class B)	Band B fine	Discharge – 26 weeks' custody
Category 3 (class C)	Band A fine	Discharge – medium level community order

The table below contains a **non-exhaustive** list of additional factual elements providing the context of the offence and factors relating to the offender. Identify whether any combination of these, or other relevant factors, should result in an upward or downward adjustment from the starting point. **In particular, possession of drugs in prison is likely to result in an upward adjustment.** In some cases, having considered these factors, it may be appropriate to move outside the identified category range.

Where appropriate, consider the custody threshold as follows:
has the custody threshold been passed?

- if so, is it unavoidable that a custodial sentence be imposed?
- if so, can that sentence be suspended?

Where appropriate, the court should also consider the community threshold as follows:

- has the community threshold been passed?

Factors increasing seriousness   *Statutory aggravating factors:*
Previous convictions, having regard to a) nature of the offence to which conviction relates and relevance to current offence; and b) time elapsed since conviction
Offence committed on bail
Other aggravating factors include:
Possession of drug in prison
Presence of others, especially children and/or non-users
Possession of drug in a school or licensed premises
Failure to comply with current court orders
Offence committed on licence
Attempts to conceal or dispose of evidence, where not charged separately
Charged as importation of a very small amount
Established evidence of community impact
Factors reducing seriousness or reflecting personal mitigation   No previous convictions **or** no relevant or recent convictions
Remorse
Good character and/or exemplary conduct
Offender is using cannabis to help with a diagnosed medical condition
Determination and/or demonstration of steps having been taken to address addiction or offending behaviour

Serious medical conditions requiring urgent, intensive or long-term treatment
Isolated incident
Age and/or lack of maturity where it affects the responsibility of the offender
Mental disorder or learning disability
Sole or primary carer for dependent relatives

STEP THREE Consider any factors which indicate a reduction, such as assistance to the prosecution
The court should take into account sections 73 and 74 of the Serious Organised Crime and Police Act 2005 (assistance by defendants: reduction or review of sentence) and any other rule of law by virtue of which an offender may receive a discounted sentence in consequence of assistance given (or offered) to the prosecutor or investigator.

STEP FOUR Reduction for guilty pleas   The court should take account of any potential reduction for a guilty plea in accordance with section 144 of the Criminal Justice Act 2003 and the *Guilty Plea* guideline.

STEP FIVE Totality principle   If sentencing an offender for more than one offence, or where the offender is already serving a sentence, consider whether the total sentence is just and proportionate to the offending behaviour.

STEP SIX Ancillary orders   In all cases, the court should consider whether to make ancillary orders.

STEP SEVEN Reasons   Section 174 of the Criminal Justice Act 2003 imposes a duty to give reasons for, and explain the effect of, the sentence.

STEP EIGHT Consideration for remand time   Sentencers should take into consideration any remand time served in relation to the final sentence at this final step. The court should consider whether to give credit for time spent on remand in custody or on bail in accordance with sections 240 and 240A of the Criminal Justice Act 2003.

Sᴇxᴜᴀʟ ᴀssᴀᴜʟᴛ
Sexual Offences Act 2003 (section 3)

Triable either way
Maximum: 10 years' custody
Offence range: Community order – 7 years' custody
For convictions on or after 3 December 2012 (irrespective of the date of commission of the offence), this is a specified offence for the purposes of section 226A (extended sentence for certain violent or sexual offences) of the Criminal Justice Act 2003.

Determining the offence category

STEP ONE   The court should determine which categories of harm and culpability the offence falls into by reference **only** to the tables below.

Category 1	• Severe psychological or physical harm
	• Abduction
	• Violence or threats of violence
	• Forced/uninvited entry into victim's home
Category 2	• Touching of naked genitalia or naked breasts
	• Prolonged detention/sustained incident
	• Additional degradation/humiliation
	• Victim is particularly vulnerable due to personal circumstances*
	* for children under 13 please refer to the guideline on page 277
Category 3	Factor(s) in categories 1 and 2 not present

Culpability   A
Significant degree of planning[Ed]
Offender acts together with others to commit the offence
Use of alcohol/drugs on victim to facilitate the offence
Abuse of trust
Previous violence against victim
Offence committed in course of burglary
Recording of offence
Commercial exploitation and/or motivation
Offence racially or religiously aggravated
Offence motivated by, or demonstrating, hostility to the victim based on his or her sexual orientation (or presumed sexual orientation) or transgender identity (or presumed transgender identity)
Offence motivated by, or demonstrating, hostility to the victim based on his or her disability (or presumed disability)
B
Factor(s) in category A not present

[Ed] 'Significant' is not an absolute concept, and in the context of an offence which can be committed without implements or tools or sophisticated planning, lying in wait in a position designed to prey on lone young women, on their way home from a night out involves a 'significant degree of planning': *R v Teklu* [2017] EWCA Crim 1477, [2018] 1 Cr App R (S) 12.

Starting point and category range

STEP TWO   Having determined the category, the court should use the corresponding starting points to reach a sentence within the category range on the next page. The starting point applies to all offenders irrespective of plea or previous convictions. Having determined the starting point, step two allows further adjustment for aggravating or mitigating features, set out on the next page.

A case of particular gravity, reflected by multiple features of culpability or harm in step one, could merit upward adjustment from the starting point before further adjustment for aggravating or mitigating features, set out on the next page.

Where there is a sufficient prospect of rehabilitation, a community order with a sex offender treatment programme requirement under section 202 of the Criminal Justice Act 2003 can be a proper alternative to a short or moderate length custodial sentence.

	A	B
Category 1	**Starting point**	**Starting point**
	4 years' custody	2 years 6 months' custody
	Category range	**Category range**
	3 – 7 years' custody	2 – 4 years' custody
Category 2	**Starting point**	**Starting point**
	2 years' custody	1 year's custody
	Category range	**Category range**

	A 1 – 4 years' custody	**B** High level community order – 2 years' custody
Category 3	**Starting point**	**Starting point**
	26 weeks' custody	High level community order
	Category range	**Category range**
	High level community order – 1 year's custody	Medium level community order – 26 weeks' custody

The table below contains a **non-exhaustive** list of additional factual elements providing the context of the offence and factors relating to the offender. Identify whether any combination of these, or other relevant factors, should result in an upward or downward adjustment from the starting point. **In particular, relevant recent convictions are likely to result in an upward adjustment.** In some cases, having considered these factors, it may be appropriate to move outside the identified category range.

When sentencing appropriate **category 2 or 3 offences**, the court should also consider the custody threshold as follows:

- has the custody threshold been passed?
- if so, is it unavoidable that a custodial sentence be imposed?
- if so, can that sentence be suspended?

Aggravating factors   *Statutory aggravating factors*

Previous convictions, having regard to a) the nature of the offence to which the conviction relates and its relevance to the current offence; and b) the time that has elapsed since the conviction

Offence committed whilst on bail

Other aggravating factors

Specific targeting of a particularly vulnerable victim

Blackmail or other threats made (where not taken into account at step one)

Location of offence

Timing of offence

Use of weapon or other item to frighten or injure

Victim compelled to leave their home (including victims of domestic violence)

Failure to comply with current court orders

Offence committed whilst on licence

Exploiting contact arrangements with a child to commit an offence

Presence of others, especially children

Any steps taken to prevent the victim reporting an incident, obtaining assistance and/or from assisting or supporting the prosecution

Attempts to dispose of or conceal evidence

Commission of offence whilst under the influence of alcohol or drugs

Mitigating factors   No previous convictions **or** no relevant/recent convictions

Remorse

Previous good character and/or exemplary conduct*

Age and/or lack of maturity where it affects the responsibility of the offender

Mental disorder or learning disability, particularly where linked to the commission of the offence

Demonstration of steps taken to address offending behaviour

---

* Previous good character/exemplary conduct is different from having no previous convictions. The more serious the offence, the less the weight which should normally be attributed to this factor. Where previous good character/exemplary conduct has been used to facilitate the offence, this mitigation should not normally be allowed and such conduct may constitute an aggravating factor.

Consider any factors which indicate a reduction, such as assistance to the prosecution

STEP THREE   The court should take into account sections 73 and 74 of the Serious Organised Crime and Police Act 2005 (assistance by defendants: reduction or review of sentence) and any other rule of law by virtue of which an offender may receive a discounted sentence in consequence of assistance given (or offered) to the prosecutor or investigator.

Reduction for guilty pleas

STEP FOUR   The court should take account of any potential reduction for a guilty plea in accordance with section 144 of the Criminal Justice Act 2003 and the *Guilty Plea* guideline.

Dangerousness

STEP FIVE   The court should consider whether having regard to the criteria contained in Chapter 5 of Part 12 of the Criminal Justice Act 2003 it would be appropriate to award an extended sentence (section 226A).

Totality principle

STEP SIX   If sentencing an offender for more than one offence, or where the offender is already serving a sentence, consider whether the total sentence is just and proportionate to the offending behaviour.

Ancillary orders

STEP SEVEN   The court must consider whether to make any ancillary orders. The court must also consider what other requirements or provisions may *automatically* apply. Further information is included on page 303.

Reasons

STEP EIGHT   Section 174 of the Criminal Justice Act 2003 imposes a duty to give reasons for, and explain the effect of, the sentence.

Consideration for time spent on bail

STEP NINE   The court must consider whether to give credit for time spent on bail in accordance with section 240A of the Criminal Justice Act 2003.

SEXUAL ASSAULT OF A CHILD UNDER 13
Sexual Offences Act 2003 (section 7)

Triable either way
Maximum: 14 years' custody
Offence range: Community order – 9 years' custody
For offences committed on or after 3 December 2012, this is an offence listed in Part 1 of Schedule 15B for the purposes of section 224A (life sentence for second listed offence) of the Criminal Justice Act 2003.
For convictions on or after 3 December 2012 (irrespective of the date of commission of the offence), this is a specified offence for the purposes of section 226A (extended sentence for certain violent or sexual offences) of the Criminal Justice Act 2003.

Determining the offence category

STEP ONE The court should determine which categories of harm and culpability the offence falls into by reference **only** to the tables below.

Category 1	• Severe psychological or physical harm
	• Abduction
	• Violence or threats of violence
	• Forced/uninvited entry into victim's home
Category 2	• Touching of naked genitalia or naked breast area
	• Prolonged detention/sustained incident
	• Additional degradation/humiliation
	• Child is particularly vulnerable due to extreme youth and/or personal circumstances
Category 3	Factor(s) in categories 1 and 2 not present

Culpability **A**
Significant degree of planning
Offender acts together with others to commit the offence
Use of alcohol/drugs on victim to facilitate the offence
Grooming behaviour used against victim
Abuse of trust
Previous violence against victim
Offence committed in course of burglary
Sexual images of victim recorded, retained, solicited or shared
Deliberate isolation of victim
Commercial exploitation and/or motivation
Offence racially or religiously aggravated
Offence motivated by, or demonstrating, hostility to the victim based on his or her sexual orientation (or presumed sexual orientation) or transgender identity (or presumed transgender identity)
Offence motivated by, or demonstrating, hostility to the victim based on his or her disability (or presumed disability)
B
Factor(s) in category A not present

Starting point and category range

STEP TWO Having determined the category, the court should use the corresponding starting points to reach a sentence within the category range on the next page. The starting point applies to all offenders irrespective of plea or previous convictions. Having determined the starting point, step two allows further adjustment for aggravating or mitigating features, set out on the next page.

A case of particular gravity, reflected by multiple features of culpability or harm in step one, could merit upward adjustment from the starting point before further adjustment for aggravating or mitigating features, set out on the next page.

Where there is a sufficient prospect of rehabilitation, a community order with a sex offender treatment programme requirement under section 202 of the Criminal Justice Act 2003 can be a proper alternative to a short or moderate length custodial sentence.

	A	B
Category 1	**Starting point**	**Starting point**
	6 years' custody	4 years' custody
	Category range	**Category range**
	4 – 9 years' custody	3 – 7 years' custody
Category 2	**Starting point**	**Starting point**
	4 years' custody	2 years' custody
	Category range	**Category range**

	A	B
	3 – 7 years' custody	1 – 4 years' custody
Category 3	**Starting point**	**Starting point**
	1 year's custody	26 weeks' custody
	Category range	**Category range**
	26 weeks' – 2 years' custody	High level community order – 1 year's custody

The table below contains a **non-exhaustive** list of additional factual elements providing the context of the offence and factors relating to the offender. Identify whether any combination of these, or other relevant factors, should result in an upward or downward adjustment from the starting point. **In particular, relevant recent convictions are likely to result in an upward adjustment.** In some cases, having considered these factors, it may be appropriate to move outside the identified category range.

Aggravating factors   *Statutory aggravating factors*

Previous convictions, having regard to a) the nature of the offence to which the conviction relates and its relevance to the current offence; and b) the time that has elapsed since the conviction

Offence committed whilst on bail

Other aggravating factors

Specific targeting of a particularly vulnerable child

Blackmail or other threats made (where not taken into account at step one)

Location of offence

Timing of offence

Use of weapon or other item to frighten or injure

Victim compelled to leave their home, school, etc

Failure to comply with current court orders

Offence committed whilst on licence

Exploiting contact arrangements with a child to commit an offence

Presence of others, especially other children

Any steps taken to prevent the victim reporting an incident, obtaining assistance and/or from assisting or supporting the prosecution

Attempts to dispose of or conceal evidence

Commission of offence whilst under the influence of alcohol or drugs

Victim encouraged to recruit others

Mitigating factors   No previous convictions **or** no relevant/recent convictions

Remorse

Previous good character and/or exemplary conduct*

Age and/or lack of maturity where it affects the responsibility of the offender

Mental disorder or learning disability, particularly where linked to the commission of the offence**

---

* Previous good character/exemplary conduct is different from having no previous convictions. The more serious the offence, the less the weight which should normally be attributed to this factor. Where previous good character/exemplary conduct has been used to facilitate the offence, this mitigation should not normally be allowed and such conduct may constitute an aggravating factor.

* In the context of this offence, previous good character/exemplary conduct should not normally be given any significant weight and will not normally justify a reduction in what would otherwise be the appropriate sentence.

** As was found to be the case, for example, in *R v Jones* [2014] EWCA Crim 1859, [2015] 1 Cr App R (S), a case where it was found that the public would be better protected by a course that might prevent further offending than by a short sentence that was unlikely to have that result.

Consider any factors which indicate a reduction, such as assistance to the prosecution

STEP THREE   The court should take into account sections 73 and 74 of the Serious Organised Crime and Police Act 2005 (assistance by defendants: reduction or review of sentence) and any other rule of law by virtue of which an offender may receive a discounted sentence in consequence of assistance given (or offered) to the prosecutor or investigator.

Reduction for guilty pleas

STEP FOUR   The court should take account of any potential reduction for a guilty plea in accordance with section 144 of the Criminal Justice Act 2003 and the *Guilty Plea* guideline.

Dangerousness

STEP FIVE   The court should consider whether having regard to the criteria contained in Chapter 5 of Part 12 of the Criminal Justice Act 2003 it would be appropriate to award a life sentence (section 224A) or an extended sentence (section 226A). When sentencing offenders to a life sentence under these provisions, the notional determinate sentence should be used as the basis for the setting of a minimum term.

Totality principle

STEP SIX   If sentencing an offender for more than one offence, or where the offender is already serving a sentence, consider whether the total sentence is just and proportionate to the offending behaviour.

Ancillary orders

STEP SEVEN The court must consider whether to make any ancillary orders. The court must also consider what other requirements or provisions may *automatically* apply. Further information is included on page 303.

Reasons

STEP EIGHT Section 174 of the Criminal Justice Act 2003 imposes a duty to give reasons for, and explain the effect of, the sentence.

Consideration for time spent on bail

STEP NINE The court must consider whether to give credit for time spent on bail in accordance with section 240A of the Criminal Justice Act 2003.

POSSESSION OF INDECENT PHOTOGRAPH OF CHILD

Criminal Justice Act 1988 (section 160)

Triable either way
Maximum: 5 years' custody
Offence range: Community order – 3 years' custody

INDECENT PHOTOGRAPHS OF CHILDREN

Protection of Children Act 1978 (section 1)

Triable either way
Maximum: 10 years' custody
Offence range: Community order – 9 years' custody
For section 1 offences committed on or after 3 December 2012, this is an offence listed in Part 1 of Schedule 15B for the purposes of section 224A (life sentence for second listed offence) of the Criminal Justice Act 2003.

For convictions on or after 3 December 2012 (irrespective of the date of commission of the offence), these are specified offences for the purposes of section 226A (extended sentence for certain violent or sexual offences) of the Criminal Justice Act 2003.

STEP ONE Determining the offence category   The court should determine the offence category using the table below.

	Possession	**Distribution**[*]	**Production**[**]
Category A	Possession of images involving penetrative sexual activity	Sharing images involving penetrative sexual activity	Creating images involving penetrative sexual activity
	Possession of images involving sexual activity with an animal or sadism	Sharing images involving sexual activity with an animal or sadism	Creating images involving sexual activity with an animal or sadism
Category B	Possession of images involving non-penetrative sexual activity	Sharing of images involving non-penetrative sexual activity	Creating images involving non-penetrative sexual activity
Category C	Possession of other indecent images not falling within categories A or B	Sharing of other indecent images not falling within categories A or B	Creating other indecent images not falling within categories A or B

[*]   Distribution includes possession with a view to distributing or sharing images.
[**]   Production includes the taking or making of any image at source, for instance the original image. Making an image by simple downloading should be treated as possession for the purposes of sentencing.

In most cases the intrinsic character of the most serious of the offending images will initially determine the appropriate category. If, however, the most serious images are unrepresentative of the offender's conduct a lower category may be appropriate. A lower category will not, however, be appropriate if the offender has produced or taken (for example photographed) images of a higher category.
See page 283.

Starting point and category range
STEP TWO   Having determined the category, the court should use the corresponding starting points to reach a sentence within the category range below. The starting point applies to all offenders irrespective of plea or previous convictions. Having determined the starting point, step two allows further adjustment for aggravating or mitigating features, set out on the next page.

Where there is a sufficient prospect of rehabilitation, a community order with a sex offender treatment programme requirement under section 202 of the Criminal Justice Act 2003 can be a proper alternative to a short or moderate length custodial sentence.[Ed]

	Possession	**Distribution**	**Production**
Category A	**Starting point**	**Starting point**	**Starting point**
	1 year's custody	3 years' custody	6 years' custody
	Category range	**Category range**	**Category range**
	26 weeks' – 3 years' custody	2 – 5 years' custody	4 – 9 years' custody
Category B	**Starting point**	**Starting point**	**Starting point**
	26 weeks' custody	1 year's custody	2 years' custody
	Category range	**Category range**	**Category range**
	High level community order – 18 months' custody	26 weeks' – 2 years' custody	1 – 4 years' custody

Category C	Possession	Distribution	Production
	Starting point	**Starting point**	**Starting point**
	High level community order	13 weeks' custody	18 months' custody
	Category range	**Category range**	**Category range**
	Medium level community order – 26 weeks' custody	High level community order – 26 weeks' custody	1 – 3 years' custody

See page 284.

The table below contains a **non-exhaustive** list of additional factual elements providing the context of the offence and factors relating to the offender. Identify whether any combination of these, or other relevant factors, should result in an upward or downward adjustment from the starting point. **In particular, relevant recent convictions are likely to result in an upward adjustment**. In some cases, having considered these factors, it may be appropriate to move outside the identified category range.

When sentencing appropriate **category 2 or 3 offences**, the court should also consider the custody threshold as follows:

- has the custody threshold been passed?
- if so, is it unavoidable that a custodial sentence be imposed?
- if so, can that sentence be suspended?

Aggravating factors   *Statutory aggravating factors*

Previous convictions, having regard to a) the nature of the offence to which the conviction relates and its relevance to the current offence; and b) the time that has elapsed since the conviction

Offence committed whilst on bail

Other aggravating factors

Failure to comply with current court orders

Offence committed whilst on licence

Age and/or vulnerability of the child depicted*

Discernable pain or distress suffered by child depicted

Period over which images were possessed, distributed or produced

High volume of images possessed, distributed or produced

Placing images where there is the potential for a high volume of viewers

Collection includes moving images

Attempts to dispose of or conceal evidence

Abuse of trust

Child depicted known to the offender

Active involvement in a network or process that facilitates or commissions the creation or sharing of indecent images of children

Commercial exploitation and/or motivation

Deliberate or systematic searching for images portraying young children, category A images or the portrayal of familial sexual abuse

Large number of different victims

Child depicted intoxicated or drugged

---

* Age and/or vulnerability of the child should be given significant weight. In cases where the actual age of the victim is difficult to determine sentencers should consider the development of the child (infant, pre-pubescent, post-pubescent).

Mitigating factors   No previous convictions **or** no relevant/recent convictions

Remorse

Previous good character and/or exemplary conduct*

Age and/or lack of maturity where it affects the responsibility of the offender

Mental disorder or learning disability, particularly where linked to the commission of the offence

Demonstration of steps taken to address offending behaviour

---

* Previous good character/exemplary conduct is different from having no previous convictions. The more serious the offence, the less the weight which should normally be attributed to this factor. Where previous good character/exemplary conduct has been used to facilitate the offence, this mitigation should not normally be allowed and such conduct may constitute an aggravating factor.

Consider any factors which indicate a reduction, such as assistance to the prosecution

STEP THREE   The court should take into account sections 73 and 74 of the Serious Organised Crime and Police Act 2005 (assistance by defendants: reduction or review of sentence) and any other rule of law by virtue of which an offender may receive a discounted sentence in consequence of assistance given (or offered) to the prosecutor or investigator.

Reduction for guilty pleas

STEP FOUR   The court should take account of any potential reduction for a guilty plea in accordance with section 144 of the Criminal Justice Act 2003 and the *Guilty Plea* guideline.

Dangerousness

STEP FIVE   The court should consider whether having regard to the criteria contained in Chapter 5 of Part 12 of the Criminal Justice Act 2003 it would be appropriate to award a life sentence (section 224A) or an extended sentence (section 226A). When sentencing offenders to a life sentence under these provisions, the notional determinate sentence should be used as the basis for the setting of a minimum term.

Totality principle
STEP SIX   If sentencing an offender for more than one offence, or where the offender is already serving a sentence, consider whether the total sentence is just and proportionate to the offending behaviour.

Ancillary orders
STEP SEVEN   The court must consider whether to make any ancillary orders. The court must also consider what other requirements or provisions may *automatically* apply. Further information is included on page 303.

Reasons
STEP EIGHT   Section 174 of the Criminal Justice Act 2003 imposes a duty to give reasons for, and explain the effect of, the sentence.

Consideration for time spent on bail
STEP NINE   The court must consider whether to give credit for time spent on bail in accordance with section 240A of the Criminal Justice Act 2003.

Ed   As was found to be the case, for example, in *R v Jones* [2014] EWCA Crim 1859, [2015] 1 Cr App R (S), a case where it was found that the public would be better protected by a course that might prevent further offending than by a short sentence that was unlikely to have that result.

CAUSING, INCITING OR CONTROLLING PROSTITUTION FOR GAIN
Sexual Offences Act 2003 (section 52)

CONTROLLING PROSTITUTION FOR GAIN
Sexual Offences Act 2003 (section 53)

Triable either way
Maximum: 7 years' custody
Offence range: Community order – 6 years' custody
For convictions on or after 3 December 2012 (irrespective of the date of commission of the offence), these are specified offences for the purposes of section 226A (extended sentence for certain violent or sexual offences) of the Criminal Justice Act 2003.
The terms "prostitute" and "prostitution" are used in this guideline in accordance with the statutory language contained in the Sexual Offences Act 2003.

Determining the offence category

STEP ONE The court should determine which categories of harm and culpability the offence falls into by reference **only** to the tables below.

Category 1	• Abduction/detention
	• Violence or threats of violence
	• Sustained and systematic psychological abuse
	• Individual(s) forced or coerced to participate in unsafe/degrading sexual activity
	• Individual(s) forced or coerced into seeing many "customers"
	• Individual(s) forced/coerced/deceived into prostitution
Category 2	Factor(s) in category 1 not present

Culpability A
Causing, inciting or controlling prostitution on significant commercial basis
Expectation of significant financial or other gain
Abuse of trust
Exploitation of those known to be trafficked
Significant involvement in limiting the freedom of prostitute(s)
Grooming of individual(s) to enter prostitution including through cultivation of a dependency on drugs or alcohol
B
Close involvement with prostitute(s), for example control of finances, choice of clients, working conditions, etc (where offender's involvement is not as a result of coercion)
C
Performs limited function under direction
Close involvement but engaged by coercion/intimidation/ exploitation

Starting point and category range

STEP TWO Having determined the category, the court should use the corresponding starting points to reach a sentence within the category range on the next page. The starting point applies to all offenders irrespective of plea or previous convictions. Having determined the starting point, step two allows further adjustment for aggravating or mitigating features, set out on the next page.

A case of particular gravity, reflected by multiple features of culpability or harm in step one, could merit upward adjustment from the starting point before further adjustment for aggravating or mitigating features, set out on the next page.

Where there is a sufficient prospect of rehabilitation, a community order with a sex offender treatment programme requirement under section 202 of the Criminal Justice Act 2003 can be a proper alternative to a short or moderate length custodial sentence.

	A	B	C
Category 1	**Starting point**	**Starting point**	**Starting point**
	4 year's custody	2 years 6 months' custody	1 years' custody
	Category range	**Category range**	**Category range**
	3 – 6 years' custody	2 – 4 years' custody	26 weeks' – 2 years' custody
Category 2	**Starting point**	**Starting point**	**Starting point**
	2 years 6 months' custody	1 year's custody	Medium level community order
	Category range	**Category range**	**Category range**
	2 – 5 years' custody	High level community order – 2 year's custody	Low level community order – High level community order

The table below contains a **non-exhaustive** list of additional factual elements providing the context of the offence and factors relating to the offender. Identify whether any combination of these, or other relevant factors, should result in an upward or downward adjustment from the starting point. **In particular, relevant recent convictions are likely to result in an upward adjustment.** In some cases, having considered these factors, it may be appropriate to move outside the identified category range.

When sentencing appropriate **category 2 offences**, the court should also consider the custody threshold as follows:

- has the custody threshold been passed?
- if so, is it unavoidable that a custodial sentence be imposed?
- if so, can that sentence be suspended?

Aggravating factors   *Statutory aggravating factors*

Previous convictions, having regard to a) the nature of the offence to which the conviction relates and its relevance to the current offence; and b) the time that has elapsed since the conviction

Offence committed whilst on bail

Other aggravating factors

Failure to comply with current court orders

Offence committed whilst on licence

Deliberate isolation of prostitute(s)

Threats made to expose prostitute(s) to the authorities (for example, immigration or police), family/friends or others

Harm threatened against the family/friends of prostitute(s)

Passport/identity documents removed

Prostitute(s) prevented from seeking medical treatment

Food withheld

Earnings withheld/kept by offender or evidence of excessive wage reduction or debt bondage, inflated travel or living expenses or unreasonable interest rates

Any steps taken to prevent the reporting of an incident, obtaining assistance and/or from assisting or supporting the prosecution

Attempts to dispose of or conceal evidence

Prostitute(s) forced or coerced into pornography

Timescale over which operation has been run

Mitigating factors   No previous convictions **or** no relevant/recent convictions

Remorse

Previous good character and/or exemplary conduct*

Age and/or lack of maturity where it affects the responsibility of the offender

Mental disorder or learning disability, particularly where linked to the commission of the offence

Demonstration of steps taken to address offending behaviour

---

* Previous good character/exemplary conduct is different from having no previous convictions. The more serious the offence, the less the weight which should normally be attributed to this factor. Where previous good character/exemplary conduct has been used to facilitate the offence, this mitigation should not normally be allowed and such conduct may constitute an aggravating factor.

Consider any factors which indicate a reduction, such as assistance to the prosecution

STEP THREE   The court should take into account sections 73 and 74 of the Serious Organised Crime and Police Act 2005 (assistance by defendants: reduction or review of sentence) and any other rule of law by virtue of which an offender may receive a discounted sentence in consequence of assistance given (or offered) to the prosecutor or investigator.

Reduction for guilty pleas

STEP FOUR   The court should take account of any potential reduction for a guilty plea in accordance with section 144 of the Criminal Justice Act 2003 and the *Guilty Plea* guideline.

Dangerousness

STEP FIVE   The court should consider whether having regard to the criteria contained in Chapter 5 of Part 12 of the Criminal Justice Act 2003 it would be appropriate to award an extended sentence (section 226A).

Totality principle

STEP SIX   If sentencing an offender for more than one offence, or where the offender is already serving a sentence, consider whether the total sentence is just and proportionate to the offending behaviour.

Ancillary orders

STEP SEVEN   The court must consider whether to make any ancillary orders. The court must also consider what other requirements or provisions may *automatically* apply. Further information is included on page 303.

Reasons

STEP EIGHT   Section 174 of the Criminal Justice Act 2003 imposes a duty to give reasons for, and explain the effect of, the sentence.

Consideration for time spent on bail
STEP NINE The court must consider whether to give credit for time spent on bail in accordance with section 240A of the Criminal Justice Act 2003.

KEEPING A BROTHEL USED FOR PROSTITUTION
Sexual Offences Act 1956 (section 33A)

Triable either way
Maximum: 7 years' custody
Offence range: Community order – 6 years' custody
The terms "prostitute" and "prostitution" are used in this guideline in accordance with the statutory language contained in the Sexual Offences Act 2003.

Determining the offence category

STEP ONE　The court should determine which categories of harm and culpability the offence falls into by reference **only** to the tables below.

Category 1	• Under 18 year olds working in brothel
	• Abduction/detention
	• Violence or threats of violence
	• Sustained and systematic psychological abuse
	• Those working in brothel forced or coerced to participate in unsafe/degrading sexual activity
	• Those working in brothel forced or coerced into seeing many "customers"
	• Those working in brothel forced/coerced/deceived into prostitution
	• Established evidence of community impact
Category 2	Factor(s) in category 1 not present

Culpability　A
Keeping brothel on significant commercial basis
Involvement in keeping a number of brothels
Expectation of significant financial or other gain
Abuse of trust
Exploitation of those known to be trafficked
Significant involvement in limiting freedom of those working in brothel
Grooming of a person to work in the brothel including through cultivation of a dependency on drugs or alcohol
B
Keeping/managing premises
Close involvement with those working in brothel, for example control of finances, choice of clients, working conditions, etc (where offender's involvement is not as a result of coercion)
C
Performs limited function under direction
Close involvement but engaged by coercion/intimidation/exploitation

Starting point and category range

STEP TWO　Having determined the category, the court should use the corresponding starting points to reach a sentence within the category range on the next page. The starting point applies to all offenders irrespective of plea or previous convictions. Having determined the starting point, step two allows further adjustment for aggravating or mitigating features, set out on the next page.

A case of particular gravity, reflected by multiple features of culpability or harm in step one, could merit upward adjustment from the starting point before further adjustment for aggravating or mitigating features, set out on the next page.

Where there is a sufficient prospect of rehabilitation, a community order with a sex offender treatment programme requirement under section 202 of the Criminal Justice Act 2003 can be a proper alternative to a short or moderate length custodial sentence.

	A	B	C
Category 1	**Starting point**	**Starting point**	**Starting point**
	5 years' custody	3 years' custody	1 year's custody
	Category range	**Category range**	**Category range**
	3 – 6 years' custody	2 – 5 years' custody	High level community order – 18 months' custody
Category 2	**Starting point**	**Starting point**	**Starting point**
	3 years' custody	12 months' custody	Medium level community order
	Category range	**Category range**	**Category range**
	2 – 5 years' custody	26 weeks' – 2 years' custody	Low level community order – High level community order

The table below contains a **non-exhaustive** list of additional factual elements providing the context of the offence and factors relating to the offender. Identify whether any combination of these, or other relevant factors, should result in an upward or downward adjustment from the starting point. **In particular, relevant recent convictions are likely to result in an upward adjustment**. In some cases, having considered these factors, it may be appropriate to move outside the identified category range.

When sentencing appropriate **category 1 offences**, the court should also consider the custody threshold as follows:

- has the custody threshold been passed?
- if so, is it unavoidable that a custodial sentence be imposed?
- if so, can that sentence be suspended?

Aggravating factors *Statutory aggravating factors*
Previous convictions, having regard to a) the nature of the offence to which the conviction relates and its relevance to the current offence; and b) the time that has elapsed since the conviction
Offence committed whilst on bail
Other aggravating factors
Failure to comply with current court orders
Offence committed whilst on licence
Deliberate isolation of those working in brothel
Threats made to expose those working in brothel to the authorities (for example, immigration or police), family/friends or others
Harm threatened against the family/friends of those working in brothel
Passport/identity documents removed
Those working in brothel prevented from seeking medical treatment
Food withheld
Those working in brothel passed around by offender and moved to other brothels
Earnings of those working in brothel withheld/kept by offender or evidence of excessive wage reduction or debt bondage, inflated travel or living expenses or unreasonable interest rates
Any steps taken to prevent those working in brothel reporting an incident, obtaining assistance and/or from assisting or supporting the prosecution
Attempts to dispose of or conceal evidence
Those working in brothel forced or coerced into pornography
Timescale over which operation has been run
Mitigating factors No previous convictions **or** no relevant/recent convictions
Remorse
Previous good character and/or exemplary conduct*
Age and/or lack of maturity where it affects the responsibility of the offender
Mental disorder or learning disability, particularly where linked to the commission of the offence
Demonstration of steps taken to address offending behaviour

---

* Previous good character/exemplary conduct is different from having no previous convictions. The more serious the offence, the less the weight which should normally be attributed to this factor. Where previous good character/exemplary conduct has been used to facilitate the offence, this mitigation should not normally be allowed and such conduct may constitute an aggravating factor.

Consider any factors which indicate a reduction, such as assistance to the prosecution
STEP THREE The court should take into account sections 73 and 74 of the Serious Organised Crime and Police Act 2005 (assistance by defendants: reduction or review of sentence) and any other rule of law by virtue of which an offender may receive a discounted sentence in consequence of assistance given (or offered) to the prosecutor or investigator.

Reduction for guilty pleas
STEP FOUR The court should take account of any potential reduction for a guilty plea in accordance with section 144 of the Criminal Justice Act 2003 and the *Guilty Plea* guideline.

Totality principle
STEP FIVE If sentencing an offender for more than one offence, or where the offender is already serving a sentence, consider whether the total sentence is just and proportionate to the offending behaviour.

Ancillary orders
STEP SIX The court must consider whether to make any ancillary orders. The court must also consider what other requirements or provisions may *automatically* apply. Further information is included on page 303.

Reasons
STEP SEVEN Section 174 of the Criminal Justice Act 2003 imposes a duty to give reasons for, and explain the effect of, the sentence.

Consideration for time spent on bail
STEP EIGHT The court must consider whether to give credit for time spent on bail in accordance with section 240A of the Criminal Justice Act 2003.

Exposure
Sexual Offences Act 2003 (section 66)

Triable either way
Maximum: 2 years' custody
Offence range: Fine – 1 year's custody
For convictions on or after 3 December 2012 (irrespective of the date of commission of the offence), this is a specified offence for the purposes of section 226A (extended sentence for certain violent or sexual offences) of the Criminal Justice Act 2003.

Determining the offence category

STEP ONE   The court should determine the offence category using the table below.

Category 1	Raised harm **and** raised culpability
Category 2	Raised harm **or** raised culpability
Category 3	Exposure **without** raised harm or culpability factors present

The court should determine culpability and harm caused or intended, by reference **only** to the factors below, which comprise the principal factual elements of the offence. Where an offence does not fall squarely into a category, individual factors may require a degree of weighting before making an overall assessment and determining the appropriate offence category.

Factors indicating raised harm   Victim followed/pursued
Offender masturbated

Factors indicating raised culpability   Specific or previous targeting of a particularly vulnerable victim

Abuse of trust

Use of threats (including blackmail)

Offence racially or religiously aggravated

Offence motivated by, or demonstrating, hostility to the victim based on his or her sexual orientation (or presumed sexual orientation) or transgender identity (or presumed transgender identity)

Offence motivated by, or demonstrating, hostility to the victim based on his or her disability (or presumed disability)

Starting point and category range

STEP TWO   Having determined the category, the court should use the corresponding starting points to reach a sentence within the category range on the next page. The starting point applies to all offenders irrespective of plea or previous convictions. Having determined the starting point, step two allows further adjustment for aggravating or mitigating features, set out on the next page.

A case of particular gravity, reflected by multiple features of culpability or harm in step one, could merit upward adjustment from the starting point before further adjustment for aggravating or mitigating features, set out on the next page.

Where there is a sufficient prospect of rehabilitation, a community order with a sex offender treatment programme requirement under section 202 of the Criminal Justice Act 2003 can be a proper alternative to a short or moderate length custodial sentence.

Category 1	**Starting point**
	26 weeks' custody
	Category range
	12 weeks' – 1 year's custody
Category 2	**Starting point**
	High level community order
	Category range
	Medium level community order – 26 weeks' custody
Category 3	**Starting point**
	Medium level community order
	Category range
	Band A fine – High level community order

The table below contains a **non-exhaustive** list of additional factual elements providing the context of the offence and factors relating to the offender. Identify whether any combination of these, or other relevant factors, should result in an upward or downward adjustment from the starting point. **In particular, relevant recent convictions are likely to result in an upward adjustment.** In some cases, having considered these factors, it may be appropriate to move outside the identified category range.

When sentencing **category 2 offences**, the court should also consider the custody threshold as follows:

- has the custody threshold been passed?
- if so, is it unavoidable that a custodial sentence be imposed?

- if so, can that sentence be suspended?

When sentencing **category 3 offences**, the court should also consider the community order threshold as follows:

- has the community order threshold been passed?

Aggravating factors   *Statutory aggravating factors*
Previous convictions, having regard to a) the nature of the offence to which the conviction relates and its relevance to the current offence; and b) the time that has elapsed since the conviction
Offence committed whilst on bail
Other aggravating factors
Location of offence
Timing of offence
Any steps taken to prevent the victim reporting an incident, obtaining assistance and/or from assisting or supporting the prosecution
Failure to comply with current court orders
Offence committed whilst on licence
Commission of offence whilst under the influence of alcohol or drugs
Presence of others, especially children
Mitigating factors   No previous convictions **or** no relevant/recent convictions
Remorse
Previous good character and/or exemplary conduct*
Age and/or lack of maturity where it affects the responsibility of the offender
Mental disorder or learning disability, particularly where linked to the commission of the offence
Demonstration of steps taken to address offending behaviour

---

* Previous good character/exemplary conduct is different from having no previous convictions. The more serious the offence, the less the weight which should normally be attributed to this factor. Where previous good character/exemplary conduct has been used to facilitate the offence, this mitigation should not normally be allowed and such conduct may constitute an aggravating factor.

Consider any factors which indicate a reduction, such as assistance to the prosecution
STEP THREE   The court should take into account sections 73 and 74 of the Serious Organised Crime and Police Act 2005 (assistance by defendants: reduction or review of sentence) and any other rule of law by virtue of which an offender may receive a discounted sentence in consequence of assistance given (or offered) to the prosecutor or investigator.

Reduction for guilty pleas
STEP FOUR   The court should take account of any potential reduction for a guilty plea in accordance with section 144 of the Criminal Justice Act 2003 and the *Guilty Plea* guideline.

Dangerousness
STEP FIVE   The court should consider whether having regard to the criteria contained in Chapter 5 of Part 12 of the Criminal Justice Act 2003 it would be appropriate to award an extended sentence (section 226A).

Totality principle
STEP SIX   If sentencing an offender for more than one offence, or where the offender is already serving a sentence, consider whether the total sentence is just and proportionate to the offending behaviour.

Ancillary orders
STEP SEVEN   The court must consider whether to make any ancillary orders. The court must also consider what other requirements or provisions may *automatically* apply. Further information is included on page 303.

Reasons
STEP EIGHT   Section 174 of the Criminal Justice Act 2003 imposes a duty to give reasons for, and explain the effect of, the sentence.

Consideration for time spent on bail
STEP NINE   The court must consider whether to give credit for time spent on bail in accordance with section 240A of the Criminal Justice Act 2003.

FAIL TO COMPLY WITH NOTIFICATION REQUIREMENTS

Sexual Offences Act 2003, s 91
Effective from: 1 October 2018
Triable either way
Maximum: 5 years' custody
Offence range: Fine – 4 years' custody

Where offence committed in a domestic context, also refer to the *Overarching principles: Domestic abuse guideline*

STEP 1 — DETERMINING THE OFFENCE CATEGORY

The court should determine the offence category with reference only to the factors in the tables below. In order to determine the category the court should assess **culpability** and **harm**.

Culpability

In assessing culpability, the court should consider the intention and motivation of the offender in committing any breach.

A	Determined attempts to avoid detection Long period of non compliance
B	Deliberate failure to comply with requirement
C	Minor breach Breach just short of reasonable excuse

Harm

The level of harm is assessed by weighing up all the factors of the case.

In assessing any risk of harm posed by the breach, consideration should be given to the original offence(s) for which the order was imposed and the circumstances in which the breach arose.

Category 1	Breach causes or risks very serious harm or distress
Category 2	Cases falling between categories 1 and 3
Category 3	Breach causes or risks little or no harm or distress

STEP 2 — STARTING POINT AND CATEGORY RANGE

Having determined the category at step one, the court should use the corresponding starting point to reach a sentence within the category range in the table below. The starting point applies to all offenders irrespective of plea or previous convictions.

Harm	Culpability		
	A	**B**	**C**
Category 1	**Starting point** 2 year's custody **Category range** 1 year's – 4 years' custody	**Starting point** 1 year's custody **Category range** 26 weeks' – 2 year's custody	**Starting point** 36 weeks' custody **Category range** 26 weeks' – 1 year 6 months'custody
Category 2	**Starting point** 1 years' custody **Category range** 26 weeks – 2 years' custody	**Starting point** 36 weeks' custody **Category range** 26 weeks' – 1 year 6 months' custody	**Starting point** High level community order **Category range** Medium level community order – 36 weeks' custody
Category 3	**Starting point** 36 weeks' custody **Category range** 26 weeks' – 1 year 6 months' custody	**Starting point** High level community order **Category range** Medium level community order – 36 weeks' custody	**Starting point** Low level community order **Category range** Band B fine – Medium level community order

The table below contains a **non-exhaustive** list of additional factual elements providing the context of the offence and factors relating to the offender. Identify whether any combination of these, or other relevant factors, should result in an upward or downward adjustment from the starting point. In some cases, having considered these factors, it may be appropriate to move outside the identified category range.

Identify whether any combination of these, or other relevant factors, should result in an upward or downward adjustment from the starting point.

Factors increasing seriousness

Statutory aggravating factors:

• Previous convictions, having regard to a) the **nature** of the offence to which the conviction

relates and its **relevance** to the current offence; and b) the **time** that has elapsed since the conviction
- Offence committed whilst on bail

Other aggravating factors:

- Breach committed shortly after order made
- History of disobedience of court orders (where not already taken into account as a previous conviction)
- Breach constitutes a further offence (where not separately prosecuted)
- Offence committed on licence or post sentence supervision

Factors reducing seriousness or reflecting personal mitigation

- Breach committed after long period of compliance
- Prompt voluntary surrender/admission of breach or failure
- Age and/or lack of maturity where it affects the responsibility of the offender
- Mental disorder or learning disability where linked to the commission of the offence
- Sole or primary carer for dependent relatives

STEP 3 — CONSIDER ANY FACTORS WHICH INDICATE A REDUCTION, SUCH AS ASSISTANCE TO THE PROSECUTION

The court should take into account sections 73 and 74 of the Serious Organised Crime and Police Act 2005 (assistance by defendants: reduction or review of sentence) and any other rule of law by virtue of which an offender may receive a discounted sentence in consequence of assistance given (or offered) to the prosecutor or investigator.

STEP 4 — REDUCTION FOR GUILTY PLEAS

The court should take account of any potential reduction for a guilty plea in accordance with section 144 of the Criminal Justice Act 2003 and the *Guilty Plea* guideline.

STEP 5 — TOTALITY PRINCIPLE

If sentencing an offender for more than one offence, or where the offender is already serving a sentence, consider whether the total sentence is just and proportionate to the overall offending behaviour in accordance with the *Offences Taken into Consideration and Totality* guideline.

STEP 6 — COMPENSATION AND ANCILLARY ORDERS

In all cases, the court must consider whether to make a compensation order and/or other ancillary orders.

Compensation order

The court should consider compensation orders in all cases where personal injury, loss or damage has resulted from the offence. The court must give reasons if it decides not to award compensation in such cases.

Other ancillary orders available include: Restraining order Where an offender is convicted of any offence, the court may make a restraining order (section 5 of the Protection from Harassment Act 1997).

The order may prohibit the offender from doing anything for the purpose of protecting the victim of the offence, or any other person mentioned in the order, from further conduct which amounts to harassment or will cause a fear of violence.

The order may have effect for a specified period or until further order.

STEP 7 — REASONS

Section 174 of the Criminal Justice Act 2003 imposes a duty to give reasons for, and explain the effect of, the sentence.

STEP 8 — CONSIDERATION FOR TIME SPENT ON BAIL

The court must consider whether to give credit for time spent on bail in accordance with section 240A of the Criminal Justice Act 2003.

FAILURE TO SURRENDER TO BAIL

Bail Act 1976, s 6
Effective from: 1 October 2018
Triable either way
Maximum: 12 months' custody
Offence range: Discharge – 26 weeks' custody

Where offence committed in a domestic context, also refer to the *Overarching principles: Domestic abuse guideline*

STEP 1 — DETERMINING THE OFFENCE CATEGORY

The court should determine the offence category with reference only to the factors listed in the tables below. In order to determine the category the court should assess **culpability** and **harm**.

Culpability

A	Failure to surrender represents deliberate attempt to evade or delay justice
B	Cases falling between categories A and C
C	Reason for failure to surrender just short of reasonable cause

Harm

The level of **harm** is determined by weighing up all the factors of the case to determine the harm that has been caused or was intended to be caused.

In assessing any risk of harm posed by the breach, consideration should be given to the original offence(s) for which the order was imposed and the circumstances in which the breach arose.

Category 1	Failure to attend Crown Court hearing results in substantial delay and/or interference with the administration of justice
Category 2	Failure to attend magistrates' court hearing results in substantial delay and/or interference with the administration of justice*
Category 3	Cases in either the magistrates' court or Crown Court not in categories 1 and 2

* In particularly serious cases where the failure to attend is in the magistrates' court and the consequences of the delay have a severe impact on victim(s) and /or witness(es) warranting a sentence outside of the powers of the magistrates' court, the case should be committed to the Crown Court pursuant to section 6(6)(a) of the Bail Act 1976 and the Crown Court should sentence the case according to the range in Category A1.

STEP 2 — STARTING POINT AND CATEGORY RANGE

Having determined the category at step one, the court should use the corresponding starting point to reach a sentence within the category range in the table below. The starting point applies to all offenders irrespective of plea or previous convictions.

Where a custodial sentence is available within the category range and the substantive offence attracts a custodial sentence, a consecutive custodial sentence should normally be imposed for the failure to surrender offence.

Harm	Culpability		
	A	**B**	**C**
Category 1	**Starting point** 6 weeks' custody **Category range** 28 days' – 26 weeks' custody[1]	**Starting point** 21 days' custody **Category range** High level community order* – 13 weeks' custody	**Starting point** Medium level community order* **Category range** Low level community order* – 6 weeks' custody
Category 2	**Starting point** 21 days' custody **Category range** High level community order* – 13 weeks' custody	**Starting point** Medium level community order* **Category range** Band B fine – 6 weeks' custody	**Starting point** Band B fine **Category range** Band A fine – Low level community order*
Category 3	**Starting point** 14 days' custody **Category range** Low level community order* – 6 weeks' custody	**Starting point** Band C fine **Category range** Band A fine – Medium level community order*	**Starting point** Band A fine **Category range** Discharge – Band B fine

* To include a curfew and/or unpaid work requirement only

[1] In A1 cases which are particularly serious and where the consequences of the delay have a severe impact on victim(s) and /or witness(es), a sentence in excess of the specified range may be appropriate.

Maximum sentence in magistrates' court – 3 months' imprisonment

Maximum sentence in Crown Court – 12 months' imprisonment

The table below contains a **non-exhaustive** list of additional factual elements providing the context of the offence and factors relating to the offender. Identify whether any combination of these, or other relevant factors, should result in an upward or downward adjustment from the starting point. In some cases, having considered these factors, it may be appropriate to move outside the identified category range.

Factors increasing seriousness

Statutory aggravating factors:

- Previous convictions, having regard to a) the **nature** of the offence to which the conviction relates and its **relevance** to the current offence; and b) the **time** that has elapsed since the conviction
- Offence committed whilst on bail

Other aggravating factors:

- History of breach of court orders or police bail
- Distress to victim(s) and /or witness(es)
- Offence committed on licence or while subject to post sentence supervision

Factors reducing seriousness or reflecting personal mitigation

- Genuine misunderstanding of bail or requirements
- Prompt voluntary surrender
- Sole or primary carer for dependent relatives

STEP 3 — CONSIDER ANY FACTORS WHICH INDICATE A REDUCTION, SUCH AS ASSISTANCE TO THE PROSECUTION

The court should take into account sections 73 and 74 of the Serious Organised Crime and Police Act 2005 (assistance by defendants: reduction or review of sentence) and any other rule of law by virtue of which an offender may receive a discounted sentence in consequence of assistance given (or offered) to the prosecutor or investigator.

STEP 4 — REDUCTION FOR GUILTY PLEAS

The court should take account of any potential reduction for a guilty plea in accordance with section 144 of the Criminal Justice Act 2003 and the *Guilty Plea* guideline.

STEP 5 — TOTALITY PRINCIPLE

If sentencing an offender for more than one offence, or where the offender is already serving a sentence, consider whether the total sentence is just and proportionate to the overall offending behaviour in accordance with the *Offences Taken into Consideration and Totality* guideline.

STEP 6 — ANCILLARY ORDERS

In all cases, the court must consider whether to make a compensation order and/or other ancillary orders.

STEP 7 — REASONS

Section 174 of the Criminal Justice Act 2003 imposes a duty to give reasons for, and explain the effect of, the sentence.

STEP 8 — CONSIDERATION FOR TIME SPENT ON BAIL

The court must consider whether to give credit for time spent on bail in accordance with section 240A of the Criminal Justice Act 2003.

Voyeurism

Sexual Offences Act 2003 (section 67)

Triable either way

Maximum: 2 years' custody

Offence range: Fine – 18 months' custody

For convictions on or after such date (irrespective of the date of commission of the offence), these are specified offences for the purposes of section 226A (extended sentence for certain violent or sexual offences) of the Criminal Justice Act 2003.Effective from 1 April 2014

Determining the offence category

STEP ONE The court should determine the offence category using the table below.

Category 1	Raised harm **and** raised culpability
Category 2	Raised harm **or** raised culpability
Category 3	Voyeurism **without** raised harm or culpability factors present

The court should determine culpability and harm caused or intended, by reference **only** to the factors below, which comprise the principal factual elements of the offence. Where an offence does not fall squarely into a category, individual factors may require a degree of weighting before making an overall assessment and determining the appropriate offence category.

Factors indicating raised harm Image(s) available to be viewed by others

Victim observed or recorded in their own home or residence

Factors indicating raised culpability Significant degree of planning

Image(s) recorded

Abuse of trust

Specific or previous targeting of a particularly vulnerable victim

Commercial exploitation and/or motivation

Offence racially or religiously aggravated

Offence motivated by, or demonstrating, hostility to the victim based on his or her sexual orientation (or presumed sexual orientation) or transgender identity (or presumed transgender identity)

Offence motivated by, or demonstrating, hostility to the victim based on his or her disability (or presumed disability)

Starting point and category range

STEP TWO Having determined the category, the court should use the corresponding starting points to reach a sentence within the category range on the next page. The starting point applies to all offenders irrespective of plea or previous convictions. Having determined the starting point, step two allows further adjustment for aggravating or mitigating features, set out on the next page.

A case of particular gravity, reflected by multiple features of culpability or harm in step one, could merit upward adjustment from the starting point before further adjustment for aggravating or mitigating features, set out on the next page.

Where there is a sufficient prospect of rehabilitation, a community order with a sex offender treatment programme requirement under section 202 of the Criminal Justice Act 2003 can be a proper alternative to a short or moderate length custodial sentence.

Category 1	**Starting point**
	26 weeks' custody
	Category range
	12 weeks' – 18 months' custody
Category 2	**Starting point**
	High level community order
	Category range
	Medium level community order – 26 weeks' custody
Category 3	**Starting point**
	Medium level community order
	Category range
	Band A fine – High level community order

The table below contains a **non-exhaustive** list of additional factual elements providing the context of the offence and factors relating to the offender. Identify whether any combination of these, or other relevant factors, should result in an upward or downward adjustment from the starting point. **In particular, relevant recent convictions are likely to result in an upward adjustment.** In some cases, having considered these factors, it may be appropriate to move outside the identified category range.

When sentencing **category 2 offences**, the court should also consider the custody threshold as follows:

- has the custody threshold been passed?
- if so, is it unavoidable that a custodial sentence be imposed?
- if so, can that sentence be suspended?

When sentencing **category 3 offences**, the court should also consider the community order threshold as follows:

- has the community order threshold been passed?

Aggravating factors   *Statutory aggravating factors*
Previous convictions, having regard to a) the nature of the offence to which the conviction relates and its relevance to the current offence; and b) the time that has elapsed since the conviction
Offence committed whilst on bail
Other aggravating factors
Location of offence
Timing of offence
Failure to comply with current court orders
Offence committed whilst on licence
Distribution of images, whether or not for gain
Placing images where there is the potential for a high volume of viewers
Period over which victim observed
Period over which images were made or distributed
Any steps taken to prevent victim reporting an incident, obtaining assistance and/or from assisting or supporting the prosecution
Attempts to dispose of or conceal evidence
Mitigating factors   No previous convictions **or** no relevant/recent convictions
Remorse
Previous good character and/or exemplary conduct*
Age and/or lack of maturity where it affects the responsibility of the offender
Mental disorder or learning disability, particularly where linked to the commission of the offence
Demonstration of steps taken to address offending behaviour

---

* Previous good character/exemplary conduct is different from having no previous convictions. The more serious the offence, the less the weight which should normally be attributed to this factor. Where previous good character/exemplary conduct has been used to facilitate the offence, this mitigation should not normally be allowed and such conduct may constitute an aggravating factor.

Consider any factors which indicate a reduction, such as assistance to the prosecution
STEP THREE   The court should take into account sections 73 and 74 of the Serious Organised Crime and Police Act 2005 (assistance by defendants: reduction or review of sentence) and any other rule of law by virtue of which an offender may receive a discounted sentence in consequence of assistance given (or offered) to the prosecutor or investigator.

Reduction for guilty pleas
STEP FOUR   The court should take account of any potential reduction for a guilty plea in accordance with section 144 of the Criminal Justice Act 2003 and the *Guilty Plea* guideline.

Dangerousness
STEP FIVE   The court should consider whether having regard to the criteria contained in Chapter 5 of Part 12 of the Criminal Justice Act 2003 it would be appropriate to award an extended sentence (section 226A).

Totality principle
STEP SIX   If sentencing an offender for more than one offence, or where the offender is already serving a sentence, consider whether the total sentence is just and proportionate to the offending behaviour.

Ancillary orders
STEP SEVEN   The court must consider whether to make any ancillary orders. The court must also consider what other requirements or provisions may *automatically* apply. Further information is included on page 303.

Reasons
STEP EIGHT   Section 174 of the Criminal Justice Act 2003 imposes a duty to give reasons for, and explain the effect of, the sentence.

Consideration for time spent on bail
STEP NINE   The court must consider whether to give credit for time spent on bail in accordance with section 240A of the Criminal Justice Act 2003.

SEXUAL OFFENCES – ANCILLARY ORDERS

This summary of the key provisions is correct as at the date of publication but will be subject to subsequent changes in law. If necessary, seek legal advice.

ANCILLARY ORDER	STATUTORY REFERENCE
Compensation	
The court must consider making a compensation order in any case in which personal injury, loss or damage has resulted from the offence. The court must give reasons if it decides not to make an order in such cases.	Section 130 of the Powers of Criminal Courts (Sentencing) Act 2000
Confiscation	
A confiscation order may be made by the Crown Court in circumstances in which the offender has obtained a financial benefit as a result of, or in connection with, his criminal conduct.	Section 6 and Schedule 2 of the Proceeds of Crime Act 2002
Deprivation of property	
The court may order the offender is deprived of property used for the purpose of committing, or facilitating the commission of, any offence, or intended for that purpose.	Section 143 of the Powers of Criminal Courts (Sentencing) Act 2000
Disqualification from working with children	
From 17 June 2013 courts **no longer** have the power to disqualify offenders from working with children pursuant to the Criminal Justice and Court Services Act 2000.	Schedule 10 of the Safeguarding Vulnerable Groups Act 2006
	Safeguarding Vulnerable Groups Act 2006 (Commencement No. 8 and Saving) Order 2012 (SI 2012/2231)
	Protection of Freedoms Act 2012 (Commencement No. 6) Order 2013 (SI 2013/1180)
Restraining order	
Following a conviction *or an acquittal*, a court may make a restraining order for the purpose of protecting the victim or another person from harassment or a fear of violence.	Sections 5 and 5A of the Protection from Harassment Act 1997
Serious crime prevention order (SCPO)	
An SCPO may be made by the Crown Court in respect of qualifying offenders, if the court is satisfied such an order would protect the public by preventing, restricting or disrupting the involvement of the offender in serious crime.	Section 19 and Schedule 1 of the Serious Crime Act 2007
Sexual offences prevention order (SOPO)	
A SOPO may be made against qualifying offenders if the court is satisfied such an order is necessary to protect the public or any particular member of the public from serious sexual harm from the offender. The terms of the SOPO must be proportionate to the objective of protecting the public and consistent with the sentence and other ancillary orders, conditions and requirements to which the offender is subject.	Section 104 and Schedules 3 and 5 of the Sexual Offences Act 2003

AUTOMATIC ORDERS ON CONVICTION

The following requirements or provisions are **not** part of the sentence imposed by the court but apply automatically by operation of law. The role of the court is to inform the offender of the applicable requirements and/or prohibition.

REQUIREMENT OR PROVISION	STATUTORY REFERENCE
Notification requirements	
A relevant offender automatically becomes subject to notification requirements, obliging him to notify the police of specified information for a specified period. The court should inform the offender accordingly.	Sections 80 to 88 and Schedule 3 of the Sexual Offences Act 2003
The operation of the notification requirement is not a relevant consideration in determining the sentence for the offence.	

REQUIREMENT OR PROVISION	STATUTORY REFERENCE
Protection for children and vulnerable adults	
A statutory scheme pursuant to which offenders *will* or *may* be barred from regulated activity relating to children or vulnerable adults, with or without the right to make representations, depending on the offence. The court should inform the offender accordingly.	Section 2 and Schedule 3 of the Safeguarding Vulnerable Groups Act 2006
	Safeguarding Vulnerable Groups Act 2006 (Prescribed Criteria and Miscellaneous Provisions) Regulations 2009 (SI 2009/37) (as amended)

Guidance for offences pre-dating those under the Sexual Offences Act 2003 can be found at www.sentencingcouncil.org.uk

Environmental Offences – Organisations

Unauthorised or harmful deposit, treatment or disposal etc of waste
Illegal discharges to air, land and water

Environmental Protection Act 1990 (section 33)

Environmental Permitting (England and Wales) Regulations 2010 (regulations 12 and 38(1), (2) and (3))

Also relevant, with adjustments, to certain related offences (see page 316)
Triable either way

Maxi-   when tried on indictment: unlimited fine
mum:

when tried summarily: £50,000 fine

Offence range: £100 fine – £3 million fine

Use this guideline when the offender is an organisation. If the offender is an individual, please refer to the guideline for individuals.

Confiscation

Committal to the Crown Court for sentence is mandatory if confiscation (see step two) is to be considered: Proceeds of Crime Act 2002 section 70. In such cases magistrates should state whether they would otherwise have committed for sentence.

Financial orders must be considered in this order: (1) compensation, (2) confiscation, and (3) fine (see Proceeds of Crime Act 2002 section 13).

Compensation

STEP ONE The court must consider making a compensation order requiring the offender to pay compensation for any personal injury, loss or damage resulting from the offence in such an amount as the court considers appropriate, having regard to the evidence and to the means of the offender.

Where the means of the offender are limited, priority should be given to the payment of compensation over payment of any other financial penalty.

Reasons should be given if a compensation order is not made.

(See section 130 Powers of Criminal Courts (Sentencing) Act 2000)

Confiscation (Crown Court only)

STEP TWO Confiscation must be considered if either the Crown asks for it or the court thinks that it may be appropriate. Confiscation must be dealt with before any other fine or financial order (except compensation).

(See sections 6 and 13 Proceeds of Crime Act 2002)

See page 307.

Determining the offence category

STEP THREE The court should determine the offence category using only the culpability and harm factors in the tables below. The culpability and harm categories are on a sliding scale; there is inevitable overlap between the factors described in adjacent categories. Where an offence does not fall squarely into a category, individual factors may require a degree of weighting before making an overall assessment and determining the appropriate offence category.

Dealing with a **risk of harm** involves consideration of both the likelihood of harm occurring and the extent of it if it does. Risk of harm is less serious than the same actual harm. Where the offence has caused risk of harm but no (or less) actual harm the normal approach is to move down to the next category of harm. This may not be appropriate if either the likelihood or extent of potential harm is particularly high.

Culpability Deliberate

Intentional breach of or flagrant disregard for the law by person(s) whose position of responsibility in the organisation is such that their acts/omissions can properly be attributed to the organisation;

OR

deliberate failure by organisation to put in place and to enforce such systems as could reasonably be expected in all the circumstances to avoid commission of the offence.

Reckless

Actual foresight of, or wilful blindness to, risk of offending but risk nevertheless taken by person(s) whose position of responsibility in the organisation is such that their acts/omissions can properly be attributed to the organisation;

OR

reckless failure by organisation to put in place and to enforce such systems as could reasonably be expected in all the circumstances to avoid commission of the offence.

Negligent

Failure by the organisation as a whole to take reasonable care to put in place and enforce proper systems for avoiding commission of the offence.

Low or no culpability

Offence committed with little or no fault on the part of the organisation as a whole, for example by accident or the act of a rogue employee and despite the presence and due enforcement of all reasonably required preventive measures, or where such proper preventive measures were unforeseeably overcome by exceptional events.

Category 1	• Polluting material of a dangerous nature, for example, hazardous chemicals or sharp objects
	• Major adverse effect or damage to air or water quality, amenity value, or property
	• Polluting material was noxious, widespread or pervasive with long-lasting effects on human health or quality of life, animal health or flora
	• Major costs incurred through clean-up, site restoration or animal rehabilitation
	• Major interference with, prevention or undermining of other lawful activities or regulatory regime due to offence
Category 2	• Significant adverse effect or damage to air or water quality, amenity value, or property
	• Significant adverse effect on human health or quality of life, animal health or flora
	• Significant costs incurred through clean-up, site restoration or animal rehabilitation
	• Significant interference with or undermining of other lawful activities or regulatory regime due to offence
	• Risk of category 1 harm
Category 3	• Minor, localised adverse effect or damage to air or water quality, amenity value, or property
	• Minor adverse effect on human health or quality of life, animal health or flora
	• Low costs incurred through clean-up, site restoration or animal rehabilitation
	• Limited interference with or undermining of other lawful activities or regulatory regime due to offence
	• Risk of category 2 harm
Category 4	• Risk of category 3 harm

Starting point and category range

STEP FOUR   Having determined the category, the court should refer to the tables on pages 309 to 312. There are four tables of starting points and ranges: one for large[Ed 1] organisations, one for medium organisations, one for small organisations and one for micro-organisations. The court should refer to the table that relates to the size of the offending organisation.

The court should use the corresponding starting point to reach a sentence within the category range. The court should then consider further adjustment within the category range for aggravating and mitigating features, set out on page 313.

General principles to follow in setting a fine

The court should determine the appropriate level of fine in accordance with section 164 of the Criminal Justice Act 2003, which requires that the fine must reflect the seriousness of the offence and the court to take into account the financial circumstances of the offender.

The level of fine should reflect the extent to which the offender fell below the required standard. The fine should meet, in a fair and proportionate way, the objectives of punishment, deterrence and the removal of gain derived through the commission of the offence; it should not be cheaper to offend than to take the appropriate precautions.

Obtaining financial information

Offenders which are companies, partnerships or bodies delivering a public or charitable service, are expected to provide comprehensive accounts for the last three years, to enable the court to make an accurate assessment of its financial status. In the absence of such disclosure, or where the court is not satisfied that it has been given sufficient reliable information, the court will be entitled to draw reasonable inferences as to the offender's means from evidence it has heard and from all the circumstances of the case.

Normally, only information relating to the organisation before the court will be relevant, unless it is demonstrated to the court that the resources of a linked organisation are available and can properly be taken into account.

(1)   *For companies*: annual accounts. Particular attention should be paid to turnover; profit before tax; directors' remuneration, loan accounts and pension provision; and assets as disclosed by the balance sheet. Most companies are required to file audited accounts at Companies House. **Failure to produce relevant recent accounts on request may properly lead to the conclusion that the company can pay any appropriate fine.**

(2)   *For partnerships*: annual accounts. Particular attention should be paid to turnover; profit

before tax; partners' drawings, loan accounts and pension provision; assets as above. Limited Liability Partnerships (LLPs) may be required to file audited accounts with Companies House. **If adequate accounts are not produced on request, see paragraph 1.**

(3) *For local authorities, fire authorities and similar public bodies*: the Annual Revenue Budget ("ARB") is the equivalent of turnover and the best indication of the size of the defendant organisation. It is unlikely to be necessary to analyse specific expenditure or reserves (where relevant) unless inappropriate expenditure is suggested.

(4) *For health trusts*: the independent regulator of NHS Foundation Trusts is Monitor. It publishes quarterly reports and annual figures for the financial strength and stability of trusts from which the annual income can be seen, available via www.monitor-nhsft.gov.uk. Detailed analysis of expenditure or reserves is unlikely to be called for.

(5) *For charities*: it will be appropriate to inspect annual audited accounts. Detailed analysis of expenditure or reserves is unlikely to be called for unless there is a suggestion of unusual or unnecessary expenditure.

At step four, the court will be required to focus on the organisation's annual turnover or equivalent to reach a starting point for a fine. At step six, the court may be required to refer to the other financial factors listed above to ensure that the proposed fine is proportionate.

Ed 1 The guidelines to do not apply to very large organisations and the court is not bound, or even bound by, or even bound to start with, the ranges of fines suggested for organisations which are merely 'large': *R v Thames Water Utilities Ltd Practice Note* [2015] EWCA Crim 960, [2015] 1 WLR 4411, [2015] 2 Cr App R (S) 63.

Very large organisations Where a defendant company's turnover or equivalent very greatly exceeds the threshold for large companies, it may be necessary to move outside the suggested range to achieve a proportionate sentence.

Large

Turnover or equivalent: £50 million and over.

Large	Starting Point	Range
Deliberate		
Category 1	£1,000,000	£450,000 – £3,000,000
Category 2	£500,000	£180,000 – £1,250,000
Category 3	£180,000	£100,000 – £450,000
Category 4	£100,000	£55,000 – £250,000
Reckless		
Category 1	£550,000	£250,000 – £1,500,000
Category 2	£250,000	£100,000 – £650,000
Category 3	£100,000	£60,000 – £250,000
Category 4	£60,000	£35,000 – £160,000
Negligent		
Category 1	£300,000	£140,000 – £750,000
Category 2	£140,000	£60,000 – £350,000
Category 3	£60,000	£35,000 – £150,000
Category 4	£35,000	£22,000 – £100,000
Low / No culpability		
Category 1	£50,000	£25,000 – £130,000
Category 2	£25,000	£14,000 – £70,000
Category 3	£14,000	£10,000 – £40,000
Category 4	£10,000	£7,000 – £25,000

Medium

Turnover or equivalent: between £10 million and £50 million.

Medium	Starting Point	Range
Deliberate		
Category 1	£400,000	£170,000 – £1,000,000
Category 2	£170,000	£70,000 – £450,000
Category 3	£70,000	£40,000 – £180,000
Category 4	£40,000	£22,000 – £100,000
Reckless		
Category 1	£220,000	£100,000 – £500,000
Category 2	£100,000	£40,000 – £250,000
Category 3	£40,000	£24,000 – £100,000
Category 4	£24,000	£14,000 – £60,000
Negligent		

Medium	Starting Point	Range
Category 1	£120,000	£55,000 – £300,000
Category 2	£55,000	£25,000 – £140,000
Category 3	£25,000	£14,000 – £60,000
Category 4	£14,000	£8,000 – £35,000
Low / No culpability		
Category 1	£20,000	£10,000 – £50,000
Category 2	£10,000	£5,500 – £25,000
Category 3	£5,000	£3,500 – £14,000
Category 4	£3,000	£2,500 – £10,000

See page 311.
Small
Turnover or equivalent: between £2 million and £10million.

Small	Starting Point	Range
Deliberate		
Category 1	£100,000	£45,000 – £400,000
Category 2	£45,000	£17,000 – £170,000
Category 3	£17,000	£10,000 – £70,000
Category 4	£10,000	£5,000 – £40,000
Reckless		
Category 1	£55,000	£24,000 – £220,000
Category 2	£24,000	£10,000 – £100,000
Category 3	£10,000	£5,000 – £40,000
Category 4	£5,000	£3,000 – £24,000
Negligent		
Category 1	£30,000	£13,000 – £120,000
Category 2	£13,000	£6,000 – £55,000
Category 3	£6,000	£3,000 – £23,000
Category 4	£3,000	£1,500 – £14,000
Low / No culpability		
Category 1	£5,000	£2,500 – £20,000
Category 2	£2,500	£1,000 – £10,000
Category 3	£1,000	£700 – £5,000
Category 4	£700	£400 – £3,500

See page 312.
Micro
Turnover or equivalent: not more than £2 million.

Micro	Starting Point	Range
Deliberate		
Category 1	£50,000	£9,000 – £95,000
Category 2	£22,000	£3,000 – £45,000
Category 3	£9,000	£2,000 – £17,000
Category 4	£5,000	£1,000 – £10,000
Reckless		
Category 1	£30,000	£3,000 – £55,000
Category 2	£12,000	£1,500 – £24,000
Category 3	£5,000	£1,000 – £10,000
Category 4	£3,000	£500 – £5,500
Negligent		
Category 1	£15,000	£1,500 – £30,000
Category 2	£6,500	£1,000 – £13,000
Category 3	£2,500	£500 – £5,500
Category 4	£1,400	£350 – £3,000
Low / No culpability		

Micro	Starting Point	Range
Category 1	£2,500	£500 – £5,000
Category 2	£1,000	£350 – £2,400
Category 3	£400	£175 – £1,000
Category 4	£200	£100 – £700

See page 313.

The table below contains a **non-exhaustive** list of factual elements providing the context of the offence and factors relating to the offender. Identify whether any combination of these, or other relevant factors, should result in an upward or downward adjustment from the starting point. **In particular, relevant recent convictions and/or a history of non-compliance are likely to result in a substantial upward adjustment**. In some cases, having considered these factors, it may be appropriate to move outside the identified category range.

Factors increasing seriousness *Statutory aggravating factors:*

Previous convictions, having regard to a) the nature of the offence to which the conviction relates and its relevance to the current offence; and b) the time that has elapsed since the conviction

Other aggravating factors include:

History of non-compliance with warnings by regulator

Location of the offence, for example, near housing, schools, livestock or environmentally sensitive sites

Repeated incidents of offending or offending over an extended period of time, where not charged separately

Deliberate concealment of illegal nature of activity

Ignoring risks identified by employees or others

Established evidence of wider/community impact

Breach of any order

Offence committed for financial gain

Obstruction of justice

Factors reducing seriousness or reflecting mitigation No previous convictions or no relevant/recent convictions

Evidence of steps taken to remedy problem

Remorse

Compensation paid voluntarily to remedy harm caused

One-off event not commercially motivated

Little or no financial gain

Effective compliance and ethics programme

Self-reporting, co-operation and acceptance of responsibility

Good character and/or exemplary conduct

See page 314.

Steps five to seven

The court should now 'step back' and, using the factors set out in steps five, six and seven, **review whether the sentence as a whole meets, in a fair way, the objectives of punishment, deterrence and removal of gain derived through the commission of the offence**. At steps five to seven, the court may increase or reduce the proposed fine reached at step four, if necessary moving outside the range.

Ensure that the combination of financial orders (compensation, confiscation if appropriate, and fine) removes any economic benefit derived from the offending

STEP FIVE The court should remove any economic benefit the offender has derived through the commission of the offence including:

- avoided costs;
- operating savings;
- any gain made as a direct result of the offence.

Where the offender is fined, the amount of economic benefit derived from the offence should normally be added to the fine arrived at in step four. If a confiscation order is made, in considering economic benefit, the court should avoid double recovery.

Economic benefit will not always be an identifiable feature of a case. For example, in some water pollution cases there may be strict liability but very little obvious gain. However, even in these cases there may be some avoidance of cost, for example alarms not installed and maintained, inadequate bunding or security measures not installed. Any costs avoided will be considered as economic benefit.

Where it is not possible to calculate or estimate the economic benefit, the court may wish to draw on information from the enforcing authorities about the general costs of operating within the law.

Check whether the proposed fine based on turnover is proportionate to the means of the offender

STEP SIX The combination of financial orders must be sufficiently substantial to have a real economic impact which will bring home to both management and shareholders the need to improve regulatory compliance. Whether the fine will have the effect of putting the offender out of business will be relevant; in some bad cases this may be an acceptable consequence.

It will be necessary to examine the financial circumstances of the organisation in the round. If an organisation has a small profit margin relative to its turnover, downward adjustment may be needed. If it has a large profit margin, upward adjustment may be needed.

In considering the ability of the offending organisation to pay any financial penalty, the court can take into account **the power to allow time for payment or to order that the amount be paid in instalments**.

Consider other factors that may warrant adjustment of the proposed fine

STEP SEVEN The court should consider any further factors that are relevant to ensuring that the proposed fine is proportionate having regard to the means of the offender and the seriousness of the offence.

Where the fine will fall on public or charitable bodies, the fine should normally be substantially reduced if the offending organisation is able to demonstrate the proposed fine would have a significant impact on the provision of their services.

The **non-exhaustive** list below contains additional factual elements the court should consider in deciding whether an increase or reduction to the proposed fine is required:

- fine impairs offender's ability to make restitution to victims;
- impact of fine on offender's ability to improve conditions in the organisation to comply with the law;
- impact of fine on employment of staff, service users, customers and local economy.

Consider any factors which indicate a reduction, such as assistance to the prosecution

STEP EIGHT The court should take into account sections 73 and 74 of the Serious Organised Crime and Police Act 2005 (assistance by defendants: reduction or review of sentence) and any other rule of law by virtue of which an offender may receive a discounted sentence in consequence of assistance given (or offered) to the prosecutor or investigator.

Reduction for guilty pleas

STEP NINE The court should take account of any potential reduction for a guilty plea in accordance with section 144 of the Criminal Justice Act 2003 and the *Guilty Plea* guideline.

Ancillary orders

STEP TEN In all cases, the court must consider whether to make ancillary orders. These may include:

Forfeiture of vehicle

The court may order the forfeiture of a vehicle used in or for the purposes of the commission of the offence in accordance with section 33C of the Environmental Protection Act 1990.

Deprivation of property

Where section 33C of the Environmental Protection Act 1990 does not apply, the court may order the offender be deprived of property used to commit crime or intended for that purpose in accordance with section 143 of the Powers of Criminal Courts (Sentencing) Act 2000. In considering whether to make an order under section 143, the court must have regard to the value of the property and the likely effects on the offender of making the order taken together with any other order the court makes.

Remediation

Where an offender is convicted of an offence under regulation 38(1), (2) or (3) of the Environmental Permitting (England and Wales) Regulations 2010, a court may order the offender to take steps to remedy the cause of the offence within a specified period in accordance with regulation 44 of the Environmental Permitting (England and Wales) Regulations 2010.

Totality principle

STEP ELEVEN If sentencing an offender for more than one offence, or where the offender is already serving a sentence, consider whether the total sentence is just and proportionate to the offending behaviour.

Reasons

STEP TWELVE Section 174 of the Criminal Justice Act 2003 imposes a duty to give reasons for, and explain the effect of, the sentence.

Other environmental offences

In sentencing other relevant and analogous environmental offences, the court should refer to the sentencing approach in steps one to three and five to seven of the guideline, **adjusting the starting points and ranges bearing in mind the statutory maxima** for those offences. An indicative list of such offences is set out below.

Offence	Mode of trial	Statutory maxima
Section 1 Control of Pollution (Amendment) Act 1989 – transporting controlled waste without registering	Triable summarily only	• level 5 fine
Section 34 Environmental Protection Act 1990 – breach of duty of care	Triable either way	• when tried on indictment: unlimited fine • when tried summarily: level 5 fine

Offence	Mode of trial	Statutory maxima
Section 80 Environmental Protection Act 1990 – breach of an abatement notice	Triable summarily only	• where the offence is committed on industrial, trade or business premises: £20,000 fine
		• where the offence is committed on non-industrial etc premises: level 5 fine with a further fine of an amount equal to one-tenth of that level for each day on which the offence continues after the conviction
Section 111 Water Industry Act 1991 – restrictions on use of public sewers	Triable either way	• when tried on indictment: imprisonment for a term not exceeding two years or a fine or both
		• when tried summarily: a fine not exceeding the statutory maximum and a further fine not exceeding £50 for each day on which the offence continues after conviction
Offences under the Transfrontier Shipment of Waste Regulations 2007	Triable either way	• when tried on indictment: a fine or two years imprisonment or both
		• when tried summarily: a fine not exceeding the statutory maximum or three months' imprisonment or both

ENVIRONMENTAL OFFENCES – INDIVIDUALS

UNAUTHORISED OR HARMFUL DEPOSIT, TREATMENT OR DISPOSAL ETC OF WASTE
ILLEGAL DISCHARGES TO AIR, LAND AND WATER

Environmental Protection Act 1990 (section 33)
Environmental Permitting (England and Wales) Regulations 2010 (regulations 12 and 38(1), (2) and (3))

Also relevant, with adjustments, to certain related offences (see page 325)
Triable either way

Maxi- when tried on indictment: unlimited fine and/or 5 years' custody
mum:

when tried summarily: £50,000 fine and/or 6 months' custody

Offence range: conditional discharge – 3 years' custody
Use this guideline when the offender is an individual. If the offender is an organisation, please refer to the guideline for organisations.
Confiscation
Committal to the Crown Court for sentence is mandatory if confiscation (see step two) is to be considered: Proceeds of Crime Act 2002 section 70. In such cases magistrates should state whether they would otherwise have committed for sentence.
If a fine is imposed, the financial orders must be considered in this order: (1) compensation, (2) confiscation, and (3) fine (see Proceeds of Crime Act 2002 section 13).

Compensation
STEP ONE The court must consider making a compensation order requiring the offender to pay compensation for any personal injury, loss or damage resulting from the offence in such an amount as the court considers appropriate, having regard to the evidence and to the means of the offender.
Where the means of the offender are limited, priority should be given to the payment of compensation over payment of any other financial penalty.
Reasons should be given if a compensation order is not made.
(See section 130 Powers of Criminal Courts (Sentencing) Act 2000)

Confiscation (Crown Court only)
STEP TWO Confiscation must be considered if either the Crown asks for it or the court thinks that it may be appropriate. Confiscation must be dealt with before any other fine or financial order (except compensation).
(See sections 6 and 13 Proceeds of Crime Act 2002)
See page 319.

Determining the offence category
STEP THREE The court should determine the offence category using only the culpability and harm factors in the tables below. The culpability and harm categories are on a sliding scale; there is inevitable overlap between the factors described in adjacent categories. Where an offence does not fall squarely into a category, individual factors may require a degree of weighting before making an overall assessment and determining the appropriate offence category.
Dealing with a **risk of harm** involves consideration of both the likelihood of harm occurring and the extent of it if it does. Risk of harm is less serious than the same actual harm. Where the offence has caused risk of harm but no (or less) actual harm the normal approach is to move down to the next category of harm. This may not be appropriate if either the likelihood or extent of potential harm is particularly high.
Culpability Deliberate
Where the offender intentionally breached, or flagrantly disregarded, the law
Reckless
Actual foresight of, or wilful blindness to, risk of offending but risk nevertheless taken
Negligent
Offence committed through act or omission which a person exercising reasonable care would not commit
Low or no culpability
Offence committed with little or no fault, for example by genuine accident despite the presence of proper preventive measures, or where such proper preventive measures were unforeseeably overcome by exceptional events

Category 1	• Polluting material of a dangerous nature, for example, hazardous chemicals or sharp objects
	• Major adverse effect or damage to air or water quality, amenity value, or property
	• Polluting material was noxious, widespread or pervasive with long-lasting effects on human health or quality of life, animal health, or flora

	• Major costs incurred through clean-up, site restoration or animal rehabilitation
	• Major interference with, prevention or undermining of other lawful activities or regulatory regime due to offence
Category 2	• Significant adverse effect or damage to air or water quality, amenity value, or property
	• Significant adverse effect on human health or quality of life, animal health or flora
	• Significant costs incurred through clean-up, site restoration or animal rehabilitation
	• Significant interference with or undermining of other lawful activities or regulatory regime due to offence
	• Risk of category 1 harm
Category 3	• Minor, localised adverse effect or damage to air or water quality, amenity value, or property
	• Minor adverse effect on human health or quality of life, animal health or flora
	• Low costs incurred through clean-up, site restoration or animal rehabilitation
	• Limited interference with or undermining of other lawful activities or regulatory regime due to offence
	• Risk of category 2 harm
Category 4	• Risk of category 3 harm

Starting point and category range

STEP FOUR   Having determined the category, the court should refer to the starting points on page 321 to reach a sentence within the category range. The court should then consider further adjustment within the category range for aggravating and mitigating features, set out on page 322.

General principles to follow in setting a fine

The court should determine the appropriate level of fine in accordance with section 164 of the Criminal Justice Act 2003, which requires that the fine must reflect the seriousness of the offence and the court to take into account the financial circumstances of the offender.

The level of fine should reflect the extent to which the offender fell below the required standard. The fine should meet, in a fair and proportionate way, the objectives of punishment, deterrence and the removal of gain derived through the commission of the offence; it should not be cheaper to offend than to take the appropriate precautions.

Obtaining financial information

In setting a fine, the court may conclude that the offender is able to pay any fine imposed unless the offender has supplied any financial information to the contrary. It is for the offender to disclose to the court such data relevant to their financial position as will enable it to assess what they can reasonably afford to pay. If necessary, the court may compel the disclosure of an individual offender's financial circumstances pursuant to section 162 of the Criminal Justice Act 2003. **In the absence of such disclosure, or where the court is not satisfied that it has been given sufficient reliable information, the court will be entitled to draw reasonable inferences as to the offender's means from evidence it has heard and from all the circumstances of the case.**

See page 321.

Starting points and ranges

Where the range includes a potential sentence of custody, the court should consider the custody threshold as follows:

*   has the custody threshold been passed?
*   if so, is it unavoidable that a custodial sentence be imposed?
*   if so, can that sentence be suspended?

Where the range includes a potential sentence of a community order, the court should consider the community order threshold as follows:

*   has the community order threshold been passed?

However, even where the community order threshold has been passed, a fine will normally be the most appropriate disposal. Where confiscation is not applied for, consider, if wishing to remove any economic benefit derived through the commission of the offence, combining a fine with a community order.

Offence category	Starting Point	Range
Deliberate		
Category 1	18 months' custody	1 – 3 years' custody
Category 2	1 year's custody	26 weeks' – 18 months' custody

Offence category	Starting Point	Range
Category 3	Band F fine	Band E fine or medium level community order – 26 weeks' custody
Category 4	Band E fine	Band D fine or low level community order– Band E fine
Reckless		
Category 1	26 weeks' custody	Band F fine or high level community order – 12 months' custody
Category 2	Band F fine	Band E fine or medium level community order – 26 weeks' custody
Category 3	Band E fine	Band D fine or low level community order – Band E fine
Category 4	Band D fine	Band C fine – Band D fine
Negligent		
Category 1	Band F fine	Band E fine or medium level community order – 26 weeks' custody
Category 2	Band E fine	Band D fine or low level community order – Band E fine
Category 3	Band D fine	Band C fine – Band D fine
Category 4	Band C fine	Band B fine – Band C fine
Low / No culpability		
Category 1	Band D fine	Band C fine – Band D fine
Category 2	Band C fine	Band B fine – Band C fine
Category 3	Band B fine	Band A fine – Band B fine
Category 4	Band A fine	Conditional discharge – Band A fine

The table below contains a **non-exhaustive** list of factual elements providing the context of the offence and factors relating to the offender. Identify whether any combination of these, or other relevant factors, should result in an upward or downward adjustment from the starting point. **In particular, relevant recent convictions and/or a history of non-compliance are likely to result in a substantial upward adjustment.** In some cases, having considered these factors, it may be appropriate to move outside the identified category range.

Factors increasing seriousness *Statutory aggravating factors:*

Previous convictions, having regard to a) the nature of the offence to which the conviction relates and its relevance to the current offence; and b) the time that has elapsed since the conviction

Offence committed whilst on bail

Other aggravating factors include:

History of non-compliance with warnings by regulator

Location of the offence, for example, near housing, schools, livestock or environmentally sensitive sites

Repeated incidents of offending or offending over an extended period of time, where not charged separately

Deliberate concealment of illegal nature of activity

Ignoring risks identified by employees or others

Established evidence of wider/community impact

Breach of any order

Offence committed for financial gain

Obstruction of justice

Offence committed whilst on licence

Factors reducing seriousness or reflecting personal mitigation No previous convictions **or** no relevant/recent convictions

Remorse

Compensation paid voluntarily to remedy harm caused

Evidence of steps taken to remedy problem

One-off event not commercially motivated

Little or no financial gain

Self-reporting, co-operation and acceptance of responsibility

Good character and/or exemplary conduct

Mental disorder or learning disability, where linked to the commission of the offence

Serious medical conditions requiring urgent, intensive or long-term treatment

Age and/or lack of maturity where it affects the responsibility of the offender

Sole or primary carer for dependent relatives

See page 323.

STEPS FIVE AND SIX Where the sentence is or includes a fine, the court should 'step back' and, using the factors set out in steps five and six, **review whether the sentence as a whole meets, in a fair way, the objectives of punishment, deterrence and removal of gain derived through the commission of the offence.** At steps five and six, the court may increase or reduce the proposed fine reached at step four, if necessary moving outside the range.

Ensure that the combination of financial orders (compensation, confiscation if appropriate, and fine) removes any economic benefit derived from the offending

STEP FIVE   The court should remove any economic benefit the offender has derived through the commission of the offence including:

- avoided costs;
- operating savings;
- any gain made as a direct result of the offence.

Where the offender is fined, the amount of economic benefit derived from the offence should normally be added to the fine arrived at in step four. If a confiscation order is made, in considering economic benefit, the court should avoid double recovery.

Economic benefit will not always be an identifiable feature of a case. For example, in some water pollution cases there may be strict liability but very little obvious gain. However, even in these cases there may be some avoidance of cost, for example alarms not installed and maintained, inadequate bunding or security measures not installed. Any costs avoided will be considered as economic benefit.

Where it is not possible to calculate or estimate the economic benefit derived from the offence, the court may wish to draw on information from the enforcing authorities about the general costs of operating within the law.

Consider other factors that may warrant adjustment of the proposed fine

STEP SIX   The court should consider any further factors that are relevant to ensuring that the proposed fine is proportionate having regard to the means of the offender and the seriousness of the offence.

The **non-exhaustive** list below contains additional factual elements the court should consider in deciding whether an increase or reduction to the proposed fine is required:

- fine impairs offender's ability to make restitution to victims;
- impact of fine on offender's ability to improve conditions to comply with the law;
- impact of fine on employment of staff, service users, customers and local economy.

Consider any factors which indicate a reduction, such as assistance to the prosecution

STEP SEVEN   The court should take into account sections 73 and 74 of the Serious Organised Crime and Police Act 2005 (assistance by defendants: reduction or review of sentence) and any other rule of law by virtue of which an offender may receive a discounted sentence in consequence of assistance given (or offered) to the prosecutor or investigator.

Reduction for guilty pleas

STEP EIGHT   The court should take account of any potential reduction for a guilty plea in accordance with section 144 of the Criminal Justice Act 2003 and the *Guilty Plea* guideline.

Ancillary orders

STEP NINE   In all cases, the court must consider whether to make ancillary orders. These may include:

Disqualification of director

An offender may be disqualified from being a director of a company in accordance with section 2 of the Company Directors Disqualification Act 1986. The maximum period of disqualification is 15 years (Crown Court) or 5 years (magistrates' court).

Disqualification from driving

The court may order disqualification from driving where a vehicle has been used in connection with the commission of the offence (section 147 of the Powers of Criminal Courts (Sentencing) Act 2000).

The court may disqualify an offender from driving on conviction for any offence either in addition to any other sentence or instead of any other sentence (section 146 of the Powers of Criminal Courts (Sentencing) Act 2000).

The court should inform the offender of its intention to disqualify and hear representations.

Forfeiture of vehicle

The court may order the forfeiture of a vehicle used in or for the purposes of the commission of the offence in accordance with section 33C of the Environmental Protection Act 1990.

Deprivation of property

Where section 33C of the Environmental Protection Act 1990 does not apply, the court may order the offender to be deprived of property used to commit crime or intended for that purpose in accordance with section 143 of the Powers of Criminal Courts (Sentencing) Act 2000. In considering whether to make an order under section 143, the court must have regard to the value of the property and the likely effects on the offender of making the order taken together with any other order the court makes.

Remediation

Where an offender is convicted of an offence under regulation 38(1), (2) or (3) of the Environmental Permitting (England and Wales) Regulations 2010, a court may order the offender to take steps to remedy the cause of the offence within a specified period in accordance with regulation 44 of the Environmental Permitting (England and Wales) Regulations 2010.

Totality principle
STEP TEN   If sentencing an offender for more than one offence, or where the offender is already serving a sentence, consider whether the total sentence is just and proportionate to the offending behaviour.

Reasons
STEP ELEVEN   Section 174 of the Criminal Justice Act 2003 imposes a duty to give reasons for, and explain the effect of, the sentence.

Consideration for time spent on bail
STEP TWELVE   The court must consider whether to give credit for time spent on bail in accordance with section 240A of the Criminal Justice Act 2003.

Other environmental offences

In sentencing other relevant and analogous environmental offences, the court should refer to the sentencing approach in steps one to three and five and six of the guideline, **adjusting the starting points and ranges bearing in mind the statutory maxima** for those offences. An indicative list of such offences is set out below.

Offence	Mode of trial	Statutory maxima
Section 1 Control of Pollution (Amendment) Act 1989 – transporting controlled waste without registering	Triable summarily only	• level 5 fine
Section 34 Environmental Protection Act 1990 – breach of duty of care	Triable either way	• when tried on indictment: unlimited fine • when tried summarily: level 5 fine
Section 80 Environmental Protection Act 1990 – breach of an abatement notice	Triable summarily only	• where the offence is committed on industrial, trade or business premises: £20,000 fine • where the offence is committed on non-industrial etc premises: level 5 fine with a further fine of an amount equal to one-tenth of that level for each day on which the offence continues after the conviction
Section 111 Water Industry Act 1991 – restrictions on use of public sewers	Triable either way	• when tried on indictment: imprisonment for a term not exceeding two years or a fine or both • when tried summarily: a fine not exceeding the statutory maximum and a further fine not exceeding £50 for each day on which the offence continues after conviction
Offences under the Transfrontier Shipment of Waste Regulations 2007	Triable either way	• when tried on indictment: a fine or two years imprisonment or both • when tried summarily: a fine not exceeding the statutory maximum or three months' imprisonment or both

Environmental offences – Fine bands and community orders

Fine Bands
In this guideline, fines are expressed as one of six fine bands (A, B, C, D, E or F).

Fine Band	Starting point *(applicable to all offenders)*	Category range *(applicable to all offenders)*
Band A	50% of relevant weekly income	25–75% of relevant weekly income
Band B	100% of relevant weekly income	75–125% of relevant weekly income
Band C	150% of relevant weekly income	125–175% of relevant weekly income
Band D	250% of relevant weekly income	200–300% of relevant weekly income
Band E	400% of relevant weekly income	300–500% of relevant weekly income
Band F	600% of relevant weekly income	500–700% of relevant weekly income

Band F is provided as an alternative to a community order or custody in the context of this guideline.

Community Orders
In this guideline, community sentences are expressed as one of three levels (low, medium or high). An illustrative description of examples of requirements that might be appropriate for each level is provided below.

Where two or more requirements are ordered, they must be compatible with each other. Save in exceptional circumstances, the court must impose at least one requirement for the purpose of punishment, or combine the community order with a fine, or both (see section 177 Criminal Justice Act 2003).

LOW	MEDIUM	HIGH
In general, only one requirement will be appropriate and the length may be curtailed if additional requirements are necessary		More intensive sentences which combine two or more requirements may be appropriate
Suitable requirements might include one or more of:	Suitable requirements might include one or more of:	Suitable requirements might include one or more of:
• 40–80 hours unpaid work;	• greater number of hours of unpaid work (for example, 80–150 hours);	• 150–300 hours unpaid work;
• prohibited activity requirement;	• prohibited activity requirement.	• activity requirement up to the maximum of 60 days;
• curfew requirement within the lowest range (for example, up to 12 hours per day for a few weeks).	• an activity requirement in the middle range (20–30 days);	• curfew requirement up to 12 hours per day for 4–6 months;
	• curfew requirement within the middle range (for example, up to 12 hours for 2–3 months).	• exclusion order lasting in the region of 12 months.

Fraud

Fraud by false representation, Fraud by failing to disclose information, Fraud by abuse of position
Fraud Act 2006 (section 1)
Triable either way

Conspiracy to defraud

Common law
Triable on indictment only
Maximum: 10 years' custody
Offence range: Discharge – 8 years' custody

False accounting

Theft Act 1968 (section 17)
Triable either way
Maximum: 7 years' custody
Offence range: Discharge – 6 years and 6 months' custody

Determining the offence category

STEP ONE The court should determine the offence category with reference to the tables below. In order to determine the category the court should assess **culpability** and **harm**.

The level of **culpability** is determined by weighing up all the factors of the case to determine the offender's role and the extent to which the offending was planned and the sophistication with which it was carried out.

Culpability demonstrated by one or more of the following: **A – High culpability**
    A leading role where offending is part of a group activity
    Involvement of others through pressure, influence
    Abuse of position of power or trust or responsibility
    Sophisticated nature of offence/significant planning
    Fraudulent activity conducted over sustained period of time
    Large number of victims
    Deliberately targeting victim on basis of vulnerability
B – Medium culpability
    Other cases where characteristics for categories A or C are not present
    A significant role where offending is part of a group activity
C – Lesser culpability
    Involved through coercion, intimidation or exploitation
    Not motivated by personal gain
    Peripheral role in organised fraud
    Opportunistic 'one-off' offence; very little or no planning
    Limited awareness or understanding of the extent of fraudulent activity

Where there are characteristics present which fall under different levels of culpability, the court should balance these characteristics to reach a fair assessment of the offender's culpability.

Harm is initially assessed by the actual[Ed 1], intended or risked loss as may arise from the offence. The values in the table below are to be used for **actual** or **intended** loss only.

Intended loss relates to offences where circumstances prevent the actual loss that is intended to be caused by the fraudulent activity.

Risk of loss (for instance in mortgage frauds) involves consideration of both the likelihood of harm occurring and the extent of it if it does. Risk of loss is less serious than actual or intended loss. Where the offence has caused risk of loss but no (or much less) actual loss the normal approach is to move down to the corresponding point in the next category. This may not be appropriate if either the likelihood or extent of risked loss is particularly high.

[Ed 1] Where consequential loss is alleged it must be proved to the criminal standard that it was caused as a direct result of the offending: *R v Green* [2016] EWCA Crim 1888, [2017] 1 Cr App R (S) 22.

Category 1	£500,000 or more	Starting point based on £1 million
Category 2	£100,000 – £500,000 **or** Risk or category 1 harm	Starting point based on £300,000
Category 3	£20,000 – £100,000 **or** Risk of category 2 harm	Starting point based on £50,000
Category 4	£5,000 – £20,000 **or** Risk of category 3 harm	Starting point based on £12,500
Category 5	Less than £5,000 **or** Risk of category 4 harm	Starting point based on £2,500
Risk of category 5 harm, move down the range within the category		

Harm B – Victim impact demonstrated by one or more of the following: The court should then take into account the level of harm caused to the victim(s) or others to determine whether it warrants the sentence being moved up to the corresponding point in the next category or further up the range of the initial category.

    High impact[Ed] – move up a category; if in category 1 move up the range

Serious detrimental effect on the victim whether financial or otherwise, for example substantial damage to credit rating

Victim particularly vulnerable (due to factors including but not limited to their age, financial circumstances, mental capacity)

Medium impact – move upwards within the category range

Considerable detrimental effect on the victim whether financial or otherwise

Lesser impact – no adjustment

Some detrimental impact on victim, whether financial or otherwise

---

[Ed] For an example of a 'high impact' (and high culpability) case, see *R v Churchill & Ward* [2017] EWCA Crim 841, 2 Cr App R (S) 34, [2017] Crim L R 1003 where a combination of entrapping the victim, chasing his car late at night and threatening to reveal false information justified moving the case into category 3 even though the sum demanded was £5,000.

Starting point and category range

STEP TWO   Having determined the category at step one, the court should use the appropriate starting point (as adjusted in accordance with step one above) to reach a sentence within the category range in the table below. The starting point applies to all offenders irrespective of plea or previous convictions.

Where the value is larger or smaller than the amount on which the starting point is based, this should lead to upward or downward adjustment as appropriate.

Where the value greatly exceeds the amount of the starting point in category 1, it may be appropriate to move outside the identified range.

TABLE 1
Section 1 Fraud Act 2006 conspiracy to defraud

Maximum: 10 years' custody

Harm	Culpability		
	A	**B**	**C**
Category 1	**Starting point**	**Starting point**	**Starting point**
£500,000 or more	7 years' custody	5 years' custody	3 years' custody
Starting point based	**Category range**	**Category range**	**Category range**
on £1 million	5 – 8 years' custody	3 – 6 years' custody	18 months' – 4 years' custody
Category 2	**Starting point**	**Starting point**	**Starting point**
£100,000–£500,000	5 years' custody	3 years' custody	18 months' custody
Starting point based	**Category range**	**Category range**	**Category range**
on £300,000	3 – 6 years' custody	18 months' – 4 years' custody	26 weeks' – 3 years' custody
Category 3	**Starting point**	**Starting point**	**Starting point**
£20,000 – £100,000	3 years' custody	18 months' custody	26 weeks' custody
Starting point based	**Category range**	**Category range**	**Category range**
on £50,000	18 months' – 4 years' custody	26 weeks' – 3 years' custody	Medium level community order – 1 year's custody
Category 4	**Starting point**	**Starting point**	**Starting point**
£5,000 – £20,000	18 months' custody	26 weeks' custody	Medium level community order
Starting point based	**Category range**	**Category range**	**Category range**
on £12,500	26 weeks' – 3 years' custody	Medium level community order – 1 year's custody	Band B fine – High level community order
Category 5	**Starting point**	**Starting point**	**Starting point**
Less than £5,000	36 weeks' custody	Medium level community order	Band B fine
Starting point based	**Category range**	**Category range**	**Category range**

| Harm | Culpability | | |
	A	B	C
on £2,500	High level community order – 1 year's custody	Band B fine – 26 weeks' custody	Discharge – Medium level community order

TABLE 2
Section 17 Theft Act 1968: false accounting

Maximum: 7 years' custody

| Harm | Culpability | | |
	A	B	C
Category 1	**Starting point**	**Starting point**	**Starting point**
£500,000 or more	5 years 6 months' custody	4 years' custody	2 years 6 months' custody
Starting point based	**Category range**	**Category range**	**Category range**
on £1 million	4 years' –	2 years 6 months' –	15 months' –
	6 years 6 months' custody	5 years' custody	3 years 6 months' custody
Category 2	**Starting point**	**Starting point**	**Starting point**
£100,000–£500,000	4 years' custody	2 years 6 months' custody	15 months' custody
Starting point based	**Category range**	**Category range**	**Category range**
on £300,000	2 years 6 months' –	15 months' –	26 weeks' –
	5 years' custody	3 years 6 months' custody	2 years 6 months' custody
Category 3	**Starting point**	**Starting point**	**Starting point**
£20,000–£100,000	2 years 6 months' custody	15 months' custody	High level community order
Starting point based	**Category range**	**Category range**	**Category range**
on £50,000	15 months' –	High level community order –	Low level community order –
	3 years 6 months' custody	2 years 6 months' custody	36 weeks' custody
Category 4	**Starting point**	**Starting point**	**Starting point**
£5,000–£20,000	15 months' custody	High level community order	Low level community order
Starting point based	**Category range**	**Category range**	**Category range**
on £12,500	High level community order –	Low level community order –	Band B fine –
	2 years 6 months' custody	36 weeks' custody	Medium level community order
Category 5	**Starting point**	**Starting point**	**Starting point**
Less than £5,000	26 weeks' custody	Low level community order	Band B fine
Starting point based	**Category range**	**Category range**	**Category range**
on £2,500	Medium level community order – 36 weeks' custody	Band B fine – Medium level community order	Discharge – Low level community order

See page 332.

The table below contains a non-exhaustive list of additional factual elements providing the context of the offence and factors relating to the offender.

Identify whether any combination of these or other relevant factors should result in an upward or downward adjustment from the sentence arrived at so far.

Consecutive sentences for multiple offences may be appropriate where large sums are involved.

Factors increasing seriousness *Statutory aggravating factors:*

Previous convictions, having regard to a) the nature of the offence to which the conviction relates and its relevance to the current offence; and b) the time that has elapsed since the conviction

Offence committed whilst on bail
Other aggravating factors:
Steps taken to prevent the victim reporting or obtaining assistance and/or from assisting or supporting the prosecution
Attempts to conceal/dispose of evidence
Established evidence of community/wider impact
Failure to comply with current court orders
Offence committed on licence
Offences taken into consideration
Failure to respond to warnings about behaviour
Offences committed across borders
Blame wrongly placed on others
Factors reducing seriousness or reflecting personal mitigation   No previous convictions **or** no relevant/recent convictions
Remorse
Good character and/or exemplary conduct
Little or no prospect of success
Serious medical conditions requiring urgent, intensive or long-term treatment
Age and/or lack of maturity where it affects the responsibility of the offender
Lapse of time since apprehension where this does not arise from the conduct of the offender
Mental disorder or learning disability
Sole or primary carer for dependent relatives
Offender co-operated with investigation, made early admissions and/or voluntarily reported offending
Determination and/or demonstration of steps having been taken to address addiction or offending behaviour
Activity originally legitimate
See page 333.

Consider any factors which indicate a reduction, such as assistance to the prosecution

STEP THREE   The court should take into account sections 73 and 74 of the Serious Organised Crime and Police Act 2005 (assistance by defendants: reduction or review of sentence) and any other rule of law by virtue of which an offender may receive a discounted sentence in consequence of assistance given (or offered) to the prosecutor or investigator.

Reduction for guilty pleas

STEP FOUR   The court should take account of any potential reduction for a guilty plea in accordance with section 144 of the Criminal Justice Act 2003 and the *Guilty Plea* guideline.

Totality principle

STEP FIVE   If sentencing an offender for more than one offence, or where the offender is already serving a sentence, consider whether the total sentence is just and proportionate to the overall offending behaviour.

Confiscation, compensation and ancillary orders

STEP SIX   The court must proceed with a view to making a confiscation order if it is asked to do so by the prosecutor or if the court believes it is appropriate for it to do so.

Where the offence has resulted in loss or damage the court must consider whether to make a compensation order.

If the court makes both a confiscation order and an order for compensation and the court believes the offender will not have sufficient means to satisfy both orders in full, the court must direct that the compensation be paid out of sums recovered under the confiscation order (section 13 of the Proceeds of Crime Act 2002).

The court may also consider whether to make ancillary orders. These may include a deprivation order, a financial reporting order, a serious crime prevention order and disqualification from acting as a company director.

Reasons

STEP SEVEN   Section 174 of the Criminal Justice Act 2003 imposes a duty to give reasons for, and explain the effect of, the sentence.

Consideration for time spent on bail

STEP EIGHT   The court must consider whether to give credit for time spent on bail in accordance with section 240A of the Criminal Justice Act 2003.

POSSESSING, MAKING OR SUPPLYING ARTICLES FOR USE IN FRAUD

POSSESSION OF ARTICLES FOR USE IN FRAUDS

Fraud Act 2006 (section 6)
Triable either way
Maximum: 5 years' custody
Offence range: Band A fine – 3 years' custody

Making or supplying articles for use in frauds

Fraud Act 2006 (section 7)
Triable either way
Maximum: 10 years' custody
Offence range: Band C fine – 7 years' custody

Determining the offence category

STEP ONE The court should determine the offence category with reference to the tables below. In order to determine the category the court should assess **culpability** and **harm**.

The level of **culpability** is determined by weighing up all the factors of the case to determine the offender's role and the extent to which the offending was planned and the sophistication with which it was carried out.

Culpability demonstrated by one or more of the following: A – High culpability
A leading role where offending is part of a group activity
Involvement of others through pressure, influence
Abuse of position of power or trust or responsibility
Sophisticated nature of offence/significant planning
Fraudulent activity conducted over sustained period of time
Articles deliberately designed to target victims on basis of vulnerability[Ed 1]
B – Medium culpability
Other cases where characteristics for categories A or C are not present
A significant role where offending is part of a group activity
C – Lesser culpability
Performed limited function under direction
Involved through coercion, intimidation or exploitation
Not motivated by personal gain
Opportunistic 'one-off' offence; very little or no planning
Limited awareness or understanding of extent of fraudulent activity
Where there are characteristics present which fall under different levels of culpability, the court should balance these characteristics to reach a fair assessment of the offender's culpability.
Harm This guideline refers to preparatory offences where no substantive fraud has been committed. The level of **harm** is determined by weighing up all the factors of the case to determine the harm that would be caused if the article(s) were used to commit a substantive offence.
Greater harm
Large number of articles created/supplied/in possession
Article(s) have potential to facilitate fraudulent acts affecting large number of victims
Article(s) have potential to facilitate fraudulent acts involving significant sums
Use of third party identities
Offender making considerable gain as result of the offence
Lesser harm
All other offences
STEP TWO Starting point and category range Having determined the category at step one, the court should use the appropriate starting point to reach a sentence within the category range in the table below. The starting point applies to all offenders irrespective of plea or previous convictions.

Section 6 Fraud Act 2006: Possessing articles for use in fraud

Maximum: 5 years' custody

| Harm | Culpability | | |
	A	B	C
Greater	**Starting point**	**Starting point**	**Starting point**
	18 months' custody	36 weeks' custody	High level community order
	Category range	**Category range**	**Category range**
	36 weeks' custody –	High level community order –	Medium level community order –
	3 years' custody	2 years' custody	26 weeks' custody
Lesser	**Starting point**	**Starting point**	**Starting point**
	26 weeks' custody	Medium level community order	Band B fine
	Category range	**Category range**	**Category range**
	High level community order –	Low level community order –	Band A fine –

Harm	Culpability		
	A	B	C
	18 months' custody	26 weeks' custody	Medium level community order

Section 7 Fraud Act 2006: Making or adapting or supplying articles for use in fraud

Maximum: 10 years' custody

Harm	Culpability		
	A	B	C
Greater	**Starting point**	**Starting point**	**Starting point**
	4 years 6 months' custody	2 years 6 months' custody	1 year's custody
	Category range	**Category range**	**Category range**
	3 – 7 years' custody	18 months' – 5 years' custody	High level community order – 3 years' custody
Lesser	**Starting point**	**Starting point**	**Starting point**
	2 years' custody	36 weeks' custody	Medium level community order
	Category range	**Category range**	**Category range**
	26 weeks' –	Low level community order –	Band C fine –
	4 years' custody	2 years' custody	26 weeks' custody

The table below contains a non-exhaustive list of additional factual elements providing the context of the offence and factors relating to the offender.

Identify whether any combination of these or other relevant factors should result in an upward or downward adjustment from the starting point

Consecutive sentences for multiple offences may be appropriate where large sums are involved.

Factors increasing seriousness   *Statutory aggravating factors:*

Previous convictions, having regard to a) the nature of the offence to which the conviction relates and its relevance to the current offence; and b) the time that has elapsed since the conviction

Offence committed whilst on bail

Other aggravating factors:

Steps taken to prevent the victim reporting or obtaining assistance and/or from assisting or supporting the prosecution

Attempts to conceal/dispose of evidence

Established evidence of community/wider impact

Failure to comply with current court orders

Offence committed on licence

Offences taken into consideration

Failure to respond to warnings about behaviour

Offences committed across borders

Blame wrongly placed on others

Factors reducing seriousness or reflecting personal mitigation   No previous convictions **or** no relevant/recent convictions

Remorse

Good character and/or exemplary conduct

Little or no prospect of success

Serious medical conditions requiring urgent, intensive or long-term treatment

Age and/or lack of maturity where it affects the responsibility of the offender

Lapse of time since apprehension where this does not arise from the conduct of the offender

Mental disorder or learning disability

Sole or primary carer for dependent relatives

Offender co-operated with investigation, made early admissions and/or voluntarily reported offending

Determination and/or demonstration of steps having been taken to address addiction or offending behaviour

Activity originally legitimate

See page 339.

Consider any factors which indicate a reduction, such as assistance to the prosecution

STEP THREE   The court should take into account sections 73 and 74 of the Serious Organised Crime and Police Act 2005 (assistance by defendants: reduction or review of sentence) and any other rule of law by virtue of which an offender may receive a discounted sentence in consequence of assistance given (or offered) to the prosecutor or investigator.

Reduction for guilty pleas
STEP FOUR The court should take account of any potential reduction for a guilty plea in accordance with section 144 of the Criminal Justice Act 2003 and the *Guilty Plea* guideline.

Totality principle
STEP FIVE If sentencing an offender for more than one offence, or where the offender is already serving a sentence, consider whether the total sentence is just and proportionate to the overall offending behaviour.

Confiscation, compensation and ancillary orders
STEP SIX The court must proceed with a view to making a confiscation order if it is asked to do so by the prosecutor or if the court believes it is appropriate for it to do so.

Where the offence has resulted in loss or damage the court must consider whether to make a compensation order.

If the court makes both a confiscation order and an order for compensation and the court believes the offender will not have sufficient means to satisfy both orders in full, the court must direct that the compensation be paid out of sums recovered under the confiscation order (section 13 of the Proceeds of Crime Act 2002).

The court may also consider whether to make any ancillary orders.

Reasons
STEP SEVEN Section 174 of the Criminal Justice Act 2003 imposes a duty to give reasons for, and explain the effect of, the sentence.

Consideration for time spent on bail
STEP EIGHT The court must consider whether to give credit for time spent on bail in accordance with section 240A of the Criminal Justice Act 2003.

Ed 1 Seeking to make fraudulent use of a weakness in the Oyster card system does not amount to deliberate targeting of a victim on the basis of vulnerability within the meaning of the guidelines: *R v Bouferache* [2015] EWCA Crim 1611, [2016] 1 Cr App R (S) 25.

REVENUE FRAUD

FRAUD

Conspiracy to defraud (common law)
Triable on indictment only
Fraud Act 2006 (section 1)
Triable either way
Maximum: 10 years' custody
Offence range: Low level community order – 8 years' custody

FRAUD

Cheat the public revenue (common law)
Triable on indictment only
Maximum: Life imprisonment
Offence range: 3 – 17 years' custody

Determining the offence category

STEP ONE The court should determine the offence category with reference to the tables below. In order to determine the category the court should assess **culpability** and **harm**.

The level of **culpability** is determined by weighing up all the factors of the case to determine the offender's role and the extent to which the offending was planned and the sophistication with which it was carried out.

Culpability demonstrated by one or more of the following: A – High culpability

A leading role where offending is part of a group activity
Involvement of others through pressure/influence
Abuse of position of power or trust or responsibility
Sophisticated nature of offence/significant planning
Fraudulent activity conducted over sustained period of time
B – Medium culpability
Other cases where characteristics for categories A or C are not present
A significant role where offending is part of a group activity
C – Lesser culpability
Involved through coercion, intimidation or exploitation
Not motivated by personal gain
Opportunistic 'one-off' offence; very little or no planning
Performed limited function under direction
Limited awareness or understanding of extent of fraudulent activity
Where there are characteristics present which fall under different levels of culpability, the court should balance these characteristics to reach a fair assessment of the offender's culpability.

Category 1	
£50 million or more	
Starting point based on £80 million	
Category 2	
£10 million–£50 million	
Starting point based on £30 million	
Category 3	
£2 million–£10 million	
Starting point based on £5 million	
Category 4	
£500,000–£2 million	
Starting point based on £1 million	
Category 5	
£100,000–£500,000	
Starting point based on £300,000	
Category 6	
£20,000–£100,000	
Starting point based on £50,000	
Category 7	
Less than £20,000	
Starting point based on £12,500	

Starting point and category range

STEP TWO Having determined the category at step one, the court should use the appropriate starting point to reach a sentence within the category range in the table below. The starting point applies to all offenders irrespective of plea or previous convictions.

Where the value is larger or smaller than the amount on which the starting point is based, this should lead to upward or downward adjustment as appropriate.

Where the value greatly exceeds the amount of the starting point in category 1, it may be appropriate to move outside the identified range.

TABLE 1
Section 1 Fraud Act 2006 Conspiracy to defraud (common law)

Maximum: 10 years' custody

For offences where the value of the fraud is over £2 million refer to the corresponding category in Table 3 subject to the maximum sentence of 10 years for this offence.

		Culpability	
Harm	**A**	**B**	**C**
Category 4	**Starting point**	**Starting point**	**Starting point**
£500,000–£2 million	7 years' custody	5 years' custody	3 years' custody
Starting point based	**Category range**	**Category range**	**Category range**
on £1 million	5 – 8 years' custody	3 – 6 years' custody	18 months' – 4 years' custody
Category 5	**Starting point**	**Starting point**	**Starting point**
£100,000–£500,000	5 years' custody	3 years' custody	18 months' custody
Starting point based	**Category range**	**Category range**	**Category range**
on £300,000	3 – 6 years' custody	18 months' – 4 years' custody	26 weeks' – 3 years' custody
Category 6	**Starting point**	**Starting point**	**Starting point**
£20,000–£100,000	3 years' custody	18 months' custody	26 weeks' custody
Starting point based	**Category range**	**Category range**	**Category range**
on £50,000	18 months' – 4 years' custody	26 weeks' – 3 years' custody	Medium level community order – 1 year's custody
Category 7	**Starting point**	**Starting point**	**Starting point**
Less than £20,000	18 months' custody	36 weeks' custody	Medium level community order
Starting point based	**Category range**	**Category range**	**Category range**
on £12,500	36 weeks' – 3 years' custody	Medium level community order – 18 months' custody	Low level community order – High level community order

TABLE 2
Section 17 Theft Act 1968: False Accounting
Section 72(1) Value Added Tax Act 1994: Fraudulent evasion of VAT
Section 72(3) Valued Added Tax Act 1994: False statement for VAT purposes
Section 72(8) Value Added Tax Act 1994: Conduct amounting to an offence Section 106(a) Taxes Management Act 1970: Fraudulent evasion of income tax
Section 170(1)(a)(i), (ii), (b), 170(2)(a), 170B Customs and Excise Management Act 1979: Fraudulent evasion of excise duty
Section 50(1)(a), (2) Customs and Excise Management Act 1979: Improper importation of goods

Maximum: 7 years' custody

		Culpability	
Harm	**A**	**B**	**C**
Category 4	**Starting point**	**Starting point**	**Starting point**
£500,000–£2 million	5 years 6 months' custody	4 years' custody	2 years 6 months' custody
Starting point based	**Category range**	**Category range**	**Category range**
on £1 million	4 years' – 6 years 6 months' custody	2 years 6 months' – 5 years' custody	15 months' – 3 years 6 months' custody

Harm	Culpability		
	A	**B**	**C**
Category 5	**Starting point**	**Starting point**	**Starting point**
£100,000–£500,000	4 years' custody	2 years 6 months' custody	15 months' custody
Starting point based	**Category range**	**Category range**	**Category range**
on £300,000	2 years 6 months' – 5 years' custody	15 months' – 3 years 6 months' custody	26 weeks' – 2 years 6 months' custody
Category 6	**Starting point**	**Starting point**	**Starting point**
£20,000–£100,000	2 years 6 months' custody	15 months' custody	High level community order
Starting point based	**Category range**	**Category range**	**Category range**
on £50,000	15 months' – 3 years 6 months' custody	High level community order - 2 years 6 months' custody	Low level community order – 36 weeks' custody
Category 7	**Starting point**	**Starting point**	**Starting point**
Less than £20,000	15 months' custody	26 weeks' custody	Medium level community order
Starting point based	**Category range**	**Category range**	**Category range**
on £12,500	26 weeks' – 2 years 6 months' custody	Medium level community order – 15 months' custody	Band C fine – High level community order

See page 345.

TABLE 3
Cheat the Revenue (common law)

Maximum: Life imprisonment
Where the offending is on the most serious scale, involving sums significantly higher than the starting point in category 1, sentences of 15 years and above may be appropriate depending on the role of the offender. In cases involving sums below £2 million the court should refer to Table 1.

Harm	Culpability		
	A	**B**	**C**
Category 1	**Starting point**	**Starting point**	**Starting point**
£50 million or more	12 years' custody	8 years' custody	6 years' custody
Starting point based on	**Category range**	**Category range**	**Category range**
£80 million	10 – 17 years' custody	7 – 12 years' custody	4 – 8 years' custody
Category 2	**Starting point**	**Starting point**	**Starting point**
£10 million–£50 million	10 years' custody	7 years' custody	5 years' custody
Starting point based on	**Category range**	**Category range**	**Category range**
£30 million	8 – 13 years' custody	5 – 9 years' custody	3 – 6 years' custody
Category 3	**Starting point**	**Starting point**	**Starting point**
£2 million–£10 million	8 years' custody	6 years' custody	4 years' custody
Starting point based on	**Category range**	**Category range**	**Category range**
£5 million	6 – 10 years' custody	4 – 7 years' custody	3 – 5 years' custody

See page 346.

The table below contains a non-exhaustive list of additional factual elements providing the context of the offence and factors relating to the offender.

Identify whether any combination of these or other relevant factors should result in any further upward or downward adjustment from the starting point.

Consecutive sentences for multiple offences may be appropriate where large sums are involved.

Factors increasing seriousness *Statutory aggravating factors:*

Previous convictions, having regard to a) the nature of the offence to which the conviction relates and its relevance to the current offence; and b) the time that has elapsed since the conviction

Offence committed whilst on bail

Other aggravating factors:

Involves multiple frauds

Number of false declarations

Attempts to conceal/dispose of evidence

Failure to comply with current court orders

Offence committed on licence

Offences taken into consideration

Failure to respond to warnings about behaviour

Blame wrongly placed on others

Damage to third party (for example as a result of identity theft)

Dealing with goods with an additional health risk

Disposing of goods to under age purchasers

Factors reducing seriousness or reflecting personal mitigation No previous convictions **or** no relevant/recent convictions

Remorse

Good character and/or exemplary conduct

Little or no prospect of success

Serious medical condition requiring urgent, intensive or long term treatment

Age and/or lack of maturity where it affects the responsibility of the offender

Lapse of time since apprehension where this does not arise from the conduct of the offender

Mental disorder or learning disability

Sole or primary carer for dependent relatives

Offender co-operated with investigation, made early admissions and/or voluntarily reported offending

Determination and/or demonstration of steps having been taken to address addiction or offending behaviour

Activity originally legitimate

See page 347.

Consider any factors which indicate a reduction, such as assistance to the prosecution

STEP THREE   The court should take into account sections 73 and 74 of the Serious Organised Crime and Police Act 2005 (assistance by defendants: reduction or review of sentence) and any other rule of law by virtue of which an offender may receive a discounted sentence in consequence of assistance given (or offered) to the prosecutor or investigator.

Reduction for guilty pleas

STEP FOUR   The court should take account of any potential reduction for a guilty plea in accordance with section 144 of the Criminal Justice Act 2003 and the *Guilty Plea* guideline.

Totality principle

STEP FIVE   If sentencing an offender for more than one offence, or where the offender is already serving a sentence, consider whether the total sentence is just and proportionate to the overall offending behaviour.

Confiscation, compensation and ancillary orders

STEP SIX   The court must proceed with a view to making a confiscation order if it is asked to do so by the prosecutor or if the court believes it is appropriate for it to do so.

Where the offence has resulted in loss or damage the court must consider whether to make a compensation order.

If the court makes both a confiscation order and an order for compensation and the court believes the offender will not have sufficient means to satisfy both orders in full, the court must direct that the compensation be paid out of sums recovered under the confiscation order (section 13 of the Proceeds of Crime Act 2002).

The court may also consider whether to make ancillary orders. These may include a deprivation order, a financial reporting order, a serious crime prevention order and disqualification from acting as a company director.

Reasons

STEP SEVEN   Section 174 of the Criminal Justice Act 2003 imposes a duty to give reasons for, and explain the effect of, the sentence.

Consideration for time spent on bail

STEP EIGHT   The court must consider whether to give credit for time spent on bail in accordance with section 240A of the Criminal Justice Act 2003.

BENEFIT FRAUD

DISHONEST REPRESENTATIONS FOR OBTAINING BENEFIT ETC

Social Security Administration Act 1992 (section 111A)

TAX CREDIT FRAUD

Tax Credits Act 2002 (section 35)

FALSE ACCOUNTING

Theft Act 1968 (section 17)
Triable either way
Maximum: 7 years' custody
Offence range: Discharge – 6 years 6 months' custody

FALSE REPRESENTATIONS FOR OBTAINING BENEFIT ETC

Social Security Administration Act 1992 (section 112)
Triable summarily only
Maximum: Level 5 fine and/or 3 months' custody
Offence range: Discharge – 12 weeks' custody

FRAUD BY FALSE REPRESENTATION, FRAUD BY FAILING TO DISCLOSE INFORMATION, FRAUD BY ABUSE OF POSITION
Fraud Act 2006 (section 1)
Triable either way

CONSPIRACY TO DEFRAUD

Common law
Triable on indictment only
Maximum: 10 years' custody
Offence range: Discharge – 8 years' custody

Determining the offence category

STEP ONE The court should determine the offence category with reference to the tables below. In order to determine the category the court should assess **culpability** and **harm**.

The level of **culpability** is determined by weighing up all the factors of the case to determine the offender's role and the extent to which the offending was planned and the sophistication with which it was carried out.

Culpability demonstrated by one or more of the following: A – High culpability
A leading role where offending is part of a group activity
Involvement of others through pressure/influence
Abuse of position of power or trust or responsibility
Sophisticated nature of offence/significant planning
B – Medium culpability
Other cases where characteristics for categories A or C are not present
Claim not fraudulent from the outset
A significant role where offending is part of a group activity
C – Lesser culpability
Involved through coercion, intimidation or exploitation
Performed limited function under direction
Where there are characteristics present which fall under different levels of culpability, the court should balance these characteristics to reach a fair assessment of the offender's culpability.

Category 1
£500,000–£2 million
Starting point based on £1 million

Category 2
£100,000–£500,000
Starting point based on £300,000

Category 3
£50,000–£100,000
Starting point based on £75,000

Category 4
£10,000–£50,000
Starting point based on £30,000

Category 5
£2,500–£10,000
Starting point based on £5,000

Category 6
Less than £2,500
Starting point based on £1,000

Starting point and category range

STEP TWO   Having determined the category at step one, the court should use the appropriate starting point to reach a sentence within the category range in the table below. The starting point applies to all offenders irrespective of plea or previous convictions.

Where the value is larger or smaller than the amount on which the starting point is based, this should lead to upward or downward adjustment as appropriate.

Where the value greatly exceeds the amount of the starting point in category 1, it may be appropriate to move outside the identified range.

TABLE 1
Section 111A Social Security Administration Act 1992: Dishonest representations to obtain benefit etc
Section 35 Tax Credits Act 2002: Tax Credit fraud
Section 17 Theft Act 1968: False accounting

Maximum: 7 years' custody

Harm	Culpability		
	A	**B**	**C**
Category 1 £500,000 or more	**Starting point** 5 years 6 months' custody	**Starting point** 4 years' custody	**Starting point** 2 years 6 months' custody
Starting point based on £1 million	**Category range** 4 years' – 6 years 6 months' custody	**Category range** 2 years 6 months' – 5 years' custody	**Category range** 15 months' – 3 years 6 months' custody
Category 2 £100,000–£500,000	**Starting point** 4 years' custody	**Starting point** 2 years 6 months' custody	**Starting point** 1 year's custody
Starting point based on £300,000	**Category range** 2 years 6 months' – 5 years' custody	**Category range** 15 months' – 3 years 6 months' custody	**Category range** 26 weeks' – 2 years 6 months' custody
Category 3 £50,000–£100,000	**Starting point** 2 years 6 months' custody	**Starting point** 1 year's custody	**Starting point** 26 weeks' custody
Starting point based on £75,000	**Category range** 2 years' – 3 years 6 months' custody	**Category range** 26 weeks' – 2 years 6 months' custody	**Category range** High level community order – 36 weeks' custody
Category 4 £10,000–£50,000	**Starting point** 18 months' custody	**Starting point** 36 weeks' custody	**Starting point** Medium level community order
Starting point based on £30,000	**Category range** 36 weeks' – 2 years 6 months' custody	**Category range** Medium level community order – 21 months' custody	**Category range** Low level community order – 26 weeks' custody
Category 5 £2,500–£10,000	**Starting point** 36 weeks' custody	**Starting point** Medium level community order	**Starting point** Low level community order
Starting point based on £5,000	**Category range** Medium level community order – 18 months' custody	**Category range** Low level community order – 26 weeks' custody	**Category range** Band B fine – Medium level community order
Category 6	**Starting point**	**Starting point**	**Starting point**

| | | Culpability | |
Harm	A	B	C
Less than £2,500	Medium level community order	Low level community order	Band A fine
Starting point based	**Category range**	**Category range**	**Category range**
on £1,000	Low level community order –	Band A fine –	Discharge –
	26 weeks' custody	Medium level community order	Band B fine

TABLE 2
Section 112 Social Security Administration Act 1992: False representations for obtaining benefit etc

Maximum: Level 5 fine and/or 3 months' custody

| | | Culpability | |
Harm	A	B	C
Category 5	**Starting point**	**Starting point**	**Starting point**
Above £2,500	High level community order	Medium level community order	Low level community order
Starting point based	**Category range**	**Category range**	**Category range**
on £5,000	Medium level community order	Band B fine –	Band A fine –
	– 12 weeks' custody	High level community order	Medium level community order
Category 6	**Starting point**	**Starting point**	**Starting point**
Less than £2,500	Medium level community order	Band B fine	Band A fine
Starting point based	**Category range**	**Category range**	**Category range**
on £1,000	Low level community order –	Category range	Discharge –
	High level community order	Band C fine	Band B fine

See page 353.

TABLE 3
Section 1 Fraud Act 2006
Conspiracy to defraud (common law)

Maximum: 10 years' custody

| | | Culpability | |
Harm	A	B	C
Category 1	**Starting point**	**Starting point**	**Starting point**
£500,000 or more	7 years' custody	5 years' custody	3 years' custody
Starting point based	**Category range**	**Category range**	**Category range**
on £1 million	5 – 8 years' custody	3 – 6 years' custody	18 months' – 4 years' custody
Category 2	**Starting point**	**Starting point**	**Starting point**
£100,000–£500,000	5 years' custody	3 years' custody	15 months' custody
Starting point based	**Category range**	**Category range**	**Category range**
on £300,000	3 – 6 years' custody	18 months' – 4 years' custody	26 weeks' – 3 years' custody
Category 3	**Starting point**	**Starting point**	**Starting point**
£50,000–£100,000	3 years' custody	15 months' custody	36 weeks' custody

| Harm | **Culpability** | | |
	A	**B**	**C**
Starting point based on £75,000	**Category range** 2 years 6 months' – 4 years' custody	**Category range** 36 weeks' – 3 years' custody	**Category range** 26 weeks' – 1 year's custody
Category 4 £10,000–£50,000	**Starting point** 21 months' custody	**Starting point** 1 year's custody	**Starting point** High level community order
Starting point based on £30,000	**Category range** 1 year's – 3 years' custody	**Category range** High level community order – 2 years' custody	**Category range** Low level community order – 26 weeks' custody
Category 5 £2,500–£10,000	**Starting point** 1 year's custody	**Starting point** High level community order	**Starting point** Medium level community order
Starting point based on £5,000	**Category range** High level community order – 2 years' custody	**Category range** Low level community order – 26 weeks' custody	**Category range** Band C fine – High level community order
Category 6 Less than £2,500	**Starting point** High level community order	**Starting point** Low level community order	**Starting point** Band B fine
Starting point based on £1,000	**Category range** Low level community order – 26 weeks' custody	**Category range** Band B fine – Medium level community order	**Category range** Discharge – Band C fine

The table below contains a non-exhaustive list of additional factual elements providing the context of the offence and factors relating to the offender.

Identify whether any combination of these or other relevant factors should result in any further upward or downward adjustment from the starting point.

Consecutive sentences for multiple offences may be appropriate where large sums are involved.

Factors increasing seriousness   *Statutory aggravating factors:*

Previous convictions, having regard to a) the nature of the offence to which the conviction relates and its relevance to the current offence; and b) the time that has elapsed since the conviction

Offence committed whilst on bail

Other aggravating factors:

Claim fraudulent from the outset

Proceeds of fraud funded lavish lifestyle

Length of time over which the offending was committed

Number of false declarations

Attempts to conceal/dispose of evidence

Failure to comply with current court orders

Offence committed on licence

Offences taken into consideration

Failure to respond to warnings about behaviour

Blame wrongly placed on others

Damage to third party (for example as a result of identity theft)

Factors reducing seriousness or reflecting personal   mitigation

No previous convictions **or** no relevant/recent convictions

Remorse

Good character and/or exemplary conduct

Serious medical condition requiring urgent, intensive or long term treatment

Legitimate entitlement to benefits not claimed

Little or no prospect of success

Age and/or lack of maturity where it affects the responsibility of the offender

Lapse of time since apprehension where this does not arise from the conduct of the offender

Mental disorder or learning disability

Sole or primary carer for dependent relatives

Offender co-operated with investigation, made early admissions and/or voluntarily reported offending

Determination and/or demonstration of steps having been taken to address addiction or offending behaviour

Offender experiencing significant financial hardship or pressure at time fraud was committed due to **exceptional** circumstances
See page 355.

Consider any factors which indicate a reduction, such as assistance to the prosecution
STEP THREE   The court should take into account sections 73 and 74 of the Serious Organised Crime and Police Act 2005 (assistance by defendants: reduction or review of sentence) and any other rule of law by virtue of which an offender may receive a discounted sentence in consequence of assistance given (or offered) to the prosecutor or investigator.

Reduction for guilty pleas
STEP FOUR   The court should take account of any potential reduction for a guilty plea in accordance with section 144 of the Criminal Justice Act 2003 and the *Guilty Plea* guideline.

Totality principle
STEP FIVE   If sentencing an offender for more than one offence, or where the offender is already serving a sentence, consider whether the total sentence is just and proportionate to the overall offending behaviour.

Confiscation, compensation and ancillary orders
STEP SIX   The court must proceed with a view to making a confiscation order if it is asked to do so by the prosecutor or if the court believes it is appropriate for it to do so.

Where the offence has resulted in loss or damage the court must consider whether to make a compensation order.

If the court makes both a confiscation order and an order for compensation and the court believes the offender will not have sufficient means to satisfy both orders in full, the court must direct that the compensation be paid out of sums recovered under the confiscation order (section 13 of the Proceeds of Crime Act 2002).

The court may also consider whether to make any ancillary orders.

Reasons
STEP SEVEN   Section 174 of the Criminal Justice Act 2003 imposes a duty to give reasons for, and explain the effect of, the sentence.

Consideration for time spent on bail
STEP EIGHT   The court must consider whether to give credit for time spent on bail in accordance with section 240A of the Criminal Justice Act 2003.

Money laundering

Concealing/disguising/converting/transferring/removing criminal property from England & Wales
Proceeds of Crime Act 2002 (section 327)

Entering into arrangements concerning criminal property
Proceeds of Crime Act 2002 (section 328)

Acquisition, use and possession of criminal property
Proceeds of Crime Act 2002 (section 329)

Triable either way
Maximum: 14 years' custody
Offence range: Band B fine – 13 years' imprisonment

Determining the offence category

STEP ONE The court should determine the offence category with reference to the tables below. In order to determine the category the court should assess **culpability** and **harm**.

The level of **culpability** is determined by weighing up all the factors of the case to determine the offender's role and the extent to which the offending was planned and the sophistication with which it was carried out.

Culpability demonstrated by one or more of the following: **A – High culpability**

A leading role where offending is part of a group activity

Involvement of others through pressure, influence

Abuse of position of power or trust or responsibility

Sophisticated nature of offence/significant planning

Criminal activity conducted over sustained period of time

B – Medium culpability

Other cases where characteristics for categories A or C are not present

A significant role where offending is part of a group activity

C – Lesser culpability

Performed limited function under direction

Involved through coercion, intimidation or exploitation

Not motivated by personal gain

Opportunistic 'one-off' offence; very little or no planning

Limited awareness or understanding of extent of criminal activity

Where there are characteristics present which fall under different levels of culpability, the court should balance these characteristics to reach a fair assessment of the offender's culpability.

Harm A   **Harm is initially assessed by the value of the money laundered.**

Category 1
£10 million or more
Starting point based on £30 million
Category 2
£2 million–£10 million
Starting point based on £5 million
Category 3
£500,000–£2 million
Starting point based on £1 million
Category 4
£100,000–£500,000
Starting point based on £300,000
Category 5
£10,000–£100,000
Starting point based on £50,000
Category 6
Less than £10,000
Starting point based on £5,000

Harm B   Money laundering is an integral component of much serious criminality. **To complete the assessment of harm, the court should take into account the level of harm associated with the underlying offence to determine whether it warrants upward adjustment of the starting point within the range, or in appropriate cases, outside the range.**

Where it is possible to identify the underlying offence, regard should be given to the relevant sentencing levels for that offence.

Starting point and category range

STEP TWO   Having determined the category at step one, the court should use the appropriate starting point (as adjusted in accordance with step one above) to reach a sentence within the category range in the table below. The starting point applies to all offenders irrespective of plea or previous convictions.

Where the value is larger or smaller than the amount on which the starting point is based, this should lead to upward or downward adjustment as appropriate.

Where the value greatly exceeds the amount of the starting point in category 1, it may be appropriate to move outside the identified range.

Section 327 Proceeds of Crime Act 2002: Concealing/disguising/converting/transferring/removing criminal property from England & Wales

Section 328 Proceeds of Crime Act 2002: Entering into arrangements concerning criminal property

Section 329 Proceeds of Crime Act 2002: Acquisition, use and possession of criminal property
Maximum: 14 years' custody

Harm	Culpability		
	A	**B**	**C**
Category 1	**Starting point**	**Starting point**	**Starting point**
£10 million or more	10 years' custody	7 years' custody	4 years' custody
Starting point based	**Category range**	**Category range**	**Category range**
on £30 million	8 – 13 years' custody	5 – 10 years' custody	3 – 6 years' custody
Category 2	**Starting point**	**Starting point**	**Starting point**
£2 million–£10 million	8 years' custody	5 years' custody	3 years 6 months' custody
Starting point based	**Category range**	**Category range**	**Category range**
on £5 million	6 – 9 years' custody	3 years 6 months' – 7 years' custody	2 – 5 years' custody
Category 3	**Starting point**	**Starting point**	**Starting point**
£500,000–£2 million	7 years' custody	5 years' custody	3 years' custody
Starting point based	**Category range**	**Category range**	**Category range**
on £1 million	5 – 8 years' custody	3 – 6 years' custody	18 months' – 4 years' custody
Category 4	**Starting point**	**Starting point**	**Starting point**
£100,000–£500,000	5 years' custody	3 years' custody	18 months' custody
Starting point based	**Category range**	**Category range**	**Category range**
on £300,000	3 – 6 years' custody	18 months' – 4 years' custody	26 weeks' – 3 years' custody
Category 5	**Starting point**	**Starting point**	**Starting point**
£10,000–£100,000	3 years' custody	18 months' custody	26 weeks' custody
Starting point based	**Category range**	**Category range**	**Category range**
on £50,000	18 months' – 4 years' custody	26 weeks' – 3 years' custody	Medium level community order – 1 year's custody
Category 6	**Starting point**	**Starting point**	**Starting point**
Less than £10,000	1 year's custody	High level community order	Low level community order
Starting point based	**Category range**	**Category range**	**Category range**
on £5,000	26 weeks' – 2 years' custody	Low level community order – 1 year's custody	Band B fine – Medium level community order[Ed 1]

[Ed 1] In *R v Fulton, R v Wood* [2017] EWCA Crim 308, [2017] 2 Cr App R (S) 11 the defendants were convicted of money laundering, which was part of a Missing Trader intra Community fraud. The sole issue in the appeal was whether the total figure passing through the various accounts or the underlying tax loss should determine the offence category. By analogy with confiscation proceedings (see *R v Ahmad* [2012] EWCA Crim 391, [2012] 1 WLR 2335) the appellants argued it should be the latter. The Court of Appeal disagreed. In money laundering it is the whole of the money involved which impacts on the financial system. Money laundering offences can be committed by people who are unaware of the underlying criminality. The court may not know what the underlying offence was, or how much the criminal proceeds were before they became mixed in the money laundering operation.

> "'25 This approach is reflected in the Sentencing Council Guideline which provides tables categorising harm by reference to the scale of the money laundering activity, not the underlying offence which provides the criminal proceeds which are being laundered. On page 36 of the Guideline, harm is to be identified by reference to two boxes, Harm A and Harm B....
> 27 The guidance therefore distinguishes between (1) the money laundering amount and (2) the harm caused by the underlying offence. The wording of Harm B recognises that the second may be something which the court cannot identify. The table at page 37 of the Guideline is set out by reference to the six categories of harm determined by applying the Harm A criteria. They are clearly based on the amount of the money laundering activity, not the amount of the criminal proceeds being laundered. This is as one would expect and in accordance with principle for the reasons we have identified.
> 28 The appellant's reliance on the case of *R v Ahmad* is misplaced. That was a case involving the substantive offence for cheating the Revenue, not a money laundering offence. Moreover, and critically, the present case is not concerned with any question of benefit for the purpose of confiscation proceedings which is what was in issue in *Ahmad*. It is concerned with sentencing and the sentencing guidelines. The sentencing exercise starts by examining the scale of the offence which these defendants conspired to commit. That was the offence of money laundering. The Guideline therefore directs attention to the scale of that criminal activity. What benefit each defendant may have received from that activity is a consideration which falls to be taken into account at a later stage, in determining the defendant's role and culpability and in taking into account all the circumstances of the case." (per Popplewell J)

Ed 1   See further *R v Campbell* [2017] EWCA Crim 213, [2017] 1 Cr App R (S) 57, where some of the criminal property had come from drug dealing, but the Court of Appeal held that the judge had been wrong to sentence the defendant by reference to the sentencing guideline for drug offences rather than straddling the starting points in that guideline and the guideline for fraud, bribery and money laundering, having regard to the guidance in *R v Ogden* [2016] EWCA Crim 6, [2017] 1 WLR 1224.

Ed 1   Where the underlying offence is charged, the offenders are the same and the POCA offence in reality adds nothing to the culpability of the conduct involved in the underlying offence, there should be no additional penalty to avoid 'double punishment': *R v Greaves* [2010] EWCA Crim 709, [2011] 1 Cr App R (S) 8, *R v Dowse* [2017] EWCA Crim 598, [2017] 2 Cr App R (S) 26.

The table below contains a non-exhaustive list of additional factual elements providing the context of the offence and factors relating to the offender.

Identify whether any combination of these or other relevant factors should result in an upward or downward adjustment of the sentence arrived at thus far.

Consecutive sentences for multiple offences may be appropriate where large sums are involved.

Factors increasing seriousness   *Statutory aggravating factors:*

Previous convictions, having regard to a) the nature of the offence to which the conviction relates and its relevance to the current offence; and b) the time that has elapsed since the conviction

Offence committed whilst on bail

Other aggravating factors:

Attempts to conceal/dispose of evidence

Established evidence of community/wider impact

Failure to comply with current court orders

Offence committed on licence

Offences taken into consideration

Failure to respond to warnings about behaviour

Offences committed across borders

Blame wrongly placed on others

Damage to third party for example loss of employment to legitimate employees

Factors reducing seriousness or reflecting personal mitigation   No previous convictions **or** no relevant/recent convictions

Remorse

Little or no prospect of success

Good character and/or exemplary conduct

Serious medical conditions requiring urgent, intensive or long-term treatment

Age and/or lack of maturity where it affects the responsibility of the offender

Lapse of time since apprehension where this does not arise from the conduct of the offender

Mental disorder or learning disability

Sole or primary carer for dependent relatives

Offender co-operated with investigation, made early admissions and/or voluntarily reported offending

Determination and/or demonstration of steps having been taken to address addiction or offending behaviour

Activity originally legitimate

See page 361.

Consider any factors which indicate a reduction, such as assistance to the prosecution

STEP THREE   The court should take into account sections 73 and 74 of the Serious Organised Crime and Police Act 2005 (assistance by defendants: reduction or review of sentence) and any other rule of law by virtue of which an offender may receive a discounted sentence in consequence of assistance given (or offered) to the prosecutor or investigator.

Reduction for guilty pleas

STEP FOUR The court should take account of any potential reduction for a guilty plea in accordance with section 144 of the Criminal Justice Act 2003 and the *Guilty Plea* guideline.

Totality principle

STEP FIVE If sentencing an offender for more than one offence, or where the offender is already serving a sentence, consider whether the total sentence is just and proportionate to the overall offending behaviour.

Confiscation, compensation and ancillary orders

STEP SIX The court must proceed with a view to making a confiscation order if it is asked to do so by the prosecutor or if the court believes it is appropriate for it to do so.

Where the offence has resulted in loss or damage the court must consider whether to make a compensation order.

If the court makes both a confiscation order and an order for compensation and the court believes the offender will not have sufficient means to satisfy both orders in full, the court must direct that the compensation be paid out of sums recovered under the confiscation order (section 13 of the Proceeds of Crime Act 2002).

The court may also consider whether to make ancillary orders. These may include a deprivation order, a financial reporting order, a serious crime prevention order and disqualification from acting as a company director.

Reasons

STEP SEVEN Section 174 of the Criminal Justice Act 2003 imposes a duty to give reasons for, and explain the effect of, the sentence.

Consideration for time spent on bail

STEP EIGHT The court must consider whether to give credit for time spent on bail in accordance with section 240A of the Criminal Justice Act 2003.

BRIBERY

BRIBING ANOTHER PERSON

Bribery Act 2010 (section 1)

BEING BRIBED

Bribery Act 2010 (section 2)

BRIBERY OF FOREIGN PUBLIC OFFICIALS

Bribery Act 2010 (section 6)
Triable either way
Maximum: 10 years' custody
Offence range: Discharge – 8 years' custody

Determining the offence category

STEP ONE   The court should determine the offence category with reference to the tables below. In order to determine the category the court should assess **culpability** and **harm**.

The level of **culpability** is determined by weighing up all the factors of the case to determine the offender's role and the extent to which the offending was planned and the sophistication with which it was carried out.

Culpability demonstrated by one or more of the following: A – High culpability

A leading role where offending is part of a group activity

Involvement of others through pressure, influence

Abuse of position of significant power or trust or responsibility

Intended corruption (directly or indirectly) of a senior official performing a public function

Intended corruption (directly or indirectly) of a law enforcement officer

Sophisticated nature of offence/significant planning

Offending conducted over sustained period of time

Motivated by expectation of substantial financial, commercial or political gain

B – Medium culpability

All other cases where characteristics for categories A or C are not present

A significant role where offending is part of a group activity

C – Lesser culpability

Involved through coercion, intimidation or exploitation

Not motivated by personal gain

Peripheral role in organised activity

Opportunistic 'one-off' offence; very little or no planning

Limited awareness or understanding of extent of corrupt activity

Where there are characteristics present which fall under different levels of culpability, the court should balance these characteristics to reach a fair assessment of the offender's culpability.

Harm is assessed in relation to any impact caused by the offending (whether to identifiable victims or in a wider context) and the actual or intended gain to the offender.

Category 1	• Serious detrimental effect on individuals (for example by provision of substandard goods or services resulting from the corrupt behaviour)
	• Serious environmental impact
	• Serious undermining of the proper function of local or national government, business or public services
	• Substantial actual or intended financial gain to offender or another or loss caused to others
Category 2	• Significant detrimental effect on individuals
	• Significant environmental impact
	• Significant undermining of the proper function of local or national government, business or public services
	• Significant actual or intended financial gain to offender or another or loss caused to others
	• Risk of category 1 harm
Category 3	• Limited detrimental impact on individuals, the environment, government, business or public services
	• Risk of category 2 harm
Category 4	• Risk of category 3 harm

Risk of harm involves consideration of both the likelihood of harm occurring and the extent of it if it does. Risk of harm is less serious than the same actual harm. Where the offence has caused risk of harm but no (or much less) actual harm, the normal approach is to move to the next category of harm down. This may not be appropriate if either the likelihood or extent of potential harm is particularly high.

Starting point and category range

STEP TWO   Having determined the category at step one, the court should use the corresponding starting point to reach a sentence within the category range below. The starting point applies to all offenders irrespective of plea or previous convictions.

    Section 1 Bribery Act 2010: Bribing another person
    Section 2 Bribery Act 2010: Being bribed
    Section 6 Bribery Act 2010: Bribery of foreign public officials
    Maximum: 10 years' custody

Harm	Culpability		
	A	**B**	**C**
Category 1	**Starting point** 7 years' custody **Category range** 5 – 8 years' custody	**Starting point** 5 years' custody **Category range** 3 – 6 years' custody	**Starting point** 3 years' custody **Category range** 18 months' – 4 years' custody
Category 2	**Starting point** 5 years' custody **Category range** 3 – 6 years' custody	**Starting point** 3 years' custody **Category range** 18 months' – 4 years' custody	**Starting point** 18 months' custody **Category range** 26 weeks' – 3 years' custody
Category 3	**Starting point** 3 years' custody **Category range** 18 months' – 4 years' custody	**Starting point** 18 months' custody **Category range** 26 weeks' – 3 years' custody	**Starting point** 26 weeks' custody **Category range** Medium level community order – 1 year's custody
Category 4	**Starting point** 18 months' custody **Category range** 26 weeks' – 3 years' custody	**Starting point** 26 weeks' custody **Category range** Medium level community order – 1 year's custody	**Starting point** Medium level community order **Category range** Band B fine – High level community order

See page 366.

The table below contains a non-exhaustive list of additional factual elements providing the context of the offence and factors relating to the offender.

Identify whether any combination of these or other relevant factors should result in an upward or downward adjustment from the starting point.

Consecutive sentences for multiple offences may be appropriate where large sums are involved.

Factors increasing seriousness   *Statutory aggravating factors:*

Previous convictions, having regard to a) the nature of the offence to which the conviction relates and its relevance to the current offence; and b) the time that has elapsed since the conviction

    Offence committed whilst on bail

Other aggravating factors:

Steps taken to prevent victims reporting or obtaining assistance and/or from assisting or supporting the prosecution

    Attempts to conceal/dispose of evidence
    Established evidence of community/wider impact
    Failure to comply with current court orders
    Offence committed on licence
    Offences taken into consideration
    Failure to respond to warnings about behaviour
    Offences committed across borders
    Blame wrongly placed on others
    Pressure exerted on another party
    Offence committed to facilitate other criminal activity

Factors reducing seriousness or reflecting personal mitigation   No previous convictions **or** no relevant/recent convictions

    Remorse
    Good character and/or exemplary conduct
    Little or no prospect of success
    Serious medical conditions requiring urgent, intensive or long-term treatment
    Age and/or lack of maturity where it affects the responsibility of the offender

Lapse of time since apprehension where this does not arise from the conduct of the offender
Mental disorder or learning disability
Sole or primary carer for dependent relatives
Offender co-operated with investigation, made early admissions and/or voluntarily reported offending
See page 367.

Consider any factors which indicate a reduction, such as assistance to the prosecution
STEP THREE The court should take into account sections 73 and 74 of the Serious Organised Crime and Police Act 2005 (assistance by defendants: reduction or review of sentence) and any other rule of law by virtue of which an offender may receive a discounted sentence in consequence of assistance given (or offered) to the prosecutor or investigator.

Reduction for guilty pleas
STEP FOUR The court should take account of any potential reduction for a guilty plea in accordance with section 144 of the Criminal Justice Act 2003 and the *Guilty Plea* guideline.

Totality principle
STEP FIVE If sentencing an offender for more than one offence, or where the offender is already serving a sentence, consider whether the total sentence is just and proportionate to the overall offending behaviour.

Confiscation, compensation and ancillary orders
STEP SIX The court must proceed with a view to making a confiscation order if it is asked to do so by the prosecutor or if the court believes it is appropriate for it to do so.

Where the offence has resulted in loss or damage the court must consider whether to make a compensation order.

If the court makes both a confiscation order and an order for compensation and the court believes the offender will not have sufficient means to satisfy both orders in full, the court must direct that the compensation be paid out of sums recovered under the confiscation order (section 13 of the Proceeds of Crime Act 2002).

The court may also consider whether to make ancillary orders. These may include a deprivation order, a financial reporting order, a serious crime prevention order and disqualification from acting as a company director.

Reasons
STEP SEVEN Section 174 of the Criminal Justice Act 2003 imposes a duty to give reasons for, and explain the effect of, the sentence.

Consideration for time spent on bail
STEP EIGHT The court must consider whether to give credit for time spent on bail in accordance with section 240A of the Criminal Justice Act 2003.

Corporate Offenders: Fraud, Bribery and Money Laundering

Fraud

Conspiracy to defraud (common law)
Cheat the public revenue (common law)
Triable only on indictment
Fraud Act 2006 (sections 1, 6 and 7)
Theft Act 1968 (section 17)
Value Added Tax Act 1994 (section 72)
Customs and Excise Management Act 1979 (section 170)
Triable either way

Bribery

Bribery Act 2010 (sections 1, 2, 6 and 7)
Triable either way

Money laundering

Proceeds of Crime Act 2002 (sections 327, 328 and 329)
Triable either way
Maximum: Unlimited fine
Most cases of corporate offending in this area are likely to merit allocation for trial to the Crown Court.
Committal for sentence is mandatory if confiscation (see step two) is to be considered. (Proceeds of Crime Act 2002 section 70).

Compensation
STEP ONE   The court must consider making a compensation order requiring the offender to pay compensation for any personal injury, loss or damage resulting from the offence in such an amount as the court considers appropriate, having regard to the evidence and to the means of the offender.
Where the means of the offender are limited, priority should be given to the payment of compensation over payment of any other financial penalty.
Reasons should be given if a compensation order is not made.
(See section 130 Powers of Criminal Courts (Sentencing) Act 2000)

Confiscation
STEP TWO   Confiscation must be considered if either the Crown asks for it or the court thinks that it may be appropriate.
Confiscation must be dealt with before, and taken into account when assessing, any other fine or financial order (except compensation).
(See Proceeds of Crime Act 2002 sections 6 and 13)
See page 371.

Determining the offence category
STEP THREE   The court should determine the offence category with reference to **culpability** and **harm**.
Culpability   The sentencer should weigh up all the factors of the case to determine **culpability. Where there are characteristics present which fall under different categories, the court should balance these characteristics to reach a fair assessment of the offender's culpability.**
Culpability demonstrated by the offending corporation's role and motivation. May be demonstrated by one or more of the following **non-exhaustive** characteristics.
A – High culpability
Corporation plays a leading role in organised, planned unlawful activity (whether acting alone or with others)
Wilful obstruction of detection (for example destruction of evidence, misleading investigators, suborning employees)
Involving others through pressure or coercion (for example employees or suppliers)
Targeting of vulnerable victims or a large number of victims
Corruption of local or national government officials or ministers
Corruption of officials performing a law enforcement role
Abuse of dominant market position or position of trust or responsibility
Offending committed over a sustained period of time
Culture of wilful disregard of commission of offences by employees or agents with no effort to put effective systems in place (section 7 Bribery Act only)
B – Medium culpability
Corporation plays a significant role in unlawful activity organised by others
Activity not unlawful from the outset
Corporation reckless in making false statement (section 72 VAT Act 1994)
All other cases where characteristics for categories A or C are not present
C – Lesser culpability
Corporation plays a minor, peripheral role in unlawful activity organised by others
Some effort made to put bribery prevention measures in place but insufficient to amount to a defence (section 7 Bribery Act only)
Involvement through coercion, intimidation or exploitation
Harm   Harm is represented by a financial sum calculated by reference to the table below

Amount obtained or intended to be obtained (or loss avoided or intended to be avoided)

Fraud	For offences of fraud, conspiracy to defraud, cheating the Revenue and fraudulent evasion of duty or VAT, harm will normally be the actual or intended gross gain to the offender.
Bribery	For offences under the Bribery Act the appropriate figure will normally be the gross profit from the contract obtained, retained or sought as a result of the offending. An alternative measure for offences under section 7 may be the likely cost avoided by failing to put in place appropriate measures to prevent bribery.
Money laundering	For offences of money laundering the appropriate figure will normally be the amount laundered or, alternatively, the likely cost avoided by failing to put in place an effective anti-money laundering programme if this is higher.
General	Where the actual or intended gain cannot be established, the appropriate measure will be the amount that the court considers was likely to be achieved in all the circumstances.
	In the absence of sufficient evidence of the amount that was likely to be obtained, 10–20 per cent of the relevant revenue (for instance between 10 and 20 per cent of the worldwide revenue derived from the product or business area to which the offence relates for the period of the offending) **may** be an appropriate measure.
	There may be large cases of fraud or bribery in which the true harm is to commerce or markets generally. That may justify adopting a harm figure beyond the normal measures here set out.

Starting point and category range

STEP FOUR Having determined the culpability level at step three, the court should use the table below to determine the starting point within the category range below. The starting point applies to all offenders irrespective of plea or previous convictions.

The harm figure at step three is multiplied by the relevant percentage figure representing culpability.

	Culpability Level		
	A	**B**	**C**
	Starting point	**Starting point**	**Starting point**
Harm figure	300%	200%	100%
multiplier	**Category range**	**Category range**	**Category range**
	250% to 400%	100% to 300%	20% to 150%

Having determined the appropriate starting point, the court should then consider adjustment within the category range for aggravating or mitigating features. In some cases, having considered these factors, it may be appropriate to move outside the identified category range. (See below for a **non-exhaustive** list of aggravating and mitigating factors.)

Factors increasing seriousness Previous relevant convictions or subject to previous relevant civil or regulatory enforcement action

   Corporation or subsidiary set up to commit fraudulent activity
   Fraudulent activity endemic within corporation
   Attempts made to conceal misconduct
   Substantial harm (whether financial or otherwise) suffered by victims of offending or by third parties affected by offending
   Risk of harm greater than actual or intended harm (for example in banking/credit fraud)
   Substantial harm caused to integrity or confidence of markets
   Substantial harm caused to integrity of local or national governments
   Serious nature of underlying criminal activity (money laundering offences)
   Offence committed across borders or jurisdictions

Factors reducing seriousness or reflecting mitigation No previous relevant convictions or previous relevant civil or regulatory enforcement action

   Victims voluntarily reimbursed/compensated
   No actual loss to victims
   Corporation co-operated with investigation, made early admissions and/or voluntarily reported offending
   Offending committed under previous director(s)/ manager(s)
   Little or no actual gain to corporation from offending

GENERAL PRINCIPLES TO FOLLOW IN SETTING A FINE

The court should determine the appropriate level of fine in accordance with section 164 of the Criminal Justice Act 2003, which requires that the fine must reflect the seriousness of the offence and requires the court to take into account the financial circumstances of the offender.

Companies and bodies delivering public or charitable services

Where the offender is a company or a body which delivers a public or charitable service, it is expected to provide comprehensive accounts for the last three years, to enable the court to make an accurate assessment of its financial status. In the absence of such disclosure, or where the court is not satisfied that it has been given sufficient reliable information, the court will be entitled to draw reasonable inferences as to the offender's means from evidence it has heard and from all the circumstances of the case.

(1) *For companies*: annual accounts. Particular attention should be paid to turnover; profit before tax; directors' remuneration, loan accounts and pension provision; and assets as disclosed by the balance sheet. Most companies are required to file audited accounts at Companies House. Failure to produce relevant recent accounts on request may properly lead to the conclusion that the company can pay any appropriate fine.

(2) *For partnerships*: annual accounts. Particular attention should be paid to turnover; profit before tax; partners' drawings, loan accounts and pension provision; assets as above. Limited liability partnerships (LLPs) may be required to file audited accounts with Companies House. If adequate accounts are not produced on request, see paragraph 1.

(3) *For local authorities, fire authorities and similar public bodies*: the Annual Revenue Budget ("ARB") is the equivalent of turnover and the best indication of the size of the defendant organisation. It is unlikely to be necessary to analyse specific expenditure or reserves unless inappropriate expenditure is suggested.

(4) *For health trusts*: the independent regulator of NHS Foundation Trusts is Monitor. It publishes quarterly reports and annual figures for the financial strength and stability of trusts from which the annual income can be seen, available via www.monitor-nhsft.gov.uk. Detailed analysis of expenditure or reserves is unlikely to be called for.

(5) *For charities*: it will be appropriate to inspect annual audited accounts. Detailed analysis of expenditure or reserves is unlikely to be called for unless there is a suggestion of unusual or unnecessary expenditure.

Adjustment of fine

STEP FIVE Having arrived at a fine level, the court should consider whether there are any further factors which indicate an adjustment in the level of the fine. The court should 'step back' and consider the overall effect of its orders. The combination of orders made, compensation, confiscation and fine ought to achieve:

- the removal of all gain
- appropriate additional punishment, and
- deterrence

The fine may be adjusted to ensure that these objectives are met in a fair way. The court should consider any further factors relevant to the setting of the level of the fine to ensure that the fine is proportionate, having regard to the size and financial position of the offending organisation and the seriousness of the offence.

The fine must be substantial enough to have a real economic impact which will bring home to both management and shareholders the need to operate within the law. Whether the fine will have the effect of putting the offender out of business will be relevant; in some bad cases this may be an acceptable consequence.

In considering the ability of the offending organisation to pay any financial penalty the court can take into account the power to allow time for payment or to order that the amount be paid in instalments.

The court should consider whether the level of fine would otherwise cause unacceptable harm to third parties. In doing so the court should bear in mind that the payment of any compensation determined at step one should take priority over the payment of any fine.

The table below contains a **non-exhaustive** list of additional factual elements for the court to consider. The Court should identify whether any combination of these, or other relevant factors, should result in a proportionate increase or reduction in the level of fine.

Factors to consider in adjusting the level of fine Fine fulfils the objectives of punishment, deterrence and removal of gain

The value, worth or available means of the offender

Fine impairs offender's ability to make restitution to victims

Impact of fine on offender's ability to implement effective compliance programmes

Impact of fine on employment of staff, service users, customers and local economy (but not shareholders)

Impact of fine on performance of public or charitable function

Consider any factors which would indicate a reduction, such as assistance to the prosecution

STEP SIX The court should take into account sections 73 and 74 of the Serious Organised Crime and Police Act 2005 (assistance by defendants: reduction or review of sentence) and any other rule of law by virtue of which an offender may receive a discounted sentence in consequence of assistance given (or offered) to the prosecutor or investigator.

Reduction for guilty pleas

STEP SEVEN The court should take into account any potential reduction for a guilty plea in accordance with section 144 of the Criminal Justice Act 2003 and the *Guilty Plea* guideline.

Ancillary Orders
STEP EIGHT   In all cases the court must consider whether to make any ancillary orders.

Totality principle
STEP NINE   If sentencing an offender for more than one offence, consider whether the total sentence is just and proportionate to the offending behaviour.

Reasons
STEP TEN   Section 174 of the Criminal Justice Act 2003 imposes a duty to give reasons for, and explain the effect of, the sentence.

GENERAL THEFT
Theft Act 1968 (section 1)

Including:

**Theft from the person
Theft in a dwelling
Theft in breach of trust
Theft from a motor vehicle
Theft of a motor vehicle
Theft of a pedal bicycle
and all other section 1 Theft Act 1968 offences,
excluding theft from a shop or stall**

**Triable either way
Maximum: 7 years' custody
Offence range: Discharge – 6 years' custody**

Determining the offence category

STEP ONE   The court should determine the offence category with reference **only** to the factors identified in the following tables. In order to determine the category the court should assess **culpability** and **harm.**

The level of culpability is determined by weighing up all the factors of the case to determine the offender's role and the extent to which the offending was **planned** and the **sophistication** with which it was carried out.

CULPABILITY demonstrated by one or more of the following: **A – High culpability**
A leading role where offending is part of a group activity
Involvement of others through coercion, intimidation or exploitation
Breach of a high degree of trust or responsibility
Sophisticated nature of offence/significant planning
Theft involving intimidation or the use or threat of force
Deliberately targeting victim on basis of vulnerability
B – Medium culpability
A significant role where offending is part of a group activity
Some degree of planning involved
Breach of some degree of trust or responsibility
All other cases where characteristics for categories A or C are not present
C – Lesser culpability
Performed limited function under direction
Involved through coercion, intimidation or exploitation
Little or no planning
Limited awareness or understanding of offence
Where there are characteristics present which fall under different levels of culpability, the court should balance these characteristics to reach a fair assessment of the offender's culpability.
HARM   Harm is assessed by reference to the **financial loss** that results from the theft **and any significant additional harm** suffered by the victim or others – examples of significant additional harm may include **but are not limited to:**
Items stolen were of substantial value to the loser – regardless of monetary worth
High level of inconvenience caused to the victim or others
Consequential financial harm to victim or others
Emotional distress
Fear/loss of confidence caused by the crime
Risk of or actual injury to persons or damage to property
Impact of theft on a business
Damage to heritage assets
Disruption caused to infrastructure
Intended loss should be used where actual loss has been prevented.

Category 1	Very high value goods stolen (above £100,000) **or** High value with significant additional harm to the victim or others
Category 2	High value goods stolen (£10,000 to £100,000) **and** no significant additional harm **or** Medium value with significant additional harm to the victim or others
Category 3	Medium value goods stolen (£500 to £10,000) **and** no significant additional harm **or** Low value with significant additional harm to the victim or others
Category 4	Low value goods stolen (up to £500) **and** Little or no significant additional harm to the victim or others

Starting point and category range

STEP TWO   Having determined the category at step one, the court should use the starting point to reach a sentence within the appropriate category range in the table below.

The starting point applies to all offenders irrespective of plea or previous convictions.

Harm	Culpability		
	A	**B**	**C**
Category 1	**Starting point**	**Starting point**	**Starting point**
Adjustment should be made for any significant additional harm factors where very high value goods are stolen.	3 years 6 months' custody	2 years' custody	1 year's custody
	Category range	**Category range**	**Category range**
	2 years 6 months' – 6 years' custody	1 – 3 years 6 months' custody	26 weeks' – 2 years' custody
Category 2	**Starting point**	**Starting point**	**Starting point**
	2 years' custody	1 year's custody	High level community order
	Category range	**Category range**	**Category range**
	1 – 3 years 6 months' custody	26 weeks' – 2 years' custody	Low level community order – 36 weeks' custody
Category 3	**Starting point**	**Starting point**	**Starting point**
	1 years' custody	High level community order	Band C fine
	Category range	**Category range**	**Category range**
	26 weeks' – 2 years' custody	Low level community order – 36 weeks' custody	Band B fine – Low level community order
Category 4	**Starting point**	**Starting point**	**Starting point**
	High level community order	Low level community order	Band B fine
	Category range	**Category range**	**Category range**
	Medium level community order – 36 weeks' custody	Band C fine – Medium level community order	Discharge – Band C fine

The table above refers to single offences. Where there are multiple offences, consecutive sentences may be appropriate: please refer to the *Offences Taken Into Consideration and Totality* guideline. Where multiple offences are committed in circumstances which justify consecutive sentences, and the total amount stolen is in excess of £1 million, then an aggregate sentence in excess of 7 years may be appropriate.

Where the offender is dependent on or has a propensity to misuse drugs or alcohol and there is sufficient prospect of success, a community order with a drug rehabilitation requirement under section 209, or an alcohol treatment requirement under section 212 of the Criminal Justice Act 2003 may be a proper alternative to a short or moderate custodial sentence.

Where the offender suffers from a medical condition that is susceptible to treatment but does not warrant detention under a hospital order, a community order with a mental health treatment requirement under section 207 of the Criminal Justice Act 2003 may be a proper alternative to a short or moderate custodial sentence.

The court should then consider further adjustment for any aggravating or mitigating factors. The following is a **non-exhaustive** list of additional factual elements providing the context of the offence and factors relating to the offender. Identify whether any combination of these, or other relevant factors, should result in an upward or downward adjustment from the sentence arrived at so far.

Factors increasing seriousness   *Statutory aggravating factors*

Previous convictions, having regard to a) the **nature** of the offence to which the conviction relates and its **relevance** to the current offence; and b) the **time** that has elapsed since the conviction

Offence committed whilst on bail

Offence motivated by, or demonstrating hostility based on any of the following characteristics or presumed characteristics of the victim: religion, race, disability, sexual orientation or transgender identity

Other aggravating factors

Stealing goods to order

Steps taken to prevent the victim reporting or obtaining assistance and/or from assisting or supporting the prosecution

Offender motivated by intention to cause harm or out of revenge

Offence committed over sustained period of time

Attempts to conceal/dispose of evidence

Failure to comply with current court orders

Offence committed on licence

Offences taken into consideration
Blame wrongly placed on others
Established evidence of community/wider impact (for issues other than prevalence)
Prevalence – see below
Factors reducing seriousness or reflecting personal mitigation No previous convictions **or** no relevant/recent convictions
Remorse, particularly where evidenced by voluntary reparation to the victim
Good character and/or exemplary conduct
Serious medical condition requiring urgent, intensive or long-term treatment
Age and/or lack of maturity where it affects the responsibility of the offender
Mental disorder or learning disability
Sole or primary carer for dependent relatives
Determination and/or demonstration of steps having been taken to address addiction or offending behaviour
Inappropriate degree of trust or responsibility
Prevalence There may be exceptional local circumstances that arise which may lead a court to decide that prevalence should influence sentencing levels. The pivotal issue in such cases will be the harm caused to the community.
It is essential that the court before taking account of prevalence:

- has supporting evidence from an external source, for example, Community Impact Statements, to justify claims that a particular crime is prevalent in their area, **and** is causing particular harm in that community, **and**
- is satisfied that there is a compelling need to treat the offence more seriously than elsewhere.

Consider any factors which indicate a reduction, such as assistance to the prosecution
STEP THREE The court should take into account sections 73 and 74 of the Serious Organised Crime and Police Act 2005 (assistance by defendants: reduction or review of sentence) and any other rule of law by virtue of which an offender may receive a discounted sentence in consequence of assistance given (or offered) to the prosecutor or investigator.

Reduction for guilty pleas
STEP FOUR The court should take account of any potential reduction for a guilty plea in accordance with section 144 of the Criminal Justice Act 2003 and the *Guilty Plea* guideline.

Totality principle
STEP FIVE If sentencing an offender for more than one offence, or where the offender is already serving a sentence, consider whether the total sentence is just and proportionate to the overall offending behaviour in accordance with the *Offences Taken into Consideration and Totality* guideline.

Confiscation, compensation and ancillary orders
STEP SIX The court must proceed with a view to making a confiscation order if it is asked to do so by the prosecutor or if the court believes it is appropriate for it to do so.
Where the offence has resulted in loss or damage the court must consider whether to make a compensation order.
If the court makes both a confiscation order and an order for compensation and the court believes the offender will not have sufficient means to satisfy both orders in full, the court must direct that the compensation be paid out of sums recovered under the confiscation order (section 13 of the Proceeds of Crime Act 2002).
The court may also consider whether to make ancillary orders. These may include a deprivation order, or a restitution order.

Reasons
STEP SEVEN Section 174 of the Criminal Justice Act 2003 imposes a duty to give reasons for, and explain the effect of, the sentence.

Consideration for time spent on bail
STEP EIGHT The court must consider whether to give credit for time spent on bail in accordance with section 240A of the Criminal Justice Act 2003.

THEFT FROM A SHOP OR STALL
Theft Act 1968 (section 1)

Triable either way
Maximum: 7 years' custody
(except for an offence of low-value shoplifting which is treated as a summary only offence in accordance with section 22A of the Magistrates' Courts Act 1980 where the maximum is 6 months' custody).
Offence range: Discharge – 3 years' custody

Determining the offence category

STEP ONE   The court should determine the offence category with reference **only** to the factors identified in the following tables. In order to determine the category the court should assess **culpability** and **harm**.

The level of culpability is determined by weighing up all the factors of the case to determine the offender's role and the extent to which the offending was **planned** and the **sophistication** with which it was carried out.

CULPABILITY demonstrated by one or more of the following: A – High culpability

A leading role where offending is part of a group activity

Involvement of others through coercion, intimidation or exploitation

Sophisticated nature of offence/significant planning

Significant use or threat of force

Offender subject to a banning order from the relevant store

Child accompanying offender is actively used to **facilitate** the offence (not merely present when offence is committed)

B – Medium culpability

A significant role where offending is part of a group activity

Some degree of planning involved

Limited use or threat of force

All other cases where characteristics for categories A or C are not present

C – Lesser culpability

Performed limited function under direction

Involved through coercion, intimidation or exploitation

Little or no planning

Mental disorder/learning disability where linked to commission of the offence

Where there are characteristics present which fall under different levels of culpability, the court should balance these characteristics to reach a fair assessment of the offender's culpability.

HARM   Harm is assessed by reference to the **financial loss** that results from the theft **and any significant additional harm** suffered by the victim – examples of significant additional harm may include **but are not limited to:**

Emotional distress

Damage to property

Effect on business

A greater impact on the victim due to the size or type of their business

A particularly vulnerable victim

Intended loss should be used where actual loss has been prevented.

Category 1	High value goods stolen (above £1,000) **or** Medium value with significant additional harm to the victim
Category 2	Medium value goods stolen (£200 to £1,000) **and** no significant additional harm **or** Low value with significant additional harm to the victim
Category 3	Low value goods stolen (up to £200) **and** Little or no significant additional harm to the victim

Starting point and category range

STEP TWO   Having determined the category at step one, the court should use the starting point to reach a sentence within the appropriate category range in the table below.

The starting point applies to all offenders irrespective of plea or previous convictions.

Harm	Culpability		
	A	B	C
Category 1	Starting point	Starting point	Starting point

Harm	Culpability		
	A	**B**	**C**
Where the value greatly exceeds £1,000 it may be appropriate to move outside the identified range. Adjustment should be made for any significant additional harm where high value goods are stolen.	26 weeks' custody	Medium level community order	Band C fine
	Category range	**Category range**	**Category range**
	12 weeks' – 3 years' custody	Low level community order – 26 weeks' custody	Band B fine – Low level community order
Category 2	**Starting point**	**Starting point**	**Starting point**
	12 weeks' custody	Low level community order	Band B fine
	Category range	**Category range**	**Category range**
	High level community order – 26 weeks' custody	Band C fine – Medium level community order	Band A fine – Band C fine
Category 3	**Starting point**	**Starting point**	**Starting point**
	High level community order	Band C fine	Band A fine
	Category range	**Category range**	**Category range**
	Low level community order – 12 weeks' custody	Band B fine – Low level community order	Discharge – Band B fine

Consecutive sentences for multiple offences may be appropriate – please refer to the *Offences Taken Into Consideration and Totality* guideline.

Previous diversionary work with an offender does not preclude the court from considering this type of sentencing option again if appropriate.

Where the offender is dependent on or has a propensity to misuse drugs or alcohol and there is sufficient prospect of success, a community order with a drug rehabilitation requirement under section 209, or an alcohol treatment requirement under section 212 of the Criminal Justice Act 2003 may be a proper alternative to a short or moderate custodial sentence.

Where the offender suffers from a medical condition that is susceptible to treatment but does not warrant detention under a hospital order, a community order with a mental health treatment requirement under section 207 of the Criminal Justice Act 2003 may be a proper alternative to a short or moderate custodial sentence.

The court should then consider further adjustment for any aggravating or mitigating factors. The following is a **non-exhaustive** list of additional factual elements providing the context of the offence and factors relating to the offender. Identify whether any combination of these, or other relevant factors, should result in an upward or downward adjustment from the sentence arrived at so far.

Factors increasing seriousness *Statutory aggravating factors*

Previous convictions, having regard to a) the **nature** of the offence to which the conviction relates and its **relevance** to the current offence; and b) the **time** that has elapsed since the conviction

Relevant recent convictions **may** justify an upward adjustment, including outside the category range. In cases involving significant persistent offending, the community and custodial thresholds may be crossed even though the offence otherwise warrants a lesser sentence. Any custodial sentence must be kept to the necessary minimum

Offence committed whilst on bail

Offence motivated by, or demonstrating hostility based on any of the following characteristics or presumed characteristics of the victim: religion, race, disability, sexual orientation or transgender identity

Other aggravating factors

Stealing goods to order

Steps taken to prevent the victim reporting or obtaining assistance and/or from assisting or supporting the prosecution

Attempts to conceal/dispose of evidence

Offender motivated by intention to cause harm or out of revenge

Failure to comply with current court orders

Offence committed on licence

Offences taken into consideration

Established evidence of community/wider impact (for issues other than prevalence)

Prevalence – see below

Factors reducing seriousness or reflecting personal mitigation   No previous convictions **or** no relevant/recent convictions

Remorse, particularly where evidenced by voluntary reparation to the victim

Good character and/or exemplary conduct

Serious medical condition requiring urgent, intensive or long-term treatment

Age and/or lack of maturity where it affects the responsibility of the offender

Mental disorder or learning disability (where not linked to the commission of the offence)

Sole or primary carer for dependent relatives

Determination and/or demonstration of steps having been taken to address addiction or offending behaviour

Offender experiencing **exceptional** financial hardship

Prevalence   There may be exceptional local circumstances that arise which may lead a court to decide that prevalence should influence sentencing levels. The pivotal issue in such cases will be the harm caused to the community.

It is essential that the court before taking account of prevalence:

- has supporting evidence from an external source, for example, Community Impact Statements, to justify claims that a particular crime is prevalent in their area, **and** is causing particular harm in that community, **and**
- is satisfied that there is a compelling need to treat the offence more seriously than elsewhere.

Consider any factors which indicate a reduction, such as assistance to the prosecution

STEP THREE   The court should take into account sections 73 and 74 of the Serious Organised Crime and Police Act 2005 (assistance by defendants: reduction or review of sentence) and any other rule of law by virtue of which an offender may receive a discounted sentence in consequence of assistance given (or offered) to the prosecutor or investigator.

Reduction for guilty pleas

STEP FOUR   The court should take account of any potential reduction for a guilty plea in accordance with section 144 of the Criminal Justice Act 2003 and the *Guilty Plea* guideline.

Totality principle

STEP FIVE   If sentencing an offender for more than one offence, or where the offender is already serving a sentence, consider whether the total sentence is just and proportionate to the overall offending behaviour in accordance with the *Offences Taken into Consideration and Totality* guideline.

Confiscation, compensation and ancillary orders

STEP SIX   The court must proceed with a view to making a confiscation order if it is asked to do so by the prosecutor or if the court believes it is appropriate for it to do so.

Where the offence has resulted in loss or damage the court must consider whether to make a compensation order.

If the court makes both a confiscation order and an order for compensation and the court believes the offender will not have sufficient means to satisfy both orders in full, the court must direct that the compensation be paid out of sums recovered under the confiscation order (section 13 of the Proceeds of Crime Act 2002).

The court may also consider whether to make ancillary orders. These may include a deprivation order, or a restitution order.

Reasons

STEP SEVEN   Section 174 of the Criminal Justice Act 2003 imposes a duty to give reasons for, and explain the effect of, the sentence.

Consideration for time spent on bail

STEP EIGHT   The court must consider whether to give credit for time spent on bail in accordance with section 240A of the Criminal Justice Act 2003.

HANDLING STOLEN GOODS
Theft Act 1968 (section 22)

Triable either way
Maximum: 14 years' custody
Offence range: Discharge – 8 years' custody

Determining the offence category

STEP ONE   The court should determine the offence category with reference **only** to the factors identified in the following tables. In order to determine the category the court should assess **culpability** and **harm**.

The level of culpability is determined by weighing up all the factors of the case to determine the offender's role and the extent to which the offending was **planned** and the **sophistication** with which it was carried out.

CULPABILITY demonstrated by one or more of the following: A – High culpability

A leading role where offending is part of a group activity

Involvement of others through coercion, intimidation or exploitation

Abuse of position of power or trust or responsibility

Professional and sophisticated offence

Advance knowledge of the primary offence

Possession of very recently stolen goods from a domestic burglary or robbery

B – Medium culpability

A significant role where offending is part of a group activity

Offender acquires goods for resale

All other cases where characteristics for categories A or C are not present

C – Lesser culpability

Performed limited function under direction

Involved through coercion, intimidation or exploitation

Little or no planning

Limited awareness or understanding of offence

Goods acquired for offender's personal use

Where there are characteristics present which fall under different levels of culpability, the court should balance these characteristics to reach a fair assessment of the offender's culpability.

HARM   Harm is assessed by reference to the **financial value** (to the loser) of the handled goods **and any significant additional harm** associated with the underlying offence on the victim or others – examples of additional harm may include **but are not limited to:**

Property stolen from a domestic burglary or a robbery (unless this has already been taken into account in assessing culpability)

Items stolen were of substantial value to the loser, regardless of monetary worth

Metal theft causing disruption to infrastructure

Damage to heritage assets

Category 1	Very high value goods stolen (above £100,000) **or** High value with significant additional harm to the victim or others
Category 2	High value goods stolen (£10,000 to £100,000) **and** no significant additional harm **or** Medium value with significant additional harm to the victim or others
Category 3	Medium value goods stolen (£1,000 to £10,000) **and** no significant additional harm **or** Low value with significant additional harm to the victim or others
Category 4	Low value goods stolen (up to £1,000) **and** Little or no significant additional harm to the victim or others

Starting point and category range

STEP TWO   Having determined the category at step one, the court should use the starting point to reach a sentence within the appropriate category range in the table below.

The starting point applies to all offenders irrespective of plea or previous convictions.

Harm	Culpability		
	A	**B**	**C**
Category 1	**Starting point**	**Starting point**	**Starting point**

Harm	Culpability		
	A	**B**	**C**
Where the value greatly exceeds £100,000, it may be appropriate to move outside the identified range. Adjustment should be made for any significant additional harm where very high value stolen goods are handled	5 years' custody	3 years' custody	1 year's custody
	Category range	**Category range**	**Category range**
	3 – 8 years' custody	1 year 6 months' – 4 years' custody	26 weeks' – 1 year 6 months' custody
Category 2	**Starting point**	**Starting point**	**Starting point**
	3 years' custody	1 year's custody	High level community order
	Category range	**Category range**	**Category range**
	1 year 6 months' – 4 years' custody	26 weeks' – 1 year 6 months' custody	Low level community order – 26 weeks' custody
Category 3	**Starting point**	**Starting point**	**Starting point**
	1 year's custody	High level community order	Band C fine
	Category range	**Category range**	**Category range**
	26 weeks' – 2 years' custody	Low level community order – 26 weeks' custody	Band B fine – Low level community order
Category 4	**Starting point**	**Starting point**	**Starting point**
	High level community order	Low level community order	Band B fine
	Category range	**Category range**	**Category range**
	Medium level community order – 26 weeks' custody	Band C fine – High level community order	Discharge – Band C fine

Consecutive sentences for multiple offences may be appropriate – please refer to the *Offences Taken Into Consideration and Totality* guideline.

The court should then consider further adjustment for any aggravating or mitigating factors. The following is a **non-exhaustive** list of additional factual elements providing the context of the offence and factors relating to the offender. Identify whether any combination of these, or other relevant factors, should result in an upward or downward adjustment from the starting point.

Factors increasing seriousness *Statutory aggravating factors*

Previous convictions, having regard to a) the **nature** of the offence to which the conviction relates and its **relevance** to the current offence; and b) the **time** that has elapsed since the conviction

Offence committed whilst on bail

Other aggravating factors

Seriousness of the underlying offence, for example, armed robbery

Deliberate destruction, disposal or defacing of stolen property

Damage to a third party

Failure to comply with current court orders

Offence committed on licence

Offences taken into consideration

Established evidence of community/wider impact

Factors reducing seriousness or reflecting personal mitigation No previous convictions **or** no relevant/recent convictions

Good character and/or exemplary conduct

Serious medical condition requiring urgent, intensive or long-term treatment

Age and/or lack of maturity where it affects the responsibility of the offender

Mental disorder or learning disability

Sole or primary carer for dependent relatives

Determination and/or demonstration of steps having been taken to address addiction or offending behaviour

Consider any factors which indicate a reduction, such as assistance to the prosecution
STEP THREE   The court should take into account sections 73 and 74 of the Serious Organised Crime and Police Act 2005 (assistance by defendants: reduction or review of sentence) and any other rule of law by virtue of which an offender may receive a discounted sentence in consequence of assistance given (or offered) to the prosecutor or investigator.

Reduction for guilty pleas
STEP FOUR   The court should take account of any potential reduction for a guilty plea in accordance with section 144 of the Criminal Justice Act 2003 and the *Guilty Plea* guideline.

Totality principle
STEP FIVE   If sentencing an offender for more than one offence, or where the offender is already serving a sentence, consider whether the total sentence is just and proportionate to the overall offending behaviour in accordance with the *Offences Taken into Consideration and Totality* guideline.

Confiscation, compensation and ancillary orders
STEP SIX   The court must proceed with a view to making a confiscation order if it is asked to do so by the prosecutor or if the court believes it is appropriate for it to do so.

Where the offence has resulted in loss or damage the court must consider whether to make a compensation order.

If the court makes both a confiscation order and an order for compensation and the court believes the offender will not have sufficient means to satisfy both orders in full, the court must direct that the compensation be paid out of sums recovered under the confiscation order (section 13 of the Proceeds of Crime Act 2002).

The court may also consider whether to make ancillary orders. These may include a deprivation order, or a restitution order.

Reasons
STEP SEVEN   Section 174 of the Criminal Justice Act 2003 imposes a duty to give reasons for, and explain the effect of, the sentence.

Consideration for time spent on bail
STEP EIGHT   The court must consider whether to give credit for time spent on bail in accordance with section 240A of the Criminal Justice Act 2003.

GOING EQUIPPED FOR THEFT OR BURGLARY
Theft Act 1968 (section 25)

Triable either way
Maximum: 3 years' custody
Offence range: Discharge – 18 months' custody

Determining the offence category

STEP ONE The court should determine the offence category with reference **only** to the factors identified in the following tables. In order to determine the category the court should assess **culpability** and **harm**.

The level of culpability is determined by weighing up all the factors of the case to determine the offender's role and the extent to which the offending was **planned** and the **sophistication** with which it was carried out.

CULPABILITY demonstrated by one or more of the following: **A – High culpability**

A leading role where offending is part of a group activity
Involvement of others through coercion, intimidation or exploitation
Significant steps taken to conceal identity and/or avoid detection
Sophisticated nature of offence/significant planning
Offender equipped for robbery or domestic burglary

B – Medium culpability

A significant role where offending is part of a group activity
All other cases where characteristics for categories A or C are not present

C – Lesser culpability

Involved through coercion, intimidation or exploitation
Limited awareness or understanding of offence
Little or no planning

Where there are characteristics present which fall under different levels of culpability, the court should balance these characteristics to reach a fair assessment of the offender's culpability.

HARM This guideline refers to preparatory offences where no theft has been committed. The level of harm is determined by weighing up all the factors of the case to determine the harm that would be caused if the item(s) were used to commit a substantive offence.

Greater harm

Possession of item(s) which have the potential to facilitate an offence affecting a large number of victims
Possession of item(s) which have the potential to facilitate an offence involving high value items

Lesser harm

All other cases

Starting point and category range

STEP TWO Having determined the category at step one, the court should use the starting point to reach a sentence within the appropriate category range in the table below.

The starting point applies to all offenders irrespective of plea or previous convictions.

Harm	Culpability		
	A	**B**	**C**
Greater	**Starting point**	**Starting point**	**Starting point**
	1 year's custody	18 weeks' custody	Medium level community order
	Category range	**Category range**	**Category range**
	26 weeks' – 1 year 6 months' custody	High level community order – 36 weeks' custody	Low level community order – High level community order
Lesser	**Starting point**	**Starting point**	**Starting point**
	26 weeks' custody	High level community order	Band C fine
	Category range	**Category range**	**Category range**
	12 weeks' – 36 weeks' custody	Medium level community order – 12 weeks' custody	Discharge – Medium level community order

Consecutive sentences for multiple offences may be appropriate – please refer to the *Offences Taken Into Consideration and Totality* guideline.

The court should then consider further adjustment for any aggravating or mitigating factors. The following is a **non-exhaustive** list of additional factual elements providing the context of the offence and factors relating to the offender. Identify whether any combination of these, or other relevant factors, should result in an upward or downward adjustment from the starting point.

Factors increasing seriousness   *Statutory aggravating factors*

Previous convictions, having regard to a) the **nature** of the offence to which the conviction relates and its **relevance** to the current offence; and b) the **time** that has elapsed since the conviction
Offence committed whilst on bail

Other aggravating factors
Attempts to conceal/dispose of evidence
Established evidence of community/wider impact
Failure to comply with current court orders
Offence committed on licence
Offences taken into consideration
Factors reducing seriousness or reflecting personal mitigation No previous convictions **or** no relevant/recent convictions
Good character and/or exemplary conduct
Serious medical condition requiring urgent, intensive or long-term treatment
Age and/or lack of maturity where it affects the responsibility of the offender
Mental disorder or learning disability
Sole or primary carer for dependent relatives
Determination and/or demonstration of steps having been taken to address addiction or offending behaviour

Consider any factors which indicate a reduction, such as assistance to the prosecution
STEP THREE The court should take into account sections 73 and 74 of the Serious Organised Crime and Police Act 2005 (assistance by defendants: reduction or review of sentence) and any other rule of law by virtue of which an offender may receive a discounted sentence in consequence of assistance given (or offered) to the prosecutor or investigator.

Reduction for guilty pleas
STEP FOUR The court should take account of any potential reduction for a guilty plea in accordance with section 144 of the Criminal Justice Act 2003 and the *Guilty Plea* guideline.

Totality principle
STEP FIVE If sentencing an offender for more than one offence, or where the offender is already serving a sentence, consider whether the total sentence is just and proportionate to the overall offending behaviour in accordance with the *Offences Taken into Consideration and Totality* guideline.

Confiscation, compensation and ancillary orders
STEP SIX The court must proceed with a view to making a confiscation order if it is asked to do so by the prosecutor or if the court believes it is appropriate for it to do so.
Where the offence has resulted in loss or damage the court must consider whether to make a compensation order.
If the court makes both a confiscation order and an order for compensation and the court believes the offender will not have sufficient means to satisfy both orders in full, the court must direct that the compensation be paid out of sums recovered under the confiscation order (section 13 of the Proceeds of Crime Act 2002).
The court may also consider whether to make any ancillary orders, such as a deprivation order.

Reasons
STEP SEVEN Section 174 of the Criminal Justice Act 2003 imposes a duty to give reasons for, and explain the effect of, the sentence.

Consideration for time spent on bail
STEP EIGHT The court must consider whether to give credit for time spent on bail in accordance with section 240A of the Criminal Justice Act 2003.

Abstracting electricity
Theft Act 1968 (section 13)

Triable either way
Maximum: 5 years' custody
Offence range: Discharge – 1 year's custody

Determining the offence category

STEP ONE The court should determine the offence category with reference **only** to the factors identified in the following tables. In order to determine the category the court should assess **culpability** and **harm**.

The level of culpability is determined by weighing up all the factors of the case to determine the offender's role and the extent to which the offending was **planned** and the **sophistication** with which it was carried out.

CULPABILITY demonstrated by one or more of the following: **A – High culpability**

A leading role where offending is part of a group activity
Involvement of others through coercion, intimidation or exploitation
Sophisticated nature of offence/significant planning
Abuse of position of power or trust or responsibility
Commission of offence in association with or to further other criminal activity

B – Medium culpability

A significant role where offending is part of a group activity
All other cases where characteristics for categories A or C are not present

C – Lesser culpability

Performed limited function under direction
Involved through coercion, intimidation or exploitation
Limited awareness or understanding of offence

Where there are characteristics present which fall under different levels of culpability, the court should balance these characteristics to reach a fair assessment of the offender's culpability.

HARM The level of harm is assessed by weighing up all the factors of the case to determine the level of harm caused.

Greater harm

A significant risk of, or actual injury to persons or damage to property
Significant volume of electricity extracted as evidenced by length of time of offending and/or advanced type of illegal process used

Lesser harm

All other cases

Starting point and category range

STEP TWO Having determined the category at step one, the court should use the starting point to reach a sentence within the appropriate category range in the table below.

The starting point applies to all offenders irrespective of plea or previous convictions.

Harm	Culpability		
	A	**B**	**C**
Greater	**Starting point**	**Starting point**	**Starting point**
	12 weeks's custody	Medium level community order	Band C fine
	Category range	**Category range**	**Category range**
	High level community order – 1 year's custody	Low level community order – 12 weeks' custody	Band B fine – Low level community order
Lesser	**Starting point**	**Starting point**	**Starting point**
	High level community order	Low level community order	Band A fine
	Category range	**Category range**	**Category range**
	Medium level community order – 12 weeks' custody	Band C fine – Medium level community order	Discharge – Band C fine

The court should then consider further adjustment for any aggravating or mitigating factors. The table below contains a **non-exhaustive** list of additional factual elements providing the context of the offence and factors relating to the offender.

Identify whether any combination of these, or other relevant factors, should result in an upward or downward adjustment from the starting point.

Factors increasing seriousness *Statutory aggravating factors*

Previous convictions, having regard to a) the **nature** of the offence to which the conviction relates and its **relevance** to the current offence; and b) the **time** that has elapsed since the conviction

Offence committed whilst on bail

Other aggravating factors

Electricity abstracted from another person's property
Attempts to conceal/dispose of evidence

Failure to comply with current court orders
Offence committed on licence
Offences taken into consideration
Blame wrongly placed on others
Established evidence of community/wider impact
Factors reducing seriousness or reflecting personal mitigation   No previous convictions **or** no relevant/recent convictions
Good character and/or exemplary conduct
Serious medical condition requiring urgent, intensive or long-term treatment
Age and/or lack of maturity where it affects the responsibility of the offender
Mental disorder or learning disability
Sole or primary carer for dependent relatives
Determination and/or demonstration of steps having been taken to address addiction or offending behaviour

Consider any factors which indicate a reduction, such as assistance to the prosecution

STEP THREE   The court should take into account sections 73 and 74 of the Serious Organised Crime and Police Act 2005 (assistance by defendants: reduction or review of sentence) and any other rule of law by virtue of which an offender may receive a discounted sentence in consequence of assistance given (or offered) to the prosecutor or investigator.

Reduction for guilty pleas

STEP FOUR   The court should take account of any potential reduction for a guilty plea in accordance with section 144 of the Criminal Justice Act 2003 and the *Guilty Plea* guideline.

Totality principle

STEP FIVE   If sentencing an offender for more than one offence, or where the offender is already serving a sentence, consider whether the total sentence is just and proportionate to the overall offending behaviour in accordance with the *Offences Taken into Consideration and Totality* guideline.

Confiscation, compensation and ancillary orders

STEP SIX   The court must proceed with a view to making a confiscation order if it is asked to do so by the prosecutor or if the court believes it is appropriate for it to do so.

Where the offence has resulted in loss or damage the court must consider whether to make a compensation order.

If the court makes both a confiscation order and an order for compensation and the court believes the offender will not have sufficient means to satisfy both orders in full, the court must direct that the compensation be paid out of sums recovered under the confiscation order (section 13 of the Proceeds of Crime Act 2002).

The court may also consider whether to make ancillary orders. These may include a deprivation order, or a restitution order.

Reasons

STEP SEVEN   Section 174 of the Criminal Justice Act 2003 imposes a duty to give reasons for, and explain the effect of, the sentence.

Consideration for time spent on bail

STEP EIGHT   The court must consider whether to give credit for time spent on bail in accordance with section 240A of the Criminal Justice Act 2003.

Making off without payment
Theft Act 1978 (section 3)

Triable either way
Maximum: 2 years' custody
Offence range: Discharge – 36 weeks' custody

Determining the offence category

STEP ONE The court should determine the offence category with reference **only** to the factors identified in the following tables. In order to determine the category the court should assess **culpability** and **harm**.

The level of culpability is determined by weighing up all the factors of the case to determine the offender's role and the extent to which the offending was **planned** and the **sophistication** with which it was carried out.

CULPABILITY demonstrated by one or more of the following: A – High culpability

A leading role where offending is part of a group activity
Involvement of others through coercion, intimidation or exploitation
Sophisticated nature of offence/significant planning
Offence involving intimidation or the use or threat of force
Deliberately targeting victim on basis of vulnerability

B – Medium culpability

A significant role where offending is part of a group activity
Some degree of planning involved
All other cases where characteristics for categories A or C are not present

C – Lesser culpability

Performed limited function under direction
Involved through coercion, intimidation or exploitation
Little or no planning
Limited awareness or understanding of offence

Where there are characteristics present which fall under different levels of culpability, the court should balance these characteristics to reach a fair assessment of the offender's culpability.

HARM Harm is assessed by reference to the **actual loss** that results from the offence **and any significant additional harm** suffered by the victim – examples of additional harm may include **but are not limited to:**

A high level of inconvenience caused to the victim
Emotional distress
Fear/loss of confidence caused by the crime
A greater impact on the victim due to the size or type of their business

Category 1	Goods or services obtained above £200 **or** Goods/services up to £200 with significant additional harm to the victim
Category 2	Goods or services obtained up to £200 **and** Little or no significant additional harm to the victim

Starting point and category range

STEP TWO Having determined the category at step one, the court should use the starting point to reach a sentence within the appropriate category range in the table below.

The starting point applies to all offenders irrespective of plea or previous convictions.

Harm	Culpability		
	A	**B**	**C**
Category 1	**Starting point**	**Starting point**	**Starting point**
Where the value greatly exceeds £200, it may be appropriate to move outside the identified range. Adjustment should be made for any significant additional harm for offences above £200.	12 weeks' custody	Low level community order	Band B fine
	Category range	**Category range**	**Category range**
	High level community order – 36 weeks' custody	Band C fine – High level community order	Band A fine – Low level community order
Category 2	**Starting point**	**Starting point**	**Starting point**
	Medium level community order	Band C fine	Band A fine

Harm	Culpability		
	A	**B**	**C**
	Category range	**Category range**	**Category range**
	Low level community order – 12 weeks' custody	Band B fine – Low level community order	Discharge – Band B fine

Consecutive sentences for multiple offences may be appropriate – please refer to the *Offences Taken Into Consideration and Totality* guideline.

The court should then consider further adjustment for any aggravating or mitigating factors. The following list is a **non-exhaustive** list of additional factual elements providing the context of the offence and factors relating to the offender.

Identify whether any combination of these, or other relevant factors, should result in an upward or downward adjustment from the starting point.

Factors increasing seriousness *Statutory aggravating factors*

Previous convictions, having regard to a) the **nature** of the offence to which the conviction relates and its **relevance** to the current offence; and b) the **time** that has elapsed since the conviction

Offence committed whilst on bail

Offence motivated by, or demonstrating hostility based on any of the following characteristics or presumed characteristics of the victim: religion, race, disability, sexual orientation or transgender identity

Other aggravating factors

Steps taken to prevent the victim reporting or obtaining assistance and/or from assisting or supporting the prosecution

Attempts to conceal/dispose of evidence

Failure to comply with current court orders

Offence committed on licence

Offences taken into consideration

Established evidence of community/wider impact

Factors reducing seriousness or reflecting personal mitigation No previous convictions **or** no relevant/recent convictions

Remorse, particularly where evidenced by voluntary reparation to the victim

Good character and/or exemplary conduct

Serious medical condition requiring urgent, intensive or long-term treatment

Age and/or lack of maturity where it affects the responsibility of the offender

Mental disorder or learning disability

Sole or primary carer for dependent relatives

Determination and/or demonstration of steps having been taken to address addiction or offending behaviour

Consider any factors which indicate a reduction, such as assistance to the prosecution

STEP THREE The court should take into account sections 73 and 74 of the Serious Organised Crime and Police Act 2005 (assistance by defendants: reduction or review of sentence) and any other rule of law by virtue of which an offender may receive a discounted sentence in consequence of assistance given (or offered) to the prosecutor or investigator.

Reduction for guilty pleas

STEP FOUR The court should take account of any potential reduction for a guilty plea in accordance with section 144 of the Criminal Justice Act 2003 and the *Guilty Plea* guideline.

Totality principle

STEP FIVE If sentencing an offender for more than one offence, or where the offender is already serving a sentence, consider whether the total sentence is just and proportionate to the overall offending behaviour in accordance with the *Offences Taken into Consideration and Totality* guideline.

Confiscation, compensation and ancillary orders

STEP SIX The court must proceed with a view to making a confiscation order if it is asked to do so by the prosecutor or if the court believes it is appropriate for it to do so.

Where the offence has resulted in loss or damage the court must consider whether to make a compensation order.

If the court makes both a confiscation order and an order for compensation and the court believes the offender will not have sufficient means to satisfy both orders in full, the court must direct that the compensation be paid out of sums recovered under the confiscation order (section 13 of the Proceeds of Crime Act 2002).

The court may also consider whether to make ancillary orders. These may include a deprivation order, or a restitution order.

Reasons

STEP SEVEN Section 174 of the Criminal Justice Act 2003 imposes a duty to give reasons for, and explain the effect of, the sentence.

Consideration for time spent on bail

STEP EIGHT   The court must consider whether to give credit for time spent on bail in accordance with section 240A of the Criminal Justice Act 2003.

HEALTH AND SAFETY – ORGANISATIONS

BREACH OF DUTY OF EMPLOYER TOWARDS EMPLOYEES AND NON-EMPLOYEES

BREACH OF DUTY OF SELF-EMPLOYED TO OTHERS

Health and Safety at Work Act 1974 (section 33(1)(a) for breaches of sections 2 and 3)

BREACH OF HEALTH AND SAFETY REGULATIONS

Health and Safety at Work Act 1974 (section 33(1)(c))

Triable either way

Maximum: when tried on indictment: unlimited fine

when tried summarily: unlimited fine

Offence range: £50 fine – £10 million fine

Determining the offence category

STEP ONE The court should determine the offence category using only the culpability and harm factors in the tables below.

Culpability Where there are factors present in the case that fall in different categories of culpability, the court should balance these factors to reach a fair assessment of the offender's culpability.

Very high

Deliberate breach of or flagrant disregard for the law

High

Offender fell far short of the appropriate standard; for example, by:

- failing to put in place measures that are recognised standards in the industry
- ignoring concerns raised by employees or others
- failing to make appropriate changes following prior incident(s) exposing risks to health and safety
- allowing breaches to subsist over a long period of time

Serious and/or systemic failure within the organisation to address risks to health and safety

Medium

Offender fell short of the appropriate standard in a manner that falls between descriptions in 'high' and 'low' culpability categories

Systems were in place but these were not sufficiently adhered to or implemented

Low

Offender did not fall far short of the appropriate standard; for example, because:

- significant efforts were made to address the risk although they were inadequate on this occasion
- there was no warning/circumstance indicating a risk to health and safety

Failings were minor and occurred as an isolated incident

Harm Health and safety offences are concerned with failures to manage risks to health and safety and do not require proof that the offence caused any actual harm[Ed 1]. **The offence is in creating a risk of harm.**

(1) Use the table below to identify an initial harm category based on the **risk of harm created by the offence.** The assessment of harm requires a consideration of **both**:
- – the seriousness of the harm risked (A, B or C) by the offender's breach; **and**
- – the likelihood of that harm arising (high, medium or low).

Seriousness of harm risked

	Level A	Level B	Level C
	• Death	• Physical or mental impairment, not amounting to Level A, which has a substantial and long-term effect on the sufferer's ability to carry out normal day-to-day activities or on their ability to return to work	• All other cases not falling within Level A or Level B

	• Physical or mental impairment resulting in lifelong dependency on third party care for basic needs • Significantly reduced life expectancy	• A progressive, permanent or irreversible condition	
High likelihood of harm	Harm category 1	Harm category 2	Harm category 3
Medium likelihood of harm	Harm category 2	Harm category 3	Harm category 4
Low likelihood of harm	Harm category 3	Harm category 4	Harm category 4 (start towards bottom of range)

(2) **Next, the court must consider if the following factors apply. These two factors should be considered in the round in assigning the final harm category.**
   (i) **Whether the offence exposed a number of workers or members of the public to the risk of harm.** The greater the number of people, the greater the risk of harm.
   (ii) **Whether the offence was a significant cause of actual harm**[Ed 1]. Consider whether the offender's breach was a **significant cause*** of actual harm and the extent to which other factors contributed to the harm caused. Actions of victims are unlikely to be considered contributory events for sentencing purposes. Offenders are required to protect workers or others who may be neglectful of their own safety in a way which is reasonably foreseeable.

If one or both of these factors apply the court must consider either moving up a harm category or substantially moving up within the category range at step two overleaf. If already in harm category 1 and wishing to move higher, move up from the starting point at step two on the following pages. The court should not move up a harm category[Ed 2] if actual harm was caused but to a lesser degree than the harm that was risked, as identified on the scale of seriousness above.

Ed 1 The second stage of the assessment of harm at Step One brings in actual harm caused by the offence, and the fact of death justifies a move not only into the next category of harm, but to the top of that category see *Whirlpool UK Appliances Limited v R* [2017] EWCA Crim 2186.

Ed 2 While this precludes in these circumstances moving up a category it does not preclude moving up within the range: *R v Havering BC* [2017] EWCA Crim 242, [2017] 2 Cr App R (S) 9.

Starting point and category range

STEP TWO Having determined the offence category, the court should identify the relevant table for the offender on the following pages. There are tables for different sized organisations.

At step two, the court is required to focus on the organisation's annual turnover or equivalent to reach a starting point for a fine. The court should then consider further adjustment within the category range for aggravating and mitigating features.

At step three, the court may be required to refer to other financial factors listed below to ensure that the proposed fine is proportionate.

Obtaining financial information The offender is expected to provide comprehensive accounts for the last three years, to enable the court to make an accurate assessment of its financial status. In the absence of such disclosure, or where the court is not satisfied that it has been given sufficient reliable information, the court will be entitled to draw reasonable inferences as to the offender's means from evidence it has heard and from all the circumstances of the case, **which may include the inference that the offender can pay any fine.**

Normally, only information relating to the organisation before the court will be relevant, unless exceptionally it is demonstrated to the court that the resources of a linked organisation are available and can properly be taken into account.

(1) *For companies*: annual accounts. Particular attention should be paid to turnover; profit before tax; directors' remuneration, loan accounts and pension provision; and assets as

disclosed by the balance sheet. Most companies are required to file audited accounts at Companies House. **Failure to produce relevant recent accounts on request may properly lead to the conclusion that the company can pay any appropriate fine.**

(2) *For partnerships*: annual accounts. Particular attention should be paid to turnover; profit before tax; partners' drawings, loan accounts and pension provision; assets as above. Limited liability partnerships (LLPs) may be required to file audited accounts with Companies House. *If adequate accounts are not produced on request, see paragraph 1.*

(3) *For local authorities, fire authorities and similar public bodies*: the Annual Revenue Budget ('ARB') is the equivalent of turnover and the best indication of the size of the organisation. It is unlikely to be necessary to analyse specific expenditure or reserves (where relevant) unless inappropriate expenditure is suggested.

(4) *For health trusts*: the independent regulator of NHS Foundation Trusts is Monitor. It publishes quarterly reports and annual figures for the financial strength and stability of trusts from which the annual income can be seen, available via www.monitor-nhsft.gov.uk. Detailed analysis of expenditure or reserves is unlikely to be called for.

(5) *For charities*: it will be appropriate to inspect annual audited accounts. Detailed analysis of expenditure or reserves is unlikely to be called for unless there is a suggestion of unusual or unnecessary expenditure.

Where an offending organisation's turnover or equivalent very greatly exceeds[Ed 1] the threshold for large organisations, it may be necessary to move outside the suggested range to achieve a proportionate sentence.

Large
Turnover or equivalent: £50 million and over

	Starting point	Category range
Very high culpability		
Harm category 1	£4,000,000	£2,600,000 – £10,000,000
Harm category 2	£2,000,000	£1,000,000 – £5,250,000
Harm category 3	£1,000,000	£500,000 – £2,700,000
Harm category 4	£500,000	£240,000 – £1,300,000
High culpability		
Harm category 1	£2,400,000	£1,500,000 – £6,000,000
Harm category 2	£1,100,000	£550,000 – £2,900,000
Harm category 3	£540,000	£250,000 – £1,450,000
Harm category 4	£240,000	£120,000 – £700,000
Medium culpability		
Harm category 1	£1,300,000	£800,000 – £3,250,000
Harm category 2	£600,000	£300,000 – £1,500,000
Harm category 3	£300,000	£130,000 – £750,000
Harm category 4	£130,000	£50,000 – £350,000
Low culpability		
Harm category 1	£300,000	£180,000 – £700,000
Harm category 2	£100,000	£35,000 – £250,000
Harm category 3	£35,000	£10,000 – £140,000
Harm category 4	£10,000	£3,000 – £60,000

[Ed 1] See *Whirlpool UK Appliances Limited v R* [2017] EWCA Crim 2186. The case involved a fatality, and the company had a turnover of £700m. The case was judged to be one of 'low culpability' and 'harm category 3', but it was held that the fact of death took the starting point to the top of the next category, ie £250,000. The large turnover of the company and its status as a very large organisation to the starting point up to within the next range, and a starting point of £500,000 was identified before adjustment on account mitigating and aggravating factors. The former led the court to reduce the starting points to £450,000. With full credit for the guilty plea this reduced to £300,000. It was emphasised that the case was unusual because of its combination of low culpability and low risk of harm. The fine would otherwise have been very much larger.

[Ed 1] As to the approach where a company has a very large turnover, but is sustaining losses and is being kept alive as an operational concern by its parent company, see *R v Tata Steel Ltd* [2017] EWCA Crim 704, [2017] 2 Cr App R (S) 29.

Medium
Turnover or equivalent: between £10 million and £50 million

	Starting point	Category range
Very high culpability		
Harm category 1	£1,600,000	£1,000,000 – £4,000,000

	Starting point	Category range
Harm category 2	£800,000	£400,000 – £2,000,000
Harm category 3	£400,000	£180,000 – £1,000,000
Harm category 4	£190,000	£90,000 – £500,000
High culpability		
Harm category 1	£950,000	£600,000 – £2,500,000
Harm category 2	£450,000	£220,000 – £1,200,000
Harm category 3	£210,000	£100,000 – £550,000
Harm category 4	£100,000	£50,000 – £250,000
Medium culpability		
Harm category 1	£540,000	£300,000 – £1,300,000
Harm category 2	£240,000	£100,000 – £600,000
Harm category 3	£100,000	£50,000 – £300,000
Harm category 4	£50,000	£20,000 – £130,000
Low culpability		
Harm category 1	£130,000	£75,000 – £300,000
Harm category 2	£40,000	£14,000 – £100,000
Harm category 3	£14,000	£3,000 – £60,000
Harm category 4	£3,000	£1,000 – £10,000

Small
Turnover or equivalent: between £2 million and £10 million

	Starting point	Category range
Very high culpability		
Harm category 1	£450,000	£300,000 – £1,600,000
Harm category 2	£200,000	£100,000 – £800,000
Harm category 3	£100,000	£50,000 – £400,000
Harm category 4	£50,000	£20,000 – £190,000
High culpability		
Harm category 1	£250,000	£170,000 – £1,000,000
Harm category 2	£100,000	£50,000 – £450,000
Harm category 3	£54,000	£25,000 – £210,000
Harm category 4	£24,000	£12,000 – £100,000
Medium culpability		
Harm category 1	£160,000	£100,000 – £600,000
Harm category 2	£54,000	£25,000 – £230,000
Harm category 3	£24,000	£12,000 – £100,000
Harm category 4	£12,000	£4,000 – £50,000
Low culpability		
Harm category 1	£45,000	£25,000 – £130,000
Harm category 2	£9,000	£3,000 – £40,000
Harm category 3	£3,000	£700 – £14,000
Harm category 4	£700	£100 – £5,000

Micro
Turnover or equivalent: not more than £2 million

	Starting point	Category range
Very high culpability		
Harm category 1	£250,000	£150,000 – £450,000
Harm category 2	£100,000	£50,000 – £200,000
Harm category 3	£50,000	£25,000 – £100,000
Harm category 4	£24,000	£12,000 – £50,000
High culpability		

	Starting point	Category range
Harm category 1	£160,000	£100,000 – £250,000
Harm category 2	£54,000	£30,000 – £110,000
Harm category 3	£30,000	£12,000 – £54,000
Harm category 4	£12,000	£5,000 – £21,000
Medium culpability		
Harm category 1	£100,000	£60,000 – £160,000
Harm category 2	£30,000	£14,000 – £70,000
Harm category 3	£14,000	£6,000 – £25,000
Harm category 4	£6,000	£2,000 – £12,000
Low culpability		
Harm category 1	£30,000	£18,000 – £60,000
Harm category 2	£5,000	£1,000 – £20,000
Harm category 3	£1,200	£200 – £7,000
Harm category 4	£200	£50 – £2,000

The table below contains a **non-exhaustive** list of factual elements providing the context of the offence and factors relating to the offender. Identify whether any combination of these, or other relevant factors, should result in an upward or downward adjustment from the starting point. **In particular, relevant recent convictions are likely to result in a substantial upward adjustment.** In some cases, having considered these factors, it may be appropriate to move outside the identified category range.

Factors increasing seriousness *Statutory aggravating factor:*
Previous convictions, having regard to a) the nature of the offence to which the conviction relates and its relevance to the current offence; and b) the time that has elapsed since the conviction
Other aggravating factors include:
Cost-cutting at the expense of safety
Deliberate concealment of illegal nature of activity
Breach of any court order
Obstruction of justice
Poor health and safety record
Falsification of documentation or licences
Deliberate failure to obtain or comply with relevant licences in order to avoid scrutiny by authorities
Targeting vulnerable victims

Factors reducing seriousness or reflecting mitigation No previous convictions **or** no relevant/recent convictions
Evidence of steps taken voluntarily to remedy problem
High level of co-operation with the investigation, beyond that which will always be expected
Good health and safety record
Effective health and safety procedures in place
Self-reporting, co-operation and acceptance of responsibility

STEPS THREE AND FOUR The court should 'step back', review and, if necessary, adjust the initial fine based on turnover to **ensure that it fulfils the objectives of sentencing** for these offences. The court may adjust the fine upwards or downwards, including outside the range.

Check whether the proposed fine based on turnover is proportionate to the overall means of the offender

General principles to follow in setting a fine The court should finalise the appropriate level of fine in accordance with section 164 of the Criminal Justice Act 2003, which requires that the fine must reflect the seriousness of the offence and that the court must take into account the financial circumstances of the offender.

The level of fine should reflect the extent to which the offender fell below the required standard. The fine should meet, in a fair and proportionate way, the objectives of punishment, deterrence and the removal of gain derived through the commission of the offence; it should not be cheaper to offend than to take the appropriate precautions.

The fine must be **sufficiently substantial to have a real economic impact which will bring home to both management and shareholders the need to comply with health and safety legislation.**

Review of the fine based on turnover The court should 'step back', review and, if necessary, adjust the initial fine reached at step two to *ensure that it fulfils the general principles* set out above. The court may adjust the fine upwards or downwards including outside of the range.

The court should examine the financial circumstances of the offender in the round to assess the economic realities of the organisation and the most efficacious way of giving effect to the purposes of sentencing.

In finalising the sentence, the court should have regard to the following factors:

• The profitability of an organisation will be relevant. If an organisation has a small profit margin relative to its turnover, downward adjustment may be needed. If it has a large profit margin, upward adjustment may be needed.
• Any quantifiable economic benefit derived from the offence, including through avoided costs or operating savings, should normally be added to the fine arrived at in step two.

Where this is not readily available, the court may draw on information available from enforcing authorities and others about the general costs of operating within the law.

- Whether the fine will have the effect of putting the offender out of business will be relevant; in some bad cases this may be an acceptable consequence.

In considering the ability of the offending organisation to pay any financial penalty, the court can take into account the **power to allow time for payment or to order that the amount be paid in instalments**, if necessary over a number of years.

Consider other factors that may warrant adjustment of the proposed fine

STEP FOUR   The court should consider any wider impacts of the fine within the organisation or on innocent third parties; such as (but not limited to):

- the fine impairs offender's ability to make restitution to victims;
- impact of the fine on offender's ability to improve conditions in the organisation to comply with the law;
- impact of the fine on employment of staff, service users, customers and local economy (but not shareholders or directors).

Where the fine will fall on public or charitable bodies, the fine should normally be substantially reduced if the offending organisation is able to demonstrate the proposed fine would have a significant impact on the provision of its services.

Consider any factors which indicate a reduction, such as assistance to the prosecution

STEP FIVE   The court should take into account sections 73 and 74 of the Serious Organised Crime and Police Act 2005 (assistance by defendants: reduction or review of sentence) and any other rule of law by virtue of which an offender may receive a discounted sentence in consequence of assistance given (or offered) to the prosecutor or investigator.

Reduction for guilty pleas

STEP SIX   The court should take account of any potential reduction for a guilty plea in accordance with section 144 of the Criminal Justice Act 2003 and the *Guilty Plea* guideline.

Compensation and ancillary orders

STEP SEVEN   In all cases, the court must consider whether to make ancillary orders. These may include:

Remediation

Under section 42(1) of the Health and Safety at Work Act 1974, the court may impose a remedial order in addition to or instead of imposing any punishment on the offender.

An offender ought by the time of sentencing to have remedied any specific failings involved in the offence and if it has not, will be deprived of significant mitigation.

The cost of compliance with such an order should not ordinarily be taken into account in fixing the fine; the order requires only what should already have been done.

Forfeiture

Where the offence involves the acquisition or possession of an explosive article or substance, section 42(4) enables the court to order forfeiture of the explosive.

Compensation

Where the offence has resulted in loss or damage, the court must consider whether to make a compensation order. The assessment of compensation in cases involving death or serious injury will usually be complex and will ordinarily be covered by insurance. In the great majority of cases the court should conclude that compensation should be dealt with in the civil court, and should say that no order is made for that reason.

If compensation is awarded, priority should be given to the payment of compensation over payment of any other financial penalty where the means of the offender are limited.

Where the offender does not have sufficient means to pay the total financial penalty considered appropriate by the court, compensation and fine take priority over prosecution costs.

Totality principle

STEP EIGHT   If sentencing an offender for more than one offence, consider whether the total sentence is just and proportionate to the offending behaviour in accordance with the *Offences Taken into Consideration and Totality* guideline.

Reasons

STEP NINE   Section 174 of the Criminal Justice Act 2003 imposes a duty to give reasons for, and explain the effect of, the sentence.

---

* A significant cause is one which more than minimally, negligibly or trivially contributed to the outcome. It does not have to be the sole or principal cause.

HEALTH AND SAFETY – INDIVIDUALS

BREACH OF DUTY OF EMPLOYER TOWARDS EMPLOYEES AND NON-EMPLOYEES

BREACH OF DUTY OF SELF-EMPLOYED TO OTHERS

BREACH OF DUTY OF EMPLOYEES AT WORK
Health and Safety at Work Act 1974 (section 33(1)(a) for breaches of sections 2, 3 and 7)

BREACH OF HEALTH AND SAFETY REGULATIONS
Health and Safety at Work Act 1974 (section 33(1)(c))

SECONDARY LIABILITY
Health and Safety at Work Act 1974 (sections 36 and 37(1) for breaches of sections 2 and 3 and section 33(1)(c))

Triable either way

Maximum: when tried on indictment: unlimited fine and/or 2 years' custody

when tried summarily: unlimited fine and/or 6 months' custody

Offence range: Conditional discharge - 2 years' custody

Determining the offence category

STEP ONE The court should determine the offence category using only the culpability and harm factors in the tables below.

Culpability Where there are factors present in the case that fall in different categories of culpability, the court should balance these factors to reach a fair assessment of the offender's culpability.

Very high

Where the offender intentionally breached, or flagrantly disregarded, the law

High

Actual foresight of, or wilful blindness to, risk of offending but risk nevertheless taken

Medium

Offence committed through act or omission which a person exercising reasonable care would not commit

Low

Offence committed with little fault, for example, because:

- significant efforts were made to address the risk although they were inadequate on this occasion
- there was no warning/circumstance indicating a risk to health and safety
- failings were minor and occurred as an isolated incident

Harm Health and safety offences are concerned with failures to manage risks to health and safety and do not require proof that the offence caused any actual harm. **The offence is in creating a risk of harm**.

(1) Use the table below to identify an initial harm category based on the **risk of harm created by the offence**. The assessment of harm requires a consideration of **both**:
 – the seriousness of the harm risked (A, B or C) by the offender's breach; **and**
 – the likelihood of that harm arising (high, medium or low).

Seriousness of harm risked

	Level A	Level B	Level C
	• Death	• Physical or mental impairment, not amounting to Level A, which has a substantial and long-term effect on the sufferer's ability to carry out normal day-to-day activities or on their ability to return to work	• All other cases not falling within Level A or Level B

	• Physical or mental impairment resulting in lifelong dependency on third party care for basic needs • Significantly reduced life expectancy	• A progressive, permanent or irreversible condition	
High likelihood of harm	Harm category 1	Harm category 2	Harm category 3
Medium likelihood of harm	Harm category 2	Harm category 3	Harm category 4
Low likelihood of harm	Harm category 3	Harm category 4	Harm category 4 (start towards bottom of range)

(2) **Next, the court must consider if the following factors apply. These two factors should be considered in the round in assigning the final harm category.**
  (i) **Whether the offence exposed a number of workers or members of the public to the risk of harm.** The greater the number of people, the greater the risk of harm.
  (ii) **Whether the offence was a significant cause of actual harm.** Consider whether the offender's breach was a **significant cause*** of actual harm[Ed 1] and the extent to which other factors contributed to the harm caused. Actions of victims are unlikely to be considered contributory events for sentencing purposes. Offenders are required to protect workers or others who may be neglectful of their own safety in a way which is reasonably foreseeable.

If one or both of these factors apply the court must consider either moving up a harm category or substantially moving up within the category range at step two overleaf. If already in harm category 1 and wishing to move higher, move up from the starting point at step two overleaf. The court should not move up a harm category if actual harm was caused but to a lesser degree than the harm that was risked, as identified on the scale of seriousness above.

Ed 1 The second stage of the assessment of harm at Step One brings in actual harm caused by the offence, and the fact of death justifies a move not only into the next category of harm, but to the top of that category: *Whirlpool UK Appliances Limited v R* [2017] EWCA Crim 2186.

Starting point and category range
STEP TWO Having determined the category, the court should refer to the starting points on the following page to reach a sentence within the category range. The court should then consider further adjustment within the category range for aggravating and mitigating features, set out on page 18.

Obtaining financial information In setting a fine, the court may conclude that the offender is able to pay any fine imposed unless the offender has supplied any financial information to the contrary. It is for the offender to disclose to the court such data relevant to his financial position as will enable it to assess what he can reasonably afford to pay. If necessary, the court may compel the disclosure of an individual offender's financial circumstances pursuant to section 162 of the Criminal Justice Act 2003. In the absence of such disclosure, or where the court is not satisfied that it has been given sufficient reliable information, the court will be entitled to draw reasonable inferences as to the offender's means from evidence it has heard and from all the circumstances of the case **which may include the inference that the offender can pay any fine.**

Starting points and ranges Where the range includes a potential sentence of custody, the court should consider the custody threshold as follows:
- has the custody threshold been passed?
- if so, is it unavoidable that a custodial sentence be imposed?
- if so, can that sentence be suspended?

Where the range includes a potential sentence of a community order, the court should consider the community order threshold as follows:

- has the community order threshold been passed?

Even where the community order threshold has been passed, a fine will normally be the most appropriate disposal where the offence was committed for economic benefit. Or, if wishing to remove economic benefit derived through the commission of the offence, consider combining a fine with a community order.

	Starting point	Category range
Very high culpability		
Harm category 1	18 months' custody	1 – 2 years' custody
Harm category 2	1 year's custody	26 weeks' – 18 months' custody
Harm category 3	26 weeks' custody	Band F fine or high level community order – 1 year's custody
Harm category 4	Band F fine	Band E fine – 26 weeks' custody
High culpability		
Harm category 1	1 year's custody	26 weeks' – 18 months' custody
Harm category 2	26 weeks' custody	Band F fine or high level community order – 1 year's custody
Harm category 3	Band F fine	Band E fine or medium level community order – 26 weeks' custody
Harm category 4	Band E fine	Band D fine – Band E fine
Medium culpability		
Harm category 1	26 weeks' custody	Band F fine or high level community order – 1 year's custody
Harm category 2	Band F fine	Band E fine or medium level community order – 26 weeks' custody
Harm category 3	Band E fine	Band D fine or low level community order – Band E fine
Harm category 4	Band D fine	Band C fine – Band D fine
Low culpability		
Harm category 1	Band F fine	Band E fine or medium level community order – 26 weeks' custody
Harm category 2	Band D fine	Band C fine – Band D fine
Harm category 3	Band C fine	Band B fine – Band C fine
Harm category 4	Band A fine	Conditional discharge – Band A fine

The table below contains a **non-exhaustive** list of factual elements providing the context of the offence and factors relating to the offender. Identify whether any combination of these, or other relevant factors, should result in an upward or downward adjustment from the starting point. **In particular, relevant recent convictions are likely to result in a substantial upward adjustment**. In some cases, having considered these factors, it may be appropriate to move outside the identified category range.

Factors increasing seriousness *Statutory aggravating factors:*

Previous convictions, having regard to a) the nature of the offence to which the conviction relates and its relevance to the current offence; and b) the time that has elapsed since the conviction

Offence committed whilst on bail

Other aggravating factors include:

Cost-cutting at the expense of safety

Deliberate concealment of illegal nature of activity

Breach of any court order

Obstruction of justice

Poor health and safety record

Falsification of documentation or licences

Deliberate failure to obtain or comply with relevant licences in order to avoid scrutiny by authorities

Targeting vulnerable victims

Factors reducing seriousness or reflecting personal mitigation No previous convictions **or** no relevant/recent convictions

Evidence of steps taken voluntarily to remedy problem

High level of co-operation with the investigation, beyond that which will always be expected

Good health and safety record

Effective health and safety procedures in place

Self-reporting, co-operation and acceptance of responsibility

Good character and/or exemplary conduct

Inappropriate degree of trust or responsibility

Mental disorder or learning disability, where linked to the commission of the offence

Serious medical conditions requiring urgent, intensive or long term treatment
Age and/or lack of maturity where it affects the responsibility of the offender
Sole or primary carer for dependent relatives

Review any financial element of the sentence

STEP THREE   Where the sentence is or includes a fine, the court should 'step back' and, using the factors set out below, review whether the sentence as a whole meets the objectives of sentencing for these offences. The court may increase or reduce the proposed fine reached at step two, if necessary moving outside of the range.

General principles to follow in setting a fine   The court should finalise the appropriate level of fine in accordance with section 164 of the Criminal Justice Act 2003, which requires that the fine must reflect the seriousness of the offence and that the court must take into account the financial circumstances of the offender.

The level of fine should reflect the extent to which the offender fell below the required standard. The fine should meet, in a fair and proportionate way, the objectives of punishment, deterrence and the removal of gain derived through the commission of the offence; it should not be cheaper to offend than to take the appropriate precautions.

Review of the fine   Where the court proposes to impose a fine it should 'step back', review and, if necessary, adjust the initial fine reached at step two to **ensure that it fulfils the general principles** set out above.

Any quantifiable economic benefit derived from the offence, including through avoided costs or operating savings, should normally be added to the fine arrived at in step two. Where this is not readily available, the court may draw on information available from enforcing authorities and others about the general costs of operating within the law.

In finalising the sentence, the court should have regard to the following factors relating to the wider impacts of the fine on innocent third parties; such as (but not limited to):

- impact of the fine on offender's ability to comply with the law;
- impact of the fine on employment of staff, service users, customers and local economy.

Consider any factors which indicate a reduction, such as assistance to the prosecution

STEP FOUR   The court should take into account sections 73 and 74 of the Serious Organised Crime and Police Act 2005 (assistance by defendants: reduction or review of sentence) and any other rule of law by virtue of which an offender may receive a discounted sentence in consequence of assistance given (or offered) to the prosecutor or investigator.

Reduction for guilty pleas

STEP FIVE   The court should take account of any potential reduction for a guilty plea in accordance with section 144 of the Criminal Justice Act 2003 and the *Guilty Plea* guideline.

Compensation and ancillary orders

STEP SIX   In all cases, the court must consider whether to make ancillary orders. These may include:

Disqualification of director

An offender may be disqualified from being a director of a company in accordance with section 2 of the Company Directors Disqualification Act 1986. The maximum period of disqualification is 15 years (Crown Court) or 5 years (magistrates' court).

Remediation

Under section 42(1) of the Health and Safety at Work Act 1974, the court may impose a remedial order in addition to or instead of imposing any punishment on the offender.

An offender ought by the time of sentencing to have remedied any specific failings involved in the offence and if not, will be deprived of significant mitigation.

The cost of compliance with such an order should not ordinarily be taken into account in fixing the fine; the order requires only what should already have been done.

Forfeiture

Where the offence involves the acquisition or possession of an explosive article or substance, section 42(4) enables the court to order forfeiture of the explosive.

Compensation

Where the offence has resulted in loss or damage, the court must consider whether to make a compensation order. The assessment of compensation in cases involving death or serious injury will usually be complex and will ordinarily be covered by insurance. In the great majority of cases the court should conclude that compensation should be dealt with in the civil courts, and should say that no order is made for that reason.

If compensation is awarded, priority should be given to the payment of compensation over payment of any other financial penalty where the means of the offender are limited.

Where the offender does not have sufficient means to pay the total financial penalty considered appropriate by the court, compensation and fine take priority over prosecution costs.

Totality principle

STEP SEVEN   If sentencing an offender for more than one offence, or where the offender is already serving a sentence, consider whether the total sentence is just and proportionate to the offending behaviour in accordance with the *Offences Taken into Consideration and Totality* guideline.

Reasons

STEP EIGHT   Section 174 of the Criminal Justice Act 2003 imposes a duty to give reasons for, and explain the effect of, the sentence.

Consideration for time spent on bail

STEP NINE   The court must consider whether to give credit for time spent on bail in accordance with section 240A of the Criminal Justice Act 2003.

---

  * A significant cause is one which more than minimally, negligibly or trivially contributed to the outcome. It does not have to be the sole or principal cause.

Food Safety – Organisations

Breach of food safety and food hygiene regulations

England

Food Safety and Hygiene (England) Regulations 2013 (regulation 19(1))

Triable either way

Maximum: when tried on indictment: unlimited fine

when tried summarily: unlimited fine

Wales

Food Hygiene (Wales) Regulations 2006 (regulation 17(1))

The General Food Regulations 2004 (regulation 4)

Triable either way

Maximum: when tried on indictment: unlimited fine

when tried summarily: unlimited fine

Determining the offence category

STEP ONE The court should determine the offence category using only the culpability and harm factors in the tables below. Where an offence does not fall squarely into a category, individual factors may require a **degree of weighting** to make an overall assessment.

Culpability   Very high

Deliberate breach of or flagrant disregard for the law

High

Offender fell far short of the appropriate standard; for example, by:

- failing to put in place measures that are recognised standards in the industry
- ignoring concerns raised by regulators, employees or others
- allowing breaches to subsist over a long period of time

Serious and/or systemic failure within the organisation to address risks to health and safety

Medium

Offender fell short of the appropriate standard in a manner that falls between descriptions in 'high' and 'low' culpability categories

Systems were in place but these were not sufficiently adhered to or implemented

Low

Offender did not fall far short of the appropriate standard; for example, because:

- significant efforts were made to secure food safety although they were inadequate on this occasion
- there was no warning/circumstance indicating a risk to food safety

Failings were minor and occurred as an isolated incident

Harm The table below contains factors relating to both actual harm and risk of harm. Dealing with a **risk of harm** involves consideration of both the likelihood of harm occurring and the extent of it if it does.

Category 1	• Serious adverse effect(s) on individual(s) and/or having a widespread impact
	• High risk of an adverse effect on individual(s) including where supply was to groups that are vulnerable
Category 2	• Adverse effect on individual(s) (not amounting to Category 1)
	• Medium risk of an adverse effect on individual(s) or low risk of serious adverse effect
	• Regulator and/or legitimate industry substantially undermined by offender's activities
	• Relevant authorities unable to trace products in order to investigate risks to health, or are otherwise inhibited in identifying or addressing risks to health
	• Consumer misled regarding food's compliance with religious or personal beliefs
Category 3	• Low risk of an adverse effect on individual(s)
	• Public misled about the specific food consumed, but little or no risk of actual adverse effect on individual(s)

Starting point and category range

STEP TWO Having determined the offence category, the court should identify the relevant table for the offender on the following pages. There are tables for different sized organisations.

At step two, the court is required to focus on the organisation's annual turnover or equivalent to reach a starting point for a fine. The court should then consider further adjustment within the category range for aggravating and mitigating features.

At step three, the court may be required to refer to other financial factors listed below to ensure that the proposed fine is proportionate.

At step three, the court may be required to refer to other financial factors listed below to ensure that the proposed fine is proportionate.

Obtaining financial information   Offenders which are companies, partnerships or bodies delivering a public or charitable service are expected to provide comprehensive accounts for the last three years, to enable the court to make an accurate assessment of its financial status. In the absence of such disclosure, or where the court is not satisfied that it has been given sufficient reliable information, the court will be entitled to draw reasonable inferences as to the offender's means from evidence it has heard and from all the circumstances of the case, **which may include the inference that the offender can pay any fine**.

Normally, only information relating to the organisation before the court will be relevant, unless it is demonstrated to the court that the resources of a linked organisation are available and can properly be taken into account.

(1) *For companies*: annual accounts. Particular attention should be paid to turnover; profit before tax; directors' remuneration, loan accounts and pension provision; and assets as disclosed by the balance sheet. Most companies are required to file audited accounts at Companies House. Failure to produce relevant recent accounts on request may properly lead to the conclusion that the company can pay any appropriate fine.

(2) *For partnerships*: annual accounts. Particular attention should be paid to turnover; profit before tax; partners' drawings, loan accounts and pension provision; assets as above. Limited liability partnerships (LLPs) may be required to file audited accounts with Companies House. If adequate accounts are not produced on request, see paragraph 1.

(3) *For local authorities, police and fire authorities and similar public bodies*: the Annual Revenue Budget ('ARB') is the equivalent of turnover and the best indication of the size of the organisation. It is unlikely to be necessary to analyse specific expenditure or reserves unless inappropriate expenditure is suggested.

(4) *For health trusts*: the independent regulator of NHS Foundation Trusts is Monitor. It publishes quarterly reports and annual figures for the financial strength and stability of trusts from which the annual income can be seen, available via www.monitor-nhsft.gov.uk. Detailed analysis of expenditure or reserves is unlikely to be called for.

(5) *For charities*: it will be appropriate to inspect annual audited accounts. Detailed analysis of expenditure or reserves is unlikely to be called for unless there is a suggestion of unusual or unnecessary expenditure.

Where an offending organisation's turnover or equivalent very greatly exceeds the threshold for large organisations, it may be necessary to move outside the suggested range to achieve a proportionate sentence.

Turnover or equivalent: £50 million and over

	Starting point	Range
Very high culpability		
Harm category 1	£1,200,000	£500,000 – £3,000,000
Harm category 2	£500,000	£200,000 – £1,400,000
Harm category 3	£200,000	£90,000 – £500,000
High culpability		
Harm category 1	£500,000	£200,000 – £1,400,000
Harm category 2	£230,000	£90,000 – £600,000
Harm category 3	£90,000	£50,000 – £240,000
Medium culpability		
Harm category 1	£200,000	£80,000 – £500,000
Harm category 2	£90,000	£35,000 – £220,000
Harm category 3	£35,000	£20,000 – £100,000
Low culpability		
Harm category 1	£35,000	£18,000 – £90,000
Harm category 2	£18,000	£9,000 – £50,000
Harm category 3	£10,000	£6,000 – £25,000

Turnover or equivalent: between £10 million and £50 million

	Starting point	Range
Very high culpability		
Harm category 1	£450,000	£200,000 – £1,200,000
Harm category 2	£200,000	£80,000 – £500,000
Harm category 3	£80,000	£40,000 – £200,000
High culpability		

	Starting point	Range
Harm category 1	£200,000	£90,000 – £500,000
Harm category 2	£90,000	£35,000 – £220,000
Harm category 3	£35,000	£18,000 – £90,000
Medium culpability		
Harm category 1	£80,000	£35,000 – £190,000
Harm category 2	£35,000	£14,000 – £90,000
Harm category 3	£14,000	£7,000 – £35,000
Low culpability		
Harm category 1	£12,000	£7,000 – £35,000
Harm category 2	£7,000	£3,500 – £18,000
Harm category 3	£3,500	£2,000 – £10,000

Turnover or equivalent: between £2 million and £10 million

	Starting point	Range
Very high culpability		
Harm category 1	£120,000	£50,000 – £450,000
Harm category 2	£50,000	£18,000 – £200,000
Harm category 3	£18,000	£9,000 – £80,000
High culpability		
Harm category 1	£50,000	£22,000 – £200,000
Harm category 2	£24,000	£8,000 – £90,000
Harm category 3	£9,000	£4,000 – £35,000
Medium culpability		
Harm category 1	£18,000	£7,000 – £70,000
Harm category 2	£8,000	£3,000 – £35,000
Harm category 3	£3,000	£1,500 – £12,000
Low culpability		
Harm category 1	£3,000	£1,400 – £12,000
Harm category 2	£1,400	£700 – £7,000
Harm category 3	£700	£300 – £3,000

Turnover or equivalent: not more than £2 million

	Starting point	Range
Very high culpability		
Harm category 1	£60,000	£25,000 – £120,000
Harm category 2	£25,000	£10,000 – £50,000
Harm category 3	£10,000	£5,000 – £18,000
High culpability		
Harm category 1	£25,000	£10,000 – £50,000
Harm category 2	£12,000	£4,000 – £22,000
Harm category 3	£4,000	£2,000 – £9,000
Medium culpability		
Harm category 1	£10,000	£3,000 – £18,000
Harm category 2	£4,000	£1,400 – £8,000
Harm category 3	£1,400	£700 – £3,000
Low culpability		
Harm category 1	£1,200	£500 – £3,000
Harm category 2	£500	£200 – £1,400
Harm category 3	£200	£100 – £7,000

Micro   The table below contains a **non-exhaustive** list of factual elements providing the context of the offence and factors relating to the offender. Identify whether any combination of these, or other relevant factors, should result in an upward or downward adjustment from the starting point. **In**

particular, relevant recent convictions are likely to result in a substantial upward adjustment. In some cases, having considered these factors, it may be appropriate to move outside the identified category range.

Factors increasing seriousness   *Statutory aggravating factors:*

Previous convictions, having regard to a) the nature of the offence to which the conviction relates and its relevance to the current offence; and b) the time that has elapsed since the conviction

Other aggravating factors include:

Motivated by financial gain

Deliberate concealment of illegal nature of activity

Established evidence of wider/community impact

Breach of any court order

Obstruction of justice

Poor food safety or hygiene record

Refusal of free advice or training

Factors reducing seriousness or reflecting mitigation No previous convictions **or** no relevant/recent convictions

Steps taken voluntarily to remedy problem

High level of co-operation with the investigation, beyond that which will always be expected

Good food safety/hygiene record

Self-reporting, co-operation and acceptance of responsibility

STEPS THREE AND FOUR   The court should 'step back', review and, if necessary, adjust the initial fine based on turnover to **ensure that it fulfils the objectives of sentencing** for these offences. The court may adjust the fine upwards or downwards, including outside the range. Full regard should be given to the totality principle at step eight where multiple offences are involved.

Check whether the proposed fine based on turnover is proportionate to the overall means of the offender

General principles to follow in setting a fine   The court should finalise the fine in accordance with section 164 of the Criminal Justice Act 2003, which requires that the fine must reflect the seriousness of the offence and that the court must take into account the financial circumstances of the offender.

The level of fine should reflect the extent to which the offender fell below the required standard. **The fine should meet, in a fair and proportionate way, the objectives of punishment, deterrence and the removal of gain derived through the commission of the offence;** it should not be cheaper to offend than to take the appropriate precautions.

The fine must be **sufficiently substantial to have a real economic impact which will bring home to both management and shareholders the need to operate within the law.**

Review of the fine based on turnover   The court should 'step back', review and, if necessary, adjust the initial fine reached at step two to **ensure that it fulfils the general principles** set out above. The court may adjust the fine upwards or downwards including outside of the range.

The court should examine the financial circumstances of the offender in the round to enable the court to assess the economic realities of the company and the most efficacious way of giving effect to the purposes of sentencing.

In finalising the sentence, the court should have regard to the following factors:

- The profitability of an organisation will be relevant. If an organisation has a small profit margin relative to its turnover, downward adjustment may be needed. If it has a large profit margin, upward adjustment may be needed.
- Any quantifiable economic benefit derived from the offence, including through avoided costs or operating savings, should normally be added to the total fine arrived at in step two. Where this is not readily available, the court may draw on information available from enforcing authorities and others about the general costs of operating within the law.
- Whether the fine will have the effect of putting the offender out of business will be relevant; in some bad cases this may be an acceptable consequence.

In considering the ability of the offending organisation to pay any financial penalty, the court can take into account the **power to allow time for payment or to order that the amount be paid in instalments**, if necessary over a number of years.

Consider other factors that may warrant adjustment of the proposed fine

STEP FOUR   Where the fine will fall on public or charitable bodies, the fine should normally be substantially reduced if the offending organisation is able to demonstrate the proposed fine would have a significant impact on the provision of their services.

The court should consider any wider impacts of the fine within the organisation or on innocent third parties; such as (but not limited to):

- impact of the fine on offender's ability to improve conditions in the organisation to comply with the law;
- impact of the fine on employment of staff, service users, customers and local economy (but not shareholders or directors).

Consider any factors which indicate a reduction, such as assistance to the prosecution

STEP FIVE   The court should take into account sections 73 and 74 of the Serious Organised Crime and Police Act 2005 (assistance by defendants: reduction or review of sentence) and any other rule of law by virtue of which an offender may receive a discounted sentence in consequence of assistance given (or offered) to the prosecutor or investigator.

Reduction for guilty pleas

STEP SIX   The court should take account of any potential reduction for a guilty plea in accordance with section 144 of the Criminal Justice Act 2003 and the Guilty Plea guideline.

Compensation and ancillary orders

Hygiene Prohibition Order

These orders are available under both the Food Safety and Hygiene (England) Regulations 2013 and the Food Hygiene (Wales) Regulations 2006.

If the court is satisfied that the health risk condition in Regulation 7(2) is fulfilled it shall impose the appropriate prohibition order in Regulation 7(3).

Where a food business operator is convicted of an offence under the Regulations and the court thinks it is proper to do so in all the circumstances of the case, the court may impose a prohibition on the operator pursuant to Regulation 7(4). An order under Regulation 7(4) is not limited to cases where there is an immediate risk to public health; the court might conclude that there is such a risk of some future breach of the regulations or the facts of any particular offence or combination of offences may alone justify the imposition of a Hygiene Prohibition Order. In deciding whether to impose an order, the court will want to consider the history of convictions or a failure to heed warnings or advice in deciding whether an order is proportionate to the facts of the case. Deterrence may also be an important consideration.

Compensation

Where the offence results in the loss or damage the court must consider whether to make a compensation order. If compensation is awarded, priority should be given to the payment of compensation over payment of any other financial penalty where the means of the offender are limited.

Where the offender does not have sufficient means to pay the total financial penalty considered appropriate by the court, compensation and fine take priority over prosecution costs.

Totality principle

STEP EIGHT   If sentencing an offender for more than one offence, consider whether the total sentence is just and proportionate to the offending behaviour in accordance with the *Offences Taken into Consideration and Totality* guideline from which the following guidance is taken:

"The total fine is inevitably cumulative.

The court should determine the fine for each individual offence based on the seriousness of the offence and taking into account the circumstances of the case including the financial circumstances of the offender so far as they are known, or appear, to the court.

The court should add up the fines for each offence and consider if they are just and proportionate.

If the aggregate total is not just and proportionate the court should consider how to reach a just and proportionate fine. There are a number of ways in which this can be achieved.

For example:

- where an offender is to be fined for two or more offences that arose out of the same incident or where there are multiple offences of a repetitive kind, especially when committed against the same person, it will often be appropriate to impose for the most serious offence a fine which reflects the totality of the offending where this can be achieved within the maximum penalty for that offence. No separate penalty should be imposed for the other offences;
- where an offender is to be fined for two or more offences that arose out of different incidents, it will often be appropriate to impose a separate fine for each of the offences. The court should add up the fines for each offence and consider if they are just and proportionate. If the aggregate amount is not just and proportionate the court should consider whether all of the fines can be proportionately reduced. Separate fines should then be passed.

Where separate fines are passed, the court must be careful to ensure that there is no double-counting.

Where compensation is being ordered, that will need to be attributed to the relevant offence as will any necessary ancillary orders."

Reasons

STEP NINE   Section 174 of the Criminal Justice Act 2003 imposes a duty to give reasons for, and explain the effect of, the sentence.

Food Safety – Individuals

Breach of food safety and food hygiene regulations

England
Food Safety and Hygiene (England) Regulations 2013 (regulation 19(1))
Triable either way
Maximum: when tried on indictment: unlimited fine and/or 2 years' custody
when tried summarily: unlimited fine

Wales
Food Hygiene (Wales) Regulations 2006 (regulation 17(1))
Triable either way
Maximum: when tried on indictment: unlimited fine and/or 2 years' custody
when tried summarily: unlimited fine

The General Food Regulations 2004 (regulation 4)
Triable either way
Maximum: when tried on indictment: unlimited fine and/or 2 years' custody
when tried summarily: unlimited fine and/or 6 months' custody
Offence range: Conditional discharge – 18 months' custody

Determining the offence category
STEP ONE   The court should determine the offence category using only the culpability and harm factors in the tables below. Where an offence does not fall squarely into a category, individual factors may require a degree of weighting to make an overall assessment.
Culpability   **Very high**
Where the offender intentionally breached, or flagrantly disregarded, the law
High
Actual foresight of, or wilful blindness to, risk of offending but risk nevertheless taken
Medium
Offence committed through act or omission which a person exercising reasonable care would not commit
Low
Offence committed with little fault, for example, because:
- significant efforts were made to address the risk although they were inadequate on this occasion
- there was no warning/circumstance indicating a risk to food safety
- failings were minor and occurred as an isolated incident

Harm   The table below contains factors relating to both actual harm and risk of harm. Dealing with a **risk of harm** involves consideration of both the likelihood of harm occurring and the extent of it if it does.

Category 1	• Serious adverse effect(s) on individual(s) and/or having a widespread impact
	• High risk of an adverse effect on individual(s) – including where supply was to persons that are vulnerable
Category 2	• Adverse effect on individual(s) (not amounting to Category 1)
	• Medium risk of an adverse effect on individual(s) or low risk of serious adverse effect
	• Regulator and/or legitimate industry substantially undermined by offender's activities
	• Relevant authorities unable to trace products in order to investigate risks to health, or are otherwise inhibited in identifying or addressing risks to health
	• Consumer misled regarding food's compliance with religious or personal beliefs
Category 3	• Low risk of an adverse effect on individual(s)
	• Public misled about the specific food consumed, but little or no risk of actual adverse effect on individual(s)

Starting point and category range
STEP TWO   Having determined the category, the court should refer to the starting points on the next page to reach a sentence within the category range. The court should then consider further adjustment within the category range for aggravating and mitigating features, set out on page 42.
Obtaining financial information   In setting a fine, the court may conclude that the offender is able to pay any fine imposed unless the offender has supplied any financial information to the contrary. It is for the offender to disclose to the court such data relevant to his financial position as will enable it to assess what he can reasonably afford to pay. If necessary, the court may compel the disclosure of an individual offender's financial circumstances pursuant to section 162 of the Criminal Justice Act 2003. In the absence of such disclosure, or where the court is not satisfied that it has been given

sufficient reliable information, the court will be entitled to draw reasonable inferences as to the offender's means from evidence it has heard and from all the circumstances of the case **which may include the inference that the offender can pay any fine**.

Starting points and ranges Where the range includes a potential sentence of custody, the court should consider the custody threshold as follows:

- has the custody threshold been passed?
- if so, is it unavoidable that a custodial sentence be imposed?
- if so, can that sentence be suspended?

Where the range includes a potential sentence of a community order, the court should consider the community order threshold as follows:

- has the community order threshold been passed?

Even where the community order threshold has been passed, a fine will normally be the most appropriate disposal. Or, consider, if wishing to remove economic benefit derived through the commission of the offence, combining a fine with a community order.

	Starting point	Range
Very high culpability		
Harm category 1	9 months' custody	Band F fine – 18 months' custody
Harm category 2	Band F fine	Band E fine – 9 months' custody
Harm category 3	Band E fine	Band D fine – 26 weeks' custody
High culpability		
Harm category 1	Band F fine	Band E fine – 9 months' custody
Harm category 2	Band E fine	Band D fine – 26 weeks' custody
Harm category 3	Band D fine	Band C fine – Band E fine
Medium culpability		
Harm category 1	Band E fine	Band D fine – Band F fine
Harm category 2	Band D fine	Band C fine – Band E fine
Harm category 3	Band C fine	Band B fine – Band C fine
Low culpability		
Harm category 1	Band C fine	Band B fine – Band C fine
Harm category 2	Band B fine	Band A fine – Band B fine
Harm category 3	Band A fine	Conditional discharge – Band A fine

Note on statutory maxima on summary conviction. For offences under *regulation 19(1) Food Safety and Hygiene (England) Regulations 2013 and regulation 17(1) Food Hygiene (Wales) Regulations 2006*, the maximum sentence magistrates may pass on summary conviction is an unlimited fine; therefore for these offences, magistrates may not pass a community order. *Regulation 4* of *The General Food Regulations 2004* is in force in Wales but not in England. For offences under *regulation 4*, the maximum sentence on summary conviction is 6 months' custody and/or an unlimited fine.

The table below contains a **non-exhaustive** list of factual elements providing the context of the offence and factors relating to the offender. Identify whether any combination of these, or other relevant factors, should result in an upward or downward adjustment from the starting point. **In particular, relevant recent convictions are likely to result in a substantial upward adjustment**. In some cases, having considered these factors, it may be appropriate to move outside the identified category range.

Factors increasing seriousness *Statutory aggravating factors:*
Previous convictions, having regard to a) the nature of the offence to which the conviction relates and its relevance to the current offence; and b) the time that has elapsed since the conviction
Offence committed whilst on bail
Other aggravating factors include:
Motivated by financial gain
Deliberate concealment of illegal nature of activity
Established evidence of wider/community impact
Breach of any court order
Obstruction of justice
Poor food safety or hygiene record
Refusal of free advice or training
Factors reducing seriousness or reflecting personal mitigation No previous convictions **or** no relevant/recent convictions
Steps voluntarily taken to remedy problem
High level of co-operation with the investigation, beyond that which will always be expected
Good food safety/hygiene record
Self-reporting, co-operation and acceptance of responsibility
Good character and/or exemplary conduct
Mental disorder or learning disability, where linked to the commission of the offence
Serious medical conditions requiring urgent, intensive or long-term treatment
Age and/or lack of maturity where it affects the responsibility of the offender

Sole or primary carer for dependent relatives

Review any financial element of the sentence

STEP THREE Where the sentence is or includes a fine, the court should 'step back' and, using the factors set out in step three, review whether the sentence as a whole meets the objectives of sentencing for these offences. The court may increase or reduce the proposed fine reached at step two, if necessary moving outside of the range.

Full regard should be given to the totality principle at step seven where multiple offences are involved.

General principles to follow in setting a fine The court should finalise the appropriate level of fine in accordance with section 164 of the Criminal Justice Act 2003, which requires that the fine must reflect the seriousness of the offence and that the court must take into account the financial circumstances of the offender.

The level of fine should reflect the extent to which the offender fell below the required standard. **The fine should meet, in a fair and proportionate way, the objectives of punishment, deterrence and the removal of gain derived through the commission of the offence**; it should not be cheaper to offend than to take the appropriate precautions.

Review of the fine Where the court proposes to impose a fine it should 'step back', review and, if necessary, adjust the initial fine reached at step two to **ensure that it fulfils the general principles** set out above.

Any quantifiable economic benefit derived from the offence, including through avoided costs or operating savings, should normally be added to the total fine arrived at in step two. Where this is not readily available, the court may draw on information available from enforcing authorities and others about the general costs of operating within the law.

In finalising the sentence, the court should have regard to the following factors relating to the wider impacts of the fine on innocent third parties; such as (but not limited to):

- impact of the fine on offender's ability to comply with the law;
- impact of the fine on employment of staff, service users, customers and local economy.

Consider any factors which indicate a reduction, such as assistance to the prosecution

STEP FOUR The court should take into account sections 73 and 74 of the Serious Organised Crime and Police Act 2005 (assistance by defendants: reduction or review of sentence) and any other rule of law by virtue of which an offender may receive a discounted sentence in consequence of assistance given (or offered) to the prosecutor or investigator.

Reduction for guilty pleas

STEP FIVE The court should take account of any potential reduction for a guilty plea in accordance with section 144 of the Criminal Justice Act 2003 and the *Guilty Plea* guideline.

Compensation and ancillary orders

Ancillary orders In all cases the court must consider whether to make ancillary orders. These may include:

Hygiene Prohibition Order

These orders are available under both the Food Safety and Hygiene (England) Regulations 2013 and the Food Hygiene (Wales) Regulations 2006.

If the court is satisfied that the health risk condition in Regulation 7(2) is fulfilled it **shall** impose the appropriate prohibition order in Regulation 7(3).

Where a food business operator is convicted of an offence under the Regulations and the court thinks it proper to do so in all the circumstances of the case, the court **may** impose a prohibition on the operator pursuant to Regulation 7(4). An order under Regulation 7(4) is not limited to cases where there is an immediate risk to public health; the court might conclude that there is such a risk of some future breach of the regulations or the facts of any particular offence or combination of offences may alone justify the imposition of a Hygiene Prohibition Order. In deciding whether to impose an order the court will want to consider the history of convictions or a failure to heed warnings or advice in deciding whether an order is proportionate to the facts of the case. Deterrence may also be an important consideration.

Disqualification of director

An offender may be disqualified from being a director of a company in accordance with section 2 of the Company Directors Disqualification Act 1986. The maximum period of disqualification is 15 years (Crown Court) or 5 years (magistrates' court).

Compensation

Where the offence results in loss or damage the court must consider whether to make a compensation order. If compensation is awarded, priority should be given to the payment of compensation over payment of any other financial penalty where the means of the offender are limited.

Where the offender does not have sufficient means to pay the total financial penalty considered appropriate by the court, compensation and fine take priority over prosecution costs.

Totality principle
STEP SEVEN   If sentencing an offender for more than one offence, or where the offender is already serving a sentence, consider whether the total sentence is just and proportionate to the offending behaviour in accordance with the *Offences Taken into Consideration and Totality* guideline.

Where the offender is convicted of more than one offence where a fine is appropriate, the court should consider the following guidance from the definitive guideline on *Offences Taken into Consideration and Totality*.

"The total fine is inevitably cumulative.

The court should add up the fines for each offence and consider if they are just and proportionate.

If the aggregate total is not just and proportionate the court should consider how to reach a just and proportionate fine. There are a number of ways in which this can be achieved.

For example:

- where an offender is to be fined for two or more offences that arose out of the same incident or where there are multiple offences of a repetitive kind, especially when committed against the same person, it will often be appropriate to impose for the most serious offence a fine which reflects the totality of the offending where this can be achieved within the maximum penalty for that offence. No separate penalty should be imposed for the other offences;
- where an offender is to be fined for two or more offences that arose out of different incidents, it will often be appropriate to impose a separate fine for each of the offences. The court should add up the fines for each offence and consider if they are just and proportionate. If the aggregate amount is not just and proportionate the court should consider whether all of the fines can be proportionately reduced. Separate fines should then be passed.

Where separate fines are passed, the court must be careful to ensure that there is no double-counting.

Where compensation is being ordered, that will need to be attributed to the relevant offence as will any necessary ancillary orders."

Reasons
STEP EIGHT   Section 174 of the Criminal Justice Act 2003 imposes a duty to give reasons for, and explain the effect of, the sentence.

STEP NINE

Consideration for time spent on bail

The court must consider whether to give credit for time spent on bail in accordance with section 240A of the Criminal Justice Act 2003.

OWNER OR PERSON IN CHARGE OF A DOG DANGEROUSLY OUT OF CONTROL IN ANY PLACE IN ENGLAND OR WALES (WHETHER OR NOT A PUBLIC PLACE) WHERE DEATH IS CAUSED[Ed 1]

Dangerous Dogs Act 1991 (section 3 (1))

Triable either way
Maximum: 14 years' custody
Offence range: High level community order – 14 years' custody

Determining the offence category

STEP ONE   In order to determine the category the court should assess **culpability** and **harm**. The court should determine the offence category with reference only to the factors in the tables below.

The level of culpability is determined by weighing up all the factors of the case. **Where there are characteristics present which fall under different levels of culpability, the court should balance these characteristics to reach a fair assessment of the offender's culpability.**

CULPABILITY demonstrated by one or more of the following: **A – High culpability**

Dog used as a weapon or to intimidate people

Dog known to be prohibited

Dog trained to be aggressive

Offender disqualified from owning a dog, or failed to respond to official warnings, or to comply with orders concerning the dog

B – Medium culpability

All other cases where characteristics for categories A or C are not present, and in particular:

Failure to respond to warnings or concerns expressed by others about the dog's behaviour

Failure to act on prior knowledge of the dog's aggressive behaviour

Lack of safety or control measures taken in situations where an incident could reasonably have been foreseen

Failure to intervene in the incident (where it would have been reasonable to do so)

Ill treatment or failure to ensure welfare needs of the dog (where connected to the offence and where not charged separately)

C – Lesser culpability

Attempts made to regain control of the dog and/or intervene

Provocation of the dog without fault of the offender

Evidence of safety or control measures having been taken

Incident could not have reasonably been foreseen by the offender

Momentary lapse of control/attention

HARM   There is no variation in the level of harm caused, as by definition the harm involved in an offence where a death is caused is always of the utmost seriousness.

Starting point and category range

STEP TWO   Having determined the category at step one, the court should use the corresponding starting point to reach a sentence within the category range below. The starting point applies to all offenders irrespective of plea or previous convictions.

High culpa-bility	Starting point	Category range
	8 years' custody	6 – 14 year's custody
Medium cul-pability	**Starting point**	**Category range**
	4 years' custody	2 – 7 years' custody
Lesser culpa-bility	**Starting point**	**Category range**
	1 year's custody	High level community order – 2 years' custody

The table is for single offences. Concurrent sentences reflecting the overall criminality of offending will ordinarily be appropriate where offences arise out of the same incident or facts: please refer to the *Offences Taken into Consideration and Totality* guideline.

The court should then consider any adjustment for any aggravating or mitigating factors. On the next page is a **non-exhaustive** list of additional factual elements providing the context of the offence and factors relating to the offender.

Identify whether any combination of these, or other relevant factors, should result in an upward or downward adjustment from the starting point.

Factors increasing seriousness   *Statutory aggravating factors:*

Previous convictions, having regard to a) the **nature** of the offence to which the conviction relates and its **relevance** to the current offence; and b) the **time** that has elapsed since the conviction

Offence committed whilst on bail

Offence motivated by, or demonstrating hostility based on any of the following characteristics or presumed characteristics of the victim: religion, race, disability, sexual orientation or transgender identity

Other aggravating factors:

Victim is a child or otherwise vulnerable because of personal circumstances

Location of the offence

Sustained or repeated attack

Significant ongoing effect on witness(es) to the attack

Serious injury caused to others (where not charged separately)

Allowing person insufficiently experienced or trained, to be in charge of the dog

Lack or loss of control of the dog due to influence of alcohol or drugs

Offence committed against those working in the public sector or providing a service to the public

Injury to other animals

Established evidence of community/wider impact

Failure to comply with current court orders (except where taken into account in assessing culpability)

Offence committed on licence

Offences taken into consideration

Factors reducing seriousness or reflecting personal mitigation: No previous convictions **or** no relevant/recent convictions

No previous complaints against, or incidents involving the dog

Evidence of responsible ownership

Remorse

Good character and/or exemplary conduct

Serious medical condition requiring urgent, intensive or long-term treatment

Age and/or lack of maturity where it affects the responsibility of the offender

Mental disorder or learning disability

Sole or primary carer for dependent relatives

Determination and/or demonstration of steps having been taken to address offending behaviour

Consider any factors which indicate a reduction, such as assistance to the prosecution

STEP THREE   The court should take into account sections 73 and 74 of the Serious Organised Crime and Police Act 2005 (assistance by defendants: reduction or review of sentence) and any other rule of law by virtue of which an offender may receive a discounted sentence in consequence of assistance given (or offered) to the prosecutor or investigator.

Reduction for guilty pleas

STEP FOUR   The court should take account of any potential reduction for a guilty plea in accordance with section 144 of the Criminal Justice Act 2003 and the *Guilty Plea* guideline.

Totality principle

STEP FIVE   If sentencing an offender for more than one offence, or where the offender is already serving a sentence, consider whether the total sentence is just and proportionate to the overall offending behaviour in accordance with the *Offences Taken into Consideration and Totality* guideline.

Compensation and ancillary orders

STEP SIX   In all cases, the court must consider whether to make a compensation order and/or other ancillary orders.

Compensation order

The court should consider compensation orders in all cases where personal injury, loss or damage has resulted from the offence. The court must give reasons if it decides not to award compensation in such cases.

Other ancillary orders available include:

Disqualification from having a dog

The court *may* disqualify the offender from having custody of a dog. The test the court should consider is whether the offender is a fit and proper person to have custody of a dog.

Destruction order/contingent destruction order

In any case where the offender is not the owner of the dog, the owner must be given an opportunity to be present and make representations to the court.

If the dog is a **prohibited dog** refer to the guideline for possession of a prohibited dog in relation to destruction/contingent destruction orders.

The court **shall** make a destruction order unless the court is satisfied that the dog would not constitute a danger to public safety.

In reaching a decision, the court should consider the relevant circumstances which **must** include:

- the temperament of the dog and its past behaviour;
- whether the owner of the dog, or the person for the time being in charge of it is a fit and proper person to be in charge of the dog;

and **may** include:

- other relevant circumstances.

If the court is satisfied that the dog would not constitute a danger to public safety and the dog is not prohibited, it **may** make a contingent destruction order requiring the dog be kept under proper control. A contingent destruction order may specify the measures to be taken by the owner for keeping the dog under proper control, which include:

- muzzling;
- keeping on a lead;
- neutering in appropriate cases; and
- excluding it from a specified place.

Where the court makes a destruction order, it **may** appoint a person to undertake destruction and order the offender to pay what it determines to be the reasonable expenses of destroying the dog and keeping it pending its destruction.

Fit and proper person

In determining whether a person is a fit and proper person to be in charge of a dog the following non-exhaustive factors may be relevant:

- any relevant previous convictions, cautions or penalty notices;
- the nature and suitability of the premises that the dog is to be kept at by the person;
- where the police have released the dog pending the court's decision whether the person has breached conditions imposed by the police; and
- any relevant previous breaches of court orders.

Reasons

STEP SEVEN   Section 174 of the Criminal Justice Act 2003 imposes a duty to give reasons for, and explain the effect of, the sentence.

Consideration for time spent on bail

STEP EIGHT   The court must consider whether to give credit for time spent on bail in accordance with section 240A of the Criminal Justice Act 2003.

Ed 1 The guidelines on dangerous dogs have been taken from 'Dangerous Dog Offences Definitive Guideline', which is effective from 1 July 2016.

OWNER OR PERSON IN CHARGE OF A DOG DANGEROUSLY OUT OF CONTROL IN ANY PLACE IN ENGLAND OR WALES (WHETHER OR NOT A PUBLIC PLACE) WHERE A PERSON IS INJURED

Dangerous Dogs Act 1991 (section 3 (1))

Triable either way
Maximum: 5 years' custody
Offence range: Discharge – 4 years' custody

Determining the offence category

STEP ONE In order to determine the category the court should assess **culpability** and **harm**. The court should determine the offence category with reference only to the factors in the tables below.

The level of culpability is determined by weighing up all the factors of the case. **Where there are characteristics present which fall under different levels of culpability, the court should balance these characteristics to reach a fair assessment of the offender's culpability.**

CULPABILITY demonstrated by one or more of the following: A – High culpability

Dog used as a weapon or to intimidate people
Dog known to be prohibited
Dog trained to be aggressive
Failure to respond to official warnings or to comply with orders concerning the dog
Offender disqualified from owning a dog, or failed to respond to official warnings, or to comply with orders concerning the dog

B – Medium culpability

All other cases where characteristics for categories A or C are not present, and in particular:
Failure to respond to warnings or concerns expressed by others about the dog's behaviour
Failure to act on prior knowledge of the dog's aggressive behaviour
Lack of safety or control measures taken in situations where an incident could reasonably have been foreseen
Failure to intervene in the incident (where it would have been reasonable to do so)
Ill treatment or failure to ensure welfare needs of the dog (where connected to the offence and where not charged separately)

C – Lesser culpability

Attempts made to regain control of the dog and/or intervene
Provocation of the dog without fault of the offender
Evidence of safety or control measures having been taken
Incident could not have reasonably been foreseen by the offender
Momentary lapse of control/attention

HARM The level of **harm** is assessed by weighing up all the factors of the case.

Category 1	Serious injury (which includes disease transmission) Serious psychological harm
Category 2	Harm that falls between categories 1 and 3
Category 3	Minor injury and no significant psychological harm

Starting point and category range

STEP TWO Having determined the category at step one, the court should use the corresponding starting point to reach a sentence within the category range below. The starting point applies to all offenders irrespective of plea or previous convictions.

Culpability

Harm	A	B	C
Category 1	**Starting point**	**Starting point**	**Starting point**
	3 years' custody	1 year 6 months' custody	High level community order
	Category range	**Category range**	**Category range**
	2 years 6 months' – 4 years' custody	6 months' – 2 years 6 months' custody	Medium level community order – 6 months' custody
Category 2	**Starting point**	**Starting point**	**Starting**
	2 years' custody	6 months' custody	Band C fine
	Category range	**Category range**	**Category range**
	1 year – 3 years' custody	Medium level community order – 1 year's custody	Band B fine – High level community order
Category 3	**Starting point**	**Starting point**	**Starting point**
	6 months' custody	Low level community order	Band B fine
	Category range	**Category range**	**Category range**

Harm	A	B	C
	High level commu- nity order – 1 year 6 months' custody	Band C fine – 6 months' custody	Discharge – Band C fine

The table is for single offences. Concurrent sentences reflecting the overall criminality of offending will ordinarily be appropriate where offences arise out of the same incident or facts: please refer to the *Offences Taken into Consideration and Totality* guideline.

The court should then consider any adjustment for any aggravating or mitigating factors. On the next page is a **non-exhaustive** list of additional factual elements providing the context of the offence and factors relating to the offender.

Identify whether any combination of these, or other relevant factors, should result in an upward ordownward adjustment from the starting point.

Factors increasing seriousness *Statutory aggravating factors:*

Previous convictions, having regard to a) the**nature** of the offence to which the conviction relates and its **relevance** to the current offence; and b) the **time** that has elapsed since the conviction

Offence committed whilst on bail

Offence motivated by, or demonstrating hostility based on any of the following characteristics or presumedcharacteristics of the victim: religion, race, disability, sexual orientation or transgender identity.

Other aggravating factors:

Victim is a child or otherwise vulnerable because of personal circumstances

Location of the offence

Sustained or repeated attack

Significant ongoing effect on witness(es) to the attack

Serious injury caused to others (where not charged separately)

Significant practical and financial effects of offence on relatives/carers

Allowing person insufficiently experienced or trained, to be in charge of the dog

Lack or loss of control of dog due to influence of alcohol or drugs

Offence committed against those working in the public sector or providing a service to the public

Injury to other animals

Established evidence of community/wider impact

Failure to comply with current court orders (except where taken into account in assessing culpability)

Offence committed on licence

Offences taken into consideration

Factors reducing seriousness or reflecting personal mitigation No previous convictions **or** no relevant/recent convictions

Isolated incident

No previous complaints against, or incidents involving the dog

Evidence of responsible ownership

Remorse

Good character and/or exemplary conduct

Serious medical condition requiring urgent, intensive or long-term treatment

Age and/or lack of maturity where it affects the responsibility of the offender

Mental disorder or learning disability

Sole or primary carer for dependent relatives

Determination and/or demonstration of steps having been taken to address offending behaviour

Consider any factors which indicate a reduction, such as assistance to the prosecution

STEP THREE The court should take into account sections 73 and 74 of the Serious Organised Crime and Police Act 2005 (assistance by defendants: reduction or review of sentence) and any other rule of law by virtue of which an offender may receive a discounted sentence in consequence of assistance given (or offered) to the prosecutor or investigator.

Reduction for guilty pleas

STEP FOUR The court should take account of any potential reduction for a guilty plea in accordance with section 144 of the Criminal Justice Act 2003 and the *Guilty Plea* guideline.

Totality principle

STEP FIVE If sentencing an offender for more than one offence, or where the offender is already serving a sentence, consider whether the total sentence is just and proportionate to the overall offending behaviour in accordance with the *Offences Taken into Consideration and Totality* guideline.

Compensation and ancillary orders

STEP SIX In all cases, the court must consider whether to make a compensation order and/or other ancillary orders.

Compensation order

The court should consider compensation orders in all cases where personal injury, loss or damage has resulted from the offence. The court must give reasons if it decides not to award compensation in such cases.

Other ancillary orders available include:

Disqualification from having a dog

The court **may** disqualify the offender from having custody of a dog. The test the court should consider is whether the offender is a fit and proper person to have custody of a dog.

Destruction order/contingent destruction order

In any case where the offender is not the owner of the dog, the owner must be given an opportunity to be present and make representations to the court.

If the dog is a **prohibited dog** refer to the guideline for possession of a prohibited dog in relation to destruction/contingent destruction orders.

The court **shall** make a destruction order unless the court is satisfied that the dog would not constitute a danger to public safety.

In reaching a decision, the court should consider the relevant circumstances which **must** include:

- the temperament of the dog and its past behaviour;
- whether the owner of the dog, or the person for the time being in charge of it is a fit and proper person to be in charge of the dog;

and **may** include:

- other relevant circumstances.

If the court is satisfied that the dog would not constitute a danger to public safety and the dog is not prohibited, it **may** make a contingent destruction order requiring the dog be kept under proper control. A contingent destruction order may specify the measures to be taken by the owner for keeping the dog under proper control, which include:

- muzzling;
- keeping on a lead;
- neutering in appropriate cases; and
- excluding it from a specified place.

Where the court makes a destruction order, it **may** appoint a person to undertake destruction and order the offender to pay what it determines to be the reasonable expenses of destroying the dog and keeping it pending its destruction.

Fit and proper person

In determining whether a person is a fit and proper person to be in charge of a dog the followingnon-exhaustive factors may be relevant:

- any relevant previous convictions, cautions or penalty notices;
- the nature and suitability of the premises that the dog is to be kept at by the person;
- where the police have released the dog pending the court's decision whether the person has breached conditions imposed by the police; and
- any relevant previous breaches of court orders.

Reasons
STEP SEVEN   Section 174 of the Criminal Justice Act 2003 imposes a duty to give reasons for, and explain the effect of, the sentence.

Consideration for time spent on bail
STEP EIGHT   The court must consider whether to give credit for time spent on bail in accordance with section 240A of the Criminal Justice Act 2003.

OWNER OR PERSON IN CHARGE OF A DOG DANGEROUSLY OUT OF CONTROL IN ANY PLACE IN ENGLAND OR WALES (WHETHER OR NOT A PUBLIC PLACE) WHERE AN ASSISTANCE DOG IS INJURED OR KILLED

Dangerous Dogs Act 1991 (section 3 (1))

Triable either way
Maximum: 3 years' custody
Offence range: Discharge – 2 years 6 months' custody

Determining the offence category

STEP ONE   In order to determine the category the court should assess **culpability** and **harm**. The court should determine the offence category with reference only to the factors in the tables below.

The level of culpability is determined by weighing up all the factors of the case. **Where there are characteristics present which fall under different levels of culpability, the court should balance these characteristics to reach a fair assessment of the offender's culpability.**

Culpability demonstrated by one or more of the following: A – High culpability

Dog used as a weapon or to intimidate people or dogs

Dog known to be prohibited

Dog trained to be aggressive

Offender disqualified from owning a dog, or failed to respond to official warnings, or to comply with orders concerning the dog

Offence motivated by, or demonstrating hostility to the victim (assisted person) based on the victim's disability (or presumed disability)

B – Medium culpability

All other cases where characteristics for categories A or C are not present, and in particular:

Failure to respond to warnings or concerns expressed by others about the dog's behaviour

Failure to act on prior knowledge of the dog's aggressive behaviour

Lack of safety or control measures taken in situations where an incident could reasonably have been foreseen

Failure to intervene in the incident (where it would have been reasonable to do so)

Ill treatment or failure to ensure welfare needs of the dog (where connected to the offence and where not charged separately)

C – Lesser culpability

Attempts made to regain control of the dog and/or intervene

Provocation of the dog without fault of the offender

Evidence of safety or control measures having been taken

Incident could not have reasonably been foreseen by the offender

Momentary lapse of control/attention

HARM   The level of **harm** is assessed by weighing up all the factors of the case.

Category 1	Fatality or serious injury to an assistance dog and/or Serious impact on the assisted person (whether psychological or other harm caused by the offence)
Category 2	Harm that falls between categories 1 and 3
Category 3	Minor injury to assistance dog and impact of the offence on the assisted person is limited

Starting point and category range

STEP TWO   Having determined the category at step one, the court should use the corresponding starting point to reach a sentence within the category range below. The starting point applies to all offenders irrespective of plea or previous convictions.

Culpability

Harm	A	B	C
Category 1	**Starting point**	**Starting point**	**Starting point**
	2 years' custody	9 months' custody	Medium level community order
	Category range	**Category range**	**Category range**
	1 year – 2 years 6 months' custody	Medium level community order – 1 year's custody	Low level community order – High level community order
Category 2	**Starting point**	**Starting point**	**Starting point**
	1 years' custody	High level community order	Band B fine
	Category range	**Category range**	**Category range**
	6 months' – 1 year 6 months' custody	Low level community order – 6 months' custody	Band A fine – Low level community order
Category 3	**Starting point**	**Starting point**	**Starting point**

Harm	A	B	C
	High level community order	Band C fine	Band A fine
	Category range	**Category range**	**Category range**
	Medium level community order – 6 months' custody	Band B fine – High level community order	Discharge – Band B fine

The court should then consider any adjustment for any aggravating or mitigating factors. On the next page is a **non-exhaustive** list of additional factual elements providing the context of the offence and factors relating to the offender.

Identify whether any combination of these, or other relevant factors, should result in an upward or downward adjustment from the starting point.

Factors increasing seriousness   *Statutory aggravating factors:*

Previous convictions, having regard to a) the **nature** of the offence to which the conviction relates and its **relevance** to the current offence; and b) the **time** that has elapsed since the conviction

Offence committed whilst on bail

Offence motivated by, or demonstrating hostility based on any of the following characteristics or presumedcharacteristics of the victim: religion, race, sexual orientation or transgender identity

Other aggravating factors:

Location of the offence

Sustained or repeated attack

Significant ongoing effect on witness(es) to the attack

Allowing person insufficiently experienced or trained, to be in charge of the dog

Lack or loss of control of the dog due to influence of alcohol or drugs

Offence committed against those working in the public sector or providing a service to the public

Injury to other animals

Cost of retraining an assistance dog

Established evidence of community/wider impact

Failure to comply with current court orders (except where taken into account in assessing culpability)

Offence committed on licence

Offences taken into consideration

Factors reducing seriousness or reflecting personal mitigation   No previous convictions **or** no relevant/recent convictions

Isolated incident

No previous complaints against, or incidents involving the dog

Evidence of responsible ownership

Remorse

Good character and/or exemplary conduct

Serious medical condition requiring urgent, intensive or long-term treatment

Age and/or lack of maturity where it affects the responsibility of the offender

Mental disorder or learning disability

Sole or primary carer for dependent relatives

Determination and/or demonstration of steps having been taken to address offending behaviour

Consider any factors which indicate a reduction, such as assistance to the prosecution

STEP THREE   The court should take into account sections 73 and 74 of the Serious Organised Crime and Police Act 2005 (assistance by defendants: reduction or review of sentence) and any other rule of law by virtue of which an offender may receive a discounted sentence in consequence of assistance given (or offered) to the prosecutor or investigator.

Reduction for guilty pleas

STEP FOUR   The court should take account of any potential reduction for a guilty plea in accordance withsection 144 of the Criminal Justice Act 2003 and the *Guilty Plea* guideline.

Totality principle

STEP FIVE   If sentencing an offender for more than one offence, or where the offender is already serving a sentence, consider whether the total sentence is just and proportionate to the overall offending behaviour in accordance with the *Offences Taken into Consideration and Totality* guideline.

Compensation and ancillary orders

STEP SIX   In all cases, the court must consider whether to make a compensation order and/or other ancillary orders.

Compensation order

The court should consider compensation orders in all cases where personal injury, loss or damage has resulted from the offence. The court must give reasons if it decides not to award compensation in such cases.

Other ancillary orders available include:

Disqualification from having custody of a dog

The court **may** disqualify the offender from having custody of a dog. The test the court should consider is whether the offender is a fit and proper person to have custody of a dog.

Destruction order/contingent destruction order

In any case where the offender is not the owner of the dog, the owner must be given an opportunity to be present and make representations to the court.

If the dog is a **prohibited dog** refer to the guideline for possession of a prohibited dog in relation to destruction/contingent destruction orders.

The court **shall** make a destruction order unless the court is satisfied that the dog would not constitute a danger to public safety.

In reaching a decision, the court should consider the relevant circumstances which **must** include:

- the temperament of the dog and its past behaviour;
- whether the owner of the dog, or the person for the time being in charge of it is a fit and proper person to be in charge of the dog;

and **may** include:

- other relevant circumstances.

If the court is satisfied that the dog would not constitute a danger to public safety and the dog is not prohibited, it **may** make a contingent destruction order requiring the dog be kept under proper control. A contingent destruction order may specify the measures to be taken by the owner for keeping the dog under proper control, which include:

- muzzling;
- keeping on a lead;
- neutering in appropriate cases; and
- excluding it from a specified place.

Where the court makes a destruction order, it **may** appoint a person to undertake destruction and order the offender to pay what it determines to be the reasonable expenses of destroying the dog and keeping it pending its destruction.

Fit and proper person

In determining whether a person is a fit and proper person to be in charge of a dog the following non-exhaustive factors may be relevant:

- any relevant previous convictions, cautions or penalty notices;
- the nature and suitability of the premises that the dog is to be kept at by the person;
- where the police have released the dog pending the court's decision whether the person has breached conditions imposed by the police; and
- any relevant previous breaches of court orders.

Reasons
STEP SEVEN   Section 174 of the Criminal Justice Act 2003 imposes a duty to give reasons for, and explain the effect of, the sentence.

Consideration for time spent on bail
STEP EIGHT   The court must consider whether to give credit for time spent on bail in accordance with section 240A of the Criminal Justice Act 2003.

OWNER OR PERSON IN CHARGE OF A DOG DANGEROUSLY OUT OF CONTROL IN ANY PLACE IN ENGLAND OR WALES (WHETHER OR NOT A PUBLIC PLACE)

Dangerous Dogs Act 1991 (section 3(1))

Triable only summarily
Maximum: 6 months' custody
Offence range: Discharge – 6 months' custody

Determining the offence category

STEP ONE In order to determine the category the court should assess **culpability** and **harm**. The court should determine the offence category with reference only to the factors in the tables below.

The level of culpability is determined by weighing up all the factors of the case. **Where there are characteristics present which fall under different levels of culpability, the court should balance these characteristics to reach a fair assessment of the offender's culpability.**

CULPABILITY demonstrated by one or more of the following: A – Higher culpability

Dog used as a weapon or to intimidate people
Dog known to be prohibited
Dog trained to be aggressive
Offender disqualified from owning a dog, or failed to respond to official warnings, or to comply with orders concerning the dog

B – Lower culpability

Attempts made to regain control of the dog and/or intervene
Provocation of dog without fault of the offender
Evidence of safety or control measures having been taken
Incident could not have reasonably been foreseen by the offender
Momentary lapse of control/attention

HARM The level of harm is assessed by weighing up all the factors of the case.

Greater harm	Presence of children or others who are vulnerable because of personal Greater harm circumstances Injury to other animals
Lesser harm	Low risk to the public

Starting point and category range

STEP TWO Having determined the category at step one, the court should use the corresponding starting point to reach a sentence within the category range below. The starting point applies to all offenders irrespective of plea or previous convictions.

Culpability

Harm	A	B
Greater harm	**Starting point**	**Starting point**
	Medium level community order	Band B fine
	Category range	**Category range**
	Band C fine – 6 months' custody	Band A fine – Band C fine
Lesser harm	**Starting point**	**Starting point**
	Band C fine	Band A fine
	Category range	**Category range**
	Band B fine – Low level community order	Discharge – Band B fine

The court should then consider any adjustment for any aggravating or mitigating factors. On the next page is a **non-exhaustive** list of additional factual elements providing the context of the offence and factors relating to the offender.

Identify whether any combination of these, or other relevant factors, should result in an upward or downward adjustment from the starting point.

Factors increasing seriousness *Statutory aggravating factors:*

Previous convictions, having regard to a) the **nature** of the offence to which the conviction relates and its **relevance** to the current offence; and b) the **time** that has elapsed since the conviction
Offence committed whilst on bail
Offence motivated by, or demonstrating hostility based on any of the following characteristics or presumed characteristics of the victim: religion, race, disability, sexual orientation or transgender identity

Other aggravating factors:

Location of the offence
Significant ongoing effect on the victim and/or others
Failing to take adequate precautions to prevent the dog from escaping
Allowing person insufficiently experienced or trained, to be in charge of the dog

Ill treatment or failure to ensure welfare needs of the dog (where connected to the offence and where not charged separately)

Lack or loss of control of the dog due to influence of alcohol or drugs

Offence committed against those working in the public sector or providing a service to the public

Established evidence of community/wider impact

Failure to comply with current court orders (unless this has already been taken into account in assessing culpability)

Offence committed on licence

Offences taken into consideration

Factors reducing seriousness or reflecting personal mitigation No previous convictions or no relevant/recent convictions

Isolated incident

No previous complaints against, or incidents involving the dog

Evidence of responsible ownership

Remorse

Good character and/or exemplary conduct

Serious medical condition requiring urgent, intensive or long-term treatment

Age and/or lack of maturity where it affects the responsibility of the offender

Mental disorder or learning disability

Sole or primary carer for dependent relatives

Determination and/or demonstration of steps having been taken to address offending behaviour

Consider any factors which indicate a reduction, such as assistance to the prosecution

STEP THREE The court should take into account sections 73 and 74 of the Serious Organised Crime and Police Act 2005 (assistance by defendants: reduction or review of sentence) and any other rule of law by virtue of which an offender may receive a discounted sentence in consequence of assistance given (or offered) to the prosecutor or investigator.

Reduction for guilty pleas

STEP FOUR The court should take account of any potential reduction for a guilty plea in accordance with section 144 of the Criminal Justice Act 2003 and the *Guilty Plea* guideline.

Totality principle

STEP FIVE If sentencing an offender for more than one offence, or where the offender is already serving a sentence, consider whether the total sentence is just and proportionate to the overall offending behaviour in accordance with the *Offences Taken into Consideration and Totality* guideline.

Compensation and ancillary orders

STEP SIX In all cases, the court must consider whether to make a compensation order and/or other ancillary orders.

Compensation order

The court should consider compensation orders in all cases where personal injury, loss or damage has resulted from the offence. The court must give reasons if it decides not to award compensation in such cases.

Other ancillary orders available include:

Disqualification from having a dog

The court **may** disqualify the offender from having custody of a dog. The test the court should consider is whether the offender is a fit and proper person to have custody of a dog.

Destruction order/contingent destruction order

In any case where the offender is not the owner of the dog, the owner must be given an opportunity to be present and make representations to the court.

If the dog is a **prohibited dog** refer to the guideline for possession of a prohibited dog in relation to destruction/contingent destruction orders.

If the dog is not prohibited and the court is satisfied that the dog would constitute a danger to public safety the court **may** make a destruction order.

In reaching a decision, the court should consider the relevant circumstances which **must** include:

- temperament of the dog and its past behaviour;
- whether the owner of the dog, or the person for the time being in charge of it is a fit and proper person to be in charge of the dog;

and **may** include:

- other relevant circumstances.

If the court is satisfied that the dog would not constitute a danger to public safety and the dog is not prohibited, it **may** make a contingent destruction order requiring the dog be kept under proper control. A contingent destruction order may specify the measures to be taken by the owner for keeping the dog under proper control, which include:

- muzzling;
- keeping on a lead;
- neutering in appropriate cases; and
- excluding it from a specified place.

Where the court makes a destruction order, it **may** appoint a person to undertake destruction and order the offender to pay what it determines to be the reasonable expenses of destroying the dog and keeping it pending its destruction.

Fit and proper person

In determining whether a person is a fit and proper person to be in charge of a dog the following non-exhaustive factors may be relevant:

- any relevant previous convictions, cautions or penalty notices;
- the nature and suitability of the premises that the dog is to be kept at by the person;
- where the police have released the dog pending the court's decision whether the person has breached conditions imposed by the police; and
- any relevant previous breaches of court orders.

Reasons

STEP SEVEN　　Section 174 of the Criminal Justice Act 2003 imposes a duty to give reasons for, and explain the effect of, the sentence.

Consideration for time spent on bail

STEP EIGHT　　The court must consider whether to give credit for time spent on bail in accordance with section 240A of the Criminal Justice Act 2003.

POSSESSION OF A PROHIBITED DOG
Dangerous Dogs Act 1991 (section 1 (7))

BREEDING, SELLING, EXCHANGING OR ADVERTISING A PROHIBITED DOG
Dangerous Dogs Act 1991 (section 1 (7))

Triable only summarily
Maximum: 6 months' custody
Offence range: Discharge – 6 months' custody

Determining the offence category

STEP ONE In order to determine the category the court should assess **culpability** and **harm**. The court should determine the offence category with reference only to the factors in the tables below.

The level of culpability is determined by weighing up all the factors of the case. **Where there are characteristics present which fall under different levels of culpability, the court should balance these characteristics to reach a fair assessment of the offender's culpability.**

CULPABILITY demonstrated by one or more of the following: A – Higher culpability:
Possessing a dog known to be prohibited
Breeding from a dog known to be prohibited
Selling, exchanging or advertising a dog known to be prohibited
Offence committed for gain
Dog used to threaten or intimidate
Permitting fighting
Training and/or possession of paraphernalia for dog fighting
B – Lower culpability:
All other cases
HARM The level of harm is assessed by weighing up all the factors of the case.

Greater harm	High risk to the public and/or animals
Lesser harm	Low risk to the public and/or animals

Starting point and category range

STEP TWO Having determined the category at step one, the court should use the corresponding starting point to reach a sentence within the category range below. The starting point applies to all offenders irrespective of plea or previous convictions.

Culpability

Harm	A	B
Greater harm	**Starting point**	**Starting point**
	Medium level community order	Band B fine
	Category range	**Category range**
	Band C fine – 6 months' custody	Band A fine – Low level community order
Lesser harm	**Starting point**	**Starting point**
	Band C fine	Band A fine
	Category range	**Category range**
	Band B fine – Medium level community order	Discharge – Band B fine

The court should then consider any adjustment for any aggravating or mitigating factors. Below is a **non-exhaustive** list of additional factual elements providing the context of the offence and factors relating to the offender.

Identify whether any combination of these, or other relevant factors, should result in an upward or downward adjustment from the starting point.

Factors increasing seriousness *Statutory aggravating factors:*
Previous convictions, having regard to a) the **nature** of the offence to which the conviction relates and its **relevance** to the current offence; and b) the **time** that has elapsed since the conviction
Offence committed whilst on bail
Other aggravating factors:
Presence of children or others who are vulnerable because of personal circumstances
Ill treatment or failure to ensure welfare needs of the dog (where connected to the offence and where not charged separately)
Established evidence of community/wider impact
Failure to comply with current court orders
Offence committed on licence
Offences taken into consideration

Factors reducing seriousness or reflecting personal mitigation   No previous convictions **or** no relevant/recent convictions

Unaware that dog was prohibited type despite reasonable efforts to identify type
Evidence of safety or control measures having been taken by owner
Prosecution results from owner notification
Evidence of responsible ownership
Remorse
Good character and/or exemplary conduct
Serious medical condition requiring urgent, intensive or long-term treatment
Age and/or lack of maturity where it affects the responsibility of the offender
Mental disorder or learning disability
Sole or primary carer for dependent relatives
Determination and/or demonstration of steps having been taken to address offending behaviour
Lapse of time since the offence where this is not the fault of the offender

Consider any factors which indicate a reduction, such as assistance to the prosecution

STEP THREE   The court should take into account sections 73 and 74 of the Serious Organised Crime and Police Act 2005 (assistance by defendants: reduction or review of sentence) and any other rule of law by virtue of which an offender may receive a discounted sentence in consequence of assistance given (or offered) to the prosecutor or investigator.

Reduction for guilty pleas

STEP FOUR   The court should take account of any potential reduction for a guilty plea in accordance with section 144 of the Criminal Justice Act 2003 and the *Guilty Plea* guideline.

Totality principle

STEP FIVE   If sentencing an offender for more than one offence, or where the offender is already serving a sentence, consider whether the total sentence is just and proportionate to the overall offending behaviour in accordance with the *Offences Taken into Consideration and Totality* guideline.

Compensation and ancillary orders

STEP SIX   In all cases, the court must consider whether to make a compensation order and/or other ancillary orders.

Compensation order

The court should consider compensation orders in all cases where personal injury, loss or damage has resulted from the offence. The court must give reasons if it decides not to award compensation in such cases.

Other ancillary orders available include:

Disqualification from having a dog

The court **may** disqualify the offender from having custody of a dog for such period as it thinks fit. The test the court should consider is whether the offender is a fit and proper person to have custody of a dog.

Destruction order/contingent destruction order

In any case where the offender is not the owner of the dog, the owner must be given an opportunity to be present and make representations to the court.

The court **shall** make a destruction order unless the court is satisfied that the dog would not constitute a danger to public safety.

In reaching a decision, the court should consider the relevant circumstances which **must** include:

- the temperament of the dog and its past behaviour;
- whether the owner of the dog, or the person for the time being in charge of it is a fit and proper person to be in charge of the dog;

and **may** include:

- other relevant circumstances.

If the court is satisfied that the dog would not constitute a danger to public safety, it **shall** make a contingent destruction order requiring that the dog be exempted from the prohibition on possession or custody within the requisite period.

Where the court makes a destruction order, it **may** appoint a person to undertake destruction and order the offender to pay what it determines to be the reasonable expenses of destroying the dog and keeping it pending its destruction.

Fit and proper person

In determining whether a person is a fit and proper person to be in charge of a dog the following non-exhaustive factors may be relevant:

- any relevant previous convictions, cautions or penalty notices;
- the nature and suitability of the premises that the dog is to be kept at by the person;
- where the police have released the dog pending the court's decision whether the person has breached conditions imposed by the police; and
- any relevant previous breaches of court orders.

Note: the court must be satisfied that the person who is assessed by the court as a fit and proper person can demonstrate that they are the owner or the person ordinarily in charge of that dog at the time the court is considering whether the dog is a danger to public safety. Someone who has previously not been in charge of the dog should not be considered for this assessment because it is an offence under the Dangerous Dogs Act 1991 to make a gift of a prohibited dog.

Reasons
STEP SEVEN　Section 174 of the Criminal Justice Act 2003 imposes a duty to give reasons for, and explain the effect of, the sentence.

Consideration for time spent on bail
STEP EIGHT　The court must consider whether to give credit for time spent on bail in accordance with section 240A of the Criminal Justice Act 2003.

EXPLANATORY MATERIAL

APPROACH TO THE ASSESSMENT OF FINES

Introduction

C.7　**1.**　The amount of a fine must reflect the seriousness **of the offence.**[1]
　2.　The court must also take into account the financial circumstances **of the offender; this applies whether it has the effect of increasing or reducing the fine.**[2]
　3.　The aim is for the fine to have an equal impact on offenders with different financial circumstances; it should be a hardship but should not force the offender below a reasonable 'subsistence' level. Normally a fine should be of an amount that is capable of being paid within 12 months though there may be exceptions to this.
　4.　The guidance below aims to establish a clear, consistent and principled approach to the assessment of fines that will apply fairly in the majority of cases. However, it is impossible to anticipate every situation that may be encountered and in each case the court will need to exercise its judgement to ensure that the fine properly reflects the seriousness of the offence **and takes into account the** financial circumstances **of the offender.**

---

[1]　Criminal Justice Act 2003, s 164(2)
[2]　Criminal Justice Act 2003, ss 164(3) and 164(4).

Fine bands

　5.　For the purpose of the offence guidelines, a fine is usually based on one of three bands (A, B or C). The selection of the relevant fine band, and the position of the individual offence within that band, is determined by the seriousness of the offence. In some cases fine bands D–F may be used even where the community or custody threshold have been passed.

	Starting point	Range
Fine Band A	50% of relevant weekly income	25–75% of relevant weekly income
Fine Band B	100% of relevant weekly income	75–125% of relevant weekly income
Fine Band C	150% of relevant weekly income	125–175% of relevant weekly income
Fine Band D	250% of relevant weekly income	200–300% of relevant weekly income
Fine Band E	400% of relevant weekly income	300–500% of relevant weekly income
Fine Band F	600% of relevant weekly income	500–700% of relevant weekly income

　6.　For an explanation of the meaning of starting point and range, both generally and in relation to fines, see pages 16–17.

Definition of relevant weekly income

　7.　The seriousness **of an offence determines the choice of fine band and the position of the offence within the range for that band. The offender's** financial circumstances **are taken into account by expressing that position as a proportion of the offender's** relevant weekly income.
　8.　Where:

- an offender is in receipt of income from employment or is self-employed **and**
- that income is **more than £120** per week after deduction of tax and national insurance (or equivalent where the offender is self-employed),

the actual income is the **relevant weekly income.**
　9.　Where:

- an offender's only source of income is state benefit (including where there is relatively low additional income as permitted by the benefit regulations) **or**
- the offender is in receipt of income from employment or is self-employed but the amount of income after deduction of tax and national insurance is **£120 or less,**

the **relevant weekly income is deemed to be £120.**
Additional information about the basis for this approach is set out in paragraphs 26–31 below.
　10.　In calculating relevant weekly income, no account should be taken of tax credits, housing benefit, child benefit or similar.

No reliable information

　11.　Where an offender has failed to provide information, or the court is not satisfied that it has been given sufficient reliable information, it is entitled to make such determination as it thinks fit regarding the financial circumstances of the offender.[1] Any determination should be clearly stated on the court records for use in any subsequent variation or enforcement proceedings. In such cases, a record should also be made of the applicable fine band and the court's assessment of the position of the offence within that band based on the seriousness of the offence.

12. Where there is no information on which a determination can be made, the court should proceed on the basis of an assumed **relevant weekly income of £440.** This is derived from national median pre-tax earnings; a gross figure is used as, in the absence of financial information from the offender, it is not possible to calculate appropriate deductions.[2]

13. Where there is some information that tends to suggest a significantly lower or higher income than the recommended £440 default sum, the court should make a determination based on that information.

14. A court is empowered to remit a fine in whole or part if the offender subsequently provides information as to means.[3] The assessment of offence seriousness and, therefore, the appropriate fine band and the position of the offence within that band are not affected by the provision of this information.

---

[1] Criminal Justice Act 2003, s 164(5).

[2] This figure is a projected estimate' based upon the 2012-13 Survey of Personal Incomes using economic assumptions consistent with the Office for Budget Responsibility's March 2015 economic and fiscal outlook. The latest actual figure is for 2012-13, when median pre-tax income was £ 404 per week (https://www.gov.uk/government/statistics/shares-of-total-income-before-and-after-tax-and-income-tax-for-percentile-groups).

[3] Criminal Justice Act 2003, s 165(2).

Assessment of financial circumstances

15. While the initial consideration for the assessment of a fine is the offender's relevant weekly income, the court is required to take account of the offender's financial circumstances including assets more broadly. Guidance on important parts of this assessment is set out below.

16. An offender's financial circumstances may have the effect of increasing or reducing the amount of the fine; however, they are not relevant to the assessment of offence seriousness. They should be considered separately from the selection of the appropriate fine band and the court's assessment of the position of the offence within the range for that band.

Out of the ordinary expenses

17. In deciding the proportions of relevant weekly income that are the starting points and ranges for each fine band, account has been taken of reasonable living expenses. Accordingly, no further allowance should normally be made for these. In addition, no allowance should normally be made where the offender has dependants.

18. Outgoings will be relevant to the amount of the fine only where the expenditure is out of the ordinary and substantially **reduces the ability to pay a financial penalty so that the requirement to pay a fine based on the standard approach would lead to** undue **hardship.**

Unusually low outgoings

19. Where the offender's living expenses are substantially lower **than would normally be expected, it may be appropriate to adjust the amount of the fine to reflect this. This may apply, for example, where an offender does not make any financial contribution towards his or her living costs.**

Savings

20. Where an offender has savings these will not normally be relevant to the assessment of the amount of a fine although they may influence the decision on time to pay.

21. However, where an offender has little or no income but has substantial savings, the court may consider it appropriate to adjust the amount of the fine to reflect this.

Household has more than one source of income

22. Where the household of which the offender is a part has more than one source of income, the fine should normally be based on the income of the offender alone.

23. However, where the offender's part of the income is very small (or the offender is wholly dependent on the income of another), the court may have regard to the extent of the household's income and assets which will be available to meet any fine imposed on the offender.[1]

Potential earning capacity

24. Where there is reason to believe that an offender's potential earning capacity is greater than his or her current income, the court may wish to adjust the amount of the fine to reflect this.[2] This may apply, for example, where an unemployed offender states an expectation to gain paid employment within a short time. The basis for the calculation of fine should be recorded in order to ensure that there is a clear record for use in variation or enforcement proceedings.

High income offenders

25. Where the offender is in receipt of very high income, a fine based on a proportion of relevant weekly income may be disproportionately high when compared with the seriousness of the offence. In such cases, the court should adjust the fine to an appropriate level; as a general indication, in most cases the fine for a first time offender pleading not guilty should not exceed 75% of the maximum fine. In the case of fines which are unlimited the court should decide the appropriate level with the guidance of the legal adviser.

---

[1] *R v Engen* [2004] EWCA Crim 1536 (CA).

[2] *R v Little* (unreported) 14 April 1976 (CA).

Approach to offenders on low income

26. An offender whose primary source of income is state benefit will generally receive a base level of benefit (eg jobseeker's allowance, a relevant disability benefit or income support) and may also be eligible for supplementary benefits depending on his or her individual circumstances (such as child tax credits, housing benefit, council tax benefit and similar). In some cases these benefits may have been replaced by Universal Credit.

27. If relevant weekly income were defined as the amount of benefit received, this would usually result in higher fines being imposed on offenders with a higher level of need; in most circumstances that would not properly balance the seriousness of the offence with the financial circumstances of the offender. While it might be possible to exclude from the calculation any allowance above the basic entitlement of a single person, that could be complicated and time consuming.

28. Similar issues can arise where an offender is in receipt of a low earned income since this may trigger eligibility for means related benefits such as working tax credits and housing benefit depending on the particular circumstances. It will not always be possible to determine with any confidence whether such a person's financial circumstances are significantly different from those of a person whose primary source of income is state benefit.

29. For these reasons, a simpler and fairer approach to cases involving offenders in receipt of low income (whether primarily earned or as a result of benefit) is to identify an amount that is deemed to represent the offender's relevant weekly income.

30. While a precise calculation is neither possible nor desirable, it is considered that an amount that is approximately half-way between the base rate for jobseeker's allowance and the net weekly income of an adult earning the minimum wage for 30 hours per week represents a starting point that is both realistic and appropriate; this is currently £120[1] The calculation is based on a 30 hour working week in recognition of the fact that many of those on minimum wage do not work a full 37 hour week and that lower minimum wage rates apply to younger people.

31. It is expected that this figure will remain in use until 31 March 2016. Future revisions of the guideline will update the amount in accordance with current benefit and minimum wage levels.

---

[1] With effect from 1 October 2014, the minimum wage is £6.50 per hour for an adult aged 21 or over. Based on a 30 hour week, this equates to approximately £189 after deductions for tax and national insurance. To ensure equivalence of approach, the level of job seeker's allowance for a single person aged 18 to 24 has been used for the purpose of calculating the mid point; this is currently £57.90.

Offence committed for 'commercial' purposes

32. Some offences are committed with the intention of gaining a significant commercial benefit. These often occur where, in order to carry out an activity lawfully, a person has to comply with certain processes which may be expensive. They include, for example, 'taxi-touting' (where unauthorised persons seek to operate as taxi drivers) and 'fly-tipping' (where the cost of lawful disposal is considerable).

33. In some of these cases, a fine based on the standard approach set out above may not reflect the level of financial gain achieved or sought through the offending. Accordingly:

(a) where the offender has generated income or avoided expenditure to a level that can be calculated or estimated, the court may wish to consider that amount when determining the financial penalty;

(b) where it is not possible to calculate or estimate that amount, the court may wish to draw on information from the enforcing authorities about the general costs of operating within the law.

Offence committed by an organisation

34. Where an offence is committed by an organisation, guidance on fines can be found at in the environmental offences guideline at page 308.

35. See the Criminal Practice Direction CPD XIII Listing Annex 3 for directions on dealing with cases involving very large fines in the magistrates' court.[1]

---

[1] www.justice.gov.uk/courts/procedure-rules/criminal/rulesmenu

Reduction for a guilty plea

36. Where a guilty plea has been entered, the amount of the fine should be reduced by the appropriate proportion. Courts should refer to the *Guilty Plea* guideline.

Maximum fines

37. A fine must not exceed the statutory limit. Where this is expressed in terms of a 'level', the maxima are:

Level 1	£200
Level 2	£500
Level 3	£1,000
Level 4	£2,500
Level 5	unlimited[1]

See the Criminal Practice Direction XIII Listing Annex 3 for directions on dealing with cases involving very large fines in the magistrates' court.[2]

---

[1] For offences committed after 13 March 2015. For offences committed before that date the level's maximum is £5,000.
[2] www.justice.gov.uk/courts/procedure-rules/criminal/rulesmenu

Multiple offences

38. Where an offender is to be fined for two or more offences that arose out of the same incident, it will often be appropriate to impose on the most serious offence a fine which reflects the totality of the offending where this can be achieved within the maximum penalty for that offence. 'No separate penalty' should be imposed for the other offences.

39. Where compensation is being ordered, that will need to be attributed to the relevant offence as will any necessary ancillary orders.

Imposition of fines with custodial sentences

40. A fine and a custodial sentence may be imposed for the same offence although there will be few circumstances in which this is appropriate, particularly where the custodial sentence is to be served immediately. One example might be where an offender has profited financially from an offence but there is no obvious victim to whom compensation can be awarded. Combining these sentences is most likely to be appropriate only where the custodial sentence is short and/or the offender clearly has, or will have, the means to pay.

41. Care must be taken to ensure that the overall sentence is proportionate to the seriousness of the offence and that better off offenders are not able to 'buy themselves out of custody'.

42. Consult your legal adviser if considering lodging fines or costs on the imposition of a custodial sentence.

Consult your legal adviser in any case in which you are considering combining a fine with a custodial sentence.

Payment

43. A fine is payable in full on the day on which it is imposed. The offender should always be asked for immediate payment when present in court and some payment on the day should be required wherever possible.

44. Where that is not possible, the court may, in certain circumstances,[1] require the offender to be detained. More commonly, a court will allow payments to be made over a period set by the court:

(a) if periodic payments are allowed, the fine should normally be payable within a maximum of 12 months.

(b) compensation should normally be payable within 12 months. However, in exceptional circumstances it may be appropriate to allow it to be paid over a period of up to 3 years.

45. Where fine bands D, E and F apply (see paragraph 5 above), it may be appropriate for the fine to be of an amount that is larger than can be repaid within 12 months. In such cases, the fine should normally be payable within a maximum of 18 months (band D) or 2 years (bands E and F).

46. When allowing payment by instalments **payments should be set at a realistic rate taking into account the offender's disposable income.** The following approach may be useful:

Net weekly income	Suggested Starting point for weekly payment
£60	£5
£120	£10
£200	£25
£250	£30
£300	£50
£400	£80

If the offender has dependants or larger than usual commitments, the weekly payment is likely to be decreased.

47. The payment terms must be included in any collection order made in respect of the amount imposed; see [pages 156–157].

The payment terms must be included in any collection order made in respect of the amount imposed; see below.

[1] See section 82 of the Magistrates' Court Act for restrictions on the power to impose imprisonment on default.

Collection Orders

48. The Courts Act 2003 created a fines collection scheme which provides for greater administrative enforcement of fines. Consult your legal adviser for further guidance.

Attachment of earnings orders/applications for benefit deductions

49. Unless it would be impracticable or inappropriate to do so, the court must make an attachment of earnings or (AEO) or application for benefit deductions (ABD) whenever:

- compensation is imposed;[1] or
- the court concludes that the offender is an existing defaulter and that the existing default cannot be disregarded.[2]

50. In other cases, the court may make an AEO or ABD with the offender's consent.[3]

51. The court must make a collection order in every case in which a fine or compensation order is imposed unless this would be impracticable or inappropriate.[4] The collection order must state:

- the amount of the sum due, including the amount of any fine, compensation order or other sum;
- whether the court considers the offender to be an existing defaulter;

- whether an AEO or ABD has been made and information about the effect of the order;
- if the court has not made an AEO or ABD, the payment terms;
- if an AEO or ABD has been made, the reserve terms (ie the payment terms that will apply if the AEO or ABD fails). It will often be appropriate to set a reserve term of payment in full within 14 days.

---

[1] Courts Act 2003, sch. 5, para. 7A.
[2] Ibid., para. 8.
[3] Ibid., para. 9.
[4] Ibid., para. 12.

COMPENSATION

Introduction

C.8 **1.** The court must consider making a compensation order in any case where personal injury, loss or damage has resulted from the offence. It can either be a sentence in its own right or an ancillary order. The court must give reasons if it decides not to order compensation[1]

2. There is no statutory limit on the amount of compensation that may be imposed in respect of offences for an offender aged 18 or over. Compensation may also be ordered in respect of offences taken into consideration.[2]

3. Where the personal injury, loss or damage arises from a road accident, a compensation order may be made only if there is a conviction for an offence under the Theft Act 1968, or the offender is uninsured and the Motor Insurers' Bureau will not cover the loss.

4. Subject to consideration of the victim's views (see paragraph 6 below), the court must order compensation wherever possible and should not have regard to the availability of other sources such as civil litigation or the Criminal Injuries Compensation Scheme. Any amount paid by an offender under a compensation order will generally be deducted from a subsequent civil award or payment under the Scheme to avoid double compensation.

5. Compensation may be ordered for such amount as the court considers appropriate having regard to any evidence and any representations made by the offender or prosecutor. The court must also take into account the offender's means (see also paragraphs 9–11 below).

6. Compensation should benefit, not inflict further harm on, the victim. Any financial recompense from the offender may cause distress. A victim may or may not want compensation from the offender and assumptions should not be made either way. The victim's views are properly obtained through sensitive discussion by the police or witness care unit, when it can be explained that the offender's ability to pay will ultimately determine whether, and how much, compensation is ordered and whether the compensation will be paid in one lump sum or by instalments. If the victim does not want compensation, this should be made known to the court and respected.

7. In cases where it is difficult to ascertain the full amount of the loss suffered by the victim, consideration should be given to making a compensation order for an amount representing the agreed or likely loss. Where relevant information is not immediately available, it may be appropriate to grant an adjournment for it to be obtained.

8. The court should consider two types of loss:

- financial loss sustained as a result of the offence such as the cost of repairing damage or, in case of injury, any loss of earnings or medical expenses;
- pain and suffering caused by the injury (including terror, shock or distress) and any loss of facility. This should be assessed in light of all factors that appear to the court to be relevant, including any medical evidence, the victim's age and personal circumstances.

9. Once the court has formed a preliminary view of the appropriate level of compensation, it must have regard to the means of the offender so far as they are known. Where the offender has little money, the order may have to be scaled down or additional time allowed to pay; the court may allow compensation to be paid over a period of up to three years in appropriate cases.

10. The fact that a custodial sentence is imposed does not, in itself, make it inappropriate to order compensation; however, it may be relevant to whether the offender has the means to satisfy the order. Consult your legal adviser in any case where you are considering combining compensation with a custodial sentence.

11. Where the court considers that it would be appropriate to impose a fine and a compensation order but the offender has insufficient means to pay both, priority should be given to compensation. Compensation also takes priority over the victim surcharge where the offender's means are an issue.

---

[1] Powers of Criminal Courts (Sentencing) Act 2000, s 130.
[2] Powers of Criminal Courts (Sentencing) Act 2000, s 131.

Suggested starting points for physical and mental injuries

12. The table below suggests starting points for compensating physical and mental injuries commonly encountered in a magistrates' court. They have been developed to be consistent with the approach in the Criminal Injuries Compensation Authority (CICA) tariff (revised 2012). The CICA tariff makes no award for minor injuries which result in short term disability; the suggested starting points for these injuries are adapted from an earlier tariff.

Type of injury	Description	Starting point
Graze	Depending on size	Up to £75
Bruise	Depending on size	Up to £100

Type of injury	Description	Starting point
Cut: no permanent scar	Depending on size and whether stitched	£100–300
Black eye		£125
Eye	Blurred or double vision lasting up to 6 weeks	£500
	Blurred or double vision lasting for 6 to 13 weeks	£1,000
	Blurred or double vision lasting for more than 13 weeks (recovery expected)	£1,500
Brain	Concussion lasting one week	£1,500
Nose	Undisplaced fracture of nasal bone	£1,000
	Displaced fracture requiring manipulation	£2,000
	Deviated nasal septum requiring septoplasty	£2,000
Loss of non-front tooth	Depending on cosmetic effect	£750 per tooth
Loss of front tooth		£1,500 per tooth
Facial scar	Minor disfigurement (permanent)	£1,000
Arm	Fractured humerus, radius, ulna (substantial recovery)	£1,500
Shoulder	Dislocated (substantial recovery)	£900
Wrist	Dislocated/fractured – including scaphoid fracture (substantial recovery)	£2,400
	Fractured – colles type (substantial recovery)	£2,400
Sprained wrist, ankle	Disabling for up to 6 weeks	500
	Disabling for 6 to 13 weeks	£800
	Disabling for more than 13 weeks	£1000
Finger	Fractured finger other than index finger (substantial recovery)	£300
	Fractured index finger (substantial recovery)	£1,200
	Fractured thumb (substantial recovery)	£1,750
Leg	Fractured fibula (substantial recovery)	£1,000
	Fractured femur, tibia (substantial recovery)	£1,800
Abdomen	Injury requiring laparotomy	£1,800
Temporary mental anxiety (including terror, shock, distress), not medically verified		Up to £500
Disabling mental anxiety, lasting more than 6 weeks, medically verified*		£1,000
Disability mental illness, lasting up to 28 weeks, confirmed by psychiatric diagnosis*		£1,500

* In this context, 'disabling' means a person's functioning is significantly impaired in some important aspect of his or her life, such as impaired work or school performance or significant adverse effects on social relationships.

13. The following table, which is also based on the Criminal Injuries Compensation Authority tariff, sets out suggested starting points for compensating physical and sexual abuse. It will be rare for cases involving this type of harm to be dealt with in a magistrates' court and it will be important to **consult your legal adviser for guidance in these situations**.

Type of injury	Description	Starting point
Physical abuse of adult	Intermittent physical assaults resulting in accumulation of healed wounds, burns or scalds, but with no appreciable disfigurement	£2,000
Physical abuse of child	Isolated or intermittent assault(s) resulting in weals, hair pulled from scalp etc.	£1,000
	Intermittent physical assaults resulting in accumulation of healed wounds, burns or scalds, but with no appreciable disfigurement	£2,000
Sexual abuse of adult	Non-penetrative indecent physical acts over clothing	£1,000
	Non-penetrative indecent act(s) under clothing	£2,000

Type of injury	Description	Starting point
Sexual abuse of child (under 18)	Non-penetrative indecent physical act(s) over clothing	£1,000
	Non-penetrative frequent assaults over clothing or non-penetrative indecent act under clothing	£1500–£2,00
	Repetitive indecent acts under clothing	£3,300

PROSECUTION COSTS

C.9   Where an offender is convicted of an offence, the court has discretion to make such order as to costs as it considers just and reasonable.[1]

The Court of Appeal has given the following guidance:[2]

(i)   an order for costs should never exceed the sum which, having regard to the offender's means and any other financial order imposed, he or she is able to pay and which it is reasonable to order him or her to pay;

(ii)   an order for costs should never exceed the sum which the prosecutor actually and reasonably incurred;

(iii)   the purpose of the order is to compensate the prosecutor. Where the conduct of the defence has put the prosecutor to avoidable expense, the offender may be ordered to pay some or all of that sum to the prosecutor but the offender must not be punished for exercising the right to defend himself or herself;

(iv)   the costs ordered to be paid should not be grossly disproportionate to any fine imposed for the offence. This principle was affirmed in *BPS Advertising Limited v London Borough of Barnet* [3] in which the Court held that, while there is no question of an arithmetical relationship, the question of costs should be viewed in the context of the maximum penalty considered by Parliament to be appropriate for the seriousness of the offence;

(v)   if the combined total of the proposed fine and the costs sought by the prosecutor exceeds the sum which the offender could reasonably be ordered to pay, the costs order should be reduced rather than the fine;

(vi)   it is for the offender to provide details of his or her financial position so as to enable the court to assess what he or she can reasonably afford to pay. If the offender fails to do so, the court is entitled to draw reasonable inferences as to means from all the circumstances of the case;

(vii)   if the court proposes to make any financial order against the offender, it must give him or her fair opportunity to adduce any relevant financial information and to make appropriate submissions.

Where the prosecutor is the Crown Prosecution Service, prosecution costs exclude the costs of the investigation, which are met by the police. In non-CPS cases where the costs of the investigation are incurred by the prosecutor a costs award may cover the costs of investigation as well as prosecution.[4] However, where the investigation was carried out as part of a council officer's routine duties, for which he or she would have been paid in the normal way, this is a relevant factor to be taken into account when deciding the appropriate amount of any costs order[5]

Where the court wishes to impose costs in addition to a fine, compensation and/or the victim surcharge but the offender has insufficient resources to pay the total amount, the order of priority is:

1. compensation;
2. victim surcharge;
3. fine;
4. costs.

---

[1] Prosecution of Offences Act 1985, s 18.
[2] *R v Northallerton Magistrates' Court, ex parte Dove* [2000] 1 Cr App R (S) 136 (CA).
[3] [2006] EWCA 3335 (Admin) QBD.
[4] Further guidance is provided in the Criminal Costs Practice Direction and the Criminal Procedure Rules Part 76 see https://www.iustice.gov.uktcourtst/procedure-rules/criminal/rules/menu
[5] ibid.

VICTIM SURCHARGE

C.10   **1.**   When sentencing for offences committed on or after 1 October 2012 a court must order the Victim Surcharge in the following ways:[1]

Victim Surcharge		
Offenders aged 18 and older at the date of the offence		
Disposal type	**One or more offences committed before 8 April 2016**	**All offence(s) committed on or after 8 April 2016**
Conditional discharge	£15	£20

Fine	10% of the fine value with a £20 minimum and a £120 maximum (*rounded up or down to the nearest pound*)	10% of the fine value with a £30 minimum and a £170 maximum (*rounded up or down to the nearest pound*)
Community order	£60	£85
Suspended sentence order	£80 (six months or less)	115 (six months or less)
Immediate custody[2]	£80 (six months or less) *	

Victim Surcharge

Offenders aged under 18 at the date of the offence

Disposal type	One or more offences committed before 8 April 2016	All offences committed on or after 8 April 2016
Conditional discharge	£10	£15
Fine, Youth Rehabilitation Order, Community Order or Referral Order	£15	£20
Suspended sentence order	£20	£30
Immediate custody[3]	£20*	£30

* * When sentencing an offender to immediate custody for a single offence committed before 1 September 2014 or more than one offence, at least one of which was committed before 1 September 2014, no surcharge is payable.

Person who is not an individual (for example, a company or other legal person)

Victim Surcharge

Disposal type	One or more offences committed before 8 April 2016	All offences committed on or after 8 April 2016
Conditional discharge	£15	£20
Fine	10% of the fine value with a £20 minimum and a £120 maximum (*rounded up or down to the nearest pound*)	10% of the fine value with a £30 minimum and a £170 maximum (*rounded up or down to the nearest pound*)

2.   Where an offender is dealt with in different ways only one surcharge (whichever attracts the higher sum) will be paid. Where there is more than one fine ordered, then the surcharge for the highest individual fine is assessed, <u>NOT</u> the total of all fines ordered. Where a custodial sentence is imposed the surcharge is based upon the longest individual sentence, <u>NOT</u> the aggregate term imposed.

3.   Where the court dealing with an offender for more than one offence and at least one offence was committed when the offender was under 18, the surcharge should be ordered at the rate for under 18s.[4]

4.   The surcharge should not be repeated when dealing with breach of a community order, suspended sentence order or conditional discharge.

5.   Where the offender has the means to pay the financial impositions of the court, there should be no reduction in compensation or fines whenever the surcharge is ordered. However, when the court:

- orders the offender to pay both a surcharge and compensation, but the offender is unable to pay both, the court must reduce the amount of the surcharge (if necessary to nil);[5] or
- orders the offender to pay both a fine and a surcharge, the court may only reduce the fine to the extent that the offender is unable to pay both[6]

6. Where the offender does not have sufficient means to pay the total financial penalty considered appropriate by the court, the order of priority is: compensation, surcharge, fine, costs.

6. When sentencing for one or more offences anyone of which was committed **after 1 April 2007 but before 1 October 2012**, a surcharge is payable only if the offender is dealt with by way of a fine at a flat rate of £15.[7]

---

[1] Criminal Justice Act 2003, s 161A; Criminal Justice Act 2003 (Surcharge) Order 2012.
[2] The Criminal Justice Act (2003) Surcharge Order 2014
[3] Ibid.
[4] Criminal Justice Act 2003 (Surcharge) Order 2012 art. 5(3).
[5] Criminal Justice Act 2003, s. 161A(3)
[6] Criminal Justice Act 2003, s. 164(4A).
[7] Criminal Justice Act 2003 (Surcharge) Order 2012 art. 7(2)

ANCILLARY ORDERS (IN ALPHABETICAL ORDER)

C.11 **1.** There are several ancillary orders available in a magistrates' court which should be considered in appropriate cases. Annex A lists the offences in respect of which certain orders are available. The individual offence guidelines above also identify ancillary orders particularly likely to be relevant to the offence. **In all cases, consult your legal adviser regarding available orders and their specific requirements and effects.**

2. Ancillary orders should be taken into account when assessing whether the overall penalty is commensurate with offence seriousness.

Anti-social behaviour orders

These have now been replaced by Criminal Behaviour Orders (see below)

Binding over orders

- The court has the power to bind an individual over to keep the peace.[1]
- The order is designed to prevent future misconduct and requires the individual to promise to pay a specified sum if the terms of the order are breached. Exercise of the power does not depend upon conviction.
- Guidance on the making of binding over orders is set out in the Criminal Practice Directions VII: Sentencing[2] Kev principles include:
  (1) before imposing the order, the court must be satisfied beyond reasonable doubt that a breach of the peace involving violence or an imminent threat of violence has occurred, or that there is a real risk of violence in the future. The court should hear evidence and the parties before making any order;
  (2) the court should state its reasons for making the order;
  (3) the order should identify the specific conduct or activity from which the individual must refrain, the length of the order and the amount of the recognisance;
  (4) the length of the order should be proportionate to the harm sought to be avoided and should not generally exceed 12 months;
  (5) when fixing the amount of the recognisance, the court should have regard to the individual's financial resources.

Confiscation orders

- Confiscation orders under the Proceeds of Crime Act 2002 may only be made by the Crown Court.
- An offender convicted of an offence in a magistrates' court must be committed to the Crown Court where this is requested by the prosecution with a view to a confiscation order being considered.[3]
- If the committal is made in respect of an either way offence, the court must state whether it would have committed the offender to the Crown Court for sentencing had the issue of a confiscation order not arisen.

Criminal Behaviour Orders

A Criminal Behaviour Order (CBO) is an order which is available on conviction for any criminal offence by any criminal court, introduced by the Anti-social Behaviour, Crime and Policing Act 2014[4] with effect from 20 October 2014. It replaces the former powers of the court to make orders such as an ASBO or a drinking banning order on conviction.

A CBO is an order designed to tackle the most serious and persistent anti-social individuals where their behaviour has brought them before a criminal court. The anti-social behaviour to be addressed does not need to be connected to the criminal behaviour, or activity which led to the conviction. However, if there is no link the court will need to reflect on the reasons for making the order.

A CBO can deal with a wide range of anti-social behaviours following the offender's conviction, for example threatening violence against others in the community, or persistently being drunk and aggressive in public. However, the order should not be designed to stop reasonable, trivial or benign behaviours that have not caused, or are not likely to cause anti-social behaviour.

Any application will be made by the prosecution.[5] The majority of applications will therefore be made by the CPS, either at their own initiative, or at the request of the police. However, it may also be applied for by local councils, providing they are the prosecuting authority in the case. **The court cannot make a CBO of its own volition.**

A CBO may only be made against an offender when they have been sentenced to at least a conditional discharge for the substantive offence[6] **A CBO cannot be made where the offender has been given an absolute discharge.**

The court may only make a CBO if it is satisfied that two conditions are met:[7]

(1) The court must be satisfied, beyond reasonable doubt, that the offender has engaged in behaviour that caused, or was likely to cause, harassment, alarm or distress to one or more persons,[8] **and**

(2) That making the order will help in preventing the offender from engaging in such behaviour[9]

For the first condition, the burden of proof on the prosecution is to the criminal standard, beyond reasonable doubt. (There is **no** test of necessity as with ASBOs.)

A CBO may:

(1) Prohibit the offender from doing anything described in the order ('a prohibition'), and/or

(2) Require the offender to do anything described in the order ('a requirement').[10]

However, any prohibitions and/or requirements must, so far as practicable, avoid any interference with times an offender would normally work, attend school or other educational establishment and any conflict with any other court order or injunction.[11]

If the order requires the offender to do anything, then the order must specify the individual or organisation that is responsible for supervising compliance with the requirement[12] and must hear from them about both the suitability and enforceability of a requirement, before including it in the CBO.[13]

The order must be proportionate and reasonable. It will be for the court to decide the measures which are most appropriate and available to tackle the underlying cause of the anti-social behaviour. The order should be tailored to the specific needs of each perpetrator.

When deciding whether or not to make a CSO, the court is entitled to consider evidence submitted by the prosecution and by the offender.[14] It does not matter whether the evidence would have been admissible, or has been heard as part of the criminal proceedings in which the offender was convicted,[15] but it should be relevant to the test to be applied to the making of the order (i.e. that the offender has engaged in behaviour that caused, or was likely to cause, harassment, alarm or distress to any person, and that the court considers that making the order will assist in preventing the offender from engaging in such behaviour). This evidence could include hearsay or bad character evidence. Special measures are available for witnesses who are vulnerable and intimidated witnesses in accordance with Section 16 and 17 Youth Justice and Criminal Evidence Act 1999.[16]

A CSO takes effect on the day it is made[17] unless the offender is already subject to an existing CSO, in which case it may take effect on the day in which the previous order expires.[18] The order must specify the period for which it has effect.[19] In the case of an adult, the order must be for a fixed period of not less than two years or it may be an indefinite period, so that it is made until further order.[20] An order may specify different periods for which particular prohibitions or requirements have effect within the order.[21]

The court can impose an **interim order** in cases where the offender is convicted but the court is adjourning the hearing of the application for a CBO[22] before or after sentence for the offence. The offender need not be sentenced to be made subject to an interim order[23] The court can make an interim order if the court thinks it is just to do so. An interim order can be made until final hearing or further order[24] When making an interim order the court has the same powers as if it were making a final order.[25]

It is likely that the hearing for a CBO will take place at the same time as the sentencing for the criminal case. For adult offenders, there is no formal consultation requirement. However, in order to ensure that applications are made appropriately and efficiently, there is an expectation that any relevant agencies will have been consulted so that the prosecution have the relevant information to decide whether to make an order or not and if so, in what terms. The prosecution should be prepared to deal with an application on the date of hearing.

The court may deal with the application for a CBO at the same time as it imposes sentence for the offence. Alternatively, the court may sentence the offender for the criminal offence and adjourn the application for a CBO to a later date[26] However, the court cannot hear an application once sentence has taken place, unless the application was made by the prosecution before sentence was concluded, as an application cannot be made retrospectively.

If the offender does not appear at an adjourned hearing for a CBO, the court may further adjourn the proceedings, issue a warrant for the offender's arrest, or hear the proceedings in the offender's absence[27] To issue a warrant for the offender's arrest, the court must be satisfied that the offender has been given adequate notice of the time and place for the hearing.[28] To proceed in the offender's absence, the court must be satisfied that the offender has been given adequate notice of the time and place for the hearing and been told if they do not attend, the court may hear the application in their absence.[29]

Further guidance is provided by the Home Office in *Anti-social Behaviour, Crime and Policing Act 2014: Reform of anti-social behaviour powers; Statutory guidance for frontline professionals. July 2014.*[30]

Deprivation orders

The court has the power to deprive an offender of property used for the purpose of committing or facilitating the commission of an offence, whether or not it deals with the offender in any other way.[31]

Before making the order, the court must have regard to the value of the property and the likely financial and other effects on the offender.

Without limiting the circumstances in which the court may exercise the power, a vehicle is deemed to have been used for the purpose of committing the offence where the offence is punishable by imprisonment and consists of:

(1) driving, attempting to drive, or being in charge of a motor vehicle;

(2) failing to provide a specimen; or

(3)　failing to stop and/or report an accident.[32]

Deprivation of ownership of animal

Where an offender is convicted of one of the following offences under the Animal Welfare Act 2006, the court may make an order depriving him or her of ownership of the animal and for its disposal:[33]

(1)　causing unnecessary suffering (s 4);
(2)　mutilation (s 5);
(3)　docking of dogs' tails (ss 6(1) and 6(2));
(4)　fighting etc. (s 8);
(5)　breach of duty to ensure welfare (s 9);
(6)　breach of disqualification order (s 36(9)).

The court is required to give reasons if it decides not to make such an order.

Deprivation of ownership may be ordered instead of or in addition to dealing with the offender in any other way.

DESTRUCTION ORDERS AND CONTINGENT DESTRUCTION ORDERS FOR DOGS

See the Dangerous Dogs Guideline at page 255 (however note that this guideline is due to be updated – consult your legal adviser)

Disqualification from ownership of animals

Where an offender is convicted of one of the following offences under the Animal Welfare Act 2006, the court may disqualify him or her from owning or keeping animals, dealing in animals, and/or transporting animals:[34]

(1)　causing unnecessary suffering (s 4);
(2)　mutilation (s 5);
(3)　docking of dogs' tails (ss 6(1) and 6(2));
(4)　administration of poisons etc. (s 7);
(5)　fighting etc. (s 8);
(6)　breach of duty to ensure welfare (s 9);
(7)　breach of licensing or registration requirements (s 13(6));
(8)　breach of disqualification order (s 36(9)).

The court is required to give reasons if it decides not to make such an order.

The court may specify a period during which an offender may not apply for termination of the order under section 43 of the Animal Welfare Act 2006; if no period is specified, an offender may not apply for termination of the order until one year after the order was made.

Disqualification may be imposed instead of or in addition to dealing with the offender in any other way.

Disqualification from driving – general power

The court may disqualify any person convicted of an offence from driving for such period as it thinks fit.[35] This may be instead of or in addition to dealing with the offender in any other way.

The section does not require the offence to be connected to the use of a vehicle. The Court of Appeal has held that the power is available as part of the overall punitive element of a sentence, and the only restrictions on the exercise of the power are those in the statutory provision.[36]

Disqualification of company directors

The Company Directors Disqualification Act 1986 empowers the court to disqualify an offender from being a director or taking part in the promotion, formation or management of a company for up to five years.

An order may be made in two situations:

(1)　where an offender has been convicted of an indictable offence in connection with the promotion, formation, management, liquidation or striking off of a company;[37] or
(2)　where an offender has been convicted of an offence involving a failure to file documents with, or give notice to, the registrar of companies. If the offence is triable only summarily, disqualification can be ordered only where the offender has been the subject of three default orders or convictions in the preceding five years.[38]

Drinking banning orders

These have now been replaced by Criminal Behaviour Orders (see above)

Exclusion orders

The court may make an exclusion order where an offender has been convicted of an offence committed on licensed premises involving the use or threat of violence.[39]

The order prohibits the offender from entering **specified** licensed premises without the consent of the licensee. The term of the order must be between three months and two years.

Football banning orders

The court must make a football banning order where an offender has been convicted of a relevant offence and it is satisfied that there are reasonable grounds to believe that making a banning order would help to prevent violence or disorder.[40] If the court is not so satisfied, it must state that fact and give its reasons.

Relevant offences are those set out in schedule 1 of the Football Spectators Act 1989; see Annex A.

The order requires the offender to report to a police station within five days, may require the offender to surrender his or her passport, and may impose requirements on the offender in relation to any regulated football matches.

Where the order is imposed in addition to a sentence of immediate imprisonment, the term of the order must be between six and ten years. In other cases, the term of the order must be between three and five years.

Forfeiture and destruction of drugs
Where an offender is convicted of an offence under the Misuse of Drugs Act 1971, the court may order forfeiture and destruction of anything shown to the satisfaction of the court to relate to the offence.[41]

FORFEITURE AND DESTRUCTION OF WEAPONS ORDERS
A court convicting a person of possession of an offensive weapon may make an order for the forfeiture or disposal of the weapon (Prevention of Crime Act 1953, s1 (2)).
See also deprivation orders above.

Forfeiture and destruction of goods bearing unauthorised trade mark
Where the court is satisfied that an offence under section 92 of the Trade Marks Act 1994 has been committed, it must (on the application of a person who has come into possession of the goods in connection with the investigation or prosecution of the offence) order forfeiture of the goods.[42]

If it considers it appropriate, instead of ordering destruction of the goods, the court may direct that they be released to a specified person on condition that the offending sign is erased, removed or obliterated.

Forfeiture or suspension of liquor licence
Where an offender who holds a personal licence to supply alcohol is charged with a 'relevant offence', he or she is required to produce the licence to the court, or inform the court of its existence, no later than his or her first appearance.[43]

'Relevant offences' are listed in schedule 4 of the Licensing Act 2003; see Annex A.

Where the offender is convicted, the court may order forfeiture of the licence or suspend it for up to six months.[44] When deciding whether to order forfeiture or suspension, the court may take account of the offender's previous convictions for 'relevant offences'.[45]

Whether or not forfeiture or suspension is ordered, the court is required to notify the licensing authority of the offender's conviction and the sentence imposed.[46]

Parenting orders
The court may make a parenting order where an offender has been convicted of an offence under section 444 of the Education Act 1996 (failing to secure regular attendance at school) and the court is satisfied that the order would be desirable in the interests of preventing the commission of any further offence under that section.[47]

The order may impose such requirements that the court considers desirable in the interests of preventing the commission of a further offence under section 444.

A requirement to attend a counselling or guidance programme may be included only if the offender has been the subject of a parenting order on a previous occasion.

The term of the order must not exceed 12 months.

Restitution orders
Where goods have been stolen and an offender is convicted of any offence with reference to theft of those goods, the court may make a restitution order.[48]
The court may:

(1) order anyone in possession or control of the stolen goods to restore them to the victim;
(2) on the application of the victim, order that goods directly or indirectly representing the stolen goods (as being the proceeds of any disposal or realisation of the stolen goods) be transferred to the victim; or
(3) order that a sum not exceeding the value of the stolen goods be paid to the victim out of any money taken out of the offender's possession on his or her apprehension.

Restraining orders
Where an offender is convicted of any offence, the court may make a restraining order.[49]

The order may prohibit the offender from doing anything for the purpose of protecting the victim of the offence, or any other person mentioned in the order, from further conduct which amounts to harassment or will cause a fear of violence.

The order may have effect for a specified period or until further order.

A court before which a person is **acquitted** of an offence may make a restraining order if the court considers that it is necessary to protect a person from harassment by the defendant.[50] **Consult your legal adviser for guidance**.

Sexual harm prevention orders
Orders can be made in relation to a person who has been convicted, found not guilty by reason of insanity or found to be under a disability and to have done the act charged, or cautioned etc. for an offence listed in either Schedule 3 or Schedule 5 to the Sexual Offences Act 2003 either in the UK or overseas (see Annex A). This includes offenders whose convictions etc. pre-date the commencement of the 2003 Act.

No application is necessary for the court to make a SHPO at the point of sentence although the prosecutor may wish to invite the court to consider making an order in appropriate cases. The court may ask pre-sentence report writers to consider the suitability of a SHPO on a non-prejudicial basis.

In order to make a SHPO, the court must be satisfied that the offender presents a risk of sexual harm to the public (or particular members of the public) and that an order is necessary to protect against this risk. The details of the offence are likely to be a key factor in the court's decision, together with the offender's previous convictions and the assessment of risk presented by the national probation service in any pre-sentence report. The court may take into consideration the range of other options available to it in respect of protecting the public. The court may want to consider:

(1) would an order minimise the risk of harm to the public or to any particular members of the public?
(2) is it proportionate?
(3) can it be policed effectively?

The only prohibitions which can be imposed by a SHPO are those which are necessary for the purpose of protecting the public from sexual harm from the defendant. These can, however, be wide ranging. An order may, for example, prohibit someone from undertaking certain forms of employment such as acting as a home tutor to children. It may also prohibit the offender from engaging in particular activities on the internet. The decision of the Court of Appeal in *R v Smith and Others* [2011] EWCA Crim 1772 reinforces the need for the terms of a SHPO to be tailored to the exact requirements of the case. SHPOs may be used to limit and manage internet use by an offender, where it is considered proportionate and necessary to do so. The behaviour prohibited by the order might well be considered unproblematic if exhibited by another member of the public –it is the offender's previous offending behaviour and subsequent demonstration that they may pose a risk of further such behaviour, which will make them eligible for an order.

The order may include only negative prohibitions; there is no power to impose positive obligations. The order may have effect for a fixed period (not less than five years) or until further order. **Consult your legal adviser for guidance.**

---

[1] Justices of the Peace Act 1361, Justices of the Peace Act 1968, s.1 (7), Magistrates Court Act 1980, s.115.
[2] www.justice.gov.uk/courts/procedure-rules/criminal/rulesmenu
[3] Proceeds of Crime Act 2002, s 70.
[4] Anti-social Behaviour, Crime and Policing Act 2014, s 22.
[5] Anti-social Behaviour, Crime and Policing Act 2014, s 22(7).
[6] Anti-social Behaviour, Crime and Policing Act 2014, s 22(6)..
[7] Anti-social Behaviour, Crime and Policing Act 2014, s 22(2).
[8] Anti-social Behaviour, Crime and Policing Act 2014, s 22(3).
[9] Anti-social Behaviour, Crime and Policing Act 2014, s 22(4).
[10] Anti-social Behaviour, Crime and Policing Act 2014, s 22(5).
[11] Anti-social Behaviour, Crime and Policing Act 2014, s 22(9).
[12] Anti-social Behaviour, Crime and Policing Act 2014, s 24(1).
[13] Anti-social Behaviour, Crime and Policing Act 2014, s 24(2).
[14] Anti-social Behaviour, Crime and Policing Act 2014, s 23(1).
[15] Anti-social Behaviour, Crime and Policing Act 2014, s 23(2).
[16] Anti-social Behaviour, Crime and Policing Act 2014, s 31.
[17] Anti-social Behaviour, Crime and Policing Act 2014, s 25(1).
[18] Anti-social Behaviour, Crime and Policing Act 2014, s 25(2).
[19] Anti-social Behaviour, Crime and Policing Act 2014, s 25(3).
[20] Anti-social Behaviour, Crime and Policing Act 2014, s 25(5).
[21] Anti-social Behaviour, Crime and Policing Act 2014, s 25(6).
[22] Anti-social Behaviour, Crime and Policing Act 2014, s 26(1).
[23] Anti-social Behaviour, Crime and Policing Act 2014, s 26(3).
[24] Anti-social Behaviour, Crime and Policing Act 2014, s 26(2).
[25] Anti-social Behaviour, Crime and Policing Act 2014, s 26(4).
[26] Anti-social Behaviour, Crime and Policing Act 2014, s 22(3).
[27] Anti-social Behaviour, Crime and Policing Act 2014, s 23(4).
[28] Anti-social Behaviour, Crime and Policing Act 2014, s 23(5).
[29] Anti-social Behaviour, Crime and Policing Act 2014, s 23(6).
[30] https://www.gov.uk/government/uploads/system/uploads/attachmentdatalfile/332839/StatutoryGuidanceFrontline.pdf
[31] Powers of Criminal Courts (Sentencing) Act 200, s 143.
[32] Powers of Criminal Courts (Sentencing) Act 200, s 143(6) and 143 (7).
[33] Animal Welfare Act 2006, s 33.
[34] Animal Welfare Act 2006, s 34.
[35] Powers of Criminal Courts (Sentencing) Act 2000, s 146.
[36] *R v Cliff* [2004] EWCA Crim 3139.
[37] Company Directors Disqualification Act 1988, s 2.
[38] Company Directors Disqualification Act 1988, s 5.
[39] Licensed Premises (Exclusion of Certain Persons) Act 1980 40 Football Spectators Act 1989, s 14A
[40] Football Spectators Act 1989, s 14A
[41] Misuse of Drugs Act 1971, s 27(1)
[42] Trade Marks Act 1994, s 97.
[43] Licensing Act 2003, s 128(1).
[44] Licensing Act 2003, s 129(2).
[45] Licensing Act 2003, s 129(3).
[46] Licensing Act 2003, s 131.
[47] Crime and Disorder 1998, s .8.
[48] Powers of Criminal Courts (Sentencing) Act 2000, s 148; Criminal Procedure Rules 2013 (SI 2013 No 1554), r.42.7.
[49] Protection from Harassment Act 1997, s 5.
[50] Protection from Harassment Act 1997, s 5A.

SEXUAL OFFENCES PREVENTION ORDERS

These have now been replaced by Sexual Harm Prevention Orders. A Sexual Offences Prevention Order may only be made if the order was applied for before 8 March 2015.
Consult your legal adviser for guidance.

DEFERRED SENTENCES

Always consult your legal adviser if you are considering deferring a sentence.

The court is empowered to defer passing sentence for up to six months.[1] The court may impose any conditions during the period of deferment that it considers appropriate. These could be specific requirements as set out in the provisions for community sentences, restorative justice activities[2] or requirements that are drawn more widely. The purpose of deferment is to enable the court to have regard to the offender's conduct after conviction or any change in his or her circumstances, including the extent to which the offender has complied with any requirements imposed by the court.

Three conditions must be satisfied before sentence can be deferred:

(1) the offender must consent (and in the case of restorative justice activities the other participants must consent);[3]
(2) the offender must undertake to comply with requirements imposed by the court; and
(3) the court must be satisfied that deferment is in the interests of justice.

Deferred sentences will be appropriate in very limited circumstances;

- deferred sentences will be appropriate in very limited circumstances;
- deferred sentences are likely to be relevant predominantly in a small group of cases close to either the community or custodial sentence threshold where, should the offender be prepared to adapt his behaviour in a way clearly specified by the sentencer, the court may be prepared to impose a lesser sentence;
- sentencers should impose specific and measurable conditions that do not involve a serious restriction on liberty;
- the court should give a clear indication of the type of sentence it would have imposed if it had decided not to defer;
- the court should also ensure that the offender understands the consequences of failure to comply with the court's wishes during the deferment period.

If the offender fails to comply with any requirement imposed in connection with the deferment, or commits another offence, he or she can be brought back to court before the end of the deferment period and the court can proceed to sentence.

---

[1] Powers of Criminal Courts (Sentencing) Act 2000, s 1 as amended by Criminal Justice Act 2003, s 278 and Sch 23, para.1.
[2] ibid s 1ZA as inserted by the Crime and Courts Act 2013, s 44, Sch 16, pt 2, para 5.
[3] ibid s 1ZA(3).

OFFENCES COMMITTED IN A DOMESTIC CONTEXT

1. Domestic violence is defined as:

Any incident or pattern of incidents of controlling, coercive or threatening behaviour, violence or abuse between those aged 16 or over who are or have been intimate partners or family members regardless of gender or sexuality. This can encompass but is not limited to the following types of abuse:

- psychological
- physical
- sexual
- financial
- emotional

Controlling behaviour is: a range of acts designed to make a person subordinate and/or dependent by isolating them from sources of support, exploiting their resources and capacities for personal gain, depriving them of the means needed for independence, resistance and escape and regulating their everyday behaviour.

Coercive behaviour is: an act or a pattern of acts of assault, threats, humiliation and intimidation or other abuse that is used to harm, punish, or frighten the victim.

This definition includes so called 'honour' based violence, female genital mutilation (FGM) and forced marriage. Victims of domestic violence are not confined to one gender or ethnic group.

2. When sentencing an offence committed in a domestic context, refer to the Sentencing Guidelines Council's definitive guideline Overarching Principles: Domestic Violence, published 7 December 2006. The guideline emphasises that:

- as a starting point for sentence, offences committed in a domestic context should be regarded as no less serious than offences committed in a non-domestic context;
- many offences of violence in a domestic context are dealt with in a magistrates' court as an offence of common assault or assault occasioning actual bodily harm because the injuries sustained are relatively minor. Offences involving serious violence will warrant a custodial sentence in the majority of cases;
- a number of aggravating factors may commonly arise by virtue of the offence being committed in a domestic context (see list below);
- since domestic violence takes place within the context of a current or past relationship, the history of the relationship will often be relevant in assessing the gravity of the offence. A court is entitled to take into account anything occurring within the relationship as a whole, which may reveal relevant aggravating or mitigating factors;
- since domestic violence takes place within the context of a current or past relationship, the history of the relationship will often be relevant in assessing the gravity of the offence. A court is entitled to take into account anything occurring within the relationship as a whole, which may reveal relevant aggravating or mitigating factors;
- in respect of an offence of violence in a domestic context, an offender's good character in relation to conduct outside the home should generally be of no relevance where there is a proven pattern of behaviour;

- assertions that the offence has been provoked by conduct of the victim need to be treated with great care, both in determining whether they have a factual basis and in considering whether the circumstances of the alleged conduct amounts to provocation sufficient to mitigate the seriousness of the offence;
- where the custody threshold is only just crossed, so that if a custodial sentence is imposed it will be a short sentence, the court will wish to consider whether the better option is a suspended sentence order or a community order, including in either case a requirement to attend an accredited domestic violence programme. Such an option will only be appropriate where the court is satisfied that the offender genuinely intends to reform his or her behaviour and that there is a real prospect of rehabilitation being successful. A pre-sentence report should be requested to assess the suitability of such an option.

Refer to paragraphs 4.1 to 4.4 of the SGC guideline for guidance regarding the relevance of the victim's wishes as to sentence.

Aggravating factors

3. The following aggravating factors may be of particular relevance to offences committed in a domestic context and should be read alongside the general factors set out on the pullout card:

Factors indicating higher culpability

(1) Abuse of trust and abuse of power
(2) Using contact arrangements with a child to instigate an offence
(3) Proven history of violence or threats by the offender in a domestic setting
(4) History of disobedience to court orders

Factors indicating a greater degree of harm

(1) Victim is particularly vulnerable
(2) Impact on children

Hate Crime

Racial or religious aggravation – statutory provisions

1. Sections 29 to 32 of the Crime and Disorder Act 1998 create specific racially or religiously aggravated offences, which have higher maximum penalties than the non-aggravated versions of those offences. The individual offence guidelines indicate whether there is a specifically aggravated form of the offence.

2. An offence is racially or religiously aggravated for the purposes of sections 29–32 of the Act if the offender demonstrates hostility towards the victim based on his or her membership (or presumed membership) of a racial or religious group, or if the offence is racially or religiously motivated.[2]

3. For all other offences, section 145 of the Criminal Justice Act 2003 provides that the court must regard racial or religious aggravation as an aggravating factor.

4. The court should not treat an offence as racially or religiously aggravated for the purposes of section 145 where a racially or religiously aggravated form of the offence was charged but resulted in an acquittal. The court should not normally treat an offence as racially or religiously aggravated if a racially or religiously aggravated form of the offence was available but was not charged.[4] **Consult your legal adviser for further guidance in these situations.**

Aggravation related to disability, sexual orientation or transgender identity – statutory provisions

5. Under section 146 of the Criminal Justice Act 2003, the court must treat as an aggravating factor the fact that:

- an offender demonstrated hostility towards the victim based on his or her disability, sexual orientation or transgender identity (or presumed disability, sexual orientation or transgender identity); or
- the offence was motivated by hostility towards persons who have a particular disability, who are of a particular sexual orientation or who are transgender.

Approach to sentencing

6. A court should not conclude that offending involved aggravation related to race, religion, disability, sexual orientation or transgender identity without first putting the offender on notice and allowing him or her to challenge the allegation.

7. When sentencing any offence where such aggravation is found to be present, the following approach should be followed. This applies both to the specific racially or religiously aggravated offences under the Crime and Disorder Act 1998 and to offences which are regarded as aggravated under section 145 or 146 of the Criminal Justice Act 2003:

- sentencers should first determine the appropriate sentence, leaving aside the element of aggravation related to race, religion, disability, sexual orientation or transgender identity but taking into account all other aggravating or mitigating factors;
- the sentence should then be increased to take account of the aggravation related to race, religion, disability, sexual orientation or transgender identity;
- the increase may mean that a more onerous penalty of the same type is appropriate, or that the threshold for a more severe type of sentence is passed;
- the sentencer must state in open court that the offence was aggravated by reason of race, religion, disability, sexual orientation or transgender identity;
- the sentencer should state what the sentence would have been without that element of aggravation.

8. The extent to which the sentence is increased will depend on the seriousness of the aggravation. The following factors could be taken as indicating a high level of aggravation:

Offender's intention

- The element of aggravation based on race, religion, disability, sexual orientation or transgender identity was planned
- The offence was part of a pattern of offending by the offender
- The offender was a member of, or was associated with, a group promoting hostility based on race, religion, disability, sexual orientation or transgender identity
- The incident was deliberately set up to be offensive or humiliating to the victim or to the group of which the victim is a member

Impact on the victim or others

- The offence was committed in the victim's home
- The victim was providing a service to the public
- The timing or location of the offence was calculated to maximise the harm or distress it caused
- The expressions of hostility were repeated or prolonged
- The offence caused fear and distress throughout a local community or more widely
- The offence caused particular distress to the victim and/or the victim's family.

9. At the lower end of the scale, the aggravation may be regarded as less serious if:

- It was limited in scope or duration
- The offence was not motivated by hostility on the basis of race, religion, disability, sexual orientation or transgender identity, and the element of hostility or abuse was minor or incidental

10. In these guidelines, the specific racially or religiously aggravated offences under the Crime and Disorder Act 1998 are addressed on the same page as the 'basic offence'; the starting points and ranges indicated on the guideline relate to the 'basic' (ie non-aggravated) offence. The increase for the element of racial or religious aggravation may result in a sentence above the range; **this will not constitute a departure from the guideline for which reasons must be given.**

ROAD TRAFFIC OFFENCES – DISQUALIFICATION

Obligatory disqualification

1. Some offences carry obligatory disqualification for a minimum of 12 months.[1] The minimum period is automatically increased where there have been certain previous convictions and disqualifications

2. An offender must be disqualified for at least two years if he or she has been disqualified two or more times for a period of at least 56 days in the three years preceding the commission of the offence.[2] The following disqualifications are to be disregarded for the purposes of this provision:

- interim disqualification;
- disqualification where vehicle used for the purpose of crime;
- disqualification for stealing or taking a vehicle or going equipped to steal or take a vehicle.

3. An offender must be disqualified for at least three years if he or she is convicted of one of the following offences *and* has within the ten years preceding the commission of the offence been convicted of any of these offences:[3]

- causing death by careless driving when under the influence of drink or drugs;
- driving or attempting to drive while unfit;
- driving or attempting to drive with excess alcohol;
- failing to provide a specimen (drive/attempting to drive).

4. The individual offence guidelines above indicate whether disqualification is mandatory for the offence and the applicable minimum period. **Consult your legal adviser for further guidance.**

Special Reasons

5. The period of disqualification may be reduced or avoided if there are special reasons.[4] These must relate to the offence; circumstances peculiar to the offender cannot constitute special reasons.[5] The Court of Appeal has established that, to constitute a special reason, a matter must:[6]

- be a mitigating or extenuating circumstance;
- not amount in law to a defence to the charge;
- be directly connected with the commission of the offence;
- be one which the court ought properly to take into consideration when imposing sentence.

Consult your legal adviser for further guidance on special reasons applications

'Totting up' disqualification

6. Disqualification for a **minimum** of six months must be ordered if an offender incurs 12 penalty points or more within a three-year period.[7] The minimum period may be automatically increased if the offender has been disqualified within the preceding three years. Totting up disqualifications, unlike other disqualifications, erase all penalty points.

7. The period of a totting up disqualification can be reduced or avoided for exceptional hardship or other mitigating circumstances. No account is to be taken of hardship that is not exceptional hardship or circumstances alleged to make the offence not serious. Any circumstances taken into account in the preceding three years to reduce or avoid a totting disqualification must be disregarded.[8]

8. **Consult your legal adviser for further guidance on exceptional hardship applications.**

Discretionary disqualification

9. Whenever an offender is convicted of an endorsable offence or of taking a vehicle without consent, the court has a discretionary power to disqualify instead of imposing penalty points. The individual offence guidelines above indicate whether the offence is endorsable and the number or range of penalty points it carries.

10. The number of variable points or the period of disqualification should reflect the seriousness of the offence. Some of the individual offence guidelines above include penalty points and/or periods of disqualification in the sentence starting points and ranges; however, the court is not precluded from sentencing outside the range where the facts justify it. Where a disqualification is for less than 56 days, there are some differences in effect compared with disqualification for a longer period; in particular, the licence will automatically come back into effect at the end of the disqualification period (instead of requiring application by the driver) and the disqualification is not taken into account for the purpose of increasing subsequent obligatory periods of disqualification.[9]

11. In some cases in which the court is considering discretionary disqualification, the offender may already have sufficient penalty points on his or her licence that he or she would be liable to a 'totting up' disqualification if further points were imposed. In these circumstances, the court should impose penalty points rather than discretionary disqualification so that the minimum totting up disqualification period applies (see paragraph 7 above).

Disqualification until a test is passed

12. Where an offender is convicted of dangerous driving, the court must order disqualification until an extended driving test is passed.

13. The court has discretion to disqualify until a test is passed where an offender is convicted of any endorsable offence.[10] Where disqualification is obligatory, the extended test applies. In other cases, it will be the ordinary test.

14. An offender disqualified as a 'totter' under the penalty points provisions may also be ordered to re-take a driving test; in this case, the extended test applies.

15. The discretion to order a re-test is likely to be exercised where there is evidence of inexperience, incompetence or infirmity, or the disqualification period is lengthy (that is, the offender is going to be 'off the road' for a considerable time).

Reduced period of disqualification for completion of rehabilitation course

16. Where an offender is disqualified for 12 months or more in respect of an alcohol-related driving offence, the court may order that the period of disqualification will be reduced if the offender satisfactorily completes an approved rehabilitation course.[11]

17. Before offering an offender the opportunity to attend a course, the court must be satisfied that an approved course is available and must inform the offender of the effect of the order, the fees that the offender is required to pay, and when he or she must pay them.

18. The court should also explain that the offender may be required to satisfy the Secretary of State that he or she does not have a drink problem and is fit to drive before the offender's licence will be returned at the end of the disqualification period.[12]

19. In general, a court should consider offering the opportunity to attend a course to all offenders convicted of a relevant offence for the first time. The court should be willing to consider offering an offender the opportunity to attend a second course where it considers there are good reasons. It will not usually be appropriate to give an offender the opportunity to attend a third course.

20. The reduction must be at least three months but cannot be more than one quarter of the total period of disqualification:

- a period of 12 months disqualification must be reduced to nine months;
- in other cases, a reduction of one week should be made for every month of the disqualification so that, for example, a disqualification of 24 months will be reduced by 24 weeks.

21. When it makes the order, the court must specify a date for completion of the course which is at least two months before the end of the reduced period of disqualification.

Disqualification in the offender's absence

22. When considering disqualification in absence the starting point should be that disqualification in absence should be imposed if there is no reason to believe the defendant is not aware of the proceedings, and after the statutory notice has been served pursuant to section 11(4) of the 1980 Act where appropriate. Disqualification should not be imposed in absence where there is evidence that the defendant has an acceptable reason for not attending or where there are reasons to believe it would be contrary to the interests of justice to do so.

New drivers

23. Drivers who incur six points or more during the two-year probationary period after passing the driving test will have their licence revoked automatically by the Secretary of State; they will be able to drive only after application for a provisional licence pending the passing of a further test.[13]

24. An offender liable for an endorsement which will cause the licence to be revoked under the new drivers' provisions may ask the court to disqualify rather than impose points. This will avoid the requirement to take a further test. Generally, this would be inappropriate since it would circumvent the clear intention of Parliament.

Extension period of disqualification from driving where a custodial sentence is also imposed

25. Where a court imposes disqualification in addition to a custodial sentence or a detention and training order, the court must extend the disqualification period by one half of the custodial sentence or detention or training order to take into account the period the offender will spend in custody. This will avoid a driving ban expiring, or being significantly diminished, during the period the offender is in custody (s 35a Criminal Justice and Courts Act, 2015). Periods of time spent on remand or subject to an electronically monitored curfew do not apply.

26. Where a rehabilitation course is completed, any extension period is disregarded when reducing the ban.

27. For example where a court imposes a 6 month custodial sentence and a disqualification period of 12 months, the ban will be extended to 15 months. Where a rehabilitation course is completed, the reduction will remain at a maximum of 3 months.

[1] Road Traffic Offenders Act 1988, s 34.
[2] Road Traffic Offenders Act 1988, s 34(4).
[3] Road Traffic Offenders Act 1988, s 34(3).
[4] Road Traffic Offenders Act 1988, s 34(1).
[5] *Whittal v Kirby* [1946] 2 All ER 552 (CA).
[6] *R v Wickens* (1958) 42 Cr App R 436 (CA).
[7] Road Traffic Offenders Act 1988, s 35.
[8] Road Traffic Offenders Act 1988, s 35.
[9] Road Traffic Offenders Act 1988, ss 34(4), 35(2), 37(1A).
[10] Road Traffic Offenders Act 1988, s 36(4).
[11] Road Traffic Offenders Act 1988, s 34A.
[12] Road Traffic Act 1988.
[13] Road Traffic (New Drivers) Act 1995.

OUT OF COURT DISPOSALS

1. There are several alternatives to formal charges available to police and CPS when dealing with adults, including cannabis and khat warnings, penalty notices for disorder, community resolution, simple cautions and conditional cautions.

Cannabis or khat warning

2. A cannabis or khat warning may be given where the offender is found in possession of a small amount of cannabis or khat consistent with personal use and the offender admits the elements of the offence. The drug is confiscated and a record of the warning will be made on local systems. The warning is not a conviction and should not be regarded as an aggravating factor when sentencing for subsequent offences.

Simple caution

3. A simple caution may be issued where there is evidence that the offender has committed an offence, the offender admits to the offence, it is not in the public interest to prosecute and the offender agrees to being given the caution.

4. When sentencing an offender who has received a simple caution on a previous occasion:

- the caution is not a previous conviction and, therefore, is not a statutory aggravating factor;
- however, the caution will form part of the offender's criminal record and if the caution is recent and is relevant to the current offence it may be considered to be an aggravating factor.

Conditional caution

5. A **conditional caution**[1] requires an offender to comply with conditions, as an alternative to prosecution. The conditions that can be attached must be rehabilitative, reparative and/or a financial penalty. (If the offender is a "relevant foreign offender" – that is someone without permission to enter or stay in the UK, conditions can be offered that have the object of effecting departure from and preventing return to the UK.) Before the caution can be given, the offender must admit the offence and consent to the conditions.

6. When sentencing an offender who has received a conditional caution in respect of an earlier offence:

- a conditional caution is not a previous conviction and, therefore, is not a statutory aggravating factor;
- however, if the conditional caution is recent and is relevant to the current offence it may be considered to be an aggravating factor;
- the offender's response to the caution may properly influence the court's assessment of the offender's suitability for a particular sentence, so long as it remains within the limits established by the seriousness of the current offence.

Approach to sentencing for offence for which offender was cautioned but failed to comply
with conditions

7. If the offender fails, without reasonable cause, to comply with the conditional caution, he or she may be prosecuted for the original offence. When sentencing in such a case:

- the offender's non-compliance with the conditional caution does not increase the seriousness of the original offence and must not be regarded as an aggravating factor;
- the offender's non-compliance may be relevant to selection of the type of sentence. For example, it may indicate that it is inappropriate to include certain requirements as part of a community order. The circumstances of the offender's failure to satisfy the conditions, and any partial compliance, will be relevant to this assessment.

Penalty notices - fixed penalty notices and penalty notices for disorder

8. Penalty notices may be issued as an alternative to prosecution in respect of a range of offences. Unlike conditional cautions, an admission of guilt is not a prerequisite to issuing a penalty notice.

9. An offender who is issued with a penalty notice may nevertheless be prosecuted for the offence if he or she:

- asks to be tried for the offence; or
- fails to pay the penalty within the period stipulated in the notice and the prosecutor decides to proceed with charges.[2]

10. When sentencing in cases in which a penalty notice was available:

- the fact that the offender did not take advantage of the penalty (whether that was by requesting a hearing or failing to pay within the specified timeframe) does not increase the seriousness of the offence and must not be regarded as an aggravating factor. The appropriate sentence must be determined in accordance with the sentencing principles set out above (including the amount of any fine, which must take an offender's financial circumstances into account), disregarding the availability of the penalty;

- where a penalty notice could not be offered or taken up for reasons unconnected with the offence itself, such as administrative difficulties outside the control of the offender, the starting point should be a fine equivalent to the amount of the penalty and no order of costs should be imposed. The offender should not be disadvantaged by the unavailability of the penalty notice in these circumstances. A list of offences for which penalty notices are available, and the amount of the penalty, is set out in Annex B.

11. Where an offender has had previous penalty notice(s), the fact that an offender has previously been issued with a penalty notice does not increase the seriousness of the current offence and must not be regarded as an aggravating factor. It may, however, properly influence the court's assessment of the offender's suitability for a particular sentence, so long as it remains within the limits established by the seriousness of the current offence.

Community Resolution

12. Community resolution is an informal non-statutory disposal used for dealing with less serious crime and anti-social behaviour where the offender accepts responsibility. The views of the victim (where there is one) are taken into account in reaching an informal agreement between the parties which can involve restorative justice techniques.

13. When sentencing an offender who has received a community resolution for an earlier offence:

- A community resolution is not a conviction and is therefore not a statutory aggravating factor, but if recent and relevant to the offence it may be considered to be an aggravating factor.

---

[1] 6riminal Justice Act 2003, s 22.

[2] 1n some cases of non-payment, the penalty is automatically registered and enforceable as a fine without need for recourse to the courts. This procedure applies to penalty notices for disorder and fixed penalty notices issued in respect of certain road traffic offences but not to fixed penalty notices issued for most other criminal offences.

Victim personal statements

Victim personal statements (VPS) give victims a formal opportunity to say how a crime has affected them. Where the victim has chosen to make such a statement, a court should consider and take it into account prior to passing sentence.

The Criminal Practice Directions[1] emphasise that:

- evidence of the effects of an offence on the victim must be in the form of a witness statement under section 9 of the Criminal Justice Act 1967 or an expert's report;
- the statement must be served on the defence prior to sentence;
- except where inferences can properly be drawn from the nature of or circumstances surrounding the offence, the court must not make assumptions unsupported by evidence about the effects of an offence on the victim;
- at the discretion of the court the VPS may also be read aloud in whole or in part or it may be summarised. If it is to be read aloud the court should also determine who should do so. In making these decisions the court should take into account the victim's preferences, and follow them unless there is a good reason not to do so (for example, inadmissible or potentially harmful content). Court hearings should not be adjourned solely to allow the victim to attend court to read the VPS;
- the court must pass what it judges to be the appropriate sentence having regard to the circumstances of the offence and the offender, taking into account, so far as the court considers it appropriate, the consequences to the victim;
- the opinions of the victim or the victim's close relatives as to what the sentence should be are not relevant.

See also the guidance on page 155 particularly with reference to the victim's views as to any compensation order that may be imposed.

---

[1] https://www.justice.gov.uk/courts/procedure-rules/criminal/rulesmenu

Prevalence and community impact statements

Taken from the Sentencing Guidelines Council's definitive guideline *Overarching Principles: Seriousness.*

The seriousness of an individual case should be judged on its own dimensions of harm and culpability rather than as part of a collective social harm.

However, there may be exceptional local circumstances that arise which may lead a court to decide that prevalence should influence sentencing levels. The pivotal issue in such cases will be the harm being caused to the community. It is essential that sentencers both have supporting evidence from an external source (for example a community impact statement compiled by the police) to justify claims that a particular crime is prevalent in their area and are satisfied that there is a compelling need to treat the offence more seriously than elsewhere. A community impact statement is a document providing information to the court about the impact of offences on the community.

The key factor in determining whether sentencing levels should be enhanced in response to prevalence will be the level of harm being caused in the locality. Enhanced sentences should be exceptional and in response to exceptional circumstances. Sentencers must sentence within the sentencing guidelines once the prevalence has been addressed.

ANNEX A

C.12 The lists below identify offences covered in the MCSG for which particular ancillary orders are available. In all cases, consult your legal adviser regarding available orders and their specific requirements and effects.

Football banning orders – Football Spectators Act 1989, s 14A

Available on conviction of a 'relevant offence', listed in schedule 1 of the Football Spectators Act 1989. These include:

- possession of alcohol or being drunk while entering/trying to enter ground – Sporting Events (Control of Alcohol etc) Act 1985, s 2;
- disorderly behaviour – Public Order Act 1986, s 5 – committed:
  (a) during a period relevant to a football match (see below) at any premises while the offender was at, or was entering or leaving or trying to enter or leave, the premises;
  (b) on a journey to or from a football match and the court makes a declaration that the offence related to football matches; or
  (c) during a period relevant to a football match (see below) and the court makes a declaration that the offence related to that match;
- any offence involving the use or threat of violence towards another person committed:
  (a) during a period relevant to a football match (see below) at any premises while the offender was at, or was entering or leaving or trying to enter or leave, the premises;
  (b) on a journey to or from a football match and the court makes a declaration that the offence related to football matches; or
  (c) during a period relevant to a football match (see below) and the court makes a declaration that the offence related to that match;
- any offence involving the use or threat of violence towards property committed:
  (a) during a period relevant to a football match (see below) at any premises while the offender was at, or was entering or leaving or trying to enter or leave, the premises;
  (b) on a journey to or from a football match and the court makes a declaration that the offence related to football matches; or
  (c) during a period relevant to a football match (see below) and the court makes a declaration that the offence related to that match;
- any offence involving the use, carrying or possession of an offensive weapon or firearm committed:
  (a) during a period relevant to a football match (see below) at any premises while the offender was at, or was entering or leaving or trying to enter or leave, the premises;
  (b) on a journey to or from a football match and the court makes a declaration that the offence related to football matches; or
  (c) during a period relevant to a football match (see below) and the court makes a declaration that the offence related to that match;
- drunk and disorderly – Criminal Justice Act 1967, s 91(1) – committed on a journey to or from a football match and the court makes a declaration that the offence related to football matches;
- driving/attempting to drive when unfit through drink or drugs – Road Traffic Act 1988, s 4 – committed on a journey to or from a football match and the court makes a declaration that the offence related to football matches;
- in charge of a vehicle when unfit through drink or drugs – Road Traffic Act 1988, s 4 – committed on a journey to or from a football match and the court makes a declaration that the offence related to football matches;
- driving/attempting to drive with excess alcohol – Road Traffic Act 1988, s 5 – committed on a journey to or from a football match and the court makes a declaration that the offence related to football matches;
- in charge of a vehicle with excess alcohol – Road Traffic Act 1988, s 5 – committed on a journey to or from a football match and the court makes a declaration that the offence related to football matches;
- any offence under the Football (Offences) Act 1991;
- unauthorised sale of tickets – Criminal Justice and Public Order Act 1994, s 166.

The following periods are 'relevant' to a football match[1]:

(a) the period beginning:
  (i) two hours before the start of the match; or
  (ii) two hours before the time at which it is advertised to start; or
  (iii) with the time at which spectators are first admitted to the premises, whichever is the earliest, and ending one hour after the end of the match;
(b) where a match advertised to start at a particular time on a particular day is postponed to a later day, or does not take place, the period in the advertised day beginning two hours before and ending one hour after that time.

Forfeiture or suspension of personal liquor licence – Licensing Act 2003, s 129

Available on conviction of a 'relevant offence', listed in schedule 4 of the Licensing Act 2003. These include:

- an offence under the Licensing Act 2003;
- an offence under the Firearms Act 1968;
- theft – Theft Act 1968, s 1;
- burglary – Theft Act 1968, s 9;
- abstracting electricity – Theft Act 1968, s 13;
- handling stolen goods – Theft Act 1968, s 22;
- going equipped for theft – Theft Act 1968, s 25;
- production of a controlled drug – Misuse of Drugs Act 1971, s 4(2);
- supply of a controlled drug – Misuse of Drugs Act 1971, s 4(3);

- possession of a controlled drug with intent to supply – Misuse of Drugs Act 1971, s 5(3);
- evasion of duty – Customs and Excise Management Act 1979, s 170 (excluding s 170(1)(*a*));
- driving/attempting to drive when unfit through drink or drugs – Road Traffic Act 1988, s 4;
- in charge of a vehicle when unfit through drink or drugs – Road Traffic Act 1988, s 4;
- driving/attempting to drive with excess alcohol – Road Traffic Act 1988, s 5;
- in charge of a vehicle with excess alcohol – Road Traffic Act 1988, s 5;
- unauthorised use of trade mark where the goods in question are or include alcohol – Trade Marks Act 1994, ss 92(1) and 92(2);
- sexual assault – Sexual Offences Act 2003, s 3;
- exploitation of prostitution – Sexual Offences Act 2003, ss 52 and 53;
- exposure – Sexual Offences Act 2003, s 66;
- voyeurism – Sexual Offences Act 2003, s 67;
- a violent offence, being any offence which leads, or is intended or likely to lead, to death or to physical injury.

Sexual Harm Prevention Orders

Available in respect of an offence listed in schedule 3[2] or 5 of the Sexual Offences Act 2003. These include:

- possession of indecent photograph of a child – Criminal Justice Act 1988, s 160;
- sexual assault – Sexual Offences Act 2003, s 3
- exposure – Sexual Offences Act 2003, s 66
- voyeurism – Sexual Offences Act 2003, s. 67
- threats to kill – Offences against the Person Act 1861, s. 16;
- wounding/causing grievous bodily harm – Offences against the Person Act 1861, s. 20;
- assault with intent to resist arrest – Offences against the Person Act 1861, s. 38;
- assault occasioning actual bodily harm – Offences against the Person Act 1861, s. 47;
- burglary with intent to inflict grievous bodily harm or to do unlawful damage to a building/anything within it – Theft Act 1968, s. 9;
- arson – Criminal Damage Act 1971, s. 1;
- violent disorder – Public Order Act 1986, s. 2;
- affray – Public Order Act 1986, s. 3;
- harassment – conduct causing fear of violence – Protection from Harassment Act 1994, s. 4;
- racially or religiously aggravated wounding/causing grievous bodily harm – Crime and Disorder Act 1998, s. 29;
- racially or religiously aggravated assault occasioning actual bodily harm – Crime and Disorder Act 1998, s. 29;
- racially or religiously aggravated common assault – Crime and Disorder Act 1998, s. 29;
- racially or religiously aggravated threatening behaviour – Crime and Disorder Act 1998, s. 31(1)(*a*);
- racially or religiously aggravated disorderly behaviour with intent to cause harassment, alarm or distress – Crime and Disorder Act 1998, s. 31(1)(*b*);
- exploitation of prostitution – Sexual Offences Act 2003, ss. 52 and 53.

---

[1] Football Spectators Act 1989, Sch.1 para.4.
[2] Sexual Offences Act s 106(14) provides that any conditions in Sch. 3 relating to the age of the offender or the victim, or the sentence imposed on the offender may be disregarded in making a Sexual Offences Prevention Order and Sexual Offences Act s 1038 (9) contains the same provision in respect of Sexual Harm Prevention Orders.

ANNEX B: OFFENCES FOR WHICH PENALTY NOTICES ARE AVAILABLE

C.13 The tables below list the offences covered in the MCSG for which penalty notices are available and the amount of the penalty. **Consult your legal adviser for further guidance.**

Penalty notices for disorder

Offence	Legislation	Amount
Criminal damage (where damage under £500 in value, and not normally where damage over £300)	Criminal Damage Act 1971, s. 1	£90
Disorderly behaviour	Public Order Act 1986, s. 5	£90
Drunk and disorderly	Criminal Justice Act 1967, s. 91	£90
Sale of alcohol to drunk person on relevant premises (not including off-licenses)	Licensing Act 2003, s. 141	£90
Sale of alcohol to person under 18 (staff only; licensees should be subject of a summons)	Licensing Act 2003, s. 146	£90
Theft from a shop (where goods under £200 in value, and not normally where goods over £100)	Theft Act 1968, s. 1	£90

Fixed penalty notices

Offence	Legislation	Amount	Penalty points
Brakes, steering or tyres defective	Road Traffic Act 1988, s. 41A	£100	3
Breach of other construction and use requirements	Road Traffic Act 1988, s. 42	£100 or £200	3
Careless driving	Road Traffic Act 1988, s. 3	£100	3
Driving other than in accordance with licence	Road Traffic Act 1988, s. 87(1)	£100	3
Failing to comply with police officer signal	Road Traffic Act 1988, s. 35	£100	3
Failing to comply with traffic sign	Road Traffic Act 1988, s. 36	£100	3
Failing to supply details of driver's identity	Road Traffic Act 1988, s. 172	£200	6
No insurance	Road Traffic Act 1988, s. 143	£300	6
No test certificate	Road Traffic Act 1988, s. 47	£100	–
Overloading/exceeding axle weight	Road Traffic Act 1988, s. 41B	£100 to £300	–
Pelican/zebra crossing contravention	Road Traffic Regulation Act 1984, s. 25(5)	£100	3
Railway fare evasion (where penalty notice scheme in operation by train operator)	Railways (Penalty Fares) Regulations 1994	£20 or twice the full single fare to next stop, whichever is greater	–
Seat belt offences	Road Traffic Act 1988, s. 14 and s. 15(2) or 15(4)	£100	–
School non-attendance	Education Act 1996, s. 444(1)	£60 if paid within 21 days; £120 if paid within 28 days	–
Speeding	Road Traffic Regulation Act 1984, s. 89(1)	£100	3
Using hand-held mobile phone while driving	Road Traffic Act 1988, s. 41D	£100	3
Using vehicle in dangerous condition	Road Traffic Act 1988, s. 40A	£100	3

PART I
MAGISTRATES' COURTS, PROCEDURE

MAGISTRATES' COURTS

CONTEMPT OF COURT

1.30 Initial procedure to be followed *At the end of Note 1 add the following text:* 'Rules had existed in civil and family proceedings long before they were introduced into the Criminal Procedure Rules, and the courts had considered in a number of cases the effect of non-compliance to the letter of the prescribed procedures; there is no justification for adopting a different approach to failure to comply with the requirements of Part 48 of the Criminal Procedure Rules 2015: In *Re Yaxley-Lennon (aka Tommy Robinson)* [2018] EWCA Crim 1856, (2018) The Times, August 9.'

DISQUALIFICATION OF MAGISTRATES

1.40 Apparent bias *Insert text on the last para of page 26 after footnote marker 16, create Note, and renumber subsequent Notes accordingly and continue narrative in new para:* 'It is quite proper for a judge to express preliminary views about the strength or weakness of each party's case during the proceedings, and this will only indicate bias if they suggested the judge had already come to a final decision before hearing the whole of the evidence and arguments[17].'

---

[17] *Bubbles and Wine Ltd v Lusha* [2018] EWCA Civ 468, [2018] BLR 341.

INVESTIGATION OF OFFENCES

POWERS OF ENTRY TO PREMISES, SEARCH AND SEIZURE

1.72 Search warrants *At the end of note 3 in a new para insert the following new text:* 'See also *R (on the application of Brook and others) v Preston Crown Court and another* [2018] EWHC 2024 (Admin) which, despite the name, relates to search warrants issued by justices.

This was a case where the evidence before the Crown Court included material obtained under three search warrants. The High Court identified a series of procedural failures in the issue of the warrants. All three warrants were held to be unlawful, and so, therefore, were the resulting searches. As a result the evidence obtained under one of the warrants was ruled inadmissible; the decision re admissibility on the remainder was left to the Crown Court.

The following defects were identified in the warrant procedure:

(1) No note was made of additional information given orally by the applicant.
(2) The identification of the material sought in the warrant was expressed insufficiently precisely, to the extent that the warrant was unlawful.
(3) However the High Court accepted that the list of items to be sought could not always be very specific at the beginning of an investigation. So it did not disapprove of references to "electronic communication equipment, electronic data storage equipment, or mobile communication devices, including telephones and tablets".
(4) But it did consider that items such as "all records of communication whether physical, electronic or otherwise, between x, y and z " or "Financial documentation" were far too broad, particularly bearing in mind that x and y were father and son, and so likely to be communicating daily about all sorts of things;
(5) Some attempt should have been made to circumscribe those items, either in terms of their content or in terms of timescale, and the nature of the financial dealings.
(6) The items sought must always been set out in such a way that the householder would know what could and could not be taken in the search.
(7) The Justice's reasons on the third warrant were defective in that she had received no evidence of one of the two grounds she gave. It was therefore unclear if the Justice would have issued the warrant if restricted to a single ground.'

In existing Note 11 replace the ALL ER (D) citation of R (Haralambous) v Crown Court at St Albans as follows: [2018] 2 ALL ER 303, [2018] 1 Cr App R 26, [2018] Crim L R 672.

CRIMINAL LAW: GENERAL

GUILTY MIND (MENS REA)

1.128   Automatism, insanity, mental malfunction   *In existing Note 3 replace the All ER (D) citation of Loake v CPS as follows:* '[2018] 2 WLR 1159, [2018] 1 Cr App R 15, [2018] Crim LR 336.'

PARTICIPATION IN CRIME

1.131   Liability of principals   *Add to existing Note 12:* 'See also *R v Crilly* [2018] EWCA Crim 168, [2018] 2 Cr App R 12.'

DEFENCES

1.140   Self defence and the use of force in the prevention of crime or the making of an arrest   *After the fourth para (ending 'unlawful force*[8]*') .insert the following new paras.):*

Section 76(5) Criminal Justice and Immigration Act 2008 provides that the defence of self-defence is not available where a mistaken belief is attributable to intoxication that was voluntarily induced.

The Court considered the wording of s 76(5) in the case of *R v. Taj* [2018] EWCA Crim 1743.

The Court held that the word "attributable" extended the scope of s 76(5) to encompass both (a) intoxication at the time of the incident; and (b) a state of mind immediately and proximately consequent upon earlier drink or drug-taking.

Insert text after reference to existing Note 13 in new para, create Note and continue narrative in new para: 'Self-defence is available as a defence to obstructing a police officer in the execution of his duty[14].

---

[14] *Oraki v Crown Prosecution Service* [2018] EWHC 115 (Admin), [2018 1 Cr App R 27.

CRIMINAL PROCEEDINGS IN MAGISTRATES' COURTS

STARTING A PROSECUTION IN A MAGISTRATES' COURT

1.152   Application for summons, etc *Time limits*   *Insert text after reference to existing Note 2, create note and renumber subsequent Notes accordingly:* It is permissible to amend an information for an indictable offence to a summary only offence outside the six-month time limit provided the original information was laid within that time limit[3].

---

[3] *Dougall v Crown Prosecution Service* [2018] EWHC 1367 (Admin), [2018] Crim L R 763 (the original charge of assault occasioning actual bodily harm, which was sought to be amended to assault by beating, was laid eight months after the alleged offence; the proposed substitution was, consequently, time-barred by s 127 of the MCA 1980).

CRIMINAL PROCEDURE RULES AND THE OVERRIDING OBJECTIVE

1.165B   Case management *Case management where the defendant may be suffering from mental health*   *Insert this new material after para 1.165A:*

Unlike the Crown Court[1], there is no statutory scheme in the magistrates' court for determining fitness to stand trial. However, the mental health of the defendant may bear on whether or not he/she can raise a defence of lack of mens rea or insanity. Mental disorder can also result in the making of a hospital or guardianship order on conviction, or without a conviction where the court is satisfied that the defendant did the act or made the omission charged[2].

It is, accordingly, important to identify as early as possible the appropriate course to take where there are grounds to believe the defendant may be suffering from mental disorder. Consequently, r 3.28 has been added to the Criminal Procedure Rules 2015[3]. This imposes detailed procedural requirements for commissioning a medical report about a defendant's mental health other than for sentencing purposes[4]. (Reports for sentencing purposes are covered by new r 28.8.)

---

[1] Where the Criminal Procedure (Insanity) Act 1964 applies.
[2] See the Mental Health Act 1983, s 37, in PART VII, MISCELLANEOUS OFFENCES AND CIVIL PROCEEDINGS.
[3] By the Criminal Procedure (Amendment No 2) Rules 2018, SI 2019/847.
[4] As to payment, the view is taken that section 19(3B)(b)(i)of the Prosecution of Offences Act 1985 (in this PART, post) embraces not only reports concerned with final disposal but also reports to assist in determining the appropriate procedural course to that stage.

PRELIMINARY ISSUES FOR CRIMINAL PROCEEDINGS IN MAGISTRATES' COURTS

1.191   Objection to the information or charge *Amendment of information or summons*   *Insert text after reference to existing Note 14, create note and renumber subsequent Notes accordingly:* 'Where the amendment is from an indictable offence to a summary only offence, the original information must, however, have been laid within six months[15].'

¹⁵ *Dougall v Crown Prosecution Service* [2018] EWHC 1367 (Admin), [2018] Crim L R 763 (the original charge of assault occasioning actual bodily, which was sought to be amended to assault by beating, was laid eight months after the alleged offence; the proposed substitution was, consequently, time-barred by s 127 of the MCA 1980.

ABUSE OF THE PROCESS OF THE COURT

1.196   General principles and magistrates' courts' jurisdiction   *At the end of Note 9 in a new para add the following new material as follows:*

'For a further case on entrapment and whether that might amount to an abuse of process see *R v TL* [2018] EWCA Crim 1821.

The issue in this case was whether the trial judge, in staying proceedings in the Crown Court against *TL*, had erred in applying the entrapment principles articulated by the House of Lords in *R v. Loosely* [2001] UKHL 53; [2001] 1 WLR 2060 to non-state actors. The Court of Appeal concluded that the judge had erred; the test was essentially whether the conduct of the non-state actor would compromise the court's integrity.

On the application of the defence at trial, proceedings against *TL* were stayed as an abuse of process. *TL* faced one count on the indictment, namely that he attempted to meet a child following sexual grooming, contrary to s 1(1) of the Criminal Attempts Act 1981. The essence of the allegation was that he communicated via WhatsApp with a person he believed to be a girl of 14 years old and arranged for that girl to attend his flat and take part in a threesome with his girlfriend. *TL* was in fact communicating with an adult male, Mr U, who, a member of a group of "Predator Hunters" had pretended to be that 14-year-old girl. The application relied on the entrapment principles set out in the House of Lords decision in *R v. Loosely* [2001] UKHL 53; [2001] 1 WLR 2060.

The prosecutor appealed against the judge's terminating ruling, contending that: (a) the judge erred in concluding that the principles articulated in *Loosely* could be applied, without modification, to non-state actors and (b), in any event, if the activities of Mr U had been undertaken by the police, there would have been no abuse of process.

Loosely was a case which concerned police conduct and the use of undercover officers, in which it was held that the court was required to:

" . . . balance the need to uphold the rule of law by convicting and punishing those who committed crimes and the need to prevent law enforcement agencies from acting in a manner which constituted an affront to the public conscience or offended ordinary notions of fairness."

The judge's approach allowed no distinction between the conduct of Mr U, a private citizen, and agents of the state in considering whether to stay proceedings as an abuse of process. Since he erred in that respect, the judge's conclusion could not be supported.

The Court endorsed the approach of Golding J in *Council for the Regulation of Health Care Professionals v The General Medical Council and Saluja* [2006] EWHC 2784 (Admin); [2007] 1 WLR 3094, [81]: 'so serious would the conduct of the non-state actor have to be that reliance upon it in the court's proceedings would compromise the court's integrity'.

In the present case Mr U had committed no offences in his course of conduct which led to *TL's* arrest. Thus, the case was far removed from a case of incitement and there was nothing in Mr U's conduct which would make it inappropriate for the prosecution to proceed.

In any event, the court concluded that if police officers had engaged in the same conduct as Mr U, an application to stay proceedings as an abuse of process would have failed.'

1.206   Res judicata; estoppel; autrefois convict/acquit; functus officio*Double jeopardy*   *Add to existing Note 1:* 'See also *R (SY) v Director of Public Prosecutions* [2018] EWHC 795 (Admin), [2018] 2 Cr App R 15, [2018] Crim L R 742 in which it was affirmed that where the proposed second charge would involve a slightly different factual matrix, but arose from the same set of circumstances, the same principles were engaged.'

REMANDS AND BAIL

1.231   Absconding or breaking conditions of bail   *Add to existing Note 1 in new para:* 'Where a defendant commits a Bail Act offence before being sent for trial, the only means by which that offence can end up in the Crown Court is by committal for sentence under s 6(6)(b) of the Bail Act 1976: *R v Osman* [2017] EWCA Crim 2178, [2018] 1 Cr App R (S) 23.'

THE COURSE OF EVIDENCE IN A CRIMINAL TRIAL

1.316   Examination in chief*Refreshing memory*   *In the third para of the narrative, add to the citation of DPP v Sugden:* '[2018] 2 Cr App R 8, [2018] RTR 17'.

1.338   Adjudication   *In existing Note 5, insert text before the ante-penultimate sentence, ie the sentence which begins 'Where the Crown Court upholds an appeal against sentence:* 'See also *R (Arthur) v*

Crown Court at Blackfriars [2017] EWHC 3416 (Admin), [2018] 2 Cr App R 4. As to amplifying reasons in a case stated, see *Marshall v Crown Prosecution Service* [2015] EWCA 2333, (2016) 180 JP 33, considered at 1.384, post.'

1.344   Conviction   *Add text to end in new para and create Note:* 'The Court of Appeal does not have the power to declare a summary trial a nullity or to quash a conviction recorded in such proceedings[15].

---

[15]   In *Re Bahbahani* [2018] EWCA Crim 95, [2018] 1 Cr App R 29, [2018] Crim L R 682.

APPEAL AND JUDICIAL REVIEW

APPEALS TO THE ADMINISTRATIVE COURT BY CASE STATED

1.381   Time limit   *In existing Note 1 insert before Crim L R citation of Mishra v Colchester Magistrates' Court:* '[2018] 1 Cr App R 24'.

1.382   When appropriate   *Insert text in new para after footnote marker 2, create Note, then renumber subsequent Notes accordingly and continue narrative in new para:* 'Where justices (or the Crown Court on appeal) refuse to state a case, the aggrieved should apply without delay for permission to bring judicial review, either to compel the justices to state a case and/or to quash the order sought to be appealed. Where the court below has already given a reasoned judgment containing all the necessary findings of fact and/or explained its refusal to state a case in terms which clearly raise the true point of law in issue, the correct course is for the single judge, if they thinks the point is properly arguable, to grant permission for judicial review which directly challenges the order complained of and thereby avoids the need for a case stated at all[3].'

---

[3]   *R v Blackfriars Crown Court ex p Sunworld* [2000] 1 WLR 2102, followed in *R (Arthur) v Crown Court* at Blackfriars [2017] EWHC 3416 (Admin), [2018] 2 Cr App R 4.'

CLAIMS FOR JUDICIAL REVIEW

1.388   *At the end of Note 3 insert the following new text:* 'Detailed legal guidance on bringing a judicial review case in the Administrative division of the High Court is available online at: www.gov.uk/government/publications/administrative-court-judicial-review-guide. The latest edition (July 2018) reflects relevant and recent legislative and practice changes.'

1.389   Discretionary remedy   *Insert text at the end and create Notes:* 'However, "Given the danger of opening unintended floodgates, my conclusion as to the application of material mistake of fact leading to unfairness being available as a ground of judicial review in the context of criminal proceedings is strictly limited to applications concerned with the determination of applications to adjourn trials in the Magistrates' Courts – which, as *Balogun v DPP* already makes clear, should only be made if the circumstances are exceptional."[11]

Mistake of fact does not extend to decision making in relation to search warrants, and subsequently established mistake of fact cannot invalidate a search warrant otherwise properly obtained[12].

---

[11]   *R (DPP) v Sunderland Magistrates' Court*, supra, per Sweeney J at para 116.
[12]   *R (Daly) v Commissioner of Police of the Metropolis* [2018] EWHC 438 (Admin), [2018] 1 WLR 2221, [2018] 2 Cr App R 19.

STATUTES

STATUTES ON PROCEDURE

1.571   Magistrates' Courts Act 1980, s 24   *At the end of Note 1 add the following new text:*

'To use s 24 of the Magistrates' Courts Act 1980, the defendant must be aged 17 or under when the court determines mode of trial. This was emphasised in the case of *R v Ford* (2018) EWCA Crim 1751, where the correct approach to take to defendants charged with indictable only offences and who turn 18 during proceedings was also set out.

In this case *D* was charged with a s 18 of the OAPA 1861 offence and appeared at the Youth Court aged 17. The case was adjourned for a few days so that the defence could read the papers. On the next appearance before a Youth court *D* was aged 18.

D pleaded to the s 18 charge (and also to possession of an offensive weapon). *D* was committed for sentence under the Powers of Criminal Courts (Sentencing) Act 2000, s 3. At the Crown Court, *D* received a 6 and a half years custodial sentence in all.

On appeal the Court of Appeal held that this decision was a nullity, assuming *inter alia* that the magistrates purported to commit *D* to the Crown Court under s 3B (because that is the section for those who require additional sentencing powers).

To use the Magistrates' Court Act 1980, s 24 (which enables those who subsequently turn 18 to be dealt with in the Youth Court) the defendant must be aged 17 when the court determines mode of trial – see *R v Islington North Juvenile Court ex parte Daley* (1982) 75 Cr App R 280 (House of Lords).

So as D was already 18 years old at mode of trial the Youth court had no power to take D's plea or commit him to the Crown Court for sentence. Everything thereafter was invalid and D's sentence was quashed and replaced by the Divisional Court.'

1.727   Senior Courts Act 1981, s 29   *At end of second para of existing Note 2, insert after the official citation of AF v Kingston CC:* '[2018] 1 Cr App R 32'.

1.764   Police and Criminal Evidence Act 1984, s 15   *At the end of para 3 in Note 10 insert the following in a new para:* In *R (Superior Import/Export Ltd) v Revenue and Customs Commissioners* [2017] EWHC 3172 (Admin), the High Court ruled that search warrants issued by a Justice were unlawful because the applicant HMRC had failed to meet the requirements of s 15 of PACE 1984 and provide sufficient information such that the Justice could properly be satisfied for the purposes of s 8(1) of PACE 1984.

First, the applicant had made no attempt whatsoever to identify the nature of the suspected fraud.

Nor was there any attempt to set out the reasonable grounds for believing that the material sought was likely to be relevant evidence.

The High Court also found that there was an unlawful delegation by the Justice, as the warrants authorised not a search for relevant material, but rather material "deemed relevant". The Court accepted the submission for the Claimants that by the use of the word "deemed" the warrants impermissibly delegated the responsibility of applying the access criteria of s 8 of PACE 1984 to HMRC officers.

1.874   Police and Criminal Evidence Act 1984, s 67   *At the end of Note 2 in a new para insert the following:* 'The Police and Criminal Evidence Act 1984 (Codes of Practice) (Revision of Codes C, E, F, and H) Order 2018, SI 2018/829 brought in to force the revised codes of practice (audio and visual recording of interviews with suspects – Codes E and F) (detention, treatment and questioning of persons by police officers – Codes C and H) with effect from 1 August 2018.'

1.882   Prosecution of Offences Act 1985, s 3   *In existing Note 1, third para replace the All ER (D) citation of R (Hayes) v CPS with:* '[2018] 2 Cr App R 7'.

Add text to the end of existing Note 1 in a new para: 'For the purposes of any right of appeal, a decision of the High Court on an application for judicial review of a decision by a prosecutor either to prosecute or not to prosecute a particular person for a particular alleged crime is a decision "in a criminal cause or matter": *Belhaj and another v DPP and another* [2018] UKSC 33. As to the application of this to an appeal against refusal to grant permission to apply for a judicial review rather than permission to appeal against a refusal, see *R (Purvis) v DPP* [2018] EWHC 1844 (Admin), [2018] ALL ER (D) 156 (Jul) (where the court declined an application for a late amendment to challenge the decision of the Court of Appeal to grant permission – this gave rise to difficult issues which should have been properly identified at the appropriate stage of the proceedings to enable the claimant to prepare submissions on those issues).'

1.894   Prosecution of Offences Act 1985, s 19   *Create Note to 'offender' at the end of s 19(3B)(a)(i):* '[5] The view is taken that section 19(3B)(*b*)(i)of the Prosecution of Offences Act 1985 embraces not only reports concerned with final disposal but also reports to assist in determining the appropriate procedural course to that stage, for example, whether a case should proceed to a normal trial, or to a fact finding inquiry with a view to the possible making of a hospital order under the Mental Health Act 1983, s 37.'

In the last para of existing Note 4 replace the All ER (D) citation of R (DPP) v Aylesbury Crown Court: '[2018] 1 Cr App R 22, [2018] Crim L R 333'.

1.1087   Crime and Disorder Act 1998, s 51E   *Add to Note in new para:* 'Where is a defendant commits a Bail Act offence before being sent for trial, the only means by which that offence can end up in the Crown Court is by committal for sentence under s 6(6)(*b*) of the Bail Act 1976: *R v Osman* [2017] EWCA Crim 2178, [2018] 1 Cr App R (S) 23.'

1.1625   Coroners and Justice Act 2009, s 33   *Add to the list of commencement orders in existing Note 1:* '; Coroners and Justice Act 2009 (Commencement No. 18) Order 2018, SI 2018/733; and Coroners and Justice Act 2009 (Commencement No. 19) Order 2018, SI 2018/727.'

1.1891   Criminal Justice and Courts Act 2015   *Add to the second para of Note 1:* 'The Civil Legal Aid (Procedure, Remuneration and Statutory Charge) (Amendment) Regulations 2018, SI 2018/803 amend: the Civil Legal Aid (Procedure) Regulations 2012, SI 2012/3098; the Civil Legal Aid (Remuneration) Regulations 2013, SI 2013/422; and the Civil Legal Aid (Statutory Charge) Regulations 2013, SI 2013/503 as a result of the coming into force of the 2018 Standard Civil Contract and the 2018 Civil Legal Advice Contract on 1st September 2018.'

STATUTORY INSTRUMENTS ON LEGAL SERVICES

STATUTORY INSTRUMENTS

1.2014   Civil Legal Aid (Procedure) Regulations 2012, reg 1   *Add to the end of existing Note 1*: 'The Civil Legal Aid (Procedure, Remuneration and Statutory Charge) (Amendment) Regulations 2018, SI 2018/803 amend: the Civil Legal Aid (Procedure) Regulations 2012, SI 2012/3098; the Civil Legal Aid (Remuneration) Regulations 2013, SI 2013/422; and the Civil Legal Aid (Statutory Charge) Regulations 2013, SI 2013/503 as a result of the coming into force of the 2018 Standard Civil Contract and the 2018 Civil Legal Advice Contract on 1st September 2018.'

1.2086   Criminal Legal Aid (General) Regulations 2013   *Add to the list of amending SIs as follows:* 'and SI 2018/587'. Note amendments to reg 12.

1.2202   Legal Aid (Disclosure of Information) Regulations 2013   *Add to the list of amending SIs as follows:* 'and SI 2018/587'. Note amendments to reg 7..

STATUTORY INSTRUMENTS AND PRACTICE DIRECTIONS ON PRACTICE AND PROCEDURE

STATUTORY INSTRUMENTS

1.2847   Magistrates' Courts Fees Order 2008   *Add to the list of amending SIs as follows:* 'SI 2018/812.' *Note the following:*

The following amendments to the Magistrates' Courts Fees Order 2008, SI 2008/1052 were made by SI 2018/812:

'(4)(1) The table in Schedule 1 (fees to be taken) to the Magistrates' Courts Fees Order 2008(1) is amended as follows.

(2)   In the entry for fee 1.1 (attendance of a justice of the peace away from court), for the amount in column 2 substitute "£30".

(3)   In the entry for fee 2.1 (application to state case to High Court), for the amount in column 2 substitute "£155".

(4)   In the entry for fee 2.3 (licensing appeal), for the amount in column 2 substitute "£70".

(5)   In the entry for fee 2.4 (appeal where no other fee specified), for the amount in column 2 substitute "£70".

(6)   In the entry for fee 3.3 (request for certified copy memorandum of conviction), for the amount in column 2 substitute "£25".

(7)   In the entry for fee 3.4 (request for certified copy where no other fee specified), for the amount in column 2 substitute "£25".

(8)   In the entry for fee 4.1 (application for liability order), for the amount in column 2 substitute "50p".

(9)   In the entry for fee 10.2 (application for warrant for commitment made in proceedings under the Child Support Act 1991(2)), for the amount in column 2 substitute "£45".'

PART II
EVIDENCE

GENERAL PRINCIPLES OF THE LAW OF EVIDENCE

SOURCES OF EVIDENCE: WITNESSES

PRIVILEGE: WITNESS PROTECTED BY PUBLIC POLICY AND GENERALLY

2.34 **Professional privilege** *In existing Note 14, insert after official citation of R v Jukes:* '[2018] 2 Cr App R 9, [2018] Crim L R 658, [2018] Lloyd's Rep F C 157'.

Add text to end in new para and create Note: 'Whether or not legal professional privilege has been waived is to be determined by reference to an objective analysis of the conduct of the person asserting, and waiver may be restricted to a limited purpose[33].

---

[33] *R (Belhaj) v DPP* [2018] EWHC 513 (Admin), [2018] 1 WLR 3602 (The Foreign and Commonwealth Office provided certain documents to the police and the CPS "for the sole purpose of assisting with (an) investigation" and the FCO did "not consider (itself) to have waived legal privilege for any other purpose, including any future prosecution or civil claim". This was held to have been an effective limited waiver and it did not extend to a subsequent application for judicial review of a decision by the DPP not to prosecute persons for alleged misconduct in a public office arising from the unlawful rendition of the claimants from Libya.)

EVIDENCE OF BAD CHARACTER OF THE DEFENDANT

GATEWAYS FOR THE ADMISSIBILITY OF EVIDENCE OF DEFENDANT'S BAD CHARACTER

2.88 **Meaning of "important matter" and "matter in issue between the defendant and the prosecution"** *Insert text after existing footnote marker 8, create note and renumber subsequent notes accordingly* ', or to rebut a defence of innocent association or coincidence[9].'

---

[9] *R v Hay* [2017] EWCA Crim 1851, [2018] Crim L R 400.

RELEVANCE OF GOOD CHARACTER TO CREDIBILITY AND PROPENSITY

2.101 *Insert text in new para after reference to existing Note 1, create Note, renumber subsequent Notes accordingly and continue narrative in new para* 'Where a defendant was accused of sexual offences against his half-sister, the judge should not have followed his direction as to the defendant's good character by adding, when dealing with the complainant's evidence, that there was, in a sense, a "level playing field" as between the parties since there was no suggestion the complainant had ever offended or had a reputation for untruthfulness. This watered down the protection which the good character direction afforded the accused[2].'

---

[2] *R v G(T)* [2018] EWCA Crim 1774, [2018] 4 WLR 39, [2018] 1 Cr App R 14, [2018] Crim L R 600.

SPECIAL RULES OF EVIDENCE IN CRIMINAL PROCEEDINGS

DRAWING INFERENCES FROM THE ACCUSED'S SILENCE

2.132 **Effect of accused's failure to mention facts when questioned or charged** *In existing Note 19 replace the All ER (D) citation of AB v CPS*: '[2018] Crim L R 576'.

STATUTORY INSTRUMENTS, CODES OF PRACTICE AND PRACTICE DIRECTIONS ON EVIDENCE

POLICE AND CRIMINAL EVIDENCE ACT 1984 CODES OF PRACTICE

Police and Criminal Evidence Act 1984 (PACE)
Code C

2.371   Revised Code of Practice for the detention, treatment and questioning of persons by Police Officers   *Replace the existing Code C with the revised 2018 versions as follows:*

Revised Code of Practice for the detention, treatment and questioning of persons by Police Officers
Police and Criminal Evidence Act 1984 (PACE)
Code C
July 2018

COMMENCEMENT – TRANSITIONAL ARRANGEMENTS
This Code applies to people in police detention after 00:00 on 31 July 2018, notwithstanding that their period of detention may have commenced before that time.

Contents

1 GENERAL

1.0 The powers and procedures in this Code must be used fairly, responsibly, with respect for the people to whom they apply and without unlawful discrimination. Under the Equality Act 2010, section 149 (Public sector Equality Duty), police forces must, in carrying out their functions, have due regard to the need to eliminate unlawful discrimination, harassment, victimisation and any other conduct which is prohibited by that Act, to advance equality of opportunity between people who share a relevant protected characteristic and people who do not share it, and to foster good relations between those persons. The Equality Act *also* makes it unlawful for police officers to discriminate against, harass or victimise any person on the grounds of the 'protected characteristics' of age, disability, gender reassignment, race, religion or belief, sex and sexual orientation, marriage and civil partnership, pregnancy and maternity, when using their powers. See *Notes 1A* and *1AA*.

1.1 All persons in custody must be dealt with expeditiously, and released as soon as the need for detention no longer applies.

1.1A A custody officer must perform the functions in this Code as soon as practicable. A custody officer will not be in breach of this Code if delay is justifiable and reasonable steps are taken to prevent unnecessary delay. The custody record shall show when a delay has occurred and the reason. See *Note 1H*.

1.2 This Code of Practice must be readily available at all police stations for consultation by:

- police officers;
- police staff;
- detained persons;
- members of the public.

1.3 The provisions of this Code:

- include the *Annexes*
- do not include the *Notes for Guidance* which form guidance to police officers and others about its application and interpretation.

1.4 If at any time an officer has any reason to suspect that a person of any age may be vulnerable (see *paragraph 1.13(d)*), in the absence of clear evidence to dispel that suspicion, that person shall be treated as such for the purposes of this Code and to establish whether any such reason may exist in relation to a person suspected of committing an offence (see *paragraph 10.1* and *Note 10A*), the custody officer in the case of a detained person, or the officer investigating the offence in the case of a person who has not been arrested or detained, shall take, or cause to be taken, (see *paragraph 3.5* and *Note 3F*) the following action:

    (a) reasonable enquiries shall be made to ascertain what information is available that is relevant to any of the factors described in *paragraph 1.13(d)* as indicating that the person may be vulnerable might apply;

(b) a record shall be made describing whether any of those factors appear to apply and provide any reason to suspect that the person may be vulnerable or (as the case may be) may not be vulnerable; and

(c) the record mentioned in sub-paragraph (b) shall be made available to be taken into account by police officers, police staff and any others who, in accordance with the provisions of this or any other Code, are required or entitled to communicate with the person in question. This would include any solicitor, appropriate adult and health care professional and is particularly relevant to communication by telephone or by means of a live link (see *paragraphs 12.9A* (interviews), *13.12* (interpretation), and *15.3C*, *15.11A*, 15.11B, *15.11C* and *15.11D* (reviews and extension of detention)).

See *Notes 1G, 1GA, 1GB* and *1GC*.

1.5 Anyone who appears to be under 18, shall, in the absence of clear evidence that they are older, be treated as a juvenile for the purposes of this Code and any other Code. See *Note 1L*.

1.5A *Not used*

1.6 If a person appears to be blind, seriously visually impaired, deaf, unable to read or speak or has difficulty orally because of a speech impediment, they shall be treated as such for the purposes of this Code in the absence of clear evidence to the contrary.

1.7 'The appropriate adult' means, in the case of a:

(a) juvenile:
(i) the parent, guardian or, if the juvenile is in the care of a local authority or voluntary organisation, a person representing that authority or organisation (see *Note 1B*);
(ii) a social worker of a local authority (see *Note 1C*);
(iii) failing these, some other responsible adult aged 18 or over who is *not*:
– a police officer;
– employed by the police;
– under the direction or control of the chief officer of a police force; or
– a person who provides services under contractual arrangements (but without being employed by the chief officer of a police force), to assist that force in relation to the discharge of its chief officer's functions,
whether or not they are on duty at the time.
See *Note 1F*.

(b) person who is vulnerable (see *paragraph 1.4* and *Note 1D*.
(i) a relative, guardian or other person responsible for their care or custody;
(ii) someone experienced in dealing with vulnerable persons but who is *not*:
– a police officer;
– employed by the police;
– under the direction or control of the chief officer of a police force; or
– a person who provides services under contractual arrangements (but without being employed by the chief officer of a police force), to assist that force in relation to the discharge of its chief officer's functions,
whether or not they are on duty at the time;
(iii) failing these, some other responsible adult aged 18 or over who is other than a person described in the bullet points in *sub-paragraph (b)(ii)* above.
See *Note 1F*.

1.7A The role of the appropriate adult is to safeguard the rights, entitlements and welfare of juveniles and vulnerable persons (see *paragraphs 1.4* and *1.5*) to whom the provisions of this and any other Code of Practice apply. For this reason, the appropriate adult is expected, amongst other things, to:

• support, advise and assist them when, in accordance with this Code or any other Code of Practice, they are given or asked to provide information or participate in any procedure;
• observe whether the police are acting properly and fairly to respect their rights and entitlements, and inform an officer of the rank of inspector or above if they consider that they are not;
• assist them to communicate with the police whilst respecting their right to say nothing unless they want to as set out in the terms of the caution (see *paragraphs 10.5* and *10.6*);
• help them to understand their rights and ensure that those rights are protected and respected (see *paragraphs 3.15, 3.17, 6.5A* and *11.17*).

1.8 If this Code requires a person be given certain information, they do not have to be given it if at the time they are incapable of understanding what is said, are violent or may become violent or in urgent need of medical attention, but they must be given it as soon as practicable.

1.9 References to a custody officer include any police officer who, for the time being, is performing the functions of a custody officer.

1.9A When this Code requires the prior authority or agreement of an officer of at least inspector or superintendent rank, that authority may be given by a sergeant or chief inspector authorised to perform the functions of the higher rank under the Police and Criminal Evidence Act 1984 (PACE), section 107.

1.10 Subject to *paragraph 1.12*, this Code applies to people in custody at police stations in England and Wales, whether or not they have been arrested, and to those removed to a police station as a place of safety under the Mental Health Act 1983, sections 135 and 136, as amended by the Policing and Crime Act 2017 (see *paragraph 3.16*). *Section 15* applies solely to people in police detention, e.g. those brought to a police station under arrest or arrested at a police station for an offence after going there voluntarily.

1.11 No part of this Code applies to a detained person:

(a) to whom PACE Code H applies because:
• they are detained following arrest under section 41 of the Terrorism Act 2000 (TACT) and not charged; or

- an authorisation has been given under section 22 of the Counter-Terrorism Act 2008 (CTACT) (post-charge questioning of terrorist suspects) to interview them.
(b) to whom the Code of Practice issued under paragraph 6 of Schedule 14 to TACT applies because they are detained for examination under Schedule 7 to TACT.

1.12 This Code does not apply to people in custody:

(i) arrested by officers under the Criminal Justice and Public Order Act 1994, section 136(2) on warrants issued in Scotland, or arrested or detained without warrant under section 137(2) by officers from a police force in Scotland. In these cases, police powers and duties and the person's rights and entitlements whilst at a police station in England or Wales are the same as those in Scotland;
(ii) arrested under the Immigration and Asylum Act 1999, section 142(3) in order to have their fingerprints taken;
(iii) whose detention has been authorised under Schedules 2 or 3 to the Immigration Act 1971 or section 62 of the Nationality, Immigration and Asylum Act 2002;
(iv) who are convicted or remanded prisoners held in police cells on behalf of the Prison Service under the Imprisonment (Temporary Provisions) Act 1980;
(v) Not used.
(vi) detained for searches under stop and search powers except as required by Code A.

The provisions on conditions of detention and treatment in *sections 8* and *9* must be considered as the minimum standards of treatment for such detainees.

1.13 In this Code:

(a) 'designated person' means a person other than a police officer, who has specified powers and duties conferred or imposed on them by designation under section 38 or 39 of the Police Reform Act 2002;
(b) reference to a police officer includes a designated person acting in the exercise or performance of the powers and duties conferred or imposed on them by their designation;
(c) where a search or other procedure to which this Code applies may only be carried out or observed by a person of the same sex as the detainee, the gender of the detainee and other parties present should be established and recorded in line with Annex L of this Code.
(d) 'vulnerable' applies to any person who, because of a mental health condition or mental disorder (see *Notes 1G and 1GB)*:
    (i) may have difficulty understanding or communicating effectively about the full implications for them of any procedures and processes connected with:
        • their arrest and detention; or (as the case may be)
        • their voluntary attendance at a police station or their presence elsewhere (see *paragraph 3.21)*, for the purpose of a voluntary interview; and
        • the exercise of their rights and entitlements.
    (ii) does not appear to understand the significance of what they are told, of questions they are asked or of their replies:
    (iii) appears to be particularly prone to:
        • becoming confused and unclear about their position;
        • providing unreliable, misleading or incriminating information without knowing or wishing to do so;
        • accepting or acting on suggestions from others without consciously knowing or wishing to do so; or
        • readily agreeing to suggestions or proposals without any protest or question.
(e) 'Live link' means:
    (i) for the purpose of *paragraph 12.9A;* an arrangement by means of which the *interviewing officer* who is not present at the police station where the detainee is held, is able to see and hear, and to be seen and heard by, the detainee concerned, the detainee's solicitor, appropriate adult and interpreter (as applicable) and the officer who has custody of that detainee (see *Note 1N)*.
    (ii) for the purpose of *paragraph 15.9A;* an arrangement by means of which the *review officer* who is not present at the police station where the detainee is held, is able to see and hear, and to be seen and heard by, the detainee concerned and the detainee's solicitor, appropriate adult and interpreter (as applicable) (see *Note 1N)*. The use of live link for decisions about detention under *section 45A of PACE* is subject to regulations made by the Secretary of State being in force.
    (iii) for the purpose of *paragraph 15.11A;* an arrangement by means of which the *authorising officer* who is not present at the police station where the detainee is held, is able to see and hear, and to be seen and heard by, the detainee concerned and the detainee's solicitor, appropriate adult and interpreter (as applicable) (see *Note 1N)*.
    (iv) for the purpose of *paragraph 15.11C;* an arrangement by means of which the *detainee* when not present in the court where the hearing is being held, is able to see and hear, and to be seen and heard by, the court during the hearing (see *Note 1N)*.
    Note: Chief officers must be satisfied that live link used in their force area for the above purposes provides for accurate and secure communication between the detainee, the detainee's solicitor, appropriate adult and interpreter (as applicable). This includes ensuring that at any time during which the live link is being used: a person cannot see, hear or otherwise obtain access to any such communications unless so authorised or allowed by the custody officer or, in the case of an interview, the interviewer and that as applicable, the confidentiality of any private consultation between a suspect and their solicitor and appropriate adult is maintained.

1.14 Designated persons are entitled to use reasonable force as follows:

(a) when exercising a power conferred on them which allows a police officer exercising that power to use reasonable force, a designated person has the same entitlement to use force; and

(b)   at other times when carrying out duties conferred or imposed on them that also entitle them to use reasonable force, for example:
- when at a police station carrying out the duty to keep detainees for whom they are responsible under control and to assist any police officer or designated person to keep any detainee under control and to prevent their escape;
- when securing, or assisting any police officer or designated person in securing, the detention of a person at a police station;
- when escorting, or assisting any police officer or designated person in escorting, a detainee within a police station;
- for the purpose of saving life or limb; or
- preventing serious damage to property.

1.15   Nothing in this Code prevents the custody officer, or other police officer or designated person (see *paragraph 1.13(a)*) given custody of the detainee by the custody officer, from allowing another person (see *(a)* and *(b)* below) to carry out individual procedures or tasks at the police station if the law allows. However, the officer or designated person given custody remains responsible for making sure the procedures and tasks are carried out correctly in accordance with the Codes of Practice (see *paragraph 3.5* and *Note 3F*). The other person who is allowed to carry out the procedures or tasks must be someone who *at that time*, is:

(a)   under the direction and control of the chief officer of the force responsible for the police station in question; or
(b)   providing services under contractual arrangements (but without being employed by the chief officer the police force), to assist a police force in relation to the discharge of its chief officer's functions.

1.16   Designated persons and others mentioned in *sub-paragraphs (a)* and *(b)* of *paragraph 1.15*, must have regard to any relevant provisions of the Codes of Practice.

1.17   In any provision of this or any other Code which allows or requires police officers or police staff to make a record in their report book, the reference to report book shall include any official report book or electronic recording device issued to them that enables the record in question to be made and dealt with in accordance with that provision. References in this and any other Code to written records, forms and signatures include electronic records and forms and electronic confirmation that identifies the person making the record or completing the form.

Chief officers must be satisfied as to the integrity and security of the devices, records and forms to which this paragraph applies and that use of those devices, records and forms satisfies relevant data protection legislation.

NOTES FOR GUIDANCE

1A   *Although certain sections of this Code apply specifically to people in custody at police stations, a person who attends a police station or other location voluntarily to assist with an investigation should be treated with no less consideration, e.g. offered or allowed refreshments at appropriate times, and enjoy an absolute right to obtain legal advice or communicate with anyone outside the police station or other location (see paragraphs 3.21 and 3.22.*

1AA   *In paragraph 1.0, under the Equality Act 2010, section 149, the 'relevant protected characteristics' are age, disability, gender reassignment, pregnancy and maternity, race, religion/belief and sex and sexual orientation. For further detailed guidance and advice on the Equality Act, see: https://www.gov.uk/guidance/equality-act-2010-guidance.*

1B   *A person, including a parent or guardian, should not be an appropriate adult if they:*

- are:
  - *suspected of involvement in the offence;*
  - *the victim;*
  - *a witness;*
  - *involved in the investigation.*
- received admissions prior to attending to act as the appropriate adult.
  Note: If a juvenile's parent is estranged from the juvenile, they should not be asked to act as the appropriate adult if the juvenile expressly and specifically objects to their presence.

1C   *If a juvenile admits an offence to, or in the presence of, a social worker or member of a youth offending team other than during the time that person is acting as the juvenile's appropriate adult, another appropriate adult should be appointed in the interest of fairness.*

1D   *In the case of someone who is vulnerable, it may be more satisfactory if the appropriate adult is someone experienced or trained in their care rather than a relative lacking such qualifications. But if the person prefers a relative to a better qualified stranger or objects to a particular person their wishes should, if practicable, be respected.*

1E   *A detainee should always be given an opportunity, when an appropriate adult is called to the police station, to consult privately with a solicitor in the appropriate adult's absence if they want. An appropriate adult is not subject to legal privilege.*

1F   *An appropriate adult who is not a parent or guardian in the case of a juvenile, or a relative, guardian or carer in the case of a vulnerable person, must be independent of the police as their role is to safeguard the person's rights and entitlements. Additionally, a solicitor or independent custody visitor who is present at the police station and acting in that capacity, may not be the appropriate adult.*

1G   *A person may be vulnerable as a result of a having a mental health condition or mental disorder. Similarly, simply because an individual does not have, or is not known to have, any such condition or disorder, does not mean that they are not vulnerable for the purposes of this Code. It is therefore important that the custody officer in the case of a detained person or the officer investigating the offence in the case of a person who has not been arrested or detained, as appropriate, considers on a case by case basis, whether any of the factors described in paragraph 1.13(d) might apply to the person in question. In doing so, the officer must take into account the particular circumstances of the individual and how the nature of the investigation might affect them and bear in mind that juveniles, by virtue of their age will always require an appropriate adult.*

1GA *For the purposes of paragraph 1.4(a), examples of relevant information that may be available include:*

- *the behaviour of the adult or juvenile;*
- *the mental health and capacity of the adult or juvenile;*
- *what the adult or juvenile says about themselves;*
- *information from relatives and friends of the adult or juvenile;*
- *information from police officers and staff and from police records;*
- *information from health and social care (including liaison and diversion services) and other professionals who know, or have had previous contact with, the individual and may be able to contribute to assessing their need for help and support from an appropriate adult. This includes contacts and assessments arranged by the police or at the request of the individual or (as applicable) their appropriate adult or solicitor.*

1GB *The Mental Health Act 1983 Code of Practice at page 26 describes the range of clinically recognised conditions which can fall with the meaning of mental disorder for the purpose of paragraph 1.13(d). The Code is published here: https://www.gov.uk/government/publications/code-of-practice-mental-health-act-1983.*

1GC *When a person is under the influence of drink and/or drugs, it is not intended that they are to be treated as vulnerable and requiring an appropriate adult for the purpose of paragraph 1.4 unless other information indicates that any of the factors described in paragraph 1.13(d) may apply to that person. When the person has recovered from the effects of drink and/or drugs, they should be re-assessed in accordance with paragraph 1.4. See paragraph 15.4A for application to live link.*

1H *Paragraph 1.1A is intended to cover delays which may occur in processing detainees e.g. if:*

- *a large number of suspects are brought into the station simultaneously to be placed in custody;*
- *interview rooms are all being used;*
- *there are difficulties contacting an appropriate adult, solicitor or interpreter.*

1I *The custody officer must remind the appropriate adult and detainee about the right to legal advice and record any reasons for waiving it in accordance with section 6.*

1J *Not used.*

1K *This Code does not affect the principle that all citizens have a duty to help police officers to prevent crime and discover offenders. This is a civic rather than a legal duty; but when police officers are trying to discover whether, or by whom, offences have been committed they are entitled to question any person from whom they think useful information can be obtained, subject to the restrictions imposed by this Code. A person's declaration that they are unwilling to reply does not alter this entitlement.*

1L *Paragraph 1.5 reflects the statutory definition of 'arrested juvenile' in section 37(15) of PACE. This section was amended by section 42 of the Criminal Justice and Courts Act 2015 with effect from 26 October 2015, and includes anyone who appears to be under the age of 18. This definition applies for the purposes of the detention and bail provisions in sections 34 to 51 of PACE. With effect from 3 April 2017, amendments made by the Policing and Crime Act 2017 require persons under the age of 18 to be treated as juveniles for the purposes of all other provisions of PACE and the Codes.*

1M *Not used.*

1N *For the purpose of the provisions of PACE that allow a live link to be used, any impairment of the detainee's eyesight or hearing is to be disregarded. This means that if a detainee's eyesight or hearing is impaired, the arrangements which would be needed to ensure effective communication if all parties were physically present in the same location, for example, using sign language, would apply to the live link arrangements.*

2 CUSTODY RECORDS

2.1A When a person:

- is brought to a police station under arrest;
- is arrested at the police station having attended there voluntarily; or
- attends a police station to answer bail.

they must be brought before the custody officer as soon as practicable after their arrival at the station or if applicable, following their arrest after attending the police station voluntarily. This applies to both designated and non-designated police stations. A person is deemed to be "at a police station" for these purposes if they are within the boundary of any building or enclosed yard which forms part of that police station.

2.1 A separate custody record must be opened as soon as practicable for each person brought to a police station under arrest or arrested at the station having gone there voluntarily or attending a police station in answer to street bail. All information recorded under this Code must be recorded as soon as practicable in the custody record unless otherwise specified. Any audio or video recording made in the custody area is not part of the custody record.

2.2 If any action requires the authority of an officer of a specified rank, subject to *paragraph 2.6A*, their name and rank must be noted in the custody record.

2.3 The custody officer is responsible for the custody record's accuracy and completeness and for making sure the record or copy of the record accompanies a detainee if they are transferred to another police station. The record shall show the:

- time and reason for transfer;
- time a person is released from detention.

2.3A If a person is arrested and taken to a police station as a result of a search in the exercise of any stop and search power to which PACE Code A (Stop and search) or the 'search powers code' issued under TACT applies, the officer carrying out the search is responsible for ensuring that the record of that stop and search is made as part of the person's custody record. The custody officer must then ensure that the person is asked if they want a copy of the search record and if they do, that they are given a copy as soon as practicable. The person's entitlement to a copy of the search record which is made as part of their custody record is in addition to, and does not affect, their entitlement to a copy of their custody record or any other provisions of section 2 (Custody records) of this Code. (See Code A *paragraph 4.2B* and the TACT search powers code *paragraph 5.3.5*).

2.4   The detainee's solicitor and appropriate adult must be permitted to inspect the whole of the detainee's custody record as soon as practicable after their arrival at the station and at any other time on request, whilst the person is detained. This includes the following *specific* records relating to the reasons for the detainee's arrest and detention and the offence concerned to which *paragraph 3.1(b)* refers:

(a)   The information about the circumstances and reasons for the detainee's arrest as recorded in the custody record in accordance with *paragraph 4.3 of Code G*. This applies to any further offences for which the detainee is arrested whilst in custody;

(b)   The record of the grounds for each authorisation to keep the person in custody. The authorisations to which this applies are the same as those described at items *(i)(a)* to *(d)* in the table in *paragraph 2* of *Annex M* of this Code.

Access to the records in *sub-paragraphs (a)* and *(b)* is *in addition* to the requirements in *paragraphs 3.4(b), 11.1A, 15.0, 15,7A(c)* and *16.7A* to make certain documents and materials available and to provide information about the offence and the reasons for arrest and detention.

Access to the custody record for the purposes of this paragraph must be arranged and agreed with the custody officer and may not unreasonably interfere with the custody officer's duties. A record shall be made when access is allowed and whether it includes the records described in *sub-paragraphs (a)* and *(b)* above.

2.4A   When a detainee leaves police detention or is taken before a court they, their legal representative or appropriate adult shall be given, on request, a copy of the custody record as soon as practicable. This entitlement lasts for 12 months after release.

2.5   The detainee, appropriate adult or legal representative shall be permitted to inspect the original custody record after the detainee has left police detention provided they give reasonable notice of their request. Any such inspection shall be noted in the custody record.

2.6   Subject to *paragraph 2.6A*, all entries in custody records must be timed and signed by the maker. Records entered on computer shall be timed and contain the operator's identification.

2.6A   Nothing in this Code requires the identity of officers or other police staff to be recorded or disclosed:

(a)   *Not used.*

(b)   if the officer or police staff reasonably believe recording or disclosing their name might put them in danger.

In these cases, they shall use their warrant or other identification numbers and the name of their police station. See *Note 2A*.

2.7   The fact and time of any detainee's refusal to sign a custody record, when asked in accordance with this Code, must be recorded.

NOTE FOR GUIDANCE

2A   *The purpose of paragraph 2.6A(b) is to protect those involved in serious organised crime investigations or arrests of particularly violent suspects when there is reliable information that those arrested or their associates may threaten or cause harm to those involved. In cases of doubt, an officer of inspector rank or above should be consulted.*

3   INITIAL ACTION

(A)   DETAINED PERSONS - NORMAL PROCEDURE

3.1   When a person is brought to a police station under arrest or arrested at the station having gone there voluntarily, the custody officer must make sure the person is told clearly about:

(a)   the following continuing rights, which may be exercised at any stage during the period in custody:
   (i)   their right to consult privately with a solicitor and that free independent legal advice is available as in *section 6*;
   (ii)   their right to have someone informed of their arrest as in *section 5*;
   (iii) their right to consult the Codes of Practice (see *Note 3D*); and
   (iv)   if applicable, their right to interpretation and translation (see *paragraph 3.12*) and their right to communicate with their High Commission, Embassy or Consulate (see *paragraph 3.12A*).

(b)   their right to be informed about the offence and (as the case may be) any further offences for which they are arrested whilst in custody and why they have been arrested and detained in accordance with *paragraphs 2.4, 3.4(a)* and *11.1A* of this Code and *paragraph 3.3* of *Code G*.

3.2   The detainee must also be given a written notice, which contains information:

(a)   to allow them to exercise their rights by setting out:
   (i)   their rights under *paragraph 3.1, paragraph 3.12* and *3.12A;*
   (ii)   the arrangements for obtaining legal advice, see *section 6*;
   (iii) their right to a copy of the custody record as in *paragraph 2.4A*;
   (iv)   their right to remain silent as set out in the caution in the terms prescribed in *section 10*;
   (v)   their right to have access to materials and documents which are essential to effectively challenging the lawfulness of their arrest and detention for any offence and (as the case may be) any further offences for which they are arrested whilst in custody, in accordance with *paragraphs 3.4(b), 15.0, 15.7A(c)* and *16.7A* of this Code;
   (vi)   the maximum period for which they may be kept in police detention without being charged, when detention must be reviewed and when release is required;
   (vii) their right to medical assistance in accordance with *section 9* of this Code;

(viii) their right, if they are prosecuted, to have access to the evidence in the case before their trial in accordance with the Criminal Procedure and Investigations Act 1996, the Attorney General's Guidelines on Disclosure, the common law and the Criminal Procedure Rules; and
(b) briefly setting out their other entitlements while in custody, by:
    (i) mentioning:
        – the provisions relating to the conduct of interviews;
        – the circumstances in which an appropriate adult should be available to assist the detainee and their statutory rights to make representations whenever the need for their detention is reviewed;
    (ii) listing the entitlements in this Code, concerning;
        – reasonable standards of physical comfort;
        – adequate food and drink;
        – access to toilets and washing facilities, clothing, medical attention, and exercise when practicable.

See *Note 3A*.

3.2A The detainee must be given an opportunity to read the notice and shall be asked to sign the custody record to acknowledge receipt of the notice. Any refusal to sign must be recorded on the custody record.

3.3 Not used.

3.3A An 'easy read' illustrated version should also be provided if available (see *Note 3A*).

(i) The custody officer shall:
- record the offence(s) that the detainee has been arrested for and the reason(s) for the arrest on the custody record. See *paragraph 10.3 and Code G paragraphs 2.2 and 4.3*;
- note on the custody record any comment the detainee makes in relation to the arresting officer's account but shall not invite comment. If the arresting officer is not physically present when the detainee is brought to a police station, the arresting officer's account must be made available to the custody officer remotely or by a third party on the arresting officer's behalf. If the custody officer authorises a person's detention, subject to *paragraph 1.8*, that officer must record the grounds for detention in the detainee's presence and at the same time, inform them of the grounds. The detainee must be informed of the grounds for their detention before they are questioned about any offence;
- note any comment the detainee makes in respect of the decision to detain them but shall not invite comment;
- not put specific questions to the detainee regarding their involvement in any offence, nor in respect of any comments they may make in response to the arresting officer's account or the decision to place them in detention. Such an exchange is likely to constitute an interview as in *paragraph 11.1A* and require the associated safeguards in *section 11*.

Note: This *sub-paragraph* also applies to any further offences and grounds for detention which come to light whilst the person is detained.
See *paragraph 11.13* in respect of unsolicited comments.

(ii) Documents and materials which are essential to effectively challenging the lawfulness of the detainee's arrest and detention must be made available to the detainee or their solicitor. Documents and materials will be "essential" for this purpose if they are capable of undermining the reasons and grounds which make the detainee's arrest and detention *necessary*. The decision about whether particular documents or materials must be made available for the purpose of this requirement therefore rests with the custody officer who determines whether detention is necessary, in consultation with the investigating officer who has the knowledge of the documents and materials in a particular case necessary to inform that decision. A note should be made in the detainee's custody record of the *fact* that documents or materials have been made available under this sub-paragraph and when. The investigating officer should make a separate note of what is made available and how it is made available in a particular case. This sub-paragraph also applies (with modifications) for the purposes of *sections 15 (Reviews and extensions of detention)* and *16 (Charging detained persons)*. See *Note 3ZA* and *paragraphs 15.0 and 16.7A*.

3.5 The custody officer or other custody staff as directed by the custody officer shall:
(a) ask the detainee whether at this time, they:
    (i) would like legal advice, see *paragraph 6.5*;
    (ii) want someone informed of their detention, see *section 5*;
(b) ask the detainee to sign the custody record to confirm their decisions in respect of (*a*);
(c) determine whether the detainee:
    (i) is, or might be, in need of medical treatment or attention, see *section 9*;
    (ii) is a juvenile and/or vulnerable and therefore requires an appropriate adult (see *paragraphs 1.4, 1.5, and 3.15*);
    (iii) requires:
        • help to check documentation (see *paragraph 3.20*);
        • an interpreter (see *paragraph 3.12 and Note 13B*).
(d) record the decision in respect of (*c*).

Where any duties under this paragraph have been carried out by custody staff at the direction of the custody officer, the outcomes shall, as soon as practicable, be reported to the custody officer who retains overall responsibility for the detainee's care and treatment and ensuring that it complies with this Code. See *Note 3F*.

3.6 When the needs mentioned in *paragraph 3.5(c)* are being determined, the custody officer is responsible for initiating an assessment to consider whether the detainee is likely to present specific risks to custody staff, any individual who may have contact with detainee (e.g. legal advisers, medical staff) or themselves. This risk assessment must include the taking of reasonable steps to establish the detainee's identity and to obtain information about the detainee that is relevant to their safe custody, security and welfare and risks to others. Such assessments should therefore always include a check on the Police National Computer (PNC), to be carried out as soon as practicable, to identify any risks that have been highlighted in relation to the detainee. Although such assessments are primarily the custody officer's responsibility, it may be necessary for them to consult and involve others, e.g. the arresting officer or an appropriate healthcare professional, see *paragraph 9.13*. Other records held by or on behalf of the police and other UK law enforcement authorities that might provide information relevant to the detainee's safe custody, security and welfare and risk to others and to confirming their identity should also be checked. Reasons for delaying the initiation or completion of the assessment must be recorded.

3.7   Chief officers should ensure that arrangements for proper and effective risk assessments required by *paragraph 3.6* are implemented in respect of all detainees at police stations in their area.

3.8   Risk assessments must follow a structured process which clearly defines the categories of risk to be considered and the results must be incorporated in the detainee's custody record. The custody officer is responsible for making sure those responsible for the detainee's custody are appropriately briefed about the risks. If no specific risks are identified by the assessment, that should be noted in the custody record. See *Note 3E* and *paragraph 9.14*.

3.8A   The content of any risk assessment and any analysis of the level of risk relating to the person's detention is not required to be shown or provided to the detainee or any person acting on behalf of the detainee. But information should not be withheld from any person acting on the detainee's behalf, for example, an appropriate adult, solicitor or interpreter, if to do so might put that person at risk.

3.9   The custody officer is responsible for implementing the response to any specific risk assessment, e.g.:

- reducing opportunities for self harm;
- calling an appropriate healthcare professional;
- increasing levels of monitoring or observation;
- reducing the risk to those who come into contact with the detainee.

See *Note 3E*.

3.10   Risk assessment is an ongoing process and assessments must always be subject to review if circumstances change.

3.11   If video cameras are installed in the custody area, notices shall be prominently displayed showing cameras are in use. Any request to have video cameras switched off shall be refused.

(B) DETAINED PERSONS – SPECIAL GROUPS

3.12   If the detainee appears to be someone who does not speak or understand English or who has a hearing or speech impediment, the custody officer must ensure:

(a)   that without delay, arrangements (see *paragraph 13.1ZA*) are made for the detainee to have the assistance of an interpreter in the action under *paragraphs 3.1* to *3.5*. If the person appears to have a hearing or speech impediment, the reference to 'interpreter' includes appropriate assistance necessary to comply with *paragraphs 3.1* to *3.5*. See *paragraph 13.1C* if the detainee is in Wales. See *section 13* and *Note 13B*;

(b)   that in addition to the continuing rights set out in *paragraph 3.1(a)(i)* to *(iv)*, the detainee is told clearly about their right to interpretation and translation;

(c)   that the written notice given to the detainee in accordance with *paragraph 3.2* is in a language the detainee understands and includes the right to interpretation and translation together with information about the provisions in *section 13* and *Annex M*, which explain how the right applies (see *Note 3A*); and

(d)   that if the translation of the notice is not available, the information in the notice is given through an interpreter and a written translation provided without undue delay.

3.12A   If the detainee is a citizen of an independent Commonwealth country or a national of a foreign country, including the Republic of Ireland, the custody officer must ensure that in addition to the continuing rights set out in *paragraph 3.1(a)(i)* to *(iv)*, they are informed as soon as practicable about their rights of communication with their High Commission, Embassy or Consulate set out in *section 7*. This right must be included in the written notice given to the detainee in accordance with *paragraph 3.2*.

3.13   If the detainee is a juvenile, the custody officer must, if it is practicable, ascertain the identity of a person responsible for their welfare. That person:

- may be:
  ~ the parent or guardian;
  ~ if the juvenile is in local authority or voluntary organisation care, or is otherwise being looked after under the Children Act 1989, a person appointed by that authority or organisation to have responsibility for the juvenile's welfare;
  ~ any other person who has, for the time being, assumed responsibility for the juvenile's welfare.
- must be informed as soon as practicable that the juvenile has been arrested, why they have been arrested and where they are detained. This right is in addition to the juvenile's right in *section 5* not to be held incommunicado. See *Note 3C*.

3.14   If a juvenile is known to be subject to a court order under which a person or organisation is given any degree of statutory responsibility to supervise or otherwise monitor them, reasonable steps must also be taken to notify that person or organisation (the 'responsible officer'). The responsible officer will normally be a member of a Youth Offending Team, except for a curfew order which involves electronic monitoring when the contractor providing the monitoring will normally be the responsible officer.

3.15   If the detainee is a juvenile or a vulnerable person, the custody officer must, as soon as practicable, ensure that:

- the detainee is informed of the decision that an appropriate adult is required and the reason for that decision (see *paragraph 3.5(c)(ii)* and;
- the detainee is advised:
  - of the duties of the appropriate adult as described in *paragraph 1.7A;* and
  - that they can consult privately with the appropriate adult at any time.
- the appropriate adult, who in the case of a juvenile may or may not be a person responsible for their welfare, as in *paragraph 3.13*, is informed of:
  - the grounds for their detention;
  - their whereabouts; and
- the attendance of the appropriate adult at the police station to see the detainee is secured.

3.16 It is imperative that a person detained under the Mental Health Act 1983, section 135 or 136, be assessed as soon as possible within the permitted period of detention specified in that Act. A police station may only be used as a place of safety in accordance with The Mental Health Act 1983 (Places of Safety) Regulations 2017. If that assessment is to take place at the police station, an approved mental health professional and a registered medical practitioner shall be called to the station as soon as possible to carry it out. See *Note 9D.* The appropriate adult has no role in the assessment process and their presence is not required. Once the detainee has been assessed and suitable arrangements made for their treatment or care, they can no longer be detained under section 135 or 136. A detainee must be immediately discharged from detention if a registered medical practitioner, having examined them, concludes they are not mentally disordered within the meaning of the Act.

3.17 If the appropriate adult is:

- already at the police station, the provisions of *paragraphs 3.1* to *3.5* must be complied with in the appropriate adult's presence;
- not at the station when these provisions are complied with, they must be complied with again in the presence of the appropriate adult when they arrive,

and a copy of the notice given to the detainee in accordance with *paragraph 3.2*, shall also be given to the appropriate adult.

3.17A The custody officer must ensure that at the time the copy of the notice is given to the appropriate adult, or as soon as practicable thereafter, the appropriate adult is advised of the duties of the appropriate adult as described in *paragraph 1.7A*.

3.18 *Not used.*

3.19 If the detainee, or appropriate adult on the detainee's behalf, asks for a solicitor to be called to give legal advice, the provisions of *section 6* apply (see *paragraph 6.5A* and *Note 3H*).

3.20 If the detainee is blind, seriously visually impaired or unable to read, the custody officer shall make sure their solicitor, relative, appropriate adult or some other person likely to take an interest in them and not involved in the investigation is available to help check any documentation. When this Code requires written consent or signing the person assisting may be asked to sign instead, if the detainee prefers. This paragraph does not require an appropriate adult to be called solely to assist in checking and signing documentation for a person who is not a juvenile, or is not vulnerable (see *paragraph 3.15* and *Note 13C*).

3.20A The Children and Young Persons Act 1933, section 31, requires that arrangements must be made for ensuring that a girl under the age of 18, while detained in a police station, is under the care of a woman. See *Note 3G.* It also requires that arrangements must be made for preventing any person under 18, while being detained in a police station, from associating with an adult charged with any offence, unless that adult is a relative or the adult is jointly charged with the same offence as the person under 18.

(C) Detained persons - Documentation

3.20B The grounds for a person's detention shall be recorded, in the person's presence if practicable. See *paragraph 1.8*.

3.20C Action taken under *paragraphs 3.12* to *3.20A* shall be recorded.

(D) Persons attending a police station or elsewhere voluntarily

3.21 Anybody attending a police station or other location (see *paragraph 3.22* and *Note 3I*) voluntarily to assist police with the investigation of an offence may leave at will unless arrested. See *Notes 1A* and *1K*. The person may only be prevented from leaving at will if their arrest on suspicion of committing the offence is necessary in accordance with Code G. See *Code G Note 2G.*

Action if arrest becomes necessary

(a) If during a person's voluntary attendance at a police station or other location it is decided for any reason that their arrest is necessary, they must:
  - be informed at once that they are under arrest and of the grounds and reasons as required by *Code G*, and
  - be brought before the custody officer at the police station where they are arrested or (as the case may be) at the police station to which they are taken after being arrested elsewhere. The custody officer is then responsible for making sure that a custody record is opened and that they are notified of their rights in the same way as other detainees as required by this Code.

Information to be given when arranging a voluntary interview:

(b) If the suspect's arrest is not necessary but they are cautioned as required in *section 10*, the person who, after describing the nature and circumstances of the suspected offence, gives the caution must at the same time, inform them that they are not under arrest and that they are not obliged to remain at the station or other location (see *paragraph 3.22* and *Note 3I*). The rights, entitlements and safeguards that apply to the conduct and recording of interviews with suspects are not diminished simply because the interview is arranged on a voluntary basis. For the purpose of arranging a voluntary interview (see *Code G Note 2F*), the duty of the interviewer reflects that of the custody officer with regard to detained suspects. As a result:

(i)   the requirement in *paragraph 3.5(c)(ii)* to determine whether a detained suspect requires an appropriate adult, help to check documentation or an interpreter shall apply equally to a suspect who has not been arrested; and

(ii) the suspect must not be asked to give their informed consent to be interviewed until *after* they have been informed of the rights, entitlements and safeguards that apply to voluntary interviews. These are set out in *paragraph 3.21A* and the interviewer is responsible for ensuring that the suspect is so informed and for explaining these rights, entitlements and safeguards.

3.21A   The interviewer must inform the suspect that the purpose of the voluntary interview is to question them to obtain evidence about their involvement or suspected involvement in the offence(s) described when they were cautioned and told that they were not under arrest. The interviewer shall then inform the suspect that the following matters will apply if they agree to the voluntary interview proceeding:

(a) Their right to information about the offence(s) in question by providing sufficient information to enable them to understand the nature of any such offence(s) and why they are suspected of committing it. This is in order to allow for the effective exercise of the rights of the defence as required by *paragraph 11.1A*. It applies whether or not they ask for legal advice and includes any further offences that come to light and are pointed out during the voluntary interview and for which they are cautioned.

(b) Their right to free *(see Note 3J)* legal advice by:

(i)   explaining that they may obtain free and independent legal advice if they want it, and that this includes the right to speak with a solicitor on the telephone and to have the solicitor present during the interview;

(ii) asking if they want legal advice and recording their reply; and

(iii) if the person requests advice, securing its provision before the interview by contacting the Defence Solicitor Call Centre and explaining that the time and place of the interview will be arranged to enable them to obtain advice and that the interview will be delayed until they have received the advice unless, in accordance with *paragraph 6.6(c)* (Nominated solicitor not available and duty solicitor declined) or *paragraph 6.6(d)* (Change of mind), an officer of the rank of inspector or above agrees to the interview proceeding; or

(iv) if the person declines to exercise the right, asking them why and recording any reasons given (see *Note 6K*).

Note: When explaining the right to legal advice and the arrangements, the interviewer must take care not to indicate, except to answer a direct question, that the time taken to arrange and complete the voluntary interview might be reduced if:

•   the suspect does not ask for legal advice or does not want a solicitor present when they are interviewed; or

•   the suspect asks for legal advice or (as the case may be) asks for a solicitor to be present when they are interviewed, but changes their mind and agrees to be interviewed without waiting for a solicitor.

(c) Their right, if in accordance with *paragraph 3.5(c)(ii)* the interviewer determines:

(i)   that they are a juvenile or are vulnerable; or

(ii) that they need help to check documentation (see *paragraph 3.20*),

to have the appropriate adult present or (as the case may be) to have the necessary help to check documentation; and that the interview will be delayed until the presence of the appropriate adult or the necessary help, is secured.

(d) If they are a juvenile or vulnerable and do not want legal advice, their appropriate adult has the right to ask for a solicitor to attend if this would be in their best interests and the appropriate adult must be so informed. In this case, action to secure the provision of advice if so requested by their appropriate adult will be taken without delay in the same way as if requested by the person (see *sub-paragraph (b)(iii)*). However, they cannot be forced to see the solicitor if they are adamant that they do not wish to do so (see *paragraphs 3.19* and *6.5A*).

(e) Their right to an interpreter, if in accordance with, *paragraphs 3.5(c)(ii)* and *3.12*, the interviewer determines that they require an interpreter and that if they require an interpreter, making the necessary arrangements in accordance with *paragraph 13.1ZA* and that the interview will be delayed to make the arrangements.

(f) That interview will be arranged for a time and location (see *paragraph 3.22* and *Note 3I*) that enables:

(i)   the suspect's rights described above to be fully respected; and

(ii) the whole of the interview to be recorded using an authorised recording device in accordance with Code E (Code of Practice on Audio recording of interviews with suspects) or (as the case may be) Code F (Code of Practice on visual recording with sound of interviews with suspects); and

(g) That their agreement to take part in the interview also signifies their agreement for that interview to be audio-recorded or (as the case may be) visually recorded with sound.

3.21B   The provision by the interviewer of factual information described in *paragraph 3.21A* and, if asked by the suspect, further such information, does not constitute an interview for the purpose of this Code and *when that information is provided*:

(a) the interviewer must remind the suspect about the caution as required in *section 10* but must not *invite* comment about the offence or put specific questions to the suspect regarding their involvement in any offence, nor in respect of any comments they may make when given the information. Such an exchange is itself likely to constitute an interview as in *paragraph 11.1A* and require the associated interview safeguards in *section 11*.

(b) Any comment the suspect makes when the information is given which might be relevant to the offence, must be recorded and dealt with in accordance with *paragraph 11.13*.

   (c)   The suspect must be given a notice summarising the matters described in *paragraph 3.21A* and which includes the arrangements for obtaining legal advice. If a specific notice is not available, the notice given to detained suspects with references to detention-specific requirements and information redacted, may be used.

   (d)   For juvenile and vulnerable suspects (see *paragraphs 1.4* and *1.5*):

      (i)   the information must be provided or (as the case may be) provided again, together with the notice, in the presence of the appropriate adult;

      (ii)   if cautioned in the absence of the appropriate adult, the caution must be repeated in the appropriate adult's presence (see *paragraph 10.12*);

      (iii)   the suspect must be informed of the decision that an appropriate is required and the reason (see *paragraph 3.5(c)(ii)*;

      (iv)   the suspect *and* the appropriate adult shall be advised:
- that the duties of the appropriate adult include giving advice and assistance in accordance with *paragraphs 1.7A* and *11.17*; and
- that they can consult privately at any time.

      (v)   their informed agreement to be interviewed voluntarily must be sought and given in the *presence* of the appropriate adult and for a juvenile, the agreement of a parent or guardian of the juvenile is also required.

3.22   If the other location mentioned in *paragraph 3.21* is any place or premises for which the interviewer requires the informed consent of the suspect and/or occupier (if different) to remain, for example, the suspect's home (see *Note 3I*), then the references that the person is 'not obliged to remain' and that they 'may leave at will' mean that the suspect and/or occupier (if different) may also withdraw their consent and require the interviewer to leave.

Commencement of voluntary interview – general

3.22A   Before asking the suspect any questions about their involvement in the offence they are suspected of committing, the interviewing officer must ask them to confirm that they agree to the interview proceeding. This confirmation shall be recorded in the interview record made in accordance with section 11 of this Code (written record) or Code E or Code F.

Documentation

3.22B   Action taken under *paragraphs 3.21A* to *3.21B* shall be recorded. The record shall include the date time and place the action was taken, who was present and anything said to or by the suspect and to or by those present.

3.23   *Not* used.

3.24   *Not* used.

(E) Persons answering street bail

3.25   When a person is answering street bail, the custody officer should link any documentation held in relation to arrest with the custody record. Any further action shall be recorded on the custody record in accordance with *paragraphs 3.20B* and *3.20C* above.

(F) Requirements for suspects to be informed of certain rights

3.26   The provisions of this section identify the information which must be given to suspects who have been cautioned in accordance with *section 10 of this Code* according to whether or not they have been arrested and detained. It includes information required by *EU Directive 2012/13* on the right to information in criminal proceedings. If a complaint is made by or on behalf of such a suspect that the information and (as the case may be) access to records and documents has not been provided as required, the matter shall be reported to an inspector to deal with as a complaint for the purposes of *paragraph 9.2*, or *paragraph 12.9* if the challenge is made during an interview. This would include, for example:

   (a)   in the case of a detained suspect:
- not informing them of their rights (see *paragraph 3.1*);
- not giving them a copy of the Notice (see *paragraph 3.2(a)*);
- not providing an opportunity to read the notice (see *paragraph 3.2A*);
- not providing the required information (see *paragraphs 3.2(a)*, *3.12(b)* and, *3.12A*;
- not allowing access to the custody record (see *paragraph 2.4*);
- not providing a translation of the Notice (see *paragraph 3.12(c)* and *(d)*); and

   (b)   in the case of a suspect who is not detained:
- not informing them of their rights or providing the required information (see *paragraphs 3.21(b)* to *3.21B*).

Notes for Guidance

3ZA   *For the purposes of paragraphs 3.4(b) and 15.0:*

   (a)   *Investigating officers are responsible for bringing to the attention of the officer who is responsible for authorising the suspect's detention or (as the case may be) continued detention (before or after charge), any documents and materials in their possession or control which appear to undermine the need to keep the suspect in custody. In accordance with Part IV of PACE, this officer will be either the custody officer, the officer reviewing the need for detention before or after charge (PACE, section 40), or the officer considering the need to extend detention without charge from 24 to 36 hours (PACE, section 42) who is then responsible for determining, which, if any, of those documents and materials are capable of undermining the need to detain the suspect and must therefore be made available to the suspect or their solicitor.*

   (b)   *the way in which documents and materials are 'made available', is a matter for the investigating officer to determine on a case by case basis and having regard to the nature and volume of the documents and materials involved. For example, they may be made available by supplying a copy or allowing supervised access to view. However, for view only access, it will be necessary to demonstrate that sufficient time is allowed for the suspect and solicitor to view and consider the documents and materials in question.*

3A   *For access to currently available notices, including 'easy-read' versions, see https://www.gov.uk/guidance/notice-of-rights-and-entitlements-a-persons-rights-in-police-detention.*

3B   *Not used.*

3C   *If the juvenile is in local authority or voluntary organisation care but living with their parents or other adults responsible for their welfare, although there is no legal obligation to inform them, they should normally be contacted, as well as the authority or organisation unless they are suspected of involvement in the offence concerned. Even if the juvenile is not living with their parents, consideration should be given to informing them.*

3D   *The right to consult the Codes of Practice does not entitle the person concerned to delay unreasonably any necessary investigative or administrative action whilst they do so. Examples of action which need not be delayed unreasonably include:*

- *procedures requiring the provision of breath, blood or urine specimens under the Road Traffic Act 1988 or the Transport and Works Act 1992;*
- *searching detainees at the police station;*
- *taking fingerprints, footwear impressions or non-intimate samples without consent for evidential purposes.*

3E   *The Detention and Custody Authorised Professional Practice (APP) produced by the College of Policing (see http://www.app.college.police.uk) provides more detailed guidance on risk assessments and identifies key risk areas which should always be considered. See* Home Office Circular 34/2007 *(Safety of solicitors and probationary representatives at police stations).*

3F   *A custody officer or other officer who, in accordance with this Code, allows or directs the carrying out of any task or action relating to a detainee's care, treatment, rights and entitlements to another officer or any other person, must be satisfied that the officer or person concerned is suitable, trained and competent to carry out the task or action in question.*

3G   *Guidance for police officers and police staff on the operational application of section 31 of the Children and Young Persons Act 1933 has been published by the College of Policing and is available at:*

https://www.app.college.police.uk/app-content/detention-and-custody-2/detainee-care/children-andyoung-persons/#girls.

3H   *The purpose of the provisions at paragraphs 3.19 and 6.5A is to protect the rights of juvenile and vulnerable persons who may not understand the significance of what is said to them. They should always be given an opportunity, when an appropriate adult is called to the police station, to consult privately with a solicitor in the absence of the appropriate adult if they want.*

3I   *An interviewer who is not sure, or has any doubt, about whether a place or location elsewhere than a police station is suitable for carrying out a voluntary interview, particularly in the case of a juvenile or vulnerable person, should consult an officer of the rank of sergeant or above for advice. Detailed guidance for police officers and staff concerning the conduct and recording of voluntary interviews is being developed by the College of Policing. It follows a review of operational issues arising when voluntary interviews need to be arranged. The aim is to ensure the effective implementation of the safeguards in paragraphs 3.21 to 3.22B particularly concerning the rights of suspects, the location for the interview and supervision.*

3J   *For voluntary interviews conducted by non-police investigators, the provision of legal advice is set out by the Legal Aid Agency at paragraph 9.54 of the 2017 Standard Crime Contract Specification. This is published at https://www.gov.uk/government/publications/standardcrime-contract-2017 and the rules mean that a non-police interviewer who does not have their own statutory power of arrest would have to inform the suspect that they have a right to seek legal advice if they wish, but payment would be a matter for them to arrange with the solicitor.*

4   DETAINEE'S PROPERTY

(A)   ACTION

4.1   The custody officer is responsible for:

(a)   ascertaining what property a detainee:
  (i)   has with them when they come to the police station, whether on:
- arrest or re-detention on answering to bail;
- commitment to prison custody on the order or sentence of a court;
- lodgement at the police station with a view to their production in court from prison custody;
- transfer from detention at another station or hospital;
- detention under the Mental Health Act 1983, section 135 or 136;
- remand into police custody on the authority of a court.
  (ii)   might have acquired for an unlawful or harmful purpose while in custody;
(b)   the safekeeping of any property taken from a detainee which remains at the police station.

The custody officer may search the detainee or authorise their being searched to the extent they consider necessary, provided a search of intimate parts of the body or involving the removal of more than outer clothing is only made as in *Annex A*. A search may only be carried out by an officer of the same sex as the detainee. See *Note 4A* and *Annex L*.

4.2   Detainees may retain clothing and personal effects at their own risk unless the custody officer considers they may use them to cause harm to themselves or others, interfere with evidence, damage property, effect an escape or they are needed as evidence. In this event the custody officer may withhold such articles as they consider necessary and must tell the detainee why.

4.3   Personal effects are those items a detainee may lawfully need, use or refer to while in detention but do not include cash and other items of value.

(B) Documentation

4.4 It is a matter for the custody officer to determine whether a record should be made of the property a detained person has with him or had taken from him on arrest. Any record made is not required to be kept as part of the custody record but the custody record should be noted as to where such a record exists and that record shall be treated as being part of the custody record for the purpose of this and any other Code of Practice (see *paragraphs 2.4, 2.4A* and *2.5*). Whenever a record is made the detainee shall be allowed to check and sign the record of property as correct. Any refusal to sign shall be recorded.

4.5 If a detainee is not allowed to keep any article of clothing or personal effects, the reason must be recorded.

Notes for Guidance

4A *PACE, Section 54(1) and paragraph 4.1 require a detainee to be searched when it is clear the custody officer will have continuing duties in relation to that detainee or when that detainee's behaviour or offence makes an inventory appropriate. They do not require every detainee to be searched, e.g. if it is clear a person will only be detained for a short period and is not to be placed in a cell, the custody officer may decide not to search them. In such a case the custody record will be endorsed 'not searched', paragraph 4.4 will not apply, and the detainee will be invited to sign the entry. If the detainee refuses, the custody officer will be obliged to ascertain what property they have in accordance with paragraph 4.1.*

4B *Paragraph 4.4 does not require the custody officer to record on the custody record property in the detainee's possession on arrest if, by virtue of its nature, quantity or size, it is not practicable to remove it to the police station.*

4C *Paragraph 4.4 does not require items of clothing worn by the person to be recorded unless withheld by the custody officer as in paragraph 4.2.*

5 Right not to be held incommunicado

(A) Action

5.1 Subject to *paragraph 5.7B*, any person arrested and held in custody at a police station or other premises may, on request, have one person known to them or likely to take an interest in their welfare informed at public expense of their whereabouts as soon as practicable. If the person cannot be contacted the detainee may choose up to two alternatives. If they cannot be contacted, the person in charge of detention or the investigation has discretion to allow further attempts until the information has been conveyed. See *Notes 5C* and *5D*.

5.2 The exercise of the above right in respect of each person nominated may be delayed only in accordance with *Annex B*.

5.3 The above right may be exercised each time a detainee is taken to another police station.

5.4 If the detainee agrees, they may at the custody officer's discretion, receive visits from friends, family or others likely to take an interest in their welfare, or in whose welfare the detainee has an interest. See *Note 5B*.

5.5 If a friend, relative or person with an interest in the detainee's welfare enquires about their whereabouts, this information shall be given if the suspect agrees and *Annex B* does not apply. See *Note 5D*.

5.6 The detainee shall be given writing materials, on request, and allowed to telephone one person for a reasonable time, see *Notes 5A* and *5E*. Either or both of these privileges may be denied or delayed if an officer of inspector rank or above considers sending a letter or making a telephone call may result in any of the consequences in:

(a) *Annex B paragraphs 1* and *2* and the person is detained in connection with an indictable offence;
(b) *Not used.*

Nothing in this paragraph permits the restriction or denial of the rights in *paragraphs 5.1* and *6.1*.

5.7 Before any letter or message is sent, or telephone call made, the detainee shall be informed that what they say in any letter, call or message (other than in a communication to a solicitor) may be read or listened to and may be given in evidence. A telephone call may be terminated if it is being abused. The costs can be at public expense at the custody officer's discretion.

5.7A Any delay or denial of the rights in this section should be proportionate and should last no longer than necessary.

5.7B In the case of a person in police custody for specific purposes and periods in accordance with a direction under the *Crime (Sentences) Act 1997, Schedule 1* (productions from prison etc.), the exercise of the rights in this section shall be subject to any additional conditions specified in the direction for the purpose of regulating the detainee's contact and communication with others whilst in police custody. See *Note 5F*.

(B) Documentation

5.8 A record must be kept of any:

(a) request made under this section and the action taken;
(b) letters, messages or telephone calls made or received or visit received;
(c) refusal by the detainee to have information about them given to an outside enquirer. The detainee must be asked to countersign the record accordingly and any refusal recorded.

Notes for Guidance

5A *A person may request an interpreter to interpret a telephone call or translate a letter.*

5B *At the custody officer's discretion and subject to the detainee's consent, visits should be allowed when possible, subject to having sufficient personnel to supervise a visit and any possible hindrance to the investigation.*

5C *If the detainee does not know anyone to contact for advice or support or cannot contact a friend or relative, the custody officer should bear in mind any local voluntary bodies or other organisations who might be able to help. Paragraph 6.1 applies if legal advice is required.*

5D *In some circumstances it may not be appropriate to use the telephone to disclose information under paragraphs 5.1 and 5.5.*

5E *The telephone call at paragraph 5.6 is in addition to any communication under paragraphs 5.1 and 6.1.*

5F *Prison Service Instruction 26/2012 (Production of Prisoners at the Request of Warranted Law Enforcement Agencies) provides detailed guidance and instructions for police officers and Governors and Directors of Prisons regarding applications for prisoners to be transferred to police custody and their safe custody and treatment while in police custody.*

6 RIGHT TO LEGAL ADVICE

(A) ACTION

6.1 Unless *Annex B* applies, all detainees must be informed that they may at any time consult and communicate privately with a solicitor, whether in person, in writing or by telephone, and that free independent legal advice is available. See *paragraph 3.1, Notes 1I, 6B and 6J*

6.2 *Not used.*

6.3 A poster advertising the right to legal advice must be prominently displayed in the charging area of every police station. See *Note 6H.*

6.4 No police officer should, at any time, do or say anything with the intention of dissuading any person who is entitled to legal advice in accordance with this Code, whether or not they have been arrested and are detained, from obtaining legal advice. See *Note 6ZA.*

6.5 The exercise of the right of access to legal advice may be delayed only as in *Annex B*. Whenever legal advice is requested, and unless *Annex B* applies, the custody officer must act without delay to secure the provision of such advice. If the detainee has the right to speak to a solicitor in person but declines to exercise the right the officer should point out that the right includes the right to speak with a solicitor on the telephone. If the detainee continues to waive this right, or a detainee whose right to free legal advice is limited to telephone advice from the Criminal Defence Service (CDS) Direct (*see Note 6B*) declines to exercise that right, the officer should ask them why and any reasons should be recorded on the custody record or the interview record as appropriate. Reminders of the right to legal advice must be given as in *paragraphs 3.5, 11.2, 15.4, 16.4, 16.5, 2B of Annex A, 3 of Annex K and 5 of Annex M* of this Code and Code D, *paragraphs 3.17(ii)* and *6.3*. Once it is clear a detainee does not want to speak to a solicitor in person or by telephone they should cease to be asked their reasons. See *Note 6K.*

6.5A In the case of a person who is a juvenile or is vulnerable, an appropriate adult should consider whether legal advice from a solicitor is required. If such a detained person wants to exercise the right to legal advice, the appropriate action should be taken and should not be delayed until the appropriate adult arrives. If the person indicates that they do not want legal advice, the appropriate adult has the right to ask for a solicitor to attend if this would be in the best interests of the person and must be so informed. In this case, action to secure the provision of advice if so requested by the appropriate adult shall be taken without delay in the same way as when requested by the person. However, the person cannot be forced to see the solicitor if they are adamant that they do not wish to do so.

6.6 A detainee who wants legal advice may not be interviewed or continue to be interviewed until they have received such advice unless:

(a) *Annex B* applies, when the restriction on drawing adverse inferences from silence in *Annex C* will apply because the detainee is not allowed an opportunity to consult a solicitor; or

(b) an officer of superintendent rank or above has reasonable grounds for believing that:
　　(i) the consequent delay might:
　　　　• lead to interference with, or harm to, evidence connected with an offence;
　　　　• lead to interference with, or physical harm to, other people;
　　　　• lead to serious loss of, or damage to, property;
　　　　• lead to alerting other people suspected of having committed an offence but not yet arrested for it;
　　　　• hinder the recovery of property obtained in consequence of the commission of an offence.
　　　　See Note 6A
　　(ii) when a solicitor, including a duty solicitor, has been contacted and has agreed to attend, awaiting their arrival would cause unreasonable delay to the process of investigation.
　　Note: In these cases the restriction on drawing adverse inferences from silence in *Annex C* will apply because the detainee is not allowed an opportunity to consult a solicitor.

(c) the solicitor the detainee has nominated or selected from a list:
　　(i) cannot be contacted;
　　(ii) has previously indicated they do not wish to be contacted; or
　　(iii) having been contacted, has declined to attend; and
　　　　• the detainee has been advised of the Duty Solicitor Scheme but has declined to ask for the duty solicitor;
　　　　• in these circumstances the interview may be started or continued without further delay provided an officer of inspector rank or above has agreed to the interview proceeding.
　　Note: The restriction on drawing adverse inferences from silence in *Annex C* will not apply because the detainee is allowed an opportunity to consult the duty solicitor;

(d) the detainee changes their mind about wanting legal advice or (as the case may be) about wanting a solicitor present at the interview and states that they no longer wish to speak to a solicitor. In these circumstances, the interview may be started or continued without delay provided that:

   (i)   an officer of inspector rank or above:
- speaks to the detainee to enquire about the reasons for their change of mind (see *Note 6K*), and
- makes, or directs the making of, reasonable efforts to ascertain the solicitor's expected time of arrival and to inform the solicitor that the suspect has stated that they wish to change their mind and the reason (if given);

   (ii) the detainee's reason for their change of mind (if given) and the outcome of the action in (i) are recorded in the custody record;

   (iii) the detainee, after being informed of the outcome of the action in (i) above, confirms in writing that they want the interview to proceed without speaking or further speaking to a solicitor or (as the case may be) without a solicitor being present and do not wish to wait for a solicitor by signing an entry to this effect in the custody record;

   (iv) an officer of inspector rank or above is satisfied that it is proper for the interview to proceed in these circumstances and:
- gives authority in writing for the interview to proceed and, if the authority is not recorded in the custody record, the officer must ensure that the custody record shows the date and time of the authority and where it is recorded, and
- takes, or directs the taking of, reasonable steps to inform the solicitor that the authority has been given and the time when the interview is expected to commence and records or causes to be recorded, the outcome of this action in the custody record.

   (v) When the interview starts and the interviewer reminds the suspect of their right to legal advice (see *paragraph 11.2*, Code E *paragraph 4.5* and Code F *paragraph 4.5*), the interviewer shall then ensure that the following is recorded in the written interview record or the interview record made in accordance with Code E or F:
- confirmation that the detainee has changed their mind about wanting legal advice or (as the case may be) about wanting a solicitor present and the reasons for it if given;
- the fact that authority for the interview to proceed has been given and, subject to *paragraph 2.6A*, the name of the authorising officer;
- that if the solicitor arrives at the station before the interview is completed, the detainee will be so informed without delay and *a break will be taken* to allow them to speak to the solicitor if they wish, unless *paragraph 6.6(a)* applies, and
- that at any time during the interview, the detainee may again ask for legal advice and that if they do, a break will be taken to allow them to speak to the solicitor, unless *paragraph 6.6(a), (b), or (c)* applies.

Note: In these circumstances, the restriction on drawing adverse inferences from silence in *Annex C* will not apply because the detainee is allowed an opportunity to consult a solicitor if they wish.

6.7 If *paragraph 6.6(a)* applies, where the reason for authorising the delay ceases to apply, there may be no further delay in permitting the exercise of the right in the absence of a further authorisation unless *paragraph 6.6(b), (c)* or *(d)* applies. If *paragraph 6.6(b)(i)* applies, once sufficient information has been obtained to avert the risk, questioning must cease until the detainee has received legal advice unless *paragraph 6.6(a), (b)(ii), (c)* or *(d)* applies.

6.8 A detainee who has been permitted to consult a solicitor shall be entitled on request to have the solicitor present when they are interviewed unless one of the exceptions in *paragraph 6.6* applies.

6.9 The solicitor may only be required to leave the interview if their conduct is such that the interviewer is unable properly to put questions to the suspect. See *Notes 6D* and *6E*.

6.10 If the interviewer considers a solicitor is acting in such a way, they will stop the interview and consult an officer not below superintendent rank, if one is readily available, and otherwise an officer not below inspector rank not connected with the investigation. After speaking to the solicitor, the officer consulted will decide if the interview should continue in the presence of that solicitor. If they decide it should not, the suspect will be given the opportunity to consult another solicitor before the interview continues and that solicitor given an opportunity to be present at the interview. See *Note 6E*.

6.11 The removal of a solicitor from an interview is a serious step and, if it occurs, the officer of superintendent rank or above who took the decision will consider if the incident should be reported to the Solicitors Regulatory Authority. If the decision to remove the solicitor has been taken by an officer below superintendent rank, the facts must be reported to an officer of superintendent rank or above, who will similarly consider whether a report to the Solicitors Regulatory Authority would be appropriate. When the solicitor concerned is a duty solicitor, the report should be both to the Solicitors Regulatory Authority and to the Legal Aid Agency.

6.12 'Solicitor' in this Code means:
- a solicitor who holds a current practising certificate;
- an accredited or probationary representative included on the register of representatives maintained by the Legal Aid Agency.

6.12A An accredited or probationary representative sent to provide advice by, and on behalf of, a solicitor shall be admitted to the police station for this purpose unless an officer of inspector rank or above considers such a visit will hinder the investigation and directs otherwise. Hindering the investigation does not include giving proper legal advice to a detainee as in *Note 6D*. Once admitted to the police station, *paragraphs 6.6* to *6.10* apply.

6.13 In exercising their discretion under *paragraph 6.12A*, the officer should take into account in particular:
- whether:
  - the identity and status of an accredited or probationary representative have been satisfactorily established;
  - they are of suitable character to provide legal advice, e.g. a person with a criminal

record is unlikely to be suitable unless the conviction was for a minor offence and not recent.

- any other matters in any written letter of authorisation provided by the solicitor on whose behalf the person is attending the police station. See *Note 6F*.

6.14 If the inspector refuses access to an accredited or probationary representative or a decision is taken that such a person should not be permitted to remain at an interview, the inspector must notify the solicitor on whose behalf the representative was acting and give them an opportunity to make alternative arrangements. The detainee must be informed and the custody record noted.

6.15 If a solicitor arrives at the station to see a particular person, that person must, unless *Annex B* applies, be so informed whether or not they are being interviewed and asked if they would like to see the solicitor. This applies even if the detainee has declined legal advice or, having requested it, subsequently agreed to be interviewed without receiving advice. The solicitor's attendance and the detainee's decision must be noted in the custody record.

(B) Documentation

6.16 Any request for legal advice and the action taken shall be recorded.

6.17 A record shall be made in the interview record if a detainee asks for legal advice and an interview is begun either in the absence of a solicitor or their representative, or they have been required to leave an interview.

Notes for Guidance

6ZA *No police officer or police staff shall indicate to any suspect, except to answer a direct question, that the period for which they are liable to be detained, or if not detained, the time taken to complete the interview, might be reduced:*

- *if they do not ask for legal advice or do not want a solicitor present when they are interviewed; or*
- *if they have asked for legal advice or (as the case may be) asked for a solicitor to be present when they are interviewed but change their mind and agree to be interviewed without waiting for a solicitor.*

6A *In considering if paragraph 6.6(b) applies, the officer should, if practicable, ask the solicitor for an estimate of how long it will take to come to the station and relate this to the time detention is permitted, the time of day (i.e. whether the rest period under paragraph 12.2 is imminent) and the requirements of other investigations. If the solicitor is on their way or is to set off immediately, it will not normally be appropriate to begin an interview before they arrive. If it appears necessary to begin an interview before the solicitor's arrival, they should be given an indication of how long the police would be able to wait before 6.6(b) applies so there is an opportunity to make arrangements for someone else to provide legal advice.*

6B *A detainee has a right to free legal advice and to be represented by a solicitor. This Note for Guidance explains the arrangements which enable detainees to obtain legal advice. An outline of these arrangements is also included in the Notice of Rights and Entitlements given to detainees in accordance with paragraph 3.2. The arrangements also apply, with appropriate modifications, to persons attending a police station or other location (see paragraph 3.22 and Notes 3I and 3J) voluntarily who are cautioned prior to being interviewed. See paragraph 3.21.*

When a detainee asks for free legal advice, the Defence Solicitor Call Centre (DSCC) must be informed of the request.

Free legal advice will be limited to telephone advice provided by CDS Direct if a detainee is:

- *detained for a non-imprisonable offence;*
- *arrested on a bench warrant for failing to appear and being held for production at court (except where the solicitor has clear documentary evidence available that would result in the client being released from custody);*
- *arrested for drink driving (driving/in charge with excess alcohol, failing to provide a specimen, driving/in charge whilst unfit through drink), or*
- *detained in relation to breach of police or court bail conditions*

unless one or more exceptions apply, in which case the DSCC should arrange for advice to be given by a solicitor at the police station, for example:

- *the police want to interview the detainee or carry out an eye-witness identification procedure;*
- *the detainee needs an appropriate adult;*
- *the detainee is unable to communicate over the telephone;*
- *the detainee alleges serious misconduct by the police;*
- *the investigation includes another offence not included in the list,*
- *the solicitor to be assigned is already at the police station.*

When free advice is not limited to telephone advice, a detainee can ask for free advice from a solicitor they know or if they do not know a solicitor or the solicitor they know cannot be contacted, from the duty solicitor.

To arrange free legal advice, the police should telephone the DSCC. The call centre will decide whether legal advice should be limited to telephone advice from CDS Direct, or whether a solicitor known to the detainee or the duty solicitor should speak to the detainee.

When a detainee wants to pay for legal advice themselves:

- *the DSCC will contact a solicitor of their choice on their behalf;*
- *they may, when free advice is only available by telephone from CDS Direct, still speak to a solicitor of their choice on the telephone for advice, but the solicitor would not be paid by legal aid and may ask the person to pay for the advice;*
- *they should be given an opportunity to consult a specific solicitor or another solicitor from that solicitor's firm. If this solicitor is not available, they may choose up to two alternatives. If these alternatives are not available, the custody officer has discretion to allow further*

attempts until a solicitor has been contacted and agreed to provide advice;
- they are entitled to a private consultation with their chosen solicitor on the telephone or the solicitor may decide to come to the police station;
- If their chosen solicitor cannot be contacted, the DSCC may still be called to arrange free legal advice.

Apart from carrying out duties necessary to implement these arrangements, an officer must not advise the suspect about any particular firm of solicitors.

6B1 *Not used.*

6B2 *Not used.*

6C *Not used.*

6D *The solicitor's only role in the police station is to protect and advance the legal rights of their client. On occasions this may require the solicitor to give advice which has the effect of the client avoiding giving evidence which strengthens a prosecution case. The solicitor may intervene in order to seek clarification, challenge an improper question to their client or the manner in which it is put, advise their client not to reply to particular questions, or if they wish to give their client further legal advice. Paragraph 6.9 only applies if the solicitor's approach or conduct prevents or unreasonably obstructs proper questions being put to the suspect or the suspect's response being recorded. Examples of unacceptable conduct include answering questions on a suspect's behalf or providing written replies for the suspect to quote.*

6E *An officer who takes the decision to exclude a solicitor must be in a position to satisfy the court the decision was properly made. In order to do this they may need to witness what is happening.*

6F *If an officer of at least inspector rank considers a particular solicitor or firm of solicitors is persistently sending probationary representatives who are unsuited to provide legal advice, they should inform an officer of at least superintendent rank, who may wish to take the matter up with the Solicitors Regulation Authority.*

6G *Subject to the constraints of Annex B, a solicitor may advise more than one client in an investigation if they wish. Any question of a conflict of interest is for the solicitor under their professional code of conduct. If, however, waiting for a solicitor to give advice to one client may lead to unreasonable delay to the interview with another, the provisions of paragraph 6.6(b) may apply.*

6H *In addition to a poster in English, a poster or posters containing translations into Welsh, the main minority ethnic languages and the principal European languages should be displayed wherever they are likely to be helpful and it is practicable to do so.*

6I *Not used.*

6J *Whenever a detainee exercises their right to legal advice by consulting or communicating with a solicitor, they must be allowed to do so in private. This right to consult or communicate in private is fundamental. If the requirement for privacy is compromised because what is said or written by the detainee or solicitor for the purpose of giving and receiving legal advice is overheard, listened to, or read by others without the informed consent of the detainee, the right will effectively have been denied. When a detainee speaks to a solicitor on the telephone, they should be allowed to do so in private unless this is impractical because of the design and layout of the custody area or the location of telephones. However, the normal expectation should be that facilities will be available, unless they are being used, at all police stations to enable detainees to speak in private to a solicitor either face to face or over the telephone.*

6K *A detainee is not obliged to give reasons for declining legal advice and should not be pressed to do so.*

7 CITIZENS OF INDEPENDENT COMMONWEALTH COUNTRIES OR FOREIGN NATIONALS

(A) ACTION

7.1 A detainee who is a citizen of an independent Commonwealth country or a national of a foreign country, including the Republic of Ireland, has the right, upon request, to communicate at any time with the appropriate High Commission, Embassy or Consulate. That detainee must be informed as soon as practicable of this right and asked if they want to have their High Commission, Embassy or Consulate told of their whereabouts and the grounds for their detention. Such a request should be acted upon as soon as practicable. See *Note 7A*.

7.2 A detainee who is a citizen of a country with which a bilateral consular convention or agreement is in force requiring notification of arrest must also be informed that subject to *paragraph 7.4*, notification of their arrest will be sent to the appropriate High Commission, Embassy or Consulate as soon as practicable, whether or not they request it. A list of the countries to which this requirement currently applies and contact details for the relevant High Commissions, Embassies and Consulates can be obtained from the Consular Directorate of the Foreign and Commonwealth Office (FCO) as follows:

- from the FCO web pages:
  - *https://gov.uk/government/publications/ table-of-consular-conventions-and-mandatory-notificationobligations*, and
  - *https://www.gov.uk/government/publications/foreign-embassies-in-the-uk*
- by telephone to 020 7008 3100,
- by email to *fcocorrespondence@fco.gov.uk.*
- by letter to the Foreign and Commonwealth Office, King Charles Street, London, SW1A 2AH.

7.3 Consular officers may, if the detainee agrees, visit one of their nationals in police detention to talk to them and, if required, to arrange for legal advice. Such visits shall take place out of the hearing of a police officer.

7.4 Notwithstanding the provisions of consular conventions, if the detainee claims that they are a refugee or have applied or intend to apply for asylum, the custody officer must ensure that UK Visas and Immigration (UKVI) (formerly the UK Border Agency) is informed as soon as practicable of the claim. UKVI will then determine whether compliance with relevant international obligations requires notification of the arrest to be sent and will inform the custody officer as to what action police need to take.

(B) Documentation

7.5 A record shall be made:

* when a detainee is informed of their rights under this section and of any requirement in paragraph 7.2;
* of any communications with a High Commission, Embassy or Consulate, and
* of any communications with UKVI about a detainee's claim to be a refugee or to be seeking asylum and the resulting action taken by police.

Note for Guidance

7A *The exercise of the rights in this section may not be Interfered with even though Annex B applies.*

8 Conditions of detention

(A) Action

8.1 So far as it is practicable, not more than one detainee should be detained in each cell. See *Note 8C.*

8.2 Cells in use must be adequately heated, cleaned and ventilated. They must be adequately lit, subject to such dimming as is compatible with safety and security to allow people detained overnight to sleep. No additional restraints shall be used within a locked cell unless absolutely necessary and then only restraint equipment, approved for use in that force by the chief officer, which is reasonable and necessary in the circumstances having regard to the detainee's de-meanour and with a view to ensuring their safety and the safety of others. If a detainee is deaf or a vulnerable person, particular care must be taken when deciding whether to use any form of approved restraints.

8.3 Blankets, mattresses, pillows and other bedding supplied shall be of a reasonable standard and in a clean and sanitary condition. See *Note 8A.*

8.4 Access to toilet and washing facilities must be provided.

8.5 If it is necessary to remove a detainee's clothes for the purposes of investigation, for hygiene, health reasons or cleaning, replacement clothing of a reasonable standard of comfort and cleanliness shall be provided. A detainee may not be interviewed unless adequate clothing has been offered.

8.6 At least two light meals and one main meal should be offered in any 24-hour period. See *Note 8B.* Drinks should be provided at meal times and upon reasonable request between meals. Whenever necessary, advice shall be sought from the appropriate healthcare professional, see *Note 9A,* on medical and dietary matters. As far as practicable, meals provided shall offer a varied diet and meet any specific dietary needs or religious beliefs the detainee may have. The detainee may, at the custody officer's discretion, have meals supplied by their family or friends at their expense. See *Note 8A.*

8.7 Brief outdoor exercise shall be offered daily if practicable.

8.8 A juvenile shall not be placed in a police cell unless no other secure accommodation is available and the custody officer considers it is not practicable to supervise them if they are not placed in a cell or that a cell provides more comfortable accommodation than other secure accommodation in the station. A juvenile may not be placed in a cell with a detained adult.

(B) Documentation

8.9 A record must be kept of replacement clothing and meals offered.

8.10 If a juvenile is placed in a cell, the reason must be recorded.

8.11 The use of any restraints on a detainee whilst in a cell, the reasons for it and, if appropriate, the arrangements for enhanced supervision of the detainee whilst so restrained, shall be recorded. See *paragraph 3.9.*

Notes for Guidance

8A *The provisions in paragraph 8.3 and 8.6 respectively are of particular importance in the case of a person likely to be detained for an extended period. In deciding whether to allow meals to be supplied by family or friends, the custody officer is entitled to take account of the risk of items being concealed in any food or package and the officer's duties and responsibilities under food handling legislation.*

8B *Meals should, so far as practicable, be offered at recognised meal times, or at other times that take account of when the detainee last had a meal.*

8C *The Detention and Custody Authorised Professional Practice (APP) produced by the College of Policing (see http://www.app.college.police.uk) provides more detailed guidance on matters concerning detainee healthcare and treatment and associated forensic issues which should be read in conjunction with sections 8 and 9 of this Code.*

9 Care and treatment of detained persons

(A) General

9.1 Nothing in this section prevents the police from calling an appropriate healthcare professional to examine a detainee for the purposes of obtaining evidence relating to any offence in which the detainee is suspected of being involved. See *Notes 9A and 8C.*

9.2 If a complaint is made by, or on behalf of, a detainee about their treatment since their arrest, or it comes to notice that a detainee may have been treated improperly, a report must be made as soon as practicable to an officer of inspector rank or above not connected with the investigation. If the matter concerns a possible assault or the possibility of the unnecessary or unreasonable use of force, an appropriate healthcare professional must also be called as soon as practicable.

9.3 Subject to *paragraph 9.6* in the case of a person to whom The Mental Health Act 1983 (Places of Safety) Regulations 2017 apply, detainees should be visited at least every hour. If no reasonably foreseeable risk was identified in a risk assessment, see *paragraphs 3.6* to *3.10*, there is no need to wake a sleeping detainee. Those suspected of being under the influence of drink or drugs or both or of having swallowed drugs, see *Note 9CA*, or whose level of consciousness causes concern must, subject to any clinical directions given by the appropriate healthcare professional, see *paragraph 9.13*:

- be visited and roused at least every half hour;
- have their condition assessed as in *Annex H*;
- and clinical treatment arranged if appropriate.

See *Notes 9B, 9C* and *9H*

9.4 When arrangements are made to secure clinical attention for a detainee, the custody officer must make sure all relevant information which might assist in the treatment of the detainee's condition is made available to the responsible healthcare professional. This applies whether or not the healthcare professional asks for such information. Any officer or police staff with relevant information must inform the custody officer as soon as practicable.

(B) Clinical treatment and attention

9.5 The custody officer must make sure a detainee receives appropriate clinical attention as soon as reasonably practicable if the person:

(a) appears to be suffering from physical illness; or
(b) is injured; or
(c) appears to be suffering from a mental disorder; or
(d) appears to need clinical attention.

9.5A This applies even if the detainee makes no request for clinical attention and whether or not they have already received clinical attention elsewhere. If the need for attention appears urgent, e.g. when indicated as in *Annex H*, the nearest available healthcare professional or an ambulance must be called immediately.

9.5B The custody officer must also consider the need for clinical attention as set out in *Note 9C* in relation to those suffering the effects of alcohol or drugs.

9.6 *Paragraph 9.5* is not meant to prevent or delay the transfer to a hospital if necessary of a person detained under the Mental Health Act 1983, sections 135 and 136, as amended by the Policing and Crime Act 2017. See *Note 9D*. When an assessment under that Act is to take place at a police station (see *paragraph 3.16*) the custody officer must also ensure that in accordance with *The Mental Health Act 1983 (Places of Safety) Regulations 2017*, a health professional is present and available to the person throughout the period they are detained at the police station and that at the welfare of the detainee is checked by the health professional at least once every thirty minutes and any appropriate action for the care and treatment of the detainee taken.

9.7 If it appears to the custody officer, or they are told, that a person brought to a station under arrest may be suffering from an infectious disease or condition, the custody officer must take reasonable steps to safeguard the health of the detainee and others at the station. In deciding what action to take, advice must be sought from an appropriate healthcare professional. See *Note 9E*. The custody officer has discretion to isolate the person and their property until clinical directions have been obtained.

9.8 If a detainee requests a clinical examination, an appropriate healthcare professional must be called as soon as practicable to assess the detainee's clinical needs. If a safe and appropriate care plan cannot be provided, the appropriate healthcare professional's advice must be sought. The detainee may also be examined by a medical practitioner of their choice at their expense.

9.9 If a detainee is required to take or apply any medication in compliance with clinical directions prescribed before their detention, the custody officer must consult the appropriate healthcare professional before the use of the medication. Subject to the restrictions in *paragraph 9.10*, the custody officer is responsible for the safekeeping of any medication and for making sure the detainee is given the opportunity to take or apply prescribed or approved medication. Any such consultation and its outcome shall be noted in the custody record.

9.10 No police officer may administer or supervise the self-administration of medically pre-scribed controlled drugs of the types and forms listed in the Misuse of Drugs Regulations 2001, Schedule 2 or 3. A detainee may only self-administer such drugs under the personal supervision of the registered medical practitioner authorising their use or other appropriate healthcare profes-sional. The custody officer may supervise the self-administration of, or authorise other custody staff to supervise the self-administration of, drugs listed in Schedule 4 or 5 if the officer has consulted the appropriate healthcare professional authorising their use and both are satisfied self-administration will not expose the detainee, police officers or anyone else to the risk of harm or injury.

9.11 When appropriate healthcare professionals administer drugs or authorise the use of other medications, supervise their self-administration or consult with the custody officer about allowing self-administration of drugs listed in Schedule 4 or 5, it must be within current medicines legislation and the scope of practice as determined by their relevant statutory regulatory body.

9.12 If a detainee has in their possession, or claims to need, medication relating to a heart condition, diabetes, epilepsy or a condition of comparable potential seriousness then, even though *paragraph 9.5* may not apply, the advice of the appropriate healthcare professional must be obtained.

9.13 Whenever the appropriate healthcare professional is called in accordance with this sec-tion to examine or treat a detainee, the custody officer shall ask for their opinion about:

- any risks or problems which police need to take into account when making decisions about the detainee's continued detention;
- when to carry out an interview if applicable; and
- the need for safeguards.

9.14 When clinical directions are given by the appropriate healthcare professional, whether orally or in writing, and the custody officer has any doubts or is in any way uncertain about any aspect of the directions, the custody officer shall ask for clarification. It is particularly important that directions concerning the frequency of visits are clear, precise and capable of being implemented. See *Note 9F*.

(C) D<small>OCUMENTATION</small>

9.15 A record must be made in the custody record of:
- (a) the arrangements made for an examination by an appropriate healthcare professional under *paragraph 9.2* and of any complaint reported under that paragraph together with any relevant remarks by the custody officer;
- (b) any arrangements made in accordance with *paragraph 9.5*;
- (c) any request for a clinical examination under *paragraph 9.8* and any arrangements made in response;
- (d) the injury, ailment, condition or other reason which made it necessary to make the arrangements in (*a*) to (*c*); See *Note 9G*.
- (e) any clinical directions and advice, including any further clarifications, given to police by a healthcare professional concerning the care and treatment of the detainee in connection with any of the arrangements made in (*a*) to (*c*); See *Notes 9E* and *9F*.
- (f) if applicable, the responses received when attempting to rouse a person using the procedure in *Annex H*. See *Note 9H*.

9.16 If a healthcare professional does not record their clinical findings in the custody record, the record must show where they are recorded. See *Note 9G*. However, information which is necessary to custody staff to ensure the effective ongoing care and well being of the detainee must be recorded openly in the custody record, see *paragraph 3.8* and *Annex G, paragraph 7*.

9.17 Subject to the requirements of *Section 4*, the custody record shall include:
- a record of all medication a detainee has in their possession on arrival at the police station;
- a note of any such medication they claim to need but do not have with them.

N<small>OTES FOR</small> G<small>UIDANCE</small>

9A *A 'healthcare professional' means a clinically qualified person working within the scope of practice as determined by their relevant statutory regulatory body. Whether a healthcare professional is 'appropriate' depends on the circumstances of the duties they carry out at the time.*

9B *Whenever possible, detained juveniles and vulnerable persons should be visited more frequently.*

9C *A detainee who appears drunk or behaves abnormally may be suffering from illness, the effects of drugs or may have sustained injury, particularly a head injury which is not apparent. A detainee needing or dependent on certain drugs, including alcohol, may experience harmful effects within a short time of being deprived of their supply. In these circumstances, when there is any doubt, police should always act urgently to call an appropriate healthcare professional or an ambulance. Paragraph 9.5 does not apply to minor ailments or injuries which do not need attention. However, all such ailments or injuries must be recorded in the custody record and any doubt must be resolved in favour of calling the appropriate healthcare professional.*

9CA *Paragraph 9.3 would apply to a person in police custody by order of a magistrates' court under the Criminal Justice Act 1988, section 152 (as amended by the Drugs Act 2005, section 8) to facilitate the recovery of evidence after being charged with drug possession or drug trafficking and suspected of having swallowed drugs. In the case of the healthcare needs of a person who has swallowed drugs, the custody officer, subject to any clinical directions, should consider the necessity for rousing every half hour. This does not negate the need for regular visiting of the suspect in the cell.*

9D *Except as allowed for under The Mental Health Act 1983 (Places of Safety) Regulations 2017, a police station must not be used as a place of safety for persons detained under section 135 or 136 of that Act. Chapter 16 of the Mental Health Act 1983 Code of Practice (as revised), provides more detailed guidance about arranging assessments under the Mental Health Act and transferring detainees from police stations to other places of safety. Additional guidance in relation to amendments made to the Mental Health Act in 2017 are published at https://www.gov.uk/government/publications/mental-health-act-1983-implementing-changes-to-police-powers.*

9E *It is important to respect a person's right to privacy and information about their health must be kept confidential and only disclosed with their consent or in accordance with clinical advice when it is necessary to protect the detainee's health or that of others who come into contact with them.*

9F *The custody officer should always seek to clarify directions that the detainee requires constant observation or supervision and should ask the appropriate healthcare professional to explain precisely what action needs to be taken to implement such directions.*

9G *Paragraphs 9.15 and 9.16 do not require any information about the cause of any injury, ailment or condition to be recorded on the custody record if it appears capable of providing evidence of an offence.*

9H *The purpose of recording a person's responses when attempting to rouse them using the procedure in Annex H is to enable any change in the individual's consciousness level to be noted and clinical treatment arranged if appropriate.*

10 C<small>AUTIONS</small>

(A) W<small>HEN A CAUTION MUST BE GIVEN</small>

10.1 A person whom there are grounds to suspect of an offence, see *Note 10A*, must be cautioned before any questions about an offence, or further questions if the answers provide the grounds for suspicion, are put to them if either the suspect's answers or silence, (i.e. failure or refusal to answer or answer satisfactorily) may be given in evidence to a court in a prosecution. A person need not be cautioned if questions are for other necessary purposes, e.g.:

  (a) solely to establish their identity or ownership of any vehicle;
  (b) to obtain information in accordance with any relevant statutory requirement, see *paragraph 10.9*;
  (c) in furtherance of the proper and effective conduct of a search, e.g. to determine the need to search in the exercise of powers of stop and search or to seek co-operation while carrying out a search; or
  (d) to seek verification of a written record as in *paragraph 11.13*.
  (e) *Not used.*

10.2 Whenever a person not under arrest is initially cautioned, or reminded that they are under caution, that person must at the same time be told they are not under arrest and must be informed of the provisions of *paragraphs 3.21 to 3.21B* which explain that they need to agree to be interviewed, how they may obtain legal advice according to whether they are at a police station or elsewhere and the other rights and entitlements that apply to a voluntary interview. See *Note 10C*.

10.3 A person who is arrested, or further arrested, must be informed at the time if practicable or, if not, as soon as it becomes practicable thereafter, that they are under arrest and of the grounds and reasons for their arrest, see *paragraph 3.4, Note 10B* and *Code G, paragraphs 2.2 and 4.3*.

10.4 As required by *Code G, section 3*, a person who is arrested, or further arrested, must also be cautioned unless:

  (a) it is impracticable to do so by reason of their condition or behaviour at the time;
  (b) they have already been cautioned immediately prior to arrest as in *paragraph 10.1*.

(B) Terms of the cautions

10.5 The caution which must be given on:

  (a) arrest; or
  (b) all other occasions before a person is charged or informed they may be prosecuted; see *section 16*,

should, unless the restriction on drawing adverse inferences from silence applies, see *Annex C*, be in the following terms:

"You do not have to say anything. But it may harm your defence if you do not mention when questioned something which you later rely on in Court. Anything you do say may be given in evidence."

Where the use of the Welsh Language is appropriate, a constable may provide the caution directly in Welsh in the following terms:

"*Does dim rhaid i chi ddweud dim byd. Ond gall niweidio eich amddiffyniad os na fyddwch chi'n sôn, wrth gael eich holi, am rywbeth y byddwch chi'n dibynnu arno nes ymlaen yn y Llys. Gall unrhyw beth yr ydych yn ei ddweud gael ei roi fel tystiolaeth.*"

See *Note 10G*

10.6 *Annex C, paragraph 2* sets out the alternative terms of the caution to be used when the restriction on drawing adverse inferences from silence applies.

10.7 Minor deviations from the words of any caution given in accordance with this Code do not constitute a breach of this Code, provided the sense of the relevant caution is preserved. See *Note 10D*.

10.8 After any break in questioning under caution, the person being questioned must be made aware they remain under caution. If there is any doubt the relevant caution should be given again in full when the interview resumes. See *Note 10E*.

10.9 When, despite being cautioned, a person fails to co-operate or to answer particular questions which may affect their immediate treatment, the person should be informed of any relevant consequences and that those consequences are not affected by the caution. Examples are when a person's refusal to provide:

  • their name and address when charged may make them liable to detention;
  • particulars and information in accordance with a statutory requirement, e.g. under the Road Traffic Act 1988, may amount to an offence or may make the person liable to a further arrest.

(C) Special warnings under the Criminal Justice and Public Order Act 1994, sections 36 and 37

10.10 When a suspect interviewed at a police station or authorised place of detention after arrest fails or refuses to answer certain questions, or to answer satisfactorily, after due warning, see *Note 10F*, a court or jury may draw such inferences as appear proper under the Criminal Justice and Public Order Act 1994, sections 36 and 37. Such inferences may only be drawn when:

  (a) the restriction on drawing adverse inferences from silence, see *Annex C*, does not apply; and
  (b) the suspect is arrested by a constable and fails or refuses to account for any objects, marks or substances, or marks on such objects found:
    • on their person;
    • in or on their clothing or footwear;
    • otherwise in their possession; or
    • in the place they were arrested;
  (c) the arrested suspect was found by a constable at a place at or about the time the offence for which that officer has arrested them is alleged to have been committed, and the suspect fails or refuses to account for their presence there.

When the restriction on drawing adverse inferences from silence applies, the suspect may still be asked to account for any of the matters in (*b*) or (*c*) but the special warning described in *paragraph 10.11* will not apply and must not be given.

10.11 For an inference to be drawn when a suspect fails or refuses to answer a question about one of these matters or to answer it satisfactorily, the suspect must first be told in ordinary language:

(a) what offence is being investigated;
(b) what fact they are being asked to account for;
(c) this fact may be due to them taking part in the commission of the offence;
(d) a court may draw a proper inference if they fail or refuse to account for this fact; and
(e) a record is being made of the interview and it may be given in evidence if they are brought to trial.

(D) Juveniles and vulnerable persons

10.11A The information required in paragraph 10.11 must not be given to a suspect who is a juvenile or a vulnerable person unless the appropriate adult is present.

10.12 If a juvenile or a vulnerable person is cautioned in the absence of the appropriate adult, the caution must be repeated in the appropriate adult's presence.

10.12A *Not used.*

(E) Documentation

10.13 A record shall be made when a caution is given under this section, either in the interviewer's report book or in the interview record.

Notes for Guidance

10A *There must be some reasonable, objective grounds for the suspicion, based on known facts or information which are relevant to the likelihood the offence has been committed and the person to be questioned committed it.*

10B *An arrested person must be given sufficient information to enable them to understand that they have been deprived of their liberty and the reason they have been arrested, e.g. when a person is arrested on suspicion of committing an offence they must be informed of the suspected offence's nature, when and where it was committed. The suspect must also be informed of the reason or reasons why the arrest is considered necessary. Vague or technical language should be avoided.*

10C *The restriction on drawing inferences from silence, see Annex C, paragraph 1, does not apply to a person who has not been detained and who therefore cannot be prevented from seeking legal advice if they want, see paragraph 3.21.*

10D *If it appears a person does not understand the caution, the person giving it should explain it in their own words.*

10E *It may be necessary to show to the court that nothing occurred during an interview break or between interviews which influenced the suspect's recorded evidence. After a break in an interview or at the beginning of a subsequent interview, the interviewer should summarise the reason for the break and confirm this with the suspect.*

10F *The Criminal Justice and Public Order Act 1994, sections 36 and 37 apply only to suspects who have been arrested by a constable or an officer of Revenue and Customs and are given the relevant warning by the police or Revenue and Customs officer who made the arrest or who is investigating the offence. They do not apply to any interviews with suspects who have not been arrested.*

10G *Nothing in this Code requires a caution to be given or repeated when informing a person not under arrest they may be prosecuted for an offence. However, a court will not be able to draw any inferences under the Criminal Justice and Public Order Act 1994, section 34, if the person was not cautioned.*

11 Interviews - general

(A) Action

11.1A An interview is the questioning of a person regarding their involvement or suspected involvement in a criminal offence or offences which, under paragraph 10.1, must be carried out under caution. Before a person is interviewed, they and, if they are represented, their solicitor must be given sufficient information to enable them to understand the nature of any such offence, and why they are suspected of committing it (see *paragraphs 3.4(a)* and *10.3*), in order to allow for the effective exercise of the rights of the defence. However, whilst the information must always be sufficient for the person to understand the nature of any offence (see *Note 11ZA*), this does not require the disclosure of details at a time which might prejudice the criminal investigation. The decision about what needs to be disclosed for the purpose of this requirement therefore rests with the investigating officer who has sufficient knowledge of the case to make that decision. The officer who discloses the information shall make a record of the information disclosed and when it was disclosed. This record may be made in the interview record, in the officer's report book or other form provided for this purpose. Procedures under the Road Traffic Act 1988, section 7 or the Transport and Works Act 1992, section 31 do not constitute interviewing for the purpose of this Code.

11.1 Following a decision to arrest a suspect, they must not be interviewed about the relevant offence except at a police station or other authorised place of detention, unless the consequent delay would be likely to:

(a) lead to:
  • interference with, or harm to, evidence connected with an offence;
  • interference with, or physical harm to, other people; or
  • serious loss of, or damage to, property;
(b) lead to alerting other people suspected of committing an offence but not yet arrested for it; or
(c) hinder the recovery of property obtained in consequence of the commission of an offence.

Interviewing in any of these circumstances shall cease once the relevant risk has been averted or the necessary questions have been put in order to attempt to avert that risk.

11.2 Immediately prior to the commencement or re-commencement of any interview at a police station or other authorised place of detention, the interviewer should remind the suspect of their entitlement to free legal advice and that the interview can be delayed for legal advice to be obtained, unless one of the exceptions in *paragraph 6.6* applies. It is the interviewer's responsibility to make sure all reminders are recorded in the interview record.

11.3 *Not used.*

11.4 At the beginning of an interview the interviewer, after cautioning the suspect, see *section 10*, shall put to them any significant statement or silence which occurred in the presence and hearing of a police officer or other police staff before the start of the interview and which have not been put to the suspect in the course of a previous interview. See *Note 11A*. The interviewer shall ask the suspect whether they confirm or deny that earlier statement or silence and if they want to add anything.

11.4A A significant statement is one which appears capable of being used in evidence against the suspect, in particular a direct admission of guilt. A significant silence is a failure or refusal to answer a question or answer satisfactorily when under caution, which might, allowing for the restriction on drawing adverse inferences from silence, see *Annex C*, give rise to an inference under the Criminal Justice and Public Order Act 1994, Part III.

11.5 No interviewer may try to obtain answers or elicit a statement by the use of oppression. Except as in *paragraph 10.9*, no interviewer shall indicate, except to answer a direct question, what action will be taken by the police if the person being questioned answers questions, makes a statement or refuses to do either. If the person asks directly what action will be taken if they answer questions, make a statement or refuse to do either, the interviewer may inform them what action the police propose to take provided that action is itself proper and warranted.

11.6 The interview or further interview of a person about an offence with which that person has not been charged or for which they have not been informed they may be prosecuted, must cease when:

(a) the officer in charge of the investigation is satisfied all the questions they consider relevant to obtaining accurate and reliable information about the offence have been put to the suspect, this includes allowing the suspect an opportunity to give an innocent explanation and asking questions to test if the explanation is accurate and reliable, e.g. to clear up ambiguities or clarify what the suspect said;

(b) the officer in charge of the investigation has taken account of any other available evidence; and

(c) the officer in charge of the investigation, or in the case of a detained suspect, the custody officer, see *paragraph 16.1*, reasonably believes there is sufficient evidence to provide a realistic prospect of conviction for that offence. See *Note 11B*.

This paragraph does not prevent officers in revenue cases or acting under the confiscation provisions of the Criminal Justice Act 1988 or the Drug Trafficking Act 1994 from inviting suspects to complete a formal question and answer record after the interview is concluded.

(B) Interview records

(a) An accurate record must be made of each interview, whether or not the interview takes place at a police station.

(b) The record must state the place of interview, the time it begins and ends, any interview breaks and, subject to *paragraph 2.6A*, the names of all those present; and must be made on the forms provided for this purpose or in the interviewer's report book or in accordance with Codes of Practice E or F.

(c) Any written record must be made and completed during the interview, unless this would not be practicable or would interfere with the conduct of the interview, and must constitute either a verbatim record of what has been said or, failing this, an account of the interview which adequately and accurately summarises it.

11.8 If a written record is not made during the interview it must be made as soon as practicable after its completion.

11.9 Written interview records must be timed and signed by the maker.

11.10 If a written record is not completed during the interview the reason must be recorded in the interview record.

11.11 Unless it is impracticable, the person interviewed shall be given the opportunity to read the interview record and to sign it as correct or to indicate how they consider it inaccurate. If the person interviewed cannot read or refuses to read the record or sign it, the senior interviewer present shall read it to them and ask whether they would like to sign it as correct or make their mark or to indicate how they consider it inaccurate. The interviewer shall certify on the interview record itself what has occurred. See *Note 11E*.

11.12 If the appropriate adult or the person's solicitor is present during the interview, they should also be given an opportunity to read and sign the interview record or any written statement taken down during the interview.

11.13 A record shall be made of any comments made by a suspect, including unsolicited comments, which are outside the context of an interview but which might be relevant to the offence. Any such record must be timed and signed by the maker. When practicable the suspect shall be given the opportunity to read that record and to sign it as correct or to indicate how they consider it inaccurate. See *Note 11E*.

11.14 Any refusal by a person to sign an interview record when asked in accordance with this Code must itself be recorded.

(C) Juveniles and vulnerable persons

11.15 A juvenile or vulnerable person must not be interviewed regarding their involvement or suspected involvement in a criminal offence or offences, or asked to provide or sign a written statement under caution or record of interview, in the absence of the appropriate adult unless *paragraphs 11.1* or *11.18* to *11.20* apply. See *Note 11C*.

11.16 Juveniles may only be interviewed at their place of education in exceptional circumstances and only when the principal or their nominee agrees. Every effort should be made to notify the parent(s) or other person responsible for the juvenile's welfare and the appropriate adult, if this is a different person, that the police want to interview the juvenile and reasonable time should be allowed to enable the appropriate adult to be present at the interview. If awaiting the appropriate adult would cause unreasonable delay, and unless the juvenile is suspected of an offence against the educational establishment, the principal or their nominee can act as the appropriate adult for the purposes of the interview.

11.17 If an appropriate adult is present at an interview, they shall be informed:

- that they are not expected to act simply as an observer; and
- that the purpose of their presence is to:
  - advise the person being interviewed;
  - observe whether the interview is being conducted properly and fairly; and
  - facilitate communication with the person being interviewed.

See *paragraph 1.7A*.

11.17A The appropriate adult may be required to leave the interview if their conduct is such that the interviewer is unable properly to put questions to the suspect. This will include situations where the appropriate adult's approach or conduct prevents or unreasonably obstructs proper questions being put to the suspect or the suspect's responses being recorded (see *Note 11F*). If the interviewer considers an appropriate adult is acting in such a way, they will stop the interview and consult an officer not below superintendent rank, if one is readily available, and otherwise an officer not below inspector rank not connected with the investigation. After speaking to the appropriate adult, the officer consulted must remind the adult that their role under *paragraph 11.17* does not allow them to obstruct proper questioning and give the adult an opportunity to respond. The officer consulted will then decide if the interview should continue without the attendance of that appropriate adult. If they decide it should, another appropriate adult must be obtained before the interview continues, unless the provisions of *paragraph 11.18* below apply.

(D) Vulnerable suspects – urgent interviews at police stations

11.18 The following interviews may take place only if an officer of superintendent rank or above considers delaying the interview will lead to the consequences in *paragraph 11.1(a) to (c)*, and is satisfied the interview would not significantly harm the person's physical or mental state (see *Annex G*):

(a) an interview of a detained juvenile or vulnerable person without the appropriate adult being present (see *Note 11C*);

(b) an interview of anyone detained other than in (*a*) who appears unable to:
- appreciate the significance of questions and their answers; or
- understand what is happening because of the effects of drink, drugs or any illness, ailment or condition;

(c) an interview, without an interpreter having been arranged, of a detained person whom the custody officer has determined requires an interpreter (see *paragraphs 3.5(c)(ii)* and *3.12*) which is carried out by an interviewer speaking the suspect's own language or (as the case may be) otherwise establishing effective communication which is sufficient to enable the necessary questions to be asked and answered in order to avert the consequences. See *paragraphs 13.2* and *13.5*.

11.19 These interviews may not continue once sufficient information has been obtained to avert the consequences in *paragraph 11.1(a)* to (c).

11.20 A record shall be made of the grounds for any decision to interview a person under *paragraph 11.18*.

(E) Conduct and recording of Interviews at police stations - use of live link

11.21 When a suspect in police detention is interviewed using a live link by a police officer who is not at the police station where the detainee is held, the provisions of this section that govern the conduct and making a written record of that interview, shall be subject to *paragraph 12.9B* of this Code.

(F) Witnesses

11.22 The provisions of this Code and Codes E and F which govern the conduct and recording of interviews do not apply to interviews with, or taking statements from, witnesses.

Notes for Guidance

11ZA *The requirement in paragraph 11.1A for a suspect to be given sufficient information about the offence applies prior to the interview and whether or not they are legally represented. What is sufficient will depend on the circumstances of the case, but it should normally include, as a minimum, a description of the facts relating to the suspected offence that are known to the officer, including the time and place in question. This aims to avoid suspects being confused or unclear about what they are supposed to have done and to help an innocent suspect to clear the matter up more quickly.*

11A *Paragraph 11.4 does not prevent the interviewer from putting significant statements and silences to a suspect again at a later stage or a further interview.*

11B *The Criminal Procedure and Investigations Act 1996 Code of Practice, paragraph 3.5 states 'In conducting an investigation, the investigator should pursue all reasonable lines of enquiry, whether these point towards or away from the suspect. What is reasonable will depend on the particular circumstances.' Interviewers should keep this in mind when deciding what questions to ask in an interview.*

11C *Although juveniles or vulnerable persons are often capable of providing reliable evidence, they may, without knowing or wishing to do so, be particularly prone in certain circumstances to* providing information that may be unreliable, misleading or self-incriminating. Special care should always be taken when questioning such a person, and the appropriate adult should be involved if there is any doubt about a person's age, mental state or capacity. Because of the risk of unreliable evidence it is also important to obtain corroboration of any facts admitted whenever possible. Because of the risks, which the presence of the appropriate adult is intended to minimise, officers of superintendent rank or above should exercise their discretion under paragraph 11.18(a) to authorise the commencement of an interview in the appropriate adult's absence only in exceptional cases, if it is necessary to avert one or more of the specified risks in paragraph 11.1.

11D Juveniles should not be arrested at their place of education unless this is unavoidable. When a juvenile is arrested at their place of education, the principal or their nominee must be informed.

11E Significant statements described in paragraph 11.4 will always be relevant to the offence and must be recorded. When a suspect agrees to read records of interviews and other comments and sign them as correct, they should be asked to endorse the record with, e.g. 'I agree that this is a correct record of what was said' and add their signature. If the suspect does not agree with the record, the interviewer should record the details of any disagreement and ask the suspect to read these details and sign them to the effect that they accurately reflect their disagreement. Any refusal to sign should be recorded.

11F The appropriate adult may intervene if they consider it is necessary to help the suspect understand any question asked and to help the suspect to answer any question. Paragraph 11.17A only applies if the appropriate adult's approach or conduct prevents or unreasonably obstructs proper questions being put to the suspect or the suspect's response being recorded. Examples of unacceptable conduct include answering questions on a suspect's behalf or providing written replies for the suspect to quote. An officer who takes the decision to exclude an appropriate adult must be in a position to satisfy the court the decision was properly made. In order to do this they may need to witness what is happening and give the suspect's solicitor (if they have one) who witnessed what happened, an opportunity to comment.

12 Interviews in police stations

(A) Action

When interviewer and suspect are present at the same police station

12.1 If a police officer wants to interview or conduct enquiries which require the presence of a detainee, the custody officer is responsible for deciding whether to deliver the detainee into the officer's custody. An investigating officer who is given custody of a detainee takes over responsibility for the detainee's care and safe custody for the purposes of this Code until they return the detainee to the custody officer when they must report the manner in which they complied with the Code whilst having custody of the detainee.

12.2 Except as below, in any period of 24 hours a detainee must be allowed a continuous period of at least 8 hours for rest, free from questioning, travel or any interruption in connection with the investigation concerned. This period should normally be at night or other appropriate time which takes account of when the detainee last slept or rested. If a detainee is arrested at a police station after going there voluntarily, the period of 24 hours runs from the time of their arrest and not the time of arrival at the police station. The period may not be interrupted or delayed, except:

(a) when there are reasonable grounds for believing not delaying or interrupting the period would:
   (i) involve a risk of harm to people or serious loss of, or damage to, property;
   (ii) delay unnecessarily the person's release from custody; or
   (iii) otherwise prejudice the outcome of the investigation;
(b) at the request of the detainee, their appropriate adult or legal representative;
(c) when a delay or interruption is necessary in order to:
   (i) comply with the legal obligations and duties arising under section 15; or
   (ii) to take action required under *section 9* or in accordance with medical advice.

If the period is interrupted in accordance with *(a)*, a fresh period must be allowed. Interruptions under *(b)* and *(c)* do not require a fresh period to be allowed.

12.3 Before a detainee is interviewed, the custody officer, in consultation with the officer in charge of the investigation and appropriate healthcare professionals as necessary, shall assess whether the detainee is fit enough to be interviewed. This means determining and considering the risks to the detainee's physical and mental state if the interview took place and determining what safeguards are needed to allow the interview to take place. See *Annex G*. The custody officer shall not allow a detainee to be interviewed if the custody officer considers it would cause significant harm to the detainee's physical or mental state. Vulnerable suspects listed at *paragraph 11.18* shall be treated as always being at some risk during an interview and these persons may not be interviewed except in accordance with *paragraphs 11.18 to 11.20*.

12.4 As far as practicable interviews shall take place in interview rooms which are adequately heated, lit and ventilated.

12.5 A suspect whose detention without charge has been authorised under PACE because the detention is necessary for an interview to obtain evidence of the offence for which they have been arrested may choose not to answer questions but police do not require the suspect's consent or agreement to interview them for this purpose. If a suspect takes steps to prevent themselves being questioned or further questioned, e.g. by refusing to leave their cell to go to a suitable interview room or by trying to leave the interview room, they shall be advised that their consent or agreement to be interviewed is not required. The suspect shall be cautioned as in *section 10*, and informed if they fail or refuse to co-operate, the interview may take place in the cell and that their failure or refusal to co-operate may be given in evidence. The suspect shall then be invited to co-operate and go into the interview room. If they refuse and the custody officer considers, on reasonable grounds, that the interview should not be delayed, the custody officer has discretion to direct that the interview be conducted in a cell.

12.6 People being questioned or making statements shall not be required to stand.
12.7 Before the interview commences each interviewer shall, subject to *paragraph 2.6A*, identify themselves and any other persons present to the interviewee.
12.8 Breaks from interviewing should be made at recognised meal times or at other times that take account of when an interviewee last had a meal. Short refreshment breaks shall be provided at approximately two hour intervals, subject to the interviewer's discretion to delay a break if there are reasonable grounds for believing it would:

  (i)   involve a:
         •   risk of harm to people;
         •   serious loss of, or damage to, property;
  (ii)   unnecessarily delay the detainee's release; or
  (iii) otherwise prejudice the outcome of the investigation.

See Note 12B
12.9 If during the interview a complaint is made by or on behalf of the interviewee concerning the provisions of any of the Codes, or it comes to the interviewer's notice that the interviewee may have been treated improperly, the interviewer should:

  (i)   record the matter in the interview record; and
  (ii)   inform the custody officer, who is then responsible for dealing with it as in *section 9*.

Interviewer not present at the same station as the detainee– use of live link

12.9A Amendments to PACE, section 39, allow a person in police detention to be interviewed using a live link (see *paragraph 1.13(e)(i)*) by a police officer who is not at the police station where the detainee is held. Subject to *sub-paragraphs (a)* to *(f)* below, the custody officer is responsible for deciding on a case by case basis whether a detainee is fit to be interviewed (see *paragraph 12.3*) and should be delivered into the physical custody of an officer who is not involved in the investigation, for the purpose of enabling another officer who is investigating the offence for which the person is detained and who is not at the police station where the person is detained, to interview the detainee by means of a live link (see *Note 12ZA*).

  (a)   The custody officer must be satisfied that the live link to be used provides for accurate and secure communication with the suspect. The provisions of *paragraph 13.13* shall apply to communications between the interviewing officer, the suspect and anyone else whose presence at the interview or, (as the case may be) whose access to any communications between the suspect and the interviewer, has been authorised by the custody officer or the interviewing officer.
  (b)   Each decision must take account of the age, gender and vulnerability of the suspect, the nature and circumstances of the offence and the investigation and the impact on the suspect of carrying out the interview by means of a live link. For this reason, the custody officer must consider whether the ability of the particular suspect, to communicate confidently and effectively for the purpose of the interview is likely to be adversely affected or otherwise undermined or limited if the interviewing officer is not physically present and a live-link is used (see *Note 12ZB*). Although a suspect for whom an appropriate adult is required may be more likely to be adversely affected as described, it is important to note that a person who does not require an appropriate adult may also be adversely impacted if interviewed by means of a live link.
  (c)   If the custody officer is satisfied that interviewing the detainee by means of a live link *would not* adversely affect or otherwise undermine or limit the suspect's ability to communicate confidently and effectively for the purpose of the *interview*, the officer must so inform the suspect, their solicitor and (if applicable) the appropriate adult. At the same time, the operation of the live-link must be explained and demonstrated to them (see *Note 12ZC*), they must be advised of the chief officer's obligations concerning the security of live-link communications under *paragraph 13.13* and they must be asked if they wish to make representations that the live-link should not be used or if they require more information about the operation of the arrangements. They must also be told that at any time live-link is in use, they may make representations to the custody officer or the interviewer that its operation should cease and that the physical presence of the interviewer should be arranged.

When the authority of an inspector is required

  (d)   If:
         (i)   representations are made that a live-link should not be used to carry out the interview, or that at any time it is in use, its operation should cease and the physical presence of the interviewer arranged; and
         (ii) the custody officer in consultation with the interviewer is unable to allay the concerns raised;
         then live-link may not be used, or (as the case may be) continue to be used, unless authorised in writing by an officer of the rank of inspector or above in accordance with *sub-paragraph (e)*.
  (e)   Authority may be given if the officer is satisfied that interviewing the detainee by means of a live link is necessary and justified. In making this decision, the officer must have regard to:
         (i)   the circumstances of the suspect;
         (ii)   the nature and seriousness of the offence;
         (iii) the requirements of the investigation, including its likely impact on both the suspect and any victim(s);
         (iv)   the representations made by the suspect, their solicitor and (if applicable) the appropriate adult that a live-link should not be used (see *sub-paragraph (b)*;
         (v)   the impact on the investigation of making arrangements for the physical presence of the interviewer (see *Note 12ZD*); and
         (vi)   the risk if the interviewer is not *physically* present, evidence obtained using link

interpretation might be excluded in subsequent criminal proceedings; and

    (vii) the likely impact on the suspect and the investigation of any consequential delay to arrange for the interviewer to be *physically* present with the suspect.

(f) The officer given custody of the detainee *and* the interviewer take over responsibility for the detainee's care, treatment and safe custody for the purposes of this Code until the detainee is returned to the custody officer. On that return, both must report the manner in which they complied with the Code during period in question.

12.9B When a suspect detained at a police station is interviewed using a live link in accordance with *paragraph 12.9A*, the officer given custody of the detainee at the police station *and* the interviewer who is not present at the police station, take over responsibility for ensuring compliance with the provisions of *sections 11* and *12* of this Code, or *Code E* (Audio recording) or *Code F* (Audio visual recording) that govern the conduct and recording of that interview. In these circumstances:

(a) *the interviewer who is not at the police station where the detainee is held* must direct the officer having physical custody of the suspect at the police station, to take the action required by those provisions and which the interviewer would be required to take if they were present at the police station.

(b) *the officer having physical custody of the suspect at the police station* must take the action required by those provisions and which would otherwise be required to be taken by the interviewer if they were present at the police station. This applies whether or not the officer has been so directed by the interviewer but in such a case, the officer must inform the interviewer of the action taken.

(c) *during the course of the interview*, the officers in (a) and (b) may consult each other as necessary to clarify any action to be taken and to avoid any misunderstanding. Such consultations must, if in the hearing of the suspect and any other person present with the suspect (for example, a solicitor, appropriate adult or interpreter) be recorded in the interview record.

(B) Documentation

12.10 A record must be made of the:

- time a detainee is not in the custody of the custody officer, and why
- reason for any refusal to deliver the detainee out of that custody.

12.11 A record shall be made of the following:

(a) the reasons it was not practicable to use an interview room;

(b) any action taken as in *paragraph 12.5*; and

(c) the actions, decisions, authorisations, representations and outcomes arising from the requirements of *paragraphs 12.9A* and *12.9B*.

The record shall be made on the custody record or in the interview record for action taken whilst an interview record is being kept, with a brief reference to this effect in the custody record.

12.12 Any decision to delay a break in an interview must be recorded, with reasons, in the interview record.

12.13 All written statements made at police stations under caution shall be written on forms provided for the purpose.

12.14 All written statements made under caution shall be taken in accordance with *Annex D*. Before a person makes a written statement under caution at a police station, they shall be reminded about the right to legal advice. See *Note 12A*.

Notes for Guidance

12ZA *'Live link' means an arrangement by means of which the interviewing officer who is not at the police station is able to see and hear, and to be seen and heard by, the detainee concerned, the detainee's solicitor, any appropriate adult present and the officer who has custody of that detainee. See paragraphs 13.12 to 13.14 and Annex N for application to live-link interpretation.*

12ZB *In considering whether the use of the live link is appropriate in a particular case, the custody officer, in consultation with the interviewer, should make an assessment of the detainee's ability to understand and take part in the interviewing process and make a record of the outcome. If the suspect has asked for legal advice, their solicitor should be involved in the assessment and in the case of a juvenile or vulnerable person, the appropriate adult should be involved.*

12ZC *The explanation and demonstration of live-link interpretation is intended to help the suspect, solicitor and appropriate adult make an informed decision and to allay any concerns they may have.*

12ZD *Factors affecting the arrangements for the interviewer to be physically present will include the location of the police station where the interview would take place and the availability of an interviewer with sufficient knowledge of the investigation who can attend that station and carry out the interview.*

12A *It is not normally necessary to ask for a written statement if the interview was recorded in writing and the record signed in accordance with paragraph 11.11 or audibly or visually recorded in accordance with Code E or F. Statements under caution should normally be taken in these circumstances only at the person's express wish. A person may however be asked if they want to make such a statement.*

12B *Meal breaks should normally last at least 45 minutes and shorter breaks after two hours should last at least 15 minutes. If the interviewer delays a break in accordance with paragraph 12.8 and prolongs the interview, a longer break should be provided. If there is a short interview and another short interview is contemplated, the length of the break may be reduced if there are reasonable grounds to believe this is necessary to avoid any of the consequences in paragraph 12.8(i) to (iii).*

13 Interpreters

(A) General

13.1   Chief officers are responsible for making arrangements (see *paragraph 13.1ZA*) to provide appropriately qualified independent persons to act as interpreters and to provide translations of essential documents for:

(a)   detained suspects who, in accordance with *paragraph 3.5(c)(ii)*, the custody officer has determined require an interpreter, and

(b)   suspects who are not under arrest but are cautioned as in *section 10* who, in accordance with *paragraph 3.21(b)*, the interviewer has determined require an interpreter. In these cases, the responsibilities of the custody officer are, if appropriate, assigned to the interviewer. An interviewer who has any doubts about whether and what arrangements for an interpreter must be made or about how the provisions of this section should be applied to a suspect who is not under arrest should seek advice from an officer of the rank of sergeant or above.

If the suspect has a hearing or speech impediment, references to 'interpreter' and 'interpretation' in this Code include arrangements for appropriate assistance necessary to establish effective communication with that person. See *paragraph 13.1C* below if the person is in Wales.

13.1ZA   References in *paragraph 13.1* above and elsewhere in this Code (see *paragraphs 3.12(a), 13.2, 13.2A, 13.5, 13.6, 13.9, 13.10, 13.10A, 13.10D* and *13.11 below* and in any other Code, to making arrangements for an interpreter to assist a suspect, mean making arrangements for the interpreter to be *physically* present in the same location as the suspect *unless* the provisions in *paragraph 13.12* below, and Part 1 of *Annex N*, allow live-link interpretation to be used.

13.1A   The arrangements *must* comply with the minimum requirements set out in *Directive 2010/64/EU* of the European Parliament and of the Council of 20 October 2010 on the right to interpretation and translation in criminal proceedings (see *Note 13A*). The provisions *of this* Code implement the requirements for those to whom this Code applies. These requirements include the following:

*   That the arrangements made and the quality of interpretation and translation provided shall be sufficient to '*safeguard the fairness of the proceedings, in particular by ensuring that suspected or accused persons have knowledge of the cases against them and are able to exercise their right of defence*'. This term which is used by the Directive means that the suspect must be able to understand their position and be able to communicate effectively with police officers, interviewers, solicitors and appropriate adults as provided for by this and any other Code in the same way as a suspect who can speak and understand English and who does not have a hearing or speech impediment and who would therefore not require an interpreter. See *paragraphs 13.12* to *13.14* and *Annex N* for application to live-link interpretation.
*   The provision of a written translation of all documents considered essential for the person to exercise their right of defence and to '*safeguard the fairness of the proceedings*' as described above. For the purposes of this Code, this includes any decision to authorise a person to be detained and details of any offence(s) with which the person has been charged or for which they have been told they may be prosecuted, see *Annex M*.
*   Procedures to help determine:
    *   whether a suspect can speak and understand English and needs the assistance of an interpreter, see *paragraph 13.1* and *Notes 13B* and *13C*; and
    *   whether another interpreter should be arranged or another translation should be provided when a suspect complains about the quality of either or both, see *paragraphs 13.10A* and *13.10C*.

13.1B   All reasonable attempts should be made to make the suspect understand that interpretation and translation will be provided at public expense.

13.1C   With regard to persons in Wales, nothing in this or any other Code affects the application of the Welsh Language Schemes produced by police and crime commissioners in Wales in accordance with the Welsh Language Act 1993. See *paragraphs 3.12 and 13.1*.

(B) Interviewing suspects - foreign languages

13.2   Unless *paragraphs 11.1 or 11.18(c)* apply, a suspect who for the purposes of this Code requires an interpreter because they do not appear to speak or understand English (see *paragraphs 3.5(c)(ii)* and *3.12*) must not be interviewed unless arrangements are made for a person capable of interpreting to assist the suspect to understand and communicate.

13.2A   If a person who is a juvenile or a vulnerable person is interviewed and the person acting as the appropriate adult does not appear to speak or understand English, arrangements must be made for an interpreter to assist communication between the person, the appropriate adult and the interviewer, unless the interview is urgent and *paragraphs 11.1 or 11.18(c)* apply.

13.3   When a written record of the interview is made (see *paragraph 11.7*), the interviewer shall make sure the interpreter makes a note of the interview at the time in the person's language for use in the event of the interpreter being called to give evidence, and certifies its accuracy. The interviewer should allow sufficient time for the interpreter to note each question and answer after each is put, given and interpreted. The person should be allowed to read the record or have it read to them and sign it as correct or indicate the respects in which they consider it inaccurate. If an audio or visual record of the interview is made, the arrangements in Code E or F shall apply. See *paragraphs 13.12* to *13.14* and *Annex N* for application to live-link interpretation.

13.4   In the case of a person making a statement under caution (see *Annex D*) to a police officer or other police staff in a language other than English:

(a)   the interpreter shall record the statement in the language it is made;

(b)   the person shall be invited to sign it;

(c)   an official English translation shall be made in due course. See *paragraphs 13.12* to *13.14* and Annex N for application to live-link interpretation.

(C) Interviewing suspects who have a hearing or speech impediment

13.5 Unless *paragraphs 11.1 or 11.18(c)* (urgent interviews) apply, a suspect who for the purposes of this Code requires an interpreter or other appropriate assistance to enable effective communication with them because they appear to have a hearing or speech impediment (see *paragraphs 3.5(c)(ii)* and *3.12*) must not be interviewed without arrangements having been made to provide an independent person capable of interpreting or of providing other appropriate assistance.

13.6 An interpreter should also be arranged if a person who is a juvenile or a vulnerable person is interviewed and the person who is present as the appropriate adult, appears to have a hearing or speech impediment, unless the interview is urgent and *paragraphs 11.1 or 11.18(c)* apply.

13.7 If a written record of the interview is made, the interviewer shall make sure the interpreter is allowed to read the record and certify its accuracy in the event of the interpreter being called to give evidence. If an audio or visual recording is made, the arrangements in Code E or F apply.

See *paragraphs 13.12* to *13.14* and *Annex N* for application to live-link interpretation.

(D) Additional rules for detained persons

13.8 *Not used.*

13.9 If *paragraph 6.1* applies and the detainee cannot communicate with the solicitor because of language, hearing or speech difficulties, arrangements must be made for an interpreter to enable communication. A police officer or any other police staff may not be used for this purpose.

13.10 After the custody officer has determined that a detainee requires an interpreter (see *paragraph 3.5(c)(ii)*) and following the initial action in *paragraphs 3.1 to 3.5*, arrangements must also be made for an interpreter to:

- explain the grounds and reasons for any authorisation for their *continued* detention, before or after charge and any information about the authorisation given to them by the authorising officer and which is recorded in the custody record. See *paragraphs 15.3, 15.4* and *15.16(a)* and *(b)*;
- to provide interpretation at the magistrates' court for the hearing of an application for a warrant of further detention or any extension or further extension of such warrant to explain any grounds and reasons for the application and any information about the authorisation of their further detention given to them by the court (see PACE, sections 43 and 44 and *paragraphs 15.2* and *15.16(c)*); and
- explain any offence with which the detainee is charged or for which they are informed they may be prosecuted and any other information about the offence given to them by or on behalf of the custody officer, see *paragraphs 16.1* and *16.3*.

13.10A If a detainee complains that they are not satisfied with the quality of interpretation, the custody officer or (as the case may be) the interviewer, is responsible for deciding whether to make arrangements for a different interpreter in accordance with the procedures set out in the arrangements made by the chief officer, *see paragraph 13.1A*.

(E) Translations of essential documents

13.10B Written translations, oral translations and oral summaries of essential documents in a language the detainee understands shall be provided in accordance with Annex M (Translations of documents and records).

13.10C If a detainee complains that they are not satisfied with the quality of the translation, the custody officer or (as the case may be) the interviewer, is responsible for deciding whether a further translation should be provided in accordance with the procedures set out in the arrangements made by the chief officer, see *paragraph 13.1A*.

(F) Decisions not to provide interpretation and translation.

13.10D If a suspect challenges a decision:

- made by the custody officer or (as the case may be) by the interviewer, in accordance with this Code (see *paragraphs 3.5(c)(ii)* and *3.21(b)*) that they do not require an interpreter, or
- made in accordance with *paragraphs 13.10A, 13.10B* or *13.10C* not to make arrangements to provide a different interpreter or another translation or not to translate a requested document,

the matter shall be reported to an inspector to deal with as a complaint for the purposes of *paragraph 9.2* or *paragraph 12.9* if the challenge is made during an interview.

(G) Documentation

13.11 The following must be recorded in the custody record or, as applicable, the interview record:

- (a) Action taken to arrange for an interpreter, including the live-link requirements in *Annex N* as applicable;
- (b) Action taken when a detainee is not satisfied about the standard of interpretation or translation provided, see *paragraphs 13.10A* and *13.10C*;
- (c) When an urgent interview is carried out in accordance with *paragraph 13.2* or *13.5* in the absence of an interpreter;
- (d) When a detainee has been assisted by an interpreter for the purpose of providing or being given information or being interviewed;
- (e) Action taken in accordance with *Annex M* when:
  - a written translation of an essential document is provided;
  - an oral translation or oral summary of an essential document is provided instead of a written translation and the authorising officer's reason(s) why this would not prejudice the fairness of the proceedings (see *Annex M, paragraph 3*);
  - a suspect waives their right to a translation of an essential document (see *Annex M, paragraph 4*);

- when representations that a document which is not included in the table is essential and that a translation should be provided are refused and the reason for the refusal (see *Annex M, paragraph 8*).

(H) Live link interpretation

13.12 In this section and in *Annex N*, 'live-link interpretation' means an arrangement to enable communication between the suspect and an interpreter who is not *physically* present with the suspect. The arrangement must ensure that anything said by any person in the suspect's presence and hearing can be interpreted in the same way as if the interpreter was physically present at that time. The communication must be by audio *and* visual means for the purpose of an interview, and for all other purposes it may be *either*, by audio and visual means, or by audio means *only*, as follows:(a)

Audio and visual communication

This applies for the purposes of an interview conducted and recorded in accordance with Code E (Audio recording) or Code F (Visual recording) and during that interview, live link interpretation must *enable:*

(i)   the suspect, the interviewer, solicitor, appropriate adult and any other person *physically* present with the suspect at any time during the interview and an interpreter who is not *physically* present, to *see* and *hear* each other; and

(ii)   the interview to be conducted and recorded in accordance with the provisions of Codes C, E and F, subject to the modifications in *Part 2 of Annex N.*

(b)

Audio and visual or audio without visual communication.

This applies to communication for the purposes of any provision of this or any other Code except as described in (a), which requires or permits information to be given to, sought from, or provided by a suspect, whether orally or in writing, which would include communication between the suspect and their solicitor and/or appropriate adult, and for these cases, live link interpretation must:

(i)   *enable* the suspect, the person giving or seeking that information, any other person *physically* present with the suspect at that time and an interpreter who is not so present, to either *see* and *hear* each other, or to *hear without seeing* each other (for example by using a telephone); and

(ii)   enable that information to be given to, sought from, or provided by, the suspect in accordance with the provisions of this or any other Code that apply to that information, as modified for the purposes of the live-link, by *Part 2 of Annex N.*

13.12A   The requirement in *sub-paragraphs 13.12(a)(ii)* and *(b)(ii)*, that live-link interpretation must enable compliance with the relevant provisions of the Codes C, E and F, means that the arrangements must provide for any written or electronic record of what the suspect says in their own language which is made by the interpreter, to be securely transmitted without delay so that the suspect can be invited to read, check and if appropriate, sign or otherwise confirm that the record is correct or make corrections to the record.

13.13   Chief officers must be satisfied that live-link interpretation used in their force area for the purposes of *paragraphs 3.12(a)* and *(b)*, provides for accurate and secure communication with the suspect. This includes ensuring that at any time during which live link interpretation is being used: a person cannot see, hear or otherwise obtain access to any communications between the suspect and interpreter or communicate with the suspect or interpreter unless so authorised or allowed by the custody officer or, in the case of an interview, the interviewer and that as applicable, the confidentiality of any private consultation between a suspect and their solicitor and appropriate adult (see *paragraphs 13.2A, 13.6* and *13.9*) is maintained. See *Annex N paragraph 4.*

Notes for Guidance

13A   *Chief officers have discretion when determining the individuals or organisations they use to provide interpretation and translation services for their forces provided that these are compatible with the requirements of the Directive. One example which chief officers may wish to consider is the Ministry of Justice commercial agreements for interpretation and translation services.*

13B   *A procedure for determining whether a person needs an interpreter might involve a telephone interpreter service or using cue cards or similar visual aids which enable the detainee to indicate their ability to speak and understand English and their preferred language. This could be confirmed through an interpreter who could also assess the extent to which the person can speak and understand English.*

13C   *There should also be a procedure for determining whether a suspect who requires an interpreter requires assistance in accordance with paragraph 3.20 to help them check and if applicable, sign any documentation.*

14 Questioning - special restrictions

14.1   If a person is arrested by one police force on behalf of another and the lawful period of detention in respect of that offence has not yet commenced in accordance with PACE, section 41, no questions may be put to them about the offence while they are in transit between the forces except to clarify any voluntary statement they make.

14.2   If a person is in police detention at a hospital, they may not be questioned without the agreement of a responsible doctor. See *Note 14A.*

Note for Guidance

14A   *If questioning takes place at a hospital under paragraph 14.2, or on the way to or from a hospital, the period of questioning concerned counts towards the total period of detention permitted.*

15 Reviews and extensions of detention

(A) Persons detained under PACE

15.0   The requirement in *paragraph 3.4(b)* that documents and materials essential to challenging the lawfulness of the detainee's arrest and detention must be made available to the detainee or their solicitor, applies for the purposes of this section as follows:

(a)   The officer reviewing the need for detention without charge (*PACE, section 40*), or (as the case may be) the officer considering the need to extend detention without charge from 24 to 36 hours (*PACE, section 42*), is responsible, in consultation with the investigating officer, for deciding which documents and materials are essential and must be made available.

(b)   When *paragraph 15.7A* applies (application for a warrant of further detention or extension of such a warrant), the officer making the application is responsible for deciding which documents and materials are essential and must be made available *before* the hearing. See *Note 3ZA*.

15.1   The review officer is responsible under PACE, section 40 for periodically determining if a person's detention, before or after charge, continues to be necessary. This requirement continues throughout the detention period and, except when a telephone or a live link is used in accordance with *paragraphs 15.9* to *15.11C*, the review officer must be present at the police station holding the detainee. See *Notes 15A* and *15B*.

15.2   Under PACE, section 42, an officer of superintendent rank or above who is responsible for the station holding the detainee may give authority any time after the second review to extend the maximum period the person may be detained without charge by up to 12 hours. Except when a live link is used as in *paragraph 15.11A*, the superintendent must be present at the station holding the detainee. Further detention without charge may be authorised only by a magistrates' court in accordance with PACE, sections 43 and 44 and unless the court has given a live link direction as in *paragraph 15.11B*, the detainee must be brought before the court for the hearing. See *Notes 15C, 15D* and *15E*.

15.2A   An authorisation under section 42(1) of PACE extends the maximum period of detention permitted before charge for indictable offences from 24 hours to 36 hours. Detaining a juvenile or a vulnerable person for longer than 24 hours will be dependent on the circumstances of the case and with regard to the person's:

(a)   special vulnerability;

(b)   the legal obligation to provide an opportunity for representations to be made prior to a decision about extending detention;

(c)   the need to consult and consider the views of any appropriate adult; and

(d)   any alternatives to police custody.

15.3   Before deciding whether to authorise continued detention the officer responsible under *paragraph 15.1* or *15.2* shall give an opportunity to make representations about the detention to:

(a)   the detainee, unless in the case of a review as in *paragraph 15.1*, the detainee is asleep;

(b)   the detainee's solicitor if available at the time; and

(c)   the appropriate adult if available at the time.

See *Note 15CA*

15.3A   Other people having an interest in the detainee's welfare may also make representations at the authorising officer's discretion.

15.3B   Subject to *paragraph 15.10*, the representations may be made orally in person or by telephone or in writing. The authorising officer may, however, refuse to hear oral representations from the detainee if the officer considers them unfit to make representations because of their condition or behaviour. See *Note 15C*.

15.3C   The decision on whether the review takes place in person or by telephone or by live link (see *paragraph 1.13(e)(ii)*) is a matter for the review officer. In determining the form the review may take, the review officer must always take full account of the needs of the person in custody. The benefits of carrying out a review in person should always be considered, based on the individual circumstances of each case with specific additional consideration if the person is:

(a)   a juvenile (and the age of the juvenile); or

(b)   a vulnerable person; or

(c)   in need of medical attention for other than routine minor ailments; or

(d)   subject to presentational or community issues around their detention.

See *paragraph 1.4(c)*

15.4   Before conducting a review or determining whether to extend the maximum period of detention without charge, the officer responsible must make sure the detainee is reminded of their entitlement to free legal advice, see *paragraph 6.5*, unless in the case of a review the person is asleep. When determining whether to extend the maximum period of detention without charge, it should also be pointed out that for the purposes of *paragraph 15.2*, the superintendent or (as the case may be) the court, responsible for authorising any such extension, will not be able to use a live link unless the detainee has *received* legal advice on the use of the live link (see *paragraphs 15.11A(ii)* and *15.11C(ii)*) and given consent to its use (see *paragraphs 15.11A(iii)* and *15.11C(iii)*. The detainee must also be given information about how the live link is used.

15.4A   Following sections 45ZA and 45ZB of PACE, when the reminder and information concerning legal advice and about the use of the live link is given and the detainee's consent is sought, the presence of an appropriate adult is required if the detainee in question is a juvenile (see *paragraph 1.5*) or is a *vulnerable adult* by virtue of being a person aged 18 or over who, because of a mental disorder established in accordance *paragraphs 1.4* and *1.13(d)* or for <u>any other reason</u> (see *paragraph 15.4B*), may have difficulty understanding the purpose of:

(a)   an authorisation under section 42 of PACE or anything that occurs in connection with a decision whether to give it (see *paragraphs 15.2* and *15.2A*); or

(b)   a court hearing under section 43 or 44 of PACE or what occurs at the hearing it (see *paragraphs 15.2* and *15.7A*).

15.4B For the purpose of using a live link in accordance with sections 45ZA and 45ZB of PACE to authorise detention without charge (see *paragraphs 15.11A* and *15.11C*), the reference to '*any other reason*' would extend to difficulties in understanding the purposes mentioned in paragraph 15.4A that might arise if the person happened to be under the influence of drink or drugs at the time the live link is to be used. This does not however apply for the purposes of *paragraphs 1.4* and *1.13(d)* (see *Note 1GC*).

15.5 If, after considering any representations, the review officer under *paragraph 15.1* decides to keep the detainee in detention or the superintendent under *paragraph 15.2* extends the maximum period for which they may be detained without charge, then any comment made by the detainee shall be recorded. If applicable, the officer shall be informed of the comment as soon as practicable. See also *paragraphs 11.4* and *11.13*.

15.6 No officer shall put specific questions to the detainee:

- regarding their involvement in any offence; or
- in respect of any comments they may make:
  - when given the opportunity to make representations; or
  - in response to a decision to keep them in detention or extend the maximum period of detention.

Such an exchange could constitute an interview as in *paragraph 11.1A* and would be subject to the associated safeguards in *section 11* and, in respect of a person who has been charged, *paragraph 16.5*. See also *paragraph 11.13*.

15.7 A detainee who is asleep at a review, see *paragraph 15.1*, and whose continued detention is authorised must be informed about the decision and reason as soon as practicable after waking.

15.7A When an application is made to a magistrates' court under PACE, section 43 for a warrant of further detention to extend detention without charge of a person arrested for an *indictable offence*, or under section 44, to extend or further extend that warrant, the detainee:

(a) (a) must, unless the court has given a live link direction as in *paragraph 15.11C*, be brought to court for the hearing of the application (see *Note 15D*);
(b) (b) is entitled to be legally represented if they wish, in which case, *Annex B* cannot apply; and
(c) (c) must be given a copy of the information which supports the application and states:
   (i) (i) the nature of the offence for which the person to whom the application relates has been arrested;
   (ii) (ii) the general nature of the evidence on which the person was arrested;
   (iii) (iii) what inquiries about the offence have been made and what further inquiries are proposed;
   (iv) (iv) the reasons for believing continued detention is necessary for the purposes of the further inquiries;

Note: A warrant of further detention can only be issued or extended if the court has reasonable grounds for believing that the person's further detention is necessary for the purpose of obtaining evidence of an indictable offence for which the person has been arrested and that the investigation is being conducted diligently and expeditiously.

See *paragraph 15.0(b)*.

15.8 *Not used.*

(B) Review of detention by telephone or by using a live link (section 40A and 45A)

15.9 PACE, section 40A provides that the officer responsible under section 40 for reviewing the detention of a person who has not been charged, need not attend the police station holding the detainee and may carry out the review by telephone.

15.9A PACE, section 45A(2) provides that the officer responsible under section 40 for reviewing the detention of a person who has not been charged, need not attend the police station holding the detainee and may carry out the review using a live link. See *paragraph 1.13(e)(ii)*.

15.9B A telephone review is not permitted where facilities for review using a live link exist and it is practicable to use them.

15.9C The review officer can decide at any stage that a telephone review or review by live link should be terminated and that the review will be conducted in person. The reasons for doing so should be noted in the custody record. See *Note 15F*.

15.10 When a review is carried out by telephone or by using a live link, an officer at the station holding the detainee shall be required by the review officer to fulfil that officer's obligations under PACE, section 40 and this Code by:

(a) making any record connected with the review in the detainee's custody record;
(b) if applicable, making the record in (*a*) in the presence of the detainee; and
(c) for a review by telephone, giving the detainee information about the review.

15.11 When a review is carried out by telephone or by using a live link, or the requirement in *paragraph 15.3* will be satisfied:

(a) if facilities exist for the immediate transmission of written representations to the review officer, e.g. fax or email message, by allowing those who are given the opportunity to make representations, to make their representations:
   (i) orally by telephone or (as the case may be) by means of the live link; or
   (ii) in writing using the facilities for the immediate transmission of written representations; and
(b) in all other cases, by allowing those who are given the opportunity to make representations, to make their representations orally by telephone or by means of the live link.

(C) Authorisation to extend detention using live link (sections 45ZA and 45ZB)

15.11A For the purpose of *paragraphs 15.2* and *15.2A*, a superintendent who is not present at the police station where the detainee is being held but who has access to the use of a live link (see *paragraph 1.13(e)(iii))* may, using that live link, give authority to extend the maximum period of detention permitted before charge, if, and only if, the following conditions are satisfied:

(i)   the custody officer considers that the use of the live link is appropriate (see *Note 15H*);
(ii) the detainee in question has requested and received legal advice on the use of the live link (see *paragraph 15.4*).
(iii) the detainee has given their consent to the live link being used (see *paragraph 15.11D*)

15.11B   When a live link is used:

(a)   the authorising superintendent shall, with regard to any record connected with the authorisation which PACE, section 42 and this Code require to be made by the authorising officer, require an officer at the station holding the detainee to make that record in the detainee's custody record;

(b)   the requirement in *paragraph 15.3* (allowing opportunity to make representations) will be satisfied:
   (i)   if facilities exist for the immediate transmission of written representations to the authorising officer, e.g. fax or email message, by allowing those who are given the opportunity to make representations, to make their representations:
      •   in writing by means of those facilities or
      •   orally by means of the live link; or
   (ii) in all other cases, by allowing those who are given the opportunity to make representations, to make their representations orally by means of the live link.

(c)   The authorising officer can decide at any stage to terminate the live link and attend the police station where the detainee is held to carry out the procedure in person. The reasons for doing so should be noted in the custody record.

15.11C   For the purpose of *paragraph 15.7A* and the hearing of an application to a magistrates' court under PACE, section 43 for a warrant of further detention to extend detention without charge of a person arrested for an *indictable offence*, or under PACE, section 44, to extend or further extend that warrant, the magistrates' court may give a direction that a live link (see *paragraph 1.13(e)(iv)*) be used for the purposes of the hearing if, and only if, the following conditions are satisfied:

(i)   the custody officer considers that the use of the live link for the purpose of the hearing is appropriate (see *Note 15H*);
(ii) the detainee in question has requested and received legal advice on the use of the live link (see *paragraph 15.4*);
(iii) the detainee has given their consent to the live link being used (see *paragraph 15.11D*); and
(iv) it is not contrary to the interests of justice to give the direction.

15.11D   References in *paragraphs 15.11A(iii)* and *15.11C(iii)* to the consent of the detainee mean:

(a)   if detainee is aged 18 or over, the consent of that detainee;
(b)   if the detainee is aged 14 and under 18, the consent of the detainee *and* their parent or guardian; and
(c)   if the detainee is aged under 14, the consent of their parent or guardian.

15.11E   The consent described in *paragraph 15.11D* will only be valid if:

(i)   in the case of a detainee aged 18 or over *who is a vulnerable adult* as described in *paragraph 15.4A*), information about how the live link is used and the reminder about their right to legal advice mentioned in *paragraph 15.4* and their consent, are given in the *presence of the appropriate adult*; and

(ii) in the case of a *juvenile:*
      •   if information about how the live link is used and the reminder about their right to legal advice mentioned in *paragraph 15.4* are given in the *presence of the appropriate adult* (who may or may not be their parent or guardian); and
      •   if the juvenile is aged 14 or over, their consent is given in the *presence of the appropriate adult* (who may or may not be their parent or guardian).

Note: If the juvenile is aged under 14, the consent of their parent or guardian is sufficient in its own right (see *Note 15I*).

(D) Documentation

15.12   It is the officer's responsibility to make sure all reminders given under *paragraph 15.4* are noted in the custody record.

15.13   The grounds for, and extent of, any delay in conducting a review shall be recorded.

15.14   When a review is carried out by telephone or video conferencing facilities, a record shall be made of:

(a)   the reason the review officer did not attend the station holding the detainee;
(b)   the place the review officer was;
(c)   the method representations, oral or written, were made to the review officer, see *paragraph 15.11*.

15.15   Any written representations shall be retained.

15.16   A record shall be made as soon as practicable of:

(a)   the outcome of each review of detention before or after charge, and if *paragraph 15.7* applies, of when the person was informed and by whom;
(b)   the outcome of any determination under PACE, section 42 by a superintendent whether to extend the maximum period of detention without charge beyond 24 hours from the relevant time. If an authorisation is given, the record shall state the number of hours and minutes by which the detention period is extended or further extended.
(c)   the outcome of each application under PACE, section 43, for a warrant of further detention or under section 44, for an extension or further extension of that warrant. If a warrant for further detention is granted under section 43 or extended or further extended under 44, the record shall state the detention period authorised by the warrant and the date and time it

was granted or (as the case may be) the period by which the warrant is extended or further extended.

Note: Any period during which a person is released on bail does not count towards the maximum period of detention without charge allowed under PACE, sections 41 to 44.

NOTES FOR GUIDANCE

15A *Review officer for the purposes of:*

- PACE, sections 40, 40A and 45A means, in the case of a person arrested but not charged, an officer of at least inspector rank not directly involved in the investigation and, if a person has been arrested and charged, the custody officer.

15B *The detention of persons in police custody not subject to the statutory review requirement in paragraph 15.1 should still be reviewed periodically as a matter of good practice. Such reviews can be carried out by an officer of the rank of sergeant or above. The purpose of such reviews is to check the particular power under which a detainee is held continues to apply, any associated conditions are complied with and to make sure appropriate action is taken to deal with any changes. This includes the detainee's prompt release when the power no longer applies, or their transfer if the power requires the detainee be taken elsewhere as soon as the necessary arrangements are made. Examples include persons:*

(a) *arrested on warrant because they failed to answer bail to appear at court;*
(b) *arrested under the Bail Act 1976, section 7(3) for breaching a condition of bail granted after charge;*
(c) *in police custody for specific purposes and periods under the Crime (Sentences) Act 1997, Schedule 1;*
(d) *convicted, or remand prisoners, held in police stations on behalf of the Prison Service under the Imprisonment (Temporary Provisions) Act 1980, section 6;*
(e) *being detained to prevent them causing a breach of the peace;*
(f) *detained at police stations on behalf of Immigration Enforcement (formerly the UK Immigration Service);*
(g) *detained by order of a magistrates' court under the Criminal Justice Act 1988, section 152 (as amended by the Drugs Act 2005, section 8) to facilitate the recovery of evidence after being charged with drug possession or drug trafficking and suspected of having swallowed drugs.*

The detention of persons remanded into police detention by order of a court under the Magistrates' Courts Act 1980, section 128 is subject to a statutory requirement to review that detention. This is to make sure the detainee is taken back to court no later than the end of the period authorised by the court or when the need for their detention by police ceases, whichever is the sooner.

15C *In the case of a review of detention, but not an extension, the detainee need not be woken for the review. However, if the detainee is likely to be asleep, e.g. during a period of rest allowed as in paragraph 12.2, at the latest time a review or authorisation to extend detention may take place, the officer should, if the legal obligations and time constraints permit, bring forward the procedure to allow the detainee to make representations. A detainee not asleep during the review must be present when the grounds for their continued detention are recorded and must at the same time be informed of those grounds unless the review officer considers the person is incapable of understanding what is said, violent or likely to become violent or in urgent need of medical attention.*

15CA *In paragraph 15.3(b) and (c), 'available' includes being contactable in time to enable them to make representations remotely by telephone or other electronic means or in person by attending the station. Reasonable efforts should therefore be made to give the solicitor and appropriate adult sufficient notice of the time the decision is expected to be made so that they can make themselves available.*

15D *An application to a Magistrates' Court under PACE, sections 43 or 44 for a warrant of further detention or its extension should be made between 10am and 9pm, and if possible during normal court hours. It will not usually be practicable to arrange for a court to sit specially outside the hours of 10am to 9pm. If it appears a special sitting may be needed outside normal court hours but between 10am and 9pm, the clerk to the justices should be given notice and informed of this possibility, while the court is sitting if possible.*

15E *In paragraph 15.2, the officer responsible for the station holding the detainee includes a superintendent or above who, in accordance with their force operational policy or police regulations, is given that responsibility on a temporary basis whilst the appointed long-term holder is off duty or otherwise unavailable.*

15F *The provisions of PACE, section 40A allowing telephone reviews do not apply to reviews of detention after charge by the custody officer. When use of a live link is not required, they allow the use of a telephone to carry out a review of detention before charge.*

15G *Not used.*

15H *In considering whether the use of the live link is appropriate in the case of a juvenile or vulnerable person, the custody officer and the superintendent should have regard to the detainee's ability to understand the purpose of the authorisation or (as the case may be) the court hearing, and be satisfied that the suspect is able to take part effectively in the process (see paragraphs 1.4(c)). The appropriate adult should always be involved.*

15I *For the purpose of paragraphs 15.11D and 15.11E, the consent required from a parent or guardian may, for a juvenile in the care of a local authority or voluntary organisation, be given by that authority or organisation. In the case of a juvenile, nothing in paragraphs 15.11D and 15.11E require the parent, guardian or representative of a local authority or voluntary organisation to be present with the juvenile to give their consent, unless they are acting as the appropriate adult. However, it is important that the parent, guardian or representative of a local authority or voluntary organisation who is not present is fully informed before being asked to consent. They must be given the same information as that given to the juvenile and the appropriate adult in accordance with* *paragraph 15.11E. They must also be allowed to speak to the juvenile and the appropriate adult if they wish. Provided the consent is fully informed and is not withdrawn, it may be obtained at any time before the live link is used.*

16 CHARGING DETAINED PERSONS

(A) ACTION

16.1 When the officer in charge of the investigation reasonably believes there is sufficient evidence to provide a realistic prospect of conviction for the offence (see *paragraph 11.6)*, they shall without delay, and subject to the following qualification, inform the custody officer who will be responsible for considering whether the detainee should be charged. See *Notes 11B* and *16A*. When a person is detained in respect of more than one offence it is permissible to delay informing the custody officer until the above conditions are satisfied in respect of all the offences, but see *paragraph 11.6*. If the detainee is a juvenile or a vulnerable person, any resulting action shall be taken in the presence of the appropriate adult if they are present at the time.
See *Notes 16B* and *16C*.

16.1A Where guidance issued by the Director of Public Prosecutions under PACE, section 37A is in force the custody officer must comply with that Guidance in deciding how to act in dealing with the detainee. See *Notes 16AA* and *16AB*.

16.1B Where in compliance with the DPP's Guidance the custody officer decides that the case should be immediately referred to the CPS to make the charging decision, consultation should take place with a Crown Prosecutor as soon as is reasonably practicable. Where the Crown Prosecutor is unable to make the charging decision on the information available at that time, the detainee may be released without charge and on bail (with conditions if necessary) under section 37(7)(a). In such circumstances, the detainee should be informed that they are being released to enable the Director of Public Prosecutions to make a decision under section 37B.

16.2 When a detainee is charged with or informed they may be prosecuted for an offence, see *Note 16B*, they shall, unless the restriction on drawing adverse inferences from silence applies, see *Annex C*, be cautioned as follows:

'You do not have to say anything. But it may harm your defence if you do not mention now something which you later rely on in court. Anything you do say may be given in evidence.'

Where the use of the Welsh Language is appropriate, a constable may provide the caution directly in Welsh in the following terms:

'Does dim rhaid i chi ddweud dim byd. Ond gall niweidio eich amddiffyniad os na fyddwch chi'n sôn, yn awr, am rywbeth y byddwch chi'n dibynnu arno nes ymlaen yn y llys. Gall unrhyw beth yr ydych yn ei ddweud gael ei roi fel tystiolaeth.'

Annex C, paragraph 2 sets out the alternative terms of the caution to be used when the restriction on drawing adverse inferences from silence applies.

16.3 When a detainee is charged they shall be given a written notice showing particulars of the offence and, subject to *paragraph 2.6A*, the officer's name and the case reference number. As far as possible the particulars of the charge shall be stated in simple terms, but they shall also show the precise offence in law with which the detainee is charged. The notice shall begin:

'You are charged with the offence(s) shown below.' Followed by the caution.

If the detainee is a juvenile, mentally disordered or otherwise mentally vulnerable, a copy of the notice should also be given to the appropriate adult.

16.4 If, after a detainee has been charged with or informed they may be prosecuted for an offence, an officer wants to tell them about any written statement or interview with another person relating to such an offence, the detainee shall either be handed a true copy of the written statement or the content of the interview record brought to their attention. Nothing shall be done to invite any reply or comment except to:

(a) caution the detainee, *'You do not have to say anything, but anything you do say may be given in evidence.'*;
Where the use of the Welsh Language is appropriate, caution the detainee in the following terms:
'Does dim rhaid i chi ddweud dim byd, ond gall unrhyw beth yr ydych yn ei ddweud gael ei roi fel tystiolaeth.'
and

(b) remind the detainee about their right to legal advice.

16.4A If the detainee:

- cannot read, the document may be read to them;
- is a juvenile, mentally disordered or otherwise mentally vulnerable, the appropriate adult shall also be given a copy, or the interview record shall be brought to their attention.

16.5 A detainee may not be interviewed about an offence after they have been charged with, or informed they may be prosecuted for it, unless the interview is necessary:

- to prevent or minimise harm or loss to some other person, or the public
- to clear up an ambiguity in a previous answer or statement
- in the interests of justice for the detainee to have put to them, and have an opportunity to comment on, information concerning the offence which has come to light since they were charged or informed they might be prosecuted

Before any such interview, the interviewer shall:

(a) caution the detainee, *'You do not have to say anything, but anything you do say may be given in evidence.'*

Where the use of the Welsh Language is appropriate, the interviewer shall caution the detainee: '*Does dim rhaid i chi ddweud dim byd, ond gall unrhyw beth yr ydych yn ei ddweud gael ei roi fel tystiolaeth.*'

(b)   remind the detainee about their right to legal advice.

See *Note 16B*

16.6   The provisions of *paragraphs 16.2* to *16.5* must be complied with in the appropriate adult's presence if they are already at the police station. If they are not at the police station then these provisions must be complied with again in their presence when they arrive unless the detainee has been released. See *Note 16C.*

16.7   When a juvenile is charged with an offence and the custody officer authorises their continued detention after charge, the custody officer must make arrangements for the juvenile to be taken into the care of a local authority to be detained pending appearance in court *unless* the custody officer certifies in accordance with PACE, section 38(6), that:

(a)   for any juvenile; it is impracticable to do so and the reasons why it is impracticable must be set out in the certificate that must be produced to the court; or,

(b)   in the case of a juvenile of at least 12 years old, no secure accommodation is available and other accommodation would not be adequate to protect the public from serious harm from that juvenile. See *Note 16D.*

Note: Chief officers should ensure that the operation of these provisions at police stations in their areas is subject to supervision and monitoring by an officer of the rank of inspector or above. See *Note 16E.*

16.7A   The requirement in *paragraph 3.4(b)* that documents and materials essential to effectively challenging the lawfulness of the detainee's arrest and detention must be made available to the detainee and, if they are represented, their solicitor, applies for the purposes of this section and a person's detention after charge. This means that the custody officer making the bail decision (*PACE, section 38*) or reviewing the need for detention after charge (*PACE, section 40*), is responsible for determining what, if any, documents or materials are essential and must be made available to the detainee or their solicitor. See *Note 3ZA.*

(B)   DOCUMENTATION

16.8   A record shall be made of anything a detainee says when charged.

16.9   Any questions put in an interview after charge and answers given relating to the offence shall be recorded in full during the interview on forms for that purpose and the record signed by the detainee or, if they refuse, by the interviewer and any third parties present. If the questions are audibly recorded or visually recorded the arrangements in Code E or F apply.

16.10   If arrangements for a juvenile's transfer into local authority care as in *paragraph 16.7* are not made, the custody officer must record the reasons in a certificate which must be produced before the court with the juvenile. See *Note 16D.*

NOTES FOR GUIDANCE

16A   *The custody officer must take into account alternatives to prosecution under the Crime and Disorder Act 1998 applicable to persons under 18, and in national guidance on the cautioning of offenders applicable to persons aged 18 and over.*

16AA   *When a person is arrested under the provisions of the Criminal Justice Act 2003 which allow a person to be re-tried after being acquitted of a serious offence which is a qualifying offence specified in Schedule 5 to that Act and not precluded from further prosecution by virtue of section 75(3) of that Act the detention provisions of PACE are modified and make an officer of the rank of superintendent or above who has not been directly involved in the investigation responsible for determining whether the evidence is sufficient to charge.*

16AB   *Where Guidance issued by the Director of Public Prosecutions under section 37B is in force, a custody officer who determines in accordance with that Guidance that there is sufficient evidence to charge the detainee, may detain that person for no longer than is reasonably necessary to decide how that person is to be dealt with under PACE, section 37(7)(a) to (d), including, where appropriate, consultation with the Duty Prosecutor. The period is subject to the maximum period of detention before charge determined by PACE, sections 41 to 44. Where in accordance with the Guidance the case is referred to the CPS for decision, the custody officer should ensure that an officer involved in the investigation sends to the CPS such information as is specified in the Guidance.*

16B   *The giving of a warning or the service of the Notice of Intended Prosecution required by the Road Traffic Offenders Act 1988, section 1 does not amount to informing a detainee they may be prosecuted for an offence and so does not preclude further questioning in relation to that offence.*

16C   *There is no power under PACE to detain a person and delay action under paragraphs 16.2 to 16.5 solely to await the arrival of the appropriate adult. Reasonable efforts should therefore be made to give the appropriate adult sufficient notice of the time the decision (charge etc.) is to be implemented so that they can be present. If the appropriate adult is not, or cannot be, present at that time, the detainee should be released on bail to return for the decision to be implemented when the adult is present, unless the custody officer determines that the absence of the appropriate adult makes the detainee unsuitable for bail for this purpose. After charge, bail cannot be refused, or release on bail delayed, simply because an appropriate adult is not available, unless the absence of that adult provides the custody officer with the necessary grounds to authorise detention after charge under PACE, section 38.*

16D   *Except as in paragraph 16.7, neither a juvenile's behaviour nor the nature of the offence provides grounds for the custody officer to decide it is impracticable to arrange the juvenile's transfer to local authority care. Impracticability concerns the transport and travel requirements and the lack of secure accommodation which is provided for the purposes of restricting liberty does not make it impracticable to transfer the juvenile. Rather, 'impracticable' should be taken to mean that exceptional circumstances render movement of the child impossible or that the juvenile is due at court in such a short space of time that transfer would deprive them of rest or cause them to miss a court appearance. When the reason for not transferring the juvenile is an imminent court* appearance, details of the travelling and court appearance times which justify the decision should be included in the certificate. The availability of secure accommodation is only a factor in relation to a juvenile aged 12 or over when other local authority accommodation would not be adequate to protect the public from serious harm from them. The obligation to transfer a juvenile to local authority accommodation applies as much to a juvenile charged during the daytime as to a juvenile to be held overnight, subject to a requirement to bring the juvenile before a court under PACE, section 46.

16E *The Concordat on Children in Custody published by the Home Office in 2017 provides detailed guidance with the aim of preventing the detention of children in police stations following charge. It is available here: https://www.gov.uk/government/publications/concordat-on-children-in-custody.*

17 Testing Persons for the Presence of Specified Class A Drugs

(A) Action

17.1 This section of Code C applies only in selected police stations in police areas where the provisions for drug testing under section 63B of PACE (as amended by section 5 of the Criminal Justice Act 2003 and section 7 of the Drugs Act 2005) are in force and in respect of which the Secretary of State has given a notification to the relevant chief officer of police that arrangements for the taking of samples have been made. Such a notification will cover either a police area as a whole or particular stations within a police area. The notification indicates whether the testing applies to those arrested or charged or under the age of 18 as the case may be and testing can only take place in respect of the persons so indicated in the notification. Testing cannot be carried out unless the relevant notification has been given and has not been withdrawn. See *Note 17F.*

17.2 A sample of urine or a non-intimate sample may be taken from a person in police detention for the purpose of ascertaining whether they have any specified Class A drug in their body only where they have been brought before the custody officer and:

(a) either the arrest condition, see *paragraph 17.3*, or the charge condition, see *paragraph 17.4* is met;

(b) the age condition see *paragraph 17.5*, is met;

(c) the notification condition is met in relation to the arrest condition, the charge condition, or the age condition, as the case may be. (Testing on charge and/or arrest must be specifically provided for in the notification for the power to apply. In addition, the fact that testing of under 18s is authorised must be expressly provided for in the notification before the power to test such persons applies.). See *paragraph 17.1*; and

(d) a police officer has requested the person concerned to give the sample (the request condition).

17.3 The arrest condition is met where the detainee:

(a) has been arrested for a trigger offence, see *Note 17E*, but not charged with that offence; or

(b) has been arrested for any other offence but not charged with that offence and a police officer of inspector rank or above, who has reasonable grounds for suspecting that their misuse of any specified Class A drug caused or contributed to the offence, has authorised the sample to be taken.

17.4 The charge condition is met where the detainee:

(a) has been charged with a trigger offence, or

(b) has been charged with any other offence and a police officer of inspector rank or above, who has reasonable grounds for suspecting that the detainee's misuse of any specified Class A drug caused or contributed to the offence, has authorised the sample to be taken.

17.5 The age condition is met where:

(a) in the case of a detainee who has been arrested but not charged as in *paragraph 17.3*, they are aged 18 or over;

(b) in the case of a detainee who has been charged as in *paragraph 17.4*, they are aged 14 or over.

17.6 Before requesting a sample from the person concerned, an officer must:

(a) inform them that the purpose of taking the sample is for drug testing under PACE. This is to ascertain whether they have a specified Class A drug present in their body;

(b) warn them that if, when so requested, they fail without good cause to provide a sample they may be liable to prosecution;

(c) where the taking of the sample has been authorised by an inspector or above in accordance with *paragraph 17.3(b)* or *17.4(b)* above, inform them that the authorisation has been given and the grounds for giving it;

(d) remind them of the following rights, which may be exercised at any stage during the period in custody:

(i) the right to have someone informed of their arrest [see section 5];

(ii) the right to consult privately with a solicitor and that free independent legal advice is available [see section 6]; and

(iii) the right to consult these Codes of Practice [see section 3].

17.7 In the case of a person who has not attained the age specified in section 63B(5A) of PACE—

(a) the making of the request for a sample under *paragraph 17.2(d)* above;

(b) the giving of the warning and the information under *paragraph 17.6* above; and

(c) the taking of the sample,

may not take place except in the presence of an appropriate adult. See *Note 17G.*

17.8 Authorisation by an officer of the rank of inspector or above within *paragraph 17.3(b)* or *17.4(b)* may be given orally or in writing but, if it is given orally, it must be confirmed in writing as soon as practicable.

17.9 If a sample is taken from a detainee who has been arrested for an offence but not charged with that offence as in *paragraph 17.3*, no further sample may be taken during the same continuous period of detention. If during that same period the charge condition is also met in respect of that detainee, the sample which has been taken shall be treated as being taken by virtue of the charge condition, see *paragraph 17.4*, being met.

17.10 A detainee from whom a sample may be taken may be detained for up to six hours from the time of charge if the custody officer reasonably believes the detention is necessary to enable a sample to be taken. Where the arrest condition is met, a detainee whom the custody officer has decided to release on bail without charge may continue to be detained, but not beyond 24 hours from the relevant time (as defined in section 41(2) of PACE), to enable a sample to be taken.

17.11 A detainee in respect of whom the arrest condition is met, but not the charge condition, see *paragraphs 17.3* and *17.4*, and whose release would be required before a sample can be taken had they not continued to be detained as a result of being arrested for a further offence which does not satisfy the arrest condition, may have a sample taken at any time within 24 hours after the arrest for the offence that satisfies the arrest condition.

(B) Documentation

17.12 The following must be recorded in the custody record:

(a) if a sample is taken following authorisation by an officer of the rank of inspector or above, the authorisation and the grounds for suspicion;

(b) the giving of a warning of the consequences of failure to provide a sample;

(c) the time at which the sample was given; and

(d) the time of charge or, where the arrest condition is being relied upon, the time of arrest and, where applicable, the fact that a sample taken after arrest but before charge is to be treated as being taken by virtue of the charge condition, where that is met in the same period of continuous detention. See *paragraph 17.9*.

(C) General

17.13 A sample may only be taken by a prescribed person. See *Note 17C*.

17.14 Force may not be used to take any sample for the purpose of drug testing.

17.15 The terms "Class A drug" and "misuse" have the same meanings as in the Misuse of Drugs Act 1971. "Specified" (in relation to a Class A drug) and "trigger offence" have the same meanings as in Part III of the Criminal Justice and Court Services Act 2000.

17.16 Any sample taken:

(a) may not be used for any purpose other than to ascertain whether the person concerned has a specified Class A drug present in his body; and

(b) can be disposed of as clinical waste unless it is to be sent for further analysis in cases where the test result is disputed at the point when the result is known, including on the basis that medication has been taken, or for quality assurance purposes.

(D) Assessment of misuse of drugs

17.17 Under the provisions of Part 3 of the Drugs Act 2005, where a detainee has tested positive for a specified Class A drug under section 63B of PACE a police officer may, at any time before the person's release from the police station, impose a requirement on the detainee to attend an initial assessment of their drug misuse by a suitably qualified person and to remain for its duration. Where such a requirement is imposed, the officer must, at the same time, impose a second requirement on the detainee to attend and remain for a follow-up assessment. The officer must inform the detainee that the second requirement will cease to have effect if, at the initial assessment they are informed that a follow-up assessment is not necessaryThese requirements may only be imposed on a person if:

(a) they have reached the age of 18

(b) notification has been given by the Secretary of State to the relevant chief officer of police that arrangements for conducting initial and follow-up assessments have been made for those from whom samples for testing have been taken at the police station where the detainee is in custody.

17.18 When imposing a requirement to attend an initial assessment and a follow-up assessment the police officer must:

(a) inform the person of the time and place at which the initial assessment is to take place;

(b) explain that this information will be confirmed in writing; and

(c) warn the person that they may be liable to prosecution if they fail without good cause to attend the initial assessment and remain for its duration and if they fail to attend the follow-up assessment and remain for its duration (if so required).

17.19 Where a police officer has imposed a requirement to attend an initial assessment and a follow-up assessment in accordance with *paragraph 17.17*, he must, before the person is released from detention, give the person notice in writing which:

(a) confirms their requirement to attend and remain for the duration of the assessments; and

(b) confirms the information and repeats the warning referred to in *paragraph 17.18*.

17.20 The following must be recorded in the custody record:

(a) that the requirement to attend an initial assessment and a follow-up assessment has been imposed; and

(b) the information, explanation, warning and notice given in accordance with *paragraphs 17.17* and *17.19*.

17.21 Where a notice is given in accordance with paragraph 17.19, a police officer can give the person a further notice in writing which informs the person of any change to the time or place at which the initial assessment is to take place and which repeats the warning referred to in *paragraph 17.18(c)*.

17.22 Part 3 of the Drugs Act 2005 also requires police officers to have regard to any guidance issued by the Secretary of State in respect of the assessment provisions.

NOTES FOR GUIDANCE

17A *When warning a person who is asked to provide a urine or non-intimate sample in accordance with paragraph 17.6(b), the following form of words may be used:*

"You do not have to provide a sample, but I must warn you that if you fail or refuse without good cause to do so, you will commit an offence for which you may be imprisoned, or fined, or both".

Where the Welsh language is appropriate, the following form of words may be used:

"Does dim rhaid i chi roi sampl, ond mae'n rhaid i mi eich rhybuddio y byddwch chi'n cyflawni trosedd os byddwch chi'n methu neu yn gwrthod gwneud hynny heb reswm da, ac y gellir, oherwydd hynny, eich carcharu, eich dirwyo, neu'r ddau."

17B *A sample has to be sufficient and suitable. A sufficient sample is sufficient in quantity and quality to enable drug-testing analysis to take place. A suitable sample is one which by its nature, is suitable for a particular form of drug analysis.*

17C *A prescribed person in paragraph 17.13 is one who is prescribed in regulations made by the Secretary of State under section 63B(6) of the Police and Criminal Evidence Act 1984. [The regulations are currently contained in regulation SI 2001 No. 2645, the Police and Criminal Evidence Act 1984 (Drug Testing Persons in Police Detention) (Prescribed Persons) Regulations 2001.]*

17D *Samples, and the information derived from them, may not be subsequently used in the investigation of any offence or in evidence against the persons from whom they were taken.*

17E *Trigger offences are:*

1. Offences under the following provisions of the Theft Act 1968:

section 1	*(theft)*
section 8	*(robbery)*
section 9	*(burglary)*
section 10	*(aggravated burglary)*
section 12	*(taking a motor vehicle or other conveyance without authority)*
section 12A	*(aggravated vehicle-taking)*
section 22	*(handling stolen goods)*
section 25	*(going equipped for stealing etc.)*

2. Offences under the following provisions of the Misuse of Drugs Act 1971, if committed in respect of a specified Class A drug:–

section 4	*(restriction on production and supply of controlled drugs)*
section 5(2)	*(possession of a controlled drug)*
section 5(3)	*(possession of a controlled drug with intent to supply)*

3. Offences under the following provisions of the Fraud Act 2006:

section 1	*(fraud)*
section 6	*(possession etc. of articles for use in frauds)*
section 7	*(making or supplying articles for use in frauds)*

3A. An offence under section 1(1) of the Criminal Attempts Act 1981 if committed in respect of an offence under
(a) any of the following provisions of the Theft Act 1968:

section 1	*(theft)*
section 8	*(robbery)*
section 9	*(burglary)*
section 22	*(handling stolen goods)*

(b) section 1 of the Fraud Act 2006 (fraud)
4. Offences under the following provisions of the Vagrancy Act 1824:

section 3	*(begging)*
section 4	*(persistent begging)*

17F *The power to take samples is subject to notification by the Secretary of State that appropriate arrangements for the taking of samples have been made for the police area as a whole or for the particular police station concerned for whichever of the following is specified in the notification:*

(a) persons in respect of whom the arrest condition is met;
(b) persons in respect of whom the charge condition is met;
(c) persons who have not attained the age of 18.

Note: Notification is treated as having been given for the purposes of the charge condition in relation to a police area, if testing (on charge) under section 63B(2) of PACE was in force immediately before section 7 of the Drugs Act 2005 was brought into force; and for the purposes of the age condition, in relation to a police area or police station, if immediately before that day, notification that arrangements had been made for the taking of samples from persons under the age of 18 (those aged 14–17) had been given and had not been withdrawn.

17G   Appropriate adult in paragraph 17.7 means the person's–

(a) parent or guardian or, if they are in the care of a local authority or voluntary organisation, a person representing that authority or organisation; or
(b) a social worker of a local authority; or
(c) if no person falling within (a) or (b) above is available, any responsible person aged 18 or over who is not:
– a police officer;
– employed by the police;
– under the direction or control of the chief officer of police force; or
– a person who provides services under contractual arrangements (but without being employed by the chief officer of a police force), to assist that force in relation to the discharge of its chief officer's functions;
whether or not they are on duty at the time.

Note: Paragraph 1.5 extends this Note to the person called to fulfil the role of the appropriate adult for a 17-year old detainee for the purposes of paragraph 17.7.

Annex A   Intimate and Strip Searches

A   Intimate Search

1.   An intimate search consists of the physical examination of a person's body orifices other than the mouth. The intrusive nature of such searches means the actual and potential risks associated with intimate searches must never be underestimated.(a)

Action

2.   Body orifices other than the mouth may be searched only:

(a) if authorised by an officer of inspector rank or above who has reasonable grounds for believing that the person may have concealed on themselves:
(i) anything which they could and might use to cause physical injury to themselves or others at the station; or
(ii) a Class A drug which they intended to supply to another or to export;
and the officer has reasonable grounds for believing that an intimate search is the only means of removing those items; and
(b) if the search is under paragraph 2(a)(ii) (a drug offence search), the detainee's appropriate consent has been given in writing.

2A.   Before the search begins, a police officer or designated detention officer, must tell the detainee:-

(a) that the authority to carry out the search has been given;
(b) the grounds for giving the authorisation and for believing that the article cannot be removed without an intimate search.

2B.   Before a detainee is asked to give appropriate consent to a search under paragraph 2(a)(ii) (a drug offence search) they must be warned that if they refuse without good cause their refusal may harm their case if it comes to trial, see Note A6. This warning may be given by a police officer or member of police staff. In the case of a juvenile or a vulnerable person, the seeking and giving of consent must take place in the presence of the appropriate adult. A juvenile's consent is only valid if their parent's or guardian's consent is also obtained unless the juvenile is under 14, when their parent's or guardian's consent is sufficient in its own right. A detainee who is not legally represented must be reminded of their entitlement to have free legal advice, see Code C, paragraph 6.5, and the reminder noted in the custody record.

3.   An intimate search may only be carried out by a registered medical practitioner or registered nurse, unless an officer of at least inspector rank considers this is not practicable and the search is to take place under paragraph 2(a)(i), in which case a police officer may carry out the search. See Notes A1 to A5.

3A.   Any proposal for a search under paragraph 2(a)(i) to be carried out by someone other than a registered medical practitioner or registered nurse must only be considered as a last resort and when the authorising officer is satisfied the risks associated with allowing the item to remain with the detainee outweigh the risks associated with removing it. See Notes A1 to A5.

4.   An intimate search under:

• paragraph 2(a)(i) may take place only at a hospital, surgery, other medical premises or police station;
• paragraph 2(a)(ii) may take place only at a hospital, surgery or other medical premises and must be carried out by a registered medical practitioner or a registered nurse.

5.   An intimate search at a police station of a juvenile or vulnerable person may take place only in the presence of an appropriate adult of the same sex (see Annex L), unless the detainee specifically requests a particular appropriate adult of the opposite sex who is readily available. In the case of a juvenile, the search may take place in the absence of the appropriate adult only if the juvenile signifies in the presence of the appropriate adult they do not want the appropriate adult present during the search and the appropriate adult agrees. A record shall be made of the juvenile's decision and signed by the appropriate adult.

6.   When an intimate search under *paragraph 2(a)(i)* is carried out by a police officer, the officer must be of the same sex as the detainee (see *Annex L*). A minimum of two people, other than the detainee, must be present during the search. Subject to *paragraph 5*, no person of the opposite sex who is not a medical practitioner or nurse shall be present, nor shall anyone whose presence is unnecessary. The search shall be conducted with proper regard to the sensitivity and vulnerability of the detainee.(b)

Documentation

7.   In the case of an intimate search, the following shall be recorded as soon as practicable in the detainee's custody record:

(a)   for searches under paragraphs 2(a)(i) and (ii);
- the authorisation to carry out the search;
- the grounds for giving the authorisation;
- the grounds for believing the article could not be removed without an intimate search;
- which parts of the detainee's body were searched;
- who carried out the search;
- who was present;
- the result.

(b)   for searches under paragraph 2(a)(ii):
- the giving of the warning required by *paragraph 2B*;
- the fact that the appropriate consent was given or (as the case may be) refused, and if refused, the reason given for the refusal (if any).

8.   If an intimate search is carried out by a police officer, the reason why it was impracticable for a registered medical practitioner or registered nurse to conduct it must be recorded.

B STRIP SEARCH

9.   A strip search is a search involving the removal of more than outer clothing. In this Code, outer clothing includes shoes and socks.(a)

Action

10.   A strip search may take place only if it is considered necessary to remove an article which a detainee would not be allowed to keep and the officer reasonably considers the detainee might have concealed such an article. Strip searches shall not be routinely carried out if there is no reason to consider that articles are concealed.

The conduct of strip searches

11.   When strip searches are conducted:

(a)   a police officer carrying out a strip search must be the same sex as the detainee (see *Annex L*);

(b)   the search shall take place in an area where the detainee cannot be seen by anyone who does not need to be present, nor by a member of the opposite sex (see *Annex L*) except an appropriate adult who has been specifically requested by the detainee;

(c)   except in cases of urgency, where there is risk of serious harm to the detainee or to others, whenever a strip search involves exposure of intimate body parts, there must be at least two people present other than the detainee, and if the search is of a juvenile or vulnerable person, one of the people must be the appropriate adult. Except in urgent cases as above, a search of a juvenile may take place in the absence of the appropriate adult only if the juvenile signifies in the presence of the appropriate adult that they do not want the appropriate adult to be present during the search and the appropriate adult agrees. A record shall be made of the juvenile's decision and signed by the appropriate adult. The presence of more than two people, other than an appropriate adult, shall be permitted only in the most exceptional circumstances;

(d)   the search shall be conducted with proper regard to the sensitivity and vulnerability of the detainee in these circumstances and every reasonable effort shall be made to secure the detainee's co-operation and minimise embarrassment. Detainees who are searched shall not normally be required to remove all their clothes at the same time, e.g. a person should be allowed to remove clothing above the waist and redress before removing further clothing;

(e)   if necessary to assist the search, the detainee may be required to hold their arms in the air or to stand with their legs apart and bend forward so a visual examination may be made of the genital and anal areas provided no physical contact is made with any body orifice;

(f)   if articles are found, the detainee shall be asked to hand them over. If articles are found within any body orifice other than the mouth, and the detainee refuses to hand them over, their removal would constitute an intimate search, which must be carried out as in *Part A*;

(g)   a strip search shall be conducted as quickly as possible, and the detainee allowed to dress as soon as the procedure is complete.

(b)

Documentation

12.   A record shall be made on the custody record of a strip search including the reason it was considered necessary, those present and any result.

NOTES FOR GUIDANCE

A1   *Before authorising any intimate search, the authorising officer must make every reasonable effort to persuade the detainee to hand the article over without a search. If the detainee agrees, a registered medical practitioner or registered nurse should whenever possible be asked to assess the risks involved and, if necessary, attend to assist the detainee.*

A2   *If the detainee does not agree to hand the article over without a search, the authorising officer must carefully review all the relevant factors before authorising an intimate search. In particular, the officer must consider whether the grounds for believing an article may be concealed are reasonable.*

A3   *If authority is given for a search under paragraph 2(a)(i), a registered medical practitioner or registered nurse shall be consulted whenever possible. The presumption should be that the search will be conducted by the registered medical practitioner or registered nurse and the authorising officer must make every reasonable effort to persuade the detainee to allow the medical practitioner or nurse to conduct the search.*

A4   *A constable should only be authorised to carry out a search as a last resort and when all other approaches have failed. In these circumstances, the authorising officer must be satisfied the detainee might use the article for one or more of the purposes in paragraph 2(a)(i) and the physical injury likely to be caused is sufficiently severe to justify authorising a constable to carry out the search.*

A5   *If an officer has any doubts whether to authorise an intimate search by a constable, the officer should seek advice from an officer of superintendent rank or above.*

A6   *In warning a detainee who is asked to consent to an intimate drug offence search, as in paragraph 2B, the following form of words may be used:*

> *"You do not have to allow yourself to be searched, but I must warn you that if you refuse without good cause, your refusal may harm your case if it comes to trial."*

Where the use of the Welsh Language is appropriate, the following form of words may be used:

> *"Nid oes rhaid i chi roi caniatad i gael eich archwilio, ond mae'n rhaid i mi eich rhybuddio os gwrthodwch heb reswm da, y gallai eich penderfyniad i wrthod wneud niwed i'ch achos pe bai'n dod gerbron llys."*

Annex B   Delay in notification of arrest and whereabouts or allowing access to legal advice

A   Persons detained under PACE

1.   The exercise of the rights in *Section 5* or *Section 6*, or both, may be delayed if the person is in police detention, as in PACE, section 118(2), in connection with an indictable offence, has not yet been charged with an offence and an officer of superintendent rank or above, or inspector rank or above only for the rights in *Section 5*, has reasonable grounds for believing their exercise will:

(i)   lead to:
  - interference with, or harm to, evidence connected with an indictable offence; or
  - interference with, or physical harm to, other people; or
(ii)   lead to alerting other people suspected of having committed an indictable offence but not yet arrested for it; or
(iii)   hinder the recovery of property obtained in consequence of the commission of such an offence.

2.   These rights may also be delayed if the officer has reasonable grounds to believe that:

(i)   the person detained for an indictable offence has benefited from their criminal conduct (decided in accordance with Part 2 of the Proceeds of Crime Act 2002); and
(ii)   the recovery of the value of the property constituting that benefit will be hindered by the exercise of either right.

3.   Authority to delay a detainee's right to consult privately with a solicitor may be given only if the authorising officer has reasonable grounds to believe the solicitor the detainee wants to consult will, inadvertently or otherwise, pass on a message from the detainee or act in some other way which will have any of the consequences specified under *paragraphs 1 or 2*. In these circumstances, the detainee must be allowed to choose another solicitor. See *Note B3*.

4.   If the detainee wishes to see a solicitor, access to that solicitor may not be delayed on the grounds they might advise the detainee not to answer questions or the solicitor was initially asked to attend the police station by someone else. In the latter case, the detainee must be told the solicitor has come to the police station at another person's request, and must be asked to sign the custody record to signify whether they want to see the solicitor.

5.   The fact the grounds for delaying notification of arrest may be satisfied does not automatically mean the grounds for delaying access to legal advice will also be satisfied.

6.   These rights may be delayed only for as long as grounds exist and in no case beyond 36 hours after the relevant time as in PACE, section 41. If the grounds cease to apply within this time, the detainee must, as soon as practicable, be asked if they want to exercise either right, the custody record must be noted accordingly, and action taken in accordance with the relevant section of the Code.

7.   A detained person must be permitted to consult a solicitor for a reasonable time before any court hearing.

B   Not used

C   Documentation

13.   The grounds for action under this Annex shall be recorded and the detainee informed of them as soon as practicable.

14.   Any reply given by a detainee under *paragraphs 6 or 11* must be recorded and the detainee asked to endorse the record in relation to whether they want to receive legal advice at this point.

D   Cautions and special warnings

15.   When a suspect detained at a police station is interviewed during any period for which access to legal advice has been delayed under this Annex, the court or jury may not draw adverse inferences from their silence.

NOTES FOR GUIDANCE

B1 *Even if Annex B applies in the case of a juvenile, or a vulnerable person, action to inform the appropriate adult and the person responsible for a juvenile's welfare, if that is a different person, must nevertheless be taken as in paragraph 3.13 and 3.15.*

B2 *In the case of Commonwealth citizens and foreign nationals, see Note 7A.*

B3 *A decision to delay access to a specific solicitor is likely to be a rare occurrence and only when it can be shown the suspect is capable of misleading that particular solicitor and there is more than a substantial risk that the suspect will succeed in causing information to be conveyed which will lead to one or more of the specified consequences.*

ANNEX C RESTRICTION ON DRAWING ADVERSE INFERENCES FROM SILENCE AND TERMS OF THE CAUTION WHEN THE RESTRICTION APPLIES

(A) THE RESTRICTION ON DRAWING ADVERSE INFERENCES FROM SILENCE

1. The Criminal Justice and Public Order Act 1994, sections 34, 36 and 37 as amended by the Youth Justice and Criminal Evidence Act 1999, section 58 describe the conditions under which adverse inferences may be drawn from a person's failure or refusal to say anything about their involvement in the offence when interviewed, after being charged or informed they may be prosecuted. These provisions are subject to an overriding restriction on the ability of a court or jury to draw adverse inferences from a person's silence. This restriction applies:

(a) to any detainee at a police station, see *Note 10C* who, before being interviewed, see *section 11* or being charged or informed they may be prosecuted, see *section 16,* has:
- (i) asked for legal advice, see *section 6, paragraph 6.1*;
- (ii) not been allowed an opportunity to consult a solicitor, including the duty solicitor, as in this Code; and
- (iii) not changed their mind about wanting legal advice, see *section 6, paragraph 6.6(d)*. Note the condition in (ii) will:
  - – apply when a detainee who has asked for legal advice is interviewed before speaking to a solicitor as in *section 6, paragraph 6.6(a)* or *(b)*;
  - – not apply if the detained person declines to ask for the duty solicitor, see *section 6, paragraphs 6.6(c)* and *(d)*.

(b) to any person charged with, or informed they may be prosecuted for, an offence who:
- (i) has had brought to their notice a written statement made by another person or the content of an interview with another person which relates to that offence, see *section 16, paragraph 16.4*;
- (ii) is interviewed about that offence, see *section 16, paragraph 16.5*; or
- (iii) makes a written statement about that offence, see *Annex D paragraphs 4* and *9*.

(B) TERMS OF THE CAUTION WHEN THE RESTRICTION APPLIES

2. When a requirement to caution arises at a time when the restriction on drawing adverse inferences from silence applies, the caution shall be:

> *'You do not have to say anything, but anything you do say may be given in evidence.'*

Where the use of the Welsh Language is appropriate, the caution may be used directly in Welsh in the following terms:

> *'Does dim rhaid i chi ddweud dim byd, ond gall unrhyw beth yr ydych chi'n ei ddweud gael ei roi fel tystiolaeth.'*

3. Whenever the restriction either begins to apply or ceases to apply after a caution has already been given, the person shall be re-cautioned in the appropriate terms. The changed position on drawing inferences and that the previous caution no longer applies shall also be explained to the detainee in ordinary language. See *Note C2.*

NOTES FOR GUIDANCE

C1 *The restriction on drawing inferences from silence does not apply to a person who has not been detained and who therefore cannot be prevented from seeking legal advice if they want to, see paragraphs 10.2 and 3.21.*

C2 *The following is suggested as a framework to help explain changes in the position on drawing adverse inferences if the restriction on drawing adverse inferences from silence:*

(a) *begins to apply:*

> *'The caution you were previously given no longer applies. This is because after that caution:*

(i) *you asked to speak to a solicitor but have not yet been allowed an opportunity to speak to a solicitor. See paragraph 1(a); or*

(ii) *you have been charged with/informed you may be prosecuted. See paragraph 1(b).*

> *'This means that from now on, adverse inferences cannot be drawn at court and your defence will not be harmed just because you choose to say nothing. Please listen carefully to the caution I am about to give you because it will apply from now on. You will see that it does not say anything about your defence being harmed.'*

(b) *ceases to apply before or at the time the person is charged or informed they may be prosecuted, see paragraph 1(a);*

> *'The caution you were previously given no longer applies. This is because after that caution you have been allowed an opportunity to speak to a solicitor. Please listen carefully to the caution I am about to give you because it will apply from now on. It explains how your defence at court may be affected if you choose to say nothing.'*

Annex D Written Statements Under Caution

(A) Written by a person under caution

1. A person shall always be invited to write down what they want to say.

2. A person who has not been charged with, or informed they may be prosecuted for, any offence to which the statement they want to write relates, shall:

(a) unless the statement is made at a time when the restriction on drawing adverse inferences from silence applies, see Annex C, be asked to write out and sign the following before writing what they want to say:

> '*I make this statement of my own free will. I understand that I do not have to say anything but that it may harm my defence if I do not mention when questioned something which I later rely on in court. This statement may be given in evidence.*';

(b) if the statement is made at a time when the restriction on drawing adverse inferences from silence applies, be asked to write out and sign the following before writing what they want to say;

> '*I make this statement of my own free will. I understand that I do not have to say anything. This statement may be given in evidence.*'

3. When a person, on the occasion of being charged with or informed they may be prosecuted for any offence, asks to make a statement which relates to any such offence and wants to write it they shall:

(a) unless the restriction on drawing adverse inferences from silence, see *Annex C*, applied when they were so charged or informed they may be prosecuted, be asked to write out and sign the following before writing what they want to say:

> '*I make this statement of my own free will. I understand that I do not have to say anything but that it may harm my defence if I do not mention when questioned something which I later rely on in court. This statement may be given in evidence.*';

(b) if the restriction on drawing adverse inferences from silence applied when they were so charged or informed they may be prosecuted, be asked to write out and sign the following before writing what they want to say:

> '*I make this statement of my own free will. I understand that I do not have to say anything. This statement may be given in evidence.*'

4. When a person who has already been charged with or informed they may be prosecuted for any offence asks to make a statement which relates to any such offence and wants to write it, they shall be asked to write out and sign the following before writing what they want to say:

> '*I make this statement of my own free will. I understand that I do not have to say anything. This statement may be given in evidence.*';

5. Any person writing their own statement shall be allowed to do so without any prompting except a police officer or other police staff may indicate to them which matters are material or question any ambiguity in the statement.

(B) Written by a police officer or other police staff

6. If a person says they would like someone to write the statement for them, a police officer, or other police staff shall write the statement.

7. If the person has not been charged with, or informed they may be prosecuted for, any offence to which the statement they want to make relates they shall, before starting, be asked to sign, or make their mark, to the following:

(a) unless the statement is made at a time when the restriction on drawing adverse inferences from silence applies, see *Annex C*:

> '*I, ... , wish to make a statement. I want someone to write down what I say. I understand that I do not have to say anything but that it may harm my defence if I do not mention when questioned something which I later rely on in court. This statement may be given in evidence.*'

(b) if the statement is made at a time when the restriction on drawing adverse inferences from silence applies:

> '*I, ... , wish to make a statement. I want someone to write down what I say. I understand that I do not have to say anything. This statement may be given in evidence.*'

8. If, on the occasion of being charged with or informed they may be prosecuted for any offence, the person asks to make a statement which relates to any such offence they shall before starting be asked to sign, or make their mark to, the following:

(a) unless the restriction on drawing adverse inferences from silence applied, see *Annex C*, when they were so charged or informed they may be prosecuted:

> '*I, ... , wish to make a statement. I want someone to write down what I say. I understand that I do not have to say anything but that it may harm my defence if I do not mention when questioned something which I later rely on in court. This statement may be given in evidence.*';

(b) if the restriction on drawing adverse inferences from silence applied when they were so charged or informed they may be prosecuted:

> '*I, ... , wish to make a statement. I want someone to write down what I say. I understand that I do not have to say anything. This statement may be given in evidence.*'

9. If, having already been charged with or informed they may be prosecuted for any offence, a person asks to make a statement which relates to any such offence they shall before starting, be asked to sign, or make their mark to:

'I, ..., *wish to make a statement. I want someone to write down what I say. I understand that I do not have to say anything. This statement may be given in evidence.*'

10. The person writing the statement must take down the exact words spoken by the person making it and must not edit or paraphrase it. Any questions that are necessary, e.g. to make it more intelligible, and the answers given must be recorded at the same time on the statement form.
11. When the writing of a statement is finished the person making it shall be asked to read it and to make any corrections, alterations or additions they want. When they have finished reading they shall be asked to write and sign or make their mark on the following certificate at the end of the statement:

'*I have read the above statement, and I have been able to correct, alter or add anything I wish. This statement is true. I have made it of my own free will.*'

12. If the person making the statement cannot read, or refuses to read it, or to write the above mentioned certificate at the end of it or to sign it, the person taking the statement shall read it to them and ask them if they would like to correct, alter or add anything and to put their signature or make their mark at the end. The person taking the statement shall certify on the statement itself what has occurred.

ANNEX E SUMMARY OF PROVISIONS RELATING TO VULNERABLE PERSON

1. If at any time, an officer has reason to suspect that a person of any age may be vulnerable (see *paragraph 1.13(d)*), in the absence of clear evidence to dispel that suspicion that person shall be treated as such for the purposes of this Code and to establish whether any such reason may exist in relation to a person suspected of committing an offence (see *paragraph 10.1* and *Note 10A*), the custody officer in the case of a detained person, or the officer investigating the offence in the case of a person who has not been arrested or detained, shall take, or cause to be taken, (see *paragraph 3.5* and *Note 3F*) the following action:

(a) reasonable enquiries shall be made to ascertain what information is available that is relevant to any of the factors described in *paragraph 1.13(d)* as indicating that the person may be vulnerable might apply;
(b) a record shall be made describing whether any of those factors appear to apply and provide any reason to suspect that the person may be vulnerable or (as the case may be) may not be vulnerable; and
(c) the record mentioned in sub-paragraph (b) shall be made available to be taken into account by police officers, police staff and any others who, in accordance with the provisions of this or any other Code, are entitled to communicate with the person in question. This would include any solicitor, appropriate adult and health care professional and is particularly relevant to communication by telephone or by means of a live link (see *paragraphs 12.9A* (interviews), *13.12* (interpretation), and *15.3C, 15.11A, 15.11B, 15.11C* and *15.11D* (reviews and extension of detention)).

See *Notes 1G, E5, E6* and *E7*.
2. In the case of a person who is vulnerable, 'the appropriate adult' means:

(i) a relative, guardian or other person responsible for their care or custody;
(ii) someone experienced in dealing with vulnerable persons but who is not:
   – a police officer;
   – employed by the police;
   – under the direction or control of the chief officer of a police force;
   – a person who provides services under contractual arrangements (but without being employed by the chief officer of a police force), to assist that force in relation to the discharge of its chief officer's functions,
   whether or not they are on duty at the time.
(iii) failing these, some other responsible adult aged 18 or over who is other than a person described in the bullet points in *sub-paragraph (ii)* above.

See *paragraph 1.7(b)* and *Notes 1D* and *1F*.
2A The role of the appropriate adult is to safeguard the rights, entitlements and welfare of 'vulnerable persons' (see *paragraph 1*) to whom the provisions of this and any other Code of Practice apply. For this reason, the appropriate adult is expected, amongst other things, to:

• support, advise and assist them when, in accordance with this Code or any other Code of Practice, they are given or asked to provide information or participate in any procedure;
• observe whether the police are acting properly and fairly to respect their rights and entitlements, and inform an officer of the rank of inspector or above if they consider that they are not;
• assist them to communicate with the police whilst respecting their right to say nothing unless they want to as set out in the terms of the caution (see *paragraphs 10.5* and *10.6*); and
• help them understand their rights and ensure that those rights are protected and respected (see *paragraphs 3.15, 3.17, 6.5A* and *11.17*).

See *paragraph 1.7A*.
3. If the custody officer authorises the detention of a vulnerable person, the custody officer must as soon as practicable inform the appropriate adult of the grounds for detention and the person's whereabouts, and secure the attendance of the appropriate adult at the police station to see the detainee. If the appropriate adult:

• is already at the station when information is given as in *paragraphs 3.1* to *3.5* the information must be given in their presence;

- is not at the station when the provisions of *paragraph 3.1* to *3.5* are complied with these provisions must be complied with again in their presence once they arrive.

See *paragraphs 3.15* to *3.17*

4. If the appropriate adult, having been informed of the right to legal advice, considers legal advice should be taken, the provisions of *section 6* apply as if the vulnerable person had requested access to legal advice. See *paragraphs 3.19, 6.5A* and *Note E1*.

5. The custody officer must make sure a person receives appropriate clinical attention as soon as reasonably practicable if the person appears to be suffering from a mental disorder or in urgent cases immediately call the nearest appropriate healthcare professional or an ambulance. See Code C *paragraphs 3.16, 9.5* and *9.6* which apply when a person is detained under the Mental Health Act 1983, sections 135 and 136, as amended by the Policing and Crime Act 2017.

6. *Not used.*

7. If a vulnerable person is cautioned in the absence of the appropriate adult, the caution must be repeated in the appropriate adult's presence. See *paragraph 10.12*.

8. A vulnerable person must not be interviewed or asked to provide or sign a written statement in the absence of the appropriate adult unless the provisions of *paragraphs 11.1* or *11.18* to *11.20* apply. Questioning in these circumstances may not continue in the absence of the appropriate adult once sufficient information to avert the risk has been obtained. A record shall be made of the grounds for any decision to begin an interview in these circumstances. See *paragraphs 11.1, 11.15* and *11.18* to *11.20*.

9. If the appropriate adult is present at an interview, they shall be informed they are not expected to act simply as an observer and the purposes of their presence are to:

- advise the interviewee;
- observe whether or not the interview is being conducted properly and fairly;
- facilitate communication with the interviewee.

See *paragraph 11.17*

10. If the detention of a vulnerable person is reviewed by a review officer or a superintendent, the appropriate adult must, if available at the time, be given an opportunity to make representations to the officer about the need for continuing detention. See *paragraph 15.3*.

11. If the custody officer charges a vulnerable person with an offence or takes such other action as is appropriate when there is sufficient evidence for a prosecution this must be carried out in the presence of the appropriate adult if they are at the police station. A copy of the written notice embodying any charge must also be given to the appropriate adult. See *paragraphs 16.1* to *16.4A*

12. An intimate or strip search of a vulnerable person may take place only in the presence of the appropriate adult of the same sex, unless the detainee specifically requests the presence of a particular adult of the opposite sex. A strip search may take place in the absence of an appropriate adult only in cases of urgency when there is a risk of serious harm to the detainee or others. See *Annex A, paragraphs 5* and *11(c)*.

13. Particular care must be taken when deciding whether to use any form of approved restraints on a vulnerable person in a locked cell. See *paragraph 8.2*.

NOTES FOR GUIDANCE

E1 *The purpose of the provisions at paragraphs 3.19 and 6.5A is to protect the rights of a vulnerable person who does not understand the significance of what is said to them. A vulnerable person should always be given an opportunity, when an appropriate adult is called to the police station, to consult privately with a solicitor in the absence of the appropriate adult if they want.*

E2 *Although vulnerable persons are often capable of providing reliable evidence, they may, without knowing or wanting to do so, be particularly prone in certain circumstances to provide information that may be unreliable, misleading or self-incriminating. Special care should always be taken when questioning such a person, and the appropriate adult should be involved if there is any doubt about a person's mental state or capacity. Because of the risk of unreliable evidence, it is important to obtain corroboration of any facts admitted whenever possible.*

E3 *Because of the risks referred to in Note E2, which the presence of the appropriate adult is intended to minimise, officers of superintendent rank or above should exercise their discretion to authorise the commencement of an interview in the appropriate adult's absence only in exceptional cases, if it is necessary to avert one or more of the specified risks in paragraph 11.1. See paragraphs 11.1 and 11.18 to 11.20.*

E4 *When a person is detained under section 136 of the Mental Health Act 1983 for assessment, the appropriate adult has no role in the assessment process and their presence is not required.*

E5 *For the purposes of Annex E paragraph 1, examples of relevant information that may be available include:*

- *the behaviour of the adult or juvenile;*
- *the mental health and capacity of the adult or juvenile;*
- *what the adult or juvenile says about themselves;*
- *information from relatives and friends of the adult or juvenile;*
- *information from police officers and staff and from police records;*
- *information from health and social care (including liaison and diversion services) and other professionals who know, or have had previous contact with, the individual and may be able to contribute to assessing their need for help and support from an appropriate adult. This includes contacts and assessments arranged by the police or at the request of the individual or (as applicable) their appropriate adult or solicitor.*

E6 *The Mental Health Act 1983 Code of Practice at page 26 describes the range of clinically recognised conditions which can fall with the meaning of mental disorder for the purpose of paragraph 1.13(d). The Code is published here: https://www.gov.uk/government/publications/code-of-practice-mental-health-act-1983.*

E7 *When a person is under the influence of drink and/or drugs, it is not intended that they are to be treated as vulnerable and requiring an appropriate adult for the purpose of Annex E paragraph 1 unless other information indicates that any of the factors described in* paragraph 1.13(d) may apply to that person. When the person has recovered from the effects of drink and/or drugs, they should be re-assessed in accordance with Annex E paragraph 1. See paragraph 15.4A for application to live link.

ANNEX F NOT USED

ANNEX G FITNESS TO BE INTERVIEWED

1.   This Annex contains general guidance to help police officers and healthcare professionals assess whether a detainee might be at risk in an interview.

2.   A detainee may be at risk in a interview if it is considered that:

(a)   conducting the interview could significantly harm the detainee's physical or mental state;

(b)   anything the detainee says in the interview about their involvement or suspected involvement in the offence about which they are being interviewed **might** be considered unreliable in subsequent court proceedings because of their physical or mental state.

3.   In assessing whether the detainee should be interviewed, the following must be considered:

(a)   how the detainee's physical or mental state might affect their ability to understand the nature and purpose of the interview, to comprehend what is being asked and to appreciate the significance of any answers given and make rational decisions about whether they want to say anything;

(b)   the extent to which the detainee's replies may be affected by their physical or mental condition rather than representing a rational and accurate explanation of their involvement in the offence;

(c)   how the nature of the interview, which could include particularly probing questions, might affect the detainee.

4.   It is essential healthcare professionals who are consulted consider the functional ability of the detainee rather than simply relying on a medical diagnosis, e.g. it is possible for a person with severe mental illness to be fit for interview.

5.   Healthcare professionals should advise on the need for an appropriate adult to be present, whether reassessment of the person's fitness for interview may be necessary if the interview lasts beyond a specified time, and whether a further specialist opinion may be required.

6.   When healthcare professionals identify risks they should be asked to quantify the risks. They should inform the custody officer:

- whether the person's condition:
  - is likely to improve;
  - will require or be amenable to treatment; and
- indicate how long it may take for such improvement to take effect.

7.   The role of the healthcare professional is to consider the risks and advise the custody officer of the outcome of that consideration. The healthcare professional's determination and any advice or recommendations should be made in writing and form part of the custody record.

8.   Once the healthcare professional has provided that information, it is a matter for the custody officer to decide whether or not to allow the interview to go ahead and if the interview is to proceed, to determine what safeguards are needed. Nothing prevents safeguards being provided in addition to those required under the Code. An example might be to have an appropriate healthcare professional present during the interview, in addition to an appropriate adult, in order constantly to monitor the person's condition and how it is being affected by the interview.

ANNEX H DETAINED PERSON: OBSERVATION LIST

1.   If any detainee fails to meet any of the following criteria, an appropriate healthcare professional or an ambulance must be called.

2.   When assessing the level of rousability, consider:

Rousability - can they be woken?

- go into the cell
- call their name
- shake gently

Response to questions - can they give appropriate answers to questions such as:

- What's your name?
- Where do you live?
- Where do you think you are?

Response to commands - can they respond appropriately to commands such as:

- Open your eyes!
- Lift one arm, now the other arm!

3.   Remember to take into account the possibility or presence of other illnesses, injury, or mental condition; a person who is drowsy and smells of alcohol may also have the following:

- Diabetes
- Epilepsy
- Head injury
- Drug intoxication or overdose
- Stroke

Annex I Not used

ANNEX J Not used

Annex K X-rays and Ultrasound Scans

(a) Action

1. PACE, section 55A allows a person who has been arrested and is in police detention to have an X-ray taken of them or an ultrasound scan to be carried out on them (or both) if:

(a) authorised by an officer of inspector rank or above who has reasonable grounds for believing that the detainee:
(i)   may have swallowed a Class A drug; and
(ii) was in possession of that Class A drug with the intention of supplying it to another or to export; and
(b) the detainee's appropriate consent has been given in writing.

2. Before an x-ray is taken or an ultrasound scan carried out, a police officer or designated detention officer must tell the detainee:-

(a) that the authority has been given; and
(b) the grounds for giving the authorisation.

3. Before a detainee is asked to give appropriate consent to an x-ray or an ultrasound scan, they must be warned that if they refuse without good cause their refusal may harm their case if it comes to trial, see *Notes K1* and *K2*.This warning may be given by a police officer or member of police staff. In the case of juveniles and vulnerable persons, the seeking and giving of consent must take place in the presence of the appropriate adult. A juvenile's consent is only valid if their parent's or guardian's consent is also obtained unless the juvenile is under 14, when their parent's or guardian's consent is sufficient in its own right. A detainee who is not legally represented must be reminded of their entitlement to have free legal advice, see Code C, *paragraph 6.5*, and the reminder noted in the custody record.

4. An x-ray may be taken, or an ultrasound scan may be carried out, only by a registered medical practitioner or registered nurse, and only at a hospital, surgery or other medical premises.

(b) Documentation

5. The following shall be recorded as soon as practicable in the detainee's custody record:

(a) the authorisation to take the x-ray or carry out the ultrasound scan (or both);
(b) the grounds for giving the authorisation;
(c) the giving of the warning required by *paragraph 3*; and
(d) the fact that the appropriate consent was given or (as the case may be) refused, and if refused, the reason given for the refusal (if any); and
(e) if an x-ray is taken or an ultrasound scan carried out:
 •   where it was taken or carried out;
 •   who took it or carried it out;
 •   who was present;
 •   the result.

6 Not used.

Notes for Guidance

K1 *If authority is given for an x-ray to be taken or an ultrasound scan to be carried out (or both), consideration should be given to asking a registered medical practitioner or registered nurse to explain to the detainee what is involved and to allay any concerns the detainee might have about the effect which taking an x-ray or carrying out an ultrasound scan might have on them. If appropriate consent is not given, evidence of the explanation may, if the case comes to trial, be relevant to determining whether the detainee had a good cause for refusing.*

K2 *In warning a detainee who is asked to consent to an X-ray being taken or an ultrasound scan being carried out (or both), as in paragraph 3, the following form of words may be used:*

"You do not have to allow an x-ray of you to be taken or an ultrasound scan to be carried out on you, but I must warn you that if you refuse without good cause, your refusal may harm your case if it comes to trial."

Where the use of the Welsh Language is appropriate, the following form of words may be provided in Welsh:

"Does dim rhaid i chi ganiatáu cymryd sgan uwchsain neu belydr-x (neu'r ddau) arnoch, ond mae'n rhaid i mi eich rhybuddio os byddwch chi'n gwrthod gwneud hynny heb reswm da, fe allai hynny niweidio eich achos pe bai'n dod gerbron llys."

Annex L Establishing Gender of Persons for the Purpose of Searching

1. Certain provisions of this and other PACE Codes explicitly state that searches and other procedures may only be carried out by, or in the presence of, persons of the same sex as the person subject to the search or other procedure. See *Note L1*.

2. All searches and procedures must be carried out with courtesy, consideration and respect for the person concerned. Police officers should show particular sensitivity when dealing with transgender individuals (including transsexual persons) and transvestite persons (see *Notes L2, L3 and L4*).

(A) Consideration

3. In law, the gender (and accordingly the sex) of an individual is their gender as registered at birth unless they have been issued with a Gender Recognition Certificate (GRC) under the Gender Recognition Act 2004 (GRA), in which case the person's gender is their acquired gender. This means that if the acquired gender is the male gender, the person's sex becomes that of a man and, if it is the female gender, the person's sex becomes that of a woman and they must be treated as their acquired gender.

4. When establishing whether the person concerned should be treated as being male or female for the purposes of these searches and procedures, the following approach which is designed to minimise embarrassment and secure the person's co-operation should be followed:

(a) The person must not be asked whether they have a GRC (see paragraph 8);

(b) If there is no doubt as to as to whether the person concerned should be treated as being male or female, they should be dealt with as being of that sex.

(c) If at any time (including during the search or carrying out the procedure) there is doubt as to whether the person should be treated, or continue to be treated, as being male or female:

    (i) the person should be asked what gender they consider themselves to be. If they express a preference to be dealt with as a particular gender, they should be asked to indicate and confirm their preference by signing the custody record or, if a custody record has not been opened, the search record or the officer's notebook. Subject to (ii) below, the person should be treated according to their preference;

    (ii) if there are grounds to doubt that the preference in (i) accurately reflects the person's predominant lifestyle, for example, if they ask to be treated as a woman but documents and other information make it clear that they live predominantly as a man, or vice versa, they should be treated according to what appears to be their predominant lifestyle and not their stated preference;

    (iii) If the person is unwilling to express a preference as in (i) above, efforts should be made to determine their predominant lifestyle and they should be treated as such. For example, if they appear to live predominantly as a woman, they should be treated as being female; or

    (iv) if none of the above apply, the person should be dealt with according to what reasonably appears to have been their sex as registered at birth.

5. Once a decision has been made about which gender an individual is to be treated as, each officer responsible for the search or procedure should where possible be advised before the search or procedure starts of any doubts as to the person's gender and the person informed that the doubts have been disclosed. This is important so as to maintain the dignity of the person and any officers concerned.

(B) Documentation

6. The person's gender as established under *paragraph 4(c)(i)* to *(iv)* above must be recorded in the person's custody record or, if a custody record has not been opened, on the search record or in the officer's notebook.

7. Where the person elects which gender they consider themselves to be under *paragraph 4(b)(i)* but, following *4(b)(ii)* is not treated in accordance with their preference, the reason must be recorded in the search record, in the officer's notebook or, if applicable, in the person's custody record.

(C) Disclosure of information

8. Section 22 of the GRA defines any information relating to a person's application for a GRC or to a successful applicant's gender before it became their acquired gender as 'protected information'. Nothing in this Annex is to be read as authorising or permitting any police officer or any police staff who has acquired such information when acting in their official capacity to disclose that information to any other person in contravention of the GRA. Disclosure includes making a record of 'protected information' which is read by others.

Notes for Guidance

L1 *Provisions to which paragraph 1 applies include:*

- *In Code C; paragraph 4.1 and Annex A paragraphs 5, 6, and 11 (searches, strip and intimate searches of detainees under sections 54 and 55 of PACE);*
- *In Code A; paragraphs 2.8 and 3.6 and Note 4;*
- *In Code D; paragraph 5.5 and Note 5F (searches, examinations and photographing of detainees under section 54A of PACE) and paragraph 6.9 (taking samples);*
- *In Code H; paragraph 4.1 and Annex A paragraphs 6, 7 and 12 (searches, strip and intimate searches under sections 54 and 55 of PACE of persons arrested under section 41 of the Terrorism Act 2000).*

L2 *While there is no agreed definition of transgender (or trans), it is generally used as an umbrella term to describe people whose gender identity (self-identification as being a woman, man, neither or both) differs from the sex they were registered as at birth. The term includes, but is not limited to, transsexual people.*

L3 *Transsexual means a person who is proposing to undergo, is undergoing or has undergone a process (or part of a process) for the purpose of gender reassignment, which is a protected characteristic under the Equality Act 2010 (see paragraph 1.0), by changing physiological or other attributes of their sex. This includes aspects of gender such as dress and title. It would apply to a woman making the transition to being a man and a man making the transition to being a woman, as well as to a person who has only just started out on the process of gender reassignment and to a person who has completed the process. Both would share the characteristic of gender reassignment with each having the characteristics of one sex, but with certain characteristics of the other sex.*

L4 *Transvestite means a person of one gender who dresses in the clothes of a person of the opposite gender. However, a transvestite does not live permanently in the gender opposite to their birth sex.*

L5 *Chief officers are responsible for providing corresponding operational guidance and instructions for the deployment of transgender officers and staff under their direction and control to duties which involve carrying out, or being present at, any of the searches and procedures described in paragraph 1. The guidance and instructions must comply with the Equality Act 2010 and should therefore complement the approach in this Annex.*

ANNEX M DOCUMENTS AND RECORDS TO BE TRANSLATED

1. For the purposes of Directive 2010/64/EU of the European Parliament and of the Council of 20 October 2010 and this Code, essential documents comprise records required to be made in accordance with this Code which are relevant to decisions to deprive a person of their liberty, to any charge and to any record considered necessary to enable a detainee to defend themselves in criminal proceedings and to safeguard the fairness of the proceedings. Passages of essential documents which are not relevant need not be translated. See *Note M1*

2. The table below lists the documents considered essential for the purposes of this Code and when (subject to paragraphs 3 to 7) written translations must be created and provided. See *paragraphs 13.12* to *13.14* and *Annex N* for application to live-link interpretation.

Table of essential documents:

	ESSENTIAL DOCUMENTS FOR THE PURPOSES OF THIS CODE		WHEN TRANS-LATION TO BE CREATED	WHEN TRANS-LATION TO BE PROVIDED.
(i)	The grounds for each of the following authorisations to keep the person in custody as they are described and referred to in the custody record:		As soon as practicable after each authorisation has been recorded in the custody record.	As soon as practicable after the translation has been created, whilst the person is detained or after they have been released (see Note M3).
	(a)	Authorisation for detention before and after charge given by the custody officer and by the review officer, see Code C paragraphs 3.4 and 15.16(a).		
	(b)	Authorisation to extend detention without charge beyond 24 hours given by a superintendent, see Code C paragraph 15.16(b).		
	(c)	A warrant of further detention issued by a magistrates' court and any extension(s) of the warrant, see Code C paragraph 15.16(c).		
	(d)	An authority to detain in accordance with the directions in a warrant of arrest issued in connection with criminal proceedings including the court issuing the warrant.		

	ESSENTIAL DOCUMENTS FOR THE PURPOSES OF THIS CODE	WHEN TRANS-LATION TO BE CREATED	WHEN TRANS-LATION TO BE PROVIDED.
(ii)	Written notice showing particulars of the offence charged required by Code C paragraph 16.3 or the offence for which the suspect has been told they may be prosecuted.	As soon as practicable after the person has been charged or reported.	
(iii)	Written interview records: Code C11.11, 13.3, 13.4 & Code E4.7 Written statement under caution: Code C Annex D	To be created contemporaneously by the interpreter for the person to check and sign.	As soon as practicable after the person has been charged or told they may be prosecuted.

3. The custody officer may authorise an oral translation or oral summary of documents (i) to (ii) in the table (but not (iii)) to be provided (through an interpreter) instead of a written translation. Such an oral translation or summary may only be provided if it would not prejudice the fairness of the proceedings by in any way adversely affecting or otherwise undermining or limiting the ability of the suspect in question to understand their position and to communicate effectively with police officers, interviewers, solicitors and appropriate adults with regard to their detention and the investigation of the offence in question and to defend themselves in the event of criminal proceedings. The quantity and complexity of the information in the document should always be considered and specific additional consideration given if the suspect is vulnerable or is a juvenile (see *Code C paragraph 1.5*). The reason for the decision must be recorded (see *paragraph 13.11(e)*)

4. Subject to paragraphs 5 to 7 below, a suspect may waive their right to a written translation of the essential documents described in the table but only if they do so voluntarily after receiving legal advice or having full knowledge of the consequences and give their unconditional and fully informed consent in writing (see *paragraph 9*).

5. The suspect may be asked if they wish to waive their right to a written translation and before giving their consent, they must be reminded of their right to legal advice and asked whether they wish to speak to a solicitor.

6. No police officer or police staff should do or say anything with the intention of persuading a suspect who is entitled to a written translation of an essential document to waive that right. See *Notes M2 and M3.*

7. For the purpose of the waiver:

(a) the consent of a vulnerable person is only valid if the information about the circumstances under which they can waive the right and the reminder about their right to legal advice mentioned in *paragraphs 3* to *5* and their consent is given in the presence of the appropriate adult.

(b) the consent of a juvenile is only valid if their parent's or guardian's consent is also obtained unless the juvenile is under 14, when their parent's or guardian's consent is sufficient in its own right and the information and reminder mentioned in *sub-paragraph (a)* above and their consent is also given in the presence of the appropriate adult (who may or may not be a parent or guardian).

8. The detainee, their solicitor or appropriate adult may make representations to the custody officer that a document which is not included in the table is essential and that a translation should be provided. The request may be refused if the officer is satisfied that the translation requested is not essential for the purposes described in *paragraph 1* above.

9. If the custody officer has any doubts about

• providing an oral translation or summary of an essential document instead of a written translation (see paragraph 3);
• whether the suspect fully understands the consequences of waiving their right to a written translation of an essential document (see *paragraph 4*), or
• about refusing to provide a translation of a requested document (see *paragraph 7*),

the officer should seek advice from an inspector or above.

DOCUMENTATION

10. Action taken in accordance with this Annex shall be recorded in the detainee's custody record or interview record as appropriate (see *Code C paragraph 13.11(e)*).

NOTES FOR GUIDANCE

M1 *It is not necessary to disclose information in any translation which is capable of undermining or otherwise adversely affecting any investigative processes, for example, by enabling the suspect to fabricate an innocent explanation or to conceal lies from the interviewer.*

M2 *No police officer or police staff shall indicate to any suspect, except to answer a direct question, whether the period for which they are liable to be detained or if not detained, the time taken to complete the interview, might be reduced:*

• *if they do not ask for legal advice before deciding whether they wish to waive their right to a written translation of an essential document; or*
• *if they decide to waive their right to a written translation of an essential document.*

M3 *There is no power under PACE to detain a person or to delay their release solely to create and provide a written translation of any essential document.*

Annex N Live-Link Interpretation (Para. 13.12)

Part 1: When the physical presence of the interpreter is not required.

1. EU Directive 2010/64 (see *paragraph 13.1*), Article 2(6) provides "Where appropriate, communication technology such as videoconferencing, telephone or the Internet may be used, unless the physical presence of the interpreter is required in order to safeguard the fairness of the proceedings." This Article permits, but does not require the use of a live-link, and the following provisions of this Annex determine whether the use of a live-link is appropriate in any particular case.

2. Decisions in accordance with this Annex that the physical presence of the interpreter is not required and to permit live-link interpretation, must be made on a case by case basis. Each decision must take account of the age, gender and vulnerability of the suspect, the nature and circumstances of the offence and the investigation and the impact on the suspect according to the particular purpose(s) for which the suspect requires the assistance of an interpreter and the time(s) when that assistance is required (see *Note N1*). For this reason, the custody officer in the case of a detained suspect, or in the case of a suspect who has not been arrested, the interviewer (subject to *paragraph 13.1(b)*), must consider whether the ability of the particular suspect, to communicate confidently and effectively for the purpose in question (see *paragraph 3*) is likely to be adversely affected or otherwise undermined or limited if the interpreter is not physically present and live-link interpretation is used. Although a suspect for whom an appropriate adult is required may be more likely to be adversely affected as described, it is important to note that a person who does not require an appropriate adult may also be adversely impacted by the use of live-link interpretation.

3. Examples of purposes referred to in *paragraph 2* include:

(a)   understanding and appreciating their position having regard to any information given to them, or sought from them, in accordance with this or any other Code of Practice which, in particular, include:
- the caution (see *paragraphs C10.1* and *10.12*).
- the special warning (see *paragraphs 10.10* to *10.12*).
- information about the offence (see *paragraphs 10.3, 11.1A* and *Note 11ZA*).
- the grounds and reasons for detention (see *paragraphs 13.10* and *13.10A*).
- the translation of essential documents (see *paragraph 13.10B* and *Annex M*).
- their rights and entitlements (see *paragraph 3.12* and *C3.21(b)*).
- intimate and non-intimate searches of detained persons at police stations.
- provisions and procedures to which Code D (Identification) applies concerning, for example, eye-witness identification, taking fingerprints, samples and photographs.

(b)   understanding and seeking clarification from the interviewer of questions asked during an interview conducted and recorded in accordance with Code E or Code F and of anything else that is said by the interviewer and answering the questions.

(c)   consulting privately with their solicitor and (if applicable) the appropriate adult (see *paragraphs 3.18, 13.2A, 13.6* and *13.9*):
   (i)   to help decide whether to answer questions put to them during interview; and
   (ii) about any other matter concerning their detention and treatment whilst in custody.

(d)   communicating with practitioners and others who have some formal responsibility for, or an interest in, the health and welfare of the suspect. Particular examples include appropriate healthcare professionals (see *section 9* of this Code), Independent Custody Visitors and drug arrest referral workers.

4. If the custody officer or the interviewer (subject to *paragraph 13.1(b)*) is satisfied that for a particular purpose as described in *paragraphs 2 and 3 above*, the live-link interpretation *would not* adversely affect or otherwise undermine or limit the suspect's ability to communicate confidently and effectively for *that* purpose, they must so inform the suspect, their solicitor and (if applicable) the appropriate adult. At the same time, the operation of live-link interpretation must be explained and demonstrated to them, they must be advised of the chief officer's obligations concerning the security of live-link communications under *paragraph 13.13* (see *Note N2*) and they must be asked if they wish to make representations that live-link interpretation should not be used or if they require more information about the operation of the arrangements. They must also be told that at any time live-link interpretation is in use, they may make representations to the custody officer or the interviewer that its operation should cease and that the physical presence of an interpreter should be arranged.

When the authority of an inspector is required

5. If:

(i)   representations are made that live-link interpretation should not be used, or that at any time live-link interpretation is in use, its operation should cease and the physical presence of an interpreter arranged; and

(ii) the custody officer or interviewer (subject to *paragraph 13.1(b)*) is unable to allay the concerns raised;

then live-link interpretation may not be used, or (as the case may be) continue to be used, unless authorised in writing by an officer of the rank of inspector or above, in accordance with *paragraph 6*.

6. Authority may be given if the officer is satisfied that for the purpose(s) in question at the time an interpreter is required, live-link interpretation is necessary and justified. In making this decision, the officer must have regard to:

(a)   the circumstances of the suspect;
(b)   the nature and seriousness of the offence;
(c)   the requirements of the investigation, including its likely impact on both the suspect and any victim(s);
(d)   the representations made by the suspect, their solicitor and (if applicable) the appropriate adult that live-link interpretation should not be used (see *paragraph 5*)
(e)   the availability of a suitable interpreter to be *physically* present compared with the avail-

ability of a suitable interpreter for live-link interpretation (see *Note N3*); and
(f) the risk if the interpreter is not *physically* present, evidence obtained using link interpretation might be excluded in subsequent criminal proceedings; and
(g) the likely impact on the suspect and the investigation of any consequential delay to arrange for the interpreter to be *physically* present with the suspect.

7.   For the purposes of Code E and live-link interpretation, there is no requirement to make a visual recording which shows the interpreter as viewed by the suspect and others present at the interview. The audio recording required by that Code is sufficient. However, the authorising officer, in consultation with the officer in charge of the investigation, may direct that the interview is conducted and recorded in accordance with Code F. This will require the visual record to show the live-link interpretation arrangements and the interpreter as seen and experienced by the suspect during the interview. This should be considered if it appears that the admissibility of interview evidence might be challenged because the interpreter was not *physically* present or if the suspect, solicitor or appropriate adult make representations that Code F should be applied.

Documentation

8.   A record must be made of the actions, decisions, authorisations and outcomes arising from the requirements of this Annex. This includes representations made in accordance with *paragraphs 4* and *7*.

PART 2:   MODIFICATIONS FOR LIVE-LINK INTERPRETATION

9.   The following modification shall apply for the purposes of live-link interpretation:(a)

Code C paragraph 13.3:

For the third sentence, *substitute:* "A clear legible copy of the complete record shall be sent without delay via the live-link to the interviewer. The interviewer, after confirming with the suspect that the copy is legible and complete, shall allow the suspect to read the record, or have the record read to them by the interpreter and to sign the copy as correct or indicate the respects in which they consider it inaccurate. The interviewer is responsible for ensuring that that the signed copy and the original record made by the interpreter are retained with the case papers for use in evidence if required and must advise the interpreter of their obligation to keep the original record securely for that purpose.";(b)

Code C paragraph 13.4:

For sub-paragraph (b), *substitute:* "A clear legible copy of the complete statement shall be sent without delay via the live-link to the interviewer. The interviewer, after confirming with the suspect that the copy is legible and complete, shall invite the suspect to sign it. The interviewer is responsible for ensuring that that the signed copy and the original record made by the interpreter are retained with the case papers for use in evidence if required and must advise the interpreter of their obligation to keep the original record securely for that purpose.";(c)

Code C paragraph 13.7:

After the first sentence, *insert:* "A clear legible copy of the certified record must be sent without delay via the live-link to the interviewer. The interviewer is responsible for ensuring that the original certified record and the copy are retained with the case papers for use as evidence if required and must advise the interpreter of their obligation to keep the original record securely for that purpose." (d)

Code C paragraph 11.2, Code E paragraphs 3.4 and 4.3 and Code F paragraph 2.5.- interviews

At the beginning of each paragraph, *insert*: "Before the interview commences, the operation of live-link interpretation shall be explained and demonstrated to the suspect, their solicitor and appropriate adult, unless it has been previously explained and demonstrated (see Code C Annex N *paragraph 4*)." (e)

Code E, paragraph 3.20 (signing master recording label)

After the *third sentence*, insert, "If live-link interpretation has been used, the interviewer should ask the interpreter to observe the removal and sealing of the master recording and to confirm in writing that they have seen it sealed and signed by the interviewer. A clear legible copy of the confirmation signed by the interpreter must be sent via the livelink to the interviewer. The interviewer is responsible for ensuring that the original confirmation and the copy are retained with the case papers for use in evidence if required and must advise the interpreter of their obligation to keep the original confirmation securely for that purpose."

NOTES FOR GUIDANCE

N1   *For purposes other than an interview, audio-only live-link interpretation, for example by telephone (see Code C paragraph 13.12(b)) may provide an appropriate option until an interpreter is physically present or audio-visual live-link interpretation becomes available. A particular example would be the initial action required when a detained suspect arrives at a police station to inform them of, and to explain, the reasons for their arrest and detention and their various rights and entitlements. Another example would be to inform the suspect by telephone, that an interpreter they will be able to see and hear is being arranged. In these circumstances, telephone live-link interpretation may help to allay the suspect's concerns and contribute to the completion of the risk assessment (see Code C paragraph 3.6).*
N2   *The explanation and demonstration of live-link interpretation is intended to help the suspect, solicitor and appropriate adult make an informed decision and to allay any concerns they may have.*
N3   *Factors affecting availability of a suitable interpreter will include the location of the police station and the language and type of interpretation (oral or sign language) required.*

The Code contained in this booklet has been issued by the Home Secretary under the Police and Criminal Evidence Act 1984 and has been approved by Parliament.

Copies of the Codes issued under the Police and Criminal Evidence Act 1984 must be readily available in all police stations for consultation by police officers, detained people and members of the public.

Revised Code of Practice on audio recording interviews with suspects

2.373 Police and Criminal Evidence Act 1984 Code E *Replace the existing Code E with the revised 2018 versions as follows:*

Police and Criminal Evidence Act 1984 Code E
Revised Code of Practice on audio recording interviews with suspects

COMMENCEMENT – TRANSITIONAL ARRANGEMENTS

This Code applies to interviews carried out after 00.00 on 31 July 2018, notwithstanding that the interview may have commenced before that time.

Contents

1 GENERAL

1.0 The procedures in this Code must be used fairly, responsibly, with respect for the people to whom they apply and without unlawful discrimination. Under the Equality Act 2010, section 149 (Public Sector Equality Duty), police forces must, in carrying out their functions, have due regard to the need to eliminate unlawful discrimination, harassment, victimisation and any other conduct which is prohibited by that Act, to advance equality of opportunity between people who share a relevant protected characteristic and people who do not share it, and to foster good relations between those persons. The Equality Act also makes it unlawful for police officers to discriminate against, harass or victimise any person on the grounds of the 'protected characteristics' of age, disability, gender reassignment, race, religion or belief, sex and sexual orientation, marriage and civil partnership, pregnancy and maternity, when using their powers. See *Note 1B*.

1.1 This Code of Practice must be readily available for consultation by:
- police officers
- police staff
- detained persons
- members of the public.

1.2 The *Notes for Guidance* included are not provisions of this Code. They form guidance to police officers and others about its application and interpretation.

1.3 Nothing in this Code shall detract from the requirements of Code C, the Code of Practice for the detention, treatment and questioning of persons by police officers.

1.4 The interviews and other matters to which this Code applies are described in section 2. This Code does not apply to the conduct and recording in England and Wales, of:
- interviews of persons detained under section 41 of, or Schedule 7 to, the Terrorism Act 2000, and
- post-charge questioning of persons authorised under section 22 of the Counter-Terrorism Act 2008.

These must be video recorded with sound in accordance with the provisions of the separate Code of Practice issued under *paragraph 3 of Schedule 8 to the Terrorism Act 2000* and under *section 25 of the Counter-Terrorism Act 2008*. If, during the course of an interview or questioning under this Code, it becomes apparent that the interview or questioning should be conducted under that separate Code, the interview should only continue in accordance with that Code.

Note: The provisions of this Code and Code F which govern the conduct and recording of interviews *do not apply* to interviews with, or taking statements from, witnesses.

1.5 In this Code:
- 'appropriate adult' has the same meaning as in Code C, *paragraph 1.7*.
- 'vulnerable person' has the same meaning as described in Code C *paragraph 1.13(d)*.
- 'solicitor' has the same meaning as in Code C, *paragraph 6.12*.
- 'interview' has the same meaning as in *Code C, paragraph 11.1A*.

1.5A The provisions of this Code which require interviews with suspects to be audio recorded and the provisions of Code F which permit simultaneous visual recording provide safeguards:
- for suspects against inaccurate recording of the words used in questioning them and of their demeanour during the interview; and;
- for police interviewers against unfounded allegations made by, or on behalf of, suspects about the conduct of the interview and what took place during the interview which might otherwise appear credible.

Recording of interviews must therefore be carried out openly to instil confidence in its reliability as an impartial and accurate record of the interview.

1.5B The provisions of Code C:
- *sections 10 and 11*, and the applicable *Notes for Guidance* apply to the conduct of interviews to which this Code applies.
- *paragraphs 11.7 to 11.14* apply only when a written record is needed.

1.5C Code C, *paragraphs 10.10, 10.11* and *Annex C* describe the restriction on drawing adverse inferences from an arrested suspect's failure or refusal to say anything about their involvement in the offence when interviewed or after being charged or informed they may be prosecuted, and how it affects the terms of the caution and determines if and by whom a special warning under sections 36 and 37 of the Criminal Justice and Public Order Act 1994 can be given.

1.6 In this Code:
(a) in relation to the place where an interview of a suspect to which this Code or (as the case may be) Code F, applies, is conducted and recorded (see *Note 1A*):
  (i) '*authorised*' in relation to the recording devices described in (ii) and (iii), means any such device that the chief officer has authorised interviewers under their direction and control to use to record the interview in question at the place in question, provided that the interviewer in question has been trained to set up and operate the device, in compliance with the manufacturer's instructions and subject to the operating procedures required by the chief officer;
  (ii) '*removable recording media device*' means a recording device which, when set up and operated in accordance with the manufacturer's instructions and the operating procedures required by the chief officers, uses removable, physical recording media (such as magnetic tape, optical disc or solid state memory card) for the purpose of making a clear and accurate, audio recording or (as the case may be) audio-visual recording, of the interview in question which can then be played back and copied using that device or any other device. A sign or indicator on the device which is visible to the suspect must show when the device is recording;
  (iii) '*secure digital recording network device*' means a recording device which, when set up and operated in accordance with the manufacturer's instructions and the operating procedures required by the chief officers, enables a clear and accurate original audio recording or (as the case may be) audio-visual recording, of the interview in question, to be made and stored using non-removable storage, as a digital file or a series of such files that can be securely transferred by a wired or wireless connection to a remote secure network file server system (which may have cloud based storage) which ensures that access to interview recordings for all purposes is strictly controlled and is restricted to those whose access, either generally or in specific cases, is necessary. Examples of access include playing back the whole or part of any original recording and making one or more copies of, the whole or part of that original recording. A sign or

indicator on the device which is visible to the suspect must show when the device is recording.

(b)   'designated person' means a person other than a police officer, who has specified powers and duties conferred or imposed on them by designation under section 38 or 39 of the Police Reform Act 2002.

(c)   any reference to a police officer includes a designated person acting in the exercise or performance of the powers and duties conferred or imposed on them by their designation.

1.7   Section 2 of this Code sets out the requirement that an authorised recording device, if available, must be used to record a suspect interview and when such a device cannot be used, it allows a 'relevant officer' (see *paragraph 2.3(c)*) to decide that the interview is to be recorded in writing in accordance with Code C. For detained suspects, the 'relevant officer' is the custody officer and for voluntary interviews, the officer is determined according to the type of offence (indictable or summary only) and where the interview takes place (police station or elsewhere). Provisions in sections 3 and 4 deal with the conduct and recording of interviews according to the type of authorised recording device used. Section 3 applies to *removable recording media devices* (see *paragraph 1.6(a)(i)*) and section 4 applies to *secure digital recording network devices* (see *paragraph 1.6(a)(ii)*). The Annex applies when a voluntary interview is conducted elsewhere than at a police station about one of the four offence types specified in the Annex. For such interviews, the relevant officer is the interviewer.

1.8   Nothing in this Code prevents the custody officer, or other officer given custody of the detainee, from allowing police staff who are not designated persons to carry out individual procedures or tasks at the police station if the law allows. However, the officer remains responsible for making sure the procedures and tasks are carried out correctly in accordance with this Code. Any such police staff must be:

(a)   a person employed by a police force and under the control and direction of the Chief Officer of that force; or

(b)   employed by a person with whom a police force has a contract for the provision of services relating to persons arrested or otherwise in custody.

1.9   Designated persons and other police staff must have regard to any relevant provisions of the Codes of Practice.

1.10   References to pocket book shall include any official report book or electronic recording device issued to police officers or police staff that enables a record required to be made by any provision of this Code (but which is not an audio record to which *paragraph 2.1* applies) to be made and dealt with in accordance with that provision. References in this Code to written records, forms and signatures include electronic records and forms and electronic confirmation that identifies the person making the record or completing the form.

Chief officers must be satisfied as to the integrity and security of the devices, records and forms to which this paragraph applies and that use of those devices, records and forms satisfies relevant data protection legislation.

1.11   References to a custody officer include those performing the functions of a custody officer as in *paragraph 1.9* of Code C.

1.12   *Not used.*

1.13   Nothing in this Code requires the identity of officers or police staff conducting interviews to be recorded or disclosed if the interviewer reasonably believes recording or disclosing their name might put them in danger. In these cases, the officers and staff should use warrant or other identification numbers and the name of their police station. Such instances and the reasons for them shall be recorded in the custody record or the interviewer's pocket book. (See *Note 1C*.)

Notes for Guidance

1A   *An interviewer who is not sure, or has any doubt, about whether a place or location elsewhere than a police station is suitable for carrying out an interview of a juvenile or vulnerable person, using a particular recording device, should consult an officer of the rank of sergeant or above for advice. See Code C paragraphs 3.21, 3.22 and Note 3I*

1B   *In paragraph 1.0, under the Equality Act 2010, section 149, the 'relevant protected characteristics' are: age, disability, gender reassignment, pregnancy and maternity, race, religion/belief, and sex and sexual orientation. For further detailed guidance and advice on the Equality Act, see: https://www.gov.uk/guidance/equality-act-2010-guidance.*

1C   *The purpose of paragraph 1.13 is to protect those involved in serious organised crime investigations or arrests of particularly violent suspects when there is reliable information that those arrested or their associates may threaten or cause harm to those involved. In cases of doubt, an officer of the rank of inspector or above should be consulted.*

1D   *Attention is drawn to the provisions set out in Code C about the matters to be considered when deciding whether a detained person is fit to be interviewed.*

2   Interviews and other matters to be audio recorded under this Code

(A)   Requirement to use authorised audio-recording device when available.

2.1   Subject to *paragraph 2.3*, if an authorised recording device (see *paragraph 1.6(a)*) in working order *and* an interview room or other location (see *Note 1A*) suitable for that device to be used, are available, then that device shall be used to record the following matters:

(a)   any interview with a person cautioned in accordance with Code C, *section 10* in respect of any *summary* offence or any *indictable* offence, which includes any offence triable either way, when:

  (i)   that person (the suspect) is questioned about their involvement or suspected involvement in that offence and they have not been charged or informed they may be prosecuted for that offence; and

  (ii)   exceptionally, further questions are put to a person about any offence *after* they have been charged with, or told they may be prosecuted for, that offence (see Code C, *paragraph 16.5 and Note 2C).*

(b)   when a person who has been charged with, or informed they may be prosecuted for, any offence, is told about any written statement or interview with another person and they are handed a true copy of the written statement or the content of the interview record is brought to their attention in accordance with Code C, *paragraph 16.4 and Note 2D.*
See *Note 2A*

2.2   The whole of each of the matters described in *paragraph 2.1* shall be audio-recorded, including the taking and reading back of any statement as applicable.

2.3   A written record of the matters described in *paragraph 2.1(a)* and *(b)* shall be made in accordance with Code C, *section 11*, only if,

(a)   an authorised recording device (see *paragraph 1.6(a)*) in working order is *not available;* or

(b)   such a device is available but a location suitable for using that device to make the audio recording of the matter in question is not available; and

(c)   the 'relevant officer' described in *paragraph 2.4* considers on reasonable grounds, that the proposed interview or (as the case may be) continuation of the interview or other action, should not be delayed until an authorised recording device in working order *and* a suitable interview room or other location become available (see *Note 2E*) and decides that a written record shall be made;

(d)   if in accordance with *paragraph 3.9*, the suspect or the appropriate adult on their behalf, objects to the interview being audibly recorded and the 'relevant officer' described in *paragraph 2.4*, after having regard to the nature and circumstances of the objections (see *Note 2F*), decides that a written record shall be made;

(e)   in the case of a detainee who refuses to go into or remain in a suitable interview room and in accordance with Code C *paragraphs 12.5* and *12.11*, the custody officer directs that interview be conducted in a cell and considers that an authorised recording device cannot be safely used in the cell.

Note: When the suspect appears to have a hearing impediment, this paragraph does not affect the separate requirement in *paragraphs 3.7* and *4.4* for the interviewer to make a written note of the interview at the same time as the audio recording.

(B) Meaning of 'relevant officer'

2.4   In *paragraph 2.3(c)*:

(a)   if the person to be interviewed is arrested elsewhere than at a police station for an offence and before they arrive at a police station, an urgent interview in accordance with *Code C paragraph 11.1* is necessary to avert one or more of the risks mentioned in *sub-paragraphs (a)* to *(c)* of that paragraph, the 'relevant officer' means the *interviewer*, who may or may not be the arresting officer, who must have regard to the time, place and urgency of the proposed interview.

(b)   if the person in question has been taken to a police station after being arrested elsewhere for an offence or is arrested for an offence whilst at a police station after attending voluntarily and is detained at that police station or elsewhere in the charge of a constable, the 'relevant officer' means the *custody officer at the station where the person's detention was last authorised.* The custody officer must have regard to the nature of the investigation and in accordance with *Code C paragraph 1.1*, ensure that the detainee is dealt with expeditiously, and released as soon as the need for their detention no longer applies.

(c)   In the case of a voluntary interview (see *Code C paragraph 3.21* to *3.22*) which takes place:

    (i)   at a police station and the offence in question is an indictable offence, the 'relevant officer' means *an officer of the rank of sergeant or above*, in consultation with the investigating officer;

    (ii)   at a police station and the offence in question is a summary offence, the 'relevant officer' means *the interviewer* in consultation with the investigating officer if different,

    (iii)   elsewhere than at a police station and the offence is one of the four indictable offence types which satisfy the conditions in Part 1 of the Annex to this Code, the 'relevant officer' means *the interviewer* in consultation with the investigating officer, if different.

    (iv)   elsewhere than at a police station and the offence in question is an indictable offence which is not one of the four indictable offence types which satisfy the conditions in Part 1 of the Annex to this Code, the 'relevant officer' means an *officer of the rank of sergeant or above*, in consultation with the investigating officer.

    (v)   elsewhere than at a police station and the offence in question is a summary only offence, the 'relevant officer' means *the interviewer* in consultation with the investigating officer, if different.

See *Note 2B –Summary table – relevant officer for voluntary interviews*

(C) Duties of the 'relevant officer' and the interviewer

2.5   When, in accordance with *paragraph 2.3*, a written record is made:

(a)   the relevant officer must:

    (i)   record the reasons for not making an audio recording and the date and time the decision in *paragraph 2.3(c)* or (as applicable) *paragraph 2.3(d)* was made; and

    (ii)   ensure that the suspect is informed that a written record will be made;

(b)   the interviewer must ensure that the written record includes:

    (i)   the date and time the decision in *paragraph 2.3(c)* or (as applicable) *paragraph 2.3(d)* was made, who made it and where the decision is recorded, and

    (ii)   the fact that the suspect was informed.

(c)   the written record shall be made in accordance with Code C, *section 11;*

See *Note 2B*

(D) Remote monitoring of interviews

2.6   If the interview room or other location where the interview takes place is equipped with facilities that enable audio recorded interviews to be remotely monitored as they take place, the interviewer must ensure that suspects, their legal representatives and any appropriate adults are fully aware of what this means and that there is no possibility of privileged conversations being listened to. With this in mind, the following safeguards should be applied:

(a) The remote monitoring system should only be able to operate when the audio recording device has been turned on.

(b) The equipment should incorporate a light, clearly visible to all in the interview room, which is automatically illuminated as soon as remote monitoring is activated.

(c) Interview rooms and other locations fitted with remote monitoring equipment must contain a notice, prominently displayed, referring to the capacity for remote monitoring and to the fact that the warning light will illuminate whenever monitoring is taking place.

(d) At the beginning of the interview, the interviewer must explain the contents of the notice to the suspect and if present, to the solicitor and appropriate adult and that explanation should itself be audio recorded.

(e) The fact that an interview, or part of an interview, was remotely monitored should be recorded in the suspect's custody record or, if the suspect is not in detention, the interviewer's pocket book. That record should include the names of the officers doing the monitoring and the purpose of the monitoring (e.g. for training, to assist with the investigation, etc.)

(E) Use of live link - Interviewer not present at the same station as the detainee

2.7 Code C *paragraphs 12.9A* and *12.9B* set out the conditions which, if satisfied allow a suspect in police detention to be interviewed using a live link by a police officer who is not present at the police station where the detainee is held. These provisions also set out the duties and responsibilities of the custody officer, the officer having physical custody of the suspect and the interviewer and the modifications that apply to ensure that any such interview is conducted and audio recorded in accordance with this Code or (as the case may be) visually recorded in accordance with Code F.

Notes for guidance

2A *Nothing in this Code is intended to preclude audio-recording at police discretion at police stations or elsewhere when persons are charged with, or told they may be prosecuted for, an offence or they respond after being so charged or informed.*

2B *A decision made in accordance with paragraph 2.3 not to audio-record an interview for any reason may be the subject of comment in court. The 'relevant officer' responsible should be prepared to justify that decision.*

Table: Summary of paragraph 2.4(c) – relevant officer for voluntary interviews:

	Location of voluntary interview	Offence type	Relevant Officer
(i)	Police station	Any indictable offence.	Sergeant or above[+]
(ii)	Police station	Any summary only offence	Interviewer[+]
(iii)	Elsewhere than at a police station	Indictable offence type defined by the Annex.	Interviewer[+]
(iv)	Elsewhere than at a police station	Indictable offence type not defined by the Annex.	Sergeant or above[+]
(v)	Elsewhere than at a police station	Summary only.	Interviewer[+]

[+] *= in consultation with the investigating officer.*

2C *Code C sets out the circumstances in which a suspect may be questioned about an offence after being charged with it.*

2D *Code C sets out the procedures to be followed when a person's attention is drawn after charge, to a statement made by another person. One method of bringing the content of an interview with another person to the notice of a suspect may be to play them a recording of that interview. The person may not be questioned about the statement or interview record unless this is allowed in accordance with paragraph 16.5 of Code C.*

2E *A voluntary interview should be arranged for a time and place when it can be audio recorded and enable the safeguards and requirements set out in Code C paragraphs 3.21 to 3.22B to be implemented. It would normally be reasonable to delay the interview to enable audio recording unless the delay to do so would be likely to compromise the outcome of the interview or investigation, for example if there are grounds to suspect that the suspect would use the delay to fabricate an innocent explanation, influence witnesses or tamper with other material evidence.*

2F *Objections for the purpose of paragraphs 2.3(d) and 3.9 are meant to apply to objections based on the suspect's genuine and honestly held beliefs and to allow officers to exercise their discretion to decide that a written interview record is to be made according to the circumstances surrounding the suspect and the investigation. Objections that appear to be frivolous with the intentions of frustrating or delaying the investigation would not be relevant.*

3 Interview recording using removable recording media device

(A) Recording and sealing master recordings - general

3.1 When using an authorised *removable recording media* device (see *paragraph 1.6(a)(i)*), one recording, the master recording, will be sealed in the suspect's presence. A second recording will be used as a working copy. The master recording is any of the recordings made by a multi-deck/drive machine or the only recording made by a single deck/drive machine. The working copy is one of the other recordings made by a multi-deck/drive machine or a copy of the master recording made by a single deck/drive machine.

3.2 The purpose of sealing the master recording before it leaves the suspect's presence is to establish their confidence that the integrity of the recording is preserved. If a single deck/drive machine is used the working copy of the master recording must be made in the suspect's presence and without the master recording leaving their sight. The working copy shall be used for making further copies if needed.

(B) Commencement of interviews

3.3 When the suspect is brought into the interview room or arrives at the location where the interview is to take place, the interviewer shall, without delay but in the suspect's sight, unwrap or open the new recording media, load the recording device with new recording media and set it to record.

3.4 The interviewer must point out the sign or indicator which shows that the recording equipment is activated and is recording (see *paragraph 1.6(a)(i)*) and shall then:

(a) tell the suspect that the interview is being audibly recorded using an authorised *removable recording media* device and outline the recording process (see *Note 3A*);

(b) subject to *paragraph 1.13*, give their name and rank and that of any other interviewer present;

(c) ask the suspect and any other party present, e.g. the appropriate adult, a solicitor or interpreter, to identify themselves (see *Note 3A*);

(d) state the date, time of commencement and place of the interview;

(e) tell the suspect that:
  • they will be given a copy of the recording of the interview in the event that they are charged or informed that they will be prosecuted but if they are not charged or informed that they will be prosecuted they will only be given a copy as agreed with the police or on the order of a court; and
  • they will be given a written notice at the end of the interview setting out their right to a copy of the recording and what will happen to the recording and;

(f) if equipment for remote monitoring of interviews as described in *paragraph 2.6* is installed, explain the contents of the notice to the suspect, solicitor and appropriate adult as required by *paragraph 2.6(d)* and point out the light that illuminates automatically as soon as remote monitoring is activated.

3.5 Any person entering the interview room after the interview has commenced shall be invited by the interviewer to identify themselves for the purpose of the audio recording and state the reason why they have entered the interview room.

3.6 The interviewer shall:
  • caution the suspect, see Code C *section 10*; and
  • if they are detained, remind them of their entitlement to free legal advice, see Code C, *paragraph 11.2*; or
  • if they are not detained under arrest, explain this and their entitlement to free legal advice (see Code C, *paragraph 3.21*) and ask the suspect to confirm that they agree to the voluntary interview proceeding (see *Code C paragraph 3.22A*).

3.7 The interviewer shall put to the suspect any significant statement or silence, see Code C, *paragraph 11.4*.

(C) Interviews with suspects who appear to have a hearing impediment

3.8 If the suspect appears to have a hearing impediment, the interviewer shall make a written note of the interview in accordance with Code C, at the same time as audio recording it in accordance with this Code. (See *Notes 3B* and *3C*.)

(D) Objections and complaints by the suspect

3.9 If the suspect or an appropriate adult on their behalf, objects to the interview being audibly recorded either at the outset, during the interview or during a break, the interviewer shall explain that the interview is being audibly recorded and that this Code requires the objections to be recorded on the audio recording. When any objections have been audibly recorded or the suspect or appropriate adult have refused to have their objections recorded, the relevant officer shall decide in accordance with *paragraph 2.3(d)* (which requires the officer to have regard to the nature and circumstances of the objections) whether a written record of the interview or its continuation, is to be made and that audio recording should be turned off. Following a decision that a written record is to be made, the interviewer shall say they are turning off the recorder and shall then make a written record of the interview as in Code C, *section 11*. If, however, following a decision that a written record is not to be made, the interviewer may proceed to question the suspect with the audio recording still on. This procedure also applies in cases where the suspect has previously objected to the interview being visually recorded, see Code F *paragraph 2.7*, and the investigating officer has decided to audibly record the interview. (See *Notes 2F* and *3D*.)

3.10 If in the course of an interview a complaint is made by or on behalf of the person being questioned concerning the provisions of this or any other Codes, or it comes to the interviewer's notice that the person may have been treated improperly, the interviewer shall act as in Code C, *paragraph 12.9*. (See *Notes 3E* and *3F*.)

3.11 If the suspect indicates they want to tell the interviewer about matters not directly connected with the offence of which they are suspected and they are unwilling for these matters to be audio recorded, the suspect should be given the opportunity to tell the interviewer about these matters after the conclusion of the formal interview.

(E) Changing recording media

3.12 When the recorder shows the recording media only has a short time left to run, the interviewer shall so inform the person being interviewed and round off that part of the interview. If the interviewer leaves the room for a second set of recording media, the suspect shall not be left unattended. The interviewer will remove the recording media from the recorder and insert the new recording media which shall be unwrapped or opened in the suspect's presence. The recorder should be set to record on the new media. To avoid confusion between the recording media, the interviewer shall mark the media with an identification number immediately after it is removed from the recorder.

(F) Taking a break during interview

3.13 When a break is taken, the fact that a break is to be taken, the reason for it and the time shall be recorded on the audio recording.

3.14 When the break is taken and the interview room vacated by the suspect, the recording media shall be removed from the recorder and the procedures for the conclusion of an interview followed, see *paragraph 3.19.*

3.15 When a break is a short one and both the suspect and an interviewer remain in the interview room, the recording may be stopped. There is no need to remove the recording media and when the interview recommences the recording should continue on the same recording media. The time the interview recommences shall be recorded on the audio recording.

3.16 After any break in the interview the interviewer must, before resuming the interview, remind the person being questioned of their right to legal advice if they have not exercised it and that they remain under caution or, if there is any doubt, give the caution in full again. (See *Note 3G.*)

(G) Failure of recording equipment

3.17 If there is an equipment failure which can be rectified quickly, e.g. by inserting new recording media, the interviewer shall follow the appropriate procedures as in *paragraph 3.12.* When the recording is resumed the interviewer shall explain what happened and record the time the interview recommences. However, if it is not possible to continue recording using the same recording device or by using a replacement device, the interview should be audio-recorded using a secure digital recording network device as in *paragraph 4.1,* if the necessary equipment is available. If it is not available, the interview may continue and be recorded in writing in accordance with *paragraph 2.3* as directed by the 'relevant officer'. (See *Note 3H.*)

(H) Removing recording media from the recorder

3.18 Recording media which is removed from the recorder during the interview shall be retained and the procedures in *paragraph 3.12* followed.

(I) Conclusion of interview

3.19 At the conclusion of the interview, the suspect shall be offered the opportunity to clarify anything they have said and asked if there is anything they want to add.

3.20 At the conclusion of the interview, including the taking and reading back of any written statement, the time shall be recorded and the recording shall be stopped. The interviewer shall seal the master recording with a master recording label and treat it as an exhibit in accordance with force standing orders. The interviewer shall sign the label and ask the suspect and any third party present during the interview to sign it. If the suspect or third party refuse to sign the label an officer of at least the rank of inspector, or if not available the custody officer, or if the suspect has not been arrested, a sergeant, shall be called into the interview room and asked, subject to *paragraph 1.13,* to sign it.

3.21 The suspect shall be handed a notice which explains:

- how the audio recording will be used;
- the arrangements for access to it;
- that if they are charged or informed they will be prosecuted, a copy of the audio recording will be supplied as soon as practicable or as otherwise agreed between the suspect and the police or on the order of a court.

(J) After the interview

3.22 The interviewer shall make a note in their pocket book that the interview has taken place and that it was audibly recorded, the time it commenced, its duration and date and identification number of the master recording (see *Note 3I*).

3.23 If no proceedings follow in respect of the person whose interview was recorded, the recording media must be kept securely as in *paragraph 3.22* and *Note 3J.*

(K) Master Recording security(i)

General

3.24 The officer in charge of each police station at which interviews with suspects are recorded or as the case may be, where recordings of interviews carried out elsewhere than at a police station are held, shall make arrangements for master recordings to be kept securely and their movements accounted for on the same basis as material which may be used for evidential purposes, in accordance with force standing orders. (See *Note 3J.*)(ii)

Breaking master recording seal for criminal proceedings

3.25 A police officer has no authority to break the seal on a master recording which is required for criminal trial or appeal proceedings. If it is necessary to gain access to the master recording, the police officer shall arrange for its seal to be broken in the presence of a representative of the Crown Prosecution Service. The defendant or their legal adviser should be informed and given a reasonable opportunity to be present. If the defendant or their legal representative is present they shall be invited to re-seal and sign the master recording. If either refuses or neither is present this should be done by the representative of the Crown Prosecution Service. (See *Notes 3K* and *3L.*)(iii)

Breaking master recording seal: other cases

3.26 The chief officer of police is responsible for establishing arrangements for breaking the seal of the master copy where no criminal proceedings result, or the criminal proceedings to which the interview relates, have been concluded and it becomes necessary to break the seal. These arrangements should be those which the chief officer considers are reasonably necessary to demonstrate to the person interviewed and any other party who may wish to use or refer to the interview record that the master copy has not been tampered with and that the interview record remains accurate. (See *Note 3M.*)

3.27 Subject to *paragraph 3.29*, a representative of each party must be given a reasonable opportunity to be present when the seal is broken and the master recording copied and resealed.

3.28 If one or more of the parties is not present when the master copy seal is broken because they cannot be contacted or refuse to attend or *paragraph 3.29* applies, arrangements should be made for an independent person such as a custody visitor, to be present. Alternatively, or as an additional safeguard, arrangements should be made to visually record the procedure.

3.29 *Paragraph 3.28* does not require a person to be given an opportunity to be present when;
(a) it is necessary to break the master copy seal for the proper and effective further investigation of the original offence or the investigation of some other offence; and
(b) the officer in charge of the investigation has reasonable grounds to suspect that allowing an opportunity might prejudice such an investigation or criminal proceedings which may be brought as a result or endanger any person. (See Note 3N.)(iv)

Documentation

3.30 When the master recording seal is broken, a record must be made of the procedure followed, including the date, time, place and persons present.

NOTES FOR GUIDANCE

Commencement of interviews (paragraph 3.3)

3A *When outlining the recording process, the interviewer should refer to paragraph 1.6(a)(ii) and (iii) and briefly describe how the recording device being used is operated and how recordings are made. For the purpose of voice identification the interviewer should ask the suspect and any other people present to identify themselves.*

Interviews with suspects who appear to have a hearing impediment (paragraph 3.8)

3B *This provision is to give a person who is deaf or has impaired hearing equivalent rights of access to the full interview record as far as this is possible using audio recording.*

3C *The provisions of Code C on interpreters for suspects who do not appear to speak or understand English or who appear to have a hearing or speech impediment, continue to apply.*

Objections and complaints by the suspect (paragraph 3.9)

3D *The relevant officer should be aware that a decision to continue recording against the wishes of the suspect may be the subject of comment in court.*

3E *If the custody officer, or in the case of a person who has not been arrested, a sergeant, is called to deal with the complaint, the recorder should, if possible, be left on until the officer has entered the room and spoken to the person being interviewed. Continuation or termination of the interview should be at the interviewer's discretion pending action by an inspector under Code C, paragraph 9.2.*

3F *If the complaint is about a matter not connected with this Code or Code C, the decision to continue is at the interviewer's discretion. When the interviewer decides to continue the interview, they shall tell the suspect that at the conclusion of the interview, the complaint will be brought to the attention of the custody officer, or in the case of a person who has not been arrested, a sergeant. When the interview is concluded the interviewer must, as soon as practicable, inform the custody officer or, as the case may be, the sergeant, about the existence and nature of the complaint made.*

3G *In considering whether to caution again after a break, the interviewer should bear in mind that they may have to satisfy a court that the person understood that they were still under caution when the interview resumed. The interviewer should also remember that it may be necessary to show to the court that nothing occurred during a break or between interviews which influenced the suspect's recorded evidence. After a break or at the beginning of a subsequent interview, the interviewer should consider summarising on the record the reason for the break and confirming this with the suspect.*

Failure of recording equipment (paragraph 3.17)

3H *Where the interview is being recorded and the media or the recording equipment fails the interviewer should stop the interview immediately. Where part of the interview is unaffected by the error and is still accessible on the media, that part shall be copied and sealed in the suspect's presence as a master copy and the interview recommenced using new equipment/media as required. Where the content of the interview has been lost in its entirety, the media should be sealed in the suspect's presence and the interview begun again. If the recording equipment cannot be fixed and no replacement is immediately available, subject to paragraph 2.3, the interview should be recorded in accordance with Code C, section 11.*

3I *Any written record of an audio recorded interview should be made in accordance with current national guidelines for police officers, police staff and CPS prosecutors concerned with the preparation, processing and submission of prosecution files.*

Master Recording security (paragraphs 3.24 to 3.30)

3J *This section is concerned with the security of the master recording sealed at the conclusion of the interview. Care must be taken of working copy recordings because their loss or destruction may lead unnecessarily to the need to access master recordings.*

Breaking master recording seal for criminal proceedings (paragraph 3.25)

3K *If the master recording has been delivered to the crown court for their keeping after committal for trial the crown prosecutor will apply to the chief clerk of the crown court centre for the release of the recording for unsealing by the crown prosecutor.*

3L *Reference to the Crown Prosecution Service or to the crown prosecutor in this part of the Code should be taken to include any other body or person with a statutory responsibility for the proceedings for which the police recorded interview is required.*

Breaking master recording seal: other cases (paragraphs 3.26 to 3.29)

3M *The most common reasons for needing access to master copies that are not required for criminal proceedings arise from civil actions and complaints against police and civil actions between individuals arising out of allegations of crime investigated by police.*

3N *Paragraph 3.29(b) could apply, for example, when one or more of the outcomes or likely outcomes of the investigation might be; (i) the prosecution of one or more of the original suspects; (ii) the prosecution of someone previously not suspected, including someone who was originally a witness, and (iii) any original suspect being treated as a prosecution witness and when premature disclosure of any police action, particularly through contact with any parties involved, could lead to a real risk of compromising the investigation and endangering witnesses.*

4 INTERVIEW RECORDING USING SECURE DIGITAL RECORDING NETWORK DEVICE.

(A) GENERAL

4.1 An authorised secure digital recording network device (see *paragraph 1.6(a)(iii)* does not use removable media and this section specifies the provisions which will apply when such a device is used. For ease of reference, it repeats in full some of the provisions of section 3 that apply to both types of recording device.

(B) COMMENCEMENT OF INTERVIEWS

4.2 When the suspect is brought into the interview room or arrives at the location where the interview is to take place, the interviewer shall without delay and in the sight of the suspect, switch on the recording equipment and in accordance with the manufacturer's instructions start recording.

4.3 The interviewer must point out the sign or indicator which shows that the recording equipment is activated and is recording (see *paragraph 1.6(a)(iii)*) and shall then:

(a)   tell the suspect that the interview is being audibly recorded using an authorised secure *digital recording network device* and outline the recording process (see *Note 3A*);

(b)   subject to *paragraph 1.13*, give their name and rank and that of any other interviewer present;

(c)   ask the suspect and any other party present, e.g. the appropriate adult, a solicitor or interpreter, to identify themselves (see *Note 3A*);

(d)   state the date, time of commencement and place of the interview; and

(e)   inform the person that:

- they will be given access to the recording of the interview in the event that they are charged or informed that they will be prosecuted but if they are not charged or informed that they will be prosecuted they will only be given access as agreed with the police or on the order of a court; and

- they will be given a written notice at the end of the interview setting out their rights to access the recording and what will happen to the recording.

(f)   If equipment for remote monitoring of interviews as described in *paragraph 2.6* is installed, explain the contents of the notice to the suspect, solicitor and appropriate adult as required by *paragraph 2.6(d)* and point out the light that illuminates automatically as soon as remote monitoring is activated.

4.4 *Paragraphs 3.5 to 3.7 apply.*

(C) INTERVIEWS WITH SUSPECTS WHO APPEAR TO HAVE A HEARING IMPEDIMENT

4.5 *Paragraph 3.8 applies.*

(D) OBJECTIONS AND COMPLAINTS BY THE SUSPECT

4.6 *Paragraphs 3.9, 3.10 and 3.11 apply.*

(E) TAKING A BREAK DURING INTERVIEW

4.7 When a break is taken, the fact that a break is to be taken, the reason for it and the time shall be recorded on the audio recording. The recording shall be stopped and the procedures in *paragraphs 4.11* and *4.12* for the conclusion of interview followed.

4.8 When the interview recommences the procedures in *paragraphs 4.2* to *4.3* for commencing an interview shall be followed to create a new file to record the continuation of the interview. The time the interview recommences shall be recorded on the audio recording.

4.9 After any break in the interview the interviewer must, before resuming the interview, remind the person being questioned of their right to legal advice if they have not exercised it and that they remain under caution or, if there is any doubt, give the caution in full again (see *Note 3G*).

(F) FAILURE OF RECORDING EQUIPMENT

4.10 If there is an equipment failure which can be rectified quickly, e.g. by commencing a new secure digital network recording using the same device or a replacement device, the interviewer shall follow the appropriate procedures as in *paragraphs 4.7 to 4.9 (Taking a break during interview).* When the recording is resumed, the interviewer shall explain what happened and record the time the interview recommences. However, if it is not possible to continue recording on the same device or by using a replacement device, the interview should be audio-recorded on removable media as in *paragraph 3.3*, if the necessary equipment is available. If it is not available, the interview may continue and be recorded in writing in accordance with *paragraph 2.3* as directed by the 'relevant officer'. (See *Note 3H*.)

(G) CONCLUSION OF INTERVIEW

4.11 At the conclusion of the interview, the suspect shall be offered the opportunity to clarify anything he or she has said and asked if there is anything they want to add.

4.12 At the conclusion of the interview, including the taking and reading back of any written statement:

(a) the time shall be orally recorded.

(b) the suspect shall be handed a notice (see *Note 4A*) which explains:
- how the audio recording will be used
- the arrangements for access to it
- that if they are charged or informed that they will be prosecuted, they will be given access to the recording of the interview either electronically or by being given a copy on removable recording media, but if they are not charged or informed that they will prosecuted, they will only be given access as agreed with the police or on the order of a court.

(c) the suspect must be asked to confirm that he or she has received a copy of the notice at *sub-paragraph (b)* above. If the suspect fails to accept or to acknowledge receipt of the notice, the interviewer will state for the recording that a copy of the notice has been provided to the suspect and that he or she has refused to take a copy of the notice or has refused to acknowledge receipt.

(d) the time shall be recorded and the interviewer shall ensure that the interview record is saved to the device in the presence of the suspect and any third party present during the interview and notify them accordingly. The interviewer must then explain that the record will be transferred securely to the remote secure network file server (see *paragraph 4.15*). If the equipment is available to enable the record to be transferred there and then in the suspect's presence, then it should be so transferred. If it is transferred at a later time, the time and place of the transfer must be recorded. The suspect should then be informed that the interview is terminated.

(H) AFTER THE INTERVIEW

4.13 The interviewer shall make a note in their pocket book that the interview has taken place and that it was audibly recorded, time it commenced, its duration and date and the identification number, filename or other reference for the recording (see *Note 3I*).

4.14 If no proceedings follow in respect of the person whose interview was recorded, the recordings must be kept securely as in *paragraphs 4.15* and *4.16*.

(I) SECURITY OF SECURE DIGITAL NETWORK INTERVIEW RECORDS

4.15 The recordings are first saved locally on the device before being transferred to the remote network file server system (see *paragraph 1.6(a)(iii)*). The recording remains on the local device until the transfer is complete. If for any reason the network connection fails, the recording will be transferred when the network connection is restored (see *paragraph 4.12(d)*). The interview record files are stored in read only form on non-removable storage devices, for example, hard disk drives, to ensure their integrity.

4.16 Access to interview recordings, including copying to removable media, must be strictly controlled and monitored to ensure that access is restricted to those who have been given specific permission to access for specified purposes when this is necessary. For example, police officers and CPS lawyers involved in the preparation of any prosecution case, persons interviewed if they have been charged or informed they may be prosecuted and their legal representatives.

NOTE FOR GUIDANCE

4A *The notice at paragraph 4.12(b) above should provide a brief explanation of the secure digital network and how access to the recording is strictly limited. The notice should also explain the access rights of the suspect, their legal representative, the police and the prosecutor to the recording of the interview. Space should be provided on the form to insert the date, the identification number, filename or other reference for the interview recording.*

ANNEX: PARAGRAPH 2.4(C)(III) – FOUR INDICTABLE OFFENCE TYPES FOR WHICH THE INTERVIEWER MAY DECIDE TO MAKE A WRITTEN RECORD OF A VOLUNTARY INTERVIEW ELSEWHERE THAN AT A POLICE STATION WHEN AN AUTHORISED AUDIO RECORDING DEVICE CANNOT BE USED.

[See *Notes 2* and *3*]

PART 1 FOUR SPECIFIED INDICTABLE OFFENCE TYPES — TWO CONDITIONS

1. The **first** condition is that the *indictable* offence in respect of which the person has been cautioned is *one* of the following:

(a) Possession of a controlled drug contrary to section 5(2) of the Misuse of Drugs Act 1971 if the drug is cannabis as defined by that Act and in a form commonly known as herbal cannabis or cannabis resin (see *Note 5*);

(b) Possession of a controlled drug contrary to section 5(2) of the Misuse of Drugs Act 1971 if the drug is khat as defined by that Act (see *Note 5*);

(c) Retail theft (shoplifting) contrary to section 1 of the Theft Act 1968 (see *Note 6*); and

(d) Criminal damage to property contrary to section 1(1) of the Criminal Damage Act 1971 (see *Note 6*),

and in this paragraph, the reference to each of the above offences applies to an attempt to commit that offence as defined by section 1 of the Criminal Attempts Act 1981.

2.   The **second** condition is that:

(a)   where the person has been cautioned in respect of an offence described in *paragraph 1(a)* (Possession of herbal cannabis or cannabis resin) or *paragraph 1(b)* (Possession of khat), the requirements of *paragraphs 3* and *4* are satisfied; or

(b)   where the person has been cautioned in respect of an offence described in *paragraph 1(c)* (Retail theft), the requirements of *paragraphs 3* and *5* are satisfied; or

(c)   where the person has been cautioned in respect of an offence described in *paragraph 1(d)* (criminal damage), the requirements of *paragraphs 3* and *6* are satisfied.

3.   The requirements of this paragraph that apply to all four offences described in *paragraph 1* are that:

(i)   with regard to the person suspected of committing the offence:
- •they appear to be aged 18 or over;
- •there is no reason to suspect that they are a vulnerable person for whom an appropriate adult is required (see *paragraph 1.5* of this Code);
- •they do *not* appear to be unable to understand what is happening because of the effects of drink, drugs or illness, ailment or condition;
- •they do *not* require an interpreter in accordance with *Code C section 13*; and
- •in accordance with Code G (Arrest), their arrest is *not* necessary in order to investigate the offence;

(ii)   it appears that the commission of the offence:
- •has *not* resulted in any injury to any person;
- •has *not* involved any realistic threat or risk of injury to any person; and
- •has *not* caused any *substantial* financial or material loss to the private property of any individual; and

(iii)   the person is not being interviewed about any other offence.

See *Notes 3* and *8*.

4.   The requirements of this paragraph that apply to the offences described in *paragraph 1(a)* (possession of herbal cannabis or cannabis resin) and *paragraph 1(b)* (possession of khat) are that a police officer who is experienced in the recognition of the physical appearance, texture and smell of herbal cannabis, cannabis resin or (as the case may be) khat, is able to say that the substance which has been found in the suspect's possession by that officer or, as the case may be, by any other officer not so experienced and trained:

(i)   is a controlled drug being either herbal cannabis, cannabis resin or khat; and

(ii)   the quantity of the substance found is consistent with personal use by the suspect and does not provide any grounds to suspect an intention to supply others.

See *Note 5*.

5.   The requirements of this paragraph that apply to the offence described in *paragraph 1(c)* (retail theft), are that it appears to the officer:

(i)   that the value of the property stolen does not exceed £100 inclusive of VAT;

(ii)   that the stolen property has been recovered and remains fit for sale unless the items stolen comprised drink or food and have been consumed; and

(iii)   that the person suspected of stealing the property is not employed (whether paid or not) by the person, company or organisation to which the property belongs.

See *Note 3*.

6.   The requirements of this paragraph that apply to the offence described in *paragraph 1(d)* (Criminal damage), are that it appears to the officer:

(i)   that the value of the criminal damage does *not exceed* £300; and

(ii)   that the person suspected of damaging the property is not employed (whether paid or not) by the person, company or organisation to which the property belongs.

See *Note 3*.

PART 2   OTHER PROVISIONS APPLICABLE TO ALL INTERVIEWS TO WHICH THIS ANNEX APPLIES

7.   *Paragraphs 3.21* to *3.22B* of Code C set out the responsibilities of the interviewing officer for ensuring compliance with the provisions of Code C that apply to the conduct and recording of voluntary interviews to which this Annex applies. See *Note 7*.

8.   If it appears to the interviewing officer that before the conclusion of an interview, any of the requirements in *paragraphs 3 to 6* of *Part 1* that apply to the offence in question described in *paragraph 1* of Part 1 have ceased to apply; this Annex shall cease to apply. The person being interviewed must be so informed and a break in the interview must be taken. The reason must be recorded in the written interview record and the continuation of the interview shall be audio recorded in accordance with section 2 of this Code. For the purpose of the continuation, the provisions of *paragraphs 3.3* and *4.2* (Commencement of interviews) shall apply. See *Note 8*.

NOTES FOR GUIDANCE

1   *Not used.*

2   *The purpose of allowing the interviewer to decide that a written record is to be made is to support the policy which gives police in England and Wales options for dealing with low-level offences quickly and non-bureaucratically in a proportionate manner. Guidance for police about these options is available at: https://www.app.college.police.uk/app-content/ prosecution-and-case-management/justiceoutcomes/.*

3   *A decision in relation to a particular indictable offence that the conditions and requirements in this Annex are satisfied is an operational matter for the interviewing officer according to all the particular circumstances of the case. These circumstances include the outcome of the officer's investigation at that time and any other matters that are relevant to the officer's consideration as to how to deal with the matter.*

4   *Not used.*

5 *Under the Misuse of Drugs Act 1971 as at the date this Code comes into force:*

(a) *cannabis includes any part of the cannabis plant but not mature stalks and seeds separated from the plant, cannabis resin and cannabis oil, but paragraph 1(a) applies only to the possession of herbal cannabis and cannabis resin; and*
(b) *khat includes the leaves, stems and shoots of the plant.*

6 *The power to issue a Penalty Notice for Disorder (PND) for an offence contrary to section 1 of the Theft Act 1968 applies when the value of the goods stolen does not exceed £100 inclusive of VAT. The power to issue a PND for an offence contrary to section 1(1) of the Criminal Damage Act 1971 applies when the value of the damage does not exceed £300.*

7 *The provisions of Code C that apply to the conduct and recording of voluntary interviews to which this Annex applies are described in paragraphs 3.21 to 3.22B of Code C. They include the suspect's right to free legal advice, the provision of information about the offence before the interview (see Code C paragraph 11.1A) and the right to interpretation and translation (see Code C section 13). These and other rights and entitlements are summarised in the notice that must be given to the suspect.*

8 *The requirements in paragraph 3 of Part 1 will cease to apply if, for example during the course of an interview, as a result of what the suspect says or other information which comes to the interviewing officer's notice:*

- *it appears that the suspect:*
  - *is aged under 18;*
  - *does require an appropriate adult;*
  - *is unable to appreciate the significance of questions and their answers;*
  - *is unable to understand what is happening because of the effects of drink, drugs or illness, ailment or condition; or*
  - *requires an interpreter; or*
- *the police officer decides that the suspect's arrest is now necessary (see Code G).*

Revised Code of Practice on visual recording with sound of interviews with suspects Codes

2.374 **Police and Criminal Evidence Act 1984 Code F** *Replace the existing Code F with the revised 2018 versions as follows:*

Police and Criminal Evidence Act 1984 Code F
Revised Code of Practice on visual recording with sound of interviews with suspects Codes

Commencement – Transitional Arrangements
This contents of this Code should be considered if an interviewer proposes to make a visual recording with sound of an interview with a suspect after 00.00 on 31 July 2018.
There is no statutory requirement under PACE to visually record interviews.

Contents

1 General
1.0 The procedures in this Code must be used fairly, responsibly, with respect for the people to whom they apply and without unlawful discrimination. Under the Equality Act 2010, section 149 (Public Sector Equality Duty), police forces must, in carrying out their functions, have due regard to the need to eliminate unlawful discrimination, harassment, victimisation and any other conduct which is prohibited by that Act, to advance equality of opportunity between people who share a relevant protected characteristic and people who do not share it, and to foster good relations between those persons. The Equality Act *also* makes it unlawful for police officers to discriminate against, harass or victimise any person on the grounds of the 'protected characteristics' of age, disability, gender reassignment, race, religion or belief, sex and sexual orientation, marriage and civil partnership, pregnancy and maternity, when using their powers. See *Note 1C*.
1.1 This Code of Practice must be readily available for consultation by police officers and other police staff, detained persons and members of the public.
1.2 The *Notes for Guidance* included are not provisions of this code. They form guidance to police officers and others about its application and interpretation.
1.3 Nothing in this Code shall detract from the requirements of Code C, the Code of Practice for the detention, treatment and questioning of persons by police officers.

1.4   The interviews and matters to which this Code applies and provisions that govern the conduct and recording of those interviews and other matters are described in section 2.

Note: The provisions of this Code and Code E which govern the conduct and recording of interviews *do not apply* to interviews with, or taking statements from, witnesses.

1.5   *Not used.*

1.5A   The provisions of Code E which require interviews with suspects to be audio recorded and the provisions of this Code which permit simultaneous visual recording provide safeguards:

- for suspects against inaccurate recording of the words used in questioning them and of their demeanour during the interview; and
- for police interviewers against unfounded allegations made by, or on behalf of, suspects about the conduct of the interview and what took place during the interview which might otherwise appear credible.

The visual recording of interviews must therefore be carried out openly to instil confidence in its reliability as an impartial and accurate record of the interview.

1.6   *Not used.*

1.6A   *Not used.*

1.7   *Not used.*

1.8   *Not used.*

NOTES FOR GUIDANCE

1A   *Not used.*

1B   *Not used.*

1C   *In paragraph 1.0, under the Equality Act 2010, section 149, the 'relevant protected character-istics' are: age, disability, gender reassignment, pregnancy and maternity, race, religion/belief, and sex and sexual orientation. For further detailed guidance and advice on the Equality Act, see: https://www.gov.uk/guidance/equality-act-2010-guidance.*

2   WHEN INTERVIEWS AND MATTERS TO WHICH CODE F APPLIES MAY BE VISUALLY RECORDED WITH SOUND AND PROVISIONS FOR THEIR CONDUCT AND RECORDING.

(A) GENERAL

2.1   For the purpose of this Code, a visual recording with sound means an audio recording of an interview or other matter made in accordance with the requirement in *paragraph 2.1* of the Code of Practice on audio recording interviews with suspects (Code E) (see *Note 2A*) during which a *simultaneous* visual recording is made which shows the suspect, the interviewer and those in whose presence and hearing the audio recording was made.

2.2   There is no statutory requirement to make a visual recording, however, the provisions of this Code shall be followed on any occasion that the 'relevant officer' described in *Code E paragraph 2.4* considers that a visual recording of any matters mentioned in *paragraph 2.1* should be made. Having regard to the safeguards described in *paragraph 1.5A*, examples of occasions when the relevant officer is likely to consider that a visual recording should be made include when:

(a)   the suspect (whether or not detained) requires an appropriate adult;

(b)   the suspect or their solicitor or appropriate adult requests that the interview be recorded visually;

(c)   the suspect or other person whose presence is necessary is deaf or deaf/blind or speech impaired and uses sign language to communicate;

(d)   the interviewer anticipates that when asking the suspect about their involvement in the offence concerned, they will invite the suspect to demonstrate their actions or behaviour at the time or to examine a particular item or object which is handed to them;

(e)   the officer in charge of the investigation believes that a visual recording with sound will assist in the conduct of the investigation, for example, when briefing other officers about the suspect or matters coming to light during the course of the interview; and

(f)   the authorised recording device that would be used in accordance with *paragraph 2.1 of Code E* incorporates a camera and creates a combined audio and visual recording and does not allow the visual recording function to operate independently of the audio recording function.

2.3   For the purpose of making such a visual recording, the provisions of Code E and the relevant *Notes for Guidance* shall apply equally to visual recordings with sound as they do to audio-only recordings, subject to the additional provisions in *paragraphs 2.5* to *2.12* below which apply exclusively to visual recordings. (See *Note 2E*.)

2.4   This Code does not apply to the conduct and recording in England and Wales, of:

- interviews of persons detained under section 41 of, or Schedule 7 to, the Terrorism Act 2000, and
- post-charge questioning of persons authorised under section 22 of the Counter-Terrorism Act 2008.

These must be video recorded with sound in accordance with the provisions of the separate Code of Practice issued under paragraph 3 of Schedule 8 to the Terrorism Act 2000 and under section 25 of the Counter-Terrorism Act 2008. If, during the course of an interview or questioning being visually recorded under this Code, it becomes apparent that the interview or questioning should be conducted under that separate Code, the interview should only continue in accordance with that Code (see *Code E paragraph 1.4*).

(B) APPLICATION OF CODE E – ADDITIONAL PROVISIONS THAT APPLY TO VISUAL RECORDING WITH SOUND.(i)

General

2.5   Before visual recording commences, the interviewer must inform the suspect that in accordance with *paragraph 2.2*, a visual recording is being made and explain the visual and audio recording arrangements. If the suspect is a juvenile or a vulnerable person (see Code C, *para-*

graphs 1.4, 1.5 and 1.13(d)), the information and explanation must be provided or (as the case may be) provided again, in the presence of the appropriate adult.

2.6 The device used to make the visual recording at the same time as the audio recording (see *paragraph 2.1*) must ensure coverage of as much of the room or location where the interview takes place as it is practically possible to achieve whilst the interview takes place (see *Note 2B*).

2.7 In cases to which *paragraph 1.13* of Code E (disclosure of identity of officers or police staff conducting interviews) applies:

(a)   the officers and staff may have their backs to the visual recording device; and

(b)   when in accordance with Code E *paragraph 3.21* or *4.12* as they apply to this Code, arrangements are made for the suspect to have access to the visual recording, the investigating officer may arrange for anything in the recording that might allow the officers or police staff to be identified to be concealed.

2.8 Following a decision made by the relevant officer in accordance with *paragraph 2.2* that an interview or other matter mentioned in *paragraph 2.1* above should be *visually recorded*, the relevant officer may decide that the interview is not to be visually recorded if it no longer appears that a visual recording should be made or because of a fault in the recording device. However, a decision not to make a *visual recording* does not detract in any way from the requirement for the interview to be *audio recorded* in accordance with *paragraph 2.1 of Code E*. (See *Note 2C*.)

2.9 The provisions in *Code E paragraph 2.6* for remote monitoring of interviews shall apply to visually recorded interviews.(ii)

Objections and complaints by the suspect about visual recording

2.10 If the suspect or an appropriate adult on their behalf objects to the interview being *visually* recorded either at the outset or during the interview or during a break in the interview, the interviewer shall explain that the visual recording is being made in accordance with *paragraph 2.2* and that this Code requires the objections to be recorded on the *visual* recording. When any objections have been recorded or the suspect or the appropriate adult have refused to have their objections recorded visually, the relevant officer shall decide in accordance with *paragraph 2.8* and having regard to the nature and circumstances of the objections, whether visual recording should be turned off (see *Note 2D*). Following a decision that visual recording should be turned off, the interviewer shall say that they are turning off the *visual* recording. The audio recording required to be maintained in accordance with Code E shall continue and the interviewer shall ask the person to record their objections to the interview being *visually* recorded on the audio recording. If the relevant officer considers that visual recording should not be turned off, the interviewer may proceed to question the suspect with the visual recording still on. If the suspect also objects to the interview being audio recorded, *paragraph 3.9* of Code E will apply if a removable recording media device (see Code E *paragraph 1.6(a)(ii)*) is being used and *paragraph 4.6* of Code E will apply if a secure digital recording device (see Code E *paragraph 1.6(a)(iii)*) is being used.

2.11 If the suspect indicates that they wish to tell the interviewer about matters not directly connected with the offence of which they are suspected and that they are unwilling for these matters to be visually recorded, the suspect should be given the opportunity to tell the interviewer about these matters after the conclusion of the formal interview.(ii)

Failure of visual recording device

2.12 If there is a failure of equipment and it is not possible to continue visual recording using the same type of recording device (i.e. a removable recording media device as in Code E *paragraph 1.6(a)(ii)* or a secure digital recording network device as in Code E *paragraph 1.6(a)(iii)*) or by using a replacement device of either type, the relevant officer may decide that the interview is to continue without being visually recorded. In these circumstances, the continuation of the interview must be conducted and recorded in accordance with the provisions of Code E (See *Note 2F*.)

Notes for Guidance

2A   *Paragraph 2.1 of Code E describes the requirement that authorised audio-recording devices are to be used for recording interviews and other matters.*

2B   *Interviewers will wish to arrange that, as far as possible, visual recording arrangements are unobtrusive. It must be clear to the suspect, however, that there is no opportunity to interfere with the recording equipment or the recording media.*

2C   *A decision made in accordance with paragraph 2.8 not to record an interview visually for any reason may be the subject of comment in court. The 'relevant officer' responsible should therefore be prepared to justify that decision.*

2D   *Objections for the purpose of paragraph 2.10 are meant to apply to objections based on the suspect's genuine and honestly held beliefs and to allow officers to exercise their discretion to decide whether a visual recording is to be made according to the circumstances surrounding the suspect and the investigation. Objections that appear to be frivolous with the intentions of frustrating or delaying the investigation would not be relevant.*

2E   *The visual recording made in accordance with this Code may be used for eye-witness identification procedures to which paragraph 3.21 and Annex E of Code D apply.*

2F   *Where the interview is being visually recorded and the media or the recording device fails, the interviewer should stop the interview immediately. Where part of the interview is unaffected by the error and is still accessible on the media or on the network device, that part shall be copied and sealed in the suspect's presence as a master copy or saved as a new secure digital network recording as appropriate. The interview should then be recommenced using a functioning recording device and new recording media as appropriate. Where the media content of the interview has been lost in its entirety, the media should be sealed in the suspect's presence and the interview begun again. If the visual recording equipment cannot be fixed and a replacement device is not immediately available, the interview should be audio recorded in accordance with Code E.*

2G   *The relevant officer should be aware that a decision to continue visual recording against the wishes of the suspect may be the subject of comment in court.*

The detention, treatment and questioning by Police Officers of persons in police detention under Section 41 of, and Schedule 8 to, the Terrorism Act 2000
The treatment and questioning by Police Officers of detained persons in respect of whom an authorisation to question after charge has been given under Section 22 of the Counter-Terrorism Act 2008

Police and Criminal Evidence Act 1984 (PACE) – Code H

2.375A   Revised Code of Practice in Connection with: *Replace the existing Code H with the revised 2018 versions as follows:*

Revised Code of Practice in Connection with:
The detention, treatment and questioning by Police Officers of persons in police detention under Section 41 of, and Schedule 8 to, the Terrorism Act 2000
The treatment and questioning by Police Officers of detained persons in respect of whom an authorisation to question after charge has been given under Section 22 of the Counter-Terrorism Act 2008

Police and Criminal Evidence Act 1984 (PACE) – Code H

July 2018

COMMENCEMENT - TRANSITIONAL ARRANGEMENTS

This Code applies to people detained under the terrorism provisions after 00:00 on 31 July 2018, notwithstanding that their period of detention may have commenced before that time.

Contents

1 GENERAL

1.0 The powers and procedures in this Code must be used fairly, responsibly, with respect for the people to whom they apply and without unlawful discrimination. Under the Equality Act 2010, section 149 (Public sector Equality Duty), police forces must, in carrying out their functions, have due regard to the need to eliminate unlawful discrimination, harassment, victimisation and any other conduct which is prohibited by that Act, to advance equality of opportunity between people who share a relevant protected characteristic and people who do not share it, and to foster good relations between those persons. The Equality Act also makes it unlawful for police officers to discriminate against, harass or victimise any person on the grounds of the 'protected characteristics' of age, disability, gender reassignment, race, religion or belief, sex and sexual orientation, marriage and civil partnership, pregnancy and maternity, when using their powers. See *Notes 1A* and *1AA*.

1.1 This Code of Practice applies to, and *only* to:

(a) persons in police detention after being arrested under section 41 of the Terrorism Act 2000 (TACT) and detained under section 41 of, or Schedule 8 to that Act and *not charged*, and

(b) detained persons in respect of whom an authorisation has been given under section 22 of the Counter-Terrorism Act 2008 (post-charge questioning of terrorist suspects) to interview them in which case, section 15 of this Code will apply.

1.2 The provisions in PACE Code C apply when a person:

(a) is in custody *otherwise* than as a result of being arrested under section 41 of TACT or detained for examination under Schedule 7 to TACT (see *paragraph 1.4*);

(b) is charged with an offence, or

(c) is being questioned about any offence after being charged with that offence *without* an authorisation being given under section 22 of the Counter-Terrorism Act 2008. See *Note 1N*.

1.3 In this Code references to an offence and to a person's involvement or suspected involvement in an offence where the person has not been charged with an offence, include being concerned, or suspected of being concerned, in the commission, preparation or instigation of acts of terrorism.

1.4 The Code of Practice issued under paragraph 6 of Schedule 14 to TACT applies to persons detained for examination under Schedule 7 to TACT. See *Note 1N*.

1.5 All persons in custody must be dealt with expeditiously, and released as soon as the need for detention no longer applies.

1.6 There is no provision for bail under TACT before or after charge. See *Note 1N*.

1.7 An officer must perform the assigned duties in this Code as soon as practicable. An officer will not be in breach of this Code if delay is justifiable and reasonable steps are taken to prevent unnecessary delay. The custody record shall show when a delay has occurred and the reason. See *Note 1H*.

1.8 This Code of Practice must be readily available at all police stations for consultation by:

- police officers;
- police staff;
- detained persons;
- members of the public.

1.9 The provisions of this Code:

- include the *Annexes;*
- do not include the *Notes for Guidance.*

1.10 If at any time an officer has any reason to suspect that a person of any age may be vulnerable (see *paragraph 1.17(d)*) in the absence of clear evidence to dispel that suspicion, that person shall be treated as such for the purposes of this Code and to establish whether any such reason may exist in relation to a person suspected of committing an offence (see *paragraph 10.1* and *Note 10A*), the custody officer in the case of a detained person, or the officer investigating the offence in the case of a person who has not been arrested or detained, shall take, or cause to be taken, (see *paragraph 3.5* and *Note 3I*) the following action:

(a) reasonable enquiries shall be made to ascertain what information is available that is relevant to any of the factors described in *paragraph 1.17(d)* as indicating that the person may be vulnerable might apply;

(b) a record shall be made describing whether any of those factors appear to apply and provide any reason to suspect that the person may be vulnerable or (as the case may be) may not be vulnerable; and

(c) the record mentioned in sub-paragraph (b) shall be made available to be taken into account by police officers, police staff and any others who, in accordance with the provisions of this or any other Code, are required or entitled to communicate with the person in question. This would include any solicitor, appropriate adult and health care professional and is particu-

larly relevant to communication for the purpose of interviewing and questioning after charge (see *sections 11, 12* and *15*), live link interpretation (see *paragraph 13.12*) and reviews and extensions of detention (see *section 14*).
See *Notes 1G, 1GA, 1GB* and *1GC.*

1.11   Anyone who appears to be under 18 shall, in the absence of clear evidence that they are older, be treated as a juvenile for the purposes of this Code.

1.11A   *Not used*

1.12   If a person appears to be blind, seriously visually impaired, deaf, unable to read or speak or has difficulty orally because of a speech impediment, they shall be treated as such for the purposes of this Code in the absence of clear evidence to the contrary.

1.13   'The appropriate adult' means, in the case of a:

(a)   juvenile:
  (i)   the parent, guardian or, if the juvenile is in the care of a local authority or voluntary organisation, a person representing that authority or organisation (see *Note 1B*);
  (ii)   a social worker of a local authority (see *Note 1C*);
  (iii)   failing these, some other responsible adult aged 18 or over who is *not*:
    –   a police officer;
    –   employed by the police;
    –   under the direction or control of the chief officer of a police force;
    –   a person who provides services under contractual arrangements (but without being employed by the chief officer of a police force), to assist that force in relation to the discharge of its chief officer's functions,
    whether or not they are on duty at the time.
  See *Note 1F.*

(b)   a person who is vulnerable: See *paragraph 1.10* and *Note 1D.*
  (i)   a relative, guardian or other person responsible for their care or custody;
  (ii)   someone experienced in dealing with vulnerable persons but who is *not*:
    –   a police officer;
    –   employed by the police;
    –   under the direction or control of the chief officer of a police force;
    –   a person who provides services under contractual arrangements (but without being employed by the chief officer of a police force), to assist that force in relation to the discharge of its chief officer's functions,
    whether or not they are on duty at the time;
  (iii)   failing these, some other responsible adult aged 18 or over who is other than a person described in the bullet points in sub-paragraph (b)(ii) above.

See *Note 1F.*

1.13A   The role of the appropriate adult is to safeguard the rights, entitlements and welfare of juveniles and vulnerable persons (see *paragraphs 1.10* and *1.11* to whom the provisions of this and any other Code of Practice apply. For this reason, the appropriate adult is expected, amongst other things, to:

- support, advise and assist them when, in accordance with this Code or any other Code of Practice, they are given or asked to provide information or participate in any procedure;
- observe whether the police are acting properly and fairly to respect their rights and entitlements, and inform an officer of the rank of inspector or above if they consider that they are not;
- assist them to communicate with the police whilst respecting their right to say nothing unless they want to as set out in the terms of the caution see *paragraphs 10.5* and *10.5*);
- help them understand their rights and ensure that those rights are protected and respected (see *paragraphs 3.17, 3.18, 6.6,* and *11.10.*

1.14   If this Code requires a person be given certain information, they do not have to be given it if at the time they are incapable of understanding what is said, are violent or may become violent or in urgent need of medical attention, but they must be given it as soon as practicable.

1.15   References to a custody officer include any police officer who for the time being, is performing the functions of a custody officer.

1.16   When this Code requires the prior authority or agreement of an officer of at least inspector or superintendent rank, that authority may be given by a sergeant or chief inspector authorised by section 107 of PACE to perform the functions of the higher rank under TACT.

1.17   In this Code:

(a)   'designated person' means a person other than a police officer, who has specified powers and duties conferred or imposed on them by designation under section 38 or 39 of the Police Reform Act 2002;

(b)   reference to a police officer includes a designated person acting in the exercise or performance of the powers and duties conferred or imposed on them by their designation.

(c)   where a search or other procedure to which this Code applies may only be carried out or observed by a person of the same sex as the detainee, the gender of the detainee and other parties present should be established and recorded in line with Annex L of this Code.

(d)   'vulnerable' applies to any person who, because of their mental health condition or mental disorder (see *Notes 1G* and *1GB*):
  (i)   may have difficulty understanding or communicating effectively about the full implications for them of any procedures and processes connected with:
    •   their arrest and detention at a police station or elsewhere;
    •   the exercise of their rights and entitlements.
  (ii)   does not appear to understand the significance of what they are told, of questions they are asked or of their replies.
  (iii)   appears to be particularly prone to:
    •   becoming confused and unclear about their position;

- providing unreliable, misleading or incriminating information without knowing or wishing to do so;
- accepting or acting on suggestions from others without consciously knowing or wishing to do so; or
- readily agreeing to suggestions or proposals without any protest or question.

1.18 Designated persons are entitled to use reasonable force as follows:

(a) when *exercising a power conferred on them which* allows a police officer exercising that power to use reasonable force, a designated person has the same entitlement to use force; and

(b) at other times when carrying out duties conferred or imposed on them that also entitle them to use reasonable force, for example:
- when at a police station carrying out the duty to keep detainees for whom they are responsible under control and to assist any other police officer or designated person to keep any detainee under control and to prevent their escape.
- when securing, or assisting any other police officer or designated person in securing, the detention of a person at a police station.
- when escorting, or assisting any other police officer or designated person in escorting, a detainee within a police station.
- for the purpose of saving life or limb; or
- preventing serious damage to property.

1.19 Nothing in this Code prevents the custody officer, or other police officer or designated person (see *paragraph 1.17(a)*) given custody of the detainee by the custody officer, from allowing another person (see (a) and (b) below) to carry out individual procedures or tasks at the police station if the law allows. However, the officer or designated person given custody remains responsible for making sure the procedures and tasks are carried out correctly in accordance with the Codes of Practice (see *paragraph 3.5* and *Note 3I*). The other person who is allowed to carry out the procedures or tasks must be someone who *at that time*, is:

(a) under the direction and control of the chief officer of the force responsible for the police station in question; or

(b) providing services under contractual arrangements (but without being employed by the chief officer the police force), to assist a police force in relation to the discharge of its chief officer's functions.

1.20 Designated persons and others mentioned in sub-paragraphs (a) and (b) of *paragraph 1.19* must have regard to any relevant provisions of this Code.

1.21 In any provision of this or any other Code of Practice which allows or requires police officers or police staff to make a record in their report book, the references to report book shall include any official report book or electronic recording device issued to them that enables the record in question to be made and dealt with in accordance with that provision. References in this and any other Code to written records, forms and signatures include electronic records and forms and electronic confirmation that identifies the person making the record or completing the form.

Chief officers must be satisfied as to the integrity and security of the devices, records and forms to which this paragraph applies and that use of those devices, records and forms satisfies relevant data protection legislation.

NOTES FOR GUIDANCE

1A *This Code applies specifically to people detained under terrorism legislation. See PACE Code C (Detention) for detailed provisions and guidance that apply to persons who attend police stations and other locations voluntarily to assist with an investigation.*

1AA *In paragraph 1.0, under the Equality Act 2010, section 149, the 'relevant protected characteristics' are age, disability, gender reassignment, pregnancy and maternity, race, religion/belief and sex and sexual orientation. For further detailed guidance and advice on the Equality Act, see: https://www.gov.uk/guidance/equality-act-2010-guidance.*

1B *A person, including a parent or guardian, should not be an appropriate adult if they:*

- *are:*
  - *suspected of involvement in the offence or involvement in the commission, preparation or instigation of acts of terrorism;*
  - *the victim;*
  - *a witness;*
  - *involved in the investigation.*
- *received admissions prior to attending to act as the appropriate adult.*
  Note: If a juvenile's parent is estranged from the juvenile, they should not be asked to act as the appropriate adult if the juvenile expressly and specifically objects to their presence.

1C *If a juvenile admits an offence to, or in the presence of, a social worker or member of a youth offending team other than during the time that person is acting as the juvenile's appropriate adult, another appropriate adult should be appointed in the interest of fairness.*

1D *In the case of someone who is vulnerable, it may be more satisfactory if the appropriate adult is someone experienced or trained in their care rather than a relative lacking such qualifications. But if the person prefers a relative to a better qualified stranger or objects to a particular person their wishes should, if practicable, be respected.*

1E *A detainee should always be given an opportunity, when an appropriate adult is called to the police station, to consult privately with a solicitor in the appropriate adult's absence if they want. An appropriate adult is not subject to legal privilege.*

1F *An appropriate adult who is not a parent or guardian in the case of a juvenile, or a relative, guardian or carer in the case of a vulnerable person, must be independent of the police as their role is to safeguard the rights and entitlements of a detained person. Additionally, a solicitor or independent custody visitor who is present at the police station and acting in that capacity may not be the appropriate adult.*

1G *An adult may be vulnerable as a result of a having a mental health condition or mental disorder. Similarly, simply because an individual does not have, or is not known to have, any such condition or disorder, does not mean that they are not vulnerable for the purposes of this Code. It is therefore important that the custody officer in the case of a detained person considers, on a case by case basis whether any of the factors described in paragraph 1.17(d) might apply to the person in question. In doing so, the officer must take into account the particular circumstances of the individual and how the nature of the investigation might affect them and bear in mind that juveniles, by virtue of their age will always require an appropriate adult.*

1GA *For the purposes of paragraph 1.10(a), examples of relevant information that may be available include:*

- the behaviour of the adult or juvenile;
- the mental health and capacity of the adult or juvenile;
- what the adult or juvenile says about themselves;
- information from relatives and friends of the adult or juvenile;
- information from police officers and staff and from police records;
- information from health and social care (including liaison and diversion services) and other professionals who know, or have had previous contact with, the individual and may be able to contribute to assessing their need for help and support from an appropriate adult. This includes contacts and assessments arranged by the police or at the request of the individual or (as applicable) their appropriate adult or solicitor.

1GB *The Mental Health Act 1983 Code of Practice at page 26 describes the range of clinically recognised conditions which can fall with the meaning of mental disorder for the purpose of paragraph 1.17(d). The Code is published here: https://www.gov.uk/government/publications/code-of-practice-mental-health-act-1983.*

1GC *When a person is under the influence of drink and/or drugs, it is not intended that they are to be treated as vulnerable and requiring an appropriate adult for the purpose of unless other information indicates that any of the factors described in paragraph 1.17(d) may apply to that person. When the person has recovered from the effects of drink and/or drugs, they should be re-assessed in accordance with paragraph 1.10.*

1H *Paragraph 1.7 is intended to cover delays which may occur in processing detainees e.g. if:*

- a large number of suspects are brought into the station simultaneously to be placed in custody;
- interview rooms are all being used;
- there are difficulties contacting an appropriate adult, solicitor or interpreter.

1I *The custody officer must remind the appropriate adult and detainee about the right to legal advice and record any reasons for waiving it in accordance with section 6.*

1J *Not used*

1K *This Code does not affect the principle that all citizens have a duty to help police officers to prevent crime and discover offenders. This is a civic rather than a legal duty; but when police officers are trying to discover whether, or by whom, offences have been committed, they are entitled to question any person from whom they think useful information can be obtained, subject to the restrictions imposed by this Code. A person's declaration that they are unwilling to reply does not alter this entitlement.*

1L *If a person is moved from a police station to receive medical treatment, or for any other reason, the period of detention is still calculated from the time of arrest under section 41 of TACT (or, if a person was being detained under TACT Schedule 7 when arrested, from the time at which the examination under Schedule 7 began).*

1M *Under Paragraph 1 of Schedule 8 to TACT, all police stations are designated for detention of persons arrested under section 41 of TACT. Paragraph 4 of Schedule 8 requires that the constable who arrests a person under section 41 takes them as soon as practicable to the police station which the officer considers is "most appropriate".*

1N *The powers under Part IV of PACE to detain and release on bail (before or after charge) a person arrested under section 24 of PACE for any offence (see PACE Code G (Arrest)) do not apply to persons whilst they are detained under the terrorism powers following their arrest/detention under section 41 of, or Schedule 7 to, TACT. If when the grounds for detention under these powers cease the person is arrested under section 24 of PACE for a specific offence, the detention and bail provisions of PACE will apply and must be considered from the time of that arrest.*

1O *Not used.*

1P *Not used.*

2 CUSTODY RECORDS

2.1 When a person is:

- brought to a police station following arrest under TACT section 41,
- arrested under TACT section 41 at a police station having attended there voluntarily,
- brought to a police station and there detained to be questioned in accordance with an authorisation under section 22 of the Counter-Terrorism Act 2008 (post-charge questioning) (see *Notes 15A* and *15B*), or
- at a police station and there detained when authority for post-charge questioning is given under section 22 of the Counter-Terrorism Act 2008 (see *Notes 15A* and *15B*),

they should be brought before the custody officer as soon as practicable after their arrival at the station or, if appropriate, following the authorisation of post-charge questioning or following arrest after attending the police station voluntarily *see Note 3H*. A person is deemed to be "at a police station" for these purposes if they are within the boundary of any building or enclosed yard which forms part of that police station.

2.2   A separate custody record must be opened as soon as practicable for each person described in *paragraph 2.1*. All information recorded under this Code must be recorded as soon as practicable in the custody record unless otherwise specified. Any audio or video recording made in the custody area is not part of the custody record.

2.3   If any action requires the authority of an officer of a specified rank, this must be noted in the custody record, subject to *paragraph 2.8*.

2.3A   If a person is arrested under TACT, section 41 and taken to a police station as a result of a search in the exercise of any stop and search power to which PACE Code A (Stop and search) or the 'search powers code' issued under TACT applies, the officer carrying out the search is responsible for ensuring that the record of that stop and search is made as part of the person's custody record. The custody officer must then ensure that the person is asked if they want a copy of the search record and if they do, that they are given a copy as soon as practicable. The person's entitlement to a copy of the search record which is made as part of their custody record is in addition to, and does not affect, their entitlement to a copy of their custody record or any other provisions of section 2 (Custody records) of this Code. See Code A *paragraph 4.2B* and the TACT search powers code *paragraph 5.3.5*).

2.4   The custody officer is responsible for the custody record's accuracy and completeness and for making sure the record or copy of the record accompanies a detainee if they are transferred to another police station. The record shall show the:

- time and reason for transfer;
- time a person is released from detention.

2.5   The detainees solicitor and appropriate adult must be permitted to inspect the detainee's custody record as soon as practicable after their arrival at the station and at any other time whilst the person is detained.

On request, the detainee, their solicitor and appropriate adult must be allowed to inspect the following records, as promptly as is practicable at any time whilst the person is detained:

(a)   The information about the circumstances and reasons for the detainee's arrest as recorded in the custody record in accordance with *paragraph 3.4*. This applies to any further reasons which come to light and are recorded whilst the detainee is detained;

(b)   The record of the grounds for each authorisation to keep the person in custody. The authorisations to which this applies are the same as those described in *paragraph 2* of *Annex M* of this Code.

Access to the custody record for the purposes of this paragraph must be arranged and agreed with the custody officer and may not unreasonably interfere with the custody officer's duties or the justifiable needs of the investigation. A record shall be made when access is allowed. This access is in addition to the requirements in *paragraphs 3.4(b), 11.1* and *14.0* to provide information about the reasons for arrest and detention and in *14.4A* to give the detainee written information about the grounds for continued detention when an application for a warrant of further detention (or for an extension of such a warrant) is made.

2.6   When a detainee leaves police detention or is taken before a court they, their legal representative or appropriate adult shall be given, on request, a copy of the custody record as soon as practicable. This entitlement lasts for 12 months after release.

2.7   The detainee, appropriate adult or legal representative shall be permitted to inspect the original custody record once the detained person is no longer being held under the provisions of TACT section 41 and Schedule 8 or being questioned after charge as authorised under section 22 of the Counter-Terrorism Act 2008 (see *section 15*), provided they give reasonable notice of their request. Any such inspection shall be noted in the custody record.

2.8   All entries in custody records must be timed and identified by the maker. Nothing in this Code requires the identity of officers or other police staff to be recorded or disclosed in the case of enquiries linked to the investigation of terrorism. In these cases, they shall use their warrant or other identification numbers and the name of their police station, *see Note 2A*. Records entered on computer shall be timed and contain the operator's identification.

2.9   The fact and time of any detainee's refusal to sign a custody record, when asked in accordance with this Code, must be recorded.

NOTE FOR GUIDANCE

2A   *The purpose of paragraph 2.8 is to protect those involved in terrorist investigations or arrests of terrorist suspects from the possibility that those arrested, their associates or other individuals or groups may threaten or cause harm to those involved.*

3   INITIAL ACTION

(A)   DETAINED PERSONS – NORMAL PROCEDURE

3.1   When a person to whom paragraph 2.1 applies is at a police station, the custody officer must make sure the person is told clearly about:

(a)   the following continuing rights which may be exercised at any stage during the period in custody:
  (i)   their right to consult privately with a solicitor and that free independent legal advice is available as in *section 6*;
  (ii)   their right to have someone informed of their arrest as in *section 5*;
  (iii) their right to consult this Code of Practice (see *Note 3D*);
  (iv)   their right to medical help as in *section 9*;
  (v)   their right to remain silent as set out in the caution (see *section 10*); and
  (vi)   if applicable, their right to interpretation and translation (see *paragraph 3.14*) and the right to communication with their High Commission, Embassy or Consulate (see *paragraph 3.14A*).

(b)   their right to be informed about why they have been arrested and detained on suspicion of being involved in the commission, preparation or instigation of acts of terrorism in accordance with *paragraphs 2.5, 3.4* and *11.1A* of this Code

3.2 The detainee must also be given a written notice, which contains information:

(a) to allow them to exercise their rights by setting out:
   (i) their rights under paragraph 3.1 (subject to *paragraphs 3.14* and *3.14A*);
   (ii) the arrangements for obtaining legal advice, see *section 6*;
   (iii) their right to a copy of the custody record as in *paragraph 2.6*;
   (iv) the caution in the terms prescribed in *section 10*;
   (v) their rights to:
   - information about the reasons and grounds for their arrest and detention and (as the case may be) any further grounds and reasons that come to light whilst they are in custody;
   - to have access to records and documents which are essential to effectively challenging the lawfulness of their arrest and detention; as required in accordance with *paragraphs 2.4, 2.4A, 2.5, 3.4, 11.1, 14.0* and *15.7A(c)* of this Code and *paragraph 3.3* of *Code G*;
   (vi) the maximum period for which they may be kept in police detention without being charged, when detention must be reviewed and when release is required.
   (vii) their right to communicate with their High Commission Embassy or Consulate in accordance with *section 7* of this Code, see *paragraph 3.14A*;
   (viii) their right to medical assistance in accordance with *section 9* of this Code
   (ix) their right, if they are prosecuted, to have access to the evidence in the case in accordance with the Criminal Procedure and Investigations Act 1996, the Attorney General's Guidelines on Disclosure and the common law and the Criminal Procedure Rules; and
(b) briefly setting out their entitlements while in custody, by:
   (i) mentioning:
   - the provisions relating to the conduct of interviews;
   - the circumstances in which an appropriate adult should be available to assist the detainee and their statutory rights to make representations whenever the need for their detention is reviewed.
   (ii) listing the entitlements in this Code, concerning
   - reasonable standards of physical comfort;
   - adequate food and drink;
   - access to toilets and washing facilities, clothing, medical attention, and exercise when practicable.

See *Note 3A*

3.2A The detainee must be given an opportunity to read the notice and shall be asked to sign the custody record to acknowledge receipt of the notices. Any refusal must be recorded on the custody record.

3.3 *Not used.*

3.3A An audio version of the notice and an 'easy read' illustrated version should also be provided if they are available (see *Note 3A*).

(a) The custody officer shall:
   - record that the person was arrested under section 41 ofTACT and the reason(s) for the arrest on the custody record. See *paragraph 10.2 and Note 3G*
   - note on the custody record any comment the detainee makes in relation to the arresting officer's account but shall not invite comment. If the arresting officer is not physically present when the detainee is brought to a police station, the arresting officer's account must be made available to the custody officer remotely or by a third party on the arresting officer's behalf;
   - note any comment the detainee makes in respect of the decision to detain them but shall not invite comment;
   - not put specific questions to the detainee regarding their involvement in any offence (see *paragraph 1.3*), nor in respect of any comments they may make in response to the arresting officer's account or the decision to place them in detention. *See paragraphs 14.1* and *14.2* and *Notes 3H, 14A* and *14B*. Such an exchange is likely to constitute an interview as in *paragraph 11.1* and require the associated safeguards in *section 11*.
   Note: This sub-paragraph also applies to any further reasons and grounds for detention which come to light whilst the person is detained.
   See *paragraph 11.8A* in respect of unsolicited comments.
   If the first review of detention is carried out at this time, see *paragraphs 14.1* and *14.2*, and Part II of Schedule 8 to the Terrorism Act 2000 in respect of action by the review officer.
(b) Documents and materials which are essential to effectively challenging the lawfulness the detainee's arrest and detention must be made available to the detainee or their solicitor. Documents and material will be "essential" for this purpose if they are capable of undermining the reasons and grounds which make the detainee's arrest and detention necessary. The decision about what needs to be disclosed for the purpose of this requirement rests with the custody officer in consultation with the investigating officer who has the knowledge of the documents and materials in a particular case necessary to inform that decision (see *Note 3G*). A note should be made in the detainee's custody record of the fact that action has been taken under this sub-paragraph and when. The investigating officer should make a separate note of what has been made available in a particular case. This also applies for the purposes of *section 14*, see *paragraph 14.0*.

3.5 The custody officer or other custody staff as directed by the custody officer shall:

(a) ask the detainee, whether at this time, they:

(i)   would like legal advice, see *paragraph 6.4*;
(ii)   want someone informed of their detention, see *section 5*;
(b) ask the detainee to sign the custody record to confirm their decisions in respect of (*a*);
(c) determine whether the detainee:
    (i)   is, or might be, in need of medical treatment or attention, see *section 9*;
    (ii)   is a juvenile and/or vulnerable and therefore requires an appropriate adult (see *paragraphs 1.10, 1.11* and *3.17*);
    (iii) requires:
       • help to check documentation (see *paragraph 3.21*);
       • an interpreter (see *paragraph 3.14* and *Note 13B*).
(d) record the decision in respect of (*c*).

Where any duties under this paragraph have been carried out by custody staff at the direction of the custody officer, the outcomes shall, as soon as practicable, be reported to the custody officer who retains overall responsibility for the detainee's care and safe custody and ensuring it complies with this Code. See *Note 3I*.

3.6   When the needs mentioned in *paragraph 3.5(c)* are being determined, the custody officer is responsible for initiating an assessment to consider whether the detainee is likely to present specific risks to custody staff, any individual who may have contact with detainee (e.g. legal advisers, medical staff), or themselves. This risk assessment must include the taking of reasonable steps to establish the detainee's identity and to obtain information about the detainee that is relevant to their safe custody, security and welfare and risks to others. Such assessments should therefore always include a check on the Police National Computer (PNC), to be carried out as soon as practicable, to identify any risks that have been highlighted in relation to the detainee. Although such assessments are primarily the custody officer's responsibility, it will be necessary to obtain information from other sources, especially the investigation team *see Note 3E*, the arresting officer or an appropriate healthcare professional, see *paragraph 9.15*. Other records held by or on behalf of the police and other UK law enforcement authorities that might provide information relevant to the detainee's safe custody, security and welfare and risk to others and to confirming their identity should also be checked. Reasons for delaying the initiation or completion of the assessment must be recorded.

3.7   Chief officers should ensure that arrangements for proper and effective risk assessments required by *paragraph 3.6* are implemented in respect of all detainees at police stations in their area.

3.8   Risk assessments must follow a structured process which clearly defines the categories of risk to be considered and the results must be incorporated in the detainee's custody record. The custody officer is responsible for making sure those responsible for the detainee's custody are appropriately briefed about the risks. The content of any risk assessment and any analysis of the level of risk relating to the person's detention is not required to be shown or provided to the detainee or any person acting on behalf of the detainee. If no specific risks are identified by the assessment, that should be noted in the custody record. See *Note 3F* and *paragraph 9.15*.

3.8A   The content of any risk assessment and any analysis of the level of risk relating to the person's detention is not required to be shown or provided to the detainee or any person acting on behalf of the detainee. But information should not be withheld from any person acting on the detainee's behalf, for example, an appropriate adult, solicitor or interpreter, if to do so might put that person at risk.

3.9   Custody officers are responsible for implementing the response to any specific risk assessment, which should include for example:

• reducing opportunities for self harm;
• calling an appropriate healthcare professional;
• increasing levels of monitoring or observation;
• reducing the risk to those who come into contact with the detainee.

See *Note 3F*

3.10   Risk assessment is an ongoing process and assessments must always be subject to review if circumstances change.

3.11   If video cameras are installed in the custody area, notices shall be prominently displayed showing cameras are in use. Any request to have video cameras switched off shall be refused.

3.12   A constable, prison officer or other person authorised by the Secretary of State may take any steps which are reasonably necessary for:

(a) photographing the detained person;
(b) measuring the person, or
(c) identifying the person.

3.13   *Paragraph 3.12* concerns the power in *TACT Schedule 8 Paragraph 2*. The power in TACT *Schedule 8 Paragraph 2* does not cover the taking of fingerprints, intimate samples or non-intimate samples, which is covered *in TACT Schedule 8 paragraphs 10* to *15*.

(B) Detained persons – special groups

3.14   If the detainee appears to be someone who does not speak or understand English or who has a hearing or speech impediment the custody officer must ensure:

(a) that without delay, arrangements (see *paragraph 13.1ZA*) are made for the detainee to have the assistance of an interpreter in the action under *paragraphs 3.1* to *3.5*. If the person appears to have a hearing or speech impediment, the reference to 'interpreter' includes appropriate assistance necessary to comply with *paragraphs 3.1 to 3.5*. See *paragraph 13.1C* if the detainee is in Wales. See *section 13* and *Note 13B*;
(b) that in addition to the rights set out in *paragraph 3.1(i)* to *(iii)*, the detainee is told clearly about their right to interpretation and translation;
(c) that the written notice given to the detainee in accordance with *paragraph 3.2* is in a language the detainee understands and includes the right to interpretation and translation

together with information about the provisions in *section 13* and Annex K, which explain how the right applies (see *Note 3A*); and

(d) that if the translation of the notice is not available, the information in the notice is given through an interpreter and a written translation provided without undue delay

3.14A If the detainee is a citizen of an independent Commonwealth country or a national of a foreign country, including the Republic of Ireland, the custody officer must ensure that in addition to the rights set out in *paragraph 3.1(i)* to *(v)*, they are informed as soon as practicable about their rights of communication with their High Commission, Embassy or Consulate set out in *section 7*. This right must be included in the written notice given to the detainee in accordance with *paragraph 3.2*.

3.15 If the detainee is a juvenile, the custody officer must, if it is practicable, ascertain the identity of a person responsible for their welfare. That person:

- may be:
  - the parent or guardian;
  - if the juvenile is in local authority or voluntary organisation care, or is otherwise being looked after under the *Children Act 1989*, a person appointed by that authority or organisation to have responsibility for the juvenile's welfare;
  - any other person who has, for the time being, assumed responsibility for the juvenile's welfare.
- must be informed as soon as practicable that the juvenile has been arrested, why they have been arrested and where they are detained. This right is in addition to the juvenile's right in *section 5* not to be held incommunicado. See *Note 3C*.

3.16 If a juvenile is known to be subject to a court order under which a person or organisation is given any degree of statutory responsibility to supervise or otherwise monitor them, reasonable steps must also be taken to notify that person or organisation (the 'responsible officer'). The responsible officer will normally be a member of a Youth Offending Team, except for a curfew order which involves electronic monitoring when the contractor providing the monitoring will normally be the responsible officer.

3.17 If the detainee is a juvenile or a vulnerable person, the custody officer must, as soon as practicable, ensure that:

- the detainee is informed of the decision that an appropriate adult is required and the reason for that decision (see *paragraph 3.5(c)(ii)* and;
- the detainee is advised:
  - of the duties of the appropriate adult as described in *paragraph 1.13A*; and
  - that they can consult privately with the appropriate adult at any time.
- the appropriate adult, who in the case of a juvenile may or may not be a person responsible for their welfare, as in *paragraph 3.15*, is informed of:
  - the grounds for their detention;
  - their whereabouts; and
- the attendance of the appropriate adult at the police station to see the detainee is secured.

3.18 If the appropriate adult is:

- already at the police station, the provisions of *paragraphs 3.1* to *3.5* must be complied with in the appropriate adult's presence;
- not at the station when these provisions are complied with, they must be complied with again in the presence of the appropriate adult when they arrive,

and a copy of the notice given to the detainee in accordance with *paragraph 3.2*, shall also be given to the appropriate adult if they wish to have a copy.

3.18A The custody officer must ensure that at the time the copy of the notice is given to the appropriate adult, or as soon as practicable thereafter, the appropriate adult is advised of the duties of the appropriate adult as described in *paragraph 1.13A*.

3.19 *Not used.*

3.20 If the detainee, or appropriate adult on the detainee's behalf, asks for a solicitor to be called to give legal advice, the provisions of *section 6* apply. (see *paragraph 6.6* and *Note 3K*).

3.21 If the detainee is blind, seriously visually impaired or unable to read, the custody officer shall make sure their solicitor, relative, appropriate adult or some other person likely to take an interest in them and not involved in the investigation is available to help check any documentation. When this Code requires written consent or signing the person assisting may be asked to sign instead, if the detainee prefers. This paragraph does not require an appropriate adult to be called solely to assist in checking and signing documentation for a person who is not a juvenile, or vulnerable (see *paragraph 3.17* and *Note 13C*).

3.21A The Children and Young Persons Act 1933, section 31, requires that arrangements must be made for ensuring that a girl under the age of 18, while detained in a police station, is under the care of a woman. See *Note 3J*. It also requires that arrangements must be made to prevent any person under 18 while being detained in a police station, from associating with an adult charged with any offence, unless that adult is a relative or the adult is jointly charged with the same offence as the person under 18.

(c) Documentation

3.22 The grounds for a person's detention shall be recorded, in the person's presence if practicable.

3.23 Action taken under *paragraphs 3.14* to *3.21A* shall be recorded.

(d) Requirements for suspects to be informed of certain rights

3.24 The provisions of this section identify the information which must be given to suspects who have been arrested under section 41of the Terrorism Act and cautioned in accordance with *section 10 of this Code*. It includes information required by EU Directive 2012/13 on the right to information in criminal proceedings. If a complaint is made by or on behalf of such a suspect that the information and (as the case may be) access to records and documents has not been provided as required, the matter shall be reported to an inspector to deal with as a complaint for the purposes of *paragraph 9.3*, or *paragraph 12.10* if the challenge is made during an interview. This would include, for example:

- not informing them of their rights (see *paragraph 3.1*);
- not giving them a copy of the Notice (see *paragraph 3.2(a)*);
- not providing an opportunity to read the notice (see *paragraph 3.2A*)
- not providing the required information (see *paragraphs 3.2(a), 3.14(b)* and, *3.14A*;
- not allowing access to the custody record (see *paragraph 2.5*);
- not providing a translation of the Notice (see *paragraph 3.14(c)* and *(d)*);

NOTES FOR GUIDANCE

3A   *For access to the currently available notices, including 'easy-read' versions, see* https://www.gov.uk/notice-of-rights-and-entitlements-a-persons-rights-in-police-detention.

3B   *Not used.*

3C   *If the juvenile is in local authority or voluntary organisation care but living with their parents or other adults responsible for their welfare, although there is no legal obligation to inform them, they should normally be contacted, as well as the authority or organisation unless they are suspected of involvement in the offence concerned. Even if the juvenile is not living with their parents, consideration should be given to informing them.*

3D   *The right to consult this or other relevant Codes of Practice does not entitle the person concerned to delay unreasonably any necessary investigative or administrative action whilst they do so. Examples of action which need not be delayed unreasonably include:*

- *searching detainees at the police station;*
- *taking fingerprints or non-intimate samples without consent for evidential purposes.*

3E   *The investigation team will include any officer involved in questioning a suspect, gathering or analysing evidence in relation to the offences of which the detainee is suspected of having committed. Should a custody officer require information from the investigation team, the first point of contact should be the officer in charge of the investigation.*

3F   *The Detention and Custody Authorised Professional Practice (APP) produced by the College of Policing (see http://www.app.college.police.uk) provides more detailed guidance on risk assessments and identifies key risk areas which should always be considered.*

3G   *Arrests under TACT section 41 can only be made where an officer has reasonable grounds to suspect that the individual concerned is a "terrorist". This differs from the constable's power of arrest for all offences under PACE, section 24, in that it need not be linked to a specific offence. There may also be circumstances where an arrest under TACT is made on the grounds of sensitive information which cannot be disclosed. In such circumstances, the grounds for arrest may be given in terms of the interpretation of a "terrorist" set out in TACT section 40(1)(a) or (b).*

3H   *For the purpose of arrests under TACT section 41, the review officer is responsible for authorising detention (see paragraphs 14.1 and 14.2, and Notes 14A and 14B). The review officer's role is explained in TACT Schedule 8 Part II. A person may be detained after arrest pending the first review, which must take place as soon as practicable after the person's arrest.*

3I   *A custody officer or other officer who, in accordance with this Code, allows or directs the carrying out of any task or action relating to a detainee's care, treatment, rights and entitlements by another officer or any other person must be satisfied that the officer or person concerned is suitable, trained and competent to carry out the task or action in question.*

3J   *Guidance for police officers and police staff on the operational application of section 31 of the Children and Young Persons Act 1933 has been published by the College of Policing and is available   at: https://www.app.college.police.uk/app-content/detention-and-custody-2/detainee-care/children-and-young-persons/#girls.*

3K   *The purpose of the provisions at paragraphs 3.20 and 6.6 is to protect the rights of juvenile and vulnerable persons who may not understand the significance of what is said to them. They should always be given an opportunity, when an appropriate adult is called to the police station, to consult privately with a solicitor in the absence of the appropriate adult if they want.*

4   DETAINEE'S PROPERTY

(A)   ACTION

4.1   The custody officer is responsible for:

(a)   ascertaining what property a detainee:
    (i)   has with them when they come to the police station, either on first arrival at the police station or any subsequent arrivals at a police station in connection with that detention;
    (ii)   might have acquired for an unlawful or harmful purpose while in custody.
(b)   the safekeeping of any property taken from a detainee which remains at the police station.

The custody officer may search the detainee or authorise their being searched to the extent they consider necessary, provided a search of intimate parts of the body or involving the removal of more than outer clothing is only made as in *Annex A*. A search may only be carried out by an officer of the same sex as the detainee. See *Note 4A* and *Annex I*.

4.2   Detainees may retain clothing and personal effects at their own risk unless the custody officer considers they may use them to cause harm to themselves or others, interfere with evidence, damage property, effect an escape or they are needed as evidence. In this event, the custody officer may withhold such articles as they consider necessary and must tell the detainee why.

4.3   Personal effects are those items a detainee may lawfully need, use or refer to while in detention but do not include cash and other items of value.

(B) Documentation

4.4 It is a matter for the custody officer to determine whether a record should be made of the property a detained person has with him or had taken from him on arrest (*see Note 4D*). Any record made is not required to be kept as part of the custody record but the custody record should be noted as to where such a record exists and that record shall be treated as being part of the custody record for the purpose of this Code of Practice (see *paragraphs 2.4, 2.5* and *2.7*). Whenever a record is made the detainee shall be allowed to check and sign the record of property as correct. Any refusal to sign shall be recorded.

4.5 If a detainee is not allowed to keep any article of clothing or personal effects, the reason must be recorded.

Notes for Guidance

4A *PACE, Section 54(1) and paragraph 4.1 require a detainee to be searched when it is clear the custody officer will have continuing duties in relation to that detainee or when that detainee's behaviour or offence makes an inventory appropriate. They do not require every detainee to be searched, e.g. if it is clear a person will only be detained for a short period and is not to be placed in a cell, the custody officer may decide not to search them. In such a case the custody record will be endorsed 'not searched', paragraph 4.4 will not apply, and the detainee will be invited to sign the entry. If the detainee refuses, the custody officer will be obliged to ascertain what property they have in accordance with paragraph 4.1.*

4B *Paragraph 4.4 does not require the custody officer to record on the custody record property in the detainee's possession on arrest if, by virtue of its nature, quantity or size, it is not practicable to remove it to the police station.*

4C *Paragraph 4.4 does not require items of clothing worn by the person to be recorded unless withheld by the custody officer as in paragraph 4.2.*

4D *Section 43(2) of TACT allows a constable to search a person who has been arrested under section 41 to discover whether they have anything in their possession that may constitute evidence that they are a terrorist.*

5 Right not to be held incommunicado

(A) Action

5.1 Any person to whom this Code applies who is held in custody at a police station or other premises may, on request, have one named person who is a friend, relative or a person known to them who is likely to take an interest in their welfare informed at public expense of their whereabouts as soon as practicable. If the person cannot be contacted the detainee may choose up to two alternatives. If they cannot be contacted, the person in charge of detention or the investigation has discretion to allow further attempts until the information has been conveyed. See *Notes 5D* and *5E*.

5.2 The exercise of the above right in respect of each person nominated may be delayed only in accordance with *Annex B*.

5.3 The above right may be exercised each time a detainee is taken to another police station or returned to a police station having been previously transferred to prison. This Code does not afford such a right to a person on transfer to a prison, where a detainee's rights will be governed by Prison Rules, see *Annex J paragraph 4*.

5.4 If the detainee agrees, they may at the custody officer's discretion, receive visits from friends, family or others likely to take an interest in their welfare, or in whose welfare the detainee has an interest. Custody Officers should liaise closely with the investigation team (*see Note 3E*) to allow risk assessments to be made where particular visitors have been requested by the detainee or identified themselves to police. In circumstances where the nature of the investigation means that such requests can not be met, consideration should be given, in conjunction with a representative of the relevant scheme, to increasing the frequency of visits from independent visitor schemes. See *Notes 5B and 5C*.

5.5 If a friend, relative or person with an interest in the detainee's welfare enquires about their whereabouts, this information shall be given if the suspect agrees and *Annex B* does not apply. See *Note 5E*.

5.6 The detainee shall be given writing materials, on request, and allowed to telephone one person for a reasonable time, see *Notes 5A* and *5F*. Either or both these privileges may be denied or delayed if an officer of inspector rank or above considers sending a letter or making a telephone call may result in any of the consequences in *Annex B paragraphs 1* and *2*, particularly in relation to the making of a telephone call in a language which an officer listening to the call (see paragraph 5.7) does not understand. See *Note 5G*.

Nothing in this paragraph permits the restriction or denial of the rights in *paragraphs 5.1* and *6.1*.

5.7 Before any letter or message is sent, or telephone call made, the detainee shall be informed that what they say in any letter, call or message (other than in a communication to a solicitor) may be read or listened to and may be given in evidence. A telephone call may be terminated if it is being abused see *Note 5G*. The costs can be at public expense at the custody officer's discretion.

5.8 Any delay or denial of the rights in this section should be proportionate and should last no longer than necessary.

(B) Documentation

5.9 A record must be kept of any:

(a) request made under this section and the action taken;
(b) letters, messages or telephone calls made or received or visit received;
(c) refusal by the detainee to have information about them given to an outside enquirer, or any refusal to see a visitor. The detainee must be asked to countersign the record accordingly and any refusal recorded.

5A   *A person may request an interpreter to interpret a telephone call or translate a letter.*

5B   *At the custody officer's discretion and subject to the detainee's consent, visits should be allowed when possible, subject to sufficient personnel being available to supervise a visit and any possible hindrance to the investigation. Custody Officers should bear in mind the exceptional nature of prolonged TACT detention and consider the potential benefits that visits may bring to the health and welfare of detainees who are held for extended periods.*

5C   *Official visitors should be given access following consultation with the officer who has overall responsibility for the investigation provided the detainee consents, and they do not compromise safety or security or unduly delay or interfere with the progress of an investigation. Official visitors should still be required to provide appropriate identification and subject to any screening process in place at the place of detention. Official visitors may include:*

- *An accredited faith representative;*
- *Members of either House of Parliament;*
- *Public officials needing to interview the prisoner in the course of their duties;*
- *Other persons visiting with the approval of the officer who has overall responsibility for the investigation;*
- *Consular officials visiting a detainee who is a national of the country they represent subject to section 7 of this Code.*

Visits from appropriate members of the Independent Custody Visitors Scheme should be dealt with in accordance with the separate Code of Practice on Independent Custody Visiting.

5D   *If the detainee does not know anyone to contact for advice or support or cannot contact a friend or relative, the custody officer should bear in mind any local voluntary bodies or other organisations that might be able to help. Paragraph 6.1 applies if legal advice is required.*

5E   *In some circumstances it may not be appropriate to use the telephone to disclose information under paragraphs 5.1 and 5.5.*

5F   *The telephone call at paragraph 5.6 is in addition to any communication under paragraphs 5.1 and 6.1. Further calls may be made at the custody officer's discretion.*

5G   *The nature of terrorism investigations means that officers should have particular regard to the possibility of suspects attempting to pass information which may be detrimental to public safety, or to an investigation.*

6   RIGHT TO LEGAL ADVICE

(A)   ACTION

6.1   Unless *Annex B* applies, all detainees must be informed that they may at any time consult and communicate privately with a solicitor, whether in person, in writing or by telephone, and that free independent legal advice is available from the duty solicitor. Where an appropriate adult is in attendance, they must also be informed of this right. See *paragraph 3.1, Note 1I, Notes 6B* and *6J*

6.2   A poster advertising the right to legal advice must be prominently displayed in the charging area of every police station. See *Note 6G*.

6.3   No police officer should, at any time, do or say anything with the intention of dissuading any person who is entitled to legal advice in accordance with this Code, from obtaining legal advice. See *Note 6ZA*.

6.4   The exercise of the right of access to legal advice may be delayed exceptionally only as in *Annex B*. Whenever legal advice is requested, and unless *Annex B* applies, the custody officer must act without delay to secure the provision of such advice. If, on being informed or reminded of this right, the detainee declines to speak to a solicitor in person, the officer should point out that the right includes the right to speak with a solicitor on the telephone (see *paragraph 5.6*). If the detainee continues to waive this right the officer should ask them why and any reasons should be recorded on the custody record or the interview record as appropriate. Reminders of the right to legal advice must be given as in *paragraphs 3.5, 11.3* and *5 of Annex K* of this Code and PACE Code D on the Identification of Persons by Police Officers, *paragraphs 3.17(ii)* and *6.3*. Once it is clear a detainee does not want to speak to a solicitor in person or by telephone they should cease to be asked their reasons. See *Note 6J*.

6.5   An officer of the rank of Commander or Assistant Chief Constable or above may give a direction under TACT Schedule 8 paragraph 9 that a detainee may only consult a solicitor within the sight and hearing of a qualified officer. Such a direction may only be given if the officer has reasonable grounds to believe that if it were not, it may result in one of the consequences set out in TACT Schedule 8 paragraph 8(4) or (5)(c). See *Annex B paragraph 3 and Note 6I*. A "qualified officer" means a police officer who:

- (a)   is at least the rank of inspector;
- (b)   is of the uniformed branch of the force of which the officer giving the direction is a member, and
- (c)   in the opinion of the officer giving the direction, has no connection with the detained person's case.

Officers considering the use of this power should first refer to *Home Office Circular 40/2003*.

6.6   In the case of a person who is a juvenile or is vulnerable, an appropriate adult should consider whether legal advice from a solicitor is required. If such a detained person wants to exercise the right to legal advice, the appropriate action should be taken and should not be delayed until the appropriate adult arrives. If the person indicates that they do not want legal advice, the appropriate adult has the right to ask for a solicitor to attend if this would be in the best interests of the person and must be so informed. In this case, action to secure the provision of advice if so requested by the appropriate adult shall be taken without delay in the same way as when requested by the person. However, the person cannot be forced to see the solicitor if they are adamant that they do not wish to do so.

6.7 A detainee who wants legal advice may not be interviewed or continue to be interviewed until they have received such advice unless:

(a) *Annex B* applies, when the restriction on drawing adverse inferences from silence in *Annex C* will apply because the detainee is not allowed an opportunity to consult a solicitor; or

(b) an officer of superintendent rank or above has reasonable grounds for believing that:

   (i) the consequent delay might:

- lead to interference with, or harm to, evidence connected with an offence;
- lead to interference with, or physical harm to, other people;
- lead to serious loss of, or damage to, property;
- lead to alerting other people suspected of having committed an offence but not yet arrested for it;
- hinder the recovery of property obtained in consequence of the commission of an offence.

   See *Note 6A*

   (ii) when a solicitor, including a duty solicitor, has been contacted and has agreed to attend, awaiting their arrival would cause unreasonable delay to the process of investigation.

Note: In these cases the restriction on drawing adverse inferences from silence in *Annex C* will apply because the detainee is not allowed an opportunity to consult a solicitor.

(c) the solicitor the detainee has nominated or selected from a list:

   (i) cannot be contacted;

   (ii) has previously indicated they do not wish to be contacted; or

   (iii) having been contacted, has declined to attend; and

- the detainee has been advised of the Duty Solicitor Scheme but has declined to ask for the duty solicitor;
- in these circumstances the interview may be started or continued without further delay provided an officer of inspector rank or above has agreed to the interview proceeding.

Note: The restriction on drawing adverse inferences from silence in *Annex C* will not apply because the detainee is allowed an opportunity to consult the duty solicitor;

(d) the detainee changes their mind, about wanting legal advice or (as the case may be) about wanting a solicitor present at the interview, and states that they no longer wish to speak to a solicitor. In these circumstances the interview may be started or continued without delay provided that:

   (i) an officer of inspector rank or above:

- speaks to the detainee to enquire about the reasons for their change of mind (see *Note 6J*), and
- makes, or directs the making of, reasonable efforts to ascertain the solicitor's expected time of arrival and to inform the solicitor that the suspect has stated that they wish to change their mind and the reason (if given);

   (ii) the detainee's reason for their change of mind (if given) and the outcome of the action in (i) are recorded in the custody record;

   (iii) the detainee, after being informed of the outcome of the action in (i) above, confirms in writing that they want the interview to proceed without speaking or further speaking to a solicitor or (as the case may be) without a solicitor being present and do not wish to wait for a solicitor by signing an entry to this effect in the custody record;

   (iv) an officer of inspector rank or above is satisfied that it is proper for the interview to proceed in these circumstances and:

- gives authority in writing for the interview to proceed and if the authority is not recorded in the custody record, the officer must ensure that the custody record shows the date and time of the authority and where it is recorded; and
- takes or directs the taking of, reasonable steps to inform the solicitor that the authority has been given and the time when the interview is expected to commence and records or causes to be recorded, the outcome of this action in the custody record.

   (v) When the interview starts and the interviewer reminds the suspect of their right to legal advice (see *paragraph 11.3*) and the Code of Practice issued under paragraph 3 of Schedule 8 to the Terrorism Act 2000 for the video recording with sound of interviews, the interviewer shall then ensure that the following is recorded in the interview record made in accordance with that Code:

- confirmation that the detainee has changed their mind about wanting legal advice or (as the case may be) about wanting a solicitor present and the reasons for it if given;
- the fact that authority for the interview to proceed has been given and, subject to *paragraph 2.8,* the name of the authorising officer;
- that if the solicitor arrives at the station before the interview is completed, the detainee will be so informed without delay and *a break will be taken* to allow them to speak to the solicitor if they wish, unless *paragraph 6.7(a)* applies, and
- that at any time during the interview, the detainee may again ask for legal advice and that if they do, a break will be taken to allow them to speak to the solicitor, unless *paragraph 6.7(a), (b), or (c)* applies.

Note: In these circumstances the restriction on drawing adverse inferences from silence in *Annex C* will not apply because the detainee is allowed an opportunity to consult a solicitor if they wish.

6.8 If *paragraph 6.7(a)* applies, where the reason for authorising the delay ceases to apply, there may be no further delay in permitting the exercise of the right in the absence of a further authorisation unless *paragraph 6.7(b), (c)* or *(d)* applies. If *paragraph 6.7(b)(i)* applies, once sufficient information has been obtained to avert the risk, questioning must cease until the detainee has received legal advice unless *paragraph 6.7(a), (b)(ii), (c)* or *(d)* applies.

6.9 A detainee who has been permitted to consult a solicitor shall be entitled on request to have the solicitor present when they are interviewed unless one of the exceptions in *paragraph 6.7* applies.

6.10 The solicitor may only be required to leave the interview if their conduct is such that the interviewer is unable properly to put questions to the suspect. See *Notes 6C and 6D.*

6.11 If the interviewer considers a solicitor is acting in such a way, they will stop the interview and consult an officer not below superintendent rank, if one is readily available, and otherwise an officer not below inspector rank not connected with the investigation. After speaking to the solicitor, the officer consulted will decide if the interview should continue in the presence of that solicitor. If they decide it should not, the suspect will be given the opportunity to consult another solicitor before the interview continues and that solicitor given an opportunity to be present at the interview. *See Note 6D.*

6.12 The removal of a solicitor from an interview is a serious step and, if it occurs, the officer of superintendent rank or above who took the decision will consider if the incident should be reported to the Solicitors Regulatory Authority. If the decision to remove the solicitor has been taken by an officer below superintendent rank, the facts must be reported to an officer of superintendent rank or above, who will similarly consider whether a report to the Solicitors Regulatory Authority would be appropriate. When the solicitor concerned is a duty solicitor, the report should be both to the Solicitors Regulatory Authority and to the Legal Aid Agency.

6.13 'Solicitor' in this Code means:

- a solicitor who holds a current practising certificate;
- an accredited or probationary representative included on the register of representatives maintained by the Legal Aid Agency.

6.14 An accredited or probationary representative sent to provide advice by, and on behalf of, a solicitor shall be admitted to the police station for this purpose unless an officer of inspector rank or above considers such a visit will hinder the investigation and directs otherwise. Hindering the investigation does not include giving proper legal advice to a detainee as in *Note 6C.* Once admitted to the police station, *paragraphs 6.7* to *6.11* apply.

6.15 In exercising their discretion under *paragraph 6.14*, the officer should take into account in particular:

- whether:
  - the identity and status of an accredited or probationary representative have been satisfactorily established;
  - they are of suitable character to provide legal advice,
- any other matters in any written letter of authorisation provided by the solicitor on whose behalf the person is attending the police station. See *Note 6E.*

6.16 If the inspector refuses access to an accredited or probationary representative or a decision is taken that such a person should not be permitted to remain at an interview, the inspector must notify the solicitor on whose behalf the representative was acting and give them an opportunity to make alternative arrangements. The detainee must be informed and the custody record noted.

6.17 If a solicitor arrives at the station to see a particular person, that person must, unless *Annex B* applies, be so informed whether or not they are being interviewed and asked if they would like to see the solicitor. This applies even if the detainee has declined legal advice or, having requested it, subsequently agreed to be interviewed without receiving advice. The solicitor's attendance and the detainee's decision must be noted in the custody record.

(B) DOCUMENTATION

6.18 Any request for legal advice and the action taken shall be recorded.

6.19 A record shall be made in the interview record if a detainee asks for legal advice and an interview is begun either in the absence of a solicitor or their representative, or they have been required to leave an interview.

NOTES FOR GUIDANCE

6ZA *No police officer or police staff shall indicate to any suspect, except to answer a direct question, that the period for which they are liable to be detained, or the time taken to complete the interview, might be reduced:*

- *if they do not ask for legal advice or do not want a solicitor present when they are interviewed; or*
- *if after asking for legal advice, they change their mind about wanting it or (as the case may be) wanting a solicitor present when they are interviewed and agree to be interviewed without waiting for a solicitor.*

6A *In considering if paragraph 6.7(b) applies, the officer should, if practicable, ask the solicitor for an estimate of how long it will take to come to the station and relate this to the time detention is permitted, the time of day (i.e. whether the rest period under paragraph 12.2 is imminent) and the requirements of other investigations. If the solicitor is on their way or is to set off immediately, it will not normally be appropriate to begin an interview before they arrive. If it appears necessary to begin an interview before the solicitor's arrival, they should be given an indication of how long the police would be able to wait so there is an opportunity to make arrangements for someone else to provide legal advice. Nothing within this section is intended to prevent police from ascertaining immediately after the arrest of an individual whether a threat to public safety exists (see paragraph 11.2).*

6B *A detainee has a right to free legal advice and to be represented by a solicitor. This Note for Guidance explains the arrangements which enable detainees to whom this Code applies to obtain legal advice. An outline of these arrangements is also included in the Notice of Rights and Entitlements given to detainees in accordance with paragraph 3.2.*

The detainee can ask for free advice from a solicitor they know or if they do not know a solicitor or the solicitor they know cannot be contacted, from the duty solicitor.

To arrange free legal advice, the police should telephone the Defence Solicitor Call Centre (DSCC). The call centre will contact either the duty solicitor or the solicitor requested by the detainee as appropriate.

When a detainee wants to pay for legal advice themselves:

- the DSCC will contact a solicitor of their choice on their behalf;
- they should be given an opportunity to consult a specific solicitor or another solicitor from that solicitor's firm. If this solicitor is not available, they may choose up to two alternatives. If these alternatives are not available, the custody officer has discretion to allow further attempts until a solicitor has been contacted and agreed to provide advice;
- they are entitled to a private consultation with their chosen solicitor on the telephone or the solicitor may decide to come to the police station;
- if their chosen solicitor cannot be contacted, the DSCC may still be called to arrange free legal advice.

Apart from carrying out duties necessary to implement these arrangements, an officer must not advise the suspect about any particular firm of solicitors.

6C The solicitor's only role in the police station is to protect and advance the legal rights of their client. On occasions this may require the solicitor to give advice which has the effect of the client avoiding giving evidence which strengthens a prosecution case. The solicitor may intervene in order to seek clarification, challenge an improper question to their client or the manner in which it is put, advise their client not to reply to particular questions, or if they wish to give their client further legal advice. Paragraph 6.9 only applies if the solicitor's approach or conduct prevents or unreasonably obstructs proper questions being put to the suspect or the suspect's response being recorded. Examples of unacceptable conduct include answering questions on a suspect's behalf or providing written replies for the suspect to quote.

6D An officer who takes the decision to exclude a solicitor must be in a position to satisfy the court the decision was properly made. In order to do this they may need to witness what is happening.

6E If an officer of at least inspector rank considers a particular solicitor or firm of solicitors is persistently sending probationary representatives who are unsuited to provide legal advice, they should inform an officer of at least superintendent rank, who may wish to take the matter up with the Solicitors Regulatory Authority.

6F Subject to the constraints of Annex B, a solicitor may advise more than one client in an investigation if they wish. Any question of a conflict of interest is for the solicitor under their professional code of conduct. If, however, waiting for a solicitor to give advice to one client may lead to unreasonable delay to the interview with another, the provisions of paragraph 6.7(b) may apply.

6G InIn addition to a poster in English, a poster or posters containing translations into Welsh, the main minority ethnic languages and the principal European languages should be displayed wherever they are likely to be helpful and it is practicable to do so.

6H Not used

6I Whenever a detainee exercises their right to legal advice by consulting or communicating with a solicitor, they must be allowed to do so in private. This right to consult or communicate in private is fundamental. Except as allowed by the Terrorism Act 2000, Schedule 8, paragraph 9, if the requirement for privacy is compromised because what is said or written by the detainee or solicitor for the purpose of giving and receiving legal advice is overheard, listened to, or read by others without the informed consent of the detainee, the right will effectively have been denied. When a detainee speaks to a solicitor on the telephone, they should be allowed to do so in private unless a direction under Schedule 8, paragraph 9 of the Terrorism Act 2000 has been given or this is impractical because of the design and layout of the custody area, or the location of telephones. However, the normal expectation should be that facilities will be available, unless they are being used, at all police stations to enable detainees to speak in private to a solicitor either face to face or over the telephone.

6J A detainee is not obliged to give reasons for declining legal advice and should not be pressed to do so.

7 CITIZENS OF INDEPENDENT COMMONWEALTH COUNTRIES OR FOREIGN NATIONALS

(A) ACTION

7.1 A detainee who is a citizen of an independent Commonwealth country or a national of a foreign country, including the Republic of Ireland, has the right, upon request, to communicate at any time with the appropriate High Commission, Embassy or Consulate. That detainee must be informed as soon as practicable of this right and asked if they want to have their High Commission, Embassy or Consulate told of their whereabouts and the grounds for their detention. Such a request should be acted upon as soon as practicable. See *Note 7A*.

7.2 A detainee who is a citizen of a country with which a bilateral consular convention or agreement is in force requiring notification of arrest, must also be informed that subject to *paragraph 7.4*, notification of their arrest will be sent to the appropriate High Commission, Embassy or Consulate as soon as practicable, whether or not they request it. A list of the countries to which this requirement currently applies and contact details for the relevant High Commissions, Embassies and Consulates can be obtained from the Consular Directorate of the Foreign and Commonwealth Office (FCO) as follows:

- from the FCO web pages:
  - https://gov.uk/government/publications/
    table-of-consular-conventions-and-mandatory-notification-obligations, and
  - https://www.gov.uk/government/publications/foreign-embassies-in-the-uk
- by telephone to 020 7008 3100,
- by email to fcocorrespondence@fco.gov.uk.
- by letter to the Foreign and Commonwealth Office, King Charles Street, London, SW1A 2AH.

7.3 Consular officers may, if the detainee agrees, visit one of their nationals in police detention to talk to them and, if required, to arrange for legal advice. Such visits shall take place out of the hearing of a police officer.

7.4 Notwithstanding the provisions of consular conventions, if the detainee claims that they are a refugee or have applied or intend to apply for asylum the custody officer must ensure that UK Visas and Immigration (UKVI) (formerly the UK Border Agency) are informed as soon as practicable of the claim. UKVI will then determine whether compliance with relevant international obligations requires notification of arrest to be sent and will inform the custody officer as to what action police need to take.

(B) D<small>OCUMENTATION</small>

7.5 A record shall be made:

- when a detainee is informed of their rights under this section and of any requirement in paragraph 7.2;
- of any communications with a High Commission, Embassy or Consulate, and
- of any communications with UKVI about a detainee's claim to be a refugee or to be seeking asylum and the resulting action taken by police.

N<small>OTE FOR</small> G<small>UIDANCE</small>

7A *The exercise of the rights in this section may not be interfered with even though Annex B applies.*

8 C<small>ONDITIONS OF DETENTION</small>

(A) A<small>CTION</small>

8.1 So far as it is practicable, not more than one detainee should be detained in each cell. See *Note 8E.*

8.2 Cells in use must be adequately heated, cleaned and ventilated. They must be adequately lit, subject to such dimming as is compatible with safety and security to allow people detained overnight to sleep. No additional restraints shall be used within a locked cell unless absolutely necessary and then only restraint equipment, approved for use in that force by the chief officer, which is reasonable and necessary in the circumstances having regard to the detainee's demeanour and with a view to ensuring their safety and the safety of others. If a detainee is deaf or a vulnerable person, particular care must be taken when deciding whether to use any form of approved restraints.

8.3 Blankets, mattresses, pillows and other bedding supplied shall be of a reasonable standard and in a clean and sanitary condition.

8.4 Access to toilet and washing facilities must be provided.

8.5 If it is necessary to remove a detainee's clothes for the purposes of investigation, for hygiene, health reasons or cleaning, replacement clothing of a reasonable standard of comfort and cleanliness shall be provided. A detainee may not be interviewed unless adequate clothing has been offered.

8.6 At least two light meals and one main meal should be offered in any 24-hour period. See *Note 8B.* Drinks should be provided at meal times and upon reasonable request between meals. Whenever necessary, advice shall be sought from the appropriate healthcare professional, see *Note 9A*, on medical and dietary matters. As far as practicable, meals provided shall offer a varied diet and meet any specific dietary needs or religious beliefs the detainee may have. Detainees should also be made aware that the meals offered meet such needs. The detainee may, at the custody officer's discretion, have meals supplied by their family or friends at their expense. See *Note 8A.*

8.7 Brief outdoor exercise shall be offered daily if practicable. Where facilities exist, indoor exercise shall be offered as an alternative if outside conditions are such that a detainee can not be reasonably expected to take outdoor exercise (e.g., in cold or wet weather) or if requested by the detainee or for reasons of security. See *Note 8C.*

8.8 Where practicable, provision should be made for detainees to practice religious observance. Consideration should be given to providing a separate room which can be used as a prayer room. The supply of appropriate food and clothing, and suitable provision for prayer facilities, such as uncontaminated copies of religious books, should also be considered. *See Note 8D.*

8.9 A juvenile shall not be placed in a cell unless no other secure accommodation is available and the custody officer considers it is not practicable to supervise them if they are not placed in a cell or that a cell provides more comfortable accommodation than other secure accommodation in the station. A juvenile may not be placed in a cell with a detained adult.

8.10 Police stations should keep a reasonable supply of reading material available for detainees, including but not limited to, the main religious texts. *See Note 8D.* Detainees should be made aware that such material is available and reasonable requests for such material should be met as soon as practicable unless to do so would:

(i)   interfere with the investigation; or
(ii) prevent or delay an officer from discharging his statutory duties, or those in this Code.

If such a request is refused on the grounds of (i) or (ii) above, this should be noted in the custody record and met as soon as possible after those grounds cease to apply.

(B) D<small>OCUMENTATION</small>

8.11 A record must be kept of replacement clothing and meals offered.

8.11A If a juvenile is placed in a cell, the reason must be recorded.

8.12 The use of any restraints on a detainee whilst in a cell, the reasons for it and, if appropriate, the arrangements for enhanced supervision of the detainee whilst so restrained, shall be recorded. See *paragraph 3.9*

NOTES FOR GUIDANCE

8A   In deciding whether to allow meals to be supplied by family or friends, the custody officer is entitled to take account of the risk of items being concealed in any food or package and the officer's duties and responsibilities under food handling legislation. If an officer needs to examine food or other items supplied by family and friends before deciding whether they can be given to the detainee, he should inform the person who has brought the item to the police station of this and the reasons for doing so.

8B   Meals should, so far as practicable, be offered at recognised meal times, or at other times that take account of when the detainee last had a meal.

8C   In light of the potential for detaining individuals for extended periods of time, the overriding principle should be to accommodate a period of exercise, except where to do so would hinder the investigation, delay the detainee's release or charge, or it is declined by the detainee.

8D   Police forces should consult with representatives of the main religious communities to ensure the provision for religious observance is adequate, and to seek advice on the appropriate storage and handling of religious texts or other religious items.

8E   The Detention and Custody Authorised Professional Practice (APP) produced by the College of Policing (see http://www.app.college.police.uk) provides more detailed guidance on matters concerning detainee healthcare and treatment and associated forensic issues which should be read in conjunction with sections 8 and 9 of this Code.

9   CARE AND TREATMENT OF DETAINED PERSONS

(A)   GENERAL

9.1   Notwithstanding other requirements for medical attention as set out in this section, detainees who are held for more than 96 hours must be visited by an appropriate healthcare professional at least once every 24 hours.

9.2   Nothing in this section prevents the police from calling an appropriate healthcare professional, to examine a detainee for the purposes of obtaining evidence relating to any offence in which the detainee is suspected of being involved. See *Note 9A*.

9.3   If a complaint is made by, or on behalf of, a detainee about their treatment since their arrest, or it comes to notice that a detainee may have been treated improperly, a report must be made as soon as practicable to an officer of inspector rank or above not connected with the investigation. If the matter concerns a possible assault or the possibility of the unnecessary or unreasonable use of force, an appropriate healthcare professional must also be called as soon as practicable.

9.4   Detainees should be visited at least every hour. If no reasonably foreseeable risk was identified in a risk assessment, see *paragraphs 3.6* to *3.10*, there is no need to wake a sleeping detainee. Those suspected of being under the influence of drink or drugs or both or of having swallowed drugs, see *Note 9C*, or whose level of consciousness causes concern must, subject to any clinical directions given by the appropriate healthcare professional, see *paragraph 9.15*:

- be visited and roused at least every half hour;
- have their condition assessed as in *Annex H*;
- and clinical treatment arranged if appropriate.

See *Notes 9B, 9C* and *9G*

9.5   When arrangements are made to secure clinical attention for a detainee, the custody officer must make sure all relevant information which might assist in the treatment of the detainee's condition is made available to the responsible healthcare professional. This applies whether or not the healthcare professional asks for such information. Any officer or police staff with relevant information must inform the custody officer as soon as practicable.

(B)   CLINICAL TREATMENT AND ATTENTION

9.6   The custody officer must make sure a detainee receives appropriate clinical attention as soon as reasonably practicable if the person:

(a)   appears to be suffering from physical illness; or
(b)   is injured; or
(c)   appears to be suffering from a mental disorder; or
(d)   appears to need clinical attention

9.7   This applies even if the detainee makes no request for clinical attention and whether or not they have already received clinical attention elsewhere. If the need for attention appears urgent, e.g. when indicated as in *Annex H*, the nearest available healthcare professional or an ambulance must be called immediately.

9.8   The custody officer must also consider the need for clinical attention as set out in *Note 9C* in relation to those suffering the effects of alcohol or drugs.

9.9   If it appears to the custody officer, or they are told, that a person brought to a station under arrest may be suffering from an infectious disease or condition, the custody officer must take reasonable steps to safeguard the health of the detainee and others at the station. In deciding what action to take, advice must be sought from an appropriate healthcare professional. See *Note 9D*. The custody officer has discretion to isolate the person and their property until clinical directions have been obtained.

9.10   If a detainee requests a clinical examination, an appropriate healthcare professional must be called as soon as practicable to assess the detainee's clinical needs. If a safe and appropriate care plan cannot be provided, the appropriate healthcare professional's advice must be sought. The detainee may also be examined by a medical practitioner of their choice at their expense.

9.11   If a detainee is required to take or apply any medication in compliance with clinical directions prescribed before their detention, the custody officer must consult the appropriate healthcare professional before the use of the medication. Subject to the restrictions in *paragraph 9.12*, the custody officer is responsible for the safekeeping of any medication and for making sure the detainee is given the opportunity to take or apply prescribed or approved medication. Any such consultation and its outcome shall be noted in the custody record.

9.12   No police officer may administer or supervise the self-administration of medically pre-scribed controlled drugs of the types and forms listed in the Misuse of Drugs Regulations 2001, Schedule 2 or 3. A detainee may only self-administer such drugs under the personal supervision of the registered medical practitioner authorising their use or other appropriate healthcare profes-sional. The custody officer may supervise the self-administration of, or authorise other custody staff to supervise the self-administration of, drugs listed in Schedule 4 or 5 if the officer has consulted the appropriate healthcare professional authorising their use and both are satisfied self-administration will not expose the detainee, police officers or anyone else to the risk of harm or injury.

9.13   When appropriate healthcare professionals administer drugs or authorise the use of other medications, or consult with the custody officer about allowing self administration of drugs listed in Schedule 4 or 5, it must be within current medicines legislation and the scope of practice as determined by their relevant regulatory body.

9.14   If a detainee has in their possession, or claims to need, medication relating to a heart condition, diabetes, epilepsy or a condition of comparable potential seriousness then, even though *paragraph 9.6* may not apply, the advice of the appropriate healthcare professional must be obtained.

9.15   Whenever the appropriate healthcare professional is called in accordance with this sec-tion to examine or treat a detainee, the custody officer shall ask for their opinion about:

- any risks or problems which police need to take into account when making decisions about the detainee's continued detention;
- when to carry out an interview if applicable; and
- the need for safeguards.

9.16   When clinical directions are given by the appropriate healthcare professional, whether orally or in writing, and the custody officer has any doubts or is in any way uncertain about any aspect of the directions, the custody officer shall ask for clarification. It is particularly important that directions concerning the frequency of visits are clear, precise and capable of being implemented. See *Note 9E*.

(c) Documentation

9.17   A record must be made in the custody record of:

(a) the arrangements made for an examination by an appropriate healthcare professional under *paragraph 9.3* and of any complaint reported under that paragraph together with any relevant remarks by the custody officer;

(b) any arrangements made in accordance with *paragraph 9.6*;

(c) any request for a clinical examination under *paragraph 9.10* and any arrangements made in response;

(d) the injury, ailment, condition or other reason which made it necessary to make the arrangements in (a) to (c); See *Note 9F*

(e) any clinical directions and advice, including any further clarifications, given to police by a healthcare professional concerning the care and treatment of the detainee in connection with any of the arrangements made in (a) to (c); See *Notes 9D* and *9E*

(f) if applicable, the responses received when attempting to rouse a person using the proce-dure in *Annex H*. See *Note 9G*.

9.18   If a healthcare professional does not record their clinical findings in the custody record, the record must show where they are recorded. See *Note 9F*. However, information which is necessary to custody staff to ensure the effective ongoing care and well being of the detainee must be recorded openly in the custody record, see *paragraph 3.8* and *Annex G, paragraph 7*.

9.19   Subject to the requirements of *Section 4*, the custody record shall include:

- a record of all medication a detainee has in their possession on arrival at the police station;
- a note of any such medication they claim to need but do not have with them.

Notes for Guidance

9A   *A 'healthcare professional' means a clinically qualified person working within the scope of practice as determined by their relevant statutory regulatory body. Whether a healthcare profes-sional is 'appropriate' depends on the circumstances of the duties they carry out at the time.*

9B   *Whenever possible detained juveniles and vulnerable persons should be visited more frequently.*

9C   *A detainee who appears drunk or behaves abnormally may be suffering from illness, the effects of drugs or may have sustained injury, particularly a head injury which is not apparent. A detainee needing or dependent on certain drugs, including alcohol, may experience harmful effects within a short time of being deprived of their supply. In these circumstances, when there is any doubt, police should always act urgently to call an appropriate healthcare professional or an ambulance. Paragraph 9.6 does not apply to minor ailments or injuries which do not need attention. However, all such ailments or injuries must be recorded in the custody record and any doubt must be resolved in favour of calling the appropriate healthcare professional.*

9D   *It is important to respect a person's right to privacy and information about their health must be kept confidential and only disclosed with their consent or in accordance with clinical advice when it is necessary to protect the detainee's health or that of others who come into contact with them.*

9E   *The custody officer should always seek to clarify directions that the detainee requires constant observation or supervision and should ask the appropriate healthcare professional to explain precisely what action needs to be taken to implement such directions.*

9F   *Paragraphs 9.17 and 9.18 do not require any information about the cause of any injury, ailment or condition to be recorded on the custody record if it appears capable of providing evidence of an offence.*

9G *The purpose of recording a person's responses when attempting to rouse them using the procedure in Annex H is to enable any change in the individual's consciousness level to be noted and clinical treatment arranged if appropriate.*

10 CAUTIONS

(A) WHEN A CAUTION MUST BE GIVEN

10.1 A person whom there are grounds to suspect of an offence, see *Note 10A*, must be cautioned before any questions about an offence, or further questions if the answers provide the grounds for suspicion, are put to them if either the suspect's answers or silence, (i.e. failure or refusal to answer or answer satisfactorily) may be given in evidence to a court in a prosecution.

10.2 A person who is arrested, or further arrested, must be informed at the time if practicable or, if not, as soon as it becomes practicable thereafter, that they are under arrest and of the grounds and reasons for their arrest, see paragraph 3.4, *Note 3G* and *Note 10B*.

10.3 As required by *section 3* of PACE Code G, a person who is arrested, or further arrested, must also be cautioned unless:

(a) it is impracticable to do so by reason of their condition or behaviour at the time; or
(b) they have already been cautioned immediately prior to arrest as in *paragraph 10.1*.

(B) TERMS OF THE CAUTIONS

10.4 The caution which must be given:

(a) on arrest;
(b) on all other occasions before a person is charged or informed they may be prosecuted; see *PACE Code C, section 16*, and
(c) before post-charge questioning under section 22 of the Counter-Terrorism Act 2008 (see *section 15.9*),

should, unless the restriction on drawing adverse inferences from silence applies, see *Annex C*, be in the following terms:

"You do not have to say anything. But it may harm your defence if you do not mention when questioned something which you later rely on in Court. Anything you do say may be given in evidence."

Where the use of the Welsh Language is appropriate, a constable may provide the caution directly in Welsh in the following terms:

"*Does dim rhaid i chi ddweud dim byd. Ond gall niweidio eich amddiffyniad os na fyddwch chi'n sôn, wrth gael eich holi, am rywbeth y byddwch chi'n dibynnu arno nes ymlaen yn y Llys. Gall unrhyw beth yr ydych yn ei ddweud gael ei roi fel tystiolaeth.*"

See *Note 10F*

10.5 *Annex C, paragraph 2* sets out the alternative terms of the caution to be used when the restriction on drawing adverse inferences from silence applies.

10.6 Minor deviations from the words of any caution given in accordance with this Code do not constitute a breach of this Code, provided the sense of the relevant caution is preserved. See *Note 10C*.

10.7 After any break in questioning under caution, the person being questioned must be made aware they remain under caution. If there is any doubt the relevant caution should be given again in full when the interview resumes. See *Note 10D*.

10.8 When, despite being cautioned, a person fails to co-operate or to answer particular questions which may affect their immediate treatment, the person should be informed of any relevant consequences and that those consequences are not affected by the caution. Examples are when a person's refusal to provide:

- their name and address when charged may make them liable to detention;
- particulars and information in accordance with a statutory requirement.

(C) SPECIAL WARNINGS UNDER THE CRIMINAL JUSTICE AND PUBLIC ORDER ACT 1994, SECTIONS 36 AND 37

10.9 When a suspect interviewed at a police station or authorised place of detention after arrest fails or refuses to answer certain questions, or to answer satisfactorily, after due warning, see *Note 10E*, a court or jury may draw such inferences as appear proper under the Criminal Justice and Public Order Act 1994, sections 36 and 37. Such inferences may only be drawn when:

(a) the restriction on drawing adverse inferences from silence, see *Annex C*, does not apply; and
(b) the suspect is arrested by a constable and fails or refuses to account for any objects, marks or substances, or marks on such objects found:
  - on their person;
  - in or on their clothing or footwear;
  - otherwise in their possession; or
  - in the place they were arrested;
(c) the arrested suspect was found by a constable at a place at or about the time the offence for which that officer has arrested them is alleged to have been committed, and the suspect fails or refuses to account for their presence there.

When the restriction on drawing adverse inferences from silence applies, the suspect may still be asked to account for any of the matters in (b) or (c) but the special warning described in *paragraph 10.10* will not apply and must not be given.

10.10 For an inference to be drawn when a suspect fails or refuses to answer a question about one of these matters, or to answer it satisfactorily, the suspect must first be told in ordinary language:

(a) what offence is being investigated;
(b) what fact they are being asked to account for;

(c)   this fact may be due to them taking part in the commission of the offence;
(d)   a court may draw a proper inference if they fail or refuse to account for this fact; and
(e)   a record is being made of the interview and it may be given in evidence if they are brought to trial.

(D) Juveniles and vulnerable persons

10.10A   The information required in *paragraph 10.10* must not be given to a suspect who is a juvenile or a vulnerable person unless the appropriate adult is present.
10.11   If a juvenile or a vulnerable person is cautioned in the absence of the appropriate adult, the caution must be repeated in the adult's presence.
10.11A   *Not used.*

(E) Documentation

10.12   A record shall be made when a caution is given under this section, either in the interviewer's pocket book or in the interview record.

Notes for Guidance

10A   *There must be some reasonable, objective grounds for the suspicion, based on known facts or information which are relevant to the likelihood the offence has been committed and the person to be questioned committed it.*
10B   *An arrested person must be given sufficient information to enable them to understand that they have been deprived of their liberty and the reason they have been arrested, e.g. when a person is arrested on suspicion of committing an offence they must be informed of the suspected offence's nature, when and where it was committed, see Note 3G. The suspect must also be informed of the reason or reasons why the arrest is considered necessary. Vague or technical language should be avoided.*
10C   *If it appears a person does not understand the caution, the person giving it should explain it in their own words.*
10D   *It may be necessary to show to the court that nothing occurred during an interview break or between interviews which influenced the suspect's recorded evidence. After a break in an interview or at the beginning of a subsequent interview, the interviewer should summarise the reason for the break and confirm this with the suspect.*
10E   *The Criminal Justice and Public Order Act 1994, sections 36 and 37 apply only to suspects who have been arrested by a constable or an officer of Revenue and Customs and are given the relevant warning by the police or Revenue and Customs officer who made the arrest or who is investigating the offence. They do not apply to any interviews with suspects who have not been arrested.*
10F   *Nothing in this Code requires a caution to be given or repeated when informing a person not under arrest they may be prosecuted for an offence. However, a court will not be able to draw any inferences under the Criminal Justice and Public Order Act 1994, section 34, if the person was not cautioned.*

11 Interviews – general

(A) Action

11.1   An interview in this Code is the questioning of a person arrested on suspicion of being a terrorist which, under *paragraph 10.1*, must be carried out under caution. Whenever a person is interviewed they and their solicitor must be informed of the grounds for arrest, and given sufficient information to enable them to understand the nature of their suspected involvement in the commission, preparation or instigation of acts of terrorism (see *paragraph 3.4(a)*) in order to allow for the effective exercise of the rights of the defence. However, whilst the information must always be sufficient information for the person to understand the nature of their suspected involvement in the commission, preparation or instigation of acts of terrorism, this does not require the disclosure of details at a time which might prejudice the terrorism investigation (*see Note 3G*). The decision about what needs to be disclosed for the purpose of this requirement therefore rests with the investigating officer who has sufficient knowledge of the case to make that decision. The officer who discloses the information shall make a record of the information disclosed and when it was disclosed. This record may be made in the interview record, in the officer's report book or other form provided for this purpose. See *Note 11ZA*.
11.2   Following the arrest of a person under *section 41 TACT*, that person must not be interviewed about the relevant offence except at a place designated for detention under *paragraph 1 of Schedule 8 to the Terrorism Act 2000*, unless the consequent delay would be likely to:

(a)   lead to:
   •   interference with, or harm to, evidence connected with an offence;
   •   interference with, or physical harm to, other people; or
   •   serious loss of, or damage to, property;
(b)   lead to alerting other people suspected of committing an offence but not yet arrested for it; or
(c)   hinder the recovery of property obtained in consequence of the commission of an offence.

Interviewing in any of these circumstances shall cease once the relevant risk has been averted or the necessary questions have been put in order to attempt to avert that risk.
11.3   Immediately prior to the commencement or re-commencement of any interview at a designated place of detention, the interviewer should remind the suspect of their entitlement to free legal advice and that the interview can be delayed for legal advice to be obtained, unless one of the exceptions in *paragraph 6.7* applies. It is the interviewer's responsibility to make sure all reminders are recorded in the interview record.
11.4   At the beginning of an interview the interviewer, after cautioning the suspect, see *section 10*, shall put to them any significant statement or silence which occurred in the presence and

hearing of a police officer or other police staff before the start of the interview and which have not been put to the suspect in the course of a previous interview. See *Note 11A*. The interviewer shall ask the suspect whether they confirm or deny that earlier statement or silence and if they want to add anything.

11.5 A significant statement is one which appears capable of being used in evidence against the suspect, in particular a direct admission of guilt. A significant silence is a failure or refusal to answer a question or answer satisfactorily when under caution, which might, allowing for the restriction on drawing adverse inferences from silence, see *Annex C*, give rise to an inference under the Criminal Justice and Public Order Act 1994, Part III.

11.6 No interviewer may try to obtain answers or elicit a statement by the use of oppression. Except as in *paragraph 10.8*, no interviewer shall indicate, except to answer a direct question, what action will be taken by the police if the person being questioned answers questions, makes a statement or refuses to do either. If the person asks directly what action will be taken if they answer questions, make a statement or refuse to do either, the interviewer may inform them what action the police propose to take provided that action is itself proper and warranted.

11.7 The interview or further interview of a person about an offence with which that person has not been charged or for which they have not been informed they may be prosecuted, must cease when:

(a) the officer in charge of the investigation is satisfied all the questions they consider relevant to obtaining accurate and reliable information about the offence have been put to the suspect, this includes allowing the suspect an opportunity to give an innocent explanation and asking questions to test if the explanation is accurate and reliable, e.g. to clear up ambiguities or clarify what the suspect said;

(b) the officer in charge of the investigation has taken account of any other available evidence; and

(c) the officer in charge of the investigation, or in the case of a detained suspect, the custody officer, see *PACE Code C paragraph 16.1*, reasonably believes there is sufficient evidence to provide a realistic prospect of conviction for that offence. See *Note 11B*.

(B) Interview records

11.8 Interviews of a person detained under *section 41 of, or Schedule 8 to, TACT* must be video recorded with sound in accordance with the Code of Practice issued under *paragraph 3 of Schedule 8 to the Terrorism Act 2000*, or in the case of post-charge questioning authorised under *section 22 of the Counter-Terrorism Act 2008*, the Code of Practice issued under section 25 of that Act.

11.8A A written record shall be made of any comments made by a suspect, including unsolicited comments, which are outside the context of an interview but which might be relevant to the offence. Any such record must be timed and signed by the maker. When practicable the suspect shall be given the opportunity to read that record and to sign it as correct or to indicate how they consider it inaccurate. See *Note 11E*.

(C) Juveniles and vulnerable persons

11.9 A juvenile or vulnerable person must not be interviewed regarding their involvement or suspected involvement in a criminal offence or offences, or asked to provide or sign a written statement under caution or record of interview, in the absence of the appropriate adult unless *paragraphs 11.2 or 11.11 to 11.13* apply. See *Note 11C*.

11.10 If an appropriate adult is present at an interview, they shall be informed:

• that they are not expected to act simply as an observer; and
• that the purpose of their presence is to:
  – advise the person being interviewed;
  – observe whether the interview is being conducted properly and fairly;
  – facilitate communication with the person being interviewed.

See *paragraph 1.13A*.

11.10A The appropriate adult may be required to leave the interview if their conduct is such that the interviewer is unable properly to put questions to the suspect. This will include situations where the appropriate adult's approach or conduct prevents or unreasonably obstructs proper questions being put to the suspect or the suspect's responses being recorded (see *Note 11F*). If the interviewer considers an appropriate adult is acting in such a way, they will stop the interview and consult an officer not below superintendent rank, if one is readily available, and otherwise an officer not below inspector rank not connected with the investigation. After speaking to the appropriate adult, the officer consulted must remind the adult that their role under *paragraph 11.10* does not allow them to obstruct proper questioning and give the adult an opportunity to respond. The officer consulted will then decide if the interview should continue without the attendance of that appropriate adult. If they decide it should, another appropriate adult must be obtained before the interview continues, unless the provisions of *paragraph 11.11* below apply.

(D) Vulnerable suspects - urgent interviews at police stations

11.11 The following interviews may take place only if an officer of superintendent rank or above considers delaying the interview will lead to the consequences in *paragraph 11.2(a) to (c)*, and is satisfied the interview would not significantly harm the person's physical or mental state (see *Annex G*):

(a) an interview of a detained juvenile or vulnerable person without the appropriate adult being present (see *Note 11C*);

(b) an interview of anyone other than in (a) who appears unable to:
  • appreciate the significance of questions and their answers; or
  • understand what is happening because of the effects of drink, drugs or any illness, ailment or condition;

(c) an interview without an interpreter having been arranged, of a detained person whom the custody officer has determined requires an interpreter (see *paragraphs 3.5(c)(ii)* and *3.14*) which is carried out by an interviewer speaking the suspect's own language or (as the case may be) otherwise establishing effective communication which is sufficient to enable the necessary questions to be asked and answered in order to avert the consequences. See *paragraphs 13.2* and *13.5*.

11.12   These interviews may not continue once sufficient information has been obtained to avert the consequences in *paragraph 11.2(a)* to *(c)*.

11.13   A record shall be made of the grounds for any decision to interview a person under *paragraph 11.11*.

NOTES FOR GUIDANCE

11ZA   *The requirement in paragraph 11.1 for a suspect to be given sufficient information about the nature of their suspected involvement in the commission, preparation or instigation of acts of terrorism offence applies prior to the interview and whether or not they are legally represented. What is sufficient will depend on the circumstances of the case, but it should normally include, as a minimum, a description of the facts relating to the suspected involvement that are known to the officer, including the time and place in question. This aims to avoid suspects being confused or unclear about what they are supposed to have done and to help an innocent suspect to clear the matter up more quickly.*

11A   *Paragraph 11.4 does not prevent the interviewer from putting significant statements and silences to a suspect again at a later stage or a further interview.*

11B   *The Criminal Procedure and Investigations Act 1996 Code of Practice, paragraph 3.4 states 'In conducting an investigation, the investigator should pursue all reasonable lines of enquiry, whether these point towards or away from the suspect. What is reasonable will depend on the particular circumstances.' Interviewers should keep this in mind when deciding what questions to ask in an interview.*

11C   *Although juveniles or vulnerable persons are often capable of providing reliable evidence, they may, without knowing or wishing to do so, be particularly prone in certain circumstances to providing information that may be unreliable, misleading or selfincriminating. Special care should always be taken when questioning such a person, and the appropriate adult should be involved if there is any doubt about a person's age, mental state or capacity. Because of the risk of unreliable evidence it is also important to obtain corroboration of any facts admitted whenever possible. Because of the risks, which the presence of the appropriate adult is intended to minimise, officers of superintendent rank or above should exercise their discretion under paragraph 11.11(a) to authorise the commencement of an interview in the appropriate adult's absence only in exceptional cases, if it is necessary to avert one or more of the specified risks in paragraph 11.2.*

11D   *Consideration should be given to the effect of extended detention on a detainee and any subsequent information they provide, especially if it relates to information on matters that they have failed to provide previously in response to similar questioning (see Annex G).*

11E   *Significant statements described in paragraph 11.4 will always be relevant to the offence and must be recorded. When a suspect agrees to read records of interviews and other comments and sign them as correct, they should be asked to endorse the record with, e.g. 'I agree that this is a correct record of what was said' and add their signature. If the suspect does not agree with the record, the interviewer should record the details of any disagreement and ask the suspect to read these details and sign them to the effect that they accurately reflect their disagreement. Any refusal to sign should be recorded.*

11F   *The appropriate adult may intervene if they consider it is necessary to help the suspect understand any question asked and to help the suspect to answer any question. Paragraph 11.10A only applies if the appropriate adult's approach or conduct prevents or unreasonably obstructs proper questions being put to the suspect or the suspect's response being recorded. Examples of unacceptable conduct include answering questions on a suspect's behalf or providing written replies for the suspect to quote. An officer who takes the decision to exclude an appropriate adult must be in a position to satisfy the court the decision was properly made. In order to do this they may need to witness what is happening and give the suspect's solicitor (if they have one) who witnessed what happened, an opportunity to comment.*

12 INTERVIEWS IN POLICE STATIONS

(A) ACTION

12.1   If a police officer wants to interview or conduct enquiries which require the presence of a detainee, the custody officer is responsible for deciding whether to deliver the detainee into the officer's custody. An investigating officer who is given custody of a detainee takes over responsibility for the detainee's care and treatment for the purposes of this Code until they return the detainee to the custody officer when they must report the manner in which they complied with the Code whilst having custody of the detainee.

12.2   Except as below, in any period of 24 hours a detainee must be allowed a continuous period of at least 8 hours for rest, free from questioning, travel or any interruption in connection with the investigation concerned. This period should normally be at night or other appropriate time which takes account of when the detainee last slept or rested. If a detainee is arrested at a police station after going there voluntarily, the period of 24 hours runs from the time of their arrest (or, if a person was being detained under TACT Schedule 7 when arrested, from the time at which the examination under Schedule 7 began) and not the time of arrival at the police station. The period may not be interrupted or delayed, except:

   (a)   when there are reasonable grounds for believing not delaying or interrupting the period would:
      (i)   involve a risk of harm to people or serious loss of, or damage to, property;
      (ii)   delay unnecessarily the person's release from custody; or
      (iii)   otherwise prejudice the outcome of the investigation;
   (b)   at the request of the detainee, their appropriate adult or legal representative;

(c) when a delay or interruption is necessary in order to:
    (i) comply with the legal obligations and duties arising under *section 14*; or
    (ii) to take action required under *section 9* or in accordance with medical advice.

If the period is interrupted in accordance with *(a)*, a fresh period must be allowed. Interruptions under *(b)* and *(c)* do not require a fresh period to be allowed.

12.3 Before a detainee is interviewed the custody officer, in consultation with the officer in charge of the investigation and appropriate healthcare professionals as necessary, shall assess whether the detainee is fit enough to be interviewed. This means determining and considering the risks to the detainee's physical and mental state if the interview took place and determining what safeguards are needed to allow the interview to take place. The custody officer shall not allow a detainee to be interviewed if the custody officer considers it would cause significant harm to the detainee's physical or mental state. Vulnerable suspects listed at *paragraph 11.11* shall be treated as always being at some risk during an interview and these persons may not be interviewed except in accordance with *paragraphs 11.11* to *11.13*.

12.4 As far as practicable interviews shall take place in interview rooms which are adequately heated, lit and ventilated.

12.5 A suspect whose detention without charge has been authorised under TACT Schedule 8, because the detention is necessary for an interview to obtain evidence of the offence for which they have been arrested, may choose not to answer questions but police do not require the suspect's consent or agreement to interview them for this purpose. If a suspect takes steps to prevent themselves being questioned or further questioned, e.g. by refusing to leave their cell to go to a suitable interview room or by trying to leave the interview room, they shall be advised that their consent or agreement to be interviewed is not required. The suspect shall be cautioned as in *section 10*, and informed if they fail or refuse to co-operate, the interview may take place in the cell and that their failure or refusal to co-operate may be given in evidence. If they refuse and the custody officer considers, on reasonable grounds, that the interview should not be delayed, the custody officer has discretion to direct that the interview be conducted in a cell. The suspect shall then be invited to co-operate and go into the interview room.

12.6 People being questioned or making statements shall not be required to stand.

12.7 Before the interview commences each interviewer shall, subject to the qualification at *paragraph 2.8*, identify themselves and any other persons present to the interviewee.

12.8 Breaks from interviewing should be made at recognised meal times or at other times that take account of when an interviewee last had a meal. Short refreshment breaks shall be provided at approximately two hour intervals, subject to the interviewer's discretion to delay a break if there are reasonable grounds for believing it would:

    (i) involve a:
        • risk of harm to people;
        • serious loss of, or damage to, property;
    (ii) unnecessarily delay the detainee's release;
    (iii) otherwise prejudice the outcome of the investigation.

See *Note 12B*

12.9 During extended periods where no interviews take place, because of the need to gather further evidence or analyse existing evidence, detainees and their legal representative shall be informed that the investigation into the relevant offence remains ongoing. If practicable, the detainee and legal representative should also be made aware in general terms of any reasons for long gaps between interviews. Consideration should be given to allowing visits, more frequent exercise, or for reading or writing materials to be offered *see paragraph 5.4, section 8 and Note 12C*.

12.10 If during the interview a complaint is made by or on behalf of the interviewee concerning the provisions of any of the Codes, or it comes to the interviewer's notice that the interviewee may have been treated improperly, the interviewer should:

    (i) record the matter in the interview record; and
    (ii) inform the custody officer, who is then responsible for dealing with it as in *section 9*.

(B) Documentation

12.11 A record must be made of the:

• time a detainee is not in the custody of the custody officer, and why;
• reason for any refusal to deliver the detainee out of that custody.

12.12 A record shall be made of:

• the reasons it was not practicable to use an interview room; and
• any action taken as in *paragraph 12.5*.

The record shall be made on the custody record or in the interview record for action taken whilst an interview record is being kept, with a brief reference to this effect in the custody record.

12.13 Any decision to delay a break in an interview must be recorded, with reasons, in the interview record.

12.14 All written statements made at police stations under caution shall be written on forms provided for the purpose.

12.15 All written statements made under caution shall be taken in accordance with *Annex D*. Before a person makes a written statement under caution at a police station they shall be reminded about the right to legal advice. See *Note 12A*.

Notes for Guidance

12A *It is not normally necessary to ask for a written statement if the interview was recorded in accordance with the Code of Practice issued under TACT Schedule 8 Paragraph 3. Statements under caution should normally be taken in these circumstances only at the person's express wish. A person may however be asked if they want to make such a statement.*

12B *Meal breaks should normally last at least 45 minutes and shorter breaks after two hours should last at least 15 minutes. If the interviewer delays a break in accordance with paragraph 12.8* and prolongs the interview, a longer break should be provided. If there is a short interview, and another short interview is contemplated, the length of the break may be reduced if there are reasonable grounds to believe this is necessary to avoid any of the consequences in paragraph 12.8(i) to (iii)..

12C   Consideration should be given to the matters referred to in paragraph 12.9 after a period of over 24 hours without questioning. This is to ensure that extended periods of detention without an indication that the investigation remains ongoing do not contribute to a deterioration of the detainee's well-being.

13 INTERPRETERS

(A) GENERAL

13.1   Chief officers are responsible for making arrangements (see *paragraph 13.1ZA*) to provide appropriately qualified independent persons to act as interpreters and to provide translations of essential documents for detained suspects who, in accordance with *paragraph 3.5(c)(ii)*, the custody officer has determined require an interpreter.

If the suspect has a hearing or speech impediment, references to 'interpreter' and 'interpretation' in this Code include appropriate assistance necessary to establish effective communication with that person. See *paragraph 13.1C* if the detainee is in Wales.

13.1ZA   References in *paragraph 13.1* above and elsewhere in this Code (see *paragraphs 3.14(a)*, *13.2*, *13.3*, *13.5*, *13.6*, *13.9*, *13.10A*, *13.10D* and *13.11 below* and in any other Code, to making arrangements for an interpreter to assist a suspect, mean making arrangements for the interpreter to be *physically* present in the same location as the suspect *unless* the provisions in *paragraph 13.12* below, and Part 1 of *Annex L*, allow live-link interpretation to be used.

13.1A   The arrangements must comply with the minimum requirements set out in Directive 2010/64/EU of the European Parliament and of the Council of 20 October 2010 on the right to interpretation and translation in criminal proceedings (see *Note 13A*). The provisions of this Code implement the requirements for those to whom this Code applies. These requirements include the following:

- That the arrangements made and the quality of interpretation and translation provided shall be sufficient to '*safeguard the fairness of the proceedings, in particular by ensuring that suspected or accused persons have knowledge of the cases against them and are able to exercise their right of defence*'. This term which is used by the Directive means that the suspect must be able to understand their position and be able to communicate effectively with police officers, interviewers, solicitors and appropriate adults as provided for by this and any other Code in the same way as a suspect who can speak and understand English who does not have a hearing or speech impediment and who would not require an interpreter. See *paragraphs 13.12* to *13.14* and *Annex L* for application to live-link interpretation
- The provision of a written translation of all documents considered essential for the person to exercise their right of defence and to '*safeguard the fairness of the proceedings*' as described above. For the purposes of this Code, this includes any decision to authorise a person to be detained and details of any offence(s) with which the person has been charged or for which they have been told they may be prosecuted, see *Annex K*.
- Procedures to help determine:
  - whether a suspect can speak and understand English and needs the assistance of an interpreter (*see paragraph 13.1* and *Notes 13B* and *13C*); and
  - whether another interpreter should be called or another translation should be provided when a suspect complains about the quality of either or both (see *paragraphs 13.10A* and *13.10C*).

13.1B   All reasonable attempts should be made to make the suspect understand that interpretation and translation will be provided at public expense.

13.1C   With regard to persons in Wales, nothing in this or any other Code affects the application of the Welsh Language Schemes produced by police and crime commissioners in Wales in accordance with the Welsh Language Act 1993. See paragraphs *3.14 and 13.1*.

(B) INTERVIEWING SUSPECTS - FOREIGN LANGUAGES

13.2   Unless *paragraphs 11.2 or 11.11(c)* apply, a suspect who for the purposes of this Code requires an interpreter because they do not appear to speak or understand English (see *paragraphs 3.5(c)(ii)* and *3.14*) must not be interviewed unless arrangements are made for a person capable of interpreting to assist the suspect to understand and communicate.

13.3   If a person who is a juvenile or a vulnerable person is interviewed and the person acting as the appropriate adult, does not appear to speak or understand English, arrangements must be made for an interpreter to assist communication between the between the person, the appropriate adult and the interviewer, unless the interview is urgent and *paragraphs 11.2 or 11.11(c)* apply.

13.4   In the case of a person making a statement under caution to a police officer or other police staff other than in English:

- (a)   the interpreter shall record the statement in the language it is made;
- (b)   the person shall be invited to sign it;
- (c)   an official English translation shall be made in due course.

See *paragraphs 13.12* to *13.14* and *Annex L* for application to live-link interpretation.

(C) INTERVIEWING SUSPECTS WHO HAVE A HEARING OR SPEECH IMPEDIMENT

13.5   Unless *paragraphs 11.2* or *11.11(c)* (urgent interviews) apply, a suspect who for the purposes of this Code requires an interpreter or other appropriate assistance to enable effective communication with them because they appear to have a hearing or speech impediment (see *paragraphs 3.5(c)(ii)* and *3.14)* must not be interviewed without arrangements having been made to provide an independent person capable of interpreting or of providing other appropriate assistance.

13.6 An interpreter should also be arranged if a person who is a juvenile or a vulnerable person is interviewed and the person who is present as the appropriate adult appears to have a hearing or speech impediment, unless the interview is urgent and *paragraphs 11.2* or *11.11(c)* apply.

13.7 *Not used*

(D) Additional rules for detained persons

13.8 Not used.

13.9 If *paragraph 6.1* applies and the detainee cannot communicate with the solicitor because of language, hearing or speech difficulties, arrangements must be made for an interpreter to enable communication. A police officer or any other police staff may not be used for this purpose.

13.10 After the custody officer has determined that a detainee requires an interpreter (see *paragraph 3.5(c)(ii)*) and following the initial action in *paragraphs 3.1 to 3.5*, arrangements must also be made for an interpreter to explain:

- the grounds and reasons for any authorisation of their detention under the provisions of the Terrorism Act 2000 or the Counter Terrorism Act 2008 (post-charge questioning) to which this Code applies; and
- any information about the authorisation given to them by the authorising officer or (as the case may be) the court and which is recorded in the custody record.

See *sections 14* and *15* of this Code.

13.10A If a detainee complains that they are not satisfied with the quality of interpretation, the custody officer or (as the case may be) the interviewer, is responsible for deciding whether to make arrangements for a different interpreter in accordance with the procedures set out in the arrangements made by the chief officer, *see paragraph 13.1A.*

(E) Translations of essential documents

13.10B Written translations, oral translations and oral summaries of essential documents in a language the detainee understands shall be provided in accordance with Annex K (Translations of documents and records).

13.10C If a detainee complains that they are not satisfied with the quality of the translation, the custody officer or (as the case may be) the interviewer, is responsible for deciding whether a further translation should be provided in accordance with the procedures set out in the arrangements made by the chief officer, *see paragraph 13.1A.*

(F) Decisions not to provide interpretation and translation.

13.10D If a suspect challenges a decision:

- made by the custody officer in accordance with this Code (see *paragraph 3.5(c)(ii)*) that they do not require an interpreter, or
- made in accordance with *paragraphs 13.10A, 13.10B* or *13.10C* not to make arrangements to provide a different interpreter or another translation or not to translate a requested document,

the matter shall be reported to an inspector to deal with as a complaint for the purposes of *paragraph 9.3* or *12.10* if the challenge is made during an interview.

(G) Documentation

13.11 The following must be recorded in the custody record or as applicable, interview record:

(a) Action taken to arrange for an interpreter, including the live-link requirements in *Annex L* as applicable;
(b) Action taken when a detainee is not satisfied about the standard of interpretation or translation provided, see paragraphs 13.10A and 13.10C;
(c) When an urgent interview is carried out in accordance with *paragraph 13.2* or *13.5* in the absence of an interpreter;
(d) When a detainee has been assisted by an interpreter for the purpose of providing or being given information or being interviewed;
(e) Action taken in accordance with Annex K when:
  - a written translation of an essential document is provided;
  - an oral translation or oral summary of an essential document is provided instead of a written translation and the authorising officer's reason(s) why this would not prejudice the fairness of the proceedings (see *Annex K, paragraph 3*);
  - a suspect waives their right to a translation of an essential document (see *Annex K, paragraph 4*);
  - when representations that a document which is not included in the table is essential and that a translation should be provided are refused and the reason for the refusal (see *Annex K, paragraph 8*).

(H) Live-link interpretation

13.12 In this section and in *Annex L*, 'live-link interpretation' means an arrangement to enable communication between the suspect and an interpreter who is not *physically* present with the suspect. The arrangement must ensure that anything said by any person in the suspect's presence and hearing can be interpreted in the same way as if the interpreter was physically present at that time. The communication must be by audio and visual means for the purpose of an interview, and for all other purposes it may be *either,* by audio and visual means, or by audio means *only*, as follows:

(a) **Audio and visual communication**
  This is required for interviews conducted and recorded in accordance with the Code of

Practice for the video recording with sound, of interviews of persons detained under *section 41 of the Terrorism Act 2000* and of persons for whom an authorisation to question after charge has been given under *section 22 of the Counter-Terrorism act 2008* (see *Note 13D*). In these each of these cases, the interview must be video recorded with sound and during that interview, live link interpretation must *enable*:

    (i)   the suspect, the interviewer, solicitor, appropriate adult and any other person *physically* present with the suspect at any time during the interview and an interpreter who is not *physically* present, to *see* and *hear* each other; and

    (ii) the interview to be conducted and recorded in accordance with the relevant provisions of the Code, subject to the modifications in *Part 2 of Annex L*.

(b) **Audio and visual or audio without visual communication.**

This applies to communication for the purposes of any provision of this Code except as described in (a), which requires or permits information to be given to, sought from, or provided by a suspect, whether orally or in writing, which would include communication between the suspect and their solicitor and/or appropriate adult, and for these cases, live link interpretation must:

    (i)   *enable* the suspect, the person giving or seeking that information, any other person *physically* present with the suspect at that time and an interpreter who is not so present, to either *see* and *hear* each other, or to *hear without seeing* each other (for example by using a telephone); and

    (ii) enable that information to be given to, sought from, or provided by, the suspect in accordance with the provisions of this Code that apply to that information, as modified for the purposes of the live-link, by *Part 2 of Annex L*.

13.12A The requirement in *sub-paragraphs 13.12(a)(ii)* and *(b)(ii)*, that live-link interpretation must enable compliance with the relevant provisions of the specified Codes, means that the arrangements must provide for any written or electronic record of what the suspect says in their own language which is made by the interpreter, to be securely transmitted without delay so that the suspect can be invited to read, check and if appropriate, sign or otherwise confirm that the record is correct or make corrections to the record.

13.13 Chief officers must be satisfied that live-link interpretation used in their force area for the purposes of *paragraphs 13.12(a)* and *(b)*, provides for accurate and secure communication with the suspect. This includes ensuring that at any time during which live link interpretation is being used, a person cannot see, hear or otherwise obtain access to any communications between the suspect and interpreter or communicate with the suspect or interpreter unless so authorised or allowed by the custody officer or in the case of an interview, the interviewer and that as applicable, the confidentiality of any private consultation between a suspect and their solicitor and appropriate adult (see *paragraphs 13.2A, 13.6* and *13.9*) is maintained. See *Annex L paragraph 4*.

Notes for Guidance

13A *Chief officers have discretion when determining the individuals or organisations they use to provide interpretation and translation services for their forces provided that these services are compatible with the requirements of the Directive. One example which chief officers may wish to consider is the Ministry of Justice commercial agreements for interpretation and translation services.*

13B *A procedure for determining whether a person needs an interpreter might involve a telephone interpreter service or using cue cards or similar visual aids which enable the detainee to indicate their ability to speak and understand English and their preferred language. This could be confirmed through an interpreter who could also assess the extent to which the person can speak and understand English.*

13C *There should also be a procedure for determining whether a suspect who requires an interpreter requires assistance in accordance with paragraph 3.20 to help them check and if applicable, sign any documentation.*

13D *The Code of Practice referred to in paragraph 13.12, is available here: https://www.gov.uk/ government/publications/terrorism-act-2000-video-recording-code-of-practice.*

14 Reviews and Extensions of Detention under the Terrorism Act 2000

(a) General

14.0 The requirement in *paragraph 3.4(b)* that documents and materials essential to challenging the lawfulness the detainee's arrest and detention must be made available to the detainee or their solicitor, applies for the purposes of this section.

14.1 The powers and duties of the review officer are in the Terrorism Act 2000, Schedule 8, Part II. See *Notes 14A and 14B*. A review officer should carry out their duties at the police station where the detainee is held and be allowed such access to the detainee as is necessary to exercise those duties.

14.2 For the purposes of reviewing a person's detention, no officer shall put specific questions to the detainee:

- regarding their involvement in any offence; or
- in respect of any comments they may make:
  - when given the opportunity to make representations; or
  - in response to a decision to keep them in detention or extend the maximum period of detention.

Such an exchange could constitute an interview as in *paragraph 11.1* and would be subject to the associated safeguards in *section 11*.

14.3 If detention is necessary for longer than 48 hours from the time of arrest or, if a person was being detained under *TACT Schedule 7*, from the time at which the examination under Schedule 7 began, a police officer of at least superintendent rank, or a Crown Prosecutor may apply for a warrant of further detention or for an extension or further extension of such a warrant under *paragraph 29* or (as the case may be) *36 of Part III of Schedule 8 to the Terrorism Act 2000*. See *Note 14C.*

14.4 When an application is made for a warrant as described in paragraph 14.3, the detained person and their representative must be informed of their rights in respect of the application. These include:

(i) the right to a written notice of the application (see *paragraph 14.4*);
(ii) the right to make oral or written representations to the judicial authority / High Court judge about the application;
(iii) the right to be present and legally represented at the hearing of the application, unless specifically excluded by the judicial authority / High Court judge;
(iv) their right to free legal advice (see *section 6* of this Code).

14.4A TACT *Schedule 8 paragraph 31* requires the notice of the application for a warrant of further detention to be provided before the judicial hearing of the application for that warrant and that the notice must include:

(a) notification that the application for a warrant has been made;
(b) the time at which the application was made;
(c) the time at which the application is to be heard;
(d) the grounds on which further detention is sought.

A notice must also be provided each time an application is made to extend or further extend an existing warrant.

(B) Transfer of persons detained for more than 14 days to prison

14.5 If the Detention of Terrorists Suspects (Temporary Extension) Bill is enacted and in force, a High Court judge may extend or further extend a warrant of further detention to authorise a person to be detained beyond a period of 14 days from the time of their arrest (or if they were being detained under TACT Schedule 7, from the time at which their examination under Schedule 7 began). The provisions of Annex J will apply when a warrant of further detention is so extended or further extended.

14.6 *Not used.*
14.7 *Not used.*
14.8 *Not used.*
14.9 *Not used.*
14.10 *Not used.*

(C) Documentation

14.11 It is the responsibility of the officer who gives any reminders as at *paragraph 14.4*, to ensure that these are noted in the custody record, as well any comments made by the detained person upon being told of those rights.

14.12 The grounds for, and extent of, any delay in conducting a review shall be recorded.
14.13 Any written representations shall be retained.
14.14 A record shall be made as soon as practicable about the outcome of each review and, if applicable, the grounds on which the review officer authorises continued detention. A record shall also be made as soon as practicable about the outcome of an application for a warrant of further detention or its extension.
14.15 *Not used.*

Notes for Guidance

14A TACT *Schedule 8 Part II* sets out the procedures for review of detention up to 48 hours from the time of arrest under TACT section 41 (or if a person was being detained under TACT Schedule 7, from the time at which the examination under Schedule 7 began). These include provisions for the requirement to review detention, postponing a review, grounds for continued detention, designating a review officer, representations, rights of the detained person and keeping a record. The review officer's role ends after a warrant has been issued for extension of detention under Part III of Schedule 8.

14B A review officer may authorise a person's continued detention if satisfied that detention is necessary:

(a) to obtain relevant evidence whether by questioning the person or otherwise;
(b) to preserve relevant evidence;
(c) while awaiting the result of an examination or analysis of relevant evidence;
(d) for the examination or analysis of anything with a view to obtaining relevant evidence;
(e) pending a decision to apply to the Secretary of State for a deportation notice to be served on the detainee, the making of any such application, or the consideration of any such application by the Secretary of State;
(f) pending a decision to charge the detainee with an offence.

14C Applications for warrants to extend detention beyond 48 hours, may be made for periods of 7 days at a time (initially under TACT Schedule 8 paragraph 29, and extensions thereafter under TACT Schedule 8, paragraph 36), up to a maximum period of 14 days (or 28 days if the Detention of Terrorists Suspects (Temporary Extension) Bill) is enacted and in force) from the time of their arrest (or if they were being detained under TACT Schedule 7, from the time at which their examination under Schedule 7 began). Applications may be made for shorter periods than 7 days, which must be specified. The judicial authority or High Court judge may also substitute a shorter period if they feel a period of 7 days is inappropriate.

14D Unless Note 14F applies, applications for warrants that would take the total period of detention up to 14 days or less should be made to a judicial authority, meaning a District Judge (Magistrates' Court) designated by the Lord Chief Justice to hear such applications.

14E If by virtue of the relevant provisions described in Note 14C being enacted the maximum period of detention is extended to 28 days, any application for a warrant which would take the period of detention beyond 14 days from the time of arrest (or if a person was being detained under TACT Schedule 7, from the time at which the examination under Schedule 7 began), must be made to a High Court Judge.

14F   If, when the Detention of Terrorists Suspects (Temporary Extension) Bill is enacted and in force, an application is made to a High Court judge for a warrant which would take detention beyond 14 days and the High Court judge instead issues a warrant for a period of time which would not take detention beyond 14 days, further applications for extension of detention must also be made to a High Court judge, regardless of the period of time to which they refer.

14G   Not used.

14H   An officer applying for an order under TACT Schedule 8 paragraph 34 to withhold specified information on which they intend to rely when applying for a warrant of further detention or the extension or further extension of such a warrant, may make the application for the order orally or in writing. The most appropriate method of application will depend on the circumstances of the case and the need to ensure fairness to the detainee.

14I   After hearing any representations by or on behalf of the detainee and the applicant, the judicial authority or High Court judge may direct that the hearing relating to the extension of detention under Part III of Schedule 8 is to take place using video conferencing facilities. However, if the judicial authority requires the detained person to be physically present at any hearing, this should be complied with as soon as practicable. Paragraph 33(4) to (9) of TACT Schedule 8 govern the hearing of applications via video-link or other means.

14J   Not used.

14K   Not used.

15   CHARGING AND POST-CHARGE QUESTIONING IN TERRORISM CASES

(A)   CHARGING

15.1   Charging of detained persons is covered by PACE and guidance issued under PACE by the Director of Public Prosecutions. Decisions to charge persons to whom this Code (H) applies, the charging process and related matters are subject to section 16 of PACE Code C.

(B)   POST-CHARGE QUESTIONING

15.2   Under *section 22 of the Counter-Terrorism Act 2008*, a judge of the Crown Court may authorise the questioning of a person about an offence for which they have been charged, informed that they may be prosecuted or sent for trial, if the offence:

- is a terrorism offence as set out in *section 27 of the Counter-Terrorism Act 2008*; or
- is an offence which appears to the judge to have a terrorist connection. See *Note 15C*.

The decision on whether to apply for such questioning will be based on the needs of the investigation. There is no power to detain a person solely for the purposes of post-charge questioning. A person can only be detained whilst being so questioned (whether at a police station or in prison) if they are already there in lawful custody under some existing power. If at a police station the contents of *sections 8* and *9* of this Code must be considered the minimum standards of treatment for such detainees.

15.3   The Crown Court judge may authorise the questioning if they are satisfied that:

- further questioning is necessary in the interests of justice;
- the investigation for the purposes of which the further questioning is being proposed is being conducted diligently and expeditiously; and
- the questioning would not interfere unduly with the preparation of the person's defence to the charge or any other criminal charge that they may be facing.

See *Note 15E*

15.4   The judge authorising questioning may specify the location of the questioning.

15.5   The judge may only authorise a period up to a maximum of 48 hours before further authorisation must be sought. The 48 hour period would run continuously from the commencement of questioning. This period must include breaks in questioning in accordance with *paragraphs 8.6* and *12.2* of this Code (see *Note 15B*).

15.6   Nothing in this Code shall be taken to prevent a suspect seeking a voluntary interview with the police at any time.

15.7   For the purposes of this section, any reference in *sections 6, 10, 11, 12* and *13* of this Code to:

- 'suspect' means the person in respect of whom an authorisation has been given under *section 22 of the Counter-Terrorism Act 2008* (post-charge questioning of terrorist suspects) to interview them;
- 'interview' means post-charge questioning authorised under section 22 of the Counter-Terrorism Act 2008;
- 'offence' means an offence for which the person has been charged, informed that they may be prosecuted or sent for trial and about which the person is being questioned; and
- 'place of detention' means the location of the questioning specified by the judge (see *paragraph 15.4*),

and the provisions of those sections apply (as appropriate), to such questioning (whether at a police station or in prison) subject to the further modifications in the following paragraphs:

Right to legal advice

15.8   In *section 6* of this Code, for the purposes of post-charge questioning:

- access to a solicitor may not be delayed under Annex B; and
- *paragraph 6.5* (direction that a detainee may only consult a solicitor within the sight and hearing of a qualified officer) does not apply.

Cautions

15.9   In *section 10* of this Code, unless the restriction on drawing adverse inferences from silence applies (see paragraph 15.10), for the purposes of post-charge questioning, the caution must be given in the following terms before any such questions are asked:

"You do not have to say anything. But it may harm your defence if you do not mention when questioned something which you later rely on in Court. Anything you do say may be given in evidence."

Where the use of the Welsh Language is appropriate, a constable may provide the caution directly in Welsh in the following terms:

"Does dim rhaid i chi ddweud dim byd. Ond gall niweidio eich amddiffyniad os na fyddwch chi'n sôn, wrth gael eich holi, am rywbeth y byddwch chi'n dibynnu arno nes ymlaen yn y Llys. Gall unrhyw beth yr ydych yn ei ddweud gael ei roi fel tystiolaeth."

15.10   The only restriction on drawing adverse inferences from silence, see Annex C, applies in those situations where a person has asked for legal advice and is questioned before receiving such advice in accordance with paragraph 6.7(b).

Interviews

15.11   In *section 11*, for the purposes of post-charge questioning, whenever a person is questioned, they must be informed of the offence for which they have been charged or informed that they may be prosecuted, or that they have been sent for trial and about which they are being questioned.

15.12   *Paragraph 11.2* (place where questioning may take place) does not apply to post-charge questioning.

Recording post-charge questioning

15.13   All interviews must be video recorded with sound in accordance with the separate Code of Practice issued under *section 25 of the Counter-Terrorism Act 2008* for the video recording with sound of post-charge questioning authorised under *section 22 of the Counter-Terrorism Act 2008* (see *paragraph 11.8*).

Notes for Guidance

15A   *If a person is detained at a police station for the purposes of post-charge questioning, a custody record must be opened in accordance with section 2 of this Code. The custody record must note the power under which the person is being detained, the time at which the person was transferred into police custody, their time of arrival at the police station and their time of being presented to the custody officer.*

15B   *The custody record must note the time at which the interview process commences. This shall be regarded as the relevant time for any period of questioning in accordance with paragraph 15.5 of this Code.*

15C   *Where reference is made to 'terrorist connection' in paragraph 15.2, this is determined in accordance with section 30 of the Counter-Terrorism Act 2008. Under section 30 of that Act a court must in certain circumstances determine whether an offence has a terrorist connection. These are offences under general criminal law which may be prosecuted in terrorism cases (for example explosives-related offences and conspiracy to murder). An offence has a terrorist connection if the offence is, or takes place in the course of, an act of terrorism or is committed for the purposes of terrorism (section 98 of the Act). Normally the court will make the determination during the sentencing process, however for the purposes of post-charge questioning, a Crown Court Judge must determine whether the offence could have a terrorist connection.*

15D   *The powers under section 22 of the Counter-Terrorism Act 2008 are separate from and additional to the normal questioning procedures within this code. Their overall purpose is to enable the further questioning of a terrorist suspect after charge. They should not therefore be used to replace or circumvent the normal powers for dealing with routine questioning.*

15E   *Post-charge questioning has been created because it is acknowledged that terrorist investigations can be large and complex and that a great deal of evidence can come to light following the charge of a terrorism suspect. This can occur, for instance, from the translation of material or as the result of additional investigation. When considering an application for post-charge questioning, the police must 'satisfy' the judge on all three points under paragraph 15.3. This means that the judge will either authorise or refuse an application on the balance of whether the conditions in paragraph 15.3 are all met. It is important therefore, that when making the application, to consider the following questions:*

- *What further evidence is the questioning expected to provide?*
- *Why was it not possible to obtain this evidence before charge?*
- *How and why was the need to question after charge first recognised?*
- *How is the questioning expected to contribute further to the case?*
- *To what extent could the time and place for further questioning interfere with the preparation of the person's defence (for example if authorisation is sought close to the time of a trial)?*
- *What steps will be taken to minimise any risk that questioning might interfere with the preparation of the person's defence?*

This list is not exhaustive but outlines the type of questions that could be relevant to any asked by a judge in considering an application.

16   Testing persons for the presence of specified Class A drugs

16.1   The provisions for drug testing under *section 63B of PACE* (as amended by *section 5 of the Criminal Justice Act 2003* and *section 7 of the Drugs Act 2005*), do not apply to persons to whom this Code applies. Guidance on these provisions can be found in section 17 of PACE Code C.

ANNEX A   INTIMATE AND STRIP SEARCHES

A   INTIMATE SEARCH

1.   An intimate search consists of the physical examination of a person's body orifices other than the mouth. The intrusive nature of such searches means the actual and potential risks associated with intimate searches must never be underestimated.(a)

Action

2.   Body orifices other than the mouth may be searched if authorised by an officer of inspector rank or above who has reasonable grounds for believing that the person may have concealed on themselves anything which they could and might use to cause physical injury to themselves or others at the station and the officer has reasonable grounds for believing that an intimate search is the only means of removing those items.

3.   Before the search begins, a police officer or designated detention officer, must tell the detainee:

(a)   that the authority to carry out the search has been given;
(b)   the grounds for giving the authorisation and for believing that the article cannot be removed without an intimate search.

4.   An intimate search may only be carried out by a registered medical practitioner or registered nurse, unless an officer of at least inspector rank considers this is not practicable, in which case a police officer may carry out the search. See *Notes A1 to A5.*

5.   Any proposal for a search under *paragraph 2* to be carried out by someone other than a registered medical practitioner or registered nurse must only be considered as a last resort and when the authorising officer is satisfied the risks associated with allowing the item to remain with the detainee outweigh the risks associated with removing it. See *Notes A1 to A5.*

6.   An intimate search at a police station of a juvenile or a vulnerable person may take place only in the presence of an appropriate adult of the same sex (see *Annex l*), unless the detainee specifically requests a particular adult of the opposite sex who is readily available. In the case of a juvenile the search may take place in the absence of the appropriate adult only if the juvenile signifies in the presence of the appropriate adult they do not want the adult present during the search and the adult agrees. A record shall be made of the juvenile's decision and signed by the appropriate adult.

7.   When an intimate search under *paragraph 2* is carried out by a police officer, the officer must be of the same sex as the detainee (see *Annex l*). A minimum of two people, other than the detainee, must be present during the search. Subject to *paragraph 6*, no person of the opposite sex who is not a medical practitioner or nurse shall be present, nor shall anyone whose presence is unnecessary. The search shall be conducted with proper regard to the sensitivity and vulnerability of the detainee.(b)

Documentation

8.   In the case of an intimate search under paragraph 2, the following shall be recorded as soon as practicable, in the detainee's custody record:

- the authorisation to carry out the search;
- the grounds for giving the authorisation;
- the grounds for believing the article could not be removed without an intimate search;
- which parts of the detainee's body were searched;
- who carried out the search;
- who was present;
- the result.

9.   If an intimate search is carried out by a police officer, the reason why it was impracticable for a registered medical practitioner or registered nurse to conduct it must be recorded.

B   STRIP SEARCH

10.   A strip search is a search involving the removal of more than outer clothing. In this Code, outer clothing includes shoes and socks.(a)

Action

11.   A strip search may take place only if it is considered necessary to remove an article which a detainee would not be allowed to keep, and the officer reasonably considers the detainee might have concealed such an article. Strip searches shall not be routinely carried out if there is no reason to consider that articles are concealed.

The conduct of strip searches

12.   When strip searches are conducted:

(a)   a police officer carrying out a strip search must be the same sex as the detainee (see *Annex l*);
(b)   the search shall take place in an area where the detainee cannot be seen by anyone who does not need to be present, nor by a member of the opposite sex (see Annex l) except an appropriate adult who has been specifically requested by the detainee;
(c)   except in cases of urgency, where there is risk of serious harm to the detainee or to others, whenever a strip search involves exposure of intimate body parts, there must be at least two people present other than the detainee, and if the search is of a juvenile or a vulnerable person, one of the people must be the appropriate adult. Except in urgent cases as above, a search of a juvenile may take place in the absence of the appropriate adult only if the juvenile signifies in the presence of the appropriate adult that they do not want the adult to be present during the search and the adult agrees. A record shall be made of the juvenile's decision and signed by the appropriate adult. The presence of more than two people, other than an appropriate adult, shall be permitted only in the most exceptional circumstances;

(d) the search shall be conducted with proper regard to the sensitivity and vulnerability of the detainee in these circumstances and every reasonable effort shall be made to secure the detainee's co-operation and minimise embarrassment. Detainees who are searched shall not normally be required to remove all their clothes at the same time, e.g. a person should be allowed to remove clothing above the waist and redress before removing further clothing;

(e) if necessary to assist the search, the detainee may be required to hold their arms in the air or to stand with their legs apart and bend forward so a visual examination may be made of the genital and anal areas provided no physical contact is made with any body orifice;

(f) if articles are found, the detainee shall be asked to hand them over. If articles are found within any body orifice other than the mouth, and the detainee refuses to hand them over, their removal would constitute an intimate search, which must be carried out as in Part A;

(g) a strip search shall be conducted as quickly as possible, and the detainee allowed to dress as soon as the procedure is complete.

(b)

Documentation

13. A record shall be made on the custody record of a strip search including the reason it was considered necessary, those present and any result.

Notes for Guidance

A1 *Before authorising any intimate search, the authorising officer must make every reasonable effort to persuade the detainee to hand the article over without a search. If the detainee agrees, a registered medical practitioner or registered nurse should whenever possible be asked to assess the risks involved and, if necessary, attend to assist the detainee.*

A2 *If the detainee does not agree to hand the article over without a search, the authorising officer must carefully review all the relevant factors before authorising an intimate search. In particular, the officer must consider whether the grounds for believing an article may be concealed are reasonable.*

A3 *If authority is given for a search under paragraph 2, a registered medical practitioner or registered nurse shall be consulted whenever possible. The presumption should be that the search will be conducted by the registered medical practitioner or registered nurse and the authorising officer must make every reasonable effort to persuade the detainee to allow the medical practitioner or nurse to conduct the search.*

A4 *A constable should only be authorised to carry out a search as a last resort and when all other approaches have failed. In these circumstances, the authorising officer must be satisfied the detainee might use the article for one or more of the purposes in paragraph 2 and the physical injury likely to be caused is sufficiently severe to justify authorising a constable to carry out the search.*

A5 *If an officer has any doubts whether to authorise an intimate search by a constable, the officer should seek advice from an officer of superintendent rank or above.*

Annex B Delay in Notification of Arrest and Whereabouts or Allowing Access to Legal Advice for Persons Detained Under the Terrorism Act 2000.

A DELAYS under TACT Schedule 8

1. The rights as in *sections 5* or *6*, may be delayed if the person is detained under the Terrorism Act 2000, section 41, has not yet been charged with an offence and an officer of superintendent rank or above has reasonable grounds for believing the exercise of either right will have one of the following consequences:

(a) interference with or harm to evidence of a serious offence,

(b) interference with or physical injury to any person,

(c) the alerting of persons who are suspected of having committed a serious offence but who have not been arrested for it,

(d) the hindering of the recovery of property obtained as a result of a serious offence or in respect of which a forfeiture order could be made under section 23,

(e) interference with the gathering of information about the commission, preparation or instigation of acts of terrorism,

(f) the alerting of a person and thereby making it more difficult to prevent an act of terrorism, or

(g) the alerting of a person and thereby making it more difficult to secure a person's apprehension, prosecution or conviction in connection with the commission, preparation or instigation of an act of terrorism.

2. These rights may also be delayed if the officer has reasonable grounds for believing that:

(a) the detained person has benefited from his criminal conduct (to be decided in accordance with Part 2 of the Proceeds of Crime Act 2002), and

(b) the recovery of the value of the property constituting the benefit will be hindered by—
(vi) informing the named person of the detained person's detention (in the case of an authorisation under paragraph 8(1)(a) of Schedule 8 to TACT), or
(vii) the exercise of the right under paragraph 7 (in the case of an authorisation under paragraph 8(1)(b) of Schedule 8 to TACT).

3. Authority to delay a detainee's right to consult privately with a solicitor may be given only if the authorising officer has reasonable grounds to believe the solicitor the detainee wants to consult will, inadvertently or otherwise, pass on a message from the detainee or act in some other way which will have any of the consequences specified under paragraph 8 of Schedule 8 to the Terrorism Act 2000. In these circumstances, the detainee must be allowed to choose another solicitor. See *Note B3.*

4. If the detainee wishes to see a solicitor, access to that solicitor may not be delayed on the grounds they might advise the detainee not to answer questions or the solicitor was initially asked to attend the police station by someone else. In the latter case the detainee must be told the solicitor has come to the police station at another person's request, and must be asked to sign the custody record to signify whether they want to see the solicitor.

5. The fact the grounds for delaying notification of arrest may be satisfied does not automatically mean the grounds for delaying access to legal advice will also be satisfied.

6. These rights may be delayed only for as long as is necessary but not beyond 48 hours from the time of arrest (or if a person was being detained under TACT Schedule 7, from the time at which the examination under Schedule 7 began). If the above grounds cease to apply within this time the detainee must as soon as practicable be asked if they wish to exercise either right, the custody record noted accordingly, and action taken in accordance with the relevant section of this Code.

7. A person must be allowed to consult a solicitor for a reasonable time before any court hearing.

B Documentation

8. The grounds for action under this Annex shall be recorded and the detainee informed of them as soon as practicable.

9. Any reply given by a detainee under paragraph 6 must be recorded and the detainee asked to endorse the record in relation to whether they want to receive legal advice at this point.

C Cautions and special warnings

10. When a suspect detained at a police station is interviewed during any period for which access to legal advice has been delayed under this Annex, the court or jury may not draw adverse inferences from their silence.

Notes for Guidance

B1 *Even if Annex B applies in the case of a juvenile, or a or a vulnerable person, action to inform the appropriate adult and the person responsible for a juvenile's welfare, if that is a different person, must nevertheless be taken as in paragraph 3.15 and 3.17.*

B2 *In the case of Commonwealth citizens and foreign nationals, see Note 7A.*

B3 *A decision to delay access to a specific solicitor is likely to be a rare occurrence and only when it can be shown the suspect is capable of misleading that particular solicitor and there is more than a substantial risk that the suspect will succeed in causing information to be conveyed which will lead to one or more of the specified consequences.*

Annex C Restriction on Drawing Adverse Inferences from Silence and Terms of the Caution When the Restriction Applies

(a) The restriction on drawing adverse inferences from silence

1. The Criminal Justice and Public Order Act 1994, sections 34, 36 and 37 as amended by the Youth Justice and Criminal Evidence Act 1999, section 58 describe the conditions under which adverse inferences may be drawn from a person's failure or refusal to say anything about their involvement in the offence when interviewed, after being charged or informed they may be prosecuted. These provisions are subject to an overriding restriction on the ability of a court or jury to draw adverse inferences from a person's silence. This restriction applies:

(a) to any detainee at a police station who, before being interviewed, see *section 11* or being charged or informed they may be prosecuted, see *section 15*, has:
   (viii) asked for legal advice, see *section 6, paragraph 6.1*;
   (ix) not been allowed an opportunity to consult a solicitor, including the duty solicitor, as in this Code; and
   (x) not changed their mind about wanting legal advice, see *section 6, paragraph 6.7(d)*.
   Note the condition in (ii) will:
   – apply when a detainee who has asked for legal advice is interviewed before speaking to a solicitor as in *section 6, paragraph 6.6(a) or (b)*;
   – not apply if the detained person declines to ask for the duty solicitor, see *section 6, paragraphs 6.7(b) and (c)*.
(b) to any person who has been charged with, or informed they may be prosecuted for, an offence who:
   (xi) has had brought to their notice a written statement made by another person or the content of an interview with another person which relates to that offence, see PACE Code C *section 16, paragraph 16.4*;
   (xii) is interviewed about that offence, see PACE Code C *section 16, paragraph 16.5*; or
   (xiii) makes a written statement about that offence, see *Annex D paragraphs 4 and 9*,
   unless post-charge questioning has been authorised in accordance with section 22 of the Counter-Terrorism Act 2008, in which case the restriction will apply only if the person has asked for legal advice, see *section 6, paragraph 6.1*, and is questioned before receiving such advice in accordance with *paragraph 6.7(b)*. See *paragraph 15.11*.

(b) Terms of the caution when the restriction applies

2. When a requirement to caution arises at a time when the restriction on drawing adverse inferences from silence applies, the caution shall be:

'You do not have to say anything, but anything you do say may be given in evidence.'

Where the use of the Welsh Language is appropriate, the caution may be used directly in Welsh in the following terms:

'Does dim rhaid i chi ddweud dim byd, ond gall unrhyw beth yr ydych chi'n ei ddweud gael ei roi fel tystiolaeth.'

3. Whenever the restriction either begins to apply or ceases to apply after a caution has already been given, the person shall be re-cautioned in the appropriate terms. The changed position on drawing inferences and that the previous caution no longer applies shall also be explained to the detainee in ordinary language. See *Note C1*.

NOTES FOR GUIDANCE

C1 *The following is suggested as a framework to help explain changes in the position on drawing adverse inferences if the restriction on drawing adverse inferences from silence:*

(a) *begins to apply:*

'The caution you were previously given no longer applies. This is because after that caution:
(i) you asked to speak to a solicitor but have not yet been allowed an opportunity to speak to a solicitor. See paragraph 1(a); or
(ii) you have been charged with/informed you may be prosecuted. See paragraph 1(b).

'This means that from now on, adverse inferences cannot be drawn at court and your defence will not be harmed just because you choose to say nothing. Please listen carefully to the caution I am about to give you because it will apply from now on. You will see that it does not say anything about your defence being harmed.'

(b) *ceases to apply before or at the time the person is charged or informed they may be prosecuted, see paragraph 1(a);*

'The caution you were previously given no longer applies. This is because after that caution you have been allowed an opportunity to speak to a solicitor. Please listen carefully to the caution I am about to give you because it will apply from now on. It explains how your defence at court may be affected if you choose to say nothing.'

ANNEX D WRITTEN STATEMENTS UNDER CAUTION

(A) WRITTEN BY A PERSON UNDER CAUTION

1. A person shall always be invited to write down what they want to say.
2. A person who has not been charged with, or informed they may be prosecuted for, any offence to which the statement they want to write relates, shall:

(a) unless the statement is made at a time when the restriction on drawing adverse inferences from silence applies, see Annex C, be asked to write out and sign the following before writing what they want to say:

'I make this statement of my own free will. I understand that I do not have to say anything but that it may harm my defence if I do not mention when questioned something which I later rely on in court. This statement may be given in evidence.';

(b) if the statement is made at a time when the restriction on drawing adverse inferences from silence applies, be asked to write out and sign the following before writing what they want to say;

'I make this statement of my own free will. I understand that I do not have to say anything. This statement may be given in evidence.'

3. When a person, on the occasion of being charged with or informed they may be prosecuted for any offence, asks to make a statement which relates to any such offence and wants to write it they shall:

(a) unless the restriction on drawing adverse inferences from silence, see Annex C, applied when they were so charged or informed they may be prosecuted, be asked to write out and sign the following before writing what they want to say:

'I make this statement of my own free will. I understand that I do not have to say anything but that it may harm my defence if I do not mention when questioned something which I later rely on in court. This statement may be given in evidence.';

(b) if the restriction on drawing adverse inferences from silence applied when they were so charged or informed they may be prosecuted, be asked to write out and sign the following before writing what they want to say:

'I make this statement of my own free will. I understand that I do not have to say anything. This statement may be given in evidence.'

4. When a person who has already been charged with or informed they may be prosecuted for any offence, asks to make a statement which relates to any such offence and wants to write it they shall be asked to write out and sign the following before writing what they want to say:

'I make this statement of my own free will. I understand that I do not have to say anything. This statement may be given in evidence.';

5. Any person writing their own statement shall be allowed to do so without any prompting except a police officer or other police staff may indicate to them which matters are material or question any ambiguity in the statement.

(B) WRITTEN BY A POLICE OFFICER OR OTHER POLICE STAFF

6. If a person says they would like someone to write the statement for them, a police officer, or other police staff shall write the statement.
7. If the person has not been charged with, or informed they may be prosecuted for, any offence to which the statement they want to make relates they shall, before starting, be asked to sign, or make their mark, to the following:

(a) unless the statement is made at a time when the restriction on drawing adverse inferences from silence applies, see Annex C:

'I, ., wish to make a statement. I want someone to write down what I say. I understand that I do not have to say anything but that it may harm my defence if I do not mention when questioned something which I later rely on in court. This statement may be given in evidence.';

(b) if the statement is made at a time when the restriction on drawing adverse inferences from silence applies:

'I, ., wish to make a statement. I want someone to write down what I say. I understand that I do not have to say anything. This statement may be given in evidence.'

8. If, on the occasion of being charged with or informed they may be prosecuted for any offence, the person asks to make a statement which relates to any such offence they shall before starting be asked to sign, or make their mark to, the following:

(a) unless the restriction on drawing adverse inferences from silence applied, see Annex C, when they were so charged or informed they may be prosecuted:

'I, ., wish to make a statement. I want someone to write down what I say. I understand that I do not have to say anything but that it may harm my defence if I do not mention when questioned something which I later rely on in court. This statement may be given in evidence.';

(b) if the restriction on drawing adverse inferences from silence applied when they were so charged or informed they may be prosecuted:

'I, ., wish to make a statement. I want someone to write down what I say. I understand that I do not have to say anything. This statement may be given in evidence.'

9. If, having already been charged with or informed they may be prosecuted for any offence, a person asks to make a statement which relates to any such offence they shall before starting, be asked to sign, or make their mark to:

'I, ., wish to make a statement. I want someone to write down what I say. I understand that I do not have to say anything. This statement may be given in evidence.'

10. The person writing the statement must take down the exact words spoken by the person making it and must not edit or paraphrase it. Any questions that are necessary, e.g. to make it more intelligible, and the answers given must be recorded at the same time on the statement form.

11. When the writing of a statement is finished the person making it shall be asked to read it and to make any corrections, alterations or additions they want. When they have finished reading they shall be asked to write and sign or make their mark on the following certificate at the end of the statement:

'I have read the above statement, and I have been able to correct, alter or add anything I wish. This statement is true. I have made it of my own free will.'

12. If the person making the statement cannot read, or refuses to read it, or to write the above mentioned certificate at the end of it or to sign it, the person taking the statement shall read it to them and ask them if they would like to correct, alter or add anything and to put their signature or make their mark at the end. The person taking the statement shall certify on the statement itself what has occurred.

Annex E Summary of Provisions Relating to Vulnerable Persons

1. If at any time an officer has reason to suspect that a person of any age may be vulnerable (see *paragraph 1.17(d)*), in the absence of clear evidence to dispel that suspicion in the absence of clear evidence to dispel that suspicion, that person shall be treated as such for the purposes of this Code and to establish whether any such reason may exist in relation to a person suspected of committing an offence (see *paragraph 10.1* and *Note 10A*), the custody officer shall take, or cause to be taken (see *paragraph 3.5* and *Note 3I*) the following action:

(a) reasonable enquiries shall be made to ascertain what information is available that is relevant to any of the factors described in *paragraph 1.17(d)* as indicating that the person may be vulnerable might apply;

(b) a record shall be made describing whether any of those factors appear to apply and provide any reason to suspect that the person may be vulnerable or (as the case may be) may not be vulnerable; and

(c) the record mentioned in sub-paragraph (b) shall be made available to be taken into account by police officers, police staff and any others who, in accordance with the provisions of this or any other Code, are required or entitled to communicate with the person in question. This would include any solicitor, appropriate adult and health care professional and is particularly relevant to communication for the purpose of interviewing and questioning after charge (see *sections 11, 12* and *15*), live link interpretation (see *paragraph 13.12*) and reviews and extensions of detention (see *section 14*).

See *Notes 1G, E4, E5* and *E6*.

2. In the case of a person who is vulnerable, ?the appropriate adult' means:

(i) a relative, guardian or other person responsible for their care or custody;

(ii) someone experienced in dealing with vulnerable persons but who is not:
~ a police officer;
~ employed by the police;
~ under the direction or control of the chief officer of a police force;
~ a person who provides services under contractual arrangements (but without being

employed by the chief officer of a police force), to assist that force in relation to the discharge of its chief officer's functions,
    whether or not they are on duty at the time.
(iii) failing these, some other responsible adult aged 18 or over who is other than a person described in the bullet points in sub-paragraph (ii) above.

See *paragraph 1.13(b)* and *Note 1D*
2A The role of the appropriate adult is to safeguard the rights, entitlements and welfare of 'vulnerable persons' (see *paragraph 1*) to whom the provisions of this and any other Code of Practice apply. For this reason, the appropriate adult is expected, amongst other things, to:

- support, advise and assist them when in accordance with this code or any other Code of Practice they are given or asked to provide information or participate in any procedure;
- observe whether the police are acting properly and fairly to respect their rights and entitlements , and inform an officer of the rank of inspector or above if they consider that they are not;
- assist them to communicate with the police whilst respecting their right to say nothing unless they want to as set out in the terms of the caution see *paragraphs 10.5* and *10.5*);
- help them to understand their rights and ensure that those rights are protected and respected.

See *paragraph 1.13A.*
3. If the detention of a person who is vulnerable is authorised by the review officer (see *paragraphs 14.1* and *14.2* and *Notes 14A* and *14B*), the custody officer must as soon as practicable inform the appropriate adult of the grounds for detention and the person's whereabouts, and secure the attendance of the appropriate adult at the police station to see the detainee. If the appropriate adult:

- is already at the station when information is given as in *paragraphs 3.1* to *3.5* the information must be given in their presence;
- is not at the station when the provisions of *paragraph 3.1* to *3.5* are complied with these provisions must be complied with again in their presence once they arrive.

See *paragraphs 3.15* to *3.16*
4. If the appropriate adult, having been informed of the right to legal advice, considers legal advice should be taken, the provisions of *section 6* apply as if the mentally disordered or otherwise mentally vulnerable person had requested access to legal advice. See *paragraphs 3.20, 6.6* and *Note E1.*
5. The custody officer must make sure a person receives appropriate clinical attention as soon as reasonably practicable if the person appears to be suffering from a mental disorder or in urgent cases immediately call the nearest appropriate healthcare professional or an ambulance. See *paragraphs 9.6* and *9.8.* See Code C *paragraphs 9.5* and *9.6* which when a person is detained under the Mental Health Act 1983, sections 135 and 136, as amended by the Policing and Crime Act 2017.
6. If a vulnerable person is cautioned in the absence of the appropriate adult, the caution must be repeated in the appropriate adult's presence. See *paragraph 10.11.*
7. A vulnerable person must not be interviewed or asked to provide or sign a written statement in the absence of the appropriate adult unless the provisions of *paragraphs 11.2* or *11.11* to *11.13* apply. Questioning in these circumstances may not continue in the absence of the appropriate adult once sufficient information to avert the risk has been obtained. A record shall be made of the grounds for any decision to begin an interview in these circumstances. See *paragraphs 11.2, 11.9* and *11.11* to *11.13*
8. If the appropriate adult is present at an interview, they shall be informed they are not expected to act simply as an observer and the purposes of their presence are to:

- advise the interviewee
- observe whether or not the interview is being conducted properly and fairly
- facilitate communication with the interviewee

See *paragraph 11.10*
9. If the custody officer charges a vulnerable person with an offence or takes such other action as is appropriate when there is sufficient evidence for a prosecution this must be carried out in the presence of the appropriate adult if they are at the police station. A copy of the written notice embodying any charge must be given to the appropriate adult. See *PACE Code C Section 16.*
10. An intimate or strip search of a vulnerable person may take place only in the presence of the appropriate adult of the same sex, unless the detainee specifically requests the presence of a particular adult of the opposite sex. A strip search may take place in the absence of an appropriate adult only in cases of urgency when there is a risk of serious harm to the detainee or others. See *Annex A, paragraphs 6* and *12(c)*
11. Particular care must be taken when deciding whether to use any form of approved restraints on a vulnerable person in a locked cell. See *paragraph 8.2*

NOTES FOR GUIDANCE

E1 *The purpose of the provision at paragraph 3.20 and 6.6 is to protect the rights of a mentally disordered or otherwise mentally vulnerable detained person who does not understand the significance of what is said to them. A mentally disordered or otherwise mentally vulnerable detained person should always be given an opportunity, when an appropriate adult is called to the police station, to consult privately with a solicitor in the absence of the appropriate adult if they want.*
E2 *Although vulnerable persons are often capable of providing reliable evidence, they may, without knowing or wanting to do so, be particularly prone in certain circumstances to provide information that may be unreliable, misleading or self-incriminating. Special care should always be taken when questioning such a person, and the appropriate adult should be involved if there is any doubt about a person's mental state or capacity. Because of the risk of unreliable evidence, it is important to obtain corroboration of any facts admitted whenever possible.*

E3 *Because of the risks referred to in Note E2, which the presence of the appropriate adult is intended to minimise, officers of superintendent rank or above should exercise their discretion to authorise the commencement of an interview in the appropriate adult's absence only in exceptional cases, if it is necessary to avert one or more of the specified risks in paragraph 11.2. See paragraphs 11.2 and 11.11 to 11.13.*

E4 *For the purposes of Annex E paragraph 1, examples of relevant information that may be available include:*

- the behaviour of the adult or juvenile;
- the mental health and capacity of the adult or juvenile;
- what the adult or juvenile says about themselves;
- information from relatives and friends of the adult or juvenile;
- information from police officers and staff and from police records;
- information from health and social care (including liaison and diversion services) and other professionals who know, or have had previous contact with, the individual and may be able to contribute to assessing their need for help and support from an appropriate adult. This includes contacts and assessments arranged by the police or at the request of the individual or (as applicable) their appropriate adult or solicitor.

E5 *The Mental Health Act 1983 Code of Practice at page 26 describes the range of clinically recognised conditions which can fall with the meaning of mental disorder for the purpose of paragraph 1.17(d). The Code is published here:*
https://www.gov.uk/government/publications/code-of-practice-mental-health-act-1983.

E6 When a person is under the influence of drink and/or drugs, it is not intended that they are to be treated as vulnerable and requiring an appropriate adult for the purpose of unless other information indicates that any of the factors described in paragraph 1.17(d) may apply to that person. When the person has recovered from the effects of drink and/or drugs, they should be re-assessed in accordance with Annex E paragraph 1.

ANNEX F

– Not used

ANNEX G FITNESS TO BE INTERVIEWED

1. This Annex contains general guidance to help police officers and healthcare professionals assess whether a detainee might be at risk in an interview.

2. A detainee may be at risk in a interview if it is considered that:

(a) conducting the interview could significantly harm the detainee's physical or mental state;

(b) anything the detainee says in the interview about their involvement or suspected involvement in the offence about which they are being interviewed **might** be considered unreliable in subsequent court proceedings because of their physical or mental state.

3. In assessing whether the detainee should be interviewed, the following must be considered:

(a) how the detainee's physical or mental state might affect their ability to understand the nature and purpose of the interview, to comprehend what is being asked and to appreciate the significance of any answers given and make rational decisions about whether they want to say anything;

(b) the extent to which the detainee's replies may be affected by their physical or mental condition rather than representing a rational and accurate explanation of their involvement in the offence;

(c) how the nature of the interview, which could include particularly probing questions, might affect the detainee.

4. It is essential healthcare professionals who are consulted consider the functional ability of the detainee rather than simply relying on a medical diagnosis, e.g. it is possible for a person with severe mental illness to be fit for interview.

5. Healthcare professionals should advise on the need for an appropriate adult to be present, whether reassessment of the person's fitness for interview may be necessary if the interview lasts beyond a specified time, and whether a further specialist opinion may be required.

6. When healthcare professionals identify risks they should be asked to quantify the risks. They should inform the custody officer:

- whether the person's condition:
  ~ is likely to improve;
  ~ will require or be amenable to treatment; and
- indicate how long it may take for such improvement to take effect.

7. The role of the healthcare professional is to consider the risks and advise the custody officer of the outcome of that consideration. The healthcare professional's determination and any advice or recommendations should be made in writing and form part of the custody record.

8. Once the healthcare professional has provided that information, it is a matter for the custody officer to decide whether or not to allow the interview to go ahead and if the interview is to proceed, to determine what safeguards are needed. Nothing prevents safeguards being provided in addition to those required under the Code. An example might be to have an appropriate healthcare professional present during the interview, in addition to an appropriate adult, in order constantly to monitor the person's condition and how it is being affected by the interview.

ANNEX H DETAINED PERSON: OBSERVATION LIST

1. If any detainee fails to meet any of the following criteria, an appropriate healthcare professional or an ambulance must be called.

2. When assessing the level of rousability, consider:

Rousability - can they be woken?

- go into the cell
- call their name
- shake gently

Response to questions - can they give appropriate answers to questions such as:

- What's your name?
- Where do you live?
- Where do you think you are?

Response to commands - can they respond appropriately to commands such as:

- Open your eyes!
- Lift one arm, now the other arm!

3. Remember to take into account the possibility or presence of other illnesses, injury, or mental condition; a person who is drowsy and smells of alcohol may also have the following:

- Diabetes
- Epilepsy
- Head injury
- Drug intoxication or overdose
- Stroke

Annex I Establishing Gender of Persons for the Purpose of Searching

1. Certain provisions of this and other PACE Codes explicitly state that searches and other procedures may only be carried out by, or in the presence of, persons of the same sex as the person subject to the search or other procedure. See *Note I1.*

2. All searches and procedures must be carried out with courtesy, consideration and respect for the person concerned. Police officers should show particular sensitivity when dealing with transgender individuals (including transsexual persons) and transvestite persons (see *Notes I2, I3 and I4*).

(A) Consideration

3. In law, the gender (and accordingly the sex) of an individual is their gender as registered at birth, unless they have been issued with a Gender Recognition Certificate (GRC) under the Gender Recognition Act 2004 (GRA), in which case the person's gender is their acquired gender. This means that if the acquired gender is the male gender, the person's sex becomes that of a man and, if it is the female gender, the person's sex becomes that of a woman) and they must be treated as their acquired gender.

4. When establishing whether the person concerned should be treated as being male or female for the purposes of these searches and procedures, the following approach which is designed to minimise embarrassment and secure the person's co-operation should be followed:

(a) The person must not be asked whether they have a GRC (see *paragraph 8*);

(b) If there is no doubt as to as to whether the person concerned should be treated as being male or female, they should be dealt with as being of that sex.

(c) If at any time (including during the search or carrying out the procedure) there is doubt as to whether the person should be treated, or continue to be treated, as being male or female:

    (i) the person should be asked what gender they consider themselves to be. If they express a preference to be dealt with as a particular gender, they should be asked to indicate and confirm their preference by signing the custody record or, if a custody record has not been opened, the search record or the officer's notebook. Subject to (ii) below, the person should be treated according to their preference;

    (ii) if there are grounds to doubt that the preference in (i) accurately reflects the person's predominant lifestyle, for example, if they ask to be treated as woman but documents and other information make it clear that they live predominantly as a man, or vice versa, they should be treated according to what appears to be their predominant lifestyle and not their stated preference;

    (iii) If the person is unwilling to express a preference as in (i) above, efforts should be made to determine their predominant lifestyle and they should be treated as such. For example, if they appear to live predominantly as a woman, they should be treated as being female; or

    (iv) if none of the above apply, the person should be dealt with according to what reasonably appears to have been their sex as registered at birth.

5. Once a decision has been made about which gender an individual is to be treated as, each officer responsible for the search or procedure should where possible be advised before the search or procedure starts of any doubts as to the person's gender and the person informed that the doubts have been disclosed. This is important so as to maintain the dignity of the person and any officers concerned.

(B) Documentation

6. The person's gender as established under *paragraph 4(c)(i)* to *(iv)* above must be recorded in the person's custody record, or if a custody record has not been opened, on the search record or in the officer's notebook.

7. Where the person elects which gender they consider themselves to be under *paragraph 4(b)(i)* but following *4(b)(ii)* is not treated in accordance with their preference, the reason must be recorded in the search record, in the officer's notebook or, if applicable, in the person's custody record.

(c) Disclosure of information

8.   Section 22 of the GRA defines any information relating to a person's application for a GRC or to a successful applicant's gender before it became their acquired gender as 'protected information'. Nothing in this Annex is to be read as authorising or permitting any police officer or any police staff who has acquired such information when acting in their official capacity to disclose that information to any other person in contravention of the GRA. Disclosure includes making a record of 'protected information' which is read by others.

Notes for Guidance

I1   *Provisions to which paragraph 1 applies include:*

- *In Code C; paragraph 4.1 and Annex A paragraphs 5, 6, 11 and 12 (searches, strip and intimate searches of detainees under sections 54 and 55 of PACE);*
- *In Code A; paragraphs 2.8 and 3.6 and Note 4;*
- *In Code D; paragraph 5.5 and Note 5F (searches, examinations and photographing of detainees under section 54A of PACE) and paragraph 6.9 (taking samples);*
- *In Code H; paragraph 4.1 and Annex A paragraphs 6, 7 and 12 (searches, strip and intimate searches under sections 54 and 55 of PACE of persons arrested under section 41 of the Terrorism Act 2000).*

I2   *While there is no agreed definition of transgender (or trans), it is generally used as an umbrella term to describe people whose gender identity (self-identification as being a woman, man, neither or both) differs from the sex they were registered as at birth. The term includes, but is not limited to, transsexual people.*

I3   *Transsexual means a person who is proposing to undergo, is undergoing or has undergone a process (or part of a process) for the purpose of gender reassignment which is a protected characteristic under the Equality Act 2010 (see paragraph 1.0), by changing physiological or other attributes of their sex. This includes aspects of gender such as dress and title. It would apply to a woman making the transition to being a man and a man making the transition to being a woman, as well as to a person who has only just started out on the process of gender reassignment and to a person who has completed the process. Both would share the characteristic of gender reassignment with each having the characteristics of one sex, but with certain characteristics of the other sex.*

I4   *Transvestite means a person of one gender who dresses in the clothes of a person of the opposite gender. However, a transvestite does not live permanently in the gender opposite to their birth sex.*

I5   *Chief officers are responsible for providing corresponding operational guidance and instructions for the deployment of transgender officers and staff under their direction and control to duties which involve carrying out, or being present at, any of the searches and procedures described in paragraph 1. The guidance and instructions must comply with the Equality Act 2010 and should therefore complement the approach in this Annex.*

Annex J   Transfer of Persons Detained for more than **14 Days to Prison**

1.   When a warrant of further detention is extended or further extended by a High Court judge to authorise a person's detention beyond a period of 14 days from the time of their arrest (or if they were being detained under TACT Schedule 7, from the time at which their examination under Schedule 7 began), the person must be transferred from detention in a police station to detention in a designated prison as soon as is practicable after the warrant is issued, unless:

(a)   the detainee specifically requests to remain in detention at a police station and that request can be accommodated, or

(b)   there are reasonable grounds to believe that transferring the detainee to a prison would:

(i)   significantly hinder a terrorism investigation;

(ii)   delay charging of the detainee or their release from custody, or

(iii) otherwise prevent the investigation from being conducted diligently and expeditiously.

Any grounds in (b)(i) to (iii) above which are relied upon for not transferring the detainee to prison must be presented to the senior judge as part of the application for the extension or further extension of the warrant. See *Note J1.*

2.   If at any time during which a person remains in detention at a police station under the warrant, the grounds at (b)(i) to (iii) cease to apply, the person must be transferred to a prison as soon as practicable.

3.   Police should maintain an agreement with the National Offender Management Service (NOMS) that stipulates named prisons to which individuals may be transferred under this paragraph. This should be made with regard to ensuring detainees are moved to the most suitable prison for the purposes of the investigation and their welfare, and should include provision for the transfer of male, female and juvenile detainees. Police should ensure that the Governor of a prison to which they intend to transfer a detainee is given reasonable notice of this. Where practicable, this should be no later than the point at which a warrant is applied for that would take the period of detention beyond 14 days.

4.   Following a detainee's transfer to a designated prison, their detention will be governed by the terms of Schedule 8 to TACT 2000 and the Prison Rules and this Code of Practice will not apply during any period that the person remains in prison detention. The Code will once more apply if the person is transferred back from prison detention to police detention. In order to enable the Governor to arrange for the production of the detainee back into police custody, police should give notice to the Governor of the relevant prison as soon as possible of any decision to transfer a detainee from prison back to a police station. Any transfer between a prison and a police station should be conducted by police and this Code will be applicable during the period of transit. *See Note 2J.* A detainee should only remain in police custody having been transferred back from a prison, for as long as is necessary for the purpose of the investigation.

5. The investigating team and custody officer should provide as much information as necessary to enable the relevant prison authorities to provide appropriate facilities to detain an individual. This should include, but not be limited to:

(i) medical assessments
(ii) security and risk assessments
(iii) details of the detained person's legal representatives
(iv) details of any individuals from whom the detained person has requested visits, or who have requested to visit the detained person.

6. Where a detainee is to be transferred to prison, the custody officer should inform the detainee's legal adviser beforehand that the transfer is to take place (including the name of the prison). The custody officer should also make all reasonable attempts to inform:

• family or friends who have been informed previously of the detainee's detention; and
• the person who was initially informed of the detainee's detention in accordance with *paragraph 5.1.*

7. Any decision not to transfer a detained person to a designated prison under paragraph *1,* must be recorded, along with the reasons for this decision. If a request under paragraph *1(a)* is not accommodated, the reasons for this should also be recorded.

NOTES FOR GUIDANCE

J1 *Transfer to prison is intended to ensure that individuals who are detained for extended periods of time are held in a place designed for longer periods of detention than police stations. Prison will provide detainees with a greater range of facilities more appropriate to longer detention periods.*

J2 *This Code will only apply as is appropriate to the conditions of detention during the period of transit. There is obviously no requirement to provide such things as bed linen or reading materials for the journey between prison and police station.*

ANNEX K DOCUMENTS AND RECORDS TO BE TRANSLATED

1. For the purposes of Directive 2010/64/EU of the European Parliament and of the Council of 20 October 2010 and this Code, essential documents comprise records required to be made in accordance with this Code which are relevant to decisions to deprive a person of their liberty, to any charge and to any record considered necessary to enable a detainee to defend themselves in criminal proceedings and safeguard the fairness of the proceedings. Passages of essential documents which are not relevant need not be translated. See *Note K1.*

2. The documents considered essential for the purposes of this Code and for which (subject to paragraphs 3 to 7) written translations must be created are the records made in accordance with this Code of the grounds and reasons for any authorisation of a suspects detention under the provisions of the Terrorism Act 2000 or the Counter Terrorism Act 2008 (post-charge questioning) to which this Code applies as they are described and referred to in the suspect's custody record. Translations should be created as soon as practicable after the authorisation has been recorded and provided as soon as practicable thereafter, whilst the person is detained or after they have been released (see *Note K3*). See *paragraphs 13.12* to *13.14* and *Annex L* for application to live-link interpretation.

3. The custody officer may authorise an oral translation or oral summary of the documents to be provided (through an interpreter) instead of a written translation. Such an oral translation or summary may only be provided if it would not prejudice the fairness of the proceedings by in any way adversely affecting or otherwise undermining or limiting the ability of the suspect in question to understand their position and to communicate effectively with police officers, interviewers, solicitors and appropriate adults with regard to their detention and the investigation of the offence in question and to defend themselves in the event of criminal proceedings. The quantity and complexity of the information in the document should always be considered and specific additional consideration given if the suspect is a vulnerable or is a juvenile. The reason for the decision must be recorded (see *paragraph 13.11(e)*).

4. Subject to *paragraphs 5* to *7* below, a suspect may waive their right to a written translation of the essential documents described in the table but only if they do so voluntarily after receiving legal advice or having full knowledge of the consequences and give their unconditional and fully informed consent in writing (see *paragraph 9*).

5. The suspect may be asked if they wish to waive their right to a written translation and before giving their consent, they must be reminded of their right to legal advice and asked whether they wish to speak to a solicitor.

6. No police officer or police staff should do or say anything with the intention of persuading a suspect who is entitled to a written translation of an essential document to waive that right. See *Notes K2 and K3.*

7. For the purpose of the waiver:

(a) the consent of a vulnerable person is only valid if the information about the circumstances under which they can waive the right and the reminder about their right to legal advice mentioned in *paragraphs 3* to *5* and their consent is given in the presence of the appropriate adult, and the appropriate adult also agrees.

(b) the consent of a juvenile is only valid if their parent's or guardian's consent is also obtained unless the juvenile is under 14, when their parent's or guardian's consent is sufficient in its own right and the information and reminder mentioned in *sub paragraph (a)* above and their consent is also given in the presence of the appropriate adult (who may or may not be a parent or guardian).

8. The detainee, their solicitor or appropriate adult may make representations to the custody officer that a document which is not included in the table is essential and that a translation should be provided. The request may be refused if the officer is satisfied that the translation requested is not essential for the purposes described in *paragraph 1* above.

9. If the custody officer has any doubts about:

*   providing an oral translation or summary of an essential document instead of a written translation (see *paragraph 3*);
*   whether the suspect fully understands the consequences of waiving their right to a written translation of an essential document (see *paragraph 4*); or
*   about refusing to provide a translation of a requested document (see *paragraph 7*), the officer should seek advice from an inspector or above.

DOCUMENTATION

10.   Action taken in accordance with this Annex shall be recorded in the detainee's custody record or interview record as appropriate (see *Code H paragraph 13.11(e)*).

NOTE FOR GUIDANCE

K1   *It is not necessary to disclose information in any translation which is capable of undermining or otherwise adversely affecting any investigative processes, for example, by enabling the suspect to fabricate an innocent explanation or to conceal lies from the interviewer.*

K2   *No police officer or police staff shall indicate to any suspect, except to answer a direct question whether the period for which they are liable to be detained, or if not detained, the time taken to complete the interview, might be reduced:*

*   *if they do not ask for legal advice before deciding whether they wish to waive their right to a written translation of an essential document; or*
*   *if they decide to waive their right to a written translation of an essential document.*

K3   *There is no power under TACT to detain a person or to delay their release solely to create and provide a written translation of any essential document.*

ANNEX L   LIVE-LINK INTERPRETATION (PARA. 13.12)

PART 1: WHEN THE PHYSICAL PRESENCE OF THE INTERPRETER IS NOT REQUIRED.

1.   EU Directive 2010/64 (see *paragraph 13.1*), Article 2(6) provides "Where appropriate, communication technology such as videoconferencing, telephone or the Internet may be used, unless the physical presence of the interpreter is required in order to safeguard the fairness of the proceedings." This Article permits, but does not require the use of a live-link, and the following provisions of this Annex determine whether the use of a live-link is appropriate in any particular case.

2.   Decisions in accordance with this Annex that the physical presence of the interpreter is not required and to permit live-link interpretation, must be made on a case by case basis. Each decision must take account of the age, gender and vulnerability of the suspect, the nature and circumstances of the terrorism investigation and the impact on the suspect according to the particular purpose(s) for which the suspect requires the assistance of an interpreter and the time(s) when that assistance is required (see *Note L1*). For this reason, the custody officer must consider whether the ability of the particular suspect, to communicate confidently and effectively for the purpose in question (see *paragraph 3*) is likely to be adversely affected or otherwise undermined or limited if the interpreter is not physically present and live-link interpretation is used. Although a suspect for whom an appropriate adult is required may be more likely to be adversely affected as described, it is important to note that a person who does not require an appropriate adult may also be adversely impacted by the use of live-link interpretation.

3.   Examples of purposes referred to in *paragraph 2* include:

(a)   understanding and appreciating their position having regard to any information given to them, or sought from them, in accordance with this or any other Code of Practice which, in particular, include:
*   the caution (see *paragraphs C10.1* and *10.12*).
*   the special warning (see *paragraphs 10.9* to *10.11*).
*   information about their suspected involvement in the commission, preparation or instigation of acts of terrorism offence (see *paragraphs 10.3, 11.1* and *Note 11ZA*).
*   the grounds and reasons for detention (see *paragraphs 13.10* and *13.10A*).
*   the translation of essential documents (see *paragraph 13.10B* and *Annex L*).
*   their rights and entitlements (see *paragraph 3.14*).
*   intimate and non-intimate searches of detained persons at police stations.
*   provisions and procedures that apply to taking fingerprints, samples and photographs from persons detained for the purposes of a terrorism investigation.
(b)   understanding and seeking clarification from the interviewer of questions asked during an interview that must be video recorded with sound (see *paragraph 7*) and of anything else that is said by the interviewer and answering the questions.
(c)   consulting privately with their solicitor and (if applicable) the appropriate adult (see *paragraphs 3.18, 13.3, 13.6* and *13.9*):
    (i)   to help decide whether to answer questions put to them during interview; and
    (ii)   about any other matter concerning their detention and treatment whilst in custody.
(d)   communicating with practitioners and others who have some formal responsibility for, or an interest in, the health and welfare of the suspect. Particular examples include appropriate healthcare professionals (see *section 9* of this Code) and Independent Custody Visitors.

4.   If the custody officer is satisfied that for a particular purpose as described in *paragraphs 2 and 3 above*, the live-link interpretation *would not* adversely affect or otherwise undermine or limit the suspect's ability to communicate confidently and effectively for *that* purpose, they must so inform the suspect, their solicitor and (if applicable) the appropriate adult. At the same time, the operation of live-link interpretation must be explained and demonstrated to them, they must be advised of the chief officer's obligations concerning the security of live-link communications under *paragraph 13.13* (see *Note L2*) and they must be asked if they wish to make representations that live-link interpretation should not be used or if they require more information about the operation of the

arrangements. They must also be told that at any time live-link interpretation is in use, they may make representations to the custody officer or interviewer that its operation should cease and that the physical presence of an interpreter should be arranged.

When the authority of an inspector is required

5. If representations are made that live-link interpretation should not be used, or that at anytime live-link interpretation is in use, its operation should cease and the physical presence of an interpreter arranged and the custody officer is unable to allay the concerns raised, live-link interpretation may not be used, or (as the case may be) continue to be used, *unless* authorised in writing by an officer of the rank of inspector or above, in accordance with *paragraph 6.*

6. Authority may be given if the officer is satisfied that for the purpose(s) in question at the time an interpreter is required, live-link interpretation is necessary and justified. In making this decision, the officer must have regard to:

(a) the circumstances of the suspect;
(b) the nature and seriousness of the offence;
(c) the requirements of the investigation, including its likely impact on both the suspect and any victim(s);
(d) the representations made by the suspect, their solicitor and (if applicable) the appropriate adult that live-link interpretation should not be used (see *paragraph 5*)
(e) the availability of a suitable interpreter to be *physically* present compared with the availability of a suitable interpreter for live-link interpretation (see *Note L3*); and
(f) the risk if the interpreter is not *physically* present, evidence obtained using link interpretation might be excluded in subsequent criminal proceedings.
(g) the likely impact on the suspect and the investigation of any consequential delay to arrange for the interpreter to be *physically* present with the suspect.

7. The separate Code of Practice that governs the conduct and recording of interviews of persons detained at a police station under section 41 of the Terrorism Act 2000 (TACT) and of persons in respect of whom an authorisation to question after charge has been given under section 22 of the Counter-Terrorism Act 2008 requires those interviews to be video recorded with sound. This will require the visual record to show the live-link interpretation arrangements and the interpreter as seen and experienced by the suspect during the interview (see *Note L4*).

Documentation

8. A record must be made of the actions, decisions, authorisations and outcomes arising from the requirements of this Annex. This includes representations made in accordance with *paragraphs 4* and *7.*

PART 2: MODIFICATIONS FOR LIVE-LINK INTERPRETATION

9. The following modification shall apply for the purposes of live-link interpretation:

(a) **Code H paragraph 13.4:**
For sub-paragraph (b), *substitute*: "A clear legible copy of the complete statement shall be sent without delay via the live-link to the interviewer. The interviewer, after confirming with the suspect that the copy is legible and complete, shall invite the suspect to sign it. The interviewer is responsible for ensuring that that the signed copy and the original record made by the interpreter are retained with the case papers for use in evidence if required and must advise the interpreter of their obligation to keep the original record securely for that purpose.";

(b) **Code of Practice for video recording interviews with sound – paragraph 4.4**
At the beginning of the paragraph *insert*: "Before the interview commences, the operation of live-link interpretation shall be explained and demonstrated to the suspect, their solicitor and appropriate adult, unless it has been previously explained and demonstrated (see Code H Annex L *paragraph 4*)."

(c) **Code for video recording interviews with sound – paragraph 4.22 (signing master recording label)**
After the *third sentence*, insert: "If live-link interpretation has been used, the interviewer should ask the interpreter to observe the removal and sealing of the master recording and to confirm in writing that they have seen it sealed and signed by the interviewer. A clear legible copy of the confirmation signed by the interpreter must be sent via the live-link to the interviewer. The interviewer is responsible for ensuring that the original confirmation and the copy are retained with the case papers for use in evidence if required, and must advise the interpreter of their obligation to keep the original confirmation securely for that purpose."

NOTES FOR GUIDANCE

L1 *For purposes other than an interview, audio-only live-link interpretation, for example by telephone (see Code H paragraph 13.12(b)) may provide an appropriate option until an interpreter is physically present or audio-visual live-link interpretation becomes available. A particular example would be the initial action required when a detained suspect arrives at a police station to inform them of, and to explain, the reasons for their arrest and detention and their various rights and entitlements. Another example would be to inform the suspect by telephone, that an interpreter they will be able to see and hear is being arranged. In these circumstances, telephone live-link interpretation may help to allay the suspect's concerns and contribute to the completion of the risk assessment (see Code H paragraph 3.6).*
L2 *The explanation and demonstration of live-link interpretation is intended to help the suspect, solicitor and appropriate adult make an informed decision on whether to agree to its use and to allay any concerns they may have.*
L3 *Factors affecting availability of a suitable interpreter will include the location of the police station and the language and type of interpretation (oral or sign language) required.*
L4 *The Code of Practice referred to is paragraphs 7 and 9, is available here:* https://www.gov.uk/government/publications/terrorism-act-2000-video-recording-code-of-practice.

The Code contained in this booklet has been issued by the Home Secretary under the Police and Criminal Evidence Act 1984 and has been approved by Parliament.

Copies of the Codes issued under the Police and Criminal Evidence Act 1984 must be readily available in all police stations for consultation by police officers, detained people and members of the public.

PART III
SENTENCING

PRINCIPLES OF SENTENCING

REDUCTION IN SENTENCE FOR A GUILTY PLEA – DEFINITIVE GUIDELINE

3.25 *Create Note to the end of 'C The Approach':* 'This approach must be followed and it is wrong in principle to give credit simply by suspending a sentence of imprisonment: *R v Hussain* [2018] EWCA Crim 780, [2018] 2 Cr App R (S) 12, [2018] Crim L R 770.'

OTHER EXCEPTIONAL, PERSONAL FACTORS

3.31 *Add to existing Note 2:* ', and *R v Stevenson* and *R v Minhas* [2018] EWCA Crim 318, [2018] 2 Cr App R (S) 6.'

SENTENCES AVAILABLE FOR OFFENDERS AGED 18 AND ABOVE

FINES FOR HEALTH AND SAFETY OFFENCES, CORPORATE MANSLAUGHTER AND FOOD SAFETY AND HYGIENE OFFENCES

3.40 *Add text to end in new para and create Note:* 'As to guilty pleas on a basis, see *R (Health and Safety Executive) v ATE Truck and Trailer Sales Ltd*[6]. There is much to be said for sensible agreement between the parties in an area where a specialist prosecution agency is involved. Such sensible agreement is to be encouraged and can be expected to be weighed heavily by any court before departing from it. Ultimately, however, sentencing is the function of the court. The case is also instructive as to the meaning of low likelihood of harm. An absence of accident does not persuasively tell in favour of a low likelihood; everything depends on the circumstances of the case.'

---

[6] [2018] EWCA Crim 752, [2018] 2 Cr App R (S) 29.

FIRE SAFETY CASES

3.41A *Insert new narrative as follows:* 'The following review and guidance was given by Lord Burnett CJ in *Mehmood Butt v Regina*[1]

---

[1] [2018] EWCA Crim 1617.

"The Approach to Sentencing in Fire Safety Cases

There are no sentencing guidelines applicable to fire safety cases. In *R v New Look Retailers Ltd* [2011] 1 Cr App R (S) 57 this court applied to prosecutions under the Order the principles earlier articulated in *R v F Howe & Son (Engineers) Ltd* [1999] 2 Cr App R (S) 37 for cases prosecuted under the 1974 Act. That envisaged that a similar approach to the assessment of harm and culpability would be appropriate and that aggravating and mitigating factors which weighed in health and safety cases would apply in sentencing for breach of the Order. A feature of the offences under the Order with which this appeal is concerned is that the breach must give rise to a risk of death or serious injury. Fire is an especially potent hazard. The products of combustion are capable of overcoming and killing victims quickly or doing them serious harm. The fire itself can do the same. Fire is notoriously unpredictable and can spread far from its seat. It is for these reasons that serious breaches of fire safety regulations have been met with severe penalties.

The parties helpfully placed before the judge a series of decisions of this court which assisted in locating appropriate sentences. *R v Salim Patel* [2015] EWCA Crim 2239 concerned guilty pleas to seven offences under the Order, including failure to comply with an enforcement notice, relating to an hotel. There was a bad history of compliance with fire safety legislation. The mitigation sought to shift responsibility to the hotel manager. The offender received a suspended sentence and a fine of £200,000. *R v Sandhu* [2017] EWCA Crim 908, [2017] 4 WLR 160 concerned another hotel and serious breaches of the order. Once more the mitigation included a suggestion that responsibility for the failures rested with a manager. An immediate custodial sentence was upheld. *R v Takhar* [2014] EWCA Crim 1619 also concerned an hotel with seriously defective fire safety precautions. The eight breaches of the order attracted an immediate custodial sentence.

These cases illustrate the serious nature of breaches of the order and the severe sentences that may be imposed. There is now a guideline for health and safety offences (Definitive Guideline on Health and Safety offences, Corporate Manslaughter and Food Safety and Hygiene Offences) but it does not apply to offences committed contrary to the Order. The Sentencing Council considered whether it should encompass within its scope offences contrary to the Order but decided against. In its response to the consultation on the draft Guideline (November 2015) it said:

'Other offences which were suggested for inclusion included fire safety offences. These were suggested by five respondents, including the London Fire and Emergency Planning Authority. The Council considered the inclusion of these offences, but decided against it. The Council felt that applying the factors in the Guidelines to offences involving risk of fire had the potential for distorting sentence levels.' (Pp 14/15)

The context of that observation was that the distortion of sentencing levels might be upwards. In the *Sandhu* case at paragraph 22 Judge Collier QC, having referred to sections 142 and 143 of the Criminal Justice Act 2003 dealing with the purpose of sentencing, observed that in fire safety cases the Guideline might provide a 'useful check for considering whether a sentence arrived at . . . has produced a sentence which is either unduly lenient or manifestly excessive.' That comment must be seen in the context we have just mentioned. That said, the structure of the Guideline in identifying the steps involved in determining the seriousness of the offending might usefully be followed to cases of this sort . . . .

In prosecutions for a breach of the Order the harm risked will be at the highest level, level A in the Guideline, because of the risk of death or serious injury. The level of culpability will vary depending upon the circumstances of the offending. The likelihood of harm occurring depends upon the chances of fire breaking out. In most cases there will be no evidence of special risk of a fire breaking out, although in some there may be evidence of an enhanced risk. The law imposes a high standard for precautions to guard against the risk of fire. That is not only because of the very serious consequences that can flow from fire but also because it is so unpredictable how and when it will start. The severe penalties evident in cases of the breach of the Order do not depend upon such enhanced risk. Its presence would be a seriously aggravating factor. The two factors referred to in paragraph 9 of the Guideline (risk to many and actual harm) are aggravating features when sentencing for fire safety offences.

In the *Patel* case, as we have seen, a suspended sentence was combined with a substantial fine. A combination of a fine and a suspended or community sentence is available when sentencing. The Definitive Guideline on Offences Taken into Consideration and Totality indicates:

'A fine should not generally be imposed in combination with a custodial sentence because of the effect of imprisonment on the means of the defendant. However, exceptionally, it may be appropriate to impose a fine in addition to a custodial sentence where:

- The sentence is suspended;
- A confiscation order is not contemplated, and
- There is no obvious victim to whom compensation can be awarded; and
- The offender has, or will have, resources from which a fine can be paid.'

It is particularly apt when the offending is related to a defendant's business or employment, when dealing with offenders with substantial means, or when the sentence allows an offender to continue in well-remunerated work. For many, a substantial fine coupled with a suspended sentence or community sentence will be an appropriate punishment. Indeed, there may be cases where a substantial fine would be viewed as a greater punishment by an offender than the other part of the sentence.

'Resources' include both income and capital. Many Guidelines, including the Health and Safety Guideline, identify fines by reference to bands which are calculated by taking a multiple of a defendant's disposable income. Courts will be astute to recognise that income, evidenced by tax returns, when looking at the means of those in business, and especially family businesses, may not tell the whole story. Moreover, the wealth of an offender may be reflected in substantial capital rather than high income.

We would also wish to reiterate the need for defendants in health and safety and similar cases to place detailed evidence of their financial circumstances before the sentencing court. As the Sentencing Council said in the Health and Safety Guideline:

'In setting a fine, the court may conclude that the offender is able to pay any fine imposed unless the offender has supplied financial information to the contrary. It is for the offender to disclose to the court such data relevant to his financial position as will enable it to assess what he can reasonably afford to pay. If necessary, the court may compel disclosure of an individual offender's financial circumstances pursuant to section 162 of the Criminal Justice Act 2003 . In the absence of such disclosure or where the court is not satisfied that it has been given sufficient reliable information, the court will be entitled to draw reasonable inferences as to the offender's means from evidence it has heard and from all the circumstances of the case **which may include the inference that the offender can pay any fine**.' (original emphasis)'

ENFORCEMENT OF COMMUNITY ORDERS

3.56 *Add text to end in new para.* 'The Sentencing Council has issued a definitive guideline for breach offences. This includes a guideline for 'breach of a community order'. This has been included within the Magistrates' Court Sentencing Guidelines, which are reproduced in *Key Materials*.'

Replace the penultimate paragraph with 'The Magistrates' Court Sentencing Guidelines are in *Key Materials*. Any cases dealing with the meaning of terms used within a MCSG are noted here and are marked as 'editorial notes' so that it is clear they have not been inserted by the Sentencing Council.'

IMPRISONMENT

3.67 Early release and licence *Insert text in new para above (d) Early release on home detention curfew* 'The Sentencing Council has issued a definitive guideline for "Breach Offences". This includes a guideline for "breach of post-sentence supervision". This has been included within the Magistrates' Court Sentencing Guidelines, which are reproduced in *Key Materials*.

SUSPENDED PRISON SENTENCES

3.72 (*b*) **Offences committed on or after 4 April 2005** *Insert text in new para after reference to existing Note 3, create Note, renumber subsequent Note accordingly and continue narrative in new para:* 'If a suspended sentence is activated with a reduced term it is not possible to leave the remaining balance of the suspended sentencing hanging over the defendant[4].

---

[4] *R v Bostan* [2018] EWCA Crim 494, [2018] 2 Cr App R (S) 15.

GUIDANCE OF THE SENTENCING COUNCIL ON THE IMPOSITION OF CUSTODIAL SENTENCES

3.75 *Replace this narrative:* 'The Sentencing Council has issued a definitive guideline "Breach Offences". This includes a guideline for "breach of a suspended sentence order". This has been included within the Magistrates' Court Sentencing Guidelines, which are reproduced in *Key Materials*.

COMMITTAL TO THE CROWN COURT FOR SENTENCE OTHER THAN AS A "DANGEROUS OFFENDER"

3.80 *Add text to end in new para:* 'Where a committal for sentence is, on its face, a valid order, it cannot be quashed by the Court Crown; the only means of challenge is by appeal to the High Court[5].'

---

[5] *R (Westminster City Council) v Crown Court at Southwark and others, R (Owadally and another) v Westminster Magistrates' Court* [2017] EWHC 1092 (Admin), [2017] 1 WLR 4350, [2017] 2 Cr App Rep 223, [2017] 2 Cr App R 18, [2017] Crim LR 806, (2017) Times, 22 June; *R v Bahbahani* [2018] EWCA Crim 95, [2018] 2 WLR 1658.

ANCILLARY ORDERS

DEPRIVATION

3.99 *Insert text in a new para after reference to existing Note 1, create note, renumber subsequent Notes accordingly and continue narrative in new para:* 'Where an offender pleaded guilty to an offence of possession of Class A drugs with intent to supply, and £4,600 in cash had been found in his home, and the defendant had sought to provide a legitimate explanation for the existence of the cash, a forfeiture should not have been made without a proper enquiry, including giving the defendant the opportunity to call evidence[2].'

---

[2] *R v Jones* [2017] EWCA Crim 2192, [2018] 1 Cr App R (S) 35.

ANCILLARY ORDERS IMPOSING RESTRICTIONS OR OBLIGATIONS

CRIMINAL BEHAVIOUR ORDERS ON CONVICTION

3.113 **Breach of a CBO** *Add text to end in a new para:* 'The Sentencing Council has issued a definitive guideline "Breach Offences". This includes a guideline for "breach of a criminal behaviour order (also applicable to breach of an anti-social behaviour order". This has been included within the Magistrates' Court Sentencing Guidelines, which are reproduced in *Key Materials*.'

ANCILLARY ORDERS ON CONVICTION OF SEX OFFENDERS

NOTIFICATION REQUIREMENTS

3.116 *Add text to end in new para:* 'The Sentencing Council has issued a definitive guideline "Breach Offences". This includes a guideline for "Fail to comply with notification requirements". This has been included within the Magistrates' Court Sentencing Guidelines, which are reproduced in *Key Materials*.

SEXUAL HARM PREVENTION ORDER

3.118 **Orders on conviction** *In the list ending (9) insert the following new para*: 'In *R v Parsons*; *R v Morgan* [2017] EWCA Crim 2163, [2018] 1 Cr App R (S) 43, confirmed that the guidance given in Smith remained, in general, essentially sound and should continue to be followed. In certain specific areas, developments in technology and changes in everyday living called for an adapted and targeted approach. That was so especially in relation to risk-management monitoring software, cloud storage and encryption software.'

Replace the citation of R v McLellan before Crim L R citation: '[2017] EWCA Crim 1464, [2018] 1 WLR 2969, [2018] 1 Cr App R (S) 18, [2018] Crim L R 91'

3.123 Breach *Add text to end in new para:* 'The Sentencing Council has issued a definitive guideline "Breach Offences". This includes a guideline for "breach of asexual harm prevention order (also applicable to breach of a sexual offences prevention order and to breach of a foreign travel order)". This has been included within the Magistrates' Court Sentencing Guidelines, which are reproduced in *Key Materials*.'

SENTENCING GUIDELINES AND EXAMPLES OF SENTENCING FOR PARTICULAR OFFENCES

OFFENCES UNDER THE PUBLIC ORDER ACT 1986

3.131 *Delete paras 3.131–3.135.*

DRUGS OFFENCES

3.147 Examples of sentencing decisions applying the guidelines in cases within or near to the powers of magistrates' courts *Add text to end in new para and create note:* '*Possession with intent to supply psychoactive substances* The sentencing guidelines for drug offences do not cover offences under the Psychoactive Substances Act 2016. Therefore, the guideline is not "relevant" within the meaning of s 125(1) of the Coroners and Justice Act 2009. Nevertheless, it is relevant in a broader sense when sentencing for a similar offence (in the present case the substance was a cannaboid and the offender was also charged with a separate offence of possession of cannabis with intent to supply committed four months later, and both cases fell within 'street dealing'). Therefore, the court should have regard to the guidelines and impose a sentence which reflected the drug and factual situation in the guidelines representing the closest approximation to the facts before the court. Here, the closest comparable offence was street dealing of cannabis[11].'

[11] *R v Waka (Mohammed Hussain)* [2018] EWCA Crim 125, [2018] 1 Cr App R (S) 54 (the offender was 19 at the time of sentencing and of good character, the sentence of 16 months' detention for the 2016 Act offence was reduced to seven months on the basis of a starting point of 11 months and a full reduction for the guilty pleas, bringing the total sentence down to 15 months' detention).

NON-FATAL OFFENCES OF BAD DRIVING, ETC

3.149 Causing serious injury by dangerous driving *Insert text in new para at the end and create Note:* 'In *R v Mcall*[3] the defendant (M) was a serving police officer responding to an emergency call. He drove through a red light and was driving at 74 mph when he struck another vehicle at a place where the speed limit was 40 mph. The judge accepted that, while it was dangerous to drive at such an excess speed, M was entitled to do so in an emergency, but to drive through a red light was dangerous. M pleaded guilty on the day of trial and was sentenced to suspended sentence of 15 months' imprisonment and disqualified for three years (the judge rejected a submission of "special reasons" for not imposing disqualification). He was also ordered to pay costs of £6,969.08.

The Court of Appeal rejected the submission that emergency responders convicted of offences of this kind should not go to prison as a matter of law. However, there was weighty mitigation and the term was reduced to six months, suspended for the same period. The judge had been entitled to reject the submission of special reasons, but there had been no justification for increasing the minimum period of two years and this term was substituted. The order for costs was also manifestly excessive in the circumstances and a sum of £1,800 was substituted.

[3] [2017] EWCA Crim 2024, [2018] Cr App R (S) 32.

3.153 Drug Driving – driving or being in charge of a motor vehicle with concentration of specified drug above specified limit *Replace all the narrative after the title with the following text:* 'Interim sentencing guidance has been given by the Sentencing Council. This has been included within the Magistrates' Court Sentencing Guidelines, which are reproduced in *Key Materials*.'

OTHER OFFENCES

3.159 *Add to paragraph on Breach of Fire Safety Laws after reference to exisitng Note 78 as follows:* 'In *R v Butt (Mehmood)* [2018] EWCA Crim 1617 it was stated that although there were no applicable sentencing guidelines, a similar approach to the assessment of harm and culpability would be appropriate and that aggravating and mitigating factors which weighed in health and safety cases would apply in sentencing for breach of the Regulatory Reform (Fire Safety) Order 2005. Fire gave rise to a risk of death or serious injury. Serious breaches of fire safety regulations had been met with severe penalties. The structure of that guideline for Health and Safety Offences could usefully be followed in such cases.'

Breach of an anti-social behaviour order

3.160 *After the introductory sentence above the guideline insert text:* 'The Magistrates' Court Sentencing Guideline for breach of a criminal behaviour order is also applicable to breach of an anti-social behaviour order, and this will be found in Magistrates' Court Sentencing Guidelines, which are reproduced in *Key Materials*.'

Breach of protective orders

3.162 *Insert text at the beginning and continue the narrative in a new para:* 'The magistrates' court sentencing guideline "Breach of a protective order (restraining and non-molestation orders)" is reproduced in *Key Materials*.'

3.165 **Breach of a notification requirement made under the Sexual Offences Act 2003** *Insert text at the beginning and continue the narrative in a new para:* 'The magistrates' court sentencing guideline "Fail to comply with notification requirements" is reproduced in *Key Materials*.'

Breach of other orders

3.166 **Sexual offences prevention orders** *Insert text at the beginning and continue the narrative in a new para:* 'The magistrates' court sentencing guideline "Breach of a sexual harm prevention order (also applicable to breach of a sexual offences prevention order and to breach of a foreign travel order)" is reproduced in *Key Materials*.'

STATUTES ON SENTENCING

Statutes

3.320 **Powers of Criminal Courts (Sentencing) Act 2000, s 91** *In existing Note 1 delete the text after 'para 5.84, post'.*

Delete Note marker 2 and the Note.

3.384 **Proceeds of Crime Act 2002, s 6** At the end of Note 1 add the following: 'In *R v McCool(Donna) R v Harkin (Michael)* [2018] UKSC 23; [2018] 1 WLR 2431; [2018] Crim LR 766. The Supreme Court interpreted the Proceeds of Crime Act 2002 (Commencement No 5, Transitional Provisions, Savings and Amendment) Order 2003, art.4(1). It had not been Parliament's intention that, if any of the offences on which a defendant had been committed pre-dated 24 March 2003, none of the offences, not even those committed after that date, could be treated as candidates for confiscation orders under the Proceeds of Crime Act 2002, s 156.'.

3.384 *Create Note to 'disproportionate' in s 6(5) and renumber subsequent Notes accordingly:* '[7] This amendment of s 6(5) to introduce the proportionality qualification was made in consequence of the decision in *Waya* [2012] UKSC 51; [2013] 1 AC 294; [2013] 2 Cr App (S) 20. This is to be contrasted with the qualification of the criminal lifestyle assumptions in s 10(6) of "serious risk of injustice". "Proportionality" is an even more limited restriction on the decision-making process than a general duty to avoid a serious risk of injustice. In this context it means that the order must be proportionate to the achievement of the statutory aim which is the recovery of the amount which the defendant had obtained from crime, and in almost all cases an order made in accordance with the provisions of the Act will satisfy that test. There may be exceptional cases where the court is satisfied that making an order will not recover proceeds of crime and will simply lead to a sentence of imprisonment which the defendant can do nothing about, but protestations should be treated with scepticism and the court should require the clearest, most complete and unassailable evidence before avoiding the usual statutory duty on the ground of proportionality: *R v Box* [2018] EWCA Crim 543, [2018] Crim L R 581.'

3.393 **Proceeds of Crime Act 2002, s 13A** *Add new Note to the end after 'order' as follows:* '[2] Guidance on the correct approach to making a compliance order with a travel restriction component under the Proceeds of Crime Act 2002 s.13A in *Rv Pritchard (John)* [2017] EWCA Crim 1267; [2018] 1 WLR. 1631; [2017] 2 Cr App. R (S.) 54; [2017] Lloyd's Rep. F.C. 590; [2017] Crim. L.R. 993.

3.404 **Proceeds of Crime Act 2002, s 22** *Add to existing Note 2 in new para:* 'As to the approach to re-assessment to be adopted following the decision in *R v Waya* [2012] UKSC 51, [2013] 1 AC, see *R v Cole* [2018] EWCA Crim 888, [2018] Lloyd's Rep FC 321.'

3.469 **Proceeds of Crime Act 2002, s 78** *Create Note to 'consideration' in s 78(1) and renumber subsequent Note accordingly* '[1] Any consideration which is asserted to have been provided must be capable of being ascribed a value in monetary terms in a way which can be utilised in accordance with the mathematical approach stipulated in s 78(2; non-financial considerations, such as providing the services of a wife and mother, are not, therefore, to be taken into account: *R v Hayes* [2018] EWCA Crim 682, [2018] 2 Cr App R (S) 27, [2018] Crim L R 586.'

3.748 **Criminal Justice Act 2003, s 226A**   *Create Note to the end of s 226A(8)* '[1] The limitations on licence periods apply to individual offences only and it is permissible to imposed consecutive sentences where the effect is to impose a licence period in excess of the prescribed periods: *R v Thompson (Christopher)*; *R v Cummings (Tajsham)*; *R v Fitzgerald (Oscar)*; *R v Ford (Richard)* [2018] EWCA Crim 639, [2018] Crim L R 593.'

PART IV
ROAD TRAFFIC

VEHICLES AND ROADS

Vehicles and roads to which the Acts apply

4.3   Vehicles to which the Road Traffic Act 1988 apply   *In the third para replace the text from the start of the para until 'despite its licensing as a works truck.' with the following new material* '"Intended or adapted for use on roads"-The test of whether a vehicle is "intended or adapted for use on roads" is whether a reasonable person, looking at the vehicle, and forming a view as to its general user, would say the vehicle might well be used on the road: *Chief Constable of Avon and Somerset v Fleming* [1987] 1 All ER 318, [1987] RTR 378.

The burden of proving that a vehicle is intended or adapted for use on roads is on the prosecution: *Reader v Bunyard* [1987] RTR 406, [1987] Crim LR 274. In *Macdonald v Carmichael* 1941 JC 27, 106 JP Jo 53 (considered in *McCrone v J & L Rigby (Wigan) Ltd* [1951] 2 TLR 911), it was held that in the circumstances of the case a diesel "dumper" was not intended or adapted for use on roads and was therefore not a "motor vehicle". It has been held in the absence of evidence supporting the contrary view, that a "dumper" used in the manner described in the case, was not "intended to be used on a road": Daley v Hargreaves [1961] 1 All ER 552, 125 JP 193. However, a 30-ton earth mover which because of its size was not transportable and had to move from site to site under its own power was held to be intended to be used on roads: *Childs v Coghlan* (1968) 112 Sol Jo 175. See also *Lewington v Motor Insurers' Bureau* [2017] EWHC 2848 (Comm), [2018] RTR 18, in which a dumper was held to be "intended or adapted for use on roads". The case was concerned with the compulsory insurance requirements of Part VI of the RTA 1988, where a purposive approach is required to ensure compatibility with EU law. See further *Percy v Smith* [1986] RTR 252 in which a fork lift truck was in the circumstances of the case "intended for use on roads", despite its licensing as a works truck.

In *Burns v Currell* [1963] 2 QB 433, [1963] 2 All ER 297, 127 JP 397, it was held that a Go-Kart was not "intended or adapted for use on roads".'

STATUTES ON ROAD TRAFFIC

Statutes

4.237   Road Traffic Act 1988, s 5   *Note 8 on a new line add* 'In *R (Hassani) v West London Magistrates' Court* [2017] EWHC 1270 (Admin), 181 JP 253, [2017] Crim LR 720 the Administrative Court emphasises the need for firm case management and states that this judgment is an intentional reminder to criminal courts that active case management using the Criminal Procedure Rules is their duty. Increased rigour and firmness is needed. This judgment should be cited by counsel and solicitors acting in motoring cases, for the prosecution or defence, when appropriate and it will be the professional obligation of those with the conduct of such cases, to cite this judgment when issues of adjournment or case management arise, and legal advisers to magistrates to draw this judgment to the attention of the Court and the parties when applications arise. The Administrative Court made the following points:

(1)   The criminal law is not a game to be played in the hope of a lucky outcome, a game to be played as long and in as involved a fashion as the paying client is able or prepared to afford.

(2)   Courts must practise firm case management and must consider the Criminal Procedure Rules, which are there to be employed actively so as to preclude game-playing and ensure that the courts only have to address real issues with some substance.

(3)   The Criminal Procedure Rules provisions most in question might be thought to be as follows. Each participant in a criminal case, that is to say lawyers as well as parties, must prepare and conduct their care in accordance with the rules: see CPR 1.2(1)(a) and (b). The key objective under the rules is to deal fairly with the case, and that includes dealing with the case efficiently and expeditiously: CPR 1.1(2)(e). Time wasting, extension of hearings and taking hopeless points in the hope of wearing down an opponent or the court are neither proper nor legitimate ways in which to conduct a case, for a party or for a party's lawyers. Courts must be aware of such behaviour and employ firm case management to prevent it.

(4) Each participant in a case has the obligation set out in CPR 1.2(1)(c): "At once inform the court and all parties of any significant failure (whether or not that participant is responsible for that failure) to take any procedural step required by these Rules, any practice direction or any direction of the court. A failure is significant if it might hinder the court in furthering the overriding objective."

(5) For example, if defence lawyers consider that a document is missing or service of a document has not taken place, their obligation is to say so early. Not to say so early may hinder the overriding objective because it is likely to cause an adjournment which could be avoided, and thus prevent the case being decided "efficiently and expeditiously". If the defence are going to suggest that some document or some piece of service is missing, they must do so early. If they do not, then it is open to the court to find that the point was raised late, and any direction then sought to produce a document or to apply for an adjournment may properly be refused.

(6) Critical rules affecting all parties, including defendants and their representatives, are rules 3.2, 3.3 and 3.11. The attention of a court dealing with such cases should be drawn to those rules and perhaps in particular to 3.2(2)(a) - active case management includes the early identification of the real issues; 3.3(1) – each party must (a) actively assist the court in fulfilling its duty under rule 3.2, with, or if necessary without, a direction and (b) apply for a direction if needed to further the overriding objective; 3.3(2) active assistance for the purposes of this rule includes (a) at the beginning of the case communication between the prosecutor and the defendant at the first available opportunity; (c)(ii) what is agreed and what is likely to be disputed (in other words, what is agreed and what is likely to be disputed should be the subject of active assistance and early communication); (c) (iii) likewise, what information or other material is required by one party of another and why; and (iv) what is to be done, by whom and when. CPR 3.11: in order to manage a trial or an appeal, the court (a) must establish with the active assistance of the parties what are the disputed issues; and (d) may limit (i) the examination, cross-examination or re-examination of a witness and (ii) the duration of any stage of the hearing.

The court went on to consider challenges to the reliability of the machine. This is considered further in the note to s 15 of the Road Traffic Offenders Act 1988 at para 4.447.

4.258 Road Traffic Act 1988, s 7 *Note 11, replace the All ER (D) citation of DPP v Cramp with:* ', [2018] Crim L R 406'.

Note 22, replace the All ER (D) citation of Miller v DPP with: '[2018] RTR 19'.

Note 22, replace the All ER (D) citation of DPP v Cramp with: '[2018] Crim L R 406'.

4.366 Road Traffic Act 1988, s 103 *Delete the first sentence of existing Note 2.*

4.399 Road Traffic Act 1988, s 143 *Section 143 of the RTA 1988 is prospectively amended by the Automated and Electric Vehicles Act 2018, Sch 1.*

4.400 Road Traffic Act 1988, s 144 *Section 144 of the RTA 1988 is prospectively amended by the Automated and Electric Vehicles Act 2018, Sch 1.*

4.405 Road Traffic Act 1988, s 145 *In existing Note 1, replace the WLR (D) citation with* '[2018] 1 WLR 1293, [2018] RTR 21'

4.427 Road Traffic Act 1988, s 172 *in Note 6 after the third para insert the following new para* 'In *Lord Howard of Lympe v DPP* [2018] EWHC 100, [2018] Crim L R 489 the appellant filled in Part 1 of the form, apart from the driver licence number, but struck through the words 'I was the driver at the time shown overleaf', adding in manuscript 'The driver was my wife or myself. We don't know which.' The District Judge convicted the appellant on the basis that, though he had made reference to his wife, he had not given the required information as to her full name and address, which he could have given in Part 2 of the form. In the light of this failure the Judge did not proceed to consider the defence of reasonable diligence (see below). The appeal was brought on the ground that the appellant had complied with the form. The choice it presented was to fill in Part 1 if the keeper was the driver, or Part 2 if the driver was somebody else. In the present case the appellant did not know who the driver was. The Administrative Court agreed that the offence was not committed by failing to fill out the form correctly. The form required him to name the driver and not, in the alternative, to provide any other information which may have led to the identification of the driver (the accompanying letter referred to this, but the form provided no space for this). By not naming the driver the appellant had committed an offence under s 172(3), but this was subject to the reasonable diligence defence under s 172(4), which the District Judge had wrongly failed to consider.'

4.428 Road Traffic Act 1988, s 173 *Section 173(2)(g) should be marked 'prospectively inserted by the Road Safety Act 1006, s 37, Sch 6'.*

STATUTORY INSTRUMENTS ON ROAD TRAFFIC

Statutory Instruments

4.1474 Road Vehicles (Construction and Use) Regulations 1986, reg 110 *Note amendments made by SI 2018/592.*

4.1667 Road Vehicles (Special Types) Order 2003 *After the Road Vehicles (Special Types) Order 2003, insert text and Note as follows:*

4.1667A 'The Road Vehicles (Defeat Devices, Fuel Economy and Type-Approval) (Amendment) Regulations 2018 These Regulations (not reproduced in this work) insert provisions in the Road Vehicles (Approval) Regulations 2009, SI 2009/717, the Agricultural and Forestry Vehicles (Type-Approval) Regulations 2018, SI 2018/236, and the Motorcycles (Type-Approval) Regulations 2018, SI 2018/235. While the amended regulations are not reproduced in this work, the following amendments concern fitted devices designed to defeat emission tests and are noted here:

(a) Regulation 16 inserts new regs 33A and 33B into the 2009 Regulations to provide for an offence of placing on the market or registering a vehicle that is fitted with a defeat system. A new Schedule 7 to the 2009 Regulations is inserted to provide that the offence in the new regulation 33A is to be punishable by either criminal or civil penalties and to make provision for enforcement (including in connection with false statements and obstruction of officers, powers of search, detention of goods by customs officers and recovery of expenses of enforcement).

(b) Part 7 amends the Motorcycle Regulations. In particular, reg 19 inserts a new reg 14A to support the existing prohibition on use of defeat devices found in Regulation (EU) No 168/2013 of the European Parliament and of the Council on the approval and market surveillance of two- or three-wheel vehicles and quadricycles. Regulation 20 makes amendments to Schedule 1 of the Motorcycles Regulations, inter alia, to correct the maximum period of imprisonment for an offence under those Regulations.

(c) Part 8 amends the AFV Regulations in a similar manner to the amendments in Part 7. In particular, reg 21 inserts a new reg 14A to support the existing prohibition on use of defeat devices found in Regulation (EU) No 167/2013 of the European Parliament and of the Council on the approval and market surveillance of agricultural and forestry vehicles. Regulation 22 makes similar amendments to Sch 1 of the AFV Regulations to those in reg 20 which amend the Motorcycles Regulations. Regulation 23 makes a further correcting amendment to Sch 2 of the AFV Regulations to insert a provision making a consequential amendment to the Motor Fuel (Composition and Content) Regulations 1999.

4.1711 Motor Vehicles (Driving Licences) Regulations 1999 *SI 2018/784 amends the Motor Vehicles (Driving Licences) Regulations 1999 to allow the holder of a category B licence to drive alternatively fuelled vehicles with a maximum authorised mass which exceeds 3,500 kilograms, up to a maximum authorised mass of 4,250 kilograms provided that person has undertaken five hours of training on the driving of an alternatively fuelled vehicle with a maximum authorised mass exceeding 3,500 kilograms with an instructor on the National Register of LGV Instructors or the National Vocational Driving Instructors Register.*

PART V
YOUTH COURTS

GENERAL PROVISIONS

REMANDS TO YOUTH DETENTION ACCOMMODATION

5.47 *After this para insert a new heading and para 5.47A as follows:*

5.47A **'Credit for time on remand in youth detention accommodation** Time spent on remand in youth detention accommodation is automatically deducted from a sentence of detention imposed under s 91 of the Powers of Criminal Courts (Sentencing) Act 2000[1]. Time spent on remand in local authority accommodation does not count towards such a sentence.

Anomalously, where an offender is remanded on bail with a qualifying electronic curfew, half of that time will automatically be credited to a sentence of detention under s 91, but this is not the case where an offender is remanded to local authority accommodation with an electronic curfew provision. In the latter case, the court should, therefore, correct the anomaly by making an appropriate reduction to the sentence[2].

The same anomaly applies to detention and training orders. Time spent on a qualifying remand is not automatically credited, but s 101(8) of the PCC(S)A 2000 provides that in determining the term of a detention for an offence the court shall take into account any period of remand in custody and any period on bail subject to a qualifying curfew condition. "Custody" includes police detention, remands in or committed to custody by an order of a court, remands to youth detention accommodation and remands, admission removal to hospital under certain provisions of the Mental Health Act 1983, but not remands to local authority accommodation[3].'

---

[1] By virtue of the Criminal Justice Act 2003, ss 240ZA and 242, in PART III, SENTENCING, ante.
[2] Criminal Justice Act 2003, 240A. *R v Anderson* [2017] EWCA Crim 2604, [2018] 2 Cr App R (S) 21.
[3] Powers of Criminal Courts (Sentencing) Act 2000, s 101(8), (11), (12).

DETENTION AND TRAINING ORDER

5.80 *Replace the para which ends with reference to existing Note 17 as follows:* 'Time spent on a qualifying remand is not automatically credited, but in determining the term of a detention for an offence the court shall take into account any period of remand in custody and any period on bail subject to a qualifying curfew condition. 'Custody' includes police detention, remands in or committed to custody by an order of a court, remands to youth detention accommodation and remands, admission removal to hospital under certain provisions of the Mental Health Act 1983, but not remands to local authority accommodation[17].'

---

[17] Powers of Criminal Courts (Sentencing) Act 2000, s 101(8), (11), (12), in PART III, SENTENCING, ante.

STATUTES ON YOUTH COURTS

STATUTES ON YOUTH COURTS

5.259 **Legal Aid, Sentencing and Punishment of Offenders Act 2012, s 103** *In Note 1 add to the list of amending SIs:* 'and SI 2018/498'.

PART VI
TRANSPORT

TRANSPORT

AVIATION

6.16   Civil Aviation Act 1982, s 71   *In Note 1 add to the list of amending SIs:* 'and 2018/670'.

6.17   Civil Aviation Act 1982, s 72   *After 2007/2999 insert* ', amended by SI 2018/784,'.

HIGHWAYS

6.376   Highways Act 1980, 137   Insert at the end of Note 3 in a new para: '*Buchanan v CPS* [2018] EWHC 1773 (Admin) held that the Court had been right to uphold a protester's conviction for obstructing the highway after he had blocked traffic on a busy road in Parliament Square in London. The obstruction was not de minimis, having lasted for five minutes. His use of the highway was unreasonable and without lawful excuse. His arrest and prosecution had constituted a necessary interference with his ECHR art.10 and art.11 rights in the interests of public safety and the protection of the rights and freedoms of others.'

RAILWAYS AND TRAMWAYS

6.809   European Communities Act 1972: regulations   *Replace the first bullet point with the following:* 'The Cableway Installations Regulations 2018, SI 2018/816'.

PART VII
OFFENCES, MATTERS OF COMPLAINT, ETC

ANIMALS

7.422 Animal Welfare Act 2006, s 13 *Add to the list of SIs in existing Note 1:* 'and the Animal Welfare (Licensing of Activities Involving Animals) (England) Regulations 2018, SI 2018/486. The latter introduce an updated licensing system in England for: selling animals as pets; providing for or arranging for the provision of boarding for cats or dogs; hiring out horses; dog breeding; and keeping or training animals for exhibition. The regulations are reproduced at 7.536A, post.'

7.442 Animal Welfare Act 2006, s 34 *Create Note to the end of s 34(10):* '[4] Section 34 also applies to an offence under reg 20 of the Animal Welfare (Licensing of Activities Involving Animals) (England) Regulations 2018, SI 2018/486, reproduced at 7.536A, post.'

7.450 Animal Welfare Act 2006, s 42 *CREATE Note to '13(6)' in s 42(1):* '[1] Section 42 also applies to an offence under reg 20 of the Animal Welfare (Licensing of Activities Involving Animals) (England) Regulations 2018, SI 2018/486, reproduced at 7.536A, post.'

7.536 Non-Commercial Movement of Pet Animals Order 2011 *After the Non-Commercial Movement of Pet Animals Order 2011 reproduce the Animal Welfare (Licensing of Activities Involving Animals) (England) Regulations 2018, SI 2018/486 as follows:*

Animal Welfare (Licensing of Activities Involving Animals) (England) Regulations 2018
(SI 2018/486)

PART 1 INTRODUCTION

7.536A *1. Title, commencement and application* (1) These Regulations—
(a) may be cited as the Animal Welfare (Licensing of Activities Involving Animals) (England) Regulations 2018;
(b) come into force on 1st October 2018.
(2) The following provisions of these Regulations apply in England only—
(a) regulations 2 to 24,
(b) regulations 27 to 29, and
(c) Schedules 1 to 8.

2. Interpretation In these Regulations—
"the Act" means the Animal Welfare Act 2006;
"adult dog" means a dog aged 6 months or more;
"general conditions" means the conditions set out in Schedule 2;
"horse" includes an ass, mule or hinny;
"licence", except as the context otherwise requires in regulation 11(1)(b) and Schedule 8 or where more specifically provided, means a licence to carry on a licensable activity granted or renewed under these Regulations and cognate expressions are to be construed accordingly;
"licence conditions" means—
    (a) the general conditions, and
    (b) the relevant specific conditions;
"licensable activity" means an activity described in paragraph 2, 4, 6, 8 or 10 of Schedule 1;
"listed" means for the time being listed as authorised to carry out an inspection on the list of veterinarians drawn up by the Royal College of Veterinary Surgeons;
"local authority" means—
    (a) a district council,
    (b) a London borough council,
    (c) the Common Council of the City of London (in their capacity as a local authority),
    (d) the Council of the Isles of Scilly, or
    (e) a combined authority in England established under section 103 of the Local Democracy, Economic Development and Construction Act 2009;
"operator" means an individual who—
    (a) carries on, attempts to carry on or knowingly allows to be carried on a licensable activity, or
    (b) where a licence has been granted or renewed, is the licence holder;

"pet" means an animal mainly or permanently, or intended to be mainly or permanently, kept by a person for—

    (a)   personal interest,

    (b)   companionship,

    (c)   ornamental purposes, or

    (d)   any combination of (a) to (c).

"puppy" means a dog aged less than 6 months;

"relevant specific conditions" means—

    (a)   in relation to the activity of selling animals as pets (or with a view to their being later resold as pets) as described in paragraph 2 of Schedule 1, the conditions set out in Schedule 3;

    (b)   in relation to the activity of providing or arranging for the provision of boarding for cats or dogs as described in paragraph 4 of Schedule 1, the conditions set out in the relevant Part of Schedule 4;

    (c)   in relation to the activity of hiring out horses as described in paragraph 6 of Schedule 1, the conditions set out in Schedule 5;

    (d)   in relation to the activity of breeding dogs as described in paragraph 8 of Schedule 1, the conditions set out in Schedule 6;

    (e)   in relation to the activity of keeping or training animals for exhibition as described in paragraph 10 of Schedule 1, the conditions set out in Schedule 7;

"sleeping area" means a fully-enclosed indoor area in which a dog, or, in the context of Part 1 of Schedule 4, a cat, can rest, sleep or avoid seeing other people or animals;

"veterinarian" means—

    (a)   a person who is for the time being registered in the register of veterinary surgeons maintained under section 2 of the Veterinary Surgeons Act 1966, or

    (b)   a person who is for the time being registered in the supplementary veterinary register maintained under section 8 of that Act;

"working day" means any day other than a Saturday, a Sunday, Christmas Day, Good Friday or a day which is a bank holiday in England and Wales under section 1 of the Banking and Financial Dealings Act 1971.

3. *Licensing of operators*   (1)   Each licensable activity is a specified activity for the purposes of section 13(1) of the Act.

(2)   A local authority is the licensing authority for any licensable activity carried on on premises in its area.

PART 2   GRANT, RENEWAL AND VARIATION WITH CONSENT OF A LICENCE AND INSPECTION OF PREMISES

4. *Conditions of grant or renewal of a licence*   (1)   This regulation applies where—

(a)   a local authority has received from an operator an application in writing for the grant or renewal of a licence to carry on a licensable activity on premises in the local authority's area, and

(b)   the application gives such information as the local authority has required.

(2)   The local authority must—

(a)   appoint one or more suitably qualified inspectors to inspect any premises on which the licensable activity or any part of it is being or is to be carried on, and

(b)   following that inspection, grant a licence to the operator, or renew the operator's licence, in accordance with the application if it is satisfied that—

        (i)   the licence conditions will be met,

        (ii)   any appropriate fee has been paid in accordance with regulation 13, and

        (iii)   the grant or renewal is appropriate having taken into account the report submitted to it in accordance with regulation 10.

(3)   A local authority must attach to each licence granted or renewed—

(a)   the general conditions, and

(b)   the relevant specific conditions.

(4)   On receipt of an application in writing for the grant or renewal of a licence in respect of the activity described in paragraph 6 of Schedule 1, if no inspector appointed under paragraph (2)(a) is a listed veterinarian, the local authority must appoint a listed veterinarian to inspect the premises with the inspector appointed under that paragraph.

(5)   On receipt of an application in writing for the grant of a licence in respect of the activity described in paragraph 8 of Schedule 1, if no inspector appointed under paragraph (2)(a) is a veterinarian, the local authority must appoint a veterinarian to inspect the premises with the inspector appointed under that paragraph.

(6)   Paragraph (5) does not apply where the application is for the grant of such a licence which is to have effect immediately after the remainder of the term of a licence mentioned in regulation 27(5).

(7)   In considering whether the licence conditions will be met, a local authority must take account of the applicant's conduct as the operator of the licensable activity to which the application for the grant or renewal relates, whether the applicant is a fit and proper person to be the operator of that activity and any other relevant circumstances.

(8)   A local authority must not grant a licence to an operator, or renew an operator's licence, in any circumstances other than those described in these Regulations.

(9)   All licences granted or renewed in relation to any of the licensable activities are subject to the licence conditions.

5. *Period of licence*   A local authority may grant or renew a licence—

(a)   for a period of one, two or three years in respect of the activity or any part of the activity described in paragraph 2, 4, 6 or 8 of Schedule 1 if it is satisfied that a period of one, two or three years, as the case may be, is appropriate on the basis of its assessment, having regard to such guidance as may be issued by the Secretary of State, of—

    (i)   the risk of an operator breaching any licence conditions;

    (ii)   the impact on animal welfare of any such breaches; and

    (iii)   whether the operator is already meeting higher standards of animal welfare than are required by the licence conditions;

(b)   for a period of three years in respect of the activity or any part of the activity described in paragraph 10 of Schedule 1.

6. *Power to take samples from animals*   An inspector may, for the purposes of ensuring the licence conditions are being complied with, take samples for laboratory testing from any animals on premises occupied by an operator.

7. *Duty to assist in the taking of samples from animals*   An operator must comply with any reasonable request of an inspector to facilitate the identification and examination of an animal and the taking of samples in accordance with regulation 6 and, in particular, must arrange the suitable restraint of an animal if so requested by an inspector.

8. *Hiring out horses: requirement for annual inspection of premises*   (1)   Where there is a licence in force in relation to an activity described in paragraph 6 of Schedule 1, the local authority must appoint a listed veterinarian to inspect the premises on which the activity is being carried on.
(2)   For the purposes of paragraph (1), the authority must make an appointment for an inspection to take place before the end of the first anniversary of the day on which the licence, as granted or renewed, came into force and before the end of each subsequent year in respect of which the licence remains in force.

9. *Variation of a licence on the application, or with the consent, of a licence holder*   A local authority may at any time vary a licence—

(a)   on the application in writing of the licence holder, or

(b)   on its own initiative, with the consent in writing of the licence holder.

10. *Inspector's report*   (1)   Where a local authority arranges an inspection pursuant to regulation 4(2)(a), it must arrange for the submission to it of a report by the inspector.
(2)   The inspector's report must—

(a)   contain information about the operator, any relevant premises, any relevant records, the condition of any animals and any other relevant matter, and

(b)   state whether or not the inspector considers that the licence conditions will be met.

11. *Persons who may not apply for a licence*   (1)   The following persons may not apply for a licence in respect of any licensable activity—

(a)   a person listed as a disqualified person in paragraph 4 or any of paragraphs 6 to 17 of Schedule 8 where the time limit for any appeal against that disqualification has expired or where, if an appeal was made, that appeal was refused;

(b)   a person listed in any of paragraphs 1 to 3 and 5 of Schedule 8 as having held a licence which was revoked where the time limit for any appeal against that revocation has expired or where, if an appeal was made, that appeal was refused.

(2)   Any licence granted or renewed, or held by, a person mentioned in paragraph (1)(a) or (b) is automatically revoked.

12. *Death of a licence holder*   (1)   In the event of the death of a licence holder, the licence is deemed to have been granted to, or renewed in respect of, the personal representatives of that former licence holder.
(2)   In the circumstances described in paragraph (1), the licence is to remain in force for three months beginning with the date of the death of the former licence holder or for as long as it was due to remain in force but for the death (whichever period is shorter) but remains subject to the provisions in Part 3.
(3)   The personal representatives must notify in writing the local authority which granted or renewed the licence that they are now the licence holders within 28 days beginning with the date of the death of the former licence holder.
(4)   If the personal representatives fail so to notify the local authority within the period specified in paragraph (3), the licence shall cease to have effect on the expiry of that period.
(5)   The local authority which granted or renewed the licence may, on the application of the personal representatives, extend the period specified in paragraph (2) for up to three months if it is satisfied that the extension is necessary for the purpose of winding up the estate of the former licence holder and is appropriate in all the circumstances.

13. *Fees*   (1)   A local authority may charge such fees as it considers necessary for—

(a)   the consideration of an application for the grant, renewal or variation of a licence including any inspection relating to that consideration, and for the grant, renewal or variation,

(b)   the reasonable anticipated costs of consideration of a licence holder's compliance with these Regulations and the licence conditions to which the licence holder is subject in circumstances other than those described in sub-paragraph (a) including any inspection relating to that consideration,

(c)   the reasonable anticipated costs of enforcement in relation to any licensable activity of an unlicensed operator, and

(d)   the reasonable anticipated costs of compliance with regulation 29.

(2)   The fee charged for the consideration of an application for the grant, renewal or variation of a licence and for any inspection relating to that consideration must not exceed the reasonable costs of that consideration and related inspection.

14.   *Guidance*   A local authority must have regard in the carrying out of its functions under these Regulations to such guidance as may be issued by the Secretary of State.

PART 3   ENFORCEMENT AND NOTICES

15.   *Grounds for suspension, variation without consent or revocation of a licence*   A local authority may, without any requirement for the licence holder's consent, decide to suspend, vary or revoke a licence at any time on being satisfied that—

(a)   the licence conditions are not being complied with,

(b)   there has been a breach of these Regulations,

(c)   information supplied by the licence holder is false or misleading, or

(d)   it is necessary to protect the welfare of an animal.

16.   *Procedure for suspension or variation without consent*   (1)   Except as otherwise provided in this regulation, the suspension or variation of a licence following a decision under regulation 15 has effect at the end of a period of seven working days beginning with the date on which notice of the decision is issued to the licence holder or, if that date is not a working day, the next working day.

(2)   If it is necessary to protect the welfare of an animal, the local authority may specify in the notice of its decision that the suspension or variation has immediate effect.

(3)   A decision to suspend or vary a licence must—

(a)   be notified to the licence holder in writing,

(b)   state the local authority's grounds for suspension or variation,

(c)   state when it comes into effect,

(d)   specify measures that the local authority considers are necessary in order to remedy the grounds, and

(e)   explain the right of the licence holder to make written representations in accordance with paragraph (4) and give details of the person to whom such representations may be made and the date by the end of which they must be received.

(4)   The licence holder may make written representations which must be received by the local authority within seven working days beginning with the date of issue of notice of the decision under regulation 15 to suspend or vary the licence or, if that date is not a working day, the next working day.

(5)   Except in relation to notices under paragraph (2), where a licence holder makes written representations which are received by the local authority within the period specified in paragraph (4), the suspension or variation is not to have effect unless the local authority, after considering the representations, suspends or varies the licence in accordance with paragraph (6)(a).

(6)   Within seven working days beginning with the date of receipt of any representations made in accordance with paragraph (5), the local authority must, after considering the representations—

(a)   suspend or vary the licence,

(b)   cancel its decision under regulation 15 to suspend or vary the licence,

(c)   confirm the suspension or variation of the licence under paragraph (2), or

(d)   reinstate the licence if it has been suspended, or cancel its variation if it has been varied, under paragraph (2).

(7)   The local authority must issue to the licence holder written notice of its decision under paragraph (6) and the reasons for it within seven working days beginning with the date of receipt of any representations made in accordance with paragraph (4) or, if that date is not a working day, beginning with the next working day.

(8)   The local authority's decision under paragraph (6) is to have effect on service of its notice under paragraph (7).

(9)   Paragraph (10) applies if the local authority fails to comply with paragraph (6) or (7).

(10)   Where this paragraph applies, after seven working days beginning with the date of receipt of any representations made in accordance with paragraph (4) or, if that date is not a working day, beginning with the next working day—

(a)   a licence suspended under paragraph (2) is to be deemed to be reinstated;

(b)   a licence varied under paragraph (2) is to be deemed to have effect as if it had not been so varied;

(c)   a licence suspended under paragraph (6)(a) is to be deemed to be reinstated;

(d)   a licence varied under paragraph (6)(a) is to be deemed to have effect as if it had not been so varied;

(e)   any licence held by the licence holder other than a licence suspended or varied under paragraph (2) or (6)(a) which the local authority decided to suspend or vary under regulation 15 is to be deemed to remain in force and not to be so varied.

(11)   Once a licence has been suspended for 28 days, the local authority must on the next working day—

(a)   reinstate it without varying it,

(b)   vary and reinstate it as varied, or

(c)   revoke it.
(12)   If the local authority fails to comply with paragraph (11), the licence is to be deemed to have been reinstated without variation with immediate effect.

17.   Reinstatement of a suspended licence by a local authority   (1)   A local authority must reinstate a suspended licence by way of written notice once it is satisfied that the grounds specified in the notice of suspension have been or will be remedied.
(2)   Where a local authority reinstates a licence under paragraph (1), it may reduce the period for which it is reinstated.

18.   Notice of revocation   (1)   A revocation decision must—
(a)   be notified in writing to the licence holder,
(b)   state the local authority's grounds for revocation, and
(c)   give notice of the licence holder's right of appeal to the First-tier Tribunal and the period under regulation 24 within which such an appeal may be brought.
(2)   The decision has effect on service of the notice.

19.   Obstruction of inspectors   A person must not intentionally obstruct an inspector appointed for the purposes of the enforcement of these Regulations in the exercise of any powers conferred by or under the Act.

20.   Offences   (1)   It is an offence for a person, without lawful authority or excuse—
(a)   to breach a licence condition;
(b)   to fail to comply with regulation 7 or 19.
(2)   A person who commits an offence under paragraph (1) is liable on summary conviction to a fine.

21.   Powers of entry   Breach of a licence condition must be treated as a relevant offence for the purposes of section 23 of the Act (entry and search under warrant in connection with offences).

22.   Post-conviction powers   The relevant post-conviction powers contained in sections 34 and 42 of the Act apply in relation to a conviction for an offence under regulation 20.

23.   Notices   (1)   Any notice issued by a local authority under these Regulations may be amended, suspended or revoked by the local authority in writing at any time.
(2)   A notice may be served on a person by—
(a)   personal delivery,
(b)   leaving it or sending it by post to the person's current or last known postal address, or
(c)   emailing it to the person's current or last known email address.

Part 4   Appeals

24.   Appeals   (1)   Any operator who is aggrieved by a decision by a local authority—
(a)   to refuse to grant or renew a licence, or
(b)   to revoke or vary a licence,
may appeal to the First-tier Tribunal.
(2)   The period within which an operator may bring such an appeal is 28 days beginning with the day following the date of the decision.
(3)   The First-tier Tribunal may on application and until the appeal is determined or withdrawn—
(a)   in the case of a decision to refuse to renew a licence, permit a licence holder to continue to carry on a licensable activity or any part of it subject to the licence conditions, or
(b)   suspend a revocation or variation under regulation 15.
(4)   On appeal, the First-tier Tribunal may overturn or confirm the local authority's decision, with or without modification.

Part 5   Repeals, Revocations and Consequential Amendments

25.   Repeals and consequential amendments   Schedule 9 (repeals and consequential amendments) is to have effect.

26.   Revocations and consequential amendments   Schedule 10 (revocations and consequential amendments) is to have effect.

Part 6   Transitional and Saving Provisions

27.   Transitional and saving provisions   (1)   Any unexpired licence granted in accordance with the provisions of the Pet Animals Act 1951 shall continue in force for the remainder of its term subject to the provisions of that Act as it had effect on the relevant date.
(2)   Any unexpired licence granted under the Animal Boarding Establishments Act 1963 shall continue in force for the remainder of its term subject to the provisions of that Act as it had effect on the relevant date.
(3)   Any unexpired licence granted under of the Riding Establishments Act 1964 shall continue in force for the remainder of its term subject to the provisions of that Act as it had effect on the relevant date.
(4)   Any unexpired provisional licence granted under the Riding Establishments Act 1970 shall continue in force for the remainder of its term subject to the provisions of that Act and, so far as relevant, the Riding Establishments Act 1964 as those Acts had effect on the relevant date.
(5)   Any unexpired licence granted in accordance with the provisions of the Breeding of Dogs Act 1973 shall continue in force for the remainder of its term subject to the provisions of—
(a)   that Act,

(b)   the Breeding of Dogs (Licensing Records) Regulations 1999,

(c)   the Breeding and Sale of Dogs (Welfare) Act 1999, and

(d)   the Sale of Dogs (Identification Tag) Regulations 1999,

as those enactments had effect on the relevant date.

(6)   Any registration of a person under the Performing Animals (Regulation) Act 1925 in force on the relevant date shall continue in force, subject to the provisions of that Act as it had effect on the relevant date, for a period of six months starting with the date on which these Regulations come into force.

(7)   In this regulation—

"unexpired" means still in force on, and with any of its term remaining after, the relevant date;

"the relevant date" means the day before the date on which these Regulations come into force.

Gardiner of Kimble
Parliamentary Under Secretary of State
Department for Environment, Food and Rural Affairs
16th April 2018

SCHEDULE 1
Licensable Activities   Regulation 2

PART 1   BUSINESS TEST

1.   The circumstances which a local authority must take into account in determining whether an activity is being carried on in the course of a business for the purposes of this Schedule include, for example, whether the operator—

(a)   makes any sale by, or otherwise carries on, the activity with a view to making a profit, or

(b)   earns any commission or fee from the activity.

PART 2   SELLING ANIMALS AS PETS

2.   Selling animals as pets (or with a view to their being later resold as pets) in the course of a business including keeping animals in the course of a business with a view to their being so sold or resold.

3.   The activity described in paragraph 2 does not include—

(a)   selling animals in the course of an aquacultural production business authorised under regulation 5(1) of the Aquatic Animal Health (England and Wales) Regulations 2009, or

(b)   the activity described in paragraph 8.

PART 3   PROVIDING OR ARRANGING FOR THE PROVISION OF BOARDING FOR CATS OR DOGS

4.   Providing or arranging for the provision of accommodation for other people's cats or dogs in the course of a business on any premises where the provision of that accommodation is a purpose of the business by—

(a)   providing boarding for cats;

(b)   providing boarding in kennels for dogs;

(c)   providing home boarding for dogs; or

(d)   providing day care for dogs.

5.   The activity described in paragraph 4 does not include keeping a dog or cat on any premises pursuant to a requirement imposed under, or having effect by virtue of, the Animal Health Act 1981.

PART 4   HIRING OUT HORSES

6.   Hiring out horses in the course of a business for either or both of the following purposes—

(a)   riding;

(b)   instruction in riding.

7.   The activity described in paragraph 6 does not include any activity—

(a)   solely for military or police purposes, or

(b)   involving the instruction of students at a university on a course of study and examinations leading to a veterinary degree to which a recognition order under section 3 of the Veterinary Surgeons Act 1966 relates and for as long as such an order is in force.

PART 5   BREEDING DOGS

8.   Either or both of the following—

(a)   breeding three or more litters of puppies in any 12-month period;

(b)   breeding dogs and advertising a business of selling dogs.

9.   The activity described in paragraph 8 does not include—

(a)   keeping a dog on any premises pursuant to a requirement imposed under, or having effect by virtue of, the Animal Health Act 1981,

(b)   breeding only assistance dogs or dogs intended to be used as assistance dogs within the meaning of section 173 of the Equality Act 2010, or

(c)   breeding three or more litters of puppies in any 12-month period if the person carrying on the activity provides documentary evidence that none of them have been sold (whether as puppies or as adult dogs).

PART 6   KEEPING OR TRAINING ANIMALS FOR EXHIBITION

10.   Keeping or training animals for exhibition in the course of a business for educational or entertainment purposes—

(a)   to any audience attending in person, or

(b)   by the recording of visual images of them by any form of technology that enables the display of such images.

11.   The activity described in paragraph 10 does not include—

(a)   keeping or training animals solely for military, police or sporting purposes,

(b)   any activity permitted under a licence to operate a travelling circus under the Welfare of Wild Animals in Travelling Circuses (England) Regulations 2012, or

(c)   any activity permitted under a licence for a zoo under the Zoo Licensing Act 1981.

SCHEDULE 2
General Conditions   Regulation 2

Licence display

1.   (1)   A copy of the licence must be clearly and prominently displayed on any premises on which the licensable activity is carried on.

(2)   The name of the licence holder followed by the number of the licence holder's licence must be clearly and

prominently displayed on any website used in respect of the licensable activity.

Records

2. (1) The licence holder must ensure that at any time all the records that the licence holder is required to keep as a condition of the licence are available for inspection by an inspector in a visible and legible form or, where any such records are stored in electronic form, in a form from which they can readily be produced in a visible and legible form.

(2) The licence holder must keep all such records for at least three years beginning with the date on which the record was created.

Use, number and type of animal

3. (1) No animals or types of animal other than those animals and types of animal specified in the licence may be used in relation to the relevant licensable activity.

(2) The number of animals kept for the activity at any time must not exceed the maximum that is reasonable taking into account the facilities and staffing on any premises on which the licensable activity is carried on.

Staffing

4. (1) Sufficient numbers of people who are competent for the purpose must be available to provide a level of care that ensures that the welfare needs of all the animals are met.

(2) The licence holder or a designated manager and any staff employed to care for the animals must have competence to identify the normal behaviour of the species for which they are caring and to recognise signs of, and take appropriate measures to mitigate or prevent, pain, suffering, injury, disease or abnormal behaviour.

(3) The licence holder must provide and ensure the implementation of a written training policy for all staff.

Suitable environment

5. (1) All areas, equipment and appliances to which the animals have access must present minimal risks of injury, illness and escape and must be constructed in materials that are robust, safe and durable, in a good state of repair and well maintained.

(2) Animals must be kept at all times in an environment suitable to their species and condition (including health status and age) with respect to—

(a)   their behavioural needs,

(b)   its situation, space, air quality, cleanliness and temperature,

(c)   the water quality (where relevant),

(d)   noise levels,

(e)   light levels,

(f)   ventilation.

(3) Staff must ensure that the animals are kept clean and comfortable.

(4) Where appropriate for the species, a toileting area and opportunities for toileting must be provided.

(5) Procedures must be in place to ensure accommodation and any equipment within it is cleaned as often as necessary and good hygiene standards are maintained and the accommodation must be capable of being thoroughly cleaned and disinfected.

(6) The animals must be transported and handled in a manner (including for example in relation to housing, temperature, ventilation and frequency) that protects them from pain, suffering, injury and disease.

(7) All the animals must be easily accessible to staff and for inspection and there must be sufficient light for the staff to work effectively and observe the animals.

(8) All resources must be provided in a way (for example as regards. frequency, location and access points) that minimises competitive behaviour or the dominance of individual animals.

(9) The animals must not be left unattended in any situation or for any period likely to cause them distress.

Suitable diet

6. (1) The animals must be provided with a suitable diet in terms of quality, quantity and frequency and any new feeds must be introduced gradually to allow the animals to adjust to them.

(2) Feed and (where appropriate) water intake must be monitored, and any problems recorded and addressed.

(3) Feed and drinking water provided to the animals must be unspoilt and free from contamination.

(4) Feed and drinking receptacles must be capable of being cleaned and disinfected, or disposable.

(5) Constant access to fresh, clean drinking water must be provided in a suitable receptacle for the species that requires it.

(6) Where feed is prepared on the premises on which the licensable activity is carried on, there must be hygienic facilities for its preparation, including a working surface, hot and cold running water and storage.

Monitoring of behaviour and training of animals

7. (1) Active and effective environmental enrichment must be provided to the animals in inside and any outside environments.

(2) For species whose welfare depends partly on exercise, opportunities to exercise which benefit the animals' physical and mental health must be provided, unless advice from a veterinarian suggests otherwise.

(3) The animals' behaviour and any changes of behaviour must be monitored and advice must be sought, as appropriate and without delay, from a veterinarian or, in the case of fish, any person competent to give such advice if adverse or abnormal behaviour is detected.

(4) Where used, training methods or equipment must not cause pain, suffering or injury.

(5) All immature animals must be given suitable and adequate opportunities to—

(a)   learn how to interact with people, their own species and other animals where such interaction benefits their welfare, and

(b)   become habituated to noises, objects and activities in their environment.

Animal handling and interactions

8. (1) All people responsible for the care of the animals must be competent in the appropriate handling of each animal to protect it from pain, suffering, injury or disease.

(2) The animals must be kept separately or in suitable compatible social groups appropriate to the species and individual animals and no animals from a social species may be isolated or separated from others of their species for any longer than is necessary.

(3) The animals must have at least daily opportunities to interact with people where such interaction benefits their welfare.

Protection from pain, suffering, injury and disease

9. (1) Written procedures must—

(a)   be in place and implemented covering—

           (i)   feeding regimes,

           (ii)   cleaning regimes,

           (iii)   transportation,

           (iv)   the prevention of, and control of the spread of, disease,

           (v)   monitoring and ensuring the health and welfare of all the animals,

           (vi)   the death or escape of an animal (including the storage of carcasses);

(b)   be in place covering the care of the animals following the suspension or revocation of the licence or during and following an emergency.

(2) All people responsible for the care of the animals must be made fully aware of these procedures.

(3) Appropriate isolation, in separate self-contained facilities, must be available for the care of sick, injured or

potentially infectious animals.

(4) All reasonable precautions must be taken to prevent and control the spread among the animals and people of infectious diseases, pathogens and parasites.

(5) All excreta and soiled bedding for disposal must be stored and disposed of in a hygienic manner and in accordance with any relevant legislation.

(6) Sick or injured animals must receive prompt attention from a veterinarian or, in the case of fish, an appropriately competent person and the advice of that veterinarian or, in the case of fish, that competent person must be followed.

(7) Where necessary, animals must receive preventative treatment by an appropriately competent person.

(8) The licence holder must register with a veterinarian with an appropriate level of experience in the health and welfare requirements of any animals specified in the licence and the contact details of that veterinarian must be readily available to all staff on the premises on which the licensable activity is carried on.

(9) Prescribed medicines must be stored safely and securely to safeguard against unauthorised access, at the correct temperature, and used in accordance with the instructions of the veterinarian.

(10) Medicines other than prescribed medicines must be stored, used and disposed of in accordance with the instructions of the manufacturer or veterinarian.

(11) Cleaning products must be suitable, safe and effective against pathogens that pose a risk to the animals and must be used, stored and disposed of in accordance with the manufacturer's instructions and used in a way which prevents distress or suffering of the animals.

(12) No person may euthanase an animal except a veterinarian or a person who has been authorised by a veterinarian as competent for such purpose or—

(a) in the case of fish, a person who is competent for such purpose;

(b) in the case of horses, a person who is competent, and who holds a licence or certificate, for such purpose.

(13) All animals must be checked at least once daily and more regularly as necessary to check for any signs of pain, suffering, injury, disease or abnormal behaviour and vulnerable animals must be checked more frequently.

(14) Any signs of pain, suffering, injury, disease or abnormal behaviour must be recorded and the advice and further advice (if necessary) of a veterinarian (or in the case of fish, of an appropriately competent person) must be sought and followed.

Emergencies

10. (1) A written emergency plan, acceptable to the local authority, must be in place, known and available to all the staff on the premises on which the licensable activity is carried on, and followed where necessary to ensure appropriate steps are taken to protect all the people and animals on the premises in case of fire or in case of breakdowns of essential heating, ventilation and aeration or filtration systems or other emergencies.

(2) The plan must include details of the emergency measures to be taken for the extrication of the animals should the premises become uninhabitable and an emergency telephone list that includes the fire service and police.

(3) External doors and gates must be lockable.

(4) A designated key holder with access to all animal areas must at all times be within reasonable travel distance of the premises and available to attend in an emergency.

SCHEDULE 3

Specific Conditions: Selling Animals as Pets   Regulation 2

Interpretation

1. In this Schedule—

    "prospective owner" means a person purchasing an animal to keep or to be kept as a pet;

    "premises" means the premises on which the licensable activity of selling animals as pets (or with a view to their being later resold as pets) is carried on;

    "purchaser" means a person purchasing an animal to keep as a pet or with a view to it later being resold as a pet.

Records and advertisements

2. (1) A register must be maintained for all the animals or, in the case of fish, all the groups of fish, on the premises which must include —

(a) the full name of the supplier of the animal,

(b) the animal's sex (where known),

(c) (except in the case of fish) the animal's age (where known),

(d) details of any veterinary treatment (where known),

(e) the date of birth of the animal or, if the animal was acquired by the licence holder, the date of its acquisition,

(f) the date of the sale of the animal by the licence holder, and

(g) the date of the animal's death (if applicable).

(2) Where an animal is undergoing any medical treatment—

(a) this fact must be clearly indicated—

    (i) in writing next to it, or

    (ii) (where appropriate) by labelling it accordingly, and

(b) it must not be sold.

(3) Any advertisement for the sale of an animal must—

(a) include the number of the licence holder's licence,

(b) specify the local authority that issued the licence,

(c) include a recognisable photograph of the animal being advertised,

(d) (except in the case of fish) display the age of the animal being advertised,

(e) state the country of residence of the animal from which it is being sold, and

(f) state the country of origin of the animal.

Prospective sales: pet care and advice

3. (1) The licence holder and all staff must ensure that any equipment and accessories being sold with an animal are suitable for the animal.

(2) The licence holder and all staff must ensure that the prospective owner is provided with information on the appropriate care of the animal including in relation to—

(a) feeding,

(b) housing,

(c) handling,

(d) husbandry,

(e) the life expectancy of its species,

(f) the provision of suitable accessories, and

(g) veterinary care.

(3) Appropriate reference materials on the care of all animals for sale must be on display and provided to the prospective owner.

(4) The licence holder and all staff must have been suitably trained to advise prospective owners about the animals being sold.

(5) The licence holder and all staff must ensure that the purchaser is informed of the country of origin of the animal

and the species, and where known, the age, sex and veterinary record of the animal being sold.

Suitable accommodation

4.   (1)   Animals must be kept in housing which minimises stress including from other animals and the public.

(2)   Where members of the public can view or come into contact with the animals, signage must be in place to deter disturbance of the animals.

(3)   Dangerous wild animals (if any) must be kept in cages that are secure and lockable and appropriate for the species.

(4)   For the purposes of sub-paragraph (3), "dangerous wild animal" means an animal of a kind specified in the first column of the Schedule to the Dangerous Wild Animals Act 1976.

Purchase and sale of animals

5.   (1)   The purchase, or sale, by or on behalf of the licence holder of any of the following is prohibited—

(a)   unweaned mammals;

(b)   mammals weaned at an age at which they should not have been weaned;

(c)   non-mammals that are incapable of feeding themselves;

(d)   puppies, cats, ferrets or rabbits, aged under 8 weeks.

(2)   The sale of a dog must be completed in the presence of the purchaser on the premises.

Protection from pain, suffering, injury and disease

6.   (1)   All animals for sale must be in good health.

(2)   Any animal with a condition which is likely to affect its quality of life must not be moved, transferred or offered for sale but may be moved to an isolation facility or veterinary care facility if required until the animal has recovered.

(3)   When arranging for the receipt of animals, the licence holder must make reasonable efforts to ensure that they will be transported in a suitable manner.

(4)   Animals must be transported or handed to purchasers in suitable containers for the species and expected duration of the journey.

SCHEDULE 4

Specific Conditions: Providing Boarding for Cats or Dogs   Regulation 2

PART 1   PROVIDING BOARDING FOR CATS

Interpretation

1.   In this Part—

"cat unit" means the physical structure and area that comprises a sleeping area and an exercise run;

"exercise run" means an enclosed area forming part of the cat unit attached to and with direct and permanent access to the sleeping area;

"premises" means the premises on which the licensable activity of providing boarding for cats is carried on.

Suitable environment

2.   (1)   Cats within the premises must be prevented from coming into direct contact with other animals from outside the premises.

(2)   There must be a safe, secure, waterproof roof over the entire cat unit.

(3)   A cat unit may only be shared by cats from the same household.

(4)   Communal exercise areas are not permitted.

(5)   Each cat unit must be clearly numbered and there must be a system in place which ensures that information about the cat or cats in each cat unit is available to all staff and any inspector.

(6)   Each cat unit must provide the cat with sufficient space to—

(a)   walk,

(b)   turn around,

(c)   stand on its hind legs,

(d)   hold its tail erect,

(e)   climb,

(f)   rest on the elevated area, and

(g)   lie down fully stretched out,

without touching another cat or the walls.

(7)   Each cat unit must have sufficient space for each cat to sit, rest, eat and drink away from the area where it urinates and defecates.

(8)   Cats must have constant access to their sleeping area.

(9)   A litter tray and safe and absorbent litter material must be provided at all times in each cat unit and litter trays must be regularly cleaned and disinfected.

(10)   Each cat unit must include an elevated area.

(11)   Adjoining cat units must have solid barriers covering the full height and full width of the adjoining wall.

(12)   Any gaps between cat units must be a minimum of 0.6 metres wide.

(13)   Any cat taken out of a cat unit must be secured in a suitable carrier.

(14)   The sleeping area must form part of the cat unit and be free from draughts.

Monitoring of behaviour and training of cats

3.   (1)   There must be an area within each cat unit in which the cat can avoid seeing other cats and people outside the cat unit if it so chooses.

(2)   Each cat unit must include a facility for scratching and any surface within a cat unit available for scratching must either be disinfected between uses by different cats or disposed of.

(3)   All cats must be provided with toys or feeding enrichment (or both) unless advice from a veterinarian suggests otherwise.

(4)   All toys and other enrichment items must be checked daily to ensure they remain safe and must be cleaned and disinfected at least weekly.

Records

4.   A register must be kept of all the cats on the premises which must include—

(a)   the dates of each cat's arrival and departure,

(b)   each cat's name, age, sex, neuter status and a description of it or its breed,

(c)   each cat's microchip number, where applicable,

(d)   the number of any cats from the same household,

(e)   a record of which cats (if any) are from the same household,

(f)   the name, postal address, telephone number (if any) and email address (if any) of the owner of each cat and emergency contact details,

(g)   in relation to each cat, the name, postal address, telephone number and email address of a local contact in an emergency,

(h)   the name and contact details of each cat's normal veterinarian and details of any insurance relating to the cat,

(i)   details of each cat's relevant medical and behavioural history, including details of any treatment administered against parasites and restrictions on exercise,

(j)   details of each cat's diet and related requirements,

(k)   any required consent forms,

(l)   a record of the date or dates of each cat's most recent vaccination, worming and flea treatments, and

(m)   details of any medical treatment each cat is receiving.

Protection from pain, suffering, injury and disease

5.   (1)   A cat must remain in its assigned cat unit, except when it is moved to an isolation cat unit or to a holding cat unit.

(2)   Where any other activity involving animals is undertaken on the premises, it must be kept entirely separate from the area where the activity of providing boarding for cats takes place.

(3)   All equipment must be cleaned and disinfected before a cat is first introduced into a cat unit.

(4)   A preventative healthcare plan agreed with the veterinarian with whom the licence holder has registered under paragraph 9(8) of Schedule 2 must be implemented.

(5)   A holding cat unit must only be used in an emergency and must not be used for longer than is necessary and in any event for no longer than a total of 12 hours in any 24-hour period.

(6)   In this paragraph, "holding cat unit" means a cat unit, separate from any other cat unit, in which a cat may be housed temporarily.

PART 2   PROVIDING BOARDING IN KENNELS FOR DOGS

Interpretation

6.   In this Part—

"exercise run" means an enclosed area forming part of a kennel unit attached to and with direct access to the sleeping area;

"kennel unit" means the physical structure and area that consists of a sleeping area and an exercise run;

"premises" means the premises on which the licensable activity of providing boarding in kennels for dogs is carried on.

Suitable environment

7.   (1)   Dogs within the premises must be prevented from coming into contact with other animals from outside the premises.

(2)   In each kennel unit, the sleeping area must—

(a)   be free from draughts;

(b)   provide the dog with sufficient space to—

(i)   sit and stand at full height,

(ii)   lie down fully stretched-out,

(iii)   wag its tail,

(iv)   walk, and

(v)   turn around,

without touching another dog or the walls;

(c)   have a floor area which is at least twice the area required for the dog in it to lie flat; and

(d)   if built after the date on which these Regulations come into force, have a floor area of at least 1.9 square metres.

(3)   Each kennel unit must be clearly numbered and there must be a system in place which ensures that information about the dog or dogs in each kennel unit is available to all staff and any inspector.

(4)   Each dog must have constant access to its sleeping area.

(5)   Each dog must have a clean, comfortable and warm area within its sleeping area where it can rest and sleep.

(6)   Each exercise run must have a single, safe, secure, waterproof roof over a minimum of half its total area.

(7)   Where a dog poses a health or welfare risk to other dogs, it must be kept on its own in a kennel unit and, if that kennel unit adjoins another kennel unit, any adjoining wall must be of full height and width so as to prevent the dog from coming into physical contact with any other dog.

(8)   Only dogs from the same household may share a kennel unit.

Monitoring of behaviour and training

8.   (1)   Any equipment that a dog is likely to be in contact with and any toy provided must not pose a risk of pain, suffering, disease or distress to the dog and must be correctly used.

(2)   All dogs must be provided with toys or feeding enrichment (or both) unless advice from a veterinarian suggests otherwise.

(3)   All toys and other enrichment items must be checked daily to ensure they remain safe and must be cleaned and disinfected at least weekly.

(4)   Each dog must be exercised at least once daily away from its kennel unit as appropriate for its age and health.

(5)   Any dog which, on the advice of a veterinarian, cannot be exercised must be provided with alternative forms of mental stimulation.

(6)   There must be an area within each kennel unit in which a dog can avoid seeing people and other dogs outside the kennel unit if it so chooses.

Records

9.   (1)   A register must be kept of all the dogs on the premises which must include—

(a)   the dates of each dog's arrival and departure;

(b)   each dog's name, age, sex, neuter status, microchip number and a description of it or its breed;

(c)   the number of any dogs from the same household;

(d)   a record of which dogs (if any) are from the same household;

(e)   the name, postal address, telephone number (if any) and email address (if any) of the owner of each dog and emergency contact details;

(f)   in relation to each dog, the name, postal address, telephone number and email address of a local contact in an emergency;

(g)   the name and contact details of the dog's normal veterinarian and details of any insurance relating to the dog;

(h)   details of each dog's relevant medical and behavioural history, including details of any treatment administered against parasites and restrictions on exercise;

(i)   details of the dog's diet and related requirements;

(j)   any required consent forms;

(k)   a record of the date or dates of each dog's most recent vaccination, worming and flea treatments;

(l)   details of any medical treatment each dog is receiving.

(2)   When outside the premises, each dog must wear an identity tag which includes the licence holder's name and contact details.

Protection from pain, suffering, injury and disease

10.   (1)   Where any other activity involving animals is undertaken on the premises, it must be kept entirely separate from the area where the activity of providing boarding for dogs in kennels takes place.

(2)   A preventative healthcare plan agreed with the veterinarian with whom the licence holder has registered under paragraph 9(8) of Schedule 2 must be implemented.

(3)   A holding kennel unit must only be used in an emergency and must not be used for longer than is necessary and in any event for no longer than a total of 12 hours in any 24-hour period.

(4)   In sub-paragraph (3), "holding kennel unit" means a kennel unit, separate from any other kennel unit, in which a dog may be housed temporarily.

PART 3   PROVIDING HOME BOARDING FOR DOGS

Interpretation
11.   In this Part—
   "designated room" means a room within the home allocated to a dog;
   "home" means a domestic dwelling on which the licensable activity of providing home boarding for dogs is carried on.
Home
12.   (1)   Dogs must be accommodated within the home.
(2)   The home must include—
(a)   direct access to a private, non-communal, secure and hazard-free external area, and
(b)   at least two secure physical barriers between any dog and any entrance to or exit from it.
Suitable environment
13.   (1)   Dogs from different households may only be boarded at the same time with the written consent of every owner.
(2)   Each dog must be provided with its own designated room where it can, if necessary, be kept separate from other dogs.
(3)   Each dog must have a clean, comfortable and warm area within its designated room where it can rest and sleep.
(4)   Each designated room must have a secure window to the outside that can be opened and closed as necessary.
(5)   A dog must not be confined in a crate for longer than three hours in any 24-hour period.
(6)   A dog must not be kept in a crate unless—
(a)   it is already habituated to it,
(b)   a crate forms part of the normal routine for the dog, and
(c)   the dog's owner has consented to the use of a crate.
(7)   Any crate in which a dog is kept must be in good condition and sufficiently large for the dog to sit and stand in it at full height, lie flat and turn around.
Suitable diet
14.   Each dog must be fed separately in its designated room unless its owner has given written consent to the contrary.
Monitoring of behaviour and training
15.   (1)   Any equipment that a dog is likely to be in contact with and any toy provided must not pose a risk of pain, suffering, disease or distress to the dog and must be correctly used.
(2)   Each dog must be exercised at least once daily as appropriate for its age and health.
(3)   Dogs which on the advice of a veterinarian cannot be exercised must be provided with alternative forms of mental stimulation.
Housing with or apart from other dogs
16.   (1)   Written consent must be obtained from the owner or owners (as the case may be) to keep dogs together in a designated room.
(2)   Unneutered bitches must be prevented from mating.
(3)   If any person aged under 16 years resides at the home, there must be procedures in place to regulate the interactions between the dogs and that person.
Records
17.   (1)   A register must be kept of all the dogs accommodated in the home which must include—
(a)   the dates of each dog's arrival and departure;
(b)   each dog's name, age, sex, neuter status, microchip number and a description of it or its breed;
(c)   the number of any dogs from the same household;
(d)   a record of which dogs (if any) are from the same household;
(e)   the name, postal address, telephone number (if any) and email address (if any) of the owner of each dog and emergency contact details;
(f)   in relation to each dog, the name, postal address, telephone number and email address of a local contact in an emergency;
(g)   the name and contact details of each dog's normal veterinarian and details of any insurance relating to the dog;
(h)   details of each dog's relevant medical and behavioural history, including details of any treatment administered against parasites and restrictions on exercise;
(i)   details of each dog's diet and related requirements;
(j)   any required consent forms;
(k)   a record of the date or dates of each dog's most recent vaccination, worming and flea treatments;
(l)   details of any medical treatment each dog is receiving.
(2)   When outside the premises, each dog must wear an identity tag which includes the licence holder's name and contact details.
Protection from pain, suffering, injury and disease
18.   (1)   Before a dog is admitted for boarding, all equipment to be used by or in relation to that dog must be cleaned and disinfected.
(2)   A preventative healthcare plan agreed with the veterinarian with whom the licence holder has registered under paragraph 9(8) of Schedule 2 must be implemented.

PART 4   PROVIDING DAY CARE FOR DOGS

Interpretation
19.   In this Part, "premises" means the premises on which the licensable activity of providing day care for dogs is carried on.
No overnight stay
20.   No dog may be kept on the premises overnight.
Suitable environment
21.   (1)   Each dog must be provided with—
(a)   a clean, comfortable and warm area where it can rest and sleep, and
(b)   another secure area in which water is provided and in which there is shelter.
(2)   Each dog must have access to areas where it can—
(a)   interact safely with other dogs, toys and people, and
(b)   urinate and defecate.
(3)   There must be an area where any dog can avoid seeing other dogs and people if it so chooses.
Suitable diet
22.   Any dog that requires specific feed due to a medical condition must be fed in isolation.
Monitoring of behaviour and training
23.   (1)   All dogs must be screened before being admitted to the premises to ensure that they are not afraid, anxious or stressed in the presence of other dogs or people and do not pose a danger to other dogs or staff.
(2)   Any equipment used that is likely to be in contact with the dogs and any toys provided must not pose a risk of pain, suffering, disease or distress to the dog and must be correctly used.
Housing apart from other dogs

24. (1) Unneutered bitches must be prevented from mating.

(2) Dogs which need to be isolated from other dogs must be provided with alternative forms of mental stimulation.

Records

25. (1) A register must be kept of all the dogs on the premises which must include—

(a) the date of the dog's attendance;

(b) the dog's name, age, sex, neuter status, microchip number and a description of it or its breed;

(c) the name, postal address, telephone number (if any) and email address (if any) of the owner and emergency contact details;

(d) the name and contact details of the dog's normal veterinarian and details of any insurance relating to the dog;

(e) details of the dog's relevant medical and behavioural history, including details of any treatment administered against parasites and any restrictions on exercise;

(f) details of the dog's diet and relevant requirements;

(g) any required consent forms;

(h) a record of the date or dates of the dog's most recent vaccination, worming and flea treatments;

(i) details of any medical treatment the dog is receiving.

(2) When outside the premises, each dog must wear an identity tag which includes the licence holder's name and contact details.

Protection from pain, suffering, injury and disease

26. (1) The dogs must be supervised at all times.

(2) A preventative healthcare plan agreed with the veterinarian with whom the licence holder has registered under paragraph 9(8) of Schedule 2 must be implemented.

(3) Any journeys in a vehicle must be planned to minimise the time dogs spend in the vehicle.

SCHEDULE 5

Specific Conditions: Hiring out Horses	Regulation 2

Interpretation

1. In this Schedule, "client" means a person for whose use a horse is hired out.

Eligibility

2. (1) The licence holder must—

(a) hold an appropriate formal qualification, or have sufficient demonstrable experience and competence, in the management of horses, and

(b) hold a valid certificate of public liability insurance which—

    (i) insures the licence holder against liability for any injury sustained by, and the death of, any client, and

    (ii) insures any client against liability for any injury sustained by, and the death of, any other person, caused by or arising out of the hire of the horse.

(2) The certificate mentioned in sub-paragraph (1)(b) must be clearly and prominently displayed on the premises.

Supervision

3. (1) The activity must not at any time be left in the charge of a person aged under 18 years.

(2) No horse may be hired out except under the supervision of a person aged 16 years or more unless the licence holder is satisfied that the person hiring the horse is competent to ride without supervision.

(3) The following must be clearly and prominently displayed on the premises—

(a) the full name, postal address (including postcode) and telephone number of the licence holder or other person with management responsibilities in respect of the activity;

(b) instructions as to the action to be taken in the event of a fire or other emergency.

Suitable environment

4. (1) It must be practicable to bring all the horses on the premises under cover.

(2) Suitable storage must be provided and used for feed, bedding, stable equipment and saddlery.

(3) All arena surfaces must be suitable for purpose, well drained, free of standing water and maintained regularly to keep them level.

Suitable diet

5. (1) At all times when any horses are kept at grass, adequate pasture, shelter and clean water must be available for them.

(2) Supplementary feed and nutrients must be provided to any horse when appropriate.

(3) Each horse must be fed a balanced diet of a quantity and at a frequency suitable for its age, health and workload to enable it to maintain an appropriate physical condition.

Protection from pain, suffering, injury and disease

6. (1) The horses must be maintained in good health and must be in all respects physically fit.

(2) A preventative healthcare plan agreed with the veterinarian with whom the licence holder has registered under paragraph 9(8) of Schedule 2 must be implemented

(3) A daily record of the workload of each horse must be maintained and available for inspection at any reasonable time.

(4) Each horse must be suitable for the purpose for which it is kept and must not be hired out if, due to its condition, its use would be likely to cause it to suffer.

(5) Any horse found on inspection to be in need of veterinary attention must not be returned to work until the licence holder has, at the licence holder's expense, obtained from and lodged with the local authority a veterinary certificate which confirms that the horse is fit for work.

(6) Each horse's hooves should be trimmed as often as is necessary to maintain the health, good shape and soundness of its feet and any shoes should be properly fitted and in good condition.

(7) An area suitable for the inspection of horses by a veterinarian must be provided.

(8) The following must not be hired out—

(a) a horse aged under 3 years;

(b) a mare heavy with foal;

(c) a mare whose foal has not yet been weaned.

(9) The licence holder must keep a register of all horses kept for the licensable activity on the premises, each such horse's valid passport showing its unique equine life number and a record of its microchip number (if any).

Equipment

7. All equipment provided to clients must be in good and safe condition and available for inspection at any reasonable time.

SCHEDULE 6

Specific Conditions: Breeding Dogs	Regulation 2

Advertisements and sales

1. (1) The licence holder must not advertise or offer for sale a dog—

(a) which was not bred by the licence holder;

(b) except from the premises where it was born and reared under the licence;

(c) otherwise than to—

    (i) a person who holds a licence for the activity described in paragraph 2 of Schedule 1; or

     (ii)   a keeper of a pet shop in Wales who is licensed under the Pet Animals Act 1951 to keep the shop, knowing or believing that the person who buys it intends to sell it or intends it to be sold by any other person.

(2)   Any advertisement for the sale of a dog must—

(a)   include the number of the licence holder's licence,

(b)   specify the local authority that issued the licence,

(c)   include a recognisable photograph of the dog being advertised, and

(d)   display the age of the dog being advertised.

(3)   The licence holder and all staff must ensure that any equipment and accessories being sold with a dog are suitable for it.

(4)   The licence holder and all staff must ensure that the purchaser is informed of the age, sex and veterinary record of the dog being sold.

(5)   No puppy aged under 8 weeks may be sold or permanently separated from its biological mother.

(6)   A puppy may only be shown to a prospective purchaser if it is together with its biological mother.

(7)   Sub-paragraphs (5) and (6) do not apply if separation of the puppy from its biological mother is necessary for the health or welfare of the puppy, other puppies from the same litter or its biological mother.

Suitable environment

2.   (1)   Each dog must have access to a sleeping area which is free from draughts and an exercise area.

(2)   Each dog must be provided with sufficient space to—

(a)   stand on its hind legs,

(b)   lie down fully stretched out,

(c)   wag its tail,

(d)   walk, and

(e)   turn around,

without touching another dog or the walls of the sleeping area.

(3)   The exercise area must not be used as a sleeping area.

(4)   Part or all of the exercise area must be outdoors.

(5)   There must be a separate whelping area for each breeding bitch to whelp in which contains a suitable bed for whelping.

(6)   Each whelping area must be maintained at an appropriate temperature (between and including 26 and 28 degrees centigrade) and include an area which allows the breeding bitch to move away from heat spots.

(7)   Each dog must be provided with constant access to a sleeping area.

(8)   A separate bed must be provided for each adult dog.

(9)   No puppy aged under 8 weeks may be transported without its biological mother except—

(a)   if a veterinarian agrees for health or welfare reasons that it may be so transported, or

(b)   in an emergency.

(10)   No breeding bitch may be transported later than 54 days after the date of successful mating except to a veterinarian.

(11)   No breeding bitch may be transported earlier than 48 hours after whelping except to a veterinarian where it is not otherwise practicable or appropriate for that person to attend to the bitch.

(12)   Each dog's sleeping area must be clean, comfortable, warm and free from draughts.

(13)   In this paragraph, "exercise area" means a secure area where dogs may exercise and play.

Suitable diet

3.   Staff must—

(a)   ensure that each puppy starts weaning as soon as it is capable of ingesting feed on its own,

(b)   provide each breeding bitch with feed appropriate to its needs,

(c)   provide each puppy with feed appropriate for its stage of development, and

(d)   ensure that each puppy ingests the correct share of the feed provided.

Monitoring of behaviour and training

4.   (1)   The licence holder must implement and be able to demonstrate use of a documented socialisation and habituation programme for the puppies.

(2)   Each dog must be provided with toys or feeding enrichment (or both) unless advice from a veterinarian suggests otherwise.

(3)   Except in the circumstances mentioned in sub-paragraph (4), all adult dogs must be exercised at least twice daily away from their sleeping area.

(4)   Where a veterinarian has advised against exercising a dog, the dog must be provided with alternative forms of mental stimulation.

(5)   Any equipment that a dog is likely to be in contact with and any toy provided must not pose a risk of pain, suffering, disease or distress to the dog and must be correctly used.

Housing with or apart from other dogs

5.   (1)   Each adult dog must be provided with opportunities for social contact with other dogs where such contact benefits the dogs' welfare.

(2)   Each adult dog must be given suitable and adequate opportunities to become habituated to handling by people.

(3)   Procedures must be in place for dealing with dogs that show abnormal behaviour.

(4)   There must be an area within each sleeping area in which dogs can avoid seeing people and other dogs outside the sleeping area if they so choose.

Protection from pain, suffering, injury and disease

6.   (1)   All dogs for sale must be in good health.

(2)   Any dog with a condition which is likely to affect materially its quality of life must not be moved, transferred or offered for sale but may be moved to an isolation facility or veterinary care facility if required until it has recovered.

(3)   The licence holder must ensure that no bitch—

(a)   is mated if aged less than 12 months;

(b)   gives birth to more than one litter of puppies in a 12-month period;

(c)   gives birth to more than six litters of puppies in total;

(d)   is mated if she has had two litters delivered by caesarean section.

(4)   The licence holder must ensure that each puppy is microchipped and registered to the licence holder before it is sold.

(5)   No dog may be kept for breeding if it can reasonably be expected, on the basis of its genotype, phenotype or state of health that breeding from it could have a detrimental effect on its health or welfare or the health or welfare of its offspring.

(6)   The health, safety and welfare of each dog must be checked at the start and end of every day and at least every four hours during the daytime.

(7)   Breeding bitches must be adequately supervised during whelping and the licence holder must keep a record of—

(a)   the date and time of birth of each puppy,

(b)   each puppy's sex, colour and weight,

(c)   placentae passed,

(d)   the number of puppies in the litter, and

(e)   any other significant events.
(8)   The licence holder must keep a record of each puppy sale including—
(a)   the microchip number of the puppy,
(b)   the date of the sale, and
(c)   the age of the puppy on that date.
(9)   The licence holder must keep a record of the following in relation to each breeding dog—
(a)   its name,
(b)   its sex,
(c)   its microchip and database details,
(d)   its date of birth,
(e)   the postal address where it normally resides,
(f)   its breed or type,
(g)   its description,
(h)   the date or dates of any matings, whether or not successful,
(i)   details of its biological mother and biological father,
(j)   details of any veterinary treatment it has received, and
(k)   the date and cause of its death (where applicable).
(10)   In addition to the matters mentioned in sub-paragraph (7), the licence holder must keep a record of the following in in relation to each breeding bitch—
(a)   the number of matings,
(b)   its age at the time of each mating,
(c)   the number of its litters,
(d)   the date or dates on which it has given birth, and
(e)   the number of caesarean sections it has had, if any.
(11)   Unless the licence holder keeps the dog as a pet, the licence holder must make arrangements for any dog no longer required for breeding to be appropriately rehomed.
(12)   A preventative healthcare plan agreed with the veterinarian with whom the licence holder has registered under paragraph 9(8) of Schedule 2 must be implemented.
(13)   The licence holder must keep a record of any preventative or curative healthcare (or both) given to each dog.
(14)   Where any other activity involving animals is undertaken on the premises on which the licensable activity of breeding dogs is carried on, it must be kept entirely separate from the area where that licensable activity is carried on.

SCHEDULE 7
Specific Conditions: Keeping or Training Animals for Exhibition   Regulation 2
Insurance
1.   The licence holder must hold valid public liability insurance in respect of the licensable activity of keeping or training animals for exhibition.
Emergencies
2.   A written policy detailing contingency measures in the event of the breakdown of a vehicle used to transport the animals or any other emergency must be available to all staff.
Suitable environment
3.   Suitable temporary accommodation must be provided for all the animals at any venue where they are exhibited.
Monitoring of behaviour and training
4.   The animals must be trained by competent staff and given suitable and adequate opportunities to become habituated to being exhibited, using positive reinforcement.
Housing with or apart from other animals
5.   (1)   Social animals must not be exhibited if their removal from and reintroduction to the group with which they are usually housed causes them or any other animal within that group stress, anxiety or fear.
(2)   Animals must be prevented from coming into contact with each other during any exhibition where such contact would be likely to cause any of them to show signs of aggression, fear or distress.
(3)   All persons likely to come into contact with the animals during an exhibition must be briefed about how to behave around the animals so as to minimise anxiety, fear and stress in the animals.
(4)   No female animal with unweaned offspring may be removed from its home environment and newborn, unweaned or dependent offspring must not be removed from their mothers.
Records
6.   The licence holder must keep a list of each animal kept, or trained, for exhibition with all the information necessary to identify that animal individually (including its common and scientific names) and must provide the local authority with a copy of the list and any change to it as soon as practicable after the change.
Protection from pain, suffering, injury and disease
7.   (1)   A register must be kept of each animal exhibited or to be exhibited which must include—
(a)   the full name of its supplier,
(b)   its date of birth,
(c)   the date of its arrival,
(d)   its name (if any), age, sex, neuter status, description and microchip or ring number (if applicable),
(e)   the name and contact details of the animal's normal veterinarian and details of any insurance relating to it,
(f)   details of the animal's relevant medical and behavioural history including details of any treatment administered against parasites and any restrictions on exercise or diet,
(g)   a record of the date or dates of the animal's most recent vaccination, worming and flea treatments, and
(h)   the distance to and times taken for it to travel to and from each exhibition event.
(2)   A record of when the animals are exhibited must be kept and an animal rotation policy must be put in place to ensure that the animals have enough rest between and during exhibition events.
(3)   All the animals used in exhibition events must be in good physical and mental health.
(4)   The exhibited animals must be suitable for the specific conditions, type of enclosure and actions involved in the exhibition.
(5)   Any equipment, chemicals and other materials used in the exhibition must not cause the animals pain, discomfort, fatigue or stress.
(6)   The animals must be transported in suitable, secure and appropriately labelled carriers.
(7)   The licence holder or the licence holder's staff must undertake a risk assessment before each exhibition event.
(8)   The animals must not be handled by persons whose behaviour appears at the time to be influenced by the consumption of alcohol or by any psychoactive substance.

SCHEDULE 8
Persons who may not Apply for a Licence   Regulation 11
1.   A person who has at any time held a licence which was revoked under regulation 15 of these Regulations.
2.   A person who has at any time held a licence which was revoked under regulation 17 of the Animal Welfare (Breeding of Dogs) (Wales) Regulations 2014.

3.   A person who has at any time held a licence which was revoked under regulation 13 of the Welfare of Wild Animals in Travelling Circuses (England) Regulations 2012.
4.   A person who is disqualified under section 33 of the Welfare of Animals Act (Northern Ireland) 2011.
5.   A person who has at any time held a licence which was revoked under regulation 12 of the Welfare of Racing Greyhounds Regulations 2010.
6.   A person who is disqualified under section 34 of the Act.
7.   A person who is disqualified under section 40(1) and (2) of the Animal Health and Welfare (Scotland) Act 2006.
8.   A person who is disqualified under section 4(1) of the Dangerous Dogs Act 1991.
9.   A person who is disqualified under Article 33A of the Dogs (Northern Ireland) Order 1983.
10.   A person who is disqualified under section 6(2) of the Dangerous Wild Animals Act 1976 from keeping a dangerous wild animal.
11.   A person who is disqualified under section 3(3) of the Breeding of Dogs Act 1973 from keeping a breeding establishment for dogs.
12.   A person who is disqualified under section 4(3) of the Riding Establishments Act 1964 from keeping a riding establishment.
13.   A person who is disqualified under section 3(3) of the Animal Boarding Establishments Act 1963 from keeping a boarding establishment for animals.
14.   A person who is disqualified under section 5(3) of the Pet Animals Act 1951 from keeping a pet shop.
15.   A person who is disqualified under section 1(1) of the Protection of Animals (Amendment) Act 1954 from having custody of an animal.
16.   A person who is disqualified under section 4(2) of the Performing Animals (Regulation) Act 1925.
17.   A person who is disqualified under section 3 of the Protection of Animals Act 1911 from the ownership of an animal.

SCHEDULE 9
Repeals and Consequential Amendments   Regulation 25

Performing Animals (Regulation) Act 1925
1.   (1)   The Performing Animals (Regulation) Act 1925 is amended as follows.
(2)   Section 1(1) (restriction on exhibition and training of performing animals) ceases to have effect in relation to England.
(3)   In section 1—
(a)   in subsection (1), after "animal" insert "in Wales";
(b)   in subsection (2)—
      (i)   for "Great Britain" substitute "Wales";
      (ii)   after "districts" insert "in Wales".
(4)   In section 4(1) (offences and legal proceedings), in each of paragraphs (a), (b) and (e), after "animal" insert "in Wales".
(5)   In section 5 (interpretation, rules, and expenses)—
(a)   in subsection (1), for the definition of "local authority" substitute—
"The expression "local authority" means a county council in Wales or a county borough council in Wales:";
(b)   in subsection (3), omit the words from "; and" to the end.
Pet Animals Act 1951
2.   (1)   The Pet Animals Act 1951 is amended as follows.
(2)   Section 1(1) (restriction on keeping a pet shop) ceases to have effect in relation to England.
(3)   In section 1—
(a)   in subsection (1), after "shop" insert "in Wales";
(b)   in subsection (2), after "Every local authority" insert "in Wales";
(c)   in subsection (3), after "shop" and "a local authority" insert "in Wales";
(d)   in subsection (4), after "local authority" insert "in Wales".
(4)   In section 4(1) (inspection of pet shops), after "A local authority" insert "in Wales".
(5)   In section 6 (power of local authority to prosecute)—
(a)   the existing text becomes subsection (1) and in that text omit "England or";
(b)   after subsection (1) insert—
"(2)   A local authority in England may prosecute proceedings for an offence under section 2 committed in the area of the authority.".
Animal Boarding Establishments Act 1963
3.   (1)   The Animal Boarding Establishments Act 1963 is amended as follows.
(2)   Section 1(1) (licensing of boarding establishments for animals) ceases to have effect in relation to England.
(3)   In section 1(1) after "animals" insert "in Wales".
(4)   In section 4 (power of local authorities to prosecute) omit "in England or Wales".
(5)   In section 5(2) (interpretation), in the definition of "local authority", for the words from "means the" to "London" substitute—
"means a county council in Wales or a county borough council in Wales".
Riding Establishments Act 1964
4.   (1)   The Riding Establishments Act 1964 is amended as follows.
(2)   Section 1(1) (licensing of riding establishments) ceases to have effect in relation to England.
(3)   In section 1(1) after "establishment" insert "in Wales".
(4)   In section 5 (power of local authorities to prosecute)—
(a)   in subsection (1), omit "in England or Wales".
(b)   in subsection (2), omit "In England and Wales".
(5)   In section 6 (interpretation)—
(a)   in subsection (1) omit paragraph (c);
(b)   in subsection (4), in the definition of "local authority", for the words from "means the council of a district" to "county borough", substitute—
"means a county council in Wales or a county borough council in Wales".
Breeding of Dogs Act 1973
5.   The Breeding of Dogs Act 1973 is repealed.
Local Government Act 1974
6.   In the Local Government Act 1974, in Schedule 7 (minor and consequential amendments), paragraph 15 is omitted.
Dangerous Wild Animals Act 1976
7.   (1)   The Dangerous Wild Animals Act 1976 is amended as follows.
(2)   In section 5 (exemptions)—
(a)   after paragraph (2), insert—
"(2A)   premises in England on which the activity described in paragraph 2 of Schedule 1 to the Animal Welfare (Licensing of Activities Involving Animals) (England) Regulations 2018 (read with paragraph 3 of that Schedule: selling animals as pets etc) is carried on under a licence under those Regulations;";

(b)   in paragraph (3), after "premises" insert "in Wales".

(3)   In section 6 (penalties)—

(a)   in subsection (2) omit "or the Breeding of Dogs Act 1973,";

(b)   at the end insert—

"(3C)   Where a person is convicted of an offence under section 13(6) of the Animal Welfare Act 2006 arising from the contravention of section 13(1) of that Act in relation to the carrying on of an activity in England, or of an offence under the Animal Welfare (Licensing of Activities Involving Animals) (England) Regulations 2018, subsections (2) and (3) apply as they do to convictions under this Act."

Zoo Licensing Act 1981

8.   In section 4(5) of the Zoo Licensing Act 1981 (grant or refusal of licence)—

(a)   after the entry which begins "section 13(6)" insert—

"section 13(6) of the Animal Welfare Act 2006, so far as the offence arises from the contravention of section 13(1) of that Act in relation to the carrying on of an activity in England;";

(b)   at the end insert—

";

the Animal Welfare (Licensing of Activities Involving Animals) (England) Regulations 2018."

Animals (Scientific Procedures) Act 1986

9.   In the Animals (Scientific Procedures) Act 1986, section 27(3) (repeal, consequential amendments and transitional provisions) is omitted.

Breeding of Dogs Act 1991

10.   The Breeding of Dogs Act 1991 is repealed.

Breeding and Sale of Dogs (Welfare) Act 1999

11.   The Breeding and Sale of Dogs (Welfare) Act 1999 is repealed.

Local Authorities (Functions and Responsibilities) (England) Regulations 2000

12.   Paragraph B of Schedule 1 to the Local Authorities (Functions and Responsibilities) (England) Regulations 2000 (licensing and registration functions not to be the responsibility of an authority's executive) is amended as follows—

(a)   in column (1) (function)—

      (i)   for "29. Power to license premises for the breeding of dogs." substitute "29. Power to grant or renew a licence for a licensable activity under the Animal Welfare (Licensing of Activities Involving Animals) (England) Regulations 2018 (selling animals as pets, providing or arranging for the provision of boarding for cats or dogs, hiring out horses, breeding dogs or keeping or training animals for exhibition).";

      (ii)   omit "30. Power to license pet shops and other establishments where animals are bred or kept for the purposes of carrying on a business" and "31. Power to register animal trainers and exhibitors";

(b)   in column (2) (provision of Act or statutory instrument)—

      (i)   in relation to the entry relating to item 29, for "Section 1 of the Breeding of Dogs Act 1973 (c 60), and section 1 of the Breeding and Sale of Dogs (Welfare) Act 1999 (c 11)." substitute "Regulation 4 of those Regulations.";

      (ii)   omit the entries relating to items 30 and 31.

Courts Act 2003

13.   In the Courts Act 2003, paragraphs 171 and 383 of Schedule 8 (minor and consequential amendments) are omitted.

Criminal Justice Act 2003

14.   In the Criminal Justice Act 2003, paragraph 72 of Schedule 25 (summary offences no longer punishable with imprisonment) is omitted.

Regulatory Enforcement and Sanctions Act 2008

15.   (1)   The Regulatory Enforcement and Sanctions Act 2008 is amended as follows.

(2)   In Schedule 3 (enactments specified for the purpose of Part 1), the following entries are omitted—

(a)   "Breeding and Sale of Dogs (Welfare) Act 1999 (c 11)";

(b)   "Breeding of Dogs Act 1973 (c 60)";

(c)   "Breeding of Dogs Act 1991 (c 64)".

(3)   in Schedule 6 (enactments specified for the purposes of orders under Part 3), the following entries are omitted—

(a)   "Breeding of Dogs Act 1973 (c 60)";

(b)   "Breeding of Dogs Act 1991 (c 64)".

Deregulation Act 2015

16.   In the Deregulation Act 2015, paragraphs 35, 36 and 41 of Schedule 23 (legislation no longer of practical use) are omitted.

SCHEDULE 10
Revocations and Consequential Amendments   Regulation 26

Performing Animals Rules 1925

1.   In rule 2 of the Performing Animals Rules 1925, for the first indented paragraph substitute "In Wales:—The City of Cardiff."

Sale of Dogs (Identification Tag) Regulations 1999

2.   The Sale of Dogs (Identification Tag) Regulations 1999 are revoked.

Breeding of Dogs (Licensing Records) Regulations 1999

3.   The Breeding of Dogs (Licensing Records) Regulations 1999 are revoked.

CONSERVATION

7.1835   Control of Trade in Endangered Species (Enforcement) Regulations 1997 *Delete the Control of Trade in Endangered Species (Enforcement) Regulations 1997 and replace with the Control of Trade in Endangered Species (Enforcement) Regulations 2018 as follows:*

Control of Trade in Endangered Species Regulations 2018
(SI 2018/703)

1.   *Citation and commencement* These Regulations may be cited as the Control of Trade in Endangered Species Regulations 2018 and come into force on 1st October 2018.

2.   *Interpretation* (1) In these Regulations—

"acquired" means, in relation to a specimen, taken from the wild or the point at which it was born in captivity or artificially propagated;

"acquired unlawfully" means acquired contrary to the provisions of the Principal Regulation or the Subsidiary Regulation and "acquired lawfully" is to be construed accordingly;

"import" means introduce into the European Union;

"imported unlawfully" means introduced into the European Union contrary to the provisions of the Principal Regulation or the Subsidiary Regulation;

"premises" includes any place, plant, machinery, equipment, apparatus, vehicle, vessel, aircraft, hovercraft, tent, temporary or movable building or structure;

"Principal Regulation" means Council Regulation (EC) No 338/97 on the protection of species of wild fauna and flora by regulating trade therein;

"Subsidiary Regulation" means Commission Regulation (EC) No 865/2006 laying down detailed rules concerning the implementation of the Principal Regulation.

(2)   Unless the context otherwise requires, expressions used in these Regulations which are also used in the Principal Regulation or the Subsidiary Regulation have the same meaning as in the instrument in question.

(3)   In these Regulations—

(a)   any reference to the Principal Regulation is a reference to the Principal Regulation as amended from time to time;

(b)   any reference to the Subsidiary Regulation is a reference to the Subsidiary Regulation as amended from time to time.

3.   *Offences, penalties and civil sanctions*   (1)   Schedule 1 makes provision for offences and penalties.

(2)   Schedule 2 makes provision for civil sanctions.

4.   *Liability for offences relating to Article 8 of the Principal Regulation*   (1)   A person is not guilty of an offence under paragraph 1 of Schedule 1 if that person proves that, at the time the alleged offence was committed, that person had no reason to believe that the specimen was a specimen of a species listed in Annex A or, as the case may be, Annex B.

(3)   A person is not guilty of an offence relating to Article 8 of the Principal Regulation if that person—

(a)   is a constable or a person acting at the request or on behalf of the management authority, and

(b)   purchases, or offers to purchase, a specimen for a purpose connected with the enforcement of these Regulations.

(4)   A person is not guilty of an offence under paragraph 1(2) of Schedule 1, involving contravention of Article 8.5 of the Principal Regulation, if that person proves—

(a)   that reasonable enquiries were made when that person came into possession of the specimen in order to ascertain whether it was imported lawfully or acquired lawfully, and

(b)   that at the time the alleged offence was committed that person had no reason to believe that the specimen was imported unlawfully or acquired unlawfully.

(5)   A person is to be taken to have made the enquiries mentioned in paragraph (3)(a) if that person produces a statement to the court provided by the person from whom possession of the specimen was obtained ("the supplier"), signed by the supplier or by a person authorised by the supplier, which states that—

(a)   the supplier made enquiries at the time when the specimen came into the supplier's possession in order to ascertain whether it was a specimen which had been imported lawfully or acquired lawfully, and

(b)   the supplier had no reason to believe at the time when possession passed to the accused that the specimen was at that time a specimen which had been imported unlawfully or acquired unlawfully.

(6)   A person must not provide a false statement for the purposes of paragraph (4).

5.   *Split-listed specimens*   (1)   For the purposes of an offence relating to Article 8 of the Principal Regulation, a split-listed specimen is presumed to be of a species listed in Annex A to the Principal Regulation, if—

(a)   where the specimen falls within paragraph (3), it is not reasonably practical to determine the population from which that specimen derives;

(b)   where the specimen falls within paragraph (4), it is not reasonably practical to determine the subspecies to which that specimen belongs;

(c)   where the specimen falls within paragraph (5), it is not reasonably practical to determine the species or subspecies to which that specimen belongs.

(2)   In paragraph (1), "split-listed specimen" means a specimen falling within paragraph (3), (4) or (5).

(3)   A specimen falls within this paragraph if—

(a)   the specimen is of a species or subspecies, or is included in a higher taxon than species, listed in Annex A or B to the Principal Regulation (or listed in both of those Annexes), and

(b)   one or more geographical populations of that species, subspecies or higher taxon are included in one of those Annexes and one or more other populations of that species, subspecies or higher taxon are included in the other of those Annexes.

(4)   A specimen falls within this paragraph if—

(a)   the specimen is of a species listed in Annex A or B to the Principal Regulation, and

(b)   one or more subspecies of that species are included in one of those Annexes and one or more subspecies of that species are included in the other of those Annexes.

(5)   A specimen falls within this paragraph if—

(a) the specimen is included in a higher taxon than species and that taxon is listed in either Annex A or B to the Principal Regulation, and

(b) one or more species or subspecies of that higher taxon are included in one of those Annexes, and one or more species or subspecies included in that higher taxon are included in the other of those Annexes, and all geographical populations of those species or subspecies are included in those Annexes.

6. *Advertising sale of Annex A specimens* A person offering to sell a specimen of a species listed in Annex A, in accordance with a certificate granted under Article 8(3) of the Principal Regulation, must include the reference number of the certificate in any advertisement for the sale of the specimen.

7. *Proof of lawful import or export* (1) Where a specimen—

(a) is being imported or exported,

(b) has been imported, or

(c) is brought to any place for the purpose of being imported or exported,

a general customs official may require any person possessing or having control of that specimen to provide proof that its import or export is or was not unlawful by virtue of the Principal Regulation or the Subsidiary Regulation.

(2) Until proof required under paragraph (1) is provided to the satisfaction of a general customs official, the specimen may be detained by the customs official for 30 days beginning on the day on which the specimen is first detained.

(3) If that proof is not provided to the satisfaction of the general customs official before the expiry of that period of detention, the specimen is deemed to be seized as liable to forfeiture under the Customs and Excise Management Act 1979 on expiry of that period.

(4) In this regulation, "general customs official" means a person designated as a general customs official under section 3(1) of the Borders, Citizenship and Immigration Act 2009 or a person authorised by a designated person.

8. *Powers of entry* (1) If, on an application made by a constable, a justice is satisfied that there are reasonable grounds for believing—

(a) that there is a specimen that has been imported unlawfully or acquired unlawfully on premises specified in the application, or

(b) that an offence under these Regulations has been or is being committed and that evidence of the offence may be found on any premises,

and that any of the conditions specified in paragraph (2) applies, a warrant may be issued authorising a constable, and any other persons as the constable thinks necessary, to enter and search those premises.

(2) The conditions referred to in paragraph (1) are that—

(a) admission to the premises has been refused;

(b) refusal of admission is anticipated;

(c) the case is one of urgency;

(d) an application for admission to the premises would defeat the object of the entry.

(3) An authorised person may, at any reasonable time and (if required to do so) upon producing evidence that the person is so authorised, enter and inspect any premises for the purpose of—

(a) ascertaining whether contrary to Article 8 of the Principal Regulation, the premises are being used for any of the following activities in relation to that specimen—

 (i) purchase;

 (ii) offering to purchase;

 (iii) acquisition for commercial purposes;

 (iv) use for commercial gain;

 (v) display to the public for commercial purposes;

 (vi) sale;

 (vii) keeping for sale;

 (viii) offering for sale;

 (ix) transporting for sale;

(b) verifying information supplied by a person for the purpose of obtaining a permit or certificate;

(c) ascertaining whether a live specimen is being kept on premises at the address specified in an import permit, or a certificate issued under Article 10 of the Principal Regulation for that specimen, as that at which the specimen is to be kept;

(d) ascertaining whether any condition of a permit or certificate has been or is being observed.

(4) Nothing in paragraph (3) confers power to enter a dwelling.

(5) A constable or an authorised person who is, by virtue of this regulation, lawfully on any premises may, in order to determine the identity, ancestry or (in the case of a specimen which is not living) age of any specimen, require—

(a) a sample of blood or tissue to be taken from a live animal specimen, provided that—

 (i) the sample is taken by a registered veterinary surgeon or a suitably trained authorised person, and

 (ii) taking the sample will not cause lasting harm to the specimen;

(b) a non-invasive sample to be taken from any other specimen by a suitably trained authorised person.

(6) A person must not—

(a)   obstruct an authorised person acting in accordance with the powers conferred by this regulation;

(b)   with intent to deceive, pretend to be an authorised person.

(7)   In this regulation—

"authorised person" means a person duly authorised in writing by the Secretary of State for the purposes of this regulation;

"justice" means—

(a)   in England and Wales, a justice of the peace;

(b)   in Scotland, a sheriff, summary sheriff or justice of the peace;

(c)   in Northern Ireland, a lay magistrate;

"registered veterinary surgeon" means a person who is registered in the register of veterinary surgeons under section 2 of the Veterinary Surgeons Act 1966.

9.   *Powers of seizure*   (1)   A constable who is, by virtue of regulation 8(1), lawfully on any premises, may seize any thing where the constable has reasonable grounds for believing that seizure is—

(a)   necessary for the protection of the constable or any person accompanying the constable;

(b)   otherwise necessary to effect seizure of a specimen;

(c)   necessary for the conservation of evidence;

(d)   in the interests of the welfare of a specimen.

(2)   The court which convicts a person of an offence under these Regulations may order the offender to reimburse any expenses incurred by a police force or the Police Service of Northern Ireland in connection with keeping a live specimen which has been seized by a constable under paragraph (1).

(3)   Where an order is made under paragraph (2) and the amount specified in the order is not paid, the unpaid amount is recoverable summarily as a civil debt owed to the police force or service named in the order.

10.   *Forfeiture and banning orders*   The court which convicts a person of an offence under these Regulations may order—

(a)   the forfeiture of any specimen or other thing in respect of which the offence was committed;

(b)   the forfeiture of any vessel, vehicle, equipment, apparatus or other thing which was used to commit the offence;

(c)   that the offender must not have any specimen, or a specimen of a particular description, in his or her possession or under his or her control for a specified period of up to five years.

11.   *Offences by corporations etc*   (1)   If an offence under these Regulations by a body corporate or a Scottish partnership is proved to have been committed with the consent or connivance of an officer, the officer (as well as the body corporate or partnership) is guilty of the offence and liable to be proceeded against and punished accordingly.

(2)   In relation to a body corporate, "officer" means—

(a)   a director, manager, secretary or other similar officer of the body;

(b)   a person purporting to act in any such capacity.

(3)   In relation to a Scottish partnership, "officer" means—

(a)   a partner;

(b)   a person purporting to act as a partner.

(4)   If the affairs of a body corporate are managed by its members, paragraph (1) applies in relation to the acts and defaults of a member in connection with functions of management as if the member were an officer of the body.

12.   *Management authority and scientific authority*   (1)   For the purposes of these Regulations, the Principal Regulation and the Subsidiary Regulation, the management authority is the Secretary of State.

(2)   For the purposes of the Principal Regulation and the Subsidiary Regulation, the Secretary of State may designate one or more persons as a scientific authority.

13.   *Ports of entry and exit*   For the purposes of the Principal Regulation and the Subsidiary Regulation, the Secretary of State may designate customs offices for carrying out the checks and formalities for the introduction into, and export from, the European Union of specimens.

14.   *Revocations*   (1)   The following regulations are revoked—

(a)   the Control of Trade in Endangered Species (Designation of Ports of Entry) Regulations 1985;

(b)   the Control of Trade in Endangered Species (Enforcement) Regulations 1997;

(c)   the Control of Trade in Endangered Species (Enforcement) (Amendment) Regulations 2005;

(d)   the Control of Trade in Endangered Species (Enforcement) (Amendment) Regulations 2007;

(e)   the Control of Trade in Endangered Species (Enforcement) (Amendment) Regulations 2009.

15.   *Savings and transitional provisions*   (1)   Where an act carried out before 1st October 2018 is unlawful under the 1997 Regulations, the 1997 Regulations continue to have effect in relation to that act.

(2) Where a specimen is detained before 1st October 2018 under regulation 5 of the 1997 Regulations, the 1997 Regulations continue to have effect in relation to that detention and any subsequent forfeiture.

(3) Any warrant issued before 1st October 2018 under regulation 9(1) of the 1997 Regulations continues to have effect.

(4) Where any thing is seized before 1st October 2018 under regulation 10 of the 1997 Regulations, the 1997 Regulations continue to have effect in relation to that seizure.

(5) But these Regulations apply where—

(a) an act carried out before 1st October 2018 is unlawful under the 1997 Regulations, and

(b) that act continues on or after 1st October 2018 and is unlawful under these Regulations.

(6) In this regulation, "the 1997 Regulations" means the Control of Trade in Endangered Species (Enforcement) Regulations 1997.

SCHEDULE 1

Offences and Penalties

Regulation 3(1)

Article 16(1)(j) of the Principal Regulation

1. (1) The penalty for the offence specified in sub-paragraph (2) is as follows—

(a) on summary conviction, imprisonment for a maximum term of six months or a fine (not exceeding the statutory maximum in Scotland or Northern Ireland, as the case may be) or both;

(b) on conviction on indictment, imprisonment for a maximum term of five years or a fine or both.

(2) The offence referred to in sub-paragraph (1) is the conduct specified in Article 16(1)(j) of the Principal Regulation in relation to a specimen, in contravention of Article 8 of the Principal Regulation, as follows—

(a) purchasing;

(b) offering to purchase;

(c) acquiring for commercial purposes;

(d) using for commercial gain;

(e) displaying to the public for commercial purposes;

(f) selling;

(g) keeping for sale;

(h) offering for sale;

(i) transporting for sale.

Other offences and penalties

2. The penalty for the offences described in the following table is as follows—

(a) on summary conviction, imprisonment for a maximum term of three months or a fine (not exceeding the statutory maximum in Scotland or Northern Ireland, as the case may be) or both;

(b) on conviction on indictment, imprisonment for a maximum term of two years or a fine or both.

Column 1 Provision of the Principal Regulation or these Regulations	Column 2 Subject matter
Article 9 of the Principal Regulation	Without reasonable excuse, causing any movement within the European Union of a live specimen of a species listed in Annex A from the location indicated in the import permit or in any certificate issued in compliance with the Principal Regulation, contrary to the provisions of Article 9 of the Principal Regulation, or the provisions of the Subsidiary Regulation
Article 16(1)(b) of the Principal Regulation	Knowingly contravening the stipulations specified on a permit or certificate issued in accordance with the Principal Regulation or the Subsidiary Regulation
Article 16(1)(c) of the Principal Regulation	Knowingly or recklessly making a false declaration or providing false information in order to obtain a permit or certificate
Article 16(1)(d) of the Principal Regulation	Knowingly or recklessly using a false or invalid permit or certificate or one altered without authorisation as a basis for obtaining a permit or certificate or for any other official purpose in connection with the Principal Regulation or the Subsidiary Regulation
Article 16(1)(e) of the Principal Regulation	Knowingly or recklessly making a false import notification
Article 16(1)(f) of the Principal Regulation	Without reasonable excuse, causing the shipment of live specimens not properly prepared so as to minimise the risk of injury, damage to health or cruel treatment (as required by Article 9(5) of the Principal Regulation)
Article 16(1)(g) of the Principal Regulation	Knowingly using specimens listed in Annex A to the Principal Regulation other than in accordance with the authorisation given at the time of issuance of the permit or subsequently
Article 16(1)(k) of the Principal Regulation	Knowingly using a permit or certificate for any specimen other than the one for which it was issued
Article 16(1)(l) of the Principal Regulation	Knowingly falsifying or altering any permit or certificate issued in accordance with the Principal Regulation or the Subsidiary Regulation
Article 16(1)(m) of the Principal Regulation	Without reasonable excuse failing to disclose the rejection of an application for an import, export or re-export permit or certificate, in accordance with Article 6(3) of the Principal Regulation
Regulation 4(6) of these Regulations	Knowingly or recklessly providing a false statement relating to whether a specimen was imported unlawfully or acquired lawfully
Regulation 8(6) of these Regulations	Intentionally obstructing entry or, with intent to deceive, pretending to be an authorised person

SCHEDULE 2
Civil Sanctions   Regulation 3(2)

Part 3   Stop notices

Stop notices
11. (1) This paragraph applies where the management authority is satisfied on the balance of probabilities that a person is—
(a)   carrying on an activity, and
(b)   the management authority reasonably believes that the activity as carried on by that person involves or is likely to involve a contravention of a relevant regulation.
(2) The management authority may by notice ("a stop notice") prohibit that person from carrying on an activity specified in the notice until the person has taken the steps specified in the notice.
(3) The steps referred to in sub-paragraph (2) must be steps to eliminate the risk of the contravention being committed or occurring.

Contents of a stop notice
16. If a person on whom a stop notice is served does not comply with it within the time limit specified in the notice, the person is guilty of an offence and liable on summary conviction to a fine (not exceeding the statutory maximum in Scotland or Northern Ireland, as the case may be).

Part 4   Enforcement undertakings

Enforcement undertakings
17. The management authority may accept a written undertaking ("an enforcement undertaking") given by a person to the management authority to take such action as may be specified in the undertaking within such period as may be specified where the management authority has reasonable grounds to suspect that the person has failed to comply with a relevant regulation.

Contents of an enforcement undertaking
18. (1) An enforcement undertaking must specify—
(a)   action to be taken by the person to secure that the failure to comply with a relevant regulation does not continue or recur;
(b)   action to secure that the position is, so far as possible, restored to what it would have been if the failure to comply had not occurred;
(c)   action (including the payment of a sum of money) to be taken by the person giving the undertaking to benefit any person affected by the failure to comply.
(2) It must specify the period within which the action must be completed.
(3) It must include—
(a)   a statement that the undertaking is made in accordance with this Schedule;
(b)   the terms of the undertaking;
(c)   information as to how and when a person is considered to have discharged the undertaking.
(4) An enforcement undertaking may be varied, or the period within which the action must be completed may be extended, if the management authority and the person who gave the undertaking agree in writing.

Acceptance of an enforcement undertaking
19. (1) If the management authority has accepted an enforcement undertaking from a person, it may not serve on that person a compliance notice or stop notice, or impose a non-compliance penalty or a variable monetary penalty, in respect of the act or omission that is the subject of the undertaking.
(2) Paragraph (1) does not apply if the person who gave the undertaking has failed to comply with it or any part of it.

Discharge of an enforcement undertaking
20. (1) The management authority must issue a certificate ("a discharge certificate") if it is satisfied on the balance of probabilities that an enforcement undertaking has been complied with.
(2) An enforcement undertaking ceases to have effect on the issue of a discharge certificate.
(3) The management authority may require the person who gave the undertaking to provide sufficient information to determine that the undertaking has been complied with.
(4) The person who gave the undertaking may at any time apply for a discharge certificate.
(5) The management authority must decide whether to issue a discharge certificate and give written notice of the decision to the applicant (including information as to the rights of appeal) within 14 days of the application.
(6) The applicant may appeal against a decision not to issue a discharge certificate on the grounds that the decision—
(a)   was based on an error of fact;
(b)   was wrong in law;
(c)   was unreasonable;
(d)   was wrong for any other reason.

Inaccurate, incomplete or misleading information
21. (1) A person who gives inaccurate, misleading or incomplete information in relation to an enforcement undertaking is regarded as not having complied with it.
(2) The management authority may by notice in writing revoke a discharge certificate if it was issued on the basis of inaccurate, incomplete or misleading information.

Non-compliance with an enforcement undertaking
22. (1) If a person does not comply with an enforcement undertaking, the management authority may serve a compliance notice or stop notice, or impose a non-compliance penalty or variable monetary penalty, in respect of the act or omission that was the subject of the undertaking.
(2) If a person has only complied partly with an undertaking, that partial compliance must be taken into account in the imposition of any sanction.

Part 5   Non-compliance penalties

Non-compliance penalties
23. (1) If a person fails to comply with a compliance notice, stop notice, third party undertaking or enforcement undertaking, irrespective of whether a variable monetary penalty is also imposed, the management authority may serve a notice on that person imposing a monetary penalty ("a non-compliance penalty").
(2) The amount of the non-compliance penalty must be determined by the management authority as a percentage of the costs of fulfilling the remaining requirements of the notice, third party undertaking or enforcement undertaking.
(3) The percentage must be determined by the management authority having regard to all the circumstances of the case and may, if appropriate, be 100%.
(4) A notice served under paragraph (1) must include information as to—
(a)   the grounds for imposing the penalty;
(b)   the amount to be paid;
(c)   how payment may be made;
(d)   the period within which payment must be made, which must not be less than 28 days;

(e)   the rights of appeal;

(f)   the consequences of failure to comply with the notice;

(g)   any circumstances in which the management authority may reduce the amount of the penalty.

(5)   If the requirements of the compliance notice, stop notice, third party undertaking or enforcement undertaking are fulfilled before the time specified for payment of the non-compliance penalty, the penalty is not payable.

Appeals

24.   (1)   A person on whom the notice imposing the non-compliance penalty is served may appeal against it.

(2)   The grounds of appeal are—

(a)   that the decision to serve the notice was based on an error of fact;

(b)   that the decision was wrong in law;

(c)   that the amount of the penalty is unreasonable;

(d)   that the decision was unreasonable for any reason;

(e)   that the decision was wrong for any other reason.

PART 6   WITHDRAWAL AND AMENDMENT OF NOTICES

Withdrawing or amending a notice

25.   The management authority may at any time in writing—

(a)   withdraw a compliance notice or stop notice, or amend the steps specified in such a notice in order to reduce the amount of work necessary to comply with the notice;

(b)   withdraw a notice imposing a variable monetary penalty or a non-compliance penalty notice, or reduce the amount of the penalty specified in such a notice.

PART 7   APPEALS

Appeals

26.   (1)   Any appeal under this Schedule must be made to the First-tier Tribunal.

(2)   In any appeal the Tribunal must determine the standard of proof.

(3)   All notices (other than stop notices) are suspended until determination or withdrawal of the appeal.

(4)   The Tribunal may, in relation to the imposition of a requirement or service of a notice—

(a)   withdraw the requirement or notice;

(b)   confirm the requirement or notice;

(c)   vary the requirement or notice;

(d)   take such steps as the management authority could take in relation to the act or omission giving rise to the requirement or notice;

(e)   remit the decision whether to confirm the requirement or notice, or any matter relating to that decision, to the management authority.

PART 8   GUIDANCE AND PUBLICITY

Guidance as to use of civil sanctions

27.   (1)   The management authority must publish guidance about its use of civil sanctions.

(2)   The management authority must revise and update the guidance where appropriate.

(3)   The management authority must have regard to the guidance or revised and updated guidance in exercising its functions.

(4)   In the case of guidance about compliance notices, stop notices, variable monetary penalties and non-compliance penalties, the guidance must contain information as to—

(a)   the circumstances in which the civil sanction is likely to be imposed;

(b)   the circumstances in which it is not likely to be imposed.

(5)   In the case of guidance about variable monetary penalties and non-compliance penalties, the guidance must contain information as to—

(a)   the matters likely to be taken into account by the management authority in determining the amount of the penalty (including voluntary reporting by a person of their own non-compliance);

(b)   the rights to make representations and the rights of appeal.

(6)   In the case of guidance about enforcement undertakings, the guidance must contain information as to—

(a)   the circumstances in which the management authority is likely to accept an enforcement undertaking;

(b)   the circumstances in which the management authority is not likely to accept an enforcement undertaking.

Consultation on guidance

28.   The management authority must consult such persons as it considers appropriate before publishing any guidance or revised or updated guidance.

Publication of enforcement action

29.   (1)   The management authority must from time to time publish—

(a)   the cases in which civil sanctions have been imposed;

(b)   where the civil sanction is a compliance notice, stop notice or variable monetary penalty, the cases in which a third party undertaking has been accepted;

(c)   the cases in which an enforcement undertaking has been given.

(2)   In sub-paragraph (1)(a), the reference to cases in which civil sanctions have been imposed does not include cases where the sanction has been imposed but overturned on appeal.

(3)   This paragraph does not apply in cases where the management authority considers that publication would be inappropriate.

CONSUMER PROTECTION

7.2061A   Consumer Rights Act 2015   *After the Consumer Rights Act 2015 insert the Financial Guidance and Claims Act 2018 in a new para as follows:*

Financial Guidance and Claims Act 2018[1]

(2018 c 10)

---

[1]   The introductory note states that the Act's purposes are: make provision establishing a new financial guidance body (including provision about a debt respite scheme); to make provision about the funding of debt advice in Scotland, Wales and Northern Ireland; to provide a power to make regulations prohibiting unsolicited direct marketing in relation to pensions and other consumer financial products and services; and to make provision about the regulation of claims management services. We reproduce only the provisions which establish the single financial guidance body and the offence of providing information, guidance or advice on its behalf when that is not in fact the case.

PART 1

FINANCIAL GUIDANCE ETC

Establishment of the single financial guidance body

1. The single financial guidance body (1) A body corporate with functions relating to financial guidance is established (the "single financial guidance body").

(2) Schedule 1 makes further provision about the single financial guidance body.

(3) The name of the new body is to be determined by regulations made by the Secretary of State.

(4) The regulations may—

    (a)   amend any provision of this Part, or of any Act amended by this Part, so as to replace the words "single financial guidance body" with the name of the body;

    (b)   make incidental, supplementary and consequential provision.

(5) The power to make regulations under subsection (3) is exercisable by statutory instrument; and an instrument containing such regulations is subject to annulment in pursuance of a resolution of either House of Parliament.

(6) The consumer financial education body is dissolved.

(7) Schedule 2 makes provision about schemes for the transfer of staff, property, rights and liabilities—

    (a)   from the Secretary of State and the Pensions Advisory Service Limited to the single financial guidance body;

    (b)   from the consumer financial education body to the single financial guidance body and the devolved authorities.

Offence of impersonating the single financial guidance body

15. False claims about provision of information etc (1) It is an offence for a person to hold himself or herself out (or where the person is a body, to hold itself out) as providing information, guidance or advice on behalf of the single financial guidance body when that is not in fact the case.

(2) It is a defence for a person charged with an offence under this section to prove that the person took all reasonable precautions and exercised all due diligence to avoid committing the offence.

(3) A person guilty of an offence under this section is liable on summary conviction—

    (a)   in England and Wales, to imprisonment for a term not exceeding 51 weeks or a fine, or both;

    (b)   in Scotland, to imprisonment for a term not exceeding 12 months or a fine not exceeding level 5 on the standard scale, or both;

    (c)   in Northern Ireland, to imprisonment for a term not exceeding 6 months or a fine not exceeding level 5 on the standard scale, or both.

(4) In relation to an offence committed before the commencement of section 281(5) of the Criminal Justice Act 2003, the reference in subsection (3)(a) to 51 weeks is to be read as a reference to 6 months.

(5) Proceedings for an offence under this section may be instituted in England and Wales only by or with the consent of the Director of Public Prosecutions.

(6) Proceedings for an offence under this section may be instituted in Northern Ireland only by or with the consent of the Director of Public Prosecutions for Northern Ireland.

16. Offences under section 15 committed by bodies corporate etc (1) If an offence under section 15 committed by a body corporate is proved—

    (a)   to have been committed with the consent or connivance of an officer of the body, or

    (b)   to be attributable to any neglect on the part of such an officer,

the officer, as well as the body corporate, is guilty of the offence and liable to be proceeded against and punished accordingly.

(2) In subsection (1) "officer", in relation to a body corporate, means—

    (a)   a director, member of the committee of management, chief executive, manager, secretary or other similar officer of the body, or a person purporting to act in any such capacity;

    (b)   an individual who is a controller of the body.

(3) If the affairs of a body corporate are managed by its members, subsection (1) applies in relation to the acts and defaults of a member in connection with the member's functions of management as if the member were a director of the body corporate.

(4) If an offence under section 15 committed by a partnership is proved—

    (a)   to have been committed with the consent or connivance of a partner, or

    (b)   to be attributable to any neglect on the part of the partner,

the partner, as well as the partnership, is guilty of the offence and liable to be proceeded against and punished accordingly.

(5) In subsection (4) "partner" includes a person purporting to act as a partner.

(6) If an offence under section 15 committed by an unincorporated association other than a partnership is proved—

(a)   to have been committed with the consent or connivance of an officer of the association or a member of its governing body, or

(b)   to be attributable to any neglect on the part of such an officer or member,

the officer or member, as well as the association, is guilty of the offence and liable to be proceeded against and punished accordingly.

(7)   Proceedings for an offence under section 15 must be brought—

(a)   where the offence is alleged to have been committed by a partnership, against the partnership in the firm name;

(b)   where the offence is alleged to have been committed by any other type of unincorporated association, against the association in its own name.

(8)   Rules of court relating to the service of documents have effect in relation to such proceedings as if the partnership or unincorporated association were a body corporate.

PACKAGE TRAVEL, PACKAGE HOLIDAYS AND PACKAGE TOURS REGULATIONS 1992

7.2097   *Delete the Package Travel, Package Holidays and Package Tours Regulations 1992.*

7.2250A   *Insert in a new paragraph the The Package Travel and Linked Travel Arrangements Regulations 2018 (SI 2018/634) as follows:*

Package Travel and Linked Travel Arrangements Regulations 2018[1]
(SI 2018/634)

PART 1   GENERAL

1.   Citation and commencement   (1)   These Regulations may be cited as the Package Travel and Linked Travel Arrangements Regulations 2018.

(2)   Except as set out in paragraph (3), these Regulations come into force on 1st July 2018.

(3)   Regulation 38(4) comes into force on the later of the following—

(a)   1st July 2018;

(b)   the day on which Schedule 1 to the Wales Act 2017 (which inserts Schedule 7A into the Government of Wales Act 2006, which regulation 38(4) amends) comes into force.

---

[1] Made by the Secretary of State in exercise of the powers conferred by s 2(2) of, and para 2(2) of Sch 2 to, the European Communities Act 1972. This instrument implements the EU's 2015 Package Travel Directive and replaces the existing Package Travel Regulations 1992, SI 1992/3288. It expands the definition of a package to ensure that it encompasses modern methods of purchasing package holidays, particularly online. It also creates the new concept of linked travel arrangements, which are looser combinations of travel services, and introduces a limited level of protection for consumers who purchase them.

2.   Interpretation

3.   Application   (1)   These Regulations apply to—

(a)   packages offered for sale or sold by traders to travellers, and

(b)   linked travel arrangements,

which are concluded on or after the commencement date.

(2)   These Regulations do not apply to—

(a)   packages and linked travel arrangements covering a period of less than 24 hours, unless overnight accommodation is included;

(b)   packages offered, and linked travel arrangements facilitated, occasionally on a not-for-profit basis for a limited group of travellers;

(c)   packages and linked travel arrangements purchased on the basis of a general agreement.

(3)   In paragraph (2)(c), a "general agreement" means an agreement which is concluded between a trader and another person acting for a trade, business, craft or profession, for the purpose of booking travel arrangements in connection with that trade, business, craft or profession.

PART 2   INFORMATION DUTIES AND CONTENT OF THE PACKAGE TRAVEL CONTRACT

4.   Information duties and "the relevant person"   (1)   Where a package travel contract is sold through a retailer—

(a)   the organiser and the retailer must ensure that the duties imposed by regulations 5, 6 and 7 ("the information duties") are performed;

(b)   the organiser and the retailer may agree whether the information duties are to be performed by the organiser or the retailer; and

(c)   either the organiser or the retailer must perform the information duties.

(2)   Where a package travel contract is not sold through a retailer, the organiser must perform the information duties imposed by regulations 5, 6 and 7.

(3)   In this Part, the person who, in accordance with this regulation, performs, or it is agreed is to perform, a duty imposed by a provision of regulation 5, 6 or 7, is "the relevant person" for the purposes of the provision of regulation 5, 6 or 7 under which the duty is performed or it is agreed is to be performed.

5.   Information to be provided by the relevant person before concluding a contract   (1)   Subject to paragraph (3), before a package travel contract is concluded, the relevant person must provide the traveller with the information specified in Schedule 1, where applicable to the package.

(2)   Subject to paragraph (3), before a package travel contract is concluded, the relevant person must also provide the traveller with—

(a)   where the use of hyperlinks is possible, the information in Schedule 2, using the form and wording set out in that Schedule;

(b)   where the use of hyperlinks is not possible, or the package travel contract is to be concluded by telephone, the information in Schedule 3, using the form and wording set out in that Schedule.

(3)   Before a traveller is bound by a package of the kind described in regulation 2(5)(b)(v)—

(a)   the relevant person and the trader to whom the data are transmitted must ensure that each of them provides the information specified in Schedule 1, in so far as it is relevant for the respective travel services they offer; and

(b)   the relevant person must provide, at the same time, the information in Schedule 4, using the form and wording set out in that Schedule.

(4)   Any information provided to the traveller under this regulation must be provided—

(a)   in a clear, comprehensible and prominent manner; and

(b)   where the information is provided in writing, in a legible form.

(5)   Where the relevant person fails to provide information to the traveller in accordance with this regulation, the organiser or, where the package travel contract is sold through a retailer, both the organiser and the retailer, commit an offence and are liable—

(a)   on summary conviction, to a fine in England and Wales, or in Scotland and Northern Ireland to a fine not exceeding the statutory maximum;

(b)   on conviction on indictment, to a fine.

6.   *Binding character of information provided before the conclusion of the contract*   (1)   Where the relevant person provides to the traveller the information specified in paragraphs 1 to 10, 12 to 14 and 16 of Schedule 1, that information—

(a)   forms an integral part of the package travel contract; and

(b)   must not be altered unless the traveller expressly agrees otherwise with the relevant person, as the case may be.

(2)   The relevant person must communicate to the traveller any change to the information provided under regulation 5, in a clear, comprehensible and prominent manner before the conclusion of the package travel contract.

(3)   Where, before the conclusion of the package travel contract, the relevant person does not provide the information which is required to be provided under paragraph (1) in respect of additional fees, charges or other costs referred to in paragraph 12 of Schedule 1 the traveller is not required to bear those fees, charges or other costs.

(4)   It is an implied condition (or, as regards Scotland, an implied term) of the package travel contract that the relevant person complies with the provisions of this regulation.

(5)   In Scotland, any breach of the condition implied by paragraph (4) is deemed to be a material breach justifying rescission of the contract.

7.   *Content of the package travel contract and other documents*   (1)   The relevant person must ensure that—

(a)   the package travel contract is in plain and intelligible language; and

(b)   where the contract, or part of the contract, is in writing, the contract or the part of the contract, is in a legible form.

(2)   The relevant person must ensure that the package travel contract sets out the full content of the package and includes—

(a)   the information specified in Schedule 1; and

(b)   the information specified in Schedule 5.

(3)   Subject to paragraphs (4) and (5), when the package travel contract is concluded, or without undue delay after its conclusion, the relevant person must provide the traveller with a copy or confirmation of the contract on a durable medium.

(4)   Where the contract is concluded in the simultaneous physical presence of the parties, the relevant person must provide to the traveller a paper copy of the package travel contract if the traveller so requests.

(5)   Where an off-premises contract is concluded, the relevant person must provide a copy or confirmation of that contract to the traveller on paper or, if the traveller agrees, on another durable medium.

(6)   Where a package of the kind described in regulation 2(5)(b)(v) is concluded—

(a)   the trader to whom the data are transmitted must inform the relevant person of the conclusion of the contract leading to the creation of a package; and

(b)   the trader must provide the relevant person with the information necessary to comply with their obligations as the relevant person.

(7)   As soon as the organiser is informed, under paragraph (6), that a package has been created, the relevant person must provide the information in Schedule 5 to the traveller on a durable medium.

(8)   The relevant person must provide the information referred to in paragraphs (2) and (7) in a clear, comprehensible and prominent manner.

(9)   The relevant person must provide the traveller in good time, before the start of the package, with the necessary receipts, vouchers and tickets, information on the scheduled times of departure and, where applicable, the deadline for check-in, as well as the scheduled times for intermediate stops, transport connections and arrival.

(10)   It is an implied condition (or, as regards Scotland, an implied term) of the contract that the

relevant person complies with paragraphs (1), (3) to (6) and (9).

(11)   In Scotland, any breach of the condition implied by paragraph (10) is deemed to be a material breach justifying rescission of the contract.

(12)   Where the relevant person fails to comply with paragraph (2), (7) or (8), the organiser or, where the package travel contract is sold through a retailer, both the organiser and the retailer, commit an offence and are liable—

(a)   on summary conviction, to a fine in England and Wales, or in Scotland and Northern Ireland to a fine not exceeding the statutory maximum;

(b)   on conviction on indictment, to a fine.

(13)   In paragraph (5), "off-premises contract" has the meaning given in point 8 of Article 2 of Directive 2011/83/EU of the European Parliament and the Council on consumer rights, amending Council Directive 93/13/EEC and Directive 1999/44/EC of the European Parliament and of the Council and repealing Council Directive 85/577/EEC and Directive 97/7/EC of the European Parliament and of the Council.

8.   *Burden of proof*   (1)   In case of dispute about the organiser or the retailer's compliance with any provision of this Part, it is for the organiser or the retailer, as appropriate, to show that the provision was complied with.

(2)   Paragraph (1) does not apply to proceedings for an offence under—

(a)   regulation 5(5); or

(b)   regulation 7(12).

PART 5   INSOLVENCY PROTECTION

19.   *Insolvency protection for packages*   (1)   The organiser of a package who is established in the United Kingdom must provide effective security to cover, in the event of the organiser's insolvency, the reasonably foreseeable costs of—

(a)   refunding all payments made by or on behalf of travellers for any travel service not performed as a consequence of the insolvency, taking into account the length of the period between down payments and final payments and the completion of the packages; and

(b)   if the carriage of passengers is included in the packages, and the performance of any package is affected by the insolvency, repatriating the traveller and, if necessary, financing the traveller's accommodation prior to the repatriation.

(2)   The organiser must provide the security under paragraph (1) to benefit travellers—

(a)   regardless of their place of residence, their place of departure or where the package is sold;

(b)   irrespective of the member State where the entity in charge of the insolvency protection is located.

(3)   The organiser must provide the security—

(a)   under paragraph (1)(a), without undue delay after the traveller's request;

(b)   under paragraph (1)(b), free of charge.

(4)   The organiser of a package who—

(a)   is not established in the United Kingdom or in any other member State, and

(b)   sells or offers for sale a package in the United Kingdom, or by any means directs such activities to the United Kingdom,

must provide security in accordance with this Part.

(5)   Without prejudice to paragraphs (1) to (4), and subject to paragraphs (6) to (8), the organiser must at least ensure that arrangements as described in—

(a)   regulation 20,

(b)   regulation 21,

(c)   regulation 22, or

(d)   regulations 23 and 24,

are in force.

(6)   Paragraph (5) does not apply to a package to the extent that—

(a)   the package is covered by measures adopted or retained by the member State where the organiser is established for the purpose of Article 17 of the Directive; or

(b)   the package is one—

(i)   in respect of which the organiser is required to hold a licence under the Civil Aviation (Air Travel Organisers' Licensing) Regulations 2012; or

(ii)   that is covered by the arrangements the organiser has entered into for the purposes of those Regulations.

(7)   For the purposes of regulations 20 to 24, a contract is to be treated as having been fully performed if the package or, as the case may be, the part of the package, has been completed.

(8)   For the purposes of paragraph (7), a package is to be deemed to have been completed whether or not there has been a lack of conformity.

(9)   An organiser who fails to comply with any provision of paragraphs (1) to (5) commits an offence and is liable—

(a)   on summary conviction, to a fine in England and Wales, or in Scotland and Northern Ireland to a fine not exceeding the statutory maximum;

(b)   on conviction on indictment, to a fine.

(10)   In the event of the organiser's insolvency, travellers may agree to continue the package where—

(a)   it is possible to do so; and

(b)   a person, other than that organiser, agrees to carry out the responsibilities of the organiser under the package travel contract.

(11)   The Civil Aviation Authority is designated as a central contact point for the purposes of Article 18(2) and (3) of the Directive and may perform the duties imposed on central contact points by that Article.

23.   *Monies in trust*   (1) Where an organiser, for the purpose of regulation 19(5), relies on the arrangements under this regulation, the organiser must ensure that—

(a)   all monies, or

(b)   where regulation 24(3) applies, a lesser sum in accordance with that regulation,

paid by or on behalf of a traveller under or in contemplation of a package travel contract are held in the United Kingdom or a member State by a person as trustee for the traveller.

(2)   The monies are to be held under paragraph (1) until—

(a)   the contract has been fully performed; or

(b)   any sum of money paid by or on behalf of the traveller in respect of the contract—

(i)   has been repaid to the traveller; or

(ii)   has been forfeited on cancellation by the traveller.

(3)   The person appointed as trustee for the purposes of paragraph (1) must be independent of the organiser.

(4)   The costs of administering the trust mentioned in paragraph (1) must be paid for by the organiser.

(5)   Any interest which is earned on the monies held by the trustee pursuant to paragraph (1) must be held for the organiser and must be payable to the organiser on demand.

(6)   Where there is produced to the trustee a statement signed by the organiser to the effect that—

(a)   a package travel contract, the price of which is specified in that statement, has been fully performed,

(b)   the organiser has repaid to the traveller a sum of money specified in that statement which the traveller had paid in respect of a package travel contract, or

(c)   the traveller has on cancellation forfeited a sum of money specified in that statement which the traveller had paid in respect of a package travel contract,

the trustee must release to the organiser the sum specified in the statement.

(7)   Where the trustee considers it appropriate to do so, the trustee may require the organiser to provide further information or evidence of the matters mentioned in sub-paragraph (a), (b) or (c) of paragraph (6) before the trustee releases any sum to the organiser pursuant to that paragraph.

(8)   In the event of the organiser's insolvency, the monies held in trust by the trustee pursuant to paragraph (1) of this regulation must be applied to meet the claims of travellers who are creditors of that organiser in respect of package travel contracts in respect of which the trust mentioned in paragraph (1) has been established and which have not been fully performed.

(9)   If there is a surplus after those claims have been met, it is to form part of the estate of the organiser for the purposes of insolvency law.

24.   *Insurance where monies are held in trust*   (1) This regulation applies to any organiser who, for the purpose of regulation 19(5), makes arrangements under regulation 23.

(2)   Where the organiser offers packages which include the carriage of passengers, the organiser must have insurance under one or more appropriate policies with an insurer authorised in respect of such business in accordance with regulation 22(1), under which, in the event of the insolvency of the organiser, the insurer agrees to cover the costs of—

(a)   repatriating the traveller who has purchased a relevant package; and

(b)   if necessary, financing the traveller's accommodation prior to the repatriation.

(3)   Where paragraph (4) applies, an organiser—

(a)   is not required, under regulation 23(1)(a), to ensure that all monies paid by a traveller under or in contemplation of a package travel contract are held in accordance with regulation 23; and

(b)   may, instead, ensure that a part of those monies only (the "lesser sum") is held in accordance with regulation 23, as the case may be.

(4)   This paragraph applies if the organiser has insurance under one or more appropriate policies with an insurer authorised in respect of such business in accordance with regulation 22(1), under which, in the event of the insolvency of the organiser, the insurer agrees to cover the relevant amount.

(5)   Where paragraph (2) or (4) applies, the organiser must ensure that it is a term of the relevant package travel contract that the traveller acquires the benefit of a policy of a kind mentioned in paragraph (2) or (3) in the event of the organiser's insolvency.

(6)   In this regulation, an "appropriate policy" means one which does not contain a condition which provides (in whatever terms) that no liability arises under the policy, or that any liability so arising ceases—

(a)   in the event of some specified thing being done or omitted to be done after the happening of the event giving rise to a claim under the policy;

(b)   in the event of the policy holder not making payments under or in connection with other policies; or

(c)   unless the policy holder keeps specified records or provides the insurer with, or makes available to, the insurer information from those records.

(7)   In paragraph (4), "the relevant amount" means such amount in excess of the lesser sum, as may be required to cover the costs of refunding the traveller for any travel service not fully

performed as a consequence of the insolvency, taking into account the length of the period between down payments and final payments and the completion of the package.

25. *Offences arising from breach of regulation 23* If the organiser makes a false statement under regulation 23(6), the organiser commits an offence and is liable—

(a)   on summary conviction, to a fine in England and Wales, or in Scotland and Northern Ireland to a fine not exceeding the statutory maximum;

(b)   on conviction on indictment, to a fine.

26. *Insolvency protection and information requirements for linked travel arrangements*
(1)   Any trader who facilitates a linked travel arrangement and is established in the United Kingdom must provide effective security to cover, in the event of the trader's insolvency, the reasonably foreseeable costs of—

(a)   refunding all payments the trader receives from travellers for any travel service which is part of the linked arrangement and is not performed as a consequence of the trader's insolvency, taking into account the length of the period between down payments and final payments and the completion of the linked travel arrangements; and

(b)   if the trader is the party responsible for the carriage of passengers, and the performance of the linked travel arrangement is affected by the insolvency, the traveller's repatriation and, if necessary, financing the traveller's accommodation prior to the repatriation.

(2)   The trader must provide the security under paragraph (1) to benefit travellers—

(a)   regardless of their place of residence, their place of departure or where the package is sold; and

(b)   irrespective of the member State where the entity in charge of the insolvency protection is located.

(3)   The trader must provide the security—

(a)   under paragraph (1)(a), without undue delay; and

(b)   under paragraph (1)(b), free of charge.

(4)   Any trader who—

(a)   is not established in the United Kingdom or in any other member State, and

(b)   sells or offers for sale a linked travel arrangement in the United Kingdom, or by any means directs such activities to the United Kingdom,

must provide security in accordance with this regulation in respect of those arrangements.

(5)   Without prejudice to paragraphs (1) to (4) and subject to paragraph (6), the trader must at least ensure that arrangements as described in—

(a)   regulation 20,

(b)   regulation 21,

(c)   regulation 22, or

(d)   regulations 23 and 24,

are in force and, for that purpose, a reference in those regulations to "organiser" is to be read as a reference to "trader", a reference to "package" or "package travel contract" is to be read as a reference to "linked travel arrangement" and a reference to regulation 19(5) is to be read as a reference to this paragraph.

(6)   Paragraph (5) does not apply to a linked travel arrangement to the extent that the linked travel arrangement—

(a)   is one which is covered by measures adopted or retained by the member State where the trader is established for the purpose of Article 17 of the Directive; or

(b)   includes a travel service—

      (i)   in respect of which the trader is required to hold a licence under the Civil Aviation (Air Travel Organisers' Licensing) Regulations 2012; or

      (ii)   which is covered by the arrangements the trader has entered into for the purposes of those Regulations.

(7)   Before the traveller is bound by any contract leading to the creation of a linked travel arrangement, the trader facilitating linked travel arrangements, including where the trader is not established in a member State but, by any means directs such activities to a member State, must—

(a)   state in a clear, comprehensible and prominent manner that the traveller—

      (i)   will not benefit from any of the rights applying exclusively to packages under these Regulations and that each service provider will be solely responsible for the proper contractual performance of the service;

      (ii)   will benefit from insolvency protection in accordance with paragraphs (1) to (5); and

(b)   provide the traveller with a copy of these Regulations.

(8)   In order to comply with paragraph (7), the trader facilitating a linked travel arrangement must provide the traveller with the information referred to in that paragraph—

(a)   using the form and wording set out in Schedule 6, where the trader facilitates an online linked travel arrangement within the meaning of regulation 2(3)(a) and the trader is a carrier selling a return ticket;

(b)   using the form and wording set out in Schedule 7, where the trader facilitates an online linked travel arrangement within the meaning of regulation 2(3)(a) and the trader is not a carrier selling a return ticket;

(c)   using the form and wording set out in Schedule 8, where the linked travel arrangement is an arrangement within the meaning of regulation 2(3)(a) and the contract is concluded in the simultaneous physical presence of the trader (other than a carrier selling a return ticket) and the traveller;

(d)   using the form and wording set out in Schedule 9, where the trader facilitates an online linked travel arrangement within the meaning of regulation 2(3)(b) and the trader is a carrier selling a return ticket; and

(e)   using the form and wording set out in Schedule 10, where the trader facilitates an online linked travel arrangement within the meaning of regulation 2(3)(b) and the trader not a carrier selling a return ticket.

(9)   Where a linked travel arrangement is not an arrangement of the kind described in sub-paragraphs (a) to (e) of paragraph (8), the trader must provide the information referred to in paragraph (7)—

(a)   in any form set out in Schedule 6, 7, 8, 9 or 10 which the trader considers is most appropriate for the purposes of providing the information, taking into account the particular circumstances of the linked travel arrangement being facilitated; and

(b)   if necessary, making such amendments to that form as are reasonably required to provide the information clearly.

(10)   A trader who fails to comply with any provision of paragraphs (1) to (9) commits an offence and is liable—

(a)   on summary conviction, to a fine in England and Wales, or in Scotland and Northern Ireland to a fine not exceeding the statutory maximum;

(b)   on conviction on indictment, to a fine.

(11)   Where the trader facilitating a linked travel arrangement does not comply with the requirements set out in this regulation, the rights and obligations specified in regulations 9 and 12 to 14 and in Part 4 apply in relation to the travel services included in the linked travel arrangement.

(12)   Where a linked travel arrangement is the result of the conclusion of a contract between a traveller and a trader who does not facilitate the linked travel arrangement, that trader must inform the trader facilitating the linked travel arrangement of the conclusion of the relevant contract.

Part 6   General Provisions

30.   Rights and obligations under these Regulations   (1)   A declaration by an organiser of a package or a trader facilitating a linked travel arrangement that—

(a)   the organiser or trader is acting exclusively as a travel service provider, as an intermediary or in any other capacity, or

(b)   a package or a linked travel arrangement does not constitute a package or a linked travel arrangement,

does not absolve that organiser or trader from the obligations imposed upon them under these Regulations.

(2)   A traveller may not waive any right granted to the traveller by these Regulations.

(3)   Any contractual arrangement or any statement by the traveller which—

(a)   directly or indirectly waives or restricts the rights conferred on travellers pursuant to these Regulations, or

(b)   aims to circumvent the application of these Regulations,

is not binding on the traveller.

Part 7   Enforcement

31.   Enforcement authority   (1)   Every local weights and measures authority in Great Britain is to be an enforcement authority for the purposes of regulations 5, 7, 19, 25 and 26 ("the relevant regulations"), and it is the duty of each such authority to enforce those provisions within their area.

(2)   The Civil Aviation Authority is to be an enforcement authority for the purposes of the relevant regulations.

(3)   The Department for the Economy in Northern Ireland is to be an enforcement authority for the purposes of the relevant regulations, and it is the duty of the Department to enforce those provisions within Northern Ireland.

32.   Due diligence defence   (1)   Subject to the following provisions of this regulation, in proceedings against any person for an offence under regulation 5(5), 7(12), 19(9), 25 or 26(10), it is a defence for that person to show that the person took all reasonable steps and exercised all due diligence to avoid committing the offence.

(2)   Where in any proceedings against any person for such an offence the defence provided by paragraph (1) involves an allegation that the commission of the offence was due to—

(a)   the act or default of another; or

(b)   reliance on information given by another,

that person is not, without the leave of the court, entitled to rely on the defence unless, at least 7 clear days before the hearing of the proceedings, or, in Scotland, the trial diet, the person has served a notice under paragraph (3) on the person bringing the proceedings.

(3)   A notice under this paragraph must give such information identifying or assisting in the identification of the person who committed the act or default or gave the information as is in the possession of the person serving the notice at the time the person serves it.

(4)   A person is not entitled to rely on the defence provided by paragraph (1) by reason of the

person's reliance on information supplied by another, unless the person shows that it was reasonable in all the circumstances for the person to have relied on the information, having regard in particular to—

(a)   the steps which the person took, and those which might reasonably have been taken, for the purpose of verifying the information; and

(b)   whether the person had any reason to disbelieve the information.

33.   *Liability of persons other than the principal offender*   (1)   Where the commission by any person of an offence under regulation 5(5), 7(12), 19(9), 25 or 26(10) is due to an act or default committed by some other person in the course of any business of that person, the other commits the offence and may be proceeded against and punished by virtue of this paragraph whether or not proceedings are taken against the first-mentioned person.

(2)   Where a body corporate commits an offence under any of the provisions mentioned in paragraph (1) (including where it is so committed by virtue of that paragraph) in respect of any act or default which is shown to have been committed with the consent or connivance of, or to be attributable to any neglect on the part of, any director, manager, secretary or other similar officer of the body corporate or any person who was purporting to act in any such capacity, both that person and the body corporate commit that offence and are liable to be proceeded against and punished accordingly.

(3)   Where the affairs of a body corporate are managed by its members, paragraph (2) applies in relation to the acts and defaults of a member in connection with that member's functions of management as if the member were a director of the body corporate.

(4)   Where an offence under any of the provisions mentioned in paragraph (1) committed in Scotland by a Scottish partnership is proved to have been committed with the consent or connivance of, or to be attributable to neglect on the part of, a partner, the partner (as well as the partnership) commits the offence and liable to be proceeded against and punished accordingly.

34.   *Prosecution time limit*   (1)   No proceedings for an offence under regulation 5(5), 7(12), 19(9), 25 or 26(10) is to be commenced after—

(a)   the end of the period of 3 years beginning within the date of the commission of the offence, or

(b)   the end of the period of 1 year beginning with the date of the discovery of the offence by the prosecutor,

whichever is the earlier.

(2)   For the purposes of this regulation, a certificate signed by or on behalf of the prosecutor and stating the date on which the offence was discovered by the prosecutor is conclusive evidence of that fact; and a certificate stating that matter and purporting to be so signed is to be treated as so signed unless the contrary is proved.

(3)   In relation to proceedings in Scotland, subsection (3) of section 331 of the Criminal Procedure (Scotland) Act 1975 applies for the purposes of this regulation as it applies for the purposes of that section.

35.   *Saving for civil consequences*   No contract is void or unenforceable, and no right of action in civil proceedings in respect of any loss arises, by reason only of the commission of an offence under regulations 5(5), 7(12), 19(9), 25 or 26(10).

36.   *Terms implied in contract*   Where it is provided in these Regulations that a term or condition is implied in the contract it is so implied irrespective of the law which governs the contract.

After the Package Travel and linked Travel Arrangements Regulations 2018 insert the Breaching of Limits on Ticket Sales Regulations 2018 as follows:

Breaching of Limits on Ticket Sales Regulations 2018[1]
(SI 2018/735)

1.   **Citation, commencement and extent**   (1)   These Regulations may be cited as the Breaching of Limits on Ticket Sales Regulations 2018 and come into force 21 days after the day on which they are made.

(2)   These Regulations extend to England and Wales and Scotland.

---

[1] These Regulations provide for a criminal offence of purchasing tickets for a recreational, sporting or cultural event in excess of conditions as to the maximum number of tickets that a purchaser may buy. The offence consists of using software with the intention of obtaining tickets in excess of the maximum and with a view to any person thereby making a financial gain.

2.   **Application**   These Regulations apply where—

(a)   tickets for a recreational, sporting or cultural event in the United Kingdom are offered for sale;

(b)   purchase of the tickets may be made wholly or partly by a process that the purchaser completes using an electronic communications network or an electronic communications service; and

(c)   the offer is subject to conditions that limit the number of tickets a purchaser may buy ("the sales limit").

3.   **Offence**   It is an offence for a person to—

(a)   use software that is designed to enable or facilitate completion of any part of a process within regulation 2(b); and

(b)   do so with intent to obtain tickets in excess of the sales limit, with a view to any person obtaining financial gain.

4. For the purposes of regulation 3 it does not matter whether the offer in regulation 2(a) is made, or anything is done to obtain tickets, in or outside the United Kingdom.

5. Offences: prosecution and penalties (1) An offence under these Regulations is triable summarily in England and Wales and Scotland.

(2) A person guilty of an offence under these Regulations is liable—

(a)   in England and Wales, to a fine; or

(b)   in Scotland, to a fine not exceeding £50,000.

Copyright, Designs and Patents

7.2453 Trade Marks Act 1994 *Add to existing Note 1 in new para as follows:* 'The Trade Mark Regulations 2018, SI 2018/825 prospectively amend (on 14 January 2019) the Trade Marks Act 1994, the Trade Marks Rules, the Community Trade Mark Regulations 2006 and the Trade Marks (International Registration) Order 2008. The majority of the provisions further implement Directive 2015/2436 of the European Parliament.'

Customs and Excise

7.2722A Finance Act 2003 *After the Finance Act 2003 insert the Finance Act 2017 and the Finance Act (No 2) 2017 in new paras as follows:*

Finance Act 2017[1]

(2017 c 10)

Part 2
Soft Drinks Industry Levy

Offences

50. Fraudulent evasion (1) A person commits an offence if the person is knowingly concerned in, or in the taking of steps with a view to, the fraudulent evasion (by that person or any other person) of soft drinks industry levy.

(2) The references in subsection (1) to the evasion of soft drinks industry levy include references to obtaining, in circumstances where there is no entitlement to it—

(a)   a tax credit under regulations under section 39;

(b)   a repayment of soft drinks industry levy under Schedule 8.

(3) A person guilty of an offence under this section is liable—

(a)   on summary conviction in England and Wales—

         (i)   to imprisonment for a term not exceeding 12 months, or

         (ii)   to a fine not exceeding £20,000 or (if greater) 3 times the total of the amounts of soft drinks industry levy that were, or were intended to be, evaded, or

         (iii)   to both;

(b)   on summary conviction in Scotland—

         (i)   to imprisonment for a term not exceeding 12 months, or

         (ii)   to a fine not exceeding the statutory maximum or (if greater) 3 times the total of the amounts of soft drinks industry levy that were, or were intended to be, evaded, or

         (iii)   to both;

(c)   on summary conviction in Northern Ireland—

         (i)   to imprisonment for a term not exceeding 6 months, or

         (ii)   to a fine not exceeding the statutory maximum or (if greater) 3 times the total of the amounts of soft drinks industry levy that were, or were intended to be, evaded, or

         (iii)   to both;

(d)   on conviction on indictment—

         (i)   to imprisonment for a term not exceeding 7 years,

         (ii)   to a fine, or

         (iii)   to both[2].

(4) For the purposes of subsection (3), the amounts of soft drinks industry levy that were, or were intended to be, evaded are to be taken as including—

(a)   the amount of any tax credit under regulations under section 39, and

(b)   the amount of any repayment of soft drinks industry levy under Schedule 8,

which was, or was intended to be, obtained in circumstances where there was no entitlement to it.

(5) In determining for the purposes of subsection (3) the amounts of soft drinks industry levy that were, or were intended to be, evaded, no account is to be taken of the extent to which any liability to levy of a person would be, or would have been, reduced by the amount of any tax credit or repayment of soft drinks industry levy to which the person was, or would have been, entitled.

(6) In relation to an offence committed before the commencement of section 154(1) of the Criminal Justice Act 2003 the reference in subsection (3)(a)(i) to 12 months is to be read as a reference to 6 months.

[Finance Act 2017, s 50.]

¹ Part 2 of this Act creates soft drinks industry levy and includes, in s 50, an offence of fraudulent evasion.
² For procedure in respect of offences triable either way, see ss 17A-21 of the Magistrates' Courts Act 1980 in Part I
Magistrates' Courts, Procedure, ante.

Finance (No 2) Act 2017¹
(2017 c 32)

¹ Part 3 of this Act creates an offence of carrying on a third country goods fulfilment business without approval. The
relevant provisions are reproduced below.

PART 3
FULFILMENT BUSINESSES

7.2722B **48. Carrying on a third country goods fulfilment business** (1) For the purposes
of this Part a person carries on a third country goods fulfilment business if the person, by way of
business—

    (a)   stores third country goods which are owned by a person who is not established in a
Member State, or

    (b)   stores third country goods on behalf of a person who is not established in a
Member State,

at a time when the conditions in subsection (2) are met in relation to the goods.

    (2) The conditions are that—

    (a)   there has been no supply of the goods in the United Kingdom for the purposes of VATA
1994, and

    (b)   the goods are being offered for sale in the United Kingdom or elsewhere.

    (3) But a person does not carry on a third country goods fulfilment business if the
person's activities within subsection (1) are incidental to the carriage of the goods.

    (4) Goods are "third country" goods if they have been imported from a place outside the
Member States within the meaning of section 15 of VATA 1994.

    (5) Whether a person is established in a Member State is to be determined in accordance with
Article 10 of Council Implementing Regulation (EU) No 282/2011 of 15 March 2011 laying down
implementing measures for Directive 2006/112/EC on the common system of value added tax.

[Finance (No 2) Act 2017, s 48.]

7.2722C **49. Requirement for approval** (1) A person may not carry on a third country
goods fulfilment business otherwise than in accordance with an approval given by
the Commissioners under this section.

    (2) The Commissioners may approve a person to carry on a third country goods fulfilment
business only if they are satisfied that the person is a fit and proper person to carry on the business.

    (3) The Commissioners may approve a person to carry on a third country goods fulfilment
business for such periods and subject to such conditions or restrictions as they may think fit or as
they may by regulations made by them prescribe.

    (4) The Commissioners may at any time for reasonable cause vary the terms of, or revoke, an
approval under this section.

    (5) In this Part "approved person" means a person approved under this section to carry on a
third country goods fulfilment business.

[Finance (No 2) Act 2017, s 49.]

7.2722D **50. Register of approved persons** (1) The Commissioners must maintain a
register of approved persons.

    (2) The register is to contain such information relating to approved persons as
the Commissioners consider appropriate.

    (3) The Commissioners may make publicly available such information contained in the register
as they consider necessary to enable those who deal with a person who carries on a third country
goods fulfilment business to determine whether the person in question is an approved person in
relation to that activity.

    (4) The information may be made available by such means (including the internet) as
the Commissioners consider appropriate.

[Finance (No 2) Act 2017, s 50.]

7.2722E **53. Offence** (1) A person who—

    (a)   carries on a third country goods fulfilment business, and

    (b)   is not an approved person,

commits an offence.

    (2) In proceedings for an offence under subsection (1) it is a defence to show that the person did
not know, and had no reasonable grounds to suspect, that the person—

    (a)   was carrying on a third country goods fulfilment business, or

    (b)   was not an approved person.

    (3) A person is taken to have shown the fact mentioned in subsection (2) if—

    (a)   sufficient evidence of that fact is adduced to raise an issue with respect to it, and

    (b)   the contrary is not proved beyond reasonable doubt.

    (4)   A person guilty of an offence under this section is liable on summary conviction—

      (a)   in England and Wales, to imprisonment for a term not exceeding 12 months, or a fine, or both;

      (b)   in Scotland, to imprisonment for a term not exceeding 12 months, or a fine not exceeding the statutory maximum, or both;

      (c)   in Northern Ireland, to imprisonment for a term not exceeding 6 months, or a fine not exceeding the statutory maximum, or both.

    (5)   A person guilty of an offence under this section is liable on conviction on indictment to—

      (a)   imprisonment for a period not exceeding 7 years,

      (b)   a fine, or

      (c)   both[1].

    (6)   In relation to an offence committed before the commencement of section 154(1) of the Criminal Justice Act 2003 the reference in subsection (4)(a) to 12 months is to be read as a reference to 6 months.

[Finance (No 2) Act 2017, s 53.]

---

[1] For procedure in respect of offences triable either way, see ss 17A-21 of the Magistrates' Courts Act 1980 in PART I MAGISTRATES' COURTS, PROCEDURE, ante.

7.2722F   54. Forfeiture   (1)   If a person—

      (a)   carries on a third country goods fulfilment business, and

      (b)   is not an approved person,

any goods within subsection (2) are liable to forfeiture under CEMA 1979.

    (2)   Goods are within this subsection if—

      (a)   they are stored by the person, and

      (b)   their storage by the person constitutes, or has constituted, the carrying on of a third country goods fulfilment business by the person.

[Finance (No 2) Act 2017, s 54.]

7.2722F   58. Interpretation   (1)   In this Part—

    "approved person" has the meaning given by section 49(5);

    "the Commissioners" means the Commissioners for Her Majesty's Revenue and Customs.

    (2)   For the purposes of this Part two or more bodies corporate are members of a group if—

      (a)   one of them controls each of the others,

      (b)   one person (whether a body corporate or an individual) controls all of them, or

      (c)   two or more individuals carrying on a business in partnership control all of them.

    (3)   A body corporate is to be taken to control another body corporate if—

      (a)   it is empowered by or under legislation to control that body's activities, or

      (b)   it is that body's holding company within the meaning of section 1159 of, and Schedule 6 to, the Companies Act 2006.

    (4)   An individual or individuals are to be taken to control a body corporate if the individual or individuals (were the individual or individuals a company) would be that body's holding company within the meaning of section 1159 of, and Schedule 6 to, the Companies Act 2006.

[Finance (No 2) Act 2017, s 58.]

DATA PROTECTION

7.2743   Data Protection Act 1998   Replace the Data Protection Act 1998 with the provisions of the Data Protection Act 2018 specified below.

Data Protection Act 2018[1]

(2018 c 12)

PART 1[2]
PRELIMINARY

7.2743   1. Overview   (1)   This Act makes provision about the processing of personal data.

    (2)   Most processing of personal data is subject to the GDPR.

    (3)   Part 2 supplements the GDPR (see Chapter 2) and applies a broadly equivalent regime to certain types of processing to which the GDPR does not apply (see Chapter 3).

    (4)   Part 3 makes provision about the processing of personal data by competent authorities for law enforcement purposes and implements the Law Enforcement Directive.

    (5)   Part 4 makes provision about the processing of personal data by the intelligence services.

    (6)   Part 5 makes provision about the Information Commissioner.

    (7)   Part 6 makes provision about the enforcement of the data protection legislation.

    (8)   Part 7 makes supplementary provision, including provision about the application of this Act to the Crown and to Parliament.

---

[1] This note does not purport to deal comprehensively with this long and complex statute, but it does attempt to explain some of the background and key concepts.

The Act replaces the Data Protection Act 1998, which regulated the processing of personal data. The 1998 Act protected the rights of individuals to whom the data related. The new Act provides a comprehensive legal framework for data protection in the UK, in accordance with the General Data Protection Regulation ((EU) 2016/679) ('GDPR'). It updates the rights provided for in the 1998 Act to make them easier to exercise and to ensure they continue to be relevant with the advent of more advanced data processing methods.

The GDPR has been incorporated into domestic law by the European Union Withdrawal Act 2018.

Consent is the primary way to enable processing of personal data. This needs to be freely given, specific, informed and unambiguous. Consent is not, however, the only way to enabling the processing of personal data. There may be a contractual or other legal obligation that allows data to be processed, or a necessity arising from the performance of a task carried out in the public interest or in the exercise of official authority vested in the controller. As with the 1998 Act, data may also be processed where there is a 'legitimate interest', for example, to prevent fraud or for internal administrative purposes, although this can no longer be relied upon by public authorities when performing their public tasks. Where specific consent is not obtained, there are additional limitations on when data can be lawfully processed for special categories of personal data and personal data relating to criminal convictions, etc.

As to law enforcement processing, the explanatory notes to the Act state:

"37 The GDPR does not apply to the processing of personal data by competent authorities (broadly the police and other criminal justice agencies) 'for the purposes of the prevention, investigation, detection or prosecution of criminal offences or the execution of criminal penalties, including safeguarding against and the prevention of threats to public security' (see Article 2(2)(d)). Instead, alongside the GDPR, the European Parliament and Council adopted the Law Enforcement Directive (EU) 2016/6801 'on the protection of natural persons with regard to the processing of personal data by competent authorities for the purposes of the prevention, investigation, detection or prosecution of criminal offences or the execution of criminal penalties, and on the free movement of such data, and repealing Council Framework Decision 2008/977/JHA' ('LED').

38 Unlike the GDPR, the LED is not directly applicable EU law; accordingly Part 3 of the Act (together with provisions in Parts 5 to 7 which apply across the GDPR, LED and intelligence services regimes) transposes the provisions of the LED into UK law

39 The scope of the LED is provided for in Article 1 and concerns the processing of personal data by competent authorities for law enforcement purposes. A competent authority is any public authority competent for the prevention, investigation, detection or prosecution of criminal offences or the execution of criminal penalties, including the safeguarding against and the prevention of threats to public security. Further, a competent authority may also be any other body or entity entrusted by Member State law to exercise public authority and public powers for the purposes of the prevention, investigation, detection or prosecution of criminal offences or the execution of criminal penalties, including the safeguarding against and the prevention of threats to public security. This definition covers not only all police forces, prosecutors and other criminal justice agencies in the UK, but also other organisations with incidental law enforcement functions, such as Her Majesty's Revenue and Customs, the Health and Safety Executive and the Office of the Information Commissioner.

40 While the LED only applies in relation to the cross-border processing of personal data for law enforcement purposes (see below), Part 3 of the Act also applies to the domestic law enforcement processing. This will ensure that there is a single domestic and trans-national regime for all law enforcement processing. The provisions of the GDPR, together with the derogations in Chapter 2 of Part 2 of the Act, will apply to the processing of personal data by law enforcement agencies for purposes other than law enforcement purposes, for example where the controller determines that the processing is for internal personnel management/ human resources purposes."

National security is outside the scope of EU law. Therefore, the processing of personal data in this connection is not within the scope of the GDPR or LED. This was governed by the 1998 Act, and Part 4 (not reproduced in this work) of the new Act builds on this regime.

The 1988 Act included certain criminal offences, and many of these are reproduced in the new Act with modifications to reflect the changes to the legal framework brought about by the GDPR.

The offence creating provisions of the 2018 Act are: a) summary offences: ss 119, 173, 173 and para 5 of Schedule 15; and b) either way offences: ss 132, 144, 148, 171 and 184.

Penalties are prescribed by 195, provision as to prosecutions is made by s 197 and the liability of directors is dealt with by s 198.

The Act is in 7 Parts. Section 1 sets out the content of each Part.

For commencement, see s 212. At the date at which this work states the law the following commencement orders had been made: Data Protection Act 2018 (Commencement No 1 and Transitional and Saving Provisions) Regulations 2018, SI 2018/625. Unless otherwise indicated, the provision reproduced below are in force.

² Part 1 contains ss 1-3.

2. Protection of personal data (1) The GDPR, the applied GDPR and this Act protect individuals with regard to the processing of personal data, in particular by—

- (a) requiring personal data to be processed lawfully and fairly, on the basis of the data subject's consent or another specified basis,
- (b) conferring rights on the data subject to obtain information about the processing of personal data and to require inaccurate personal data to be rectified, and
- (c) conferring functions on the Commissioner, giving the holder of that office responsibility for monitoring and enforcing their provisions.

(2) When carrying out functions under the GDPR, the applied GDPR and this Act, the Commissioner must have regard to the importance of securing an appropriate level of protection for personal data, taking account of the interests of data subjects, controllers and others and matters of general public interest.

3. Terms relating to the processing of personal data (1) This section defines some terms used in this Act.

(2) "Personal data" means any information relating to an identified or identifiable living individual (subject to subsection (14)(c)).

(3) "Identifiable living individual" means a living individual who can be identified, directly or indirectly, in particular by reference to—

- (a) an identifier such as a name, an identification number, location data or an online identifier, or
- (b) one or more factors specific to the physical, physiological, genetic, mental, economic,

cultural or social identity of the individual.

(4) "Processing", in relation to information, means an operation or set of operations which is performed on information, or on sets of information, such as—

(a) collection, recording, organisation, structuring or storage,

(b) adaptation or alteration,

(c) retrieval, consultation or use,

(d) disclosure by transmission, dissemination or otherwise making available,

(e) alignment or combination, or

(f) restriction, erasure or destruction,

(subject to subsection (14)(c) and sections 5(7), 29(2) and 82(3), which make provision about references to processing in the different Parts of this Act).

(5) "Data subject" means the identified or identifiable living individual to whom personal data relates.

(6) "Controller" and "processor", in relation to the processing of personal data to which Chapter 2 or 3 of Part 2, Part 3 or Part 4 applies, have the same meaning as in that Chapter or Part (see sections 5, 6, 32 and 83 and see also subsection (14)(d)).

(7) "Filing system" means any structured set of personal data which is accessible according to specific criteria, whether held by automated means or manually and whether centralised, decentralised or dispersed on a functional or geographical basis.

(8) "The Commissioner" means the Information Commissioner (see section 114).

(9) "The data protection legislation" means—

(a) the GDPR,

(b) the applied GDPR,

(c) this Act,

(d) regulations made under this Act, and

(e) regulations made under section 2(2) of the European Communities Act 1972 which relate to the GDPR or the Law Enforcement Directive.

(10) "The GDPR" means Regulation (EU) 2016/679 of the European Parliament and of the Council of 27 April 2016 on the protection of natural persons with regard to the processing of personal data and on the free movement of such data (General Data Protection Regulation).

(11) "The applied GDPR" means the GDPR as applied by Chapter 3 of Part 2.

(12) "The Law Enforcement Directive" means Directive (EU) 2016/680 of the European Parliament and of the Council of 27 April 2016 on the protection of natural persons with regard to the processing of personal data by competent authorities for the purposes of the prevention, investigation, detection or prosecution of criminal offences or the execution of criminal penalties, and on the free movement of such data, and repealing Council Framework Decision 2008/977/JHA.

(13) "The Data Protection Convention" means the Convention for the Protection of Individuals with regard to Automatic Processing of Personal Data which was opened for signature on 28 January 1981, as amended up to the day on which this Act is passed.

(14) In Parts 5 to 7, except where otherwise provided—

(a) references to the GDPR are to the GDPR read with Chapter 2 of Part 2 and include the applied GDPR read with Chapter 3 of Part 2 ;

(b) references to Chapter 2 of Part 2, or to a provision of that Chapter, include that Chapter or that provision as applied by Chapter 3 of Part 2;

(c) references to personal data, and the processing of personal data, are to personal data and processing to which Chapter 2 or 3 of Part 2, Part 3 or Part 4 applies;

(d) references to a controller or processor are to a controller or processor in relation to the processing of personal data to which Chapter 2 or 3 of Part 2, Part 3 or Part 4 applies.

(15) There is an index of defined expressions in section 206.

PART 2[1]
GENERAL PROCESSING

CHAPTER 1[2]
SCOPE AND DEFINITIONS

---

[1] Part 2 contains ss 4-28.
[2] Chapter 1 contains ss 4 and 5.

4. Processing to which this Part applies (1) This Part is relevant to most processing of personal data.

(2) Chapter 2 of this Part—

(a) applies to the types of processing of personal data to which the GDPR applies by virtue of Article 2 of the GDPR[1], and

(b) supplements, and must be read with, the GDPR.

(3) Chapter 3 of this Part—

(a) applies to certain types of processing of personal data to which the GDPR does not apply (see section 21), and

(b) makes provision for a regime broadly equivalent to the GDPR to apply to such processing.

---

[1] Article 2 provides:

"Material scope

This Regulation applies to the processing of personal data wholly or partly by automated means and to the processing other than by automated means of personal data which form part of a filing system or are intended to form part of a filing system.

This Regulation does not apply to the processing of personal data:

(a) in the course of an activity which falls outside the scope of Union law;
(b) by the Member States when carrying out activities which fall within the scope of Chapter 2 of Title V of the TEU;
(c) by a natural person in the course of a purely personal or household activity;
(d) by competent authorities for the purposes of the prevention, investigation, detection or prosecution of criminal offences or the execution of criminal penalties, including the safeguarding against and the prevention of threats to public security.

For the processing of personal data by the Union institutions, bodies, offices and agencies, Regulation (EC) No 45/2001 applies. Regulation (EC) No 45/2001 and other Union legal acts applicable to such processing of personal data shall be adapted to the principles and rules of this Regulation in accordance with Article 98.

This Regulation shall be without prejudice to the application of Directive 2000/31/EC, in particular of the liability rules of intermediary service providers in Articles 12 to 15 of that Directive."

5. Definitions (1) Terms used in Chapter 2 of this Part and in the GDPR have the same meaning in Chapter 2 as they have in the GDPR.

(2) In subsection (1), the reference to a term's meaning in the GDPR is to its meaning in the GDPR read with any provision of Chapter 2 which modifies the term's meaning for the purposes of the GDPR.

(3) Subsection (1) is subject to any provision in Chapter 2 which provides expressly for the term to have a different meaning and to section 204.

(4) Terms used in Chapter 3 of this Part and in the applied GDPR have the same meaning in Chapter 3 as they have in the applied GDPR.

(5) In subsection (4), the reference to a term's meaning in the applied GDPR is to its meaning in the GDPR read with any provision of Chapter 2 (as applied by Chapter 3) or Chapter 3 which modifies the term's meaning for the purposes of the applied GDPR.

(6) Subsection (4) is subject to any provision in Chapter 2 (as applied by Chapter 3) or Chapter 3 which provides expressly for the term to have a different meaning.

(7) A reference in Chapter 2 or Chapter 3 of this Part to the processing of personal data is to processing to which the Chapter applies.

(8) Sections 3 and 205 include definitions of other expressions used in this Part.

CHAPTER 2[1]

THE GDPR

Meaning of certain terms used in the GDPR

6. Meaning of "controller" (1) The definition of "controller" in Article 4(7) of the GDPR has effect subject to—

(a) subsection (2),
(b) section 209, and
(c) section 210.

(2) For the purposes of the GDPR, where personal data is processed only—

(a) for purposes for which it is required by an enactment to be processed, and
(b) by means by which it is required by an enactment to be processed,

the person on whom the obligation to process the data is imposed by the enactment (or, if different, one of the enactments) is the controller.

---

[1] Chapter 2 contains ss 6-20.

7. Meaning of "public authority" and "public body" (1) For the purposes of the GDPR, the following (and only the following) are "public authorities" and "public bodies" under the law of the United Kingdom—

(a) a public authority as defined by the Freedom of Information Act 2000,
(b) a Scottish public authority as defined by the Freedom of Information (Scotland) Act 2002 (asp 13), and
(c) an authority or body specified or described by the Secretary of State in regulations,

subject to subsections (2), (3) and (4).

(2) An authority or body that falls within subsection (1) is only a "public authority" or "public body" for the purposes of the GDPR when performing a task carried out in the public interest or in the exercise of official authority vested in it.

(3) The references in subsection (1)(a) and (b) to public authorities and Scottish public authorities as defined by the Freedom of Information Act 2000 and the Freedom of Information (Scotland) Act 2002 (asp 13) do not include any of the following that fall within those definitions—

(a) a parish council in England;
(b) a community council in Wales;
(c) a community council in Scotland;

(d)   a parish meeting constituted under section 13 of the Local Government Act 1972;

(e)   a community meeting constituted under section 27 of that Act;

(f)   charter trustees constituted—

    (i)   under section 246 of that Act,

    (ii)   under Part 1 of the Local Government and Public Involvement in Health Act 2007, or

    (iii)   by the Charter Trustees Regulations 1996 (SI 1996/263).

(4)   The Secretary of State may by regulations provide that a person specified or described in the regulations that is a public authority described in subsection (1)(a) or (b) is not a "public authority" or "public body" for the purposes of the GDPR.

(5)   Regulations under this section are subject to the affirmative resolution procedure.

Lawfulness of processing

8. Lawfulness of processing: public interest etc   In Article 6(1) of the GDPR (lawfulness of processing), the reference in point (e) to processing of personal data that is necessary for the performance of a task carried out in the public interest or in the exercise of the controller's official authority includes processing of personal data that is necessary for—

(a)   the administration of justice,

(b)   the exercise of a function of either House of Parliament,

(c)   the exercise of a function conferred on a person by an enactment or rule of law,

(d)   the exercise of a function of the Crown, a Minister of the Crown or a government department, or

(e)   an activity that supports or promotes democratic engagement.

9. Child's consent in relation to information society services   In Article 8(1) of the GDPR (conditions applicable to child's consent in relation to information society services)—

(a)   references to "16 years" are to be read as references to "13 years", and

(b)   the reference to "information society services" does not include preventive or counselling services.

Special categories of personal data

10. Special categories of personal data and criminal convictions etc data

(1)   Subsections (2) and (3) make provision about the processing of personal data described in Article 9(1) of the GDPR (prohibition on processing of special categories of personal data) in reliance on an exception in one of the following points of Article 9(2)—

(a)   point (b) (employment, social security and social protection);

(b)   point (g) (substantial public interest);

(c)   point (h) (health and social care);

(d)   point (i) (public health);

(e)   point (j) (archiving, research and statistics).

(2)   The processing meets the requirement in point (b), (h), (i) or (j) of Article 9(2) of the GDPR for authorisation by, or a basis in, the law of the United Kingdom or a part of the United Kingdom only if it meets a condition in Part 1 of Schedule 1.

(3)   The processing meets the requirement in point (g) of Article 9(2) of the GDPR for a basis in the law of the United Kingdom or a part of the United Kingdom only if it meets a condition in Part 2 of Schedule 1.

(4)   Subsection (5) makes provision about the processing of personal data relating to criminal convictions and offences or related security measures that is not carried out under the control of official authority.

(5)   The processing meets the requirement in Article 10 of the GDPR for authorisation by the law of the United Kingdom or a part of the United Kingdom only if it meets a condition in Part 1, 2 or 3 of Schedule 1.

(6)   The Secretary of State may by regulations—

(a)   amend Schedule 1—

    (i)   by adding or varying conditions or safeguards, and

    (ii)   by omitting conditions or safeguards added by regulations under this section, and

(b)   consequentially amend this section.

(7)   Regulations under this section are subject to the affirmative resolution procedure.

11. Special categories of personal data etc: supplementary   (1) For the purposes of Article 9(2)(h) of the GDPR (processing for health or social care purposes etc), the circumstances in which the processing of personal data is carried out subject to the conditions and safeguards referred to in Article 9(3) of the GDPR (obligation of secrecy) include circumstances in which it is carried out—

(a)   by or under the responsibility of a health professional or a social work professional, or

(b)   by another person who in the circumstances owes a duty of confidentiality under an enactment or rule of law.

(2) In Article 10 of the GDPR and section 10, references to personal data relating to criminal convictions and offences or related security measures include personal data relating to—

    (a)   the alleged commission of offences by the data subject, or

    (b)   proceedings for an offence committed or alleged to have been committed by the data subject or the disposal of such proceedings, including sentencing.

Rights of the data subject

12. Limits on fees that may be charged by controllers (1) The Secretary of State may by regulations specify limits on the fees that a controller may charge in reliance on—

    (a)   Article 12(5) of the GDPR (reasonable fees when responding to manifestly unfounded or excessive requests), or

    (b)   Article 15(3) of the GDPR (reasonable fees for provision of further copies).

(2) The Secretary of State may by regulations—

    (a)   require controllers of a description specified in the regulations to produce and publish guidance about the fees that they charge in reliance on those provisions, and

    (b)   specify what the guidance must include.

(3) Regulations under this section are subject to the negative resolution procedure.

13. Obligations of credit reference agencies (1) This section applies where a controller is a credit reference agency (within the meaning of section 145(8) of the Consumer Credit Act 1974).

(2) The controller's obligations under Article 15(1) to (3) of the GDPR (confirmation of processing, access to data and safeguards for third country transfers) are taken to apply only to personal data relating to the data subject's financial standing, unless the data subject has indicated a contrary intention.

(3) Where the controller discloses personal data in pursuance of Article 15(1) to (3) of the GDPR, the disclosure must be accompanied by a statement informing the data subject of the data subject's rights under section 159 of the Consumer Credit Act 1974 (correction of wrong information).

14. Automated decision-making authorised by law: safeguards (1) This section makes provision for the purposes of Article 22(2)(b) of the GDPR (exception from Article 22(1) of the GDPR for significant decisions based solely on automated processing that are authorised by law and subject to safeguards for the data subject's rights, freedoms and legitimate interests).

(2) A decision is a "significant decision" for the purposes of this section if, in relation to a data subject, it—

    (a)   produces legal effects concerning the data subject, or

    (b)   similarly significantly affects the data subject.

(3) A decision is a "qualifying significant decision" for the purposes of this section if—

    (a)   it is a significant decision in relation to a data subject,

    (b)   it is required or authorised by law, and

    (c)   it does not fall within Article 22(2)(a) or (c) of the GDPR (decisions necessary to a contract or made with the data subject's consent).

(4) Where a controller takes a qualifying significant decision in relation to a data subject based solely on automated processing—

    (a)   the controller must, as soon as reasonably practicable, notify the data subject in writing that a decision has been taken based solely on automated processing, and

    (b)   the data subject may, before the end of the period of 1 month beginning with receipt of the notification, request the controller to—

        (i)   reconsider the decision, or

        (ii)   take a new decision that is not based solely on automated processing.

(5) If a request is made to a controller under subsection (4), the controller must, within the period described in Article 12(3) of the GDPR—

    (a)   consider the request, including any information provided by the data subject that is relevant to it,

    (b)   comply with the request, and

    (c)   by notice in writing inform the data subject of—

        (i)   the steps taken to comply with the request, and

        (ii)   the outcome of complying with the request.

(6) In connection with this section, a controller has the powers and obligations under Article 12 of the GDPR (transparency, procedure for extending time for acting on request, fees, manifestly unfounded or excessive requests etc) that apply in connection with Article 22 of the GDPR.

(7) The Secretary of State may by regulations make such further provision as the Secretary of State considers appropriate to provide suitable measures to safeguard a data subject's rights, freedoms and legitimate interests in connection with the taking of qualifying significant decisions based solely on automated processing.

(8) Regulations under subsection (7)—

    (a)   may amend this section, and

    (b)   are subject to the affirmative resolution procedure.

Restrictions on data subject's rights

15. Exemptions etc   (1)   Schedules 2, 3 and 4 make provision for exemptions from, and restrictions and adaptations of the application of, rules of the GDPR.

(2)   In Schedule 2—

(a)   Part 1 makes provision adapting or restricting the application of rules contained in Articles 13 to 21 and 34 of the GDPR in specified circumstances, as allowed for by Article 6(3) and Article 23(1) of the GDPR;

(b)   Part 2 makes provision restricting the application of rules contained in Articles 13 to 21 and 34 of the GDPR in specified circumstances, as allowed for by Article 23(1) of the GDPR;

(c)   Part 3 makes provision restricting the application of Article 15 of the GDPR where this is necessary to protect the rights of others, as allowed for by Article 23(1) of the GDPR;

(d)   Part 4 makes provision restricting the application of rules contained in Articles 13 to 15 of the GDPR in specified circumstances, as allowed for by Article 23(1) of the GDPR;

(e)   Part 5 makes provision containing exemptions or derogations from Chapters II, III, IV, V and VII of the GDPR for reasons relating to freedom of expression, as allowed for by Article 85(2) of the GDPR;

(f)   Part 6 makes provision containing derogations from rights contained in Articles 15, 16, 18, 19, 20 and 21 of the GDPR for scientific or historical research purposes, statistical purposes and archiving purposes, as allowed for by Article 89(2) and (3) of the GDPR.

(3)   Schedule 3 makes provision restricting the application of rules contained in Articles 13 to 21 of the GDPR to health, social work, education and child abuse data, as allowed for by Article 23(1) of the GDPR.

(4)   Schedule 4 makes provision restricting the application of rules contained in Articles 13 to 21 of the GDPR to information the disclosure of which is prohibited or restricted by an enactment, as allowed for by Article 23(1) of the GDPR.

(5)   In connection with the safeguarding of national security and with defence, see Chapter 3 of this Part and the exemption in section 26.

16. Power to make further exemptions etc by regulations   (1)   The following powers to make provision altering the application of the GDPR may be exercised by way of regulations made by the Secretary of State under this section—

(a)   the power in Article 6(3) for Member State law to lay down a legal basis containing specific provisions to adapt the application of rules of the GDPR where processing is necessary for compliance with a legal obligation, for the performance of a task in the public interest or in the exercise of official authority;

(b)   the power in Article 23(1) to make a legislative measure restricting the scope of the obligations and rights mentioned in that Article where necessary and proportionate to safeguard certain objectives of general public interest;

(c)   the power in Article 85(2) to provide for exemptions or derogations from certain Chapters of the GDPR where necessary to reconcile the protection of personal data with the freedom of expression and information.

(2)   Regulations under this section may—

(a)   amend Schedules 2 to 4—

(i)   by adding or varying provisions, and

(ii)   by omitting provisions added by regulations under this section, and

(b)   consequentially amend section 15.

(3)   Regulations under this section are subject to the affirmative resolution procedure.

Accreditation of certification providers

17. Accreditation of certification providers   (1)   Accreditation of a person as a certification provider is only valid when carried out by—

(a)   the Commissioner, or

(b)   the national accreditation body.

(2)   The Commissioner may only accredit a person as a certification provider where the Commissioner—

(a)   has published a statement that the Commissioner will carry out such accreditation, and

(b)   has not published a notice withdrawing that statement.

(3)   The national accreditation body may only accredit a person as a certification provider where the Commissioner—

(a)   has published a statement that the body may carry out such accreditation, and

(b)   has not published a notice withdrawing that statement.

(4)   The publication of a notice under subsection (2)(b) or (3)(b) does not affect the validity of any accreditation carried out before its publication.

(5)   Schedule 5 makes provision about reviews of, and appeals from, a decision relating to accreditation of a person as a certification provider.

(6)   The national accreditation body may charge a reasonable fee in connection with, or incidental to, the carrying out of the body's functions under this section, Schedule 5 and Article 43

of the GDPR.

(7)   The national accreditation body must provide the Secretary of State with such information relating to its functions under this section, Schedule 5 and Article 43 of the GDPR as the Secretary of State may reasonably require.

(8)   In this section—

"certification provider" means a person who issues certification for the purposes of Article 42 of the GDPR;

"the national accreditation body" means the national accreditation body for the purposes of Article 4(1) of Regulation (EC) No 765/2008 of the European Parliament and of the Council of 9 July 2008 setting out the requirements for accreditation and market surveillance relating to the marketing of products and repealing Regulation (EEC) No 339/93.

Transfers of personal data to third countries etc

18.   Transfers of personal data to third countries etc   (1)   The Secretary of State may by regulations specify, for the purposes of Article 49(1)(d) of the GDPR—

    (a)   circumstances in which a transfer of personal data to a third country or international organisation is to be taken to be necessary for important reasons of public interest, and

    (b)   circumstances in which a transfer of personal data to a third country or international organisation which is not required by an enactment is not to be taken to be necessary for important reasons of public interest.

(2)   The Secretary of State may by regulations restrict the transfer of a category of personal data to a third country or international organisation where—

    (a)   the transfer is not authorised by an adequacy decision under Article 45(3) of the GDPR, and

    (b)   the Secretary of State considers the restriction to be necessary for important reasons of public interest.

(3)   Regulations under this section—

    (a)   are subject to the made affirmative resolution procedure where the Secretary of State has made an urgency statement in respect of them;

    (b)   are otherwise subject to the affirmative resolution procedure.

(4)   For the purposes of this section, an urgency statement is a reasoned statement that the Secretary of State considers it desirable for the regulations to come into force without delay.

Specific processing situations

19.   Processing for archiving, research and statistical purposes: safeguards   (1)   This section makes provision about—

    (a)   processing of personal data that is necessary for archiving purposes in the public interest,

    (b)   processing of personal data that is necessary for scientific or historical research purposes, and

    (c)   processing of personal data that is necessary for statistical purposes.

(2)   Such processing does not satisfy the requirement in Article 89(1) of the GDPR for the processing to be subject to appropriate safeguards for the rights and freedoms of the data subject if it is likely to cause substantial damage or substantial distress to a data subject.

(3)   Such processing does not satisfy that requirement if the processing is carried out for the purposes of measures or decisions with respect to a particular data subject, unless the purposes for which the processing is necessary include the purposes of approved medical research.

(4)   In this section—

"approved medical research" means medical research carried out by a person who has approval to carry out that research from—

    (a)   a research ethics committee recognised or established by the Health Research Authority under Chapter 2 of Part 3 of the Care Act 2014, or

    (b)   a body appointed by any of the following for the purpose of assessing the ethics of research involving individuals—

        (i)   the Secretary of State, the Scottish Ministers, the Welsh Ministers, or a Northern Ireland department;

        (ii)   a relevant NHS body;

        (iii)   United Kingdom Research and Innovation or a body that is a Research Council for the purposes of the Science and Technology Act 1965;

        (iv)   an institution that is a research institution for the purposes of Chapter 4A of Part 7 of the Income Tax (Earnings and Pensions) Act 2003 (see section 457 of that Act);

"relevant NHS body" means—

    (a)   an NHS trust or NHS foundation trust in England,

    (b)   an NHS trust or Local Health Board in Wales,

(c)   a Health Board or Special Health Board constituted under section 2 of the National Health Service (Scotland) Act 1978,

(d)   the Common Services Agency for the Scottish Health Service, or

(e)   any of the health and social care bodies in Northern Ireland falling within paragraphs (a) to (e) of section 1(5) of the Health and Social Care (Reform) Act (Northern Ireland) 2009 (c 1 (NI)).

(5)   The Secretary of State may by regulations change the meaning of "approved medical research" for the purposes of this section, including by amending subsection (4).

(6)   Regulations under subsection (5) are subject to the affirmative resolution procedure.

Minor definition

20.   Meaning of "court"   Section 5(1) (terms used in this Chapter to have the same meaning as in the GDPR) does not apply to references in this Chapter to a court and, accordingly, such references do not include a tribunal.

---

[1] Chapter 3 contains ss 21-28.

Chapter 3[1]
Other General Processing

Scope

21.   Processing to which this Chapter applies   (1)   This Chapter applies to the automated or structured processing of personal data in the course of—

(a)   an activity which is outside the scope of European Union law, or

(b)   an activity which falls within the scope of Article 2(2)(b) of the GDPR (common foreign and security policy activities),

provided that the processing is not processing by a competent authority for any of the law enforcement purposes (as defined in Part 3) or processing to which Part 4 (intelligence services processing) applies.

(2)   This Chapter also applies to the manual unstructured processing of personal data held by an FOI public authority.

(3)   This Chapter does not apply to the processing of personal data by an individual in the course of a purely personal or household activity.

(4)   In this section—

"the automated or structured processing of personal data" means—

(a)   the processing of personal data wholly or partly by automated means, and

(b)   the processing otherwise than by automated means of personal data which forms part of a filing system or is intended to form part of a filing system;

"the manual unstructured processing of personal data" means the processing of personal data which is not the automated or structured processing of personal data.

(5)   In this Chapter, "FOI public authority" means—

(a)   a public authority as defined in the Freedom of Information Act 2000, or

(b)   a Scottish public authority as defined in the Freedom of Information (Scotland) Act 2002 (asp 13).

(6)   References in this Chapter to personal data "held" by an FOI public authority are to be interpreted—

(a)   in relation to England and Wales and Northern Ireland, in accordance with section 3(2) of the Freedom of Information Act 2000, and

(b)   in relation to Scotland, in accordance with section 3(2), (4) and (5) of the Freedom of Information (Scotland) Act 2002 (asp 13),

but such references do not include information held by an intelligence service (as defined in section 82) on behalf of an FOI public authority.

(7)   But personal data is not to be treated as "held" by an FOI public authority for the purposes of this Chapter, where—

(a)   section 7 of the Freedom of Information Act 2000 prevents Parts 1 to 5 of that Act from applying to the personal data, or

(b)   section 7(1) of the Freedom of Information (Scotland) Act 2002 (asp 13) prevents that Act from applying to the personal data.

Application of the GDPR

22.   Application of the GDPR to processing to which this Chapter applies   (1)   The GDPR applies to the processing of personal data to which this Chapter applies but as if its Articles were part of an Act extending to England and Wales, Scotland and Northern Ireland.

(2)   Chapter 2 of this Part applies for the purposes of the applied GDPR as it applies for the purposes of the GDPR.

(3)   In this Chapter, "the applied Chapter 2 " means Chapter 2 of this Part as applied by this Chapter.

(4)   Schedule 6 contains provision modifying—

(a)   the GDPR as it applies by virtue of subsection (1) (see Part 1);

(b)   Chapter 2 of this Part as it applies by virtue of subsection (2) (see Part 2).

(5)   A question as to the meaning or effect of a provision of the applied GDPR, or the applied Chapter 2 , is to be determined consistently with the interpretation of the equivalent provision of the GDPR, or Chapter 2 of this Part, as it applies otherwise than by virtue of this Chapter, except so far as Schedule 6 requires a different interpretation.

23.   Power to make provision in consequence of regulations related to the GDPR

(1)   The Secretary of State may by regulations make provision in connection with the processing of personal data to which this Chapter applies which is equivalent to that made by GDPR regulations, subject to such modifications as the Secretary of State considers appropriate.

(2)   In this section, "GDPR regulations" means regulations made under section 2(2) of the European Communities Act 1972 which make provision relating to the GDPR.

(3)   Regulations under subsection (1) may apply a provision of GDPR regulations, with or without modification.

(4)   Regulations under subsection (1) may amend or repeal a provision of—

    (a)   the applied GDPR;

    (b)   this Chapter;

    (c)   Parts 5 to 7, in so far as they apply in relation to the applied GDPR.

(5)   Regulations under this section are subject to the affirmative resolution procedure.

Exemptions etc

24.   Manual unstructured data held by FOI public authorities   (1)   The provisions of the applied GDPR and this Act listed in subsection (2) do not apply to personal data to which this Chapter applies by virtue of section 21(2) (manual unstructured personal data held by FOI public authorities).

(2)   Those provisions are—

    (a)   in Chapter II of the applied GDPR (principles)—

        (i)   Article 5(1)(a) to (c), (e) and (f) (principles relating to processing, other than the accuracy principle),

        (ii)   Article 6 (lawfulness),

        (iii)   Article 7 (conditions for consent),

        (iv)   Article 8(1) and (2) (child's consent),

        (v)   Article 9 (processing of special categories of personal data),

        (vi)   Article 10 (data relating to criminal convictions etc), and

        (vii) Article 11(2) (processing not requiring identification);

    (b)   in Chapter III of the applied GDPR (rights of the data subject)—

        (i)   Article 13(1) to (3) (personal data collected from data subject: information to be provided),

        (ii)   Article 14(1) to (4) (personal data collected other than from data subject: information to be provided),

        (iii)   Article 20 (right to data portability), and

        (iv)   Article 21(1) (objections to processing);

    (c)   in Chapter V of the applied GDPR, Articles 44 to 49 (transfers of personal data to third countries or international organisations);

    (d)   sections 170 and 171 of this Act;

(see also paragraph 1(2) of Schedule 18).

(3)   In addition, the provisions of the applied GDPR listed in subsection (4) do not apply to personal data to which this Chapter applies by virtue of section 21(2) where the personal data relates to appointments, removals, pay, discipline, superannuation or other personnel matters in relation to—

    (a)   service in any of the armed forces of the Crown;

    (b)   service in any office or employment under the Crown or under any public authority;

    (c)   service in any office or employment, or under any contract for services, in respect of which power to take action, or to determine or approve the action taken, in such matters is vested in—

        (i)   Her Majesty,

        (ii)   a Minister of the Crown,

        (iii)   the National Assembly for Wales,

        (iv)   the Welsh Ministers,

        (v)   a Northern Ireland Minister (within the meaning of the Freedom of Information Act 2000), or

        (vi)   an FOI public authority.

(4)   Those provisions are—

    (a)   the remaining provisions of Chapters II and III (principles and rights of the data subject);

    (b)   Chapter IV (controller and processor);

(c)   Chapter IX (specific processing situations).

(5)   A controller is not obliged to comply with Article 15(1) to (3) of the applied GDPR (right of access by the data subject) in relation to personal data to which this Chapter applies by virtue of section 21(2) if—

    (a)   the request under that Article does not contain a description of the personal data, or

    (b)   the controller estimates that the cost of complying with the request so far as relating to the personal data would exceed the appropriate maximum.

(6)   Subsection (5)(b) does not remove the controller's obligation to confirm whether or not personal data concerning the data subject is being processed unless the estimated cost of complying with that obligation alone in relation to the personal data would exceed the appropriate maximum.

(7)   An estimate for the purposes of this section must be made in accordance with regulations under section 12(5) of the Freedom of Information Act 2000.

(8)   In subsections (5) and (6), "the appropriate maximum" means the maximum amount specified by the Secretary of State by regulations.

(9)   Regulations under subsection (8) are subject to the negative resolution procedure.

25.   Manual unstructured data used in longstanding historical research   (1)   The provisions of the applied GDPR listed in subsection (2) do not apply to personal data to which this Chapter applies by virtue of section 21(2) (manual unstructured personal data held by FOI public authorities) at any time when—

    (a)   the personal data—

        (i)   is subject to processing which was already underway immediately before 24 October 1998, and

        (ii)   is processed only for the purposes of historical research, and

    (b)   the processing is not carried out—

        (i)   for the purposes of measures or decisions with respect to a particular data subject, or

        (ii)   in a way that causes, or is likely to cause, substantial damage or substantial distress to a data subject.

(2)   Those provisions are—

    (a)   in Chapter II of the applied GDPR (principles), Article 5(1)(d) (the accuracy principle), and

    (b)   in Chapter III of the applied GDPR (rights of the data subject)—

        (i)   Article 16 (right to rectification), and

        (ii)   Article 17(1) and (2) (right to erasure).

(3)   The exemptions in this section apply in addition to the exemptions in section 24.

26.   National security and defence exemption   (1)   A provision of the applied GDPR or this Act mentioned in subsection (2) does not apply to personal data to which this Chapter applies if exemption from the provision is required for—

    (a)   the purpose of safeguarding national security, or

    (b)   defence purposes.

(2)   The provisions are—

    (a)   Chapter II of the applied GDPR (principles) except for—

        (i)   Article 5(1)(a) (lawful, fair and transparent processing), so far as it requires processing of personal data to be lawful;

        (ii)   Article 6 (lawfulness of processing);

        (iii)   Article 9 (processing of special categories of personal data);

    (b)   Chapter III of the applied GDPR (rights of data subjects);

    (c)   in Chapter IV of the applied GDPR—

        (i)   Article 33 (notification of personal data breach to the Commissioner);

        (ii)   Article 34 (communication of personal data breach to the data subject);

    (d)   Chapter V of the applied GDPR (transfers of personal data to third countries or international organisations);

    (e)   in Chapter VI of the applied GDPR—

        (i)   Article 57(1)(a) and (h) (Commissioner's duties to monitor and enforce the applied GDPR and to conduct investigations);

        (ii)   Article 58 (investigative, corrective, authorisation and advisory powers of Commissioner);

    (f)   Chapter VIII of the applied GDPR (remedies, liabilities and penalties) except for—

        (i)   Article 83 (general conditions for imposing administrative fines);

        (ii)   Article 84 (penalties);

    (g)   in Part 5 of this Act—

        (i)   in section 115 (general functions of the Commissioner), subsections (3) and (8);

        (ii)   in section 115, subsection (9), so far as it relates to Article 58(2)(i) of the applied GDPR;

        (iii)   section 119 (inspection in accordance with international obligations);

    (h)   in Part 6 of this Act—

      (i)   sections 142 to 154 and Schedule 15 (Commissioner's notices and powers of entry and inspection);

      (ii)   sections 170 to 173 (offences relating to personal data);

  (i)   in Part 7 of this Act, section 187 (representation of data subjects).

27. National security: certificate (1) Subject to subsection (3), a certificate signed by a Minister of the Crown certifying that exemption from all or any of the provisions listed in section 26(2) is, or at any time was, required in relation to any personal data for the purpose of safeguarding national security is conclusive evidence of that fact.

(2) A certificate under subsection (1)—

  (a)   may identify the personal data to which it applies by means of a general description, and

  (b)   may be expressed to have prospective effect.

(3) Any person directly affected by a certificate under subsection (1) may appeal to the Tribunal against the certificate.

(4) If, on an appeal under subsection (3), the Tribunal finds that, applying the principles applied by a court on an application for judicial review, the Minister did not have reasonable grounds for issuing a certificate, the Tribunal may—

  (a)   allow the appeal, and

  (b)   quash the certificate.

(5) Where, in any proceedings under or by virtue of the applied GDPR or this Act, it is claimed by a controller that a certificate under subsection (1) which identifies the personal data to which it applies by means of a general description applies to any personal data, another party to the proceedings may appeal to the Tribunal on the ground that the certificate does not apply to the personal data in question.

(6) But, subject to any determination under subsection (7), the certificate is to be conclusively presumed so to apply.

(7) On an appeal under subsection (5), the Tribunal may determine that the certificate does not so apply.

(8) A document purporting to be a certificate under subsection (1) is to be—

  (a)   received in evidence, and

  (b)   deemed to be such a certificate unless the contrary is proved.

(9) A document which purports to be certified by or on behalf of a Minister of the Crown as a true copy of a certificate issued by that Minister under subsection (1) is—

  (a)   in any legal proceedings, evidence of that certificate;

  (b)   in any legal proceedings in Scotland, sufficient evidence of that certificate.

(10) The power conferred by subsection (1) on a Minister of the Crown is exercisable only by—

  (a)   a Minister who is a member of the Cabinet, or

  (b)   the Attorney General or the Advocate General for Scotland.

28. National security and defence: modifications to Articles 9 and 32 of the applied GDPR (1) Article 9(1) of the applied GDPR (prohibition on processing of special categories of personal data) does not prohibit the processing of personal data to which this Chapter applies to the extent that the processing is carried out—

  (a)   for the purpose of safeguarding national security or for defence purposes, and

  (b)   with appropriate safeguards for the rights and freedoms of data subjects.

(2) Article 32 of the applied GDPR (security of processing) does not apply to a controller or processor to the extent that the controller or the processor (as the case may be) is processing personal data to which this Chapter applies for—

  (a)   the purpose of safeguarding national security, or

  (b)   defence purposes.

(3) Where Article 32 of the applied GDPR does not apply, the controller or the processor must implement security measures appropriate to the risks arising from the processing of the personal data.

(4) For the purposes of subsection (3), where the processing of personal data is carried out wholly or partly by automated means, the controller or the processor must, following an evaluation of the risks, implement measures designed to—

  (a)   prevent unauthorised processing or unauthorised interference with the systems used in connection with the processing,

  (b)   ensure that it is possible to establish the precise details of any processing that takes place,

  (c)   ensure that any systems used in connection with the processing function properly and may, in the case of interruption, be restored, and

  (d)   ensure that stored personal data cannot be corrupted if a system used in connection with the processing malfunctions.

PART 3[1]
LAW ENFORCEMENT PROCESSING

CHAPTER 1[2]
SCOPE AND DEFINITIONS

Scope

29. Processing to which this Part applies (1) This Part applies to—

    (a) the processing by a competent authority of personal data wholly or partly by automated means, and

    (b) the processing by a competent authority otherwise than by automated means of personal data which forms part of a filing system or is intended to form part of a filing system.

(2) Any reference in this Part to the processing of personal data is to processing to which this Part applies.

(3) For the meaning of "competent authority", see section 30.

---

[1] Part 3 contains ss 29-81.
[2] Chapter 1 contains ss 30-33.

Definitions

30. Meaning of "competent authority" (1) In this Part, "competent authority" means—

    (a) a person specified or described in Schedule 7, and

    (b) any other person if and to the extent that the person has statutory functions for any of the law enforcement purposes.

(2) But an intelligence service is not a competent authority within the meaning of this Part.

(3) The Secretary of State may by regulations amend Schedule 7—

    (a) so as to add or remove a person or description of person;

    (b) so as to reflect any change in the name of a person specified in the Schedule.

(4) Regulations under subsection (3) which make provision of the kind described in subsection (3)(a) may also make consequential amendments of section 73(4)(b).

(5) Regulations under subsection (3) which make provision of the kind described in subsection (3)(a), or which make provision of that kind and of the kind described in subsection (3)(b), are subject to the affirmative resolution procedure.

(6) Regulations under subsection (3) which make provision only of the kind described in subsection (3)(b) are subject to the negative resolution procedure.

(7) In this section—

"intelligence service" means—

        (a) the Security Service;

        (b) the Secret Intelligence Service;

        (c) the Government Communications Headquarters;

"statutory function" means a function under or by virtue of an enactment.

31. "The law enforcement purposes" For the purposes of this Part, "the law enforcement purposes" are the purposes of the prevention, investigation, detection or prosecution of criminal offences or the execution of criminal penalties, including the safeguarding against and the prevention of threats to public security.

32. Meaning of "controller" and "processor" (1) In this Part, "controller" means the competent authority which, alone or jointly with others—

    (a) determines the purposes and means of the processing of personal data, or

    (b) is the controller by virtue of subsection (2).

(2) Where personal data is processed only—

    (a) for purposes for which it is required by an enactment to be processed, and

    (b) by means by which it is required by an enactment to be processed,

the competent authority on which the obligation to process the data is imposed by the enactment (or, if different, one of the enactments) is the controller.

(3) In this Part, "processor" means any person who processes personal data on behalf of the controller (other than a person who is an employee of the controller).

33. Other definitions (1) This section defines certain other expressions used in this Part.

(2) "Employee", in relation to any person, includes an individual who holds a position (whether paid or unpaid) under the direction and control of that person.

(3) "Personal data breach" means a breach of security leading to the accidental or unlawful destruction, loss, alteration, unauthorised disclosure of, or access to, personal data transmitted, stored or otherwise processed.

(4) "Profiling" means any form of automated processing of personal data consisting of the use of personal data to evaluate certain personal aspects relating to an individual, in particular to analyse or predict aspects concerning that individual's performance at work, economic situation,

health, personal preferences, interests, reliability, behaviour, location or movements.

(5) "Recipient", in relation to any personal data, means any person to whom the data is disclosed, whether a third party or not, but it does not include a public authority to whom disclosure is or may be made in the framework of a particular inquiry in accordance with the law.

(6) "Restriction of processing" means the marking of stored personal data with the aim of limiting its processing for the future.

(7) "Third country" means a country or territory other than a member State.

(8) Sections 3 and 205 include definitions of other expressions used in this Part.

CHAPTER 2[1]

PRINCIPLES

34. Overview and general duty of controller (1) This Chapter sets out the six data protection principles as follows—

(a)   section 35(1) sets out the first data protection principle (requirement that processing be lawful and fair);

(b)   section 36(1) sets out the second data protection principle (requirement that purposes of processing be specified, explicit and legitimate);

(c)   section 37 sets out the third data protection principle (requirement that personal data be adequate, relevant and not excessive);

(d)   section 38(1) sets out the fourth data protection principle (requirement that personal data be accurate and kept up to date);

(e)   section 39(1) sets out the fifth data protection principle (requirement that personal data be kept for no longer than is necessary);

(f)   section 40 sets out the sixth data protection principle (requirement that personal data be processed in a secure manner).

(2) In addition—

(a)   each of sections 35, 36, 38 and 39 makes provision to supplement the principle to which it relates, and

(b)   sections 41 and 42 make provision about the safeguards that apply in relation to certain types of processing.

(3) The controller in relation to personal data is responsible for, and must be able to demonstrate, compliance with this Chapter.

---

[1] Chapter 2 contains ss 34-42.

35. The first data protection principle (1) The first data protection principle is that the processing of personal data for any of the law enforcement purposes must be lawful and fair.

(2) The processing of personal data for any of the law enforcement purposes is lawful only if and to the extent that it is based on law and either—

(a)   the data subject has given consent to the processing for that purpose, or

(b)   the processing is necessary for the performance of a task carried out for that purpose by a competent authority.

(3) In addition, where the processing for any of the law enforcement purposes is sensitive processing, the processing is permitted only in the two cases set out in subsections (4) and (5).

(4) The first case is where—

(a)   the data subject has given consent to the processing for the law enforcement purpose as mentioned in subsection (2)(a), and

(b)   at the time when the processing is carried out, the controller has an appropriate policy document in place (see section 42).

(5) The second case is where—

(a)   the processing is strictly necessary for the law enforcement purpose,

(b)   the processing meets at least one of the conditions in Schedule 8, and

(c)   at the time when the processing is carried out, the controller has an appropriate policy document in place (see section 42).

(6) The Secretary of State may by regulations amend Schedule 8—

(a)   by adding conditions;

(b)   by omitting conditions added by regulations under paragraph (a).

(7) Regulations under subsection (6) are subject to the affirmative resolution procedure.

(8) In this section, "sensitive processing" means—

(a)   the processing of personal data revealing racial or ethnic origin, political opinions, religious or philosophical beliefs or trade union membership;

(b)   the processing of genetic data, or of biometric data, for the purpose of uniquely identifying an individual;

(c)   the processing of data concerning health;

(d)   the processing of data concerning an individual's sex life or sexual orientation.

36. The second data protection principle (1) The second data protection principle is that—

(a)   the law enforcement purpose for which personal data is collected on any occasion must be specified, explicit and legitimate, and

(b)   personal data so collected must not be processed in a manner that is incompatible with the purpose for which it was collected.

(2)   Paragraph (b) of the second data protection principle is subject to subsections (3) and (4).

(3)   Personal data collected for a law enforcement purpose may be processed for any other law enforcement purpose (whether by the controller that collected the data or by another controller) provided that—

(a)   the controller is authorised by law to process the data for the other purpose, and

(b)   the processing is necessary and proportionate to that other purpose.

(4)   Personal data collected for any of the law enforcement purposes may not be processed for a purpose that is not a law enforcement purpose unless the processing is authorised by law.

37.   The third data protection principle   The third data protection principle is that personal data processed for any of the law enforcement purposes must be adequate, relevant and not excessive in relation to the purpose for which it is processed.

38.   The fourth data protection principle   (1)   The fourth data protection principle is that—

(a)   personal data processed for any of the law enforcement purposes must be accurate and, where necessary, kept up to date, and

(b)   every reasonable step must be taken to ensure that personal data that is inaccurate, having regard to the law enforcement purpose for which it is processed, is erased or rectified without delay.

(2)   In processing personal data for any of the law enforcement purposes, personal data based on facts must, so far as possible, be distinguished from personal data based on personal assessments.

(3)   In processing personal data for any of the law enforcement purposes, a clear distinction must, where relevant and as far as possible, be made between personal data relating to different categories of data subject, such as—

(a)   persons suspected of having committed or being about to commit a criminal offence;

(b)   persons convicted of a criminal offence;

(c)   persons who are or may be victims of a criminal offence;

(d)   witnesses or other persons with information about offences.

(4)   All reasonable steps must be taken to ensure that personal data which is inaccurate, incomplete or no longer up to date is not transmitted or made available for any of the law enforcement purposes.

(5)   For that purpose—

(a)   the quality of personal data must be verified before it is transmitted or made available,

(b)   in all transmissions of personal data, the necessary information enabling the recipient to assess the degree of accuracy, completeness and reliability of the data and the extent to which it is up to date must be included, and

(c)   if, after personal data has been transmitted, it emerges that the data was incorrect or that the transmission was unlawful, the recipient must be notified without delay.

39.   The fifth data protection principle   (1)   The fifth data protection principle is that personal data processed for any of the law enforcement purposes must be kept for no longer than is necessary for the purpose for which it is processed.

(2)   Appropriate time limits must be established for the periodic review of the need for the continued storage of personal data for any of the law enforcement purposes.

40.   The sixth data protection principle   The sixth data protection principle is that personal data processed for any of the law enforcement purposes must be so processed in a manner that ensures appropriate security of the personal data, using appropriate technical or organisational measures (and, in this principle, "appropriate security" includes protection against unauthorised or unlawful processing and against accidental loss, destruction or damage).

41.   Safeguards: archiving   (1)   This section applies in relation to the processing of personal data for a law enforcement purpose where the processing is necessary—

(a)   for archiving purposes in the public interest,

(b)   for scientific or historical research purposes, or

(c)   for statistical purposes.

(2)   The processing is not permitted if—

(a)   it is carried out for the purposes of, or in connection with, measures or decisions with respect to a particular data subject, or

(b)   it is likely to cause substantial damage or substantial distress to a data subject.

42.   Safeguards: sensitive processing   (1)   This section applies for the purposes of section 35(4) and (5) (which require a controller to have an appropriate policy document in place when carrying out sensitive processing in reliance on the consent of the data subject or, as the case may be, in reliance on a condition specified in Schedule 8).

(2)   The controller has an appropriate policy document in place in relation to the sensitive processing if the controller has produced a document which—

(a)   explains the controller's procedures for securing compliance with the data protection principles (see section 34(1)) in connection with sensitive processing in reliance on the consent of the data subject or (as the case may be) in reliance on the condition in question, and

(b)   explains the controller's policies as regards the retention and erasure of personal data processed in reliance on the consent of the data subject or (as the case may be) in reliance on the condition in question, giving an indication of how long such personal data is likely to be retained.

(3)   Where personal data is processed on the basis that an appropriate policy document is in place, the controller must during the relevant period—

(a)   retain the appropriate policy document,

(b)   review and (if appropriate) update it from time to time, and

(c)   make it available to the Commissioner, on request, without charge.

(4)   The record maintained by the controller under section 61(1) and, where the sensitive processing is carried out by a processor on behalf of the controller, the record maintained by the processor under section 61(3) must include the following information—

(a)   whether the sensitive processing is carried out in reliance on the consent of the data subject or, if not, which condition in Schedule 8 is relied on,

(b)   how the processing satisfies section 35 (lawfulness of processing), and

(c)   whether the personal data is retained and erased in accordance with the policies described in subsection (2)(b) and, if it is not, the reasons for not following those policies.

(5)   In this section, "relevant period", in relation to sensitive processing in reliance on the consent of the data subject or in reliance on a condition specified in Schedule 8, means a period which—

(a)   begins when the controller starts to carry out the sensitive processing in reliance on the data subject's consent or (as the case may be) in reliance on that condition, and

(b)   ends at the end of the period of 6 months beginning when the controller ceases to carry out the processing.

CHAPTER 3[1]

RIGHTS OF THE DATA SUBJECT

Overview and scope

43. Overview and scope (1) This Chapter—

(a)   imposes general duties on the controller to make information available (see section 44);

(b)   confers a right of access by the data subject (see section 45);

(c)   confers rights on the data subject with respect to the rectification of personal data and the erasure of personal data or the restriction of its processing (see sections 46 to 48);

(d)   regulates automated decision-making (see sections 49 and 50);

(e)   makes supplementary provision (see sections 51 to 54).

(2)   This Chapter applies only in relation to the processing of personal data for a law enforcement purpose.

(3)   But sections 44 to 48 do not apply in relation to the processing of relevant personal data in the course of a criminal investigation or criminal proceedings, including proceedings for the purpose of executing a criminal penalty.

(4)   In subsection (3), "relevant personal data" means personal data contained in a judicial decision or in other documents relating to the investigation or proceedings which are created by or on behalf of a court or other judicial authority.

(5)   In this Chapter, "the controller", in relation to a data subject, means the controller in relation to personal data relating to the data subject.

---

[1] Chapter 3 contains ss 43-54.

Information: controller's general duties

44. Information: controller's general duties (1) The controller must make available to data subjects the following information (whether by making the information generally available to the public or in any other way)—

(a)   the identity and the contact details of the controller;

(b)   where applicable, the contact details of the data protection officer (see sections 69 to 71);

(c)   the purposes for which the controller processes personal data;

(d)   the existence of the rights of data subjects to request from the controller—

      (i)   access to personal data (see section 45),

      (ii)   rectification of personal data (see section 46), and

      (iii) erasure of personal data or the restriction of its processing (see section 47);

(e)   the existence of the right to lodge a complaint with the Commissioner and the contact details of the Commissioner.

(2)   The controller must also, in specific cases for the purpose of enabling the exercise of a data subject's rights under this Part, give the data subject the following—

(a)   information about the legal basis for the processing;

(b)   information about the period for which the personal data will be stored or, where that is not possible, about the criteria used to determine that period;

(c)   where applicable, information about the categories of recipients of the personal data (including recipients in third countries or international organisations);

(d)   such further information as is necessary to enable the exercise of the data subject's rights under this Part.

(3)   An example of where further information may be necessary as mentioned in subsection (2)(d) is where the personal data being processed was collected without the knowledge of the data subject.

(4)   The controller may restrict, wholly or partly, the provision of information to the data subject under subsection (2) to the extent that and for so long as the restriction is, having regard to the fundamental rights and legitimate interests of the data subject, a necessary and proportionate measure to—

(a)   avoid obstructing an official or legal inquiry, investigation or procedure;

(b)   avoid prejudicing the prevention, detection, investigation or prosecution of criminal offences or the execution of criminal penalties;

(c)   protect public security;

(d)   protect national security;

(e)   protect the rights and freedoms of others.

(5)   Where the provision of information to a data subject under subsection (2) is restricted, wholly or partly, the controller must inform the data subject in writing without undue delay—

(a)   that the provision of information has been restricted,

(b)   of the reasons for the restriction,

(c)   of the data subject's right to make a request to the Commissioner under section 51,

(d)   of the data subject's right to lodge a complaint with the Commissioner, and

(e)   of the data subject's right to apply to a court under section 167.

(6)   Subsection (5)(a) and (b) do not apply to the extent that complying with them would undermine the purpose of the restriction.

(7)   The controller must—

(a)   record the reasons for a decision to restrict (whether wholly or partly) the provision of information to a data subject under subsection (2), and

(b)   if requested to do so by the Commissioner, make the record available to the Commissioner.

Data subject's right of access

45.   Right of access by the data subject   (1)   A data subject is entitled to obtain from the controller—

(a)   confirmation as to whether or not personal data concerning him or her is being processed, and

(b)   where that is the case, access to the personal data and the information set out in subsection (2).

(2)   That information is—

(a)   the purposes of and legal basis for the processing;

(b)   the categories of personal data concerned;

(c)   the recipients or categories of recipients to whom the personal data has been disclosed (including recipients or categories of recipients in third countries or international organisations);

(d)   the period for which it is envisaged that the personal data will be stored or, where that is not possible, the criteria used to determine that period;

(e)   the existence of the data subject's rights to request from the controller—

(i)   rectification of personal data (see section 46), and

(ii)   erasure of personal data or the restriction of its processing (see section 47);

(f)   the existence of the data subject's right to lodge a complaint with the Commissioner and the contact details of the Commissioner;

(g)   communication of the personal data undergoing processing and of any available information as to its origin.

(3)   Where a data subject makes a request under subsection (1), the information to which the data subject is entitled must be provided in writing—

(a)   without undue delay, and

(b)   in any event, before the end of the applicable time period (as to which see section 54).

(4)   The controller may restrict, wholly or partly, the rights conferred by subsection (1) to the extent that and for so long as the restriction is, having regard to the fundamental rights and legitimate interests of the data subject, a necessary and proportionate measure to—

(a)   avoid obstructing an official or legal inquiry, investigation or procedure;

(b)   avoid prejudicing the prevention, detection, investigation or prosecution of criminal offences or the execution of criminal penalties;

(c)   protect public security;

(d)   protect national security;

(e)   protect the rights and freedoms of others.

(5)   Where the rights of a data subject under subsection (1) are restricted, wholly or partly, the controller must inform the data subject in writing without undue delay—

(a)   that the rights of the data subject have been restricted,

(b)   of the reasons for the restriction,

(c)   of the data subject's right to make a request to the Commissioner under section 51,

(d)   of the data subject's right to lodge a complaint with the Commissioner, and

(e)   of the data subject's right to apply to a court under section 167.

(6)   Subsection (5)(a) and (b) do not apply to the extent that the provision of the information would undermine the purpose of the restriction.

(7)   The controller must—

(a)   record the reasons for a decision to restrict (whether wholly or partly) the rights of a data subject under subsection (1), and

(b)   if requested to do so by the Commissioner, make the record available to the Commissioner.

Data subject's rights to rectification or erasure etc

46. Right to rectification   (1)   The controller must, if so requested by a data subject, rectify without undue delay inaccurate personal data relating to the data subject.

(2)   Where personal data is inaccurate because it is incomplete, the controller must, if so requested by a data subject, complete it.

(3)   The duty under subsection (2) may, in appropriate cases, be fulfilled by the provision of a supplementary statement.

(4)   Where the controller would be required to rectify personal data under this section but the personal data must be maintained for the purposes of evidence, the controller must (instead of rectifying the personal data) restrict its processing.

47. Right to erasure or restriction of processing   (1)   The controller must erase personal data without undue delay where—

(a)   the processing of the personal data would infringe section 35, 36(1) to (3), 37, 38(1), 39(1), 40, 41 or 42, or

(b)   the controller has a legal obligation to erase the data.

(2)   Where the controller would be required to erase personal data under subsection (1) but the personal data must be maintained for the purposes of evidence, the controller must (instead of erasing the personal data) restrict its processing.

(3)   Where a data subject contests the accuracy of personal data (whether in making a request under this section or section 46 or in any other way), but it is not possible to ascertain whether it is accurate or not, the controller must restrict its processing.

(4)   A data subject may request the controller to erase personal data or to restrict its processing (but the duties of the controller under this section apply whether or not such a request is made).

48. Rights under section 46 or 47: supplementary   (1)   Where a data subject requests the rectification or erasure of personal data or the restriction of its processing, the controller must inform the data subject in writing—

(a)   whether the request has been granted, and

(b)   if it has been refused—

     (i)   of the reasons for the refusal,

     (ii)   of the data subject's right to make a request to the Commissioner under section 51,

     (iii)   of the data subject's right to lodge a complaint with the Commissioner, and

     (iv)   of the data subject's right to apply to a court under section 167.

(2)   The controller must comply with the duty under subsection (1)—

(a)   without undue delay, and

(b)   in any event, before the end of the applicable time period (see section 54).

(3)   The controller may restrict, wholly or partly, the provision of information to the data subject under subsection (1)(b)(i) to the extent that and for so long as the restriction is, having regard to the fundamental rights and legitimate interests of the data subject, a necessary and proportionate measure to—

(a)   avoid obstructing an official or legal inquiry, investigation or procedure;

(b)   avoid prejudicing the prevention, detection, investigation or prosecution of criminal offences or the execution of criminal penalties;

(c)   protect public security;

(d)   protect national security;

(e)   protect the rights and freedoms of others.

(4)   Where the rights of a data subject under subsection (1) are restricted, wholly or partly, the controller must inform the data subject in writing without undue delay—

(a)   that the rights of the data subject have been restricted,

(b)   of the reasons for the restriction,

(c)   of the data subject's right to lodge a complaint with the Commissioner, and

(d)   of the data subject's right to apply to a court under section 167.

(5)   Subsection (4)(a) and (b) do not apply to the extent that the provision of the information would undermine the purpose of the restriction.

(6)   The controller must—

(a)   record the reasons for a decision to restrict (whether wholly or partly) the provision of information to a data subject under subsection (1)(b)(i), and

(b)   if requested to do so by the Commissioner, make the record available to the Commissioner.

(7)   Where the controller rectifies personal data, it must notify the competent authority (if any) from which the inaccurate personal data originated.

(8)   In subsection (7), the reference to a competent authority includes (in addition to a competent authority within the meaning of this Part) any person that is a competent authority for the purposes of the Law Enforcement Directive in a member State other than the United Kingdom.

(9)   Where the controller rectifies, erases or restricts the processing of personal data which has been disclosed by the controller—

(a)   the controller must notify the recipients, and

(b)   the recipients must similarly rectify, erase or restrict the processing of the personal data (so far as they retain responsibility for it).

(10)   Where processing is restricted in accordance with section 47(3), the controller must inform the data subject before lifting the restriction.

Automated individual decision-making

49.   Right not to be subject to automated decision-making   (1)   A controller may not take a significant decision based solely on automated processing unless that decision is required or authorised by law.

(2)   A decision is a "significant decision" for the purpose of this section if, in relation to a data subject, it—

(a)   produces an adverse legal effect concerning the data subject, or

(b)   significantly affects the data subject.

50.   Automated decision-making authorised by law: safeguards   (1)   A decision is a "qualifying significant decision" for the purposes of this section if—

(a)   it is a significant decision in relation to a data subject, and

(b)   it is required or authorised by law.

(2)   Where a controller takes a qualifying significant decision in relation to a data subject based solely on automated processing—

(a)   the controller must, as soon as reasonably practicable, notify the data subject in writing that a decision has been taken based solely on automated processing, and

(b)   the data subject may, before the end of the period of 1 month beginning with receipt of the notification, request the controller to—

(i)   reconsider the decision, or

(ii)   take a new decision that is not based solely on automated processing.

(3)   If a request is made to a controller under subsection (2), the controller must, before the end of the period of 1 month beginning with receipt of the request—

(a)   consider the request, including any information provided by the data subject that is relevant to it,

(b)   comply with the request, and

(c)   by notice in writing inform the data subject of—

(i)   the steps taken to comply with the request, and

(ii)   the outcome of complying with the request.

(4)   The Secretary of State may by regulations make such further provision as the Secretary of State considers appropriate to provide suitable measures to safeguard a data subject's rights, freedoms and legitimate interests in connection with the taking of qualifying significant decisions based solely on automated processing.

(5)   Regulations under subsection (4)—

(a)   may amend this section, and

(b)   are subject to the affirmative resolution procedure.

(6)   In this section "significant decision" has the meaning given by section 49(2).

Supplementary

51.   Exercise of rights through the Commissioner   (1)   This section applies where a controller—

(a)   restricts under section 44(4) the information provided to the data subject under section 44(2) (duty of the controller to give the data subject additional information),

(b)   restricts under section 45(4) the data subject's rights under section 45(1) (right of access), or

(c)   refuses a request by the data subject for rectification under section 46 or for erasure or restriction of processing under section 47.

(2)   The data subject may—

(a)   where subsection (1)(a) or (b) applies, request the Commissioner to check that the restriction imposed by the controller was lawful;

(b)   where subsection (1)(c) applies, request the Commissioner to check that the refusal of the data subject's request was lawful.

(3)   The Commissioner must take such steps as appear to the Commissioner to be appropriate to respond to a request under subsection (2) (which may include the exercise of any of the powers conferred by sections 142 and 146).

(4)   After taking those steps, the Commissioner must inform the data subject—

(a)   where subsection (1)(a) or (b) applies, whether the Commissioner is satisfied that the restriction imposed by the controller was lawful;

(b)   where subsection (1)(c) applies, whether the Commissioner is satisfied that the controller's refusal of the data subject's request was lawful.

(5)   The Commissioner must also inform the data subject of the data subject's right to apply to a court under section 167.

(6)   Where the Commissioner is not satisfied as mentioned in subsection (4)(a) or (b), the Commissioner may also inform the data subject of any further steps that the Commissioner is considering taking under Part 6 .

52.   Form of provision of information etc   (1)   The controller must take reasonable steps to ensure that any information that is required by this Chapter to be provided to the data subject is provided in a concise, intelligible and easily accessible form, using clear and plain language.

(2)   Subject to subsection (3), the information may be provided in any form, including electronic form.

(3)   Where information is provided in response to a request by the data subject under section 45, 46, 47 or 50, the controller must provide the information in the same form as the request where it is practicable to do so.

(4)   Where the controller has reasonable doubts about the identity of an individual making a request under section 45, 46 or 47, the controller may—

(a)   request the provision of additional information to enable the controller to confirm the identity, and

(b)   delay dealing with the request until the identity is confirmed.

(5)   Subject to section 53, any information that is required by this Chapter to be provided to the data subject must be provided free of charge.

(6)   The controller must facilitate the exercise of the rights of the data subject under sections 45 to 50.

53.   Manifestly unfounded or excessive requests by the data subject   (1)   Where a request from a data subject under section 45, 46, 47 or 50 is manifestly unfounded or excessive, the controller may—

(a)   charge a reasonable fee for dealing with the request, or

(b)   refuse to act on the request.

(2)   An example of a request that may be excessive is one that merely repeats the substance of previous requests.

(3)   In any proceedings where there is an issue as to whether a request under section 45, 46, 47 or 50 is manifestly unfounded or excessive, it is for the controller to show that it is.

(4)   The Secretary of State may by regulations specify limits on the fees that a controller may charge in accordance with subsection (1)(a).

(5)   Regulations under subsection (4) are subject to the negative resolution procedure.

54.   Meaning of "applicable time period"   (1)   This section defines "the applicable time period" for the purposes of sections 45(3)(b) and 48(2)(b).

(2)   "The applicable time period" means the period of 1 month, or such longer period as may be specified in regulations, beginning with the relevant time.

(3)   "The relevant time" means the latest of the following—

(a)   when the controller receives the request in question;

(b)   when the controller receives the information (if any) requested in connection with a request under section 52(4);

(c)   when the fee (if any) charged in connection with the request under section 53 is paid.

(4)   The power to make regulations under subsection (2) is exercisable by the Secretary of State.

(5)   Regulations under subsection (2) may not specify a period which is longer than 3 months.

(6)   Regulations under subsection (2) are subject to the negative resolution procedure.

CHAPTER 4[1]
CONTROLLER AND PROCESSOR

Overview and scope

55. Overview and scope (1) This Chapter—

(a) sets out the general obligations of controllers and processors (see sections 56 to 65);

(b) sets out specific obligations of controllers and processors with respect to security (see section 66);

(c) sets out specific obligations of controllers and processors with respect to personal data breaches (see sections 67 and 68);

(d) makes provision for the designation, position and tasks of data protection officers (see sections 69 to 71).

(2) This Chapter applies only in relation to the processing of personal data for a law enforcement purpose.

(3) Where a controller is required by any provision of this Chapter to implement appropriate technical and organisational measures, the controller must (in deciding what measures are appropriate) take into account—

(a) the latest developments in technology,

(b) the cost of implementation,

(c) the nature, scope, context and purposes of processing, and

(d) the risks for the rights and freedoms of individuals arising from the processing.

---

[1] Chapter 4 contains ss 55-71

General obligations

56. General obligations of the controller (1) Each controller must implement appropriate technical and organisational measures to ensure, and to be able to demonstrate, that the processing of personal data complies with the requirements of this Part.

(2) Where proportionate in relation to the processing, the measures implemented to comply with the duty under subsection (1) must include appropriate data protection policies.

(3) The technical and organisational measures implemented under subsection (1) must be reviewed and updated where necessary.

57. Data protection by design and default (1) Each controller must implement appropriate technical and organisational measures which are designed—

(a) to implement the data protection principles in an effective manner, and

(b) to integrate into the processing itself the safeguards necessary for that purpose.

(2) The duty under subsection (1) applies both at the time of the determination of the means of processing the data and at the time of the processing itself.

(3) Each controller must implement appropriate technical and organisational measures for ensuring that, by default, only personal data which is necessary for each specific purpose of the processing is processed.

(4) The duty under subsection (3) applies to—

(a) the amount of personal data collected,

(b) the extent of its processing,

(c) the period of its storage, and

(d) its accessibility.

(5) In particular, the measures implemented to comply with the duty under subsection (3) must ensure that, by default, personal data is not made accessible to an indefinite number of people without an individual's intervention.

58. Joint controllers (1) Where two or more competent authorities jointly determine the purposes and means of processing personal data, they are joint controllers for the purposes of this Part.

(2) Joint controllers must, in a transparent manner, determine their respective responsibilities for compliance with this Part by means of an arrangement between them, except to the extent that those responsibilities are determined under or by virtue of an enactment.

(3) The arrangement must designate the controller which is to be the contact point for data subjects.

59. Processors (1) This section applies to the use by a controller of a processor to carry out processing of personal data on behalf of the controller.

(2) The controller may use only a processor who provides guarantees to implement appropriate technical and organisational measures that are sufficient to secure that the processing will—

(a) meet the requirements of this Part, and

(b) ensure the protection of the rights of the data subject.

(3) The processor used by the controller may not engage another processor ("a sub-processor") without the prior written authorisation of the controller, which may be specific or general.

(4) Where the controller gives a general written authorisation to a processor, the processor must inform the controller if the processor proposes to add to the number of sub-processors engaged by

it or to replace any of them (so that the controller has the opportunity to object to the proposal).

(5)   The processing by the processor must be governed by a contract in writing between the controller and the processor setting out the following—

    (a)   the subject-matter and duration of the processing;

    (b)   the nature and purpose of the processing;

    (c)   the type of personal data and categories of data subjects involved;

    (d)   the obligations and rights of the controller and processor.

(6)   The contract must, in particular, provide that the processor must—

    (a)   act only on instructions from the controller,

    (b)   ensure that the persons authorised to process personal data are subject to an appropriate duty of confidentiality,

    (c)   assist the controller by any appropriate means to ensure compliance with the rights of the data subject under this Part,

    (d)   at the end of the provision of services by the processor to the controller—

        (i)   either delete or return to the controller (at the choice of the controller) the personal data to which the services relate, and

        (ii)   delete copies of the personal data unless subject to a legal obligation to store the copies,

    (e)   make available to the controller all information necessary to demonstrate compliance with this section, and

    (f)   comply with the requirements of this section for engaging sub-processors.

(7)   The terms included in the contract in accordance with subsection (6)(a) must provide that the processor may transfer personal data to a third country or international organisation only if instructed by the controller to make the particular transfer.

(8)   If a processor determines, in breach of this Part, the purposes and means of processing, the processor is to be treated for the purposes of this Part as a controller in respect of that processing.

60. Processing under the authority of the controller or processor A processor, and any person acting under the authority of a controller or processor, who has access to personal data may not process the data except—

    (a)   on instructions from the controller, or

    (b)   to comply with a legal obligation.

61. Records of processing activities (1) Each controller must maintain a record of all categories of processing activities for which the controller is responsible.

(2)   The controller's record must contain the following information—

    (a)   the name and contact details of the controller;

    (b)   where applicable, the name and contact details of the joint controller;

    (c)   where applicable, the name and contact details of the data protection officer;

    (d)   the purposes of the processing;

    (e)   the categories of recipients to whom personal data has been or will be disclosed (including recipients in third countries or international organisations);

    (f)   a description of the categories of—

        (i)   data subject, and

        (ii)   personal data;

    (g)   where applicable, details of the use of profiling;

    (h)   where applicable, the categories of transfers of personal data to a third country or an international organisation;

    (i)   an indication of the legal basis for the processing operations, including transfers, for which the personal data is intended;

    (j)   where possible, the envisaged time limits for erasure of the different categories of personal data;

    (k)   where possible, a general description of the technical and organisational security measures referred to in section 66.

(3)   Each processor must maintain a record of all categories of processing activities carried out on behalf of a controller.

(4)   The processor's record must contain the following information—

    (a)   the name and contact details of the processor and of any other processors engaged by the processor in accordance with section 59(3);

    (b)   the name and contact details of the controller on behalf of which the processor is acting;

    (c)   where applicable, the name and contact details of the data protection officer;

    (d)   the categories of processing carried out on behalf of the controller;

    (e)   where applicable, details of transfers of personal data to a third country or an international organisation where explicitly instructed to do so by the controller, including the identification of that third country or international organisation;

    (f)   where possible, a general description of the technical and organisational security measures referred to in section 66.

(5)   The controller and the processor must make the records kept under this section available to the Commissioner on request.

62.   Logging   (1)   A controller (or, where personal data is processed on behalf of the controller by a processor, the processor) must keep logs for at least the following processing operations in automated processing systems—

(a)   collection;
(b)   alteration;
(c)   consultation;
(d)   disclosure (including transfers);
(e)   combination;
(f)   erasure.

(2)   The logs of consultation must make it possible to establish—

(a)   the justification for, and date and time of, the consultation, and
(b)   so far as possible, the identity of the person who consulted the data.

(3)   The logs of disclosure must make it possible to establish—

(a)   the justification for, and date and time of, the disclosure, and
(b)   so far as possible—
   (i)   the identity of the person who disclosed the data, and
   (ii)   the identity of the recipients of the data.

(4)   The logs kept under subsection (1) may be used only for one or more of the following purposes—

(a)   to verify the lawfulness of processing;
(b)   to assist with self-monitoring by the controller or (as the case may be) the processor, including the conduct of internal disciplinary proceedings;
(c)   to ensure the integrity and security of personal data;
(d)   the purposes of criminal proceedings.

(5)   The controller or (as the case may be) the processor must make the logs available to the Commissioner on request.

63.   Co-operation with the Commissioner   Each controller and each processor must co-operate, on request, with the Commissioner in the performance of the Commissioner's tasks.

64.   Data protection impact assessment   (1)   Where a type of processing is likely to result in a high risk to the rights and freedoms of individuals, the controller must, prior to the processing, carry out a data protection impact assessment.

(2)   A data protection impact assessment is an assessment of the impact of the envisaged processing operations on the protection of personal data.

(3)   A data protection impact assessment must include the following—

(a)   a general description of the envisaged processing operations;
(b)   an assessment of the risks to the rights and freedoms of data subjects;
(c)   the measures envisaged to address those risks;
(d)   safeguards, security measures and mechanisms to ensure the protection of personal data and to demonstrate compliance with this Part, taking into account the rights and legitimate interests of the data subjects and other persons concerned.

(4)   In deciding whether a type of processing is likely to result in a high risk to the rights and freedoms of individuals, the controller must take into account the nature, scope, context and purposes of the processing.

65.   Prior consultation with the Commissioner   (1)   This section applies where a controller intends to create a filing system and process personal data forming part of it.

(2)   The controller must consult the Commissioner prior to the processing if a data protection impact assessment prepared under section 64 indicates that the processing of the data would result in a high risk to the rights and freedoms of individuals (in the absence of measures to mitigate the risk).

(3)   Where the controller is required to consult the Commissioner under subsection (2), the controller must give the Commissioner—

(a)   the data protection impact assessment prepared under section 64, and
(b)   any other information requested by the Commissioner to enable the Commissioner to make an assessment of the compliance of the processing with the requirements of this Part.

(4)   Where the Commissioner is of the opinion that the intended processing referred to in subsection (1) would infringe any provision of this Part, the Commissioner must provide written advice to the controller and, where the controller is using a processor, to the processor.

(5)   The written advice must be provided before the end of the period of 6 weeks beginning with receipt of the request for consultation by the controller or the processor.

(6)   The Commissioner may extend the period of 6 weeks by a further period of 1 month, taking into account the complexity of the intended processing.

(7)   If the Commissioner extends the period of 6 weeks, the Commissioner must—

(a)   inform the controller and, where applicable, the processor of any such extension before the end of the period of 1 month beginning with receipt of the request for consultation, and

(b)   provide reasons for the delay.

Obligations relating to security

66. Security of processing (1) Each controller and each processor must implement appropriate technical and organisational measures to ensure a level of security appropriate to the risks arising from the processing of personal data.

(2)   In the case of automated processing, each controller and each processor must, following an evaluation of the risks, implement measures designed to—

(a)   prevent unauthorised processing or unauthorised interference with the systems used in connection with it,

(b)   ensure that it is possible to establish the precise details of any processing that takes place,

(c)   ensure that any systems used in connection with the processing function properly and may, in the case of interruption, be restored, and

(d)   ensure that stored personal data cannot be corrupted if a system used in connection with the processing malfunctions.

Obligations relating to personal data breaches

67. Notification of a personal data breach to the Commissioner (1) If a controller becomes aware of a personal data breach in relation to personal data for which the controller is responsible, the controller must notify the breach to the Commissioner—

(a)   without undue delay, and

(b)   where feasible, not later than 72 hours after becoming aware of it.

(2)   Subsection (1) does not apply if the personal data breach is unlikely to result in a risk to the rights and freedoms of individuals.

(3)   Where the notification to the Commissioner is not made within 72 hours, the notification must be accompanied by reasons for the delay.

(4)   Subject to subsection (5), the notification must include—

(a)   a description of the nature of the personal data breach including, where possible, the categories and approximate number of data subjects concerned and the categories and approximate number of personal data records concerned;

(b)   the name and contact details of the data protection officer or other contact point from whom more information can be obtained;

(c)   a description of the likely consequences of the personal data breach;

(d)   a description of the measures taken or proposed to be taken by the controller to address the personal data breach, including, where appropriate, measures to mitigate its possible adverse effects.

(5)   Where and to the extent that it is not possible to provide all the information mentioned in subsection (4) at the same time, the information may be provided in phases without undue further delay.

(6)   The controller must record the following information in relation to a personal data breach—

(a)   the facts relating to the breach,

(b)   its effects, and

(c)   the remedial action taken.

(7)   The information mentioned in subsection (6) must be recorded in such a way as to enable the Commissioner to verify compliance with this section.

(8)   Where a personal data breach involves personal data that has been transmitted by or to a person who is a controller under the law of another member State, the information mentioned in subsection (6) must be communicated to that person without undue delay.

(9)   If a processor becomes aware of a personal data breach (in relation to personal data processed by the processor), the processor must notify the controller without undue delay.

68. Communication of a personal data breach to the data subject (1) Where a personal data breach is likely to result in a high risk to the rights and freedoms of individuals, the controller must inform the data subject of the breach without undue delay.

(2)   The information given to the data subject must include the following—

(a)   a description of the nature of the breach;

(b)   the name and contact details of the data protection officer or other contact point from whom more information can be obtained;

(c)   a description of the likely consequences of the personal data breach;

(d)   a description of the measures taken or proposed to be taken by the controller to address the personal data breach, including, where appropriate, measures to mitigate its possible adverse effects.

(3)   The duty under subsection (1) does not apply where—

(a)   the controller has implemented appropriate technological and organisational protection measures which were applied to the personal data affected by the breach,

(b)   the controller has taken subsequent measures which ensure that the high risk to the rights and freedoms of data subjects referred to in subsection (1) is no longer likely to materialise, or

(c)   it would involve a disproportionate effort.

(4)   An example of a case which may fall within subsection (3)(a) is where measures that render personal data unintelligible to any person not authorised to access the data have been applied, such as encryption.

(5)   In a case falling within subsection (3)(c) (but not within subsection (3)(a) or (b)), the information mentioned in subsection (2) must be made available to the data subject in another equally effective way, for example, by means of a public communication.

(6)   Where the controller has not informed the data subject of the breach the Commissioner, on being notified under section 67 and after considering the likelihood of the breach resulting in a high risk, may—

(a)   require the controller to notify the data subject of the breach, or

(b)   decide that the controller is not required to do so because any of paragraphs (a) to (c) of subsection (3) applies.

(7)   The controller may restrict, wholly or partly, the provision of information to the data subject under subsection (1) to the extent that and for so long as the restriction is, having regard to the fundamental rights and legitimate interests of the data subject, a necessary and proportionate measure to—

(a)   avoid obstructing an official or legal inquiry, investigation or procedure;

(b)   avoid prejudicing the prevention, detection, investigation or prosecution of criminal offences or the execution of criminal penalties;

(c)   protect public security;

(d)   protect national security;

(e)   protect the rights and freedoms of others.

(8)   Subsection (6) does not apply where the controller's decision not to inform the data subject of the breach was made in reliance on subsection (7).

(9)   The duties in section 52(1) and (2) apply in relation to information that the controller is required to provide to the data subject under this section as they apply in relation to information that the controller is required to provide to the data subject under Chapter 3 .

Data protection officers

69. Designation of a data protection officer   (1)   The controller must designate a data protection officer, unless the controller is a court, or other judicial authority, acting in its judicial capacity.

(2)   When designating a data protection officer, the controller must have regard to the professional qualities of the proposed officer, in particular—

(a)   the proposed officer's expert knowledge of data protection law and practice, and

(b)   the ability of the proposed officer to perform the tasks mentioned in section 71.

(3)   The same person may be designated as a data protection officer by several controllers, taking account of their organisational structure and size.

(4)   The controller must publish the contact details of the data protection officer and communicate these to the Commissioner.

70. Position of data protection officer   (1)   The controller must ensure that the data protection officer is involved, properly and in a timely manner, in all issues which relate to the protection of personal data.

(2)   The controller must provide the data protection officer with the necessary resources and access to personal data and processing operations to enable the data protection officer to—

(a)   perform the tasks mentioned in section 71, and

(b)   maintain his or her expert knowledge of data protection law and practice.

(3)   The controller—

(a)   must ensure that the data protection officer does not receive any instructions regarding the performance of the tasks mentioned in section 71;

(b)   must ensure that the data protection officer does not perform a task or fulfil a duty other than those mentioned in this Part where such task or duty would result in a conflict of interests;

(c)   must not dismiss or penalise the data protection officer for performing the tasks mentioned in section 71.

(4)   A data subject may contact the data protection officer with regard to all issues relating to—

(a)   the processing of that data subject's personal data, or

(b)   the exercise of that data subject's rights under this Part.

(5)   The data protection officer, in the performance of this role, must report to the highest management level of the controller.

71. Tasks of data protection officer   (1)   The controller must entrust the data protection officer with at least the following tasks—

(a) informing and advising the controller, any processor engaged by the controller, and any employee of the controller who carries out processing of personal data, of that person's obligations under this Part,

(b) providing advice on the carrying out of a data protection impact assessment under section 64 and monitoring compliance with that section,

(c) co-operating with the Commissioner,

(d) acting as the contact point for the Commissioner on issues relating to processing, including in relation to the consultation mentioned in section 65, and consulting with the Commissioner, where appropriate, in relation to any other matter,

(e) monitoring compliance with policies of the controller in relation to the protection of personal data, and

(f) monitoring compliance by the controller with this Part.

(2) In relation to the policies mentioned in subsection (1)(e), the data protection officer's tasks include—

(a) assigning responsibilities under those policies,

(b) raising awareness of those policies,

(c) training staff involved in processing operations, and

(d) conducting audits required under those policies.

(3) In performing the tasks set out in subsections (1) and (2), the data protection officer must have regard to the risks associated with processing operations, taking into account the nature, scope, context and purposes of processing.

CHAPTER 5[1]

TRANSFERS OF PERSONAL DATA TO THIRD COUNTRIES ETC

Overview and interpretation

72. Overview and interpretation (1) This Chapter deals with the transfer of personal data to third countries or international organisations, as follows—

(a) sections 73 to 76 set out the general conditions that apply;

(b) section 77 sets out the special conditions that apply where the intended recipient of personal data is not a relevant authority in a third country or an international organisation;

(c) section 78 makes special provision about subsequent transfers of personal data.

(2) In this Chapter, "relevant authority", in relation to a third country, means any person based in a third country that has (in that country) functions comparable to those of a competent authority.

---

[1] Chapter 5 contains ss 72-78.

General principles for transfers

73. General principles for transfers of personal data (1) A controller may not transfer personal data to a third country or to an international organisation unless—

(a) the three conditions set out in subsections (2) to (4) are met, and

(b) in a case where the personal data was originally transmitted or otherwise made available to the controller or another competent authority by a member State other than the United Kingdom, that member State, or any person based in that member State which is a competent authority for the purposes of the Law Enforcement Directive, has authorised the transfer in accordance with the law of the member State.

(2) Condition 1 is that the transfer is necessary for any of the law enforcement purposes.

(3) Condition 2 is that the transfer—

(a) is based on an adequacy decision (see section 74),

(b) if not based on an adequacy decision, is based on there being appropriate safeguards (see section 75), or

(c) if not based on an adequacy decision or on there being appropriate safeguards, is based on special circumstances (see section 76).

(4) Condition 3 is that—

(a) the intended recipient is a relevant authority in a third country or an international organisation that is a relevant international organisation, or

(b) in a case where the controller is a competent authority specified in any of paragraphs 5 to 17, 21, 24 to 28, 34 to 51, 54 and 56 of Schedule 7—

(i) the intended recipient is a person in a third country other than a relevant authority, and

(ii) the additional conditions in section 77 are met.

(5) Authorisation is not required as mentioned in subsection (1)(b) if—

(a) the transfer is necessary for the prevention of an immediate and serious threat either to the public security of a member State or a third country or to the essential interests of a member State, and

(b)   the authorisation cannot be obtained in good time.

(6)   Where a transfer is made without the authorisation mentioned in subsection (1)(b), the authority in the member State which would have been responsible for deciding whether to authorise the transfer must be informed without delay.

(7)   In this section, "relevant international organisation" means an international organisation that carries out functions for any of the law enforcement purposes.

74. Transfers on the basis of an adequacy decision   A transfer of personal data to a third country or an international organisation is based on an adequacy decision where—

- (a)   the European Commission has decided, in accordance with Article 36 of the Law Enforcement Directive, that—
  - (i)   the third country or a territory or one or more specified sectors within that third country, or
  - (ii)   (as the case may be) the international organisation,
  ensures an adequate level of protection of personal data, and
- (b)   that decision has not been repealed or suspended, or amended in a way that demonstrates that the Commission no longer considers there to be an adequate level of protection of personal data.

75. Transfers on the basis of appropriate safeguards   (1)   A transfer of personal data to a third country or an international organisation is based on there being appropriate safeguards where—

- (a)   a legal instrument containing appropriate safeguards for the protection of personal data binds the intended recipient of the data, or
- (b)   the controller, having assessed all the circumstances surrounding transfers of that type of personal data to the third country or international organisation, concludes that appropriate safeguards exist to protect the data.

(2)   The controller must inform the Commissioner about the categories of data transfers that take place in reliance on subsection (1)(b).

(3)   Where a transfer of data takes place in reliance on subsection (1)—

- (a)   the transfer must be documented,
- (b)   the documentation must be provided to the Commissioner on request, and
- (c)   the documentation must include, in particular—
  - (i)   the date and time of the transfer,
  - (ii)   the name of and any other pertinent information about the recipient,
  - (iii)   the justification for the transfer, and
  - (iv)   a description of the personal data transferred.

76. Transfers on the basis of special circumstances   (1)   A transfer of personal data to a third country or international organisation is based on special circumstances where the transfer is necessary—

- (a)   to protect the vital interests of the data subject or another person,
- (b)   to safeguard the legitimate interests of the data subject,
- (c)   for the prevention of an immediate and serious threat to the public security of a member State or a third country,
- (d)   in individual cases for any of the law enforcement purposes, or
- (e)   in individual cases for a legal purpose.

(2)   But subsection (1)(d) and (e) do not apply if the controller determines that fundamental rights and freedoms of the data subject override the public interest in the transfer.

(3)   Where a transfer of data takes place in reliance on subsection (1)—

- (a)   the transfer must be documented,
- (b)   the documentation must be provided to the Commissioner on request, and
- (c)   the documentation must include, in particular—
  - (i)   the date and time of the transfer,
  - (ii)   the name of and any other pertinent information about the recipient,
  - (iii)   the justification for the transfer, and
  - (iv)   a description of the personal data transferred.

(4)   For the purposes of this section, a transfer is necessary for a legal purpose if—

- (a)   it is necessary for the purpose of, or in connection with, any legal proceedings (including prospective legal proceedings) relating to any of the law enforcement purposes,
- (b)   it is necessary for the purpose of obtaining legal advice in relation to any of the law enforcement purposes, or
- (c)   it is otherwise necessary for the purposes of establishing, exercising or defending legal rights in relation to any of the law enforcement purposes.

Transfers to particular recipients

77. Transfers of personal data to persons other than relevant authorities   (1)   The additional conditions referred to in section 73(4)(b)(ii) are the following four conditions.

(2)   Condition 1 is that the transfer is strictly necessary in a specific case for the performance of a task of the transferring controller as provided by law for any of the law enforcement purposes.

(3)   Condition 2 is that the transferring controller has determined that there are no fundamental rights and freedoms of the data subject concerned that override the public interest necessitating the transfer.

(4)   Condition 3 is that the transferring controller considers that the transfer of the personal data to a relevant authority in the third country would be ineffective or inappropriate (for example, where the transfer could not be made in sufficient time to enable its purpose to be fulfilled).

(5)   Condition 4 is that the transferring controller informs the intended recipient of the specific purpose or purposes for which the personal data may, so far as necessary, be processed.

(6)   Where personal data is transferred to a person in a third country other than a relevant authority, the transferring controller must inform a relevant authority in that third country without undue delay of the transfer, unless this would be ineffective or inappropriate.

(7)   The transferring controller must—

    (a)   document any transfer to a recipient in a third country other than a relevant authority, and

    (b)   inform the Commissioner about the transfer.

(8)   This section does not affect the operation of any international agreement in force between member States and third countries in the field of judicial co-operation in criminal matters and police co-operation.

Subsequent transfers

78.   Subsequent transfers   (1)   Where personal data is transferred in accordance with section 73, the transferring controller must make it a condition of the transfer that the data is not to be further transferred to a third country or international organisation without the authorisation of the transferring controller or another competent authority.

(2)   A competent authority may give an authorisation under subsection (1) only where the further transfer is necessary for a law enforcement purpose.

(3)   In deciding whether to give the authorisation, the competent authority must take into account (among any other relevant factors)—

    (a)   the seriousness of the circumstances leading to the request for authorisation,

    (b)   the purpose for which the personal data was originally transferred, and

    (c)   the standards for the protection of personal data that apply in the third country or international organisation to which the personal data would be transferred.

(4)   In a case where the personal data was originally transmitted or otherwise made available to the transferring controller or another competent authority by a member State other than the United Kingdom, an authorisation may not be given under subsection (1) unless that member State, or any person based in that member State which is a competent authority for the purposes of the Law Enforcement Directive, has authorised the transfer in accordance with the law of the member State.

(5)   Authorisation is not required as mentioned in subsection (4) if—

    (a)   the transfer is necessary for the prevention of an immediate and serious threat either to the public security of a member State or a third country or to the essential interests of a member State, and

    (b)   the authorisation cannot be obtained in good time.

(6)   Where a transfer is made without the authorisation mentioned in subsection (4), the authority in the member State which would have been responsible for deciding whether to authorise the transfer must be informed without delay.

CHAPTER 6[1]

SUPPLEMENTARY

79.   National security: certificate   (1)   A Minister of the Crown may issue a certificate certifying, for the purposes of section 44(4), 45(4), 48(3) or 68(7), that a restriction is a necessary and proportionate measure to protect national security.

(2)   The certificate may—

    (a)   relate to a specific restriction (described in the certificate) which a controller has imposed or is proposing to impose under section 44(4), 45(4), 48(3) or 68(7), or

    (b)   identify any restriction to which it relates by means of a general description.

(3)   Subject to subsection (6), a certificate issued under subsection (1) is conclusive evidence that the specific restriction or (as the case may be) any restriction falling within the general description is, or at any time was, a necessary and proportionate measure to protect national security.

(4)   A certificate issued under subsection (1) may be expressed to have prospective effect.

(5)   Any person directly affected by the issuing of a certificate under subsection (1) may appeal to the Tribunal against the certificate.

(6)   If, on an appeal under subsection (5), the Tribunal finds that, applying the principles applied by a court on an application for judicial review, the Minister did not have reasonable grounds for issuing the certificate, the Tribunal may—

    (a)   allow the appeal, and

(b)   quash the certificate.

(7)   Where in any proceedings under or by virtue of this Act, it is claimed by a controller that a restriction falls within a general description in a certificate issued under subsection (1), any other party to the proceedings may appeal to the Tribunal on the ground that the restriction does not fall within that description.

(8)   But, subject to any determination under subsection (9), the restriction is to be conclusively presumed to fall within the general description.

(9)   On an appeal under subsection (7), the Tribunal may determine that the certificate does not so apply.

(10)   A document purporting to be a certificate under subsection (1) is to be—

(a)   received in evidence, and

(b)   deemed to be such a certificate unless the contrary is proved.

(11)   A document which purports to be certified by or on behalf of a Minister of the Crown as a true copy of a certificate issued by that Minister under subsection (1) is—

(a)   in any legal proceedings, evidence of that certificate, and

(b)   in any legal proceedings in Scotland, sufficient evidence of that certificate.

(12)   The power conferred by subsection (1) on a Minister of the Crown is exercisable only by—

(a)   a Minister who is a member of the Cabinet, or

(b)   the Attorney General or the Advocate General for Scotland.

(13)   No power conferred by any provision of Part 6 may be exercised in relation to the imposition of—

(a)   a specific restriction in a certificate under subsection (1), or

(b)   a restriction falling within a general description in such a certificate.

---

[1] Chapter 6 contains ss 79–81.

80. Special processing restrictions   (1)   Subsections (3) and (4) apply where, for a law enforcement purpose, a controller transmits or otherwise makes available personal data to an EU recipient or a non-EU recipient.

(2)   In this section—

"EU recipient" means—

(a)   a recipient in a member State other than the United Kingdom, or

(b)   an agency, office or body established pursuant to Chapters 4 and 5 of Title V of the Treaty on the Functioning of the European Union;

"non-EU recipient" means—

(a)   a recipient in a third country, or

(b)   an international organisation.

(3)   The controller must consider whether, if the personal data had instead been transmitted or otherwise made available within the United Kingdom to another competent authority, processing of the data by the other competent authority would have been subject to any restrictions by virtue of any enactment or rule of law.

(4)   Where that would be the case, the controller must inform the EU recipient or non-EU recipient that the data is transmitted or otherwise made available subject to compliance by that person with the same restrictions (which must be set out in the information given to that person).

(5)   Except as provided by subsection (4), the controller may not impose restrictions on the processing of personal data transmitted or otherwise made available by the controller to an EU recipient.

(6)   Subsection (7) applies where—

(a)   a competent authority for the purposes of the Law Enforcement Directive in a member State other than the United Kingdom transmits or otherwise makes available personal data to a controller for a law enforcement purpose, and

(b)   the competent authority in the other member State informs the controller, in accordance with any law of that member State which implements Article 9(3) and (4) of the Law Enforcement Directive, that the data is transmitted or otherwise made available subject to compliance by the controller with restrictions set out by the competent authority.

(7)   The controller must comply with the restrictions.

81. Reporting of infringements   (1)   Each controller must implement effective mechanisms to encourage the reporting of an infringement of this Part.

(2)   The mechanisms implemented under subsection (1) must provide that an infringement may be reported to any of the following persons—

(a)   the controller;

(b)   the Commissioner.

(3)   The mechanisms implemented under subsection (1) must include—

(a)   raising awareness of the protections provided by Part 4A of the Employment Rights Act 1996 and Part 5A of the Employment Rights (Northern Ireland) Order 1996 (SI 1996/1919 (NI 16)), and

(b)   such other protections for a person who reports an infringement of this Part as the controller considers appropriate.

(4) A person who reports an infringement of this Part does not breach—

(a) an obligation of confidence owed by the person, or

(b) any other restriction on the disclosure of information (however imposed).

(5) Subsection (4) does not apply if or to the extent that the report includes a disclosure which is prohibited by any of Parts 1 to 7 or Chapter 1 of Part 9 of the Investigatory Powers Act 2016.

(6) Until the repeal of Part 1 of the Regulation of Investigatory Powers Act 2000 by paragraphs 45 and 54 of Schedule 10 to the Investigatory Powers Act 2016 is fully in force, subsection (5) has effect as if it included a reference to that Part.

PART 4[1]

INTELLIGENCE SERVICES PROCESSING

---

[1] Part 4 contains ss 82-113. This part is concerned with intelligence services processing and is not reproduced in this work.

PART 5[1]

THE INFORMATION COMMISSIONER

The Commissioner

114. The Information Commissioner (1) There is to continue to be an Information Commissioner.

(2) Schedule 12 makes provision about the Commissioner.

---

[1] Part 5 contains ss 114-141.

General functions

115. General functions under the GDPR and safeguards (1) The Commissioner is to be the supervisory authority in the United Kingdom for the purposes of Article 51 of the GDPR.

(2) General functions are conferred on the Commissioner by—

(a) Article 57 of the GDPR (tasks), and

(b) Article 58 of the GDPR (powers),

(and see also the Commissioner's duty under section 2).

(3) The Commissioner's functions in relation to the processing of personal data to which the GDPR applies include—

(a) a duty to advise Parliament, the government and other institutions and bodies on legislative and administrative measures relating to the protection of individuals' rights and freedoms with regard to the processing of personal data, and

(b) a power to issue, on the Commissioner's own initiative or on request, opinions to Parliament, the government or other institutions and bodies as well as to the public on any issue related to the protection of personal data.

(4) The Commissioner's functions under Article 58 of the GDPR are subject to the safeguards in subsections (5) to (9).

(5) The Commissioner's power under Article 58(1)(a) of the GDPR (power to require a controller or processor to provide information that the Commissioner requires for the performance of the Commissioner's tasks under the GDPR) is exercisable only by giving an information notice under section 142.

(6) The Commissioner's power under Article 58(1)(b) of the GDPR (power to carry out data protection audits) is exercisable only in accordance with section 146.

(7) The Commissioner's powers under Article 58(1)(e) and (f) of the GDPR (power to obtain information from controllers and processors and access to their premises) are exercisable only—

(a) in accordance with Schedule 15 (see section 154), or

(b) to the extent that they are exercised in conjunction with the power under Article 58(1)(b) of the GDPR, in accordance with section 146.

(8) The following powers are exercisable only by giving an enforcement notice under section 149—

(a) the Commissioner's powers under Article 58(2)(c) to (g) and (j) of the GDPR (certain corrective powers);

(b) the Commissioner's powers under Article 58(2)(h) to order a certification body to withdraw, or not to issue, a certification under Articles 42 and 43 of the GDPR.

(9) The Commissioner's powers under Articles 58(2)(i) and 83 of the GDPR (administrative fines) are exercisable only by giving a penalty notice under section 155.

(10) This section is without prejudice to other functions conferred on the Commissioner, whether by the GDPR, this Act or otherwise.

116. Other general functions (1) The Commissioner—

(a) is to be the supervisory authority in the United Kingdom for the purposes of Article 41 of the Law Enforcement Directive, and

(b) is to continue to be the designated authority in the United Kingdom for the purposes of

Article 13 of the Data Protection Convention.

(2)   Schedule 13 confers general functions on the Commissioner in connection with processing to which the GDPR does not apply (and see also the Commissioner's duty under section 2).

(3)   This section and Schedule 13 are without prejudice to other functions conferred on the Commissioner, whether by this Act or otherwise.

117. Competence in relation to courts etc   Nothing in this Act permits or requires the Commissioner to exercise functions in relation to the processing of personal data by—

  (a)   an individual acting in a judicial capacity, or

  (b)   a court or tribunal acting in its judicial capacity,

(and see also Article 55(3) of the GDPR).

International role

118. Co-operation and mutual assistance   (1)   Articles 60 to 62 of the GDPR confer functions on the Commissioner in relation to co-operation and mutual assistance between, and joint operations of, supervisory authorities under the GDPR.

(2)   References to the GDPR in subsection (1) do not include the applied GDPR.

(3)   Article 61 of the applied GDPR confers functions on the Commissioner in relation to co-operation with other supervisory authorities (as defined in Article 4(21) of the applied GDPR).

(4)   Part 1 of Schedule 14 makes provision as to the functions to be carried out by the Commissioner for the purposes of Article 50 of the Law Enforcement Directive (mutual assistance).

(5)   Part 2 of Schedule 14 makes provision as to the functions to be carried out by the Commissioner for the purposes of Article 13 of the Data Protection Convention (co-operation between parties).

119. Inspection of personal data in accordance with international obligations

(1)   The Commissioner may inspect personal data where the inspection is necessary in order to discharge an international obligation of the United Kingdom, subject to the restriction in subsection (2).

(2)   The power under subsection (1) is exercisable only if the personal data—

  (a)   is processed wholly or partly by automated means, or

  (b)   is processed otherwise than by automated means and forms part of a filing system or is intended to form part of a filing system.

(3)   The power under subsection (1) includes power to inspect, operate and test equipment which is used for the processing of personal data.

(4)   Before exercising the power under subsection (1), the Commissioner must by written notice inform the controller and any processor that the Commissioner intends to do so.

(5)   Subsection (4) does not apply if the Commissioner considers that the case is urgent.

(6)   It is an offence—

  (a)   intentionally to obstruct a person exercising the power under subsection (1), or

  (b)   to fail without reasonable excuse to give a person exercising that power any assistance the person may reasonably require.

(7)   Paragraphs (c) and (d) of section 3(14) do not apply to references in this section to personal data, the processing of personal data, a controller or a processor.

120. Further international role   (1)   The Commissioner must, in relation to third countries and international organisations, take appropriate steps to—

  (a)   develop international co-operation mechanisms to facilitate the effective enforcement of legislation for the protection of personal data;

  (b)   provide international mutual assistance in the enforcement of legislation for the protection of personal data, subject to appropriate safeguards for the protection of personal data and other fundamental rights and freedoms;

  (c)   engage relevant stakeholders in discussion and activities aimed at furthering international co-operation in the enforcement of legislation for the protection of personal data;

  (d)   promote the exchange and documentation of legislation and practice for the protection of personal data, including legislation and practice relating to jurisdictional conflicts with third countries.

(2)   Subsection (1) applies only in connection with the processing of personal data to which the GDPR does not apply; for the equivalent duty in connection with the processing of personal data to which the GDPR applies, see Article 50 of the GDPR (international co-operation for the protection of personal data).

(3)   The Commissioner must carry out data protection functions which the Secretary of State directs the Commissioner to carry out for the purpose of enabling Her Majesty's Government in the United Kingdom to give effect to an international obligation of the United Kingdom.

(4)   The Commissioner may provide an authority carrying out data protection functions under the law of a British overseas territory with assistance in carrying out those functions.

(5)   The Secretary of State may direct that assistance under subsection (4) is to be provided on terms, including terms as to payment, specified or approved by the Secretary of State.

(6)   In this section—

"data protection functions" means functions relating to the protection of individuals with respect to the processing of personal data;

"mutual assistance in the enforcement of legislation for the protection of personal data" includes assistance in the form of notification, complaint referral, investigative assistance and information exchange;

"third country" means a country or territory that is not a member State.

(7) Section 3(14)(c) does not apply to references to personal data and the processing of personal data in this section.

Codes of practice

121. Data-sharing code (1) The Commissioner must prepare a code of practice which contains—

(a) practical guidance in relation to the sharing of personal data in accordance with the requirements of the data protection legislation, and

(b) such other guidance as the Commissioner considers appropriate to promote good practice in the sharing of personal data.

(2) Where a code under this section is in force, the Commissioner may prepare amendments of the code or a replacement code.

(3) Before preparing a code or amendments under this section, the Commissioner must consult the Secretary of State and such of the following as the Commissioner considers appropriate—

(a) trade associations;

(b) data subjects;

(c) persons who appear to the Commissioner to represent the interests of data subjects.

(4) A code under this section may include transitional provision or savings.

(5) In this section—

"good practice in the sharing of personal data" means such practice in the sharing of personal data as appears to the Commissioner to be desirable having regard to the interests of data subjects and others, including compliance with the requirements of the data protection legislation;

"the sharing of personal data" means the disclosure of personal data by transmission, dissemination or otherwise making it available;

"trade association" includes a body representing controllers or processors.

122. Direct marketing code (1) The Commissioner must prepare a code of practice which contains—

(a) practical guidance in relation to the carrying out of direct marketing in accordance with the requirements of the data protection legislation and the Privacy and Electronic Communications (EC Directive) Regulations 2003 (SI 2003/2426), and

(b) such other guidance as the Commissioner considers appropriate to promote good practice in direct marketing.

(2) Where a code under this section is in force, the Commissioner may prepare amendments of the code or a replacement code.

(3) Before preparing a code or amendments under this section, the Commissioner must consult the Secretary of State and such of the following as the Commissioner considers appropriate—

(a) trade associations;

(b) data subjects;

(c) persons who appear to the Commissioner to represent the interests of data subjects.

(4) A code under this section may include transitional provision or savings.

(5) In this section—

"direct marketing" means the communication (by whatever means) of advertising or marketing material which is directed to particular individuals;

"good practice in direct marketing" means such practice in direct marketing as appears to the Commissioner to be desirable having regard to the interests of data subjects and others, including compliance with the requirements mentioned in subsection (1)(a);

"trade association" includes a body representing controllers or processors.

123. Age-appropriate design code (1) The Commissioner must prepare a code of practice which contains such guidance as the Commissioner considers appropriate on standards of age-appropriate design of relevant information society services which are likely to be accessed by children.

(2) Where a code under this section is in force, the Commissioner may prepare amendments of the code or a replacement code.

(3) Before preparing a code or amendments under this section, the Commissioner must consult the Secretary of State and such other persons as the Commissioner considers appropriate, including—

(a) children,

(b) parents,

(c) persons who appear to the Commissioner to represent the interests of children,

(d) child development experts, and

(e)   trade associations.

(4)   In preparing a code or amendments under this section, the Commissioner must have regard—

(a)   to the fact that children have different needs at different ages, and

(b)   to the United Kingdom's obligations under the United Nations Convention on the Rights of the Child.

(5)   A code under this section may include transitional provision or savings.

(6)   Any transitional provision included in the first code under this section must cease to have effect before the end of the period of 12 months beginning when the code comes into force.

(7)   In this section—

"age-appropriate design" means the design of services so that they are appropriate for use by, and meet the development needs of, children;

"information society services" has the same meaning as in the GDPR, but does not include preventive or counselling services;

"relevant information society services" means information society services which involve the processing of personal data to which the GDPR applies;

"standards of age-appropriate design of relevant information society services" means such standards of age-appropriate design of such services as appear to the Commissioner to be desirable having regard to the best interests of children;

"trade association" includes a body representing controllers or processors;

"the United Nations Convention on the Rights of the Child" means the Convention on the Rights of the Child adopted by the General Assembly of the United Nations on 20 November 1989 (including any Protocols to that Convention which are in force in relation to the United Kingdom), subject to any reservations, objections or interpretative declarations by the United Kingdom for the time being in force.

124.   Data protection and journalism code   (1)   The Commissioner must prepare a code of practice which contains—

(a)   practical guidance in relation to the processing of personal data for the purposes of journalism in accordance with the requirements of the data protection legislation, and

(b)   such other guidance as the Commissioner considers appropriate to promote good practice in the processing of personal data for the purposes of journalism.

(2)   Where a code under this section is in force, the Commissioner may prepare amendments of the code or a replacement code.

(3)   Before preparing a code or amendments under this section, the Commissioner must consult such of the following as the Commissioner considers appropriate—

(a)   trade associations;

(b)   data subjects;

(c)   persons who appear to the Commissioner to represent the interests of data subjects.

(4)   A code under this section may include transitional provision or savings.

(5)   In this section—

"good practice in the processing of personal data for the purposes of journalism" means such practice in the processing of personal data for those purposes as appears to the Commissioner to be desirable having regard to—

(a)   the interests of data subjects and others, including compliance with the requirements of the data protection legislation, and

(b)   the special importance of the public interest in the freedom of expression and information;

"trade association" includes a body representing controllers or processors.

125.   Approval of codes prepared under sections 121 to 124   (1)   When a code is prepared under section 121, 122, 123 or 124—

(a)   the Commissioner must submit the final version to the Secretary of State, and

(b)   the Secretary of State must lay the code before Parliament.

(2)   In relation to the first code under section 123—

(a)   the Commissioner must prepare the code as soon as reasonably practicable and must submit it to the Secretary of State before the end of the period of 18 months beginning when this Act is passed, and

(b)   the Secretary of State must lay it before Parliament as soon as reasonably practicable.

(3)   If, within the 40-day period, either House of Parliament resolves not to approve a code prepared under section 121, 122, 123 or 124, the Commissioner must not issue the code.

(4)   If no such resolution is made within that period—

(a)   the Commissioner must issue the code, and

(b)   the code comes into force at the end of the period of 21 days beginning with the day on which it is issued.

(5)   If, as a result of subsection (3), there is no code in force under section 121, 122, 123 or 124, the Commissioner must prepare another version of the code.

(6)   Nothing in subsection (3) prevents another version of the code being laid before Parliament.

(7)   In this section, "the 40-day period" means—

   (a)   if the code is laid before both Houses of Parliament on the same day, the period of 40 days beginning with that day, or

   (b)   if the code is laid before the Houses of Parliament on different days, the period of 40 days beginning with the later of those days.

(8)   In calculating the 40-day period, no account is to be taken of any period during which Parliament is dissolved or prorogued or during which both Houses of Parliament are adjourned for more than 4 days.

(9)   This section, other than subsections (2) and (5), applies in relation to amendments prepared under section 121, 122, 123 or 124 as it applies in relation to codes prepared under those sections.

126. Publication and review of codes issued under section 125(4)

(1)   The Commissioner must publish a code issued under section 125(4).

(2)   Where an amendment of a code is issued under section 125(4), the Commissioner must publish—

   (a)   the amendment, or

   (b)   the code as amended by it.

(3)   The Commissioner must keep under review each code issued under section 125(4) for the time being in force.

(4)   Where the Commissioner becomes aware that the terms of such a code could result in a breach of an international obligation of the United Kingdom, the Commissioner must exercise the power under section 121(2), 122(2), 123(2) or 124(2) with a view to remedying the situation.

127. Effect of codes issued under section 125(4)

(1)   A failure by a person to act in accordance with a provision of a code issued under section 125(4) does not of itself make that person liable to legal proceedings in a court or tribunal.

(2)   A code issued under section 125(4), including an amendment or replacement code, is admissible in evidence in legal proceedings.

(3)   In any proceedings before a court or tribunal, the court or tribunal must take into account a provision of a code issued under section 125(4) in determining a question arising in the proceedings if—

   (a)   the question relates to a time when the provision was in force, and

   (b)   the provision appears to the court or tribunal to be relevant to the question.

(4)   Where the Commissioner is carrying out a function described in subsection (5), the Commissioner must take into account a provision of a code issued under section 125(4) in determining a question arising in connection with the carrying out of the function if—

   (a)   the question relates to a time when the provision was in force, and

   (b)   the provision appears to the Commissioner to be relevant to the question.

(5)   Those functions are functions under—

   (a)   the data protection legislation, or

   (b)   the Privacy and Electronic Communications (EC Directive) Regulations 2003 (SI 2003/2426).

128. Other codes of practice

(1)   The Secretary of State may by regulations require the Commissioner—

   (a)   to prepare appropriate codes of practice giving guidance as to good practice in the processing of personal data, and

   (b)   to make them available to such persons as the Commissioner considers appropriate.

(2)   Before preparing such codes, the Commissioner must consult such of the following as the Commissioner considers appropriate—

   (a)   trade associations;

   (b)   data subjects;

   (c)   persons who appear to the Commissioner to represent the interests of data subjects.

(3)   Regulations under this section—

   (a)   must describe the personal data or processing to which the code of practice is to relate, and

   (b)   may describe the persons or classes of person to whom it is to relate.

(4)   Regulations under this section are subject to the negative resolution procedure.

(5)   In this section—

"good practice in the processing of personal data" means such practice in the processing of personal data as appears to the Commissioner to be desirable having regard to the interests of data subjects and others, including compliance with the requirements of the data protection legislation;

"trade association" includes a body representing controllers or processors.

Consensual audits

129. Consensual audits

(1)   The Commissioner's functions under Article 58(1) of the GDPR and paragraph 1 of Schedule 13 include power, with the consent of a controller or processor, to carry out an assessment of whether the controller or processor is complying with good practice in

the processing of personal data.

(2)   The Commissioner must inform the controller or processor of the results of such an assessment.

(3)   In this section, "good practice in the processing of personal data" has the same meaning as in section 128.

Records of national security certificates

130.   Records of national security certificates   (1)   A Minister of the Crown who issues a certificate under section 27, 79 or 111 must send a copy of the certificate to the Commissioner.

(2)   If the Commissioner receives a copy of a certificate under subsection (1), the Commissioner must publish a record of the certificate.

(3)   The record must contain—

(a)   the name of the Minister who issued the certificate,

(b)   the date on which the certificate was issued, and

(c)   subject to subsection (4), the text of the certificate.

(4)   The Commissioner must not publish the text, or a part of the text, of the certificate if—

(a)   the Minister determines that publishing the text or that part of the text—

(i)   would be against the interests of national security,

(ii)   would be contrary to the public interest, or

(iii)   might jeopardise the safety of any person, and

(b)   the Minister has notified the Commissioner of that determination.

(5)   The Commissioner must keep the record of the certificate available to the public while the certificate is in force.

(6)   If a Minister of the Crown revokes a certificate issued under section 27, 79 or 111, the Minister must notify the Commissioner.

Information provided to the Commissioner

131.   Disclosure of information to the Commissioner   (1)   No enactment or rule of law prohibiting or restricting the disclosure of information precludes a person from providing the Commissioner with information necessary for the discharge of the Commissioner's functions.

(2)   But this section does not authorise the making of a disclosure which is prohibited by any of Parts 1 to 7 or Chapter 1 of Part 9 of the Investigatory Powers Act 2016.

(3)   Until the repeal of Part 1 of the Regulation of Investigatory Powers Act 2000 by paragraphs 45 and 54 of Schedule 10 to the Investigatory Powers Act 2016 is fully in force, subsection (2) has effect as if it included a reference to that Part.

132.   Confidentiality of information   (1)   A person who is or has been the Commissioner, or a member of the Commissioner's staff or an agent of the Commissioner, must not disclose information which—

(a)   has been obtained by, or provided to, the Commissioner in the course of, or for the purposes of, the discharging of the Commissioner's functions,

(b)   relates to an identified or identifiable individual or business, and

(c)   is not available to the public from other sources at the time of the disclosure and has not previously been available to the public from other sources,

unless the disclosure is made with lawful authority.

(2)   For the purposes of subsection (1), a disclosure is made with lawful authority only if and to the extent that—

(a)   the disclosure was made with the consent of the individual or of the person for the time being carrying on the business,

(b)   the information was obtained or provided as described in subsection (1)(a) for the purpose of its being made available to the public (in whatever manner),

(c)   the disclosure was made for the purposes of, and is necessary for, the discharge of one or more of the Commissioner's functions,

(d)   the disclosure was made for the purposes of, and is necessary for, the discharge of an EU obligation,

(e)   the disclosure was made for the purposes of criminal or civil proceedings, however arising, or

(f)   having regard to the rights, freedoms and legitimate interests of any person, the disclosure was necessary in the public interest.

(3)   It is an offence for a person knowingly or recklessly to disclose information in contravention of subsection (1).

133.   Guidance about privileged communications   (1)   The Commissioner must produce and publish guidance about—

(a)   how the Commissioner proposes to secure that privileged communications which the Commissioner obtains or has access to in the course of carrying out the Commissioner's functions are used or disclosed only so far as necessary for carrying out those functions, and

(b)   how the Commissioner proposes to comply with restrictions and prohibitions on obtaining or having access to privileged communications which are imposed by an enactment.

(2)   The Commissioner—

(a)   may alter or replace the guidance, and

(b)   must publish any altered or replacement guidance.

(3)   The Commissioner must consult the Secretary of State before publishing guidance under this section (including altered or replacement guidance).

(4)   The Commissioner must arrange for guidance under this section (including altered or replacement guidance) to be laid before Parliament.

(5)   In this section, "privileged communications" means—

(a)   communications made—

(i)   between a professional legal adviser and the adviser's client, and

(ii)   in connection with the giving of legal advice to the client with respect to legal obligations, liabilities or rights, and

(b)   communications made—

(i)   between a professional legal adviser and the adviser's client or between such an adviser or client and another person,

(ii)   in connection with or in contemplation of legal proceedings, and

(iii)   for the purposes of such proceedings.

(6)   In subsection (5)—

(a)   references to the client of a professional legal adviser include references to a person acting on behalf of the client, and

(b)   references to a communication include—

(i)   a copy or other record of the communication, and

(ii)   anything enclosed with or referred to in the communication if made as described in subsection (5)(a)(ii) or in subsection (5)(b)(ii) and (iii).

Fees

134.   Fees for services   The Commissioner may require a person other than a data subject or a data protection officer to pay a reasonable fee for a service provided to the person, or at the person's request, which the Commissioner is required or authorised to provide under the data protection legislation.

135.   Manifestly unfounded or excessive requests by data subjects etc   (1)   Where a request to the Commissioner from a data subject or a data protection officer is manifestly unfounded or excessive, the Commissioner may—

(a)   charge a reasonable fee for dealing with the request, or

(b)   refuse to act on the request.

(2)   An example of a request that may be excessive is one that merely repeats the substance of previous requests.

(3)   In any proceedings where there is an issue as to whether a request described in subsection (1) is manifestly unfounded or excessive, it is for the Commissioner to show that it is.

(4)   Subsections (1) and (3) apply only in cases in which the Commissioner does not already have such powers and obligations under Article 57(4) of the GDPR.

136.   Guidance about fees   (1)   The Commissioner must produce and publish guidance about the fees the Commissioner proposes to charge in accordance with—

(a)   section 134 or 135, or

(b)   Article 57(4) of the GDPR.

(2)   Before publishing the guidance, the Commissioner must consult the Secretary of State.

Charges

137.   Charges payable to the Commissioner by controllers   (1)   The Secretary of State may by regulations require controllers to pay charges of an amount specified in the regulations to the Commissioner.

(2)   Regulations under subsection (1) may require a controller to pay a charge regardless of whether the Commissioner has provided, or proposes to provide, a service to the controller.

(3)   Regulations under subsection (1) may—

(a)   make provision about the time or times at which, or period or periods within which, a charge must be paid;

(b)   make provision for cases in which a discounted charge is payable;

(c)   make provision for cases in which no charge is payable;

(d)   make provision for cases in which a charge which has been paid is to be refunded.

(4)   In making regulations under subsection (1), the Secretary of State must have regard to the desirability of securing that the charges payable to the Commissioner under such regulations are sufficient to offset—

(a)   expenses   incurred   by   the   Commissioner   in   discharging the Commissioner's functions—

   (i) under the data protection legislation,

   (ii) under the Data Protection Act 1998,

   (iii) under or by virtue of sections 108 and 109 of the Digital Economy Act 2017, and

   (iv) under or by virtue of the Privacy and Electronic Communications (EC Directive) Regulations 2003 (SI 2003/2426),

 (b) any expenses of the Secretary of State in respect of the Commissioner so far as attributable to those functions,

 (c) to the extent that the Secretary of State considers appropriate, any deficit previously incurred (whether before or after the passing of this Act) in respect of the expenses mentioned in paragraph (a), and

 (d) to the extent that the Secretary of State considers appropriate, expenses incurred by the Secretary of State in respect of the inclusion of any officers or staff of the Commissioner in any scheme under section 1 of the Superannuation Act 1972 or section 1 of the Public Service Pensions Act 2013.

 (5) The Secretary of State may from time to time require the Commissioner to provide information about the expenses referred to in subsection (4)(a).

 (6) The Secretary of State may by regulations make provision—

 (a) requiring a controller to provide information to the Commissioner, or

 (b) enabling the Commissioner to require a controller to provide information to the Commissioner,

for either or both of the purposes mentioned in subsection (7).

 (7) Those purposes are—

 (a) determining whether a charge is payable by the controller under regulations under subsection (1);

 (b) determining the amount of a charge payable by the controller.

 (8) The provision that may be made under subsection (6)(a) includes provision requiring a controller to notify the Commissioner of a change in the controller's circumstances of a kind specified in the regulations.

138. Regulations under section 137: supplementary (1) Before making regulations under section 137(1) or (6), the Secretary of State must consult such representatives of persons likely to be affected by the regulations as the Secretary of State thinks appropriate (and see also section 182).

 (2) The Commissioner—

 (a) must keep under review the working of regulations under section 137(1) or (6), and

 (b) may from time to time submit proposals to the Secretary of State for amendments to be made to the regulations.

 (3) The Secretary of State must review the working of regulations under section 137(1) or (6)—

 (a) at the end of the period of 5 years beginning with the making of the first set of regulations under section 108 of the Digital Economy Act 2017, and

 (b) at the end of each subsequent 5 year period.

 (4) Regulations under section 137(1) are subject to the negative resolution procedure if—

 (a) they only make provision increasing a charge for which provision is made by previous regulations under section 137(1) or section 108(1) of the Digital Economy Act 2017, and

 (b) they do so to take account of an increase in the retail prices index since the previous regulations were made.

 (5) Subject to subsection (4), regulations under section 137(1) or (6) are subject to the affirmative resolution procedure.

 (6) In subsection (4), "the retail prices index" means—

 (a) the general index of retail prices (for all items) published by the Statistics Board, or

 (b) where that index is not published for a month, any substitute index or figures published by the Board.

 (7) Regulations under section 137(1) or (6) may not apply to—

 (a) Her Majesty in her private capacity,

 (b) Her Majesty in right of the Duchy of Lancaster, or

 (c) the Duke of Cornwall.

Reports etc

139. Reporting to Parliament (1) The Commissioner must—

 (a) produce a general report on the carrying out of the Commissioner's functions annually,

 (b) arrange for it to be laid before Parliament, and

 (c) publish it.

 (2) The report must include the annual report required under Article 59 of the GDPR.

 (3) The Commissioner may produce other reports relating to the carrying out of the Commissioner's functions and arrange for them to be laid before Parliament.

140. Publication by the Commissioner A duty under this Act for the Commissioner to publish a document is a duty for the Commissioner to publish it, or to arrange for it to be published, in such form and manner as the Commissioner considers appropriate.

141. Notices from the Commissioner (1) This section applies in relation to a notice authorised or required by this Act to be given to a person by the Commissioner.

(2)　The notice may be given to an individual—

(a)　by delivering it to the individual,

(b)　by sending it to the individual by post addressed to the individual at his or her usual or last-known place of residence or business, or

(c)　by leaving it for the individual at that place.

(3)　The notice may be given to a body corporate or unincorporate—

(a)　by sending it by post to the proper officer of the body at its principal office, or

(b)　by addressing it to the proper officer of the body and leaving it at that office.

(4)　The notice may be given to a partnership in Scotland—

(a)　by sending it by post to the principal office of the partnership, or

(b)　by addressing it to that partnership and leaving it at that office.

(5)　The notice may be given to the person by other means, including by electronic means, with the person's consent.

(6)　In this section—

"principal office", in relation to a registered company, means its registered office;

"proper officer", in relation to any body, means the secretary or other executive officer charged with the conduct of its general affairs;

"registered company" means a company registered under the enactments relating to companies for the time being in force in the United Kingdom.

(7)　This section is without prejudice to any other lawful method of giving a notice.

PART 6[1]

ENFORCEMENT

Information notices

142. Information notices (1) The Commissioner may, by written notice (an "information notice")—

(a)　require a controller or processor to provide the Commissioner with information that the Commissioner reasonably requires for the purposes of carrying out the Commissioner's functions under the data protection legislation, or

(b)　require any person to provide the Commissioner with information that the Commissioner reasonably requires for the purposes of—

(i)　investigating a suspected failure of a type described in section 149(2) or a suspected offence under this Act, or

(ii)　determining whether the processing of personal data is carried out by an individual in the course of a purely personal or household activity.

(2)　An information notice must state—

(a)　whether it is given under subsection (1)(a), (b)(i) or (b)(ii), and

(b)　why the Commissioner requires the information.

(3)　An information notice—

(a)　may specify or describe particular information or a category of information;

(b)　may specify the form in which the information must be provided;

(c)　may specify the time at which, or the period within which, the information must be provided;

(d)　may specify the place where the information must be provided;

(but see the restrictions in subsections (5) to (7)).

(4)　An information notice must provide information about—

(a)　the consequences of failure to comply with it, and

(b)　the rights under sections 162 and 164 (appeals etc).

(5)　An information notice may not require a person to provide information before the end of the period within which an appeal can be brought against the notice.

(6)　If an appeal is brought against an information notice, the information need not be provided pending the determination or withdrawal of the appeal.

(7)　If an information notice—

(a)　states that, in the Commissioner's opinion, the information is required urgently, and

(b)　gives the Commissioner's reasons for reaching that opinion,

subsections (5) and (6) do not apply but the notice must not require the information to be provided before the end of the period of 24 hours beginning when the notice is given.

(8)　The Commissioner may cancel an information notice by written notice to the person to whom it was given.

(9)　In subsection (1), in relation to a person who is a controller or processor for the purposes of the GDPR, the reference to a controller or processor includes a representative of a controller or processor designated under Article 27 of the GDPR (representatives of controllers or processors not established in the European Union).

(10)　Section 3(14)(c) does not apply to the reference to the processing of personal data in subsection (1)(b).

¹ Part 6 contains ss 142–181.

143. Information notices: restrictions (1) The Commissioner may not give an information notice with respect to the processing of personal data for the special purposes unless—

    (a)   a determination under section 174 with respect to the data or the processing has taken effect, or

    (b)   the Commissioner—

        (i)   has reasonable grounds for suspecting that such a determination could be made, and

        (ii)   the information is required for the purposes of making such a determination.

(2) An information notice does not require a person to give the Commissioner information to the extent that requiring the person to do so would involve an infringement of the privileges of either House of Parliament.

(3) An information notice does not require a person to give the Commissioner information in respect of a communication which is made—

    (a)   between a professional legal adviser and the adviser's client, and

    (b)   in connection with the giving of legal advice to the client with respect to obligations, liabilities or rights under the data protection legislation.

(4) An information notice does not require a person to give the Commissioner information in respect of a communication which is made—

    (a)   between a professional legal adviser and the adviser's client or between such an adviser or client and another person,

    (b)   in connection with or in contemplation of proceedings under or arising out of the data protection legislation, and

    (c)   for the purposes of such proceedings.

(5) In subsections (3) and (4), references to the client of a professional legal adviser include references to a person acting on behalf of the client.

(6) An information notice does not require a person to provide the Commissioner with information if doing so would, by revealing evidence of the commission of an offence expose the person to proceedings for that offence.

(7) The reference to an offence in subsection (6) does not include an offence under—

    (a)   this Act;

    (b)   section 5 of the Perjury Act 1911 (false statements made otherwise than on oath);

    (c)   section 44(2) of the Criminal Law (Consolidation) (Scotland) Act 1995 (false statements made otherwise than on oath);

    (d)   Article 10 of the Perjury (Northern Ireland) Order 1979 (SI 1979/1714 (NI 19)) (false statutory declarations and other false unsworn statements).

(8) An oral or written statement provided by a person in response to an information notice may not be used in evidence against that person on a prosecution for an offence under this Act (other than an offence under section 144) unless in the proceedings—

    (a)   in giving evidence the person provides information inconsistent with the statement, and

    (b)   evidence relating to the statement is adduced, or a question relating to it is asked, by that person or on that person's behalf.

(9) In subsection (6), in relation to an information notice given to a representative of a controller or processor designated under Article 27 of the GDPR, the reference to the person providing the information being exposed to proceedings for an offence includes a reference to the controller or processor being exposed to such proceedings.

144. False statements made in response to information notices It is an offence for a person, in response to an information notice—

    (a)   to make a statement which the person knows to be false in a material respect, or

    (b)   recklessly to make a statement which is false in a material respect.

145. Information orders (1) This section applies if, on an application by the Commissioner, a court is satisfied that a person has failed to comply with a requirement of an information notice.

(2) The court may make an order requiring the person to provide to the Commissioner some or all of the following—

    (a)   information referred to in the information notice;

    (b)   other information which the court is satisfied the Commissioner requires, having regard to the statement included in the notice in accordance with section 142(2)(b).

(3) The order—

    (a)   may specify the form in which the information must be provided,

    (b)   must specify the time at which, or the period within which, the information must be provided, and

    (c)   may specify the place where the information must be provided.

Assessment notices

146. Assessment notices (1) The Commissioner may by written notice (an "assessment notice") require a controller or processor to permit the Commissioner to carry out an assessment of whether the controller or processor has complied or is complying with the data protection legislation.

(2) An assessment notice may require the controller or processor to do any of the following—

(a) permit the Commissioner to enter specified premises;

(b) direct the Commissioner to documents on the premises that are of a specified description;

(c) assist the Commissioner to view information of a specified description that is capable of being viewed using equipment on the premises;

(d) comply with a request from the Commissioner for a copy (in such form as may be requested) of—

(i) the documents to which the Commissioner is directed;

(ii) the information which the Commissioner is assisted to view;

(e) direct the Commissioner to equipment or other material on the premises which is of a specified description;

(f) permit the Commissioner to inspect or examine the documents, information, equipment or material to which the Commissioner is directed or which the Commissioner is assisted to view;

(g) provide the Commissioner with an explanation of such documents, information, equipment or material;

(h) permit the Commissioner to observe the processing of personal data that takes place on the premises;

(i) make available for interview by the Commissioner a specified number of people of a specified description who process personal data on behalf of the controller, not exceeding the number who are willing to be interviewed.

(3) In subsection (2), references to the Commissioner include references to the Commissioner's officers and staff.

(4) An assessment notice must, in relation to each requirement imposed by the notice, specify the time or times at which, or period or periods within which, the requirement must be complied with (but see the restrictions in subsections (6) to (9)).

(5) An assessment notice must provide information about—

(a) the consequences of failure to comply with it, and

(b) the rights under sections 162 and 164 (appeals etc).

(6) An assessment notice may not require a person to do anything before the end of the period within which an appeal can be brought against the notice.

(7) If an appeal is brought against an assessment notice, the controller or processor need not comply with a requirement in the notice pending the determination or withdrawal of the appeal.

(8) If an assessment notice—

(a) states that, in the Commissioner's opinion, it is necessary for the controller or processor to comply with a requirement in the notice urgently,

(b) gives the Commissioner's reasons for reaching that opinion, and

(c) does not meet the conditions in subsection (9)(a) to (d),

subsections (6) and (7) do not apply but the notice must not require the controller or processor to comply with the requirement before the end of the period of 7 days beginning when the notice is given.

(9) If an assessment notice—

(a) states that, in the Commissioner's opinion, there are reasonable grounds for suspecting that a controller or processor has failed or is failing as described in section 149(2) or that an offence under this Act has been or is being committed,

(b) indicates the nature of the suspected failure or offence,

(c) does not specify domestic premises,

(d) states that, in the Commissioner's opinion, it is necessary for the controller or processor to comply with a requirement in the notice in less than 7 days, and

(e) gives the Commissioner's reasons for reaching that opinion,

subsections (6) and (7) do not apply.

(10) The Commissioner may cancel an assessment notice by written notice to the controller or processor to whom it was given.

(11) Where the Commissioner gives an assessment notice to a processor, the Commissioner must, so far as reasonably practicable, give a copy of the notice to each controller for whom the processor processes personal data.

(12) In this section—

"domestic premises" means premises, or a part of premises, used as a dwelling;

"specified" means specified in an assessment notice.

147. Assessment notices: restrictions (1) An assessment notice does not require a person to do something to the extent that requiring the person to do it would involve an infringement of the privileges of either House of Parliament.

(2)   An assessment notice does not have effect so far as compliance would result in the disclosure of a communication which is made—

(a)   between a professional legal adviser and the adviser's client, and

(b)   in connection with the giving of legal advice to the client with respect to obligations, liabilities or rights under the data protection legislation.

(3)   An assessment notice does not have effect so far as compliance would result in the disclosure of a communication which is made—

(a)   between a professional legal adviser and the adviser's client or between such an adviser or client and another person,

(b)   in connection with or in contemplation of proceedings under or arising out of the data protection legislation, and

(c)   for the purposes of such proceedings.

(4)   In subsections (2) and (3)—

(a)   references to the client of a professional legal adviser include references to a person acting on behalf of such a client, and

(b)   references to a communication include—

(i)   a copy or other record of the communication, and

(ii)   anything enclosed with or referred to in the communication if made as described in subsection (2)(b) or in subsection (3)(b) and (c).

(5)   The Commissioner may not give a controller or processor an assessment notice with respect to the processing of personal data for the special purposes.

(6)   The Commissioner may not give an assessment notice to—

(a)   a body specified in section 23(3) of the Freedom of Information Act 2000 (bodies dealing with security matters), or

(b)   the Office for Standards in Education, Children's Services and Skills in so far as it is a controller or processor in respect of information processed for the purposes of functions exercisable by Her Majesty's Chief Inspector of Education, Children's Services and Skills by virtue of section 5(1)(a) of the Care Standards Act 2000.

Information notices and assessment notices: destruction of documents etc

148.   Destroying or falsifying information and documents etc   (1)   This section applies where a person—

(a)   has been given an information notice requiring the person to provide the Commissioner with information, or

(b)   has been given an assessment notice requiring the person to direct the Commissioner to a document, equipment or other material or to assist the Commissioner to view information.

(2)   It is an offence for the person—

(a)   to destroy or otherwise dispose of, conceal, block or (where relevant) falsify all or part of the information, document, equipment or material, or

(b)   to cause or permit the destruction, disposal, concealment, blocking or (where relevant) falsification of all or part of the information, document, equipment or material,

with the intention of preventing the Commissioner from viewing, or being provided with or directed to, all or part of the information, document, equipment or material.

(3)   It is a defence for a person charged with an offence under subsection (2) to prove that the destruction, disposal, concealment, blocking or falsification would have occurred in the absence of the person being given the notice.

Enforcement notices

149.   Enforcement notices   (1)   Where the Commissioner is satisfied that a person has failed, or is failing, as described in subsection (2), (3), (4) or (5), the Commissioner may give the person a written notice (an "enforcement notice") which requires the person—

(a)   to take steps specified in the notice, or

(b)   to refrain from taking steps specified in the notice,

or both (and see also sections 150 and 151).

(2)   The first type of failure is where a controller or processor has failed, or is failing, to comply with any of the following—

(a)   a provision of Chapter II of the GDPR or Chapter 2 of Part 3 or Chapter 2 of Part 4 of this Act (principles of processing);

(b)   a provision of Articles 12 to 22 of the GDPR or Part 3 or 4 of this Act conferring rights on a data subject;

(c)   a provision of Articles 25 to 39 of the GDPR or section 64 or 65 of this Act (obligations of controllers and processors);

(d)   a requirement to communicate a personal data breach to the Commissioner or a data subject under section 67, 68 or 108 of this Act;

(e)   the principles for transfers of personal data to third countries, non-Convention countries and international organisations in Articles 44 to 49 of the GDPR or in sections 73 to 78 or 109 of this Act.

(3)   The second type of failure is where a monitoring body has failed, or is failing, to comply with an obligation under Article 41 of the GDPR (monitoring of approved codes of conduct).

(4)   The third type of failure is where a person who is a certification provider—

(a)   does not meet the requirements for accreditation,

(b)   has failed, or is failing, to comply with an obligation under Article 42 or 43 of the GDPR (certification of controllers and processors), or

(c)   has failed, or is failing, to comply with any other provision of the GDPR (whether in the person's capacity as a certification provider or otherwise).

(5)   The fourth type of failure is where a controller has failed, or is failing, to comply with regulations under section 137.

(6)   An enforcement notice given in reliance on subsection (2), (3) or (5) may only impose requirements which the Commissioner considers appropriate for the purpose of remedying the failure.

(7)   An enforcement notice given in reliance on subsection (4) may only impose requirements which the Commissioner considers appropriate having regard to the failure (whether or not for the purpose of remedying the failure).

(8)   The Secretary of State may by regulations confer power on the Commissioner to give an enforcement notice in respect of other failures to comply with the data protection legislation.

(9)   Regulations under this section—

(a)   may make provision about the giving of an enforcement notice in respect of the failure, including by amending this section and sections 150 to 152,

(b)   may make provision about the giving of an information notice, an assessment notice or a penalty notice, or about powers of entry and inspection, in connection with the failure, including by amending sections 142, 143, 146, 147 and 155 to 157 and Schedules 15 and 16, and

(c)   are subject to the affirmative resolution procedure.

150.   **Enforcement notices: supplementary**   (1)   An enforcement notice must—

(a)   state what the person has failed or is failing to do, and

(b)   give the Commissioner's reasons for reaching that opinion.

(2)   In deciding whether to give an enforcement notice in reliance on section 149(2), the Commissioner must consider whether the failure has caused or is likely to cause any person damage or distress.

(3)   In relation to an enforcement notice given in reliance on section 149(2), the Commissioner's power under section 149(1)(b) to require a person to refrain from taking specified steps includes power—

(a)   to impose a ban relating to all processing of personal data, or

(b)   to impose a ban relating only to a specified description of processing of personal data, including by specifying one or more of the following—

       (i)   a description of personal data;

       (ii)   the purpose or manner of the processing;

       (iii)   the time when the processing takes place.

(4)   An enforcement notice may specify the time or times at which, or period or periods within which, a requirement imposed by the notice must be complied with (but see the restrictions in subsections (6) to (8)).

(5)   An enforcement notice must provide information about—

(a)   the consequences of failure to comply with it, and

(b)   the rights under sections 162 and 164 (appeals etc).

(6)   An enforcement notice must not specify a time for compliance with a requirement in the notice which falls before the end of the period within which an appeal can be brought against the notice.

(7)   If an appeal is brought against an enforcement notice, a requirement in the notice need not be complied with pending the determination or withdrawal of the appeal.

(8)   If an enforcement notice—

(a)   states that, in the Commissioner's opinion, it is necessary for a requirement to be complied with urgently, and

(b)   gives the Commissioner's reasons for reaching that opinion,

subsections (6) and (7) do not apply but the notice must not require the requirement to be complied with before the end of the period of 24 hours beginning when the notice is given.

(9)   In this section, "specified" means specified in an enforcement notice.

151.   **Enforcement notices: rectification and erasure of personal data etc**   (1)   Subsections (2) and (3) apply where an enforcement notice is given in respect of a failure by a controller or processor—

(a)   to comply with a data protection principle relating to accuracy, or

(b)   to comply with a data subject's request to exercise rights under Article 16, 17 or 18 of the GDPR (right to rectification, erasure or restriction on processing) or section 46, 47 or 100 of this Act.

(2)　If the enforcement notice requires the controller or processor to rectify or erase inaccurate personal data, it may also require the controller or processor to rectify or erase any other data which—

(a)　is held by the controller or processor, and

(b)　contains an expression of opinion which appears to the Commissioner to be based on the inaccurate personal data.

(3)　Where a controller or processor has accurately recorded personal data provided by the data subject or a third party but the data is inaccurate, the enforcement notice may require the controller or processor—

(a)　to take steps specified in the notice to ensure the accuracy of the data,

(b)　if relevant, to secure that the data indicates the data subject's view that the data is inaccurate, and

(c)　to supplement the data with a statement of the true facts relating to the matters dealt with by the data that is approved by the Commissioner,

(as well as imposing requirements under subsection (2)).

(4)　When deciding what steps it is reasonable to specify under subsection (3)(a), the Commissioner must have regard to the purpose for which the data was obtained and further processed.

(5)　Subsections (6) and (7) apply where—

(a)　an enforcement notice requires a controller or processor to rectify or erase personal data, or

(b)　the Commissioner is satisfied that the processing of personal data which has been rectified or erased by the controller or processor involved a failure described in subsection (1).

(6)　An enforcement notice may, if reasonably practicable, require the controller or processor to notify third parties to whom the data has been disclosed of the rectification or erasure.

(7)　In determining whether it is reasonably practicable to require such notification, the Commissioner must have regard, in particular, to the number of people who would have to be notified.

(8)　In this section, "data protection principle relating to accuracy" means the principle in—

(a)　Article 5(1)(d) of the GDPR,

(b)　section 38(1) of this Act, or

(c)　section 89 of this Act.

152.　Enforcement notices: restrictions　(1)　The Commissioner may not give a controller or processor an enforcement notice in reliance on section 149(2) with respect to the processing of personal data for the special purposes unless—

(a)　a determination under section 174 with respect to the data or the processing has taken effect, and

(b)　a court has granted leave for the notice to be given.

(2)　A court must not grant leave for the purposes of subsection (1)(b) unless it is satisfied that—

(a)　the Commissioner has reason to suspect a failure described in section 149(2) which is of substantial public importance, and

(b)　the controller or processor has been given notice of the application for leave in accordance with rules of court or the case is urgent.

(3)　An enforcement notice does not require a person to do something to the extent that requiring the person to do it would involve an infringement of the privileges of either House of Parliament.

(4)　In the case of a joint controller in respect of the processing of personal data to which Part 3 or 4 applies whose responsibilities for compliance with that Part are determined in an arrangement under section 58 or 104, the Commissioner may only give the controller an enforcement notice in reliance on section 149(2) if the controller is responsible for compliance with the provision, requirement or principle in question.

153.　Enforcement notices: cancellation and variation　(1)　The Commissioner may cancel or vary an enforcement notice by giving written notice to the person to whom it was given.

(2)　A person to whom an enforcement notice is given may apply in writing to the Commissioner for the cancellation or variation of the notice.

(3)　An application under subsection (2) may be made only—

(a)　after the end of the period within which an appeal can be brought against the notice, and

(b)　on the ground that, by reason of a change of circumstances, one or more of the provisions of that notice need not be complied with in order to remedy the failure identified in the notice.

Powers of entry and inspection

154.　Powers of entry and inspection　Schedule 15 makes provision about powers of entry and inspection.

Sections 155-164 are concerned with penalty notices, guidance about regulatory action and appeals. These provisions are not reproduced in this work.

Complaints

165. Complaints by data subjects   (1)   Articles 57(1)(f) and (2) and 77 of the GDPR (data subject's right to lodge a complaint) confer rights on data subjects to complain to the Commissioner if the data subject considers that, in connection with personal data relating to him or her, there is an infringement of the GDPR.

(2)   A data subject may make a complaint to the Commissioner if the data subject considers that, in connection with personal data relating to him or her, there is an infringement of Part 3 or 4 of this Act.

(3)   The Commissioner must facilitate the making of complaints under subsection (2) by taking steps such as providing a complaint form which can be completed electronically and by other means.

(4)   If the Commissioner receives a complaint under subsection (2), the Commissioner must—

     (a)   take appropriate steps to respond to the complaint,

     (b)   inform the complainant of the outcome of the complaint,

     (c)   inform the complainant of the rights under section 166, and

     (d)   if asked to do so by the complainant, provide the complainant with further information about how to pursue the complaint.

(5)   The reference in subsection (4)(a) to taking appropriate steps in response to a complaint includes—

     (a)   investigating the subject matter of the complaint, to the extent appropriate, and

     (b)   informing the complainant about progress on the complaint, including about whether further investigation or co-ordination with another supervisory authority or foreign designated authority is necessary.

(6)   If the Commissioner receives a complaint relating to the infringement of a data subject's rights under provisions adopted by a member State other than the United Kingdom pursuant to the Law Enforcement Directive, the Commissioner must—

     (a)   send the complaint to the relevant supervisory authority for the purposes of that Directive,

     (b)   inform the complainant that the Commissioner has done so, and

     (c)   if asked to do so by the complainant, provide the complainant with further information about how to pursue the complaint.

(7)   In this section—

"foreign designated authority" means an authority designated for the purposes of Article 13 of the Data Protection Convention by a party, other than the United Kingdom, which is bound by that Convention;

"supervisory authority" means a supervisory authority for the purposes of Article 51 of the GDPR or Article 41 of the Law Enforcement Directive in a member State other than the United Kingdom.

166. Orders to progress complaints   (1)   This section applies where, after a data subject makes a complaint under section 165 or Article 77 of the GDPR, the Commissioner—

     (a)   fails to take appropriate steps to respond to the complaint,

     (b)   fails to provide the complainant with information about progress on the complaint, or of the outcome of the complaint, before the end of the period of 3 months beginning when the Commissioner received the complaint, or

     (c)   if the Commissioner's consideration of the complaint is not concluded during that period, fails to provide the complainant with such information during a subsequent period of 3 months.

(2)   The Tribunal may, on an application by the data subject, make an order requiring the Commissioner—

     (a)   to take appropriate steps to respond to the complaint, or

     (b)   to inform the complainant of progress on the complaint, or of the outcome of the complaint, within a period specified in the order.

(3)   An order under subsection (2)(a) may require the Commissioner—

     (a)   to take steps specified in the order;

     (b)   to conclude an investigation, or take a specified step, within a period specified in the order.

(4)   Section 165(5) applies for the purposes of subsections (1)(a) and (2)(a) as it applies for the purposes of section 165(4)(a).

Remedies in the court

167. Compliance orders   (1)   This section applies if, on an application by a data subject, a court is satisfied that there has been an infringement of the data subject's rights under the data protection legislation in contravention of that legislation.

(2)   A court may make an order for the purposes of securing compliance with the data

protection legislation which requires the controller in respect of the processing, or a processor acting on behalf of that controller—

    (a)   to take steps specified in the order, or

    (b)   to refrain from taking steps specified in the order.

  (3)   The order may, in relation to each step, specify the time at which, or the period within which, it must be taken.

  (4)   In subsection (1)—

    (a)   the reference to an application by a data subject includes an application made in exercise of the right under Article 79(1) of the GDPR (right to an effective remedy against a controller or processor);

    (b)   the reference to the data protection legislation does not include Part 4 of this Act or regulations made under that Part.

  (5)   In relation to a joint controller in respect of the processing of personal data to which Part 3 applies whose responsibilities are determined in an arrangement under section 58, a court may only make an order under this section if the controller is responsible for compliance with the provision of the data protection legislation that is contravened.

168. Compensation for contravention of the GDPR (1) In Article 82 of the GDPR (right to compensation for material or non-material damage), "non-material damage" includes distress.

  (2)   Subsection (3) applies where—

    (a)   in accordance with rules of court, proceedings under Article 82 of the GDPR are brought by a representative body on behalf of a person, and

    (b)   a court orders the payment of compensation.

  (3)   The court may make an order providing for the compensation to be paid on behalf of the person to—

    (a)   the representative body, or

    (b)   such other person as the court thinks fit.

169. Compensation for contravention of other data protection legislation (1) A person who suffers damage by reason of a contravention of a requirement of the data protection legislation, other than the GDPR, is entitled to compensation for that damage from the controller or the processor, subject to subsections (2) and (3).

  (2)   Under subsection (1)—

    (a)   a controller involved in processing of personal data is liable for any damage caused by the processing, and

    (b)   a processor involved in processing of personal data is liable for damage caused by the processing only if the processor—

        (i)   has not complied with an obligation under the data protection legislation specifically directed at processors, or

       (ii)   has acted outside, or contrary to, the controller's lawful instructions.

  (3)   A controller or processor is not liable as described in subsection (2) if the controller or processor proves that the controller or processor is not in any way responsible for the event giving rise to the damage.

  (4)   A joint controller in respect of the processing of personal data to which Part 3 or 4 applies whose responsibilities are determined in an arrangement under section 58 or 104 is only liable as described in subsection (2) if the controller is responsible for compliance with the provision of the data protection legislation that is contravened.

  (5)   In this section, "damage" includes financial loss and damage not involving financial loss, such as distress.

Offences relating to personal data

170. Unlawful obtaining etc of personal data (1) It is an offence for a person knowingly or recklessly—

    (a)   to obtain or disclose personal data without the consent of the controller,

    (b)   to procure the disclosure of personal data to another person without the consent of the controller, or

    (c)   after obtaining personal data, to retain it without the consent of the person who was the controller in relation to the personal data when it was obtained.

  (2)   It is a defence for a person charged with an offence under subsection (1) to prove that the obtaining, disclosing, procuring or retaining—

    (a)   was necessary for the purposes of preventing or detecting crime,

    (b)   was required or authorised by an enactment, by a rule of law or by the order of a court or tribunal, or

    (c)   in the particular circumstances, was justified as being in the public interest.

  (3)   It is also a defence for a person charged with an offence under subsection (1) to prove that—

    (a)   the person acted in the reasonable belief that the person had a legal right to do the obtaining, disclosing, procuring or retaining,

    (b)   the person acted in the reasonable belief that the person would have had the consent of the controller if the controller had known about the obtaining, disclosing, procuring or retaining and the circumstances of it, or

    (c)   the person acted—

        (i)   for the special purposes,

        (ii)   with a view to the publication by a person of any journalistic, academic, artistic or literary material, and

        (iii)   in the reasonable belief that in the particular circumstances the obtaining, disclosing, procuring or retaining was justified as being in the public interest.

    (4)   It is an offence for a person to sell personal data if the person obtained the data in circumstances in which an offence under subsection (1) was committed.

    (5)   It is an offence for a person to offer to sell personal data if the person—

    (a)   has obtained the data in circumstances in which an offence under subsection (1) was committed, or

    (b)   subsequently obtains the data in such circumstances.

    (6)   For the purposes of subsection (5), an advertisement indicating that personal data is or may be for sale is an offer to sell the data.

    (7)   In this section—

    (a)   references to the consent of a controller do not include the consent of a person who is a controller by virtue of Article 28(10) of the GDPR or section 59(8) or 105(3) of this Act (processor to be treated as controller in certain circumstances);

    (b)   where there is more than one controller, such references are references to the consent of one or more of them.

171.   Re-identification of de-identified personal data   (1)   It is an offence for a person knowingly or recklessly to re-identify information that is de-identified personal data without the consent of the controller responsible for de-identifying the personal data.

    (2)   For the purposes of this section and section 172—

    (a)   personal data is "de-identified" if it has been processed in such a manner that it can no longer be attributed, without more, to a specific data subject;

    (b)   a person "re-identifies" information if the person takes steps which result in the information no longer being de-identified within the meaning of paragraph (a).

    (3)   It is a defence for a person charged with an offence under subsection (1) to prove that the re-identification—

    (a)   was necessary for the purposes of preventing or detecting crime,

    (b)   was required or authorised by an enactment, by a rule of law or by the order of a court or tribunal, or

    (c)   in the particular circumstances, was justified as being in the public interest.

    (4)   It is also a defence for a person charged with an offence under subsection (1) to prove that—

    (a)   the person acted in the reasonable belief that the person—

        (i)   is the data subject to whom the information relates,

        (ii)   had the consent of that data subject, or

        (iii)   would have had such consent if the data subject had known about the re-identification and the circumstances of it,

    (b)   the person acted in the reasonable belief that the person—

        (i)   is the controller responsible for de-identifying the personal data,

        (ii)   had the consent of that controller, or

        (iii)   would have had such consent if that controller had known about the re-identification and the circumstances of it,

    (c)   the person acted—

        (i)   for the special purposes,

        (ii)   with a view to the publication by a person of any journalistic, academic, artistic or literary material, and

        (iii)   in the reasonable belief that in the particular circumstances the re-identification was justified as being in the public interest, or

    (d)   the effectiveness testing conditions were met (see section 172).

    (5)   It is an offence for a person knowingly or recklessly to process personal data that is information that has been re-identified where the person does so—

    (a)   without the consent of the controller responsible for de-identifying the personal data, and

    (b)   in circumstances in which the re-identification was an offence under subsection (1).

    (6)   It is a defence for a person charged with an offence under subsection (5) to prove that the processing—

    (a)   was necessary for the purposes of preventing or detecting crime,

    (b)   was required or authorised by an enactment, by a rule of law or by the order of a court or tribunal, or

    (c)   in the particular circumstances, was justified as being in the public interest.

    (7)   It is also a defence for a person charged with an offence under subsection (5) to prove that—

(a)   the person acted in the reasonable belief that the processing was lawful,

(b)   the person acted in the reasonable belief that the person—

    (i)   had the consent of the controller responsible for de-identifying the personal data, or

    (ii)   would have had such consent if that controller had known about the processing and the circumstances of it, or

(c)   the person acted—

    (i)   for the special purposes,

    (ii)   with a view to the publication by a person of any journalistic, academic, artistic or literary material, and

    (iii)   in the reasonable belief that in the particular circumstances the processing was justified as being in the public interest.

(8)   In this section—

(a)   references to the consent of a controller do not include the consent of a person who is a controller by virtue of Article 28(10) of the GDPR or section 59(8) or 105(3) of this Act (processor to be treated as controller in certain circumstances);

(b)   where there is more than one controller, such references are references to the consent of one or more of them.

172. Re-identification: effectiveness testing conditions (1) For the purposes of section 171, in relation to a person who re-identifies information that is de-identified personal data, "the effectiveness testing conditions" means the conditions in subsections (2) and (3).

(2)   The first condition is that the person acted—

(a)   with a view to testing the effectiveness of the de-identification of personal data,

(b)   without intending to cause, or threaten to cause, damage or distress to a person, and

(c)   in the reasonable belief that, in the particular circumstances, re-identifying the information was justified as being in the public interest.

(3)   The second condition is that the person notified the Commissioner or the controller responsible for de-identifying the personal data about the re-identification—

(a)   without undue delay, and

(b)   where feasible, not later than 72 hours after becoming aware of it.

(4)   Where there is more than one controller responsible for de-identifying personal data, the requirement in subsection (3) is satisfied if one or more of them is notified.

173. Alteration etc of personal data to prevent disclosure to data subject (1) Subsection (3) applies where—

(a)   a request has been made in exercise of a data subject access right, and

(b)   the person making the request would have been entitled to receive information in response to that request.

(2)   In this section, "data subject access right" means a right under—

(a)   Article 15 of the GDPR (right of access by the data subject);

(b)   Article 20 of the GDPR (right to data portability);

(c)   section 45 of this Act (law enforcement processing: right of access by the data subject);

(d)   section 94 of this Act (intelligence services processing: right of access by the data subject).

(3)   It is an offence for a person listed in subsection (4) to alter, deface, block, erase, destroy or conceal information with the intention of preventing disclosure of all or part of the information that the person making the request would have been entitled to receive.

(4)   Those persons are—

(a)   the controller, and

(b)   a person who is employed by the controller, an officer of the controller or subject to the direction of the controller.

(5)   It is a defence for a person charged with an offence under subsection (3) to prove that—

(a)   the alteration, defacing, blocking, erasure, destruction or concealment of the information would have occurred in the absence of a request made in exercise of a data subject access right, or

(b)   the person acted in the reasonable belief that the person making the request was not entitled to receive the information in response to the request.

The special purposes

174. The special purposes (1) In this Part, "the special purposes" means one or more of the following—

(a)   the purposes of journalism[1];

(b)   academic purposes;

(c)   artistic purposes;

(d)   literary purposes.

(2)   In this Part, "special purposes proceedings" means legal proceedings against a controller or

processor which relate, wholly or partly, to personal data processed for the special purposes and which are—

(a) proceedings under section 167 (including proceedings on an application under Article 79 of the GDPR), or

(b) proceedings under Article 82 of the GDPR or section 169.

(3) The Commissioner may make a written determination, in relation to the processing of personal data, that—

(a) the personal data is not being processed only for the special purposes;

(b) the personal data is not being processed with a view to the publication by a person of journalistic, academic, artistic or literary material which has not previously been published by the controller.

(4) The Commissioner must give written notice of the determination to the controller and the processor.

(5) The notice must provide information about the rights of appeal under section 162.

(6) The determination does not take effect until one of the following conditions is satisfied—

(a) the period for the controller or the processor to appeal against the determination has ended without an appeal having been brought, or

(b) an appeal has been brought against the determination and—

(i) the appeal and any further appeal in relation to the determination has been decided or has otherwise ended, and

(ii) the time for appealing against the result of the appeal or further appeal has ended without another appeal having been brought.

---

[1] For an exposition of the Data Protection Act 1998 to newspapers, see *Campbell v Mirror Group Newspapers* [2002] EWCA Civ 1373, [2003] QB 633, [2003] 1 ALL ER 224.

It was held in *NT1 v Google LLC* [2018] EWCA 799 (QB), [2018] 3 ALL ER 581 that Google was not entitled to rely on the journalism exemption in s 32 of the 1998 Act. Journalism does not extend to every activity connected with conveying information or opinions; the concepts of journalism and communication are not the same.

175. Provision of assistance in special purposes proceedings (1) An individual who is a party, or prospective party, to special purposes proceedings may apply to the Commissioner for assistance in those proceedings.

(2) As soon as reasonably practicable after receiving an application under subsection (1), the Commissioner must decide whether, and to what extent, to grant it.

(3) The Commissioner must not grant the application unless, in the Commissioner's opinion, the case involves a matter of substantial public importance.

(4) If the Commissioner decides not to provide assistance, the Commissioner must, as soon as reasonably practicable, notify the applicant of the decision, giving reasons for the decision.

(5) If the Commissioner decides to provide assistance, the Commissioner must—

(a) as soon as reasonably practicable, notify the applicant of the decision, stating the extent of the assistance to be provided, and

(b) secure that the person against whom the proceedings are, or are to be, brought is informed that the Commissioner is providing assistance.

(6) The assistance that may be provided by the Commissioner includes—

(a) paying costs in connection with the proceedings, and

(b) indemnifying the applicant in respect of liability to pay costs, expenses or damages in connection with the proceedings.

(7) In England and Wales or Northern Ireland, the recovery of expenses incurred by the Commissioner in providing an applicant with assistance under this section (as taxed or assessed in accordance with rules of court) is to constitute a first charge for the benefit of the Commissioner—

(a) on any costs which, by virtue of any judgment or order of the court, are payable to the applicant by any other person in respect of the matter in connection with which the assistance is provided, and

(b) on any sum payable to the applicant under a compromise or settlement arrived at in connection with that matter to avoid, or bring to an end, any proceedings.

(8) In Scotland, the recovery of such expenses (as taxed or assessed in accordance with rules of court) is to be paid to the Commissioner, in priority to other debts—

(a) out of any expenses which, by virtue of any judgment or order of the court, are payable to the applicant by any other person in respect of the matter in connection with which the assistance is provided, and

(b) out of any sum payable to the applicant under a compromise or settlement arrived at in connection with that matter to avoid, or bring to an end, any proceedings.

176. Staying special purposes proceedings (1) In any special purposes proceedings before a court, if the controller or processor claims, or it appears to the court, that any personal data to which the proceedings relate—

(a) is being processed only for the special purposes,

(b) is being processed with a view to the publication by any person of journalistic, academic, artistic or literary material, and

   (c)   has not previously been published by the controller,
the court must stay or, in Scotland, sist the proceedings.
   (2)   In considering, for the purposes of subsection (1)(c), whether material has previously been published, publication in the immediately preceding 24 hours is to be ignored.
   (3)   Under subsection (1), the court must stay or sist the proceedings until either of the following conditions is met—

   (a)   a determination of the Commissioner under section 174 with respect to the personal data or the processing takes effect;

   (b)   where the proceedings were stayed or sisted on the making of a claim, the claim is withdrawn.

177. Guidance about how to seek redress against media organisations
   (1)   The Commissioner must produce and publish guidance about the steps that may be taken where an individual considers that a media organisation is failing or has failed to comply with the data protection legislation.
   (2)   In this section, "media organisation" means a body or other organisation whose activities consist of or include journalism.
   (3)   The guidance must include provision about relevant complaints procedures, including—

   (a)   who runs them,

   (b)   what can be complained about, and

   (c)   how to make a complaint.

   (4)   For the purposes of subsection (3), relevant complaints procedures include procedures for making complaints to the Commissioner, the Office of Communications, the British Broadcasting Corporation and other persons who produce or enforce codes of practice for media organisations.
   (5)   The guidance must also include provision about—

   (a)   the powers available to the Commissioner in relation to a failure to comply with the data protection legislation,

   (b)   when a claim in respect of such a failure may be made before a court and how to make such a claim,

   (c)   alternative dispute resolution procedures,

   (d)   the rights of bodies and other organisations to make complaints and claims on behalf of data subjects, and

   (e)   the Commissioner's power to provide assistance in special purpose proceedings.

   (6)   The Commissioner—

   (a)   may alter or replace the guidance, and

   (b)   must publish any altered or replacement guidance.

   (7)   The Commissioner must produce and publish the first guidance under this section before the end of the period of 1 year beginning when this Act is passed.

178. Review of processing of personal data for the purposes of journalism
   (1)   The Commissioner must—

   (a)   review the extent to which, during each review period, the processing of personal data for the purposes of journalism complied with—

        (i)   the data protection legislation, and

        (ii)   good practice in the processing of personal data for the purposes of journalism,

   (b)   prepare a report of the review, and

   (c)   submit the report to the Secretary of State.

   (2)   In this section—
"good practice in the processing of personal data for the purposes of journalism" has the same meaning as in section 124;
"review period" means—

        (a)   the period of 4 years beginning with the day on which Chapter 2 of Part 2 of this Act comes into force, and

        (b)   each subsequent period of 5 years beginning with the day after the day on which the previous review period ended.

   (3)   The Commissioner must start a review under this section, in respect of a review period, within the period of 6 months beginning when the review period ends.
   (4)   The Commissioner must submit the report of a review under this section to the Secretary of State—

   (a)   in the case of the first review, before the end of the period of 18 months beginning when the Commissioner started the review, and

   (b)   in the case of each subsequent review, before the end of the period of 12 months beginning when the Commissioner started the review.

   (5)   The report must include consideration of the extent of compliance (as described in subsection (1)(a)) in each part of the United Kingdom.
   (6)   The Secretary of State must—

   (a)   lay the report before Parliament, and

   (b)   send a copy of the report to—

        (i)   the Scottish Ministers,

        (ii)   the Welsh Ministers, and

        (iii)   the Executive Office in Northern Ireland.

(7)   Schedule 17 makes further provision for the purposes of a review under this section.

179. Effectiveness of the media's dispute resolution procedures (1) The Secretary of State must, before the end of each review period, lay before Parliament a report produced by the Secretary of State or an appropriate person on—

     (a)   the use of relevant alternative dispute resolution procedures, during that period, in cases involving a failure, or alleged failure, by a relevant media organisation to comply with the data protection legislation, and

     (b)   the effectiveness of those procedures in such cases.

(2)   In this section—

"appropriate person" means a person who the Secretary of State considers has appropriate experience and skills to produce a report described in subsection (1);

"relevant alternative dispute resolution procedures" means alternative dispute resolution procedures provided by persons who produce or enforce codes of practice for relevant media organisations;

"relevant media organisation" means a body or other organisation whose activities consist of or include journalism, other than a broadcaster;

"review period" means—

        (a)   the period of 3 years beginning when this Act is passed, and

        (b)   each subsequent period of 3 years.

(3)   The Secretary of State must send a copy of the report to—

     (a)   the Scottish Ministers,

     (b)   the Welsh Ministers, and

     (c)   the Executive Office in Northern Ireland.

Jurisdiction of courts

180. Jurisdiction (1) The jurisdiction conferred on a court by the provisions listed in subsection (2) is exercisable—

     (a)   in England and Wales, by the High Court or the county court,

     (b)   in Northern Ireland, by the High Court or a county court, and

     (c)   in Scotland, by the Court of Session or the sheriff,

subject to subsections (3) and (4).

(2)   Those provisions are—

     (a)   section 145 (information orders);

     (b)   section 152 (enforcement notices and processing for the special purposes);

     (c)   section 156 (penalty notices and processing for the special purposes);

     (d)   section 167 and Article 79 of the GDPR (compliance orders);

     (e)   sections 168 and 169 and Article 82 of the GDPR (compensation).

(3)   In relation to the processing of personal data to which Part 4 applies, the jurisdiction conferred by the provisions listed in subsection (2) is exercisable only by the High Court or, in Scotland, the Court of Session.

(4)   In relation to an information notice which contains a statement under section 142(7), the jurisdiction conferred on a court by section 145 is exercisable only by the High Court or, in Scotland, the Court of Session.

(5)   The jurisdiction conferred on a court by section 164 (applications in respect of urgent notices) is exercisable only by the High Court or, in Scotland, the Court of Session.

Definitions

181. Interpretation of Part 6 In this Part—

"assessment notice" has the meaning given in section 146;

"certification provider" has the meaning given in section 17;

"enforcement notice" has the meaning given in section 149;

"information notice" has the meaning given in section 142;

"penalty notice" has the meaning given in section 155;

"penalty variation notice" has the meaning given in Schedule 16;

"representative", in relation to a controller or processor, means a person designated by the controller or processor under Article 27 of the GDPR to represent the controller or processor with regard to the controller's or processor's obligations under the GDPR.

PART 7[1]

SUPPLEMENTARY AND FINAL PROVISION

---

[1] PART 7 contains ss 182-212.

Regulations under this Act

182. Regulations and consultation
[Text not reproduced.]

Changes to the Data Protection Convention

183. Power to reflect changes to the Data Protection Convention
[Text not reproduced.]

Rights of the data subject

184. Prohibition of requirement to produce relevant records (1) It is an offence for a person ("P1") to require another person to provide P1 with, or give P1 access to, a relevant record in connection with—

(a) the recruitment of an employee by P1,

(b) the continued employment of a person by P1, or

(c) a contract for the provision of services to P1.

(2) It is an offence for a person ("P2") to require another person to provide P2 with, or give P2 access to, a relevant record if—

(a) P2 is involved in the provision of goods, facilities or services to the public or a section of the public, and

(b) the requirement is a condition of providing or offering to provide goods, facilities or services to the other person or to a third party.

(3) It is a defence for a person charged with an offence under subsection (1) or (2) to prove that imposing the requirement—

(a) was required or authorised by an enactment, by a rule of law or by the order of a court or tribunal, or

(b) in the particular circumstances, was justified as being in the public interest.

(4) The imposition of the requirement referred to in subsection (1) or (2) is not to be regarded as justified as being in the public interest on the ground that it would assist in the prevention or detection of crime, given Part 5 of the Police Act 1997 (certificates of criminal records etc).

(5) In subsections (1) and (2), the references to a person who requires another person to provide or give access to a relevant record include a person who asks another person to do so—

(a) knowing that, in the circumstances, it would be reasonable for the other person to feel obliged to comply with the request, or

(b) being reckless as to whether, in the circumstances, it would be reasonable for the other person to feel obliged to comply with the request,

and the references to a "requirement" in subsections (3) and (4) are to be interpreted accordingly.

(6) In this section—

"employment" means any employment, including—

(a) work under a contract for services or as an office-holder,

(b) work under an apprenticeship,

(c) work experience as part of a training course or in the course of training for employment, and

(d) voluntary work,

and "employee" is to be interpreted accordingly;

"relevant record" has the meaning given in Schedule 18 and references to a relevant record include—

(a) a part of such a record, and

(b) a copy of, or of part of, such a record.

185. Avoidance of certain contractual terms relating to health records (1) A term or condition of a contract is void in so far as it purports to require an individual to supply another person with a record which—

(a) consists of the information contained in a health record, and

(b) has been or is to be obtained by a data subject in the exercise of a data subject access right.

(2) A term or condition of a contract is also void in so far as it purports to require an individual to produce such a record to another person.

(3) The references in subsections (1) and (2) to a record include a part of a record and a copy of all or part of a record.

(4) In this section, "data subject access right" means a right under—

(a) Article 15 of the GDPR (right of access by the data subject);

(b) Article 20 of the GDPR (right to data portability);

(c) section 45 of this Act (law enforcement processing: right of access by the data subject);

(d) section 94 of this Act (intelligence services processing: right of access by the data subject).

186. Data subject's rights and other prohibitions and restrictions (1) An enactment or rule of law prohibiting or restricting the disclosure of information, or authorising the withholding of information, does not remove or restrict the obligations and rights provided for in the provisions listed in subsection (2), except as provided by or under the provisions listed in subsection (3).

  (2) The provisions providing obligations and rights are—

   (a)   Chapter III of the GDPR (rights of the data subject),

   (b)   Chapter 3 of Part 3 of this Act (law enforcement processing: rights of the data subject), and

   (c)   Chapter 3 of Part 4 of this Act (intelligence services processing: rights of the data subject).

  (3) The provisions providing exceptions are—

   (a)   in Chapter 2 of Part 2 of this Act, sections 15 and 16 and Schedules 2, 3 and 4,

   (b)   in Chapter 3 of Part 2 of this Act, sections 23, 24, 25 and 26,

   (c)   in Part 3 of this Act, sections 44(4), 45(4) and 48(3), and

   (d)   in Part 4 of this Act, Chapter 6 .

Sections 187-195 are concerned with: representation of data subjects; framework for data processing by government; and data sharing between HMRC and reserve forces. These provisions are not reproduced in this work.

Offences

196. Penalties for offences (1) A person who commits an offence under section 119 or 173 or paragraph 15 of Schedule 15 is liable—

   (a)   on summary conviction in England and Wales, to a fine;

   (b)   on summary conviction in Scotland or Northern Ireland, to a fine not exceeding level 5 on the standard scale[1].

  (2) A person who commits an offence under section 132, 144, 148, 170, 171 or 184 is liable—

   (a)   on summary conviction in England and Wales, to a fine;

   (b)   on summary conviction in Scotland or Northern Ireland, to a fine not exceeding the statutory maximum;

   (c)   on conviction on indictment, to a fine.

  (3) Subsections (4) and (5) apply where a person is convicted of an offence under section 170 or 184.

  (4) The court by or before which the person is convicted may order a document or other material to be forfeited, destroyed or erased if—

   (a)   it has been used in connection with the processing of personal data, and

   (b)   it appears to the court to be connected with the commission of the offence, subject to subsection (5).

  (5) If a person, other than the offender, who claims to be the owner of the material, or to be otherwise interested in the material, applies to be heard by the court, the court must not make an order under subsection (4) without giving the person an opportunity to show why the order should not be made.

[1] For procedure in respect of offences triable either way, see ss 17A-21 of the Magistrates' Courts Act 1980 in PART I MAGISTRATES' COURTS, PROCEDURE, ante.

197. Prosecution (1) In England and Wales, proceedings for an offence under this Act may be instituted only—

   (a)   by the Commissioner, or

   (b)   by or with the consent of the Director of Public Prosecutions.

  (2) In Northern Ireland, proceedings for an offence under this Act may be instituted only—

   (a)   by the Commissioner, or

   (b)   by or with the consent of the Director of Public Prosecutions for Northern Ireland.

  (3) Subject to subsection (4), summary proceedings for an offence under section 173 (alteration etc of personal data to prevent disclosure) may be brought within the period of 6 months beginning with the day on which the prosecutor first knew of evidence that, in the prosecutor's opinion, was sufficient to bring the proceedings.

  (4) Such proceedings may not be brought after the end of the period of 3 years beginning with the day on which the offence was committed.

  (5) A certificate signed by or on behalf of the prosecutor and stating the day on which the 6 month period described in subsection (3) began is conclusive evidence of that fact.

  (6) A certificate purporting to be signed as described in subsection (5) is to be treated as so signed unless the contrary is proved.

  (7) In relation to proceedings in Scotland, section 136(3) of the Criminal Procedure (Scotland) Act 1995 (deemed date of commencement of proceedings) applies for the purposes of this section as it applies for the purposes of that section.

198. Liability of directors etc (1) Subsection (2) applies where—

   (a)   an offence under this Act has been committed by a body corporate, and

   (b)   it is proved to have been committed with the consent or connivance of or to be attributable to neglect on the part of—

     (i)   a director, manager, secretary or similar officer of the body corporate, or

     (ii)   a person who was purporting to act in such a capacity.

  (2) The director, manager, secretary, officer or person, as well as the body corporate, is guilty of

the offence and liable to be proceeded against and punished accordingly.

(3) Where the affairs of a body corporate are managed by its members, subsections (1) and (2) apply in relation to the acts and omissions of a member in connection with the member's management functions in relation to the body as if the member were a director of the body corporate.

(4) Subsection (5) applies where—

(a) an offence under this Act has been committed by a Scottish partnership, and

(b) the contravention in question is proved to have occurred with the consent or connivance of, or to be attributable to any neglect on the part of, a partner.

(5) The partner, as well as the partnership, is guilty of the offence and liable to be proceeded against and punished accordingly.

199. Recordable offences (1) The National Police Records (Recordable Offences) Regulations 2000 (SI 2000/1139) have effect as if the offences under the following provisions were listed in the Schedule to the Regulations—

(a) section 119;

(b) section 132;

(c) section 144;

(d) section 148;

(e) section 170;

(f) section 171;

(g) section 173;

(h) section 184;

(i) paragraph 15 of Schedule 15.

(2) Regulations under section 27(4) of the Police and Criminal Evidence Act 1984 (recordable offences) may repeal subsection (1).

200. Guidance about PACE codes of practice (1) The Commissioner must produce and publish guidance about how the Commissioner proposes to perform the duty under section 67(9) of the Police and Criminal Evidence Act 1984 (duty to have regard to codes of practice under that Act when investigating offences and charging offenders) in connection with offences under this Act.

(2) The Commissioner—

(a) may alter or replace the guidance, and

(b) must publish any altered or replacement guidance.

(3) The Commissioner must consult the Secretary of State before publishing guidance under this section (including any altered or replacement guidance).

(4) The Commissioner must arrange for guidance under this section (including any altered or replacement guidance) to be laid before Parliament.

The Tribunal

201. Disclosure of information to the Tribunal (1) No enactment or rule of law prohibiting or restricting the disclosure of information precludes a person from providing the First-tier Tribunal or the Upper Tribunal with information necessary for the discharge of—

(a) its functions under the data protection legislation, or

(b) its other functions relating to the Commissioner's acts and omissions.

(2) But this section does not authorise the making of a disclosure which is prohibited by any of Parts 1 to 7 or Chapter 1 of Part 9 of the Investigatory Powers Act 2016.

(3) Until the repeal of Part 1 of the Regulation of Investigatory Powers Act 2000 by paragraphs 45 and 54 of Schedule 10 to the Investigatory Powers Act 2016 is fully in force, subsection (2) has effect as if it included a reference to that Part.

202. Proceedings in the First-tier Tribunal: contempt (1) This section applies where—

(a) a person does something, or fails to do something, in relation to proceedings before the First-tier Tribunal—

(i) on an appeal under section 27, 79, 111 or 162, or

(ii) for an order under section 166, and

(b) if those proceedings were proceedings before a court having power to commit for contempt, the act or omission would constitute contempt of court.

(2) The First-tier Tribunal may certify the offence to the Upper Tribunal.

(3) Where an offence is certified under subsection (2), the Upper Tribunal may—

(a) inquire into the matter, and

(b) deal with the person charged with the offence in any manner in which it could deal with the person if the offence had been committed in relation to the Upper Tribunal.

(4) Before exercising the power under subsection (3)(b), the Upper Tribunal must—

(a) hear any witness who may be produced against or on behalf of the person charged with the offence, and

(b) hear any statement that may be offered in defence.

Section 203 is a rule enabling provision and is not reproduced.

Interpretation

204. Meaning of "health professional" and "social work professional"   (1)   In this Act, "health professional" means any of the following—

    (a)   a registered medical practitioner;

    (b)   a registered nurse or midwife;

    (c)   a registered dentist within the meaning of the Dentists Act 1984 (see section 53 of that Act);

    (d)   a registered dispensing optician or a registered optometrist within the meaning of the Opticians Act 1989 (see section 36 of that Act);

    (e)   a registered osteopath with the meaning of the Osteopaths Act 1993 (see section 41 of that Act);

    (f)   a registered chiropractor within the meaning of the Chiropractors Act 1994 (see section 43 of that Act);

    (g)   a person registered as a member of a profession to which the Health *and Social Work* Professions Order 2001 (SI 2002/254) for the time being extends, *other than the social work profession in England*;

    (h)   a registered pharmacist or a registered pharmacy technician within the meaning of the Pharmacy Order 2010 (SI 2010/231) (see article 3 of that Order);

    (i)   a registered person within the meaning of the Pharmacy (Northern Ireland) Order 1976 (SI 1976/1213 (NI 22)) (see Article 2 of that Order);

    (j)   a child psychotherapist;

    (k)   a scientist employed by a health service body as head of a department.

  (2)   In this Act, "social work professional" means any of the following—

    (a)   *a person registered as a social worker in England in the register maintained under the Health and Social Work Professions Order 2001 (SI 2002/254);*

    [(a)   a person registered as a social worker in the register maintained by Social Work England under section 39(1) of the Children and Social Work Act 2017;]

    (b)   a person registered as a social worker in the register maintained by Social Care Wales under section 80 of the Regulation and Inspection of Social Care (Wales) Act 2016 (anaw 2);

    (c)   a person registered as a social worker in the register maintained by the Scottish Social Services Council under section 44 of the Regulation of Care (Scotland) Act 2001 (asp 8);

    (d)   a person registered as a social worker in the register maintained by the Northern Ireland Social Care Council under section 3 of the Health and Personal Social Services Act (Northern Ireland) 2001 (c 3 (NI)).

  (3)   In subsection (1)(a) "registered medical practitioner" includes a person who is provisionally registered under section 15 or 21 of the Medical Act 1983 and is engaged in such employment as is mentioned in subsection (3) of that section.

  (4)   In subsection (1)(k) "health service body" means any of the following—

    (a)   the Secretary of State in relation to the exercise of functions under section 2A or 2B of, or paragraph 7C, 8 or 12 of Schedule 1 to, the National Health Service Act 2006;

    (b)   a local authority in relation to the exercise of functions under section 2B or 111 of, or any of paragraphs 1 to 7B or 13 of Schedule 1 to, the National Health Service Act 2006;

    (c)   a National Health Service trust first established under section 25 of the National Health Service Act 2006;

    (d)   a Special Health Authority established under section 28 of the National Health Service Act 2006;

    (e)   an NHS foundation trust;

    (f)   the National Institute for Health and Care Excellence;

    (g)   the Health and Social Care Information Centre;

    (h)   a National Health Service trust first established under section 5 of the National Health Service and Community Care Act 1990;

    (i)   a Local Health Board established under section 11 of the National Health Service (Wales) Act 2006;

    (j)   a National Health Service trust first established under section 18 of the National Health Service (Wales) Act 2006;

    (k)   a Special Health Authority established under section 22 of the National Health Service (Wales) Act 2006;

    (l)   a Health Board within the meaning of the National Health Service (Scotland) Act 1978;

    (m)   a Special Health Board within the meaning of the National Health Service (Scotland) Act 1978;

    (n)   a National Health Service trust first established under section 12A of the National Health Service (Scotland) Act 1978;

    (o)   the managers of a State Hospital provided under section 102 of the National Health Service (Scotland) Act 1978;

(p)   the Regional Health and Social Care Board established under section 7 of the Health and Social Care (Reform) Act (Northern Ireland) 2009 (c 1 (NI));

(q)   a special health and social care agency established under the Health and Personal Social Services (Special Agencies) (Northern Ireland) Order 1990 (SI 1990/247 (NI 3));

(r)   a Health and Social Care trust established under Article 10 of the Health and Personal Social Services (Northern Ireland) Order 1991 (SI 1991/194 (NI 1)).

205. General interpretation (1) In this Act—

"biometric data" means personal data resulting from specific technical processing relating to the physical, physiological or behavioural characteristics of an individual, which allows or confirms the unique identification of that individual, such as facial images or dactyloscopic data;

"data concerning health" means personal data relating to the physical or mental health of an individual, including the provision of health care services, which reveals information about his or her health status;

"enactment" includes—

(a)   an enactment passed or made after this Act,

(b)   an enactment comprised in subordinate legislation,

(c)   an enactment comprised in, or in an instrument made under, a Measure or Act of the National Assembly for Wales,

(d)   an enactment comprised in, or in an instrument made under, an Act of the Scottish Parliament, and

(e)   an enactment comprised in, or in an instrument made under, Northern Ireland legislation;

"genetic data" means personal data relating to the inherited or acquired genetic characteristics of an individual which gives unique information about the physiology or the health of that individual and which results, in particular, from an analysis of a biological sample from the individual in question;

"government department" includes the following (except in the expression "United Kingdom government department")—

(a)   a part of the Scottish Administration;

(b)   a Northern Ireland department;

(c)   the Welsh Government;

(d)   a body or authority exercising statutory functions on behalf of the Crown;

"health record" means a record which—

(a)   consists of data concerning health, and

(b)   has been made by or on behalf of a health professional in connection with the diagnosis, care or treatment of the individual to whom the data relates;

"inaccurate", in relation to personal data, means incorrect or misleading as to any matter of fact;

"international obligation of the United Kingdom" includes—

(a)   an EU obligation, and

(b)   an obligation that arises under an international agreement or arrangement to which the United Kingdom is a party;

"international organisation" means an organisation and its subordinate bodies governed by international law, or any other body which is set up by, or on the basis of, an agreement between two or more countries;

"Minister of the Crown" has the same meaning as in the Ministers of the Crown Act 1975;

"publish" means make available to the public or a section of the public (and related expressions are to be read accordingly);

"subordinate legislation" has the meaning given in the Interpretation Act 1978;

"tribunal" means any tribunal in which legal proceedings may be brought;

"the Tribunal", in relation to an application or appeal under this Act, means—

(a)   the Upper Tribunal, in any case where it is determined by or under Tribunal Procedure Rules that the Upper Tribunal is to hear the application or appeal, or

(b)   the First-tier Tribunal, in any other case.

(2) References in this Act to a period expressed in hours, days, weeks, months or years are to be interpreted in accordance with Article 3 of Regulation (EEC, Euratom) No 1182/71 of the Council of 3 June 1971 determining the rules applicable to periods, dates and time limits, except in—

(a)   section 125(4), (7) and (8);

(b)   section 161(3), (5) and (6);

(c)   section 176(2);

(d)   section 178(2);

(e)   section 182(8) and (9);

(f)   section 183(4);

(g)   section 192(3), (5) and (6);

(h)   section 197(3) and (4);

(i)   paragraph 23(4) and (5) of Schedule 1;

(j)   paragraphs 5(4) and 6(4) of Schedule 3;
(k)   Schedule 5;
(l)   paragraph 11(5) of Schedule 12;
(m)   Schedule 15;

(and the references in section 5 to terms used in Chapter 2 or 3 of Part 2 do not include references to a period expressed in hours, days, weeks, months or years).

(3)   Section 3(14)(b) (interpretation of references to Chapter 2 of Part 2 in Parts 5 to 7) and the amendments in Schedule 19 which make equivalent provision are not to be treated as implying a contrary intention for the purposes of section 20(2) of the Interpretation Act 1978, or any similar provision in another enactment, as it applies to other references to, or to a provision of, Chapter 2 of Part 2 of this Act.

206.   **Index of defined expressions**   The Table below lists provisions which define or otherwise explain terms defined for this Act, for a Part of this Act or for Chapter 2 or 3 of Part 2 of this Act.

the affirmative resolution procedure	section 182
the applied Chapter 2 (in Chapter 3 of Part 2)	section 22
the applied GDPR	section 3
assessment notice (in Part 6)	section 181
biometric data	section 205
certification provider (in Part 6)	section 181
the Commissioner	section 3
competent authority (in Part 3)	section 30
consent (in Part 4)	section 84
controller	section 3
data concerning health	section 205
the Data Protection Convention	section 3
the data protection legislation	section 3
data subject	section 3
employee (in Parts 3 and 4)	sections 33 and 84
enactment	section 205
enforcement notice (in Part 6)	section 181
filing system	section 3
FOI public authority (in Chapter 3 of Part 2)	section 21
the GDPR	section 3
genetic data	section 205
government department	section 205
health professional	section 204
health record	section 205
identifiable living individual	section 3
inaccurate	section 205
information notice (in Part 6)	section 181
intelligence service (in Part 4)	section 82
international obligation of the United Kingdom	section 205
international organisation	section 205
the Law Enforcement Directive	section 3
the law enforcement purposes (in Part 3)	section 31
the made affirmative resolution procedure	section 182
Minister of the Crown	section 205
the negative resolution procedure	section 182
penalty notice (in Part 6)	section 181
penalty variation notice (in Part 6)	section 181
personal data	section 3
personal data breach (in Parts 3 and 4)	sections 33 and 84
processing	section 3
processor	section 3
profiling (in Part 3)	section 33

public authority (in the GDPR and Part 2)	section 7
public body (in the GDPR and Part 2)	section 7
publish	section 205
recipient (in Parts 3 and 4)	sections 33 and 84
representative (in Part 6)	section 181
representative body (in relation to a right of a data subject)	section 187
restriction of processing (in Parts 3 and 4)	sections 33 and 84
social work professional	section 204
the special purposes (in Part 6)	section 174
special purposes proceedings (in Part 6)	section 174
subordinate legislation	section 205
third country (in Part 3)	section 33
tribunal	section 205
the Tribunal	section 205

Territorial application

207. Territorial application of this Act (1) This Act applies only to processing of personal data described in subsections (2) and (3).

(2) It applies to the processing of personal data in the context of the activities of an establishment of a controller or processor in the United Kingdom, whether or not the processing takes place in the United Kingdom.

(3) It also applies to the processing of personal data to which Chapter 2 of Part 2 (the GDPR) applies where—

    (a)   the processing is carried out in the context of the activities of an establishment of a controller or processor in a country or territory that is not a member State, whether or not the processing takes place in such a country or territory,

    (b)   the personal data relates to a data subject who is in the United Kingdom when the processing takes place, and

    (c)   the processing activities are related to—

        (i)   the offering of goods or services to data subjects in the United Kingdom, whether or not for payment, or

        (ii)   the monitoring of data subjects' behaviour in the United Kingdom.

(4) Subsections (1) to (3) have effect subject to any provision in or made under section 120 providing for the Commissioner to carry out functions in relation to other processing of personal data.

(5) Section 3(14)(c) does not apply to the reference to the processing of personal data in subsection (2).

(6) The reference in subsection (3) to Chapter 2 of Part 2 (the GDPR) does not include that Chapter as applied by Chapter 3 of Part 2 (the applied GDPR).

(7) In this section, references to a person who has an establishment in the United Kingdom include the following—

    (a)   an individual who is ordinarily resident in the United Kingdom,

    (b)   a body incorporated under the law of the United Kingdom or a part of the United Kingdom,

    (c)   a partnership or other unincorporated association formed under the law of the United Kingdom or a part of the United Kingdom, and

    (d)   a person not within paragraph (a), (b) or (c) who maintains, and carries on activities through, an office, branch or agency or other stable arrangements in the United Kingdom,

and references to a person who has an establishment in another country or territory have a corresponding meaning.

General

Sections 208-210 are concerned with: children in Scotland; application to the Crown; and application to Parliament and are not reproduced in this work.

211. Minor and consequential provision (1) In Schedule 19—

    (a)   Part 1 contains minor and consequential amendments of primary legislation;

    (b)   Part 2 contains minor and consequential amendments of other legislation;

    (c)   Part 3 contains consequential modifications of legislation;

    (d)   Part 4 contains supplementary provision.

(2) The Secretary of State may by regulations make provision that is consequential on any provision made by this Act.

(3) Regulations under subsection (2)—

(a)   may include transitional, transitory or saving provision;

(b)   may amend, repeal or revoke an enactment.

(4)   The reference to an enactment in subsection (3)(b) does not include an enactment passed or made after the end of the Session in which this Act is passed.

(5)   Regulations under this section that amend, repeal or revoke primary legislation are subject to the affirmative resolution procedure.

(6)   Any other regulations under this section are subject to the negative resolution procedure.

(7)   In this section, "primary legislation" means—

(a)   an Act;

(b)   an Act of the Scottish Parliament;

(c)   a Measure or Act of the National Assembly for Wales;

(d)   Northern Ireland legislation.

Final

212.   Commencement[1]   (1)   Except as provided by subsections (2) and (3), this Act comes into force on such day as the Secretary of State may by regulations appoint.

(2)   This section and the following provisions come into force on the day on which this Act is passed—

(a)   sections 1 and 3;

(b)   section 182;

(c)   sections 204, 205 and 206;

(d)   sections 209 and 210;

(e)   sections 213(2), 214 and 215;

(f)   any other provision of this Act so far as it confers power to make regulations or Tribunal Procedure Rules or is otherwise necessary for enabling the exercise of such a power on or after the day on which this Act is passed.

(3)   The following provisions come into force at the end of the period of 2 months beginning when this Act is passed—

(a)   section 124;

(b)   sections 125, 126 and 127, so far as they relate to a code prepared under section 124;

(c)   section 177;

(d)   section 178 and Schedule 17;

(e)   section 179.

(4)   Regulations under this section may make different provision for different areas.

---

[1] For details of commencement orders made, see the note to the title of the Act.

213.   Transitional provision   (1)   Schedule 20 contains transitional, transitory and saving provision.

(2)   The Secretary of State may by regulations make transitional, transitory or saving provision in connection with the coming into force of any provision of this Act or with the GDPR beginning to apply, including provision amending or repealing a provision of Schedule 20.

(3)   Regulations under this section that amend or repeal a provision of Schedule 20 are subject to the negative resolution procedure.

214.   Extent   (1)   This Act extends to England and Wales, Scotland and Northern Ireland, subject to—

(a)   subsections (2) to (5), and

(b)   paragraph 12 of Schedule 12.

(2)   Section 199 extends to England and Wales only.

(3)   Sections 188, 189 and 190 extend to England and Wales and Northern Ireland only.

(4)   An amendment, repeal or revocation made by this Act has the same extent in the United Kingdom as the enactment amended, repealed or revoked.

(5)   This subsection and the following provisions also extend to the Isle of Man—

(a)   paragraphs 332 and 434 of Schedule 19;

(b)   sections 211(1), 212(1) and 213(2), so far as relating to those paragraphs.

(6)   Where there is a power to extend a part of an Act by Order in Council to any of the Channel Islands, the Isle of Man or any of the British overseas territories, the power may be exercised in relation to an amendment or repeal of that part which is made by or under this Act.

215.   Short title   This Act may be cited as the Data Protection Act 2018.

SCHEDULE 1
Special Categories of Personal Data and Criminal Convictions etc Data

Section 10

PART 1
CONDITIONS RELATING TO EMPLOYMENT, HEALTH AND RESEARCH ETC
Employment, social security and social protection

1.   (1)   This condition is met if—

(a)   the processing is necessary for the purposes of performing or exercising obligations or rights which are imposed or conferred by law on the controller or the data subject in connection with employment, social security or social protection, and

(b)   when the processing is carried out, the controller has an appropriate policy document in place (see paragraph 39 in Part 4 of this Schedule).

(2)   See also the additional safeguards in Part 4 of this Schedule.

(3)   In this paragraph—

"social security" includes any of the branches of social security listed in Article 3(1) of Regulation (EC) No 883/2004 of the European Parliament and of the Council on the co-ordination of social security systems (as amended from time to time);

"social protection" includes an intervention described in Article 2(b) of Regulation (EC) 458/2007 of the European Parliament and of the Council of 25 April 2007 on the European system of integrated social protection statistics (ESSPROS) (as amended from time to time).

Health or social care purposes

2.   (1)   This condition is met if the processing is necessary for health or social care purposes.

(2)   In this paragraph "health or social care purposes" means the purposes of—
     (a)   preventive or occupational medicine,
     (b)   the assessment of the working capacity of an employee,
     (c)   medical diagnosis,
     (d)   the provision of health care or treatment,
     (e)   the provision of social care, or
     (f)   the management of health care systems or services or social care systems or services.

(3)   See also the conditions and safeguards in Article 9(3) of the GDPR (obligations of secrecy) and section 11(1).

Public health

3.   This condition is met if the processing—
     (a)   is necessary for reasons of public interest in the area of public health, and
     (b)   is carried out—
         (i)   by or under the responsibility of a health professional, or
         (ii)   by another person who in the circumstances owes a duty of confidentiality under an enactment or rule of law.

Research etc

4.   This condition is met if the processing—
     (a)   is necessary for archiving purposes, scientific or historical research purposes or statistical purposes,
     (b)   is carried out in accordance with Article 89(1) of the GDPR (as supplemented by section 19), and
     (c)   is in the public interest.

Part 2
Substantial Public Interest Conditions
Requirement for an appropriate policy document when relying on conditions in this Part

5.   (1)   Except as otherwise provided, a condition in this Part of this Schedule is met only if, when the processing is carried out, the controller has an appropriate policy document in place (see paragraph 39 in Part 4 of this Schedule).

(2)   See also the additional safeguards in Part 4 of this Schedule.

Statutory etc and government purposes

6.   (1)   This condition is met if the processing—
     (a)   is necessary for a purpose listed in sub-paragraph (2), and
     (b)   is necessary for reasons of substantial public interest.

(2)   Those purposes are—
     (a)   the exercise of a function conferred on a person by an enactment or rule of law;
     (b)   the exercise of a function of the Crown, a Minister of the Crown or a government department.

Administration of justice and parliamentary purposes

7.   This condition is met if the processing is necessary—
     (a)   for the administration of justice, or
     (b)   for the exercise of a function of either House of Parliament.

Equality of opportunity or treatment

8.   (1)   This condition is met if the processing—
     (a)   is of a specified category of personal data, and
     (b)   is necessary for the purposes of identifying or keeping under review the existence or absence of equality of opportunity or treatment between groups of people specified in relation to that category with a view to enabling such equality to be promoted or maintained,

subject to the exceptions in sub-paragraphs (3) to (5).

(2)   In sub-paragraph (1), "specified" means specified in the following table—

Category of personal data	Groups of people (in relation to a category of personal data)
Personal data revealing racial or ethnic origin	People of different racial or ethnic origins
Personal data revealing religious or philosophical beliefs	People holding different religious or philosophical beliefs
Data concerning health	People with different states of physical or mental health

| Personal data concerning an individual's sexual orientation | People of different sexual orientation |

(3)   Processing does not meet the condition in sub-paragraph (1) if it is carried out for the purposes of measures or decisions with respect to a particular data subject.

(4)   Processing does not meet the condition in sub-paragraph (1) if it is likely to cause substantial damage or substantial distress to an individual.

(5)   Processing does not meet the condition in sub-paragraph (1) if—

    (a)   an individual who is the data subject (or one of the data subjects) has given notice in writing to the controller requiring the controller not to process personal data in respect of which the individual is the data subject (and has not given notice in writing withdrawing that requirement),

    (b)   the notice gave the controller a reasonable period in which to stop processing such data, and

    (c)   that period has ended.

Racial and ethnic diversity at senior levels of organisations

9.   (1)   This condition is met if the processing—

    (a)   is of personal data revealing racial or ethnic origin,

    (b)   is carried out as part of a process of identifying suitable individuals to hold senior positions in a particular organisation, a type of organisation or organisations generally,

    (c)   is necessary for the purposes of promoting or maintaining diversity in the racial and ethnic origins of individuals who hold senior positions in the organisation or organisations, and

    (d)   can reasonably be carried out without the consent of the data subject,

subject to the exception in sub-paragraph (3).

(2)   For the purposes of sub-paragraph (1)(d), processing can reasonably be carried out without the consent of the data subject only where—

    (a)   the controller cannot reasonably be expected to obtain the consent of the data subject, and

    (b)   the controller is not aware of the data subject withholding consent.

(3)   Processing does not meet the condition in sub-paragraph (1) if it is likely to cause substantial damage or substantial distress to an individual.

(4)   For the purposes of this paragraph, an individual holds a senior position in an organisation if the individual—

    (a)   holds a position listed in sub-paragraph (5), or

    (b)   does not hold such a position but is a senior manager of the organisation.

(5)   Those positions are—

    (a)   a director, secretary or other similar officer of a body corporate;

    (b)   a member of a limited liability partnership;

    (c)   a partner in a partnership within the Partnership Act 1890, a limited partnership registered under the Limited Partnerships Act 1907 or an entity of a similar character formed under the law of a country or territory outside the United Kingdom.

(6)   In this paragraph, "senior manager", in relation to an organisation, means a person who plays a significant role in—

    (a)   the making of decisions about how the whole or a substantial part of the organisation's activities are to be managed or organised, or

    (b)   the actual managing or organising of the whole or a substantial part of those activities.

(7)   The reference in sub-paragraph (2)(b) to a data subject withholding consent does not include a data subject merely failing to respond to a request for consent.

Preventing or detecting unlawful acts

10.   (1)   This condition is met if the processing—

    (a)   is necessary for the purposes of the prevention or detection of an unlawful act,

    (b)   must be carried out without the consent of the data subject so as not to prejudice those purposes, and

    (c)   is necessary for reasons of substantial public interest.

(2)   If the processing consists of the disclosure of personal data to a competent authority, or is carried out in preparation for such disclosure, the condition in sub-paragraph (1) is met even if, when the processing is carried out, the controller does not have an appropriate policy document in place (see paragraph 5 of this Schedule).

(3)   In this paragraph—

"act" includes a failure to act;

"competent authority" has the same meaning as in Part 3 of this Act (see section 30).

Protecting the public against dishonesty etc

11.   (1)   This condition is met if the processing—

    (a)   is necessary for the exercise of a protective function,

    (b)   must be carried out without the consent of the data subject so as not to prejudice the exercise of that function, and

    (c)   is necessary for reasons of substantial public interest.

(2)   In this paragraph, "protective function" means a function which is intended to protect members of the public against—

    (a)   dishonesty, malpractice or other seriously improper conduct,

    (b)   unfitness or incompetence,

    (c)   mismanagement in the administration of a body or association, or

    (d)   failures in services provided by a body or association.

Regulatory requirements relating to unlawful acts and dishonesty etc

12.   (1)   This condition is met if—

    (a)   the processing is necessary for the purposes of complying with, or assisting other persons to comply with, a regulatory requirement which involves a person taking steps to establish whether another person has—

        (i)   committed an unlawful act, or

    (ii)   been involved in dishonesty, malpractice or other seriously improper conduct,

  (b)   in the circumstances, the controller cannot reasonably be expected to obtain the consent of the data subject to the processing, and

  (c)   the processing is necessary for reasons of substantial public interest.

  (2)   In this paragraph—

"act" includes a failure to act;

"regulatory requirement" means—

    (a)   a requirement imposed by legislation or by a person in exercise of a function conferred by legislation, or

    (b)   a requirement forming part of generally accepted principles of good practice relating to a type of body or an activity.

Journalism etc in connection with unlawful acts and dishonesty etc

13. (1)   This condition is met if—

    (a)   the processing consists of the disclosure of personal data for the special purposes,

    (b)   it is carried out in connection with a matter described in sub-paragraph (2),

    (c)   it is necessary for reasons of substantial public interest,

    (d)   it is carried out with a view to the publication of the personal data by any person, and

    (e)   the controller reasonably believes that publication of the personal data would be in the public interest.

  (2)   The matters mentioned in sub-paragraph (1)(b) are any of the following (whether alleged or established)—

    (a)   the commission of an unlawful act by a person;

    (b)   dishonesty, malpractice or other seriously improper conduct of a person;

    (c)   unfitness or incompetence of a person;

    (d)   mismanagement in the administration of a body or association;

    (e)   a failure in services provided by a body or association.

  (3)   The condition in sub-paragraph (1) is met even if, when the processing is carried out, the controller does not have an appropriate policy document in place (see paragraph 5 of this Schedule).

  (4)   In this paragraph—

"act" includes a failure to act;

"the special purposes" means—

    (a)   the purposes of journalism;

    (b)   academic purposes;

    (c)   artistic purposes;

    (d)   literary purposes.

Preventing fraud

14. (1)   This condition is met if the processing—

    (a)   is necessary for the purposes of preventing fraud or a particular kind of fraud, and

    (b)   consists of—

        (i)   the disclosure of personal data by a person as a member of an anti-fraud organisation,

        (ii)   the disclosure of personal data in accordance with arrangements made by an anti-fraud organisation, or

        (iii)   the processing of personal data disclosed as described in sub-paragraph (i) or (ii).

  (2)   In this paragraph, "anti-fraud organisation" has the same meaning as in section 68 of the Serious Crime Act 2007.

Suspicion of terrorist financing or money laundering

15. This condition is met if the processing is necessary for the purposes of making a disclosure in good faith under either of the following—

    (a)   section 21CA of the Terrorism Act 2000 (disclosures between certain entities within regulated sector in relation to suspicion of commission of terrorist financing offence or for purposes of identifying terrorist property);

    (b)   section 339ZB of the Proceeds of Crime Act 2002 (disclosures within regulated sector in relation to suspicion of money laundering).

Support for individuals with a particular disability or medical condition

16. (1)   This condition is met if the processing—

    (a)   is carried out by a not-for-profit body which provides support to individuals with a particular disability or medical condition,

    (b)   is of a type of personal data falling within sub-paragraph (2) which relates to an individual falling within sub-paragraph (3),

    (c)   is necessary for the purposes of—

        (i)   raising awareness of the disability or medical condition, or

        (ii)   providing support to individuals falling within sub-paragraph (3) or enabling such individuals to provide support to each other,

    (d)   can reasonably be carried out without the consent of the data subject, and

    (e)   is necessary for reasons of substantial public interest.

  (2)   The following types of personal data fall within this sub-paragraph—

    (a)   personal data revealing racial or ethnic origin;

    (b)   genetic data or biometric data;

    (c)   data concerning health;

    (d)   personal data concerning an individual's sex life or sexual orientation.

  (3)   An individual falls within this sub-paragraph if the individual is or has been a member of the body mentioned in sub-paragraph (1)(a) and—

    (a)   has the disability or condition mentioned there, has had that disability or condition or has a significant risk of developing that disability or condition, or

(b) is a relative or carer of an individual who satisfies paragraph (a) of this sub-paragraph.

(4) For the purposes of sub-paragraph (1)(d), processing can reasonably be carried out without the consent of the data subject only where—

    (a) the controller cannot reasonably be expected to obtain the consent of the data subject, and

    (b) the controller is not aware of the data subject withholding consent.

(5) In this paragraph—

"carer" means an individual who provides or intends to provide care for another individual other than—

    (a) under or by virtue of a contract, or

    (b) as voluntary work;

"disability" has the same meaning as in the Equality Act 2010 (see section 6 of, and Schedule 1 to, that Act).

(6) The reference in sub-paragraph (4)(b) to a data subject withholding consent does not include a data subject merely failing to respond to a request for consent.

Counselling etc

17. (1) This condition is met if the processing—

    (a) is necessary for the provision of confidential counselling, advice or support or of another similar service provided confidentially,

    (b) is carried out without the consent of the data subject for one of the reasons listed in sub-paragraph (2), and

    (c) is necessary for reasons of substantial public interest.

(2) The reasons mentioned in sub-paragraph (1)(b) are—

    (a) in the circumstances, consent to the processing cannot be given by the data subject;

    (b) in the circumstances, the controller cannot reasonably be expected to obtain the consent of the data subject to the processing;

    (c) the processing must be carried out without the consent of the data subject because obtaining the consent of the data subject would prejudice the provision of the service mentioned in sub-paragraph (1)(a).

Safeguarding of children and of individuals at risk

18. (1) This condition is met if—

    (a) the processing is necessary for the purposes of—

        (i) protecting an individual from neglect or physical, mental or emotional harm, or

        (ii) protecting the physical, mental or emotional well-being of an individual,

    (b) the individual is—

        (i) aged under 18, or

        (ii) aged 18 or over and at risk,

    (c) the processing is carried out without the consent of the data subject for one of the reasons listed in sub-paragraph (2), and

    (d) the processing is necessary for reasons of substantial public interest.

(2) The reasons mentioned in sub-paragraph (1)(c) are—

    (a) in the circumstances, consent to the processing cannot be given by the data subject;

    (b) in the circumstances, the controller cannot reasonably be expected to obtain the consent of the data subject to the processing;

    (c) the processing must be carried out without the consent of the data subject because obtaining the consent of the data subject would prejudice the provision of the protection mentioned in sub-paragraph (1)(a).

(3) For the purposes of this paragraph, an individual aged 18 or over is "at risk" if the controller has reasonable cause to suspect that the individual—

    (a) has needs for care and support,

    (b) is experiencing, or at risk of, neglect or physical, mental or emotional harm, and

    (c) as a result of those needs is unable to protect himself or herself against the neglect or harm or the risk of it.

(4) In sub-paragraph (1)(a), the reference to the protection of an individual or of the well-being of an individual includes both protection relating to a particular individual and protection relating to a type of individual.

Safeguarding of economic well-being of certain individuals

19. (1) This condition is met if the processing—

    (a) is necessary for the purposes of protecting the economic well-being of an individual at economic risk who is aged 18 or over,

    (b) is of data concerning health,

    (c) is carried out without the consent of the data subject for one of the reasons listed in sub-paragraph (2), and

    (d) is necessary for reasons of substantial public interest.

(2) The reasons mentioned in sub-paragraph (1)(c) are—

    (a) in the circumstances, consent to the processing cannot be given by the data subject;

    (b) in the circumstances, the controller cannot reasonably be expected to obtain the consent of the data subject to the processing;

    (c) the processing must be carried out without the consent of the data subject because obtaining the consent of the data subject would prejudice the provision of the protection mentioned in sub-paragraph (1)(a).

(3) In this paragraph, "individual at economic risk" means an individual who is less able to protect his or her economic well-being by reason of physical or mental injury, illness or disability.

Insurance

20. (1) This condition is met if the processing—

    (a) is necessary for an insurance purpose,

    (b) is of personal data revealing racial or ethnic origin, religious or philosophical beliefs or trade union membership, genetic data or data concerning health, and

    (c)   is necessary for reasons of substantial public interest,

subject to sub-paragraphs (2) and (3).

    (2)   Sub-paragraph (3) applies where—

    (a)   the processing is not carried out for the purposes of measures or decisions with respect to the data subject, and

    (b)   the data subject does not have and is not expected to acquire—

        (i)   rights against, or obligations in relation to, a person who is an insured person under an insurance contract to which the insurance purpose mentioned in sub-paragraph (1)(a) relates, or

        (ii)   other rights or obligations in connection with such a contract.

    (3)   Where this sub-paragraph applies, the processing does not meet the condition in sub-paragraph (1) unless, in addition to meeting the requirements in that sub-paragraph, it can reasonably be carried out without the consent of the data subject.

    (4)   For the purposes of sub-paragraph (3), processing can reasonably be carried out without the consent of the data subject only where—

    (a)   the controller cannot reasonably be expected to obtain the consent of the data subject, and

    (b)   the controller is not aware of the data subject withholding consent.

    (5)   In this paragraph—

"insurance contract" means a contract of general insurance or long-term insurance;

"insurance purpose" means—

    (a)   advising on, arranging, underwriting or administering an insurance contract,

    (b)   administering a claim under an insurance contract, or

    (c)   exercising a right, or complying with an obligation, arising in connection with an insurance contract, including a right or obligation arising under an enactment or rule of law.

    (6)   The reference in sub-paragraph (4)(b) to a data subject withholding consent does not include a data subject merely failing to respond to a request for consent.

    (7)   Terms used in the definition of "insurance contract" in sub-paragraph (5) and also in an order made under section 22 of the Financial Services and Markets Act 2000 (regulated activities) have the same meaning in that definition as they have in that order.

Occupational pensions

21.   (1)   This condition is met if the processing—

    (a)   is necessary for the purpose of making a determination in connection with eligibility for, or benefits payable under, an occupational pension scheme,

    (b)   is of data concerning health which relates to a data subject who is the parent, grandparent, great-grandparent or sibling of a member of the scheme,

    (c)   is not carried out for the purposes of measures or decisions with respect to the data subject, and

    (d)   can reasonably be carried out without the consent of the data subject.

    (2)   For the purposes of sub-paragraph (1)(d), processing can reasonably be carried out without the consent of the data subject only where—

    (a)   the controller cannot reasonably be expected to obtain the consent of the data subject, and

    (b)   the controller is not aware of the data subject withholding consent.

    (3)   In this paragraph—

"occupational pension scheme" has the meaning given in section 1 of the Pension Schemes Act 1993;

"member", in relation to a scheme, includes an individual who is seeking to become a member of the scheme.

    (4)   The reference in sub-paragraph (2)(b) to a data subject withholding consent does not include a data subject merely failing to respond to a request for consent.

Political parties

22.   (1)   This condition is met if the processing—

    (a)   is of personal data revealing political opinions,

    (b)   is carried out by a person or organisation included in the register maintained under section 23 of the Political Parties, Elections and Referendums Act 2000, and

    (c)   is necessary for the purposes of the person's or organisation's political activities,

subject to the exceptions in sub-paragraphs (2) and (3).

    (2)   Processing does not meet the condition in sub-paragraph (1) if it is likely to cause substantial damage or substantial distress to a person.

    (3)   Processing does not meet the condition in sub-paragraph (1) if—

    (a)   an individual who is the data subject (or one of the data subjects) has given notice in writing to the controller requiring the controller not to process personal data in respect of which the individual is the data subject (and has not given notice in writing withdrawing that requirement),

    (b)   the notice gave the controller a reasonable period in which to stop processing such data, and

    (c)   that period has ended.

    (4)   In this paragraph, "political activities" include campaigning, fund-raising, political surveys and case-work.

Elected representatives responding to requests

23.   (1)   This condition is met if—

    (a)   the processing is carried out—

        (i)   by an elected representative or a person acting with the authority of such a representative,

        (ii)   in connection with the discharge of the elected representative's functions, and

        (iii)   in response to a request by an individual that the elected representative take action on behalf of the individual, and

    (b)   the processing is necessary for the purposes of, or in connection with, the action reasonably taken by the elected representative in response to that request,

subject to sub-paragraph (2).

    (2)   Where the request is made by an individual other than the data subject, the condition in sub-paragraph (1) is met only if the processing must be carried out without the consent of the data subject for one of the following reasons—

(a)   in the circumstances, consent to the processing cannot be given by the data subject;

(b)   in the circumstances, the elected representative cannot reasonably be expected to obtain the consent of the data subject to the processing;

(c)   obtaining the consent of the data subject would prejudice the action taken by the elected representative;

(d)   the processing is necessary in the interests of another individual and the data subject has withheld consent unreasonably.

(3)   In this paragraph, "elected representative" means—

(a)   a member of the House of Commons;

(b)   a member of the National Assembly for Wales;

(c)   a member of the Scottish Parliament;

(d)   a member of the Northern Ireland Assembly;

(e)   a member of the European Parliament elected in the United Kingdom;

(f)   an elected member of a local authority within the meaning of section 270(1) of the Local Government Act 1972, namely—

     (i)   in England, a county council, a district council, a London borough council or a parish council;

     (ii)   in Wales, a county council, a county borough council or a community council;

(g)   an elected mayor of a local authority within the meaning of Part 1A or 2 of the Local Government Act 2000;

(h)   a mayor for the area of a combined authority established under section 103 of the Local Democracy, Economic Development and Construction Act 2009;

(i)   the Mayor of London or an elected member of the London Assembly;

(j)   an elected member of—

     (i)   the Common Council of the City of London, or

     (ii)   the Council of the Isles of Scilly;

(k)   an elected member of a council constituted under section 2 of the Local Government etc (Scotland) Act 1994;

(l)   an elected member of a district council within the meaning of the Local Government Act (Northern Ireland) 1972 (c 9 (NI));

(m)   a police and crime commissioner.

(4)   For the purposes of sub-paragraph (3), a person who is—

(a)   a member of the House of Commons immediately before Parliament is dissolved,

(b)   a member of the National Assembly for Wales immediately before that Assembly is dissolved,

(c)   a member of the Scottish Parliament immediately before that Parliament is dissolved, or

(d)   a member of the Northern Ireland Assembly immediately before that Assembly is dissolved,

is to be treated as if the person were such a member until the end of the fourth day after the day on which the subsequent general election in relation to that Parliament or Assembly is held.

(5)   For the purposes of sub-paragraph (3), a person who is an elected member of the Common Council of the City of London and whose term of office comes to an end at the end of the day preceding the annual Wardmotes is to be treated as if he or she were such a member until the end of the fourth day after the day on which those Wardmotes are held.

Disclosure to elected representatives

24.   (1)   This condition is met if—

(a)   the processing consists of the disclosure of personal data—

     (i)   to an elected representative or a person acting with the authority of such a representative, and

     (ii)   in response to a communication to the controller from that representative or person which was made in response to a request from an individual,

(b)   the personal data is relevant to the subject matter of that communication, and

(c)   the disclosure is necessary for the purpose of responding to that communication,

subject to sub-paragraph (2).

(2)   Where the request to the elected representative came from an individual other than the data subject, the condition in sub-paragraph (1) is met only if the disclosure must be made without the consent of the data subject for one of the following reasons—

(a)   in the circumstances, consent to the processing cannot be given by the data subject;

(b)   in the circumstances, the elected representative cannot reasonably be expected to obtain the consent of the data subject to the processing;

(c)   obtaining the consent of the data subject would prejudice the action taken by the elected representative;

(d)   the processing is necessary in the interests of another individual and the data subject has withheld consent unreasonably.

(3)   In this paragraph, "elected representative" has the same meaning as in paragraph 23.

Informing elected representatives about prisoners

25.   (1)   This condition is met if—

(a)   the processing consists of the processing of personal data about a prisoner for the purpose of informing a member of the House of Commons, a member of the National Assembly for Wales or a member of the Scottish Parliament about the prisoner, and

(b)   the member is under an obligation not to further disclose the personal data.

(2)   The references in sub-paragraph (1) to personal data about, and to informing someone about, a prisoner include personal data about, and informing someone about, arrangements for the prisoner's release.

(3)   In this paragraph—

"prison" includes a young offender institution, a remand centre, a secure training centre or a secure college;

"prisoner" means a person detained in a prison.

Publication of legal judgments

26.   This condition is met if the processing—

(a)   consists of the publication of a judgment or other decision of a court or tribunal, or

(b)   is necessary for the purposes of publishing such a judgment or decision.

Anti-doping in sport

27. (1) This condition is met if the processing is necessary—
    (a) for the purposes of measures designed to eliminate doping which are undertaken by or under the responsibility of a body or association that is responsible for eliminating doping in a sport, at a sporting event or in sport generally, or
    (b) for the purposes of providing information about doping, or suspected doping, to such a body or association.

    (2) The reference in sub-paragraph (1)(a) to measures designed to eliminate doping includes measures designed to identify or prevent doping.

    (3) If the processing consists of the disclosure of personal data to a body or association described in sub-paragraph (1)(a), or is carried out in preparation for such disclosure, the condition in sub-paragraph (1) is met even if, when the processing is carried out, the controller does not have an appropriate policy document in place (see paragraph 5 of this Schedule).

Standards of behaviour in sport

28. (1) This condition is met if the processing—
    (a) is necessary for the purposes of measures designed to protect the integrity of a sport or a sporting event,
    (b) must be carried out without the consent of the data subject so as not to prejudice those purposes, and
    (c) is necessary for reasons of substantial public interest.

    (2) In sub-paragraph (1)(a), the reference to measures designed to protect the integrity of a sport or a sporting event is a reference to measures designed to protect a sport or a sporting event against—
    (a) dishonesty, malpractice or other seriously improper conduct, or
    (b) failure by a person participating in the sport or event in any capacity to comply with standards of behaviour set by a body or association with responsibility for the sport or event.

Part 3
Additional Conditions Relating to Criminal Convictions etc
Consent

29. This condition is met if the data subject has given consent to the processing.

Protecting individual's vital interests

30. This condition is met if—
    (a) the processing is necessary to protect the vital interests of an individual, and
    (b) the data subject is physically or legally incapable of giving consent.

Processing by not-for-profit bodies

31. This condition is met if the processing is carried out—
    (a) in the course of its legitimate activities with appropriate safeguards by a foundation, association or other not-for-profit body with a political, philosophical, religious or trade union aim, and
    (b) on condition that—
        (i) the processing relates solely to the members or to former members of the body or to persons who have regular contact with it in connection with its purposes, and
        (ii) the personal data is not disclosed outside that body without the consent of the data subjects.

Personal data in the public domain

32. This condition is met if the processing relates to personal data which is manifestly made public by the data subject.

Legal claims

33. This condition is met if the processing—
    (a) is necessary for the purpose of, or in connection with, any legal proceedings (including prospective legal proceedings),
    (b) is necessary for the purpose of obtaining legal advice, or
    (c) is otherwise necessary for the purposes of establishing, exercising or defending legal rights.

Judicial acts

34. This condition is met if the processing is necessary when a court or tribunal is acting in its judicial capacity.

Administration of accounts used in commission of indecency offences involving children

35. (1) This condition is met if—
    (a) the processing is of personal data about a conviction or caution for an offence listed in sub-paragraph (2),
    (b) the processing is necessary for the purpose of administering an account relating to the payment card used in the commission of the offence or cancelling that payment card, and
    (c) when the processing is carried out, the controller has an appropriate policy document in place (see paragraph 39 in Part 4 of this Schedule).

    (2) Those offences are an offence under—
    (a) section 1 of the Protection of Children Act 1978 (indecent photographs of children),
    (b) Article 3 of the Protection of Children (Northern Ireland) Order 1978 (SI 1978/1047 (NI 17)) (indecent photographs of children),
    (c) section 52 of the Civic Government (Scotland) Act 1982 (indecent photographs etc of children),
    (d) section 160 of the Criminal Justice Act 1988 (possession of indecent photograph of child),
    (e) Article 15 of the Criminal Justice (Evidence etc) (Northern Ireland) Order 1988 (SI 1988/1847 (NI 17)) (possession of indecent photograph of child), or
    (f) section 62 of the Coroners and Justice Act 2009 (possession of prohibited images of children),
or incitement to commit an offence under any of those provisions.

(3)   See also the additional safeguards in Part 4 of this Schedule.

(4)   In this paragraph—

"caution" means a caution given to a person in England and Wales or Northern Ireland in respect of an offence which, at the time when the caution is given, is admitted;

"conviction" has the same meaning as in the Rehabilitation of Offenders Act 1974 or the Rehabilitation of Offenders (Northern Ireland) Order 1978 (SI 1978/1908 (NI 27));

"payment card" includes a credit card, a charge card and a debit card.

Extension of conditions in Part 2 of this Schedule referring to substantial public interest

36.   This condition is met if the processing would meet a condition in Part 2 of this Schedule but for an express requirement for the processing to be necessary for reasons of substantial public interest.

Extension of insurance conditions

37.   This condition is met if the processing—

    (a)   would meet the condition in paragraph 20 in Part 2 of this Schedule (the "insurance condition"), or

    (b)   would meet the condition in paragraph 36 by virtue of the insurance condition,

but for the requirement for the processing to be processing of a category of personal data specified in paragraph 20(1)(b).

PART 4
APPROPRIATE POLICY DOCUMENT AND ADDITIONAL SAFEGUARDS
Application of this Part of this Schedule

38.   This Part of this Schedule makes provision about the processing of personal data carried out in reliance on a condition in Part 1, 2 or 3 of this Schedule which requires the controller to have an appropriate policy document in place when the processing is carried out.

Requirement to have an appropriate policy document in place

39.   The controller has an appropriate policy document in place in relation to the processing of personal data in reliance on a condition described in paragraph 38 if the controller has produced a document which—

    (a)   explains the controller's procedures for securing compliance with the principles in Article 5 of the GDPR (principles relating to processing of personal data) in connection with the processing of personal data in reliance on the condition in question, and

    (b)   explains the controller's policies as regards the retention and erasure of personal data processed in reliance on the condition, giving an indication of how long such personal data is likely to be retained.

Additional safeguard: retention of appropriate policy document

40.   (1)   Where personal data is processed in reliance on a condition described in paragraph 38, the controller must during the relevant period—

    (a)   retain the appropriate policy document,

    (b)   review and (if appropriate) update it from time to time, and

    (c)   make it available to the Commissioner, on request, without charge.

    (2)   "Relevant period", in relation to the processing of personal data in reliance on a condition described in paragraph 38, means a period which—

    (a)   begins when the controller starts to carry out processing of personal data in reliance on that condition, and

    (b)   ends at the end of the period of 6 months beginning when the controller ceases to carry out such processing.

Additional safeguard: record of processing

41.   A record maintained by the controller, or the controller's representative, under Article 30 of the GDPR in respect of the processing of personal data in reliance on a condition described in paragraph 38 must include the following information—

    (a)   which condition is relied on,

    (b)   how the processing satisfies Article 6 of the GDPR (lawfulness of processing), and

    (c)   whether the personal data is retained and erased in accordance with the policies described in paragraph 39(b) and, if it is not, the reasons for not following those policies.

SCHEDULE 2
Exemptions etc from the GDPR

Section 15

PART 1
ADAPTATIONS AND RESTRICTIONS BASED ON ARTICLES 6(3) AND 23(1)
GDPR provisions to be adapted or restricted: "the listed GDPR provisions"

1.   In this Part of this Schedule, "the listed GDPR provisions" means—

    (a)   the following provisions of the GDPR (the rights and obligations in which may be restricted by virtue of Article 23(1) of the GDPR)—

        (i)   Article 13(1) to (3) (personal data collected from data subject: information to be provided);

        (ii)   Article 14(1) to (4) (personal data collected other than from data subject: information to be provided);

        (iii)   Article 15(1) to (3) (confirmation of processing, access to data and safeguards for third country transfers);

        (iv)   Article 16 (right to rectification);

        (v)   Article 17(1) and (2) (right to erasure);

        (vi)   Article 18(1) (restriction of processing);

        (vii)   Article 19 (notification obligation regarding rectification or erasure of personal data or restriction of processing);

      (viii)   Article 20(1) and (2) (right to data portability);

      (ix)   Article 21(1) (objections to processing);

      (x)   Article 5 (general principles) so far as its provisions correspond to the rights and obligations provided for in the provisions mentioned in sub-paragraphs (i) to (ix); and

  (b)   the following provisions of the GDPR (the application of which may be adapted by virtue of Article 6(3) of the GDPR)—

      (i)   Article 5(1)(a) (lawful, fair and transparent processing), other than the lawfulness requirements set out in Article 6;

      (ii)   Article 5(1)(b) (purpose limitation).

Crime and taxation: general

2. (1)   The listed GDPR provisions and Article 34(1) and (4) of the GDPR (communication of personal data breach to the data subject) do not apply to personal data processed for any of the following purposes—

  (a)   the prevention or detection of crime,

  (b)   the apprehension or prosecution of offenders, or

  (c)   the assessment or collection of a tax or duty or an imposition of a similar nature,

to the extent that the application of those provisions would be likely to prejudice any of the matters mentioned in paragraphs (a) to (c).

  (2)   Sub-paragraph (3) applies where—

  (a)   personal data is processed by a person ("Controller 1") for any of the purposes mentioned in sub-paragraph (1)(a) to (c), and

  (b)   another person ("Controller 2") obtains the data from Controller 1 for the purpose of discharging statutory functions and processes it for the purpose of discharging statutory functions.

  (3)   Controller 2 is exempt from the obligations in the following provisions of the GDPR—

  (a)   Article 13(1) to (3) (personal data collected from data subject: information to be provided),

  (b)   Article 14(1) to (4) (personal data collected other than from data subject: information to be provided),

  (c)   Article 15(1) to (3) (confirmation of processing, access to data and safeguards for third country transfers), and

  (d)   Article 5 (general principles) so far as its provisions correspond to the rights and obligations provided for in the provisions mentioned in paragraphs (a) to (c),

to the same extent that Controller 1 is exempt from those obligations by virtue of sub-paragraph (1).

Crime and taxation: risk assessment systems

3. (1)   The GDPR provisions listed in sub-paragraph (3) do not apply to personal data which consists of a classification applied to the data subject as part of a risk assessment system falling within sub-paragraph (2) to the extent that the application of those provisions would prevent the system from operating effectively.

  (2)   A risk assessment system falls within this sub-paragraph if—

  (a)   it is operated by a government department, a local authority or another authority administering housing benefit, and

  (b)   it is operated for the purposes of—

      (i)   the assessment or collection of a tax or duty or an imposition of a similar nature, or

      (ii)   the prevention or detection of crime or apprehension or prosecution of offenders, where the offence concerned involves the unlawful use of public money or an unlawful claim for payment out of public money.

  (3)   The GDPR provisions referred to in sub-paragraph (1) are the following provisions of the GDPR (the rights and obligations in which may be restricted by virtue of Article 23(1) of the GDPR)—

  (a)   Article 13(1) to (3) (personal data collected from data subject: information to be provided);

  (b)   Article 14(1) to (4) (personal data collected other than from data subject: information to be provided);

  (c)   Article 15(1) to (3) (confirmation of processing, access to data and safeguards for third country transfers);

  (d)   Article 5 (general principles) so far as its provisions correspond to the rights and obligations provided for in the provisions mentioned in paragraphs (a) to (c).

Immigration

4. (1)   The GDPR provisions listed in sub-paragraph (2) do not apply to personal data processed for any of the following purposes—

  (a)   the maintenance of effective immigration control, or

  (b)   the investigation or detection of activities that would undermine the maintenance of effective immigration control,

to the extent that the application of those provisions would be likely to prejudice any of the matters mentioned in paragraphs (a) and (b).

  (2)   The GDPR provisions referred to in sub-paragraph (1) are the following provisions of the GDPR (the rights and obligations in which may be restricted by virtue of Article 23(1) of the GDPR)—

  (a)   Article 13(1) to (3) (personal data collected from data subject: information to be provided);

  (b)   Article 14(1) to (4) (personal data collected other than from data subject: information to be provided);

  (c)   Article 15(1) to (3) (confirmation of processing, access to data and safeguards for third country transfers);

  (d)   Article 17(1) and (2) (right to erasure);

  (e)   Article 18(1) (restriction of processing);

  (f)   Article 21(1) (objections to processing);

  (g)   Article 5 (general principles) so far as its provisions correspond to the rights and obligations provided for in the provisions mentioned in sub-paragraphs (a) to (f).

(That is, the listed GDPR provisions other than Article 16 (right to rectification), Article 19 (notification obligation regarding rectification or erasure of personal data or restriction of processing) and Article 20(1) and (2) (right to data portability) and, subject to sub-paragraph (2)(g) of this paragraph, the provisions of Article 5 listed in paragraph 1(b).)

   (3)   Sub-paragraph (4) applies where—

     (a)   personal data is processed by a person ("Controller 1"), and

     (b)   another person ("Controller 2") obtains the data from Controller 1 for any of the purposes mentioned in sub-paragraph (1)(a) and (b) and processes it for any of those purposes.

   (4)   Controller 1 is exempt from the obligations in the following provisions of the GDPR—

     (a)   Article 13(1) to (3) (personal data collected from data subject: information to be provided),

     (b)   Article 14(1) to (4) (personal data collected other than from data subject: information to be provided),

     (c)   Article 15(1) to (3) (confirmation of processing, access to data and safeguards for third country transfers), and

     (d)   Article 5 (general principles) so far as its provisions correspond to the rights and obligations provided for in the provisions mentioned in paragraphs (a) to (c),

to the same extent that Controller 2 is exempt from those obligations by virtue of sub-paragraph (1).

Information required to be disclosed by law etc or in connection with legal proceedings

5. (1)   The listed GDPR provisions do not apply to personal data consisting of information that the controller is obliged by an enactment to make available to the public, to the extent that the application of those provisions would prevent the controller from complying with that obligation.

   (2)   The listed GDPR provisions do not apply to personal data where disclosure of the data is required by an enactment, a rule of law or an order of a court or tribunal, to the extent that the application of those provisions would prevent the controller from making the disclosure.

   (3)   The listed GDPR provisions do not apply to personal data where disclosure of the data—

     (a)   is necessary for the purpose of, or in connection with, legal proceedings (including prospective legal proceedings),

     (b)   is necessary for the purpose of obtaining legal advice, or

     (c)   is otherwise necessary for the purposes of establishing, exercising or defending legal rights,

to the extent that the application of those provisions would prevent the controller from making the disclosure.

PART 2

RESTRICTIONS BASED ON ARTICLE 23(1): RESTRICTIONS OF RULES IN ARTICLES 13 TO 21 AND 34

GDPR provisions to be restricted: "the listed GDPR provisions"

6.   In this Part of this Schedule, "the listed GDPR provisions" means the following provisions of the GDPR (the rights and obligations in which may be restricted by virtue of Article 23(1) of the GDPR)—

     (a)   Article 13(1) to (3) (personal data collected from data subject: information to be provided);

     (b)   Article 14(1) to (4) (personal data collected other than from data subject: information to be provided);

     (c)   Article 15(1) to (3) (confirmation of processing, access to data and safeguards for third country transfers);

     (d)   Article 16 (right to rectification);

     (e)   Article 17(1) and (2) (right to erasure);

     (f)   Article 18(1) (restriction of processing);

     (g)   Article 19 (notification obligation regarding rectification or erasure of personal data or restriction of processing);

     (h)   Article 20(1) and (2) (right to data portability);

     (i)   Article 21(1) (objections to processing);

     (j)   Article 5 (general principles) so far as its provisions correspond to the rights and obligations provided for in the provisions mentioned in sub-paragraphs (a) to (i).

Functions designed to protect the public etc

7.   The listed GDPR provisions do not apply to personal data processed for the purposes of discharging a function that—

     (a)   is designed as described in column 1 of the Table, and

     (b)   meets the condition relating to the function specified in column 2 of the Table,

to the extent that the application of those provisions would be likely to prejudice the proper discharge of the function.

TABLE

Description of function design	Condition
1 The function is designed to protect members of the public against— (a) financial loss due to dishonesty, malpractice or other seriously improper conduct by, or the unfitness or incompetence of, persons concerned in the provision of banking, insurance, investment or other financial services or in the management of bodies corporate, or (b) financial loss due to the conduct of discharged or undischarged bankrupts.	The function is— (a) conferred on a person by an enactment, (b) a function of the Crown, a Minister of the Crown or a government department, or (c) of a public nature, and is exercised in the public interest.
2 The function is designed to protect members of the public against— (a) dishonesty, malpractice or other seriously improper conduct, or (b) unfitness or incompetence.	The function is— (a) conferred on a person by an enactment, (b) a function of the Crown, a Minister of the Crown or a government department, or (c) of a public nature, and is exercised in the public interest.

3 The function is designed— (a) to protect charities or community interest companies against misconduct or mismanagement (whether by trustees, directors or other persons) in their administration, (b) to protect the property of charities or community interest companies from loss or misapplication, or (c) to recover the property of charities or community interest companies.	The function is— (a) conferred on a person by an enactment, (b) a function of the Crown, a Minister of the Crown or a government department, or (c) of a public nature, and is exercised in the public interest.
4 The function is designed— (a) to secure the health, safety and welfare of persons at work, or (b) to protect persons other than those at work against risk to health or safety arising out of or in connection with the action of persons at work.	The function is— (a) conferred on a person by an enactment, (b) a function of the Crown, a Minister of the Crown or a government department, or (c) of a public nature, and is exercised in the public interest.
5 The function is designed to protect members of the public against— (a) maladministration by public bodies, (b) failures in services provided by public bodies, or (c) a failure of a public body to provide a service which it is a function of the body to provide.	The function is conferred by any enactment on— (a) the Parliamentary Commissioner for Administration, (b) the Commissioner for Local Administration in England, (c) the Health Service Commissioner for England, (d) the Public Services Ombudsman for Wales, (e) the Northern Ireland Public Services Ombudsman, (f) the Prison Ombudsman for Northern Ireland, or (g) the Scottish Public Services Ombudsman.
6 The function is designed— (a) to protect members of the public against conduct which may adversely affect their interests by persons carrying on a business, (b) to regulate agreements or conduct which have as their object or effect the prevention, restriction or distortion of competition in connection with any commercial activity, or (c) to regulate conduct on the part of one or more undertakings which amounts to the abuse of a dominant position in a market.	The function is conferred on the Competition and Markets Authority by an enactment.

Judicial appointments, judicial independence and judicial proceedings

14. (1) The listed GDPR provisions do not apply to personal data processed for the purposes of assessing a person's suitability for judicial office or the office of Queen's Counsel.

(2) The listed GDPR provisions do not apply to personal data processed by—
  (a) an individual acting in a judicial capacity, or
  (b) a court or tribunal acting in its judicial capacity.

(3) As regards personal data not falling within sub-paragraph (1) or (2), the listed GDPR provisions do not apply to the extent that the application of those provisions would be likely to prejudice judicial independence or judicial proceedings.

PART 3
RESTRICTION BASED ON ARTICLE 23(1): PROTECTION OF RIGHTS OF OTHERS
Protection of the rights of others: general

16. (1) Article 15(1) to (3) of the GDPR (confirmation of processing, access to data and safeguards for third country transfers), and Article 5 of the GDPR so far as its provisions correspond to the rights and obligations provided for in Article 15(1) to (3), do not oblige a controller to disclose information to the data subject to the extent that doing so would involve disclosing information relating to another individual who can be identified from the information.

(2) Sub-paragraph (1) does not remove the controller's obligation where—
  (a) the other individual has consented to the disclosure of the information to the data subject, or
  (b) it is reasonable to disclose the information to the data subject without the consent of the other individual.

(3) In determining whether it is reasonable to disclose the information without consent, the controller must have regard to all the relevant circumstances, including—
  (a) the type of information that would be disclosed,
  (b) any duty of confidentiality owed to the other individual,
  (c) any steps taken by the controller with a view to seeking the consent of the other individual,
  (d) whether the other individual is capable of giving consent, and
  (e) any express refusal of consent by the other individual.

(4) For the purposes of this paragraph—
  (a) "information relating to another individual" includes information identifying the other individual as the source of information;
  (b) an individual can be identified from information to be provided to a data subject by a controller if the individual can be identified from—
    (i) that information, or
    (ii) that information and any other information that the controller reasonably believes the data subject is likely to possess or obtain.

Assumption of reasonableness for health workers, social workers and education workers

17. (1)   For the purposes of paragraph 16(2)(b), it is to be considered reasonable for a controller to disclose information to a data subject without the consent of the other individual where—
     (a)   the health data test is met,
     (b)   the social work data test is met, or
     (c)   the education data test is met.

   (2)   The health data test is met if—
     (a)   the information in question is contained in a health record, and
     (b)   the other individual is a health professional who has compiled or contributed to the health record or who, in his or her capacity as a health professional, has been involved in the diagnosis, care or treatment of the data subject.

   (3)   The social work data test is met if—
     (a)   the other individual is—
         (i)   a children's court officer,
         (ii)   a person who is or has been employed by a person or body referred to in paragraph 8 of Schedule 3 in connection with functions exercised in relation to the information, or
         (iii)   a person who has provided for reward a service that is similar to a service provided in the exercise of any relevant social services functions, and
     (b)   the information relates to the other individual in an official capacity or the other individual supplied the information—
         (i)   in an official capacity, or
         (ii)   in a case within paragraph (a)(iii), in connection with providing the service mentioned in paragraph (a)(iii).

   (4)   The education data test is met if—
     (a)   the other individual is an education-related worker, or
     (b)   the other individual is employed by an education authority (within the meaning of the Education (Scotland) Act 1980) in pursuance of its functions relating to education and—
         (i)   the information relates to the other individual in his or her capacity as such an employee, or
         (ii)   the other individual supplied the information in his or her capacity as such an employee.

   (5)   In this paragraph—
"children's court officer" means a person referred to in paragraph 8(1)(q), (r), (s), (t) or (u) of Schedule 3;
"education-related worker" means a person referred to in paragraph 14(4)(a) or (b) or 16(4)(a), (b) or (c) of Schedule 3 (educational records);
"relevant social services functions" means functions specified in paragraph 8(1)(a), (b), (c) or (d) of Schedule 3.

PART 4

RESTRICTIONS BASED ON ARTICLE 23(1): RESTRICTIONS OF RULES IN ARTICLES 13 TO 15

GDPR provisions to be restricted: "the listed GDPR provisions"

18.   In this Part of this Schedule, "the listed GDPR provisions" means the following provisions of the GDPR (the rights and obligations in which may be restricted by virtue of Article 23(1) of the GDPR)—
     (a)   Article 13(1) to (3) (personal data collected from data subject: information to be provided);
     (b)   Article 14(1) to (4) (personal data collected other than from data subject: information to be provided);
     (c)   Article 15(1) to (3) (confirmation of processing, access to data and safeguards for third country transfers);
     (d)   Article 5 (general principles) so far as its provisions correspond to the rights and obligations provided for in the provisions mentioned in sub-paragraphs (a) to (c).

Legal professional privilege

19.   The listed GDPR provisions do not apply to personal data that consists of—
     (a)   information in respect of which a claim to legal professional privilege or, in Scotland, confidentiality of communications, could be maintained in legal proceedings, or
     (b)   information in respect of which a duty of confidentiality is owed by a professional legal adviser to a client of the adviser.

Self incrimination

20. (1)   A person need not comply with the listed GDPR provisions to the extent that compliance would, by revealing evidence of the commission of an offence, expose the person to proceedings for that offence.

   (2)   The reference to an offence in sub-paragraph (1) does not include an offence under—
     (a)   this Act,
     (b)   section 5 of the Perjury Act 1911 (false statements made otherwise than on oath),
     (c)   section 44(2) of the Criminal Law (Consolidation) (Scotland) Act 1995 (false statements made otherwise than on oath), or
     (d)   Article 10 of the Perjury (Northern Ireland) Order 1979 (SI 1979/1714 (NI 19)) (false statutory declarations and other false unsworn statements).

   (3)   Information disclosed by any person in compliance with Article 15 of the GDPR is not admissible against the person in proceedings for an offence under this Act.

Confidential references

24.   The listed GDPR provisions do not apply to personal data consisting of a reference given (or to be given) in confidence for the purposes of—
     (a)   the education, training or employment (or prospective education, training or employment) of the data subject,
     (b)   the placement (or prospective placement) of the data subject as a volunteer,
     (c)   the appointment (or prospective appointment) of the data subject to any office, or
     (d)   the provision (or prospective provision) by the data subject of any service.

SCHEDULE 3
Exemptions etc from the GDPR: Health, Social Work, Education and Child Abuse Data

Section 15

PART 1
GDPR PROVISIONS TO BE RESTRICTED

1. In this Schedule "the listed GDPR provisions" means the following provisions of the GDPR (the rights and obligations in which may be restricted by virtue of Article 23(1) of the GDPR)—

   (a) Article 13(1) to (3) (personal data collected from data subject: information to be provided);
   (b) Article 14(1) to (4) (personal data collected other than from data subject: information to be provided);
   (c) Article 15(1) to (3) (confirmation of processing, access to data and safeguards for third country transfers);
   (d) Article 16 (right to rectification);
   (e) Article 17(1) and (2) (right to erasure);
   (f) Article 18(1) (restriction of processing);
   (g) Article 20(1) and (2) (right to data portability);
   (h) Article 21(1) (objections to processing);
   (i) Article 5 (general principles) so far as its provisions correspond to the rights and obligations provided for in the provisions mentioned in sub-paragraphs (a) to (h).

PART 2
HEALTH DATA
Exemption from the listed GDPR provisions: data processed by a court

3. (1) The listed GDPR provisions do not apply to data concerning health if—
   (a) it is processed by a court,
   (b) it consists of information supplied in a report or other evidence given to the court in the course of proceedings to which rules listed in subparagraph (2) apply, and
   (c) in accordance with those rules, the data may be withheld by the court in whole or in part from the data subject.

   (2) Those rules are—
   (a) the Magistrates' Courts (Children and Young Persons) Rules (Northern Ireland) 1969 (SR (NI) 1969 No 221);
   (b) the Magistrates' Courts (Children and Young Persons) Rules 1992 (SI 1992/2071 (L 17));
   (c) the Family Proceedings Rules (Northern Ireland) 1996 (SR (NI) 1996 No 322);
   (d) the Magistrates' Courts (Children (Northern Ireland) Order 1995) Rules (Northern Ireland) 1996 (SR (NI) 1996 No 323);
   (e) the Act of Sederunt (Child Care and Maintenance Rules) 1997 (SI 1997/291 (S 19));
   (f) the Sheriff Court Adoption Rules 2009;
   (g) the Family Procedure Rules 2010 (SI 2010/2955 (L 17));
   (h) the Children's Hearings (Scotland) Act 2011 (Rules of Procedure in Children's Hearings) Rules 2013 (SSI 2013/194).

PART 3
SOCIAL WORK DATA
Definitions

7. (1) In this Part of this Schedule—
"education data" has the meaning given by paragraph 17 of this Schedule;
"Health and Social Care trust" means a Health and Social Care trust established under the Health and Personal Social Services (Northern Ireland) Order 1991 (SI 1991/194 (NI 1));
"Principal Reporter" means the Principal Reporter appointed under the Children's Hearings (Scotland) Act 2011 (asp 1), or an officer of the Scottish Children's Reporter Administration to whom there is delegated under paragraph 10(1) of Schedule 3 to that Act any function of the Principal Reporter;
"social work data" means personal data which—
   (a) is data to which paragraph 8 applies, but
   (b) is not education data or data concerning health.

   (2) For the purposes of this Part of this Schedule, the "serious harm test" is met with respect to social work data if the application of Article 15 of the GDPR to the data would be likely to prejudice carrying out social work, because it would be likely to cause serious harm to the physical or mental health of the data subject or another individual.

   (3) In sub-paragraph (2), "carrying out social work" is to be taken to include doing any of the following—
   (a) the exercise of any functions mentioned in paragraph 8(1)(a), (d), (f) to (j), (m), (p), (s), (t), (u), (v) or (w);
   (b) the provision of any service mentioned in paragraph 8(1)(b), (c) or (k);
   (c) the exercise of the functions of a body mentioned in paragraph 8(1)(e) or a person mentioned in paragraph 8(1)(q) or (r).

   (4) In this Part of this Schedule, a reference to a local authority, in relation to data processed or formerly processed by it, includes a reference to the Council of the Isles of Scilly, in relation to data processed or formerly processed by the Council in connection with any functions mentioned in paragraph 8(1)(a)(ii) which are or have been conferred on the Council by an enactment.

8. (1) This paragraph applies to personal data falling within any of the following descriptions—
   (a) data processed by a local authority—
      (i) in connection with its social services functions (within the meaning of the Local Authority Social Services Act 1970 or the Social Services and Well-being (Wales) Act 2014 (anaw 4)) or any functions exercised by local authorities under the Social Work (Scotland) Act 1968 or referred to in section 5(1B) of that Act, or
      (ii) in the exercise of other functions but obtained or consisting of information obtained in connection with any of the functions mentioned in sub-paragraph (i);

(b)   data processed by the Regional Health and Social Care Board—
      (i)   in connection with the provision of social care within the meaning of section 2(5) of the Health and Social Care (Reform) Act (Northern Ireland) 2009 (c 1 (NI)), or
      (ii)   in the exercise of other functions but obtained or consisting of information obtained in connection with the provision of that care;

(c)   data processed by a Health and Social Care trust—
      (i)   in connection with the provision of social care within the meaning of section 2(5) of the Health and Social Care (Reform) Act (Northern Ireland) 2009 (c 1 (NI)) on behalf of the Regional Health and Social Care Board by virtue of an authorisation made under Article 3(1) of the Health and Personal Social Services (Northern Ireland) Order 1994 (SI 1994/429 (NI 2)), or
      (ii)   in the exercise of other functions but obtained or consisting of information obtained in connection with the provision of that care;

(d)   data processed by a council in the exercise of its functions under Part 2 of Schedule 9 to the Health and Social Services and Social Security Adjudications Act 1983;

(e)   data processed by—
      (i)   a probation trust established under section 5 of the Offender Management Act 2007, or
      (ii)   the Probation Board for Northern Ireland established by the Probation Board (Northern Ireland) Order 1982 (SI 1982/713 (NI 10));

(f)   data processed by a local authority in the exercise of its functions under section 36 of the Children Act 1989 or Chapter 2 of Part 6 of the Education Act 1996, so far as those functions relate to ensuring that children of compulsory school age (within the meaning of section 8 of the Education Act 1996) receive suitable education whether by attendance at school or otherwise;

(g)   data processed by the Education Authority in the exercise of its functions under Article 55 of the Children (Northern Ireland) Order 1995 (SI 1995/755 (NI 2)) or Article 45 of, and Schedule 13 to, the Education and Libraries (Northern Ireland) Order 1986 (SI 1986/594 (NI 3)), so far as those functions relate to ensuring that children of compulsory school age (within the meaning of Article 46 of the Education and Libraries (Northern Ireland) Order 1986) receive efficient full-time education suitable to their age, ability and aptitude and to any special educational needs they may have, either by regular attendance at school or otherwise;

(h)   data processed by an education authority in the exercise of its functions under sections 35 to 42 of the Education (Scotland) Act 1980 so far as those functions relate to ensuring that children of school age (within the meaning of section 31 of the Education (Scotland) Act 1980) receive efficient education suitable to their age, ability and aptitude, whether by attendance at school or otherwise;

(i)   data relating to persons detained in a hospital at which high security psychiatric services are provided under section 4 of the National Health Service Act 2006 and processed by a Special Health Authority established under section 28 of that Act in the exercise of any functions similar to any social services functions of a local authority;

(j)   data relating to persons detained in special accommodation provided under Article 110 of the Mental Health (Northern Ireland) Order 1986 (SI 1986/595 (NI 4)) and processed by a Health and Social Care trust in the exercise of any functions similar to any social services functions of a local authority;

(k)   data which—
      (i)   is processed by the National Society for the Prevention of Cruelty to Children, or by any other voluntary organisation or other body designated under this paragraph by the Secretary of State or the Department of Health in Northern Ireland, and
      (ii)   appears to the Secretary of State or the Department, as the case may be, to be processed for the purposes of the provision of any service similar to a service provided in the exercise of any functions specified in paragraph (a), (b), (c) or (d);

(l)   data processed by a body mentioned in sub-paragraph (2)—
      (i)   which was obtained, or consists of information which was obtained, from an authority or body mentioned in any of paragraphs (a) to (k) or from a government department, and
      (ii)   in the case of data obtained, or consisting of information obtained, from an authority or body mentioned in any of paragraphs (a) to (k), fell within any of those paragraphs while processed by the authority or body;

(m)   data processed by a National Health Service trust first established under section 25 of the National Health Service Act 2006, section 18 of the National Health Service (Wales) Act 2006 or section 5 of the National Health Service and Community Care Act 1990 in the exercise of any functions similar to any social services functions of a local authority;

(n)   data processed by an NHS foundation trust in the exercise of any functions similar to any social services functions of a local authority;

(o)   data processed by a government department—
      (i)   which was obtained, or consists of information which was obtained, from an authority or body mentioned in any of paragraphs (a) to (n), and
      (ii)   which fell within any of those paragraphs while processed by that authority or body;

(p)   data processed for the purposes of the functions of the Secretary of State pursuant to section 82(5) of the Children Act 1989;

(q)   data processed by—
      (i)   a children's guardian appointed under Part 16 of the Family Procedure Rules 2010 (SI 2010/2955 (L 17)),
      (ii)   a guardian ad litem appointed under Article 60 of the Children (Northern Ireland) Order 1995 (SI 1995/755 (NI 2)) or Article 66 of the Adoption (Northern Ireland) Order 1987 (SI 1987/2203 (NI 22)), or
      (iii)   a safeguarder appointed under section 30(2) or 31(3) of the Children's Hearings (Scotland) Act 2011 (asp 1);

(r)   data processed by the Principal Reporter;

(s)   data processed by an officer of the Children and Family Court Advisory and Support Service for the purpose of the officer's functions under section 7 of the Children Act 1989 or Part 16 of the Family Procedure Rules 2010 (SI 2010/2955 (L 17));

(t)   data processed by the Welsh family proceedings officer for the purposes of the functions under section 7 of the Children Act 1989 or Part 16 of the Family Procedure Rules 2010;

(u)   data processed by an officer of the service appointed as guardian ad litem under Part 16 of the Family Procedure Rules 2010;

(v)   data processed by the Children and Family Court Advisory and Support Service for the purpose of its functions under section 12(1) and (2) and section 13(1), (2) and (4) of the Criminal Justice and Court Services Act 2000;

(w)   data processed by the Welsh Ministers for the purposes of their functions under section 35(1) and (2) and section 36(1), (2), (4), (5) and (6) of the Children Act 2004;

(x)   data processed for the purposes of the functions of the appropriate Minister pursuant to section 12 of the Adoption and Children Act 2002 (independent review of determinations).

(2)   The bodies referred to in sub-paragraph (1)(l) are—

(a)   a National Health Service trust first established under section 25 of the National Health Service Act 2006 or section 18 of the National Health Service (Wales) Act 2006;

(b)   a National Health Service trust first established under section 5 of the National Health Service and Community Care Act 1990;

(c)   an NHS foundation trust;

(d)   a clinical commissioning group established under section 14D of the National Health Service Act 2006;

(e)   the National Health Service Commissioning Board;

(f)   a Local Health Board established under section 11 of the National Health Service (Wales) Act 2006;

(g)   a Health Board established under section 2 of the National Health Service (Scotland) Act 1978.

Exemption from the listed GDPR provisions: data processed by a court

9.   (1)   The listed GDPR provisions do not apply to data that is not education data or data concerning health if—

(a)   it is processed by a court,

(b)   it consists of information supplied in a report or other evidence given to the court in the course of proceedings to which rules listed in subparagraph (2) apply, and

(c)   in accordance with any of those rules, the data may be withheld by the court in whole or in part from the data subject.

(2)   Those rules are—

(a)   the Magistrates' Courts (Children and Young Persons) Rules (Northern Ireland) 1969 (SR (NI) 1969 No 221);

(b)   the Magistrates' Courts (Children and Young Persons) Rules 1992 (SI 1992/2071 (L 17));

(c)   the Family Proceedings Rules (Northern Ireland) 1996 (SR (NI) 1996 No 322);

(d)   the Magistrates' Courts (Children (Northern Ireland) Order 1995) Rules (Northern Ireland) 1996 (SR (NI) 1996 No 323);

(e)   the Act of Sederunt (Child Care and Maintenance Rules) 1997 (SI 1997/291 (S 19));

(f)   the Sheriff Court Adoption Rules 2009;

(g)   the Family Procedure Rules 2010 (SI 2010/2955 (L 17));

(h)   the Children's Hearings (Scotland) Act 2011 (Rules of Procedure in Children's Hearings) Rules 2013 (SSI 2013/194).

Exemption from the listed GDPR provisions: data subject's expectations and wishes

10.   (1)   This paragraph applies where a request for social work data is made in exercise of a power conferred by an enactment or rule of law and—

(a)   in relation to England and Wales or Northern Ireland, the data subject is an individual aged under 18 and the person making the request has parental responsibility for the data subject,

(b)   in relation to Scotland, the data subject is an individual aged under 16 and the person making the request has parental responsibilities for the data subject, or

(c)   the data subject is incapable of managing his or her own affairs and the person making the request has been appointed by a court to manage those affairs.

(2)   The listed GDPR provisions do not apply to social work data to the extent that complying with the request would disclose information—

(a)   which was provided by the data subject in the expectation that it would not be disclosed to the person making the request,

(b)   which was obtained as a result of any examination or investigation to which the data subject consented in the expectation that the information would not be so disclosed, or

(c)   which the data subject has expressly indicated should not be so disclosed.

(3)   The exemptions under sub-paragraph (2)(a) and (b) do not apply if the data subject has expressly indicated that he or she no longer has the expectation mentioned there.

PART 4
EDUCATION DATA
Exemption from the listed GDPR provisions: data processed by a court

18.   (1)   The listed GDPR provisions do not apply to education data if—

(a)   it is processed by a court,

(b)   it consists of information supplied in a report or other evidence given to the court in the course of proceedings to which rules listed in subparagraph (2) apply, and

(c)   in accordance with those rules, the data may be withheld by the court in whole or in part from the data subject.

(2)   Those rules are—

(a)   the Magistrates' Courts (Children and Young Persons) Rules (Northern Ireland) 1969 (SR (NI) 1969 No 221);

(b)   the Magistrates' Courts (Children and Young Persons) Rules 1992 (SI 1992/2071 (L 17));

(c)   the Family Proceedings Rules (Northern Ireland) 1996 (SR (NI) 1996 No 322);

(d)   the Magistrates' Courts (Children (Northern Ireland) Order 1995) Rules (Northern Ireland) 1996 (SR (NI) 1996 No 323);

(e)   the Act of Sederunt (Child Care and Maintenance Rules) 1997 (SI 1997/291 (S 19));

(f)   the Sheriff Court Adoption Rules 2009;

(g)   the Family Procedure Rules 2010 (SI 2010/2955 (L 17));
(h)   the Children's Hearings (Scotland) Act 2011 (Rules of Procedure in Children's Hearings) Rules 2013 (SSI 2013/194).

PART 5
CHILD ABUSE DATA
Exemption from Article 15 of the GDPR: child abuse data

21. (1) This paragraph applies where a request for child abuse data is made in exercise of a power conferred by an enactment or rule of law and—
(a)   the data subject is an individual aged under 18 and the person making the request has parental responsibility for the data subject, or
(b)   the data subject is incapable of managing his or her own affairs and the person making the request has been appointed by a court to manage those affairs.
(2) Article 15(1) to (3) of the GDPR (confirmation of processing, access to data and safeguards for third country transfers) do not apply to child abuse data to the extent that the application of that provision would not be in the best interests of the data subject.
(3) "Child abuse data" is personal data consisting of information as to whether the data subject is or has been the subject of, or may be at risk of, child abuse.
(4) For this purpose, "child abuse" includes physical injury (other than accidental injury) to, and physical and emotional neglect, ill-treatment and sexual abuse of, an individual aged under 18.
(5) This paragraph does not apply in relation to Scotland.

SCHEDULE 4
Exemptions etc from the GDPR: Disclosure Prohibited or Restricted by an Enactment

Text of Schedule is not reproduced.

SCHEDULE 5
Accreditation of Certification Providers: Reviews and Appeals

Text of Schedule is not reproduced.

SCHEDULE 6
The Applied GDPR and the Applied Chapter 2

Text of Schedule is not reproduced.

SCHEDULE 7
Competent Authorities

Section 30

1.   Any United Kingdom government department other than a non-ministerial government department.
2.   The Scottish Ministers.
3.   Any Northern Ireland department.
4.   The Welsh Ministers.

Chief officers of police and other policing bodies

5.   The chief constable of a police force maintained under section 2 of the Police Act 1996.
6.   The Commissioner of Police of the Metropolis.
7.   The Commissioner of Police for the City of London.
8.   The Chief Constable of the Police Service of Northern Ireland.
9.   The chief constable of the Police Service of Scotland.
10.   The chief constable of the British Transport Police.
11.   The chief constable of the Civil Nuclear Constabulary.
12.   The chief constable of the Ministry of Defence Police.
13.   The Provost Marshal of the Royal Navy Police.
14.   The Provost Marshal of the Royal Military Police.
15.   The Provost Marshal of the Royal Air Force Police.
16.   The chief officer of—
(a)   a body of constables appointed under provision incorporating section 79 of the Harbours, Docks, and Piers Clauses Act 1847;
(b)   a body of constables appointed under an order made under section 14 of the Harbours Act 1964;
(c)   the body of constables appointed under section 154 of the Port of London Act 1968 (c xxxii).
17.   A body established in accordance with a collaboration agreement under section 22A of the Police Act 1996.
18.   The Director General of the Independent Office for Police Conduct.
19.   The Police Investigations and Review Commissioner.
20.   The Police Ombudsman for Northern Ireland.

Other authorities with investigatory functions

21.   The Commissioners for Her Majesty's Revenue and Customs.
22.   The Welsh Revenue Authority.
23.   Revenue Scotland.
24.   The Director General of the National Crime Agency.
25.   The Director of the Serious Fraud Office.
26.   The Director of Border Revenue.
27.   The Financial Conduct Authority.
28.   The Health and Safety Executive.
29.   The Competition and Markets Authority.
30.   The Gas and Electricity Markets Authority.

31. The Food Standards Agency.
32. Food Standards Scotland.
33. Her Majesty's Land Registry.
34. The Criminal Cases Review Commission.
35. The Scottish Criminal Cases Review Commission.

Authorities with functions relating to offender management

36. A provider of probation services (other than the Secretary of State), acting in pursuance of arrangements made under section 3(2) of the Offender Management Act 2007.
37. The Youth Justice Board for England and Wales.
38. The Parole Board for England and Wales.
39. The Parole Board for Scotland.
40. The Parole Commissioners for Northern Ireland.
41. The Probation Board for Northern Ireland.
42. The Prisoner Ombudsman for Northern Ireland.
43. A person who has entered into a contract for the running of, or part of—
    (a) a prison or young offender institution under section 84 of the Criminal Justice Act 1991, or
    (b) a secure training centre under section 7 of the Criminal Justice and Public Order Act 1994.
44. A person who has entered into a contract with the Secretary of State—
    (a) under section 80 of the Criminal Justice Act 1991 for the purposes of prisoner escort arrangements, or
    (b) under paragraph 1 of Schedule 1 to the Criminal Justice and Public Order Act 1994 for the purposes of escort arrangements.
45. A person who is, under or by virtue of any enactment, responsible for securing the electronic monitoring of an individual.
46. A youth offending team established under section 39 of the Crime and Disorder Act 1998.

Other authorities

47. The Director of Public Prosecutions.
48. The Director of Public Prosecutions for Northern Ireland.
49. The Lord Advocate.
50. A Procurator Fiscal.
51. The Director of Service Prosecutions.
52. The Information Commissioner.
53. The Scottish Information Commissioner.
54. The Scottish Courts and Tribunal Service.
55. The Crown agent.
56. A court or tribunal.

SCHEDULE 8
Conditions for Sensitive Processing under Part 3

Section 35(5)

Statutory etc purposes

1. This condition is met if the processing—
    (a) is necessary for the exercise of a function conferred on a person by an enactment or rule of law, and
    (b) is necessary for reasons of substantial public interest.

Administration of justice

2. This condition is met if the processing is necessary for the administration of justice.

Protecting individual's vital interests

3. This condition is met if the processing is necessary to protect the vital interests of the data subject or of another individual.

Safeguarding of children and of individuals at risk

4. (1) This condition is met if—
    (a) the processing is necessary for the purposes of—
        (i) protecting an individual from neglect or physical, mental or emotional harm, or
        (ii) protecting the physical, mental or emotional well-being of an individual,
    (b) the individual is—
        (i) aged under 18, or
        (ii) aged 18 or over and at risk,
    (c) the processing is carried out without the consent of the data subject for one of the reasons listed in sub-paragraph (2), and
    (d) the processing is necessary for reasons of substantial public interest.
   (2) The reasons mentioned in sub-paragraph (1)(c) are—
    (a) in the circumstances, consent to the processing cannot be given by the data subject;
    (b) in the circumstances, the controller cannot reasonably be expected to obtain the consent of the data subject to the processing;
    (c) the processing must be carried out without the consent of the data subject because obtaining the consent of the data subject would prejudice the provision of the protection mentioned in sub-paragraph (1)(a).
   (3) For the purposes of this paragraph, an individual aged 18 or over is "at risk" if the controller has reasonable cause to suspect that the individual—
    (a) has needs for care and support,
    (b) is experiencing, or at risk of, neglect or physical, mental or emotional harm, and
    (c) as a result of those needs is unable to protect himself or herself against the neglect or harm or the risk

of it.

(4)   In sub-paragraph (1)(a), the reference to the protection of an individual or of the well-being of an individual includes both protection relating to a particular individual and protection relating to a type of individual.

Personal data already in the public domain

5.   This condition is met if the processing relates to personal data which is manifestly made public by the data subject.

Legal claims

6.   This condition is met if the processing—
    (a)   is necessary for the purpose of, or in connection with, any legal proceedings (including prospective legal proceedings),
    (b)   is necessary for the purpose of obtaining legal advice, or
    (c)   is otherwise necessary for the purposes of establishing, exercising or defending legal rights.

Judicial acts

7.   This condition is met if the processing is necessary when a court or other judicial authority is acting in its judicial capacity.

Preventing fraud

8.   (1)   This condition is met if the processing—
    (a)   is necessary for the purposes of preventing fraud or a particular kind of fraud, and
    (b)   consists of—
        (i)   the disclosure of personal data by a competent authority as a member of an anti-fraud organisation,
        (ii)   the disclosure of personal data by a competent authority in accordance with arrangements made by an anti-fraud organisation, or
        (iii)   the processing of personal data disclosed as described in sub-paragraph (i) or (ii).

(2)   In this paragraph, "anti-fraud organisation" has the same meaning as in section 68 of the Serious Crime Act 2007.

Archiving etc

9.   This condition is met if the processing is necessary—
    (a)   for archiving purposes in the public interest,
    (b)   for scientific or historical research purposes, or
    (c)   for statistical purposes.

SCHEDULE 9
Conditions for Processing under Part 4

Text of Schedule is not reproduced.

SCHEDULE 10
Conditions for Sensitive Processing under Part 4

Text of Schedule is not reproduced.

Section 86

SCHEDULE 11
Other Exemptions under Part 4

Text of Schedule is not reproduced.

Section 112

SCHEDULE 12
The Information Commissioner

Section 114

Status and capacity

1.   (1)   The Commissioner is to continue to be a corporation sole.
(2)   The Commissioner and the Commissioner's officers and staff are not to be regarded as servants or agents of the Crown.

Appointment

2.   (1)   The Commissioner is to be appointed by Her Majesty by Letters Patent.
(2)   No recommendation may be made to Her Majesty for the appointment of a person as the Commissioner unless the person concerned has been selected on merit on the basis of fair and open competition.
(3)   The Commissioner is to hold office for such term not exceeding 7 years as may be determined at the time of the Commissioner's appointment, subject to paragraph 3.
(4)   A person cannot be appointed as the Commissioner more than once.

Resignation and removal

3.   (1)   The Commissioner may be relieved of office by Her Majesty at the Commissioner's own request.
(2)   The Commissioner may be removed from office by Her Majesty on an Address from both Houses of

Parliament.

(3) No motion is to be made in either House of Parliament for such an Address unless a Minister of the Crown has presented a report to that House stating that the Minister is satisfied that one or both of the following grounds is made out—

(a) the Commissioner is guilty of serious misconduct;

(b) the Commissioner no longer fulfils the conditions required for the performance of the Commissioner's functions.

Salary etc

4. (1) The Commissioner is to be paid such salary as may be specified by a resolution of the House of Commons.

(2) There is to be paid in respect of the Commissioner such pension as may be specified by a resolution of the House of Commons.

(3) A resolution for the purposes of this paragraph may—

(a) specify the salary or pension,

(b) specify the salary or pension and provide for it to be increased by reference to such variables as may be specified in the resolution, or

(c) provide that the salary or pension is to be the same as, or calculated on the same basis as, that payable to, or in respect of, a person employed in a specified office under, or in a specified capacity in the service of, the Crown.

(4) A resolution for the purposes of this paragraph may take effect from—

(a) the date on which it is passed, or

(b) from an earlier date or later date specified in the resolution.

(5) A resolution for the purposes of this paragraph may make different provision in relation to the pension payable to, or in respect of, different holders of the office of Commissioner.

(6) A salary or pension payable under this paragraph is to be charged on and issued out of the Consolidated Fund.

(7) In this paragraph, "pension" includes an allowance or gratuity and a reference to the payment of a pension includes a reference to the making of payments towards the provision of a pension.

Officers and staff

5. (1) The Commissioner—

(a) must appoint one or more deputy commissioners, and

(b) may appoint other officers and staff.

(2) The Commissioner is to determine the remuneration and other conditions of service of people appointed under this paragraph.

(3) The Commissioner may pay pensions, allowances or gratuities to, or in respect of, people appointed under this paragraph, including pensions, allowances or gratuities paid by way of compensation in respect of loss of office or employment.

(4) The references in sub-paragraph (3) to paying pensions, allowances or gratuities includes making payments towards the provision of pensions, allowances or gratuities.

(5) In making appointments under this paragraph, the Commissioner must have regard to the principle of selection on merit on the basis of fair and open competition.

(6) The Employers' Liability (Compulsory Insurance) Act 1969 does not require insurance to be effected by the Commissioner.

Carrying out of the Commissioner's functions by officers and staff

6. (1) The functions of the Commissioner are to be carried out by the deputy commissioner or deputy commissioners if—

(a) there is a vacancy in the office of the Commissioner, or

(b) the Commissioner is for any reason unable to act.

(2) When the Commissioner appoints a second or subsequent deputy commissioner, the Commissioner must specify which deputy commissioner is to carry out which of the Commissioner's functions in the circumstances referred to in sub-paragraph (1).

(3) A function of the Commissioner may, to the extent authorised by the Commissioner, be carried out by any of the Commissioner's officers or staff.

Authentication of the seal of the Commissioner

7. The application of the seal of the Commissioner is to be authenticated by—

(a) the Commissioner's signature, or

(b) the signature of another person authorised for the purpose.

Presumption of authenticity of documents issued by the Commissioner

8. A document purporting to be an instrument issued by the Commissioner and to be—

(a) duly executed under the Commissioner's seal, or

(b) signed by or on behalf of the Commissioner,

is to be received in evidence and is to be deemed to be such an instrument unless the contrary is shown.

Money

9. The Secretary of State may make payments to the Commissioner out of money provided by Parliament.

Fees etc and other sums

10. (1) All fees, charges, penalties and other sums received by the Commissioner in carrying out the Commissioner's functions are to be paid by the Commissioner to the Secretary of State.

(2) Sub-paragraph (1) does not apply where the Secretary of State, with the consent of the Treasury, otherwise directs.

(3) Any sums received by the Secretary of State under sub-paragraph (1) are to be paid into the Consolidated Fund.

Accounts

11. (1)   The Commissioner must—
    (a)   keep proper accounts and other records in relation to the accounts, and
    (b)   prepare in respect of each financial year a statement of account in such form as the Secretary of State may direct.

  (2)   The Commissioner must send a copy of the statement to the Comptroller and Auditor General—
    (a)   on or before 31 August next following the end of the year to which the statement relates, or
    (b)   on or before such earlier date after the end of that year as the Treasury may direct.

  (3)   The Comptroller and Auditor General must examine, certify and report on the statement.

  (4)   The Commissioner must arrange for copies of the statement and the Comptroller and Auditor General's report to be laid before Parliament.

  (5)   In this paragraph, "financial year" means a period of 12 months beginning with 1 April.

Scotland

12.   Paragraphs 1(1), 7 and 8 do not extend to Scotland.

SCHEDULE 13
Other General Functions of the Commissioner

Section 116

General tasks

1. (1)   The Commissioner must—
    (a)   monitor and enforce Parts 3 and 4 of this Act;
    (b)   promote public awareness and understanding of the risks, rules, safeguards and rights in relation to processing of personal data to which those Parts apply;
    (c)   advise Parliament, the government and other institutions and bodies on legislative and administrative measures relating to the protection of individuals' rights and freedoms with regard to processing of personal data to which those Parts apply;
    (d)   promote the awareness of controllers and processors of their obligations under Parts 3 and 4 of this Act;
    (e)   on request, provide information to a data subject concerning the exercise of the data subject's rights under Parts 3 and 4 of this Act and, if appropriate, co-operate with LED supervisory authorities and foreign designated authorities to provide such information;
    (f)   co-operate with LED supervisory authorities and foreign designated authorities with a view to ensuring the consistency of application and enforcement of the Law Enforcement Directive and the Data Protection Convention, including by sharing information and providing mutual assistance;
    (g)   conduct investigations on the application of Parts 3 and 4 of this Act, including on the basis of information received from an LED supervisory authority, a foreign designated authority or another public authority;
    (h)   monitor relevant developments to the extent that they have an impact on the protection of personal data, including the development of information and communication technologies;
    (i)   contribute to the activities of the European Data Protection Board established by the GDPR in connection with the processing of personal data to which the Law Enforcement Directive applies.

  (2)   Section 3(14)(c) does not apply to the reference to personal data in sub-paragraph (1)(h).

General powers

2.   The Commissioner has the following investigative, corrective, authorisation and advisory powers in relation to processing of personal data to which Part 3 or 4 of this Act applies—
    (a)   to notify the controller or the processor of an alleged infringement of Part 3 or 4 of this Act;
    (b)   to issue warnings to a controller or processor that intended processing operations are likely to infringe provisions of Part 3 or 4 of this Act;
    (c)   to issue reprimands to a controller or processor where processing operations have infringed provisions of Part 3 or 4 of this Act;
    (d)   to issue, on the Commissioner's own initiative or on request, opinions to Parliament, the government or other institutions and bodies as well as to the public on any issue related to the protection of personal data.

Definitions

3.   In this Schedule—
"foreign designated authority" means an authority designated for the purposes of Article 13 of the Data Protection Convention by a party, other than the United Kingdom, which is bound by that Convention;
"LED supervisory authority" means a supervisory authority for the purposes of Article 41 of the Law Enforcement Directive in a member State other than the United Kingdom.

SCHEDULE 14
Co-Operation and Mutual Assistance

Section 118

PART 1
LAW ENFORCEMENT DIRECTIVE
Co-operation

1. (1)   The Commissioner may provide information or assistance to an LED supervisory authority to the extent that, in the opinion of the Commissioner, providing that information or assistance is necessary for the performance of the recipient's data protection functions.

  (2)   The Commissioner may ask an LED supervisory authority to provide information or assistance which

the Commissioner requires for the performance of the Commissioner's data protection functions.

(3)   In this paragraph, "data protection functions" means functions relating to the protection of individuals with respect to the processing of personal data.

Requests for information and assistance from LED supervisory authorities

2.   (1)   This paragraph applies where the Commissioner receives a request from an LED supervisory authority for information or assistance referred to in Article 41 of the Law Enforcement Directive and the request—
    (a)   explains the purpose of and reasons for the request, and
    (b)   contains all other information necessary to enable the Commissioner to respond.
    (2)   The Commissioner must—
    (a)   take all appropriate measures required to reply to the request without undue delay and, in any event, before the end of the period of 1 month beginning with receipt of the request, and
    (b)   inform the LED supervisory authority of the results or, as the case may be, of the progress of the measures taken in order to respond to the request.
    (3)   The Commissioner must not refuse to comply with the request unless—
    (a)   the Commissioner does not have power to do what is requested, or
    (b)   complying with the request would infringe the Law Enforcement Directive, EU legislation or the law of the United Kingdom or a part of the United Kingdom.
    (4)   If the Commissioner refuses to comply with a request from an LED supervisory authority, the Commissioner must inform the authority of the reasons for the refusal.
    (5)   As a general rule, the Commissioner must provide information requested by LED supervisory authorities by electronic means using a standardised format.

Fees

3.   (1)   Subject to sub-paragraph (2), any information or assistance that is required to be provided by this Part of this Schedule must be provided free of charge.
    (2)   The Commissioner may enter into agreements with other LED supervisory authorities for the Commissioner and other authorities to indemnify each other for expenditure arising from the provision of assistance in exceptional circumstances.

Restrictions on use of information

4.   Where the Commissioner receives information from an LED supervisory authority as a result of a request under paragraph 1(2), the Commissioner may use the information only for the purposes specified in the request.

LED supervisory authority

5.   In this Part of this Schedule, "LED supervisory authority" means a supervisory authority for the purposes of Article 41 of the Law Enforcement Directive in a member State other than the United Kingdom.

Part 2
Data Protection Convention
Co-operation between the Commissioner and foreign designated authorities

6.   (1)   The Commissioner must, at the request of a foreign designated authority—
    (a)   provide that authority with such information referred to in Article 13(3)(a) of the Data Protection Convention (information on law and administrative practice in the field of data protection) as is the subject of the request, and
    (b)   take appropriate measures in accordance with Article 13(3)(b) of the Data Protection Convention for providing that authority with information relating to the processing of personal data in the United Kingdom.
    (2)   The Commissioner may ask a foreign designated authority—
    (a)   to provide the Commissioner with information referred to in Article 13(3) of the Data Protection Convention, or
    (b)   to take appropriate measures to provide such information.

Assisting persons resident outside the UK with requests under Article 14 of the Convention

7.   (1)   This paragraph applies where a request for assistance in exercising any of the rights referred to in Article 8 of the Data Protection Convention in the United Kingdom is made by a person resident outside the United Kingdom, including where the request is forwarded to the Commissioner through the Secretary of State or a foreign designated authority.
    (2)   The Commissioner must take appropriate measures to assist the person to exercise those rights.

Assisting UK residents with requests under Article 8 of the Convention

8.   (1)   This paragraph applies where a request for assistance in exercising any of the rights referred to in Article 8 of the Data Protection Convention in a country or territory (other than the United Kingdom) specified in the request is—
    (a)   made by a person resident in the United Kingdom, and
    (b)   submitted through the Commissioner under Article 14(2) of the Convention.
    (2)   If the Commissioner is satisfied that the request contains all necessary particulars referred to in Article 14(3) of the Data Protection Convention, the Commissioner must send the request to the foreign designated authority in the specified country or territory.
    (3)   Otherwise, the Commissioner must, where practicable, notify the person making the request of the reasons why the Commissioner is not required to assist.

Restrictions on use of information

9.   Where the Commissioner receives information from a foreign designated authority as a result of—
    (a)   a request made by the Commissioner under paragraph 6(2), or
    (b)   a request received by the Commissioner under paragraph 6(1) or 7,
the Commissioner may use the information only for the purposes specified in the request.

Foreign designated authority

10.　In this Part of this Schedule, "foreign designated authority" means an authority designated for the purposes of Article 13 of the Data Protection Convention by a party, other than the United Kingdom, which is bound by that Data Protection Convention.

SCHEDULE 15
Powers of Entry and Inspection

Section 154

Issue of warrants in connection with non-compliance and offences

1.　(1)　This paragraph applies if a judge of the High Court, a circuit judge or a District Judge (Magistrates' Courts) is satisfied by information on oath supplied by the Commissioner that—
　　(a)　there are reasonable grounds for suspecting that—
　　　　(i)　a controller or processor has failed or is failing as described in section 149(2), or
　　　　(ii)　an offence under this Act has been or is being committed, and
　　(b)　there are reasonable grounds for suspecting that evidence of the failure or of the commission of the offence is to be found on premises specified in the information or is capable of being viewed using equipment on such premises.
　　(2)　The judge may grant a warrant to the Commissioner.

Issue of warrants in connection with assessment notices

2.　(1)　This paragraph applies if a judge of the High Court, a circuit judge or a District Judge (Magistrates' Courts) is satisfied by information on oath supplied by the Commissioner that a controller or processor has failed to comply with a requirement imposed by an assessment notice.
　　(2)　The judge may, for the purpose of enabling the Commissioner to determine whether the controller or processor has complied or is complying with the data protection legislation, grant a warrant to the Commissioner in relation to premises that were specified in the assessment notice.

Restrictions on issuing warrants: processing for the special purposes

3.　A judge must not issue a warrant under this Schedule in respect of personal data processed for the special purposes unless a determination under section 174 with respect to the data or the processing has taken effect.

Restrictions on issuing warrants: procedural requirements

4.　(1)　A judge must not issue a warrant under this Schedule unless satisfied that—
　　(a)　the conditions in sub-paragraphs (2) to (4) are met,
　　(b)　compliance with those conditions would defeat the object of entry to the premises in question, or
　　(c)　the Commissioner requires access to the premises in question urgently.
　　(2)　The first condition is that the Commissioner has given 7 days' notice in writing to the occupier of the premises in question demanding access to the premises.
　　(3)　The second condition is that—
　　(a)　access to the premises was demanded at a reasonable hour and was unreasonably refused, or
　　(b)　entry to the premises was granted but the occupier unreasonably refused to comply with a request by the Commissioner or the Commissioner's officers or staff to be allowed to do any of the things referred to in paragraph 5.
　　(4)　The third condition is that, since the refusal, the occupier of the premises—
　　(a)　has been notified by the Commissioner of the application for the warrant, and
　　(b)　has had an opportunity to be heard by the judge on the question of whether or not the warrant should be issued.
　　(5)　In determining whether the first condition is met, an assessment notice given to the occupier is to be disregarded.

Content of warrants

5.　(1)　A warrant issued under this Schedule must authorise the Commissioner or any of the Commissioner's officers or staff—
　　(a)　to enter the premises,
　　(b)　to search the premises, and
　　(c)　to inspect, examine, operate and test any equipment found on the premises which is used or intended to be used for the processing of personal data.
　　(2)　A warrant issued under paragraph 1 must authorise the Commissioner or any of the Commissioner's officers or staff—
　　(a)　to inspect and seize any documents or other material found on the premises which may be evidence of the failure or offence mentioned in that paragraph,
　　(b)　to require any person on the premises to provide, in an appropriate form, a copy of information capable of being viewed using equipment on the premises which may be evidence of that failure or offence,
　　(c)　to require any person on the premises to provide an explanation of any document or other material found on the premises and of any information capable of being viewed using equipment on the premises, and
　　(d)　to require any person on the premises to provide such other information as may reasonably be required for the purpose of determining whether the controller or processor has failed or is failing as described in section 149(2).
　　(3)　A warrant issued under paragraph 2 must authorise the Commissioner or any of the Commissioner's officers or staff—
　　(a)　to inspect and seize any documents or other material found on the premises which may enable the Commissioner to determine whether the controller or processor has complied or is complying with the data protection legislation,

(b)   to require any person on the premises to provide, in an appropriate form, a copy of information capable of being viewed using equipment on the premises which may enable the Commissioner to make such a determination,

(c)   to require any person on the premises to provide an explanation of any document or other material found on the premises and of any information capable of being viewed using equipment on the premises, and

(d)   to require any person on the premises to provide such other information as may reasonably be required for the purpose of determining whether the controller or processor has complied or is complying with the data protection legislation.

(4)   A warrant issued under this Schedule must authorise the Commissioner or any of the Commissioner's officers or staff to do the things described in sub-paragraphs (1) to (3) at any time in the period of 7 days beginning with the day on which the warrant is issued.

(5)   For the purposes of this paragraph, a copy of information is in an "appropriate form" if—

(a)   it can be taken away, and

(b)   it is visible and legible or it can readily be made visible and legible.

Copies of warrants

6.   A judge who issues a warrant under this Schedule must—

(a)   issue two copies of it, and

(b)   certify them clearly as copies.

Execution of warrants: reasonable force

7.   A person executing a warrant issued under this Schedule may use such reasonable force as may be necessary.

Execution of warrants: time when executed

8.   A warrant issued under this Schedule may be executed only at a reasonable hour, unless it appears to the person executing it that there are grounds for suspecting that exercising it at a reasonable hour would defeat the object of the warrant.

Execution of warrants: occupier of premises

9.   (1)   If an occupier of the premises in respect of which a warrant is issued under this Schedule is present when the warrant is executed, the person executing the warrant must—

(a)   show the occupier the warrant, and

(b)   give the occupier a copy of it.

(2)   Otherwise, a copy of the warrant must be left in a prominent place on the premises.

Execution of warrants: seizure of documents etc

10.   (1)   This paragraph applies where a person executing a warrant under this Schedule seizes something.

(2)   The person must, on request—

(a)   give a receipt for it, and

(b)   give an occupier of the premises a copy of it.

(3)   Sub-paragraph (2)(b) does not apply if the person executing the warrant considers that providing a copy would result in undue delay.

(4)   Anything seized may be retained for so long as is necessary in all the circumstances.

Matters exempt from inspection and seizure: privileged communications

11.   (1)   The powers of inspection and seizure conferred by a warrant issued under this Schedule are not exercisable in respect of a communication which is made—

(a)   between a professional legal adviser and the adviser's client, and

(b)   in connection with the giving of legal advice to the client with respect to obligations, liabilities or rights under the data protection legislation.

(2)   The powers of inspection and seizure conferred by a warrant issued under this Schedule are not exercisable in respect of a communication which is made—

(a)   between a professional legal adviser and the adviser's client or between such an adviser or client and another person,

(b)   in connection with or in contemplation of proceedings under or arising out of the data protection legislation, and

(c)   for the purposes of such proceedings.

(3)   Sub-paragraphs (1) and (2) do not prevent the exercise of powers conferred by a warrant issued under this Schedule in respect of—

(a)   anything in the possession of a person other than the professional legal adviser or the adviser's client, or

(b)   anything held with the intention of furthering a criminal purpose.

(4)   The references to a communication in sub-paragraphs (1) and (2) include—

(a)   a copy or other record of the communication, and

(b)   anything enclosed with or referred to in the communication if made as described in sub-paragraph (1)(b) or in sub-paragraph (2)(b) and (c).

(5)   In sub-paragraphs (1) to (3), the references to the client of a professional legal adviser include a person acting on behalf of such a client.

Matters exempt from inspection and seizure: Parliamentary privilege

12.   The powers of inspection and seizure conferred by a warrant issued under this Schedule are not exercisable where their exercise would involve an infringement of the privileges of either House of Parliament.

Partially exempt material

13.   (1)   This paragraph applies if a person in occupation of premises in respect of which a warrant is issued under this Schedule objects to the inspection or seizure of any material under the warrant on the grounds that it consists partly of matters in respect of which those powers are not exercisable.

(2)   The person must, if the person executing the warrant so requests, provide that person with a copy of so much of the material as is not exempt from those powers.

Return of warrants

14. (1)   Where a warrant issued under this Schedule is executed—
- (a)   it must be returned to the court from which it was issued after being executed, and
- (b)   the person by whom it is executed must write on the warrant a statement of the powers that have been exercised under the warrant.

(2)   Where a warrant issued under this Schedule is not executed, it must be returned to the court from which it was issued within the time authorised for its execution.

Offences

15. (1)   It is an offence for a person—
- (a)   intentionally to obstruct a person in the execution of a warrant issued under this Schedule, or
- (b)   to fail without reasonable excuse to give a person executing such a warrant such assistance as the person may reasonably require for the execution of the warrant.

(2)   It is an offence for a person—
- (a)   to make a statement in response to a requirement under paragraph 5(2)(c) or (d) or (3)(c) or (d) which the person knows to be false in a material respect, or
- (b)   recklessly to make a statement in response to such a requirement which is false in a material respect.

Self-incrimination

16. (1)   An explanation given, or information provided, by a person in response to a requirement under paragraph 5(2)(c) or (d) or (3)(c) or (d) may only be used in evidence against that person—
- (a)   on a prosecution for an offence under a provision listed in sub-paragraph (2), or
- (b)   on a prosecution for any other offence where—
  - (i)   in giving evidence that person makes a statement inconsistent with that explanation or information, and
  - (ii)   evidence relating to that explanation or information is adduced, or a question relating to it is asked, by that person or on that person's behalf.

(2)   Those provisions are—
- (a)   paragraph 15,
- (b)   section 5 of the Perjury Act 1911 (false statements made otherwise than on oath),
- (c)   section 44(2) of the Criminal Law (Consolidation) (Scotland) Act 1995 (false statements made otherwise than on oath), or
- (d)   Article 10 of the Perjury (Northern Ireland) Order 1979 (SI 1979/1714 (NI 19)) (false statutory declarations and other false unsworn statements).

Vessels, vehicles etc

17. In this Schedule—
- (a)   "premises" includes a vehicle, vessel or other means of transport, and
- (b)   references to the occupier of premises include the person in charge of a vehicle, vessel or other means of transport.

SCHEDULE 16
Penalties

Text of Schedule is not reproduced.

SCHEDULE 17
Review of Processing of Personal Data for the Purposes of Journalism

Text of Schedule is not reproduced.

SCHEDULE 18
Relevant Records

Section 184

Relevant records

1. (1)   In section 184, "relevant record" means—
- (a)   a relevant health record (see paragraph 2),
- (b)   a relevant record relating to a conviction or caution (see paragraph 3), or
- (c)   a relevant record relating to statutory functions (see paragraph 4).

(2)   A record is not a "relevant record" to the extent that it relates, or is to relate, only to personal data which falls within section 21(2) (manual unstructured personal data held by FOI public authorities).

Relevant health records

2. "Relevant health record" means a health record which has been or is to be obtained by a data subject in the exercise of a data subject access right.

Relevant records relating to a conviction or caution

3. (1)   "Relevant record relating to a conviction or caution" means a record which—
- (a)   has been or is to be obtained by a data subject in the exercise of a data subject access right from a person listed in sub-paragraph (2), and
- (b)   contains information relating to a conviction or caution.

(2)   Those persons are—
- (a)   the chief constable of a police force maintained under section 2 of the Police Act 1996;

    (b)   the Commissioner of Police of the Metropolis;
    (c)   the Commissioner of Police for the City of London;
    (d)   the Chief Constable of the Police Service of Northern Ireland;
    (e)   the chief constable of the Police Service of Scotland;
    (f)   the Director General of the National Crime Agency;
    (g)   the Secretary of State.

    (3)   In this paragraph—

"caution" means a caution given to a person in England and Wales or Northern Ireland in respect of an offence which, at the time when the caution is given, is admitted;

"conviction" has the same meaning as in the Rehabilitation of Offenders Act 1974 or the Rehabilitation of Offenders (Northern Ireland) Order 1978 (SI 1978/1908 (NI 27)).

Relevant records relating to statutory functions

4.   (1)   "Relevant record relating to statutory functions" means a record which—
    (a)   has been or is to be obtained by a data subject in the exercise of a data subject access right from a person listed in sub-paragraph (2), and
    (b)   contains information relating to a relevant function in relation to that person.

    (2)   Those persons are—
    (a)   the Secretary of State;
    (b)   the Department for Communities in Northern Ireland;
    (c)   the Department of Justice in Northern Ireland;
    (d)   the Scottish Ministers;
    (e)   the Disclosure and Barring Service.

    (3)   In relation to the Secretary of State, the "relevant functions" are—
    (a)   the Secretary of State's functions in relation to a person sentenced to detention under—
        (i)   section 92 of the Powers of Criminal Courts (Sentencing) Act 2000,
        (ii)   section 205(2) or 208 of the Criminal Procedure (Scotland) Act 1995, or
        (iii)   Article 45 of the Criminal Justice (Children) (Northern Ireland) Order 1998 (SI 1998/1504 (NI 9));
    (b)   the Secretary of State's functions in relation to a person imprisoned or detained under—
        (i)   the Prison Act 1952,
        (ii)   the Prisons (Scotland) Act 1989, or
        (iii)   the Prison Act (Northern Ireland) 1953 (c 18 (NI));
    (c)   the Secretary of State's functions under—
        (i)   the Social Security Contributions and Benefits Act 1992,
        (ii)   the Social Security Administration Act 1992,
        (iii)   the Jobseekers Act 1995,
        (iv)   Part 5 of the Police Act 1997,
        (v)   Part 1 of the Welfare Reform Act 2007, or
        (vi)   Part 1 of the Welfare Reform Act 2012.

    (4)   In relation to the Department for Communities in Northern Ireland, the "relevant functions" are its functions under—
    (a)   the Social Security Contributions and Benefits (Northern Ireland) Act 1992,
    (b)   the Social Security Administration (Northern Ireland) Act 1992,
    (c)   the Jobseekers (Northern Ireland) Order 1995 (SI 1995/2705 (NI 15)), or
    (d)   Part 1 of the Welfare Reform Act (Northern Ireland) 2007 (c 2 (NI)).

    (5)   In relation to the Department of Justice in Northern Ireland, the "relevant functions" are its functions under Part 5 of the Police Act 1997.

    (6)   In relation to the Scottish Ministers, the "relevant functions" are their functions under
    (a)   Part 5 of the Police Act 1997, or
    (b)   Parts 1 and 2 of the Protection of Vulnerable Groups (Scotland) Act 2007 (asp 14).

    (7)   In relation to the Disclosure and Barring Service, the "relevant functions" are its functions under—
    (a)   Part 5 of the Police Act 1997,
    (b)   the Safeguarding Vulnerable Groups Act 2006, or
    (c)   the Safeguarding Vulnerable Groups (Northern Ireland) Order 2007 (SI 2007/1351 (NI 11)).

Data subject access right

5.   In this Schedule, "data subject access right" means a right under—
    (a)   Article 15 of the GDPR (right of access by the data subject);
    (b)   Article 20 of the GDPR (right to data portability);
    (c)   section 45 of this Act (law enforcement processing: right of access by the data subject);
    (d)   section 94 of this Act (intelligence services processing: right of access by the data subject).

Records stating that personal data is not processed

6.   For the purposes of this Schedule, a record which states that a controller is not processing personal data relating to a particular matter is to be taken to be a record containing information relating to that matter.

Power to amend

7.   (1)   The Secretary of State may by regulations amend this Schedule.
    (2)   Regulations under this paragraph are subject to the affirmative resolution procedure.

SCHEDULE 19
Minor and Consequential Amendments[1]

Text of Schedule is not reproduced.

---

[1] Repeals and amendments affecting provisions reproduced in this work have been taken in.

Section 211

SCHEDULE 20
Transitional Provision etc

Section 213

Part 1
General
Interpretation

1. (1)   In this Schedule—
"the 1984 Act" means the Data Protection Act 1984;
"the 1998 Act" means the Data Protection Act 1998;
"the 2014 Regulations" means the Criminal Justice and Data Protection (Protocol No 36) Regulations 2014 (SI 2014/3141);
"data controller" has the same meaning as in the 1998 Act (see section 1 of that Act);
"the old data protection principles" means the principles set out in—
     (a)   Part 1 of Schedule 1 to the 1998 Act, and
     (b)   regulation 30 of the 2014 Regulations.
(2)   A provision of the 1998 Act that has effect by virtue of this Schedule is not, by virtue of that, part of the data protection legislation (as defined in section 3).

Part 2
Rights of Data Subjects
Right of access to personal data under the 1998 Act

2. (1)   The repeal of sections 7 to 9A of the 1998 Act (right of access to personal data) does not affect the application of those sections after the relevant time in a case in which a data controller received a request under section 7 of that Act (right of access to personal data) before the relevant time.
(2)   The repeal of sections 7 and 8 of the 1998 Act and the revocation of regulation 44 of the 2014 Regulations (which applies those sections with modifications) do not affect the application of those sections and that regulation after the relevant time in a case in which a UK competent authority received a request under section 7 of the 1998 Act (as applied by that regulation) before the relevant time.
(3)   The revocation of the relevant regulations, or their amendment by Schedule 19 to this Act, and the repeals and revocation mentioned in sub-paragraphs (1) and (2), do not affect the application of the relevant regulations after the relevant time in a case described in those sub-paragraphs.
(4)   In this paragraph—
"the relevant regulations" means—
     (a)   the Data Protection (Subject Access) (Fees and Miscellaneous Provisions) Regulations 2000 (SI 2000/191);
     (b)   regulation 4 of, and Schedule 1 to, the Consumer Credit (Credit Reference Agency) Regulations 2000 (SI 2000/290);
     (c)   regulation 3 of the Freedom of Information and Data Protection (Appropriate Limit and Fees) Regulations 2004 (SI 2004/3244);
"the relevant time" means the time when the repeal of section 7 of the 1998 Act comes into force;
"UK competent authority" has the same meaning as in Part 4 of the 2014 Regulations (see regulation 27 of those Regulations).

Right to prevent processing likely to cause damage or distress under the 1998 Act

3. (1)   The repeal of section 10 of the 1998 Act (right to prevent processing likely to cause damage or distress) does not affect the application of that section after the relevant time in a case in which an individual gave notice in writing to a data controller under that section before the relevant time.
(2)   In this paragraph, "the relevant time" means the time when the repeal of section 10 of the 1998 Act comes into force.

Right to prevent processing for purposes of direct marketing under the 1998 Act

4. (1)   The repeal of section 11 of the 1998 Act (right to prevent processing for purposes of direct marketing) does not affect the application of that section after the relevant time in a case in which an individual gave notice in writing to a data controller under that section before the relevant time.
(2)   In this paragraph, "the relevant time" means the time when the repeal of section 11 of the 1998 Act comes into force.

Automated processing under the 1998 Act

5. (1)   The repeal of section 12 of the 1998 Act (rights in relation to automated decision-taking) does not affect the application of that section after the relevant time in relation to a decision taken by a person before that time if—
     (a)   in taking the decision the person failed to comply with section 12(1) of the 1998 Act, or
     (b)   at the relevant time—
          (i)   the person had not taken all of the steps required under section 12(2) or (3) of the 1998 Act, or
          (ii)   the period specified in section 12(2)(b) of the 1998 Act (for an individual to require a person to reconsider a decision) had not expired.
(2)   In this paragraph, "the relevant time" means the time when the repeal of section 12 of the 1998 Act comes into force.

Compensation for contravention of the 1998 Act or Part 4 of the 2014 Regulations

6. (1)   The repeal of section 13 of the 1998 Act (compensation for failure to comply with certain requirements) does not affect the application of that section after the relevant time in relation to damage or distress suffered at any time by reason of an act or omission before the relevant time.
(2)   The revocation of regulation 45 of the 2014 Regulations (right to compensation) does not affect the application of that regulation after the relevant time in relation to damage or distress suffered at any time by

reason of an act or omission before the relevant time.

(3) "The relevant time" means—

    (a)   in sub-paragraph (1), the time when the repeal of section 13 of the 1998 Act comes into force;

    (b)   in sub-paragraph (2), the time when the revocation of regulation 45 of the 2014 Regulation comes into force.

Rectification, blocking, erasure and destruction under the 1998 Act

7. (1)   The repeal of section 14(1) to (3) and (6) of the 1998 Act (rectification, blocking, erasure and destruction of inaccurate personal data) does not affect the application of those provisions after the relevant time in a case in which an application was made under subsection (1) of that section before the relevant time.

(2)   The repeal of section 14(4) to (6) of the 1998 Act (rectification, blocking, erasure and destruction: risk of further contravention in circumstances entitling data subject to compensation under section 13 of the 1998 Act) does not affect the application of those provisions after the relevant time in a case in which an application was made under subsection (4) of that section before the relevant time.

(3)   In this paragraph, "the relevant time" means the time when the repeal of section 14 of the 1998 Act comes into force.

Jurisdiction and procedure under the 1998 Act

8.   The repeal of section 15 of the 1998 Act (jurisdiction and procedure) does not affect the application of that section in connection with sections 7 to 14 of the 1998 Act as they have effect by virtue of this Schedule.

Exemptions under the 1998 Act

9. (1)   The repeal of Part 4 of the 1998 Act (exemptions) does not affect the application of that Part after the relevant time in connection with a provision of Part 2 of the 1998 Act as it has effect after that time by virtue of paragraphs 2 to 7 of this Schedule.

(2)   The revocation of the relevant Orders, and the repeal mentioned in sub-paragraph (1), do not affect the application of the relevant Orders after the relevant time in connection with a provision of Part 2 of the 1998 Act as it has effect as described in sub-paragraph (1).

(3)   In this paragraph—

"the relevant Orders" means—

    (a)   the Data Protection (Corporate Finance Exemption) Order 2000 (SI 2000/184);

    (b)   the Data Protection (Subject Access Modification) (Health) Order 2000 (SI 2000/413);

    (c)   the Data Protection (Subject Access Modification) (Education) Order 2000 (SI 2000/414);

    (d)   the Data Protection (Subject Access Modification) (Social Work) Order 2000 (SI 2000/415);

    (e)   the Data Protection (Crown Appointments) Order 2000 (SI 2000/416);

    (f)   Data Protection (Miscellaneous Subject Access Exemptions) Order 2000 (SI 2000/419);

    (g)   Data Protection (Designated Codes of Practice) (No 2) Order 2000 (SI 2000/1864);

"the relevant time" means the time when the repeal of the provision of Part 2 of the 1998 Act in question comes into force.

(4)   As regards certificates issued under section 28(2) of the 1998 Act, see Part 5 of this Schedule.

Prohibition by this Act of requirement to produce relevant records

10. (1)   In Schedule 18 to this Act, references to a record obtained in the exercise of a data subject access right include a record obtained at any time in the exercise of a right under section 7 of the 1998 Act.

(2)   In section 184 of this Act, references to a "relevant record" include a record which does not fall within the definition in Schedule 18 to this Act (read with sub-paragraph (1)) but which, immediately before the relevant time, was a "relevant record" for the purposes of section 56 of the 1998 Act.

(3)   In this paragraph, "the relevant time" means the time when the repeal of section 56 of the 1998 Act comes into force.

Avoidance under this Act of certain contractual terms relating to health records

11.   In section 185 of this Act, references to a record obtained in the exercise of a data subject access right include a record obtained at any time in the exercise of a right under section 7 of the 1998 Act.

Part 3
The GDPR and Part 2 of this Act
Exemptions from the GDPR: restrictions of rules in Articles 13 to 15 of the GDPR

12.   In paragraph 20(2) of Schedule 2 to this Act (self-incrimination), the reference to an offence under this Act includes an offence under the 1998 Act or the 1984 Act.

Manual unstructured data held by FOI public authorities

13.   Until the first regulations under section 24(8) of this Act come into force, "the appropriate maximum" for the purposes of that section is—

    (a)   where the controller is a public authority listed in Part 1 of Schedule 1 to the Freedom of Information Act 2000, £600, and

    (b)   otherwise, £450.

Part 4
Law Enforcement and Intelligence Services Processing
Logging

14. (1)   In relation to an automated processing system set up before 6 May 2016, subsections (1) to (3) of section 62 of this Act do not apply if and to the extent that compliance with them would involve disproportionate effort.

(2)   Sub-paragraph (1) ceases to have effect at the beginning of 6 May 2023.

Regulation 50 of the 2014 Regulations (disapplication of the 1998 Act)

15. Nothing in this Schedule, read with the revocation of regulation 50 of the 2014 Regulations, has the effect of applying a provision of the 1998 Act to the processing of personal data to which Part 4 of the 2014 Regulations applies in a case in which that provision did not apply before the revocation of that regulation.

Maximum fee for data subject access requests to intelligence services

16. Until the first regulations under section 94(4)(b) of this Act come into force, the maximum amount of a fee that may be required by a controller under that section is £10.

Part 5
National Security Certificates
National security certificates: processing of personal data under the 1998 Act

17. (1) The repeal of section 28(2) to (12) of the 1998 Act does not affect the application of those provisions after the relevant time with respect to the processing of personal data to which the 1998 Act (including as it has effect by virtue of this Schedule) applies.

(2) A certificate issued under section 28(2) of the 1998 Act continues to have effect after the relevant time with respect to the processing of personal data to which the 1998 Act (including as it has effect by virtue of this Schedule) applies.

(3) Where a certificate continues to have effect under sub-paragraph (2) after the relevant time, it may be revoked or quashed in accordance with section 28 of the 1998 Act after the relevant time.

(4) In this paragraph, "the relevant time" means the time when the repeal of section 28 of the 1998 Act comes into force.

National security certificates: processing of personal data under the 2018 Act

18. (1) This paragraph applies to a certificate issued under section 28(2) of the 1998 Act (an "old certificate") which has effect immediately before the relevant time.

(2) If and to the extent that the old certificate provides protection with respect to personal data which corresponds to protection that could be provided by a certificate issued under section 27, 79 or 111 of this Act, the old certificate also has effect to that extent after the relevant time as if—
    (a) it were a certificate issued under one or more of sections 27, 79 and 111 (as the case may be),
    (b) it provided protection in respect of that personal data in relation to the corresponding provisions of this Act or the applied GDPR, and
    (c) where it has effect as a certificate issued under section 79, it certified that each restriction in question is a necessary and proportionate measure to protect national security.

(3) Where an old certificate also has effect as if it were a certificate issued under one or more of sections 27, 79 and 111, that section has, or those sections have, effect accordingly in relation to the certificate.

(4) Where an old certificate has an extended effect because of sub-paragraph (2), section 130 of this Act does not apply in relation to it.

(5) An old certificate that has an extended effect because of sub-paragraph (2) provides protection only with respect to the processing of personal data that occurs during the period of 1 year beginning with the relevant time (and a Minister of the Crown may curtail that protection by wholly or partly revoking the old certificate).

(6) For the purposes of this paragraph—
    (a) a reference to the protection provided by a certificate issued under—
        (i) section 28(2) of the 1998 Act, or
        (ii) section 27, 79 or 111 of this Act,
    is a reference to the effect of the evidence that is provided by the certificate;
    (b) protection provided by a certificate under section 28(2) of the 1998 Act is to be regarded as corresponding to protection that could be provided by a certificate under section 27, 79 or 111 of this Act where, in respect of provision in the 1998 Act to which the certificate under section 28(2) relates, there is corresponding provision in this Act or the applied GDPR to which a certificate under section 27, 79 or 111 could relate.

(7) In this paragraph, "the relevant time" means the time when the repeal of section 28 of the 1998 Act comes into force.

Part 6
The Information Commissioner
Appointment etc

19. (1) On and after the relevant day, the individual who was the Commissioner immediately before that day—
    (a) continues to be the Commissioner,
    (b) is to be treated as having been appointed under Schedule 12 to this Act, and
    (c) holds office for the period—
        (i) beginning with the relevant day, and
        (ii) lasting for 7 years less a period equal to the individual's pre-commencement term.

(2) On and after the relevant day, a resolution passed by the House of Commons for the purposes of paragraph 3 of Schedule 5 to the 1998 Act (salary and pension of Commissioner), and not superseded before that day, is to be treated as having been passed for the purposes of paragraph 4 of Schedule 12 to this Act.

(3) In this paragraph—
"pre-commencement term", in relation to an individual, means the period during which the individual was the Commissioner before the relevant day;
"the relevant day" means the day on which Schedule 12 to this Act comes into force.

Accounts

20. (1) The repeal of paragraph 10 of Schedule 5 to the 1998 Act does not affect the duties of the Commissioner and the Comptroller and Auditor General under that paragraph in respect of the Commissioner's statement of account for the financial year beginning with 1 April 2017.

(2) The Commissioner's duty under paragraph 11 of Schedule 12 to this Act to prepare a statement of account for each financial year includes a duty to do so for the financial year beginning with 1 April 2018.

Annual report

21. (1)   The repeal of section 52(1) of the 1998 Act (annual report) does not affect the Commissioner's duty under that subsection to produce a general report on the exercise of the Commissioner's functions under the 1998 Act during the period of 1 year beginning with 1 April 2017 and to lay it before Parliament.

(2)   The repeal of section 49 of the Freedom of Information Act 2000 (annual report) does not affect the Commissioner's duty under that section to produce a general report on the exercise of the Commissioner's functions under that Act during the period of 1 year beginning with 1 April 2017 and to lay it before Parliament.

(3)   The first report produced by the Commissioner under section 139 of this Act must relate to the period of 1 year beginning with 1 April 2018.

Fees etc received by the Commissioner

22. (1)   The repeal of Schedule 5 to the 1998 Act (Information Commissioner) does not affect the application of paragraph 9 of that Schedule after the relevant time to amounts received by the Commissioner before the relevant time.

(2)   In this paragraph, "the relevant time" means the time when the repeal of Schedule 5 to the 1998 Act comes into force.

23.   Paragraph 10 of Schedule 12 to this Act applies only to amounts received by the Commissioner after the time when that Schedule comes into force.

Functions in connection with the Data Protection Convention

24. (1)   The repeal of section 54(2) of the 1998 Act (functions to be discharged by the Commissioner for the purposes of Article 13 of the Data Protection Convention), and the revocation of the Data Protection (Functions of Designated Authority) Order 2000 (SI 2000/186), do not affect the application of articles 1 to 5 of that Order after the relevant time in relation to a request described in those articles which was made before that time.

(2)   The references in paragraph 9 of Schedule 14 to this Act (Data Protection Convention: restrictions on use of information) to requests made or received by the Commissioner under paragraph 6 or 7 of that Schedule include a request made or received by the Commissioner under article 3 or 4 of the Data Protection (Functions of Designated Authority) Order 2000 (SI 2000/186).

(3)   The repeal of section 54(7) of the 1998 Act (duty to notify the European Commission of certain approvals and authorisations) does not affect the application of that provision after the relevant time in relation to an approval or authorisation granted before the relevant time.

(4)   In this paragraph, "the relevant time" means the time when the repeal of section 54 of the 1998 Act comes into force.

Co-operation with the European Commission: transfers of personal data outside the EEA

25. (1)   The repeal of section 54(3) of the 1998 Act (co-operation by the Commissioner with the European Commission etc), and the revocation of the Data Protection (International Co-operation) Order 2000 (SI 2000/190), do not affect the application of articles 1 to 4 of that Order after the relevant time in relation to transfers that took place before the relevant time.

(2)   In this paragraph—
"the relevant time" means the time when the repeal of section 54 of the 1998 Act comes into force;
"transfer" has the meaning given in article 2 of the Data Protection (International Co-operation) Order 2000 (SI 2000/190).

Charges payable to the Commissioner by controllers

26. (1)   The Data Protection (Charges and Information) Regulations 2018 (SI 2018/480) have effect after the relevant time (until revoked) as if they were made under section 137 of this Act.

(2)   In this paragraph, "the relevant time" means the time when section 137 of this Act comes into force.

Requests for assessment

27. (1)   The repeal of section 42 of the 1998 Act (requests for assessment) does not affect the application of that section after the relevant time in a case in which the Commissioner received a request under that section before the relevant time, subject to sub-paragraph (2).

(2)   The Commissioner is only required to make an assessment of acts and omissions that took place before the relevant time.

(3)   In this paragraph, "the relevant time" means the time when the repeal of section 42 of the 1998 Act comes into force.

Codes of practice

28. (1)   The repeal of section 52E of the 1998 Act (effect of codes of practice) does not affect the application of that section after the relevant time in relation to legal proceedings or to the exercise of the Commissioner's functions under the 1998 Act as it has effect by virtue of this Schedule.

(2)   In section 52E of the 1998 Act, as it has effect by virtue of this paragraph, the references to the 1998 Act include that Act as it has effect by virtue of this Schedule.

(3)   For the purposes of subsection (3) of that section, as it has effect by virtue of this paragraph, the data-sharing code and direct marketing code in force immediately before the relevant time are to be treated as having continued in force after that time.

(4)   In this paragraph—
"the data-sharing code" and "the direct marketing code" mean the codes respectively prepared under sections 52A and 52AA of the 1998 Act and issued under section 52B(5) of that Act;
"the relevant time" means the time when the repeal of section 52E of the 1998 Act comes into force.

PART 7

ENFORCEMENT ETC UNDER THE 1998 ACT

Interpretation of this Part

29. (1) In this Part of this Schedule, references to contravention of the sixth data protection principle sections are to relevant contravention of any of sections 7, 10, 11 or 12 of the 1998 Act, as they continue to have effect by virtue of this Schedule after their repeal (and references to compliance with the sixth data protection principle sections are to be read accordingly).

(2) In sub-paragraph (1), "relevant contravention" means contravention in a manner described in paragraph 8 of Part 2 of Schedule 1 to the 1998 Act (sixth data protection principle).

Information notices

30. (1) The repeal of section 43 of the 1998 Act (information notices) does not affect the application of that section after the relevant time in a case in which—

    (a) the Commissioner served a notice under that section before the relevant time (and did not cancel it before that time), or

    (b) the Commissioner requires information after the relevant time for the purposes of—

        (i) responding to a request made under section 42 of the 1998 Act before that time,

        (ii) determining whether a data controller complied with the old data protection principles before that time, or

        (iii) determining whether a data controller complied with the sixth data protection principle sections after that time.

(2) In section 43 of the 1998 Act, as it has effect by virtue of this paragraph—

    (a) the reference to an offence under section 47 of the 1998 Act includes an offence under section 144 of this Act, and

    (b) the references to an offence under the 1998 Act include an offence under this Act.

(3) In this paragraph, "the relevant time" means the time when the repeal of section 43 of the 1998 Act comes into force.

Special information notices

31. (1) The repeal of section 44 of the 1998 Act (special information notices) does not affect the application of that section after the relevant time in a case in which—

    (a) the Commissioner served a notice under that section before the relevant time (and did not cancel it before that time), or

    (b) the Commissioner requires information after the relevant time for the purposes of—

        (i) responding to a request made under section 42 of the 1998 Act before that time, or

        (ii) ascertaining whether section 44(2)(a) or (b) of the 1998 Act was satisfied before that time.

(2) In section 44 of the 1998 Act, as it has effect by virtue of this paragraph—

    (a) the reference to an offence under section 47 of the 1998 Act includes an offence under section 144 of this Act, and

    (b) the references to an offence under the 1998 Act include an offence under this Act.

(3) In this paragraph, "the relevant time" means the time when the repeal of section 44 of the 1998 Act comes into force.

Assessment notices

32. (1) The repeal of sections 41A and 41B of the 1998 Act (assessment notices) does not affect the application of those sections after the relevant time in a case in which—

    (a) the Commissioner served a notice under section 41A of the 1998 Act before the relevant time (and did not cancel it before that time), or

    (b) the Commissioner considers it appropriate, after the relevant time, to investigate—

        (i) whether a data controller complied with the old data protection principles before that time, or

        (ii) whether a data controller complied with the sixth data protection principle sections after that time.

(2) The revocation of the Data Protection (Assessment Notices) (Designation of National Health Service Bodies) Order 2014 (SI 2014/3282), and the repeals mentioned in sub-paragraph (1), do not affect the application of that Order in a case described in sub-paragraph (1).

(3) Sub-paragraph (1) does not enable the Secretary of State, after the relevant time, to make an order under section 41A(2)(b) or (c) of the 1998 Act (data controllers on whom an assessment notice may be served) designating a public authority or person for the purposes of that section.

(4) Section 41A of the 1998 Act, as it has effect by virtue of sub-paragraph (1), has effect as if subsections (8) and (11) (duty to review designation orders) were omitted.

(5) The repeal of section 41C of the 1998 Act (code of practice about assessment notice) does not affect the application, after the relevant time, of the code issued under that section and in force immediately before the relevant time in relation to the exercise of the Commissioner's functions under and in connection with section 41A of the 1998 Act, as it has effect by virtue of sub-paragraph (1).

(6) In this paragraph, "the relevant time" means the time when the repeal of section 41A of the 1998 Act comes into force.

Enforcement notices

33. (1) The repeal of sections 40 and 41 of the 1998 Act (enforcement notices) does not affect the application of those sections after the relevant time in a case in which—

    (a) the Commissioner served a notice under section 40 of the 1998 Act before the relevant time (and did not cancel it before that time), or

    (b) the Commissioner is satisfied, after that time, that a data controller—

        (i) contravened the old data protection principles before that time, or

        (ii) contravened the sixth data protection principle sections after that time.

(2) In this paragraph, "the relevant time" means the time when the repeal of section 40 of the 1998 Act comes into force.

34. (1) The repeal of section 45 of the 1998 Act (determination by Commissioner as to the special purposes) does not affect the application of that section after the relevant time in a case in which—

(a)   the Commissioner made a determination under that section before the relevant time, or

(b)   the Commissioner considers it appropriate, after the relevant time, to make a determination under that section.

(2)   In this paragraph, "the relevant time" means the time when the repeal of section 45 of the 1998 Act comes into force.

Restriction on enforcement in case of processing for the special purposes

35. (1) The repeal of section 46 of the 1998 Act (restriction on enforcement in case of processing for the special purposes) does not affect the application of that section after the relevant time in relation to an enforcement notice or information notice served under the 1998 Act—

(a)   before the relevant time, or

(b)   after the relevant time in reliance on this Schedule.

(2)   In this paragraph, "the relevant time" means the time when the repeal of section 46 of the 1998 Act comes into force.

Offences

36. (1) The repeal of sections 47, 60 and 61 of the 1998 Act (offences of failing to comply with certain notices and of providing false information etc in response to a notice) does not affect the application of those sections after the relevant time in connection with an information notice, special information notice or enforcement notice served under Part 5 of the 1998 Act—

(a)   before the relevant time, or

(b)   after that time in reliance on this Schedule.

(2)   In this paragraph, "the relevant time" means the time when the repeal of section 47 of the 1998 Act comes into force.

Powers of entry

37. (1) The repeal of sections 50, 60 and 61 of, and Schedule 9 to, the 1998 Act (powers of entry) does not affect the application of those provisions after the relevant time in a case in which—

(a)   a warrant issued under that Schedule was in force immediately before the relevant time,

(b)   before the relevant time, the Commissioner supplied information on oath for the purposes of obtaining a warrant under that Schedule but that had not been considered by a circuit judge or a District Judge (Magistrates' Courts), or

(c)   after the relevant time, the Commissioner supplies information on oath to a circuit judge or a District Judge (Magistrates' Courts) in respect of—

(i)   a contravention of the old data protection principles before the relevant time;

(ii)   a contravention of the sixth data protection principle sections after the relevant time;

(iii)   the commission of an offence under a provision of the 1998 Act (including as the provision has effect by virtue of this Schedule);

(iv)   a failure to comply with a requirement imposed by an assessment notice issued under section 41A the 1998 Act (including as it has effect by virtue of this Schedule).

(2)   In paragraph 16 of Schedule 9 to the 1998 Act, as it has effect by virtue of this paragraph, the reference to an offence under paragraph 12 of that Schedule includes an offence under paragraph 15 of Schedule 15 to this Act.

(3)   In this paragraph, "the relevant time" means the time when the repeal of Schedule 9 to the 1998 Act comes into force.

(4)   Paragraphs 14 and 15 of Schedule 9 to the 1998 Act (application of that Schedule to Scotland and Northern Ireland) apply for the purposes of this paragraph as they apply for the purposes of that Schedule.

Monetary penalties

38. (1) The repeal of sections 55A, 55B, 55D and 55E of the 1998 Act (monetary penalties) does not affect the application of those provisions after the relevant time in a case in which—

(a)   the Commissioner served a monetary penalty notice under section 55A of the 1998 Act before the relevant time,

(b)   the Commissioner served a notice of intent under section 55B of the 1998 Act before the relevant time, or

(c)   the Commissioner considers it appropriate, after the relevant time, to serve a notice mentioned in paragraph (a) or (b) in respect of—

(i)   a contravention of section 4(4) of the 1998 Act before the relevant time, or

(ii)   a contravention of the sixth data protection principle sections after the relevant time.

(2)   The revocation of the relevant subordinate legislation, and the repeals mentioned in sub-paragraph (1), do not affect the application of the relevant subordinate legislation (or of provisions of the 1998 Act applied by them) after the relevant time in a case described in sub-paragraph (1).

(3)   Guidance issued under section 55C of the 1998 Act (guidance about monetary penalty notices) which is in force immediately before the relevant time continues in force after that time for the purposes of the Commissioner's exercise of functions under sections 55A and 55B of the 1998 Act as they have effect by virtue of this paragraph.

(4)   In this paragraph—

"the relevant subordinate legislation" means—

(a)   the Data Protection (Monetary Penalties) (Maximum Penalty and Notices) Regulations 2010 (SI 2010/31);

(b)   the Data Protection (Monetary Penalties) Order 2010 (SI 2010/910);

"the relevant time" means the time when the repeal of section 55A of the 1998 Act comes into force.

Appeals

39. (1)   The repeal of sections 48 and 49 of the 1998 Act (appeals) does not affect the application of those sections after the relevant time in relation to a notice served under the 1998 Act or a determination made under section 45 of that Act—

(a)   before the relevant time, or

(b)   after that time in reliance on this Schedule.

(2)   In this paragraph, "the relevant time" means the time when the repeal of section 48 of the 1998 Act comes into force.

Exemptions

40. (1)   The repeal of section 28 of the 1998 Act (national security) does not affect the application of that section after the relevant time for the purposes of a provision of Part 5 of the 1998 Act as it has effect after that time by virtue of the preceding paragraphs of this Part of this Schedule.

(2)   In this paragraph, "the relevant time" means the time when the repeal of the provision of Part 5 of the 1998 Act in question comes into force.

(3)   As regards certificates issued under section 28(2) of the 1998 Act, see Part 5 of this Schedule.

Tribunal Procedure Rules

41. (1)   The repeal of paragraph 7 of Schedule 6 to the 1998 Act (Tribunal Procedure Rules) does not affect the application of that paragraph, or of rules made under that paragraph, after the relevant time in relation to the exercise of rights of appeal conferred by section 28 or 48 of the 1998 Act, as they have effect by virtue of this Schedule.

(2)   Part 3 of Schedule 19 to this Act does not apply for the purposes of Tribunal Procedure Rules made under paragraph 7(1)(a) of Schedule 6 to the 1998 Act as they apply, after the relevant time, in relation to the exercise of rights of appeal described in sub-paragraph (1).

(3)   In this paragraph, "the relevant time" means the time when the repeal of paragraph 7 of Schedule 6 to the 1998 Act comes into force.

Obstruction etc

42. (1)   The repeal of paragraph 8 of Schedule 6 to the 1998 Act (obstruction etc in proceedings before the Tribunal) does not affect the application of that paragraph after the relevant time in relation to an act or omission in relation to proceedings under the 1998 Act (including as it has effect by virtue of this Schedule).

(2)   In this paragraph, "the relevant time" means the time when the repeal of paragraph 8 of Schedule 6 to the 1998 Act comes into force.

Enforcement etc under the 2014 Regulations

43. (1)   The references in the preceding paragraphs of this Part of this Schedule to provisions of the 1998 Act include those provisions as applied, with modifications, by regulation 51 of the 2014 Regulations (other functions of the Commissioner).

(2)   The revocation of regulation 51 of the 2014 Regulations does not affect the application of those provisions of the 1998 Act (as so applied) as described in those paragraphs.

PART 8
ENFORCEMENT ETC UNDER THIS ACT
Information notices

44.   In section 143 of this Act—

(a)   the reference to an offence under section 144 of this Act includes an offence under section 47 of the 1998 Act (including as it has effect by virtue of this Schedule), and

(b)   the references to an offence under this Act include an offence under the 1998 Act (including as it has effect by virtue of this Schedule) or the 1984 Act.

Powers of entry

45.   In paragraph 16 of Schedule 15 to this Act (powers of entry: self-incrimination), the reference to an offence under paragraph 15 of that Schedule includes an offence under paragraph 12 of Schedule 9 to the 1998 Act (including as it has effect by virtue of this Schedule).

Tribunal Procedure Rules

46. (1)   Tribunal Procedure Rules made under paragraph 7(1)(a) of Schedule 6 to the 1998 Act (appeal rights under the 1998 Act) and in force immediately before the relevant time have effect after that time as if they were also made under section 203 of this Act.

(2)   In this paragraph, "the relevant time" means the time when the repeal of paragraph 7(1)(a) of Schedule 6 to the 1998 Act comes into force.

PART 9
OTHER ENACTMENTS
Powers to disclose information to the Commissioner

47. (1)   The following provisions (as amended by Schedule 19 to this Act) have effect after the relevant time as if the matters they refer to included a matter in respect of which the Commissioner could exercise a power conferred by a provision of Part 5 of the 1998 Act, as it has effect by virtue of this Schedule—

(a)   section 11AA(1)(a) of the Parliamentary Commissioner Act 1967 (disclosure of information by Parliamentary Commissioner);

(b)   sections 33A(1)(a) and 34O(1)(a) of the Local Government Act 1974 (disclosure of information by Local Commissioner);

(c)   section 18A(1)(a) of the Health Service Commissioners Act 1993 (disclosure of information by Health Service Commissioner);

(d)   paragraph 1 of the entry for the Information Commissioner in Schedule 5 to the Scottish Public Services Ombudsman Act 2002 (asp 11) (disclosure of information by the Ombudsman);

(e)   section 34X(3)(a) of the Public Services Ombudsman (Wales) Act 2005 (disclosure of information by the Ombudsman);

(f)   section 18(6)(a) of the Commissioner for Older People (Wales) Act 2006 (disclosure of information by the Commissioner);

(g)   section 22(3)(a) of the Welsh Language (Wales) Measure 2011 (nawm 1) (disclosure of information by the Welsh Language Commissioner);

(h)   section 49(3)(a) of the Public Services Ombudsman Act (Northern Ireland) 2016 (c 4 (NI))(disclosure of information by the Ombudsman);

(i)   section 44(3)(a) of the Justice Act (Northern Ireland) 2016 (c 21 (NI)) (disclosure of information by the Prison Ombudsman for Northern Ireland).

(2)   The following provisions (as amended by Schedule 19 to this Act) have effect after the relevant time as if the offences they refer to included an offence under any provision of the 1998 Act other than paragraph 12 of Schedule 9 to that Act (obstruction of execution of warrant)—

(a)   section 11AA(1)(b) of the Parliamentary Commissioner Act 1967;

(b)   sections 33A(1)(b) and 34O(1)(b) of the Local Government Act 1974;

(c)   section 18A(1)(b) of the Health Service Commissioners Act 1993;

(d)   paragraph 2 of the entry for the Information Commissioner in Schedule 5 to the Scottish Public Services Ombudsman Act 2002 (asp 11);

(e)   section 34X(5) of the Public Services Ombudsman (Wales) Act 2005 (disclosure of information by the Ombudsman);

(f)   section 18(8) of the Commissioner for Older People (Wales) Act 2006;

(g)   section 22(5) of the Welsh Language (Wales) Measure 2011 (nawm 1);

(h)   section 49(5) of the Public Services Ombudsman Act (Northern Ireland) 2016 (c 4 (NI));

(i)   section 44(3)(b) of the Justice Act (Northern Ireland) 2016 (c 21 (NI)).

(3)   In this paragraph, "the relevant time", in relation to a provision of a section or Schedule listed in sub-paragraph (1) or (2), means the time when the amendment of the section or Schedule by Schedule 19 to this Act comes into force.

Codes etc required to be consistent with the Commissioner's data-sharing code

48. (1)   This paragraph applies in relation to the code of practice issued under each of the following provisions—

(a)   section 19AC of the Registration Service Act 1953 (code of practice about disclosure of information by civil registration officials);

(b)   section 43 of the Digital Economy Act 2017 (code of practice about disclosure of information to improve public service delivery);

(c)   section 52 of that Act (code of practice about disclosure of information to reduce debt owed to the public sector);

(d)   section 60 of that Act (code of practice about disclosure of information to combat fraud against the public sector);

(e)   section 70 of that Act (code of practice about disclosure of information for research purposes).

(2)   During the relevant period, the code of practice does not have effect to the extent that it is inconsistent with the code of practice prepared under section 121 of this Act (data-sharing code) and issued under section 125(4) of this Act (as altered or replaced from time to time).

(3)   In this paragraph, "the relevant period", in relation to a code issued under a section mentioned in sub-paragraph (1), means the period—

(a)   beginning when the amendments of that section in Schedule 19 to this Act come into force, and

(b)   ending when the code is first reissued under that section.

49. (1)   This paragraph applies in relation to the original statement published under section 45E of the Statistics and Registration Service Act 2007 (statement of principles and procedures in connection with access to information by the Statistics Board).

(2)   During the relevant period, the statement does not have effect to the extent that it is inconsistent with the code of practice prepared under section 121 of this Act (data-sharing code) and issued under section 125(4) of this Act (as altered or replaced from time to time).

(3)   In this paragraph, "the relevant period" means the period—

(a)   beginning when the amendments of section 45E of the Statistics and Registration Service Act 2007 in Schedule 19 to this Act come into force, and

(b)   ending when the first revised statement is published under that section.

Consumer Credit Act 1974

50.   In section 159(1)(a) of the Consumer Credit Act 1974 (correction of wrong information) (as amended by Schedule 19 to this Act), the reference to information given under Article 15(1) to (3) of the GDPR includes information given at any time under section 7 of the 1998 Act.

Freedom of Information Act 2000

51.   Paragraphs 52 to 55 make provision about the Freedom of Information Act 2000 ("the 2000 Act").

52. (1)   This paragraph applies where a request for information was made to a public authority under the 2000 Act before the relevant time.

(2)   To the extent that the request is dealt with after the relevant time, the amendments of sections 2 and 40 of the 2000 Act in Schedule 19 to this Act have effect for the purposes of determining whether the authority deals with the request in accordance with Part 1 of the 2000 Act.

(3)   To the extent that the request was dealt with before the relevant time—

(a)   the amendments of sections 2 and 40 of the 2000 Act in Schedule 19 to this Act do not have effect for the purposes of determining whether the authority dealt with the request in accordance with Part 1 of the 2000 Act, but

(b)   the powers of the Commissioner and the Tribunal, on an application or appeal under the 2000 Act, do not include power to require the authority to take steps which it would not be required to take in order to comply with Part 1 of the 2000 Act as amended by Schedule 19 to this Act.

(4)   In this paragraph—

"public authority" has the same meaning as in the 2000 Act;

"the relevant time" means the time when the amendments of sections 2 and 40 of the 2000 Act in Schedule 19 to this Act come into force.

53.   (1)   Tribunal Procedure Rules made under paragraph 7(1)(b) of Schedule 6 to the 1998 Act (appeal rights under the 2000 Act) and in force immediately before the relevant time have effect after that time as if they were also made under section 61 of the 2000 Act (as inserted by Schedule 19 to this Act).

(2)   In this paragraph, "the relevant time" means the time when the repeal of paragraph 7(1)(b) of Schedule 6 to the 1998 Act comes into force.

54.   (1)   The repeal of paragraph 8 of Schedule 6 to the 1998 Act (obstruction etc in proceedings before the Tribunal) does not affect the application of that paragraph after the relevant time in relation to an act or omission before that time in relation to an appeal under the 2000 Act.

(2)   In this paragraph, "the relevant time" means the time when the repeal of paragraph 8 of Schedule 6 to the 1998 Act comes into force.

55.   (1)   The amendment of section 77 of the 2000 Act in Schedule 19 to this Act (offence of altering etc record with intent to prevent disclosure: omission of reference to section 7 of the 1998 Act) does not affect the application of that section after the relevant time in relation to a case in which—

(a)   the request for information mentioned in section 77(1) of the 2000 Act was made before the relevant time, and

(b)   when the request was made, section 77(1)(b) of the 2000 Act was satisfied by virtue of section 7 of the 1998 Act.

(2)   In this paragraph, "the relevant time" means the time when the repeal of section 7 of the 1998 Act comes into force.

Freedom of Information (Scotland) Act 2002

56.   (1)   This paragraph applies where a request for information was made to a Scottish public authority under the Freedom of Information (Scotland) Act 2002 ("the 2002 Act") before the relevant time.

(2)   To the extent that the request is dealt with after the relevant time, the amendments of the 2002 Act in Schedule 19 to this Act have effect for the purposes of determining whether the authority deals with the request in accordance with Part 1 of the 2002 Act.

(3)   To the extent that the request was dealt with before the relevant time—

(a)   the amendments of the 2002 Act in Schedule 19 to this Act do not have effect for the purposes of determining whether the authority dealt with the request in accordance with Part 1 of the 2002 Act, but

(b)   the powers of the Scottish Information Commissioner and the Court of Session, on an application or appeal under the 2002 Act, do not include power to require the authority to take steps which it would not be required to take in order to comply with Part 1 of the 2002 Act as amended by Schedule 19 to this Act.

(4)   In this paragraph—

"Scottish public authority" has the same meaning as in the 2002 Act;

"the relevant time" means the time when the amendments of the 2002 Act in Schedule 19 to this Act come into force.

Access to Health Records (Northern Ireland) Order 1993 (SI 1993/1250 (NI 4))

57.   Until the first regulations under Article 5(4)(a) of the Access to Health Records (Northern Ireland) Order 1993 (as amended by Schedule 19 to this Act) come into force, the maximum amount of a fee that may be required for giving access under that Article is £10.

Privacy and Electronic Communications (EC Directive) Regulations 2003 (SI 2003/2450)

58.   (1)   The repeal of a provision of the 1998 Act does not affect its operation for the purposes of the Privacy and Electronic Communications (EC Directive) Regulations 2003 ("the PECR 2003") (see regulations 2, 31 and 31B of, and Schedule 1 to, those Regulations).

(2)   Where subordinate legislation made under a provision of the 1998 Act is in force immediately before the repeal of that provision, neither the revocation of the subordinate legislation nor the repeal of the provision of the 1998 Act affect the application of the subordinate legislation for the purposes of the PECR 2003 after that time.

(3)   Part 3 of Schedule 19 to this Act (modifications) does not have effect in relation to the PECR 2003.

(4)   Part 7 of this Schedule does not have effect in relation to the provisions of the 1998 Act as applied by the PECR 2003.

Health and Personal Social Services (Quality, Improvement and Regulation) (Northern Ireland) Order 2003 (SI 2003/431 (NI 9))

59.   Part 3 of Schedule 19 to this Act (modifications) does not have effect in relation to the reference to an accessible record within the meaning of section 68 of the 1998 Act in Article 43 of the Health and Personal Social Services (Quality, Improvement and Regulation) (Northern Ireland) Order 2003.

Environmental Information Regulations 2004 (SI 2004/3391)

60.   (1)   This paragraph applies where a request for information was made to a public authority under the Environmental Information Regulations 2004 ("the 2004 Regulations") before the relevant time.

(2)   To the extent that the request is dealt with after the relevant time, the amendments of the 2004 Regulations in Schedule 19 to this Act have effect for the purposes of determining whether the authority deals with the request in accordance with Parts 2 and 3 of those Regulations.

(3)   To the extent that the request was dealt with before the relevant time—

(a)   the amendments of the 2004 Regulations in Schedule 19 to this Act do not have effect for the purposes of determining whether the authority dealt with the request in accordance with Parts 2 and 3 of those Regulations, but

(b)   the powers of the Commissioner and the Tribunal, on an application or appeal under the 2000 Act (as applied by the 2004 Regulations), do not include power to require the authority to take steps which it would not be required to take in order to comply with Parts 2 and 3 of those Regulations as amended by Schedule 19 to this Act.

(4)   In this paragraph—

"public authority" has the same meaning as in the 2004 Regulations;

"the relevant time" means the time when the amendments of the 2004 Regulations in Schedule 19 to this Act come into force.

Environmental Information (Scotland) Regulations 2004 (SSI 2004/520)

61. (1) This paragraph applies where a request for information was made to a Scottish public authority under the Environmental Information (Scotland) Regulations 2004 ("the 2004 Regulations") before the relevant time.

(2) To the extent that the request is dealt with after the relevant time, the amendments of the 2004 Regulations in Schedule 19 to this Act have effect for the purposes of determining whether the authority deals with the request in accordance with those Regulations.

(3) To the extent that the request was dealt with before the relevant time—

(a) the amendments of the 2004 Regulations in Schedule 19 to this Act do not have effect for the purposes of determining whether the authority dealt with the request in accordance with those Regulations, but

(b) the powers of the Scottish Information Commissioner and the Court of Session, on an application or appeal under the 2002 Act (as applied by the 2004 Regulations), do not include power to require the authority to take steps which it would not be required to take in order to comply with those Regulations as amended by Schedule 19 to this Act.

(4) In this paragraph—

"Scottish public authority" has the same meaning as in the 2004 Regulations;

"the relevant time" means the time when the amendments of the 2004 Regulations in Schedule 19 to this Act come into force.

Dogs

Dogs

7.2879 **Dangerous Dogs Act 1991** *Create Note to 'in charge of it' in s 4B(2A)(ii) and renumber subsequent Note accordingly:* '[2] The court is not permitted to find that someone who is not 'an owner' or 'a person for the time being in charge of the dog' is a fit and proper person to be in charge of it; the court can consider only someone from that limited class and only such a person can apply for a certificate of exemption. Whether or not someone is 'for the time being in charge' of a dog is fact sensitive. The concept has to relate to having responsibility for the dog and it is at least possible that somebody who walks a dog on a regular basis and has responsibility for it during that time meets that description. "For the time being" does not mean at the time of the seizure, but there are some temporal limits. The concept involves contact in the past or present, but cannot extend to the future: *Webb v Chief Constable of Avon and Somerset* [2017] EWHC 3311 (Admin), The Times, 31 January, 2018.'

Elections

Elections

7.3218 **Representation of the People Act 1983, s 90C** *To the heading to s 90C create the following note:* '[1] In *R v Mackinlay* [2018] UKSC 42; [2018] 3 WLR 556; (2018) Times, August 6, the Supreme Court held that, for the purposes of s 90C, there was no requirement that before such property, goods, services of facilities fell to be declared, they must have been authorised by the candidate or his election agent or by someone authorised by them.'

Employment

Election

7.3432 **Employment Rights Act 1996, s 50** *Note amendments introduced by the Time Off for Public Duties Order 2018, SI 2018/665.*

7.3526 **Modern Slavery Act 2015, s 45** *At the end of s 1 after 'if' create a new note 1 as follows:* '[1] Where a defendant seeks to rely on one of the defences in s 45, he bears only an evidential burden. The legal or persuasive burden rests upon the prosecution. Where evidence of any element of the defence is provided, it is for the prosecution to disprove one or more of them to the criminal standard in the usual way: see *R v MK* [2018] EWCA Crim 667; [2018] 3 All E.R. 566; [2018] 2 Cr App R 14.

Extradition, Fugitive Offenders and Backing of Warrants

Extradition, Fugitive Offenders etc

7.3927 **Extradition Act 2003, s 1** *Insert text in the Note in a new para after the para ending 'see paras 90–93 of the judgment.)', then continue text in new para:* 'Where an extradition request had been refused, and the requesting authority or the CPS had not advanced all aspects of its case as it could have done, a fresh application on a further European Arrest Warrant (EAW) to reopen an issue was not an abuse of process. However, such a case fell to be considered within the context of the statutory bars under the scheme of the 2003 Act. Balances had to be struck to reflect the public interests at stake and any unfair prejudice caused to the requested person in all the circumstances of the case. The factors to consider were: the gravity of the actual or alleged offending; the nature and cause of the failure which had led to the further EAW being issued; the effect which that might have in consequence on the public interest in that particular extradition; and the effect which that had had on the requested person both in his family and private life, and on his trial, retrial and punishment, whether through change in circumstance or passage of time: *Camaras v Baia Mare Local Court, Romania* [2016] EWHC 1766 (Admin), [2018] 1 WLR 1174.'

7.3928 **Extradition Act 2003, s 2** *In Note 2 at the end of the second para insert the following after '1427':* '(since endorsed in *Kirsanov v Viru County Court, Estonia* [2017] EWHC 2593 (Admin)'.

In Note 6 after the first para insert the following new para: 'Note, however, the decision in *Alexander v Public Prosecutor's Office, Marseille District Court of First Instance, France and Di Benedetto v Court of Palermo, Italy*, above, as to obtaining supplementary information. In the light of the latter decision, this statement of the law now appears to be doubtful. Further confirmation of the "sea change" described in Alexander (supra) is found in *Imre v District Court in Szolnok (Hungary)* [2018] EWHC 218 (Admin) (paras.35 to 37) where the Administrative Court held that where further information is provided pursuant to Article 15 of the Framework Decision, it is not to be regarded as extraneous evidence and that the European arrest warrant and the further information must be read together.'

In Note 6 delete the last para.

7.3941 **Extradition Act 2003, s 12A** *In the last para of existing Note 1 replace the All ER (D) citation of Cimeri with:* '[2018] 1 WLR 2833'

7.3953 **Extradition Act 2003, s 21** *In Note 1 before the para starting 'There is no implication insert the following new para:* 'The decision of the CJEU in *Aronyosi* (above) was considered further by the Administrative Court in *Yaser Mohammed v Comarca de Lisboa Oeste* [2017] EWHC 3237 (Admin) and *Yaser Mohammed (No 2)* [2018] EWHC 225 (Admin) when considering whether, when and in what circumstances the court in this jurisdiction is under a duty to request further information from the requesting judicial authority where there is clear cogent and compelling evidence rebutting the presumption that parties to the ECHR are willing and able to fulfil their obligations under Article 3. The effect of the decisions in the *Yaser Mohammed* cases is summarised by the Court in *Emanuel Shumba and Others v Public Prosecutor of Bobigny County Court, France, First Instance Court of Bobigny, France* [2018] EWHC 1782 (Admin)'

29 *Aranyosi* was considered and applied by the Divisional Court in *Yaser Mohammed v Comarca de Lisboa Oeste* [2017] EWHC 3237(Admin), which concerned the extradition of a person pursuant to a conviction European Arrest Warrant in circumstances where he would be returned to Lisbon Central Prison in Portugal. The main judgment was given by Beatson LJ, with whom Sir Wyn Williams agreed. Beatson LJ first considered what the CJEU had said at para. 89 in *Aranyosi*. He concluded, at para. 51 of his judgment, that there was information which was objective, reliable, specific and up-to-date of deficiencies affecting Lisbon Prison and of a real risk of inhuman or degrading treatment by reason of conditions of detention in parts of that prison. Accordingly, this Court was obliged to move to the second stage of the Aranyosi test, set out at para. 92 of the CJEU's judgment, which requires this Court to make a further assessment, specific and precise, of whether there are substantial grounds to believe that the individual concerned will be exposed to that risk because of the conditions for his detention envisaged in the issuing Member State.

30 In the circumstances of *Yaser Mohammed* , and in accordance with paras. 95-96 of *Aranyosi* , this Court considered that it was necessary to ask the Portuguese authorities for supplemental information. This Court then set out a number of questions and asked for those questions to be answered within 28 days of receipt of the request for further information.

31 In *Yaser Mohammed (No 2)* [2018] EWHC 225 (Admin) this Court then dealt with the case in the light of the further information which was filed on behalf of the requesting State. On this occasion the main judgment was given by Sir Wyn Williams, with whom Beatson LJ agreed. Having considered the supplementary information, this Court was of the view that there remained a real risk of inhuman or degrading treatment should the appellant be detained in Lisbon Central Prison: see paras. 18-19 of the judgment.

7.3961 **Extradition Act 2003, s 27** *Insert a new Note 1 at the end of s 27(1)(b) as follows:* '[1] The question that arises on appeal under s 27 has been considered by the Administrative Court in *Celinski v Poland* [2015] EWCH 124:

'24   The single question therefore for the appellate court is whether or not the district judge made the wrong decision. It is only if the court concludes that the decision was wrong, applying what Lord Neuberger PSC said, as set out above, that the appeal can be allowed. Findings of fact, especially if evidence has been heard, must ordinarily be respected. In answering the question whether the district judge, in the light of those findings of fact, was wrong to decide that extradition was or was not proportionate, the focus must be on the outcome, that is on the decision itself. Although the district judge's reasons for the proportionality decision must be considered with care, errors and omissions do not of themselves necessarily show that the decision on proportionality itself was wrong.'

7.4021 **Extradition Act 2003, s 83A** *In existing note replace the All ER (D) citation of Love v Government of the USA with:* '[2018] 1 WLR 2889'

At the end of Note 1 add the following text in a new para: 'The Administrative Court in *Love* expressed the view that the absence of any prosecutor's belief was "a factor which albeit modestly, favoured" the operation of the forum bar. This finding is to be contrasted with that in *Shaw v Government of the United States of America* [2014] EWHC 4654 (Admin) at para. 38 where a differently constituted court concluded that in the absence of a prosecutor's the judge "cannot have any further 'regard' to this factor". This apparent conflict was revisited in *Scott v Government of the United States of America* [2018] EWHC 2021 (Admin). At para. 31 the Court held

> '31   The question remains whether the dicta in Love are to be preferred over the conclusions in *Shaw* and *Atraskevic* . The general approach is that a court of concurrent jurisdiction will follow another unless the earlier court was clearly wrong. That is not the case here. *Atraskevic* was not cited in I and, on this point, we overlooked *Shaw* . For the reasons given in both cases in the paragraphs to which we have referred we conclude that they were correct. Section 83A(3)(c) is only in point if the prosecutor has expressed the relevant belief.'

7.4031   Extradition Act 2003, s 92   *In the asterisk note replace the All ER (D) citation of Love v Government of the USA:* '[2018] 1 WLR 2889'

7.4042   Extradition Act 2003, s 103   *At the end of Note 2 add the following in a new para:* 'When considering what approach to take when challenging the decision of a district judge about the existence of a real risk of a breach of a requested persons human rights under the Convention, the court must have "a very high respect for the findings of fact", "we must also have respect for the DJ's evaluation of the expert evidence", and "the decision of the DJ can only be successfully challenged if it is demonstrated that it is 'wrong'", see *United States of America v Giese (No.1)* [2015] EWHC 2733 (Admin) at paragraph 15 and *Dzgoev v Russian Federation* [2017] EWHC 735 (Admin) at paragraphs 23 and 24'.

FISHERIES

7.4544   European Communities Act 1972: Regulations   *In the bullet list of SIs, add to SI 2014/3345:* 'amended by SI 2018/643'.

7.4633   Fisheries Act 1981, s 30   *In the penultimate para of existing Note 1 add to the list of SIs amending 2009/3391:* 'and SI 2018/643'.

GAMBLING

7.4945   Gambling Act 2005, s 42   *In existing Note 2, insert in the citation of the Ivey case before the WLR citation:* '[2018] 2 ALL ER 406'.

HEALTH AND SAFETY

7.5406   Health and Safety at Work etc Act 1974, s 3   *At the end of note 1 in a new paragraph insert the following:* 'The fact that a partnership can be prosecuted under s 3 does not provide authority for the proposition that, in such circumstances, only the partnership can be prosecuted. A prosecution can also be brought against the individual partners where they are shown to be an "employer". In *Lear* [2018] EWCA Crim 69, [2018] 2 Cr. App R 11, a husband and wife who together ran a hotel were held to be jointly and severally liable for the actions of the business such that they were properly charged as individual partners.'

7.5428   Health and Safety at Work etc Act 1974, s 33   *Create Note to the title 'Provisions as to offences' and renumber subsequent Notes accordingly:* '[1] The Cableway Installations Regulations 2018, SI 2018/816 provide that the following provisions of the 1974 Act, namely ss 19-22, 23, 25A, 27, 33(1)(c) and (e) to (o),33(2), 34-42, 46, 48(1) to (3), and Sch 3A apply for the purposes of Regulation (EC) 765/2008 and Regulation 2016/424 EU as if those regulatory provisions were health and safety regulations for the purposes of the 1974 Act. Regulation 26 of SI 2018/816 provides a defence of due diligence, and reg 27 provides for the liability of persons other than the principal offender.'

7.5955A   Social Worker Regulations 2018   *Insert the following regulation after the Nicotine Inhaling Products (Age of Sale and Proxy Purchasing) Regulations 2015 as follows:*

Social Workers Regulations 2018[1]
(SI 2018/893)

PART 6   RESTRICTIONS ON PRACTICE, PROTECTED TITLES AND OFFENCES

28.   *Carrying out social work in England and use of title*   (1)   A person may not practise as a social worker in England unless they are a registered social worker.
(2)   A person must not use the title of "social worker" unless they are a registered social worker.
(3)   Paragraphs (1) and (2) do not apply to a person who is practising as a social worker in England on a temporary basis, and is registered as a social worker in a register kept by—
(a)   Social Care Wales,
(b)   the Scottish Social Services Council, or
(c)   the Northern Ireland Social Care Council.

[1] The Social Worker Regulations 2018 are created pursuant to Part 2 of the Children and Social Workers Act 2017. They will come into force on a date to be appointed. They set out the regulatory framework for the operation of Social Work England, the regulator for social workers in England. A number of summary only offences are created which are punishable by fine only.

29. *Holding out of a person as qualified to carry out social work in England* (1) A person must not falsely represent themselves to be a registered social worker, to have a qualification in relation to social work, or to be the subject of an entry in the register.

(2) A person ("A") must not make a false representation about another person ("B") which, if it was made by B, would be contrary to paragraph (1).

30. *Offences in connection with registration* A person commits an offence if they fraudulently procure, or attempt to procure, the making, amendment, removal or restoration of an entry in the register.

31. *Offences in connection with restrictions on practice and protected titles* (1) A person commits an offence if, with intent to deceive (whether expressly or by implication), they—

(a) use the title of "social worker" in breach of regulation 28(2),

(b) falsely represent themselves, in breach of regulation 29(1)—

     (i) to be registered, or to be the subject of an entry in the register, or

     (ii) to possess a qualification in relation to social work.

(2) A person ("A") commits an offence if—

(a) with intent that any person is deceived (whether expressly or by implication) they cause or permit another person ("B") to make any representation about A which, if made by A with intent to deceive, would be an offence under paragraph (1), or

(b) with intent to deceive they make any representation with regard to another person ("B") which—

     (i) A knows to be false, and

     (ii) if made by B with that intent would be an offence by B under paragraph (1).

32. *Offences in connection with the provision of information* (1) A person commits an offence if they fail, without reasonable excuse to—

(a) attend and give evidence or produce documents when required to do so by the regulator in accordance with regulation 14(3) (in connection with the removal of an entry under regulation 14(1)(a) on the grounds it was fraudulently procured or incorrectly made),

(b) attend and give evidence or produce documents when required to do so by adjudicators in accordance with regulation 15(5)(b) (in connection with an application for restoration by a person who was the subject of a removal order),

(c) attend and give evidence or produce documents when required to do so by the regulator, or adjudicators, in accordance with regulation 19(4) (in connection with a registration appeal),

(d) provide information when required to do so by the regulator under paragraph 1(3)(a), or by investigators under paragraph 4(1)(b), of Schedule 2 (in connection with fitness to practise proceedings), or

(e) attend and give evidence or produce documents when required to do so by investigators in accordance with paragraph 5(1) of Schedule 2 (in connection with fitness to practise proceedings).

33. *Offences under this Part* A person guilty of an offence under this Part is liable on summary conviction to a fine.

Housing, Landlord and Tenanat

7.6021 Housing Act 2004, s 258 *Create Note to 'Persons' at the beginning of s 258(2) and renumber subsequent Note accordingly:* '[1] Section 258 makes clear that children count as persons forming part of the same household for the purposes of s 254(2) and on that basis children count as qualifying persons for the purpose of determining whether or not an HMO is "large" (occupied by more than six residents) and therefore requires Class C4 planning permission: *Paramaguru v Ealing LBC* [2018] EWHC 373 (Admin), [2018] LLR 254.'

7.6259 Housing and Planning Act 2016, s 13 *Add to the list of commencement orders in existing Note 1:* ', and Housing and Planning Act 2016 (Commencement No. 9 and Transitional and Saving Provisions) Regulations 2018, SI 2018/805.'

7.6290 Licensing of Houses in Multiple Occupation (Prescribed Description) (England) Order 2018 *After this para reproduce the Housing Administration (England and Wales) Rules 2018, SO 2018/719 as follows and create Note to the title:*

Housing Administration (England and Wales) Rules 2018[1]
(2018/719)

SCHEDULE 1
Punishment of Offences under These Rules   Rule 1.4

Rule creating offence	General nature of offence	Mode of prosecution	Punishment	Daily default fine (if applicable)

3.13(5)	Housing administrator failing to deliver progress reports in accordance with rule 3.13	Summary	Level 3 on the standard scale.	One tenth of level 3 on the standard scale.
3.39(7)	Former housing administrator failing to file a notice of automatic end of housing administration and progress report	Summary	Level 3 on the standard scale.	One tenth of level 3 on the standard scale.
6.9(2)	Failing to comply with housing administrator's duties on vacating office	Summary	Level 3 on the standard scale.	One tenth of level 3 on the standard scale.
7.35(3)	Falsely claiming to be a person entitled to inspect a document with the intention of gaining sight of it.	1 On indictment 2 Summary	2 years, or a fine, or both. 6 months, or a fine, or both.	Not applicable.

[1] These Rules were made under a 102(5) of the Housing and Planning Act 2016 and s 411 of the Insolvency Act 1986. They set out the detailed procedures for the conduct of housing administration, as provided by Chapter 5 of Part 4 of the Housing and Planning Act 2016. Schedule 1 contains specific details of the punishment of offences under these Rules.

HUMAN RIGHTS

7.6291   Human Rights Act 1998, s 1   *At the end of note 1 in a new paragraph insert the following text:* 'In *Al-Skeini v United Kingdom* (2011) 53 EHRR 18 and *Al-Jedda v United Kingdom* (2011) 53 EHRR 23 the European court confirmed that the UK Government's human rights obligations are not limited to the territorial UK but can exceptionally extend overseas to situations in which British officials exercise "control and authority" over foreign nationals. Article 1 applies not only where a contracting state exercises effective control over foreign territory but also where the state exercises physical power and control over an individual who is situated on foreign territory. Where a state exercises control over an individual, the state is required to secure those Convention rights which are relevant to the situation of the individual. An example is *Alseran v Ministry of Defence* [2017] EWHC 3289 (QB); [2018] 3 WLR 95 where the court found in favour of four Iraqi claimants who alleged that they were unlawfully detained and mistreated by the British forces during military operations in Iraq.'

7.6297   Human Rights Act 1998, s 7   *In existing Note 3 Replace the All ER (D) citation of O'Connor v BSB:* '[2018] 2 ALL ER 779'

     At the end of s 5(b) insert new note 4 and text and renumber subsequent notes: [4] In *Alseran* [2017] EWHC 3289 (QB); [2018] 3 WLR 95, the court confirmed that it had a wide discretion in determining whether it was equitable to extend time. The court should examine in the circumstances of each case all the relevant factors and decide whether it was equitable to provide for a longer period.

7.6299   Human Rights Act 1998, s 9   *At the start of note 2 insert the following text in a new paragraph:* 'Whilst section 9(3) contemplates an award of damages for the breach of Article 5.5 by a judicial act, it does not provide for any other remedy, including a declaration. In *Mazhar v Lord Chancellor* [2018] 2 WLR 1304, the appellant pursued a claim against the Lord Chancellor seeking declaratory relief to the effect that the order of a judge authorising the use of reasonable and proportionate force by police and medical professionals to enter his home and to remove him to a specialist respiratory centre violated his Article 5 rights because he was not a person "of unsound mind" and did not fall within any other of the exceptions to the right to liberty and security outlined in Article 5. The court dismissed his claim, holding that nothing in ss 7, 8 and 9 of the Human Rights Act 1998 taken together with either the Civil Procedure Rules or the Family Procedure Rules, whether by express provision or necessary implication, created a power in a court or tribunal to grant declaratory relief against the Crown in respect of a judicial act. The HRA 1998 Act neither abrogated, nor limited, nor carved out an exception to, the constitutional principle of judicial immunity in relation to claims brought under the Act. The court also confirmed the principle that ministers of the Crown are not vicariously liable for judicial acts. To hold otherwise would be to infringe the doctrine of the separation of powers and the principle of the independence of the judiciary.'

7.6313   Human Rights Act 1998, Sch 1, Pt I, Art 3   *In the 4th para of existing Note 1 replace the All ER (D) citation of DSD case with:* '[2018] 1 Cr App R 31'.

7.6313   Human Rights Act 1998, Sch 1, Pt I, Art 5   *In the last paragraph of Note 2 insert the following new text:* 'In *R (Bowen) v Secretary of State for Justice* [2018] 1 WLR 2170, there was no breach of Article 5 where a prisoner's release was delayed for several weeks until a place became available for him in Approved Premises following a Parole Board Decision for licenced release.'

7.6313   Human Rights Act 1998, Sch 1, Pt I, Art 6   *Insert text after first para of existing Note 1 and continue Note in new para:* 'In a case where damages were awarded, Article 6 did not operate as a guarantee that the aggrieved person would recover his/her award, but rather guaranteed that an individual had proper access to justice. Thus, in a case where a legally-aided litigant failed to obtain more than a small amount of an award of damages, and this was fully absorbed by a statutory charge under section 25 of the Legal Aid, Sentencing and Punishment of Offenders Act 2012, there was no breach of the right of access to justice, and if there was any interference with that right it was proportionate and accordingly did not breach Article 6: *R (Tirkey) v Director of Legal Aid Casework* [2017] EWHC 3403 (Admin), [2018] 1 WLR 2112.'

In Note 12 at the beginning insert the following new text: 'In *Re Maguire* [2018] UKSC 17; [2018] 1 WLR 1412; [2018] 3 All ER 30, it was held that Article 6 does not give the accused the right to be represented by counsel of their choice at public expense. The interests of justice require only that the accused is properly represented. There is no right to choose counsel that is free-standing of the fair trial goal.'

7.6313 Human Rights Act 1998, Sch 1, Pt I, Art 8 *Add to the the para which begins 'As to the inclusion of an acquittal':* 'The decision was affirmed by the Supreme Court in *R (AR) v Chief Constable of Greater Manchester* [2018] UKSC 47, [2018] ALL ER (D) 166 (Jul). The Court added "Given that Parliament has clearly authorised the inclusion in ECRCs of 'soft' information, including disputed allegations, there may be no logical reason to exclude information about serious allegations of criminal conduct, merely because a prosecution has not been pursued or has failed ... However, I am concerned at the lack of information about how an ECRC is likely to be treated by a potential employer in such a case . . . We have been shown reports which emphasise the importance of not excluding the convicted from consideration for employment, but they say nothing about the acquitted, who surely deserve greater protection from unfair stigmatisation. Nor does there appear to be any guidance to employers as to how to handle such issues. Even if the ECRC is expressed in entirely neutral terms, there must be a danger that the employer will infer that the disclosure would not have been made unless the chief officer had formed a view of likely guilt. These issues require further consideration outside the scope of this appeal ..." (see [74]-[76] of the judgment).'

Add text to the para which begins 'The police policy of retention' as follows: 'See also *Hewson v Commissioner of Police of the Metropolis* [2018] EWHC 471 (Admin), [2018] 4 WLR 69 (a case of alleged harassment on social media). The issue of a prevention from harassment letter is not regulated by statute but comes within the discretion of the police in their duty to enforce the law, and the courts will interfere with the exercise of that discretion only in rare cases. The idea behind issuing a letter is that it puts the recipient on notice that his/her conduct is capable of amounting to harassment; this is particularly useful where the recipient may have thought that his/her actions were reasonable. While it constitutes an interference with the recipient's Article 8 rights, the proportionality of the interference will depend on the circumstances and the process leading to its issue; any implication as to possible damage to the recipient's reputation is tempered by the fact that such a letter is no more than a warning and does not involve any formal determination that the conduct had taken place, let alone that the offence of harassment had been committed. Fairness does not require that in every case the police should first talk to the intended recipient.'

Replace the para which begins 'There is no rule of law that the deportation' with: 'As to the relevant consideration where a court or tribunal is required to determine whether or not a decision taken under the Immigration Acts breaches art 6, see Part 5A of the Nationality, Immigration and Asylum Act 2002 in this PART, post'.

7.6313 Human Rights Act 1998, Sch 1, Pt I, Art 14 *In Note 1 at the end insert in a new paragraph the following new text:* 'In *Smith v Lancashire NHS Teaching Hospitals NHS Foundation Trust* [2017] EWCA Civ 1916; [2018] QB 804; [2018] 2 WLR 1063, which was concerned with the payment of bereavement damages in fatal accident cases, the court held that it was discriminatory to treat unmarried long-term cohabitees less favourably than those who were married or in a civil partnership. The court confirmed that the correct test for determining whether a measure fell within the ambit of Article 8 so as to engage Article 14 was that set out in *Stenfeld* [2017] EWCA Civ 81; [2018] QB 519. A claim was capable of falling within Article 14 even though there had been no infringement of Article 8 provided that it fell within the ambit of Article 8. If a state had brought into existence a positive measure which, even though not required by Article 8, was a modality of the exercise of the rights governed by article 8, the state would be in breach of Article 14 if the measure had more than a tenuous connection with the core values protected by Article 8 and was discriminatory and not justified. In the context of bereavement damages, the situation of someone who was in a long-term relationship in every respect equal to a marriage in terms of love, loyalty and commitment, was sufficiently analogous to that of a surviving spouse or civil partner to require discrimination to be justified in order to avoid infringement of Article 14 in conjunction with Article 8. The court also found it relevant to note the decline in popularity of the institution of marriage and the increase in the number of cohabiting couples.'

7.6313 Human Rights Act 1998, Sch 1, Pt II, Art 3 *Insert text in new para after the third para of existing Note 1:* 'Where a pleasure boat certificate had expired, the removal of the boat, with a requirement of payment of a sum including removal and storage fees and licence fee arrears, did not contravene art 1; it struck a fair balance between the rights of the individual and the interests of the community: *Ravenscroft v Canal & River Trust* [2017] EWHC 1874 (Ch), [2018] 1 WLR 249.'

In existing Note 1, in the last para, insert text after the first sentence as follows: '(In consequence of the decision in *Waya*, s 6(5) of the Proceeds of Crime Act 2002 was amended to include a requirement of proportionality.)'

In Note 2 at the start of the final paragraph delete the words: 'Where fishing licensing conditions' *and then insert the following new text:* 'A decision by HMRC to cancel a taxpayer's registration under the Construction Industry Scheme did not amount to a disproportionate interference to his rights under Article 1 of Protocol 1, notwithstanding the highly damaging impact it had on the company's business and was well within the wide margin of appreciation allowed to the state for the enforcement of tax: *JP Whitter (WaterWell Engineers) Ltd v Revenue and Customs Commissioners* [2018] UKSC 31; [2018] 1 WLR 3117; [2018] STC. 1394; [2018] BTC. 24; [2018] STI 1110. However, where fishing licensing conditions'

> *At the end of existing Note 2, replace AlL ER (D) citation of R (Mott) v Environment Agency with:* '[2018] UKSC 10; [2018] 1 WLR 1022; [2018] 2 All ER 663'.

IMMIGRATION

7.6385   Immigration Act 1971, Sch 2, para 27B   *In Note 1 to para 27B add to the list of amending SIs as follows:* 'and SI 2018/598'.

7.6394   British Nationality Act 1981, 41   *Replace existing Note 1 with:* 'The British Nationality (Falkland Islands) Regulations 1983, SI 1983/479, the British Nationality (Hong Kong) Order 1986, SI 1986/2175 amended by SI 2003/540 and SI 2007/3137, the British Nationality (Hong Kong) (Registration of Citizens) Regulations 1990, SI 1990/2211, the British Nationality (General) Regulations 2003, SI 2003/548 amended by SI 2005/2114 and 2785, SI 2007/3139, SI 2009/3363, SI 2010/677 and 785, SI 2012/1588, SI 2013/2541, SI 2014/1465 and SI 2015/681, 738 and 1806, SI 2018/851, the British Nationality (Fees) Regulations 2003, SI 2003/3157 amended by SI 2005/2114, the British Nationality (British Overseas Territories) Regulations 2007, SI 2007/3139 and the Registration of Overseas Births and Deaths Regulations 2014, SI 2014/511 have been made.'

7.6464   Nationality, Immigration and Asylum Act 2002   *Before Part 6 insert Part 5A of the Nationality, Immigration and Asylum Act 2002 as follows:*

Nationality, Immigration and Asylum Act 2002
(2002 c 41)

PART 5A

ARTICLE 8 OF THE ECHR: PUBLIC INTEREST CONSIDERATIONS

7.6463A   117A.   Application of this Part   (1)   This Part applies where a court or tribunal is required to determine whether a decision made under the Immigration Acts—

    (a)   breaches a person's right to respect for private and family life under Article 8, and

    (b)   as a result would be unlawful under section 6 of the Human Rights Act 1998.

(2)   In considering the public interest question, the court or tribunal must (in particular) have regard[1]—

    (a)   in all cases, to the considerations listed in section 117B, and

    (b)   in cases concerning the deportation of foreign criminals, to the considerations listed in section 117C.

(3)   In subsection (2), "the public interest question" means the question of whether an interference with a person's right to respect for private and family life is justified under Article 8(2).

---

[1] 'Having regard to' does not mandate any particular outcome in an art 8 balancing exercise: a court or tribunal has to take these considerations into account and give them considerable weight, but they are in principle capable of being outweighed by other relevant considerations which may make it disproportionate under Aticle 8 for an individual to be removed from the UK; see *Rhuppiah v Secretary of State for the Home Department* [2016] EWCA Civ 803.

117B.   Article 8: public interest considerations applicable in all cases   (1)   The maintenance of effective immigration controls is in the public interest.

(2)   It is in the public interest, and in particular in the interests of the economic well-being of the United Kingdom, that persons who seek to enter or remain in the United Kingdom are able to speak English, because persons who can speak English—

    (a)   are less of a burden on taxpayers, and

    (b)   are better able to integrate into society.

(3)   It is in the public interest, and in particular in the interests of the economic well-being of the United Kingdom, that persons who seek to enter or remain in the United Kingdom are financially independent, because such persons—

    (a)   are not a burden on taxpayers, and

    (b)   are better able to integrate into society.

(4)   Little weight should be given to—

    (a)   a private life, or

    (b)   a relationship formed with a qualifying partner,

that is established by a person at a time when the person is in the United Kingdom unlawfully.

(5)   Little weight should be given to a private life established by a person at a time when the person's immigration status is precarious.

(6)   In the case of a person who is not liable to deportation, the public interest does not require the person's removal where—

    (a)   the person has a genuine and subsisting parental relationship with a qualifying child, and

   (b)   it would not be reasonable to expect the child to leave the United Kingdom.]

117C.   Article 8: additional considerations in cases involving foreign criminals
   (1)   The deportation of foreign criminals is in the public interest.
   (2)   The more serious the offence committed by a foreign criminal, the greater is the public interest in deportation of the criminal.
   (3)   In the case of a foreign criminal ("C") who has not been sentenced to a period of imprisonment of four years or more, the public interest requires C's deportation unless Exception 1 or Exception 2 applies.
   (4)   Exception 1 applies where—
       (a)   C has been lawfully resident in the United Kingdom for most of C's life,
       (b)   C is socially and culturally integrated in the United Kingdom, and
       (c)   there would be very significant obstacles to C's integration into the country to which C is proposed to be deported.
   (5)   Exception 2 applies where C has a genuine and subsisting relationship with a qualifying partner, or a genuine and subsisting parental relationship with a qualifying child, and the effect of C's deportation on the partner or child would be unduly harsh.
   (6)   In the case of a foreign criminal who has been sentenced to a period of imprisonment of at least four years, the public interest requires deportation unless there are very compelling circumstances, over and above those described in Exceptions 1 and 2.
   (7)   The considerations in subsections (1) to (6) are to be taken into account where a court or tribunal is considering a decision to deport a foreign criminal only to the extent that the reason for the decision was the offence or offences for which the criminal has been convicted.

117D.   Interpretation of this Part   (1)   In this Part—
   "Article 8" means Article 8 of the European Convention on Human Rights;
   "qualifying child" means a person who is under the age of 18 and who—
       (a)   is a British citizen, or
       (b)   has lived in the United Kingdom for a continuous period of seven years or more;
   "qualifying partner" means a partner who—
       (a)   is a British citizen, or
       (b)   who is settled in the United Kingdom (within the meaning of the Immigration Act 1971—see section 33(2A) of that Act).
   (2)   In this Part, "foreign criminal" means a person—
       (a)   who is not a British citizen,
       (b)   who has been convicted in the United Kingdom of an offence, and
       (c)   who—
            (i)   has been sentenced to a period of imprisonment of at least 12 months,
            (ii)   has been convicted of an offence that has caused serious harm, or
            (iii)   is a persistent offender.
   (3)   For the purposes of subsection (2)(b), a person subject to an order under—
       (a)   section 5 of the Criminal Procedure (Insanity) Act 1964 (insanity etc),
       (b)   section 57 of the Criminal Procedure (Scotland) Act 1995 (insanity etc), or
       (c)   Article 50A of the Mental Health (Northern Ireland) Order 1986 (insanity etc),
   has not been convicted of an offence.
   (4)   In this Part, references to a person who has been sentenced to a period of imprisonment of a certain length of time—
       (a)   do not include a person who has received a suspended sentence (unless a court subsequently orders that the sentence or any part of it (of whatever length) is to take effect);
       (b)   do not include a person who has been sentenced to a period of imprisonment of that length of time only by virtue of being sentenced to consecutive sentences amounting in aggregate to that length of time;
       (c)   include a person who is sentenced to detention, or ordered or directed to be detained, in an institution other than a prison (including, in particular, a hospital or an institution for young offenders) for that length of time; and
       (d)   include a person who is sentenced to imprisonment or detention, or ordered or directed to be detained, for an indeterminate period, provided that it may last for at least that length of time.
   (5)   If any question arises for the purposes of this Part as to whether a person is a British citizen, it is for the person asserting that fact to prove it.[1]

---

   [1] Section 117D(4)(c) expressly refers to hospital orders, whereas s 117D(4)(d) does not. However, the latter unambiguously includes offenders sentenced to hospital orders; they are necessarily for an indeterminate period because detention lasts until a clinician considers release to be appropriate or, in the case of a restriction order, until the Secretary of State consents to discharge or the tribunal orders release: *Secretary of State for the Home Department v KE (Nigeria)* [2017] EWCA Civ 1382, [2018] INLR 147.

7.6499   Immigration, Asylum and Nationality Act 2006, s 32   *In Note 1 add to the list of amending SIs:* 'and SI 2018/598'.

Industry and Commerce

7.6666   Financial Services and Markets Act 2000, s 22   *Replace existing the text in Note 1 with the following:* 'The Financial Services and Markets Act 2000 (Regulated Activities) Order 2001, SI 2001/544 amended by SI 2001/3544, SI 2002/682 and 1776, SI 2003/1475, 1476 and 2822, SI 2004/1610, 2737 and 3379, SI 2005/593, 1518 and 2114, SI 2006/1969, 2383 and 3384, SI 2007/1339, 2157, 3254 and 3510, SI 2009/209, 1342 and 1389, SI 2010/86 and 2960, SI 2011/1265, 1613 and 2581, SI 2012/1906, SI 2013/472, 504, 655, 1881, 3115 and SI 2014/366, 1292 (amended by SI 2014/1313), 1448, 1740 and 1850, SI 2015/352, 369, 489, 575, 731 and 853, SI 2016/392 and 715 and SI 2017/488, 500, 692 and 752, 1064 and 1255 and SI 2018/134, 135 and 831, and the Risk Transformation Regulations 2017, SI 2017/2012 have been made.'

7.6822A   Scrap Metal Act 2018   *After the Scrap Metal Act 2013 Insert the following provisions of the Scrap Metal Act 2018 as follows:*

Sanctions and Anti-Money Laundering Act 2018[1]

(2018 c 13)

Part 1
Sanctions Regulations

Chapter 1
Power to Make Sanctions Regulations

Power to make sanctions regulations

1.   Power to make sanctions regulations   (1) An appropriate Minister may make sanctions regulations where that Minister considers that it is appropriate to make the regulations—

    (a)   for the purposes of compliance with a UN obligation,

    (b)   for the purposes of compliance with any other international obligation, or

    (c)   for a purpose within subsection (2).

    (2) A purpose is within this subsection if the appropriate Minister making the regulations considers that carrying out that purpose would—

    (a)   further the prevention of terrorism, in the United Kingdom or elsewhere,

    (b)   be in the interests of national security,

    (c)   be in the interests of international peace and security,

    (d)   further a foreign policy objective of the government of the United Kingdom,

    (e)   promote the resolution of armed conflicts or the protection of civilians in conflict zones,

    (f)   provide accountability for or be a deterrent to gross violations of human rights, or otherwise promote—

        (i)   compliance with international human rights law, or

        (ii)   respect for human rights,

    (g)   promote compliance with international humanitarian law,

    (h)   contribute to multilateral efforts to prevent the spread and use of weapons and materials of mass destruction, or

    (i)   promote respect for democracy, the rule of law and good governance.

    (3) Regulations under this section must state the purpose (or purposes) of the regulations, and any purpose stated must be—

    (a)   compliance with a UN obligation, or other international obligation, specified in the regulations, or

    (b)   a particular purpose that is within subsection (2).

    (4) Section 2 contains additional requirements in relation to regulations stating a purpose within subsection (2) above.

    (5) In this section "sanctions regulations" means regulations which do one or more of the following—

    (a)   impose financial sanctions (see section 3);

    (b)   impose immigration sanctions (see section 4);

    (c)   impose trade sanctions (see section 5 and Schedule 1);

    (d)   impose aircraft sanctions (see section 6);

    (e)   impose shipping sanctions (see section 7);

    (f)   impose sanctions within section 8 (other sanctions for purposes of UN obligations);

    (g)   make supplemental provision in connection with any provision of the regulations or other regulations made under this section.

    (6) In this section "supplemental provision" includes any provision authorised by any other provision of this Act to be made by regulations under this section (see in particular sections 9 to 17, 19 to 21 and 54).

    (7) In this Act any reference to a gross violation of human rights is to conduct which—

    (a)   constitutes, or

    (b)   is connected with,

the commission of a gross human rights abuse or violation; and whether conduct constitutes or is connected with the commission of such an abuse or violation is to be determined in accordance with section 241A of the Proceeds of Crime Act 2002.

(8) In this Act—

"UN obligation" means an obligation that the United Kingdom has by virtue of a UN Security Council Resolution;

"UN Security Council Resolution" means a resolution adopted by the Security Council of the United Nations;

"international obligation" means an obligation of the United Kingdom created or arising by or under any international agreement.

(9) For the purposes of any provision of this Act which refers to an "appropriate Minister", the following are appropriate Ministers—

    (a)   the Secretary of State;

    (b)   the Treasury.

(10) None of paragraphs (a) to (i) of subsection (2) is to be taken to limit the meaning of any other of those paragraphs.

[Sanctions and Anti-Money Laundering Act 2018, s 1.]

---

[1] The introductory note states that the Act's purposes are: make provision enabling sanctions to be imposed where appropriate for the purposes of compliance with United Nations obligations or other international obligations or for the purposes of furthering the prevention of terrorism or for the purposes of national security or international peace and security or for the purposes of furthering foreign policy objectives; to make provision for the purposes of the detection, investigation and prevention of money laundering and terrorist financing and for the purposes of implementing Standards published by the Financial Action Task Force relating to combating threats to the integrity of the international financial system; and for connected purposes.

Contents of sanctions regulations: further provision

17. Enforcement (1) In this section "regulations" means regulations under section 1.

(2) Regulations may make provision—

    (a)   for the enforcement of any prohibitions or requirements imposed by regulations;

    (b)   for the enforcement of any prohibitions or requirements imposed under regulations, including, in particular, prohibitions or requirements imposed by—

        (i)   conditions of a licence or direction issued by virtue of section 15, or

        (ii)   directions given by virtue of sections 6 and 7;

    (c)   for preventing any prohibitions or requirements mentioned in paragraph (a) or (b) from being circumvented.

(3) The provision that may be made by virtue of subsection (2) includes provision as to the powers and duties of any person who is to enforce the regulations.

(4) Regulations—

    (a)   may create criminal offences for the purposes of the enforcement of prohibitions or requirements mentioned in subsection (2)(a) or (b) or for the purposes of preventing such prohibitions or requirements from being circumvented, and

    (b)   may include provision dealing with matters relating to any offences created for such purposes by regulations (including provision that creates defences).

(5) Regulations may not provide for an offence under regulations to be punishable with imprisonment for a period exceeding—

    (a)   in the case of conviction on indictment, 10 years;

    (b)   in the case of summary conviction—

        (i)   in relation to England and Wales, 12 months or, in relation to offences committed before section 154(1) of the Criminal Justice Act 2003 comes into force, 6 months;

        (ii)   in relation to Scotland, 12 months;

        (iii)   in relation to Northern Ireland, 6 months.

(6) Regulations may include provision applying, for the purpose of the enforcement of any relevant prohibition or requirement, any provision of the Customs and Excise Management Act 1979 specified in the regulations, with or without modifications.

(7) In subsection (6) a "relevant prohibition or requirement" means—

    (a)   a prohibition or requirement imposed by regulations for a purpose mentioned in—

        (i)   section 3(1)(b) to (g) or (2), or

        (ii)   Part 1 of Schedule 1, or

    (b)   a prohibition or requirement imposed by a condition of a licence or direction issued by virtue of section 15 in relation to a prohibition or requirement mentioned in paragraph (a).

(8) Regulations may provide that a particular offence which is—

    (a)   created by virtue of this section, and

    (b)   specified by the regulations,

is an offence to which Chapter 1 of Part 2 of the Serious Organised Crime and Police Act 2005 (investigatory powers) applies.

(9) Regulations may provide that a particular provision of the regulations which—

    (a)   contains a prohibition or requirement imposed for a purpose mentioned in section 3(1) or (2), and

    (b)   is specified by the regulations,

is to be regarded as not being financial sanctions legislation for the purposes of Part 8 of the Policing and Crime Act 2017 (financial sanctions: monetary penalties).

[Sanctions and Anti-Money Laundering Act 2018, s 17.]

19. Enforcement: goods etc on ships (1) The provision that may be made by virtue of section 17(2) (enforcement of prohibitions or requirements) includes provision as to the powers and duties of prescribed persons in relation to—

    (a)   British ships in foreign waters or international waters,

    (b)   ships without nationality in international waters, and

    (c)   foreign ships in international waters.

(2) Regulations may make provision by virtue of this section only for the purpose of enforcing relevant prohibitions or requirements.

(3) A prohibition or requirement is a "relevant prohibition or requirement" for the purposes of this section if it is—

    (a)   a prohibition or requirement specified by the regulations which is imposed by regulations for a purpose mentioned in any of paragraphs 2 to 7, 15(a), (b) or (c) or 16(a) of Schedule 1, or

    (b)   a prohibition or requirement imposed by a condition of a licence or direction issued by virtue of section 15 in relation to a prohibition or requirement mentioned in paragraph (a).

(4) The powers that may be conferred by virtue of this section include powers to—

    (a)   stop a ship;

    (b)   board a ship;

    (c)   require any person found on a ship boarded by virtue of this section to provide information or produce documents;

    (d)   inspect and copy such documents or information;

    (e)   stop any person found on such a ship and search that person for—

        (i)   prohibited goods, or

        (ii)   any thing that might be used to cause physical injury or damage to property or to endanger the safety of any ship;

    (f)   search a ship boarded by virtue of this section, or any thing found on such a ship (including cargo), for prohibited goods;

    (g)   seize goods found on a ship, in any thing found on a ship, or on any person found on a ship (but see subsection (8));

    (h)   for the purpose of exercising a power mentioned in paragraph (e), (f) or (g), require a ship to be taken to, and remain in, a port or anchorage in the United Kingdom or any other country willing to receive it.

(5) Regulations that confer a power mentioned in subsection (4)(a) to (f) or (h) must provide that a person may not exercise the power in relation to a ship unless the person has reasonable grounds to suspect that the ship is carrying prohibited goods (and the regulations need not require the person to have reasonable grounds to suspect that an offence is being or has been committed).

(6) Regulations that confer a power mentioned in subsection (4)(e)(i) or (f) must provide that the power may be exercised only to the extent reasonably required for the purpose of discovering prohibited goods.

(7) Regulations that confer a power mentioned in subsection (4)(e)(ii) on a person ("the officer") may permit the search of a person only where the officer has reasonable grounds to believe that that person might use a thing in a way mentioned in subsection (4)(e)(ii).

(8) Regulations that confer a power mentioned in subsection (4)(g) on a person—

    (a)   must provide for the power to be exercisable on a ship only where that person is lawfully on the ship (whether in exercise of powers conferred by virtue of this section or otherwise), and

    (b)   may permit the seizure only of—

        (i)   goods which that person has reasonable grounds to suspect are prohibited goods, or

        (ii)   things within subsection (4)(e)(ii).

(9) Regulations that confer a power on a person by virtue of this section may authorise that person to use reasonable force, if necessary, in the exercise of the power.

(10) Regulations that confer a power by virtue of this section must provide that—

    (a)   the power may be exercised in relation to a British ship in foreign waters only with the authority of the Secretary of State, and

    (b)   in relation to foreign waters other than the sea and other waters within the seaward limits of the territorial sea adjacent to any relevant British possession, the Secretary of State may give authority only if the State in whose waters the power would be exercised consents to the exercise of the power.

(11) Regulations that confer a power by virtue of this section must provide that—

(a)   the power may be exercised in relation to a foreign ship only with the authority of the Secretary of State, and

(b)   the Secretary of State may give authority only if—

    (i)   the home state has requested the assistance of the United Kingdom for the purpose of enforcing relevant prohibitions or requirements,

    (ii)   the home state has authorised the United Kingdom to act for that purpose, or

    (iii)   the United Nations Convention on the Law of the Sea 1982 (Cmnd 8941) or a UN Security Council Resolution otherwise permits the exercise of the powers in relation to the ship.

(12)   The reference in subsection (11) to the United Nations Convention on the Law of the Sea includes a reference to any modifications of that Convention agreed after the passing of this Act that have entered into force in relation to the United Kingdom.

(13)   In this section—

"arrangements" includes any agreement, understanding, scheme, transaction or series of transactions (whether or not legally enforceable);

"British ship" means a ship falling within paragraph (a), (c), (d) or (e) of section 7(12);

"foreign ship" means a ship which—

(a)   is registered in a State other than the United Kingdom, or

(b)   is not so registered but is entitled to fly the flag of a State other than the United Kingdom;

"foreign waters" means the sea and other waters within the seaward limits of the territorial sea adjacent to any relevant British possession or State other than the United Kingdom;

"goods" includes technology within the meaning of Schedule 1 (see paragraph 37 of that Schedule);

"home state", in relation to a foreign ship, means—

(a)   the State in which the ship is registered, or

(b)   the State whose flag the ship is otherwise entitled to fly;

"international waters" means waters beyond the territorial sea of the United Kingdom or of any other State or relevant British possession;

"prohibited goods" means goods which have been, or are being, dealt with in contravention of a relevant prohibition or requirement (see subsection (3));

"regulations" means regulations under section 1;

"relevant British possession" has the same meaning as in section 7 (see subsection (14) of that section);

"ship" has the same meaning as in section 7 (see subsection (14) of that section);

"ship without nationality" means a ship which—

(a)   is not registered in, or otherwise entitled to fly the flag of, any State or relevant British possession, or

(b)   sails under the flags of two or more States or relevant British possessions, or under the flags of a State and relevant British possession, using them according to convenience.

(14)   In the definition of "prohibited goods" in subsection (13), the reference to goods dealt with in contravention of a relevant prohibition or requirement includes a reference to a case where—

(a)   arrangements relating to goods have been entered into that have not been fully implemented, and

(b)   if those arrangements were to be fully implemented, the goods would be dealt with in contravention of that prohibition or requirement.

[Sanctions and Anti-Money Laundering Act 2018, s 19.]

LOCAL GOVERNMENT

7.7106   Local Government (Miscellaneous Provisions) Act 1976, s 55A   Create Note to end of s 55A(1)(b): '[1] *In Milton Keynes Council v Skyline Taxis and Private Hire Ltd* [2017] EWHC 2794 (Admin), [2018] LL7 73 a private hire operator (R1) and its director (R2) held licences in neighbouring licensing authorities, operating in one in the name Skyline SNC and in the other as Skyline MK. The two entities shared the same unitary computer system. The prosecution was brought in consequence of Skyline MK taking a booking and allocating it to Skyline SNC, ie to a driver and vehicle not licensed by the appellant local authority but to a neighbouring one. The issue was whether or not this fell within s 55A, in which case there was no offence. At first instance the charges were dismissed on the ground that the prosecutor had failed to prove that the booking had not been "subcontracted".

The decision was upheld in the subsequent appeal by way of case stated. The prosecutor had contended that s 55A required that the two operators had separate controlling minds and that there had to be a positive decision by the sub-contractor to accept the booking. The Administrative Court disagreed. Section 55A(3) required the matter to be approached on the basis that the operator's licences were held by separate persons. The scheme R1 and R2 had adopted fulfilled the obvious purpose of s 55A. The provisions clearly contemplated a single operator having multiple licences in different areas. Section 55A(1)(b) was focused on the district in which the sub-contracted booking was accepted. It mattered not that the initial acceptance happened in a different area. The integrity of the scheme required that the second operator accepted the booking as one made in the district in which that operator held its licence, so that the booking would be subject to that licence.'

7.7530   Non-Domestic Rating (Collection and Enforcement) (Local Lists) Regulations 1989, reg 5   *In reg 5(1) after 'practicable' create note 2 as follows:* '[2] There are limited challenges that can be advanced to resist liability once a demand notice has been served. However, one matter that the billing authority must establish is that the demand notice was served "as soon as practicable". There are conflicting opinions as to whether this requirement is absolute or whether the respondent must also establish that they have suffered some prejudice as a result of any delay in serving the notice: see *Encon Insulation Ltd v Nottingham City Council* [1999] All ER (D) 58, *North Somerset District Council v Honda* [2010] EWHC 1505 (QB), and *R (on the application of LB Waltham Forest) v Waltham Forest Magistrates Court* [2008] EWHC 2579 (Admin).'

7.7574   Council Tax (Administration and Enforcement) Regulations 1992, reg 34   *In note 1 delete the word 'service' and replace with the following word:* 'served'.

MEDICINE AND PHARMACY

7.8199   Psychoactive Substances Act 2016, s 3   *Add to citation of R v Chapman in existing Note 1:* '[2018] 1 Cr App R 9'.

PERSONS, OFFENCES AGAINST

7.8588   Consent   *Insert text in new para after reference to existing Note 3, create Note and continue text in new para:* 'Where a registered tattooist and body piercer also did body modifications, and had no medical qualifications, and was charged with three counts of causing grievous bodily harm with intent in consequence of carrying out operations without anaesthetic: to remove an ear; to remove a nipple; and to split a person's tongue to resemble a reptile's tongue, the consent of the clients concerned did not provide a defence. There was no easily articulated principle by which novel situations could be judged, but most of the exceptions to consent as a defence had a basis in some discernible social benefit, such as sport, or dangerous exhibitions as social entertainment or religious ritual.

"41 New exceptions should not be recognised on a case by case basis, save perhaps where there is a close analogy with an existing exception to the general rule established in the Brown case. The recognition of an entirely new exception would involve a value judgement which is policy laden, and on which there may be powerful conflicting views in society. The criminal trial process is inapt to enable a wide-ranging inquiry into the underlying policy issues, which are much better explored in the political environment.

42 That said, there is, to our minds, no proper analogy between body modification, which involves the removal of parts of the body or mutilation as seen in tongue splitting, and tattooing, piercing or other body adornment. What the defendant undertook for reward in this case was a series of medical procedures performed for no medical reason. When Lord Lane referred to "reasonable surgical interference" in the Attorney General's Reference case (quoted in [23] above) it carried with the implication that elective surgery would only be reasonable if carried out by someone qualified to perform it. The professional and regulatory superstructure which governs how doctors and other medical professionals practise is there to protect the public. The protections provided to patients, some of which are referred to in the medical evidence before the judge, were not available to the appellant's customers or more widely to the customers of those who set themselves up as body modifiers. It is immaterial that this appellant took some trouble to ensure a sterile environment when he operated, or that his work was in some respects tidy and clean. Consent as a defence could not turn on the quality of the work then performed.

43 The protection of the public in this context extends beyond the risks of infection, bungled or poor surgery or an inability to deal with immediate complications. Those seeking body modification of the sort we are concerned with in this appeal invited the appellant to perform irreversible surgery without anaesthetic with profound long-term consequences. The fact that a desire to have an ear or nipple removed or tongue split is incomprehensible to most, may not be sufficient in itself to raise the question whether those who seek to do so might be in need of a mental health assessment. Yet the first response in almost every other context to those who seek to harm themselves would be to suggest medical assistance. That is not to say that all who seek body modification are suffering from any identifiable mental illness but it is difficult to avoid the conclusion that some will be, and that within the cohort will be many who are vulnerable. There are good reasons why reputable medical practitioners will not remove parts of the body simply when asked by a patient. One only has to reflect on the care, degree of inquiry and support given to a patient before gender reassignment surgery can be performed to appreciate the extensive nature of the protections provided in the medical context.

44 The personal autonomy of his customers does not provide the appellant with a justification for removing body modification from the ambit of the law of assault. It is true that Mr Lott could have cut his own left ear off and in doing so would have committed no criminal offence. So too the

other customers. But the personal autonomy of one individual does not extend to involving another in what would otherwise be a crime. We note that the European Court of Human Rights rejected the arguments advanced under article 8 of the Convention by the appellants in the Brown case, (1997) 24 EHRR 39, and remind ourselves that the level of harm engaged in that case was below really serious injury.

45 In short, we can see no good reason why body modification should be placed in a special category of exemption from the general rule that the consent of an individual to injury provides no defence to the person who inflicts that injury if the violence causes actual bodily harm or more serious injury . . . .' (Per Lord Burnet LCJ)[4]

---

[4] *R v BM; R v M* [2018] EWCA Crim 560, [2018] 2 Cr App R 1..'"

7.8627   Infanticide Act 1938, s 1   *At the end of s 1(2) change note 1 to note 3 and insert the following text in a new note 3 as follows:* '[3] For infanticide to be left as an alternative verdict to murder, s 1 does not require the effects of giving birth to be the sole cause of a mother's disturbance of balance of mind. It is sufficient if a failure to recover from the effects of birth was an operative or substantial cause of the disturbance of balance of mind, even if there were other underlying mental problems that contributed to it: see *R v Tunstill* [2018] EWCA Crim 1696, [2018] All ER (D) 26.'

7.8632   Suicide Act 1961, s 2   *At the end of note 2 delete the following text* 'R *(Conway) v Secretary of State for Justice [2017] EWHC 2447 (Admin), [2018] 2 All ER 881, [2018] 2 WLR 322.' and substitute with the following:* 'R *(on the application of Conway) v Secretary of State for Justice* [2018] EWCA Civ 1431; [2018] All ER (D) 156, (2018) *Times*, July 26.'

7.8659   Protection from Harassment Act 1997, s 1   *In existing Note 5 replace the All ER (D) citation of Loake v CPS:* '[2018] 2 WLR 1159, [2018] 1 Cr App R 15, [2018] Crim LR 336.'

7.8668   Protection from Harassment Act 1997, s 5A   Add to existing Note 2 in new para: 'R *v Smith (Mark John)* [2012] EWCA Crim 2566; [2013] 1 WLR 1399; [2013] 2 Cr App R (S) 28 the court looked at the meaning of s 5A(1) and concluded:

"29. There are other fundamental problems with the order. Since the purpose of such an order is to protect a person from harassment by an acquitted defendant, the court must first be satisfied that the defendant is likely to pursue a course of conduct which amounts to harassment within the meaning of s 1. Pursuit of a course of conduct requires intention .

30. Further, the power to make an order under s5A is circumscribed by the important words 'necessary . . . to protect a person from harassment by the defendant'. The word 'necessary' is not to be diluted. To make an order prohibiting a person who has not committed any criminal offence from doing an act which is otherwise lawful, on pain of imprisonment, is an interference with that person's freedom of action which could be justified only when it is truly necessary for the protection of some other person."

See further *R v Taylor* [2017] EWCA Crim 2209, [2018] 1 Cr App R (S) 39, where an order was quashed because the necessity test had not been made out.'

7.8687   Terrorism Act 2000, s 12   *In the last para of existing Note 1 add to the citation of R v Choudary:* '[2018] 1 Cr App R 21'.

7.8777   Terrorism Act 2000, s 120C   *Create Note to 'Order in Council' in s 120C(1) as follows:* '[1] The Terrorism Act 2000 (Enforcement in Different Parts of the United Kingdom) Order 2018, SI 2018/521, has been made.'

7.9038A   The Laser (Misuse of Vehicles) Act 2018   *After the Counter-Terrorisim and Security Act 2015 insert the Laser (Misuse of Vehicles) Act 2018 as follows:*

Laser Misuse (Vehicles) Act 2018[1]
(2018 c 9)

1.   Offence of shining or directing a laser beam towards a vehicle   (1)   A person commits an offence if—
  (a)   the person shines or directs a laser beam towards a vehicle which is moving or ready to move, and
  (b)   the laser beam dazzles or distracts, or is likely to dazzle or distract, a person with control of the vehicle.
  (2)   It is a defence to show—
  (a)   that the person had a reasonable excuse for shining or directing the laser beam towards the vehicle, or
  (b)   that the person—
    (i)   did not intend to shine or direct the laser beam towards the vehicle, and
    (ii)   exercised all due diligence and took all reasonable precautions to avoid doing so.
  (3)   A person is taken to have shown a fact mentioned in subsection (2) if—
  (a)   sufficient evidence is adduced to raise an issue with respect to it, and
  (b)   the contrary is not proved beyond reasonable doubt.
  (4)   A person who commits an offence under this section is liable—

(a)   on summary conviction in England and Wales, to imprisonment for a term not exceeding 12 months, to a fine or to both;

(b)   on summary conviction in Scotland, to imprisonment for a term not exceeding 12 months, to a fine not exceeding the statutory maximum or to both;

(c)   on summary conviction in Northern Ireland, to imprisonment for a term not exceeding six months, to a fine not exceeding the statutory maximum or to both;

(d)   on conviction on indictment, to imprisonment for a term not exceeding five years, to a fine or to both.

(5)   In relation to an offence committed before the coming into force of section 154(1) of the Criminal Justice Act 2003, the reference in subsection (4)(a) to 12 months is to be read as a reference to six months.

(6)   A mechanically propelled vehicle which is not moving or ready to move but whose engine or motor is running is to be treated for the purposes of subsection (1)(a) as ready to move.

(7)   In relation to an aircraft, the reference in subsection (1)(b) to "a person with control of the vehicle" is a reference to any person on the aircraft who is engaged in controlling it, or in monitoring the controlling of it.

(8)   In relation to a vessel, hovercraft or submarine, the reference in subsection (1)(b) to "a person with control of the vehicle" is a reference to the master, the pilot or any person engaged in navigating the vessel, hovercraft or submarine.

---

[1] The Act came into force on 10th May 2018. It creates offences of shining or directing a laser beam towards a vehicle or air traffic facility; and for connected purposes.
[Laser Misuse (Vehicles) Act 2018, s 1.]

2. Offences relating to air traffic services   (1)   A person commits an offence if—

(a)   the person shines or directs a laser beam—
         (i)   towards an air traffic facility, or
         (ii)   towards a person providing air traffic services, and

(b)   the laser beam dazzles or distracts, or is likely to dazzle or distract, a person providing air traffic services.

(2)   It is a defence to show—

(a)   that the person had a reasonable excuse for shining or directing the laser beam towards the facility or person, or

(b)   that the person—
         (i)   did not intend to shine or direct the laser beam towards the facility or person, and
         (ii)   exercised all due diligence and took all reasonable precautions to avoid doing so.

(3)   A person is taken to have shown a fact mentioned in subsection (2) if—

(a)   sufficient evidence is adduced to raise an issue with respect to it, and

(b)   the contrary is not proved beyond reasonable doubt.

(4)   A person who commits an offence under this section is liable—

(a)   on summary conviction in England and Wales, to imprisonment for a term not exceeding 12 months, to a fine or to both;

(b)   on summary conviction in Scotland, to imprisonment for a term not exceeding 12 months, to a fine not exceeding the statutory maximum or to both;

(c)   on summary conviction in Northern Ireland, to imprisonment for a term not exceeding six months, to a fine not exceeding the statutory maximum or to both;

(d)   on conviction on indictment, to imprisonment for a term not exceeding five years, to a fine or to both.

(5)   In relation to an offence committed before the coming into force of section 154(1) of the Criminal Justice Act 2003, the reference in subsection (4)(a) to 12 months is to be read as a reference to six months.

(6)   In this section—

"air traffic facility" means any building, structure, vehicle or other place from which air traffic services are provided;

"air traffic services" has the meaning given by section 98(1) of the Transport Act 2000.
[Laser Misuse (Vehicles) Act 2018, s 2.]

3. Interpretation   In this Act—

"aircraft" means any vehicle used for travel by air;

"laser beam" means a beam of coherent light produced by a device of any kind;

"vehicle" means any vehicle used for travel by land, water or air;

"vessel" has the meaning given by section 255(1) of the Merchant Shipping Act 1995.
[Laser Misuse (Vehicles) Act 2018, s 3.]

4. Extent, commencement and short title   (1)   This Act extends to England and Wales, Scotland and Northern Ireland.

(2)   This section and section 3 come into force on the day on which this Act is passed.

(3)   Section 1 comes into force, so far as extending to England and Wales and Scotland, at the end of the period of two months beginning with the day on which this Act is passed.

(4)   Section 1 comes into force, so far as extending to Northern Ireland—

(a)   in relation to aircraft, vessels, hovercraft and submarines, at the end of the period of two months beginning with the day on which this Act is passed;

(b)   in relation to other vehicles, on such day as the Secretary of State may by regulations made by statutory instrument appoint.

(5)   Section 2 comes into force at the end of the period of two months beginning with the day on which this Act is passed.

(6)   Different days may be appointed under subsection (4)(b) for different purposes.

(7)   This Act may be cited as the Laser Misuse (Vehicles) Act 2018.

[Laser Misuse (Vehicles) Act 2018, s 4.]

POLICE

7.9081   Police Act 1996, s 89   *Add to the end of existing Note 6 in new para:* 'Self- defence is available as a defence to obstructing a police officer in the execution of his duty: *Oraki v Crown Prosecution Service* [2018] EWHC 115 (Admin), [2018] 1 Cr App R 27, [2018] Crim L R 655.'

7.9094   Police Act 1997, s 113B   *Add to existing Note 3 in new para:* 'It is neither necessary nor appropriate, as a matter of domestic law or under art 8, for those responsible for an ECRC to conduct a detailed analysis of the evidence at the trial. Additional information might, in some cases, be available about the circumstances of the acquittal, including possibly the court's own statements about it, which might give reasons for treating the court's disposal as less than decisive. However, in the absence of information of that kind, it was not the officers' job to fill the gap: *R (AR) v Chief Constable of Greater Manchester* [2018] UKSC 47, [2018] ALL ER (D) 166 (Jul).'

7.9127   Police Reform Act 2002, s 13A   *Add to the next which begins 'Part 2A' in new para:* 'The Police Super-complaints (Designation and Procedure) Regulations 2018, SI 2018/748 have been made.'

PUBLIC HEALTH

7.10207   Environmental Permitting (England and Wales) Regulations 2016   *After the Environmental Permitting (England and Wakes) Regulations 2016, insert the Non-Road Mobile Machinery (Type-Approval and Emission of Gaseous and Particulate Pollutants) Regulations 2018, SI 2018/764 as follows:*

Non-Road Mobile Machinery (Type-Approval and Emission of Gaseous and Particulate Pollutants) Regulations 2018

(2018/764)

7.10207A   1.   *Citation, commencement and effect*   These Regulations—

(a)   may be cited as the Non-Road Mobile Machinery (Type-Approval and Emission of Gaseous and Particulate Pollutants) Regulations 2018;

(b)   come into force on 21st September 2018; and

(c)   are of no effect in relation to any matter to which paragraphs 3 to 11 of article 58 of the NRMM Regulation applies.

2.   *Interpretation*   (1)   In these Regulations—

"enforcement authority" means the Secretary of State;

"the NRMM Regulation" means Regulation (EU) 2016/1628 of the European Parliament and of the Council on requirements relating to gaseous and particulate pollutant emission limits and type-approval for internal combustion engines for non-road mobile machinery, as it may be amended from time to time;

"relevant products" means—

     (a)   engines;

     (b)   components or assemblies of components that go to make up engines;

     (c)   devices which are capable of forming part of emission control systems; or

     (d)   non-road mobile machinery.

(2)   Unless otherwise provided, any word or expression used in these Regulations which is defined in article 3 of the NRMM Regulation has the meaning given in that article.

3.   *Appointment of approval authority*   The Secretary of State is the approval authority for the purposes of these Regulations and the NRMM Regulation.

4.   *Market surveillance authority*   The Secretary of State is the market surveillance authority for the purposes of—

(a)   these Regulations and the NRMM Regulation; and

(b)   where applied by the NRMM Regulation, Regulation (EC) No 765/2008 of the European Parliament and of the Council setting out the requirements for accreditation and market surveillance relating to the marketing of products and repealing Regulation (EEC) No 339/93.

5.   *Requests for information: failure to comply*   Where a manufacturer who makes an application for type-approval fails to comply with a request for additional information made under paragraph 1(c) of article 21 of the NRMM Regulation, the approval authority may treat the application as having been withdrawn by the manufacturer.

6. Refusal of EU type-approval application (1)   The approval authority must refuse an EU type-approval application if the requirements of—
(a)   articles 22 and 24 to 26; or
(b)   article 35,
of the NRMM Regulation have not been complied with.
(2)   The requirements of article 24 of the NRMM Regulation are not complied with if the tests required by that article demonstrate that there is non-compliance with the technical prescriptions mentioned in paragraph 1 of that article.
(3)   The requirements of article 26 of the NRMM Regulation are not complied with if the approval authority is not satisfied that the applicant has made or will make adequate arrangements to ensure that—
(a)   production will conform to the approved type; or
(b)   where applicable, the data in the statements of conformity are correct.

7. Conformity of production: record keeping The holder of an EU type-approval mentioned in article 26 of the NRMM Regulation must compile and retain for inspection by the approval authority for a period of five years commencing with the date of compilation, such records of tests and checks undertaken that are sufficient to demonstrate—
(a)   conformity of production to the approved type;
(b)   compliance of statements of conformity to article 31 of the NRMM Regulation; and
(c)   that, where applicable, the data in statements of conformity issued by the holder are correct.

8. Review of decisions (1)   A decision to which article 41 of the NRMM Regulation applies must be given by notice in writing ("a relevant notice").
(2)   Where the approval authority has given a person a relevant notice, that person may apply to the approval authority for a reconsideration of the decision given in that notice.
(3)   An application under paragraph (2) must—
(a)   be made within the period of 28 days beginning on the date when the relevant notice is received; and
(b)   state the reasons for making the application and be accompanied by such further evidence as the person believes supports those reasons.
(4)   The approval authority may—
(a)   request evidence in support of the application;
(b)   after giving reasonable notice to the applicant, carry out a re-examination of one or more engines for the purpose of determining the issues raised by the application.
(5)   The approval authority must as soon as reasonably practicable—
(a)   give written notification to the applicant stating whether the decision is confirmed, amended or reversed; and
(b)   if the decision is reversed or amended, take the appropriate action in respect of the revised decision.
(6)   An applicant aggrieved by the approval authority's notification under paragraph (5) may by notice request the approval authority to appoint an independent assessor to review the decision to which the relevant notice relates.
(7)   A request under paragraph (6) must—
(a)   be made not later than 28 days after receipt of the approval authority's notification under paragraph (5); and
(b)   state the reasons for the request.
(8)   As soon as reasonably practicable after the date of receipt of the request under paragraph (6), the approval authority must—
(a)   appoint a person to act as assessor or, at the authority's discretion, not more than three persons to act as an assessment panel; and
(b)   notify the applicant of the appointment.
(9)   The independent assessor or assessment panel may—
(a)   request further evidence in support of the request for review;
(b)   after giving reasonable notice to the applicant, carry out a re-examination of one or more engines for the purpose of determining the issues raised by the request for review.

9. Withdrawal of approvals: mistake or error (1)   Subject to the provisions of this regulation, the approval authority may decide to withdraw any approval given by it by reason of mistake or error on the part of that authority.
(2)   A decision to withdraw an approval must be given by notice in writing ("a relevant notice") and specify—
(a)   the nature of the mistake or error; and
(b)   the date from which the approval is to be withdrawn, which must be not less than 28 days nor more than six months after the date on which the relevant notice is given.
(3)   Regulation 8(2) to (9) applies to the review of a decision under this regulation.
(4)   Any review of a decision under this regulation may, subject to the requirement in paragraph (2)(b), vary the date from which the approval is to be withdrawn.

10. Withdrawal and suspension of approvals: effect (1)   If the holder of an approval which has been withdrawn or suspended pursuant to the NRMM Regulation or these Regulations purports by virtue of that approval to—
(a)   issue a statement of conformity with respect to an engine; or
(b)   affix a statutory marking pursuant to article 32 of the NRMM Regulation,

the statement or marking is invalid.

(2)   The approval authority may, by notice given to the holder, exempt from paragraph (1) one or more engine types within an engine family specified in the notice.

11.   *Service*   (1)   Paragraphs (2) to (4) of this regulation have effect in relation to any notice or other document required or authorised by these Regulations or the NRMM Regulation to be given to or served on any person by the approval authority, market surveillance authority or enforcement authority.

(2)   Any such notice or document may be given to or served on the person in question—

(a)   by delivering it to the person;

(b)   by leaving it at that person's proper address;

(c)   by sending it by post to that person at that address;

(d)   by means of any form of electronic communication agreed with the person to whom it is to be sent.

(3)   Any such notice or document may—

(a)   in the case of a body corporate, be given to or served on an officer of that body;

(b)   in the case of a partnership, be given to or served on any partner;

(c)   in the case of an unincorporated association other than a partnership, be given to or served on any member of the governing body of that association.

(4)   For the purposes of this regulation and section 7 of the Interpretation Act 1978 (service of documents by post) in its application to this regulation, the proper address of any person is that person's last known address (whether of the person's residence or of a place where the person carries on business or is employed) and also—

(a)   in the case of a body corporate or an officer of that body, the address of the registered or principal office of that body in the United Kingdom;

(b)   in the case of an unincorporated association other than a partnership or a member of its governing body, its principal office in the United Kingdom;

(c)   an address within the United Kingdom other than that person's proper address at which that person, or another acting on that person's behalf, will accept service of any notice or document required or authorised by these Regulations or the NRMM Regulation to be given to or served on any person by the approval authority.

(5)   Any notice or other document or information required by these Regulations or the NRMM Regulation to be given to or served by any person on the approval authority, market surveillance authority or enforcement authority must be—

(a)   in writing; or

(b)   in an electronic format accepted by, and sent by means of any form of electronic communication agreed with, the approval authority, market surveillance authority or enforcement authority (as appropriate).

12.   *Provision of testing stations*   The approval authority may provide and maintain stations where examinations of relevant products may be carried out for the purposes of these Regulations or the NRMM Regulation and may provide and maintain apparatus for carrying out such examinations.

13.   *Information and instructions: loss or damage*   (1)   Where a duty is imposed on a manufacturer by article 43 of the NRMM Regulation (information and instructions intended for OEMs and end-users), any breach of the duty which causes a person to sustain loss or damage is actionable at the suit of that person.

(2)   But, in any proceedings brought against a manufacturer in pursuance of this regulation, it is a defence for the manufacturer to show that the manufacturer took all reasonable steps and exercised all due diligence to avoid the breach.

14.   *Defeat Devices*   (1)   For the purposes of articles 18 and 57 of the NRMM Regulation, "use of defeat strategies" or "using defeat strategies" is where an engine manufactured by a person—

(a)   is placed on the market in the United Kingdom; and

(b)   that engine is fitted with a defeat device.

(2)   A separate offence under article 18(4) the NRMM Regulation is committed in respect of each such engine placed on the market.

(3)   Where, following examination of engines associated with a single engine type approval, the enforcement authority is satisfied that two or more of those engines—

(a)   are engines which have been affixed with a statutory marking under article 32 of the NRMM Regulation in respect of that approval; and

(b)   are fitted with a defeat device,

each engine associated with that single engine type approval is to be taken to be similarly fitted with a defeat device unless proved otherwise by the manufacturer.

(4)   In paragraph (3), an engine is associated with an engine type approval if the statutory marking affixed to the engine under article 32 of the NRMM Regulation cites the type approval number for that type approval.

(5)   In this regulation—

"auxiliary emission control strategy" has the meaning given in article 1(10) of Commission Delegated Regulation (EU) 2017/654;

"Commission Delegated Regulation (EU) 2017/654" means Commission Delegated Regulation (EU) 2017/654 supplementing Regulation (EU) 2016/1628 of the European Parliament and of the Council on requirements relating to gaseous and particulate pollutant emission limits and type-approval for internal combustion engines for non-road mobile machinery;

"defeat device" means—

(a)　　a defeat strategy; or

(b)　　an auxiliary emission control strategy which is prohibited under point 2.3.7 of Annex IV of Commission Delegated Regulation (EU) 2017/654;

"placed on the market" means supplying to a third party or making available for distribution or use in the course of a commercial activity, whether in return for payment or free of charge, and includes exposure for sale to a third party.

15.　*Offences, enforcement and civil penalties* (1)　Schedule 1 (offences, penalties, enforcement and other matters) has effect.

(2)　Except in paragraph 2 of Schedule 1 or in relation to the expression "Officer of Revenue and Customs", a reference in Schedule 1 to an officer is a reference to any person authorised by the enforcement authority to assist the authority in enforcing these Regulations and the NRMM Regulation.

16.　*Consequential amendments and revocations* Schedule 2 (consequential amendments and revocations) has effect.

Signed by authority of the Secretary of State for Transport
Jesse Norman
Parliamentary Under Secretary of State
Department for Transport
25th June 2018

SCHEDULE 1
Offences, Penalties, Enforcement and other Matters　　　　　　　　Regulation 15

PART 1　OFFENCES

Offences and penalties

1.　A person who is an economic operator is guilty of an offence if that person—

(a)　　contravenes any prohibition in these Regulations or the NRMM Regulation; or

(b)　　fails to comply with any requirement or obligation in these Regulations or the NRMM Regulation.

Offences by bodies corporate and partnerships

2.　(1)　If an offence under these Regulations committed by a body corporate is proved to have been committed with the consent or connivance of, or to be attributable to neglect on the part of, an officer of the body corporate, or a person purporting to act as an officer of the body corporate, that officer or person (as well as the body corporate) is guilty of the offence and is liable to be proceeded against and punished accordingly.

(2)　If the affairs of a body corporate are managed by its members, sub-paragraph (1) applies in relation to the acts and omissions of a member in connection with the member's functions of management as it applies to an officer of the body corporate.

(3)　If an offence under these Regulations is—

(a)　　committed by a Scottish partnership; and

(b)　　proved to have been committed with the consent or connivance of, or to be attributable to neglect on the part of, a partner of the partnership,

the partner (as well as the partnership) is guilty of the offence and is liable to be proceeded against and punished accordingly.

(4)　In this paragraph "officer" in relation to a body corporate means a director, secretary or other similar officer of the body corporate.

PART 2　PENALTIES

Criminal penalties

3.　(1)　A person guilty of an offence under these Regulations in relation to regulation 14 or articles 18 and 57 of the NRMM Regulation is punishable on summary conviction—

(a)　　in England and Wales by a fine; or

(b)　　in Scotland or Northern Ireland by a fine not exceeding level 5 on the standard scale.

(2)　But an offence is not punishable under this paragraph if—

(a)　　the enforcement authority has required a person to pay a penalty in respect of that offence under paragraph 4; and

(b)　　that penalty has been paid to the enforcement authority.

Civil penalties

4.　(1)　The enforcement authority may require a person who is an economic operator to pay a penalty if the enforcement authority is satisfied, on a balance of probabilities, that the person has committed an offence mentioned in paragraph 1.

(2)　But the enforcement authority may not require a person to pay a penalty if—

(a)　　the person shows that there was a reasonable excuse for committing the offence; or

(b)　　criminal proceedings (where applicable) have been instituted against the person in respect of the same offence.

(3)　A penalty imposed under this paragraph may not exceed £50,000 per offence.

(4)　The penalty is payable to the enforcement authority on demand.

Notification of penalty decision

5.　(1)　If the enforcement authority decides to require a person to pay a penalty under these Regulations, the enforcement authority must give the person a penalty notice.

(2)　A penalty notice must—

(a)　　be in writing;

(b)　　state the enforcement authority's reasons for deciding to require the person to pay a penalty;

(c)　　state the amount of the penalty;

(d)　　specify the date on which it is given;

(e)　　specify the date, at least 28 days after the date specified in the notice as the date on which it is given, before which the penalty must be paid;

(f)　　specify how a penalty must be paid;

(g)　　include an explanation of the steps that the person may take if the person objects to the penalty (including specifying the manner and form in which any notice of objection must be given to the enforcement authority); and

(h)   include an explanation of the steps the enforcement authority may take to recover any unpaid penalty.

Objection to penalty decision

6.   (1)   The recipient of a penalty notice (the "recipient") may object to the penalty notice by giving a notice of objection to the enforcement authority.

(2)   A notice of objection must—

(a)   give the reasons for the objection;

(b)   be given to the enforcement authority in the manner and form specified in the penalty notice; and

(c)   be given before the end of the period of 28 days beginning with the date specified in the penalty notice as the date on which it is given.

(3)   Where the enforcement authority receives a notice of objection, the enforcement authority must consider it and—

(a)   cancel the penalty;

(b)   reduce the penalty;

(c)   increase the penalty; or

(d)   determine not to alter the penalty.

(4)   After reaching a decision as to how to proceed under sub-paragraph (3), the enforcement authority must notify the recipient of the decision in writing.

(5)   A notification under sub-paragraph (4) must be given before the end of the period of 70 days beginning with the date specified in the penalty notice as the date on which it is given, or such longer period as the enforcement authority may agree with the recipient.

(6)   A notification under sub-paragraph (4), other than one notifying the recipient that the enforcement authority has decided to cancel the penalty, must—

(a)   state the amount of the penalty following the enforcement authority's consideration of the notice of objection;

(b)   state the enforcement authority's reasons for the decision under sub-paragraph (3);

(c)   specify the date, at least 28 days after the date on which the notification is given, before which the penalty must be paid;

(d)   specify how the penalty must be paid;

(e)   include an explanation of the recipient's rights of appeal; and

(f)   include an explanation of the steps the enforcement authority may take to recover any unpaid penalty.

(7)   A notification under sub-paragraph (4) notifying the recipient that the enforcement authority has decided to cancel the penalty must state the enforcement authority's reasons for the decision under sub-paragraph (3).

Civil penalties: appeals

7.   (1)   A person (the "appellant") may appeal to the court against a decision to require the person to pay a penalty under these Regulations.

(2)   An appeal may be brought only if the appellant has given a notice of objection and the enforcement authority has—

(a)   reduced the penalty under paragraph 6(3)(b);

(b)   increased the penalty under paragraph 6(3)(c); or

(c)   determined not to alter the penalty under paragraph 6(3)(d).

(3)   An appeal must be brought within the period of 28 days beginning with the date on which the person is notified of the enforcement authority's decision on the notice of objection under paragraph 6(4).

(4)   On appeal, the court may—

(a)   allow the appeal and cancel the penalty;

(b)   allow the appeal and reduce the penalty; or

(c)   dismiss the appeal.

(5)   An appeal—

(a)   is to be a re-hearing of the enforcement authority's decision to impose a penalty; and

(b)   may be determined having regard to matters of which the enforcement authority was unaware.

(6)   Sub-paragraph (5)(a) has effect despite any provision of rules of court.

(7)   In this paragraph, a reference to "the court" is a reference—

(a)   in England and Wales, to the county court;

(b)   in Scotland, to the sheriff; and

(c)   in Northern Ireland, to a county court.

(8)   But—

(a)   the county court in England and Wales, or a county court in Northern Ireland, may transfer proceedings under this regulation to the High Court; and

(b)   the sheriff may transfer proceedings under this regulation to the Court of Session.

PART 3   ENFORCEMENT AND OTHER MATTERS

Enforcement of penalty decision

8.   (1)   This paragraph applies where a sum is payable to the enforcement authority as a penalty under these Regulations.

(2)   In England and Wales the penalty is recoverable as if it were payable under an order of the county court in England and Wales.

(3)   In Scotland the penalty may be enforced in the same manner as an extract registered decree arbitral bearing a warrant for execution issued by the sheriff court of any sheriffdom in Scotland.

(4)   In Northern Ireland the penalty is recoverable as if it were payable under an order of a county court in Northern Ireland.

(5)   Where action is taken under this paragraph for the recovery of a sum payable as a penalty under these Regulations, the penalty is—

(a)   in relation to England and Wales, to be treated for the purposes of section 98 of the Courts Act 2003 (register of judgments and orders etc) as if it were a judgment entered in the county court;

(b)   in relation to Northern Ireland, to be treated for the purposes of Article 116 of the Judgments Enforcement (Northern Ireland) Order 1981 (register of judgments) as if it were a judgment in respect of which an application has been accepted under Article 22 or 23(1) of that Order.

Obstruction of officers and false statements

9.   (1)   A person must not—

(a)   intentionally obstruct an officer when acting in pursuance of any provision of these Regulations;

(b)   intentionally fail to comply with any requirement properly made by an officer under any provision of these Regulations; or

(c)   without reasonable cause, fail to give an officer any other assistance or information which the officer may reasonably require of that person for the purposes of the exercise of the officer's functions under any provision of these Regulations.

(2)   A person must not, in giving any information which is required of that person by virtue of sub-paragraph (1)(c)—

(a)   make any statement which the person knows is false in a material particular; or

(b)   recklessly make a statement which is false in a material particular.

Powers of search, etc

10.   (1)   Officers may exercise any of the powers set out in sub-paragraph (2) at all reasonable hours provided—

(a)   the officers identify themselves and produce authority in writing from the enforcement authority for the exercise by the officers of powers conferred on the authority by these Regulations; and

(b)   state the purpose of the officers' actions and the grounds for undertaking them.

(2)   The powers referred to in sub-paragraph (1) are as follows—

(a)   an officer may for the purpose of ascertaining whether an offence under these Regulations has been committed—

    (i)   inspect any relevant products; and

    (ii)   enter any premises other than premises used wholly or mainly as a dwelling;

(b)   if an officer has reasonable cause to suspect that an offence under these Regulations has been committed, the officer may, for the purpose of ascertaining whether it has been committed, require any person carrying on, or employed in connection with, a business to produce any records relating to the relevant products and the officer may take copies of those records or any part of them;

(c)   if an officer has reasonable cause to suspect that an offence under these Regulations has been committed, the officer may seize and detain any relevant products for the purpose of ascertaining whether the offence has been committed;

(d)   an officer may seize and detain any relevant products or records which the officer has reason to believe may be required as evidence in proceedings for an offence under these Regulations;

(e)   an officer may, for the purpose of exercising the officer's powers of seizure under this sub-paragraph, but only if and to the extent that it is reasonably necessary in order to secure that the provisions of these Regulations are duly observed, require any person having authority to do so to open any container and, if that person does not comply with the requirement or if there is no person present having authority to open it, the officer may break open the container.

(3)   For the purposes of sub-paragraph (2), the officer may require information stored electronically to be made available in printed form.

(4)   An officer may, for the purpose of ascertaining whether an offence has been committed under these Regulations, make a purchase of relevant products.

(5)   If a justice is satisfied by any written information on oath—

(a)   that there are reasonable grounds for believing either—

    (i)   that any relevant products or records, which an officer has power under this paragraph to inspect, copy, seize or require to be produced, is or are on any premises and that the inspection, copying, seizure or production of that item is likely to disclose evidence of the commission of an offence under these Regulations; or

    (ii)   that any offence under these Regulations has been, is being, or is about to be committed on any premises; and

(b)   either—

    (i)   that admission to the premises has been or is likely to be refused and that notice of intention to apply for a warrant under this sub-paragraph has been given to the occupier; or

    (ii)   that an application for admission, or the giving of such a notice, would defeat the object of the entry or that the premises are unoccupied or that the occupier is temporarily absent and it might defeat the object of the entry to await the occupier's return,

the justice may by warrant under the justice's hand, which continues in force for a period of one month, authorise an officer to enter the premises, if need be by force.

(6)   On entering any premises by authority of a warrant granted under sub-paragraph (5), an officer must, if the occupier is present, give to the occupier or, if the occupier is temporarily absent, leave in a prominent place on the premises, or an appropriate part of the premises, a notice in writing—

(a)   summarising an officer's powers of seizure and detention of any relevant products or records under this paragraph;

(b)   explaining that compensation may be payable for damage caused in entering premises and seizing and removing any relevant products or records and giving the address to which an application for compensation should be directed; and

(c)   indicating at which office of the enforcement authority and within which hours a copy of these Regulations is available to be consulted.

(7)   An officer, when entering any premises by virtue of this paragraph, may be accompanied by such persons and take such equipment as appear to the officer to be necessary.

(8)   An officer, when leaving any premises which the officer entered by virtue of a warrant, must, if the premises are unoccupied or the occupier is temporarily absent, leave them in as secure a state as that in which they were found.

(9)   When exercising any power of seizure and detention under this paragraph, an officer must, as soon as practicable, give to the person against whom the power has been exercised, a written notice stating—

(a)   precisely what has been so seized and detained;

(b)   that an application for the release of a detained item may be made in accordance with paragraph 12 of this Schedule; and

(c)   the procedure for making such an application.

(10)   A person who is not an officer of the enforcement authority must not purport to act as such under this paragraph.

(11)   In sub-paragraph (5), the reference to "any written information on oath" is to be construed, in the application of this paragraph to—

(a)   Scotland, as a reference to any evidence on oath;

(b)   Northern Ireland, as a reference to any complaint on oath.

(12)   In this paragraph, "justice" means—

(a)   in England and Wales, a justice of the peace;

(b)   in Scotland, a sheriff or summary sheriff; and

(c)   in Northern Ireland, a lay magistrate.

Powers of customs officers to detain goods

11.   (1)   An Officer of Revenue and Customs may, for the purpose of facilitating the exercise by the enforcement authority, or duly authorised officer of the authority, of any powers conferred on the authority or officer by these Regulations seize any imported relevant products or any records, and detain them for not more than two working days.

(2)   Anything seized and detained under this paragraph must be dealt with during the period of its detention in such manner as the Commissioners for Her Majesty's Revenue and Customs may direct.

(3)   An Officer of Revenue and Customs seizing any relevant products or records under this paragraph must inform the person from whom they are seized that such relevant products or records have been seized.

(4)   In sub-paragraph (1) the reference to two working days is a reference to a period of forty-eight hours calculated from the time when the goods in question are seized, but disregarding so much of any period as falls on a Saturday or Sunday or on Christmas Day, Good Friday or a day which is a bank holiday under the Banking and Financial Dealings Act 1971 in the part of the United Kingdom where the goods are seized.

Applications for the release of detained items

12. (1) Any person having an interest in any relevant products or records detained for the time being under paragraph 10 may apply for an order requiring any item so detained to be released to the applicant or another person.
(2) An application under this paragraph may be made—
(a)   to any magistrates' court in which proceedings have been brought in England and Wales or Northern Ireland for an offence in respect of a contravention of any provision of these Regulations in connection with the detained item;
(b)   where no such proceedings have been so brought, by way of complaint to a magistrates' court; or
(c)   in Scotland, by summary application to the sheriff.
(3) A magistrates' court or the sheriff must not make an order under sub-paragraph (1) unless the court or sheriff is satisfied that—
(a)   proceedings have not been brought for an offence in respect of a contravention of any provision of these Regulations in connection with the detained item or, having been brought, have been concluded; and
(b)   where no such proceedings have been brought, more than six months have elapsed since the seizure was carried out.
(4) Any person aggrieved by an order made under this paragraph by a magistrates' court or sheriff, or by a decision of such a court or sheriff not to make such an order, may appeal against that order or decision—
(a)   in England and Wales, to the Crown Court;
(b)   in Scotland, to the Sheriff Appeal Court as though it were an appeal under section 110(1) of the Courts Reform (Scotland) Act 2014; or
(c)   in Northern Ireland, to a county court.
(5) In England and Wales or in Northern Ireland, an order so made may contain such provision as appears to the court to be appropriate for delaying the coming into force of the order pending the making and determination of any appeal (including any application under section 111 of the Magistrates' Courts Act 1980 or Article 146 of the Magistrates' Courts (Northern Ireland) Order 1981 (statement of case)).

Compensation for seizure and detention
13. (1) Where an officer exercises any power under paragraph 10 to seize and detain any relevant products or records, the enforcement authority is liable to pay compensation to any person having an interest in the item seized and detained in respect of any loss or damage caused by the exercise of the power if—
(a)   there has been no contravention of any provision of these Regulations; and
(b)   the exercise of the power is not attributable to any neglect or default by that person.
(2) Any disputed question as to the right to, or the amount of, any compensation payable under this paragraph must be determined by arbitration—
(a)   in England and Wales or Northern Ireland, in accordance with the Arbitration Act 1996; or
(b)   in Scotland, in accordance with the Arbitration (Scotland) Act 2010.

Recovery of the expenses of enforcement
14. (1) This paragraph applies where a court convicts a person of an offence in respect of a contravention of any provision of these Regulations in relation to any relevant products or records.
(2) The court may (in addition to any other order it may make as to costs and expenses) order the person convicted to reimburse the enforcement authority for any expenditure which has been or may be incurred by that authority in connection with any seizure or detention by or on behalf of the authority of the relevant products or records.

Power of the Commissioners for Her Majesty's Revenue and Customs to disclose information
15. (1) If they think it appropriate to do so for the purpose of facilitating the exercise by any person to whom sub-paragraph (2) applies of any functions conferred on that person by any provisions of these Regulations, the Commissioners for Her Majesty's Revenue and Customs may authorise the disclosure to that person of any information obtained for the purposes of the exercise by the Commissioners of their functions in relation to imported goods.
(2) This sub-paragraph applies to the enforcement authority and to any officer authorised by the enforcement authority.
(3) A disclosure of information made to any person under sub-paragraph (1) must be made in such manner as may be directed by the Commissioners for Her Majesty's Revenue and Customs and may be made through such persons acting on behalf of that person as may be so directed.
(4) Information may be disclosed to a person under sub-paragraph (1) whether or not the disclosure of the information has been requested by or on behalf of that person.

Savings for certain privileges
16. Nothing in these Regulations is to be taken as requiring any person—
(a)   to produce any records if that person would be entitled to refuse to produce those records in any proceedings in any court on the grounds that they are the subject of legal professional privilege or, in Scotland, a claim of confidential communications, or as authorising any person to take possession of any records which are in the possession of a person who would be so entitled; or
(b)   to answer any question or give any information if to do so would incriminate that person or that person's spouse or civil partner.

Savings for civil rights
17. A contract for the supply of relevant products is not void or unenforceable by reason only of a contravention of any provision of these Regulations.

PUBLIC MEETING AND PUBLIC ORDER

7.10237   **Public Order Act 1986, s 8**   *In Note 1 add to citation of DPP v Distill:* '[2018] 1 Cr App R 13'.

SEXUAL OFFENCES

7.10573   **Sexual Offences Act 2003, Sch 3, para 13**   *Create Note to '16' in para 13 and then renumber subsequent Notes:* '[1] Offences under the s 1 of the Protection of Children Act 1978 can relate to children aged 16 or 17; therefore, it needs to be clear that the child shown in the photograph was under 16 or a notification requirement will not arise: *R v George* [2018] EWCA Crim 417, [2018] 2 Cr App R (s) 10.'

TELECOMMUNICATIONS AND BROADCASTING

7.10979   **Regulation of Investigatory Powers Act 2000, s 71**   *Add to Note 1 in new para:* 'The Investigatory Powers (Codes of Practice and Miscellaneous Amendments) Order 2018, SI 2018/905 has been made. This brought into force three revised codes of practice regarding functions carried out under RIPA 2000. They have been updated to:

(a) bring them into line with current legislation and structures (such as the Investigatory Powers Act 2016 and its Commissioner);
(b) cover current practice;
(c) reflect changes to strengthen protection for juvenile covert human intelligence sources, and for electronic information;
(d) bring various technical elements up to date.

The Order also makes various amendments to provisions relating to the authorisation of covert investigatory powers.

7.11109 Investigatory Powers Act 2016, s 1 *Add to the list of commencement orders at the end of existing Note 1:* 'Investigatory Powers Act 2016 (Commencement No 4 and Transitional and Saving Provisions) Regulations 2018, SI 2018/341; Investigatory Powers Act 2016 (Commencement No 5 and Transitional and Saving Provisions) Regulations 2018, SI 2018/652; and Investigatory Powers Act 2016 (Commencement No 6) Regulations 2018, SI 2018/817.'

7.11135 Investigatory Powers Act 2016, s 52 *Create Note to 'regulations' in the last line of s 52(3):* '[1] Regulation 5 of the Investigatory Powers (Consequential Amendments etc.) Regulations 2018, SI 2018/682, designates the Convention on Mutual Assistance in Criminal Matters between the Member States of the European Union as an international agreement for the purposes of s 52 of the Investigatory Powers Act 2016.'

THEFT AND FRAUD

7.11318 Theft Act 1968, s 2 *In existing Note 5, insert in the citation of the Ivey case before the WLR citation:* '[2018] 2 ALL ER 406' *and then after the WLR citation insert:* '[2018] 1 Cr App R 12, [2018] Crim L R 395'.

7.11319 Theft Act 1968, s 3 *Insert text in new para after para which ends with reference to R v Williams)* 'In *R v Darroux* [2018] EWCA Crim 1009, [2018] 2 Cr App R 21 the defendant ran a residential care home operated by a housing association. She had responsibility for the payroll of all the staff, including herself. She was entitled to claim certain additional payments, such as overtime. Relevant claims were sent on a monthly basis to a company which provided payroll services. This company was permitted to operate the housing association's bank account and the sums in question were paid from that account by BACS. The defendant had no control over this account. An audit established that the defendant had submitted a number of false claims for overtime, etc. She was charged with nine counts of theft, all alleging that she had stolen "monies" belonging to the housing association. The convictions were quashed on appeal. A chose in action, here a credit balance in a bank account, could be stolen, but in submitting false claims the defendant had not assumed any of the rights of an owner with regard to the account. The forms she submitted did not, themselves, confer any rights regarding the account, she had no contact with the bank and no control over the account. Conduct which was ultimately causally operative in reducing a bank account did not necessarily become an assumption of the rights of the owner with regard to the bank balance simply and solely through the causation process. There was no evidence that the payroll company automatically had to give effect, at the behest of the defendant, to the forms she submitted.

"61 In submitting the monthly time forms and holiday forms the defendant was not, in our judgment, assuming any rights of an owner with regard to the bank account. The situation here is different from that in *Williams (Roy)* (supra). The monthly forms are not to be equated with cheques. The monthly forms of themselves conferred no rights on the defendant with regard to the bank account. Rather, the defendant was doing, albeit in some instances dishonestly, what she was employed to do as part of her employment—viz submitting to PCS the monthly forms for payroll preparation purposes. She had no contact with the bank at all and no control of the bank account. What she did, we consider, was too far removed to be an act of appropriation with regard to the bank account. It may well be that such conduct was an essential step in procuring, via the instructions of PCS to the bank, the ultimate payment out (and thence the diminution pro tanto of the credit balance). But conduct which ultimately is causally operative in reducing a bank balance does not necessarily become an assumption of rights of the owner with regard to the bank balance simply and solely because it is causally operative. Thus, in the present case the defendant dishonestly induced the Housing Association (by its agents PCS) to do acts—viz instruct the payments out—which, we accept, would be an appropriation, through PCS, by the Housing Association itself. But that did not thereby necessarily render the dishonest conduct of the defendant an appropriation by her of the relevant chose in action.

62 Cases such as *Kohn* (supra) and *Hilton* [1997] 2 Cr App R 445, CA are, in this respect, distinguishable. In those cases, the defendant was a signatory on, and had direct and authorised control of, the account in question and gave the necessary instructions. Here, however, the defendant did not. Control of the account rested solely with the Housing Association and, for payroll purposes, with PCS, the authorised agents of the Housing Association. PCS were not the agents of the defendant in any true sense. Rather, they were her dupes. The defendant successfully

deceived the Housing Association and PCS. But such deceit was not of itself, in our judgment, an appropriation, for the purposes of the 1968 Act , of the chose in action representing the Housing Association's bank balance.

63 Accordingly, given those facts, we conclude that the charges were not properly framed in theft. This was, on the facts, a clear potential case of fraud by misrepresentation. But that was not charged.

64 We add two observations:

(1)   while the above cited statement in *Naviede* (supra), as restated in *Briggs*, may in general terms frequently represent the correct position, as will be gathered we do not think that such statement should be taken as an inflexible statement of principle of invariable application. As we see it, there may be cases where a deceptive representation inducing an account holder to make payment out of his bank account could constitute an appropriation (within the meaning of the 1968 Act). It would depend on the circumstances; and

(2)   it has been suggested, most notably by Professor Sir John Smith, that cases where a cheque is dishonestly obtained and presented are different from cases where payment out of an account is procured in circumstances where the bank uses electronic or automated means. In common with the court in Hilton, we have some difficulty with that. It is at all events hard to see how or why (as is suggested) the latter scenario may give rise to a break in the chain of causation but the former not. That said, as will also be gathered, we do not regard the causative impact of a deception as of itself determinative of whether there has been an appropriation by a defendant with regard to a bank account in any particular case. (per Davis LJ)"'

7.11325   Theft Act 1968, s 9   *In existing Note 3 change the para reference from 3.355 to:* '3.343'.

Add text to the end of Note 3 as follows: 'While each case is fact specific, burglary of a communal area in a block of flats, without entering any individual flat, should be sentenced on the basis the burglary was non-domestic within the guidelines: *R v Ogungbile* [2017] EWCA Crim 1826, [2018] 4 WLR 56, [2018] 1 Cr App R (S) 31.'

7.11332   Theft Act 1968, s 15   *In existing Note 1, insert in the citation of the Ivey case before the WLR citation:* '[2018] 2 ALL ER 406' *and then after the after WLR citation insert:* '[2018] 1 Cr App R 12.'.

7.11336   Theft Act 1968, s 17   *In existing Note 1, insert in the citation of the Ivey case before the WLR citation:* '[2018] 2 ALL ER 406' *and then after the after WLR citation insert:* '2018] 1 Cr App R 12.'.

7.11339   Theft Act 1968, s 20   *In existing Note 1, insert in the citation of the Ivey case before the WLR citation:* '[2018] 2 ALL ER 406' *and then after the after WLR citation insert:* '[2018] 1 Cr App R 12.'.

7.11340   Theft Act 1968, s 21   *For note 3 substitute the following text:* 'In *R v Pogmore* [2017] EWCA Crim 925, [2018] 1 WLR 3237; [2018] 2 Cr App R 2 the court confirmed that blackmail could be tried in England and Wales where either the demand with menaces was sent from a place in England and Wales to a place elsewhere, or where it was sent from a place elsewhere to a place in England and Wales. The court rejected a submission that the "demand" and the "menaces" should be treated as severable and held that the relevant part of the actus reus of blackmail was a "demand with menaces". It was not the communication of the demand but the demand itself which was the "relevant event" for the purposes of the jurisdiction provisions in s 2 of the Criminal Justice Act 1993.'